About Pearson

Pearson is the world's learning company, with presence across 70 countries worldwide. Our unique insights and world-class expertise comes from a long history of working closely with renowned teachers, authors and thought leaders, as a result of which, we have emerged as the preferred choice for millions of teachers and learners across the world.

We believe learning opens up opportunities, creates fulfilling careers and hence better lives. We hence collaborate with the best of minds to deliver you class-leading products, spread across the Higher Education and K12 spectrum.

Superior learning experience and improved outcomes are at the heart of everything we do. This product is the result of one such effort.

Your feedback plays a critical role in the evolution of our products and you can contact us - reachus@pearson.com. *We look forward to it.*

DYNAMICS OF STRUCTURES WITH EARTHQUAKE ENGINEERING

2nd Edition

Ashok K. Jain
Former Professor of Civil Engineering
Indian Institute of Technology Roorkee
Roorkee

Pearson

Senior Manager—Product: Harsha Singh
Senior Editor—Production: C. Purushothaman

ISBN 978-93-570-5935-0

First Impression

Published by Pearson India Education Services Pvt. Ltd, CIN: U72200TN2005PTC057128.

Head Office: 1st Floor, Berger Tower, Plot No. C-001A/2, Sector 16B, Noida - 201 301, Uttar Pradesh, India.
Registered Office: Featherlite, 'The Address' 5th Floor, Survey No 203/10B, 200 Ft MMRD Road, Zamin Pallavaram, Chennai - 600044
Website: in.pearson.com, Email: companysecretary.india@pearson.com

Compositor: SRS Global, Puducherry.
Printed in India at Saurabh Printers Pvt. Ltd.

Dedicated to
my little grandchildren Dhruv, Samyukta, and Samaira who made me understand energy dissipation mechanisms in
live *dynamic systems*

Brief Contents

ONLINE CHAPTERS

Contents

ONLINE CHAPTERS

Preface

It is needless to reemphasize the significance and importance of the subject of dynamics of structures when the architects and engineers are constantly craving for lightweight but strong materials, and lean and slim structures. Among the whole family of the subjects on *Structural Engineering*, this is indeed the most mathematical and, therefore, most scary. There are umpteen number of text books available on *Dynamics of Structures*. They all discuss the derivation of equations along with their physical significance. Nevertheless, it is very difficult to visualize these equations. FORTRAN has been the most powerful and favourite programming language of structural engineers but it was without graphic commands. The subject of structural dynamics, stiffness matrix method, nonlinear behaviour of members and structures, FORTRAN language, and computer hardware and software have evolved together since early 1960s. There used to be special Tektronix and vt100 graphic terminals, and Calcomp plotters with proprietary graphics software. The biggest hurdle in understanding the subject of dynamics remained inability of easy graphical representation of equations and dynamic response of structures. Remember SAP IV, DRAIN-2D and SAKE developed in early 1970s? With the beginning of the *twenty first century* all that has changed. The desktop and laptop computers, and colour laser printers with very high resolutions are easily available and affordable. MATLAB and PYTHON are very powerful and user friendly software for carrying out solution of very complicated mathematical equations with built-in graphic functions. Another very easy and powerful tool is the electronic worksheets such as MS-EXCEL.

The writing of this book was inspired by the following objectives:

- to present the subject matter with utmost ease
- to provide necessary and detailed mathematical background
- to introduce more illustrative examples
- to present the subject matter useful to final year undergraduate and post graduate students
- to introduce MS-EXCEL and MATLAB
- to introduce nonlinear modelling and analysis
- to introduce special damping devices and their modeling
- to introduce practical applications useful to practicing engineers

During the past few years, my students have greatly appreciated the power and impact of these tools in understanding the subject. An attempt has been made to present both elementary topics as well as advanced topics including acceleration–displacement response spectra (ADRS) and performance–based seismic design of structures. The response of structures with energy dissipating devices subjected to earthquakes is also presented.

SECOND EDITION CHANGES

The changes made in the second edition is largely in response to the feedback received from students and faculty using the book in class rooms and practicing engineers using it for solving their day-to-day variety of practical problems. The breadth and depth of the subject has been increased in each chapter to have a better understanding of earthquake engineering. More information has been provided on machine foundations, over ground explosions, torsion in single storey buildings, besides physical interpretation of various terms and concepts. Two new chapters on bridges and liquid retaining structures have been incorporated. The chapter on buildings has been re-written to make it more precise and practical.

Over fifty new solved examples have been added to improve the understanding of the basic concepts and applications to earthquake engineering. Over 400 review problems have been added throughout to clarify the concepts.

ORGANIZATION OF THE BOOK

A genuine effort has been made to develop the subject from the very basics of simple harmonic motion of a pendulum and introduce the concept of equation of motion. The next step is to find its solution. There are several techniques to solve the 2nd order differential equations of motion for different types of dynamic loads. These techniques along with physical interpretation of results have been covered in Chapters 2 to 7. The estimation of earthquake force has been discussed in Chapter 8. Analyses of two-degree-of-freedom system and tuned mass dampers have been developed in Chapter 9 while that of multi-degree-of-freedom systems has been developed in Chapters 10 and 11.

The analysis of multistorey reinforced concrete and steel buildings subjected to earthquake loads has been discussed in Chapter 12; that of bridges and liquid retaining structures are discussed in Chapters 13 and 14. Under a severe earthquake loading, a structure is expected to undergo inelastic region. Modelling for nonlinear analysis, hysteresis models, solution algorithms, energy dissipating devices, concept of ductility etc., are discussed in Chapter 15. Nowadays there is a great emphasis on predicting the performance of a structure under earthquake loads. The intention is to know if the structure will remain in *immediate occupancy, damage control, life safety, limited safety, or in structural stability states* during an earthquake event. In case there is a downtime for the building after an event, then how much will it be? What it will cost to the owner and its occupants as a result of downtime? What will be the estimated extent and cost of repair? Pushover analysis is used to study the performance-based design. These issues are discussed in Chapter 16. As on today, we may not have all the answers but these do indicate the direction of further research.

Finally, the last Chapter 17 is devoted to the estimation of wind loads based on IS 875-Part 3 and IRC 6. Wind may be treated as a static load or dynamic load. The wind loads on various structures are calculated based on exhaustive studies in wind tunnels over an extended period of time in various countries. The concepts of fluid mechanics are involved in the estimation of wind loads. It is important to understand the estimation of drag coefficient for different shape and size of structures and their exposed structural elements. It is interesting to know that the dynamic wind loads are applied statically to a structure in order to understand its response.

Wherever required, IS 1893, IS 875-part 3, IS 2974, IRC 6, Eurocode 8, ASCE 7, AISC 341, NZS 1170 and ISO codes have been introduced. Federal Emergency Management Agency (FEMA), Washington, D.C., and Pacific Earthquake Engineering Research Center (PEER) have prepared several documents with detailed commentary and background notes including publications under the National Earthquake Hazards Reduction Program (NEHRP). These publications have been introduced as appropriate. It is recommended that the reader should have a copy of these codes and research reports to understand and appreciate the latest developments.

HOW TO STUDY THE SUBJECT OF DYNAMICS?

As already pointed out, this is a highly mathematical subject. It is recommended that the reader should make himself/herself familiar with the solution of 2nd order differential equations, integral calculus, and numerical integration along with computer programming. The reader should himself/herself derive each equation and make it a general practice to represent them in graphical form. It will help develop an understanding of the nature of equations, their physical meaning and interpretation, and, therefore, behaviour of the structure under a given dynamic load. MATLAB and PYTHON are very powerful tool for learning and exploring the subject. MS-EXCEL is another very powerful tool to carryout repetitive calculations and represent the data in graphical form. In addition, the dynamic response of structures subjected to earthquake loading should be understood using any popular software. The GUI in all these tools is extremely powerful and helpful in unravelling the mystery of dynamics of structures. All such tools must be fully exploited for effective computer aided learning.

ACKNOWLEDGEMENTS

I wish to thank the following students with whom I used to have short but intense brain storming sessions, *sometimes forced as is natural in dynamics*, on various aspects of structural dynamics while they were working on their research projects during their stay at Roorkee: M. R. Deshpande, S. S. Dasaka, Shri Pal, R. A. Mir, Ashok Mittal, Satish Annigeri, Jainendra Agarwal, J. Satyanarayan, P. Rajeshwari, M L Meena, Abhijit S. Niphade, Sourabh Agrawal, Yogesh Bansal, Ranjith Shetty, Sujit Ashok Gangal, Payal

Thukral, Abhinav Gupta, Shabbir Lokhandwala, Mandakini Dehuri, Pruthvik B. M., Alwin N., Ripu Daman Singh and Saurabh Khandelwal. In addition, there were several other students who worked on static problems and had very stimulating technical sessions with me.

I must admit that I learned wind loads from A.K.M. Tripathi who had a deep understanding of wind loads on TV and MW towers. Special thanks are due to Aparna K. P. who started working with me for her Master's thesis with a clean slate and in a very short time she picked up the fine points of inelastic response spectra and acceleration-displacement response spectra and helped produce numerous tables and graphs.

How can I forget my *alma mater*, the erstwhile University of Roorkee and now Indian Institute of Technology Roorkee, situated in a very small and calm town on the banks of Ganga and foothills of Himalaya for providing an excellent work environment, library, and computing facilities to *learn, learn and learn*? The University of Michigan at Ann Arbor, another *alma mater*, situated in a very small and calm town on the banks of Huron river, provided me with excellent laboratory facilities in its North Campus to generate hysteresis loops for steel bracing members, and computing facilities in its main campus to study the inelastic seismic response of concentrically and eccentrically braced steel frames.

I acknowledge the editorial and production teams at Pearson consisting of Harsha Singh, Senior Manager-Products, C. Purushothaman, Senior Production Editor and Sojan Jose, Director-Products for their untiring efforts and tolerating my last-minute changes in producing this book in the present form.

Lastly, I wish to thank my wife Sarita, our children Payal, Gaurav, son-in-law Vikash and daughter-in-law Saavy, for their unconditional support and encouragement in writing this book.

FINALLY, WHY BUILDINGS DISAPPEAR DURING AN EARTHQUAKE WITH A BLINK OF AN EYE?

In my opinion, the buildings *collapse and disappear* during an earthquake not because it was *an act of God!* or the code was not *revised* but because of *poor* materials, *poor* workmanship, *poor* detailing of reinforcement especially beam-column, and beam-wall joints, besides *careless* site supervision and *faulty* QA/QC.

Ashok K. Jain

About the Author

Dr. Ashok K. Jain is a former Professor of Civil Engineering at the Indian Institute of Technology Roorkee (Formerly University of Roorkee), obtained B.E. and M.E. degrees with Honours from the University of Roorkee in 1972 and 1974, and doctorate degree from the University of Michigan, Ann Arbor in 1978. He has over 40 years of experience in exploring the dynamic behaviour of RC buildings to bridges, bracing members to braced steel frames, steel bridges to TV towers, RC water tanks, effect of over ground explosions on airport hangars and retaining walls, and wind loads on TV and MW towers. He has conducted extensive non-linear analysis of RC and steel buildings and bridges. A recipient of several awards, he has been a Research Fellow at the University of Michigan; a Visiting Professor at the McGill University, Montreal; Director, Malaviya National Institute of Technology, Jaipur, and Head of Civil Engineering Department, I.I.T. Roorkee. Prof. Jain embodies a unique combination of teaching, research, design consultancy, as well as a mentor and a philanthropist.

Part

1

Single Degree of Freedom Systems

1 Introduction to Structural Dynamics

1.1 INTRODUCTION

There are many situations in real life when a structure is subjected to vibrations caused by *dynamic loads* due to machines, road traffic, rail traffic or air traffic, wind, earthquake, blast loading, sea waves, or tsunami. The movement of pedestrians may cause vibrations in a floor of a building and in a suspension bridge. The term *dynamic loads* includes any loading which varies with time. The manner in which a *structure* responds to a given dynamic excitation depends upon the nature of excitation and the dynamic characteristics of the structure, that is, the manner in which it stores and dissipates energy. The energy is stored in the form of potential energy and is dissipated in the form of kinetic energy through vibrations. Some of these loads could lead to catastrophic loss to lives and properties in a very short span of time while the others cause irritation to the users of the facility. If the vibrations are small but persistent, this condition may lead to cracking in joints and members of a structure. In earlier days, a simplified solution was arrived at by treating the *dynamic load* as *equivalent static load*. Under certain conditions, this idealization works quite well. However, with better understanding of dynamics of structures, it is desirable to develop more efficient solutions by realistically modelling the loads taking account of their dynamic nature. When a dynamic load is applied to the structure it produces a time-dependent response in each element of the structure. The organization of structural systems to resist such loadings has a major influence on the overall planning, design and economics of a structure.

The subject of dynamics of structures becomes quite complex because of a large number of variables involved in the problem. The term *structure* encompasses a single-storey building to a multi-storey building, small overhead water tanks to large water tanks of different shapes, small bridges to large bridges of different materials and configurations, viaducts, microwave and TV towers, industrial structures, machine foundations, theatres, stadiums, airports, jetties and so on. Mass and stiffness of a structure along with their spatial distribution define the structure. Material used in structures is another parameter that defines the structure. Damping is generally associated with materials. Finally the *amplitude, frequency* and *duration of load* lead to another complication. Earthquake loading is a complex variant of this. Some of the dynamic loads are *deterministic* while the others are *non-deterministic or probabilistic*. Some of the structures will respond to dynamic loads in *linear and elastic* range while the others may venture into *nonlinear elastic* or *nonlinear inelastic* range. The role of a structural analyst is to identify each of these parameters and determine the response of the structure as accurately as possible. The study of vibrations, that is, their cause, measurement, analysis and effect on the structure is called *dynamics of structures*.

The details of excitation, structure and response are illustrated in Figures 1.1 to 1.5. The excitation shown in Figures 1.2(b) and 1.2(c) may be static or dynamic or even slow dynamic. A slow dynamic load is also called pseudo static load. It is very helpful in conducting tests in laboratory.

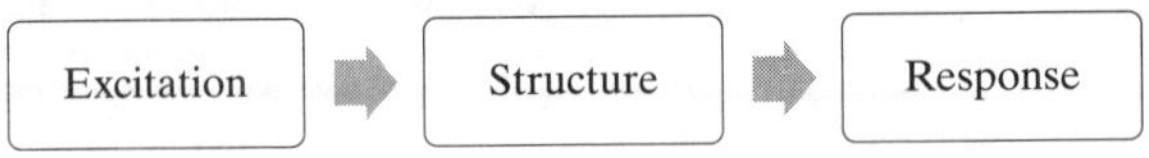

Figure 1.1 Cause and effect on a structure.

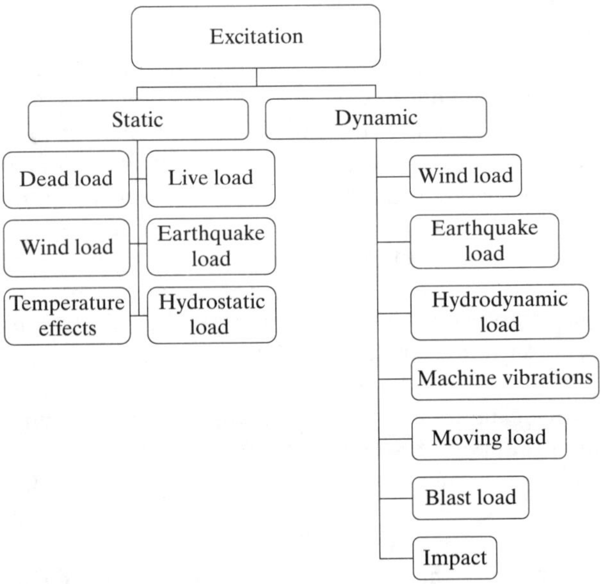

Figure 1.2(a) Source of excitation.

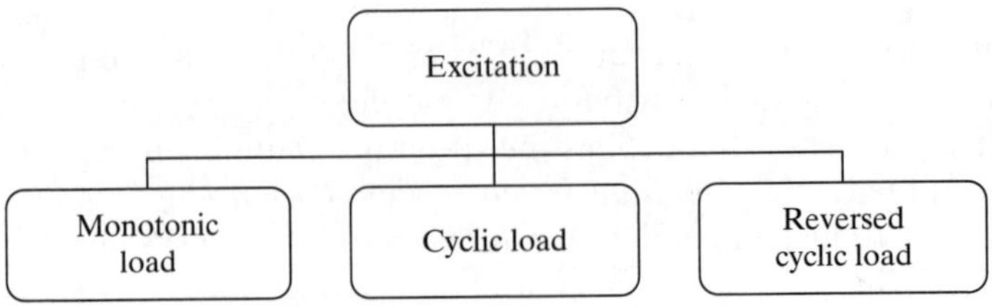

Figure 1.2(b) Nature of excitation.

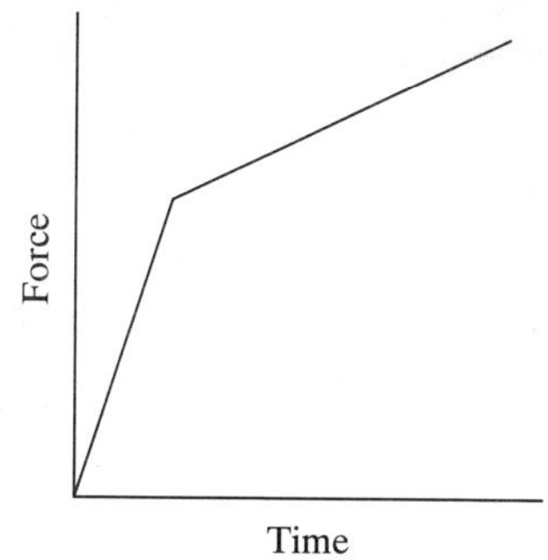

(i) Monotonic loading

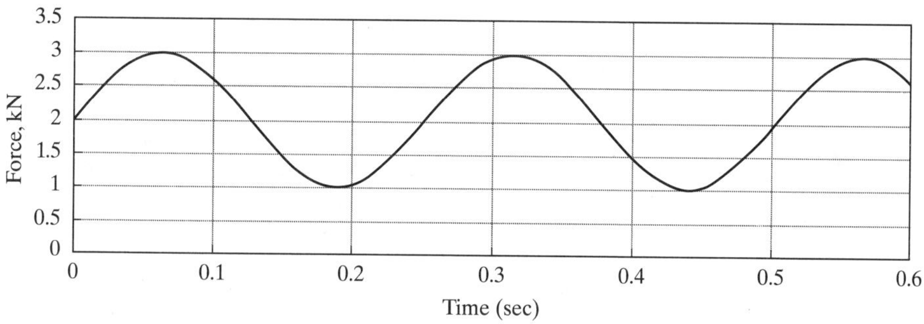

(ii) Cyclic loading

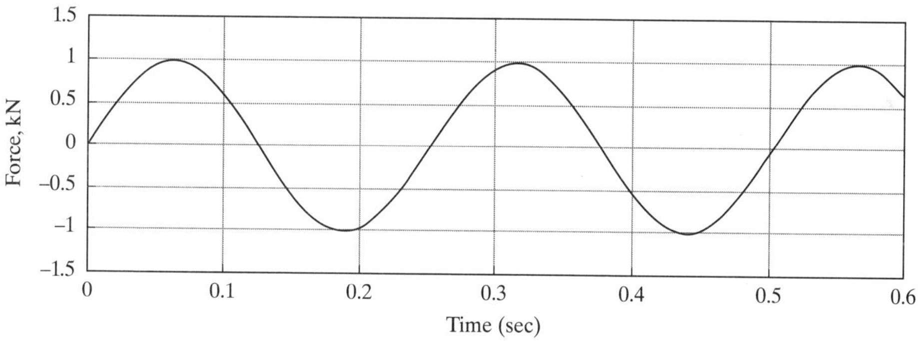

(iii) Reversed cyclic loading

Figure 1.2(c) Nature of excitation.

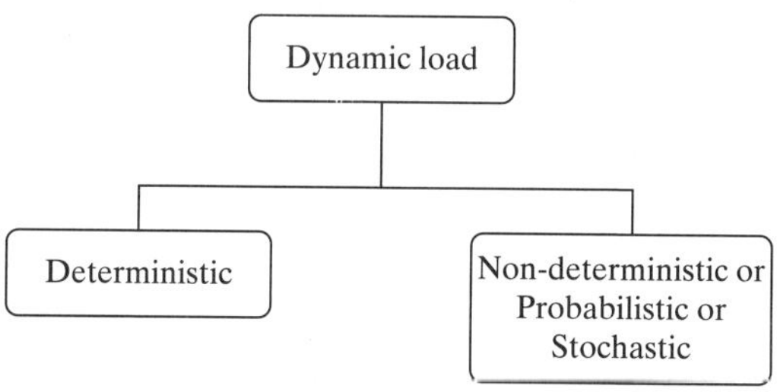

Figure 1.3 Assessment of dynamic load.

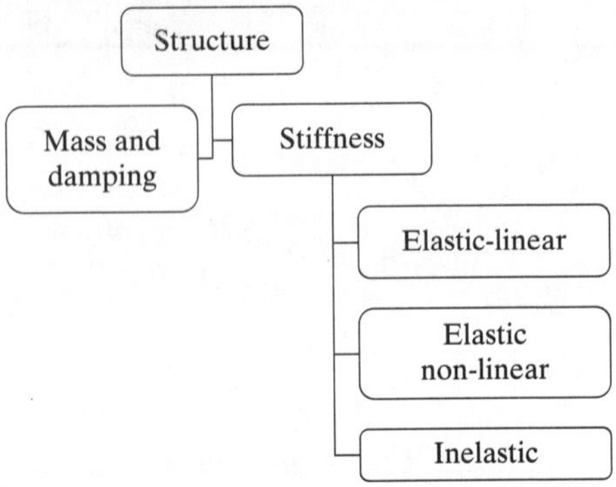

Figure 1.4 Properties of a structure.

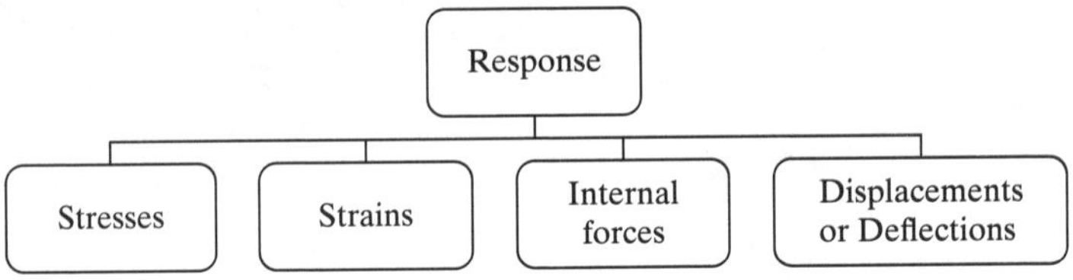

Figure 1.5 Type of response.

1.1.1 Why Dynamic Analysis?

The objective of dynamic analysis is to determine the displacement–time history, velocity–time history and acceleration–time history, and internal member force – time history due to the given force–time history. The time history provides the following information:

- Peak values (positive and negative)
- Mean value
- Nature of change in the response parameter—that is, its frequency (only qualitatively)
- Oscillations with respect to its mean position.

It is possible to determine absolute maximum displacement, absolute maximum velocity and absolute maximum acceleration. Knowing stiffness of the structure, forces in various members can be calculated. The dynamic member forces can be superimposed on those due to static loads in different load combinations. The design member forces can be estimated for the chosen design philosophy, that is, *limit state design* or *performance based design philosophy*.

Let us discuss some of the terminologies used in dynamic analysis of structures.

Amplitude The maximum value of a periodic function (which may be displacement, velocity, acceleration or force) is called amplitude.

Damping It is the dissipation of energy that causes the amplitude of motion of a freely vibrating structure to decrease with each cycle with the motion eventually dying out. The term 'damping' is widely applied to energy dissipation mechanisms that are not associated with structural damage. It may be natural or artificial, that is, external. Natural damping is an inherent property of the material. There are different types of damping such as viscous damping, friction damping and hysteretic damping.

Degree of Freedom The number of independent displacement components required to define the deflected shape of a structure is called degree of freedom. If only a single displacement is required to define its deflected shape, it is called a single-degree-of-freedom (SDOF) system. If 'n' degrees are required, it is called a multi-degrees-of-freedom system.

Deterministic When a given parameter is fully known and there are no uncertainties surrounding the values of the parameter, it is called deterministic.

Forced Vibration When a structure vibrates under the influence of an external force, it is called forced vibration.

Free Vibration When a structure vibrates without any externally applied force such as when it is pulled out of position and then released gently, it is called free vibration.

Frequency The number of cycles of motion completed during a unit time interval (i.e., radian per second or cycles per second) is called frequency. Frequency is the inverse of period (that is, a structure with a natural period of 0.5 second has a natural frequency of 2 cycles per second or 2 Hz). When a structure vibrates freely without any external force, it is said to have one or more *natural frequency* or *natural period* of vibration depending upon its degrees of freedom.

Fundamental Frequency The smallest frequency of vibration of a structure is called the fundamental frequency.

Fundamental Period The longest period of vibration of a structure is called the fundamental period.

Mode Shape A structure is assumed to vibrate in different modes depending upon its natural frequencies. The total number of modes depends upon the total active degrees of freedom of the structure. There will be a unique mode of vibration corresponding to each natural frequency.

Non-deterministic or Probabilistic When a given parameter is not fully known and there are uncertainties surrounding the values of the parameter, it is called non-deterministic or probabilistic. Thus, probability of uncertainties associated with all variables used explicitly or implicitly to define the parameter would be formally taken into account.

Period The duration of one cycle of motion in second is called period.

Resonance The amplification of response that occurs under forced vibration when period of the applied force is equal or very close to the natural period of the structure is called resonance. The amplitude of vibrations is maximum at resonance and may lead to damage to the machine, structure or its foundation.

Steady State Vibration When a structure vibrates under the influence of an external periodic force, it is said to be in a steady state.

Stochastic It is synonymous with the term 'random'. It is of Greek origin and means pertaining to chance or randomly determined sequence of observations. It is same as *non-deterministic.*

Transient Vibration These vibrations depend upon the initial conditions of the structure (displacement and velocity at time $t = 0$) and die out shortly due to the inherent damping present in a structure.

1.2 PHYSICAL AND MATHEMATICAL MODELLING

Civil engineering structures are conceived to meet the functional and aesthetical requirements. They consist of a combination of structural elements and non-structural elements. It is a standard practice to idealize a physical problem into a mathematical problem in order to study its response under the applied loads. It may be modelled as a one-, two- or a three-dimensional problem as shown in Figure 1.6. The non-structural elements are generally not modelled. Next, it is necessary to determine the *force-deformation* relationship for this mathematical model. For small deformations, the force-deformation relation is usually *linear and elastic*. The slope of this relation gives stiffness of the structure. At larger displacements, the slope may become *non-linear*. The structure may or may not remain *elastic*. Therefore, depending upon the state of the structure, stiffness may be *non-linear-elastic* or *non-linear-inelastic*. The estimation of stiffness of the structure is required, both for static analysis and dynamic analysis. For a complex structure consisting of large number of similar or different types of structural elements, stiffness is generated from the element level as done in the *matrix method of structural analysis*. The same procedure may be followed for dynamic analysis of structures. Sometimes it may not be easy to find solution of the mathematical model subjected to given loads in the absence of known appropriate boundary conditions. Therefore, it may be necessary to

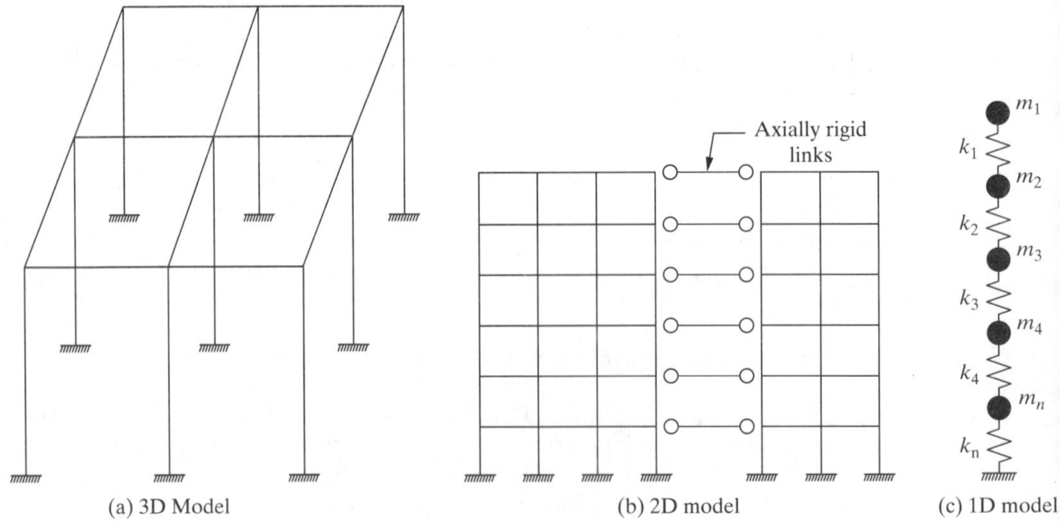

Figure 1.6 Modelling of a structure.

develop a numerical model of the problem and solve it using one or more *numerical techniques*.

Sometimes it is necessary to include soil and foundation in the model to examine the effect of soil–structure interaction. The problem now becomes very complex. The treatment requires advanced treatment that is beyond the scope of the present text.

Let us consider a simple pendulum consisting of a mass suspended from a massless rod as shown in Figure 1.7.

This pendulum can be displaced slightly vertically and released gently. It sets into simple harmonic motion whose equation is given by the principles of physics, that is, *Newton's second law of motion*:

$$\ddot{x} \propto -x \tag{1.1a}$$

or,

$$\ddot{x} = -\omega^2 x \tag{1.1b}$$

where,

$$\ddot{x} = \frac{d^2x}{dt^2} \text{ acceleration} \tag{1.1c}$$

$$\omega = \sqrt{\frac{k}{m}} \tag{1.1d}$$

k = axial stiffness of the rod = AE/L
m = total mass
ω = natural frequency of vibration in rad/sec

$$\omega = \frac{2\pi}{T} = 2\pi f \tag{1.1e}$$

f = natural frequency of vibration in cycles/sec or in Hz

$$T = \frac{1}{f} = 2\pi\sqrt{\frac{m}{k}} \tag{1.1f}$$

T = natural period of vibration in sec

The pendulum has only one degree of freedom in the vertical direction, that is, vertical displacement x. It shows that the acceleration is directed towards the mean position of the pendulum and it is proportional to the displacement.

This pendulum can be inverted upside down as shown in Figure 1.8.

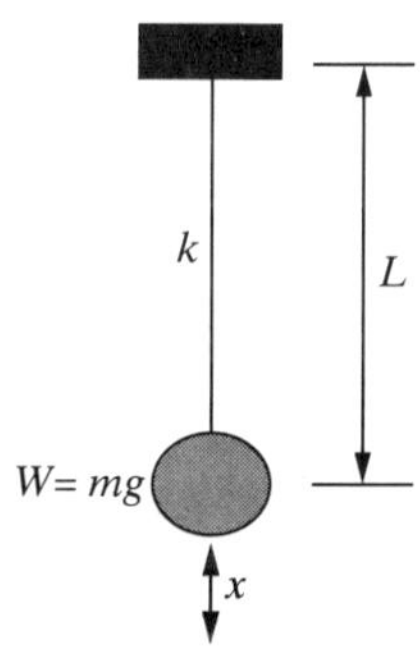

Figure 1.7 Simple pendulum.

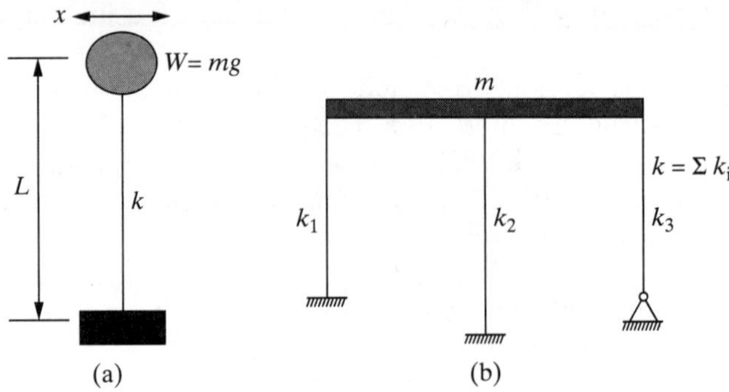

Figure 1.8 Inverted pendulum.

This inverted pendulum still vibrates in simple harmonic motion and its equation of motion remains same as before. In the inverted position, it can simulate the behaviour of an overhead water tank or that of a single-storey building. However, it needs to displace in lateral direction. In case of a water tank, mass m represents the mass of the container and the water, whereas k represents the lateral stiffness of staging of the tank. In case of a building, mass m represents mass lumped at its roof, whereas k represents the lateral stiffness of all the lateral load-resisting elements. These elements may be columns, walls or both. The natural frequency of the pendulum is the most important characteristic of a dynamic system. It is a function of the *mass* and *stiffness* of the system.

Now let us consider a simple portal frame as shown in Figure 1.9(a). There are three degrees of freedom per node: one horizontal translation, one vertical translation and one rotation. Since A and D are fixed supports, the frame has six active degrees of freedom. If axial deformation is neglected, it will have three degrees of freedom: one lateral and two rotational for static analysis. In dynamic analysis, the number of independent displacements required to define the displaced position of all the masses relative to their original position is called *dynamic degrees of freedom*. If mass of the frame is concentrated at one location, that is roof, the frame will have only one degree of freedom—lateral displacement. Thus, it is called a SDOF system. Its mathematical model is shown in Figure 1.9(b). Again, natural frequency of the frame is its most important characteristic. It is a function of the mass and lateral stiffness of the system. The lateral stiffness of this rigid jointed frame depends upon the relative stiffness of beams and columns. Let us consider two extreme cases:

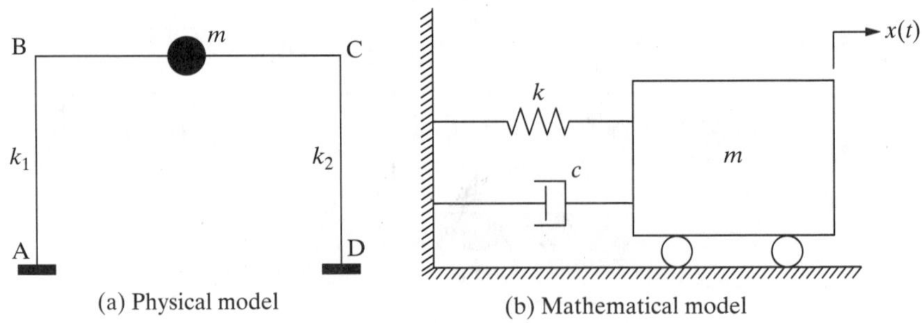

Figure 1.9 Portal frame.

***Case 1:** Rigid beam, that is, flexural stiffness of beam is infinite.*

The flexural rigidity of each column is EI. Height of each column is L. Therefore, lateral stiffness of each column is given by

$$K = \frac{12EI}{L^3} \tag{1.2a}$$

The total lateral stiffness of the frame =

$$K = 2 \times \frac{12EI}{L^3} \tag{1.2b}$$

***Case 2:** Flexible beam, that is, flexural stiffness of beam is very low*

Therefore, lateral stiffness of each column is given by

$$K = \frac{3EI}{L^3} \tag{1.3a}$$

The total lateral stiffness of the frame =

$$K = 2 \times \frac{3EI}{L^3} \tag{1.3b}$$

In case there are three identical columns, the total stiffness of the frame becomes three times the stiffness of a single column. Equations (1.2a) and (1.3a) give range of lateral stiffness of a column.

Dynamic degrees of freedom of a structure can be determined by computing the displacement due to a unit load in the desired direction. This may be done by making use of either *stiffness method* or *flexibility method* depending upon the structure. Examples 1.10 to 1.12 illustrate the application of different methods. Example 1.11 is again solved in Example 9.4 by making use of the influence coefficient method.

1.3 DISCRETE AND CONTINUUM MODELLING

In dynamics of structures, the first step is to identify dynamic degrees of freedom. In certain structures these degrees of freedom are obvious and identifiable whereas, in many other structures it is difficult to identify these degrees of freedom. Thus, depending upon the number of degrees of freedom, we may have a multi-degrees-of-freedom system. For example, consider a four-storey moment-resistant frame having rigid floors. It is a skeletal structure and it is referred to as a discrete system in matrix structural analysis terminology. The entire mass of the floor and storey can be lumped at each floor level. It can, therefore, be identified that there is only one lateral displacement at each floor, that is, there is one-degree-of-freedom per floor. Similarly, in an overhead water tank, the entire mass of water is lumped at its top. The mass of water is much more than the mass of the staging. Thus, it can be said that there is only one lateral degree of freedom at the centre of gravity of the mass. This is referred to as a lumped mass approach in a discrete system. A TV tower or a truss steel bridge is an example of discrete structural system having n-degrees-of-freedom as shown in Figure 1.10.

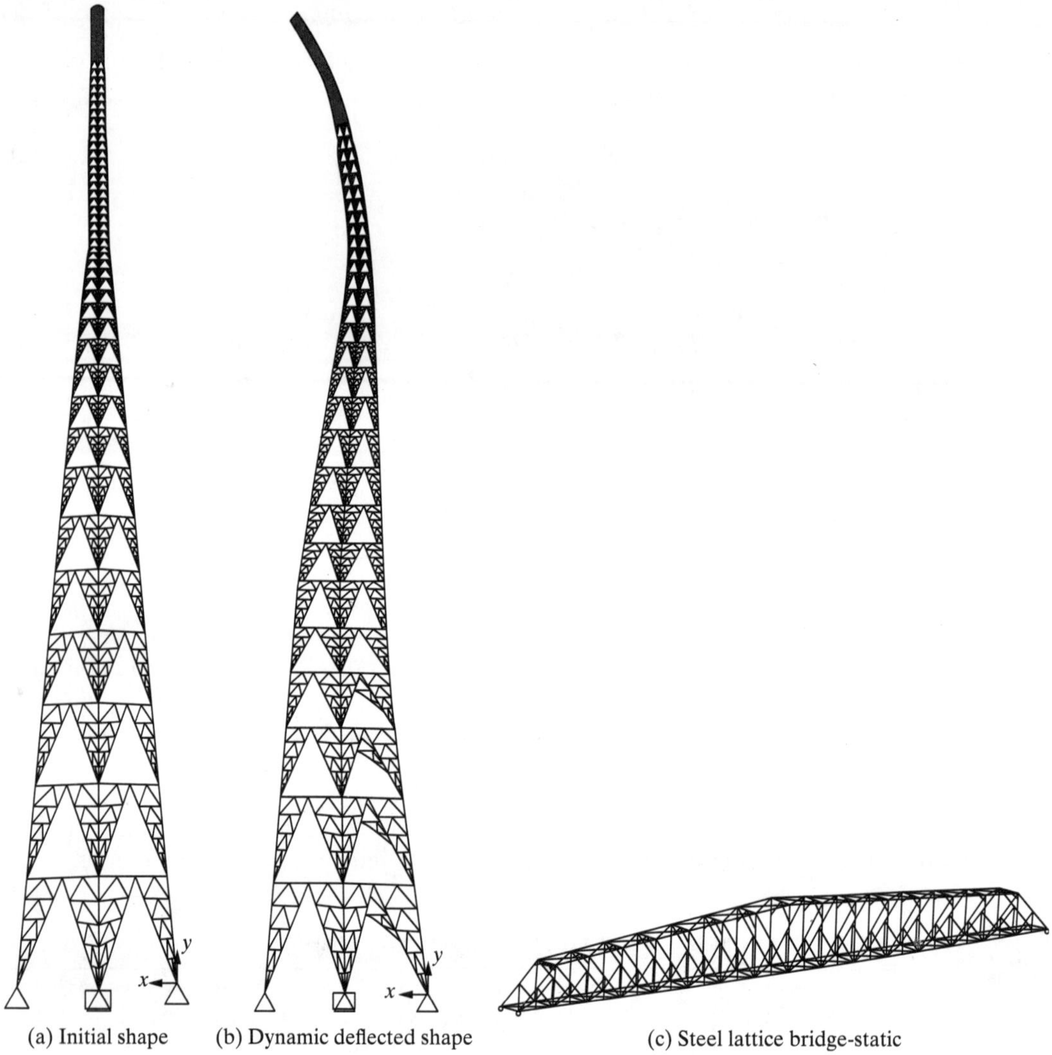

Figure 1.10 (a) Steel TV tower—static; (b) Steel TV tower—dynamic; (c) Steel truss bridge.

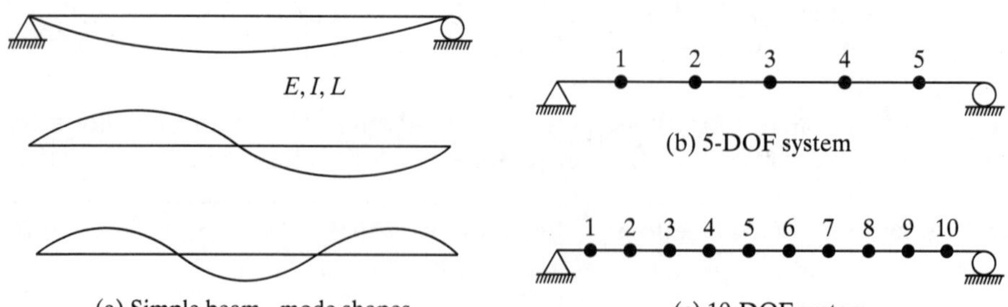

Figure 1.11 A system with distributed mass and stiffness.

Now consider a simply supported beam under its self-weight having length L as shown in Figure 1.11. Its mass and elasticity or stiffness is distributed along its length. Theoretically, it has infinite degrees of freedom. How do we identify its active degrees of freedom? There are two options. One, make use of generalized displacements. In other words, assume a deflected shape which remains constant along the entire length at any point of time. This is called a *shape function*. It represents one degree of freedom. Similarly, select other shape function compatible with its boundary conditions. It will represent another degree of freedom. Thus, 'n' shape functions can be selected for a system with distributed mass and elasticity representing n-degrees-of-freedom. Other option is to lump its mass at certain locations along its length. If it is lumped at five locations, it will result in a five-degrees-of-freedom system. If it is lumped at 10 locations, it will result in a 10-degrees-of-freedom system. More the number of discretization, better will be the accuracy.

Now consider a retaining wall as shown in Figure 1.12(a). It is again a continuum system having distributed mass and elasticity in its entire body. It has infinite-degrees-of-freedom. How do we identify its active degrees of freedom? The answer lies in making use of the finite element concept. Mesh the wall in appropriate shape and size

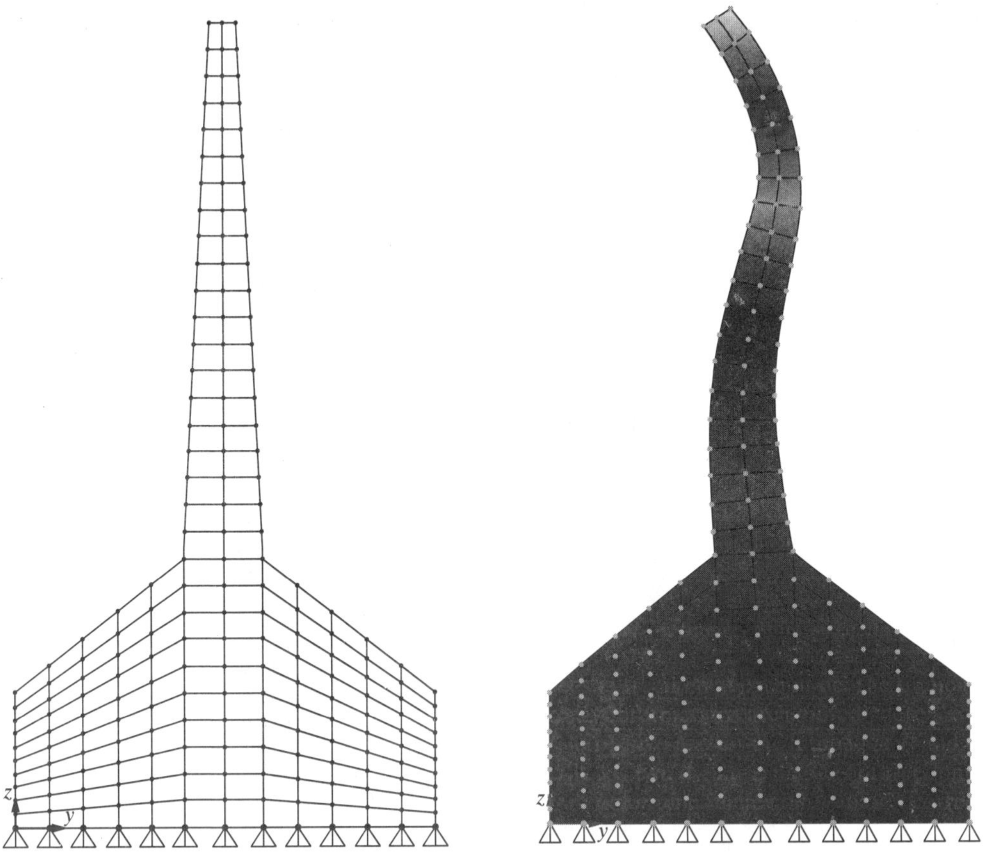

(a) Initial shape (b) Dynamic deflected shape

Figure 1.12 Retaining wall.

in each of the two directions in the vertical plane. Identify the degrees of freedom at each node and select appropriate finite element to represent structural characteristics of the wall, that is, *plane stress* element, *plane strain* element, *plate element* or a *shell element.* There are different options to discretize a structure and adopt a finite element depending upon its structural characteristics, desired accuracy and convenience. A typical mode shape under free vibration condition is shown in Figure 1.12(b). The same concept is applicable to chimneys as shown in Figure 1.13.

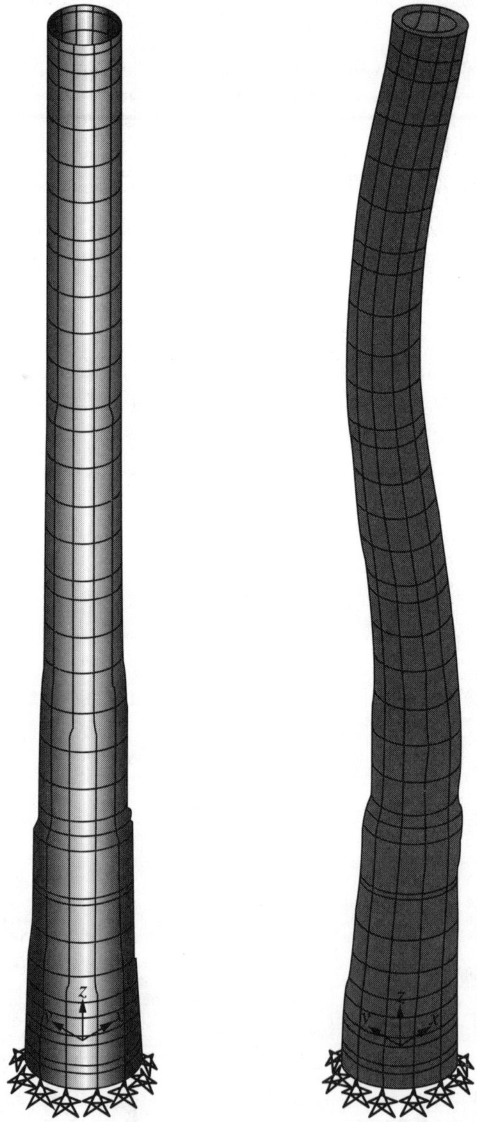

(a) Initial shape (b) Dynamic deflected shape

Figure 1.13 RC Chimney.

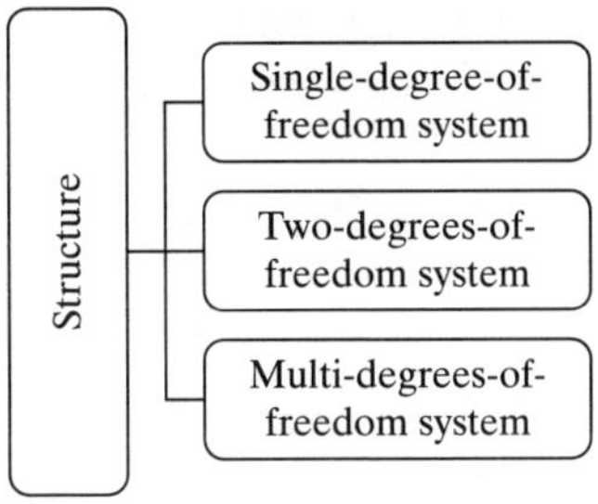

Figure 1.14 Classification of a structure for dynamic analysis.

A structure can be classified according to its degrees-of-freedom for dynamic analysis as shown in Figure 1.14, irrespective of whether it is a discrete system or a distributed system.

1.4 LAWS OF EQUILIBRIUM

In the static analysis of a structure, static equilibrium must be satisfied in order to arrive at a unique solution. It is achieved through the following conditions:

$$\sum F_x = 0, \sum F_y = 0, \sum F_z = 0, \sum M_x = 0, \sum M_y = 0, \sum M_z = 0 \tag{1.4}$$

Similarly, in dynamic analysis of a structure, equilibrium must be satisfied at each time instant. This can be accomplished with the help of *Newton's second law of motion*. The objective of dynamic analysis is to evaluate the displacement–time history of a structure when subjected to a given dynamic load. In most cases, considering only a limited degrees-of-freedom of a structure will give reasonably accurate results. The problem is reduced to the determination of time histories of these selected displacement components. The mathematical equations defining the dynamic displacements are called *equations of motion*. Naturally, these degrees of freedom need to be identified carefully.

1.4.1 Newton's Law of Motion

Consider a mass m attached to a massless spring suspended vertically. It has a vertical stiffness of k. In its unstretched position, the system is shown in Figure 1.15(a). Under its own weight, the system stretches by an amount Δ_{st} as shown in Figure 1.15(b). If the mass is pulled down by an amount x (Figure 1.15(c)) and released, the system will be subjected to vibrations. Let us consider the equilibrium of the system:

For equilibrium of Figure 1.15(b), $$k\,\Delta_{st} = mg = W \tag{1.5}$$

Let us consider the free body diagram of a system shown in Figure 1.15(c), and write the equilibrium equation by making use of Newton's second law, that is, *rate of change of momentum is proportional to the force applied on the body*,

$$\frac{d}{dt}\left(m\frac{dx}{dt}\right) = p(t) \tag{1.6a}$$

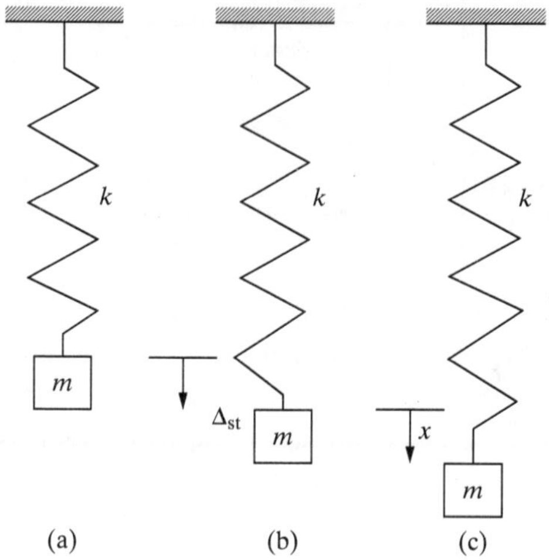

Figure 1.15 Simple spring mass system.

or, for most problems in structural dynamics, it may be assumed that mass m does not vary with time, that is,

$$m\frac{d}{dt}\left(\frac{dx}{dt}\right)=m\frac{d^2x}{dt^2}=p(t) \tag{1.6b}$$

or,
$$m\ddot{x}(t)=p(t)=mg-k\left(\Delta_{st}+x(t)\right) \tag{1.7}$$

where,
$$\ddot{x}=\text{acceleration}=\frac{d^2x}{dt^2}$$

Making use of Equation (1.5), Equation (1.7) can be written as

$$m\ddot{x}(t)+kx(t)=0 \tag{1.8}$$

Equation (1.8) can again be written as follows by dividing by m.

$$\ddot{x}(t)+\omega^2x(t)=0 \tag{1.9}$$

where,
$$\omega^2=k/m$$

or,
$$\omega=\sqrt{\frac{k}{m}} \tag{1.1d}$$

ω = undamped natural frequency of vibration in radian/sec

Equation (1.8) shows that 'mg' and $k\,\Delta_{st}$ neutralize at all instants. Therefore, we need to consider only the forces which have come into effect beyond the static equilibrium position. Thus, Equations (1.8) and (1.9) are referred to as the *equations of motion* of an *undamped SDOF system* under *free vibrations*. It is relatively easy to estimate *mass* of a structure. The challenge is to estimate its *stiffness* corresponding to the desired degrees of freedom.

1.4.2 D' Alembert's Principle

The same equation of motion can be obtained by using D' Alembert's principle. It states that:

A body which is not in static equilibrium by virtue of some acceleration which it possesses can be brought to static equilibrium by introducing on it the inertia forces which can be considered to be an extra external force. This inertia force is equal to mass times the acceleration of the body and acts through the centre of gravity of the body in the direction opposite to that of the acceleration. That is,

$$p(t) - f_I = 0 \tag{1.10a}$$

or,

$$p(t) - m\frac{d^2x}{dt^2} = 0 \tag{1.10b}$$

The mass develops an inertia force proportional to acceleration and opposes the acceleration of the mass, that is, dynamic motion. It is a very important concept in structural dynamics and permits the equation of motion to be expressed as equations of dynamic equilibrium. The force term $p(t)$ includes many types of forces acting on the mass such as, elastic force that opposes the displacement, viscous force that opposes the velocity, and other such loads. In a free vibration case, damping force is responsible for bringing the system to rest.

Equation (1.10a) may be written as follows:

$$p(t) - f_S - f_D - f_I = 0 \tag{1.11a}$$

or,

$$f_I + f_D + f_S = p(t) \tag{1.11b}$$

or,

$$m\frac{d^2x}{dt^2} + f_D + f_S = p(t) \tag{1.11c}$$

where, f_D = damping force

f_S = elastic force

Equation (1.11b) or (1.11c) is referred to as the *Equation of Motion.*

1.4.3 Principle of Virtual Displacement

Sometimes the structural system is quite complicated and it may be difficult to write equations of equilibrium involving all the forces acting on the system. In such a scenario, it may be helpful to make use of the principle of virtual work or virtual displacement. It may be stated as follows:

If a body is in equilibrium under a force system and remains in equilibrium while it is subjected to a small virtual displacement, the virtual work done by the external forces is equal to the virtual work done by the internal stresses due to those forces.

The imposed virtual displacements have to be compatible with the boundary conditions. Since the net work done due to the virtual displacement is zero, this statement is equivalent to that of a dynamic equilibrium. There is a need to identify all the forces acting on the various masses of the system. Next, equations of motion are obtained by introducing virtual displacements corresponding to each degree of freedom and equating the virtual work to zero. The inherent advantage of this method is that a virtual work is a scalar quantity whereas various forces acting on the structure are vector quantities. It is easy to work with scalars rather than with vectors.

1.5 TYPES OF DYNAMIC LOADING

There can be different types of dynamic loads on any structure such as:

(a) Harmonic load
(b) Periodic load
(c) Impulse load
(d) Earthquake load
(e) Wind load
(f) Blast load
(g) Tornado
(h) Missile or aircraft impact load
(i) Sea wave load

The last four types of loads are not discussed in the present text. Various loads are shown in Figure 1.16. It will be noticed that earthquake and wind loads are essentially

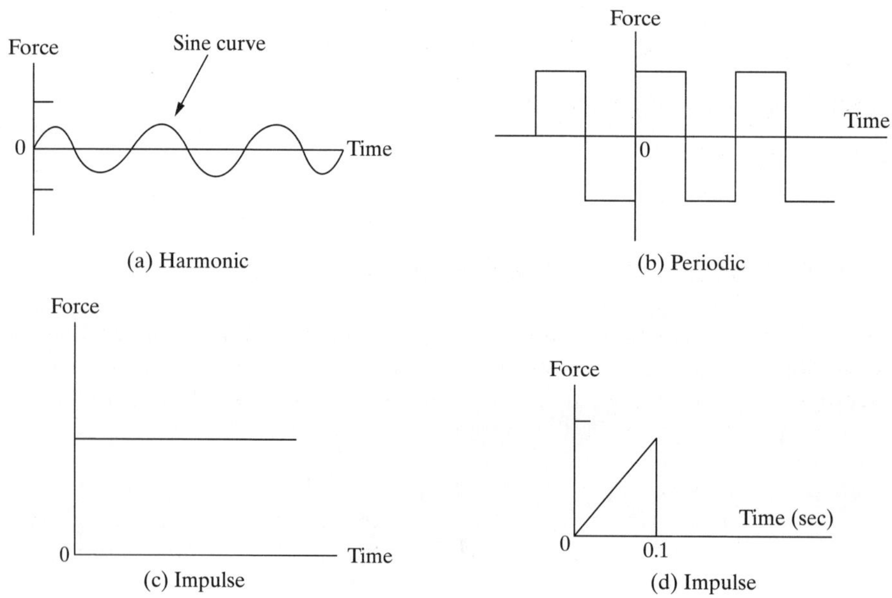

Figure 1.16 Type of dynamic loads.

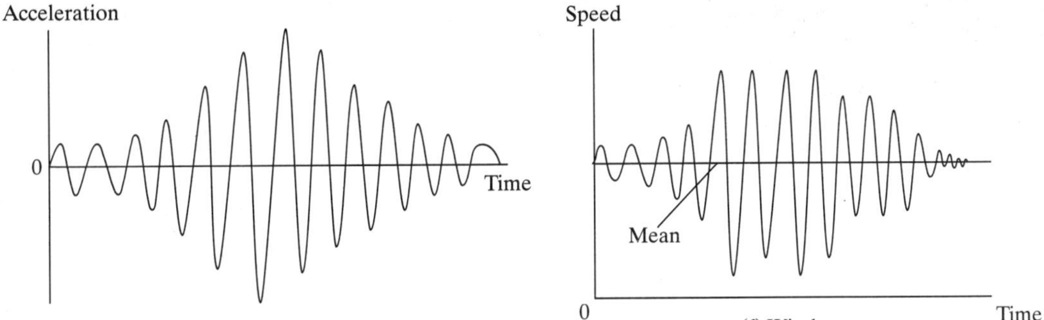

(e) Earthquake

(f) Wind

Figure 1.16 (Continued)

random loads. It means these loads are neither repeatable nor it is possible to represent them through a simple mathematical equation. Every time there is a wind load or an earthquake at a given location, it will be different from that recorded previously. Earthquake loads are *transient* in nature. It means it is a short duration load. It may last from a few seconds to a few minutes.

The above description of dynamic loads is very helpful in learning fundamentals of dynamics of structures. Harmonic load is simplest to visualize and understand. It is also easy to understand and appreciate the response of a structure subjected to a harmonic load. The other loads become more complex and, therefore, corresponding response of a structure also becomes more complex and difficult to visualize.

1.6 SOLUTION OF EQUATION OF MOTION

There are various methods to solve a second-order differential equation or a set of such equations depending upon the type of loading. Sometimes, it may be necessary to represent a loading in terms of Fourier series. For simple cases, these equations can be solved using the principles of differential calculus. For other cases, help may be taken from Green's function, Duhamel integral, eigenvalue problems, or various numerical integration schemes. These solution techniques will be discussed throughout the book.

MATLAB, owned by The MathWorks, Inc., USA, is a high-performance language for technical computing which integrates computation, visualization and programming in an easy-to-use environment. MATLAB is an interactive system and stands for *MATRIX LABORATORY*. It is the most powerful and user friendly tool to study dynamics of structures and will be discussed in detail.

Alternatively, PYTHON, a free and open source software can be used. It was created in early 1990s. PYTHON makes use of NumPy library to work with arrays. It is equally powerful software.

1.7 ILLUSTRATIVE EXAMPLES

Example 1.1

A simply supported beam of length L carries a mass m at its midspan as shown in Figure 1.17. The beam is massless. Write its equation of motion.

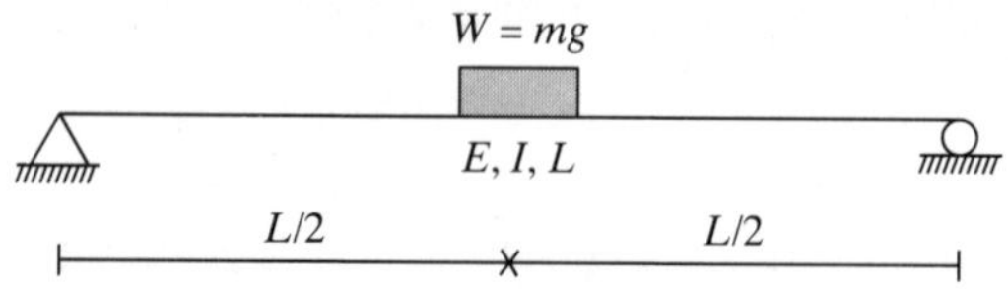

Figure 1.17 Simple supported beam.

Solution

Let us determine the flexure stiffness of the beam. It is carrying a load $W = mg$ at its midspan. It is known that under the vertical load W at its midspan, the vertical deflection is given by:

$$\Delta = \frac{WL^3}{48\text{EI}}$$

Thus, flexure stiffness of beam is given by

$$k = \frac{W}{\Delta} = \frac{48\text{EI}}{\text{L}^3}$$

The equation of motion of the beam is

$$m\ddot{x} + kx = 0 \tag{1.8}$$

or,

$$m\ddot{x} + \frac{48EI}{L^3}x = 0$$

□

Example 1.2

A cantilever beam of length L carries a mass m at its free end suspended by a spring of stiffness k as shown in Figure 1.18. The beam and spring are massless. Write the equation of motion.

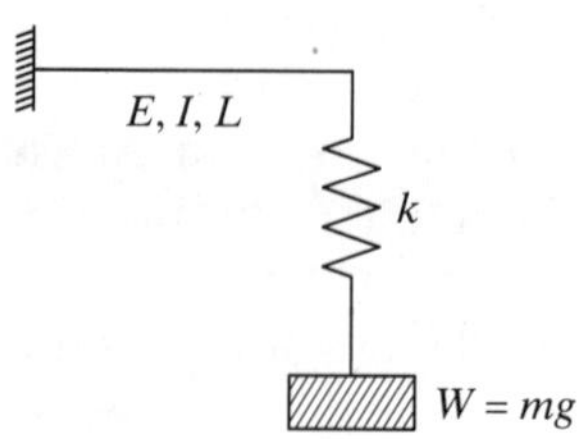

Figure 1.18 Cantilever beam with loading at free end.

Solution

In this problem, it is important to understand deflected shape of the system under different situations. Under the weight W, the beam will deflect and the spring to which this weight is attached will also elongate. Let the deflection of beam alone is x_1 and that of the spring alone is x_2 due to weight W as shown in Figure 1.19(a). Thus,

$$x_{\text{static}} = x_1 + x_2 \tag{i}$$

The same deflection can be measured from the unstretched position of both beam and spring as shown in Figure 1.19(b) for convenience. Let us now consider the free body diagram of the mass. The equilibrium condition gives

$$W = mg = k_e x_{\text{static}} \tag{ii}$$

where,

k_e = effective vertical stiffness of the beam and spring system

The deflections x_1 and x_2 can be written as follows:

$$x_1 = \frac{W}{k_{\text{beam}}} = \frac{W}{\dfrac{3EI}{L^3}} \tag{iii}$$

and

$$x_2 = \frac{W}{k} \tag{iv}$$

equation (i) can be written as:

$$\frac{W}{k_e} = \frac{W}{k_{\text{beam}}} + \frac{W}{k}$$

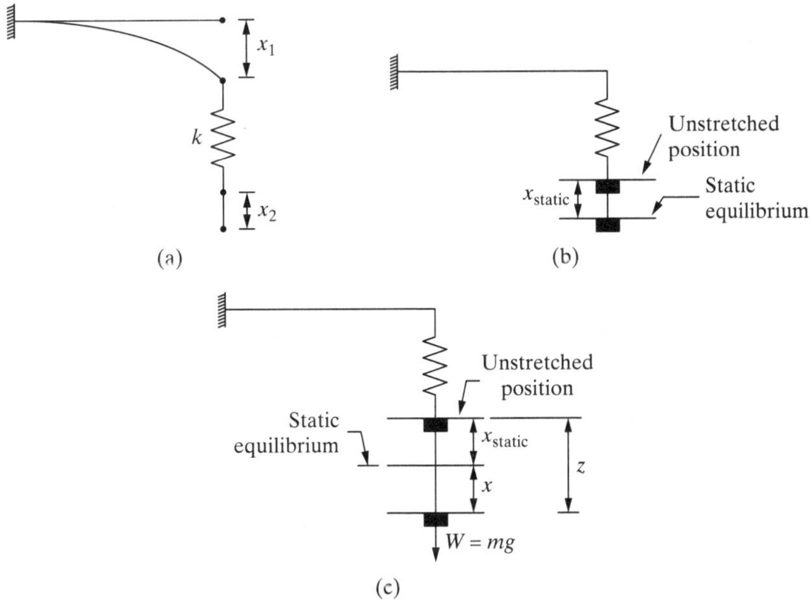

Figure 1.19 Deflected positions under different conditions.

or,

$$k_e = \frac{k_{\text{beam}} k}{k_{\text{beam}} + k} \tag{v}$$

If the mass is given a small displacement x from its static equilibrium position and then released gently, the mass will set in motion and will begin to vibrate. Its free body diagram is shown in Figure 1.19(c). The equation of dynamic equilibrium can be written as follows:

$$m\ddot{x} = mg - k_e z \tag{vi}$$

$$m\ddot{x} = mg - k_e \left(x_{\text{static}} + x\right) \tag{vii}$$

Making use of Equation (ii), Equation (vii) can be written as follows:

$$m\ddot{x} + k_e x = 0 \tag{viii}$$

This is the equation of motion where the effective stiffness k_e is given by Equation (v). It can be seen that the static displacement under the weight W does not appear in the equation of motion. Same conclusion was arrived at while writing the equation of motion for a simple spring and mass system. □

Example 1.3

Two springs are connected in series and are subjected to an axial load P_0 as in Figure 1.20(a). Determine the elongation of each spring and their equivalent stiffness.

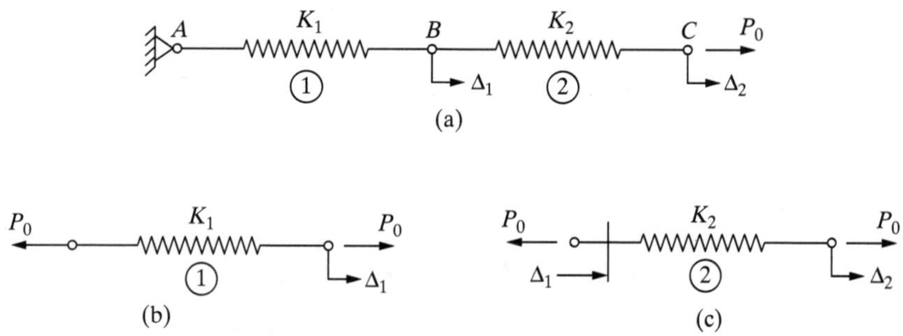

Figure 1.20 Two springs connected in series.

Solution

Let point B elongates by Δ_1 and point C elongates by Δ_2. The free body diagrams of the two springs are shown in Figures 1.20(b) and 1.20(c). The force in each spring remains P_0. Let us write the force-deformation relations:

$$\text{Force} = \text{stiffness} \times \text{displacement}$$

For spring 1,

$$P_0 = K_1 \Delta_1 \tag{i}$$

or

$$\Delta_1 = \frac{P_0}{K_1}$$

if

$$P_0 = 20 \text{ kN}, K_1 = 100 \text{ kN/m and } K_2 = 150 \text{ kN/m}$$

$$\Delta_1 = \frac{20}{100} = 0.2 \text{ m}$$

For spring 2,
The net elongation in spring 2 is $(\Delta_2 - \Delta_1)$,

$$\therefore \quad P_0 = K_2(\Delta_2 - \Delta_1) \tag{ii}$$

or
$$\Delta_2 = \frac{P_0}{K_2} + \Delta_1 \text{ or } \Delta_2 = \frac{20}{150} + 0.2 = 0.333 \text{ m}$$

To obtain the equivalent spring stiffness, let us rearrange Equations (i) and (ii),

$$\Delta_2 = \frac{P_0}{K_1} + \frac{P_0}{K_2} \text{ and } \Delta_2 = \frac{P_0}{K_{eq}}$$

or,
$$K_{eq} = \frac{K_1 K_2}{K_1 + K_2} \tag{iii}$$

Thus, springs 1 and 2 can be replaced with a single spring whose stiffness is given by Equation (iii), which will give the same displacement. □

Example 1.4

A two springs system shown in Figure 1.21 is subjected to an axial load P_0. Determine the forces produced in the two springs and displacement of joint B.

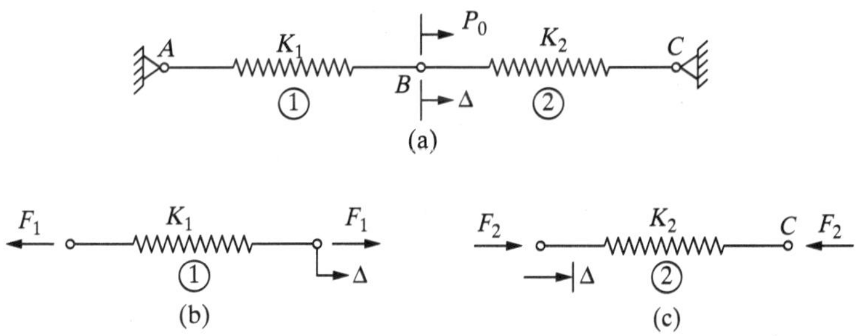

Figure 1.21 Two springs connected in parallel.

Solution

Let forces produced in the two springs be F_1 and F_2. The free body diagrams of the springs are shown in Figures 1.21(b) and 1.21(c). The force-deformation relations can be written for the two springs:

$$F_1 = K_1\Delta \quad \text{and} \quad F_2 = K_2\Delta \tag{i}$$

The equilibrium of joint B gives,

$$F_1 + F_2 = P_0 \tag{ii}$$

It may be seen that spring 1 elongates by Δ, whereas spring 2 shortens by the same amount. Substituting the values of F_1 and F_2 in Equation (ii) gives,

$$(K_1 + K_2)\,\Delta = P_0 \text{ or } \Delta = \frac{P_0}{K_1 + K_2}$$

if
$$P_0 = 20 \text{ kN}, K_1 = 100 \text{ kN/m}, K_2 = 150 \text{ kN/m},$$

$$\therefore \Delta = \frac{20}{100 + 150} = 0.08 \text{ m}$$

$$F_1 = 100 \times 0.08 = 8 \text{ kN tension}$$

and $$F_2 = 150 \times (-0.08) = -12 \text{ kN compression}$$ □

Example 1.5

A massless cantilever beam carries a mass m at its free end, and it is connected to two springs having axial stiffness k_1 and k_2 as shown in Figure 1.22. Determine its stiffness and period of vibration.

Solution

Stiffness of the beam due to load applied at its free end $k_b = \dfrac{3\,EI}{L^3}$

If the mass m is displaced vertically by an amount δ, both the springs also undergo the same displacement. Thus, both the springs are in parallel. The equivalent stiffness of beam and both springs is given by

$$k_{eq} = k_b + k_1 + k_2$$

Natural frequency of the system $\omega = \sqrt{\dfrac{k_e}{m}}$

and time period $T = 2\pi\sqrt{\dfrac{m}{k_e}}$ □

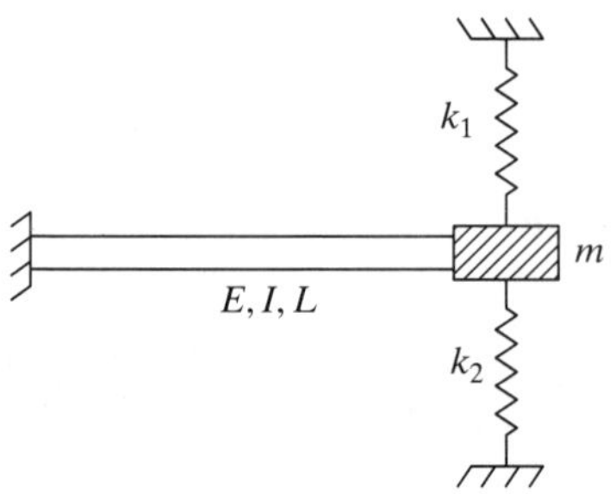

Figure 1.22 Cantilever beam with two springs at the free end.

Example 1.6

A fixed ended massless beam carries a mass m at its midspan suspended through a spring having axial stiffness k_s as shown in Figure 1.23. Determine its stiffness and period of vibration.

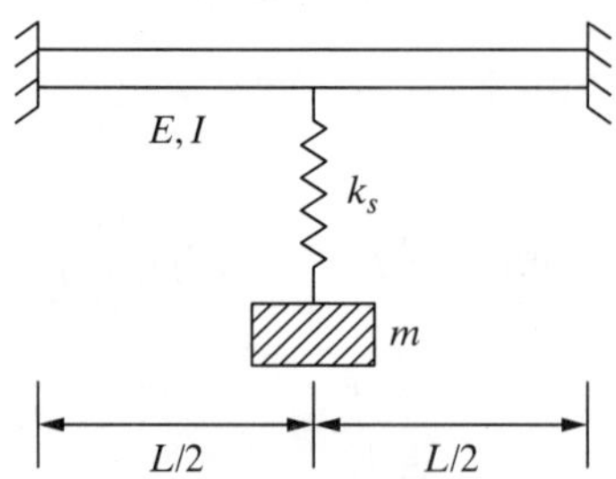

Figure 1.23 Fixed ended beam with a suspended mass.

Solution

Stiffness of the beam due to load applied at its midspan $k = \dfrac{192\,EI}{L^3}$

Effective stiffness of the beam and axial spring k_e is given by

$$\frac{1}{k_e} = \frac{1}{k} + \frac{1}{k_s}$$

or,

$$k_e = \frac{k \times k_s}{k + k_s} \text{ and } T = 2\pi\sqrt{\frac{m}{k_e}}$$ □

Example 1.7

A rigid thin rod has mass m and is supported on an elastic spring and a viscous damper besides being hinged at end A as shown in Figure 1.24. The viscous damping force is represented by a dash-pot at end C. It is subjected to a triangular load. Derive the equation of motion of a structural system.

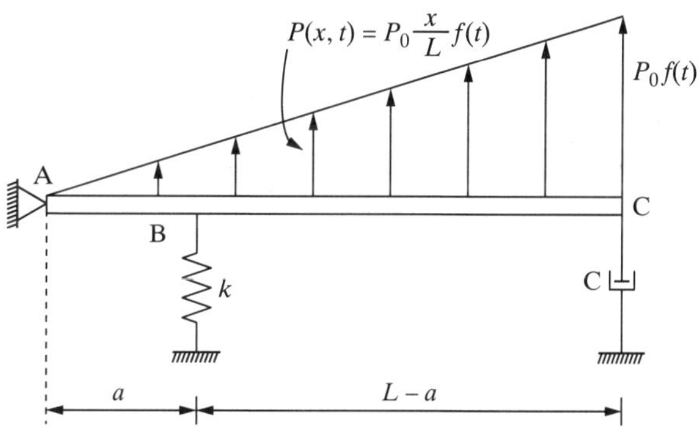

Figure 1.24 A hinged beam supported on spring and damper.

Solution

Let us give a small rotation to the rod and release it gently. It will start vibrating in the vertical plane about hinge A. It has only one-degree-of-freedom, the angular displacement θ. Its free body diagram is shown in Figure 1.25. The various forces generated are as follows:

Mass moment of inertia normal to the rod at its midspan $= \left(\dfrac{mL^2}{12}\right)$

If vertical displacement at C is x, then $x = L\theta,\ \dot{x} = L\dot{\theta},\ \ddot{x} = L\ddot{\theta}$

1. Rotational inertia force $= M_I = \left(\dfrac{mL^2}{12}\right)\ddot{\theta}$
2. Inertia force $= f_I = \dfrac{m(0 + L\ddot{\theta})}{2} = m\dfrac{L\ddot{\theta}}{2}$

   (average lateral displacement undergone by the mass m)
3. Elastic spring forcc $= f_S = ka0$

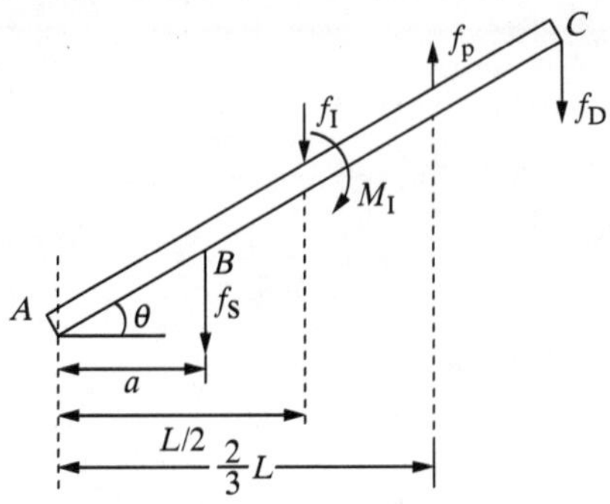

Figure 1.25 Free body diagram.

4. Viscous damping force $= f_D = cL\dot{\theta}$
5. External force $= f_p = P(x,t) = P_0 f(t)\frac{L}{2}$ (= area of the triangle)

The viscous damping force is proportional to velocity. It is a case of damped forced vibrations. Let us consider moment equilibrium by taking moment about A, the centre of rotation:

$$f_P\frac{2L}{3} - f_S a - f_D L - f_I\frac{L}{2} - M_I = 0$$

or, substituting the values,

$$\frac{mL^2}{12}\ddot{\theta} + \frac{mL^2}{4}\ddot{\theta} + cL^2\dot{\theta} + ka^2\theta = \frac{P_0L^2}{3}f(t)$$

The equation of motion becomes

$$\frac{mL^2}{3}\ddot{\theta} + cL^2\dot{\theta} + ka^2\theta = \frac{P_0L^2}{3}f(t)$$

□

Example 1.8

Consider a structure shown in Figure 1.26. A rigid thin bar is supported on two springs and a dashpot system besides being hinged at end A. The rigid rod has mass m. Determine its equation of motion.

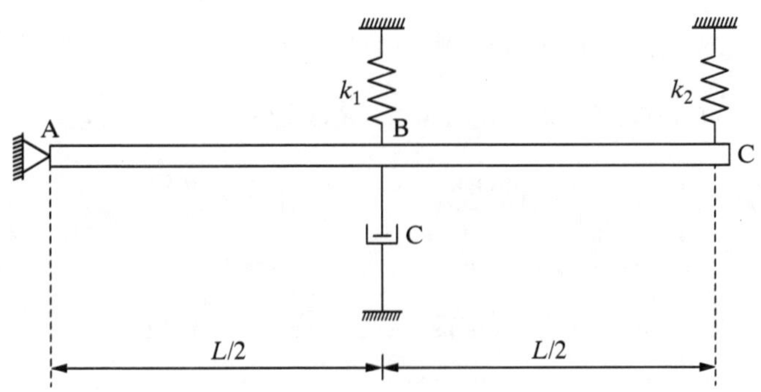

Figure 1.26 A hinged beam supported on damper and suspended from springs.

Solution

Let us give a small rotation to the rod and release it gently. It will start vibrating in the vertical plane about hinge A. It has only one-degree-of-freedom, the angular displacement θ. Its free body diagram is shown in Figure 1.27. The various forces generated are as follows:

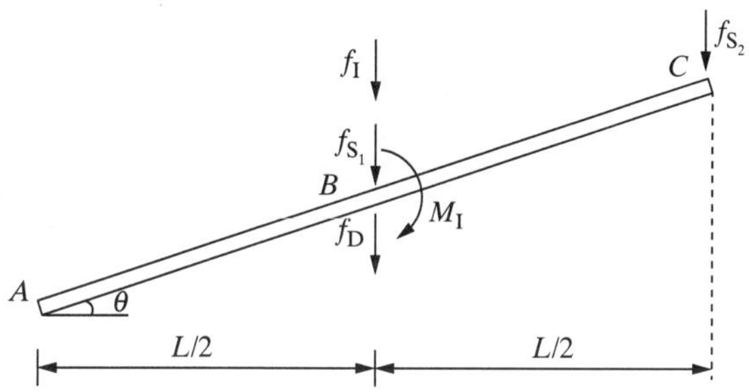

Figure 1.27 Free body diagram.

If the vertical displacement at C is x, then

$$x = L\theta,\ \dot{x} = L\dot{\theta} \text{ and } \ddot{x} = L\ddot{\theta}$$

1. Rotational inertia force $= M_I = \left(\dfrac{mL^2}{12}\right)\ddot{\theta} = \dfrac{mL}{12}\ddot{x}$

2. Inertia force $= f_I = \dfrac{m(0 + L\ddot{\theta})}{2} = \dfrac{mL}{2}\ddot{\theta} = \dfrac{m\ddot{x}}{2}$

3. Elastic spring force $= f_{S_1} = k_1\dfrac{L}{2}\theta = k_1\dfrac{x}{2}$

4. Elastic spring force $= f_{S_2} = k_2L\theta = k_2x$

5. Viscous damping force $= f_D = c\dfrac{L}{2}\dot{\theta} = c\dfrac{\dot{x}}{2}$

The rotational inertia force involves mass moment of inertia. The viscous damping force is proportional to velocity. Let us consider moment equilibrium by taking moment about A, the centre of rotation:

$$M_I + f_I\frac{L}{2} + f_D\frac{L}{2} + f_{S_1}\frac{L}{2} + f_{S_2}L = 0$$

There is no external force on the body. It is a case of damped free vibrations.

Substituting the values,

$$\frac{mL}{12}\ddot{x} + \frac{mL}{4}\ddot{x} + c\frac{L}{4}\dot{x} + k_1\frac{xL}{4} + k_2xL = 0$$

The equation of motion becomes

$$\frac{m}{3}\ddot{x} + \frac{c}{4}\dot{x} + k_1\frac{x}{4} + k_2x = 0$$

□

Example 1.9

A harmonic oscillation test gave the natural frequency of an overhead water tank to be 0.50 Hz. Given that the weight of the tank is 1000 kN, what deflection will result if a 100 kN horizontal load is applied statically? The mass of the tank staging can be neglected.

Solution

Acceleration due to gravity $g = 980$ cm/sec^2 or, 9.80 m/sec^2

$\therefore$ Mass of tank = 1000/g = 1000/9.80 kN-sec^2/m

Natural frequency $\quad f = 0.50$ Hz

or, $\quad \omega = 2\pi f$

Natural frequency $\quad \omega = \sqrt{\dfrac{k}{m}}$

or, $\quad k = m\omega^2$

or, $\quad k = \dfrac{1000}{9.80} \times (2 \times 3.14159 \times 0.5)^2 = 1007$ kN/m

$\therefore$ Lateral displacement $\Delta = P/k = 100/1007 = 0.099$ m or 99 mm □

Example 1.10

A two-hinged portal frame is shown in Figure 1.28. A mass m has been lumped at the roof level. The frame is massless. Ignore axial deformations and damping. Develop its equation of motion.

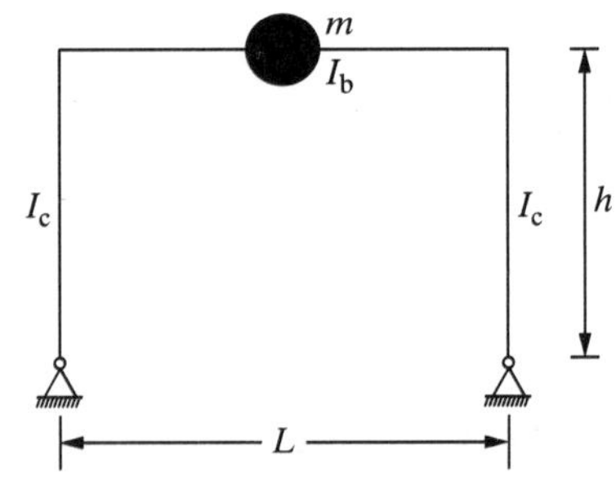

Figure 1.28 Two-hinged portal frame.

Solution

There are three degrees of freedom per node, and therefore, total of eight active degrees of freedom of the frame as shown in Figure 1.29(a). If axial deformations are ignored, the degrees of freedom are reduced to five for static analysis as shown in Figure 1.29(b).

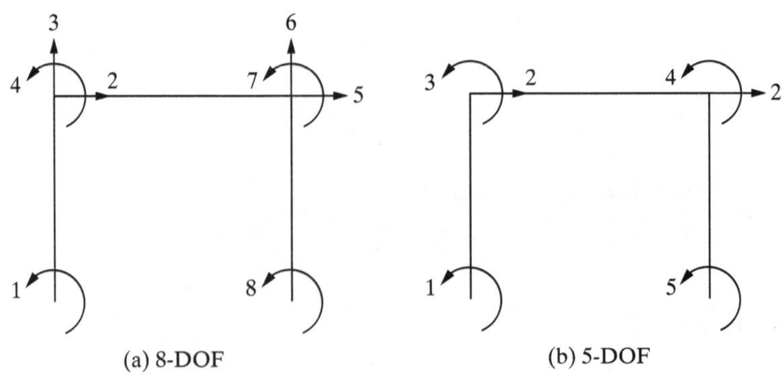

Figure 1.29 Stiffness coefficient computation.

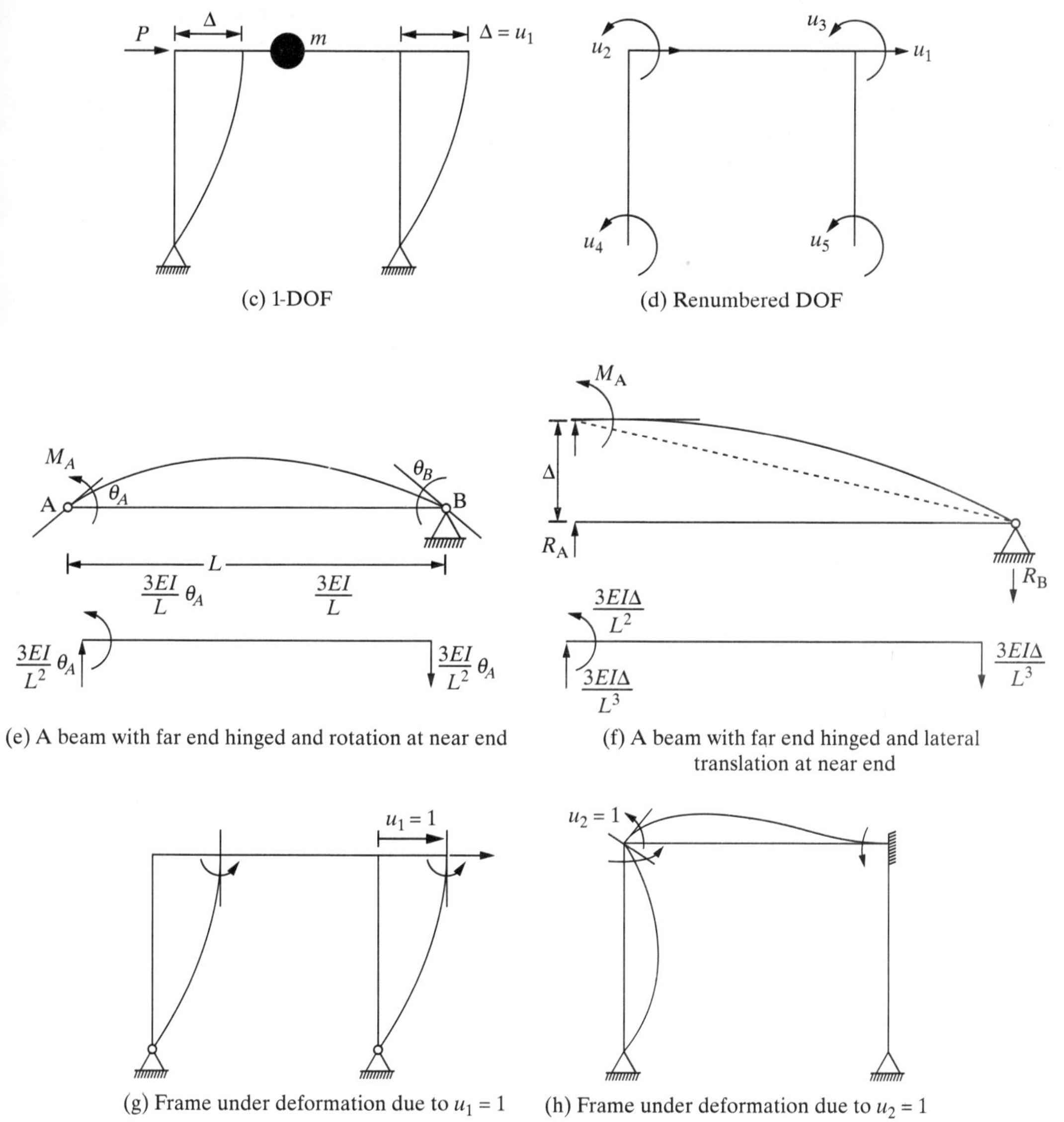

(c) 1-DOF

(d) Renumbered DOF

(e) A beam with far end hinged and rotation at near end

(f) A beam with far end hinged and lateral translation at near end

(g) Frame under deformation due to $u_1 = 1$

(h) Frame under deformation due to $u_2 = 1$

Figure 1.29 (Continued)

A mass has been lumped at the roof level. It can displace only laterally. Therefore, it is a SDOF system for dynamic analysis (Figure 1.29(c)). A lateral load P is applied at its roof level and the corresponding lateral displacement is calculated. Thus, lateral stiffness of the frame can be determined.

Let us determine 3 × 3 stiffness matrix of the structure with respect to the three degrees-of-freedom u_1, u_2 and u_3 as shown in Figure 1.29(d). The rotational degrees of freedom u_4 and u_5 can be ignored without introducing any significant error in the result.

The following two standard results for a beam can be made use of in the derivation of stiffness coefficients for the frame.

In a beam hinged at far end, if a rotation θ_A is applied at the near end while both its translations are restrained, the forces produced are shown in Figure 1.29(e).

Similarly, in a beam hinged at far end, if a lateral displacement Δ is applied at its near end while its rotation and longitudinal translation are restrained, the forces produced are shown in Figure 1.29(f).

Now, it is easy to generate the stiffness coefficients for the frame due to the following three cases:

Case 1: $u_1 = 1, u_2 = 0$, and $u_3 = 0$ (Figures 1.29(d) and 1.29(g))

Compute the coefficients k_{11}, k_{21} and k_{31} making use of the standard results shown in Figure 1.29(f).
We get,

$$k_{11} = 2 \times \frac{3EI_c}{h^3} = \frac{6EI_c}{h^3}$$

$$k_{21} = \frac{3EI_c}{h^2} = k_{31}$$

Case 2: $u_1 = 0, u_2 = 1$, and $u_3 = 0$ (Figures 1.29(d) and 1.29(h))

Compute the coefficients k_{12}, k_{22} and k_{32} making use of the standard results shown in Figure 1.29(e).
We get,

For beam, $$k_{22} = \frac{4EI_b}{L}$$

For column, $$k_{22} = \frac{3EI_c}{h}$$

Total stiffness $$k_{22} = \frac{4EI_b}{L} + \frac{3EI_c}{h}$$

Similarly, $$k_{32} = \frac{2EI_b}{L}$$

and $$k_{12} = \frac{3EI_c}{h^2}$$

Case 3: $u_1 = 0, u_2 = 0$, and $u_3 = 1$ (Figure 1.29(d))

Compute, the coefficients k_{13}, k_{23} and k_{33} making use of the standard results shown in Figure 1.29(e). These are the same as in Case 2.
We get,

$$k_{13} = \frac{3EI_c}{h^2}$$

$$k_{23} = \frac{2EI_b}{L}$$

$$k_{33} = \frac{4EI_b}{L} + \frac{3EI_c}{h}$$

The total stiffness matrix of the structure can be formulated as follows:

$$[K]=\begin{bmatrix} \dfrac{6EI_c}{h^3} & \dfrac{3EI_c}{h^2} & \dfrac{3EI_c}{h^2} \\ \dfrac{3EI_c}{h^2} & \dfrac{4EI_b}{L}+\dfrac{3EI_c}{h} & \dfrac{2EI_b}{L} \\ \dfrac{3EI_c}{h^2} & \dfrac{2EI_b}{L} & \dfrac{4EI_b}{L}+\dfrac{3EI_c}{h} \end{bmatrix}$$

Let us assume:

$$L = 1.5h, I_b = I_c = \mathrm{I}$$

The stiffness matrix of the structure can be written as follows:

$$[K]=\frac{\mathrm{EI}}{h^3}\begin{bmatrix} 6 & 3h & 3h \\ 3h & 5.67h^2 & 1.34h^2 \\ 3h & 1.34h^2 & 5.67h^2 \end{bmatrix}$$

The force-deformation relation for the portal frame can be written as follows:

$$[K]\{\Delta\}=\{P\}$$

or,

$$\Delta=\begin{Bmatrix} u_1 \\ u_2 \\ u_3 \end{Bmatrix} \text{ and } P=\begin{Bmatrix} P_1 \\ P_2 \\ P_3 \end{Bmatrix}=\begin{Bmatrix} P \\ 0 \\ 0 \end{Bmatrix}$$

Let us solve for Δ.

$$\frac{EI}{h^3}\begin{bmatrix} 6 & 3h & 3h \\ 3h & 5.67h^2 & 1.34h^2 \\ 3h & 1.34h^2 & 5.67h^2 \end{bmatrix}\begin{Bmatrix} u_1 \\ u_2 \\ u_3 \end{Bmatrix}=\begin{Bmatrix} P \\ 0 \\ 0 \end{Bmatrix}$$

The u_2 and u_3 DOFs can be eliminated by static condensation or their values can be determined in terms of u_1.

$$\begin{bmatrix} 5.67 & 1.34 \\ 1.34 & 5.67 \end{bmatrix}\begin{Bmatrix} u_2 \\ u_3 \end{Bmatrix}=-\frac{3}{h}\begin{Bmatrix} 1 \\ 1 \end{Bmatrix}u_1$$

We get,

$$\begin{Bmatrix} u_2 \\ u_3 \end{Bmatrix}=-\frac{0.428}{h}\begin{Bmatrix} 1 \\ 1 \end{Bmatrix}u_1$$

or,

$$3.432\frac{EI}{h^3}u_1 = P$$

or,

$$k=\frac{P}{u_1}=3.432\frac{EI}{h^3}$$

The equation of motion of the portal frame is given by

$$m\ddot{x} + kx = 0$$

or,

$$m\ddot{x} + 3.432\frac{EI}{h^3}x = 0$$ □

Example 1.11

Derive the stiffness matrix of the inverted L-frame shown in Figure 1.30(a).

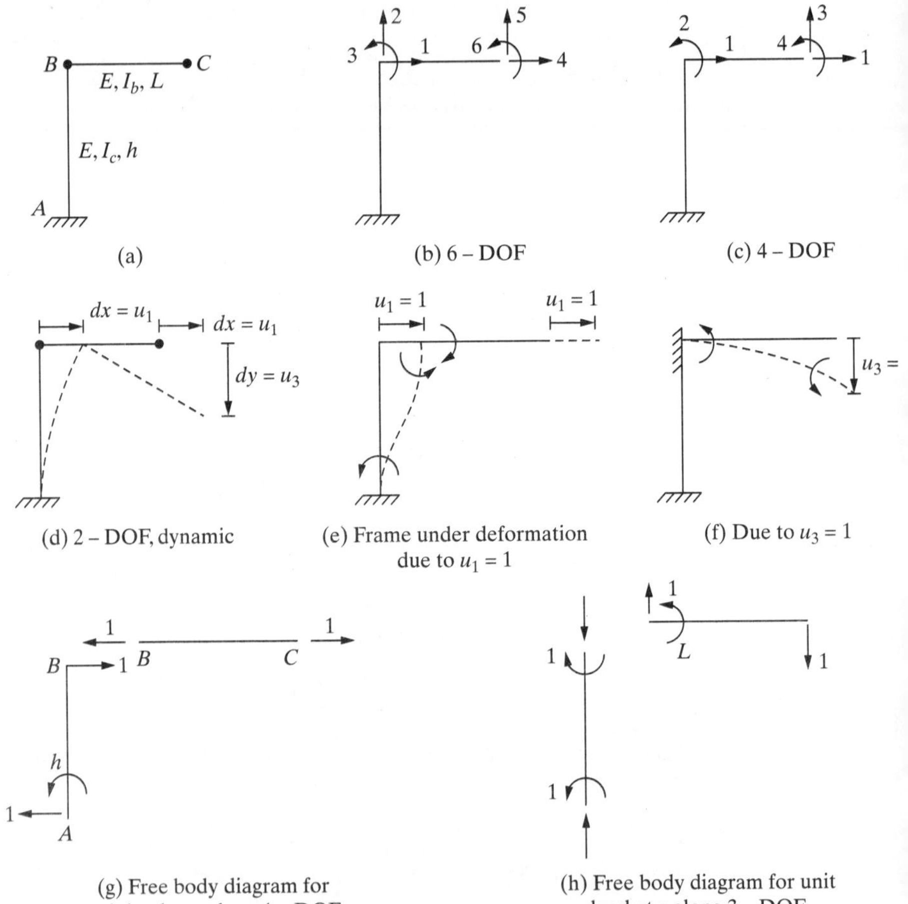

Figure 1.30 L-frame – Stiffness coefficient computation

There are three degrees of freedom at each node. The frame has six active DOF as shown in Figure 1.30(b). If axial deformations are ignored, there are four DOF for static analysis as shown in Figure 1.30(c). Two masses are lumped at B and C each. The rotational DOF can be ignored. Thus, it has two dynamic degrees of freedom as shown in Figure 1.30(d). It will be convenient to determine its flexibility matrix corresponding to each of the two DOF as shown in Figure 1.30(e) and 1.30(f). This is a *statically determinate frame*, therefore, the unit load method can be used to determine its flexibility matrix.

Deflection at any point in a desired direction can be estimated using the following equation:

$$\Delta = \int_0^L \frac{Mm\,dx}{EI}$$

Where,

M = bending moment due to external loads

m = moment due to unit load applied at the section and in the desired direction where deflection is desired

EI = flexural rigidity

Flexibility matrix is given by

$$[F] = \begin{bmatrix} f_{11} & f_{12} \\ f_{21} & f_{22} \end{bmatrix}$$

f_{11} = deflection at C, along 1-DOF due to unit load applied at C along 1-DOF
f_{21} = deflection at C, along 2-DOF due to unit load applied at C along 1-DOF
f_{22} = deflection at C along 2-DOF due to unit load applied at C along 2-DOF
Let $h = L$ and $I_b = I_c = I$ for convenience,
The influence coefficients are computed as follows:

$$f_{11} = \frac{L^3}{3EI},\quad f_{12} = \frac{L^3}{2EI},\quad f_{22} = \frac{4L^3}{3EI}$$

Thus,

$$[F] = \frac{L^3}{EI}\begin{bmatrix} \frac{1}{3} & \frac{1}{2} \\ \frac{1}{2} & \frac{4}{3} \end{bmatrix} = \frac{L^3}{6EI}\begin{bmatrix} 2 & 3 \\ 3 & 8 \end{bmatrix}$$

The stiffness matrix is inverse of the $[F]$.

$$[K] = \frac{6EI}{7L^3}\begin{bmatrix} 8 & -3 \\ -3 & 2 \end{bmatrix}$$

Example 1.12

Derive the stiffness matrix of the inverted L-frame shown in Figure 1.31(a).

Solution

There are three degrees of freedom at each node. The frame has five active DOF as shown in Figure 1.31(b). If axial deformations are ignored, there are three DOF for static analysis as shown in Figure 1.31(c). One mass is lumped at B. The rotational DOF can be ignored. Thus, it has one dynamic degree of freedom as shown in Figure 1.31(d). It will be convenient to determine its deflection corresponding to 1-DOF as shown in Figure 1.31(e). This is a *statically indeterminate frame*, therefore, the slope-deflection method can be used to determine the displacement along 1-DOF. The slope-deflection equations are as follows: Let $h = L$ and $I_c = I_b = I$ for convenience.

$$M_{AB} = \frac{2EI}{L}\left[2\theta_A + \theta_B - \frac{3\Delta}{L}\right] \quad \text{(i)}$$

$$M_{BA} = \frac{2EI}{L}\left[\theta_A + 2\theta_B - \frac{3\Delta}{L}\right] \quad \text{(ii)}$$

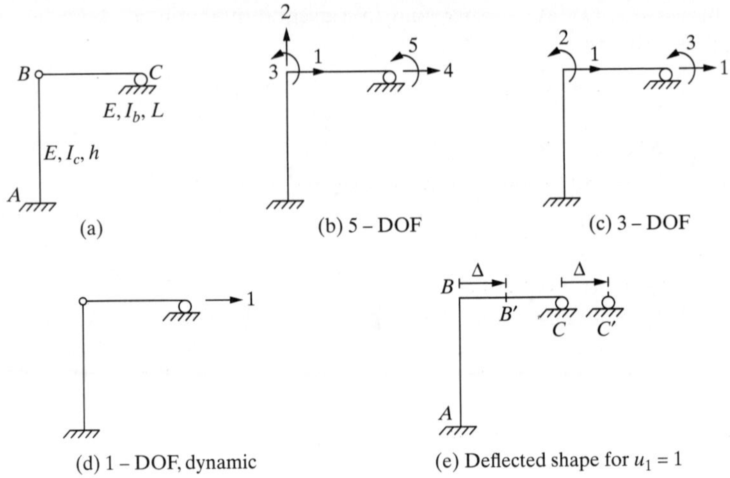

Figure 1.31 L-frame – Stiffness coefficient computation

$$M_{BC} = \frac{2EI}{L}[2\theta_B + \theta_C] \tag{iii}$$

$$M_{CB} = \frac{2EI}{L}[\theta_B + 2\theta_C] \tag{iv}$$

For joint equilibrium,

$$\Sigma M_B = 0; \Sigma M_C = 0; \text{also, } \theta_A = 0 \text{ being a fixed end}$$

We get,

$$\frac{2EI}{L}\left[4\theta_B + \theta_C - \frac{3\Delta}{L}\right] = 0 \tag{v}$$

and

$$\frac{2EI}{L}[\theta_B + 2\theta_C] = 0 \tag{vi}$$

Shear equation gives,

$$\frac{M_{AB} + M_{BA}}{L} + 1 = 0$$

or,

$$\frac{2EI}{L^2}\left[3\theta_B - \frac{6\Delta}{L}\right] + 1 = 0 \tag{vii}$$

Upon solving, Equation (v) and (vi), we get,

$$\theta_B = -2\theta_C \text{ and } \theta_C = -\frac{3}{7}\frac{\Delta}{L}$$

Substituting in Equation (vii) gives,

$$\Delta = -\frac{7}{48}\frac{L^3}{EI}$$

Ignoring the –ve sign as it indicates the direction, the stiffness is

$$k = \frac{48}{7}\frac{EI}{L^3}$$

REVIEW QUESTIONS

1.1 What do you understand by a dynamic load? What are the various sources of excitation for a structure?

1.2 Discuss the nature of different types of excitations.

1.3 What is the purpose of carrying out a dynamic analysis? What information is obtained from time-history analysis of a structure?

1.4 Explain the following terms:

(a) Amplitude

(b) Frequency of vibration

(c) Time period

(d) Resonance

(e) Free vibrations

(f) Forced vibrations

1.5 What is a simple harmonic motion? Discuss the Newton's second law of motion.

1.6 What is an inverted pendulum? Explain with examples.

1.7 Differentiate between static degrees-of-freedom and dynamic degrees-of-freedom with neat sketches.

1.8 What is an equation of motion of a simple pendulum?

1.9 Given the stiffness and mass of a pendulum, how do you estimate its natural frequency of vibration and natural period of vibration. What are the S.I. units of mass and stiffness?

1.10 What is the relationship between frequency of vibration and natural period of vibration?

1.11 How the natural frequency varies with increase in stiffness of a system?

1.12 How 0the natural frequency varies with increase in mass of a system?

1.13 How the natural period varies with increase in stiffness of a system?

1.14 How do you define an inertia force? Derive the relation between kg and Newton?

1.15 What is a single-degree-of-freedom system? Discuss its physical and mathematical models.

1.16 State the D' Alembert's principle. Hence, derive the equation of motion of free vibration of a single-degree-of-freedom system.

1.17 What do you understand by continuum and discrete modelling of a simple beam? Discuss their mode shapes.

PROBLEMS

1.1. A mass of 20 kg when suspended from a spring causes a static deflection of 1 cm. Find natural frequency of the system.

Ans: $\omega = 31.30$ rad/sec

1.2. A spring mass system has spring stiffness of 'k' N/m and mass 'm' kg. Its natural frequency of vibration is 10 Hz. An extra 4 kg mass is coupled to 'm' and the natural frequency reduces by 2 Hz. Determine 'k' and 'm'.

1.3 A SDOF system having mass m and stiffness k vibrates with a natural frequency of 20 Hz. If the stiffness is decreased by 1500 N/m, the natural frequency is decreased by 25%. Determine the mass and stiffness of the original system.

Ans: $m = 0.217$ kg, $k = 3428$ N/m

1.4. A mass 'm' is suspended from a spring system as shown in Figure P1.1. Determine natural frequency of the system. Also, derive an expression for equivalent stiffness of the system.

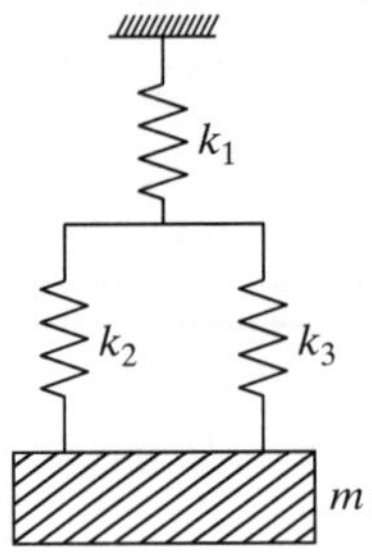

Figure P1.1

Ans: $k_{equ} = \dfrac{k_1(k_2 + k_3)}{(k_1 + k_2 + k_3)}$

1.5. A mass m is suspended through a system of three springs k_1, k_2, and k_3 as shown in Figure P1.2. The spring k_3 is attached to a rigid massless bar A at its midspan. Determine the equivalent stiffness of the system and its natural frequency.

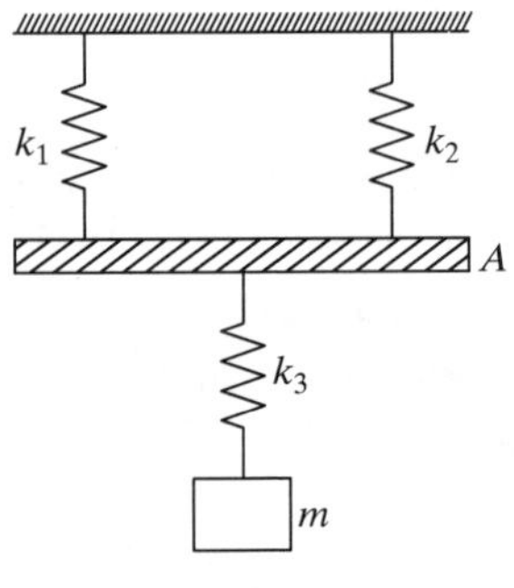

Figure P1.2

Hint: *(i) Two springs are in series if each carries the same force.*

(ii) Two springs are in parallel if each undergoes the same deformation.

1.6 A spring and mass system is shown in Figure P1.3. Estimate its natural frequency.

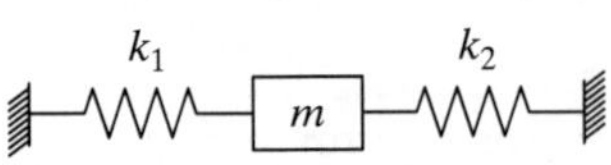

Figure P1.3

Ans: $k_{equ} = k_1 + k_2, \quad \omega = \sqrt{\dfrac{k_1 + k_2}{m}}$

1.7. (a) Develop the equation governing the longitudinal motion of the system shown in Figure P1.4. Estimate its natural frequency. Ignore the mass of the rod and measure x from the static equilibrium position.

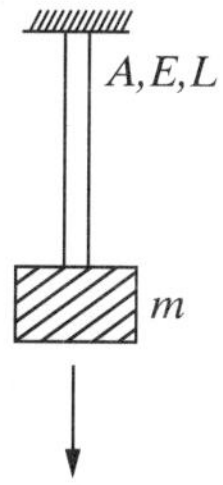

Figure P1.4

(b) If the rod is replaced with a string of length L, estimate the natural frequency of the pendulum.

1.8. Write the equation governing free vibration of the system shown in Figure P1.5, (a) beam is massless and it carries a weight ($W = mg$) at its free end, and (b) beam has a total mass m.

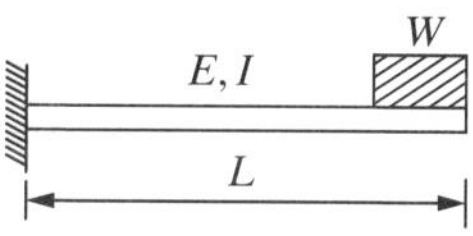

Figure P1.5

Ans: (b) $k = \frac{16}{3}\frac{EI}{L^3}$

1.9. A cylinder of cross-sectional area A and mass m floats in a liquid having a mass density of ρ as shown in Figure P1.6. If the cylinder is pushed by a distance x and released gently, what will be the natural frequency of vibration. Neglect damping effect of the liquid and inertia effect of mass of the displaced liquid.

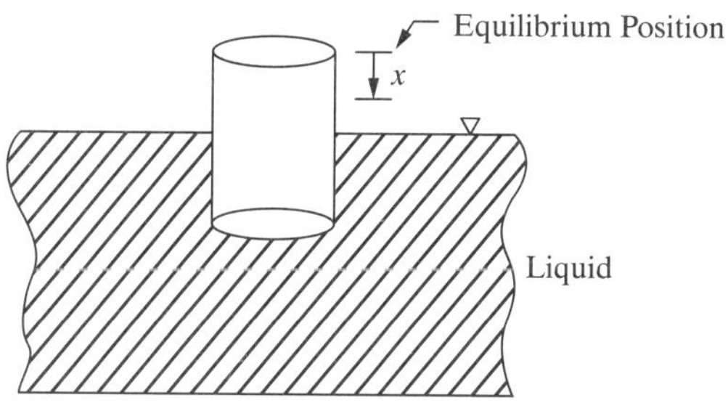

Figure P1.6

Ans: $\omega = \sqrt{\frac{\rho A g}{m}}$

1.10. A spring and mass system is shown in Figure P1.7. Determine the effect of gravity on the natural frequency and equation of motion.

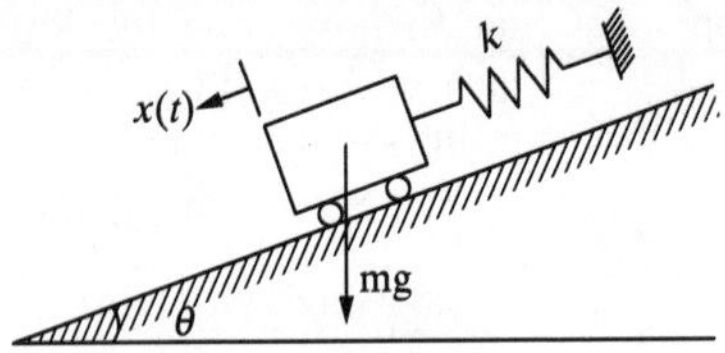

Figure P1.7

1.11. (a) A spring and mass system is shown in Figure P1.8. Assume that the rotation is small so that the spring deflects horizontally and ignore mass of the rod. Determine the frequency of vibration.

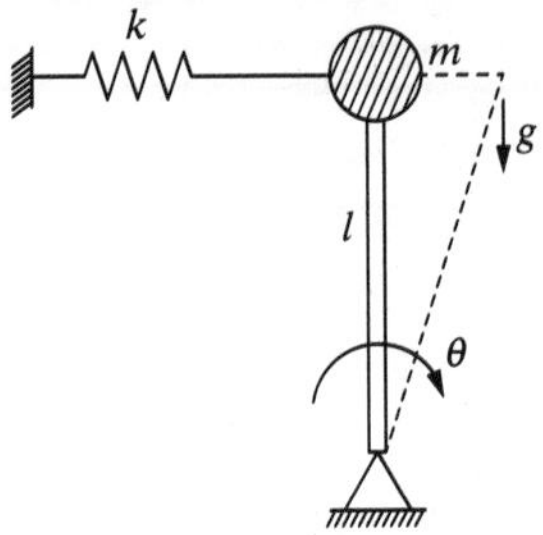

Figure P1.8

(b) If total mass of the rod is m_0, how it will affect the frequency of vibration?

1.12. Write the equation of motion of single-storey portal frame shown in Figure P1.9. Assume that the columns are massless, entire mass of the beam is lumped in the middle as shown and neglect damping.

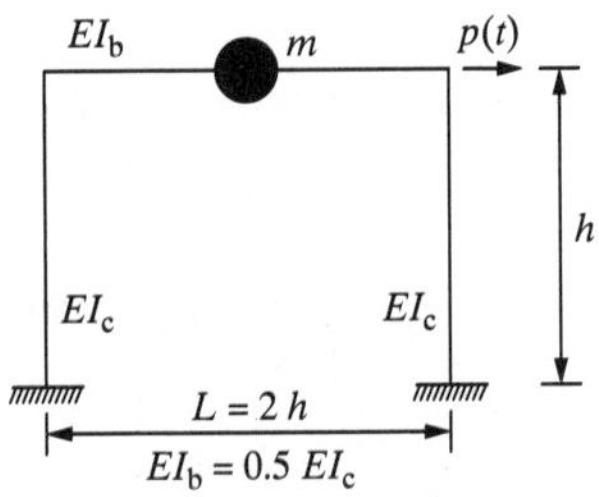

Figure P1.9

Hint: It has three static degrees of freedom and one dynamic degree of freedom. Apply a lateral force P at the beam level and compute lateral sway in the frame using slope–deflection method, or influence coefficient method – generate a 3 × 3 stiffness matrix corresponding to 3 d.o.f. at the beam level neglecting axial deformations. Finally, eliminate the two rotational degrees of freedom using static condensation.

Ans: $k = \dfrac{120}{11}\dfrac{EI}{h^3}$

1.13. A harmonic oscillation test gave the natural frequency of an overhead water tank to be 0.50 Hz. If mass of the tank is 1200 kN, what will be the lateral deflection if a 75 kN horizontal load is applied? You may neglect mass of the staging.

1.14. A 3.5 m high, 6 m wide single-bay single-storey frame is rigidly jointed with a beam of mass 8000 kg and columns of negligible mass and rigidity of $EI_c = 5000$ kNm^2. Calculate the natural frequency and period. Find the force required to deflect the frame 20 mm laterally.

Ans: k = 2.8 × 10^6 N/m, Force = 56 kN

1.15. A frame is shown in Figure P1.10. Assume that the columns are massless, entire mass of the frame is lumped at the roof level, neglect damping and axial deformations. Determine equation of motion of the frame.

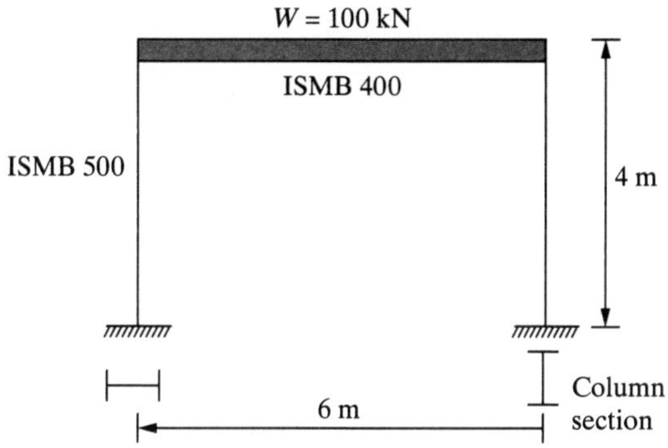

Figure P1.10

Hint: Get the member properties from Indian Standard steel tables.

1.16. A RC frame is shown in Figure P1.11. Determine the lateral stiffness of the frame in the lateral direction considering only tension brace. Neglect axial deformations. Column AB = 20 × 30 cm; Column CD = 25 × 35 cm, Bracc = 15 × 15 cm. Modulus of elasticity of concrete = 25,000 MPa.

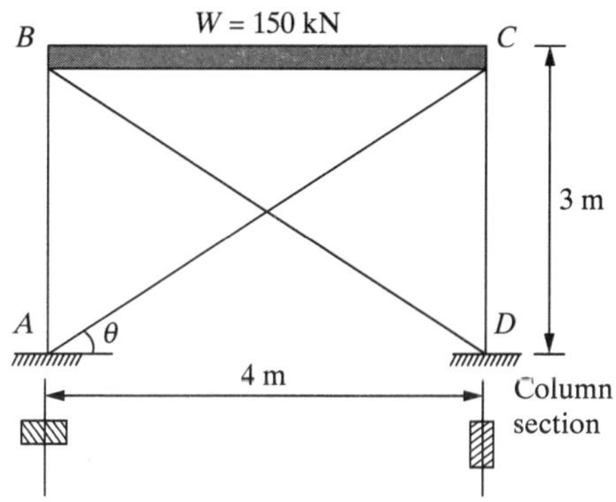

Figure P1.11

Hint: Lateral stiffness of a diagonal brace = $\dfrac{AE}{L}\cos^2\theta$*, where A is area of cross-section, L is length of brace, E is modulus of elasticity of the brace material, and* θ *is the angle a brace makes with horizontal).*

Ans: k_{col} = 10064 kN/m, k_{brace} = 72000 kN/m, k_{eq} = 82064 kN/m

2 Single Degree of Freedom System: Free Vibrations

2.1 INTRODUCTION

It is interesting to analyse a single-degree-of-freedom (SDOF) system as shown in Figure 2.1 when it vibrates freely under its own characteristics, that is, when external force $p(t)$ is absent. Naturally its motion will not be influenced by the nature, frequency and duration of the external force. It is called a *free vibration* analysis. It is assumed that the spring and damper are massless. A damper is also referred to as a dash-pot system. A SDOF system moves over a smooth and frictionless surface represented by rollers in Figure 2.1. Damping plays a very significant role in the dynamic response of a structure by dissipating vibrational energy. Damping is an inherent property of the material used to construct the structure. It does not depend upon the shape and size of the elements.

There can be different source of energy dissipation in a system, that is, damping. If damping is assumed to be proportional to velocity then it is referred to as *viscous damping*. The concept of viscous damping has been found to be quite satisfactory for structural engineering problems. It is possible to represent any other type of damping as an equivalent viscous damping. A system is said to be *underdamped, critically damped or overdamped* and exhibits characteristic vibrations in each of these three states. In this chapter, we will discuss undamped and damped free vibrations along with viscous and Coulomb damping.

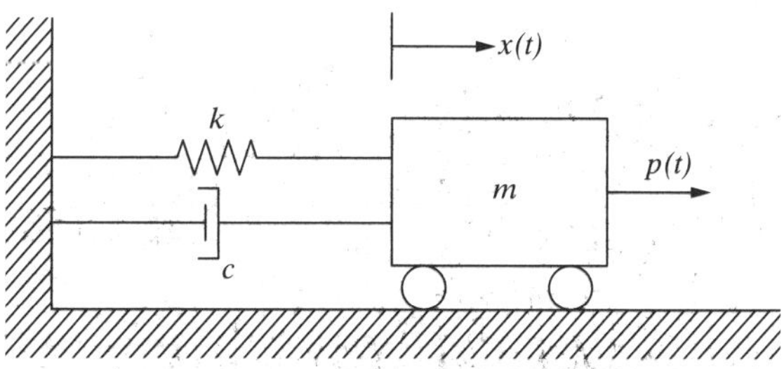

Figure 2.1 A single degree of freedom system.

2.2 SINGLE DEGREE OF FREEDOM SYSTEM (SDOF)

A SDOF system is subjected to an external force $p(t)$ as shown in Figure 2.2(a). The two models shown in Figures 2.1 and 2.2(a) are frequently used to represent the SDOF systems. Its free body diagram is shown in Figure 2.2(b). If this system is subjected to a dynamic force $p(t)$ causing an acceleration $\ddot{x}$, the equation of equilibrium can be written using the Newton's IInd law of motion as follows:

$$f_{\mathrm{I}} = p(t) - f_{\mathrm{D}} - f_{\mathrm{S}} \tag{2.1a}$$

or,

$$f_{\mathrm{I}} + f_{\mathrm{D}} + f_{\mathrm{S}} = p(t) \tag{2.1b}$$

where,

f_{I} = inertia force = $m\ddot{x}(t)$
f_{D} = damping force = $c\dot{x}(t)$
f_{S} = spring force = $kx(t)$
m = mass (in kg)
k = stiffness (in N/m)
c = damping coefficient (in N-sec/m)

It is assumed that the entire mass m is lumped at the floor level in Figure 2.2(a). The damping is represented through a dash-pot system.

Now, Equation (2.1b) can be written as follows:

$$m\,\ddot{x}(t) + c\,\dot{x}(t) + k\,x(t) = p(t) \tag{2.2}$$

This equation is referred to as the general equation of motion of a SDOF system subjected to an external force $p(t)$. Its solution consists of two parts. The first part is known as a complimentary solution or a *transient solution* in structural dynamics problems. The second part is known as a particular integral or a *steady state solution* in structural dynamics problems. The steady state solution depends upon the nature of the forcing function.

For free vibrations, $p(t) = 0$, therefore, the equation of motion becomes:

$$m\ddot{x}(t) + c\,\dot{x}(t) + k\,x(t) = 0 \tag{2.3a}$$

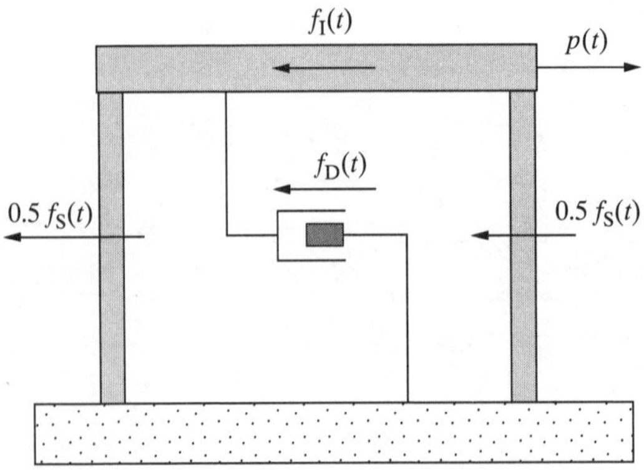

Figure 2.2(a) A single degree of freedom system.

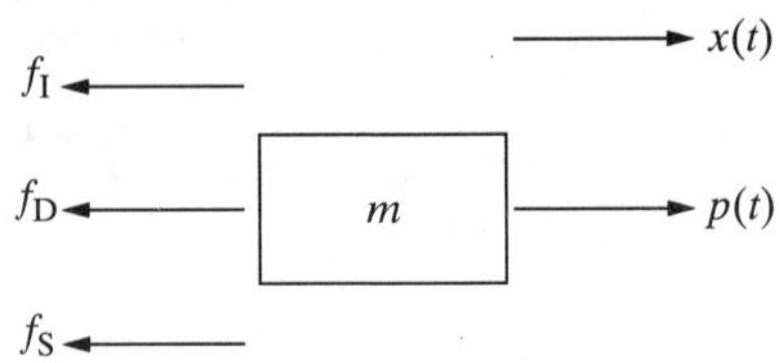

Figure 2.2(b) Free body diagram of mass.

Let its solution is given by $x(t) = Ge^{st}$ (2.4)

Complimentary solution exists but particular integral does not exist for this differential equation because right hand side is zero.

Substituting Equation (2.4) in Equation (2.3a) gives,

$$(ms^2 + cs + k)Ge^{st} = 0$$

either $G = 0, \text{ or } e^{st} = 0$

or, $$s^2 + \frac{c}{m}s + \frac{k}{m} = 0$$

For a non-trivial solution, $Ge^{st} \neq 0$

$\therefore$ $s^2 + \frac{c}{m}s + \frac{k}{m}$ must be zero

or, $$s^2 + \frac{c}{m}s + \omega^2 = 0 \tag{2.5}$$

where, $$\omega = \sqrt{\frac{k}{m}} \tag{2.6}$$

The term ω represents natural frequency of vibration of a SDOF system in radian/sec. The value of s is obtained by solving the quadratic Equation (2.5).

2.2.1 Undamped Free Vibrations

Let us first consider undamped free vibrations, that is, damping is zero.

$$m\,\ddot{x} + k\,x = 0 \tag{2.3b}$$

This is a second order differential equation. Its solution is given by Equation (2.4). Substituting $c = 0$ in Equation (2.5) gives, $s = \pm i\omega$

Its solution can be written in three different manners:

$$x(t) = G_1\,e^{i\omega t} + G_2 e^{-i\omega t} \tag{2.7a}$$

or, $$x(t) = A\sin\omega t + B\cos\omega t \tag{2.7b}$$

or, $$x(t) = G\sin(\omega t + \theta) \tag{2.7c}$$

Let us consider the first solution:

$$x(t) = G_1\,e^{i\omega t} + G_2 e^{-i\omega t}$$

Using the Euler's equation $e^{\pm i\omega t} = \cos\omega t \pm i\sin\omega t$

The solution $x(t)$ can be written as follows:

$$x(t) = G_1(\cos\omega t + i\sin\omega t) + G_2(\cos\omega t - i\sin\omega t)$$

or $$x(t) = (G_1 + G_2)\cos\omega t + i(G_1 - G_2)\sin\omega t$$

or $$x(t) = A\sin\omega t + B\cos\omega t \tag{2.7b}$$

This leads to the second solution.
where,

$$A = i\,(G_1 - G_2) \quad \text{and} \quad B = G_1 + G_2 \tag{2.8a}$$

$$G_2 = (B + i\,A)/2 \quad \text{and} \quad G_1 = (B - i\,A)/2 \tag{2.8b}$$

Thus, G_1 and G_2 are complex conjugate pair, so that both A and B are real numbers.
Let us consider the third solution:

$$x(t) = G\,sin(\omega t + \theta)$$

It can be written as follows:

$$x(t) = G\sin\omega t\cos\theta + G\cos\omega t\sin\theta$$

Let $A = G\cos\theta$ and $B = G\sin\theta$

$$\therefore \quad x(t) = A\sin\omega t + B\cos\omega t \tag{2.7b}$$

$$\therefore G = \sqrt{A^2 + B^2} \quad \text{and} \quad \theta = \tan^{-1}\left(\frac{B}{A}\right) \tag{2.8c}$$

where, G and θ are real valued constants.

Each set of two constants given by Equations (2.8) can be determined knowing the initial conditions, that is, initial displacement $x(0)$ and initial velocity $\dot{x}(0)$ at $t = 0$. Substituting the values of initial conditions in Equation (2.7b) gives,

$$x(0) = B \text{ and } \dot{x}(0) = A\omega \tag{2.8d}$$

The amplitude of displacement is given by

$$G = \sqrt{\left(\frac{\dot{x}(0)}{\omega}\right)^2 + x^2(0)} \tag{2.8e}$$

The phase angle θ is given by

$$\theta = \tan^{-1}\left(\frac{x(0)}{\dot{x}(0)/\omega}\right) \tag{2.8f}$$

Upon differentiating Equation (2.7c), velocity can be obtained:

$$\dot{x}(t) = G\omega\cos(\omega t + \theta) \tag{2.7d}$$

$$\therefore \text{ Maximum velocity } \dot{x}_{max} = G\omega \tag{2.8g}$$

Upon further differentiating Equation (2.7d), acceleration can be obtained:

$$\ddot{x}(t) = -G\omega^2\sin(\omega t + \theta) \tag{2.7e}$$

$$\therefore \text{ Maximum acceleration } \ddot{x}_{max} = G\omega^2 \tag{2.8h}$$

On substituting the values of constants A and B from Equation (2.8d) in Equation (2.7b), we get

$$x(t) = \frac{\dot{x}(0)}{\omega}\sin\omega t + x(0)\cos\omega t \quad (2.9a)$$

where,

$$\omega = 2\pi f, T = \frac{2\pi}{\omega}, f = \frac{1}{T} \quad (2.9b)$$

Upon differentiating Equation (2.9a), velocity can be obtained:

$$\dot{x}(t) = \dot{x}(0)\cos\omega t - x(0)\,\omega\sin\omega t \quad (2.9c)$$

Upon once again differentiating Equation (2.9c), acceleration can be obtained:

$$\ddot{x}(t) = -\,\omega^2 x(t) \quad (2.9d)$$

The displacement, velocity and acceleration terms can be plotted with time to understand the effect of different natural frequencies. Example 2.3 illustrates the vibration characteristics of a system undergoing undamped free vibrations.

2.2.2 Damped Free Vibrations

Let us again consider $s^2 + \frac{c}{m}s + \omega^2 = 0$ (2.5)

Solution is:

$$s = -\frac{c}{2m} \pm \sqrt{\left(\frac{c}{2m}\right)^2 - \omega^2} \quad (2.10)$$

There are three possibilities depending upon the sign of the discriminant;

If the sign is (i) – ve the solution is termed as underdamped system

(ii) 0 the solution is termed as critically damped system

(iii) + ve the solution is termed as over damped system

Let us first consider the second case, that is, critically damped system.

Critically Damped System

In this case no oscillations take place and the system quickly returns to its mean position, that is, of rest.

If $\left(\frac{c}{2m}\right)^2 - \omega^2 = 0$

or, $\frac{c}{2m} = \omega;$

or, $c = c_c = 2m\omega = 2\sqrt{km}$ (2.11)

where, c_c = critical damping

Hence, $$s=-\frac{c}{2m}=-\omega \tag{2.12}$$

Solution is: $$x(t)=(G_1+G_2t)e^{-\omega t} \quad \text{from Equation (2.4)} \tag{2.13}$$

The second term is multiplied by 't' otherwise only a single value of s is available from Equation (2.12). Introducing initial conditions, that is, displacement $x(0)$ and velocity $\dot{x}(0)$ at $t=0$, the final solution is

$$x(t)=\left[x(0)(1+\omega t)+\dot{x}(0)t\right]e^{-\omega t} \tag{2.14}$$

The critically damped vibrations are shown in Figure 2.3. It can be seen that there are no oscillations about the mean position. So, the system quickly returns to rest.

Underdamped System

If damping is less than critical, then it is obvious that $c < 2$ mw and discriminant in Equation (2.10) is –ve.

Let $$\xi=\frac{c}{c_c}=\frac{c}{2mw} \quad \text{damping ratio} \tag{2.15}$$

∴ Equation (2.10) becomes

$$s=-\xi\omega\pm\sqrt{(\xi\omega)^2-\omega^2}$$

or, $$s=-\xi\omega\pm i\,\omega_D \tag{2.16a}$$

where, $$\omega_D=\omega\sqrt{1-\xi^2} \tag{2.16b}$$

ω_D is damped frequency of vibration.

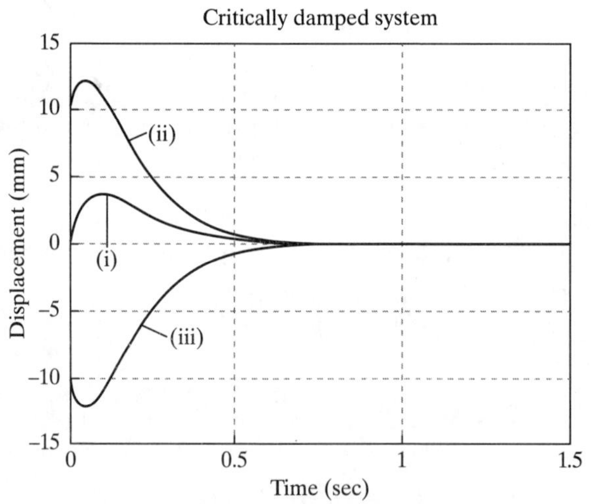

(m = 1 kg, c = 20 Ns/m, k = 100 N/m, (i) $x(0)$ = 0, $\dot{x}(0)$ = 0.1 m/s; (ii) $x(0)$ = 0.01 m, $\dot{x}(0)$ = 0.1 m/s; (iii) $x(0)$ = –0.01 m, $\dot{x}(0)$ = –0.1 m/s)

Figure 2.3 Critically damped system.

For damping ratios to be expected in typical structural systems ($\xi < 20\%$); it differs very little for the undamped frequency as is obvious from Equation (2.16b).

Free vibration response of underdamped system is obtained from Equation (2.4) by substituting the values of s given by Equation (2.16a).

$$\begin{aligned} x(t) &= G_1 e^{(-\xi\omega + i\omega_D)t} + G_2 e^{(-\xi\omega - i\omega_D)t} \\ &= e^{-\xi\omega t}(G_1 e^{i\omega_D t} + G_2 e^{-i\omega_D t}) \end{aligned}$$

It represents a simple harmonic motion

$$x(t) = e^{-\xi\omega t}(\mathrm{A}\sin\omega_D t + \mathrm{B}\cos\omega_D t) \tag{2.17}$$

If $\dot{x}(0)$ and $x(0)$ are initial velocity and displacement, the constants A and B are given by:

$$\mathrm{A} = \frac{x(0)\,\xi\,\omega + \dot{x}(0)}{\omega_D} \quad \text{and} \quad \mathrm{B} = x(0) \tag{2.18a}$$

The final solution is given by

$$x(t) = e^{-\xi\omega t}\left\{\frac{x(0)\xi\omega + \dot{x}(0)}{\omega_D}\sin\omega_D t + x(0)\cos\omega_D t\right\} \tag{2.18b}$$

On differentiating Equation (2.17), the velocity term is obtained:

$$\dot{x}(t) = e^{-\xi\omega t}[-(\mathrm{A}\xi\omega + \mathrm{B}\omega_D)\sin\omega_D t + (\mathrm{A}\omega_D - \mathrm{B}\xi\omega)\cos\omega_D t] \tag{2.18c}$$

Upon once again differentiating, the acceleration term is obtained:

$$\begin{aligned} \ddot{x}(t) = [\{&\mathrm{A}(\xi^2\omega^2 - \omega_D^2) + \mathrm{B}(2\omega\omega_D\xi)\}\sin\omega_D t - \{\mathrm{A}(2\omega\omega_D\xi) \\ &- \mathrm{B}(\xi^2\omega^2 - \omega_D^2)\}\cos\omega_D t] \end{aligned} \tag{2.18d}$$

The Equations (2.18b), (2.18c) and (2.18d) can be plotted for different values of the initial conditions and damping ratio ξ to understand the dynamic response of underdamped SDOF systems.

The amplitude of the displacement response can be written as follows:

$$x_0 = \sqrt{\left(\frac{x(0)\xi\omega + \dot{x}(0)}{\omega_D}\right)^2 + (x(0))^2} \tag{2.18e}$$

The response of an underdamped system is shown in Figure 2.4 with damping coefficient (c = 2 N-s/m). It can be seen that an underdamped system oscillates about its mean position as against no oscillation in a critically damped system.

Overdamped System

Although overdamped systems are not encountered in normal conditions, it is useful to understand thier behaviour:

In this case $\xi = \dfrac{c}{c_c} = \dfrac{c}{2m\omega} > 1$

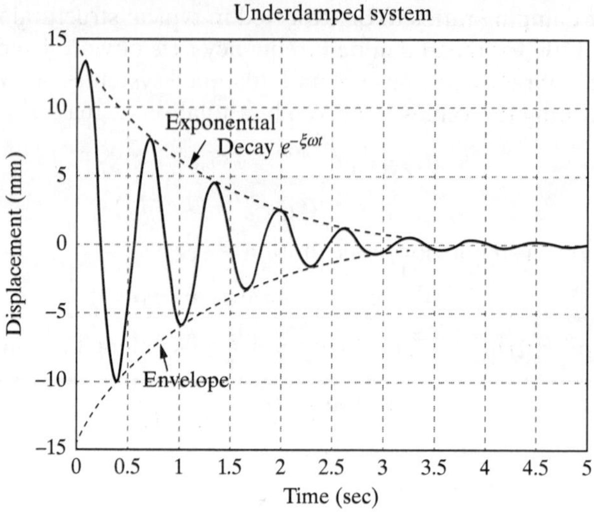

($m = 1$ kg, $c = 2$ Ns/m, $k = 100$ N/m, $x(0) = 0.01$ m, $\dot{x}(0) = 0.1$ m/s)

Figure 2.4 Underdamped system.

Hence, Equation (2.10) can be written as:

$$s = -\xi\omega \pm \omega\sqrt{\xi^2 - 1} = -\xi\omega \pm \hat{\omega}$$

where, $$\hat{\omega} = \omega\sqrt{\xi^2 - 1} \tag{2.19}$$

The solution is given by

$$x(t) = G_1 e^{(-\xi\omega + \hat{\omega})t} + G_2 e^{(-\xi\omega - \hat{\omega})t} \quad \text{from Equation (2.4)}$$

or, $$x(t) = e^{-\xi\omega t}\left(G_1 e^{\hat{\omega}t} + G_2 e^{-\hat{\omega}t}\right)$$

We know that

$$e^x = \sinh\, x + \cosh\, x$$

and

$$\sinh\, x = \left(e^x - e^{-x}\right)/2$$

$\therefore$ $$x(t) = e^{-\xi\omega t}(\text{A}\sinh\, \hat{\omega}t + \text{B}\cosh\, \hat{\omega}t) \tag{2.20a}$$

where, the constants A and B can be determined using the initial conditions.

On differentiating Equation (2.20a), the velocity term is obtained:

$$\dot{x}(t) = e^{-\xi\omega t}(-\xi\omega)[\text{A}\sinh\, \hat{\omega}t + \text{B}\cosh\, \hat{\omega}t] + e^{-\xi\omega t}(\hat{\omega})[\text{A}\cosh\, \hat{\omega}t + \text{B}\sinh\, \hat{\omega}t] \tag{2.20b}$$

The motion in over damped systems is not oscillatory, that is, it does not cross the mean position. It is similar to the motion of critically damped system but return towards the mean position is slowed as the damping ratio is increased as shown in Figure 2.5. It can be seen in Figures 2.3 and 2.5 that an over damped system comes to rest very slowly as compared to a critically damped system.

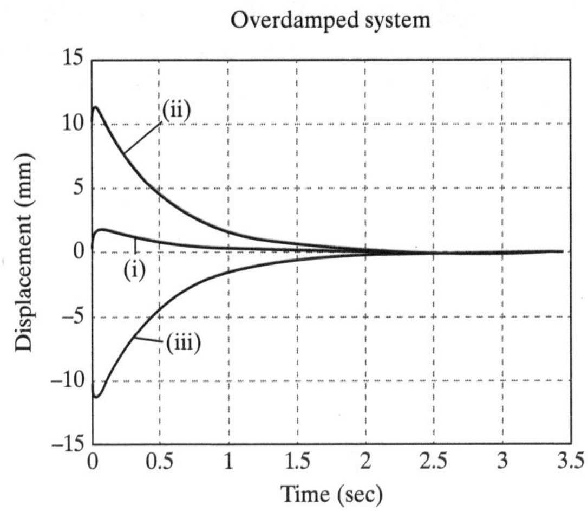

(m = 1 kg, c = 50 Ns/m, k = 100 N/m, (i) $x(0) = 0, \dot{x}(0) = 0.1$ m/s; (ii) $x(0) = 0.01$ m, $\dot{x}(0) = 0.1$ m/s; (iii) $x(0) = -0.01$ m, $\dot{x}(0) = -0.1$ m/s)

Figure 2.5 Overdamped system.

2.3 MATLAB APPLICATIONS

Let us arrange the equation of motion for a SDOF system for use with MATLAB. The equation of motion is given by Equation (2.3)

$$m\ddot{x}(t)+c\dot{x}(t)+kx(t) = 0 \tag{2.3}$$

Initial conditions are known through $x(0)$ and $\dot{x}(0)$.

MATLAB requires that the second order differential equation should be rearranged as a set of first order differential equations.

Let

$$x(t) = z(1) \text{ and } \dot{x}(\mathrm{t}) = z(2) \tag{2.21a}$$

or,

$$\dot{z}(1) = \dot{x}(\mathrm{t}) = z(2) \tag{2.21b}$$

$$\dot{z}(2) = \ddot{x}(t) = -\frac{c}{m}z(2)-\frac{k}{m}z(1) \tag{2.21c}$$

$$\begin{Bmatrix} \dot{z}(1) \\ \dot{z}(2) \end{Bmatrix} = \begin{bmatrix} 0 & 1 \\ -\left(\dfrac{k}{m}\right) & -\left(\dfrac{c}{m}\right) \end{bmatrix} \begin{Bmatrix} z(1) \\ z(2) \end{Bmatrix} \tag{2.21d}$$

or,

$$\dot{z} = Az \tag{2.21e}$$

where, $\{z\}$ is a state vector of size 2 × 1. The matrix A is called the state matrix. The position z(1) and velocity z(2) variables are called the state variables.

Now the set of first order differential equations (2.21a), (2.21b) and (2.21c) can be solved by using the MATLAB function `ode23`. It is based on Runge – Kutta method. The step size is selected automatically by the program. MATLAB Codes `DOS2_1`,

DOS2_2 and DOS2_3 compute the undamped free response of a SDOF system. The codes have been written in different styles. Code DOS2_4 computes damped free response for underdamped, critically damped or overdamped systems for the given initial conditions. Code DOS2_5 computes damped free response of a SDOF for a given initial conditions.

CODE DOS2_1

```
%    Dynamics of Structures by Ashok K. Jain I.I.T. Roorkee
%    DOS2_1
%    Undamped Free Vibrations of a SDOF System
%    Calls: DOS2_1a            Function: DOS2_1a in a separate file
%    Equation of motion of a SDOF is a second order differential equation
%    The program calls function "ode23" to solve ordinary differential eqn.
%    The program can be modified to read the initial conditions from the
%    command prompt
%
%    m=1;
%    k=10;
ic=[0;0.1];
tspan=[0 10];
fprintf ('Initial displacement at t=0, is %.3g m\n',ic(1));
fprintf ('Initial velocity at t=0, is %.3g m/s\n',ic(2));
fprintf ('Duration of vibration is %.3g sec\n',tspan(2));
%
[t,y]=ode23(@DOS2_1a,tspan,ic);
subplot 211
plot (t,y(:,1),'.-r');
title ('Displacement vs. time');
xlabel ('Time sec');
ylabel ('Displacement m');
grid on;
subplot 212
plot (t,y(:,2),'.-b');
title ('Velocity vs. time');
xlabel ('Time sec');
ylabel ('Velocity m/s');
grid on;
```

CODE DOS2_1a

```
%    Dynamics of Structures by Ashok K. Jain I.I.T. Roorkee
%    DOS2_1a
%    Called by: DOS2_1
%    Undamped Free Vibrations of a SDOF System
%
function dz = DOS2_1a(t,z)
```

```
m=1;
k=10;
w=sqrt(k/m);
if t==0
  fprintf ('\n m = %.3f, k = %.3f\n',m,k);
  fprintf ('\n natural frequency = %.3f rad/s\n',w);
end
dz = zeros(2,1); % initializes the column vector z
dz(1) =  z(2);
dz(2) = -k*z(1)/m;
end
```

CODE DOS2_2   Alternate solution I

```
%   Dynamics of Structures by Ashok K. Jain I.I.T. Roorkee
%   DOS2_2
%   Undamped Free Vibrations of a SDOF System
%   Calls:DOS2_2a
%   Equation of motion of a SDOF is a second order differential equation
%   The program calls function "ode23" to solve ordinary differential eqn.
%   The program can be modified to read the initial conditions
%        from the command prompt
%   ic=initial conditions: at t=0, x0 and v0
%   t = time duration of vibration - 0 to 5 sec
%   Alternate solution I
%
clear all;
ic=[0.02;0.05];
t=[0; 5];
fprintf('Initial displacement at t=0, is %.3g m\n',ic(1));
fprintf('Initial velocity at t=0, is %.3g m/s\n',ic(2));
fprintf('Duration of vibration is %.3g sec\n',t(2));
%
[t,z]=ode23(@DOS2_2a,t,ic)
plot(t,z(:,1));
xlabel('time');
ylabel('Displacement');
title('Displacement time History');
```

CODE DOS2_2a

```
%   Dynamics of Structures by Ashok K. Jain I.I.T. Roorkee
%   DOS2_2a
%   Called by DOS2_2
%   Undamped Free Vibrations of a SDOF System
%   m = 5
%   k = 100
```

```
%   The values of mass and stiffnes can be changed as desired
%
function q=DOS2_2a(t,z)
m =5;
k =100;
q=[z(2);(-(k/m)*z(1))]; % column vector
end
```

```
------------------
CODE DOS2_3    Alternate solution II
------------------
%   Dynamics of Structures by Ashok K. Jain I.I.T. Roorkee
%   DOS2_3
%   Undamped Free Vibrations of a SDOF System
%   The function to define first order differential equation is builtin here
%       itself.
%   Equation of motion of a SDOF is a second order differential equation
%   The program calls function "ode23" to solve ordinary differential eqn.
%   The program can be modified to read the initial conditions
%       from the command prompt
%   m=1;
%   k=10;
%   Alternate solution II
%
prompt='Pl enter the value of mass (m):';
m=input (prompt);
prompt='Pl enter the value of stiffness (k):';
k=input (prompt);
omega=sqrt(k/m);
period=2*pi()/omega;
fprintf ('Mass = %.3g kg\n',m);
fprintf ('Stiffness = %.3g N/m\n',k);
fprintf ('Natural frequency = %.3g rad/s.\n',omega);
fprintf ('Period of vibration = %.3g s\n',period);
ic=[0.2;0.1];
fprintf ('Initial displacement at t=0, is %.3g m\n',ic(1));
fprintf ('Initial velocity at t=0, is %.3g m/s\n',ic(2));
%
springmass=@(t,z)[z(2);-k*z(1)/m];
%
tspan=[0 10];
[t,y]=ode23(springmass, tspan,ic);
subplot 211
plot (t,y(:,1),'.-r');
title ('Displacement vs. time')
xlabel ('Time sec');
ylabel ('Displacement m');
grid on;
subplot 212
plot (t,y(:,2),'.-g'); title('Velocity vs. time')
```

```
xlabel ('Time sec');
ylabel ('Velocity m/s');
grid on;
```

CODE DOS2_4

```
%   Dynamics of Structures by Ashok K. Jain I.I.T. Roorkee
%   DOS2_4
%   Damped Free response of a single degree of freedom system.
%   If zai < 1.0, underdamped system
%   If zai = 1.0, critically damped system
%   If zai > 1.0, overdamped system
%   Input parameters are entered at the command prompt
%   m=1;
%   k=100;
%   c=2 for underdamped system;
%   c=20 for critically damped system;
%   c=50 for overdamped system;
%   x0=0.1;
%   v0=0.05;
%   tf=5;
prompt='Pl enter the value of mass (m):';
m=input(prompt);
prompt='Pl enter the value of stiffness (k):';
k=input(prompt);
prompt='Pl enter the value of damping coeff.(c):';
c=input(prompt);
w=sqrt(k/m);
zai=c/(2*sqrt(k*m));
wd=w*sqrt(1-zai^2);
fprintf ('Mass = %.3g \n',m);
fprintf ('Stiffness = %.3g \n',k);
fprintf ('damping coeff. = %.3g \n',c);
fprintf ('The natural frequency is %.3g rad/s.\n',w);
fprintf ('The damping ratio is %.3g.\n',zai);
fprintf ('The damped natural frequency is %.3g.\n',wd);
prompt='Pl enter initial displacement at t=0; (x0):';
x0=input(prompt);
prompt='Pl enter initial velocity at t=0; (v0):';
v0=input(prompt);
prompt='Pl enter duration of vibrations (tf):';
tf=input(prompt);
fprintf('Initial displacement at t=0, is %.3g m\n',x0);
fprintf('Initial velocity at t=0, is %.3g m/s\n',v0);
fprintf('Duration of vibrations is %.3g \n',tf);
%
t=0:0.01:tf;
if zai < 1
    g0=sqrt(((v0+zai*w*x0)^2+(x0*wd)^2)/wd^2);
```

```
    phi=atan2(x0*wd,v0+zai*w*x0);
    x=g0*exp(-zai*w*t).*sin(wd*t+phi);
    fprintf ('Underdamped system\n');
    fprintf ('Amplitude = %.3g\n',g0);
    fprintf ('Phase angle= %.3g radian\n',phi);
  elseif zai==1
    g1=x0;
    g2=v0+w*x0;
    fprintf ('Critically damped system\n');
    fprintf ('g1= %.3g\n',g1);
    fprintf ('g2= %.3g\n',g2);
    x=(g1+g2*t).*exp(-w*t);
else
    wc=w*sqrt(zai^2-1);
    g1=(-v0+(-zai*w+wc)*x0)/(2*wc);
    g2=(v0+(zai*w+wc)*x0)/(2*wc);
    fprintf ('Overdamped system\n');
    fprintf ('constant g1= %.3g\n',g1);
    fprintf ('constant g2= %.3g\n',g2);
    x=exp(-zai*w*t).*(g1*exp(-wc*t)+g2*exp(wc*t));
end
plot (t,x)
xlabel ('Time sec')
ylabel ('Displacement m')
title ('Displacement versus Time')
grid on
```

CODE DOS2_5

```
%   Dynamics of Structures by Ashok K. Jain I.I.T. Roorkee
%   DOS2_5
%   Damped Free Vibrations of a SDOF System
%   Equation of motion of a SDOF is a second order differential equation
%   The program calls function "ode23" to solve ordinary differential eqn.
%   The program can be modified to read the initial conditions
%                                       from the command prompt
%   Calls DOS2_5a
%   IC=initial conditions at time t=0, x0 and v0
%   t = time duration of vibrations; 0 to 5 sec @ 0.005 sec interval
%
clear all;
clc;
IC =[0.02;0.05];  % Initial conditions x(0) and v(0)
fprintf('\n Initial displacement = %.3f m',IC(1));
fprintf('\n Initial velocity = %.3f m/s',IC(2));
t = [0:0.005:5];
[t,z] = ode23(@DOS2_5a,t,IC);
%
[dismax, maxindex1] = max(z(:,1));
```

```
[dismin, minindex1] = min(z(:,1));
dtimemax = (maxindex1-1)*0.005;
dtimemin = (minindex1-1)*0.005;
%
[velmax, maxindex2] = max(z(:,2));
[velmin, minindex2] = min(z(:,2));
vtimemax = (maxindex2-1)*0.005;
vtimemin = (minindex2-1)*0.005;
%
fprintf('\n dismax = %.3f , at time = %.3f sec\n',dismax,dtimemax);
fprintf('\n dismin = %.3f , at time = %.3f sec\n',dismin,dtimemin);
fprintf('\n velmax = %.3f , at time = %.3f sec\n',velmax,vtimemax);
fprintf('\n velmin = %.3f , at time = %.3f sec\n',velmin,vtimemin);
subplot 211
plot(t,z(:,1))
grid on;
xlabel('time sec')
ylabel('displacement m')
title('Displacement time history')
subplot 212
plot(t,z(:,2))
xlabel('time sec')
ylabel('Velocity m/s')
title('Velocity time history')
grid on;
```

CODE DOS2_5a

```
%   Dynamics of Structures by Ashok K. Jain I.I.T. Roorkee
%   DOS2_5a
%   Called by DOS2_5
%   Damped Free Vibrations of a SDOF System
%   The program can be modified to read mass, stiffness, damping etc.
%                                               from the command prompt
%
function q=DOS2_5a(t,z)
m=5;
k = 100;
zai=0.05; % 5%
w=sqrt(k/m);
c=2*zai*sqrt(k*m);
if t==0
  fprintf ('\n m = %.3f, k = %.3f, zai = %.3f, c  = %.3f\n',m,k,zai,c);
  fprintf ('\n natural frequency = %.3f rad/s\n',w);
end
q=[z(2);(-(c/m)*z(2)-(k/m)*z(1))];
end
```

These MATLAB codes are used to generate results shown in the following examples.

2.4 ILLUSTRATIVE EXAMPLES

Example 2.1

A SDOF system has a natural period of 1.2 sec and maximum velocity of 150 mm/sec. If the initial displacement is 15 mm, determine the amplitude, initial velocity, and maximum acceleration.

Solution

Given $T = 1.2$ sec, $x(0) = 15$ mm, $\dot{x}_{max} = 150$ mm/sec

$$\omega = \frac{2\pi}{T} = \frac{2\times\pi}{1.2} \quad \therefore\ \omega = 5.236 \text{ rad/sec}$$

Maximum velocity $\dot{x}_{max} = G\omega$

$\therefore$ Amplitude $G = 150/5.236 = 28.65$ mm

Also,

$$G = \sqrt{\left(\frac{\dot{x}(0)}{\omega}\right)^2 + x^2(0)}$$

or,

$$\left(\frac{\dot{x}(0)}{\omega}\right)^2 = G^2 - x^2(0)$$

$\therefore$

$$\dot{x}(0) = \omega\sqrt{G^2 - x^2(0)}$$

$$\dot{x}(0) = 5.236\times\sqrt{28.65^2 - 15^2} = 127.8 \text{ mm/sec}$$

Maximum acceleration $\ddot{x}_{max} = G\omega^2 = 28.65\times 5.236^2 = 785.46$ mm/sec^2 □

Example 2.2

A portal frame with a rigid beam is shown in Figure 2.6. If the initial displacement and initial velocity are 20 mm and 10 mm/sec, respectively, determine the amplitude of displacement and displacement at time $t = 2$ sec. $E = 200$ GPa and $I = 300\times10^{-6}$ m^4

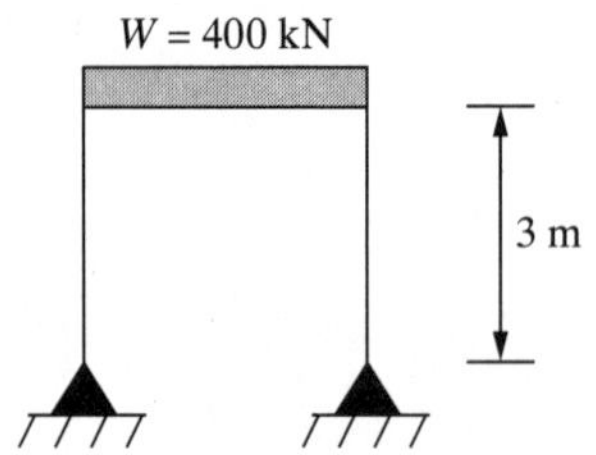

Figure 2.6 An undamped SDOF portal frame

Solution

The lateral stiffness of a column with hinged support $= \dfrac{3EI}{L^3}$

$$\text{Total lateral stiffness} = 2\times\frac{3EI}{L^3} = \frac{6\times200\times10^6\times30\times10^{-4}}{3^3} = 0.133\times10^6 \text{ kN/m}$$

Mass of the frame $m = 400$ kN/g $= 400/9.81 = 40.76$ kN-sec²/m

Natural frequency of the frame $\omega = \sqrt{\dfrac{k}{m}} = \sqrt{\dfrac{0.133\times10^6}{40.76}} = 57.1$ rad/sec

Amplitude of displacement $\quad G = \sqrt{\left(\dfrac{\dot{x}(0)}{\omega}\right)^2 + x^2(0)}$

$$= \sqrt{\left(\frac{10}{57.1}\right)^2 + 20^2} = 20 \text{ mm}$$

Displacement at 2 sec is given by

$$x(t) = A\sin\omega t + B\cos\omega t$$

$$x(2) = \frac{10}{57.1}\sin(57.1\times2) + 20\times\cos(57.1\times2) = -8.04 \text{ mm}$$

Example 2.3

Consider a SDOF system shown in Figure 2.1. It undergoes undamped free vibrations. The mass = 40 kNs²/m, stiffness k = 3500 kN/m. Determine the natural frequency and natural period of vibration. The initial conditions are given as: $x(0) = 0.01$ m, $\dot{x}(0) = 0.1$ m/s. Hence, plot a graph of displacement–time history, and inertia and elastic forces.

Solution

The complete solution is given by Equations (2.6) and (2.9). These equations can be plotted either using MS EXCEL or MATLAB.

The frequency of vibration is given by $\omega = \sqrt{\dfrac{k}{m}} = \sqrt{\dfrac{3500}{40}} = 9.3541$ rad/sec

Natural period is given by $T = \dfrac{2\pi}{\omega} = 0.6717$ sec

The plots of displacement, velocity and acceleration are shown in Figure 2.7. Knowing the displacement and acceleration, elastic force (= kx) and inertia forces (= $m\ddot{x}$) can be estimated. At any point of time, the sum of elastic and inertia forces is zero to keep the system in equilibrium. □

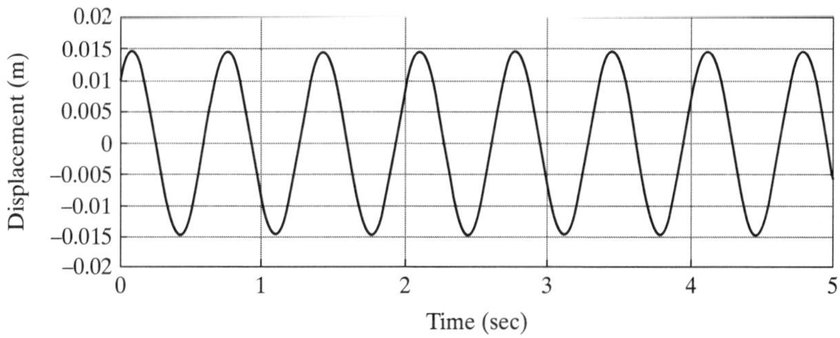

(a)

Figure 2.7 Response of SDOF system.

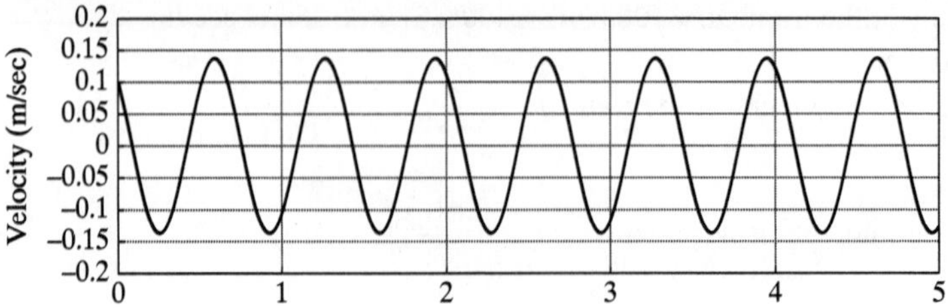

(b)

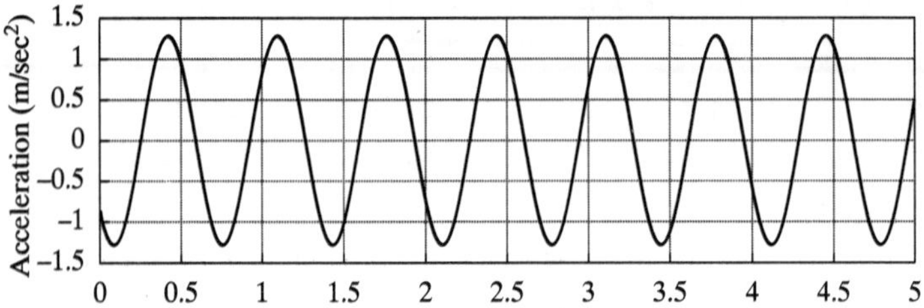

(c)

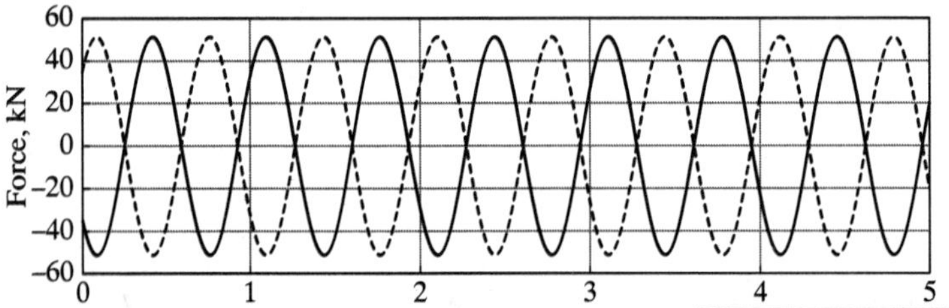

(d) Elastic and inertia force

Figure 2.7 (Continued)

Example 2.4

In the undamped SDOF system of Example 2.3, plot the response for different initial conditions as follows:

Case 1: $x(0) = 0.01$ m, $\dot{x}(0) = 0.1$ m/s

Case 2: $x(0) = 0$, $\dot{x}(0) = 0.1$ m/s

Case 3: $x(0) = 0.01$ m, $\dot{x}(0) = 0$

Solution

The solution can be found either using MS EXCEL or MATLAB as shown in Figure 2.8. It is a very interesting problem to understand the effect of initial conditions:

Case 1: $x(0) = 0.01$ m and $\dot{x}(0) = 0.1$ m/s
The curve starts from the initial displacement of 0.01 m and slope of the curve at $x = x(0)$ on the ordinate axis represents initial velocity.

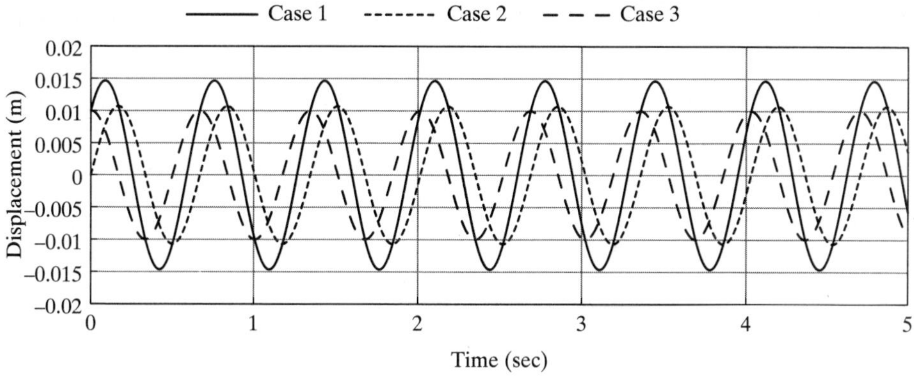

Figure 2.8 Response of a SDOF under different initial conditions.

Case 2: $x(0) = 0$ and $\dot{x}(0) = 0.1$ m/s
The curve starts from $x = 0$ and slope of the curve at $x = x(0)$ on the ordinate axis represents initial velocity.

Case 3: $x(0) = 0.01$ m and $\dot{x}(0) = 0$
The curve starts from the initial displacement of 0.01 m and slope of the curve at $x = x(0)$ on the ordinate axis is zero. The tangent is horizontal. □

Example 2.5

Consider a SDOF system shown in Figure 2.1. It undergoes underdamped free vibrations (damping $\xi = 5\%$). The mass = 5 kNs²/m, stiffness $k = 100$ kN/m. The initial conditions are given as: $x(0) = 0.02$ m, $\dot{x}(0) = 0.05$ m/s. Plot the displacement–time history and velocity–time history using MATLAB.

Solution

The plots of the displacement response and velocity response obtained using the MATLAB code presented earlier are shown in Figure 2.9. □

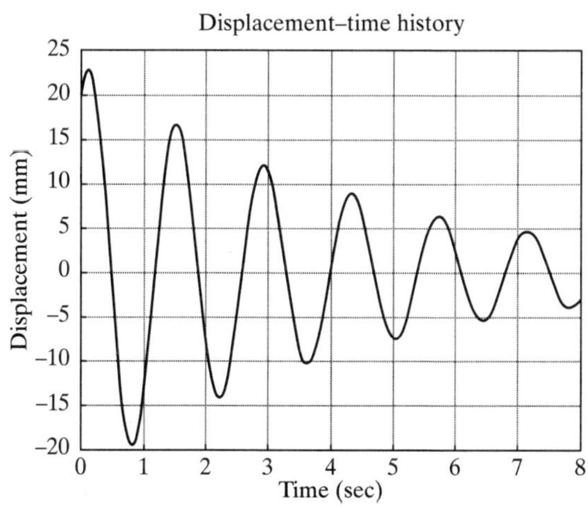

Figure 2.9(a) Displacement response of an underdamped system.

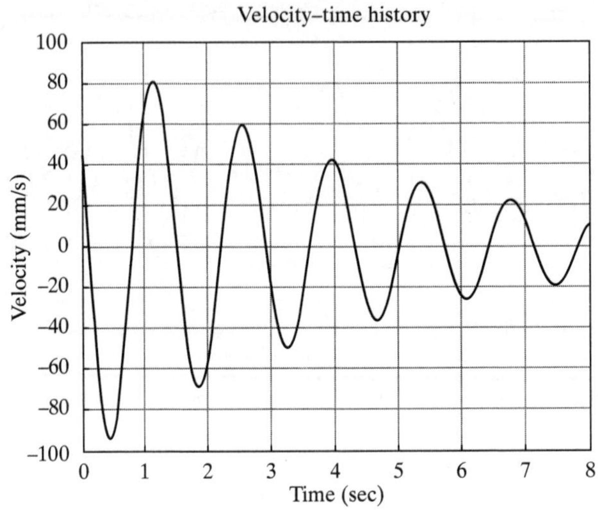

Figure 2.9(b) Velocity response of an underdamped system.

Example 2.6

Consider a SDOF system shown in Figure 2.2. It undergoes underdamped free vibrations. The mass = 40 kNs²/m and stiffness k = 3750 kN/m. The initial conditions are given as: $x(0)$ = 0.01 m, $\dot{x}(0) = 0.1$ m/s. Plot the influence of 0, 5% and 10% damping on the displacement–time history.

Solution

The response of a SDOF system can be determined using MATLAB for different damping ratios. The results are plotted in Figure 2.10. The amplitude of displacement decreases with increase in damping. In an undamped system ($\xi = 0\%$), the amplitude remains constant and the system vibrates indefinitely. Even with 5% damping, there is significant drop in the amplitude of vibration. □

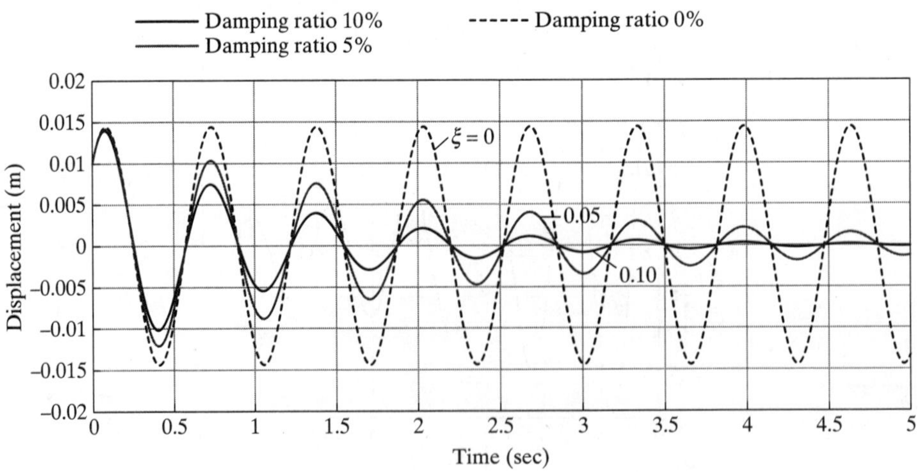

Figure 2.10 Influence of damping ratios on the free response of a SDOF system.

Example 2.7

Consider a SDOF system shown in Figure 2.2. It undergoes underdamped free vibrations. The mass = 40 kNs²/m, stiffness $k = 3750$ kN/m and $c = 50$ kNs/m. The initial conditions are given as: $x(0) = 0.01$ m, $\dot{x}(0) = 0.1$ m/s. Plot the inertia, damping and spring forces.

Solution

Mass $m = 40$ kN s²/m

Stiffness $k = 3750$ kN/m

Damping $c = 50$ kNs/m

Natural frequency of vibration $\omega = \sqrt{\frac{k}{m}} = 9.6825$ rad/s

Period of vibration $T = 2\pi/\omega = 0.6489$ sec

Critical damping $c_c = 774.5967$

Damping ratio $\xi = c/c_c = 6.45\%$

The inertia force $m\ddot{x}(t)$, damping force $c\dot{x}(t)$ and spring force $kx(t)$ are shown in Figure 2.11. The sum of these forces at any instant t is zero. It can be seen that in the present case the damping force is quite small as compared to the other two forces. □

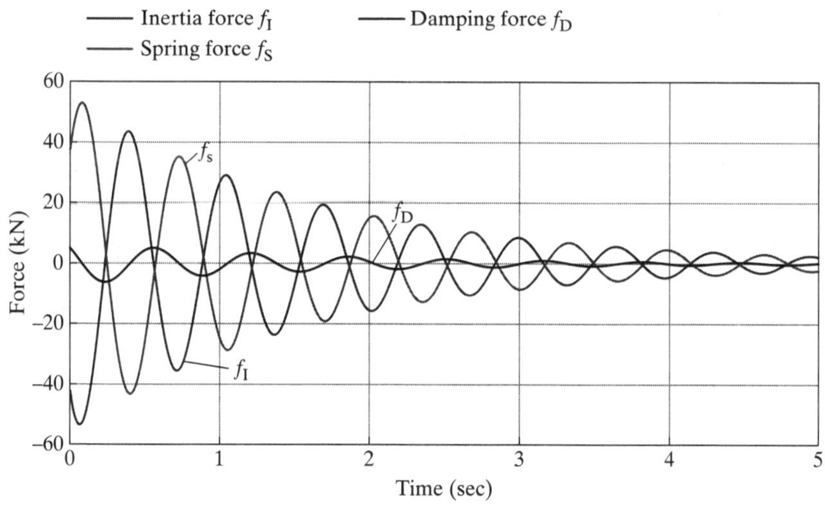

Figure 2.11 Variation of inertia, damping and spring forces.

Example 2.8

A SDOF frame has a mass = 5000 kg, lateral stiffness $k = 4 \times 10^6$ N/m and a damping ratio of 4%. Determine its undamped and damped natural frequency. If the frame is displaced by 25 mm and released suddenly, determine the peak displacements of first five cycles of vibrations.

Solution

Undamped natural frequency $\omega = \sqrt{\frac{k}{m}} = \sqrt{\frac{4\times 10^6}{5000}} = 28.28$ rad/sec

$$f = \frac{\omega}{2\pi} = 4.5 \text{ Hz}$$

$$\omega_D = \omega\sqrt{1-\xi^2}$$

ω_D is damped frequency of vibration.

$$\therefore \quad \omega_D = 28.28\sqrt{1-0.04^2} = 28.257 \text{ rad/sec or,} \quad f_D = 4.496 \text{ Hz}$$

Damped free response of a SDOF system is given by

$$x(t)=e^{-\xi\omega t}\left\{\frac{x(0)\xi\omega+\dot{x}(0)}{\omega_D}\sin\omega_D t + x(0)\cos\omega_D t\right\} \quad \text{(i)}$$

If the initial displacement $x(0) = x_0$, and initial velocity $\dot{x}(0) = 0$, damped free response can be written as:

$$x(t) = x_0 e^{-\xi\omega t}(\cos\omega t + \xi\sin\omega t) \text{ if } \omega_D \approx \omega \quad \text{(ii)}$$

Differentiating Equation (ii)

$$\frac{dx}{dt} = \dot{x}(t) = -x_0\omega e^{-\xi\omega t}((1+\xi^2)\sin\omega t)$$

For maximum displacement, velocity = 0,

or, $\sin \omega t = 0$

or, $\omega t = n\pi$

or, $t = n\pi/\omega$

For first five peak displacements, time of occurrence is given by

$$t = 0, 2\pi/\omega, 4\pi/\omega, 6\pi/\omega, 8\pi/\omega$$

and $x_{max} = x_0 e^{-2\pi\xi n} = 25\ e^{-2\pi\xi n} = 25\ e^{-0.251n}$ where $n = 0, 1, 2, 3,$ and 4

$\therefore$ Peak displacements are 25, 19.44, 15.12, 9.15 and 7.12 mm as shown in Figure 2.12. □

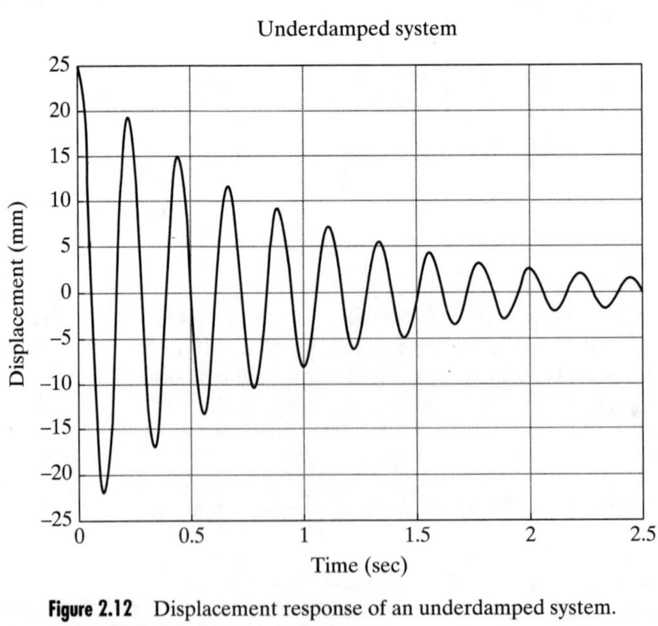

Figure 2.12 Displacement response of an underdamped system.

2.5 VISCOUS DAMPING

The mass and stiffness of a SDOF system can be estimated by static tests. However, the measurement of damping requires a dynamic test. Let us conduct a underdamped vibration test and estimate damping. Its response is given by Equation 2.17 and is shown in Figure 2.13.

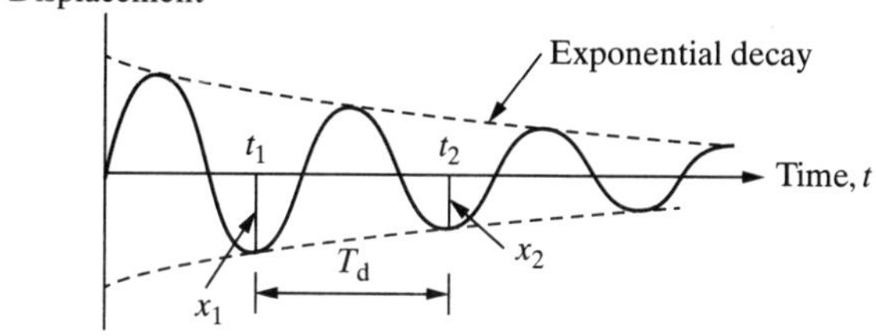

Figure 2.13 Underdamped response for measuring damping.

$$x(t)=e^{-\xi\omega t}\left(\mathrm{A}\sin\omega_{\mathrm{D}}t+\mathrm{B}\cos\omega_{\mathrm{D}}t\right) \tag{2.17}$$

Let x_1 = amplitude of motion at $t = t_1$

and x_2 = amplitude of motion at $t = t_1 + \mathrm{T_D}$

where $\mathrm{T_D}$ is time period for one cycle

$$\therefore \quad x_1 = e^{-\zeta\omega t_1}\left(\mathrm{A}\sin\omega_{\mathrm{D}}t_1+\mathrm{B}\cos\omega_{\mathrm{D}}t_1\right) \tag{2.22a}$$

$$x_2 = e^{-\xi\omega(t_1+T_{\mathrm{D}})}\left\{\mathrm{A}\sin\omega_{\mathrm{D}}(t_1+T_{\mathrm{D}})+\mathrm{B}\cos\omega_{\mathrm{D}}(t_1+T_{\mathrm{D}})\right\} \tag{2.22b}$$

$$= e^{-\xi\omega(t_1+T_{\mathrm{D}})}\left\{\mathrm{A}\sin\omega_{\mathrm{D}}t_1+\mathrm{B}\cos\omega_{\mathrm{D}}t_1\right\} \text{ because } \omega_{\mathrm{D}}=\frac{2\pi}{T_{\mathrm{D}}}$$

Dividing Equations (2.22a) and (2.22b),

$$\frac{x_1}{x_2}=e^{\xi\omega T_{\mathrm{D}}}$$

Taking natural log of both sides,

or, $$\log_e\frac{x_1}{x_2}=\xi\,\omega T_{\mathrm{D}}=\delta= \text{ logarithmic decrement}$$

or, $$\delta=\xi\,\omega\frac{2\pi}{\omega_{\mathrm{D}}}=2\pi\,\xi\,\frac{\omega}{\omega_{\mathrm{D}}} \tag{2.23a}$$

or, $$\delta=\frac{2\pi\xi}{\sqrt{1-\xi^2}} \quad \because \omega_{\mathrm{D}}=\omega\sqrt{1-\xi^2} \tag{2.23b}$$

For low damping $\delta \approx 2\pi\,\xi$ (2.23c)

Damping is a property of material. Typical values for different materials are as follows:

Material	Damping
Clay Brick	5% to 12%
Concrete	5% to 10%
Earth	20%
Steel	2% to 4%

$$\text{Log decrement} = \log_e \left[\frac{\text{amplitude in cycle } n}{\text{amplitude in cycle}(n+1)} \right] = \log_e \frac{x_1}{x_2} = \delta = 2\pi\xi \tag{2.24}$$

For lightly damped system,

$$\frac{x_1}{x_2} = e^{2\pi\xi} = 1 + 2\pi\xi + \frac{(2\pi\xi)^2}{2^2} + \ldots\ldots\ldots\ldots \infty$$

Neglecting higher order terms in ξ

$$\therefore\ \xi = \frac{x_1 - x_2}{2\pi\ x_2} \tag{2.25}$$

A structure whose damping is to be measured is subjected to free vibrations, or 'ambient vibrations'. The free vibrations are recorded as shown in Figure 2.13. The amplitude of vibrations in any two consecutive cycles is measured. The damping ratio is given by Equation (2.25). However, there is a high probability of making an error in measuring the displacement amplitudes in any two consecutive cycles as the difference in these two nearly equal quantities may be very small. Therefore, a greater accuracy can be achieved by considering response peaks which are several cycles apart, say in 'j' cycles.

The motion decreases from x_i to x_{i+j} over j cycles, that is,

$$\frac{x_i}{x_{i+j}} = \frac{x_i}{x_{i+1}} \frac{x_{i+1}}{x_{i+2}} \frac{x_{i+2}}{x_{i+3}} \cdots\cdots \frac{x_{i+j-1}}{x_{i+j}} = e^{j\delta}$$

Taking natural log of both sides,

$$\delta = \frac{1}{j} \log_e \frac{x_i}{x_{i+j}} \tag{2.26a}$$

but

$$\delta = 2\pi\xi \frac{\omega}{\omega_D} \approx 2\pi\xi$$

$\therefore$ For low damping:

$$\xi = \frac{x_i - x_{i+j}}{2j\pi\, x_{i+j}} \tag{2.26b}$$

In general for 10% damping, the amplitude is reduced by 50%.

Example 2.9

A displacement–time plot for a free vibration analysis of a SDOF system gives a displacement of 7.5 mm at time t_1 and 1 mm after 7 cycles. Determine logarithmic decrement and damping ratio.

Solution

Logarithmic decrement is given by

$$\delta = \frac{1}{j}\log_e \frac{x_i}{x_{i+j}} = 2j\pi\xi\frac{\omega}{\omega_D}$$

$$\delta = \frac{1}{7}\log_e \frac{7.5}{1.0} = 0.288$$

∴ Damping ratio $\xi = \delta/2\pi = 0.288/2\times\pi = 0.046$ or 4.6% □

Example 2.10

A SDOF system is displaced by 40 mm and released suddenly. At the end of 15 cycles, the time elapsed is 2.5 sec. The amplitude of displacement is 2.5 mm. Determine the natural period, viscous damping coefficient c, damping ratio ξ and stiffness k if mass $m = 20$ kg.

Solution

Mass $m = 20$ kg, $x_1 = 40$ mm, $x_{15} = 2.5$ mm
Damped natural period $T_d = 2.5/15 = 0.167$ sec

Damped natural frequency $\omega_D = \frac{2\pi}{T_D} = \frac{2\times\pi}{0.167} = 37.62$ rad/sec

Logarithmic decrement

$$\delta = \frac{1}{j}\log_e \frac{x_i}{x_{i+j}} = \frac{1}{15}\log_e \frac{40}{2.5} = 0.098$$

Damping ratio $\xi = \frac{\delta}{2\pi} = \frac{0.098}{2\times\pi} = 0.0156$ or, $\xi = 1.56\%$

Damped natural frequency $\omega_D = \omega\sqrt{1-\xi^2}$

∴ Undamped natural frequency $\omega = \frac{\omega_D}{\sqrt{1-\xi^2}} = \frac{37.62}{\sqrt{1-0.0156^2}} = 37.62$

Thus, the damped and undamped natural frequency are equal because damping is very small.

Also, Damping ratio $\xi = \frac{c}{c_c} = \frac{c}{2m\omega}$

Or, Damping coefficient $c = 2\,\text{m}\,\omega\,\xi = 2\times 20\times 37.62\times 0.0156 = 23.47$ Nsec/m
Stiffness $k = m\,\omega^2 = 20\times 37.62^2 = 28305$ N/m □

Example 2.11

A SDOF system has a mass of 50 kg and a spring stiffness k of 1000 N/m. It develops a damping force of 25 N at a velocity of 750 mm/sec. Determine the natural frequency, damping ratio and damping coefficient.

Solution

Undamped natural frequency $\omega = \sqrt{\frac{k}{m}} = \sqrt{\frac{1000}{50}} = 4.47$ rad/sec

Natural frequency $f = \frac{\omega}{2\pi} = \frac{4.47}{2\pi} = 0.71$ Hz

Damping force = $c\dot{x}(t)$

or, damping coefficient c = 25/0.75 = 33.34 Ns/m

Damping ratio $\xi = \frac{c}{c_c} = \frac{c}{2m\omega} = \frac{33.34}{2 \times 50 \times 4.47} = 0.074$

or, $\xi = 7.4\%$

2.6 COULOMB DAMPING

There are many situations in real life problems where damping results due to looseness of joints, dry friction between components or bolted joints, etc. This situation may lead to non-linear response of the structure. The dry friction damping is also known as Coulomb damping. Let us consider a mass *m* sliding on a rough surface which produces a force of friction as shown in Figure 2.14.

Its free body diagrams are shown in Figures 2.15(a) when the velocity is negative, and in Figure 2.15(b) when the velocity is positive. During a complete cycle, the velocity changes from zero to maximum positive, then to zero, then to maximum negative, and again to zero.

Damping force $f_D = \mu N = \mu mg$ where N is support reaction

The equilibrium of the mass can be written with respect to Figures 2.15(a) and 2.15(b):

$$f_I + f_D + f_S = 0$$

or,

$$m\ddot{x} + kx \pm f_D = 0 \tag{2.27a}$$

where, a positive sign before f_D is applicable only when the velocity is positive.

This equation cannot be solved directly using the conventional method of solution of a differential equation. This is because it is a nonlinear equation. Any solution of Equation (2.27a) will apply only during a time interval when the sign remains unchanged. Equation (2.27a) can be solved by breaking the time interval into two segments corresponding to the changes in the direction of motion in terms of velocity

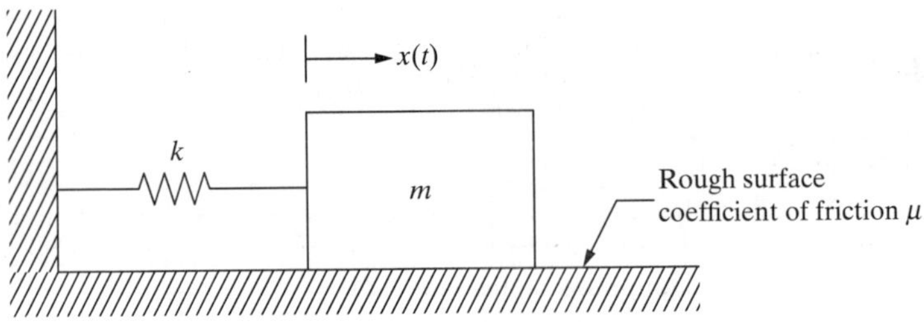

Figure 2.14 SDOF with friction damping.

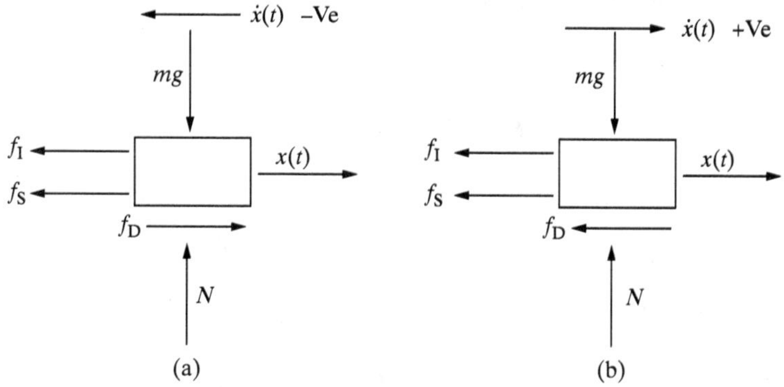

Figure 2.15 Free body diagram of the forces on sliding block.

Consider Figure 2.15(a)

$$m\ddot{x} + kx - f_D = 0 \quad \text{when the velocity is negative, } \dot{x} < 0 \tag{2.27b}$$

or, $$m\ddot{x} + kx = f_D = \mu mg$$

and, consider Figure 2.15(b)

$$m\ddot{x} + kx + f_D = 0 \quad \text{when the velocity is positive, } \dot{x} > 0 \tag{2.27c}$$

or, $$m\ddot{x} + kx = -f_D = -\mu mg$$

This block requires non-zero initial conditions to set it in motion. If the initial velocity is zero, then it requires initial displacement so that the spring force exceeds the static frictional force. Naturally, if $x(0)$ is less than the frictional force $f_D = \mu mg$, there will be no motion. If the initial velocity is non-zero, the object will move.

Let $$x_F = \frac{|f_D|}{k} = \frac{\mu mg}{k} = \frac{\mu g}{\omega^2} \tag{2.28a}$$

Therefore, Equation (2.27b) can be written as:

$$m\ddot{x} + kx = f_D = m\omega^2 x_F$$

$$\ddot{x} + \omega^2 x = \frac{f_D}{m} = \omega^2 x_F \quad \text{for } \dot{x} < 0 \tag{2.28b}$$

Similarly, Equation (2.27c) can be written as:

$$m\ddot{x} + kx = f_D = -m\omega^2 x_F$$

$$\ddot{x} + \omega^2 x = -\frac{f_D}{m} = -\omega^2 x_F \quad \text{for } \dot{x} > 0 \tag{2.28c}$$

Let us determine the solution of Equation (2.28b).

$$x(t) = A_1 \sin \omega t + B_1 \cos \omega t + x_F \tag{2.29a}$$

On differentiation,

$$\dot{x}(t) = \omega A_1 \cos \omega t - \omega B_1 \sin \omega t \tag{2.29b}$$

The initial conditions are as follows:

At $t = 0,\ x = x(0);$ and $\dot{x}(0) = 0$

Substituting in Equation (2.29a) gives,

$$B_1 = (x(0) - x_F) \text{ and } A_1 = 0$$

∴ The solution is given by

$$x(t) = (x(0) - x_F)\cos\omega t + x_F \text{ for } 0 \le t \le \frac{\pi}{\omega} \tag{2.30}$$

First negative peak given by Equation (2.30) is

At $t = \frac{\pi}{\omega} = \frac{T}{2}$

$$\therefore \quad x\left(\frac{\pi}{\omega}\right) = -x(0) + 2x_F \text{ and } \dot{x}\left(\frac{\pi}{\omega}\right) = 0 \tag{2.31}$$

In the second half cycle, the velocity is positive and the equation of motion is given by Equation (2.28c).

Its solution is given by

$$x(t) = A_2 \sin\omega t + B_2 \cos\omega t - x_F \tag{2.32}$$

The constants A_2 and B_2 can be determined by using the initial conditions at the beginning of this half cycle given by Equation (2.31).

Substituting in Equation (2.32) gives,

$$B_2 = (x(0) - 3x_F) \text{ and } A_2 = 0$$

∴ The solution is given by

$$x(t) = (x(0) - 3x_F)\cos\omega t - x_F \text{ for } \frac{\pi}{\omega} \le t \le \frac{2\pi}{\omega} \tag{2.33}$$

At $t = \frac{2\pi}{\omega}$

or $t = T$ Equation (2.33) gives

$$x\left(\frac{2\pi}{\omega}\right) = x(0) - 4x_F \text{ and } \dot{x}\left(\frac{2\pi}{\omega}\right) = 0 \tag{2.34}$$

Thus, at $t = \frac{2\pi}{\omega}$, the motion again reverses. The full motion in a cycle is described by Equations (2.30) and (2.33) and is shown in Figure 2.16. It can be seen that successive peaks are given by $\left[x(0) - 4x_F n\right]$ where n is an integer representing number of complete cycles. The damping envelope is formed by a pair of straight lines and each half cycle is a cosine function.

The solution will stop when the velocity is zero and the spring force (kx) is insufficient to overcome the maximum frictional force (μmg). In other words, the motion

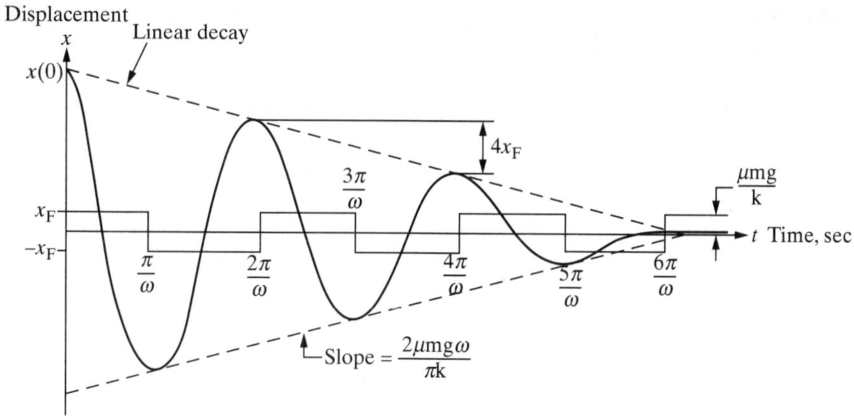

Figure 2.16 Vibrations with Coulomb damping.

stops at the end of the half-cycle for which the amplitude is less than x_F. At that point, the spring force is less than the frictional force.

The amplitude decays linearly. Its slope is given by using its displacement across any one complete cycle, say at 0.5 and 1.5 cycles (Figure 2.16)

$$\tan\theta = \left[\left(x(0) - 4x_F(1.5)\right) - \left(x(0) - 4(0.5)x_F\right)\right] / \left(\frac{2\pi}{\omega}\right)$$

$$\tan\theta = -\frac{2x_F\omega}{\pi} = -\frac{2\mu mg\omega}{\pi k} = -\frac{2\mu g}{\pi\omega} \tag{2.35}$$

The negative sign shows a decay or decrease in slope.

Coulomb damping vs Viscous damping

A few significant observations can be made for the free response of a SDOF system with these two types of damping:

1. With viscous damping, the amplitude of displacement decays exponentially, whereas with coulomb damping, the same decays linearly and comes to a complete rest.
2. A system with viscous damping continues to vibrate even at a very small displacement amplitude about its mean position, whereas, a system with coulomb damping comes to rest at a different equilibrium position than its mean position.
3. The damped natural frequency is different than the undamped natural frequency in a system with viscous damping, whereas, damped and undamped frequencies in a system with coulomb damping are the same.

Example 2.12

A SDOF system with a friction damper vibrates with an initial displacement of 50 mm. It completes 4 cycles in 0.8 second when its amplitude reduces to 5 mm. Estimate the coefficient of friction and when does the system come to rest.

Solution

Period of vibration T = 0.8/4 = 0.2 sec

Frequency of vibration $\omega = 2\pi/T = \dfrac{2\pi}{0.2} = 31.4$ rad/sec

Slope of the displacement-time envelope curve $= -\dfrac{2\mu g}{\pi\omega}$

or,

$$\text{Slope} = \frac{50-5}{0.8} = -\frac{45}{0.8} = -\frac{2\mu g}{\pi\omega}$$

or,

$$\mu = \frac{\pi\omega}{2g}\left(\frac{45}{0.8}\right) = \frac{\pi\times 31.4\times 45}{2\times 9810\times 0.8} = 0.2828$$

The displacement x_F is given by

$$x_F = \frac{\mu g}{\omega^2} = \frac{0.2828\times 9810}{31.4^2} = 2.81 \text{ mm}$$

It will come to rest when

$$x(0) - 4x_F n < x_F \text{ and velocity is zero.}$$

or,

$$n = \frac{x(0) - x_F}{4x_F} = \frac{50-2.81}{4\times 2.81} = 4.198 \text{ cycles}$$

It means the system will come to rest at the beginning of next half cycle, that is, 4.5 cycles or at 0.9 sec. The displacement at 0.9 sec will be equal to

$$x(0) - 4x_F\times 4.5 = 50 - 4\times 2.81\times 4.5 = -0.58 \text{ mm}$$

The minus sign indicates that 0.58 mm is in a direction opposite to that of the initial displacement. □

REVIEW QUESTIONS

2.1 What do you mean by free vibrations and forced vibrations of a SDOF system? Explain with the help of simple sketch. (*No mathematics*)

2.2 What do you mean by an undamped vibration and a damped vibration of a SDOF system? Explain with the help of simple sketch. (*No mathematics*)

2.3 What do you mean by free body diagram of a mass in a SDOF system?

2.4 What is a transient vibration?

2.5 What is a steady state vibration?

2.6 Explain critically damped system, underdamped system and overdamped system.

2.7 What is the difference between damping ratio and coefficient of damping?

2.8 How do you differentiate between undamped and damped frequency of vibration?

2.9 What do you understand by initial conditions of a SDOF system? Where and why do you use them?

2.10 Arrange the equation of motion of a SDOF system in terms of state matrix.

2.11 Derive an expression for logarithmic decrement and explain its physical meaning.

2.12 What is a viscous damping? How do you evaluate it?

2.13 What is a Coulomb damping?

2.14 What are different types of damping in a vibrating system?

2.15 Derive an expression for the amplitude of displacement response of a damped free vibrating system.

PROBLEMS

2.1 An overhead water tank has an effective weight of 500 kN when empty and has a 100 kL capacity. Its lateral stiffness is 600 kN/m. Determine the natural period of vibration when the tank is (a) empty and (b) when full. If the damping was 5% when the tank was empty, determine the damping when the tank is full.

Ans: (a) 1.83 sec (b) 3.17 sec, $c = 17.48$ kN-s/m, $\xi = 2.88$ %

2.2 An undamped SDOF system ($m = 30$ kg, $k = 500$ N/m) is given an initial displacement of 10 mm and initial velocity of 75 mm/s. Find
(a) the natural frequency
(b) the period of vibration
(c) the amplitude of vibration
(d) the time at which the second and third maximum peak occurs.

Ans: $\omega = 4.082$ rad/sec, $T = 1.539$ sec, $x_{max} = 20.915$ mm

2.3 An undamped SDOF system is set in motion from rest by giving it an initial velocity of 0.1 m/s. It vibrates with a maximum amplitude of 15 mm. Determine its natural frequency.

2.4 The mass of a block shown in Figure P2.1 is 100 kg and the spring stiffness is 1000 N/m. A bullet weighing 250 gm is fired at a speed of 20 m/s into the block and becomes embedded in the block. Determine the resulting undamped motion of the block.

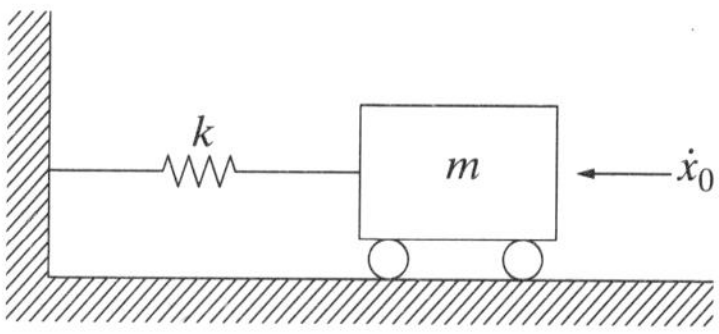

Figure P2.1

Ans: $\omega = 3.158$ rad/sec, initial velocity = 0.05 m/s

$$x(t) = \frac{0.05}{3.158}\sin 3.158t \text{ (m)}$$

2.5 A mass m_1 hangs from a massless spring k and is in static equilibrium. A second mass m_2 drops through a height h and sticks to m_1. Determine the subsequent motion $x(t)$ measured from the static position of m_1 and k.

Ans: $x(t) = A\cos\omega t + B\sin\omega t + \dfrac{m_2 g}{k}$ the last term is due to shift in the origin

or $x(t) = \dfrac{m_2 g}{k}(1 - \cos\omega t) + \dfrac{m_2\sqrt{2gh}}{(m_1 + m_2)\omega}\sin\omega t$

2.6 Consider a SDOF system having a mass m = 5 kg, damping c = 10 N-s/m and stiffness k = 20 N/m. Determine the values of undamped and damped natural frequency. Is the system overdamped, critically damped or underdamped?

2.7 Consider a SDOF system shown in Figure P2.2 where m = 20 kg, c = 125 N-s/m, k_1 = 3000 N/m, k_2 = 500 N/m and k_3 = 1200 N/m. Is the system overdamped, critically damped or underdamped?

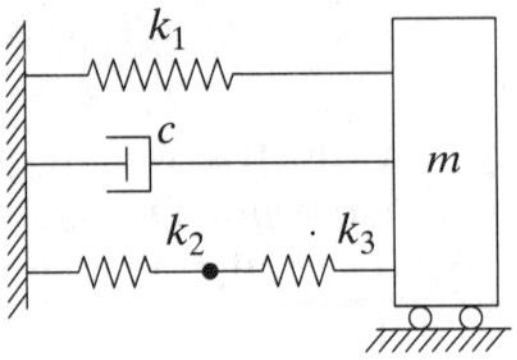

Figure P2.2

Ans: $k_{eq} = k_1 + \dfrac{k_2 k_3}{k_2 + k_3} = 3353\dfrac{\text{N}}{\text{m}},\ c_c = 2\sqrt{k_{eq} m} = 518\dfrac{\text{Ns}}{\text{m}};\ \xi = 0.24$ underdamped

2.8 Consider a SDOF system having a mass m = 30 kN s²/m, damping c = 50 kNs/m and stiffness k = 4000 kN/m. Determine natural frequency, damping ratio and critical damping. For $x(0)$ = 0.02 m, and $\dot{x}(0)$ = 0.1 m/s. Find the solution of the equation of motion. Hence, plot inertia, damping and spring force vs time for free vibration.

(Hint: Make use of MS-EXCEL)

2.9 A braced portal frame is shown in Figure P2.3. Beam and columns are of concrete of M25 grade. Size of column is 300 × 400 mm. Area of steel brace = 10 cm² and length = 5 m. Determine the natural period of vibration considering only the tension brace. If the initial displacement is 50 mm, and initial velocity is 0.5 m/s, plot the response up to 3 cycles.

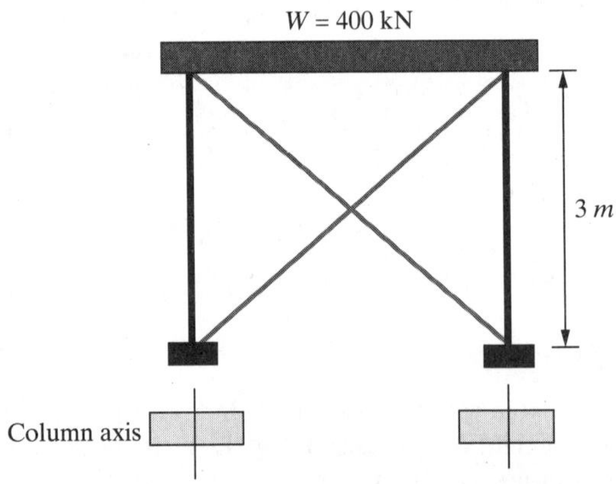

Figure P2.3

Ans: k_{col} = 35.55 kN/mm, k_{brace} = 25.6 kN/mm, k_{eq} = 61.60 kN/mm

$x(t) = 12.91 \sin \omega t + 50 \cos \omega t$

2.10 It is observed that amplitude of free vibration of a structure reduces from 100 mm to 30 mm in 10 cycles. Determine the viscous damping ratio.

2.11 A sliding block shown in Figure P2.4 has a natural period of 0.3 sec and the coefficient of friction between the block and the sliding surface is 0.25. If the block is given an initial displacement of 150 mm, what is the displacement after one cycle; what is the velocity after one cycle.

Ans: $x_F = 5.59$ mm, $\omega = 20.94$ rad/sec, 127.64 mm, zero

2.12 Consider the friction block of Figure P2.4. Mass = 50 kg, stiffness $k = 100$ kN/m and friction force is 50 N. If the initial displacement is 200 mm, determine the amplitude after two cycles.

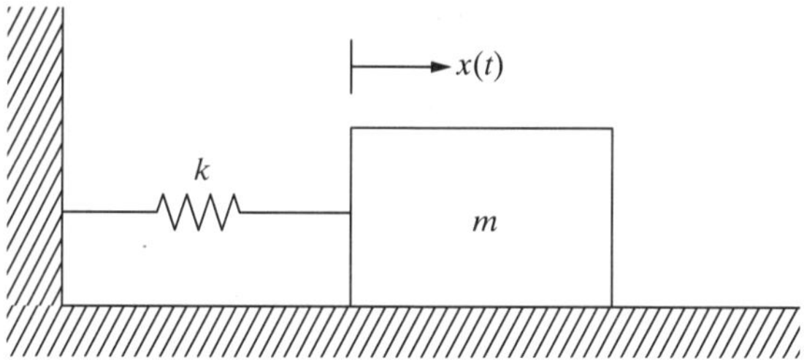

Figure P2.4

2.13 Consider a friction block having a mass = 250 kg and stiffness $k = 50$ kN/m. Coefficient of friction is 0.15 and initial displacement is 25 cm. Plot the displacement–time history. How long does it take for the system to come to rest and what is the amplitude at rest?

Ans: $x_F = 7.35$ mm, $T = 0.444$ sec, comes to rest after 8.5 cycles, –0.1 mm

MATLAB AND PYTHON APPLICATIONS

2.14 Consider a SDOF system with mass m, stiffness k and damping coefficient c. It is given an initial displacement $x(0)$ and initial velocity $\dot{x}(0)$. Write a MATLAB or PYTHON code to plot displacement–time history, velocity–time history, and acceleration–time history. Also plot inertia force, damping force and spring force–time history. Make use of MATLAB function '*diff*' to differentiate the displacement to obtain velocity and acceleration. Choose appropriate input data to make the system underdamped, critically damped and over damped.

2.15 In Problem 2.14, also show the influence of initial conditions by taking: (i) $x(0) = 10$ mm, and $\dot{x}(0) = 0$, (ii) $x(0) = 100$ mm, and $\dot{x}(0) = 0$, (iii) $x(0) = 0$, and $\dot{x}(0) = -10$ mm/sec; (iv) $x(0) = 0$, and $\dot{x}(0) = 100$ mm/sec.

2.16 The solution of an undamped free vibration SDOF system is given by the following equation:

$$x(t) = \mathrm{A}\sin(\omega t + \phi)$$

where

$$\mathrm{A} = \frac{\sqrt{\omega^2 x_0^2 + v_0^2}}{\omega} \quad \text{and} \quad \phi = \tan^{-1}\frac{\omega x_0}{v_0}$$

Make a 3D surface plot in MATLAB of the amplitude A vs x_0 and v_0 for the range of initial conditions given by $-0.1 \le x_0 \le 0.1\ m$ and $-1 \le v_0 \le 1$ m/s for a system with natural frequency of 20 rad/s.

(Hint: Make use of MATLAB functions meshgrid, grid, and mesh or surf.)

2.17 A spring and damper are attached to a mass of 100 kg to obtain a SDOF system. The initial conditions are: $x(0) = 0.1$ m, and $v(0) = 10$ mm/s. Design the spring and the damper such that the system will come to rest in 2 sec and not oscillate more than two complete cycles. Try to keep damping as small as possible.

Ans: $K = 3950$ N/m, $C = 775$ and zai = 61.7%

2.18 A sliding block has a natural period of 0.25 sec and the coefficient of friction between the block and the sliding surface is 0.15. If the block is given an initial displacement of 5 cm and an initial velocity of 50 cm/sec, plot the displacement and velocity – time history.

3 Single Degree of Freedom System: Harmonic Loading

3.1 INTRODUCTION

A harmonic loading or sinusoidal loading is the simplest dynamic force and frequently encountered in vibrations due to machines. The nature of the force is well defined in terms of magnitude, frequency, shape, as well as duration. It is, therefore, customary to begin the study of dynamics of structures with this loading. A single-degree-of-freedom (SDOF) system is subjected to harmonic loading and its response is studied without and with damping. The total response consists of two components: a *transient response,* which dies out quickly and a *steady state response,* which continues till the forcing function continues. The steady state response has a constant amplitude and frequency. The steady state response is of much interest to the analysts. The ratio of frequency of the forcing function and that of the structure plays a very significant role in dynamics. If the forcing frequency is equal to the natural frequency of the SDOF system, a *resonance* is said to have occurred. It is very enlightening to study the response at resonance. It also helps in determining damping in the system.

3.2 UNDAMPED FORCED VIBRATIONS

The general equation of motion of a single degree of freedom system is given by:

$$m\ddot{x}(t) + c\dot{x}(t) + kx(t) = p(t) \tag{3.1}$$

For an undamped system shown in Figure 3.1, $c = 0$

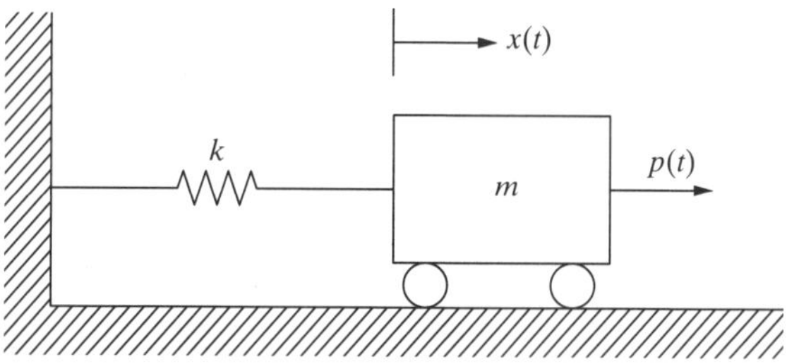

Figure 3.1 Undamped SDOF system.

Let $p(t) = p_0 \sin \bar{\omega} t$ for harmonic loading,
where $p_0 =$ amplitude of harmonic loading,
$\bar{\omega}$ = circular frequency of harmonic loading.

$\therefore$ Equation (3.1) reduces to $m\ddot{x}(t) + k\,x(t) = p_0 \sin \bar{\omega}t$ (3.2)

Its solution consists of the following two components:

(i) Complimentary solution—it is given by the free vibration analysis done earlier

(ii) Particular solution

Particular solution means the specific behaviour generated by the form of the dynamic loading. The response to the harmonic loading can be assumed to be harmonic and in phase with loading. Thus,

$$x_p(t) = G \sin \bar{\omega}t$$

Differentiating twice and substituting in Equation (3.2) gives,

$$-m\bar{\omega}^2 G \sin \bar{\omega}t + kG \sin \bar{\omega}t = p_0 \sin \bar{\omega}t$$

On rearranging the terms,

$$G\left(1 - \frac{\bar{\omega}^2}{\omega^2}\right) = \frac{p_0}{k}$$

$\therefore$ Amplitude of the response becomes,

$$G = \frac{p_0}{k} \cdot \frac{1}{1-\beta^2}$$

where

β = ratio of applied load frequency to the natural free vibration frequency.
$= \bar{\omega}/\omega$ frequency ratio.

Total response is given by $x(t) = x_c(t) + x_p(t)$ (3.3)

$$= \underbrace{A \sin \omega t + B \cos \omega t}_{\text{complimentary solution}} + \underbrace{\frac{p_0}{k} \frac{1}{1-\beta^2} \sin \bar{\omega}t}_{\text{steady state solution}} \quad (3.4)$$

The values of A and B depend on the initial conditions.
If the initial conditions are at $t = 0, x = x(0)$ and $\dot{x} = \dot{x}(0)$, the final solution becomes

$$x(t) = \underbrace{x(0)\cos \omega t + \left[\frac{\dot{x}(0)}{\omega} - \frac{p_0}{k}\frac{\beta}{(1-\beta^2)}\right] \sin \omega t}_{\text{Transient solution}} + \underbrace{\frac{p_0}{k}\frac{1}{1-\beta^2} \sin \bar{\omega}t}_{\text{Steady state solution}} \quad (3.5a)$$

If the system is *at rest* at $t = 0, x(0)=0$ and $\dot{x}(0)=0$

then $B = 0$ and $A = -p_0\,\beta/(k(1-\beta^2))$

The final solution of undamped forced vibration becomes

$$x(t) = \frac{p_0}{k}\frac{1}{(1-\beta^2)}(\sin \bar{\omega}t - \beta \sin \omega t) \quad (3.5b)$$

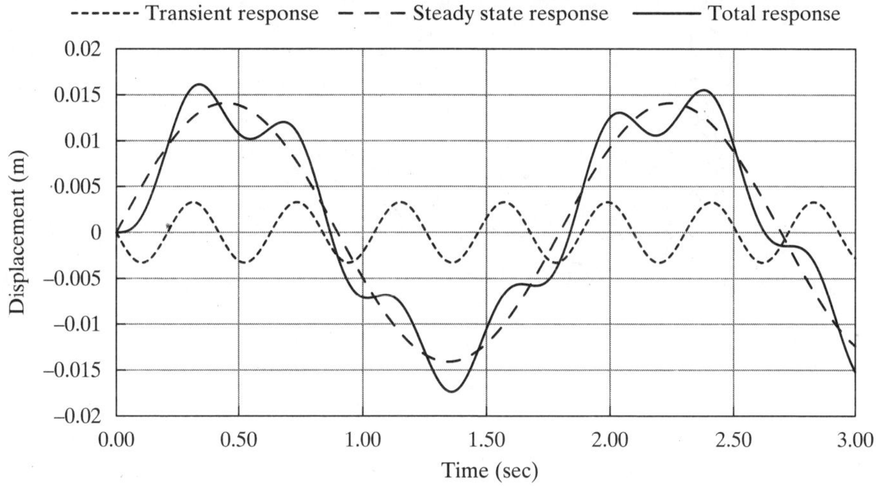

Figure 3.2 Transient, steady state and total response of an undamped SDOF system. (m = 33.33 kN-s^2/m, k = 7500 kN/m, P_0 = 100 kN, $\bar{\omega}$ = 3.5 rad/sec $x(0) = 0, \dot{x}(0) = 0$)

where,

$p_0/k = \Delta_{ST}$, that is, displacement which would be produced by the load p_0 applied statically

$\dfrac{1}{(1-\beta^2)}$ = magnification factor representing dynamic amplification effect of harmonically applied load

$\sin\bar{\omega}t$ = response component at frequency of the applied load
= steady state response directly related to the load

$\beta\sin\omega t$ = response component at natural frequency of vibration
= free vibration effect induced by the initial condition

The last term in Equation (3.5b) is also called *transient response.*

The variation of transient response, steady state response and total response with time is shown in Figure 3.2. It can be seen that in the absence of any damping, the transient response goes on indefinitely.

3.3 DAMPED FORCED VIBRATIONS

A damped SDOF system is shown in Figure 3.3. The dash-pot represents a viscous damper having damping coefficient c.

Equation (3.1) can be rewritten as:

$$\ddot{x}(t) + 2\xi\omega\dot{x}(t) + \omega^2 x(t) = \frac{p_0}{m}\sin\bar{\omega}t \tag{3.6}$$

where,

$$c/m = 2\xi\omega$$

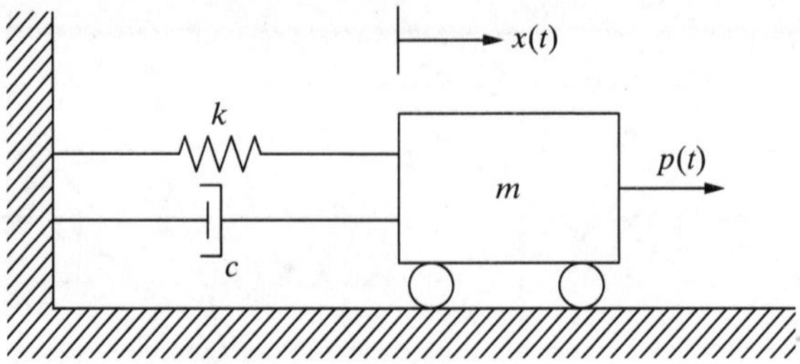

Figure 3.3 Damped SDOF system.

Complimentary solution $x_c(t) = e^{-\xi\omega t}(\mathrm{A}\sin\omega_D t + \mathrm{B}\cos\omega_D t)$ (3.7)

where, $\omega_D = \omega\sqrt{1-\xi^2}$

Let particular integral $x_p(t) = G_1 \sin\bar{\omega}t + G_2 \cos\bar{\omega}t$ (3.8)

in which the second term is required because, in general, the response of a damped system is not in phase with the loading.
The constants G_1 and G_2 are to be found using the initial conditions. Substitute Equation (3.8) in Equation (3.6) and compare the coefficients of $\sin\bar{\omega}t$ and $\cos\bar{\omega}t$. It gives

$$G_1 = \frac{p_0}{k}\frac{1-\beta^2}{(1-\beta^2)^2+(2\xi\beta)^2} \tag{3.9}$$

$$G_2 = \frac{p_0}{k}\frac{-2\xi\beta}{(1-\beta^2)^2+(2\xi\beta)^2} \tag{3.10}$$

Final solution becomes

$$x(t) = e^{-\xi\omega t}(\mathrm{A}\sin\omega_D t + \mathrm{B}\cos\omega_D t) + \frac{p_0}{k}\left\{\frac{1}{(1-\beta^2)^2+(2\xi\beta)^2}\right\}[(1-\beta^2)\sin\bar{\omega}t - 2\xi\beta\cos\bar{\omega}t] \tag{3.11}$$

The transient response dies quickly and is of little interest. The steady state response will continue till the external force continues to be applied. The variation of transient, steady state and total response for a typical SDOF system is shown in Figure 3.4. The data was as follows:

Undamped natural frequency $\omega = 15$ rad/sec, damping = 5%, force amplitude = 100 kN stiffness $k = 7500$ kN/m, forcing frequency $\bar{\omega} = 5$ rad/sec

The solution given by Equations (3.8), (3.9) and (3.10) is of interest to the analysts. The resultant ρ of the two vectors represent the amplitude of the steady state response.

$$\rho = \frac{p_0}{k}[(1-\beta^2)^2+(2\xi\beta)^2]^{-0.5} \tag{3.12}$$

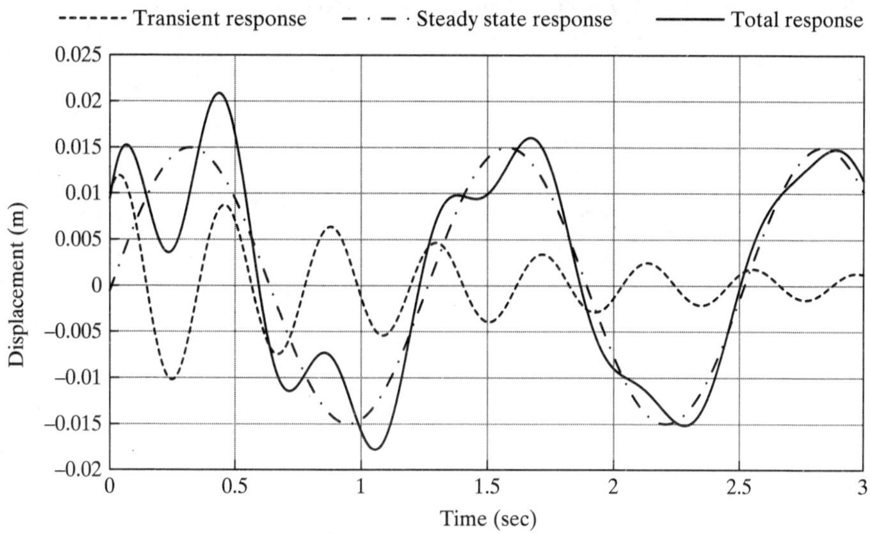

Figure 3.4 Transient, steady state and total response of a damped SDOF system.

and the phase angle θ by which the response lags behind the applied load is given by

$$\theta = \tan^{-1}\frac{2\xi\beta}{1-\beta^2} \qquad 0<\theta<180^\circ \tag{3.13}$$

The steady state response can be written as:

$$x(t) = \frac{p_0}{k}\left\{\frac{1}{\left[(1-\beta^2)^2+(2\xi\beta)^2\right]}\right\}\left[(1-\beta^2)\sin\bar{\omega}t-(2\xi\beta)\cos\bar{\omega}t\right] \tag{3.14a}$$

or,
$$x(t) = \rho\sin(\bar{\omega}t-\theta) \tag{3.14b}$$

The ratio of the resultant response amplitude to the static displacement, which would be produced by the force p_0 is called *dynamic magnification* factor D

$$D = \frac{\rho}{p_0/k} = \frac{x_{\max}}{x_{\text{static}}} \tag{3.15a}$$

or,
$$D = [(1-\beta^2)^2+(2\xi\beta)^2]^{-0.5} \tag{3.15b}$$

The variation of magnification factor with the frequency ratio β for a given damping ratio can be plotted as shown in Figure 3.5 using MATLAB.

Similarly, the variation of phase angle with the frequency ratio β for a given damping ratio can be plotted as shown in Figure 3.6 using MATLAB.

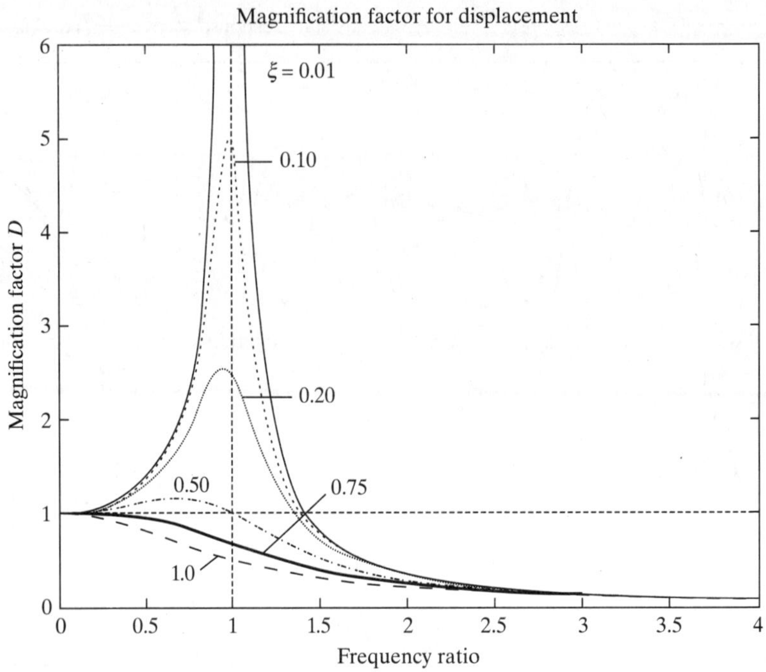

Figure 3.5 Variation of dynamic magnification factor with frequency ratio.

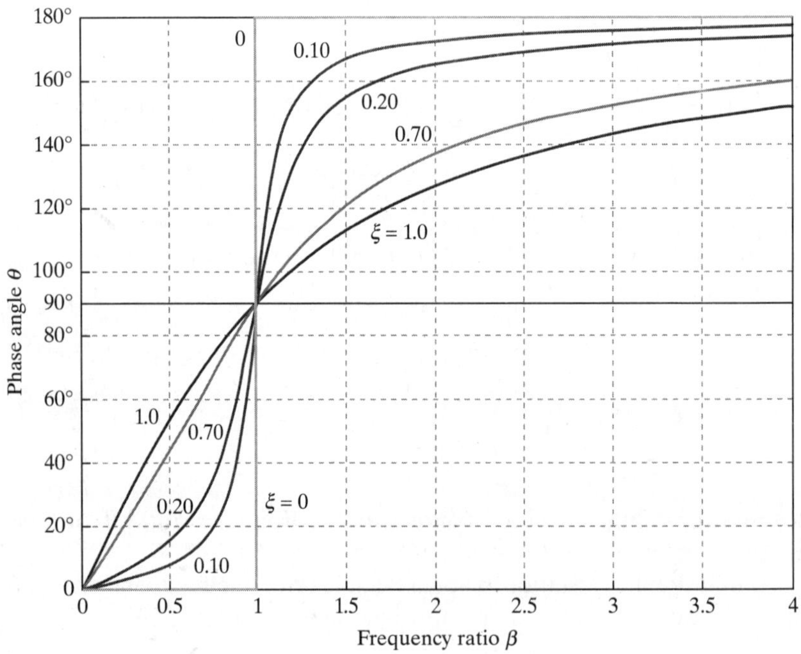

Figure 3.6 Variation of phase angle with frequency ratio.

3.3.1 Dynamic Magnification Factor – Displacement

It is interesting to understand the behaviour of the dynamic magnification factor as seen in Figure 3.5. The following observations can be made:

1. There is a decrease in amplitude of displacement with increase in damping. It is maximum for 0% damping.
2. For frequency ratio equal to 1, that is, at resonance, the displacement amplitude is maximum.
   At $\beta = 1$ and $\xi = 0, D = \infty$
   At $\beta = 1$ and $\xi \neq 0, D$ is very high
3. For frequency ratios near 1, the factor is very sensitive to damping. It can be very large depending upon the damping.

$$x_{max} = x_{static} \frac{1}{2\xi}$$

$$x_{max} = \frac{p_0}{k} \frac{1}{2\xi} = \frac{p_0}{c\omega} \tag{3.16a}$$

4. For frequency ratios less than 1 (<< 1.0), the factor is slightly more than 1 and appears to be independent of damping, that is,

$$D \approx 1, \text{or } x_{max} \approx x_{static} = \frac{p_0}{k} = \frac{p_0}{m\omega^2} \tag{3.16b}$$

5. For frequency ratios greater than 1 (>> 1.0), the factor D tends to be zero and is essentially independent of damping, that is,

$$D \approx \frac{1}{\beta^2} = \frac{\omega^2}{\bar{\omega}^2}$$

or,

$$x_{max} \approx x_{static} \times \left(\frac{k}{m}\right)\left(\frac{1}{\bar{\omega}^2}\right) = \frac{p_0}{k}\frac{k}{m}\frac{1}{\bar{\omega}^2} \tag{3.16c}$$

or,

$$x_{max} \approx \frac{p_0}{m}\frac{1}{\bar{\omega}^2} \tag{3.16d}$$

This information is very useful while designing machine foundations or structures against undesirable vibrations.

Behaviour of the Phase Angle with Frequency Ratio

Similarly, the variation of phase angle between the response and the applied force with frequency ratio and damping can be examined (Figure 3.6):

1. For frequency ratios less than 1 (<< 1.0), the phase angle is close to 0° and the displacement is in phase with the force.
2. For frequency ratios greater than 1 (>> 1.0), the phase angle is very close to 180° and the displacement is out of phase with the force. The force and the displacement are in opposite directions.
3. For frequency ratios equal to 1, the phase angle is 90° irrespective of damping. The displacement attains its peak when the force passes through zero.

3.3.2 Dynamic Magnification Factors – Velocity and Acceleration

Let us consider the steady state displacement derived earlier:

$$x(t) = \rho \sin(\bar{\omega}t - \theta) \tag{3.14b}$$

and

$$D = \frac{\rho}{p_0 / k} \tag{3.15a}$$

$$\therefore \quad \frac{x(t)}{p_0 / k} = D \sin(\bar{\omega}t - \theta) \tag{3.17a}$$

Now, let us differentiate this equation, we get

$$\frac{\dot{x}(t)}{p_0 / k} = D\bar{\omega} \cos(\bar{\omega}t - \theta) \tag{3.17b}$$

Let us define magnification factor for velocity as follows:

$$D_v = \frac{\bar{\omega}}{\omega} D \tag{3.17c}$$

We know that

$$\omega = \sqrt{\frac{k}{m}}$$

$\therefore$ Equation (3.17b) can be written as follows:

$$\frac{\dot{x}(t)}{p_0 / k} = \omega D_v \cos(\bar{\omega}t - \theta) \tag{3.17d}$$

or,

$$\frac{\dot{x}(t)}{p_0 / \sqrt{km}} = D_v \cos(\bar{\omega}t - \theta) \tag{3.17e}$$

where,

D_v = velocity response factor or, velocity magnification factor

Again differentiating Equation (3.17e) gives an equation for acceleration

$$\frac{\ddot{x}(t)}{p_0 / \sqrt{km}} = -D_v \bar{\omega} \sin(\bar{\omega}t - \theta) \tag{3.17f}$$

Let us define magnification factor for acceleration as follows:

$$D_a = \left(\frac{\bar{\omega}}{\omega}\right)^2 D = \frac{\bar{\omega}}{\omega} D_v \tag{3.17g}$$

or,

$$\frac{\ddot{x}(t)}{p_0 / \sqrt{km}} = -\omega D_a \sin(\bar{\omega}t - \theta)$$

or,

$$\frac{\ddot{x}(t)}{p_0 / m} = -D_a \sin(\bar{\omega}t - \theta) \tag{3.17h}$$

where,

D_a = ratio of amplitude of acceleration response to the acceleration due to force p_0 acting on the mass.
= acceleration response factor or, acceleration magnification factor

Equation (3.17g) can be re-written as follows:

$$\frac{D_a}{\left(\frac{\bar{\omega}}{\omega}\right)} = D_v = \left(\frac{\bar{\omega}}{\omega}\right) D \tag{3.18a}$$

or,

$$\frac{D_a}{\beta} = D_v = \beta D \tag{3.18b}$$

where,

$$D = \frac{1}{\sqrt{(1-\beta^2)^2 + (2\beta\xi)^2}} \tag{3.15b}$$

Now it is convenient to plot the three response magnifications factors, D, D_v and D_a against the frequency ratio β for a given damping ratio ξ as shown in Figure 3.5 and Figure 3.7. The following observations can be a made in these plots:

1. The displacement magnification factor D is unity at $\beta = 0$; it attains maximum value at $\beta = 1$; and approaches zero as $\beta \to \infty$.
2. The velocity magnification factor D_v is zero at $\beta = 0$; peaks at $\beta = 1$; and approaches zero as $\beta \to \infty$.
3. The acceleration magnification factor D_a is zero at $\beta = 0$; peaks at $\beta = 1$; and approaches unity as $\beta \to \infty$.
4. For a damping ratio $\xi > 1/\sqrt{2}$, both displacement and velocity magnification factors are less than unity.

It is possible to plot all the three factors in a single plot on a tripartite log paper. It will be discussed later in Chapter 8 on elastic response spectra.

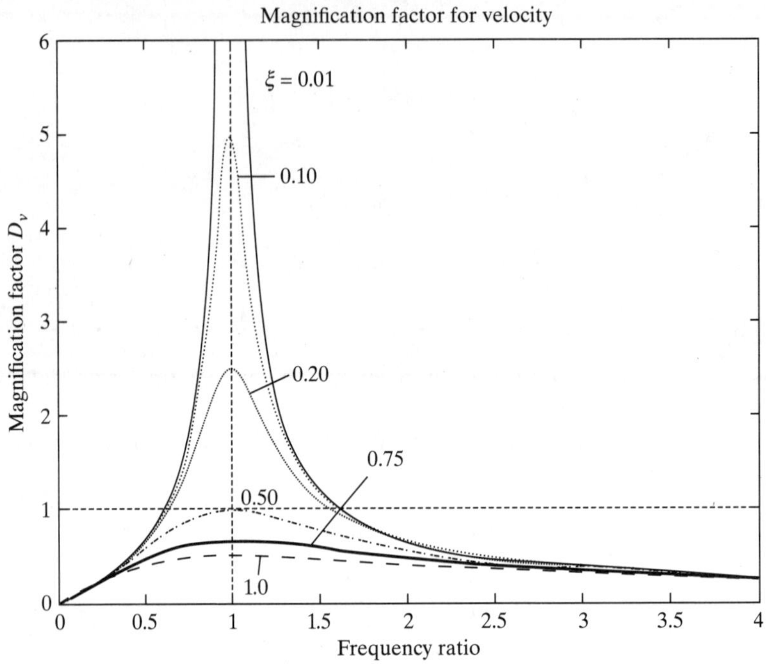

Figure 3.7(a) Magnification factor for velocity with frequency ratio

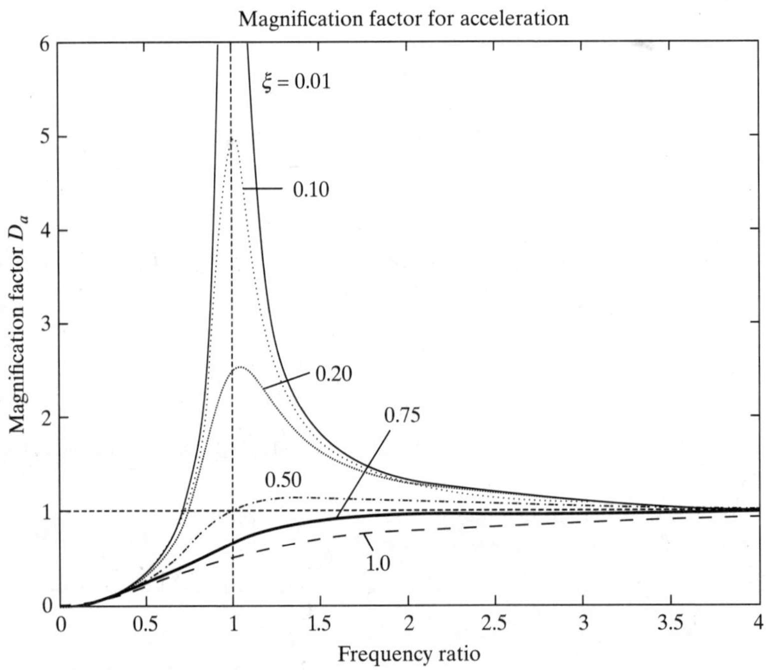

Figure 3.7(b) Magnification factor for acceleration with frequency ratio

3.4 MATLAB APPLICATIONS

Two MATLAB codes have been written. DOS3_1 computes the damped forced response of a SDOF and DOS3_2 computes dynamic magnification factor D and phase angle θ with frequency ratio β

```
------------------
CODE DOS3_1
------------------
%    Dynamics of Structures by Ashok K. Jain I. I. T. Roorkee
%    DOS3_1
%    Damped Forced Vibrations of a SDOF System
%    Calls DOS3_1a
%    The program calls function "ode23" to solve ordinary differential eqn.
%    Initial conditions are defined inside and can be changed.
%    Total duration of sinusoidal force = tf.
%
clear all;
clc;
IC = [0.02;0.05];  % Initial conditions x(0) and v(0)
tf = 15.0;
fprintf('Initial displacement at t=0, is %.3g m\n',IC(1));
fprintf('Initial velocity at t=0, is %.3g m/s\n',IC(2));
fprintf('Total duration of force = %.3g sec\n',tf);
t = [0:0.005:tf];
[t,z] = ode23(@DOS3_1a,t,IC);
% dismax=max((z(:,1)'))  % I need the max. value of displacement
% velmax=max((z(:,2)'))  % I need the maximum value of velocity
% sprintf('%s',dismax, velmax)
plot(t,z(:,1))
grid on;
xlabel('time sec')
ylabel('displacement m')
title('Displacement time history')
figure;
plot(t,z(:,2))
xlabel('time sec')
ylabel('Velocity m/sec')
title('Velocity time history')
grid on;

------------------
CODE DOS3_1a
------------------
%    Dynamics of Structures by Ashok K. Jain I. I. T. Roorkee
%    DOS3_1a
%    Damped Forced Vibrations of a SDOF System
```

```
%   Called by DOS3_1
%   force = f*sin(omegab*t)
%   Input parameters are defined inside function and can be changed
function q=DOS3_1a(t,z)
m=5;
k = 100;
zai=0.05; % 5%
c=2*zai*sqrt(k*m);
omega=sqrt(k/m);
per=2*pi/omega;
omegab=10;
f=10.;
if (t==0)
fprintf('Mass = %.3g kg\n',m);
fprintf('Stiffness = %.3g N/m\n',k);
fprintf('Damping ratio = %.3g \n',zai);
fprintf('Natural frequency = %.3g rad/s.\n',omega);
fprintf('Period of vibration = %.3g s\n',per);
fprintf('Forcing frequency = %.3g rad/s\n',omegab);
fprintf('Amplitude of force = %.3g N\n',f);
end
q=[z(2);((f/m)*sin(omegab*t)-(c/m)*z(2)-(k/m)*z(1))];
end
```

CODE DOS3_2

```
%   Dynamics of Structures by Ashok K. Jain I. I. T. Roorkee
%   DOS3_2
%   Dynamic magnification factor plot
%   Phase angle plot
%   beta = frequency ratio
clc
clear all;
close all
zai=[ 0.0001 0.10 0.20 0.70 1.0];
beta=[0:0.01:4];
for i=1:length(zai)
    for j=1:length(beta)
        d(i,j)=(1/((1-beta(j)^2)^2+(2*beta(j)*zai(i))^2))^0.5;
    end
end
for i=1:length(zai)
    plot(beta,d(i,:),'.-k')
    hold on
end
grid on
xlabel('frequency ratio')
```

```
ylabel('Magnification factor')
axis([0 4 0 10])
hold on
%
% Alternative way of plotting the same but with different colors
%
figure
plot(beta,d,'.-')
grid on
xlabel('frequency ratio')
ylabel('Magnification factor')
axis([0 4 0 10])
hold on
%
% Calculate phase angle with beta and zai
%
for i=1:length(zai)
    for j=1:length(beta)
        theta(i,j)=mod(atan(2*zai(i)*beta(j)/(1-beta(j)*beta(j))),pi);
    end
end
%
figure
for i=1:length(zai)
    plot(beta,theta*180/pi)
    hold on
end
grid on
xlabel('frequency ratio')
ylabel('Phase angle')
%axis([beta(1) beta(end) 0 180]);
--------------------------
```

These codes have been used to generate results as shown in the following examples.

Example 3.1

Consider a SDOF system shown in Figure 3.3. The mass = 5 kNs^2/m, stiffness k = 100 kN/m and damping is 5%. It is subjected to a sinusoidal force having a magnitude of 10 kN and a forcing frequency of 10 rad/sec. Determine the natural frequency and natural period of vibration. The initial conditions are given as: $x(0) = 0.02$ m and $\dot{x}(0) = 0.05$ m/s. Hence, plot its total displacement and total velocity response.

Solution

The displacement and velocity response obtained using MATLAB code are shown in Figure 3.8. It can be seen that in the initial seven seconds, the response is a combination of transient and forcing functions; later the transient response dies down and only steady state response is available. Its free damped vibration response was shown in Example 2.3.

□

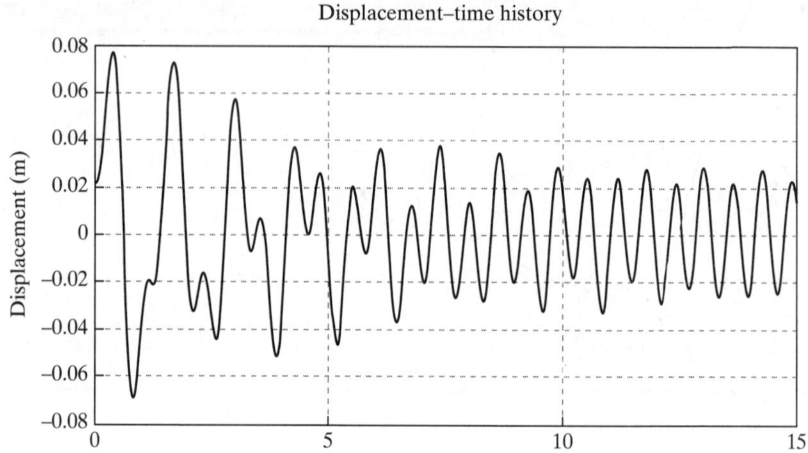

(a) Displacement response

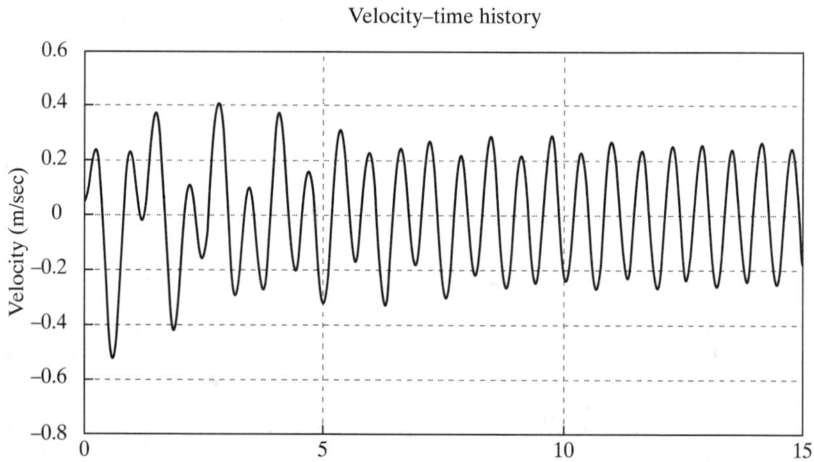

(b) Velocity response

Figure 3.8 Total displacement and velocity response of a damped SDOF system.

Example 3.2

A SDOF system has a stiffness k = 7500 kN/m, natural frequency of 15 rad/sec and a damping of 10%. The initial conditions are $x(0) = 0.01$ m and $\dot{x}(0) = 0.1$ m/sec. Plot the variation in steady state response if the frequency ratio $\beta = 0.5, 1.0$ and 2.0.

Solution

The steady state response was determined using Equation (3.14a) in MS-EXCEL for different frequency ratios and the response is plotted in Figure 3.9. It can be seen that the frequency ratio has a significant influence on the response.

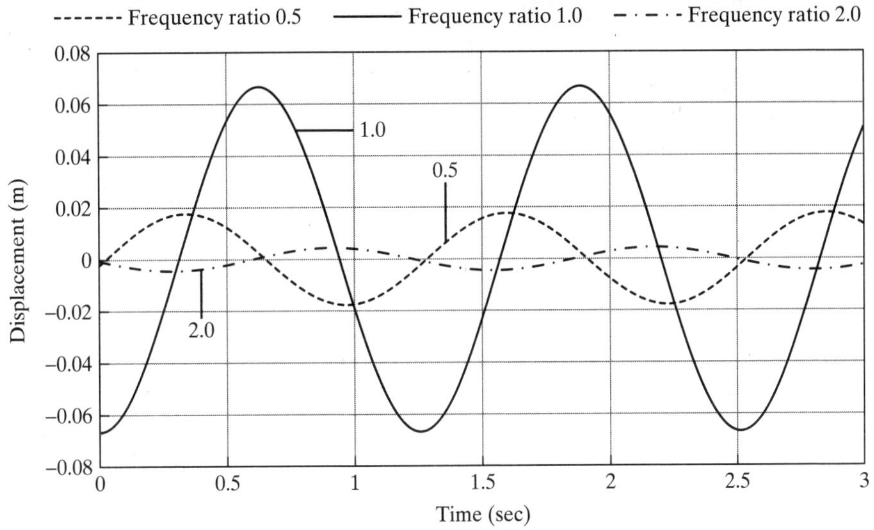

Figure 3.9 Influence of frequency ratio on the steady state response ($\xi = 10\%$).

It would be interesting to know the static response due to the force $p(t)$. It can be determined by applying the force $p(t)$ very slowly instead of at its forcing frequency $\bar{\omega}$ using the following relation:

$$x_{st}(t) = \frac{p_0}{k} \sin \bar{\omega} t$$

or,

$$\frac{x_{st}(t)}{x_0} = \sin \bar{\omega} t$$

The static displacement $x_{st}(t)$ is in phase with the forcing function $p(t)$. By plotting the steady state displacement and static displacement on the same graph for a given forcing frequency, the phase difference can be seen. □

3.5 RESONANT RESPONSE

For an undamped SDOF system subjected to harmonic loading, the dynamic magnification factor D is given by Equation (3.15b) with $\xi = 0$.

$$D = \frac{x_{max}}{x_{static}} = \frac{1}{(1-\beta^2)} \tag{3.15c}$$

At resonance, $\beta = 1, D = \infty$

For a damped system, D is given by Equation (3.15b)

$$D = \frac{1}{\sqrt{(1-\beta^2)^2 + (2\beta\xi)^2}} \tag{3.15b}$$

At resonance, $\beta = 1$, that is,

$$D_{\max} = \frac{1}{2\xi} \tag{3.19a}$$

Let us differentiate D in Equation (3.15b) with respect to β and equate it to zero, it gives, $\beta_{\max} = \sqrt{1-2\xi^2}$ and the corresponding $D_{\max}$ is given by

$$D_{\max} = \frac{1}{2\xi\sqrt{1-\xi^2}} \tag{3.19b}$$

For reasonable amounts of damping, the difference between Equation (3.19a) and (3.19b) is negligible.

Let us consider the nature of resonant response of a SDOF system to harmonic loading. Its total response at $\beta = 1$ is given by Equation (3.11)

$$x(t) = e^{-\xi\omega t}(\mathrm{A}\sin\omega_{\mathrm{D}}t + \mathrm{B}\cos\omega_{\mathrm{D}}t) - \frac{p_0}{k}\frac{\cos\bar{\omega}t}{2\xi} \tag{3.20a}$$

If the system is *at rest* at $t = 0$, $x(0) = 0$ and $\dot{x}(0) = 0$, then

The constants $\quad \mathrm{A} = \frac{p_0}{k}\frac{1}{2\sqrt{1-\xi^2}}$ and $\mathrm{B} = \frac{p_0}{k}\frac{1}{2\xi}$ (3.20b)

Equation (3.20) can be re-written as follows:

For $\beta = 1$ means $\omega = \bar{\omega}$; and if ξ^2 can be neglected, $\omega = \omega_{\mathrm{D}}$; also the term $(\xi \sin \omega_D t)$ will contribute very little and, therefore, ignored.

$$x(t) = \frac{1}{2\xi}\frac{p_0}{k}(e^{-\xi\omega t} - 1)\cos\omega t \tag{3.21}$$

$$\therefore \quad D(t) = \frac{x(t)}{p_0/k} = \frac{1}{2\xi}(e^{-\xi\omega t} - 1)\cos\omega t \tag{3.22}$$

If damping ratio ξ becomes zero, Equation (3.22) becomes indeterminate. Using the principles of differential calculus, the resonant response of an undamped system is given by

$$D(t) = \frac{1}{2}(\sin\omega t - \omega t\cos\omega t) \tag{3.23}$$

A MATLAB code `DOS3_3` is written using Equation (3.22) and (3.23). The plots of Equation (3.22) and (3.23) are shown in Figure 3.10.

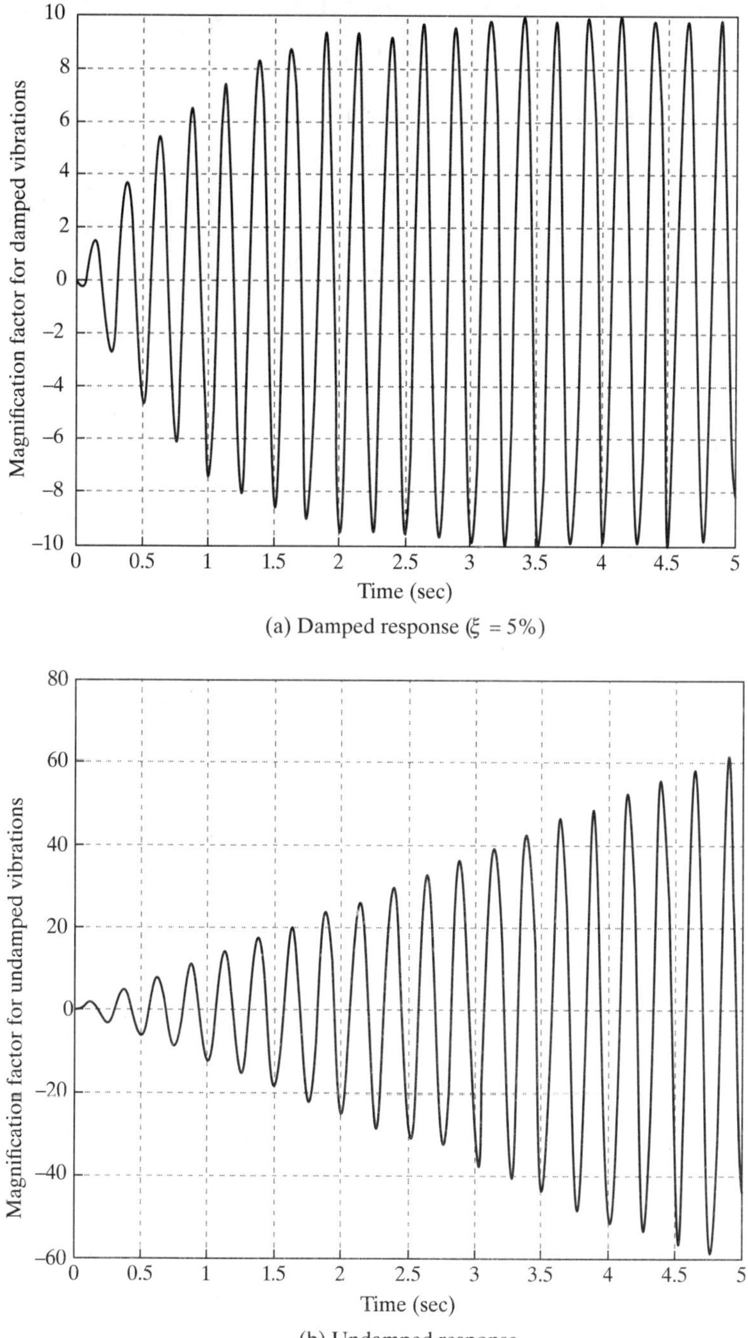

(a) Damped response (ξ = 5%)

(b) Undamped response

Figure 3.10 Resonant response of a SDOF system (ω = 25 rad/sec).

CODE DOS3_3

```
%   Dynamics of Structures by Ashok K. Jain I. I. T. Roorkee
%   DOS3_3
%   Dynamic magnification factor for damped/undamped resonant response
%   Damping ratio = 5%
%   Natural frequency = 25 rad/sec - it can be changed in program
%
clc
clear all;
close all
zai=0.05;
omega=25;
t=[0:0.01:5];
yy=length(t);
for i=1:length(t)
   dd(i)=(1/(2*zai))*(exp(-zai*omega*t(i))-1)*cos(omega*t(i));
end
plot(t,dd,'-r')
hold on
grid on
xlabel('Time, sec')
ylabel('Magnification factor for Damped Vibrations')
%
for i=1:length(t)
yy(i)=0.5*(sin(omega*t(i))-omega*t(i)*cos(omega*t(i)));
end
figure;
plot(t,yy,'-b')
grid on
xlabel('Time, sec')
ylabel('Magnification factor for undamped Vibrations')
```

3.6 MEASUREMENT OF VISCOUS DAMPING

The viscous damping in a SDOF system can be measured as follows:

(a) Free vibration analysis—exponent decay or logarithmic decay method
(b) Resonant amplification method
(c) Half power (Bandwidth) method
(d) Resonant testing or energy loss per cycle method

The exponent decay or logarithmic method has already been discussed earlier in Section 2.5. Let us discuss the other methods.

3.6.1 Resonant Amplification Method

A SDOF system can be subjected to a harmonic loading and under steady state, its vibrations can be recorded. The amplitude and frequency of the harmonic loading can be adjusted to obtain the desired response. The forcing frequency can be varied spanning the resonance and the resulting displacement amplitude can be plotted against frequency ratio. At resonance,

$$\text{Dynamic amplification factor } D = \frac{1}{2\xi} \quad \text{or} \quad \xi = \frac{1}{2D} = \frac{x_{\text{static}}}{2x_{\max}} \tag{3.24}$$

where $x_{\max}$ is measured at resonance.

Sometimes it may be difficult to subject the SDOF system to resonate. Let us rewrite Equation (3.19b) as follows:

$$D_{\max} = \frac{1}{2\xi}\frac{\omega}{\omega_D} \tag{3.25}$$

Thus, damping can be measured.

3.6.2 Half Power (Bandwidth) Method

In this method, the damping is measured at frequencies at which the amplitude is reduced to 1/√2 of that at resonance (Figure 3.11), that is,

$$\text{The displacement amplitude} = \frac{1}{\sqrt{2}} \text{ of } x_{\max} \text{ at } \beta = 1.$$

$$x_{\max} = x_{\text{static}} \times D$$

$$= x_{\text{static}} \times \frac{1}{2\xi} \qquad \text{using Equation (3.24)}$$

The values of these frequency ratios β_1 and β_2 can be determined by setting the response amplitude in Equation (3.15b) equal to $\frac{1}{\sqrt{2}}$ times the resonant amplitude given by Equation (3.24), that is,

$$\therefore \quad \frac{x_{\max}}{\sqrt{2}} = \frac{1}{\sqrt{2}} \times x_{\text{static}} \times \frac{1}{2\xi} \tag{i}$$

$$= x_{\text{static}} \times \frac{1}{\sqrt{(1-\beta^2)^2 + (2\beta\xi)^2}} \tag{ii}$$

Solving for frequency ratio then given

or,
$$\beta^2 = 1 - 2\xi^2 \pm 2\xi\sqrt{1+\xi^2}$$

Neglecting ξ^2 term being too small,

$$\beta^2 \approx 1 \pm 2\xi \quad \text{or} \quad \beta \approx (1 \pm 2\xi)^{\frac{1}{2}}$$

Expanding using the Taylor series and taking only the first term,

$$\beta_1 \approx 1 - \xi \tag{i}$$

Similarly,
$$\beta_2 \approx 1 + \xi \tag{ii}$$

Equations (i) and (ii) give, $\xi = (\beta_2 - \beta_1)/2$ (3.26a)

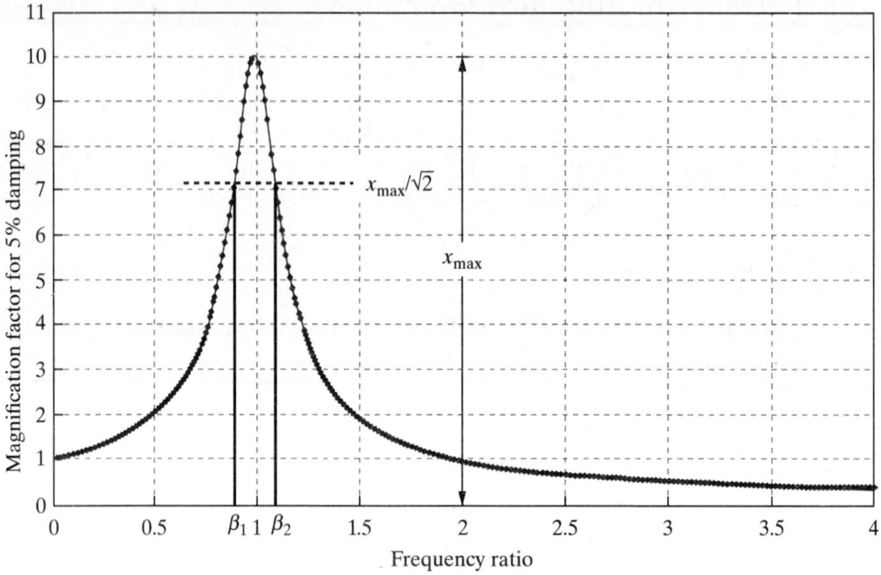

Figure 3.11 Half band frequency response curve.

This can also be written as follows:

$$\xi = \frac{\omega_2 - \omega_1}{2\omega} \tag{3.26b}$$

This is known as *bandwidth method* or *half power method* as illustrated in Figure 3.11.

3.6.3 Energy Loss per Cycle: Resonant Testing Method

Force-deformation curve for a SDOF system when subjected to a force can be plotted in each cycle. The area under the force-deformation curve represents energy dissipation in each cycle. The shape of the force-deformation curve depends upon the nature of the force and system properties. The energy loss per cycle due to elastic force and damping force are shown in Figure 3.12.

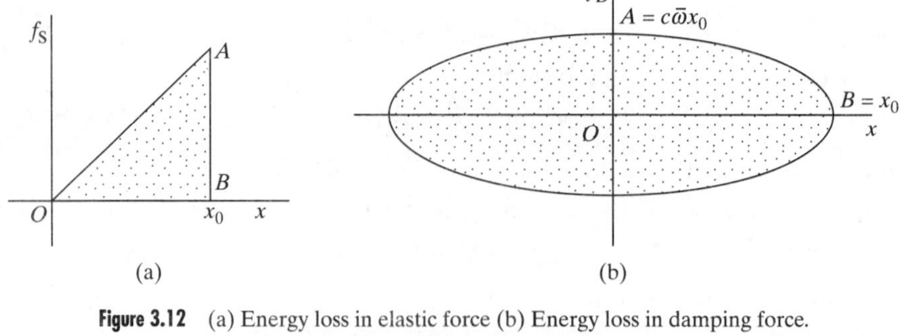

Figure 3.12 (a) Energy loss in elastic force (b) Energy loss in damping force.

Consider the response of a damped SDOF due to sinusoidal loading $p(t) = p_0 \sin \bar{\omega}t$. The input frequency is adjusted until the response is 90° out of phase with the applied loading and the system resonates, that is, $\omega = \bar{\omega}$. Now the applied load is balanced exactly by the damping force. The relation between the applied load and the resulting displacement in one loading cycle is as shown in Figure 3.12(b). This result can be interpreted as the damping force-displacement diagram.

Viscous damping force $f_D = c\dot{x}(t)$

But $x(t) = x_0 \sin \bar{\omega}t$ and $\dot{x}(t) = \bar{\omega}x_0 \cos \bar{\omega}t$

$$\therefore \qquad f_D = c\,\bar{\omega}\,x_0 \cos \bar{\omega}t = c\,\bar{\omega}\,x_0 \sqrt{1-\sin^2 \bar{\omega}t}$$

or,
$$f_D = c\,\bar{\omega}\sqrt{x_0^2 - x^2(t)} \tag{3.27a}$$

This equation can be rewritten as follows:

$$\left(\frac{f_D}{c\,\bar{\omega}}\right)^2 = x_0^2 - x^2(t)$$

or,
$$\left(\frac{x(t)}{x_0}\right)^2 + \left(\frac{f_D}{c\,\bar{\omega}\,x_0}\right)^2 = 1 \tag{3.27b}$$

This represents an ellipse.

Area of the ellipse $= \pi\, a\, b = \pi$ (semi-major axis) $\times$ (semi-minor axis)

$$= \pi\, x_0\, c\,\bar{\omega}\, x_0 = \pi\, c\,\bar{\omega}\, x_0^2 \tag{3.28}$$

Thus, energy loss per cycle in a SDOF due to viscous damping is proportional to:

(i) Damping coefficient c,
(ii) Forcing frequency $\bar{\omega}$, and
(iii) Square of amplitude.

The total spring and damping force $= f_S + f_D = k\,x(t) + c\,\dot{x}(t)$

$$f_S + f_D = k\,x(t) + c\,\bar{\omega}\sqrt{x_0^2 - x^2(t)} \tag{3.29}$$

Let us compute its ordinates as follows:

If $x(t) = 0$, $\quad f_S + f_D = \pm\, c\,\bar{\omega} x_0$ (i)

If $x(t) = x_0$, $\quad f_S + f_D = k\,x_0$ (ii)

If $x(t) = -x_0$, $\quad f_S + f_D = -k\,x_0$ (iii)

If $f_S + f_D = 0$,

$$(k\,x(t))^2 = (c\,\bar{\omega})^2 \left(x_0^2 - x^2(t)\right)$$

or,
$$(k^2 + (c\,\bar{\omega})^2)\,x^2(t) = (c\,\bar{\omega}\,x_0)^2$$

or,
$$x(t) = \pm \frac{c\bar{\omega}x_0}{\sqrt{k^2 + (c\,\bar{\omega})^2}}$$

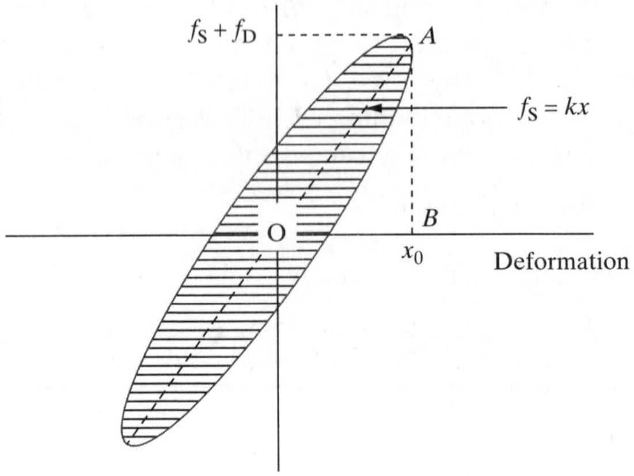

Figure 3.13 Definition of loss of energy E_D and E_S under harmonic vibrations.

$$= \pm \frac{x_0}{\sqrt{1 + \left(\frac{k}{c\bar{\omega}}\right)^2}} \tag{iv}$$

Knowing the various ordinates, Equation (3.29) can be plotted as shown in Figure 3.13. The elliptic curve represents energy dissipated per cycle by the damping force f_D, that is, work done. Similarly, the area OAB represents the energy dissipated per cycle by the spring force f_S. The ordinate OB represents x_0 while the slope OA represents the elastic stiffness k.

If the structure has linear viscous damping, the curve will be an ellipse as shown in Figure 3.12(b). Damping coefficient is given by

$$f_{D\,max} = c\dot{x}_{max}$$

or,

$$c = \frac{f_{D\,max}}{\dot{x}_{max}} = \frac{p_0}{\bar{\omega} x_{max}} \tag{3.30}$$

(given that $p(t) = p_0 \sin \bar{\omega} t, \dot{x}(t) = \bar{\omega} x_0 \cos \bar{\omega} t$ and $x_{max} = x_0$)

If the damping is not linear viscous damping, the shape of the force-deformation curve will not be elliptic but some other shape. However, it is possible to determine equivalent viscous damping by drawing an elliptic force-displacement diagram having the same area and maximum displacement as that of the original curve as shown in Figure 3.14.

If W_D = area under the non-elliptic force-deformation curve
= work done by the equivalent damping force

then W_D = area under the elliptic curve = $\pi a b$.

where, a = amplitude of equivalent applied force = p_0 (say)
b = maximum displacement of the actual force-deformation curve
= x_{max} (say)

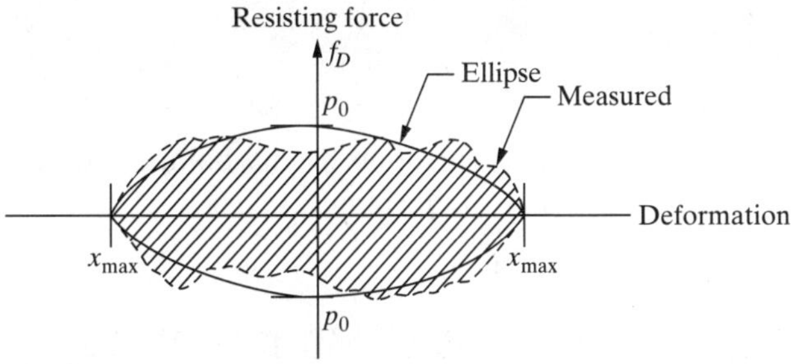

Figure 3.14 Measured and Equivalent damping energy per cycle.

$\therefore$ Amplitude of equivalent applied force $= p_0 = \dfrac{W_D}{\pi x_{max}}$ (v)

$\therefore$ Equivalent viscous damping $C_{eq} = \dfrac{p_0}{\bar{\omega} x_{max}}$ from Equation (3.30)

$$= \frac{1}{\bar{\omega} x_{max}} p_0 = \frac{1}{\bar{\omega} x_{max}} \frac{W_D}{\pi x_{max}} \text{ from (v)}$$

or,
$$C_{eq} = \frac{W_D}{\pi \bar{\omega} x_{max}^2} \quad \text{(vi)}$$

If
$$C_c = 2m\omega = \frac{2k}{\omega} \quad \text{(vii)}$$

The equivalent elastic stiffness can be measured by the area under the linear elastic force-deformation curve, that is, work done by the spring force W_S

$$W_S = \frac{1}{2} x_{max} f_S = \frac{1}{2} k\, x_{max}^2$$

or,
$$k = \frac{2W_S}{x_{max}^2} \quad \text{(viii)}$$

The damping ratio is given by $\xi = C_{eq}/C_c$
Making use of Equations (vi) and (vii),

$$\xi = \frac{W_D}{\pi \bar{\omega} x_{max}^2} \Big/ \frac{2k}{\omega}$$

Again, making use of Equation (viii),

$$\xi = \frac{\dfrac{W_D}{\pi \bar{\omega} x_{max}^2}}{\dfrac{2}{\omega} \dfrac{2W_S}{x_{max}^2}}$$

or, $$\xi = \frac{W_D}{4\pi W_S} \text{ where } \omega = \bar{\omega} \text{ at resonance} \tag{3.31}$$

Knowing the area under the work done by the damped force and elastic force, the equivalent damping ratio can be determined.

3.7 MEASUREMENT OF COULOMB DAMPING

Let us determine equivalent viscous damping for a system with Coulomb damping. Equation (vi) can be re-written as:

$$W_D = \pi\, \bar{\omega} x_{max}^2 C_{eq}$$

or, $$W_D = \pi\, \bar{\omega} x_{max}^2 \xi_{eq} 2\frac{k}{\omega} = 2\pi\xi_{eq}\frac{\bar{\omega}}{\omega} k\, x_{max}^2 = 4\pi\xi_{eq}\frac{\bar{\omega}}{\omega} W_S \tag{3.32}$$

or, $$\xi_{eq} = \frac{1}{4\pi\left(\dfrac{\bar{\omega}}{\omega}\right)}\frac{W_D}{W_S} \tag{3.33}$$

Coulomb damping will produce a rectangular hysteresis loop as shown in Figure 3.15.

The area under the curve is given by

$$W_D = 4Fx_{max}$$

$$\xi_{eq} = \frac{4Fx_{max}}{4\pi\left(\dfrac{\bar{\omega}}{\omega}\right)\dfrac{1}{2}kx_{max}^2} = \frac{2}{\pi}\frac{1}{\left(\dfrac{\bar{\omega}}{\omega}\right)}\frac{F}{k}\frac{1}{x_{max}} = \frac{2}{\pi}\frac{1}{\left(\dfrac{\bar{\omega}}{\omega}\right)}\frac{x_F}{x_{max}} \tag{3.34}$$

where $$x_F = \frac{F}{k} = \frac{\mu mg}{k}$$

For a system subjected to harmonic loading, the maximum dynamic displacement can be determined from the dynamic amplification factor discussed earlier.

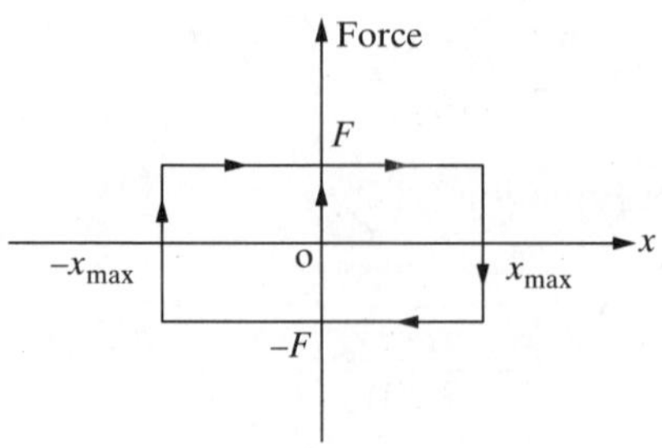

Figure 3.15 Hysteresis loop for Columb friction.

3.8 ILLUSTRATIVE EXAMPLES

Example 3.3

A SDOF system is subjected to a sinusoidal force. At resonance, the displacement amplitude is 70 mm. At an exciting frequency of one-fifth of the natural frequency of the system, the displacement amplitude was measured to be 10 mm. Determine the damping ratio.

Solution

Dynamic amplification factor $D = \dfrac{1}{\sqrt{(1-\beta^2)^2+(2\beta\xi)^2}}$

At frequency ratio $\beta = 1$,

$$D = \frac{70}{x_{\text{static}}} = \frac{1}{\sqrt{(2\times 1\times\xi)^2}} \quad \text{(i)}$$

At a frequency ratio $\beta = 1/5$,

$$D = \frac{10}{x_{\text{static}}} = \frac{1}{\sqrt{(1-0.2^2)^2+(2\times 0.2\times\xi)^2}} \quad \text{(ii)}$$

Dividing Equations (i) and (ii) and solving for ξ gives, $\xi = 6.85\%$

If at an exciting frequency of 2.5 times natural frequency, the same displacement amplitude of 10 mm is again observed, determine the damping ratio.

At a frequency ratio $\beta = 2.5$

$$D = \frac{10}{x_{\text{static}}} = \frac{1}{\sqrt{(1-2.5^2)^2+(2\times 2.5\times\xi)^2}} \quad \text{(iii)}$$

Dividing Equations (i) and (iii), and solving for ξ gives, $\xi = 0.40$ or 40%.

The damping plays a very significant role on the magnification depending upon the frequency ratio. □

Example 3.4

A SDOF system has a mass m = 35 kN s²/m, damping c = 27.5 kN s/m and stiffness k = 6000 kN/m. It is subjected to a sinusoidal force having amplitude p_0 = 100 kN. Determine the peak response if the forcing frequency is (i) 12.5 rad/sec and (ii) 3.5 rad/sec.

Solution

Natural frequency of vibration $\omega = \sqrt{\dfrac{k}{m}} = \sqrt{\dfrac{6000}{35}} = 13.09$ rad/sec

or, Period T = 0.48 sec

Critical damping $c_c = 2m\omega = 2\sqrt{km} = 2\sqrt{35\times 6000} = 916.5$ kNs/m

Damping ratio $\xi = c/c_c = 27.5/916.5 = 0.03$ or 3%

Case 1: Frequency ratio $\beta = \bar{\omega}/\omega = 12.5/13.09 = 0.955$

Dynamic amplification factor $D = \dfrac{1}{\sqrt{(1-\beta^2)^2+(2\beta\xi)^2}} = 9.52$

Static displacement $D_{ST} = p_0/k = 100/6000 = 0.0167$ m
$\therefore$ Peak dynamic displacement $= 9.52 \times 0.0167 = 0.159$ m
This is quite close to resonance.

Case 2: Frequency ratio $\beta = \bar{\omega}/\omega = 3.5/13.09 = 0.267$

Dynamic amplification factor $D = \dfrac{1}{\sqrt{(1-\beta^2)^2 + (2\beta\xi)^2}} = 1.077$

$\therefore$ Peak dynamic displacement $= 1.077 \times 0.0167 = 0.018$ m
Thus, there is little amplification as the forcing frequency is quite away from resonance. □

Example 3.5

A damped SDOF having a mass of 10 kg and a period of 0.1 sec undergoes resonant amplitude of 0.025 m. It was excited by a harmonic force having 50 N amplitude. Determine the damping coefficient.

Solution

Natural frequency $\omega = \dfrac{2\pi}{T} = \dfrac{2\times\pi}{0.1}$ $\quad\therefore \omega = 62.83$ rad/sec

At resonance, the forcing frequency $\bar{\omega} = \omega = 62.83$ rad/sec

Also, $\omega = \sqrt{\dfrac{k}{m}}$ or, $62.83 = \sqrt{\dfrac{k}{10}}$ or, $k = 39470$ N/m

Static displacement $x_{static} = \dfrac{F}{k} = \dfrac{50}{39470} = 0.00126$ m

Dynamic magnification factor D at resonance $= \dfrac{x_{max}}{x_{static}} = \dfrac{1}{2\xi}$

$\therefore \xi = \dfrac{x_{static}}{2x_{max}} = \dfrac{0.00126}{2\times 0.025} = 0.025$, or, damping ratio $\xi = 2.5\%$

Damping ratio $\xi = \dfrac{c}{c_c} = \dfrac{c}{2m\omega}$

or, damping coefficient $c = 2\text{ m }\omega\xi = 2 \times 10 \times 62.83 \times 0.025 = 31.66$ Ns/m □

Example 3.6

A portal frame supports a machine that exerts a sinusoidal force of 8.5 kN at a frequency of 1.75 Hz. The mass of the machine is 4000 kg and is added to that of the frame. The mass of the frame at the floor level is 5000 kg and lateral stiffness of the frame is 4×10^6 N/m.

(a) Determine the steady state amplitude of vibration, if damping ratio is 4%.
(b) What would be the steady state amplitude if the forcing frequency was in resonance with the supporting structure?

Solution

Given $p_0 = 8.5$ kN $= 8500$ N, $\bar{f} = 1.75$ Hz or, $\bar{\omega} = 2\pi\, 1.75$ rad/sec

Lateral stiffness $k = 4 \times 10^6$ N/m

The applied force $p(t) = p_0 \sin \bar{\omega} t = 8500 \sin (2\pi 1.75\, t)$

or, $p(t) = 8500 \sin 11\, t$

Maximum static deflection $\Delta st = p_0/k = 8500/4 \times 10^6 = 0.002125\, m = 2.125$ mm

Total mass = 5000 + 4000 = 9000 kg

Natural frequency of the total system $\omega = \sqrt{\dfrac{k}{m}} = \sqrt{\dfrac{4\times 10^6}{9000}} = 21.08$ rad/sec

or, $f = \omega/2\,\pi = 3.356$ Hz

$\therefore$ Frequency ratio $\beta = \bar{\omega}/\omega = \bar{f}/f = 1.75/3.356 = 0.521$

Dynamic amplification factor $D = \dfrac{1}{\sqrt{(1-\beta^2)^2 + (2\beta\xi)^2}} = 1.371$ for $\xi = 4\%$

$\therefore$ Steady state amplitude = $D\, x_{st} = 1.371 \times 2.125 = 2.92$ mm

At resonance, $\beta = 1$

$\therefore$ Dynamic amplification factor $D = \dfrac{1}{2\xi} = 1/0.08 = 12.5$

$\therefore$ Steady state amplitude = $D\, x_{st} = 12.5 \times 2.125 = 26.56$ mm □

Example 3.7

In a SDOF system, the damping force is proportional to the square of speed. Determine the equivalent viscous damping for this system.

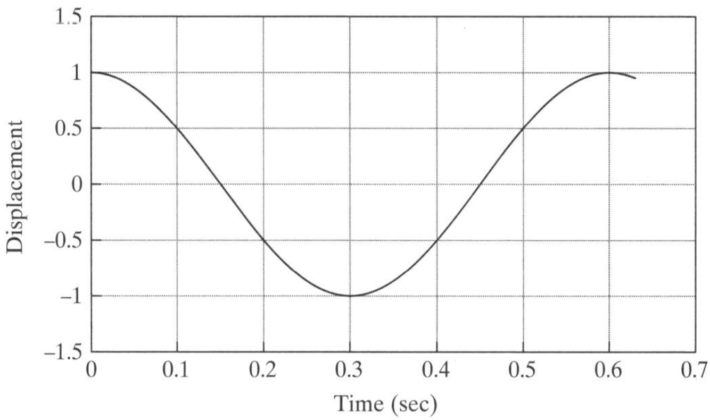

Figure 3.16 Cosine function.

Solution

It is given that $f_D \propto \pm(\dot{x}(t))^2$ or $f_D = \pm\alpha\,(\dot{x}(t))^2$ (i)

where α = damping coefficient

The energy dissipated per cycle = $W_D = 2\int_{-x_0}^{x_0} (\alpha \dot{x}^2)\, dx$

Let $x(t) = x_0 \cos \bar{\omega} t$ (Figure 3.16)

$\therefore$ $dx = -\bar{\omega} x_0 \sin \bar{\omega} t\; dt$

or, $\quad dx = \dot{x}\, dt$

$$\therefore \quad W_D = 2\int_{-x_0}^{x_0} (\alpha \dot{x}^3) dt \tag{ii}$$

Let us find the limits in terms of $\bar{\omega}$.

When $\quad x = -x_0$

$$\cos \bar{\omega} t = -1$$

or, $\quad \cos \frac{2\pi}{\bar{T}} t = -1$

or, $\quad t = \frac{\bar{T}}{2} = \frac{\pi}{\bar{\omega}}$

When $\quad x = x_0$

$$\cos \bar{\omega} t = 1$$

or, $\quad t = 0$

$$\therefore \quad W_D = 2\int_{\frac{\pi}{\bar{\omega}}}^{0} (\alpha \dot{x}^3) dt = 2\int_{\frac{\pi}{\bar{\omega}}}^{0} \alpha(-x_0 \bar{\omega} \sin \bar{\omega} t)^3 dt$$

$$= -2\alpha x_0^3 \bar{\omega}^3 \int_{\frac{\pi}{\bar{\omega}}}^{0} \sin^3 \bar{\omega} t\, dt$$

$$= -2\alpha x_0^3 \bar{\omega}^3 \left| \frac{-1}{3\bar{\omega}} \cos \bar{\omega} t\, (\sin^2 \bar{\omega} t + 2) \right|_{\frac{\pi}{\omega}}^{0}$$

$$= \frac{8}{3} \alpha \bar{\omega}^2 x_0^3$$

$$\therefore \text{ Equivalent damping} \quad C_{eq} = \frac{W_D}{\pi \bar{\omega} x_{max}^2} = \frac{8/3 \alpha \bar{\omega}^2 x_0^3}{\pi \bar{\omega} x_0^2}$$

or, $\quad C_{eq} = \frac{8}{3\pi} \alpha \bar{\omega} x_0$ □

Example 3.8

A system of mass 20 kg and stiffness 15000 N/m is subjected to Coulomb damping. If the mass is driven harmonically by a 100 N force at 6 Hz, determine the equivalent viscous damping coefficient if the coefficient of friction is 0.35.

Solution

Forcing frequency $\bar{\omega} = 2\pi f = 2\pi(6) = 37.70$ rad/sec

Natural frequency $\omega = \sqrt{(k/m)} = \sqrt{(15000/20)} = 27.38$ rad/sec

Frequency ratio $\beta = 37.70/27.38 = 1.37$

$$x_F = \frac{F}{k} = \frac{\mu m g}{k} = \frac{0.35 \times 20 \times 9.81}{15000} = 4.578 \times 10^{-3}\text{m}$$

$$x_{static} = 100/15000 = 6.666 \times 10^{-3}\text{ m}$$

$$D = [(1-\beta^2)^2 + (2\xi\beta)^2]^{-0.5}$$

$$\frac{x_{max}}{x_{static}} = \frac{1}{\sqrt{(1-\beta^2)^2 + (2\beta\xi)^2}}$$

$$\therefore \quad x_{max} = \frac{6.666\times 10^{-3}}{\sqrt{(1-1.37^2)^2 + (2\times 1.37\times \xi_{eq})^2}}$$

Also,

$$\xi_{eq} = \frac{2}{\pi}\frac{1}{\left(\dfrac{\bar{\omega}}{\omega}\right)}\frac{x_F}{x_{max}} = \frac{2\times 4.578\times 10^{-3}}{\pi\times 1.37\times x_{max}}$$

Equating the value of x_{max} from these two equations, we obtain,

$$\xi_{eq} = 0.57 \quad \text{or} \quad \xi_{eq} = 57\%$$ □

REVIEW QUESTIONS

3.1 Why a study of the response of a SDOF system is critical in structural dynamics?

3.2 Derive an expression for transient response of an undamped SDOF system subjected to a harmonic loading $p(t) = p_0 \sin \bar{\omega}t$.

3.3 Write a note on dynamic magnification factor.

3.4 Derive an expression for dynamic magnification factor for an undamped SDOF system subjected to a harmonic loading $p(t) = p_0 \sin \bar{\omega}t$.

3.5 Derive an expression for the total response of a damped SDOF system subjected to a harmonic loading $p(t) = p_0 \sin \bar{\omega}t$.

3.6 Derive an expression for dynamic magnification factor for displacement of a damped SDOF system subjected to a harmonic loading $p(t) = p_0 \sin \bar{\omega}t$. Discuss its salient features.

3.7 What do you understand by the dynamic magnification factors for displacement, velocity, and acceleration of a SDOF system subjected to a harmonic loading $p(t) = p_0 \sin \bar{\omega}t$.

3.8 What is the relationship between dynamic magnification factors for displacement, velocity, and acceleration?

3.9 What are the values of dynamic magnification factors for displacement, velocity, and acceleration for the frequency ratio (i) $\beta = 0$, (ii) $\beta = 1$, and (iii) $\beta = \propto$?

3.10 Plot variation of dynamic magnification factor D vs. frequency ratio β for 0%, 20% and 70% damping ratio ξ. Discuss its salient features.

3.11 Plot variation of phase angle θ vs. frequency ratio β for 0%, 20% and 100% damping ratio ξ for a SDOF system. Discuss its salient features.

3.12 What do you understand by resonant response of a damped SDOF system? What is the maximum dynamic magnification factor?

3.13 What do you understand by resonant response of an undamped SDOF system? What is the maximum dynamic magnification factor?

3.14 How do you measure viscous damping using half power method?

3.15 How do you measure viscous damping using resonant amplification method?

3.16 How do you measure Coulomb damping?

PROBLEMS

3.1 Consider a SDOF system having a mass $m = 8$ kg and stiffness $k = 3000$ N/m. It is subjected to a harmonic force $p_0 \cos \bar{\omega}t$, where $p_0 = 50$ N and forcing frequency is 3 Hz. If the system is initially at rest, plot the steady state response time history.

3.2 How the response will change in Problem 3.1, if the initial conditions are $x(0) = 0$ and $\dot{x}(0) = 0.1$ m/s?

3.3 How the response in Problem 3.1 will change if the damping ratio is 5%?

3.4 Consider a SDOF system having a mass $m = 30$ kN s²/m, damping $c = 50$ kN s/m and stiffness $k = 4000$ kN/m. It is subjected to a harmonic force having an amplitude of $p_0 = 150$ kN. For $x(0) = 0.02$ m and $\dot{x}(0) = 0.1$ m/s. Plot

(a) the transient response time history

(b) the steady state response time history

(c) total response time history

(d) inertia, damping and spring force time history

(Hint: You may make use of MS-EXCEL worksheet)

3.5 In Problem 3.4 determine the magnification factor if (i) $\bar{\omega} = 20$ rad/sec and (ii) $\bar{\omega} = 5$ rad sec.

Ans: $\omega = 11.55$ rad/sec, (i) $D = 0.498$, (ii) $D = 1.22$

3.6 A SDOF system is subjected to a sinusoidal force. At resonance, the displacement amplitude is 100 mm. At an exciting frequency of one-third of the natural frequency of the system, the displacement amplitude was measured to be 25 mm. Determine the damping ratio.

Ans: $\xi = 11.1\%$

3.7 A SDOF system is subjected to a sinusoidal excitation. It was observed that at resonance the amplitude is eight times of that at a frequency ratio of 3. Estimate the damping ratio.

Ans: $\xi = 54$ %

3.8 The mass m, stiffness k and natural frequency of an undamped SDOF system are unknown. These properties are to be determined by harmonic excitation tests. At an excitation frequency of 4 Hz, the response tends to increase without any bound. Next, a mass $\Delta m = 15$ kg is attached to the mass m and the resonance test is repeated. This time resonance occurs at $f = 3$ Hz. Determine the mass and stiffness of the system.

Ans: $m = 19.28$ kg, $k = 12180$ N/m

3.9 A system of mass 12 kg and stiffness 15000 N/m exhibits Coulomb damping. If the mass is driven harmonically by a 120 N force at 25 Hz, determine the equivalent viscous damping coefficient if the coefficient of friction is 0.15.

Ans: $\xi_{eq} = 40.2$ %

3.10 In a resonant vibration test, it was noted that at frequency ratios of 0.97 and 1.05, the maximum amplitude was $1/\sqrt{2}$ of that at the resonance. Estimate the damping ratio.

Ans: $\xi = 4\ \%$

3.11 A SDOF system was subjected to sinusoidal loading at different frequencies and the steady state amplitude of acceleration was recorded as follows:

Frequency Hz	Acceleration amplitude, (10^{-2}) g	Frequency Hz	Acceleration amplitude, (10^{-2})g
2.10	0.55	2.21	7.2
2.11	0.7	2.22	6.2
2.12	0.9	2.23	5.3
2.13	1.3	2.24	4.7
2.14	1.9	2.25	3.95
2.15	2.5	2.26	3.4
2.16	3.4	2.27	2.7
2.17	6.5	2.28	2.1
2.18	9.4	2.29	1.7
2.19	10.2	2.30	1.6
2.20	8.5		

Determine the natural frequency of vibration and damping ratio.

MATLAB AND PYTHON APPLICATIONS

3.12 A single degree of freedom system has a mass of 40 kg, damping ratio of 5% and stiffness of 2000 N/m. It is subjected to a periodic forcing function $P_0 \sin \bar{\omega} t$, where $P_0 = 1000$ N and forcing frequency $\bar{\omega} = 10$ rad/sec. Using MATLAB function 'diff' determine

(a) the maximum displacement from rest position, $x(0) = 0$ and $v(0) = 5$ mm/s.

(b) the response of the system at 2 sec.

(c) the maximum force applied to dash pot.

(d) the angle by which the displacement lags the applied force.

3.13 A single degree of freedom system has a mass of 75 kg and stiffness of 1500 N/m and exhibits Coulomb damping with coefficient of friction of 0.12. The initial conditions are $x(0) = 0.2$ m, and $\dot{x}(0) = 0$. Plot its response and determine how long does it take for the system to come to rest.

4 Single Degree of Freedom System: Periodic Loading

4.1 INTRODUCTION

Sometimes it is very difficult to express dynamic loading in terms of an equation. If this loading happens to be periodic as shown in Figure 4.1, then it is possible to express it in the form of Fourier trigonometric series. Each term of the Fourier series represents a harmonic component. The response of a SDOF system due to harmonic loading has already been computed earlier. The response to each term of the series is then merely the response to a harmonic loading, and by the principle of superposition the total response is sum of response of each individual harmonic term. The response of a SDOF system to a periodic loading is examined with the help of Fourier series. The load and response terms are expressed in terms of trigonometric series or exponential series. The response of a SDOF system can be studied in frequency domain through a Fourier transform pair. The Fourier series representation involves intensive mathematics and integration. The final expressions may sometimes be quite lengthy. Therefore, it is highly recommended that these equations should be developed in graphics form using MS Excel or MATLAB in order to appreciate the power of the Fourier series.

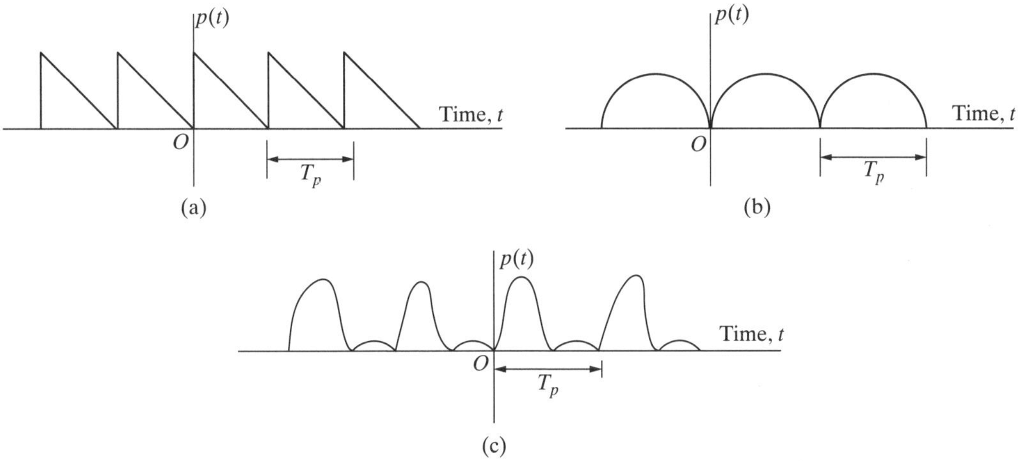

Figure 4.1 Periodic loading.

4.2 FOURIER SERIES

A periodic function $p(t)$ can be expressed by the Fourier series:

$$p(t) = a_0 + \sum_{n=1}^{\infty} a_n \cos n\bar{\omega}_1 t + \sum_{n=1}^{\infty} b_1 \sin n\bar{\omega}_1 t \tag{4.1a}$$

or,

$$p(t) = a_0 + \sum_{n=1}^{\infty} a_n \cos \frac{2\pi n}{T_p} t + \sum_{n=1}^{\infty} b_n \sin \frac{2\pi n}{T_p} t \tag{4.1b}$$

where

n = number of harmonics and varies from 1 to ∝

$\bar{\omega}_1$ = first harmonic frequency of the load function $= \dfrac{2\pi}{T_p}$

$\bar{\omega}_n = n\bar{\omega}_1$

T_p = period of the load function

The coefficients a_0, a_n and b_n can be expressed in terms of $p(t)$ because the sine and cosine functions are orthogonal:

$$a_0 = \frac{1}{T_p} \int_0^{T_p} p(t)\, dt$$

$$a_n = \frac{2}{T_p} \int_0^{T_p} p(t) \cos \frac{2\pi n}{T_p} t \qquad n = 1, 2, 3.... \tag{4.2}$$

and

$$b_n = \frac{2}{T_p} \int_0^{T_p} p(t) \sin \frac{2\pi n}{T_p} t \qquad n = 1, 2, 3, ...$$

The orthogonality property of the trigonometric functions can be stated as follows:

$$\int_0^T \sin n\omega_1 t \, \sin m\omega_1 t \, dt = \begin{cases} 0 & m \neq n \\ T/2 & m = n \end{cases}$$

$$\int_0^T \cos n\omega_1 t \, \cos m\omega_1 t \, dt = \begin{cases} 0 & m \neq n \\ T/2 & m = n \end{cases}$$

$$\int_0^T \cos n\omega_1 t \, \sin m\omega_1 t \, dt = 0 \tag{4.3}$$

where, n and m are integers.

When an arbitrary periodic loading has been expressed in the Fourier series in the form of Equation (4.1), it is apparent that it consists of a

(i) constant load – average load value represented by coefficient a_0, plus
(ii) a series of harmonic loads of frequencies $n\bar{\omega}_1$ and amplitudes a_n and b_n

4.3 UNDAMPED SYSTEM

The total response produced in an undamped SDOF structure by each sine term of the harmonic loading series is given as follows:

$$x(t) = \frac{p_0}{k}\frac{1}{(1-\beta^2)}(\sin\bar{\omega}t - \beta\sin\omega t) \tag{4.4}$$

The steady state response can be determined by omitting the transient term (sin ωt), as follows:

Sine terms

$$x_n(t) = \frac{b_n}{k}\frac{1}{1-\beta_n^2}\sin n\bar{\omega}_1 t \tag{4.5a}$$

where

$$\beta_n = \frac{n\bar{\omega}_1}{\omega} = \frac{nT}{T_p} \tag{4.5b}$$

Cosine terms

Similarly, the response due to the cosine terms can be determined:

$$x_n(t) = \frac{a_n}{k}\frac{1}{1-\beta_n^2}\cos n\bar{\omega}_1 t \tag{4.5c}$$

Constant term

$$x_0 = a_0/k \tag{4.5d}$$

The total periodic steady state response of the undamped structure can be expressed as follows:

$$x(t) = \frac{1}{k}[a_0 + \sum_{n=1}^{\infty}\frac{1}{1-\beta_n^2}(a_n\cos n\bar{\omega}_1 t + b_n\sin n\bar{\omega}_1 t)] \tag{4.6}$$

where the load amplitude coefficients are given by Equation (4.2).

4.4 DAMPED SYSTEM

To take account of damping in evaluating the response of a SDOF structure to a periodic loading, it is necessary merely to substitute the damped harmonic response expression in the form of Equation (3.11) for the undamped response expressions in Equation (4.6). The total steady state response is given by:

$$x(t) = \frac{1}{k}(a_0 + \sum_{n=1}^{\infty}\frac{1}{(1-\beta_n^2)^2 + (2\xi\beta_n)^2}$$

$$\{[a_n 2\xi\beta_n + b_n(1-\beta_n^2)]\sin n\bar{\omega}_1 t$$

$$+[a_n(1-\beta_n^2) - b_n 2\xi\beta_n]\cos n\bar{\omega}_1 t\} \tag{4.7}$$

4.5 EXPONENTIAL FORM OF FOURIER SERIES SOLUTION

The Fourier series expressions of Equations (4.1) and (4.2) can also be written in exponential form by substituting for the trigonometric functions, the corresponding exponential terms given by Euler's equation, namely

$$\sin x = -i\frac{(e^{ix} - e^{-ix})}{2}$$

$$\cos x = \frac{(e^{ix} + e^{-ix})}{2} \tag{4.8}$$

The result is

$$p(t) = \sum_{n=-\infty}^{\infty} C_n\, e^{in\bar{\omega}_1 t} \tag{4.9a}$$

where,

$$C_n = \frac{1}{T_p}\int_0^{T_p} p(t)e^{-in\bar{\omega}_1 t}dt \tag{4.9b}$$

Having expressed the arbitrary periodic loading in the exponential Fourier series form, by means of Equations (4.9a) and (4.9b), let us write the response in the exponential form.

The equation of motion can be written as follows:

$$m\ddot{x}(t) + c\dot{x}(t) + kx(t) = p(t) = e^{i\bar{\omega}t} \tag{4.10}$$

↑ unit complex forcing function

Its steady state solution is of the form

$$x(t) = H(\bar{\omega})\, p(t) \tag{4.11a}$$

$$x(t) = H(\bar{\omega})e^{i\bar{\omega}t} \tag{4.11b}$$

where $H(\bar{\omega})$ = complex frequency response function.
Let us differentiate Equation (4.11b) twice

$$\dot{x}(t) = i\bar{\omega}H(\bar{\omega})e^{i\bar{\omega}t} \tag{4.11c}$$

and

$$\ddot{x}(t) = -\bar{\omega}^2 H(\bar{\omega})e^{i\bar{\omega}t} \tag{4.11d}$$

Substituting Equations (4.11c) and (4.11d) in Equation (4.10) gives

$$\left(-\bar{\omega}^2 m + i\bar{\omega}c + k\right)H(\bar{\omega})e^{i\bar{\omega}t} = e^{i\bar{\omega}t}$$

or,

$$H(\bar{\omega}) = \frac{1}{-\bar{\omega}^2 m + i\bar{\omega}c + k} \tag{4.12a}$$

$$= \frac{1}{k(-\beta^2 + 2i\xi\beta + 1)} \tag{4.12b}$$

Consequently, the complex frequency response to a forcing frequency $\bar{\omega} = n\bar{\omega}_1$ will be

$$H(n\bar{\omega}_1) = \frac{1}{k(-n^2\beta_1^2 + 2in\beta_1\xi + 1)} \tag{4.13}$$

where, $\beta_1 = \bar{\omega}_1 / \omega$

Equation (4.13) shows that $H(n\bar{\omega}_1)$ is complex conjugate of $H(-n\bar{\omega}_1)$. Hence, it is possible to express the steady state response of a SDOF system to the forcing function which represents each term of the Fourier series. From the principle of superposition, it follows that the total steady state response of the system to any periodic forcing function can be written as:

$$x(t) = \sum_{n=-\infty}^{\infty} H(n\bar{\omega}_1) C_n e^{in\bar{\omega}_1 t} \tag{4.14}$$

where $H(n\bar{\omega}_1)$ is given by Equation (4.13) and C_n is given by Equation (4.9b).
Alternatively,
The equation of motion given by Equation (4.10a) can be written as follows:

$$\ddot{x}(t) + 2\xi\omega\dot{x}(t) + \omega^2 x(t) = e^{i\bar{\omega}t} \tag{4.10b}$$

Substituting Equation (4.11) in Equation (4.10b),

$$\left(-\bar{\omega}^2 + i2\xi\omega\bar{\omega} + \omega^2\right) H(\bar{\omega}) e^{i\bar{\omega}t} = e^{i\bar{\omega}t}$$

or, for a damped system,

$$H(\bar{\omega}) = \frac{1}{(\omega^2 + i2\xi\omega\bar{\omega} - \bar{\omega}^2)} \tag{4.12c}$$

and for an undamped system,

$$H(\bar{\omega}) = \frac{1}{(\omega^2 - \bar{\omega}^2)} \tag{4.12d}$$

Physical Significance of $H(\bar{\omega})$

Let us substitute Equation (4.12b) in Equation (4.11a),

$$x(t) = \frac{1}{k(1 - \beta^2 + 2i\beta\xi)} \cdot p(t)$$

$$= \frac{1}{(1 - \beta^2 + 2i\beta\xi)} \frac{p(t)}{k}$$

$$= \frac{1}{(1 - \beta^2 + 2i\beta\xi)} x'(t)$$

or,

$$x(t) = H'(\bar{\omega})\, x'(t) \tag{4.15a}$$

where,

$$H'(\bar{\omega}) = \frac{1}{(1-\beta^2+2i\beta\xi)} \tag{4.15b}$$

$$x'(t) = \frac{p(t)}{k} \tag{4.15c}$$

It means when a periodic force $p(t)$ is applied statically to the SDOF system, the resulting displacement becomes $x'(t)$. Hence, $H(\bar{\omega})$ can be assumed to be a magnification factor representing the complex ratio of the steady state dynamic displacement to the displacement which results when the exciting force is applied statically.

The frequency response $H'(\bar{\omega})$ contains information regarding the phase lag of the response with respect to the exciting force function. The term $H'(\bar{\omega})$ can be written as the vector sum of the real part $R(\bar{\omega})$ and imaginary part $I(\bar{\omega})$

$$H'(\bar{\omega}) = R(\bar{\omega}) + I(\bar{\omega}) \tag{4.16a}$$

or,

$$H'(\bar{\omega}) = |H(\bar{\omega})|\, e^{i\psi} \tag{4.16b}$$

where $|H(\bar{\omega})|$ and ψ are the amplitude and phase of the response $x(t)$ of the SDOF when it is excited by the simple harmonic forcing function $p(t)$

$$\therefore \qquad x(t) = |H(\bar{\omega})|\, e^{i(\bar{\omega}t+\psi)} \tag{4.17}$$

Multiplying both the numerator and denominator in Equation (4.15b) by $(1-\beta^2-2i\beta\xi)$, we get

$$H'(\bar{\omega}) = \frac{1}{[(1-\beta^2)^2+(2\beta\xi)^2]}(1-\beta^2-i2\beta\xi)$$

The amplitude $|H(\bar{\omega})|$ is found to be

$$|H(\bar{\omega})| = \{(1-\beta^2)^2 + (2\xi\beta)^2\}^{-0.5} \tag{4.18a}$$

and phase angle

$$\psi = \tan^{-1}\frac{2\xi\beta}{1-\beta^2} \tag{4.18b}$$

4.6 ILLUSTRATIVE EXAMPLES

Example 4.1

A square pulse is shown in Figure 4.2. Develop the Fourier series representation of $p(t)$.

Solution

The square pulse is having a period of T_p. It can be assumed to vary from $-T_p/2$ to $T_p/2$ for convenience. The Fourier series constants can be evaluated as follows:

$$a_0 = \frac{1}{T_p}\int_{-T_p/2}^{T_p/2} p(t)\,dt \tag{i}$$

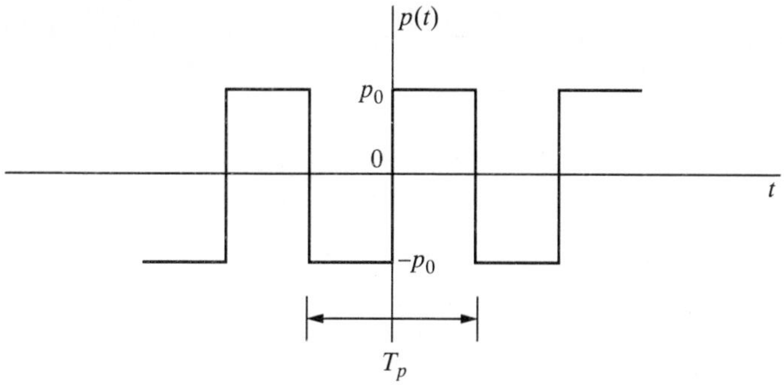

Figure 4.2 Square pulse loading.

$$a_n = \frac{2}{T_p}\int_{-T_p/2}^{T_p/2} \cos(n\bar{\omega}_1 t)\,dt \tag{ii}$$

and

$$b_n = \frac{2}{T_p}\int_{-T_p/2}^{T_p/2} \sin(n\bar{\omega}_1 t)\,dt \tag{iii}$$

where
$$p(t) = -p_0 \qquad \text{for } -T_p/2 < t < 0$$
$$= p_0 \qquad \text{for } 0 < t < T_p/2 \tag{iv}$$

Substituting the value of $p(t)$ from Equation (iv) in Equations (i) and (ii), gives $a_0 = 0$ and $a_n = 0$ because $p(t)$ is an odd function of t, that is, $p(t) = -p(-t)$ while a_0 and a_n are coefficients of even terms in the Fourier series.

Equations (iii) and (iv) give

$$b_n = \frac{4p_0}{T_p}\int_0^{Tp/2} \sin(n\bar{\omega}_1 t)\,dt$$

But
$$\bar{\omega}_1 = \frac{2\pi}{T_p}$$

∴
$$b_n = -\frac{2p_0}{n\pi}(\cos(n\pi) - 1)$$

or,
$$b_n = \frac{4p_0}{n\pi} \text{ for } n = 1, 3, 5, \text{ etc.}$$

The Fourier series representation of the square pulse is given by

$$p(t) = \frac{4p_0}{\pi}\sum_{n=1,3,5,}^{\infty} \frac{1}{n}\sin(n\bar{\omega}_1 t)$$

It can be plotted for different values of $n = 1, 3, 5,$ etc. in MS-EXCEL. The convergence of different harmonic components of sine to the square pulse can be seen in Figure 4.3. The convergence will improve further by taking more number of harmonic terms. □

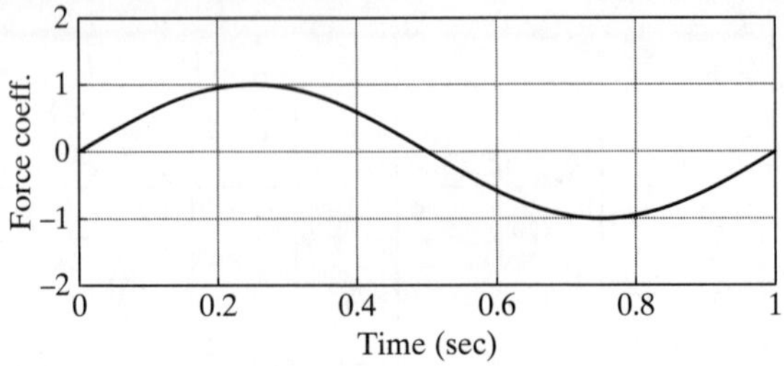

(a) First harmonic

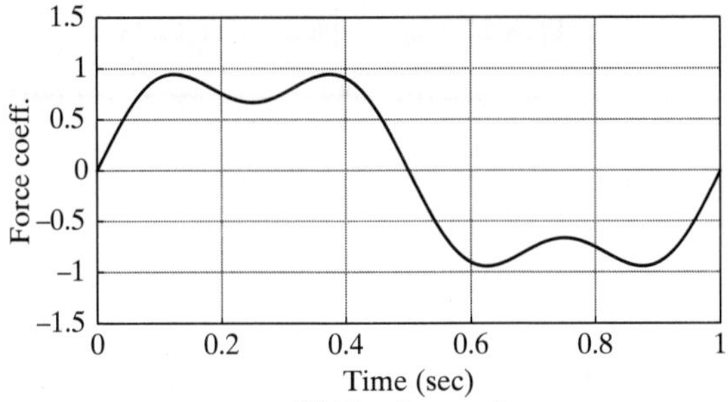

(b) Two harmonics

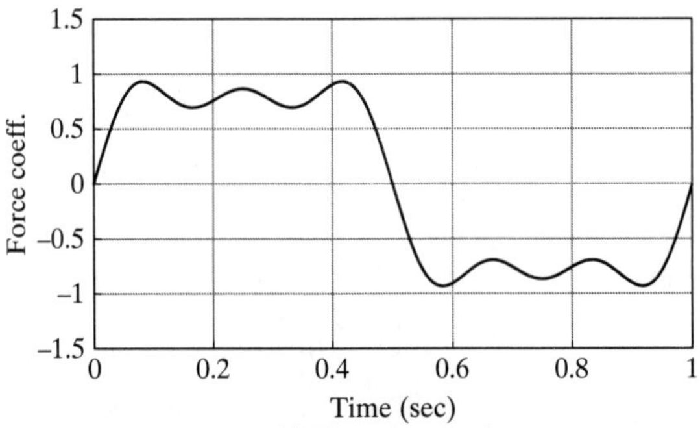

(c) Three harmonics

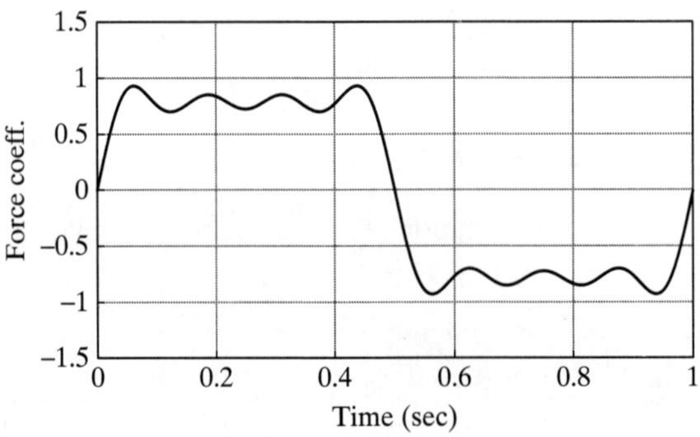

(d) Four harmonics

Figure 4.3 Fourier representation of the square pulse loading.

Example 4.2

Find the steady state response of an undamped SDOF system to a square pulse. Given $\omega = 4\ \bar{\omega}_1$.

Solution

The steady state response of an undamped SDOF subjected to a harmonic excitation p_0 sin $\bar{\omega}t$ is given as follows:

$$x(t) = \frac{p_0}{k}\frac{1}{\left(1-\beta^2\right)}\sin\bar{\omega}t$$

where $\beta = \bar{\omega}/\omega = n\ \bar{\omega}_1/\omega = \beta_n$

The load term can be written as follows:

$$p(t) = \frac{4p_0}{\pi}\sum_{n=1,3,5,}^{\infty}\frac{1}{n}\sin(n\bar{\omega}_1 t) \qquad \text{for } n = 1, 3, 5, \text{etc.}$$

$$= 0 \qquad \text{for } n = 0, 2, 4, \text{etc.}$$

The nth term of the steady state response is of the form:

$$x_n = \frac{4p_0}{n\pi}\left(\frac{1}{k}\right)\frac{\sin(n\bar{\omega}_1 t)}{\left(1-\beta_n^2\right)}$$

Hence, the steady state response is given by

$$x(t) = \sum_{n=1,3,5}^{\infty}\frac{4p_0}{k\pi}\frac{1}{n}\frac{\sin(n\bar{\omega}_1 t)}{\left(1-\left(\frac{n\bar{\omega}_1}{\omega}\right)^2\right)}$$

Let us plot the amplitude of each harmonic term of load as well as displacement versus frequency.

$$p_n = \frac{4p_0}{n\pi} \quad \text{or} \quad \frac{p_n}{p_0} = \frac{4}{n\pi}$$

or $$\frac{p_n}{p_0}\frac{\pi}{4} = \frac{1}{n}, \quad \text{where } n = 1, 3, 5, \text{etc.}$$

$$= 0 \qquad n = 0, 2, 4, \text{etc.}$$

Its plot is shown in Figure 4.4(a).

Similarly, the amplitude of each harmonic of the response term can be plotted as follows:

$$\frac{x_n}{\frac{p_0}{k}} = \frac{4}{n\pi\left(1-\left(\frac{n\bar{\omega}_1}{\omega}\right)^2\right)} \qquad \text{for } n = 1, 3, 5$$

$$= 0 \qquad \text{for } n = 0, 2, 4, 6$$

Given $\bar{\omega}_1/\omega = ¼$,

$$\therefore \quad \frac{x_n}{\frac{p_0}{k}} = \frac{4}{n\pi\left(1-\left(\frac{n}{4}\right)^2\right)} \qquad \text{for } n = \text{odd}$$

Its plot is shown in Figure 4.4(b). □

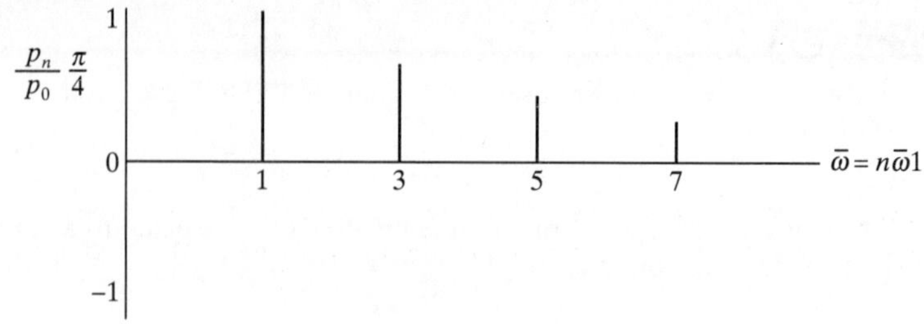

Figure 4.4(a) Amplitude of Fourier force function.

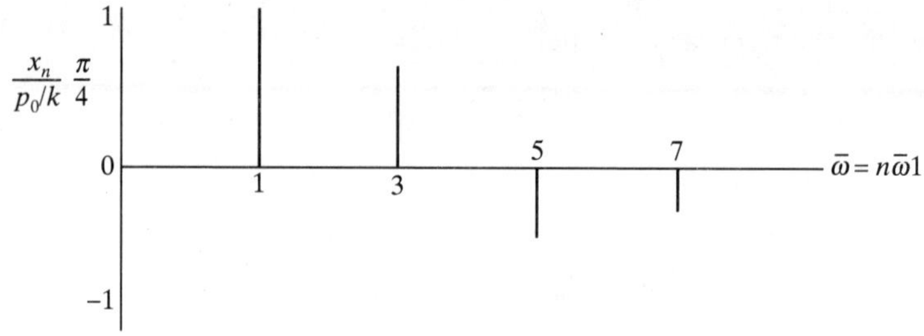

Figure 4.4(b) Amplitude of Fourier response function.

Example 4.3

Express the square pulse of Example (4.1) in exponential form.

Solution

The Fourier pair is given by Equation (4.9):

$$p(t) = \sum_{n=-\infty}^{\infty} C_n e^{in\bar{\omega}_1 t} \tag{4.9a}$$

where,

$$C_n = \frac{1}{T_p}\int_0^{T_p} p(t) e^{-in\bar{\omega}_1 t} dt \tag{4.9b}$$

The constant term C_n can be written as follows:

$$C_n = \frac{1}{T_p}\int_0^{T_{p/2}} p_0 e^{-i\bar{\omega}t} dt + \frac{1}{T_p}\int_{T_{p/2}}^{T_p} (-p_0) e^{-i\bar{\omega}t} dt$$

$$= \frac{-p_0}{i\bar{\omega}T_p}\left[\left|e^{-i\bar{\omega}t}\right|_0^{T_{p/2}} + \left|-e^{-i\bar{\omega}t}\right|_{T_{p/2}}^{T_p}\right]$$

But

$$\bar{\omega} = n\,\bar{\omega}_1 = n\,\frac{2\pi}{T_p}$$

∴

$$e^{-in\bar{\omega}_1 T_p/2} = e^{-in\pi} = 1 \qquad \text{for } n \text{ even}$$

and

$$e^{-in\bar{\omega}_1 T_p} = e^{-i2\pi n} = -1 \qquad \text{for } n \text{ odd}$$

Hence,

$$C_n = \frac{i\,p_0}{2\pi n}\left[2e^{-in\pi} - 2\right]$$

or, $$C_n = \frac{-2p_0 i}{n\pi} \quad \text{for } n \text{ odd}$$
$$= 0 \quad \text{for } n \text{ even}$$

This can also be written as follows as amplitude of imaginary and real terms:

$$\mathrm{I}(C_n) = \frac{-2p_0}{n\pi} \quad \text{for } n \text{ odd} \qquad \text{(i)}$$

$$\mathrm{R}(C_n) = 0 \quad \text{for } n \text{ even} \qquad \text{(ii)}$$

The expression (i) and the amplitude of the Fourier force function can be depicted as shown in Figures 4.5(a) and 4.5(b). □

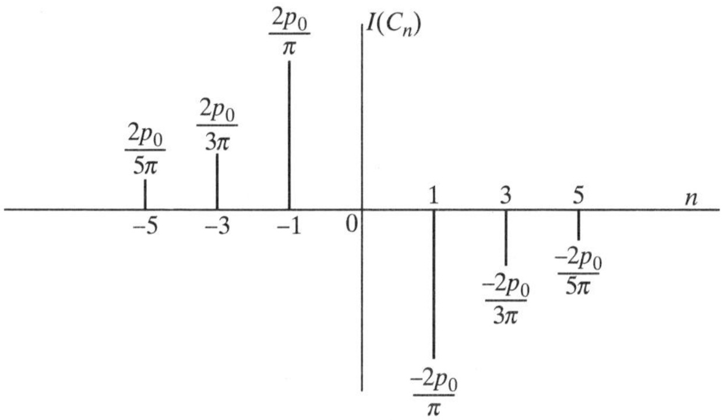

Figure 4.5(a) Amplitude of imaginary harmonic terms.

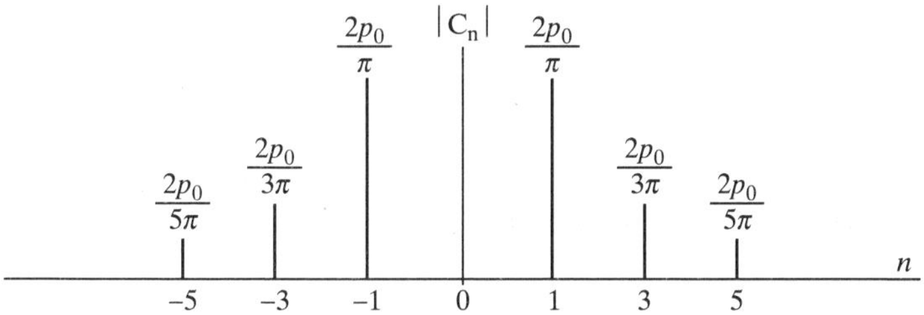

Figure 4.5(b) Amplitude of Fourier force function.

Example 4.4

Determine an expression for steady state response of an undamped SDOF system subjected to a square pulse with $\omega = 4\ \bar{\omega}_1$ in exponential form.

Solution

Let us write the expression for the steady state response of SDOF system as given in Equations 4.10(a) and 4.10(b).

$$x(t) = H(\bar{\omega})p(t)$$

or, $$x(t) = H(\bar{\omega})C_n e^{i\bar{\omega}t}$$

where, $$H(\bar{\omega}) = \frac{1}{k\left(1 - \beta^2 + i2\beta\xi\right)}$$

For an undamped system, $\xi = 0$,

$$\therefore \qquad H(\bar{\omega}) = \frac{1}{k(1-\beta^2)} = \frac{1}{k\left[1-\left(\frac{n\bar{\omega}_1}{\omega}\right)^2\right]}$$

or,

$$H(\bar{\omega}) = \frac{1}{k\left[1-\left(\frac{n}{4}\right)^2\right]}$$

Also, derived earlier, $C_n = 0$ for n even

$$C_n = \frac{-2p_0 i}{n\pi} \qquad \text{for } n \text{ odd}$$

$\therefore$ n[th] term of response can be written as $x_n = H(\bar{\omega})C_n$

or,

$$x_n = \frac{-i2p_0}{n\pi k\left[1-\left(\frac{n}{4}\right)^2\right]} \qquad \text{for } n \text{ odd}$$

$$= 0 \qquad \text{for } n \text{ even}$$

$$\therefore \qquad |x_n| = \left|\frac{2p_0/\pi k}{n\left[1-\left(\frac{n}{4}\right)^2\right]}\right| \qquad \text{for } n \text{ odd}$$

Alternatively, this can be re-written as follows:

$$\frac{x_n\pi/2}{p_0/k} = \frac{1}{n\left[1-\left(\frac{n}{4}\right)^2\right]} = \alpha \qquad \text{for } n \text{ odd}$$

This can be plotted as shown in Figure 4.6. □

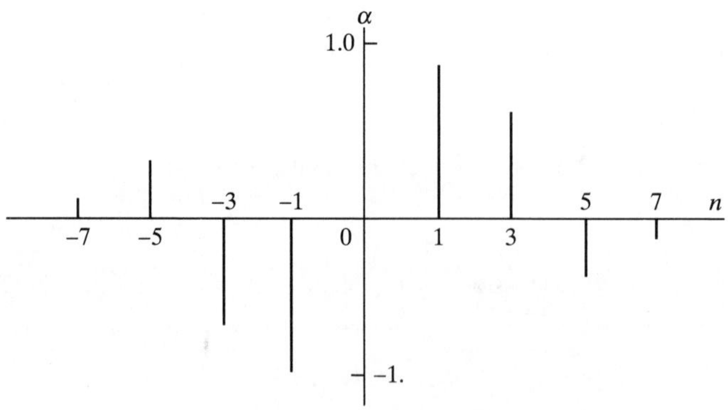

Figure 4.6 Amplitude of Fourier response function.

Example 4.5

A SDOF system has a mass of 100 kg, stiffness of 100 kN/m and a damping of 10 per cent. It is subjected to a force as shown in Figure 4.7. Period of the forcing function is 0.12 sec and its duration is also 0.12 sec. Determine the Fourier constants of force and displacement up to 20 terms. Also, plot the steady state response.

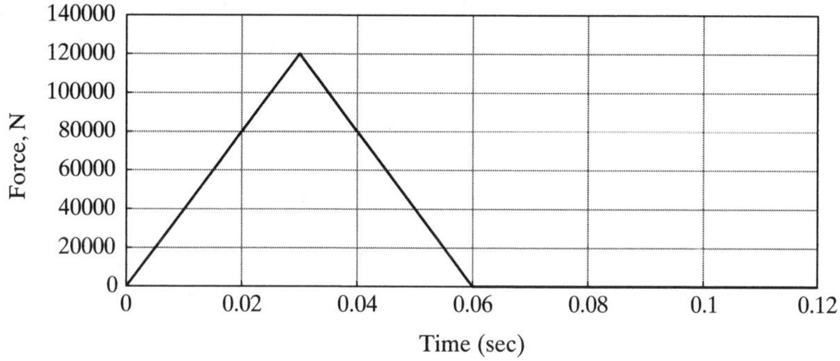

Figure 4.7 Forcing function

Solution

Natural frequency of SDOF = 31.623 rad/sec
Forcing frequency = $2\pi/0.12$ = 52.36 rad/sec

A computer code was written in FORTRAN using Equations (4.2) and (4.7), and the results are shown in Table 4.1.

Fourier force coefficient $A_0 = 30000.000$
Fourier displacement coefficient $X_0 = 0.300$

The plot of the Fourier periodic force due to first 20 terms is shown in Figure 4.8 and that of the response in Figure 4.9. □

TABLE 4.1 FOURIER CONSTANTS FOR FORCE AND DISPLACEMENT TERMS

			Fourier Force Coeff.		Fourier Displacement Coeff.	
N	Frequency	Frequency Ratio	A(N) COS term	B(N) SINE term	X1(N) COS term	X2(N) SINE term
1	52.36	1.656	−2.13E − 03	4.86E + 04	−2.70E − 01	−5.12E − 02
2	104.72	3.312	−2.43E + 04	−2.13E − 03	−1.61E − 03	2.43E − 02
3	157.08	4.967	7.09E − 04	−5.40E + 03	2.28E − 03	9.56E − 05
4	209.44	6.623	0.00E + 00	0.00E + 00	0.00E + 00	0.00E + 00
5	261.799	8.279	−4.25E − 04	1.95E + 03	−2.88E − 04	−7.06E − 06
6	314.159	9.935	−2.70E + 03	−7.09E − 04	−5.62E − 06	2.76E − 04
7	366.519	11.59	3.04E − 04	−9.93E + 02	7.44E − 05	1.29E − 06
8	418.879	13.246	0.00E + 00	0.00E + 00	0.00E + 00	0.00E + 00
9	471.239	14.902	−2.36E − 04	6.00E + 02	−2.72E − 05	−3.66E − 07
10	523.599	16.558	−9.73E + 02	−4.25E − 04	−4.32E − 07	3.56E − 05

(Continued)

			Fourier Force Coeff.		Fourier Displacement Coeff.	
N	Frequency	Frequency Ratio	A(N) COS term	B(N) SINE term	X1(N) COS term	X2(N) SINE term
11	575.959	18.213	1.93E – 04	–4.02E + 02	1.22E – 05	1.34E – 07
12	628.319	19.869	0.00E + 00	0.00E + 00	0.00E + 00	0.00E + 00
13	680.678	21.525	–1.64E – 04	2.88E + 02	–6.22E – 06	–5.80E – 08
14	733.038	23.181	–4.96E + 02	–3.04E – 04	–8.00E – 08	9.25E – 06
15	785.398	24.836	1.42E – 04	–2.16E + 02	3.51E – 06	2.83E – 08
16	837.758	26.492	0.00E + 00	0.00E + 00	0.00E + 00	0.00E + 00
17	890.118	28.148	–1.25E – 04	1.68E + 02	–2.13E – 06	–1.51E – 08
18	942.478	29.804	–3.00E + 02	–2.36E – 04	–2.27E – 08	3.38E–06
19	994.838	31.46	1.12E – 04	–1.35E + 02	1.36E – 06	8.67E – 09
20	1047.198	33.115	0.00E + 00	0.00E + 00	0.00E + 00	0.00E + 00

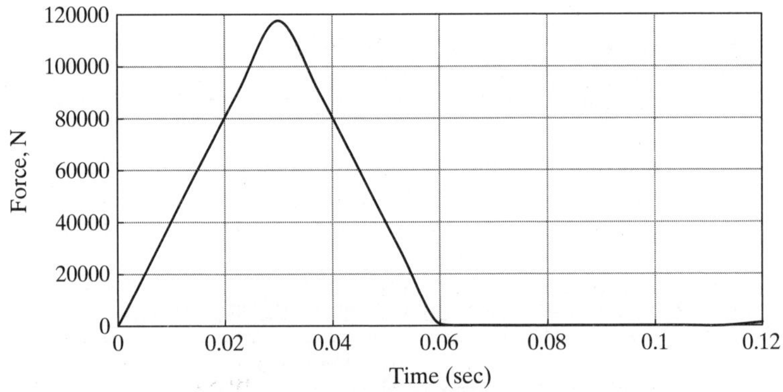

Figure 4.8 Fourier periodic force.

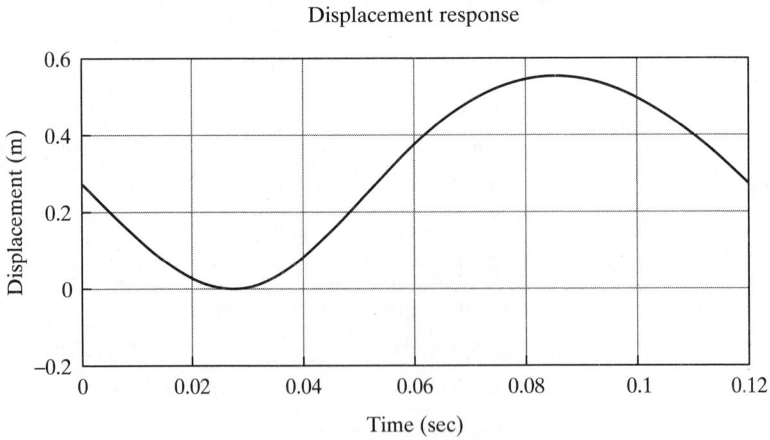

Figure 4.9 Steady state response.

4.7 FREQUENCY DOMAIN ANALYSIS

In the preceding sections, the force was known in the time domain, that is, the variation of the force with time was known. The response was also formulated in the time domain, that is, variation of response with time was determined. This is referred to as the *time domain* analysis. The time-domain analysis is completely general and can be used to evaluate the response of any linear SDOF system to any *periodic* or *non-periodic* force input. A forcing function may consist of number of frequencies over its entire duration. Yet, the time domain analysis is easy to perform and easy to understand. However, there is a drawback. It does not give any idea about the *frequency contents* of the forcing function. The spectral information of a forcing function is critical, for example, in certain situations in machine vibrations and analysis of accelerograms. It helps in determining which frequencies are dominating and critical for *resonance*. This information is available if the analysis is performed in the *frequency domain*. The force and response are expressed in terms of frequency varying from 0 to 2π or 0 to $2n\pi$. It means both the force and the response will repeat after one complete 2π cycle. The frequency domain approach is similar in concept to the Fourier analysis procedure. Both these methods involve

(i) expressing the applied loading in terms of harmonic components,
(ii) evaluating the response of the structure to each component,
(iii) then superposing the harmonic responses to obtain the total structural response.

However, to apply the periodic load technique to non-periodic loading, it is necessary to extend the Fourier series concept to the representation of non-periodic functions. Consider non-periodic loading shown by solid line in Figure 4.10. If this function was to be represented by a Fourier series, the coefficients C_n obtained by Equation (4.9b) over the interval $0 < t < T_p$ would define the periodic function shown in the figure by dash as well as solid lines. As a matter of fact, the loading in dash lines does not exist and must be eliminated. It is possible to eliminate the spurious repetitive loadings by extending loading period to infinity. Therefore, there is a need to reformulate the Fourier series expression so that it extends over an infinite time range. This is achieved by making the frequency increment infinitesimal ($\Delta\bar{\omega} \rightarrow d\bar{\omega}$) so that discrete frequencies $\bar{\omega}_n$ become a continuous function $\bar{\omega}$.

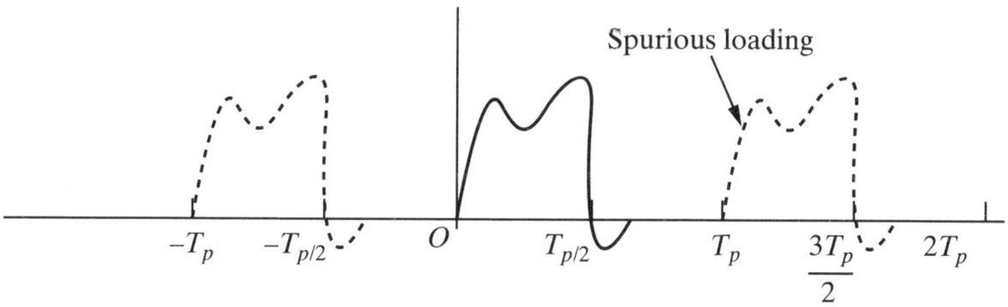

Figure 4.10 Non-periodic loading.

The Fourier series expression of Equation (4.9) eventually becomes the following Fourier integral:

$$F(\omega) = \int_{-\infty}^{\infty} f(t)e^{-i\omega t}dt \tag{4.19a}$$

and

$$f(t) = \frac{1}{2\pi}\int_{-\infty}^{\infty} F(\omega)e^{i\omega t}\, d\omega \tag{4.19b}$$

[Note: change of notation ω for $\bar{\omega}$ for convenience in use of standard results. However, in the text, forcing frequency is represented by $\bar{\omega}$. It will continue to be used for uniformity.]

The two integrals of Equations (4.19a) and (4.19b) are known as a *Fourier Transform Pair* because the frequency function can be derived from the time function or vice versa by equivalent processes. A necessary condition for the existence of the *Fourier Transform* is that

$$\text{The integral } I = \int_{-\infty}^{\infty} |f(t)|\; dt \text{ should be finite} \tag{4.20}$$

In other words, the function $f(t)$ is defined for all real numbers $t \in R$.
Equation (4.19a) has a very interesting implication. For any $\omega \in R$, integrating $f(t)$ against $e^{-i\omega t}$ with respect to t, produces a complex valued function of ω. That is, the Fourier transform $F(\omega)$ is a complex valued function of $\omega \in R$. Equation (4.19b) represents *inverse Fourier transform* as it recovers $f(t)$ from $F(\omega)$.

There is yet another very interesting observation. The Fourier transform or spectrum of a periodic function is always a discrete set of frequencies. By contrast, the Fourier transform of a nonperiodic signal produces a continuous spectrum, or a continuum of frequencies.

The Fourier transform analyzes a signal into its frequency components. The Fourier integral of Equation (4.19b) may be interpreted as representing an arbitrary loading as an infinite sum of harmonic components. Multiplying this by the complex frequency response function $H(\bar{\omega})$, therefore, yields the amplitude per unit $\bar{\omega}$ of the response component at frequency $\bar{\omega}$. Hence, the total response can be obtained by summing these response components over the entire frequency range

$$x(t) = \frac{1}{2\pi}\int_{-\infty}^{\infty} H(\bar{\omega})F(\bar{\omega})e^{i\bar{\omega}t}\, d\bar{\omega} \tag{4.21}$$

where $F(\bar{\omega})$ is given by Equation (4.19a)
and $H(\bar{\omega})$ is given by Equation (4.12).
Let us find *steady state response* of an undamped SDOF system having a natural frequency ω subjected to an earthquake excitation given by $a_0 \sin(\bar{\omega}t)$.

Step 1: First find the Fourier transform of the excitation force from time domain to frequency domain using Equation (4.19a).

$$F(\bar{\omega}) = \int_{-\infty}^{\infty} (a_0 \sin \bar{\omega}t)e^{-i\bar{\omega}t}\, dt \tag{4.22a}$$

Step 2: Now find the response of the SDOF system in time domain using Equation (4.21) and (4.22a) in frequency domain.

$$x(t) = \frac{1}{2\pi}\int_{-\infty}^{\infty}\left(\frac{1}{\omega^2 - \bar{\omega}^2}\right)F(\bar{\omega})e^{i\bar{\omega}t}d\bar{\omega} \tag{4.22b}$$

Thus, for any given forcing function in the time domain or frequency domain, the response can be determined by making use of the Fourier transform pair. Similarly, response of a damped system can be obtained.

4.7.1 Dirac Delta Function

It is a very important function and it is desirable to understand its properties for use with Fourier transform applications. It represents an abbreviation just like the symbol π represents a value 22/7. It is a single value function. At a single value of t, it is infinity, elsewhere it is zero.

$$\delta(t) = \begin{cases} \infty & \text{if } t = 0 \\ 0 & \text{if } t \neq 0 \end{cases} \tag{4.23}$$

where, t = real variable

The Dirac delta function is shown in Figure 4.11.

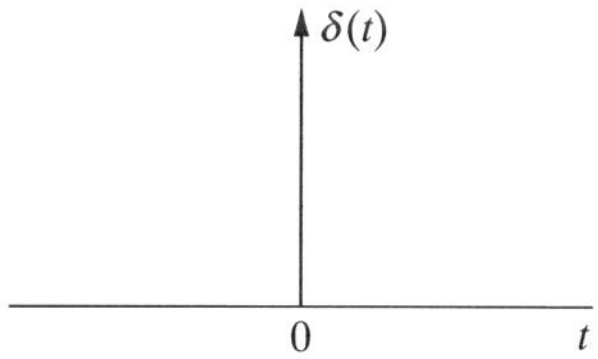

Figure 4.11 Dirac Delta function plot

The properties of Dirac Delta function are as follows:

Area under the plot is unity.

$$\int_{-\infty}^{\infty}\delta(t)dt = 1 \tag{4.24a}$$

$$\int_{-\infty}^{\infty}\delta(t-a)f(t)dt = \int_{-\infty}^{\infty}\delta(t-a)f(a)dt = f(a) \tag{4.24b}$$

$$\int_{-\infty}^{\infty}e^{\pm i\omega t}dt = 2\pi\,\delta(\omega) \tag{4.24c}$$

$$\int_{-\infty}^{\infty}e^{\pm i(\omega-\bar{\omega})t}dt = 2\pi\,\delta(\omega-\bar{\omega}) \tag{4.24d}$$

4.8 ILLUSTRATIVE EXAMPLES

Example 4.6

Find the Fourier transform of the following functions:

1. Dirac Delta function
2. Unity
3. $e^{i\bar{\omega}t}$
4. $\sin\bar{\omega}t$

Solution

1. Fourier transform of the Dirac Delta function is given by

$$f(t) = \delta(t)$$

$$F(\omega) = \int_{-\infty}^{\infty} \delta(t) e^{-i\omega t} dt$$

At $t = 0$, $e^{-i\omega(0)} = 1$, $\therefore$ $F(\omega) = 1$
Its plot is as shown in Figure 4.12.

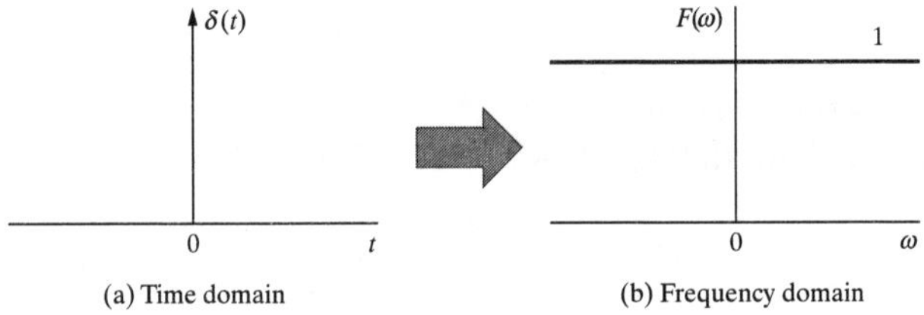

Figure 4.12 Fourier transform of Dirac Delta function

2. Fourier transform of constant unity is given by

$$f(t) = 1$$

$$F(\omega) = \int_{-\infty}^{\infty} 1.e^{-i\omega t} dt = 2\pi\,\delta(\omega)$$

by making use of the basic properties.
Its plot is as shown in Figure 4.13.

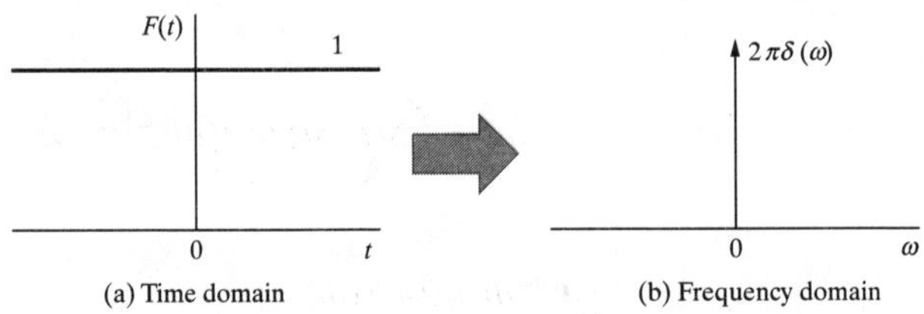

Figure 4.13 Fourier transform of constant unity

3. Fourier transform of $e^{i\bar{\omega}t}$ is given by

$$f(t) = e^{i\bar{\omega}t}$$

$$F(\omega)=\int_{-\infty}^{\infty} e^{i\bar{\omega}t}e^{-i\omega t}dt=\int_{-\infty}^{\infty} e^{-i(\omega-\bar{\omega})t}dt$$

$F(\omega)=2\pi\delta(\omega-\bar{\omega})$ by making use of the basic properties.

$$e^{i\bar{\omega}t}=\cos\bar{\omega}t+i\sin\bar{\omega}t$$

Here the cosine term is real while the sine term is imaginary. It can be plotted as shown in Figure 4.14.

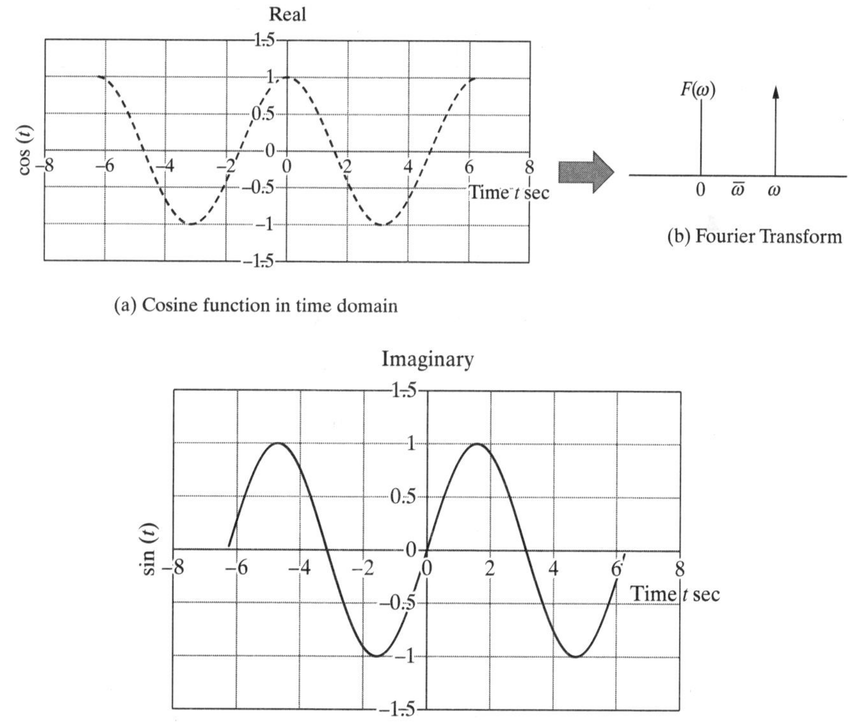

(a) Cosine function in time domain

(b) Fourier Transform

(c) Sine function in time domain

Figure 4.14 Fourier transform of $e^{i\bar{\omega}t}$

4. Fourier transform of $\sin\bar{\omega}t$

$$f(t)=\sin\bar{\omega}t$$

$$F(\omega)=\int_{-\infty}^{\infty}\sin\bar{\omega}t\,e^{-i\omega t}\,dt$$

We know that $$\sin\bar{\omega}t=\frac{e^{i\bar{\omega}t}-e^{-i\bar{\omega}t}}{2i}$$

$$F(\omega)=\int_{-\infty}^{\infty}\frac{\left(e^{i\bar{\omega}t}-e^{-i\bar{\omega}t}\right)e^{-i\omega t}}{2i}dt$$

$$F(\omega) = -\frac{i}{2}\int_{-\infty}^{\infty}\left(e^{-i(\omega-\bar{\omega})t} - e^{-i(\omega+\bar{\omega})t}\right)dt$$

or, by making use of properties,

$$F(\omega) = -i\left[\pi\delta(\omega-\bar{\omega}) - \pi\delta(\omega+\bar{\omega})\right]$$

Its plot is shown in Figure 4.15.

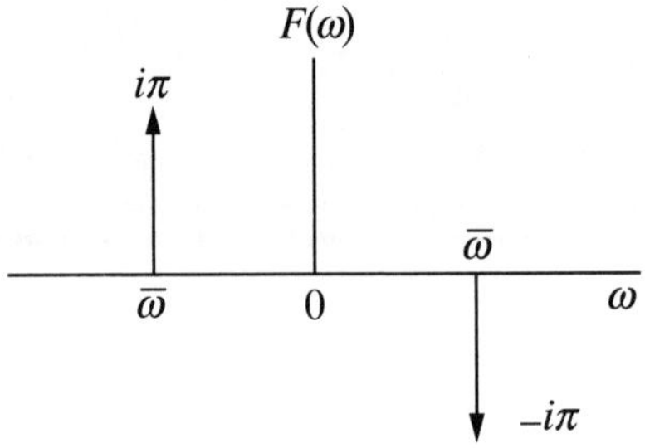

Figure 4.15 Fourier transform of $\sin\bar{\omega}t$

Similarly, the Fourier transform of $\cos\bar{\omega}t$ can be shown as in Figure 4.16.

$$f(t) = \cos\bar{\omega}t$$

$$F(\omega) = \left[\pi\delta(\omega-\bar{\omega}) + \pi\delta(\omega+\bar{\omega})\right]$$ □

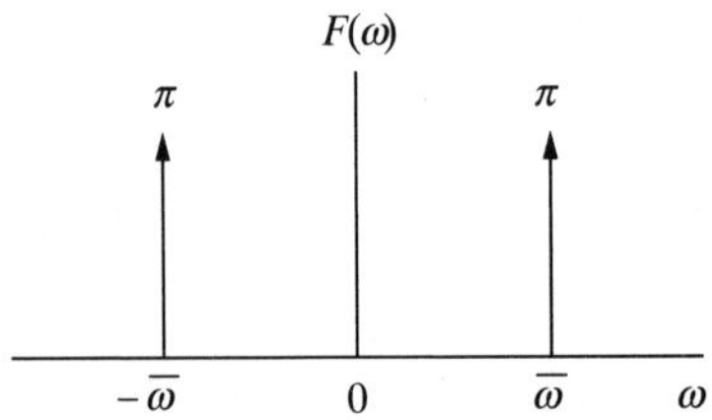

Figure 4.16 Fourier transform of $\cos\bar{\omega}t$

Example 4.7

Determine the Fourier Transform of the rectangular pulse which is symmetric about t = 0 as shown in Figure 4.17 in frequency domain.

Solution

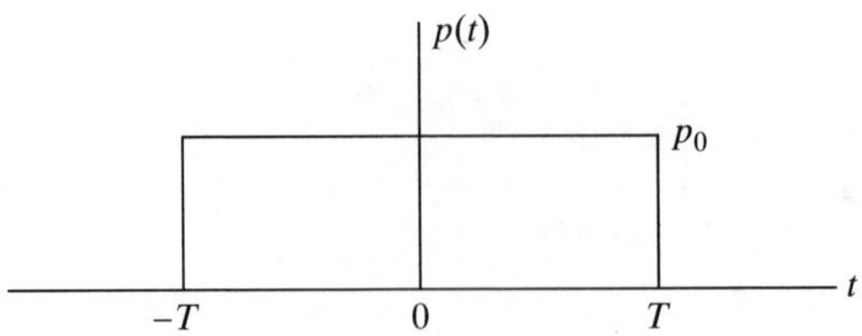

Figure 4.17 Square pulse

The Fourier transform pairs are as follows:

$$F(\omega)=\int_{-\infty}^{\infty} f(t)e^{-i\omega t}dt \tag{4.19a}$$

and

$$f(t)=\frac{1}{2\pi}\int_{-\infty}^{\infty} F(\omega)e^{i\omega t}d\omega \tag{4.19b}$$

Equation (4.19a) gives,

$$F(\omega) = \int_{-T}^{T} p_0\, e^{-i\omega t}dt$$

or,

$$= -\frac{p_0}{i\omega}\left(e^{-i\omega T} - e^{i\omega T}\right)$$

or,

$$= \frac{ip_0}{\omega}[(\cos\omega T - i\sin\omega T) - (\cos\omega T + i\sin\omega T)]$$

$$F(\omega) = 2p_0T\left(\frac{\sin\omega T}{\omega T}\right)$$

It is a real function and can be plotted as shown in Figure 4.18 (a).

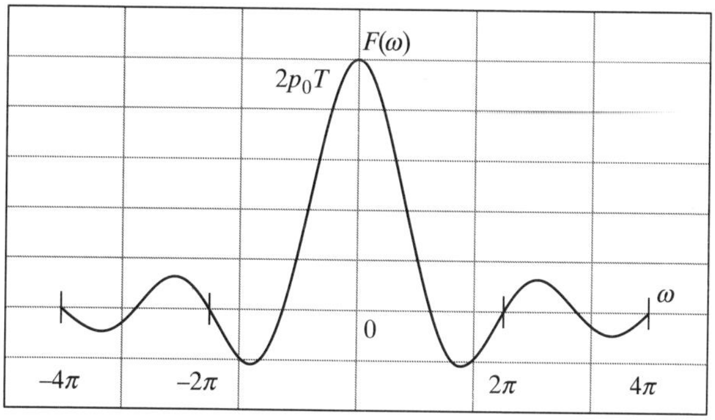

Figure 4.18 (a) Plot of Fourier Transform pair $F(\omega)$

Let us consider two rectangular pulses:

1. Magnitude $p_0 = 1.0$, and duration $= \pm T = \pm 0.25$ sec → Short pulse
2. Magnitude $p_0 = 0.50$, and duration $= \pm T = \pm 1.0$ sec → Long pulse

Therefore, the scale factor becomes 1 : 4 between short and long pulse.
The Fourier transform of a rectangular pulse is given by

$$F(\omega) = 2p_0T\left(\frac{\sin\omega T}{\omega T}\right)$$

The rectangular functions and their Fourier transforms are shown in Figures 4.18(b) and 4.18(c). The spectrum is broader in the case of short pulse as compared to that of the long pulse.

□

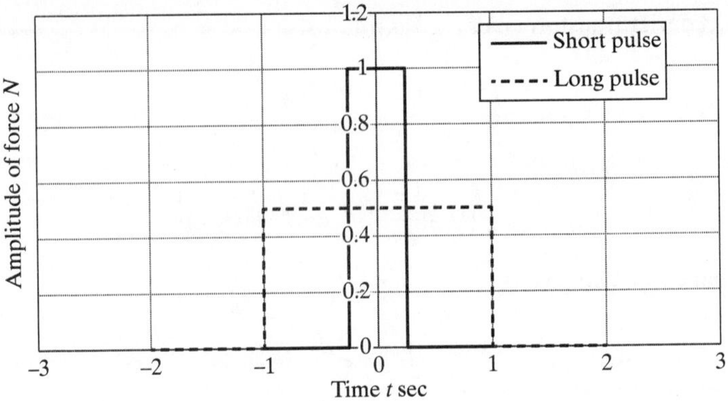

Figure 4.18 (b) Rectangular pulse in time domain ($T = 0.25$ and 1.0 sec)

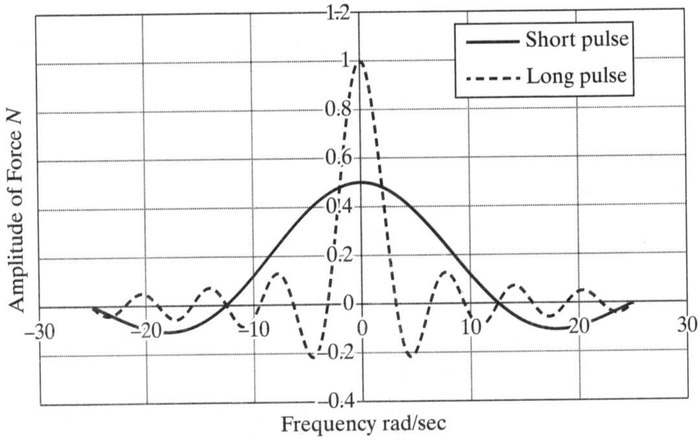

Figure 4.18 (c) Fourier Transform of Rectangular Pulse ($T = 0.25$ and 1.0 sec)

Example 4.8

Determine the Fourier Transform of the triangular function as shown in Figure 4.19.

$$f(t) = \begin{cases} p_0\left(1+\dfrac{t}{T}\right), -T \le t \le 0 \\ p_0\left(1-\dfrac{t}{T}\right), 0 \le t \le T \end{cases}$$

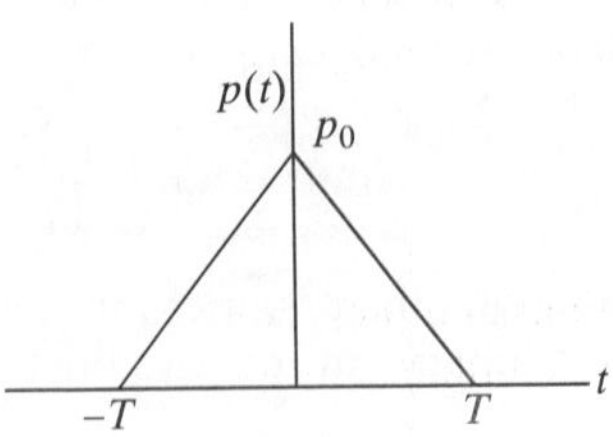

Figure 4.19 Triangular Function

Solution

The function in the time domain is given as follows:

$$f(t)=\begin{cases} p_0\left(1+\dfrac{t}{T}\right), -T\le t\le 0 \\ p_0\left(1-\dfrac{t}{T}\right), 0\le t\le T \end{cases}$$

The Fourier transform can be written as

$$F(\omega)=\int_{-\infty}^{\infty} f(t)e^{-i\omega t}dt$$

or,

$$F(\omega)=\int_{-T}^{0} f(t)e^{-i\omega t}dt+\int_{0}^{T} f(t)e^{-i\omega t}dt$$

$$F(\omega)=\int_{-T}^{0} p_0\left(1+\frac{t}{T}\right)e^{-i\omega t}dt+\int_{0}^{T} p_0\left(1-\frac{t}{T}\right)e^{-i\omega t}dt$$

Recall the formula for integration by parts:

$$\int u\,dv=uv-\int v\,du$$

= first function x integrate the second function – ∫ differentiate the first function x integrate the second function

$$F(\omega)=\left|p_0\left(\frac{e^{-i\omega t}}{-i\omega}\right)+p_0\frac{t}{T}\left(\frac{e^{-i\omega t}}{-i\omega}\right)-p_0\int\frac{1}{T}dt\left(\frac{e^{-i\omega t}}{-i\omega}\right)\right|_{-T}^{0}+$$

$$\left|p_0\left(\frac{e^{-i\omega t}}{-i\omega}\right)-p_0\frac{t}{T}\left(\frac{e^{-i\omega t}}{-i\omega}\right)+p_0\int\frac{1}{T}dt\left(\frac{e^{-i\omega t}}{-i\omega}\right)\right|_{0}^{T}$$

$$F(\omega)=\left|p_0\left(\frac{e^{-i\omega t}}{-i\omega}\right)+p_0\frac{t}{T}\left(\frac{e^{-i\omega t}}{-i\omega}\right)-p_0\frac{1}{T}\frac{e^{-i\omega t}}{(-i\omega)^2}\right|_{-T}^{0}+$$

$$\left|p_0\left(\frac{e^{-i\omega t}}{-i\omega}\right)-p_0\frac{t}{T}\left(\frac{e^{-i\omega t}}{-i\omega}\right)+p_0\frac{1}{T}\frac{e^{-i\omega t}}{(-i\omega)^2}\right|_{0}^{T}$$

$$F(\omega)=\left\{\frac{p_0}{T\omega^2}(1+i\omega T)-e^{i\omega T}\right\}+\left\{\frac{p_0}{T\omega^2}(1-i\omega T)-e^{-i\omega T}\right\}$$

$$F(\omega)=\frac{p_0}{T\omega^2}\left\{2-e^{i\omega T}-e^{-i\omega T}\right\}$$

Now onwards, it is a tricky solution

$$F(\omega)=-\frac{p_0e^{-i\omega T}}{T\omega^2}\left[1-2e^{i\omega T}+e^{2i\omega T}\right]$$

$$= -\frac{p_0 e^{-i\omega T}}{T\omega^2}[e^{i\omega T} - 1]^2$$

$$= -\frac{p_0 e^{-i\omega T}}{T\omega^2}\left[e^{\frac{i\omega T}{2}}\left\{e^{(i\omega T)/2} - e^{(-i\omega T)/2}\right\}\right]^2$$

$$= -\frac{p_0 e^{-i\omega T}}{T\omega^2} e^{i\omega T}(2i)^2 sin^2\left(\frac{\omega T}{2}\right)$$

$$= \frac{4p_0}{T\omega^2} sin^2\left(\frac{\omega T}{2}\right)$$

or,

$$F(\omega) = \frac{1}{2}(2p_0 T)\left[\frac{sin\left(\frac{\omega T}{2}\right)}{\left(\frac{\omega T}{2}\right)}\right]^2$$

where, Area of the triangle = $\frac{1}{2}(p_0 2T)$

Its Fourier transform is shown in Figure 4.20.

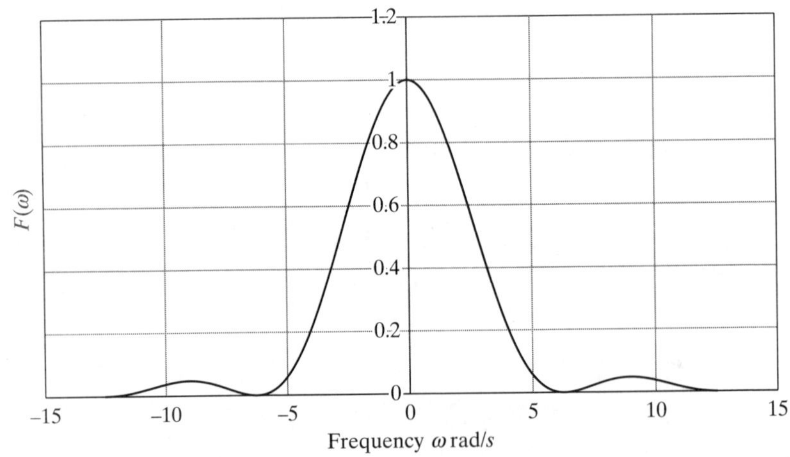

Figure 4.20 Fourier Transform of sinc$(x)^2$ ($p_0 = 1, T = 1$)

4.9 MATLAB APPLICATIONS

MATLAB codes are written to represent periodic loading using Fourier series. Thereafter, response of a SDOF system can be obtained by using the results obtained in Chapter 3. The MATLAB codes DOS4_1 and DOS4_2 are available on the web.

Example 4.9

Represent the triangular function shown in Figure 4.21 in terms of Fourier series using MATLAB.

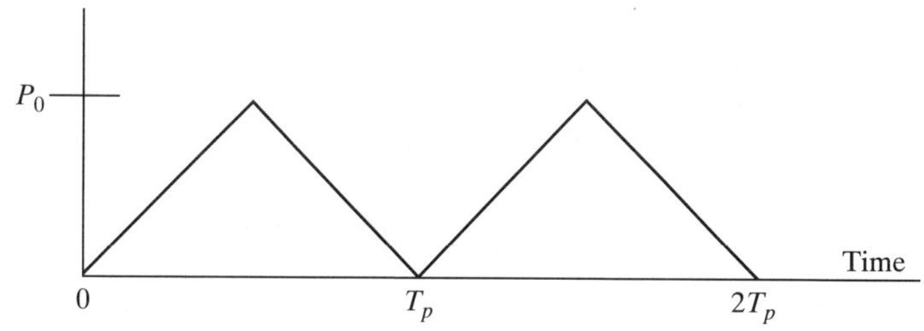

Figure 4.21 Triangular function.

Solution

The MATLAB code is written in the following parts:

Main module DOS4_1 calls MATLAB function 'quad'. The function 'quad' numerically evaluates an integral using Simpson rule.

Function curve1 calculates the constant term a_0

Function curve1c calculates the a_n coefficients of cosine terms

Function curve1s calculates the b_n coefficients of sine terms

The Fourier representation with 15 terms is shown in Figure 4.22. □

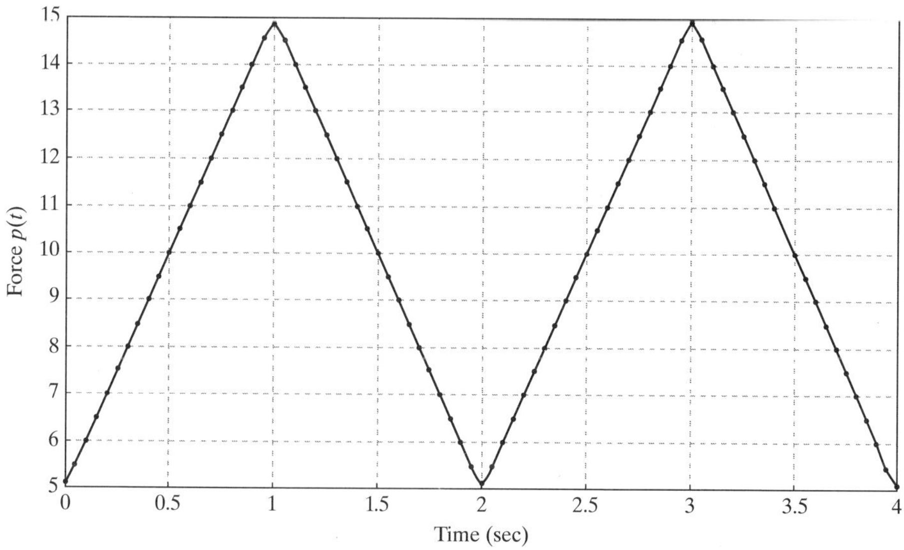

Figure 4.22 Fourier representation of triangular pulse.

Example 4.10

Represent the ramp function shown in Figure 4.23 in terms of Fourier series using MATLAB.

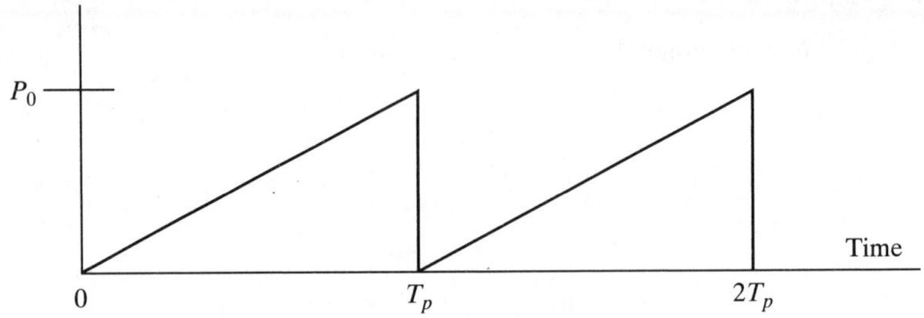

Figure 4.23 Ramp function.

Solution

The MATLAB code for ramp function is written in the following parts:

Main module DOS4_2 calls MATLAB function 'quad'. The function 'quad' numerically evaluates an integral using Simpson rule.

Function curve2 calculates the constant term a_0

Function curve2c calculates the a_n coefficients of cosine terms

Function curve2s calculates the b_n coefficients of sine terms

The Fourier representation of the ramp function with 15 terms is shown in Figure 4.24. □

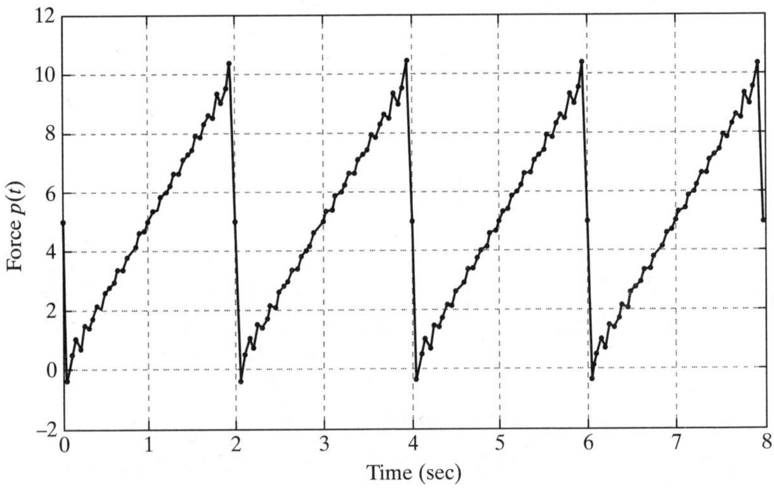

Figure 4.24 Fourier representation of the ramp function.

4.10 HUMAN-INDUCED VIBRATIONS IN STRUCTURES

With the development of new materials, improvement in understanding of the behaviour of structures, construction technologies, and development of GUI-based analysis and design software, there is a demand for more slender and lighter structures such as large span building floors and footbridges. Forces are induced due to movement of the pedestrians. They may be walking slowly, normally or faster. They may be walking, running, jumping or dancing. There may be a single person or a group of persons (density) irrespective of age and built-up. The other feature is the synchronization of the walking pattern among the pedestrians and synchronization of human with the structure. The mass and damping of thin and slender structures can have significant influence due to human loading.

The human response to floor vibrations is a very complex phenomenon depending upon the magnitude and frequency of the motion, the environment and the human sensor itself. A continuous motion (steady state) may be more disturbing than an intermittent impact (transient). The reaction of a person depends very strongly as to what he was doing. The vibration frequencies between 2 and 8 Hz are more annoying. People sitting in offices or at home do not like vibrations having peak accelerations of about 0.5 per cent due to gravity. People engaged in some activity may accept vibrations about 10 times greater, that is 5 per cent of the acceleration due to gravity. People dining besides a dance floor, or exercising in a gym, or enjoying in a shopping mall will accept about 1.5 per cent of the acceleration due to gravity. The sensitivity within each occupancy also depends upon the duration of the vibration and remoteness of the source. Outside the frequency range of 2–8 Hz, people accept higher vibration accelerations.

The study of *human induced resonant vibrations* in the floors of structures consists of the following three components:

- Characteristics of the force induced in a structure,
- Characteristics of the floor, and
- Acceptance criteria.

4.10.1 Force Characteristics

The human-induced force has three components: vertical, longitudinal, and lateral. The vertical component is about 40 per cent of the weight of the body. It is the largest component. The lateral component is much smaller while the longitudinal component is the least. During normal walking, the vertical forces have a frequency in the range of 1.3–2.4 Hz depending on the pace; while running, the frequency is in the range of 2–3.5 Hz. During walking, at least one foot is always in contact with the ground. While running, both foot may be off the ground at the same instant; also, the duration of contact while a foot is on the ground is relatively small.

During walking, the vertical component shows a typical double hump as shown in Figures 4.25(a) and 4.25(b). The first hump is the result of impact of the heel on the ground; while the second hump is due to push off by the toe. The amplitude of the force increases with the step frequency. Also, the next footfall begins just before the earlier one has finished. The load model for running or jumping can be represented by a half sine curve as shown in Figure 4.25(c). The net force during walking is shown in Figure 4.26. The walking load is much more complex than the running load. Both are periodic forces. The vertical component of the walking or running loads due to a single pedestrian can be represented by the Fourier series. The building floor or a pedestrian bridge can be represented by a single degree of freedom system. The steady state response can be determined using the equations derived earlier.

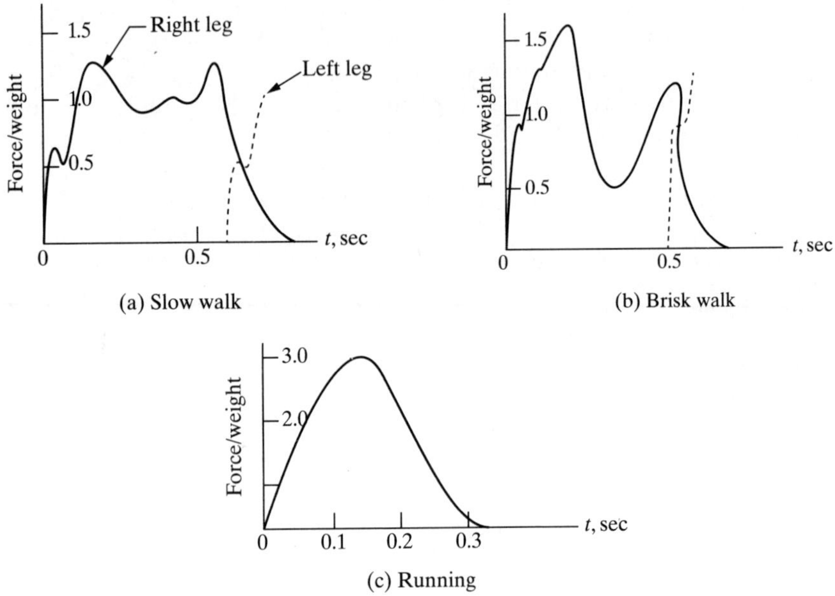

Figure 4.25 Force due to walking and running.

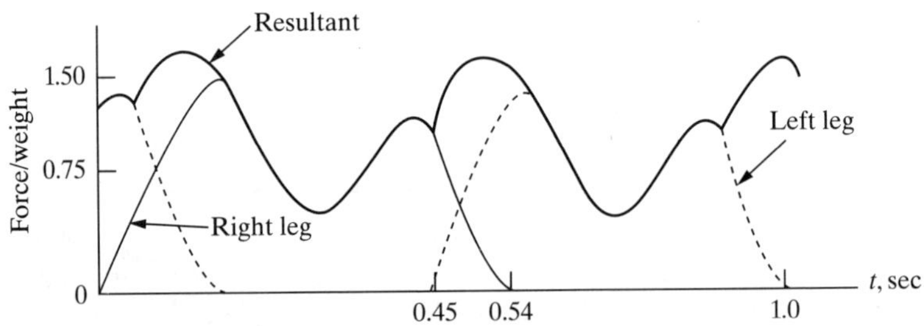

Figure 4.26 Combined force due to both legs while walking.

4.10.2 Floor Characteristics

The determination of floor characteristics is a very complex issue. The floor of a building is quite different than that of a bridge. Each requires a different treatment. Floor characteristics depend upon materials, type of construction, boundary conditions, mass, stiffness, and damping, The floor may consist of simple RC slab, a composite slab, an isotropic plate, and orthotropic plate. It may rest on a network of beams and girders. It may have different boundary conditions. The floor will have different frequencies of vibrations in different modes. In simple cases, the floor characteristics can be determined by simple calculations. However, in other cases, a finite element modelling and analysis will be required.

In the determination of the dynamic floor characteristics, a realistic fraction of imposed load should be considered towards the total mass of the floor. For residential and office buildings, 10% to 20% of the imposed load is considered satisfactory.

Damping has a huge influence on the vibrations of a floor and consist of three components:

- viscous damping of the system ξ_1,
- damping due to furniture ξ_2, and
- damping due to finishes or false ceiling ξ_3.

The system damping ξ is obtained by summing up the appropriate values for ξ_1 to ξ_3. The damping values for different causes can be determined by actual field measurements or from a code. Typical values are shown in Table 4.2.

TABLE 4.2 TYPICAL DAMPING RATIOS

Particulars		Damping ratio ξ
Structural Damping		
	Wood	6%
	Concrete	2%
	Steel	1%
	Composite RC and steel floor	1%
Damping due to furniture		
	Traditional office for 1 to 3 persons with separation walls	2%
	Paperless office	0%
	Library	1%
	Houses	1%
	School	0%
	Gymnastic	0%
Damping due to finishes		
	Ceiling under floor	1%
	Free floating floor	0%

Natural Frequency of Steel Framed Floor System

The following simplified procedure is suggested by Murray et al in AISC Steel Design Guide Series 11 (1997) for determining the fundamental frequency of vertical vibration of a steel frame floor system.

A floor is assumed to consist of concrete deck supported on steel beams which are supported on walls or steel girders between columns. The natural frequency is estimated by first considering a "beam or joist panel" mode and a "girder panel" mode separately and then combining them. Alternatively, finite element method can be used to estimate the natural frequency.

$$f = \frac{1}{T} = \frac{1}{2\pi}\sqrt{\frac{k}{m}} \tag{1.1f}$$

For a simply supported beam, maximum deflection at its midspan due to a uniform load w per unit length,

$$\Delta = \frac{5wL^4}{384\, E_s I} \tag{4.25}$$

Natural frequency of a simply supported steel beam in the first mode is as follows:

$$\omega = \pi^2 \sqrt{\frac{E_s I}{mL^4}} = \pi^2 \sqrt{\left(\frac{E_s I}{L^3}\right) / \left(\frac{wL}{g}\right)} \tag{4.26}$$

Equation 1.1f can be written as follows:

$$f = \frac{\pi}{2} \times \sqrt{\frac{5}{384}} \sqrt{\frac{g}{\Delta}} = 0.18\sqrt{\frac{g}{\Delta}} \tag{4.27}$$

where,

I = effective moment of inertia
w = uniformly distributed load per unit length
L = member span
g = acceleration due to gravity
f = fundamental natural frequency, Hz

Similarly, the girder panel mode natural frequency can be estimated from the same equation. The combined mode or system frequency can be estimated using the Dunkerley relationship:

$$\frac{1}{f^2} = \frac{1}{f_j^2} + \frac{1}{f_g^2} \tag{4.28}$$

where,

f_j = beam or joist panel mode frequency
f_g = girder panel mode frequency

4.10.3 Vibration Modes of a Bridge Deck

The modes of vibration of a RC bridge deck supported along the two opposite short supports are shown in Figure 4.27. The deck vibrates in vertical (flexure), lateral and torsional modes due to its flexibility. These vibration modes are very critical for its safety. The frequency of vibration for this deck varies from 0.33 Hz in the first mode to 8 Hz in the 12th mode. In 1940, the Tacoma Narrows bridge in the State of Washington, USA, collapsed within four months of its opening under a wind speed of only 64 kmph because of flexure – torsional mode also known as flutter mechanism.

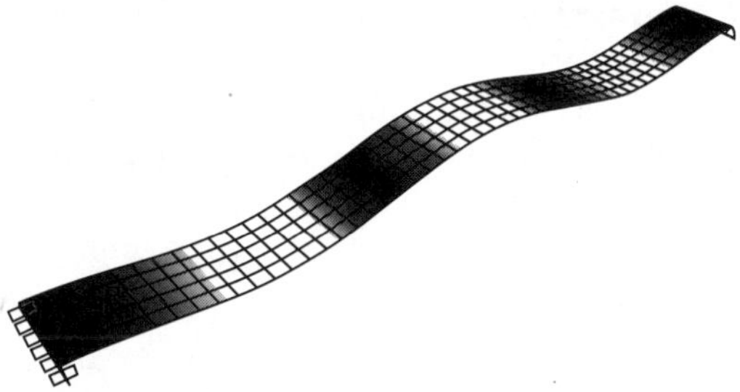

Figure 4.27(a) Mode 3 – Frequency = 1.75 Hz.

Figure 4.27(b) Mode 5 – Frequency = 3 Hz.

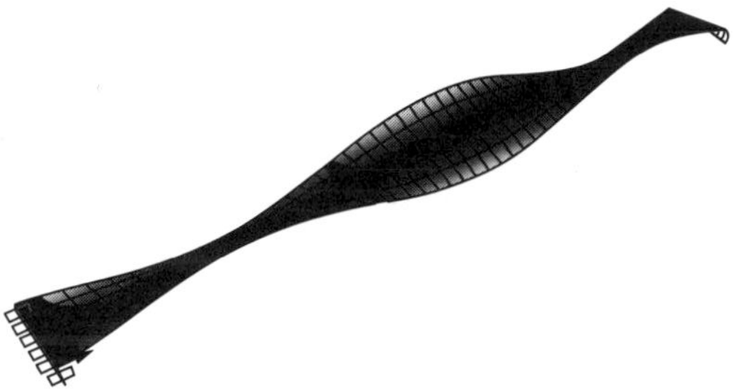

Figure 4.27(c) Mode 10 – Frequency = 6 Hz.

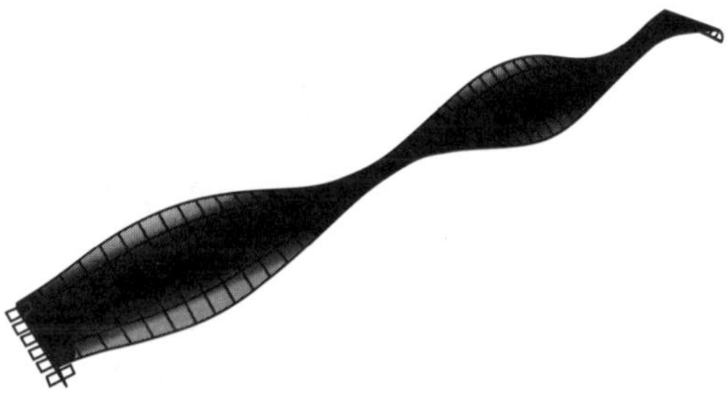

Figure 4.27(d) Mode 12 – Frequency = 8 Hz.

The London Millennium footbridge spans over 332 m divided into a north span of 80 m, a central span of 144 m and a southern span of 108 m. On the opening day in June 2000, unexpected large lateral vibrations occurred mainly in the south span of the bridge and the bridge had to be closed. The frequencies of the movements were around 0.8 Hz, the first lateral mode of the south span. In the central span, movements took place at barely 0.5 Hz and 1.1 Hz, respectively, the first and second lateral modes. At the north side, movements occurred at a frequency around 1.0 Hz, the first lateral mode of the north span. The maximum lateral acceleration on the south and north span was about 2.5 m/s^2. Later special dampers were fitted to control the undesirable vibrations. Therefore, it is important to examine the frequencies and modes of vibrations of slender bridge decks.

4.11 CODAL PROVISIONS FOR HUMAN INDUCED VIBRATIONS

The estimated natural frequency of the floor system must be less than the permissible value of the natural frequency for the given comfort level. AISC Design Guide 11, Eurocode 1990, 1991 and 1993, ISO 2631, ISO 10137 and IS:800 codes have detailed provisions for measurement and estimating the human induced vibrations as well as comfort and performance criteria.

4.11.1 AISC Design Guide 11 Provisions

The design criterion for walking excitations states that the floor system is satisfactory if the peak acceleration due to walking excitation given by the following equation remains within the permissible value:

$$\frac{a_0}{g} = \frac{P_0 \exp(-0.35 f_n)}{\xi W} \tag{4.29}$$

where

P_0 = a constant force representing the excitation
f_n = natural frequency of the joist panel, girder panel or a combined panel as per the case
ξ = modal damping ratio
W = effective weight supported by the joist panel, girder panel or a combined panel as per the case

For concrete, the dynamic modulus of elasticity of concrete should be taken 35% higher than the static modulus *Ec*.

The permissible values of limiting accelerations are shown in Table 4.3.

TABLE 4.3 PERMISSIBLE ACCELERATION LIMITS

	Recommended values of parameters		
	Constant force P0	Damping ratio ξ%	Acceleration limit % g
Offices, residences	0.29 kN	2 to 5	0.5%
Shopping Malls	0.29 kN	2	1.5%
Foot bridges – indoor	0.41 kN	1	1.5%
Foot bridges – outdoor	0.41 kN	1	5%

4.11.2 ISO 2631 Provisions

Part 1 of this Code defines methods for the measurements of periodic, random and transient whole body vibration. It provides guidance on the possible effects of the vibration on health, comfort, and perception and motion sickness. The frequency range considered is 0.5 Hz to 80 Hz for health, comfort, and perception; and 0.1 Hz to 0.5 Hz for motion sickness. The Code considers motions transmitted to the human body through the supporting surface: the feet of a standing person, the buttocks, back and seat of a seated person or the supporting area of a recumbent person.

Clause C.2.3 specifies acceptable values of vibration magnitude for comfort in public transport as shown in Table 4.4 depending on passenger expectations about trip duration and the type of activities passengers expect to accomplish (for example, reading, eating, writing etc.).

TABLE 4.4 VIBRATION MAGNITUDE FOR COMFORT

Acceleration in m/s^2	Reaction
Less than 0.315	Not uncomfortable
0.315 to 0.63	A little uncomfortable
0.5 to 1	Fairly uncomfortable
0.8 to 1.6	Uncomfortable
1.25 to 2.5	Very uncomfortable
>2	Extremely uncomfortable

Example 4.11

A simply supported pedestrian outdoor bridge has a 15 m span and 3 m width. Its cross-section is shown in Figure 4.28. The RC deck is 150 mm thick and supported on 2 no. ISMB 500 beams. Check it for human induced vibrations.

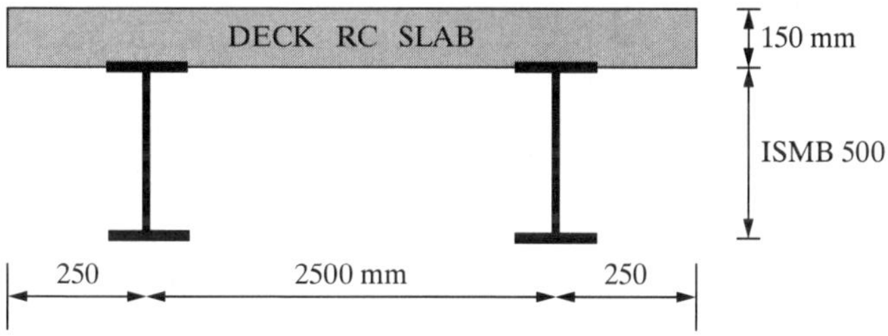

Figure 4.28 Floor section

Solution

Deck concrete properties: $f_{ck} = 30$ MPa, $Ec = 5000\sqrt{30} = 27380$ MPa
Area of cross-section = 15 × 300 = 4500 cm^2/m length
Steel beam properties, ISMB 500: Overall depth = 500 mm, Area = 110.74 cm^2, weight $w = 86.9$ kg/m, I = 45218 cm^4
Weight of deck slab = 0.15 × 25 = 3.75 kN/m^2

Modular ratio $$m = \frac{E_s}{1.35E_c} = \frac{200000}{1.35 \times 27380} = 5.40$$

Center of gravity of the floor above the bottom of the steel beam,

$$\bar{y} = \frac{2 \times 110.74 \times 25 + \left(\frac{4500}{5.4}\right) \times (50 + 7.5)}{2 \times 110.74 + 4500/5.40} = 50.66 \text{ cm}$$

Moment of inertia of the composite deck

$$I = 2\left[45218 + 110.74 \times (25 + 0.66)^2\right] + \frac{300}{5.4} \times \frac{15^3}{12} + \frac{4500}{5.4} \times (7.50 - 0.66)^2$$

$= 291 \times 10^3$ cm^4

Weight of the deck system $w = 3.75 \times 3 + 2 \times 86.9 \times 10/1000 = 13$ kN/m
Maximum deflection at the midspan is

$$\Delta = \frac{5wL^4}{384E_sI} = \frac{5\times 13\times 15000^4}{384\times 200000\times 291\times 10^7} = 14.72 \text{ mm}$$

Natural frequency of vibration of the beam (joist)

$$f_j = 0.18\sqrt{\frac{9810}{14.72}} = 4.6 \text{ Hz} = f_n$$

Total weight of the footbridge $W = 13 \times 15 = 195$ kN
$P_0 = 0.41$ kN, Damping = 1% as per Table 4.3
Peak acceleration is given by

$$\frac{a_0}{g} = \frac{P_0 \exp(-0.35 f_n)}{\xi W} = \frac{0.41 e^{-0.35\times 4.6}}{0.01\times 195} = 0.042 \text{ or, } 4.2\% \text{ of g}$$

The permissible peak acceleration limit for outdoor bridge is 5% from Table 4.3. Hence, the footbridge is satisfactory.

REVIEW QUESTIONS

4.1 What is a periodic loading?

4.2 How a periodic loading can be expressed by a Fourier series?

4.3 What is the orthogonality property of trigonometric functions?

4.4 What is the steady state response of an undamped SDOF system when subjected to a periodic loading represented by a Fourier series?

4.5 How a periodic loading can be expressed by exponential form of a Fourier series?

4.6 What is the general form of steady state response of an undamped SDOF system subjected to a unit complex forcing function?

4.7 What is the physical significance of complex frequency response function?

4.8 What is the concept behind frequency domain analysis of a SDOF system?

4.9 How do you represent a forcing function from time domain to frequency domain?

4.10 What is a Fourier transform pair? What is the necessary condition for a Fourier transform pair to exist?

4.11 What is a Dirac Delta function? Graphically illustrate the Fourier transform of Dirac Delta function.

4.12 Graphically illustrate the Fourier transform of constant unity.

4.13 Graphically illustrate the Fourier transform of sin ($\bar{\omega} t$).

4.14 Describe the salient features of human induced vibrations when a person (i) walks slowly, (ii) briskly, or (iii) runs.

4.15 List the parameters that need to be examined while designing a pedestrian bridge for human induced vibrations.

4.16 List the parameters that need to be examined while designing floor of a steel building for human induced vibrations.

4.17 What is Dunkerley relationship for estimating the natural frequency of a floor system?

4.18 What is the maximum acceleration recommended by Eurocode 1990 Annexure A2 for any part of the deck for pedestrian comfort?

[0.2 m/s^2 under normal use and 0.4 m/s^2 under exceptional crowd conditions]

4.19 What is the maximum acceleration recommended by ISO 2631-part 1 for passenger comfort in public transport?

[0.315 m/s^2]

4.20 Discuss the IS 800 code provision for natural frequency of a steel floor due to pedestrian loads.

MATLAB APPLICATIONS

4.1 (a) Represent the triangular periodic loading shown in Figure 4.1(a) having an amplitude p_0 and period T_p by Fourier series using MATLAB.

(b) How many terms are necessary to obtain a reasonable convergence? Show the plots for different number of terms.

(c) Find the steady state response of an undamped SDOF system having a frequency ratio of (i) 0.5 and (ii) 2. Show the plots for different number of terms.

4.2 Repeat Problem 4.1 for the half sine wave shown in Figure 4.1(b).

4.3 (a) Represent the periodic loading shown in Figure 4.1(a) having an amplitude of p_0 and period T_p using the exponential form of Fourier series. Show the amplitude of real and imaginary Fourier terms.

(b) Find the steady state response of an undamped SDOF system having a frequency ratio of (i) 0.5 and (ii) 2 using the exponential form of Fourier series. Show the amplitude of real and imaginary Fourier terms.

4.4 Determine the Fourier transform of a triangular pulse which is symmetric about $t = 0$ as shown in Figure 4.21 in frequency domain.

4.5 A SDOF system has a mass of 100 kg, stiffness of 250 kN/m and a damping of 5 per cent. It is subjected to a force as shown in Figure P4.1. The amplitude and period of the periodic forcing function is 100 kN and 0.20 sec, respectively. Determine the Fourier constants of displacement and response up to 25 terms. Also, plot the steady state response.

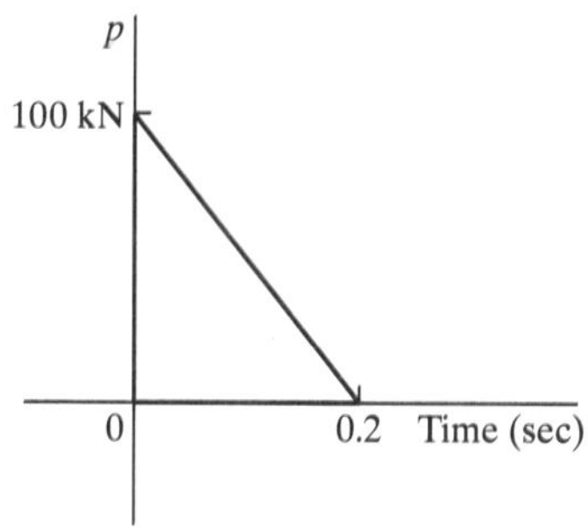

Figure P4.1

4.6 The force due to one leg of a person walking on a floor is shown in Figure P4.2. Discretize the load function so as to capture its salient features. Illustrate the first four Fourier harmonics using MATLAB or MS-EXCEL.

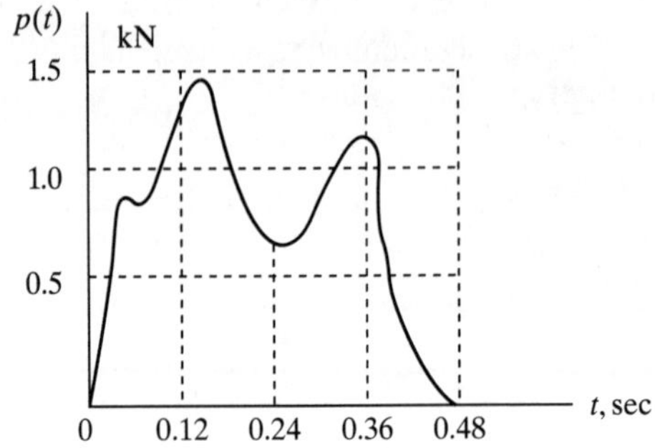

Figure P4.2

4.7 The force due to both legs of a person walking on a floor is shown in Figure P4.3. Discretize the load function so as to capture its salient features. Illustrate the first four Fourier harmonics using MATLAB or MS-EXCEL.

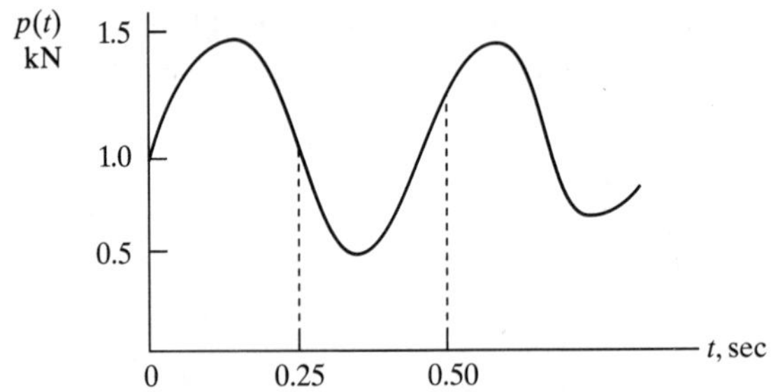

Figure P4.3

4.8 Determine the response of a damped SDOF system due to the force shown in Figure P4.2, if natural frequency of vibration of the system is 2Hz and damping is 1.5 per cent. Illustrate the first four Fourier harmonics using MATLAB or MS-EXCEL.

4.9 Determine the response of a damped SDOF system due to the force shown in Figure P4.3, if natural frequency of vibration of the system is 2.5 Hz and damping is 1.5 per cent. Illustrate the first four Fourier harmonics using MATLAB or MS-EXCEL.

REFERENCES

Bachmann, H. (2002) Lively Footbridges a Real Challenge, Proceedings of the International Conference on the Design and Dynamic Behaviour of Footbridges, Paris, France, November 20–22, pp. 18–30.

Ellis, B.R. (2004) The Response of Structures to Dynamic Crowd Loads, BRE Digest 426, London.

Eurocode 1990 (2002) Basis of Structural Design, European Standard, Brussels.

Eurocode 1991- part 2 (2003) Actions on structures – Part 2: Traffic loads on bridges, and UK National Annex, European Standard, Brussels.

Eurocode 1993-part 2 (2004): Design of Steel Structures – Part 2: Steel Bridges, European Standard, Brussels.

IS:800 (2007) General Construction in Steel – Code of Practice, Bureau of Indian Standards, New Delhi.

ISO 2631-part 1 (1997) Mechanical Vibration and Shock — Evaluation of Human Exposure to Wholebody Vibration — Part 1: General Requirements, International Standardization Organization, Geneva.

ISO 2631-part 2 (2003) Mechanical Vibration and Shock — Evaluation of Human Exposure to Wholebody Vibration — Part 2: Vibration in buildings (1 Hz to 80 Hz), International Standardization Organization, Geneva.

ISO 10137 (2007)Bases for Design of Structures: Serviceability of Buildings and Pedestrian Walkways against Vibration, International Standardization Organization, Geneva.

Kala, J., Salajka, V. and Hradil, P. (2009) Footbridge Response on Single Pedestrian Induced Vibration Analysis, International Science Index, Vol 3, No.2, pp. 548–559.

Murray, T.M., Allen, D.E., and Ungar, E.E. (1997) Floor Vibrations Due to Human Activities, Steel Design Guide Series-11, American Institute of Steel Construction, Chicago.

SETRA (2006) Footbridges, Assessment of Vibrational Behaviour of Footbridges Under Pedestrian Loading, *Technical guide SETRA*, Paris.

5 Single Degree of Freedom System: Impulse Loading

5.1 INTRODUCTION

In many practical situations, the forcing function is neither harmonic nor periodic. It may be a single impulse loading having a very large magnitude but a very short duration t_d. It may be a sine impulse, a rectangular impulse, a ramp impulse or any other similar impulse having a total duration of t_d as shown in Figure 5.1. Such impulses may be produced by a blast loading. The response of such an impulse depends upon the ratio t_d/T, where T is a natural period of the SDOF system. The response of such arbitrary single impulse excitation is presented for an undamped SDOF system because the effect of damping on the response of a SDOF system due to single impulse excitation is usually not significant. The maximum response to an impulse force will be reached in a very short time. The damping force will not be able to absorb energy from the structure during this time. Duhamel integral is used to determine the response of a SDOF system subjected to such loadings. The concept of *shock spectrum* is introduced to represent the response in graphical form, which is very easy to understand.

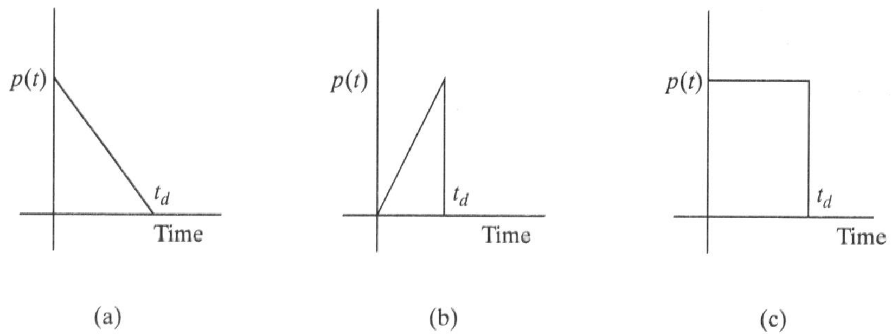

Figure 5.1 Impulse loading.

5.2 IMPULSIVE FORCE

Consider a single impulse shown in Figure 5.2. This is a rectangular pulse of very large magnitude and a very short duration. It may be expressed mathematically as follows:

$$p(t)\begin{cases} = 0 & t-\varepsilon \le \tau \\ = \dfrac{p}{2\varepsilon} & \tau-\varepsilon \le t \le \tau+\varepsilon \\ = 0 & t \ge \tau+\varepsilon \end{cases}$$

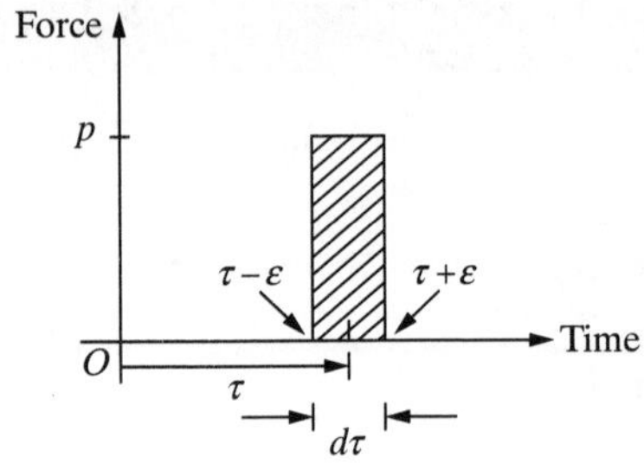

Figure 5.2 Unit impulse force

The impulse is defined as follows:

$$\text{Impulse} = \text{force} \times \text{duration}$$

$$I(\varepsilon) = \int_{t-\varepsilon}^{t+\varepsilon} p(t)dt \tag{5.1a}$$

Since the force is zero outside the limits $(\tau - \varepsilon)$ to $(\tau + \varepsilon)$, the limits of integration may be extended from $-\infty$ to $+\infty$, that is,

$$I(\varepsilon) = \int_{-\infty}^{\infty} p(t)dt \tag{5.1b}$$

As the duration of the force $2\varepsilon \to 0$, the force becomes infinite. However, the magnitude of the impulse given by the time integral of $p(t)$ remains equal to p. In case, the magnitude p is unity, such a force is called the *unit impulse*.

According to the Newton's second law of motion, if a force p acts on a body, the rate of change of momentum is equal to the force applied on the body.

$$\frac{d}{dt}\left(m\frac{dx}{dt}\right) = p$$

If the mass is constant, it can be written as

$$m\frac{d^2x}{dt^2} = p \tag{5.2a}$$

$$m\ddot{x} = p \tag{5.2b}$$

Integrating both sides with respect to t gives,

$$\int_{t_1}^{t_2} pdt = m(\dot{x}_2 - \dot{x}_1) \tag{5.2c}$$

where,

$\dot{x}_1$ = initial velocity prior to the application of the force, that is, impulse
$\dot{x}_2$ = final velocity after the application of the force

The integral on the left side of the equation represents *magnitude of the impulse*. The quantity on the right side of the equation represents *change in momentum* of the body. If the system is at rest just prior to the application of the impulse, this equation can be written as

$$\int_{t_1}^{t_2} p\,dt = m\dot{x}_2 = m\dot{x}$$

If the force acts for a very short duration at $t = \tau$, it can be written as

$$p d\tau = m\dot{x}$$

$$\dot{x} = \frac{p d\tau}{m} \tag{5.2d}$$

Undamped Free Vibrations

For undamped free vibrations in a SDOF, it was shown in Chapter 2 that:

$$x(t) = A\sin\omega t + B\cos\omega t \tag{2.7b}$$

Constants A and B can be expressed in terms of initial conditions, that is, $x(0)$ and $\dot{x}(0)$ at $t = 0$

$$x(t) = \frac{\dot{x}(0)}{\omega}\sin\omega t + x(0)\cos\omega t \tag{2.9a}$$

The initial displacement is zero prior to and up to the impulse, therefore, the response is given by

$$\therefore \qquad x(t) = \frac{\dot{x}(0)}{\omega}\sin[\omega(t-\tau)] \quad \text{for} \quad t \geq \tau$$

The impulse imparts initial velocity to the mass given by Equation (5.2d). Therefore, the response becomes

$$x(t) = \frac{p d\tau}{m\omega}\sin[\omega(t-\tau)] \quad \text{for} \quad t \geq \tau \tag{5.3a}$$

or,

$$x(t) = p d\tau\left[h(t-\tau)\right] \quad \text{for} \quad t \geq \tau \tag{5.3b}$$

If the magnitude of the impulse is unity, that is, $p\,d\tau = 1$, the response of the undamped system is given by

$$h(t-\tau) = x(t) = \frac{1}{m\omega}\sin[\omega(t-\tau)] \tag{5.3c}$$

where $h(t-\tau)$ is referred to as the *unit impulse response function*.

Damped Free Vibrations

For damped free vibrations in a SDOF, it was shown in Chapter 2 that:

$$x(t) = e^{-\xi\omega t}\left(A\sin\omega_D t + B\cos\omega_D t\right) \tag{2.17}$$

Constants A and B can be expressed in terms of initial conditions, that is, $x(0)$ and $\dot{x}(0)$ at $t = 0$

$$x(t) = e^{-\xi\omega t}\left\{\frac{x(0)\xi\omega + \dot{x}(0)}{\omega_D}\sin\omega_D t + x(0)\cos\omega_D t\right\} \tag{2.18b}$$

The initial displacement is zero prior to and up to the impulse, therefore, the response is given by

$$x(t) = e^{-\xi\omega(t-\tau)}\left\{\frac{\dot{x}(0)}{\omega_D}\sin\omega_D(t-\tau)\right\} \quad \text{for} \quad t \ge \tau$$

or,

$$x(t) = \frac{p d\tau}{m\omega_D}e^{-\xi\omega(t-\tau)}\sin\omega_D(t-\tau) \quad \text{for} \quad t \ge \tau \tag{5.4a}$$

For a single impulse, the total response is given by

$$x(t) = p_0 h(t-\tau)$$

where

$$p_0 = p\, d\tau = \text{magnitude of impulse} \tag{5.4b}$$

If there is a series of three impulses of magnitude, p_1, p_2, and p_3, at different instants, τ_1, τ_2 and τ_3, respectively, the total response can be written as:

$$x(t) = p_1 h(t-\tau_1) + p_2 h(t-\tau_2) + p_3 h(t-\tau_3)$$

For a general solution consisting of n impulses, the total response is given by

$$x(t) = \sum_i p_i h(t-\tau_i) \tag{5.4c}$$

5.3 RESPONSE TO ARBITRARY FORCE

Consider a unit impulse at instant $t = 0$ and again at instant $t = t_1$ as shown in Figure 5.3(a) and 5.3(b). The steady state response of a SDOF system, with zero damping and 5% damping, subjected to these two impulses are shown in Figure 5.3(c) and 5.3(d), respectively by making use of Equations (5.3a) and (5.4a). The total response is obtained by superimposing the two responses, if the system is linear, as shown in Figure 5.3(e) and 5.3(f). In this illustration, undamped natural frequency was 5 rad/sec, or the fundamental natural period was 1.257 sec, and duration of the pulse was 0.01 sec. The shift t_1 is 1.5 sec. There is a discontinuity at $t = 5$ sec due to superimposition of the two responses ($t = 0$ and $t = 1.5$ sec) as seen in Figure 5.3(e) and 5.3(f).

The effect of spring stiffness and damping is negligible on the overall response because they are unable to respond in view of very short duration of each impulse, that is, when $t_d/T << 1$. This leads to a very important conclusion. An arbitrary loading such as shown in Figure 5.4 may be considered to consist of a series of short impulses of duration $d\tau$ each producing its own response. If the SDOF system is linear, its response can be found by superimposition of the individual response to each impulse.

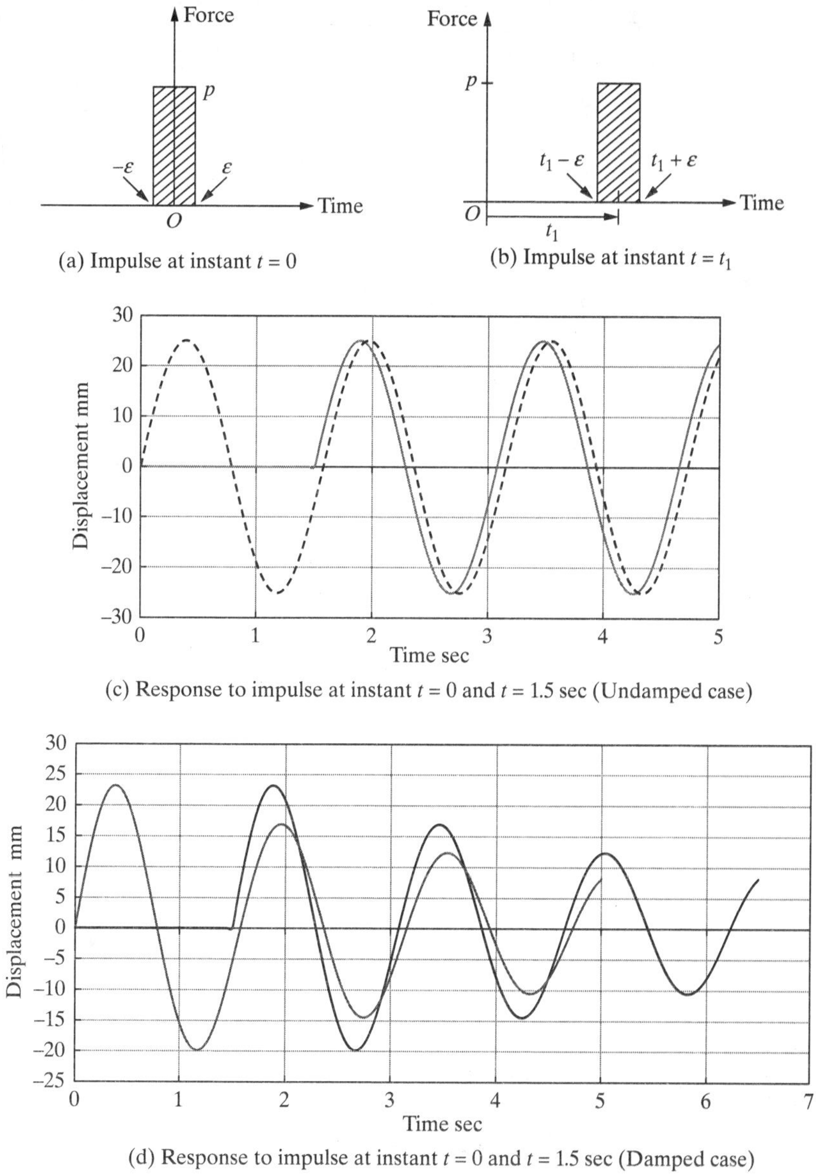

Figure 5.3 Impulse and its response

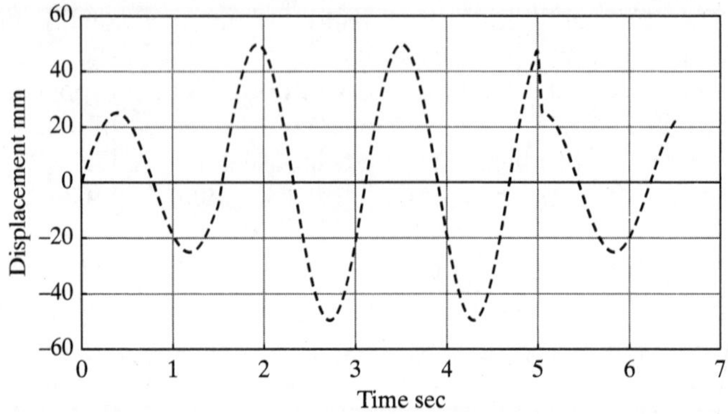

(e) Total response for undamped case

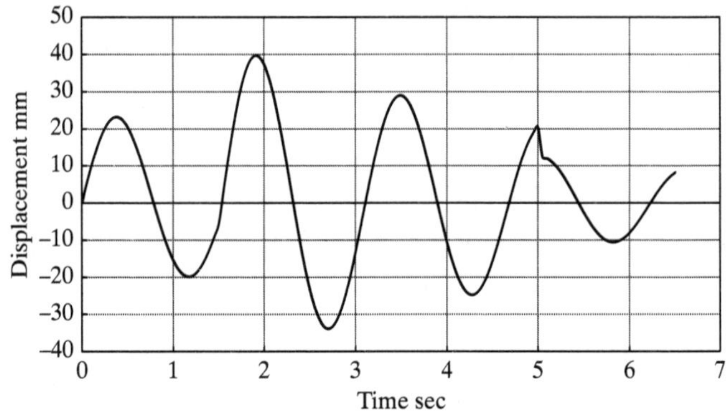

(f) Total response for 5% damping

Figure 5.3 (Continued)

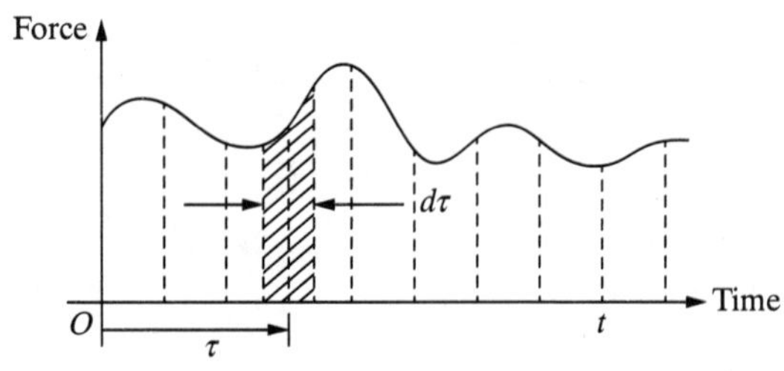

Figure 5.4 An arbitrary force

5.4 DUHAMEL INTEGRAL

5.4.1 Undamped SDOF System

The response of an undamped SDOF system due to an infinitesimally short impulse can be written as follows:

$$dx(t)=\frac{p(\tau)d\tau}{m\omega}\sin[\omega(t-\tau)] \text{ for } t>\tau \tag{5.5}$$

The total steady state response is the sum of the responses to all the impulses up to that time as shown in Figure 5.4. Therefore,

$$x(t)=\frac{1}{m\omega}\int_{o}^{t} p(\tau)\sin[\omega(t-\tau)]d\tau \tag{5.6}$$

It is known as Duhamel integral. It can also be written as

$$x(t)=\int_{o}^{t} p(\tau)h(t-\tau)d\tau \tag{5.7a}$$

where

$$h(t-\tau)=\frac{1}{m\omega}\sin[\omega(t-\tau)] \tag{5.7b}$$

Equation (5.7a) is called the *convolution integral*. It is a general solution applicable to any linear dynamic system. The function $h\ (t-\tau)$ is called *unit impulse response* for undamped systems. Equation (5.6) or (5.7) can be evaluated using numerical integration. In these equations, it is implicit that initial conditions of the SDOF system is at rest, that is, $x(0) = 0$, and $\dot{x}(0) = 0$. If not, then the resulting free vibration response given by Equation (2.9a) should also be considered.

5.4.2 Damped SDOF System

The steady state response of a damped SDOF system for an infinitesimally short pulse of magnitude p and duration $d\tau$ at instant τ can be written as follows:

$$dx(t)=\frac{p(\tau)d\tau}{m\omega_D}e^{-\xi\omega(t-\tau)}\sin[\omega_D(t-\tau)] \text{ for } t\geq\tau \tag{5.8a}$$

If a continuous function can be finely divided as a sequence of infinitesimally short impulses, its total response can be written as

$$x(t)=\frac{1}{m\omega_D}\int_{o}^{t} p(\tau)e^{-\xi\omega(t-\tau)}\sin[\omega_D(t-\tau)]d\tau \qquad \text{for } t\geq\tau \tag{5.8b}$$

or,

$$x(t)=\int_{0}^{t} p(\tau)h(t-\tau)d\tau$$

This is again Duhamel integral. The unit impulse response for a damped system is given by

$$h(t-\tau)=\frac{1}{m\omega_D}e^{-\xi\omega(t-\tau)}\sin[\omega_D(t-\tau)] \tag{5.8c}$$

The unit impulse response function $h(t-\tau)$ can be evaluated using the convolution function `conv` in MATLAB.

5.5 WHAT IS CONVOLUTION?

Let us rewrite Equation (5.7a) as follows:

$$(h \times f)(t) = \int_{-\infty}^{\infty} h(t-\tau) f(\tau) d\tau \tag{5.9a}$$

$$= \int_{-\infty}^{\infty} f(t-\tau) h(\tau) d\tau \tag{5.9b}$$

The limits are more often taken over an infinite range instead of 0 to t. The symbol $(h \times f)(t)$ denotes convolution of functions h and f.

The convolution is defined as the integral of the product of the two functions after one is reversed and shifted. As such, it is a special kind of integral transform. It can be understood as follows:

(a) Let us first fix a value t. The graph of the function $h(\tau - t)$ has the same shape as $h(\tau)$ but shifted to the right by t. Then forming $h(t - \tau)$ flips the graph (left to right) about the line $\tau = t$. If the most important feature of $h(\tau)$ is near $\tau = 0$, for example, it has a sharp peak, then this feature is shifted to $\tau = t$ for the function $h(t - \tau)$.

(b) Multiply the two functions $f(\tau)$ and $h(t - \tau)$ and integrate with respect to τ. The value of the convolution $(h \times f)(t)$ is not just the product of the values of f and the flipped and shifted h, but it is the *integral* of the product. Integrating the product sums up these values.

Convolution is a formal mathematical operation, just as multiplication, addition, and integration. Addition takes two *numbers* and produces a third *number*, while convolution takes two *functions* or *signals* and produces a third *function* or *signal*. This is typically viewed as a modified version of one of the original functions. A convolution is an integral that expresses the amount of overlap of one function as it is shifted over another function. It, therefore, *blends* one function with another.

5.6 SHOCK SPECTRA

If a SDOF system is subjected to an impulse of duration t_d, its maximum response can be obtained using the Duhamel's integral. The dynamic magnification factor can be computed. By changing the duration of the impulse of a given shape, different values of the dynamic magnification factor can be obtained. A plot can be made between dynamic magnification factor and t_d/T for a given shape of the impulse. Such a plot is referred to as *shock spectra*. Similar plots can be made for other shapes of the impulse function. Shock spectra is very useful in designing SDOF systems subjected to impulse loading. The Duhamel integral can be easily evaluated using MATLAB.

5.7 ILLUSTRATIVE EXAMPLES

Example 5.1

Find the steady state response of an undamped SDOF system subjected to a constant step impulse as shown in Figure 5.5.

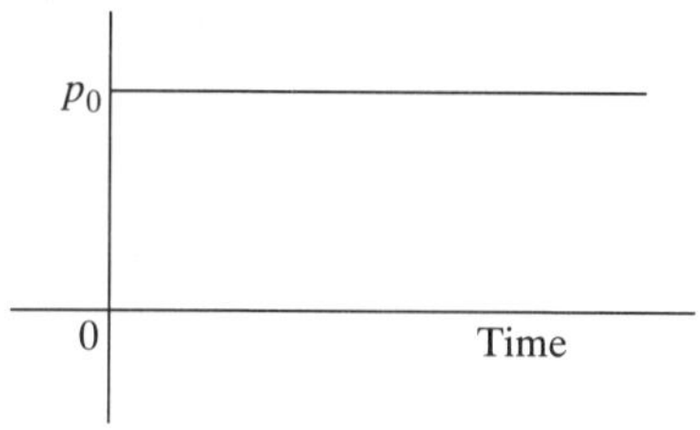

Figure 5.5 Step impulse.

Solution

The steady state response can be written as follows:

$$x(t) = \frac{1}{m\omega}\int_0^t p(\tau)\sin\omega(t-\tau)\,d\tau \tag{1}$$

$$x(t) = \int_0^t \frac{p_0}{m\omega}\sin\omega(t-\tau)\,d\tau$$

Upon integration,

$$x(t) = \frac{p_0}{m\omega^2}(1-\cos\omega t) = \frac{p_0}{k}(1-\cos\omega t) \tag{2}$$

It is implicit that the initial conditions $x(0)$ and $\dot{x}(0)$ are zero.
Equation (2) leads to a very important conclusion.
The maximum value of $x(t)$ is equal to

$$x_{\max} = \frac{2p_0}{k} \quad \text{when } \cos\omega t = -1$$

It shows that if a constant load p_0 is applied suddenly, the maximum dynamic displacement is twice that of the static displacement. □

Example 5.2

An undamped SDOF system is subjected to an earthquake excitation given by $\ddot{x}_g(t) = \ddot{x}_0 e^{-\bar{\omega}t}$. Determine its steady state response.

Solution

The undamped steady state response of a SDOF system by Duhamel integral is given as follows:

$$x(t) = \int_0^t p(\tau)h(t-\tau)\,d\tau \tag{5.7a}$$

where,

$$h(t-\tau)=\frac{1}{m\omega}\sin[\omega(t-\tau)] \tag{5.7b}$$

The response $x(t)$ can be written as follows:

$$x(t)=-\int_0^t m\ddot{x}_g(t)\frac{1}{m\omega}\sin[\omega(t-\tau)]d\tau$$

or,

$$x(t)=-\int_0^t \ddot{x}_0 e^{-\bar{\omega}\tau}\frac{1}{\omega}\sin[\omega(t-\tau)]d\tau$$

$$x(t)=-\frac{\ddot{x}_0}{\omega}\int_0^t e^{-\bar{\omega}\tau}\sin[\omega(t-\tau)]d\tau$$

This integral can be evaluated by making use of integration by parts as shown in earlier examples.

$$\int u\,dv = uv-\int v\,du$$

Let $u=\sin\omega(t-\tau)$, $du=-\omega\cos\omega(t-\tau)d\tau$

$$dv=e^{-\bar{\omega}\tau},\quad v=-\frac{e^{-\bar{\omega}\tau}}{\bar{\omega}}$$

$$\begin{aligned}
x(t)&=-\frac{\ddot{x}_0}{\omega}\left|-\frac{e^{-\bar{\omega}\tau}}{\bar{\omega}}\sin\omega(t-\tau)\right|_0^t+\frac{\ddot{x}_0}{\omega}\int_0^t\frac{e^{-\bar{\omega}\tau}}{\bar{\omega}}\omega\cos\omega(t-\tau)d\tau\\
&=-\frac{\ddot{x}_0}{\omega}\left(\frac{\sin\omega t}{\bar{\omega}}\right)+\frac{\ddot{x}_0}{\bar{\omega}}\int_0^t e^{-\bar{\omega}\tau}\cos\omega(t-\tau)d\tau\\
&=-\frac{\ddot{x}_0}{\omega}\left(\frac{\sin\omega t}{\bar{\omega}}\right)+\frac{\ddot{x}_0}{\bar{\omega}}\left|-\frac{e^{-\bar{\omega}\tau}}{\bar{\omega}}\cos\omega(t-\tau)\right|_0^t-\frac{\ddot{x}_0}{\bar{\omega}}\int_0^t-\frac{e^{-\bar{\omega}\tau}}{\bar{\omega}}\omega\sin\omega(t-\tau)d\tau\\
&=-\frac{\ddot{x}_0}{\omega}\left(\frac{\sin\omega t}{\bar{\omega}}\right)+\frac{\ddot{x}_0}{\bar{\omega}}\left[-\frac{e^{-\bar{\omega}t}}{\bar{\omega}}+\frac{\cos\omega t}{\bar{\omega}}\right]+\frac{\ddot{x}_0\omega}{\bar{\omega}^2}\int_0^t e^{-\bar{\omega}\tau}\sin\omega(t-\tau)d\tau
\end{aligned}$$

$$x(t)=-\frac{\ddot{x}_0}{\omega}\left(\frac{\sin\omega t}{\bar{\omega}}\right)-\frac{\ddot{x}_0}{\bar{\omega}^2}e^{-\bar{\omega}t}+\frac{\ddot{x}_0}{\bar{\omega}^2}\cos\omega t-\left(\frac{\omega}{\bar{\omega}}\right)^2x(t)$$

$$x(t)=-\left(\frac{\ddot{x}_0}{\omega^2+\bar{\omega}^2}\right)\left[\frac{\bar{\omega}}{\omega}\sin\omega t-\cos\omega t+e^{-\bar{\omega}t}\right]$$ □

Example 5.3

A damped SDOF system is subjected to an earthquake excitation given by $\ddot{x}_g(t)=\dot{x}_0\,\delta(t)$. Determine its maximum steady state response.

Solution

The damped steady state response of a SDOF system by Duhamel integral is given as follows:

$$x(t) = \int_0^t p(\tau)h(t-\tau)d\tau \tag{5.7a}$$

where,

$$h(t-\tau) = \frac{1}{m\omega_D}e^{-\xi\omega(t-\tau)}\sin\omega_D(t-\tau) \tag{5.8c}$$

The response $x(t)$ can be written as follows:

$$x(t) = -\int_0^t m\dot{x}_0\delta(t)\frac{1}{m\omega_D}e^{-\xi\omega(t-\tau)}\sin\omega_D(t-\tau)d\tau$$

or,

$$x(t) = -\frac{\dot{x}_0}{\omega_D}e^{-\xi\omega t}\sin\omega_D t \quad \text{for} \quad \delta(t) = 1$$

Maximum displacement occurs when velocity is zero, that is,

$$\dot{x}(t) = 0$$

Differentiating Equation (i) and setting it to zero gives

$$\frac{dx(t)}{dt} = -\frac{\dot{x}_0}{\omega_D}e^{-\xi\omega t}(-\xi\omega\sin\omega_D t + \omega_D\cos\omega_D t) = 0$$

or,

$$\tan\omega_D t = \frac{\omega_D}{\xi\omega} = \frac{\sqrt{1-\xi^2}}{\xi}$$

$$\therefore \sin\omega_D t = \sqrt{1-\xi^2}$$

Time t_0 at which maximum displacement occurs is given by

$$t_0 = \frac{1}{\omega_D}\tan^{-1}\frac{\sqrt{1-\xi^2}}{\xi}$$

$\therefore$ Maximum absolute displacement x_{max} is given by

$$x_{max} = \frac{\dot{x}_0}{\omega_D}e^{-\xi\omega t_0}\sin\omega_D t_0$$ □

Example 5.4

An undamped SDOF system is subjected to a ramp impulse as shown in Figure 5.6. Find (a) steady state response in the forced and free vibration states using Duhamel integral and (b) shock spectra.

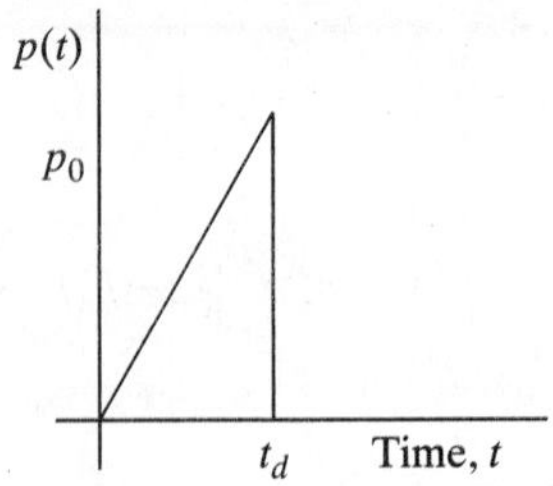

Figure 5.6 Ramp impulse.

Solution

(a) Steady State Response

The forcing function can be expressed as

$$p(\tau)=\frac{\tau}{t_d}p_0 \qquad 0\le t\le t_d \tag{1a}$$

and

$$=0 \qquad t\ge t_d \tag{1b}$$

Duhamel integral of Equation (1a) gives,

$$x(t)=\frac{p_0}{m\omega}\int_0^t\frac{\tau}{t_d}\sin\omega(t-\tau)d\tau \tag{2}$$

On integration, $$x(t)=\frac{p_0}{m\omega t_d}\left|\tau\cos\omega(t-\tau)-\sin\omega(t-\tau)\right|$$

or, $$x(t)=x_{st}\left[\frac{t}{t_d}-\frac{\sin\omega t}{\omega t_d}\right] \quad \text{for} \quad t\le t_d \tag{3}$$

and velocity is given by $$\dot{x}(t)=x_{st}\left[\frac{1}{t_d}-\frac{\cos\omega t}{t_d}\right] \quad \text{for} \quad t\le t_d \tag{4}$$

The vibrations after the loading has ceased to zero may be found by the response of the free vibration analysis with proper boundary conditions. It means we need to know the displacement and velocity at the end of the force function, at time t_d. These can be obtained by substituting $t = t_d$ in Equations (3) and (4).

Free vibration response is given by

$$x(t)=\frac{\dot{x}(t_d)}{\omega}\sin\omega(t-t_d)+x(t_d)\cos\omega(t-t_d) \quad \text{for} \quad t>t_d \tag{5}$$

Upon substituting the values of initial conditions at $t = t_d$ from Equations (3) and (4) in Equation (5), we obtain

$$x(t)=\frac{x_{st}}{\omega t_d}\left[sin\omega(t-t_d)(1-\cos\omega t_d)+\cos\omega(t-t_d)(\omega t_d-\sin\omega t_d)\right] \quad \text{for} \quad t>t_d \tag{6}$$

It is now possible to plot $x(t)/x_{st}$ vs t_d/T for the ramp impulse for a SDOF system and develop a shock spectra using Equations (3) and (6).

Let us rewrite Equation (3) as follows:

$$\frac{x(t)}{x_{st}}=\left[\frac{t}{T}\frac{T}{t_d}-\frac{\sin 2\pi\frac{t}{T}}{2\pi\frac{t_d}{T}}\right] \quad \text{for} \quad t\le t_d \tag{7}$$

Similarly, Equation (6) can be re-written as follows:

$$\frac{x(t)}{x_{st}}=\frac{T}{2\pi t_d}\left[\sin\frac{2\pi}{T}(t-t_d)\left(1-\cos 2\pi\frac{t_d}{T}\right)+\cos\frac{2\pi}{T}(t-t_d)\left(2\pi\frac{t_d}{T}-\sin 2\pi\frac{t_d}{T}\right)\right] \quad (8)$$

$$\text{for } t \geq t_d$$

Now a plot can be drawn between the steady state response $x(t)/x_{st}$ and (t/T) for given value of (t_d/T) using Equations (7) and (8) using MATLAB code DOS5_1.

The maximum response may occur either in the forced vibration phase or in the free vibration phase depending up on the ratio t_d/T.
The static displacement at any instant t can be estimated as follows:

$$x_{st}(t)=\frac{p(t)}{k}=\frac{p_0}{k}\frac{t}{t_d}=x_{st}^0\frac{t}{t_d} \quad \text{for} \quad t<t_d \quad (9)$$

where x_{st}^0 is maximum static displacement due to p_0.
This equation can also be plotted on the dynamic response graphs in order to compare static and dynamic displacements. □

The net dynamic response for $t_d/T = 0.1, 0.2, 0.5, 1, 2, 3$ and 4.0 are shown in Figures 5.7(a) to 5.7(g); respectively. The arrow in these graphs indicates the demarcation between forced and free vibrations. The following observations can be made in these plots:

1. The dynamic response consists of two parts: forced response and free response. The forced response acts till the duration of the ramp force, after this, it undergoes free vibrations.
2. The dynamic response depends upon the ratio t_d/T and not on the individual values of t_d and T because of the presence of the term $\omega t_d = 2\pi(t_d/T)$ in the expression for dynamic response.
3. During the forced response phase, the system oscillates about its static solution. During the free vibration phase, the SDOF system vibrates about its mean zero position.
4. As t_d/T increases from 0.1 to 1.0, the ratio of dynamic displacement to static displacement increases up to 1.0, thereafter, with the increase in t_d/T, there is no further increase in the magnitude of $x_{\text{dynamic}}/x_{\text{static}}$. It means there is no dynamic effect in the present pulse loading.

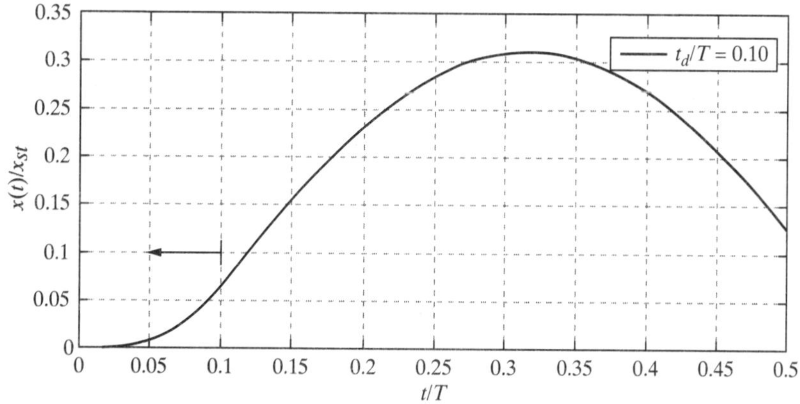

Figure 5.7(a) Dynamic response for $t_d/T = 0.1$.

Note: The MATLAB codes DOS5_1, DOS5_2, DOS5_3, DOS5_4 and DOS5_5 are available on the web.

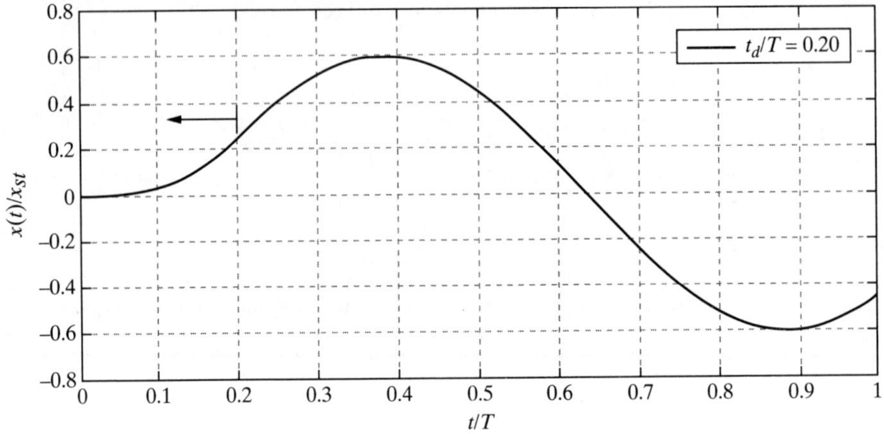

Figure 5.7(b) Dynamic response for $t_d/T = 0.2$.

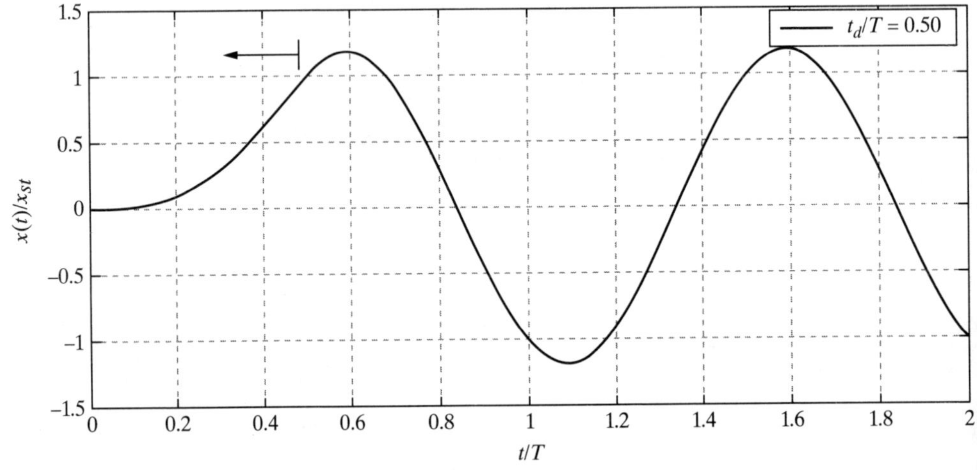

Figure 5.7(c) Dynamic response for $t_d/T = 0.5$.

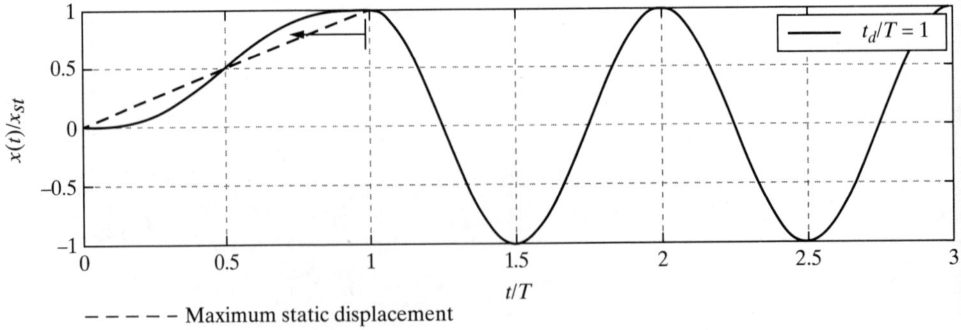

Figure 5.7(d) Dynamic response for $t_d/T = 1.0$.

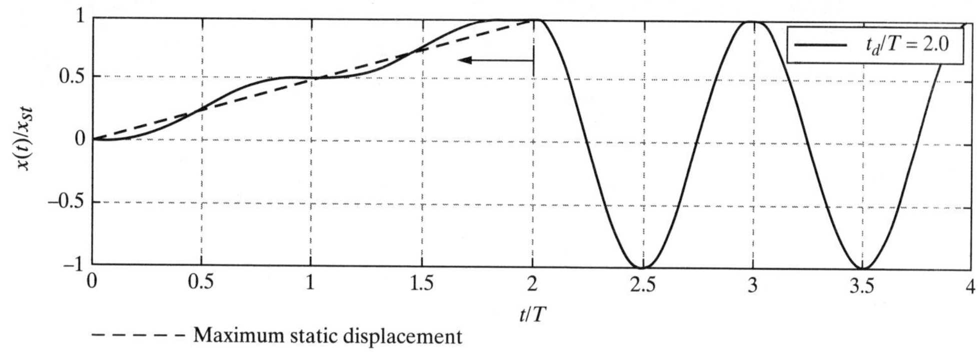

Figure 5.7(e) Dynamic response for $t_d/T = 2.0$.

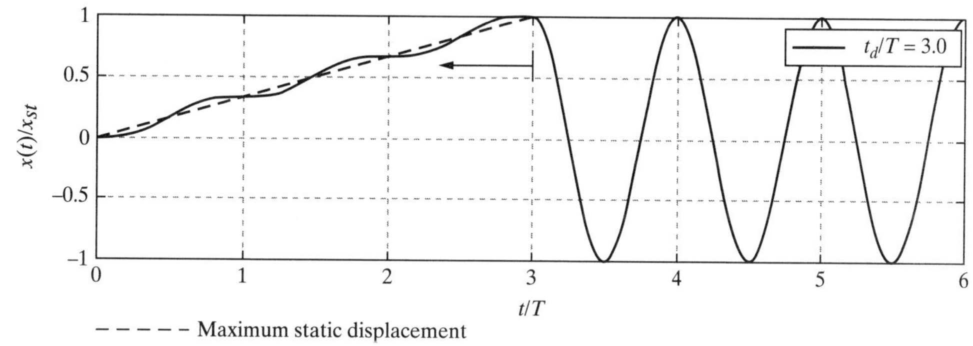

Figure 5.7(f) Dynamic response for $t_d/T = 3.0$.

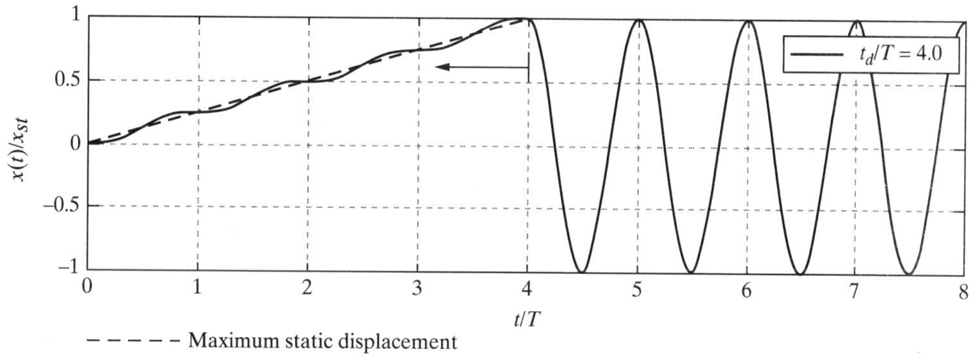

Figure 5.7(g) Dynamic response for $t_d/T = 4.0$.

(b) Shock Spectra

The maximum response of a SDOF system is obtained for a given t_d/T value. The MATLAB code developed earlier is modified. Using the MATLAB code `DOS5_2`, shock spectra is plotted in Figure 5.8(a) and (b) on semi-log and normal scales. It shows the ratio of absolute maximum displacement and static displacement versus t_d/T. For short duration pulse up to $t_d/T \leq 0.5$, there is an increase in the maximum displacement ratio up to about 1.25, thereafter, the dynamic magnification factor reduces continuously, and the system vibrates about its mean static position.

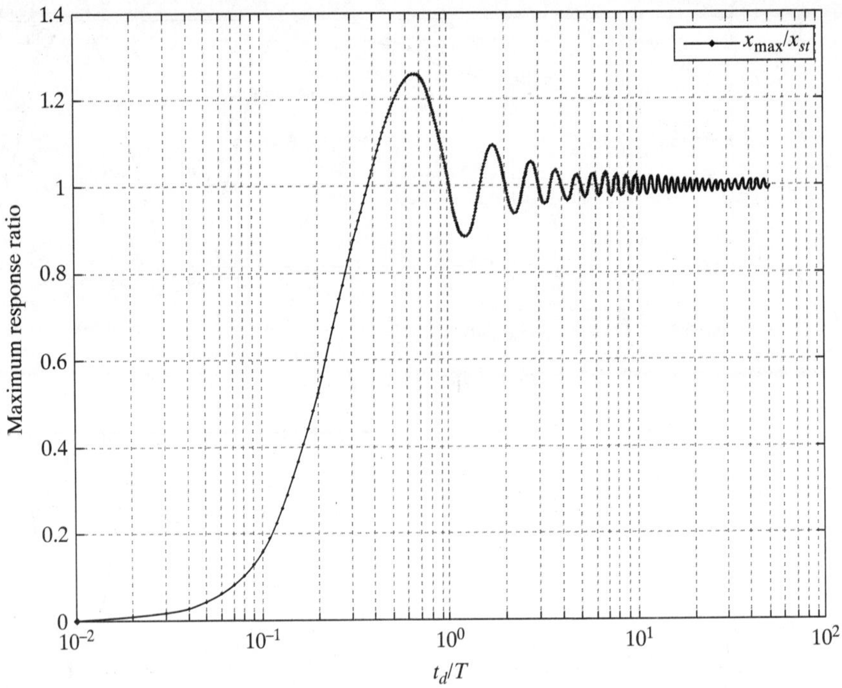

Figure 5.8(a) Shock spectra on log scale.

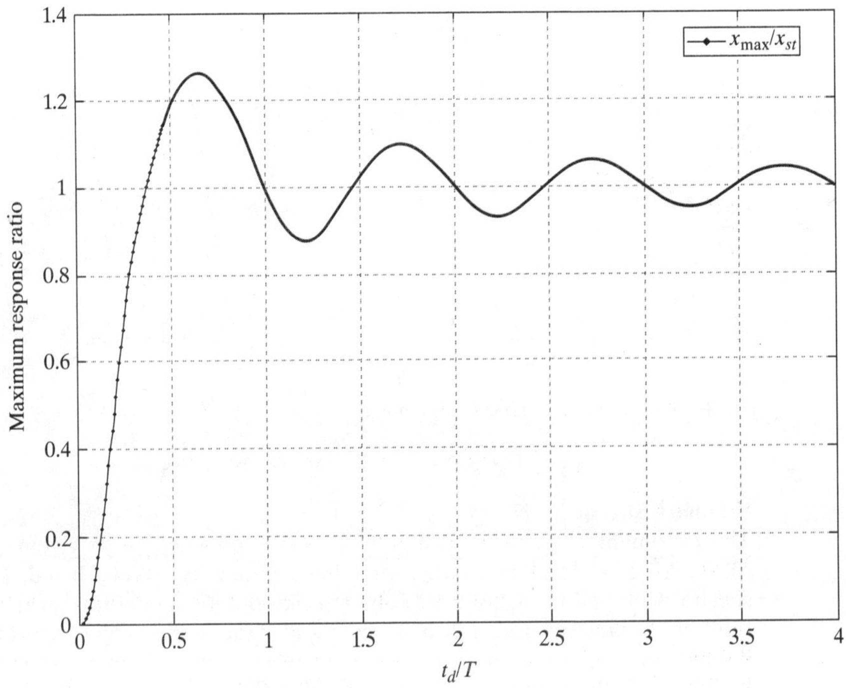

Figure 5.8(b) Shock spectra-normal scale.

Example 5.5

An undamped SDOF system is subjected to a ramp + step impulse as shown in Figure 5.9. Find (a) steady state response in the forced and free vibration states using Duhamel integral and (b) shock spectra.

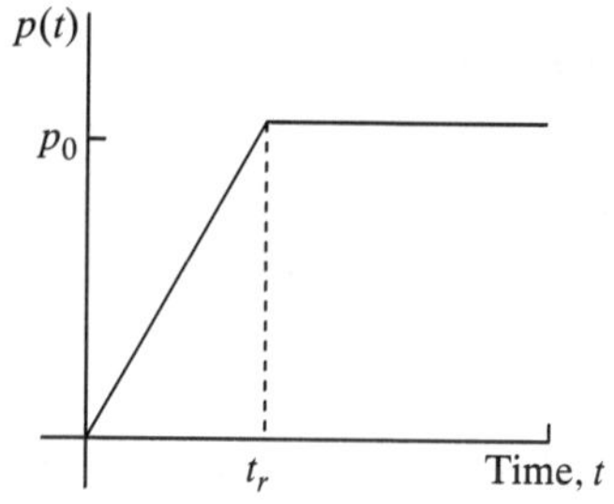

Figure 5.9 Ramp + step impulse.

Solution

(a) Steady State Response

For $t \le t_r$,

The solution was obtained in Example 5.4 through Equation (3).

$$x(t) = x_{st}\left[\frac{t}{t_r} - \frac{\sin\omega t}{\omega t_r}\right] \qquad \text{for } t \le t_r \tag{1}$$

For the step part, the response can be determined using the solution obtained in Example 5.1.

For $t \ge t_r$

The total response consists of two components: free vibration response $x_1(t)$ and forced vibration response $x_2(t)$, that is,

$$x(t) = x_1(t) + x_2(t) \tag{2}$$

For the free vibration part, Equation (6) of Example 5.4 gives,

$$x_1(t) = \frac{x_{st}}{\omega t_r}[\sin\omega(t-t_r)(1-\cos\omega t_r) + \cos\omega(t-t_r)(\omega t_r - \sin\omega t_r) \tag{3a}$$

and, for the step force part, Equation (2) of Example 5.1 gives,

$$x_2(t) = \frac{p_0}{k}(1-\cos\omega(t-t_r)) = x_{st}(1-\cos\omega(t-t_r)) \tag{3b}$$

Substituting the values of $x_1(t)$ and $x_2(t)$ in Equation (2), gives

$$x(t) = \frac{x_{st}}{\omega t_r}\Big[\sin\omega(t-t_r)(1-\cos\omega t_r) + \cos\omega(t-t_r)(\omega t_r - \sin\omega t_r) + \omega t_r(1-\cos\omega(t-t_r))\Big] \tag{4}$$

This can be simplified to

$$x(t) = x_{st}\left[1 + \frac{1}{\omega t_r}\left[\sin\omega(t-t_r)(1-\cos\omega t_r) - \cos\omega(t-t_r)(\sin\omega t_r)\right]\right]$$

or, $$x(t) = x_{st}\left[1 - \frac{1}{\omega t_r}\{\sin \omega t - \sin \omega (t - t_r)\}\right] \qquad t \geq t_r \tag{5}$$

It is possible to generate the dynamic response as well as shock spectra using Equations (1) and (5).

The maximum response may occur either in the ramp phase or in the step phase. □

The response of a SDOF system subjected to the ramp + step force impulse using Equations (1) and (5) in MATLAB code `DOS5_3` are shown in Figures 5.10(a) to 5.10(f) for t_r/T = 0.2, 0.5, 1.0, 1.5, 2.0 and 3.0. The following observations can be made:

1. For short duration pulse $t_r/T = 0.2$ and 0.5, the system achieves maximum response in its step force phase.
2. During the ramp phase, the system oscillates at its natural period about the static solution.
3. During the step force phase, the system oscillates at the natural period about its static solution.
4. If the velocity is zero at the end of ramp, the system does not oscillate during the constant force phase (Figures 5.10(c), 5.10(e) and 5.10(f)).
5. For large t_d/T, the dynamic displacement is close to its static displacement. It shows that dynamic effect is small.

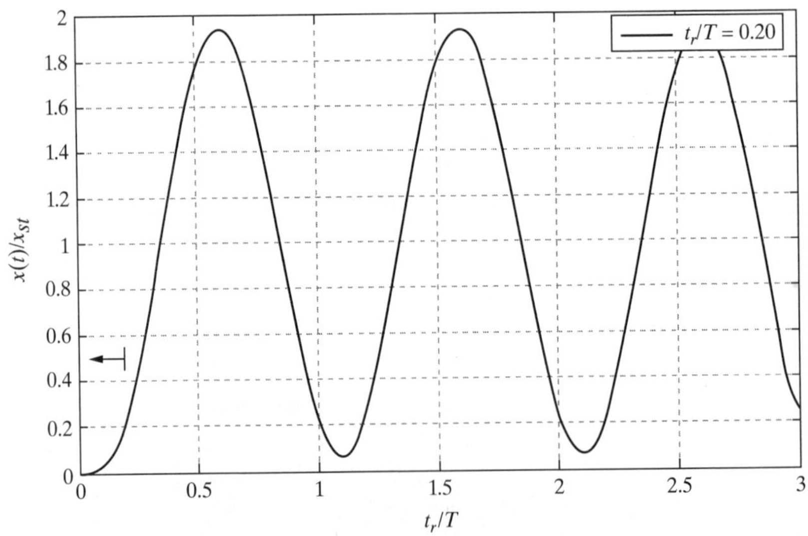

Figure 5.10(a) Dynamic response for $t_r/T = 0.20$.

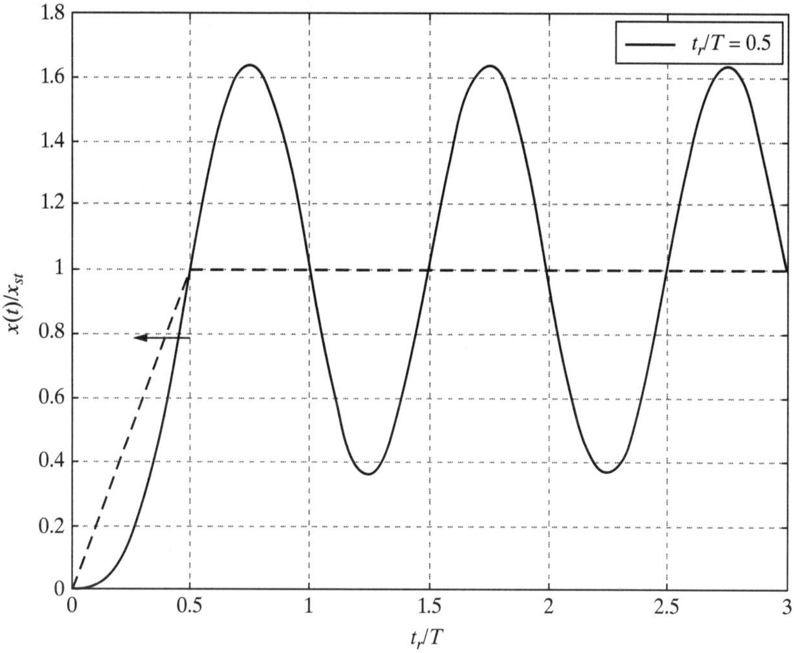

– – – – – Maximum static response

Figure 5.10(b) Dynamic response for $t_r/T = 0.5$.

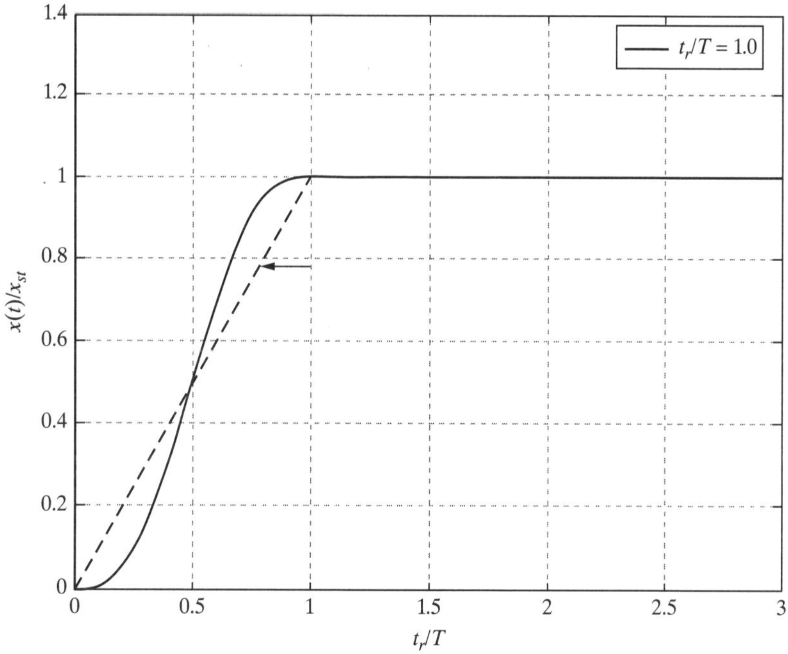

– – – – – Maximum static response

Figure 5.10(c) Dynamic response for $t_r/T = 1.0$.

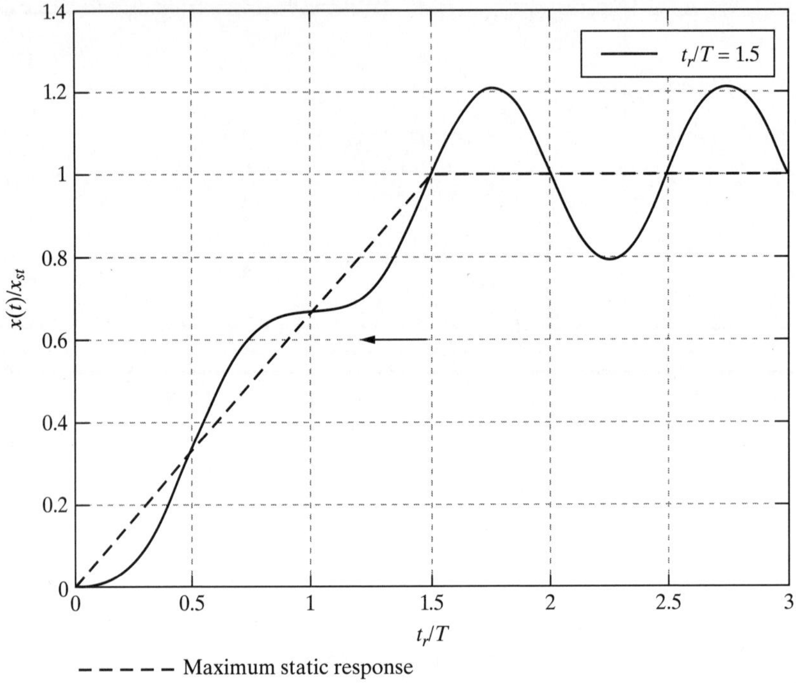

Figure 5.10(d) Dynamic response for $t_r/T = 1.5$.

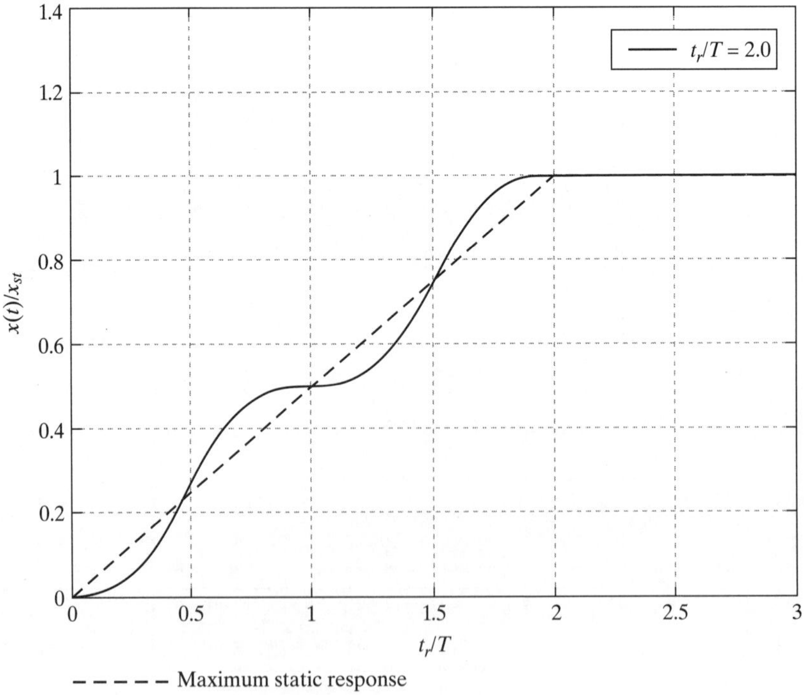

Figure 5.10(e) Dynamic response for $t_r/T = 2.0$.

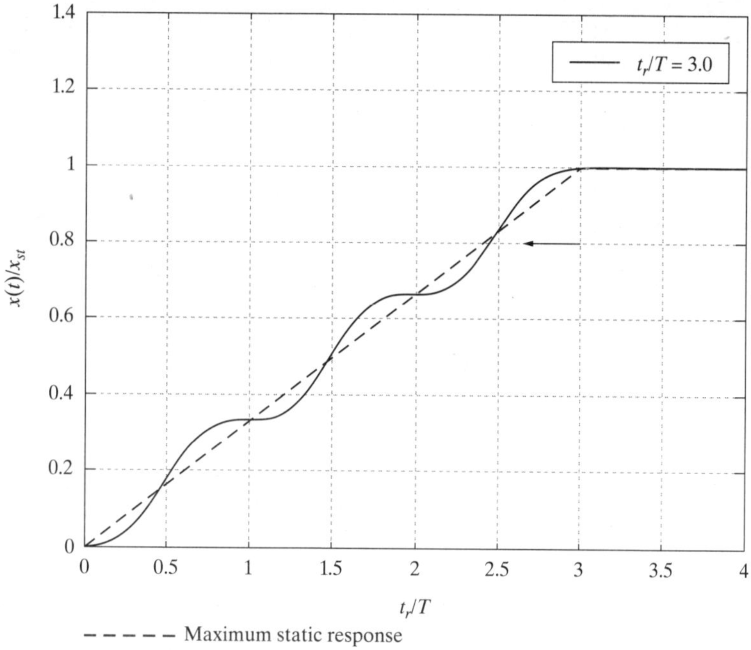

Figure 5.10(f) Dynamic response for $t_r/T = 3.0$.

(b) Shock Spectra

The shock spectra is generated by slightly modifying the MATLAB code `DOS5_3` as `DOS5_4`. The shock spectra is shown in Figures 5.11(a) and 5.11(b) on log and normal scales.

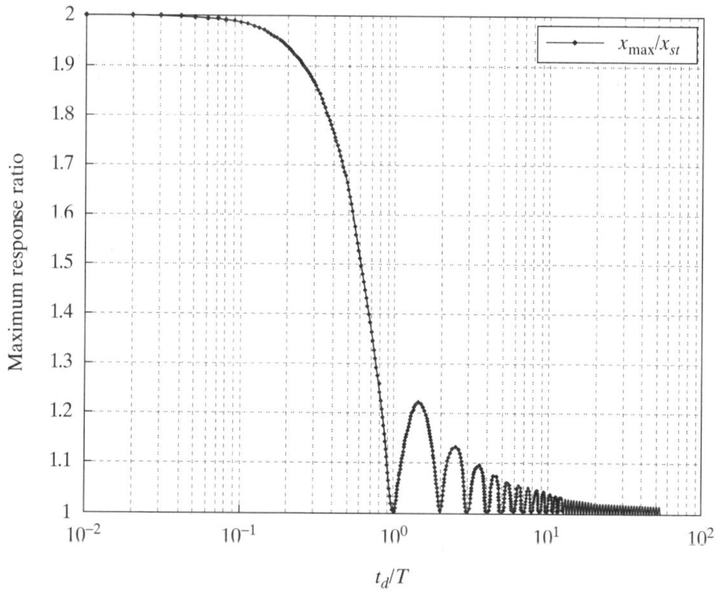

Figure 5.11(a) Dynamic response factor for impulse – log scale.

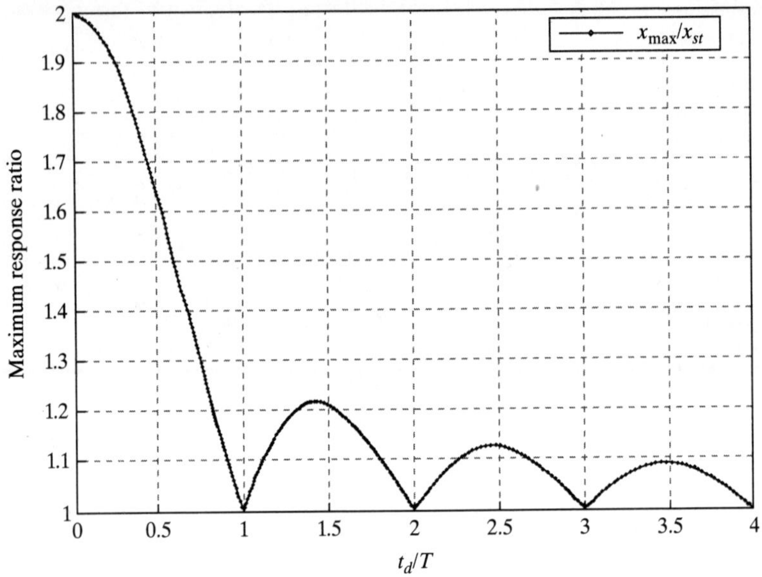

Figure 5.11(b) Dynamic response factor for impulse – normal scale.

Example 5.6

An undamped SDOF system is subjected to a down ramp impulse as shown in Figure 5.12. Find its steady state response in the forced and free vibration states. Determine the maximum response if peak load is 50 kN and duration of the impulse is 0.16 sec, stiffness $k = 4000$ kN/m and natural frequency of vibration is 4.5 Hz. Also, determine the maximum spring force.

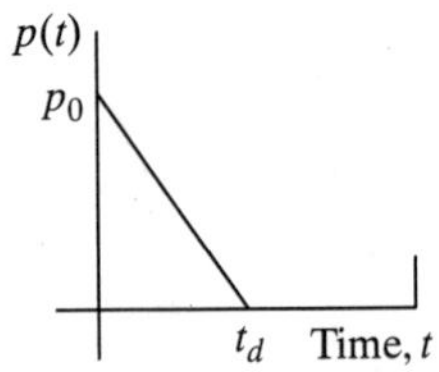

Figure 5.12 Down ramp impulse.

Solution

(a) Steady State Response

The forcing function can be written as follows:

$$p(t) = p_0\left(1 - \frac{t}{t_d}\right) \quad 0 \le t \le t_d \tag{1}$$

$$= 0 \quad t \ge t_d \tag{2}$$

Duhamel integral gives

$$x(t) = \int_0^t \frac{p_0}{m\omega}\left(1 - \frac{\tau}{t_d}\right)\sin\omega(t-\tau)\,d\tau \tag{3}$$

Upon integration,

$$x(t) = x_{st}\left(1 - \frac{t}{t_d} + \frac{1}{\omega t_d}\sin\omega t - \cos\omega t\right) \qquad 0 \le t \le t_d \tag{4}$$

where, $$x_{st} = \frac{p_0}{k} = \frac{p_0}{m\omega^2}$$

The vibrations after the loading has ceased to zero may be found by the response of the free vibration analysis with proper boundary conditions. It means we need to know the displacement and velocity at the end of the force function, at time t_d.
Displacement at $t = t_d$ is given by

$$x(t_d) = x_{st}\left(\frac{1}{\omega t_d}\sin\omega t_d - \cos\omega t_d\right) \tag{5a}$$

Similarly, the velocity at $t = t_d$ is given by

$$\dot{x}(t_d) = x_{st}\left(\omega\sin\omega t_d + \frac{1}{t_d}\cos\omega t_d - \frac{1}{t_d}\right)$$

or,

$$\dot{x}(t_d) = x_{st}\omega\left(\sin\omega t_d + \frac{1}{\omega t_d}\cos\omega t_d - \frac{1}{\omega t_d}\right) \tag{5b}$$

Free vibration response is given by

$$x(t) = \frac{\dot{x}(0)}{\omega}\sin\omega(t - t_d) + x(0)\cos\omega(t - t_d) \quad \text{for} \quad t > t_d \tag{6}$$

where, $x(0) = x(t_d)$ given by Equation (5a)

$\dot{x}(0) = \dot{x}(t_d)$ given by Equation (5b)

Upon substituting the values of initial conditions at $t = t_d$ in Equation (6), we obtain

$$x(t) = \frac{x_{st}}{\omega t_d}[\sin\omega(t - t_d)\times(\omega t_d\sin\omega t_d + \cos\omega t_d - 1) + \cos\omega(t - t_d)\times$$

$$(\sin\omega t_d - \omega t_d\cos\omega t_d)] \quad \text{for} \quad t > t_d \tag{7}$$

It is now possible to plot the steady state response $x(t)/x_{st}$ versus t_d/T for the down ramp impulse for a SDOF system and develop a shock spectra using Equations (4) and (7). The MATLAB code `DOS5_5` is written to compute it. The shock spectra is shown in Figures 5.13(a) and 5.13(b) on log and normal scales.

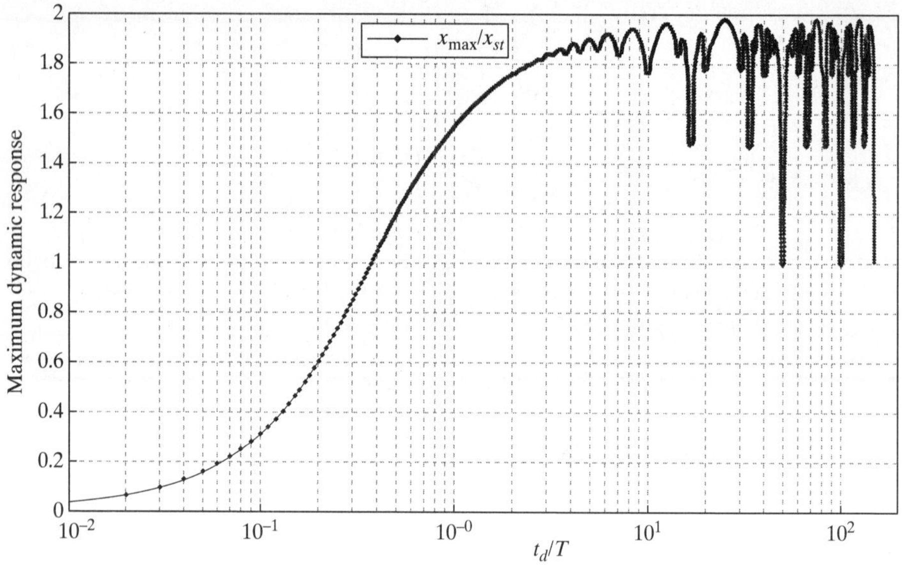

Figure 5.13(a) Dynamic response factor for impulse – log scale.

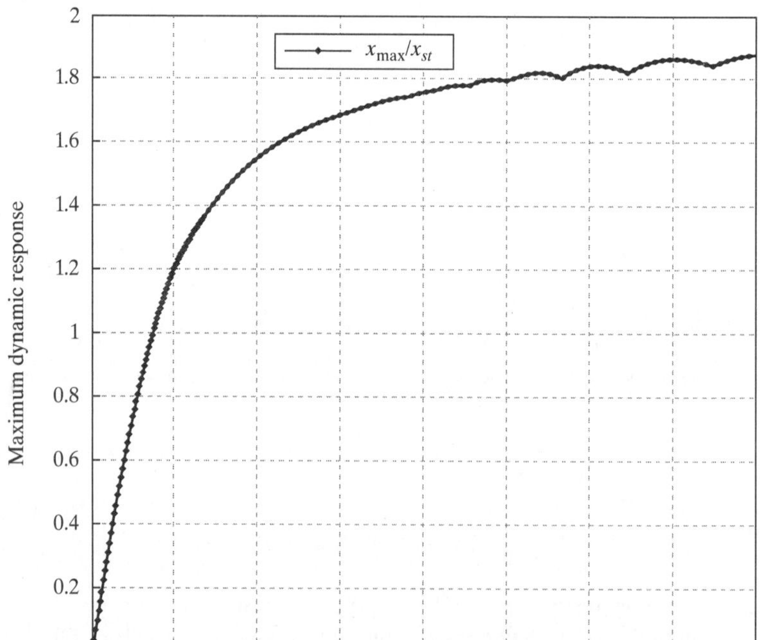

Figure 5.13(b) Dynamic response factor for impulse – normal scale.

(b)

Given: spring stiffness $k = 4 \times 10^6$ N/m, natural frequency $f = 4.5$ Hz, peak force = 50 kN and duration of triangular impulse = 0.16 sec.

Period of vibration $T = 1/f = 1/4.5 = 0.22$ sec

$$\frac{t_d}{T} = \frac{0.16}{0.22} = 0.72$$

∴ The dynamic amplification factor for the down ramp impulse for the given $t_d/T = 1.40$.

$$\text{Static displacement } x_{st} = \frac{p_0}{k} = \frac{50}{4000} = 0.0125 \text{ m} = 12.5 \text{ mm}$$

$$\therefore \text{ Dynamic displacement } x_{\max} = Dx_{st} = 1.40 \times 12.5 = 17.5 \text{ mm}$$

$$\text{Elastic spring force} = k\,x_{\max} = 4000 \times 0.0175 = 70 \text{ kN}$$

□

Example 5.7

An undamped SDOF system is subjected to a down ramp impulse as shown in Figure 5.14. The maximum amplitude of the force is 5 kN and its duration is 0.04 sec. Estimate the elastic force developed in the system. If the duration of the impulse is reduced to 0.01 sec only, what is the elastic force?

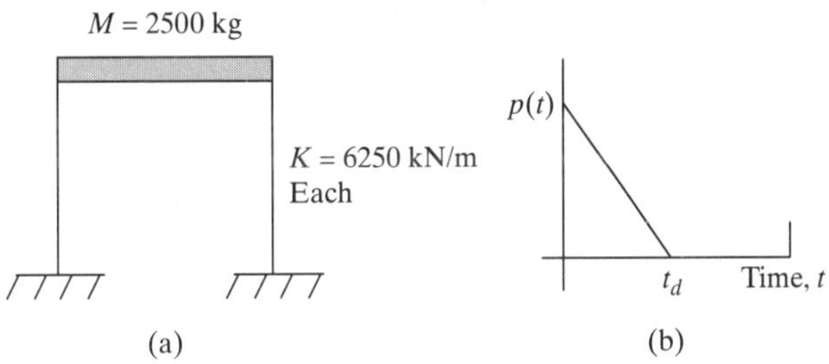

Figure 5.14 (a) SDOF system; (b) Down ramp impulse.

Solution

(a) For two columns, the total lateral stiffness = $2 \times 6250 \times 10^3 = 12500000$ N/m

$$\text{Natural frequency } \omega = \sqrt{\frac{k}{m}} = \sqrt{\frac{125 \times 100000}{2500}} = 70.70 \text{ rad/sec}$$

$$\text{Period} \qquad T = \frac{2\pi}{\omega} = \frac{2\pi}{70.70} = 0.0888 \text{ sec}$$

$$\therefore \qquad \frac{t_d}{T} = \frac{0.04}{0.0888} = 0.45$$

Shock spectra for down ramp impulse (Figure 5.11(b)) gives, $D = 1.12$

$$\text{Static deflection } \Delta_{st} = \frac{P_0}{k} = \frac{5000}{125 \times 10^5} = 0.4 \text{ mm}$$

∴ Dynamic displacement amplitude $x_{\max} = 0.4 \times 1.12 = 0.448$ mm

Corresponding maximum elastic force produced $- kx_{\max} - 125 \times 10^5 \times (0.448 \times 10^{-3})$ = 5600 N

(b) If duration of the impulse loading was only 0.01 sec, then

$$\frac{t_d}{T} = \frac{0.010}{0.0888} = 0.11$$

$$\therefore \qquad D = 0.38$$

$\therefore$ Dynamic displacement amplitude $x_{max} = 0.40 \times 0.38 = 0.152$ mm

Corresponding maximum elastic force produced $= k\,x_{max} = 125 \times 10^5 \times (0.152 \times 10^{-3})$

$= 1900$ N

$<< 5650$ N in case (a)

For an impulse of very small duration, a large part of the load is resisted by inertia of the system. □

Example 5.8

An overhead water tank (Figure 5.15(a)) has an effective weight of 1800 kN at its top when filled with water. Its lateral stiffness is 20000 kN/m. Estimate the maximum lateral displacement of its top when it is subjected to a dynamic force as shown in (i) Figure 5.15(b) and (ii) Figure 5.15(c). Maximum amplitude of force $p(t) = 200$ kN and duration of impulse is 0.15 sec. Determine the bending moment at its base in each case if its height is 15 m.

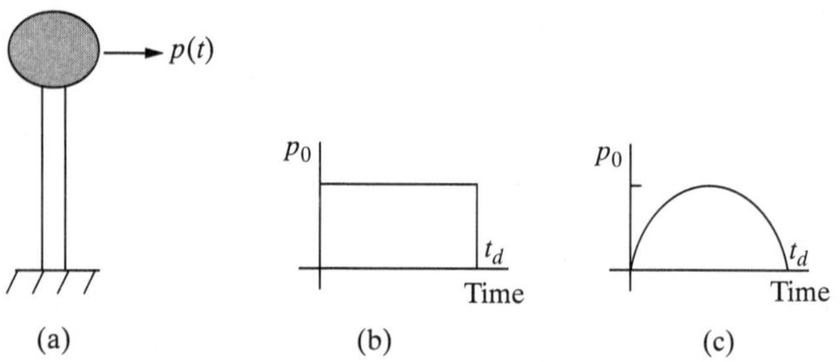

Figure 5.15 Overhead water tank under impulse loading.

Solution

For the water tank, lateral stiffness = 20000 kN/m

$$\text{Natural frequency of the OHT } \omega = \sqrt{\frac{k}{m}} = \sqrt{\frac{20000}{1800/10}} = 10.54 \text{ rad/sec}$$

$$\text{Period } T = \frac{2\pi}{\omega} = \frac{2\pi}{10.54} = 0.60 \text{ sec}$$

Amplitude of pulse $p_0 = 200$ kN, duration of the pulse is 0.15 sec.

$$\frac{t_d}{T} = \frac{0.15}{0.60} = 0.25$$

$$\text{Maximum static displacement } x_{st} = \frac{p_0}{k} = \frac{200}{20000} = 0.01 \text{ m}$$

(a) When subjected to the step impulse shown in Figure 5.15(b)
$p(t) = 200$ kN and duration of impulse $t_d = 0.15$ sec.
Upon derivation, it can be shown that

$$D = \frac{x_{\max}}{x_{st}} = 2\sin\left(\pi\frac{t_d}{T}\right) \quad \text{for} \quad \frac{t_d}{T} \le 0.50$$

$$D = \frac{x_{\max}}{x_{st}} = 2 \quad \text{for} \quad \frac{t_d}{T} \ge 0.50$$

where, D = dynamic magnification factor.
∴ Dynamic displacement for $td/T = 0.25$, $x_{\max} = x_{st} \times 2 \times \sin(\pi \times 0.25)$

$$= 0.01 \times 2 \times 0.707 = 0.0141 \text{ m or, } 14.10 \text{ mm}$$

Equivalent Static force at the top of the tank $F_{st} = p_0 \times \left(\frac{x_{max}}{x_{st}}\right) = 200 \times 1.414 = 282.8$ kN

Maximum shear at the base = 282.8 kN
Maximum bending moment at the base = 282.8 × 15 = 4242 kNm

(b) When subjected to the half sine impulse shown in Figure 5.15(c)

$$p = p_0 \sin\left(\frac{\pi t}{t_d}\right) \quad \text{for} \quad t \le t_d$$

$$= 0 \text{ for } t \ge t_d$$

Response analysis shows that no peak develops during the forced vibrations. Upon derivation,

$$D = \frac{x_{\max}}{x_{st}} = \left[\frac{1}{1-\left(\frac{T}{2t_d}\right)^2}\right]\left[\sin\left(\frac{\pi t}{t_d}\right) - \frac{T}{2t_d}\sin\left(\frac{2\pi t}{T}\right)\right] \quad \text{for} \quad t \le t_d$$

For $t = t_d$, this equation becomes,

$$D = \frac{x_{\max}}{x_{st}} = \left[\frac{1}{1-\left(\frac{T}{2t_d}\right)^2}\right] \times \frac{T}{2t_d}\sin\left(\frac{2\pi t_d}{T}\right)$$

For $t_d/T = 0.25$,

$$D = \frac{x_{\max}}{x_{st}} = \left[\frac{1}{1-\left(\frac{1}{2\times 0.25}\right)^2}\right] \times \frac{1}{2\times 0.25}\sin(2\pi \times 0.25) = 0.67$$

where, D = dynamic magnification factor
∴ Dynamic displacement $x_{\max} = x_{st} \times 0.67 = 0.01 \times 0.67 = 0.0067$ m or, 6.70 mm

Equivalent Static force at the top of the tank $F_{st} = p_0 \times \left(\frac{x_{max}}{x_{st}}\right) = 200 \times 0.67 = 134$ kN

Maximum shear at the base = 134 kN
Maximum bending moment at the base = 134 × 15 = 2010 kNm □

Example 5.9

A 1 kg missile hits a target at 60 kmph. The target consists of an aluminum vertical cantilever of height 0.5 m having a cross-section of 25 × 25 mm as shown in Figure 5.16. An instrument weighing 2 kg is attached to its free end. Compute the maximum lateral deflection due to the impact ($E_{AL} = 7.1 \times 10^{10}$ N/m²).

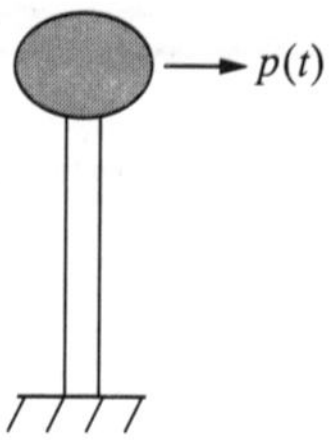

Figure 5.16 A vertical cantilever model

Solution

Lateral stiffness of the cantilever $k = \frac{3EI}{L^3}$
Cross-section of the cantilever = 25 × 25 mm
Moment of inertia $I = bD^3/12 = 25 \times 25^3/12$
Length of cantilever = 0.5 m

$$\therefore \text{stiffness } k = \frac{3EI}{L^3} = \frac{EbD^3}{4L^3} = \frac{7.1 \times 10^{10} \times (0.025)^4}{4 \times (0.5)^3} = 55468 \text{ N/m}$$

Natural frequency of the system $\omega = \sqrt{\frac{k}{m}} = \sqrt{\frac{55468}{2}} = 166.5$ rad/s

An impact may be represented as $F[\delta(t)]$ where $\delta(t)$ is Dirac Delta function.
For an undamped system

$$m\ddot{x} + kx = F(t)$$

The response of a SDOF system can be written as follows:

$$dx(t) = \frac{pd\tau}{m\omega}\sin\omega(t-\tau)$$

For maximum response,

$$dx(t) = \frac{pd\tau}{m\omega}$$

Momentum due to the impact of missile of 1 kg mass

$$pd\tau = m_0 v_0$$

where,
$m_0 = 1$ kg

Initial velocity of impact $v_0 = 60$ kmph $= \dfrac{60 \times 1000}{60 \times 60} = 16.67$ m/s

Therefore, maximum response can be written as

$$dx(t) = \left|\frac{m_0 v_0}{m\omega}\right| = \frac{1 \times 16.67}{2 \times 166.5} = 0.05 \text{ m}$$

The maximum lateral deflection due to impact = 5 cm. □

Example 5.10

A 15 m high overhead water tank has an effective weight of 17500 kN and a lateral stiffness of 1500 kN/m. Damping may be taken as 1%. It is subjected to a force $p(t)$ as shown below caused by an above ground explosion. Determine the maximum base shear and bending moment at the base of the staging supporting the tank.

Time sec	0	0.05	0.10	0.15	0.20	0.25
$P(t)$, kN	0	160	225	75	0	0

Solution

Natural frequency $\omega = \sqrt{\dfrac{k}{m}} = \sqrt{\dfrac{60000}{17500/9.81}} = 5.8$ rad/sec

Natural period $T = \dfrac{2\pi}{\omega} = \dfrac{2\pi}{5.8} = 1.08$ sec

Duration of the impulse = 0.20 sec

Ratio $\dfrac{t_d}{T} = \dfrac{0.2}{1.08} = 0.18 < 0.25$ ∴ the forcing function may be treated as a pure impulse.

Impulse $I = \int_0^t p(t)\,dt$

This integral may be evaluated using the trapezoidal rule.

$$I = \frac{0.05}{2}(0 + 2 \times 160 + 2 \times 225 + 2 \times 75 + 0) = 23 \text{ kN sec}$$

Ignoring damping, maximum displacement is given by

$$x_{max} = \frac{I}{m\omega} = \frac{23}{\left(\dfrac{17500}{9.81}\right) \times 5.8} = 0.0022 \text{ m}$$

The equivalent static force associated with this displacement = $k\ x$ = 60000 × 0.0022 = 132 kN
The shear force in the staging = 132 kN constant throughout its height
Bending moment at its base = 132 × 15 = 1980 kNm
It varies linearly from zero at the top to the maximum at the base.
The shear force and bending moment diagrams are shown in Figure 5.17. □

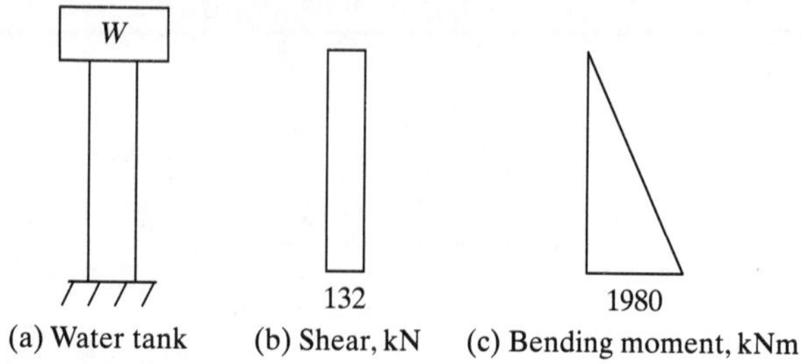

Figure 5.17 Forces on a water tank

5.8 EXPLOSIONS

An explosion is defined as a large-scale, rapid and sudden release of energy characterized by an audible blast. Explosions can be categorized on the basis of their nature as physical, nuclear or chemical events. In physical explosions, energy may be released from the catastrophic failure of a cylinder of compressed gas, volcanic eruptions or even mixing of two liquids at different temperatures. In a nuclear explosion, energy is released from the formation of different atomic nuclei. The rapid oxidation of carbon and hydrogen atoms is the main source of energy in the case of chemical explosions. Explosive materials can be classified according to their physical state as solids, liquids or gases. The blast effects of lethal explosives such as RDX, TNT (Trinitrotoluene), Gelatin, and Nitroglycerin are well known.

In an explosion part of the energy is released as thermal radiation, and part is coupled into the air (air-blast) and soil (ground-shock) as radially expanding shock waves. Air-blast is the principal damage mechanism. Air-blast phenomena occur within milliseconds and the local effects of the blast are often over before the building structure can globally react to the effects of the blast. The sudden release of energy initiates a pressure wave in the surrounding medium, known as a *shock wave* or *blast wave* with a sudden increase in pressure at the front termed as *shock front*. This is referred to as the *side-on overpressure* that decays as the shock wave expands outward from the explosion source. The pressure in the shock wave decreases rapidly as the shock is propagated outward. The pressure behind the front may drop below the ambient pressure (Figure 5.18). During such a negative phase, a partial vacuum is created and air is sucked in. This is also accompanied by high suction winds that carry the debris for long distances away from the explosion source. In many cases, the effect of the negative phase is ignored because it usually has little effect on the maximum response. The maximum impulse delivered to the structure is the area under the positive phase of the reflected pressure-time curve. Both the pressure and impulse (or duration time) are required to define the blast loading.

A secondary effect of the air-blast is dynamic pressure or drag loading which is a very high velocity wind. It propels the debris generated by the air-blast, creating secondary projectiles. Also, the building is subject to the ground-shock which produces ground motions sometimes similar to a short duration earthquake.

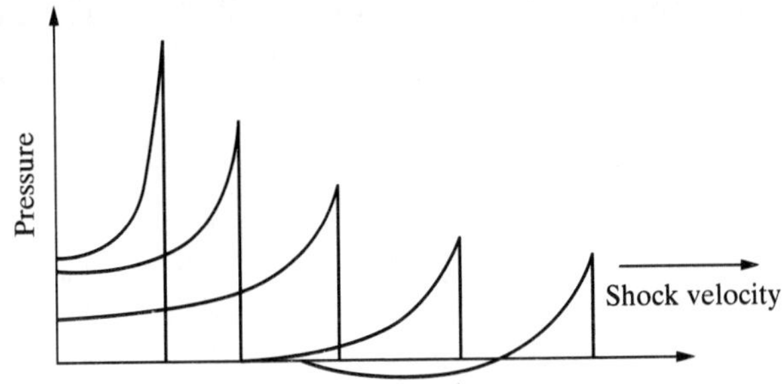

Figure 5.18 Blast wave propagation

The shape of the building can affect the overall damage to the structure. For example, "U"- or "L-shaped" buildings may trap the shock wave, which may increase blast pressure locally because of the complex reflections created. Large or gradual re-entrant corners have less effect than small or sharp re-entrant corners. In general, convex rather than concave shapes are preferred for the exterior of the building. The reflected pressure on the surface of a circular building is less intense than on a flat building.

The phenomenon immediately associated with explosions vary with the location of the point of burst in relation to the surface of the earth. The types of bursts are usually classified as:

(a) High altitude burst
(b) Air burst
(c) Under water burst
(d) Underground burst
(e) Near surface burst, and
(f) Surface burst

Blast Resistant Design

The blast wave duration t_d is typically in the range of 0.1 to 0.001 seconds. This is often much shorter than, or at most of the order of the natural period T of typical structural elements. For situations where $t_d < 0.4T$ (or may be $t_d < 0.1T$), the blast wave effectively imparts an initial velocity to a structural element and the element then continues to respond at its natural frequency. In this response regime, the mass of the structural element is the only system parameter that controls the magnitude of the initial motion of the system – the more massive the structural element, the less it will be excited by the impulse from the blast wave. In this regard, the larger mass of the structures can be used to great advantage. Thus, response to a blast loading is significantly different from the response to a seismic event. In the latter case, the natural frequency of the structure, rather than the mass alone, is the crucial factor in deciding the response.

The structural engineers would be interested in knowing the nature of impulsive loading, that is, overpressure distribution – time history due to different kinds of explosives in order to design blast resistant structures. There are four main considerations for design:

- Defining the blast load characteristics
- Blast and shock resistant design of structures including architectural layout and planning etc.
- Isolation of structure contents from the effects of shock.
- Protection of the contents of the facility from the effects of radiation, dust and debris

The main objective of this section is to understand the dynamics of blast pressure wave and to estimate the overpressure distribution – time history.

5.8.1 Definitions

Let us become familiar with some of the terms used in blast loading.

Blast Wind It is the moving air mass along with the over-pressures resulting from pressure difference behind the shock wave front. The blast wind movement during the positive phase of the overpressures is in the direction of shock front propagation.

Decay Parameter It is the coefficient of the negative power of exponent *e* governing the fall of pressure with time in the pressure-time curves.

Drag Force It is the force on a structure or structural element due to the blast wind. On any structural element, the drag force equals dynamic pressure multiplied by the drag coefficient of the element.

Dynamic Pressure It is the pressure effect of air mass movement called the blast wind.

Equivalent Bare Charge It is the weight of a bare high explosive charge geometrically similar to any given cased charge, which produces the same blast field as the given cased charge.

Ground Zero It is the point on the earth surface vertically below the explosion.

Mach Number It is the ratio of the speed of the shock front propagation to the speed of sound in standard atmosphere at sea level.

Overpressure It is the rise in pressure above atmospheric pressure due to the shock wave from an air blast.

Reflected Overpressure It is the overpressure resulting due to reflection of a shock wave front striking any surface. If the shock front is parallel to the surface, the reflection is normal.

Shock Wave Front It is the discontinuity between the blast wave and the surrounding atmosphere. It propagates away from the point of explosion in all directions at a speed greater than the speed of sound in the undisturbed atmosphere.

Side-on Overpressure It is the overpressure if it is not reflected by any surface.

Stagnation Time This is the time in which the reflected pressure decays down to the sum of the side-on overpressure and the drag pressure. It is also referred to as the clearance time.

Transit Time It is the time required for the shock front to travel across the structure or its element under consideration.

Yield It is a measure of the size of the explosion expressed in equivalent weight of reference explosive.

The air blast loading on the surfaces of the above ground structures is a function of the free-field overpressure and dynamic pressure, the size, shape and orientation of surfaces; and the location and orientation of other surfaces in the vicinity. In computation of blast loading on structure surfaces, the following components of air blast loading are normally considered:

- **(a)** Overpressure
- **(b)** Reflected pressure
- **(c)** Dynamic pressure
- **(d)** Yield scaling, and
- **(e)** Height of burst.

Overpressure Characteristics

When an explosion takes place, the expansion of hot gasses produces a pressure wave in the surrounding air. The transient pressure greater than the ambient (surrounding atmospheric) pressure is defined as *overpressure.* The *peak overpressure* is the maximum value of the overpressure at a given location. As the blast wave arrives at a given point, the overpressure rapidly increases to the peak overpressure. If nothing interferes with the blast wave, the rise time to peak overpressure will be less than a microsecond. The formation of a shock front and variation of overpressure with distance from center of explosion at various times are shown in Figure 5.19.

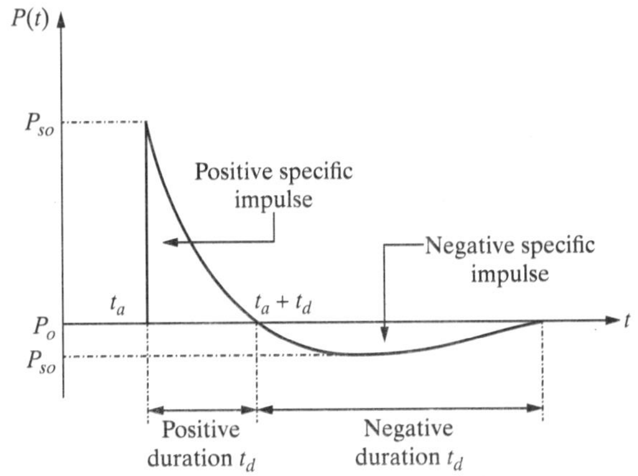

Figure 5.19 Blast wave pressure – time history

The equation for decay of peak overpressure with time is given by

$$P(t) = P_{so}\left(1 - \frac{t - t_a}{t_d}\right)e^{-\alpha\left(\frac{t-t_a}{t_d}\right)} \text{ for } t \geq t_a \tag{5.10}$$

where
$P(t)$ = pressure at any time t
α = wave form parameter
t_a = arrival time
t_d = positive phase duration

The following parameters are of interest:

(a) time of arrival
(b) peak pressure
(c) positive phase duration
(d) positive phase impulse (the time integral of the pressure history).

A finite time elapses between the detonation and the arrival of the blast front at a given location. This time of arrival is dependent primarily upon the weapon yield and the distance from the point of burst. The duration of blast wave is characterized by two distinct phases, the overpressure rises very rapidly from ambient to peak value and then subsides more slowly to ambient once again. For some heights of burst (HOB) in the Mach reflection region, a second pressure increase may occur which may be higher or lower than the first pulse.

In the negative phase a partial vacuum is created and the air is sucked in rather than being pushed away, as when the over pressure is positive. Consequently, the wind blows towards the point of detonation during the negative phase. Peak values of under pressure during the negative phase rarely exceed 28 to 35 kPa below ambient. Like peak overpressure, under pressure peak values also decrease with distance from the explosion, although at a slower rate.

Dynamic Pressure Characteristics

As the blast wave moves outward from the explosion, the flow of mass of the air behind the blast front produces a wind. The resulting pressure is termed as *dynamic pressure* which is a function of density of the air through which the blast wave passes, and the wind velocity behind the shock front. The shock wave compresses the air, raising its density above normal. Under some circumstances, the density may be further increased by the dust, smoke and other materials picked up by the blast wave as it moves across the earth's surface.

Like overpressure, the dynamic pressure also decays down with time and has the positive and negative phases. As the distance from the explosion increases, the positive phase of dynamic pressure becomes somewhat longer than that of overpressure. During the negative phase, peak values of both dynamic pressure and under pressure are typically much smaller than those during the positive phase, but should not be overlooked in design of latches or hold down devices for doors etc.

The equation for decay of dynamic pressure with time is given by

$$q(t) = q_0\left(1-\frac{t-t_a}{t_d}\right)^2 e^{-2\alpha\left(\frac{t-t_a}{t_d}\right)} \text{ for } t \geq t_a \tag{5.11}$$

It shows that the dynamic pressure decays much faster than the side-on overpressure P_s.

Reflected Overpressure

Whenever the blast wave strikes a surface which is not parallel to its direction of propagation, a reflection process takes place that causes an increase in the peak overpressure. This reflection process is caused by the momentum change when the moving air changes direction as a result of striking the surface. The ratio of reflected overpressure to incident pressure is called the *reflection factor*. The reflection factor varies with both the peak overpressure in the incident wave and the angle at which the blast wave strikes the surface.

Yield Scaling

In order to calculate the characteristic properties of the blast wave from an explosion of any given yield, if those for another yield or known, appropriate scaling laws are applied. If suitable assumptions are made regarding the properties of air and shock wane propagation, it can be concluded that a given pressure will occur at a distance from the explosion that is proportional to the cube root of the energy yield. High explosives and nuclear tests have shown this relation to hold approximately true for yields up to the megaton range. Accordingly, the equivalent range (distance) R at which a particular overpressure or dynamic pressure will occur is known as a result of the detonation of a weapon of standard yield (tonne) W. The range R_o due to the detonation of a weapon of yield Wo may be found from the relation:

$$\frac{R}{R_0} = \left(\frac{W}{W_0}\right)^{1/3} \tag{5.12}$$

where

R = equivalent range at which the blast of standard yield W occurs.

Similarly, cube root scaling law can be applied to the air blast time of arrival, positive phase duration and impulse such as:

$$\frac{t}{t_0} = \left(\frac{W}{W_0}\right)^{1/3} \tag{5.13}$$

where t = equivalent time of arrival or positive phase duration due to detonation of standard yield W

t_0 = equivalent time of arrival or positive phase duration due to detonation of yield W_0

5.8.2 Blast Pressure on a Closed Structure

Dynamic pressures associated with air flow behind the shock cause drag and lift on objects that interface with the flow of such air. An approximate assumption made in the computation of blast loading on structures is that the shock loading is ideal and the structure is in the Mach reflection region where the air burst front is propagating parallel to the ground surface. As an ideal blast wave encounters the front face of a closed rectangular structure (Figure 5.20, such as a nuclear shelter), it is reflected to some higher value as a function of peak incident over pressure and the orientation of the surface with respect to direction of propagation of shock front. The blast wave then bends or diffracts around the structure, subjecting first the sides and roof and finally the rear face to pressure equal to the incident overpressure. At the same time, these surfaces are also subjected to drag pressures that are a function of the dynamic pressure and drag coefficient for the surface. NBC 2016 and IS:4991-1968 gives detailed equations for estimating the pressures on front, side and rear walls in different types of structures besides giving detailed design criteria.

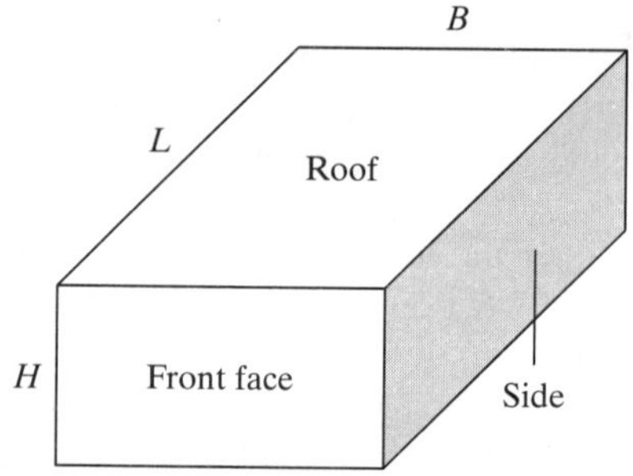

Figure 5.20 A closed structure with less than 5% opening

Figures 5.21(a) and (b) show an idealized loading history on the front face of a closed rectangular structure. The maximum pressure is equal to the peak reflected over pressure P_{ro} on the front face given by:

$$P_{ro} \geq 2P_{so}\left(\frac{7P_a + 4P_{so}}{7P_a + P_{so}}\right) \text{ MPa} \tag{5.14a}$$

$$\geq P_{so} + C_d q_o \tag{5.14b}$$

where

P_{so} = peak side-on over pressure and
P_a = atmospheric pressure = 100 kPa = 0.1 MPa = 1 kg/cm^2
q_o = peak dynamic pressure

For an overpressure pulse that rises instantaneously from zero to its peak value, the rise time t_r to peak reflected pressure on the wall surface can also be taken at zero. In the time t_c known as stagnation time or clearance time, the reflected pressure may be assumed to decay linearly from the peak value P_{ro} to a value given by

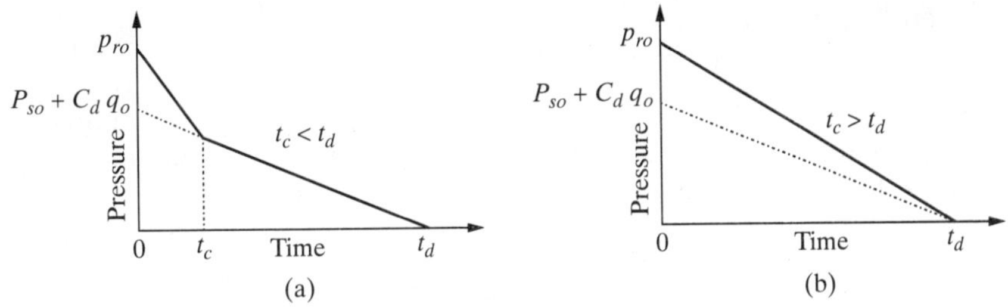

Figure 5.21(a) and (b) Idealized loading history on front face

$$P_{so}(t) + C_{df}q(t) \tag{5.15}$$

where

$P_{so}(t)$ = incident overpressure as a function of time
C_{df} = drag coefficient for front surface; and
$q(t)$ = dynamic pressure as a function of time.
t_c = clearance time

A reasonable approximation of the clearance time t_c is

$$t_c = \frac{3S}{U} \text{ or } t_d \text{ whichever is less} \tag{5.16a}$$

Transit time
$$t_t = \frac{L}{U} \tag{5.16b}$$

where

S = height of the structure H or one-half the structure width ($B/2$) whichever is less
U = air blast shock front velocity = $M \times a$
M = Mach number of the incident pulse

$$M = \sqrt{1 + \frac{6P_{so}}{7P_a}} \tag{5.17}$$

a = velocity of sound in air = 344 m/s at mean sea level at 20° C
t_d = duration of the equivalent triangular pulse
B = width of the structure across the direction of wave propagation
L = length of the structure along the direction of wave propagation

No pressure is transmitted to the rear face until the shock front reaches that face. Using the same time reference as for the front face, average pressure begins to build up on the back face at time L/U. At some later time after the rear face has become completely engulfed in the blast, the pressure reaches a maximum value equal to the side-on overpressure reduced by an amount equal to the drag pressure, which acts as a suction on the rear surface, that is, a pressure equal to

$$P_{so}(t) - C_{db}q(t) \tag{5.18}$$

where
C_{db} = drag coefficient for the rear face.

The pressure on the rear face is assumed to build up linearly in a time equal to $4S/U$ where S and U are defined in the same manner as for the front face. The pressure then drops down to zero depending upon the overpressure values.

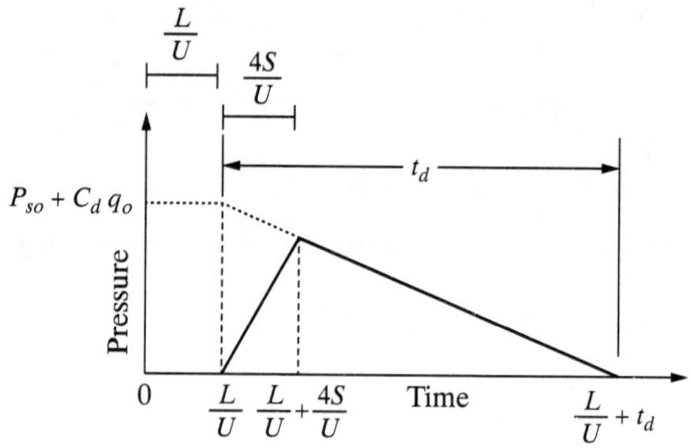

Figure 5.21(c) Overpressure on the rear wall

As the blast wave pressure over the structures, the roof loading at any time is equal to the overpressure reduced by a *negative drag pressure,* or *suction,* associated with the flow of air around the structure. The total pressure rises linearly from zero to a maximum value in a time equal to the transient time L/U $(= t_t)$ of the shock front across the roof. Pressure at any time after this is given by

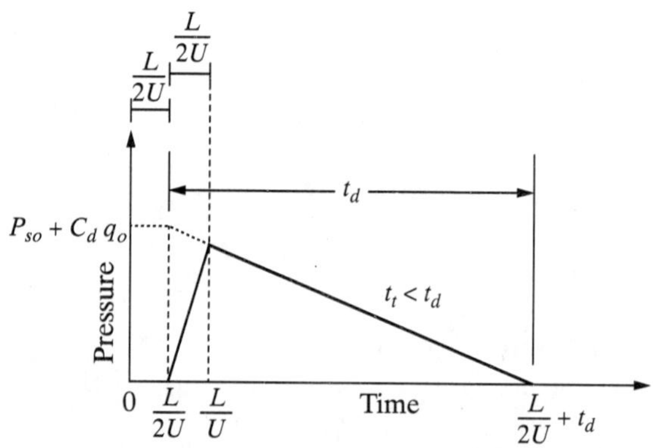

Figure 5.21(d) Overpressure on the sides and roof for $t_t < t_d$

$$P_{so}(t) + C_{dr}q(t) \tag{5.19}$$

where
C_{dr} = drag coefficient for the roof.
t_t = transit time

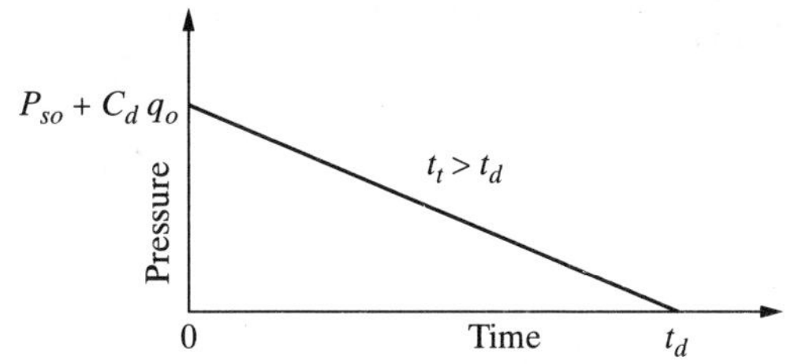

Figure 5.21(e) Overpressure on the roof for $t_t > t_d$

If the values of pressure on the back face are subtracted from the corresponding values of the front face, the net horizontal pressure on the structure is obtained,

$$P_{net} = P_{front} - P_{back} \tag{5.20}$$

5.8.3 Blast Load on Below-Ground Structures

The below-ground structures are classified depending upon the earth cover and slopes of earth berms as follows:

- buried structures
- semi-buried structures

A buried structure is the one that satisfies the condition shown in Figure 5.22 (a) and 5.22 (b). A buried structure is subjected only to the general overpressure p_{so}, while the reflected and dynamic pressures are neglected. Semi-buried structures are those that do not have the minimum earth cover or the slopes are steeper than those specified in Figure 5.22. These are subjected to dynamic pressures besides the general overpressures. Both are acted upon by air-induced ground shock also. IS 4991 provides detailed pressure diagrams for different faces of such structures.

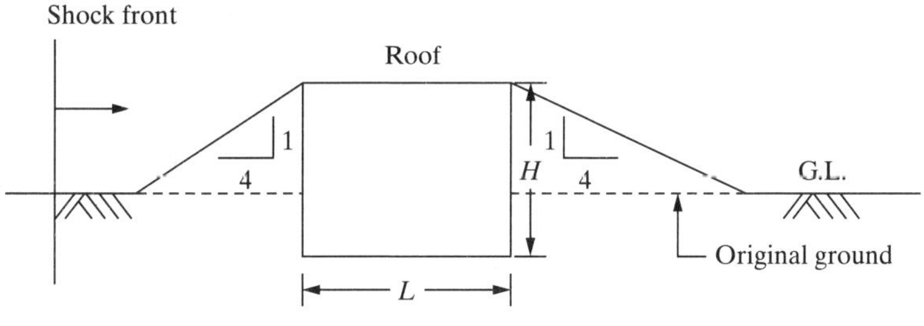

(a) Buried rectangular structure

Figure 5.22 (Continued)

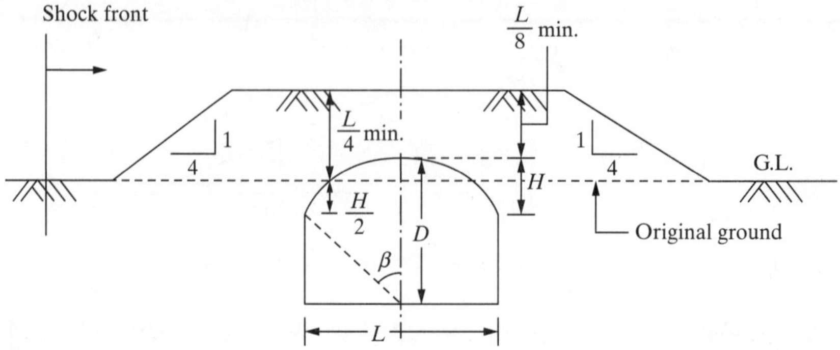

(b) Buried arch or dome structure

Figure 5.22

5.9 HOW TO MITIGATE POTENTIAL TERRORIST ATTACKS AGAINST BUILDINGS?

The damage sequence of a building due to a nearby blast is shown schematically in Figures 5.23 (a) to (d).

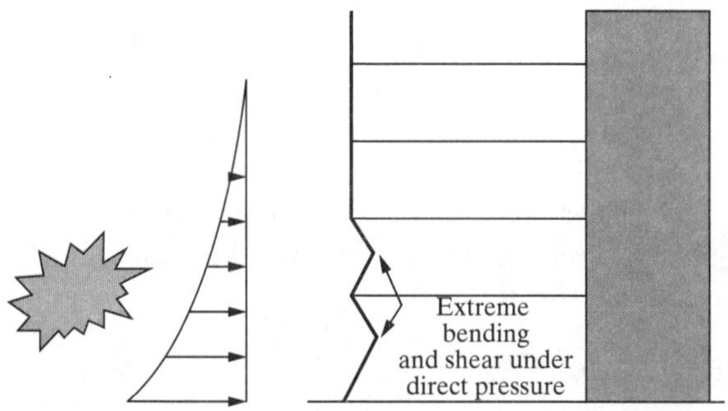

(a) The blast waves break the glass on the façade and extreme loading is applied on the front columns and walls

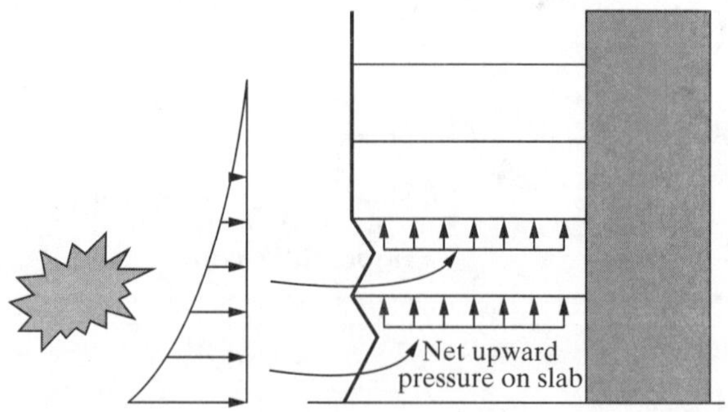

(b) The blast waves exert upward pressure on the floor slabs

Figure 5.23 Failure sequence of a building due to blast loading

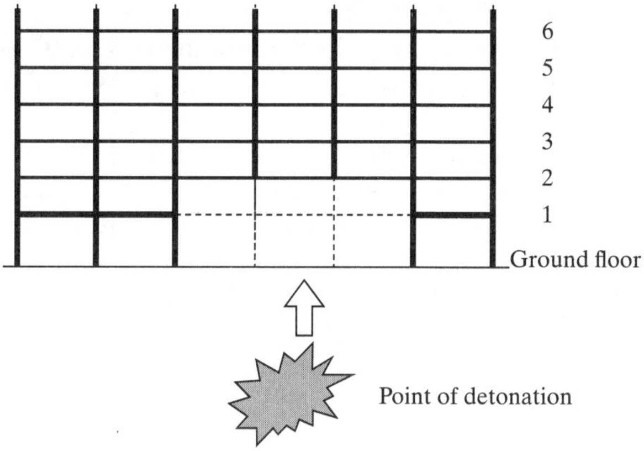

(c) Damage to perimeter beams, columns and slabs due to blast pressure (in dotted lines)

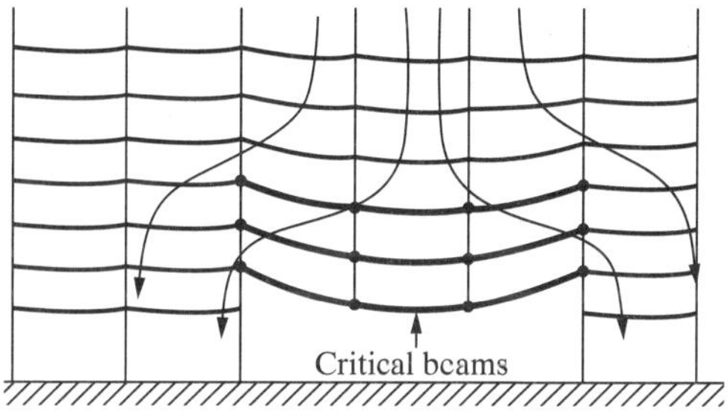

(d) Progressive collapse due to failure of perimeter columns due to blast pressure

Figure 5.23 (Continued)

US Army Engineers Corps and Federal Emergency Management Agency, USA have published several reports highlighting and detailing various steps necessary to design blast proof structures especially in view of higher threat from terrorists. FEMA 426, 427 and 428 details several methodologies to quantify risk and to identify the most effective mitigation measures to achieve a desired level of protection against terrorist acts at a reasonable cost. It includes assessment process, asset value assessment, threat/hazard assessment, vulnerability assessment, risk assessment and risk management etc.

5.10 DESIGN PROCEDURE

For a safe and efficient design of a blast proof structure, it is essential to consider the following comprehensive architectural and engineering design considerations (mitigation measures) for the site: *from the property line to the building, including land use, site planning, stand-off distance, controlled access zones, entry control and vehicular access, signage, parking, loading docks and service access, physical security lighting, and site utilities*. The intent here is to provide concepts for integrating mitigation strategies to the design basis threats as identified during the risk assessment. Integrating security requirements into a larger, more comprehensive approach necessitates achieving a balance among many objectives such as reducing risk and facilitating all the required functional requirements.

To assure a very high strength and ductility in the basic materials used in the construction of such structures, it is essential to specify materials with demonstrated and reliable characteristics. It is desirable to estimate the minimum specified strength or other characteristics of the material in different failure modes and to *amplify* that property as appropriate to account for the expected dynamic effects. All modes of failure, separately and in combination where appropriate (buckling, shear, bond, etc.) with appropriate material strengths or yield points should be considered. In the design, consideration must be given not only to the direct loading but also to the *rebound* or other sources of load reversal. In every case, a check must be made for radiation shielding requirements; and in some cases, especially for aboveground structures– doors and windows – a check must be made for thermal effects arising from the weapon.

After the initial proportions are defined, the strength, ductility, absolute displacements, and related parameters can be determined. The initial design may be modified where ever necessary. For special structures, complete structure may be analyzed using more sophisticated nonlinear methods to establish *ductility demand and capacity*. From this analysis, it will be obvious if modifications need to be made in the structure in order to improve its performance. Analytical aspects are discussed in Chapters 8, 12, 15 and 16. The force-deformation behaviour of the structure may be idealized as *elasto-plastic* or *tri-linear* as discussed in Chapter 15.

National Building Code of India 2016, part 6, section 1, Annexure N recommends IS 4991-1968 for *over ground blast resistant design*. For elasto-plastic design of reinforced concrete members subjected to direct stress and bending, the ductility ratio may be assumed as shown in Table 5.1 provided that the steel ratio remains less than balanced steel ratio for plastic design.

TABLE 5.1 DUCTILITY RATIOS IN RC MEMBERS (IS 4991 – CL. 10.3.3)

Extent of damage	Ductility Ratio μ
Minor damage	$0.04/(pt - pc) \not> 5$
Moderate damage	$0.07/(pt - pc) \not> 10$
Severe damage	$0.10/(pt - pc) \not> 15$

pt = percent steel in tension; pc = percent steel in compression

5.11 ILLUSTRATIVE EXAMPLES

Example 5.11

A 0.5 *t* blast takes place at 20 m in front of an above ground closed building (Figure 5.24) with less than 5% permeability. Its width, length and height are 15 m, 12 m, and 9 m, respectively. Estimate the pressures on the building due to the blast.

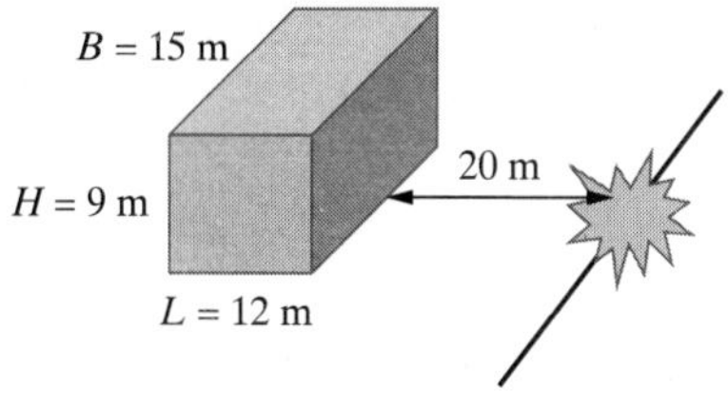

Figure 5.24 An above ground closed building under blast

Solution

Distance $R_o = 20$ m; Yield of blast $W_o = 0.5\ t$
For a standard blast yield of $W = 1\ t$, the reference distance R is given by

$$\frac{R}{R_0} = \left(\frac{W}{W_0}\right)^{1/3} \tag{5.12}$$

$$R = R_0\left(\frac{W}{W_0}\right)^{1/3} = 20 \times \left(\frac{1}{0.5}\right)^{1/3} = 25.2 \text{ m}$$

Let us obtain the standard blast parameters from IS 4991-1968 by interpolation for 25.2 m distance corresponding to 1 t blast.

Blast Characteristics

Peak side-on over-pressure ratio $P_{so}/P_a = 2.16$
Dynamic pressure ratio $q_0/P_a = 1.287$
Peak reflected over-pressure $P_{ro}/P_a = 7.41$
Positive phase duration $t_0 = 19.56$ millisec for standard 1 t blast
Duration of equivalent triangular pulse $t_d = 12.05$ millisec for standard 1 t blast
Mach number $M = 1.69$
where,
P_a = atmospheric pressure = 0.1 MPa (= 1 kg/cm^2)
The duration of positive phase due to the actual blast is given by

$$\frac{t}{t_0} = \left(\frac{W}{W_0}\right)^{1/3} \tag{5.13}$$

$$\therefore t_0 = t\left(\frac{W_0}{W}\right)^{1/3} = 19.56 \times \left(\frac{0.5}{1}\right)^{1/3} = 15.52 \text{ millisec}$$

Similarly, the duration of the equivalent triangular pulse due to the actual blast is given by

$$\therefore t_d = t\left(\frac{W_0}{W}\right)^{1/3} = 12.05 \times \left(\frac{0.5}{1}\right)^{1/3} = 9.56 \text{ millisec}$$

U = air blast shock front velocity = $M \times a$
= 1.69 × 344 = 581.36 m/s = 0.581 m/millisec
where a = velocity of sound in air = 344 m/s

Pressure on the Building

The distance S = min of (H and B/2) = min (9, 15/2) = 7.5 m

$$\text{Clearance time } t_c = \frac{3S}{U} = \frac{3 \times 7.5}{0.581} = 38.72 > t_d\,(= 9.56 \text{ millisec})$$

$$\text{Transit time } t_t = \frac{L}{U} = \frac{12}{0.581} = 20.65 > t_d\,(= 9.56 \text{ millisec})$$

$$\text{Time to reach the rear wall } t_r = \frac{4S}{U} = \frac{4 \times 7.5}{0.581} = 51.635 > t_d\,(= 9.56 \text{ millisec})$$

Since $t_r > t_d$, no pressure is considered on the rear wall
The drag coefficient for front wall = 1
For $q_0 = 0.1287$ MPa, IS 4998 gives drag coefficient for side wall and roof = – 0.4
Pressure on the side wall and roof is given by

$$P_{so} + C_d q_0 = (2.16 - 0.4 \times 1.287) \times 0.1 = 1.645 \text{ MPa}$$

The pressure diagrams are shown in Figure 5.25. □

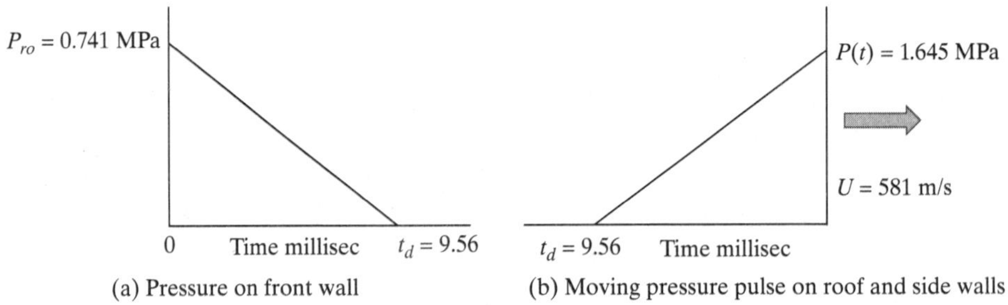

Figure 5.25 Pressure on walls and roof due to blast loading

Example 5.12

A 5 *t* blast takes place at 100 m in front of an above ground closed building (Figure 5.26) with less than 5% permeability. Its width, length and height are 15m, 12 m, and 3.5 m, respectively. Estimate the pressures on the building due to the blast.

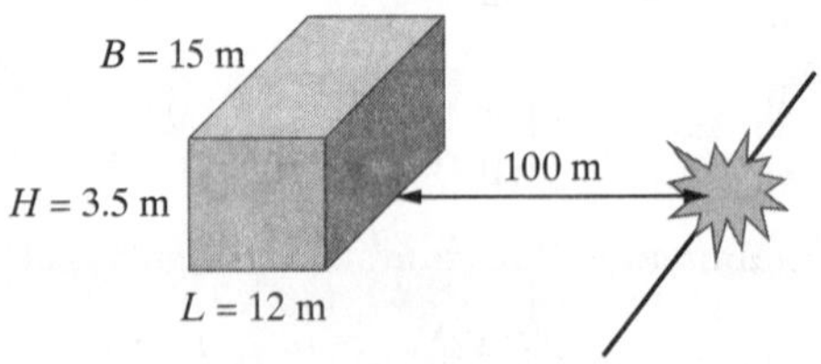

Figure 5.26 An above ground closed building under blast

Solution

Distance R_o = 100 m; Yield of blast W_o = 5 t
For a standard blast yield of W = 1 t, the reference distance R is given by

$$\frac{R}{R_0} = \left(\frac{W}{W_0}\right)^{1/3} \tag{5.12}$$

$$R = R_0\left(\frac{W}{W_0}\right)^{1/3} = 100 \times \left(\frac{1}{5}\right)^{1/3} = 58.4 \text{ m}$$

Let us obtain the standard blast parameters from IS 4991-1968 by interpolation for 58.4 m distance corresponding to 1 *t* blast.

Blast Characteristics

Peak side-on over-pressure ratio $P_{so}/P_a = 0.415$
Dynamic pressure ratio $q_0/P_a = 0.058$
Peak reflected over-pressure $P_{ro}/P_a = 0.971$
Positive phase duration $t_0 = 35.91$ millisec for standard 1 *t* blast
Duration of equivalent triangular pulse $t_d = 26.50$ millisec for standard 1 *t* blast
Mach number $M = 1.165$
Where,
P_a = atmospheric pressure = 0.1 MPa (= 1 kg/cm^2)
The duration of positive phase due to the actual blast is given by

$$\frac{t}{t_0} = \left(\frac{W}{W_0}\right)^{1/3} \tag{5.13}$$

$$\therefore t_0 = t\left(\frac{W_0}{W}\right)^{1/3} = 35.91 \times \left(\frac{5}{1}\right)^{1/3} = 61.41 \text{ millisec}$$

Similarly, the duration of the equivalent triangular pulse due to the actual blast is given by

$$\therefore t_d = t\left(\frac{W_0}{W}\right)^{1/3} = 26.50 \times \left(\frac{5}{1}\right)^{1/3} = 45.31 \text{ millisec}$$

U = airblast shock front velocity = M × a
= 1.165 × 344 = 400 m/s = 0.4 m/millisec
Where, a = velocity of sound in air = 344 m/s

Pressure on the Building

The distance S = min of (H and B/2) = min (3.5, 15/2) = 3.5 m

$$\text{Clearance time } t_c = \frac{3S}{U} = \frac{3 \times 3.5}{0.4} = 26.25 < t_d (= 45.31 \text{ millisec})$$

$$\text{Transit time } t_t = \frac{L}{U} = \frac{12}{0.4} = 30 < t_d (= 45.31 \text{ millisec})$$

$$\text{Time to reach the rear wall } t_r = \frac{4S}{U} = \frac{4 \times 3.5}{0.4} = 35 < t_d (= 45.31 \text{ millisec})$$

The drag coefficient for front wall = 1
For $q_0 = 0.0058$ MPa, IS 4998 gives drag coefficient for side wall, rear wall, and roof = – 0.4
Pressure on the front wall is given by

$$P_{ro} = 0.0971 \text{ MPa}$$

$$P_{so} + C_d q_0 = (0.415 + 1 \times 0.058) \times 0.1 = 0.0473 \text{ MPa}$$

Pressure on the side wall, rear wall and roof is given by

$$P_{so} + C_d q_0 = (0.415 - 0.4 \times 0.058) \times 0.1 = 0.0392 \text{ MPa}$$

The pressure diagrams are shown in Figure 5.27. □

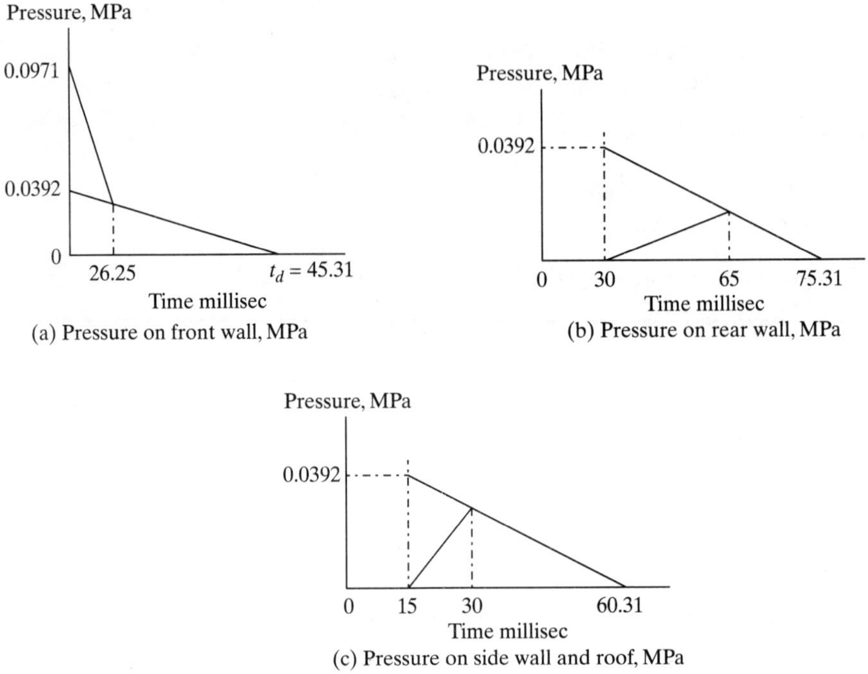

(a) Pressure on front wall, MPa

(b) Pressure on rear wall, MPa

(c) Pressure on side wall and roof, MPa

Figure 5.27 Pressure on walls and roof due to blast loading

REVIEW QUESTIONS

5.1 Graphically illustrate a single impulse. How can it be represented mathematically?

5.2 How do you define an impulse? What is a unit impulse.

5.3 Derive the following relation using the Newton's law of momentum.

$$\int_{t_1}^{t_2} p\,dt = m(\dot{x}_2 - \dot{x}_1)$$

Where,

p = applied force

m = mass of the system

$\dot{x}_1$ and $\dot{x}_2$ = initial and final velocity of the mass

5.4 Derive the response of an undamped SDOF system due to impulse p.

$$x(t) = p\,d\tau\,h(t-\tau) \quad \text{for} \quad t \geq \tau$$

5.5 What is unit impulse response function for an undamped system?

5.6 What is unit impulse response function for a damped system?

5.7 What is a Duhamel integral? How does it give the response of an undamped SDOF system subjected to a short impulse? What are the initial conditions?

5.8 What is the steady state response of a damped system using Duhamel integral?

5.9 What is convolution? Explain its physical meaning.

5.10 What is convolution integral?

5.11 What is a shock spectrum? How it is useful in dynamic analysis of a SDOF system?

5.12 An undamped SDOF system is subjected to a short impulse. Why it is necessary to find its steady state response in both forced and free vibration states?

5.13 What is an explosion? What are different kinds of explosions?

5.14 Write short note on the following:

- Types of explosions
- Shock wave or blast wave front
- Overpressure
- Reflected overpressure
- Yield of explosion
- Blast wave propagation
- Types of bursts
- Stagnation time
- Transit time
- Cube root scaling law

5.15 Sketch idealized loading history on the front face of a closed structure due to blast.

5.16 Sketch idealized loading history on the rear face of a closed structure due to blast.

5.17 Sketch idealized loading history on the roof of a closed structure due to blast.

5.18 Write a note on blast load on below ground structure.

5.19 Discuss how to mitigate potential terrorist attack against buildings.

5.20 Discuss salient features of blast resistant design.

PROBLEMS

MATLAB APPLICATIONS

5.1 An undamped system is subjected to a rectangular impulse force of amplitude p_0 and duration t_d as shown in Figure P5.1. Derive the equations for the response to this impulse starting from rest during the forced vibration phase and free vibration phase.

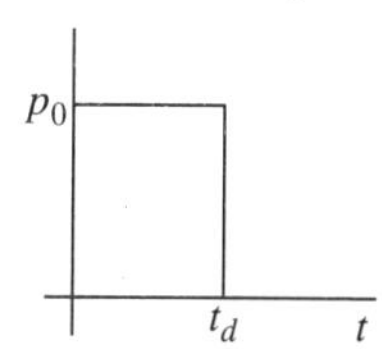

Figure P5.1

(a) Plot the response $x(t)/x_{st}$ vs. t/T for various values of t_d/T.

(b) Plot the maximum response ratio x_{max}/x_{st} against t_d/T, where x_{max} is defined as the absolute value of $x(t)$ during (i) the forced vibration phase and (ii) the free vibration phase.

(c) Plot the shock spectra.

5.2 An undamped system is subjected to a symmetric triangular impulse force as shown in Figure P5.2. Derive the equations for the response to this impulse starting from rest during the forced vibration phase and free vibration phase.

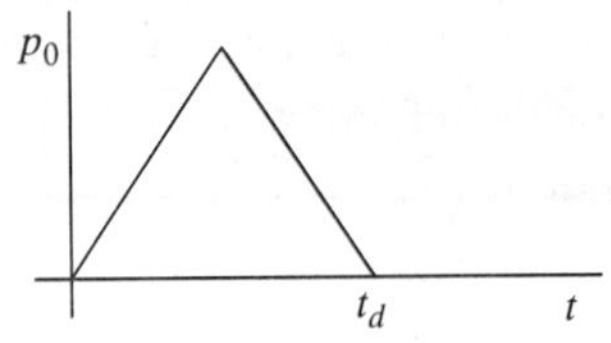

Figure P5.2

(a) Plot the response $x(t)/x_{st}$ vs. t/T for various values of t_d/T.

(b) Plot the maximum response ratio x_{max}/x_{st} against t_d/T, where x_{max} is defined as the absolute value of $x(t)$ during (i) the forced vibration phase and (ii) the free vibration phase.

(c) Plot the shock spectra.

5.3 An undamped system is subjected to a half sine impulse force as shown in Figure P5.3. Derive the equations for the response to this impulse starting from rest during the forced vibration phase and free vibration phase. Plot the maximum response ratio against t_d/T.

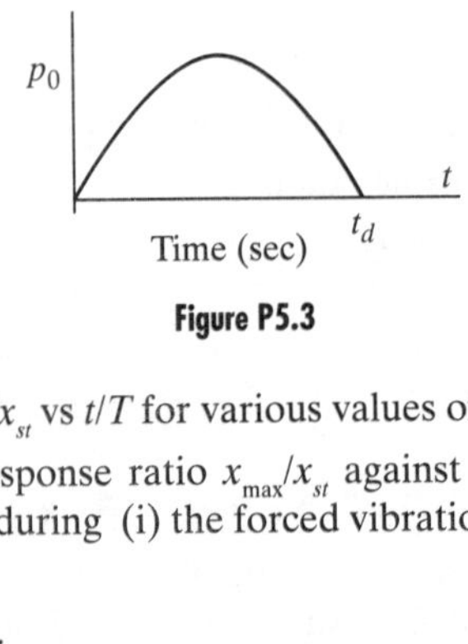

Figure P5.3

(a) Plot the response $x(t)/x_{st}$ vs t/T for various values of t_d/T.

(b) Plot the maximum response ratio x_{max}/x_{st} against t_d/T, where x_{max} is defined as the absolute value of $x(t)$ during (i) the forced vibration phase and (ii) the free vibration phase.

(c) Plot the shock spectra.

5.4 An undamped system is subjected to a full sine impulse force as shown in Figure P5.4. Derive the equations for the response to this impulse starting from rest during the forced vibration phase and free vibration phase. Plot the maximum response ratio against t_d/T.

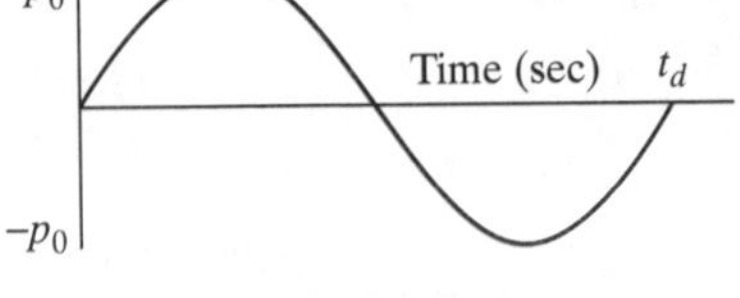

Figure P5.4

(a) Plot the response $x(t)/x_{st}$ vs t/T for various values of t_d/T.

(b) Plot the maximum response ratio x_{max}/x_{st} against t_d/T, where x_{max} is defined as the absolute value of $x(t)$ during (i) the forced vibration phase and (ii) the free vibration phase.

(c) Plot the shock spectra.

5.5 A damped SDOF system with mass = 1 kg, natural frequency = 10 rad/sec, and damping = 10% is subjected to a set of three impulses each having a duration of 0.1 sec as shown in Fig. P5.5(a). Determine the response of the SDOF system due to each impulse separately and combined response up to 10 sec using an EXCEL sheet.

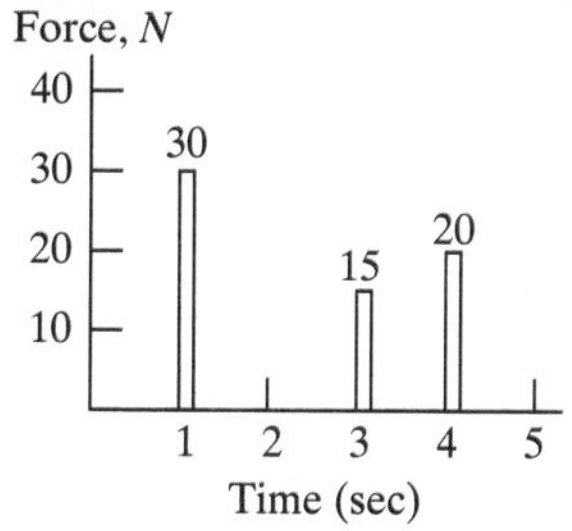

Figure P5.5(a)

Ans: The results are shown in figure P5.5(b)and (c).

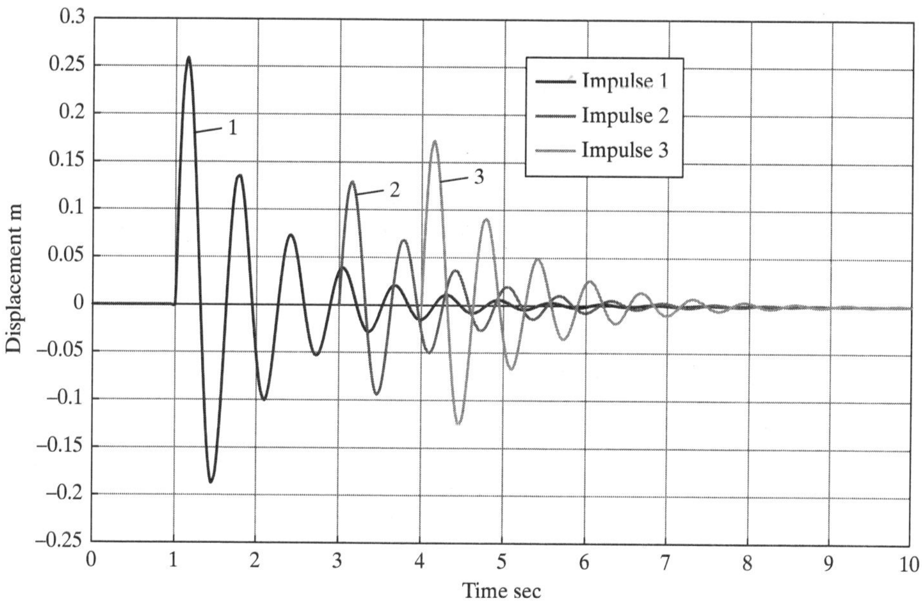

Figure P5.5(b) Response due to each impulse

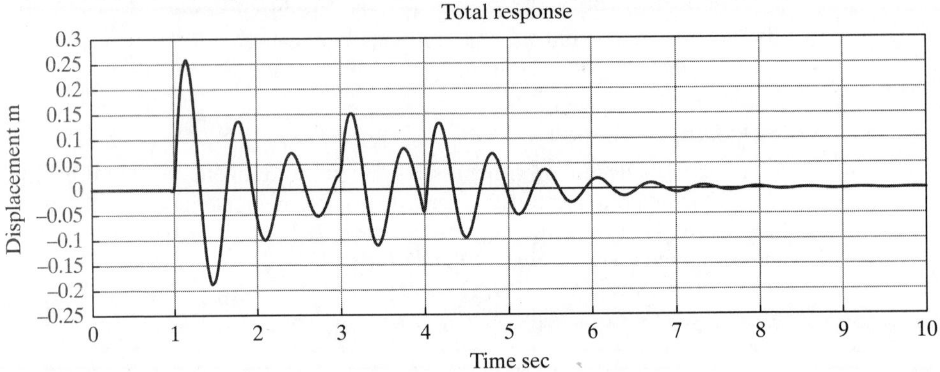

Figure P5.5(c) Total response due to all the three impulses

5.6 A damped system with $\xi = 5\%$ and mass = 1 kg is subjected to an impulse force as shown in Figure P5.6. Derive the equations for the response to this impulse starting from rest and valid for $t > t_d$

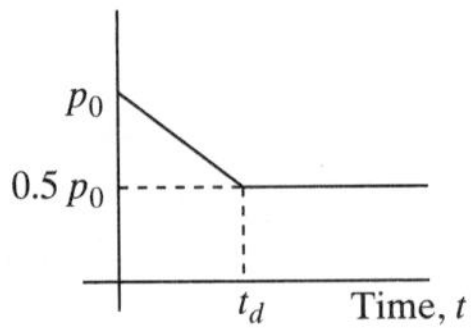

Figure P5.6

Plot the response $x(t)/x_{st}$ vs t/T for various values of t_d/T using MATLAB or PYTHON.

5.7 A damped system with $\xi = 10\%$ and mass = 1 kg is subjected to an impulse force as shown in Figure P5.7. Derive the equations for the response to this impulse starting from rest during the forced vibration phase and free vibration phase. Plot the maximum response ratio against t_d/T using MATLAB.

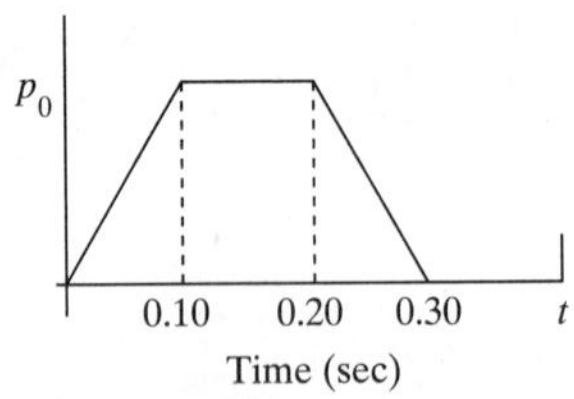

Figure P5.7

5.8 A 11.5 m high counterfort retaining wall is to be designed for use by army for an over ground blast of 1 t at 50 m. Its general arrangement is shown in Figure P5.8. It is located in seismic zone V. Density of soil = 19 kN/m^3, Angle of repose = 30°, coefficient of friction = 0.50. Net Safe bearing capacity of soil = 150 kN/m^2 at 2.5 m depth. Water table is 5 m below the ground level. Design the retaining wall.

[This problem should be attempted after understanding the dynamic earth pressure discussed in Chapter 14, concept of ductility and non-linear behaviour discussed in Chapter 15.]

Spacing of front counterforts = 1200 mm clear

Spacing of small rear counterforts = 1200 mm clear

Height of small real counterforts = 2000 mm

Spacing of main rear counterforts = 2750 mm clear

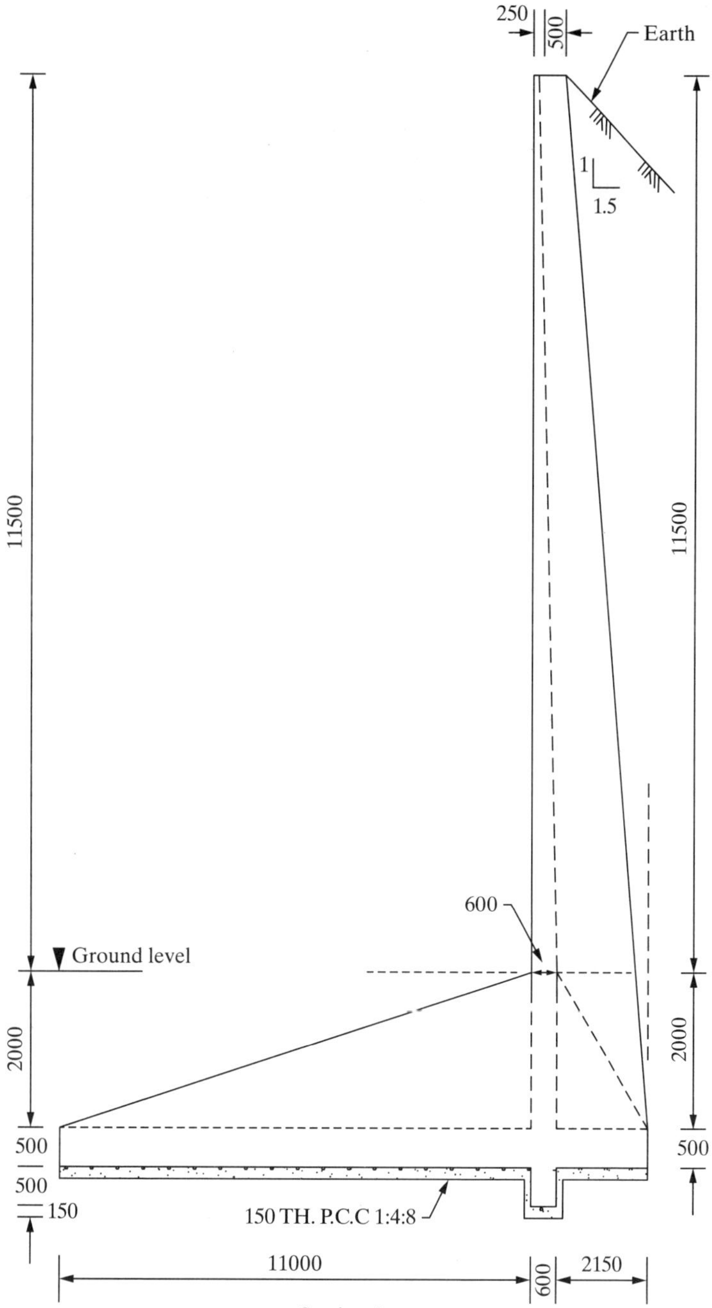

Figure P5.8 General arrangement of the retaining wall

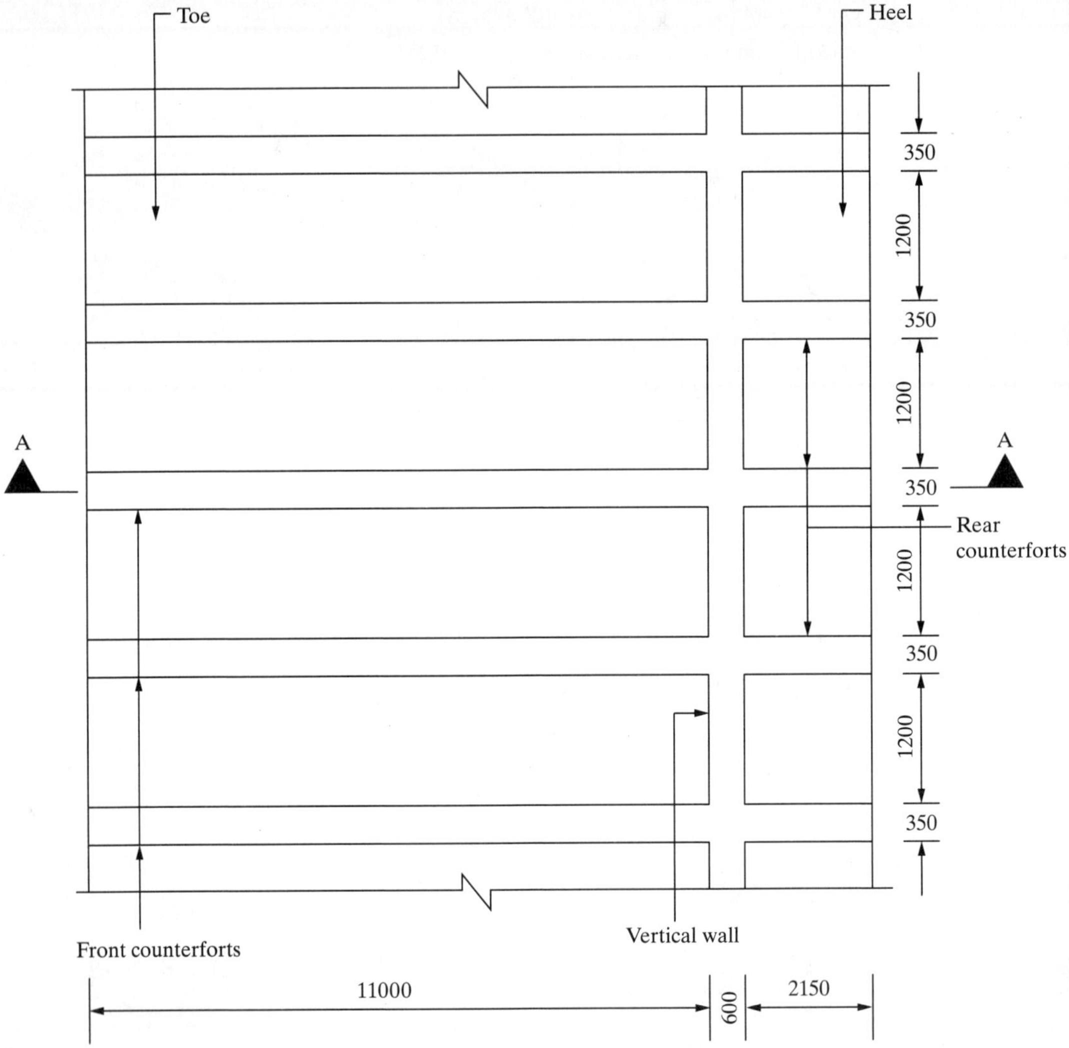

Plan of counterforts

Figure P5.8 (Continued)

Hint: This retaining wall is to be designed so that it may be able to resist the highly indeterminate earthquake and blast loadings, and protect the equipment and personnel enclosed by it. Therefore, high strength concrete (say M40 grade) and Fe500D grade steel should be used in the design. The moment of inertia of the wall may be taken as 70% of the gross.

The retaining wall is designed for the following load combinations:

(1) Earth pressure
(2) Earth pressure + Earthquake force
(3) Earth pressure + Blast force

(1) Check for Stability of the Wall

The counterfort wall is checked for conventional stability checks as per IS 456 under gravity and earth pressure:

- Check for bearing pressure below the counterforts at heel and toe
- Check for overturning – factor of safety more than 2
- Check for sliding – factor of safety more than 2

Modify the dimensions, if necessary.

(2) Estimate the static and dynamic earth pressure on the wall

The static earth pressure and dynamic earth pressure due to earthquake can be estimated in accordance with IS 1893-part 3 and discussed in Chapter 14. The static earth pressure acts at a height of h/3 above the base, while dynamic earth pressure acts at a height of h/2 above the base of the wall. Thus, shear force and bending moment at different sections of the wall may be estimated.

(3) Estimate the static and dynamic earth pressure on the wall

National Building Code of India 2016, part 6, section 1, Annexure N recommends IS 4991-1968 for *over ground blast resistant design*. You may obtain the standard blast parameters from IS 4991-1968, Table 1 by interpolation for 50 m distance corresponding to 1 t blast.

(5) Estimate the dynamic force due to blast loading

The blast loading is usually quite intense. If the retaining wall is assumed to be elastic to resist this force, it will require a huge cross-section and reinforcement. Therefore, the concept of ductility or inelastic deformations is introduced in the design. A reduction factor R is applied on the force to get a reduced force in lieu of ductile detailing of the structure. The concept of ductility and reduction factor R are discussed in Chapters 12 and 15. For the present, it is sufficient to note that for a given ductility μ, the response reduction factor R is given by the following equation:

$$\text{Reduction factor } R = \frac{F_0}{F_y} = \sqrt{2\mu - 1}$$

For a ductility of 5, the reduction factor $R = \sqrt{2 \times 5 - 1} = 3$

Thus, design force acting on the wall = maximum elastic force / R

This load is applied at each node of the wall in horizontal direction in proportion to the length of each element. A 2D time-history analysis can be carried out to estimate the design forces at different heights in the retaining wall for the impact loading shown in Figure P5.9 for a total duration of t, (say 0.5 sec). A higher duration of analysis is chosen to take care of free vibrations after the impact dies down.

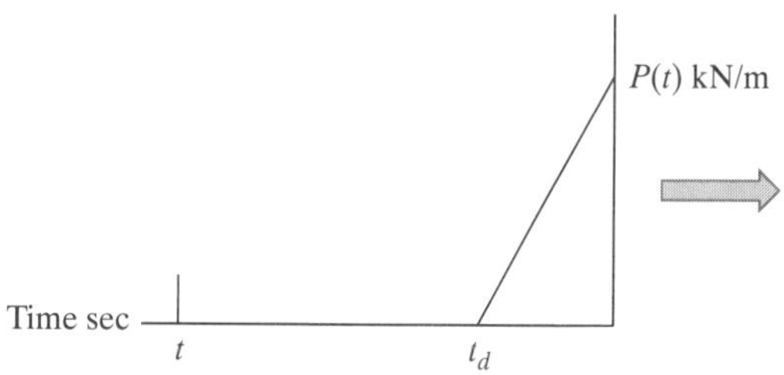

Figure P5.9 Blast force on the retaining wall

Damping may be taken as 5%. The maximum positive and negative values of shear force and bending moment can be obtained at different heights.

(6) Design of the Retaining Wall

Thus, shear force and bending moment can be calculated. at different heights of the wall. The limit state design of the various elements of the structure is carried out for the worst combination. The ties between the counterforts and the vertical wall, and between the counterforts and the base slab are very crucial.

The curtailment of reinforcement and ductile detailing of the reinforcement is carried out in accordance with IS 456 and IS 13920 codes.

REFERENCES

Biggs, J.M. (1964) Introduction to Structural Dynamics, McGraw Hill Book Co., New York.

ASCE Manual 42 (1985), Design of Structures to Resist Nuclear Weapon Effects, ASCE, New York.

Biggs, J.M. (1964) Introduction to Structural Dynamics, McGraw Hill Book Co., New York.

FEMA 426 (2003) Reference Manual to Mitigate Potential Terrorist Attacks against Buildings, Federal Emergency Management Agency, Washington, DC.

IS 4991 (1968) Blast Resistant Design of Structures for Explosions above Ground, BIS, New Delhi.

IS 6922 (1973) Safety and Design of Structures Subjected to Underground Blasts, BIS, New Delhi.

Mays, G.C. and Smith, P.D. (1995), Blast effects on Building Design to Optimize Resistance to Blast Loading, Thomas Telford, London.

NBC (2016) National Building Code of India, Bureau of Indian Standards, New Delhi.

6 Single Degree of Freedom System: Machine Vibrations

6.1 INTRODUCTION

Installation of heavy machinery has assumed increased importance in view of increased sophistication in mechanics and electronics of machines. Foundations for these machines have to be specially designed taking into consideration the impact of the load, vibration characteristics of the machine, and properties of the soil. For different types of machines, different types of foundations are required to satisfy their individual requirements and characteristics. There are machines having static characteristics. Their foundations are designed using the limit states of collapse and serviceability design philosophy. The pressure on the soil cannot exceed their safe bearing capacity. Other critical criteria include deformations in the foundations, and settlement under serviceability conditions depending upon the geotechnical considerations. Sometimes, such machines may experience undesirable vibrations induced due to base excitation. The base is excited due to either a machine operating in nearby room or building, or due to nearby road or rail traffic, or an earthquake.

There are machines having dynamic characteristics. Depending upon the type of motion produced, these machines may be classified as follows:

- Rotary machines
- Reciprocating machines
- Impact type machines.

Further, based on the speed of operation, these machines may be grouped as follows:

- Very low speed machines (< 100 rpm)
- Low speed machines (100 to 1500 rpm)
- Medium speed machines (1500 to 3000 rpm)
- High speed machines. (> 3000 rpm)

Most used foundations for such machines are as follows:

- Block foundation, Figure 6.1(a)
- Framed foundation, Figure 6.1(b)

In any case, a machine is treated as a rigid body. Only its mass is considered in assessing the static and dynamic characteristics of the foundation. The machine is usually connected to the foundation through foundation bolts. Soil is treated as a massless elastic body. It means only its stiffness is considered but not the inertial force. The soil stiffness is represented through *elastic translational and rotational springs*. It is assumed that a machine foundation undergoes elastic vibrations as long as the total static and dynamic pressure on the soil below is within its elastic limit.

A block foundation is usually made up of concrete. The stiffness of the concrete block is much higher than that of the soil below. Therefore, it is also treated as a rigid body and only its mas is considered in the analysis. In case of a framed foundation, both mass and stiffness of beams and columns are considered as both of them are elastic bodies.

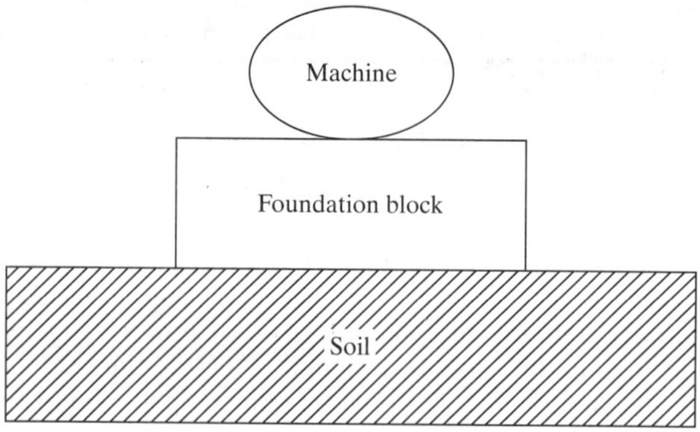

Figure 6.1 (a) Block foundation

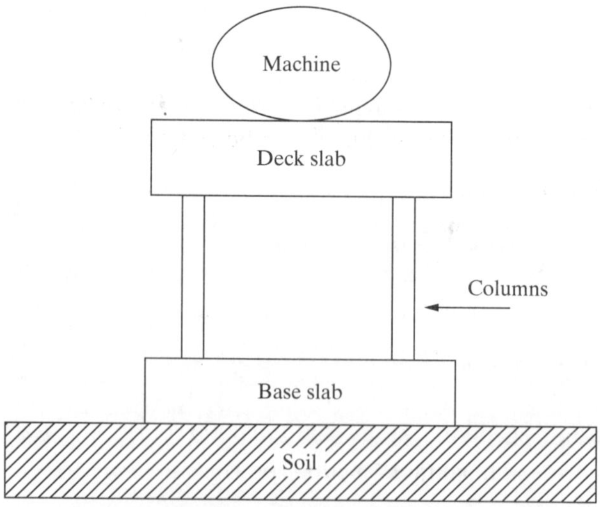

Figure 6.1 (b) Frame Foundation

Here, it is important to understand the term *machine foundation*. Generally, in the civil engineering terminology, a foundation is understood to be below the ground level. But in the case of machines, a machine foundation is usually above the ground. A machine foundation may be in the form of a space frame consisting of beams, columns, and slabs as shown in Figure 6.1(c). Both the RC block and the space frame may have a conventional foundation below the ground level in the form of a raft or pile foundation depending upon the geotechnical considerations.

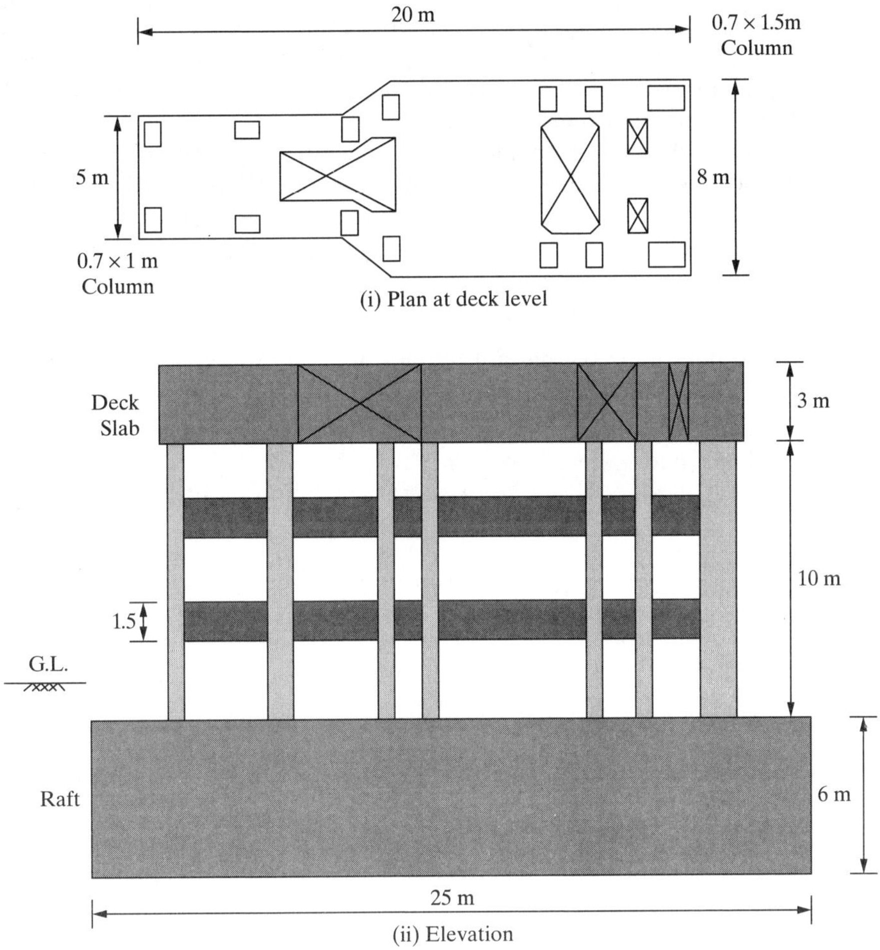

Figure 6.1 (c) A typical turbogenerator foundation.

The vibrations are caused whenever a machine is in operation. These vibrations are transmitted through its foundation to adjoining areas and vice versa. Such situations are unwelcome. In terms of displacements, the permissible displacements may be as low as about 10^{-4} mm at between 0.1 and 10 Hz for very delicate electronic or medical components, or CNC machine foundations, to several cm (say 10 cm to 50 cm) in tall buildings at between 0.05 and 0.50 Hz. Machine vibrations can range between 10 and 1000 Hz. Vibrations of the foundation may be injurious to the safety and working of the machine as well as foundation itself. Therefore, there is a need to control and/or isolate such undesirable vibrations. This isolation is achieved by suitably designing the stiffness and damping of the foundation.

These vibrations can be measured with the help of very tiny but powerful sensors in three orthogonal directions simultaneously, and the real time data can be easily recorded in a laptop. These sensors are based on the micro-electro-mechanical sensor (MEMS) technology. A triaxial accelerometer is small and thin, it is only 5 mm × 3 mm × 1 mm or even smaller (2 mm × 2 mm × 1 mm) in size; has low power consumption, variable range, and high resolution characteristics. It is capable of measuring vibrations in various selectable ranges: ± 2, ± 4, ± 8 g and up to ± 400 g as well as different frequency range.

The subject of machine foundations and machine vibrations is very vast and complicated. A machine foundation can be modeled as a single-degree-of-freedom system, or a multi-degree-of-freedom system depending upon the type of machine and its foundation. In certain situations, it may be necessary to incorporate soil–structure interaction, especially in the case of soft soils. The study of the subject of machine foundations consists of the following aspects:

1. To determine the natural frequency of vibrations of the machine foundation in different modes,
2. To determine the response of the mass of the machine under given dynamic loads, and
3. To determine the forces transmitted to the foundation, or displacements transmitted by the foundation to the machine.

The discussion in this chapter covers only single-degree-of-freedom systems but without soil–structure interaction. The analysis of a two-degree-of-freedom system and multi-degree-of-freedom system will be discussed in Chapters 9 and 10. The Indian standard code IS 2974 deals with different types of machine foundations.

6.2 DYNAMIC SOIL PARAMETERS

It needs to be recalled that a machine foundation system is a 3D system. It can be visualized as consisting of three orthogonal axes x, y and z as shown in Figure 6.2. There can be overall six degrees of freedom for the complete system: three translations (x, y,

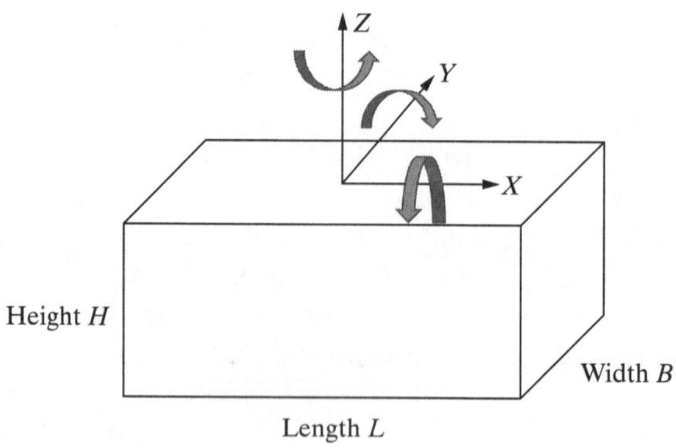

Figure 6.2 Axes of vibrations of a machine foundation

and z) and three rotations (θ, ϕ and ψ). The deformations and vibrations can take place along these axes. It is essential to monitor and control each of these six components in any machine foundation. The translation z along the vertical axis Z represents the *uniform compression* of the soil; the translations x and y along the horizontal axes X and Y represent *uniform shear* of the soil; rotations θ and ϕ about the horizontal axes X and Y, respectively, represent *non-uniform compression* of the soil; and rotation ψ about the vertical axis Z represent *non-uniform shear* of the soil. The rotational components are referred to as *rocking, pitching and yawing,* about the shorter dimension, about the longer dimension and about the vertical axis, respectively. Sometimes, the rotational components about the shorter and longer dimensions are both referred to as *rocking*.

Thus, there are four independent soil deformation modes: uniform compression, uniform shear, non-uniform compression and non-uniform shear. There are four coefficients of subgrade reaction corresponding to each of these four modes as follows:

1. Coefficient of uniform compression C_u
2. Coefficient of uniform shear C_τ
3. Coefficient of non-uniform compression C_θ
4. Coefficient of non-uniform shear C_ψ

The three basic properties of the soil: modulus of elasticity E, shear modulus G and Poisson's ratio v are related as follows:

$$G = \frac{E}{2(1+\upsilon)} \tag{6.1}$$

All the above properties of soil at any site can be determined by carrying out appropriate laboratory and field tests. For details, reader may refer any text book on soil mechanics or foundation engineering. It will be noticed that the two parameters *dynamic shear modulus G* and *coefficient of uniform compression* Cu are independent while the rest are inter-related.

6.2.1 Equivalent Soil Springs

In order to analyze a machine foundation, different soil subgrade systems are employed:

1. foundation supported directly on soil
2. foundation supported directly on an elastic pad such as rubber pad or cork pad or isolation pad
3. foundation supported directly on piles

It is a common practice to model the soil subgrade system in a machine foundation using springs: *translational springs and rotational springs*. The foundation may have any shape in plan (linear, square, rectangular, triangular or circular) and form (beam or rod, circular cylinder, cubical block, frame or piles) depending upon the machine requirements.

Soil Springs When Foundation is Supported Directly on Soil

If the area of the foundation in contact with the soil is $L \times B$, its mechanical properties are as follows:

$$\text{Area } A = L \times B$$

$$\text{Moment of inertia about } X\text{-axis, } Ixx = \frac{L \times B^3}{12}$$

$$\text{Moment of inertia about } Y\text{-axis, } Iyy = \frac{B \times L^3}{12}$$

$$\text{Moment of inertia about } Z\text{-axis, } Izz = Ixx + I\,yy$$

$$\text{Spring stiffness } kx = C_\tau \times A$$

$$\text{Spring stiffness } ky = C_\tau \times A$$

$$\text{Spring stiffness } kz = C_u \times A$$

$$\text{Spring stiffness } k\theta = C_\theta \times Ixx$$

$$\text{Spring stiffness } k\phi = C_\phi \times Iyy$$

$$\text{Spring stiffness } k\psi = C_\psi \times Izz$$

Similarly, the soil springs for other cases can be developed. The reader may refer any text book on soil mechanics or foundation engineering.

The equation of motion for a SDOF system machine foundation may be written by direct analogy as follows:

Vertical or Sliding Modes

$$m\ddot{x}(t) + c\dot{x}(t) + kx(t) = p_x(t) \tag{6.2a}$$

$$m\ddot{y}(t) + c\dot{y}(t) + ky(t) = p_y(t) \tag{6.2b}$$

$$m\ddot{z}(t) + c\dot{z}(t) + kz(t) = p_z(t) \tag{6.2c}$$

Rocking Mode

$$I_\theta\ddot{\theta}(t) + c_\theta\dot{\theta}(t) + k_\theta\theta(t) = p_\theta(t) \tag{6.2d}$$

6.3 UNBALANCED FORCE IN MACHINES

Let us understand the salient features of commonly used machines: rotary machines, reciprocating machines and impact machines as to how they produce unbalanced force and, therefore, vibrations. A machine would necessarily have three components:

- A drive unit
- A driven unit, and
- A coupling unit.

They may be arranged in different configurations depending upon the machine.

6.3.1 Rotary Machine

A typical single cylinder rotary machine is shown in Figure 6.3(a). It has a total mass m and an unbalanced mass m' acting at a radius of r from its center. It is rotating at an angular velocity $\bar{\omega}$. The unbalanced force acts in a plane normal to the rotor axis and radially outward from the center of the rotor. At any instant t, the dynamic force is given by

$$F(t) = m' r \bar{\omega}^2$$

This unbalanced force can be resolved along the horizontal and vertical axes X and Z, as follows (Figure 6.3b):

$$\text{Along horizontal direction, } Fx(t) = m' r \bar{\omega}^2 \cos\theta = m' r \bar{\omega}^2 \cos(t) \tag{6.3b}$$

$$\text{Along vertical direction } Fz(t) = m' r \bar{\omega}^2 \sin\theta = m' r \bar{\omega}^2 \sin(t) \tag{6.3c}$$

These forces are transferred from rotor to the bearings as per static equilibrium.

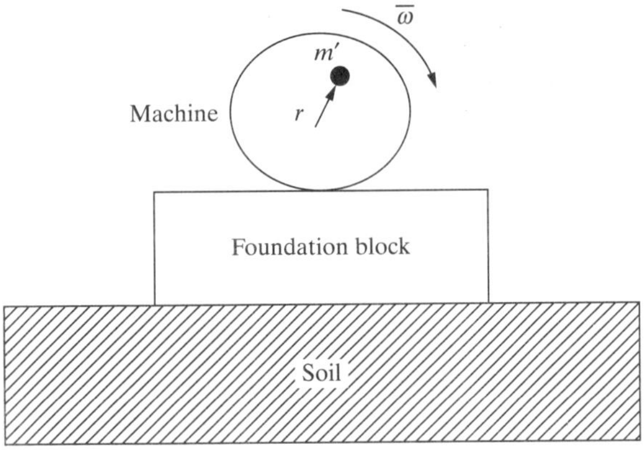

Figure 6.3 (a) Rotary machine foundation

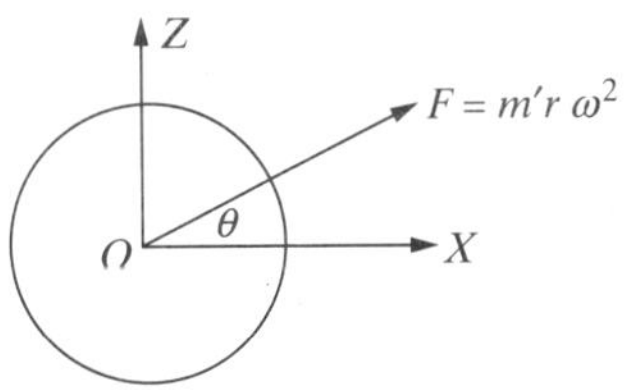

(b)

Figure 6.3 (b) Unbalanced force acting in the plane normal to the rotor axis

The following points needs to be considered while developing model for dynamic analysis of the machine foundation:

- The foundation should be modelled as a three dimensional space frame. Slabs and walls, if present, may be modelled using thin shell (plate bending) elements.

- The columns should be assumed to be fixed at the base disregarding the base mat.
- Lumped-mass approach should be used for computing modal masses of the foundation. The machine should be modelled to lump its mass together with the mass of the foundation. The stiffness and damping of the shaft and casing etc. can be disregarded.
- Soil-structure interaction must be accounted for in the dynamic analysis.
- Uncracked sections may be used for calculating moments of inertia of the members. The rotational inertia may be disregarded. However, shear rigidity should be considered.

6.3.2 Reciprocating Machine

A reciprocating machine consists of a crack rod, a connecting rod and a piston with piston rod. It may be arranged vertically or horizontally as per requirement. Let us consider a single cylinder machine in *Y-Z* plane as shown in Figure 6.4. Let us derive the expression for unbalanced force. The motion of the connecting rod is very interesting: one end of the rod undergoes linear motion while the other end undergoes rotary motion. The engine produces both primary and secondary forces.

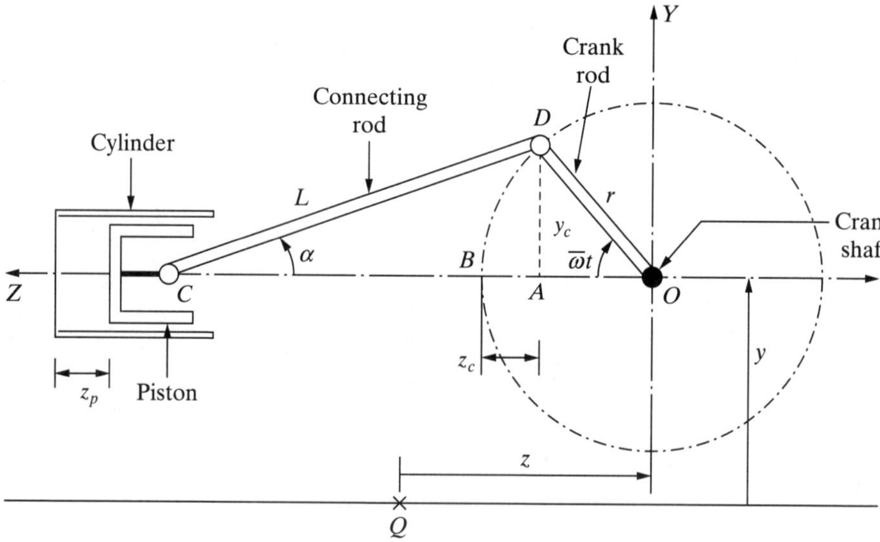

Figure 6.4 Moving parts of a typical reciprocating machine

Let us define the various parameters:

Crank Rod

Length $= r$, mass $= m_r$, speed of rotation $= \overline{\omega}$

Distance of its center of gravity from the center of rotation point $= r_1$

Vertical component of the displacement of crank rod $DA = y_c$

Horizontal component of the displacement of crank rod $BA = z_c$

Connecting Rod

Length = L, mass = m_c,

Distance of its center of gravity from point $C = l_1$

Piston assembly

Mass = m_p

Let the displacement of the piston from its extreme position (when $\bar{\omega}\ t = 0) = z_p$

The maximum value of z_p occurs at $\bar{\omega}\, t = \pi$ radian counterclockwise.

At any time *t*,

$$z_p = r\,(1 - \cos \bar{\omega} t\,) + L\,(\,1 - \cos \alpha) \tag{1}$$

But angle $\alpha = f(\bar{\omega} t\,)$ since y_c is common to both the crank rod and connecting rod

$$\sin \alpha = \frac{r \sin \bar{\omega} t}{L} \tag{2}$$

Using the trigonometric identity, $\sin^2\theta + \cos^2\theta = 1$, we get

$$\cos\theta = (1 - \sin^2\theta)^{0.5} \tag{3}$$

On expanding this series, we get

$$\cos\theta = 1 - \frac{1}{2}\sin^2\theta + \frac{1}{8}\sin^4\theta \text{ and so on} \tag{4}$$

Neglecting higher order terms, we get

$$\cos\theta = 1 - \frac{1}{2}\sin^2\theta$$

or,

$$1 - \cos\theta = \frac{1}{2}\sin^2\theta \tag{5}$$

Substituting the value of α from Equation (2) in Equation (5), we get

$$1 - \cos\alpha = \frac{1}{2}\left(\frac{r \sin \bar{\omega} t}{L}\right)^2 = \frac{1}{2}\left(\frac{r}{L}\right)^2 \sin^2 \bar{\omega} t$$

Making use of $\cos 2\theta = 1 - 2\sin^2\theta$, we obtain,

$$1 - \cos\alpha = \frac{1}{2}\left(\frac{r}{L}\right)^2 \times \left(\frac{1 - \cos 2\bar{\omega} t}{2}\right) \tag{6}$$

Making use of Equation (6), Equation (1) can be written as follows:

$$z_p = r\,(1 - \cos \bar{\omega} t\,) + \frac{1}{2} \times \frac{r^2}{L} \times \left(\frac{1 - \cos 2\bar{\omega} t}{2}\right)$$

or,

$$z_p = \left(r + \frac{r^2}{4L}\right) - r\left(\cos \bar{\omega} t + \frac{r}{4L}\cos 2\bar{\omega} t\right) \tag{6.4a}$$

Differentiating it twice,

$$\dot{z}_p = r\bar{\omega}\left(\sin\bar{\omega}t + \frac{r}{2L}\sin 2\bar{\omega}t\right) \tag{6.4b}$$

$$\ddot{z}_p = r\bar{\omega}^2\left(\cos\bar{\omega}t + \frac{r}{L}\cos 2\bar{\omega}t\right) \tag{6.4c}$$

Similarly, the following relations for the crank can be obtained:

$$y_c = -r\sin\bar{\omega}t \tag{6.5a}$$

$$\dot{y}_c = -r\bar{\omega}\cos\bar{\omega}t \tag{6.5b}$$

$$\ddot{y}_c = r\bar{\omega}^2\sin\bar{\omega}t \tag{6.5c}$$

and

$$z_c = r\left(1-\cos\bar{\omega}t\right) \tag{6.6a}$$

$$\dot{z}_c = r\bar{\omega}\sin\bar{\omega}t \tag{6.6b}$$

$$\ddot{z}_c = r\bar{\omega}^2\cos\bar{\omega}t \tag{6.6c}$$

The mass of the connecting rod is lumped at C and D, and mass of the crank rod is lumped at O and D. The mass of the piston is also lumped at C.

$$\text{Total mass lumped at } C = \text{reciprocating mass } m_{rec} = \frac{m_c\left(L-l_1\right)}{L} + m_p \tag{6.7a}$$

$$\text{Total mass lumped at } D = \text{rotating mass } m_{rot} = \frac{m_c l_1}{L} + \frac{m_r r_1}{r} \tag{6.7b}$$

The unbalanced forces are as follows:

Horizontal: $$F_z = m_{rec}\ddot{z}_p + m_{rot}\ddot{z}_c \tag{6.8a}$$

or,

$$F_z = m_{rec}r\bar{\omega}^2\left(\cos\bar{\omega}t + \frac{r}{L}\cos 2\bar{\omega}t\right) + m_{rot}\, r\bar{\omega}^2\cos\bar{\omega}t$$

or,

$$F_z = \left(m_{rec} + m_{rot}\right)r\bar{\omega}^2\cos\bar{\omega}t + m_{rec}\frac{r^2\bar{\omega}^2}{L}\cos 2\bar{\omega}t \tag{6.8b}$$

Vertical: $$F_y = m_{rot}\ddot{y}_c = m_{rot}r\bar{\omega}^2\sin\bar{\omega}t \tag{6.8c}$$

Equation (6.8b) consists of force in two parts:
A primary force at machine speed, $\bar{\omega}$:

$$F_1 = \left(m_{rec} + m_{rot}\right)r\bar{\omega}^2\cos\bar{\omega}t \tag{6.8d}$$

A secondary force at twice the machine speed, $2\bar{\omega}$:

$$F_2 = m_{rec}\frac{r^2\bar{\omega}^2}{L}\cos 2\bar{\omega}t \tag{6.8e}$$

These are horizontal primary and secondary forces and are a maximum at $\bar{\omega}t = 2\bar{\omega}t = 0$ and multiple of π so that the cos term is 1 with the same sign. These forces are machine frequency dependent. Equation (6.8a) gives a primary vertical force as there is only one term. This force is maximum at $\bar{\omega}t = \pi/4, 5\pi/4$ etc. It acts at some distance y above the base-ground interface of the machine and, therefore, it will produce a moment (that is, a rocking motion) about x-axis (which is normal to the plane of the paper).

These dynamic forces are transferred to the foundation through the base frame of the machine. Let center of gravity of the machine is at point Q as shown in Figure 6.4. Let y and z be the vertical and horizontal distances QO. The moment at Q is as follows:

$$M_Q = F_z \times y + F_y \times z \tag{6.9}$$

At Q, the horizontal force Fz will produce a sliding mode and a rocking mode which may be independent or coupled.

6.3.3 Impact Machine

A typical impact machine is shown in Figure 6.5(a). It is subjected to an impulse load. A typical drop hammer foundation is shown in Figure 6.5(b). Its solution consists of two parts:

1. A falling mass from height h producing an impact on the anvil. The *first part* is to calculate the initial velocity of the anvil after impact.
2. The foundation system has to absorb this impact. The *second part* is to calculate the response of the anvil and foundation in order to ensure that the maximum displacements are within the permissible limits.

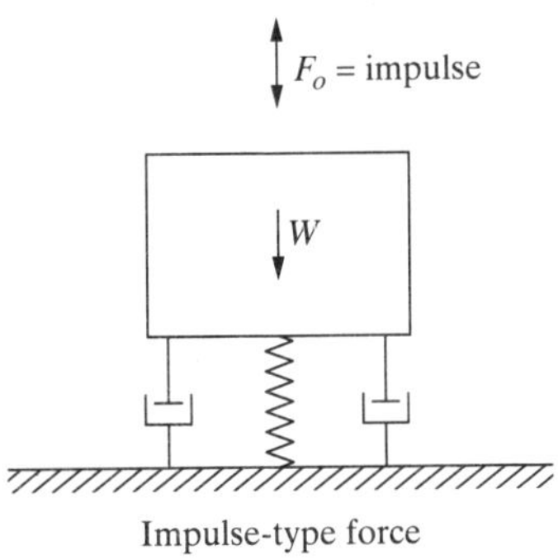

Figure 6.5 (a) Impact type machine

An elastic cushioning of suitable material and thickness is provided between the anvil and thc foundation block in order to prevent bouncing of anvil and creation of large impact stresses and consequent damage to the top surface of the concrete in the foundation block. The cushion may consist of timber sleepers, cork layer, or springs. A coefficient of restitution 'e' is used to determine the velocity of the anvil and the foundation block after the tup strikes. This coefficient is governed by the condition $0 < e < 1$ and its average value for design purposes may be taken up to 0.6.

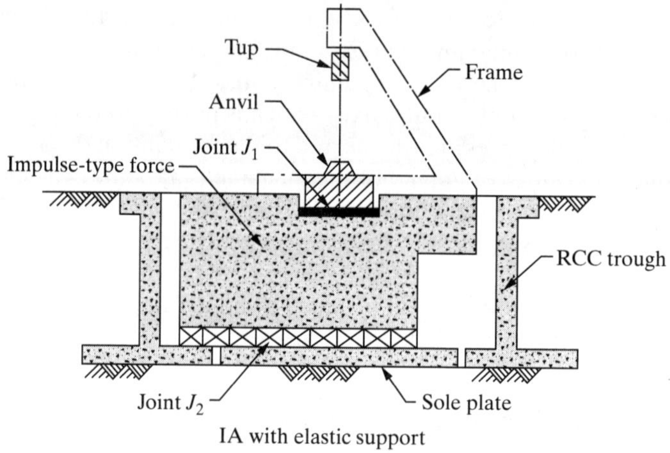

Figure 6.5 (b) Typical hammer foundation

The machine foundation system is modeled as a two-DOF system with anvil forming one mass m_2 and the foundation block as the second mass m_1. Let us derive the expression for final velocity of mass m_2 just after the impact. A mass m_0 drops freely from height h on a two-DOF system and impacts mass m_2 as shown in Figure 6.6.

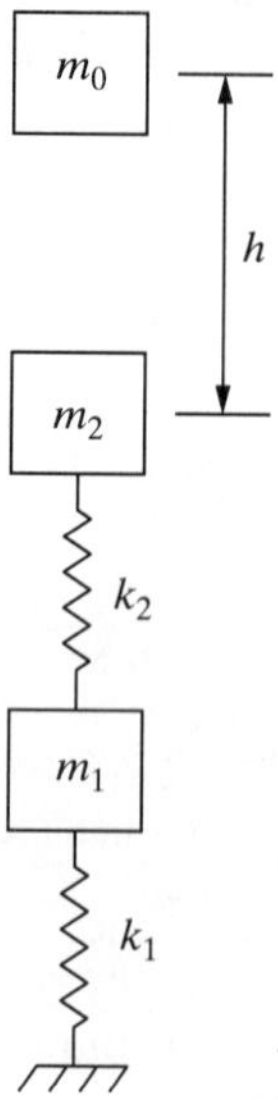

Figure 6.6 Model of a drop hammer foundation

Let velocity of mass m_0 and m_2 just *before* impact = v_0 and v_2, respectively,
Let velocity of mass m_0 and m_2 just *after* impact = v_0' and v_2', respectively,

The velocity of mass $m_0 = v_0 = \sqrt{2gh}$

An efficiency factor χ is used to account to overcome friction to the tup's movement and the resistance of the steam/air counter pressure. Its value is taken as 0.65. Thus, initial velocity of mass m_0 is modified as χv_0.
Momentum equation gives

$$m_0 v_0 = m_0 v_0' + m_2 v_2' \tag{6.10a}$$

The coefficient of restitution $e = \dfrac{\text{speed of separation}}{\text{speed of approach}}$

$$\therefore v_2' = \frac{m_0}{m_2}(v_0 - e v_0') \quad \text{where} \quad 0 < e < 1$$

$$\begin{aligned} e &= 1 \text{ for elastic collision} \\ &= 0 \text{ for inelastic collision} \end{aligned}$$

Relative initial speed of mass A with respect to mass $B = v_B - v_A = v_2 - v_0$

Relative final speed of mass A with respect to mass $B = v_B' - v_A' = v_2' - v_0'$

$$\therefore e = \left|\frac{v_2' - v_0'}{v_2 - v_0}\right| = \frac{v_2' - v_0'}{v_0} \tag{6.11a}$$

Equation (6.10a) gives

$$v_2' = \frac{m_0}{m_2}(v_0 - v_0') \tag{6.10b}$$

Equation (6.11a) gives

$$v_0' = v_2' - e v_0 \tag{6.11b}$$

$\therefore$ Equation (6.10b) becomes

$$v_2' = \frac{m_0}{m_2}(v_0 - v_2' + e v_0) \tag{6.10c}$$

or,

$$v_2' = \frac{(1+e)}{\left(1 + \dfrac{m_2}{m_0}\right)} v_0 \tag{6.11c}$$

Thus, we know the final velocity v_2' of mass m_2 in terms of the velocity v_0 of mass m_0 just before impact.

The equations of motion for the two masses can be written as follows:

$$m_1\ddot{x}_1 + k_1x_1 + k_2(x_1 - x_2) = 0 \tag{6.12a}$$

and

$$m_2\ddot{x}_2 + k_2(x_2 - x_1) = 0 \tag{6.12b}$$

or,

$$\begin{bmatrix} m_1 & 0 \\ 0 & m_2 \end{bmatrix}\begin{Bmatrix} \ddot{x}_1 \\ \ddot{x}_2 \end{Bmatrix} + \begin{bmatrix} k_1 + k_2 & -k_2 \\ -k_2 & k_2 \end{bmatrix}\begin{Bmatrix} x_1 \\ x_2 \end{Bmatrix} = \begin{Bmatrix} 0 \\ 0 \end{Bmatrix} \tag{6.12c}$$

The initial conditions are:
At $t = 0; x_1 = 0, x_2 = 0, \dot{x}_1 = 0$, and $\dot{x}_2 = v_2'$
There are two degrees-of-freedom x_1 and x_2. The analysis of a two-mass system or 2-DOF system is explained in Chapter 9.
The characteristic equation of vibration of the two-DOF system is follows:

$$\omega^4 - \left(\frac{k_2}{m_2} + \frac{k_1 + k_2}{m_1}\right)\omega^2 + \frac{k_1}{m_1}\frac{k_2}{m_2} = 0 \tag{6.13}$$

Its solution will give four values of ω, two positive values and two negative values. However, we are not interested in the negative frequencies since they are not admissible.

The solution for the response of the system will be discussed in Chapters 9 and 10.

6.4 DESIGN CRITERIA FOR MACHINE FOUNDATIONS

All machine foundations must satisfy *three criteria*:

1. that resonance does not occur between the frequencies of the pulsating loads and natural frequency of foundation/soil system,
2. the amplitude of vibration does not exceed safe limits as prescribed by the machine manufacturer, and
3. The foundations should be so dimensioned that the resultant force due to the mass of the machine and mass of the foundation passes through the center of gravity of the base contact area. In other words, there should be no *eccentricity* between the center of mass and center of rigidity to avoid torsional vibrations.

There are two interpretations for *eccentricity* for a framed foundation:

1. *Overall eccentricity:* It is defined as the distance between the center of mass of the complete system covering machine and foundation, and center of gravity of the base contact area of the foundation and soil.
2. *Top deck eccentricity:* It is defined as the distance between the center of mass (mass of top deck, machine, and about 25% of the column mass) and center of stiffness of frames.

The eccentricity must be checked along both *x*- and *y*- axes in plan.

The foundation of machine needs to be isolated at all levels from the main building and from other foundations as far as possible. In case there are any overhanging cantilevers, they should be designed to ensure rigidity against vibration. Design criteria based on frequency and amplitude limits can be classified as follows:

1. Limits set by the possibility of damage or uneconomic wear to machinery or associated equipment or both,
2. Limits set by the possibility of damage to building structures,
3. Limits of structural borne vibrations to ensure comfort of person, and
4. Limits set by possibility of disturbance of ground resulting in unacceptable settlement of foundation.

Frequency Ratio

The natural frequency of the foundation soil-system should be higher than the highest disturbing frequency. Alternatively, natural frequency of the foundation-soil system should be kept lower than the lowest disturbing frequency. A foundation may be either *under tuned* and *over tuned* as follows:

$$\frac{\bar{\omega}}{\omega} \leq 0.60 \text{ Under tuned} \tag{6.14a}$$

$$\frac{\bar{\omega}}{\omega} \geq 1.50 \text{ Over tuned} \tag{6.14b}$$

The intent is to keep the frequency ratio away from resonance.

Codes on Machine Foundations

IS 2974 code on machine foundations has five parts for analysis and design of different kinds of machines. These codes give the data on machines to be provided by the machine manufacturer, data required for the site, mass and geometric constraints on the foundation, desirable static and dynamic characteristics, modeling, limiting deflection and frequency ratios, load combinations, damping, minimum grade of concrete, and minimum reinforcement etc. Salient features for various kinds of machine foundations are specified in each of the five parts of IS 2974.

6.4.1 Reciprocating Type Machines

The following data needs to be provided by the machine manufacturer:

- Description of driving and driven machinery,
- Operating speed or speed ranges,
- Number and arrangement of cylinders,
- Distance between axis of main shaft of the machine and the top face of foundation,
- Maximum rated output,
- Gear box ratio where applicable, and
- Maximum operating temperature in the bases of the machine.

For Static Design

A detailed loading diagram comprising plan, elevation and section showing details of communication and point of all loads on foundation.

For Dynamic Design

Details of out of balance forces and couples together with associated frequencies for all possible modes of vibration for driving and driven machinery. These include the following:

- External forces,
- External primary couples,
- External secondary couples, and
- Harmonic torques.

Mass moments of inertia of driving and driven machine about three principal axes should be indicated. Additional information relating to specific machines should be provided where necessary:

1. Loads due to dynamic short circuit conditions, and
2. Loads due to an abnormal sudden stoppage.

6.4.2 Impact Type Machines (Hammer Foundations)

The following data is necessary in order to design such a foundation.

Hammer Details

- Total mass of hammer, that is, mass of frame and falling parts;
- Mass of falling parts, that is, mass of tup and top die;
- Mass of anvil (in case guide frame of the hammer is attached to the anvil, the mass of the frame should be added);
- Energy of impact;
- Number of blows per minute (this may vary depending on full stroke and short stroke);
- Base dimensions of the anvil;
- Manufacturer's drawing showing general cross section, plan, elevation of anvil, frame base, anvil base, etc, including details of anchor bolts;. and
- Coefficient of impact of anvil in extreme case for die-to-die blow.

Details of the Cushion Pad Between Anvil and Block

- Material,
- Elastic modulus,
- Maximum allowable deformation, and
- Allowable stress intensity.

Details of Cushioning Between Foundation Block and Soil, If Provided

1. If resilient pad is used:
    - Material,
    - Elastic modulus,
    - Maximum allowable deformation, and
    - Allowable stress intensity.
2. If springs and dampers are used:
    - Maximum allowable spring deflections for normal working as well as for extreme conditions and also for static loads as well as for dynamic loads,
    - Details of springs, and
    - Details of dampers.

6.4.3 Rotary Type Machines with Medium and High Frequency

The following data must be made available to the designer by the machine manufacturer:

- Loading diagram of the machine showing the location, magnitude and direction of all loads including dynamic loads;
- Speed of the machine;
- Critical speeds of the machine;
- Outline dimensions of the foundation;
- Mass moment of inertia of the machine components;
- Details of inserts and embedments;
- Layout of piping, ducting, etc. and their supporting details;
- Temperatures in various zones during operation; and
- Allowable displacements at the machine bearing points during normal operation.

The following loads should be considered for the foundation design:

- Dead loads which include the self–weight of the foundation and dead weight of the machine;
- Operation loads supplied by the machine manufacturer which include friction forces, power torque, thermal elongation forces, vacuum in the condenser, piping forces, etc;
- Unbalance forces during normal operation;
- Temperature forces caused by uniform temperature change and gradient temperature;
- Short circuit breaker;
- Loss of blade unbalance forces/bearing failure load;
- Seismic forces; and
- Erection loads.

IS 2974 part III gives further guidelines on how to size the foundation, top deck, girders, columns and base mat etc.

6.4.4 Rotary Type Machines with Low Frequency

IS 2974 part IV specifies machine data, design data, load combinations and other details. As a rule, the equipment foundation must not be allowed to serve as a support for other structures or for machineries not related to the particular equipment.

Isolation To avoid transmission of vibration to adjoining parts of buildings or other foundations, it is necessary to provide a suitable isolation between the equipment foundation and the adjoining structures. This may commonly be achieved by providing sand trench around the foundation block, the thickness and depth of which should be determined for each individual case.

The natural frequencies of the foundation depend upon the size of foundation in terms of total mass and contact area. Therefore, the mass and contact area should be decided taking into consideration the dynamic characteristics. The mass of the foundation should be at least 2.5 times the mass of the whole machine.

6.4.5 Impact Machines Other Than Hammer (Forging and Stamping Press, Pig Breaker, Drop Crusher and Jolter)

IS 2974 part V gives necessary data required for static and dynamic analysis, load cases for dynamic analysis, general provisions of design, and construction details.

More details can be seen in IS:13301, ISO 4866 (IS:4866), ISO 10811 and ISO 10816 codes.

6.5 UNDAMPED VIBRATIONS

Let us idealize a machine foundation as a 2D system for motion in each of the following planes:

1. Motion in *X*-*Z* plane
2. Motion in *Y*-*Z* plane, and
3. Motion in *X*-*Y* plane (torsional vibration).

6.5.1 Free Vibrations

Motion in X-Z Plane or Y-Z Plane

Consider a machine foundation supported on translational spring k_s connected at the center of gravity of the base area of the RC block as shown in Figure 6.7. The equation of motion of free vibrations of such an undamped SDOF system is given by Equation (2.3b) as derived earlier in Chapter 2. Its solution is given by Equation (2.9).

$$m\ddot{x}(t)+k_s x(t)=0 \tag{2.3b}$$

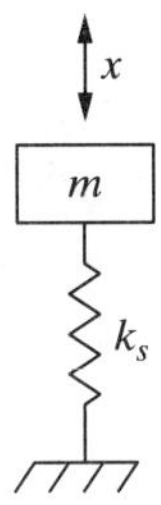

Figure 6.7 Machine foundation on translational spring

Motion in X-Z plane

Consider a machine foundation supported on a rotational spring k_θ connected at the center of the base area of the RC block as shown in Figure 6.8(a). The block is constrained to rotate only in the *X*-*Z* plane about *Y*-axis passing through *O*.

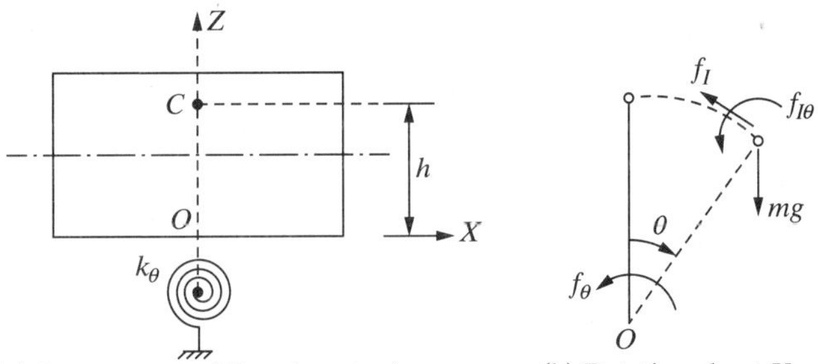

(a) System at rest (Elevation view) (b) Rotation about *Y*-axis

Figure 6.8 Machine foundation in *X*-*Z* plane

Let us consider the following:

Mass of RC block including machine = m acting at the centroid C

Mass moment of inertia of RC block

= M_{cy} acting about *Y*-axis passing through the centroid C

= M_{oy} acting about *Y*-axis passing through point O, center of the base

$$M_{oy} = M_{cy} + mh^2 \tag{6.15a}$$

h = height between centroid of the machine foundation C and center of the base O

The displaced position of the center line of the block is shown in Figure 6.8(b). The free body diagram shows:

$$\text{Inertia force } f_{I\theta} = M_{cy}\ddot{\theta}$$

$$\text{Inertia force } f_I = mh\ddot{\theta}$$

$$\text{Spring force (rotational) } f_s = k_\theta \theta$$

$$\text{Self weight} = mg$$

Equilibrium of the moments about point O gives,

$$f_{I\theta} + f_I h + f_s - mgh\sin\theta = 0 \tag{6.15b}$$

or,

$$M_{cy}\ddot{\theta}(t) + mh^2\ddot{\theta}(t) + k_\theta\theta(t) - mgh\theta(t) = 0 \text{ if } \sin\theta \approx \theta \tag{6.15c}$$

or,

$$(M_{cy} + mh^2)\ddot{\theta}(t) + (k_\theta - mgh)\theta(t) = 0 \tag{6.15d}$$

This is the *equation of motion* of the undamped vibrations of a SDOF system. Rocking natural frequency of the foundation system about y-axis (parallel to the shorter dimension) is given by

$$\omega_{\theta y} = \sqrt{\frac{k_\theta - mgh}{M_{cy} + mh^2}} \text{ rad/s} \tag{6.16}$$

The undamped free vibration response of the block in X-Z plane is given by

$$\theta(t) = A\cos\omega_\theta t + B\sin\omega_\theta t \tag{6.17}$$

where the constants A and B can be evaluated using the initial conditions.

Motion in Y-Z plane

An expression similar to Equations (6.15) to (6.17) can be derived for undamped free vibrations in Y-Z plane. The natural frequency of vibration about X-axis (parallel to the longer dimension) is referred to as the *pitching* frequency.

Motion in X-Y plane (Torsional vibration)

The rotational spring k_ψ is connected at the center of the base area of the RC block in plan as shown in Figure 6.9(a). It rotates about the vertical axis Z.

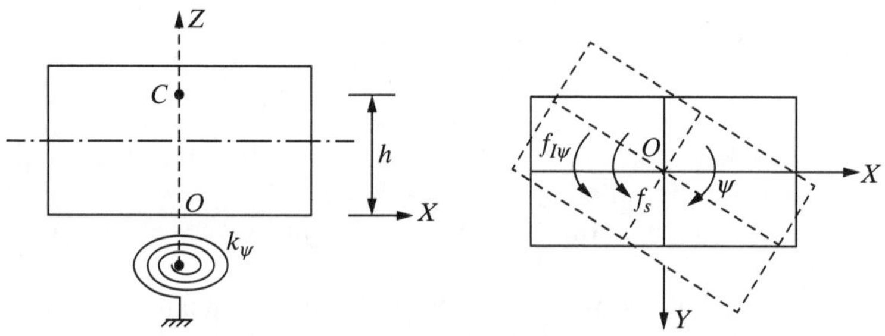

(a) System at rest (Elevation view) (b) Rotation about Z-axis (Plan view)

Figure 6.9 Machine foundation in X-Y plane

Mass of RC block including machine = M acting at the centroid C

Mass moment of inertia of RC block

= M_{cz} acting about Z-axis passing through the centroid C

= M_{oz} acting about Z-axis passing through the point O, center of the base

$$M_{oz} = M_{cz} \tag{6.18a}$$

The displaced position of the center line of the block is shown in Figure 6.9(b). The free body diagram shows:

$$\text{Inertia force } f_{I\psi} = M_{oz}\ddot{\psi}$$

Spring force (rotational) $f_s = k_\psi \psi$

k_ψ = torsional stiffness of the spring about Z-axis passing through point O, at the center of the base (in plan) where the spring is attached

Equilibrium of the forces gives,

$$f_{I\psi} + f_s = 0 \tag{6.18b}$$

or,

$$M_{oz}\ddot{\psi}(t) + k_\psi \psi(t) = 0 \tag{6.18c}$$

This is the *equation of motion* of the undamped vibrations of a SDOF system. Yawing natural frequency of the foundation system about z-axis is given by

$$\omega_{\psi z} = \sqrt{\frac{k_\psi}{M_{oz}}} = \sqrt{\frac{k_\psi}{M_{cz}}} \text{ rad/s} \tag{6.19}$$

The undamped free vibration response of the block in X-Y plane is given by

$$\psi(t) = A\cos\omega_\psi t + B\sin\omega_\psi t \tag{6.20}$$

6.5.2 Forced Vibrations

The equations of motion for undamped and damped forced vibrations can be derived as discussed in Chapter 3.

Motion in X-Z plane

For a machine supported on translational springs and subjected to a sinusoidal force $p(t) = p_0 \sin\bar{\omega} t$, the equation of motion can be written as follows:

$$m\ddot{x}(t) + k_s x(t) = p_0 \sin\bar{\omega}t \tag{3.2}$$

Its solution is given by Equation (3.4).

Motion in X-Z plane

For a machine supported on rotational springs and subjected to a sinusoidal moment force.

$M(t) = M_0 \sin\bar{\omega} t$, applied at point O, the equation of motion can be written as follows:

$$(M_{cy} + mh^2)\ddot{\theta}(t) + (k_\theta - mgh)\theta(t) = M_0 \sin\bar{\omega}t \tag{6.21}$$

Its solution is similar to that given by Equation (3.4).

$$\theta(t) = A\sin\omega t + B\cos\omega t + \frac{M_0}{(k_\theta - mgh)} \times \frac{1}{1-\beta_\theta^2}\sin\bar{\omega}t \tag{6.22}$$

6.5.3 MDOF Systems

If the foundation block is supported on more than one spring, for example, translational spring k_x and rotational spring $k_{\theta y}$, it will have two degrees of freedom. If it is supported on three springs, that is, vertical, lateral and a rotational spring, it will have three degrees of freedom. Accordingly, its equation of motion can be derived as discussed in Chapter 10.

6.6 ILLUSTRATIVE EXAMPLES

Example 6.1

A machine having a weight of 40 kN is supported on a RC block which is supported on a vertical translational spring shown in Figure 6.10. A dynamic force of 5 kN at 500 r.p.m. is applied to the machine through the center of gravity of the mass. Design the block foundation if the permissible displacement amplitude is 80 microns.

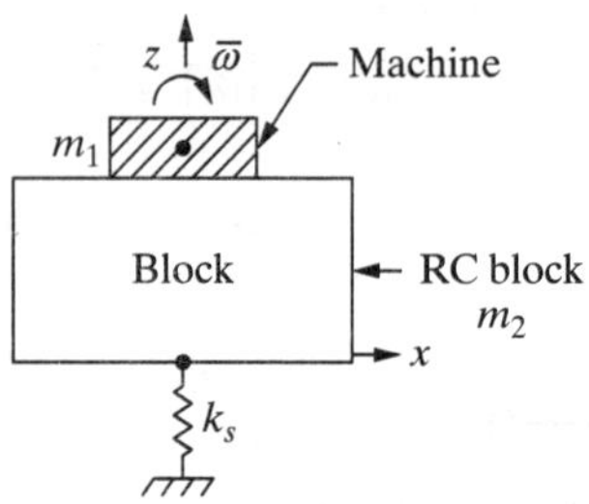

Figure 6.10 2D model of RC block in *X-Z* plane

Solution

Forcing frequency = 500 rpm or $\bar{\omega} = \dfrac{2\pi 500}{60} = 52.36$ rad/s

Dynamic force $P(t) = P_0 \sin \bar{\omega}t = 5000 \sin(52.36t)\ N$

Let frequency ratio $\beta = 2$

∴ Natural frequency of the foundation system is given by

$$\beta = \frac{\bar{\omega}}{\omega} = 2, \text{ or } \omega = \frac{52.36}{2} = 26.18 \text{ rad/s}$$

Let us assume that the mass of the foundation is 8 times the mass of the machine, that is,
Mass of machine $m_1 = 40$ kN/g = 40000/9.81 = 4077 kg
Mass of foundation $m_2 = 8 \times 4077 = 32620$ kg
Total mass = $m_1 + m_2 = 36700$ kg
∴ Translational spring stiffness is given by

$$\omega = \sqrt{\frac{k_s}{m}}$$

or, $$k_s = m\omega^2 = 36700 \times 26.18^2 = 25.15 \times 10^6 \text{ N/m}$$

Density of concrete = 25 kN/m^3
∴ Volume of concrete block = (8 × 40)/25 = 12.8 m^3
Let the thickness of concrete block =1 m, ∴ area of concrete block = 12.8 m^2
Let us provide an area of 3.6 × 3.6 m in plan.

In an undamped system,

Steady state amplitude $= x_0 = Dx_{st} = \dfrac{P_0 / k}{|1-\beta^2|}$

$$\therefore \qquad x_0 = \frac{5000 / 25.15 \times 10^6}{|1-2^2|} = 6.63 \times 10^{-5}\,\text{m} \equiv 0.0663\ \text{mm}$$

or, $\qquad x_0 = 66\,\mu < 80\,\mu$ OK

Thus, a foundation block of 3.6 × 3.6 × 1 m satisfies the design requirements. □

Example 6.2

A machine having a weight of 40 kN is supported on a RC block (3 m × 4 m × 1 m high) which is supported on a rotational spring having a stiffness of 70 × 10³ kNm/rad. The height of c.g. of machine above the top of foundation block is 150 mm as shown in Figure 6.11. A dynamic force of 5 kN at 50 rad/s is acting at the c.g. of the machine. Find the natural frequency and maximum amplitude of vibration at the c.g. of the machine.

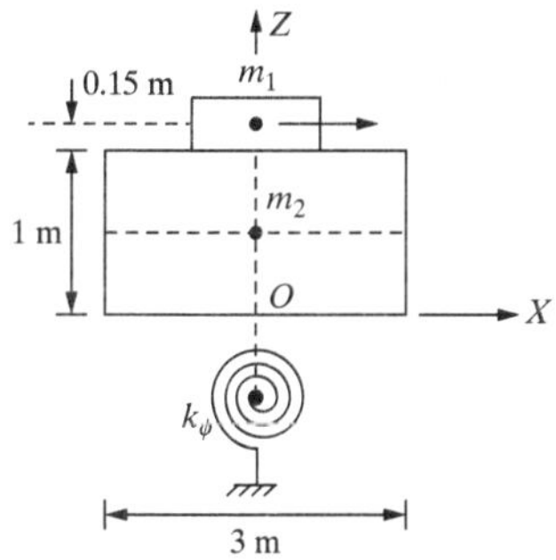

Figure 6.11 2D model of the machine in *X-Z* plane

Solution

Weight of the machine $W_1 = 40$ kN

∴ Mass of the machine $m_1 = 40000/\text{g} = 4077$ kg

Weight of RC block $W_2 = 3 \times 4 \times 1 \times 25 = 300$ kN

∴ Mass of the RC block $m_2 = 300 \times 1000/\text{g} = 30580$ kg

Total mass $= m_1 + m_2 = 4077 + 30580 = 34657$ kg

The system rotates about the *Y*-axis passing through the point *O* at the bottom of the base. Let us compute mass moment of inertia about point *O*.

$$I_{my} = 3058\left\{\frac{(3^2+1^2)}{12} + 0.5^2\right\} + 4077 \times (1+0.15)^2 = 38520\ \text{kg m}^2$$

where,

$$\text{Mass moment of inertia of a rectangular plate} = m\left(\frac{a^2+b^2}{12}\right)$$

$$\text{Natural frequency of vibration } \omega_{y\phi} = \sqrt{\frac{k_\phi}{I_{my}}} = \sqrt{\frac{70 \times 10^6}{38520}} = 42.63\ \text{rad/s}$$

The dynamic force $P(t)$ acting at the machine center causes a dynamic moment M_ϕ about O

$$\therefore\ M_\phi = P(t)\,(1 + 0.15) = 5 \times 1.15 = 5.75 \text{ kNm}$$

Dynamic amplification ratio for vibration about point O

$$D_\phi = \frac{\phi_{max}}{M_\phi / k_\phi} = \frac{1}{1-\beta_\phi^2}.$$

Or, maximum dynamic amplitude ϕ_{max} is given by

$$\phi_{max} = \frac{M_\phi}{k_\phi}\left|\frac{1}{1-\beta_\phi^2}\right|$$

$$\phi_{max} = \frac{5.75}{70\times10^3}\left|\frac{1}{1-\left(\dfrac{50}{42.63}\right)^2}\right| = 8.214\times2.66\times10^{-5} = 2.185\times10^{-4} \text{ rad}$$

Amplitude at the c.g. of the machine along x-direction $= 2.185 \times 10^{-4} \times (1 + 0.15)$
$= 2.51 \times 10^{-4}$ m $= 251$ microns □

Example 6.3

A drop hammer foundation has the following data:

Mass of tup $m_0 = 1500$ kg

Mass of anvil $m_2 = 32000$ kg

Mass of foundation $m_1 = 135000$ kg

Stiffness of elastic pad below anvil $k_2 = 6.10\text{E}05$ kN/m

Stiffness of soil below foundation base $k_1 = 7.5\text{E}05$ kN/m

Factor for impact efficiency $\chi = 0.65$

Coefficient of restitution $e = 0.60$

Height fall of tup $h = 1.7$ m

Determine the final velocity of anvil just after impact, frequencies, and mode shapes of the 2-DOF system.

Solution

The velocity of mass $m_0 = v_0 = \sqrt{2gh}$

$$v_0 = \sqrt{2\times9.81\times1.7} = 5.60 \text{ m/s}$$

Thus, initial velocity of mass $m_0 = \chi\, v_0 = 0.65 \times 5.6 = 3.64$ m/s

Let velocity of mass just *after* impact $= v_2'$

$$v_2' = \frac{(1+e)}{\left(1+\dfrac{m_2}{m_0}\right)} v_0$$

or,
$$v_2' = \frac{(1+0.6)}{\left(1+\dfrac{32000}{1500}\right)} \times 3.64 = 0.26 \text{ m/s}$$

The equation of motion of the 2-DOF system is

$$\begin{bmatrix} m_1 & 0 \\ 0 & m_2 \end{bmatrix} \begin{Bmatrix} \ddot{x}_1 \\ \ddot{x}_2 \end{Bmatrix} + \begin{bmatrix} k_1+k_2 & -k_2 \\ -k_2 & k_2 \end{bmatrix} \begin{Bmatrix} x_1 \\ x_2 \end{Bmatrix} = \begin{Bmatrix} 0 \\ 0 \end{Bmatrix}$$

$$\text{Mass matrix } [M] \text{ in kg} = \begin{bmatrix} m_1 & 0 \\ 0 & m_2 \end{bmatrix} = \begin{bmatrix} 135000 & 0 \\ 0 & 32000 \end{bmatrix}$$

$$\text{Stiffness matrix } [K] \text{ in N/m} = \begin{bmatrix} k_1+k_2 & -k_2 \\ -k_2 & k_2 \end{bmatrix} = \begin{bmatrix} 13.6E08 & -6.1E08 \\ -6.1E08 & 6.1E08 \end{bmatrix}$$

MATLAB solution using function *eig* gives the natural frequencies and mode shapes as follows:

$$\{\omega\} = \begin{Bmatrix} 65.24 \\ 157.74 \end{Bmatrix} \text{ rad/sec}$$

The mode shapes are as follows and shown in Figure 6.12.

$$\{\phi_1\} = \begin{Bmatrix} 0.766 \\ 1.0 \end{Bmatrix} \text{ and } \{\phi_2\} = \begin{Bmatrix} -0.30 \\ 1 \end{Bmatrix}$$

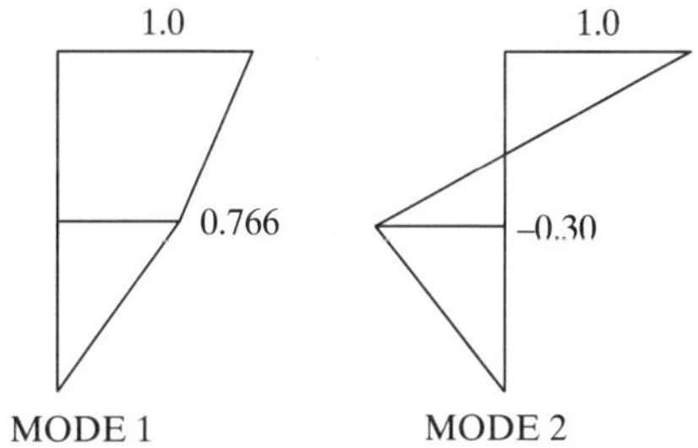

Figure 6.12 Mode shapes

Initial conditions after the impact are as follows:

$$\{x(0)\} = \begin{Bmatrix} x_1(0) \\ x_2(0) \end{Bmatrix} = \begin{Bmatrix} 0 \\ 0 \end{Bmatrix} \text{ and } \{\dot{x}(0)\} = \begin{Bmatrix} \dot{x}_1(0) \\ \dot{x}_2(0) \end{Bmatrix} = \begin{Bmatrix} 0 \\ 0.26 \end{Bmatrix}$$

The response of the anvil $x_2(t)$ and foundation $x_1(t)$ in the each of the two modes will be calculated using modal analysis in Chapter 10. □

6.7 VIBRATION ISOLATION DUE TO BASE EXCITATION

Let us consider a single-degree-of-freedom system as shown in Figure 6.13(a). Let the motion of the mass be $x(t)$ and that of the base be $y(t) = y_0 \sin \bar{\omega} t$. The free body diagram of the system is shown in Figure 6.13(b) The equation of motion can be written by taking into account the relative motion between the mass and the base, that is,

$$m\ddot{x} + c(\dot{x} - \dot{y}) + k(x - y) = 0 \tag{6.23a}$$

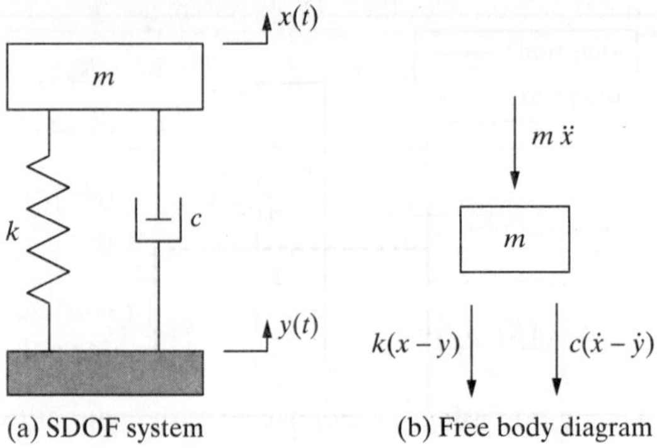

Figure 6.13 SDOF system under base excitation.

The force of inertia is not dependent on the ground motion. That is why it is taken as its absolute value. Equation (6.1a) can be re-written as follows:

$$m\ddot{x} + c\dot{x} + kx = c\dot{y} + ky \tag{6.23b}$$

where,

$$y = y_0 \sin \bar{\omega} t \tag{6.23c}$$

Substituting the values of $y(t)$ and $\dot{y}(t)$, we get

$$m\ddot{x} + c\dot{x} + kx = c\,\bar{\omega}\,y_0 \cos \bar{\omega} t + k\,y_0 \sin \bar{\omega} t \tag{6.24}$$

The right-hand side term can be re-written in terms of its amplitude

$$= y_0 \sqrt{(c\bar{\omega})^2 + k^2}\ \sin(\bar{\omega} t + \phi) \tag{6.25a}$$

or,

$$m\ddot{x} + c\dot{x} + kx = p_0 \sin(\bar{\omega} t + \phi) \tag{6.25b}$$

where,

$p_0 = y_0\sqrt{(c\bar{\omega})^2 + k^2}$ It has the unit of force

$$\phi = \tan^{-1}\frac{c\bar{\omega}}{k} \tag{6.25c}$$

= phase lag between ground motion and system response

Equation (6.25a) is similar to the equation of a forced vibration problem derived in Chapter 3. The only difference is the amplitude of the forcing function and the existence of a phase difference ϕ. The phase difference can be ignored if we choose to measure time from a different origin. Thus, the amplitude of vibration of the motion can be obtained. The equation of motion, Equation (6.25b), can be written as follows:

$$m\ddot{x} + c\dot{x} + kx = p_0 \sin \bar{\omega} t' \tag{6.26}$$

The time t' is measured from a different origin so that the phase difference ϕ is zero. Let us drop the symbol (′) for ease while retaining its definition.

The steady state solution can be written as follows:

$$x = y_0 \sin\bar{\omega}t \; \frac{\sqrt{k^2 + c^2\bar{\omega}^2}}{\sqrt{(k - m\bar{\omega})^2 + c^2\bar{\omega}^2}} \tag{6.27a}$$

Phase difference

$$\phi = \tan^{-1}\frac{c\bar{\omega}}{(k - m\bar{\omega})} \tag{6.27b}$$

Dividing by m in denominator as well as numerator and taking maximum displacement

$$\frac{x_{\max}}{y_0} = \frac{\sqrt{\dfrac{k^2}{m^2} + \dfrac{c^2\bar{\omega}^2}{m^2}}}{\sqrt{\left(\dfrac{k}{m} - \bar{\omega}\right)^2 + \dfrac{c^2\bar{\omega}^2}{m^2}}}$$

or,

$$\frac{x_{\max}}{y_0} = \frac{\sqrt{\omega^4 + (2\xi\omega\bar{\omega})^2}}{\sqrt{(\omega^2 - \bar{\omega}^2)^2 + (2\xi\omega\bar{\omega})^2}}$$

or,

$$\frac{x_{\max}}{y_0} = \frac{\sqrt{1 + (2\beta\xi)^2}}{\sqrt{(1 - \beta^2)^2 + (2\beta\xi)^2}} \tag{6.28}$$

or,

$$\text{TR} = D\sqrt{1 + (2\beta\xi)^2} \tag{6.29}$$

where,

$$\text{TR} = \text{Transmissibility ratio} = \frac{\text{amplitude of motion of mass}}{\text{amplitude of ground motion}} \tag{6.30}$$

D = dynamic magnification factor obtained earlier for steady state response due to harmonic loading.

β = ratio of the frequency of the forcing function to that of the natural vibration of the foundation.

The frequency of the forcing function means frequency of vibration of the ground motion or ground vibrations.

Transmissibility ratio is a measure of how much vibration is transmitted to the mass from the foundation below. Thus, (1 – TR) is a measure of effectiveness of the isolation system. A plot of TR vs. frequency ratio β is shown in Figure 6.14 for different damping ratios.

If TR = 1,

$$\sqrt{1 + (2\beta\xi)^2} = \sqrt{\left(1 - \beta^2\right)^2 + (2\beta\xi)^2}$$

or,

$$1 = \left(1 - \beta^2\right)^2$$

or,

$$1 - \beta^2 = \pm 1$$

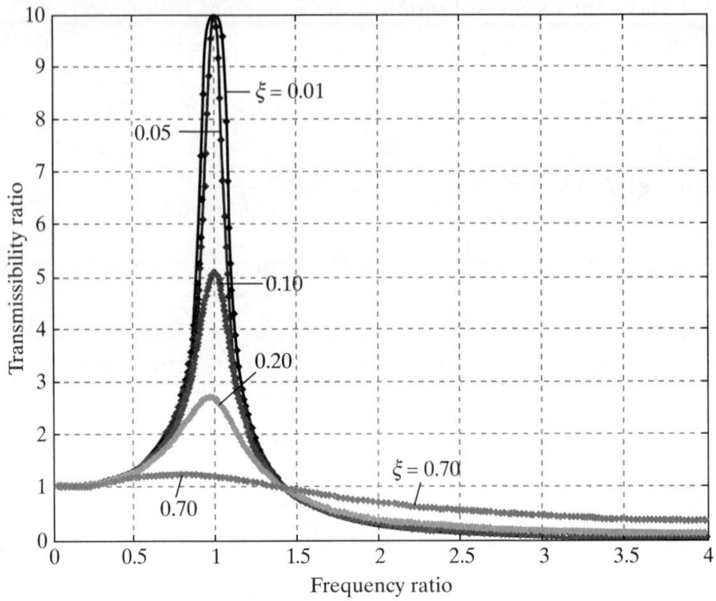

Figure 6.14 Transmissibility ratio vs. frequency ratio for different damping.

or,
$$\beta = 0 \text{ or } \sqrt{2} \tag{6.31}$$

It can be seen in Figure 6.14 that for a frequency ratio β greater than $\sqrt{2}$, TR is always less than 1. Hence there is no magnification of the ground vibrations.

It is interesting to understand the curves of Figure 6.14. The following observations can be made:

(a) For a frequency ratio $\beta > \sqrt{2}$, the transmissibility ratio TR is always less than 1 irrespective of damping ξ.
(b) For a frequency ratio $\beta < \sqrt{2}$, increase in damping reduces the displacement amplitude. However, for a frequency ratio $\beta > \sqrt{2}$, increase in damping increases the displacement amplitude.
(c) For TR < 1, the frequency ratio β should be >> 1. It means the natural frequency of the foundation should be very small, that is, it should have a very low stiffness. Again, damping should also be very low in this region.

There is a need to carefully choose the stiffness and damping parameters in order to arrive at a satisfactory solution meeting all the specified design criteria under static and dynamic operating conditions.

6.7.1 Isolation of Ground Acceleration

An alternative formulation in terms of ground acceleration can also be derived. If the SDOF system is subjected to harmonic ground motion, that is,

$$\ddot{y}(t) = \ddot{y}_0 \sin(\bar{\omega} t) \tag{6.32}$$

and the total acceleration of the mass is given by

$$\ddot{x}^t(t) = \ddot{x}(t) + \ddot{y}(t) \tag{6.33}$$

where,

$$x(t) = \frac{p_0}{k} D \sin(\bar{\omega}t - \phi) \tag{6.34a}$$

and

$$p_0 = |-m\,\ddot{y}|_{\max} \tag{6.34b}$$

∴ Equation (6.34a) can be written as follows:

$$x(t) = \frac{-m\ddot{y}_0}{k} D \sin(\bar{\omega}t - \phi) \tag{6.34c}$$

Substituting the values of accelerations from Equations (6.34c) and (6.32) into Equation (6.33), and rearranging the equation leads to Equation (6.28). Thus,

$$\text{TR} = \frac{\ddot{x}_0^t}{\ddot{y}_0} = \frac{\text{acceleration transmitted to the mass}}{\text{amplitude of ground acceleration}} \tag{6.35}$$

The transmissibility is defined in terms of displacement transmitted to the mass or acceleration transmitted to the mass. The undesirable ground vibrations can be isolated by properly designing the vertical stiffness and damping of the foundation system, that is, k and c. The expression given by Equation (6.35) is significant while designing vibration measuring instruments.

6.8 VIBRATION ISOLATION DUE TO ROTATING UNBALANCE

A machine is mounted on a foundation as shown in Figure 6.15. It is quite possible that when the machine is in motion at $\bar{\omega}$ rotations per minute (rpm), it may transmit vibrations through its foundation to the adjoining areas. The machine has an unbalanced mass of m' acting at a radius of r from its center of rotation. It will produce a

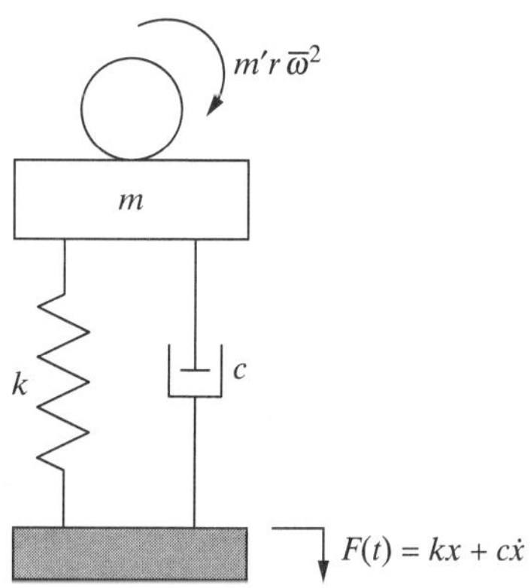

Figure 6.15 A machine foundation under rotating unbalance.

centrifugal force equal to $m' r \bar{\omega}^2$. Even though a machine is always designed to be balanced, there may still be some small unbalance causing significant vibrations. This is a problem of designing a machine foundation.

$$\text{Vertical component of centrifugal force} = m' r \bar{\omega}^2 \sin \bar{\omega} t \tag{6.36}$$

Therefore, the equation of motion of a SDOF system is given by

$$m\ddot{x} + c\dot{x} + kx = m' r \bar{\omega}^2 \sin \bar{\omega} t \tag{6.37a}$$

$$= p_0 \sin(\bar{\omega} t) \tag{6.37b}$$

Steady state response $$x(t) = \frac{p_0}{k} D \sin(\bar{\omega} t - \phi) \tag{6.34a}$$

The amplitude of the motion is given by

$$x_{\max} = \frac{p_0}{k} D = \frac{m' r \bar{\omega}^2}{m\omega^2} D \tag{6.38a}$$

$$= \left(\frac{m'}{m}\right) r \left(\frac{\bar{\omega}}{\omega}\right)^2 \frac{1}{\sqrt{\left(1 - \left(\frac{\bar{\omega}}{\omega}\right)^2\right)^2 + \left(2\xi \frac{\bar{\omega}}{\omega}\right)^2}}$$

or, $$x_{\max} = \frac{(m'/m) r \beta^2}{\sqrt{(1-\beta^2)^2 + (2\xi\beta)^2}} \tag{6.38b}$$

At resonance, $$x_{\max} = \frac{m' r}{2m\xi} \tag{6.38c}$$

For very large values of the frequency ratio β, Equation (6.38b) reduces to

$$x_{\max} = \frac{m' r}{m} \tag{6.38d}$$

Force transmitted to foundation through the spring and dash-pot system is equal to

$$F_t = c\dot{x} + kx \tag{6.39a}$$

∴ $$\dot{x}(t) = \frac{p_0}{k} D \cos(\bar{\omega} t - \phi) \bar{\omega} \tag{6.39b}$$

The spring force $f_s = k\,x(t)$ and damping force $f_d = c\dot{x}(t)$
Total force transmitted to the foundation is given by

$$f(t) = f_s(t) + f_d(t) \tag{6.40a}$$

or, $$= p_0 D \sin(\bar{\omega} t - \phi) + 2\beta\xi\, p_0 D \cos(\bar{\omega} t - \phi) \tag{6.40b}$$

Its amplitude is given by

$$F_{t\max} = \sqrt{(p_0 D)^2 + (2\beta\xi p_0 D)^2}$$

or, $$= p_0 D\sqrt{1+(2\beta\xi)^2}$$

or, $$\frac{F_{t\,max}}{m'r\bar{\omega}^2} = \frac{\sqrt{1+(2\beta\xi)^2}}{\sqrt{(1-\beta^2)^2+(2\beta\xi)^2}} \quad (6.41)$$

This is same as Equation (6.28).

β is ratio of forcing frequency of the machine to natural frequency of the system. Transmissibility ratio is defined as follows:

$$\text{TR} = \frac{\text{Maximum force applied on the base}}{\text{amplitude of the force}} \quad (6.42a)$$

or, $$\text{TR} = D\sqrt{1+(2\xi\beta)^2} \quad (6.42b)$$

The Equation (6.42b) is the same as Equation (6.29) plotted in Figure 6.14. Although the quantity being transmitted is different.

Let us consider Equation 6.38b and plot the dimensionless steady state displacement as follows:

$$\frac{x_{max}}{(m'/m)r} = \frac{\beta^2}{\sqrt{(1-\beta^2)^2+(2\xi\beta)^2}} \quad (6.38b)$$

Its plot for various values of damping ratio is shown in Figure 6.16. The following observations can be made:

1. The maximum displacement ratio is less than or equal to 1 for any system with $\xi > 1$. This indicates that the increase in displacement caused by unbalance can be eliminated by increasing damping in the system. Although it is not practically possible to have a very large damping.

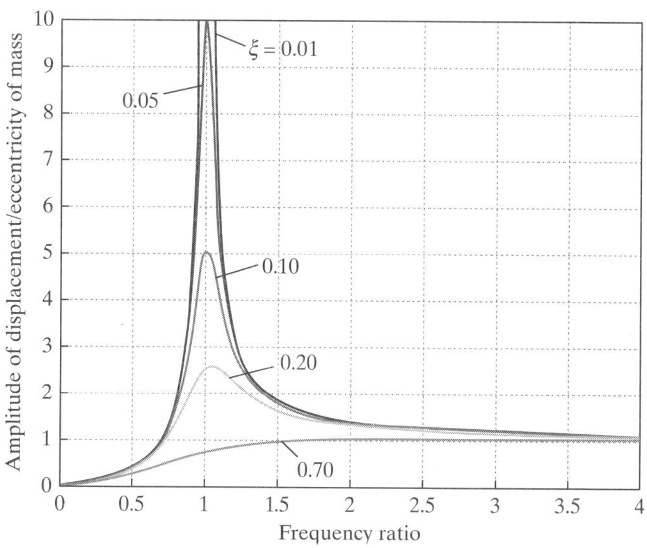

Figure 6.16 Ratio of displacement to eccentricity of mass vs. frequency ratio for different damping

2. The magnitude of displacement approaches unity if the frequency ratio β is large. It means at large frequency ratios; the effect of unbalance is limited.
3. At large values of frequency ratio β, all the displacement curves for each value of damping ξ approach unity. It means the choice of damping coefficient for large β is not important.

This information is quite useful in the design of foundations for rotating machines. The undesirable vibrations are isolated from being transmitted to the foundation by designing the vertical stiffness k and damping c of the foundation.

The effectiveness for zero damping is given by Equation (6.28):

$$\text{TR} = \pm\frac{1}{(1-\beta^2)}$$

For β greater than 1, it can be written as follows:

$$\text{TR} = \frac{1}{\beta^2 - 1} \tag{6.43a}$$

or,

$$1 - \text{TR} = \frac{\beta^2 - 2}{\beta^2 - 1} = E, \text{ say (where } \beta > \sqrt{2}) \tag{6.43b}$$

The term ($E = 1 - \text{TR}$) is a measure of effectiveness of the vibration isolation system, that is, degree of vibration cut-off. If TR is 15%, it means 85% vibrations were isolated or cut-off.

If frequency ratio

$$\beta = \frac{\bar{\omega}}{\omega} = \frac{\bar{\omega}}{\sqrt{\frac{k}{m}}}$$

Equation (6.43b) can be re-written as follows:

$$\beta^2 = \frac{2-E}{1-E} \tag{6.44a}$$

or,

$$\beta = \frac{\bar{\omega}}{\omega} = \frac{\bar{\omega}}{\sqrt{\frac{k}{m}}} = \sqrt{\frac{2-E}{1-E}} \tag{6.44b}$$

or,

$$\bar{\omega} = \sqrt{\frac{k}{m}\left(\frac{2-E}{1-E}\right)} \tag{6.45}$$

Stiffness is given by $k = \dfrac{mg}{\Delta_{st}}$ where Δ_{st} is static deflection

The forcing frequency, that is, frequency of rotation of the machine in rpm ($\bar{f}$) can be written as follows:

$$\bar{\omega} = 2\pi \bar{f}$$

and

$$\bar{f} = \frac{1}{2\pi}\sqrt{\frac{g}{\Delta_{st}}\frac{2-E}{1-E}} \tag{6.46}$$

If $g = 980$ cm/sec^2, Equation (6.46) can be written as follows:

$$\bar{f} = 4.98\sqrt{\frac{1}{\Delta_{st}}\frac{2-E}{1-E}} \tag{6.47}$$

The static displacement is given in cm and the machine frequency is in radians per sec or in rotation per second. For a given percentage reduction of force transmitted E, a plot can be drawn between frequency of rotation and static displacement. This plot can be used for design of such foundations. For a given machine frequency and desired effectiveness, the support deflection can be estimated from the graph. These curves can also be plotted on a log-log scale.

$$\log \bar{f} = -\frac{1}{2}\log \Delta_{st} + \log\left(4.98\sqrt{\frac{2-E}{1-E}}\right) \tag{6.48}$$

The design curves are shown in Figure 6.17.

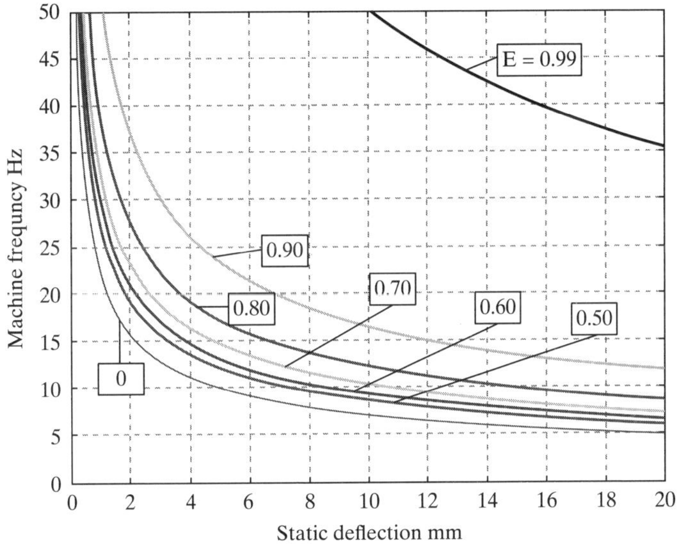

Figure 6.17 Effectiveness of vibration isolation system.

6.9 MONITORING HEALTH OF MACHINE FOUNDATION

The displacement, velocity and acceleration characteristics of vibration are measured to monitor the health of a machine foundation. The amplitude of vibration gives an indication of the condition of the machine and the foundation. Higher the vibration amplitude, greater are the chances of possible defects. The dynamic force created by the vibration of a rotating member can lead to the failure of machine bearings and also that of the foundation. The question arises how to decide if one should measure displacement, velocity or acceleration in a given situation? A motion below 10 Hz (600 rpm) produces very little vibration in terms of acceleration, moderate vibration in terms of velocity and relatively large vibrations in terms of displacement. Hence, displacement is used in this range. In the high frequency range, acceleration is more significant than velocity or displacement. Therefore, measurement of acceleration is preferred for frequencies over 1000 Hz (60k rpm). Between 10 Hz (600 rpm) and 1000 Hz (60k rpm) velocity gives a good indication of the severity of vibration. Since majority of the rotating machinery operates in the 10 to 1000 Hz range, velocity is commonly used for vibration measurements and analysis.

The International Standards Organization (ISO) suggested velocity – root mean square (rms) as the appropriate standard unit of measurement. This was decided in an attempt to develop criteria that would determine an effective value for the varying velocity function. *Velocity – rms* tends to provide the energy content in the vibration signal, whereas the *velocity – peak* correlated better with the intensity of vibration. A higher velocity – rms is generally more damaging than a similar magnitude of velocity – peak. The crest factor of a waveform is the ratio of the peak value of the waveform to its rms value, that is, *peak-to-rms ratio*. The crest factor of a sine wave is $\sqrt{2}$.

The vibration measuring instrument may either give a velocity vs time history or velocity – rms vs frequency history. The natural frequencies of the foundation-machine system and that of the machine are known. Therefore, it is directly possible to take immediate corrective steps as necessary. A typical velocity vs time history plot is shown in Figure 6.18(a). It does not give much meaningful information. Therefore, it is necessary to convert it into frequency domain and make some sense out of the measurements. This is done using *Fast Fourier Transform* (FFT). A computer code may be written in Fortran making use of standard FFT subroutine or MATLAB may be used. The details of the procedure may be found in any text book on *Digital Signal*

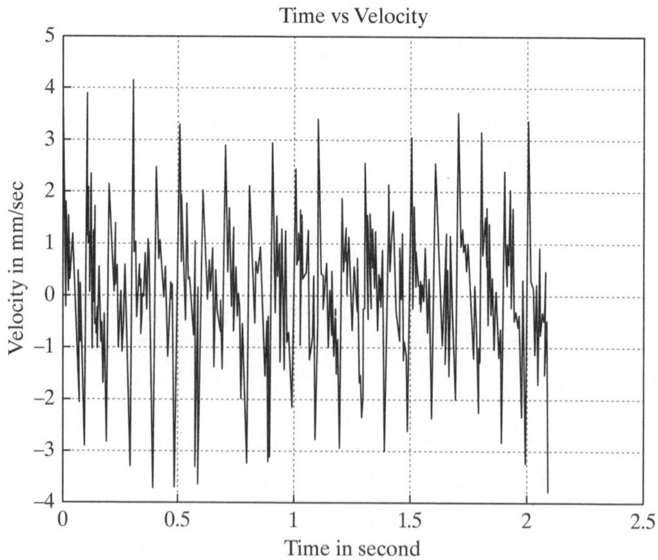

Figure 6.18 (a) Velocity – time series as recorded on a machine foundation

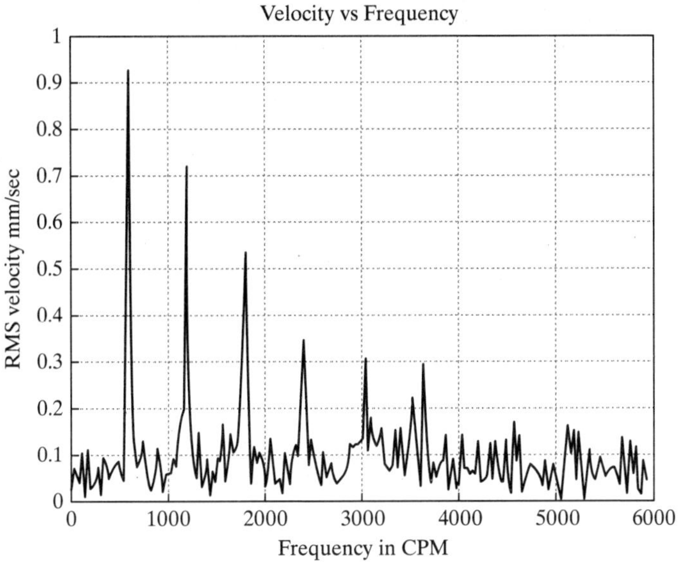

Figure 6.18 (b) Fourier transform of the time series in frequency domain

Processing. A MATLAB code DOS6_3 converts a velocity – time series in velocity – frequency series as shown in Figure 6.18(b). The time series shows that the peak velocity is 4.1 mm/sec and continues to oscillate. However, the frequency response shows distinct rms velocity at different frequencies. The maximum rms velocity is 0.92 mm/sec at 10 Hz (600 rpm), 0.71 mm/sec at 20 Hz (1200 rpm) and 0.53 mm/sec at 30 Hz (1800 rpm) etc. It clearly shows the frequencies at which the response is dominating. Appropriate steps can now be taken to adjust the stiffness and/or damping in order to control the velocity.

Note: The MATLAB code 6_3 is available on the web.

6.10 APPLICATION TO EARTHQUAKE ENGINEERING

In Equation (6.23a), the base motion could be due to an earthquake. This equation can be modified to model the earthquake motion. In vibrations due to earthquakes, we are more interested in the relative displacement of a mass with respect to ground rather than its absolute displacement as shown in Figure 6.19.

Let us re-write Equation (6.23a)

$$m\ddot{x} + c(\dot{x} - \dot{y}) + k(x - y) = 0 \tag{6.23a}$$

Let $x_r = x - y$, $\dot{x}_r = \dot{x} - \dot{y}$ and $\ddot{x}_r = \ddot{x} - \ddot{y}$ (6.49a)

where $x_r, \dot{x}_r$ and $\ddot{x}_r$ are relative displacement, relative velocity and relative acceleration, respectively, of the mass m.

Substituting Equation (6.49a) in Equation (6.23a) gives,

$$m\ddot{x}_r(t)+c\dot{x}_r(t)+kx_r(t)=-m\ddot{y}(t) \tag{6.49b}$$

or, for convenience, the subscript r is dropped, and $\ddot{y}$ is replaced with $\ddot{y}_g$

Thus, we get
$$m\,\ddot{x}(t)+c\dot{x}(t)+k\,x(t)=-m\,\ddot{y}_g(t) \tag{6.50a}$$

or,
$$m\ddot{x}+c\dot{x}+k\,x=-m\,\ddot{y}_g \tag{6.50b}$$

This is the equation of motion of a SDOF system subjected to ground motion $\ddot{y}_g(t)$. It's solution is discussed in Chapters 7 and 8.

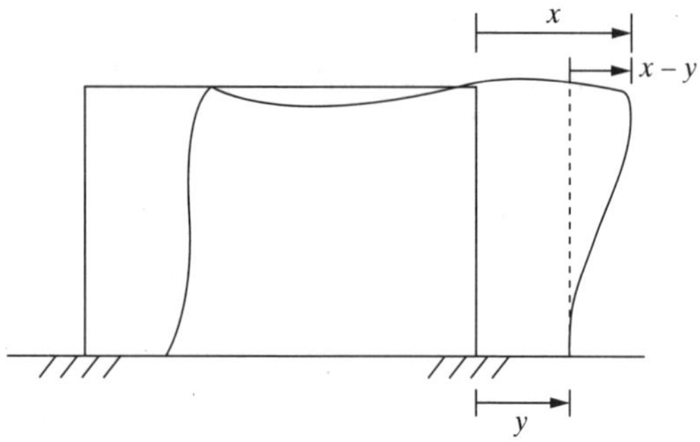

Figure 6.19 A SDOF system under ground displacement.

6.11 ILLUSTRATIVE EXAMPLES

Example 6.4

A machine is supported on a pedestal which can tolerate a vertical deflection of 1×10^{-3} mm under operating conditions. It is subjected to a forcing function causing a base displacement amplitude of 20×10^{-3} mm at a frequency of 10 Hz. Damping may be taken as 2%.

(a) Determine the natural frequency of the system.

(b) If the mass of the machine including platform is 1500 kg, what will be its static deflection?

Solution

(a) Transmissibility ratio (TR) $= \dfrac{\text{amplitude of motion of mass}}{\text{amplitude of ground motion}} = \dfrac{1\times10^{-3}}{20\times10^{-3}} = \dfrac{1}{20}$

$$= \frac{\sqrt{1+(2\beta\xi)^2}}{\sqrt{(1-\beta^2)^2+(2\beta\xi)^2}}$$

For damping ratio $\xi = 2\%$, β can be estimated from Equation (6.7).

It gives frequency ratio $\beta = 4.62 = \dfrac{\overline{\omega}}{\omega} = \dfrac{\overline{f}}{f} = 4.62$

The natural frequency ω or $f = 10/4.62 = 2.16$ Hz

(b) Stiffness of the foundation $k = \text{m}\ \omega^2 = 1500 \times (2\ \pi f)^2 = 276.3$ kN/m

Hence, static deflection under self-weight $\Delta_{st} = \text{mg/k} = \dfrac{1500 \times 9.8}{276.3 \times 10^3} = 53.1 \times 10^{-3}$ m
or, $\Delta_{st} = 53.1$ mm □

Example 6.5

A foundation block is to be installed in a plant such that the vibration from the adjacent areas will not affect it. The mass of the foundation system is 2000 kg and the surrounding floor vibrates at 2500 cycles per minute. Estimate the stiffness of the foundation so that the transmissibility ratio is not more than 10%, if

(a) Damping is ignored
(b) Damping is taken as 30%

Solution

(a) Damping is zero

$$\text{TR} = \pm\frac{1}{1-\beta^2} = 10\%$$

or, $0.1 - 0.1\ \beta^2 = -1$, or, $\beta = \pm\ 3.32 > \sqrt{2}$ OK

Frequency ratio $\beta = \overline{\omega}/\omega = 3.32$

But forcing frequency = $\overline{f}$ = 2500 c.p.m. = 41.67 Hz or, $\overline{\omega} = 6.63$ rad/sec

∴ Natural frequency $\omega = 6.63/3.32 = 2$ rad/sec

∴ Stiffness of the isolated system = $k = \text{m}\ \omega^2 = 2000 \times 2^2 = 8000$ N/m

(b) Damping is 30%

$$\text{TR} = \frac{\sqrt{1+(2\beta\xi)^2}}{\sqrt{(1-\beta^2)^2+(2\beta\xi)^2}}$$

For TR = 0.1, and damping ratio 30%, frequency ratio β is calculated as 6.33

Frequency ratio $\beta = \overline{\omega}/\omega = 6.33$

But forcing frequency = $\overline{\omega} = 6.63$ rad/sec

∴ Natural frequency $\omega = 6.63/6.33 = 1.047$ rad/sec

∴ Stiffness of the isolated system = $k = \text{m}\ \omega^2 = 2000 \times 1.047^2 = 2192$ N/m

It shows that if a highly damped isolation system such as a rubber pad or rubber tyre is used to isolate the vibrations, it will require a very low stiffness. □

Example 6.6

A machine foundation has a mass of 500 kg with a vertical stiffness of 400 kN/m. If the base displacement amplitude is 5 mm, the displacement amplitude of the mass is 10 mm while it is vibrating at its natural frequency. Calculate the damping ratio and damping coefficient.

Solution

It is a problem of base excitation.

$$\text{TR} = \frac{\sqrt{1+(2\beta\xi)^2}}{\sqrt{(1-\beta^2)^2+(2\beta\xi)^2}}$$

At resonance, $\beta = 1$,

$$\text{TR} = \frac{\sqrt{1+(2\xi)^2}}{2\xi} = \frac{10}{5} = 2$$

or,

$$1 + (2\xi)^2 = (4\,\xi)^2$$

or,

$$\xi = 0.288 \text{ or } 28.8\%$$

Natural frequency of the system $\omega = \sqrt{\dfrac{k}{m}} = \sqrt{\dfrac{400\times 1000}{500}} = 63.24$ rad/sec

Damping coefficient $c = 2\,\text{m}\,\omega\,\xi = 2\times 500\times 63.24\times 0.288 = 18213$ kg/sec □

Example 6.7

In Example 6.6, also calculate the force transmitted to the base.

Solution

The force acting at the base $F_t = k(x-y) + c(\dot{x}-\dot{y})$
At equilibrium,

$$m\ddot{x} + c(\dot{x}-\dot{y}) + k(x-y) = 0$$

∴

$$F_t = -m\ddot{x}$$

Let us find the acceleration of the mass by twice differentiating its displacement. The steady state solution is given by Equation (6.27a),

$$x = y_0 \sin\bar{\omega}t \frac{\sqrt{k^2+c^2\bar{\omega}^2}}{\sqrt{(k-m\bar{\omega})^2+c^2\bar{\omega}^2}}$$

∴

$$\ddot{x}(t) = -\bar{\omega}^2 y_0 \sin\bar{\omega}t \frac{\sqrt{k^2+c^2\bar{\omega}^2}}{\sqrt{(k-m\bar{\omega})^2+c^2\bar{\omega}^2}}$$

Thus, force acting at its base $F(t)$ is given by

$$F(t) = -m\ddot{x}(t) = m\bar{\omega}^2 y_0 \sin\bar{\omega}t \frac{\sqrt{k^2+c^2\bar{\omega}^2}}{\sqrt{(k-m\bar{\omega})^2+c^2\bar{\omega}^2}}$$

or,

$$F(t) = k\beta^2 y_0 \sin\bar{\omega}t \frac{\sqrt{k^2+c^2\bar{\omega}^2}}{\sqrt{(k-m\bar{\omega})^2+c^2\bar{\omega}^2}}$$

The amplitude of the force transmitted to the base is given by

$$F = ky_0\beta^2 \frac{\sqrt{k^2 + c^2\bar{\omega}^2}}{\sqrt{(k - m\bar{\omega})^2 + c^2\bar{\omega}^2}}$$

This can be rearranged as follows:
Force transmissibility

$$\frac{F}{ky_0} = \beta^2 \frac{\sqrt{k^2 + c^2\bar{\omega}^2}}{\sqrt{(k - m\bar{\omega})^2 + c^2\bar{\omega}^2}}$$

$$\frac{F}{ky_0} = \beta^2 \frac{\sqrt{1 + (2\beta\xi)^2}}{\sqrt{(1 - \beta^2)^2 + (2\beta\xi)^2}}$$

In the present example, $\beta = 1$, $\xi = 0.288$, $k = 400$ kN/m and $y_0 = 5$ mm
∴ Amplitude of force transmitted

$$F = 400 \times (5/1000) \times \frac{\sqrt{1 + (2 \times 0.288)^2}}{2 \times 0.288}$$

or, $$F = 4 \text{ kN}$$ □

Example 6.8

A SDOF system is subjected to base excitation. At a frequency ratio of 2.5, it is desired to keep the transmissibility ratio to less than 0.40. Determine the damping ratio.

Solution

The displacement transmissibility ratio (TR)

$$\text{TR} = \frac{x_{max}}{y_0} = \frac{\sqrt{1 + (2\beta\xi)^2}}{\sqrt{(1 - \beta^2)^2 + (2\beta\xi)^2}}$$

$$0.40 = \frac{\sqrt{1 + (2 \times 2.5 \times \xi)^2}}{\sqrt{(1 - 2.5^2)^2 + (2 \times 2.5 \times \xi)^2}}$$

or, $$\xi = 0.40 \text{ or } 40\%$$

Any damping ratio less than 40% will ensure a transmissibility ratio of less than 0.40 because the frequency ratio is more than √2. □

Example 6.9

A building is modeled as a SDOF system having a mass of 250 kN and a lateral stiffness of 5000 kN/m. If the base amplitude is 0.20 m at a frequency of 10 rad/sec during an earthquake, estimate the lateral displacement at its top.

Solution

Natural frequency of the building $\omega = \sqrt{\frac{k}{m}} = \sqrt{\frac{5000 \times 1000}{250 \times 1000 / 9.8}} = 14$ rad/sec

Period of vibration $T = \frac{2\pi}{\omega} = 0.448$ sec

$$\text{TR} = \frac{x_{\max}}{y_0} = \frac{\sqrt{1+(2\beta\xi)^2}}{\sqrt{\left(1-\beta^2\right)^2+(2\beta\xi)^2}}$$

Frequency ratio $\beta = 10/14 = 0.714$
Let us assume a damping ratio of 2% for a steel building,

$$\therefore \text{TR} = \frac{\sqrt{1+(2\times 0.714\times 0.02)^2}}{\sqrt{(1-0.714^2)^2+(2\times 0.714\times 0.02)^2}} = 1.96$$

∴ Displacement at the top of the building = 1.96 × 0.20 = 0.392 m □

Example 6.10

A machine is mounted on a foundation and rotates at 1250 rpm, its unbalance mass is 15 kg (10% of the total mass) at an eccentricity of 50 mm from its centre. The stiffness of the foundation is 250000 N/m and damping is 10%. Determine the amplitude of vertical vibrations.

Solution

Natural frequency of the foundation $\omega = \sqrt{\frac{k}{m}} = \sqrt{\frac{250000}{(150+15)}} = 38.90$ rad/sec

Forcing frequency $\bar{\omega} = 1250$ rpm = 1250/60 = 20.83 cps = 20.83 Hz
$\therefore \bar{\omega} = 2\,\pi\, 20.83 = 130.90$ rad/sec
∴ Frequency ratio $\beta = 130.90/38.90 = 3.36$
Its steady state response is given by

$$x(t) = \frac{p_0}{k} D \sin(\bar{\omega}t - \phi)$$

Its amplitude
$$x_0 = \frac{p_0}{k} D = \frac{p_0}{k} \frac{1}{\sqrt{\left(1-\beta^2\right)^2+(2\beta\xi)^2}}$$

$$x_0 = \frac{m' r \bar{\omega}^2}{k} \frac{1}{\sqrt{\left(1-\beta^2\right)^2+(2\beta\xi)^2}}$$

$$x_0 = \frac{15\times 50/1000\times 130.9^2}{250000} \frac{1}{\sqrt{(1-3.36^2)^2+(2\times 3.36\times 0.10)^2}}$$

$$x_0 = 0.00494 \text{ m} = 4.94 \text{ mm}$$ □

Example 6.11

A machine is mounted on a framed foundation whose 2D model is shown in Figure 6.8. The mass at the deck level is 750 kN and the three columns are rigidly connected at top and bottom with the slabs. The column size is 30 cm × 50 cm and a clear height is 3 m. The machine has an unbalanced mass of 40 kg acting at a radius of 25 cm and operates at 3000 rpm. Determine the amplitude of vertical vibrations neglecting damping. Grade of concrete = M30.

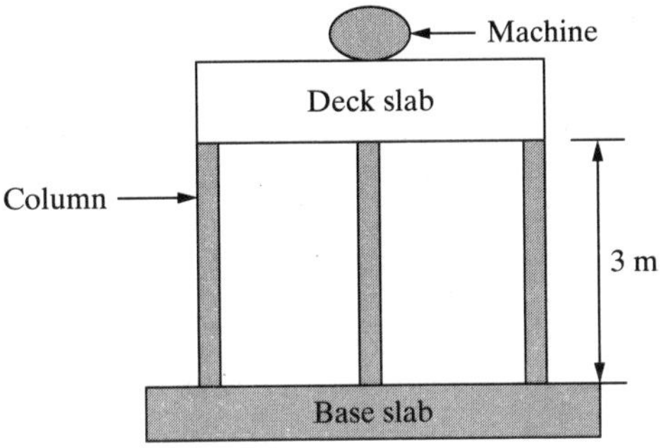

Figure 6.8 Machine foundation.

Solution

Modulus of elasticity of concrete $= 5000\sqrt{f_{ck}} = 5000 \times \sqrt{30} = 27380$ MPa

$= 27380 \times 10^3$ kN/m²

Vertical stiffness of columns $= 3\dfrac{AE}{L} = \dfrac{3\times 0.30\times 0.50\times 27380\times 10^3}{3} = 4107000 \text{ kN/m}$

Natural frequency of the foundation $\omega = \sqrt{\dfrac{k}{m}} = \sqrt{\dfrac{4107000\times 1000}{750\times 1000/9.80}} = 231$ rad/sec

Period of vibration in vertical direction $T = \dfrac{2\pi}{\omega} = \dfrac{2\pi}{231} = 0.027$ sec

Forcing frequency $\bar{\omega} = 3000 \text{ rpm} = \dfrac{3000}{60}\times 2\pi = 314 \text{ rad/sec}$

Frequency ratio $\beta = 314/231 = 1.36$

Centrifugal force $p_0 = m'r\bar{\omega}^2 = 40\times 0.25\times 314^2 = 985960 \text{ N}$

Steady state displacement amplitude x_0 is given by

$$\frac{p_0}{k}D = \frac{p_0}{k}\frac{1}{\sqrt{(1-\beta^2)^2 + (2\beta\xi)^2}}$$

$$x_0 = \frac{985960}{4107000\times 10^3}\times\frac{1}{(1-1.36^2)} = 204\times 10^{-6} \text{ m}$$

or, amplitude of vertical vibrations = 0.204 mm □

Example 6.12

A machine foundation is supporting a machine. It exhibits an amplitude of 20 mm at resonance. At very high machine frequencies, an amplitude of 2.5 mm is observed. Estimate the damping in the system.

Solution

At resonance

$$x_{\max} = \frac{m'r}{2m\xi} = 20 \tag{6.38c}$$

At very high frequencies,

$$x_{\max} = \frac{m'r}{m} = 2.5 \tag{6.38d}$$

∴ Dividing Equation (6.38d) by Equation (6.38c) gives

$$2\xi = \frac{2.5}{20} \quad \text{or} \quad \xi = 0.0625 \quad \text{or} \quad 6.25\%$$

□

Example 6.13

A motor weighing 10 kN is supported by four springs each of stiffness 5000 N/m. The system has a viscous damping. Estimate the minimum damping coefficient such that there is no oscillation.

Solution

For no oscillation, minimum damping = critical damping C_c

Critical damping $C_c = 2\sqrt{k\,m}$

Mass $m = 10 \times 1000/9.81 = 1019.37$ kg

Stiffness $k = 4 \times 5000 = 20000$ N/m

Natural frequency $\omega = \sqrt{\frac{k}{m}} = \sqrt{\frac{20000}{1019.37}} = 4.43$ rad/sec

Period $T = \frac{2\pi}{\omega} = 1.42$ sec

Critical damping $C_c = 2\sqrt{20000 \times 1019.37} = 4515 \text{ Ns/m}$

or, $C_c = 4.52 \text{ kNs/m}$

□

Example 6.14

An instrument weighs 0.1 kN and mounted on a base having spring stiffness of 5 kN/m and damping of 15%. The ground is transmitting a vertical acceleration of 0.1 g at a frequency of 50 rad/sec.

(a) What acceleration is transmitted to the instrument?

(b) If the instrument can tolerate an acceleration of 0.004 g, advice how to modify the foundation using the same support system.

Solution

(a) Natural frequency of the base $\omega = \sqrt{\frac{k}{m}} = \sqrt{\frac{5000}{0.1 \times 1000/9.80}} = 22.14$ rad/sec

The frequency ratio $\beta = \bar{\omega}/\omega = 50/22.14 = 2.258$

$$\text{TR} = \frac{\ddot{x}^t_{\max}}{\ddot{y}_0} = \frac{\sqrt{1+(2\beta\xi)^2}}{\sqrt{\left(1-\beta^2\right)^2+(2\beta\xi)^2}}$$

$$= \left[\frac{1 + (2 \times 2.258 \times 0.15)^2}{(1 - 2.258^2)^2 + (2 \times 2.258 \times 0.15)^2} \right]^{0.50}$$

$$\frac{\ddot{x}^t_{max}}{\ddot{y}_0} = 0.29$$

$$\therefore \quad \ddot{x}^t = 0.29 \times 0.1 g = 0.029 g$$

(b) The machine can tolerate a transmissibility ratio given by

$$TR = 0.004\, g / 0.1\, g = 0.04$$

In order to achieve such a low TR ratio, the frequency ratio β needs to be very high, that is, the natural frequency of the supporting system needs to be very low since the base excitation frequency cannot be controlled.

(i) Let us try and add a mass of 0.3 kN on to the foundation
Revised natural frequency of the base is given by

$$\omega_1 = \sqrt{\frac{k}{m + m'}} = \sqrt{\frac{5}{(0.1 + 0.3)/g}} = 11.068 \text{ rad/sec}$$

Revised frequency ratio $\beta = \bar{\omega}/\omega_1 = 50/11.068 = 4.52$
Let us calculate revised damping ratio for the system with added mass
Earlier damping ratio $\xi = c/c_c$

Revised damping ratio $\xi' = \dfrac{c}{c_c'}$

$$\therefore \quad \frac{\xi}{\xi'} = \frac{c_c'}{c_c} = \frac{2(m + m')\omega_1}{2m\omega}$$

$$\xi' = \frac{m\omega\xi}{(m + m')\omega_1} = \frac{0.1 \times 22.14 \times 0.15}{(0.1 + 0.3) \times 11.068} = 0.075$$

$$TR = \frac{\ddot{x}^t_{max}}{\ddot{y}_0} = \frac{\sqrt{1 + (2\beta\xi)^2}}{\sqrt{(1 - \beta^2)^2 + (2\beta\xi)^2}}$$

$$= \left[\frac{1 + (2 \times 4.52 \times 0.075)^2}{(1 - 4.52^2)^2 + (2 \times 4.52 \times 0.075)^2} \right]^{0.50} = 0.062$$

$$\ddot{x}^t = 0.062 \times 0.1\text{ g} = 0.0062\text{ g} > 0.004\text{ g} \qquad \text{No Good}$$

(ii) Therefore, there is a need to revise the design. Let us add a mass of 0.6 kN
Revised natural frequency of the base

$$\omega_1 = \sqrt{\frac{k}{m + m'}} = \sqrt{\frac{5}{(0.1 + 0.6)/g}} = 8.36 \text{ rad/sec}$$

Revised frequency ratio $\beta = \bar{\omega}/\omega_1 = 50/8.36 = 5.98$
Revised damping ratio ξ' is given by

$$\xi' = \frac{m\omega\xi}{(m + m')\omega_1} = \frac{0.1 \times 22.14 \times 0.15}{(0.1 + 0.6) \times 8.36} = 0.0567$$

$$\text{TR} = \frac{\ddot{x}^{t}_{\max}}{\ddot{y}_0} = 0.0348$$

$$\ddot{x}^{t} = 0.0348 \times 0.1\,\text{g} = 0.00348\,\text{g} < 0.004\,\text{g} \qquad \text{OK}$$

Therefore, there is a need to add a mass of 0.6 kN to the base in order to control the acceleration transmitted to the instrument. □

REVIEW QUESTIONS

6.1 What are different types of machines from the point of their foundations?

6.2 How can you group various machines based on their speed of operations from the point of their foundations?

6.3 What is a block foundation for a machine? Show with the help of a neat sketch.

6.4 What is a frame foundation for a machine? Show with the help of a neat sketch.

6.5 List the dynamic soil parameters for use in machine foundations.

6.6 What are different types of soil springs? Discuss a soil spring when foundation is supported directly on the soil.

6.7 What is the expression for unbalanced force in a rotary machine?

6.8 Derive the expression for unbalanced force in a reciprocating machine? Explain it with the help of a neat sketch.

6.9 What is the basic criteria for the design of a machine foundation?

6.10 How do you determine mass moment of inertia of a rectangular block foundation in *X-Z* plane?

6.11 Draw free body diagram of a block foundation having torsional vibration in *X-Y* horizontal plane.

6.12 What is coefficient of restitution with reference to impact loading.

6.13 Derive an expression for the final velocity of mass m_2 in terms of the initial velocity of the falling mass m_0.

6.14 What is an under tuned and over tuned foundation? Discuss their physical significance.

6.15 Discuss is the modeling criteria for the foundation of a high frequency rotary machine.

6.16 How do you monitor the health of a machine foundation?

6.17 Develop the equation of motion for undamped free vibrations of a block foundation having rotational motion in *X-Z* vertical plane. What is the expression for its natural pitching frequency?

6.18 What is transmissibility ratio in machine foundations? Derive an expression for the force transmitted to the foundation by a damped SDOF system subjected to a harmonic load $p_0 \sin(\bar{\omega}t)$.

6.19 What is the physical significance of the frequency ratio $\sqrt{2}$ in terms of transmissibility ratio and damping for a machine foundation?

6.20 Derive an expression for the amplitude of motion of a SDOF system due to the vibration $y_0 \sin(\bar{\omega}t)$.caused by the ground.

PROBLEMS

6.1 A machine is supported on a pedestal which can tolerate a vertical deflection of 1×10^{-3} mm under operating conditions. It is subjected to a forcing function causing a base displacement of amplitude 50×10^{-3} mm at a frequency of 15 Hz. Damping may be taken as 4%.

(a) Determine the natural frequency of the system.

(b) If the mass of the machine including platform is 2500 kg, what will be its static deflection?

Ans: $\omega = 12.18$ rad/sec, $k = 371260$ N/m, $\Delta_{st} = 6.7$ mm

6.2 A foundation block is to be installed in a plant such that the vibration from the adjacent areas will not affect it. The mass of the foundation system is 3000 kg, and the surrounding floor vibrates at 2500 cycles per minute. Estimate the stiffness of the foundation so that the transmissibility ratio is not more than 5%, if

(a) Damping is ignored and

(b) Damping is taken as 20%.

Ans: (a) $k = 9.8 \times 10^6$ N/m, (b) $k = 2.87 \times 10^6$ N/m

6.3 A machine foundation has a mass of 1500 kg with a vertical stiffness of 650 kN/m. If the base displacement amplitude is 10 mm, the displacement amplitude of the mass is 20 mm while it is vibrating at its natural frequency. Calculate the damping ratio and damping coefficient. Also, calculate the force transmitted to the base.

Ans: $\xi = 28.8\%$, $c = 17985$ Ns/m

6.4 A SDOF system is subjected to base excitation. At a frequency ratio of 2.75, it is desired to keep the transmissibility ratio to less than 0.30. Determine the damping ratio.

Ans: $\xi = 32\%$

6.5 A building is modelled as a SDOF system having a mass of 350 kN, damping 5%, and a lateral stiffness of 5000 kN/m. If the base amplitude is 0.10 m at a frequency of 12.5 rad/sec during an earthquake, estimate the lateral displacement at its top.

6.6 A machine is mounted on a foundation and rotates at 1800 rpm, its unbalance mass is 25 kg (10% of the total mass) at an eccentricity of 35 mm from its center. The stiffness of the foundation is 350000 N/m and damping is 15%. Determine the amplitude of vertical vibrations.

Ans: $x_{max} = 3.63$ mm

6.7 An instrument weighs 0.25 kN and mounted on a base having spring stiffness of 10 kN/m and damping of 10%. The ground is transmitting a vertical acceleration of 0.3 g at a frequency of 50 rad/sec.

(a) What acceleration is transmitted to the instrument?

(b) If the instrument can tolerate an acceleration of 0.005 g, advice how to modify the foundation using the same support system.

6.8 A machine weighing 500 kg is mounted at the midspan of a simply supported beam. It produces a harmonic force $F_0 \sin \bar{\omega} t$ where $F_0 = 150$ kN, and $\bar{\omega} = 50$ rad/sec. Assuming 10% critical damping and neglecting the self weight of the beam, determine the amplitude of the motion of the machine and the force transmitted to the foundation. $EI = 50 \times 10^5$ Nm^2

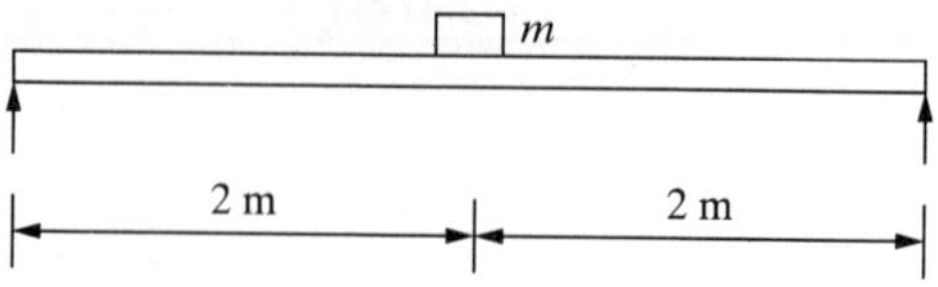

Figure P6.1 Simply supported beam

Ans: $TR = \frac{F_{max}}{F_0} = \frac{\sqrt{1+(2\beta\xi)^2}}{\sqrt{(1-\beta^2)^2+(2\beta\xi)^2}}$

6.9 An instrument is mounted on a vibrating platform using rubber pad as an isolator. Total mass of the instrument and isolator is 200 kg. Stiffness and damping of the isolators are 500 kN/m and 15% respectively. The platform vibrates at a frequency of 15 Hz with an amplitude of 2 mm. Determine the displacement transmitted to the instrument.

Ans: $TR = \frac{y_{max}}{y_0} = \frac{\sqrt{1+(2\beta\xi)^2}}{\sqrt{(1-\beta^2)^2+(2\beta\xi)^2}}$

REFERENCES

Bhatia, K. G. (2015) Foundations for Industrial Machines – Handbook for Practicing Engineers, 2nd ed., D-CAD Publishers, New Delhi.

Bowles, J E (1997) Foundation Analysis and Design, McGraw-Hill Books, New York.

IS/ISO 4866 (2010) Mechanical Vibration and Shock — Vibration of Fixed Structures — Guidelines for the Measurement of Vibrations and Evaluation of Their Effects on Structures, BIS, New Delhi

IS: 2974

Part 1: Foundation for reciprocating type machines

Part 2: Foundations for impact type machines (Hammer foundations)

Part 3: Foundation for rotary type machines with medium and high frequency

Part 4: Foundations for rotary type machines of low frequency

Part 5: Foundations for impact machines other than hammer (forging and stamping press, pig breaker, drop crusher and jolter)

Bureau of Indian Standards, New Delhi.

IS: 13301 (1992) Vibration Isolation for Machine Foundation – Guidelines, Bureau of Indian Standards, New Delhi.

ISO 2631 (1997) Mechanical Vibration and Shock – Evaluation of Human Exposure to Whole-Body Vibration – Part 1: General Requirements, ISO, Geneva.

ISO 2631 (2003) Mechanical Vibration and Shock – Evaluation of Human Exposure to Whole-Body Vibration – Part 2: Vibration in Buildings (1 Hz to 80 Hz), ISO, Geneva.

ISO/TS 10811:2000 Mechanical Vibration and Shock – Vibration and Shock in buildings with Sensitive Equipment – Part 1: Measurements and Evaluation, Part 2: Classification, International Organization for Standardization, Geneva.

Murray, T. M., Allen, D. E., and Ungar, E. E. (1997) Floor Vibrations Due to Human Activity, Steel Design Guide 11, AISC, Chicago.

7 Direct Integration of Equation of Motion

7.1 INTRODUCTION

In the previous chapters, the second-order differential equation of motion has been solved using the basic principles of calculus. The forcing function had a simple nature and it was convenient to solve the differential equation. In case a single-degree-of-freedom (SDOF) system or a multi-degree-of-freedom (MDOF) system is subjected to a random acceleration-time history or if the system is nonlinear, it will be very difficult to solve its differential equation using the methods discussed so far. Direct integration methods or step-by-step integration methods are used for the solution of such problems as illustrated in Figure 7.1. A very small time step Δt is chosen and the solution is obtained from one step to the next step. The force is linearly interpolated as shown in Figure 7.2. The term direct means prior to numerical integration no transformation of the equations of motion has been carried out. These methods are based on two essential features:

1. Variation of displacement, velocity and acceleration is assumed within each time step. Hence, the accuracy and stability of the final solution depends upon this variation.
2. The equilibrium is satisfied at all discrete time points within the interval of solution instead of at any time t.

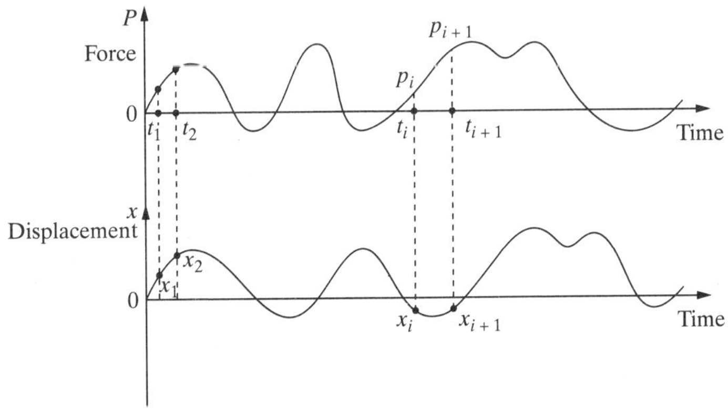

Figure 7.1 Force and displacement variation with time stepping.

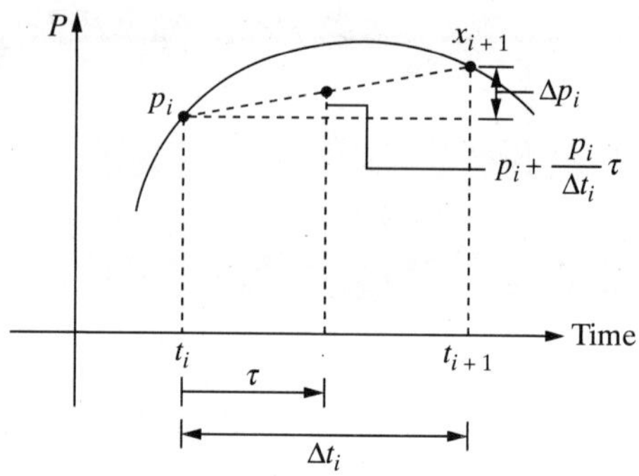

Figure 7.2 Interpolation of force.

The main advantage of these methods is that they are applicable to linear as well as nonlinear analysis of SDOF systems as well as MDOF systems. A very large number of algorithms are available in the literature for the solution of various types of differential equations. The mathematical development, accuracy, convergence and stability criteria of these methods are discussed in the literature. In the present study, only a few commonly used algorithms will be discussed in order to make the reader familiar and aware of these procedures.

7.2 ALGORITHMS

The solution is obtained step-by-step starting from the initial condition at time $t = t_0$. The most critical factor is the selection of the time step 'h'. The solution is known at a time step t, and the problem is to obtain the solution at the next time step $(t + h)$. The expressions at time step $(t + h)$ may be either entirely in terms of the quantities at time step t or both at time step t and $(t + h)$. This gives rise to two types of algorithms: *explicit algorithm* and *implicit algorithm*. In the former, the expressions at time step $(t + h)$ are in terms of time step t only, whereas, in the latter, the expressions at time step $(t + h)$ are in terms of both at time t and $(t + h)$. The solution using the explicit algorithms is easy as compared to those using the implicit algorithms.

These methods may be classified as follows:

1. Conditionally stable
2. Unconditionally stable

These numerical methods are based on any of the three approaches:

1. Numerical interpolation of the excitation function,
2. Finite difference expressions for velocity and acceleration, and
3. Assumed variation of acceleration in a time step.

Notation The solution at the current time step is denoted by either t or t_n, and the solution at next time step is denoted by $(t + h)$ or t_{n+1}. The time step is denoted by h or Δt, and it is taken as a very small value for better accuracy, stability and fast convergence.

Explicit Algorithms The response at time t_{n+1} is known in terms of the known variables at time t_n. Thus, the response values displacement, velocity and acceleration can be determined directly.

$$
\begin{aligned}
x_{n+1} &= f(x_n) \\
\dot{x}_{n+1} &= f(\dot{x}_n) \\
\ddot{x}_{n+1} &= f(\ddot{x}_n) \qquad (7.1)
\end{aligned}
$$

There are two methods for the solution:

1. Euler method or constant acceleration method
2. Central difference method

Implicit Algorithms The response at time t_{n+1} is known in terms of the known variables at time t_n and unknown variables at time t_{n+1}. Such algorithms involve either an iterative scheme or solution of linear simultaneous equations because the unknown quantities are appearing on both sides of the equations.

$$
\begin{aligned}
x_{n+1} &= f(x_n, x_{n+1}) \\
\dot{x}_{n+1} &= f(\dot{x}_n, \dot{x}_{n+1}) \\
\ddot{x}_{n+1} &= f(\ddot{x}_n, \ddot{x}_{n+1}) \qquad (7.2)
\end{aligned}
$$

Some of these algorithms are as follows:

1. Linear acceleration method
2. Newmark β method
3. Wilson θ method
4. Houbolt method
5. Hilber–Hughes–Taylor method

Convergence means the solution should approach the exact solution with the decrease in time step.

Stability means the solution should not destabilize in the presence of numerical round-off errors. Any error in displacement, velocity and acceleration at time t do not grow in integration due to numerical round off error.

Accuracy means a numerical method should provide an accurate solution which is close enough with the exact solution. It is measured in terms of amplitude accuracy or amplitude decay or period accuracy or period elongation.

7.3 CONSTANT ACCELERATION METHOD

The equation of motion of a SDOF system at time step t or t_n is given as follows:

$$m\ddot{x}(t) + c\dot{x}(t) + kx(t) = p(t) \qquad (7.3)$$

or, it may be written for convenience as follows:

$$m\ddot{x} + c\dot{x} + kx = p(t)$$

or,
$$\ddot{x} = \frac{1}{m}[p(t) - c\dot{x} - kx] \tag{7.4}$$

Let us write the Taylor's series:

$$x(t+h) = x(t) + h\dot{x}(t) + \frac{h^2}{2}\ddot{x}(t) + \frac{h^3}{6}\dddot{x}(t) + \ldots \quad h << 1 \tag{7.5}$$

On differentiating Equation (7.5),

$$\dot{x}(t+h) = \dot{x}(t) + h\ddot{x}(t) + \frac{h^2}{2}\dddot{x}(t) + \ldots \tag{7.6}$$

Since time increment h is small, and we are interested in $\ddot{x}$, dropping all the terms higher than $\ddot{x}$,

we get,

$$x(t+h) = x(t) + h\dot{x}(t) + \frac{h^2}{2}\ddot{x}(t) \tag{7.7}$$

$$\dot{x}(t+h) = \dot{x}(t) + h\ddot{x}(t) \tag{7.8}$$

$$\ddot{x}(t+h) = \frac{1}{m}[p(t+h) - c\dot{x}(t+h) - kx(t+h)] \tag{7.9}$$

The new response values at time $(t+h)$ can be obtained directly from Equations (7.7), (7.8) and (7.9) knowing the displacement, velocity and acceleration values at the previous time step. The dynamic equilibrium of the system is satisfied through Equation (7.9) at each time step. The variation of acceleration, velocity and displacement is shown in Figure 7.3.

This method is called constant acceleration method because in Equation (7.8), the term $\dddot{x}(t)$ is taken as zero, that is, the acceleration $\ddot{x}(t)$ is constant, therefore, its derivative is zero. It is essential to keep the time step size small in order to get good results from the constant acceleration method. It is recommended that

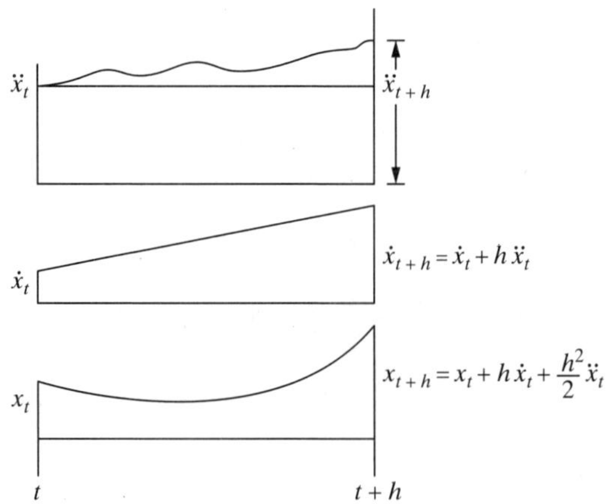

Figure 7.3 Variation of response parameters – constant acceleration method.

$$\frac{\Delta t}{T} \leq \frac{1}{10} \tag{7.10}$$

Typically, Δt is chosen as 0.01 sec or 0.02 sec or sometimes even still smaller, say 0.005 sec.

7.4 CENTRAL DIFFERENCE METHOD

This method is based on the finite difference approximation of the time derivative of displacement, that is, velocity and acceleration. The central finite difference expressions for velocity and acceleration at time i are as follows:

$$\dot{x}_i = \frac{x_{i+1} - x_{i-1}}{2\Delta t} \tag{7.11}$$

and

$$\ddot{x}_i = \frac{x_{i+1} - 2x_i + x_{i-1}}{(\Delta t)^2} \tag{7.12}$$

Both velocity and acceleration terms are now expressed in terms of displacement terms. The equation of motion can be written as:

$$m\frac{x_{i+1} - 2x_i + x_{i-1}}{(\Delta t)^2} + c\frac{x_{i+1} - x_{i-1}}{2\Delta t} + kx_i = p_i \tag{7.13}$$

Equation (7.13) is in terms of displacements only. The values x_i and x_{i-1} are known, and x_{i+1} is unknown. Let us re-write this equation in terms of known and unknown quantities:

$$\left[\frac{m}{(\Delta t)^2} + \frac{c}{2\Delta t}\right]x_{i+1} = p_i - \left[\frac{m}{(\Delta t)^2} - \frac{c}{2\Delta t}\right]x_{i-1} - \left[k - \frac{2m}{(\Delta t)^2}\right]x_i \tag{7.14}$$

Or,

$$\bar{k}x_{i+1} = \bar{p}_i \tag{7.15}$$

where,

$$\bar{k} = \left[\frac{m}{(\Delta t)^2} + \frac{c}{2\Delta t}\right] \tag{7.16a}$$

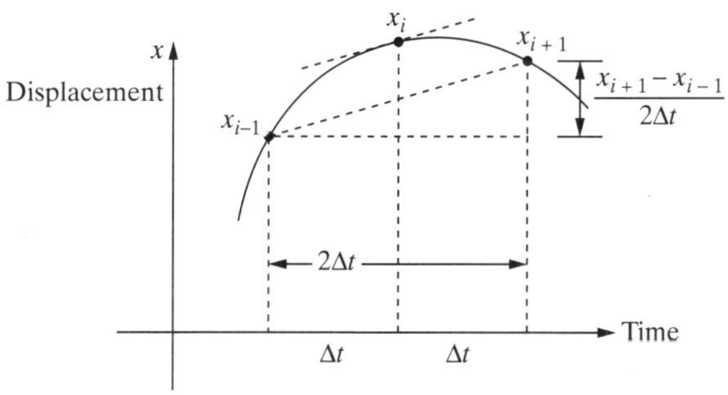

Figure 7.4 Variation of displacement – central difference method.

and

$$\bar{p}_i = p_i - \left[\frac{m}{(\Delta t)^2} - \frac{c}{2\Delta t}\right] x_{i-1} - \left[k - \frac{2m}{(\Delta t)^2}\right] x_i \tag{7.16b}$$

or,

$$\bar{p}_i = p_i - a x_{i-1} - b x_i \tag{7.16c}$$

where,

$$a = \left[\frac{m}{(\Delta t)^2} - \frac{c}{2\Delta t}\right] \tag{7.16d}$$

$$b = \left[k - \frac{2m}{(\Delta t)^2}\right] \tag{7.16e}$$

The unknown displacement x_{i+1} is given by Equation (7.15).

In this approach, the problem will arise at the first time step to determine x_{i-1}. The initial displacement must be known, that is, x_0. To determine x_{i-1}, Equations (7.11) and (7.12) give for $i = 0$,

$$\dot{x}_0 = \frac{x_1 - x_{-1}}{2\Delta t}$$

and

$$\ddot{x}_0 = \frac{x_1 - 2x_0 + x_{-1}}{(\Delta t)^2}$$

The first equation will give x_1 and the second equation will give x_{-1}, that is,

$$x_{-1} = x_0 - \Delta t\, \dot{x}_0 + \frac{(\Delta t)^2}{2} \ddot{x}_0 \tag{7.17a}$$

In this equation, initial displacement x_0 and initial velocity $\dot{x}_0$ are known. The initial acceleration $\ddot{x}_0$ can be determined from the equation of motion at time $t = 0$:

$$\ddot{x}_0 = \frac{p_0 - c\dot{x}_0 - kx_0}{m} \tag{7.17b}$$

Again, for stability, the time step should be chosen small as follows:

$$\frac{\Delta t}{T} < \frac{1}{\pi} \tag{7.17c}$$

Equation (7.10) gives still smaller step size.

Algorithm:

Step 1: Initial displacement and velocity are known as initial conditions of the problem at time $t = 0$

Step 2: Damping c and stiffness k are computed from the system properties

Step 3: Acceleration at time $t = 0$ is computed from Equation (7.17b)

Step 4: Compute equivalent stiffness $\bar{k}$ from Equation (7.16a)

Step 5: Compute constants a and b from Equation (7.16d) and (7.16e)

Step 6: For time step i, compute equivalent force $\bar{p}_i$ from Equation (7.16c)

Step 7: Solve for new displacement x_{i+1} from Equation (7.15)

$$x_{i+1} = \frac{\bar{p}_i}{\bar{k}}$$

Step 8: Compute velocity and acceleration at time step i from Equations (7.11) and (7.12)

Step 9: Repeat Steps 6 to 8 for the next time step

Example 7.1

An undamped SDOF system has a mass of 4900 N and stiffness of 20 kN/m. It is subjected to a triangular force as shown in Figure 7.5. The initial displacement and velocity are zero. Determine the displacement-time history.

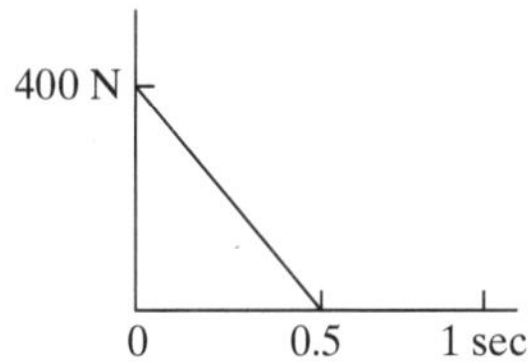

Figure 7.5 Triangular force.

Solution Acceleration due to gravity = 9.8 m/sec^2

$$\text{Mass} = W/g = 4900/9.8 = 500 \text{ kg}$$

Natural frequency of vibration $\omega = \sqrt{\frac{k}{m}} = \sqrt{\frac{20000}{500}} = 6.32$ rad/sec

Therefore, period of vibration $T = 0.994 \approx 1$ sec

$$m\ddot{x} + c\dot{x} + kx = p(t)$$

or,

$$\ddot{x} = \frac{1}{m}[p(t) - c\dot{x} - kx] \tag{7.4}$$

Since it is an undamped system, $c = 0$,

$$\ddot{x}(t) = \frac{1}{m}(p(t) - kx(t))$$

$$x(t+h) = x(t) + h\dot{x}(t) + \frac{h^2}{2}\ddot{x}(t) \tag{7.7}$$

$$\dot{x}(t+h) = \dot{x}(t) + h\ddot{x}(t) \tag{7.8}$$

Equations (7.4), (7.7) and (7.8) can also be written as follows:

$$\ddot{x}_n = \frac{1}{m}(p_n - kx_n)$$

$$\dot{x}_{n+1} = \dot{x}_n + h\ddot{x}_n$$

$$x_{n+1} = x_n + h\dot{x}_n + \frac{h^2}{2}\ddot{x}_n$$

Equation (7.4) is valid for time t_n as well as t_{n+1}.

Step size $h = T/10 = 0.1$ sec

It is convenient to solve these equations in tabular form in MS-EXCEL as shown in Table 7.1.

TABLE 7.1 CONSTANT ACCELERATION METHOD

t	x_n	$20000x_n$	p	$\ddot{x}_n$	$\dot{x}_n$	$h\dot{x}_n$	$h\ddot{x}_n$	$\frac{h^2}{2}\ddot{x}_n$	x_{n+1}	$\dot{x}_{n+1}$
sec	m		N	m²/s	m/s				m	m/s
(1)	(2)	(3)	(4)	(5)	(6)	(7)	(8)	(9)	(10)	(11)
0	0.0000	0.00	400.00	0.8000	0.0000	0.0000	0.0800	0.0040	0.0040	0.0800
0.1	0.0040	80.00	320.00	0.4800	0.0800	0.0080	0.0480	0.0024	0.0144	0.1280
0.2	0.0144	288.00	240.00	–0.0960	0.1280	0.0128	–0.0096	–0.0005	0.0267	0.1184
0.3	0.0267	534.40	160.00	–0.7488	0.1184	0.0118	–0.0749	–0.0037	0.0348	0.0435
0.4	0.0348	696.32	80.00	–1.2326	0.0435	0.0044	–0.1233	–0.0062	0.0330	–0.0797
0.5	0.0330	660.10	0.00	–1.3202	–0.0797	–0.0080	–0.1320	–0.0066	0.0184	–0.2118
0.6	0.0184	368.59	0.00	–0.7372	–0.2118	–0.0212	–0.0737	–0.0037	–0.0064	–0.2855
0.7	–0.0064	–128.66	0.00	0.2573	–0.2855	–0.0285	0.0257	0.0013	–0.0337	–0.2597
0.8	–0.0337	–673.89	0.00	1.3478	–0.2597	–0.0260	0.1348	0.0067	–0.0529	–0.1250
0.9	–0.0529	–1058.61	0.00	2.1172	–0.1250	–0.0125	0.2117	0.0106	–0.0548	0.0867
1	–0.0548	–1096.83	0.00	2.1937	0.0867	0.0087	0.2194	0.0110	–0.0352	0.3061

The displacement-time history, velocity-time history and acceleration-time history are shown in Figure 7.6.

The problem is again solved using a smaller time step $h = 0.05$ sec to see the effect of step size. The results are shown in the same figure. It can be seen that there is appreciable difference in the two sets of results. It means a smaller time step is more desirable. □

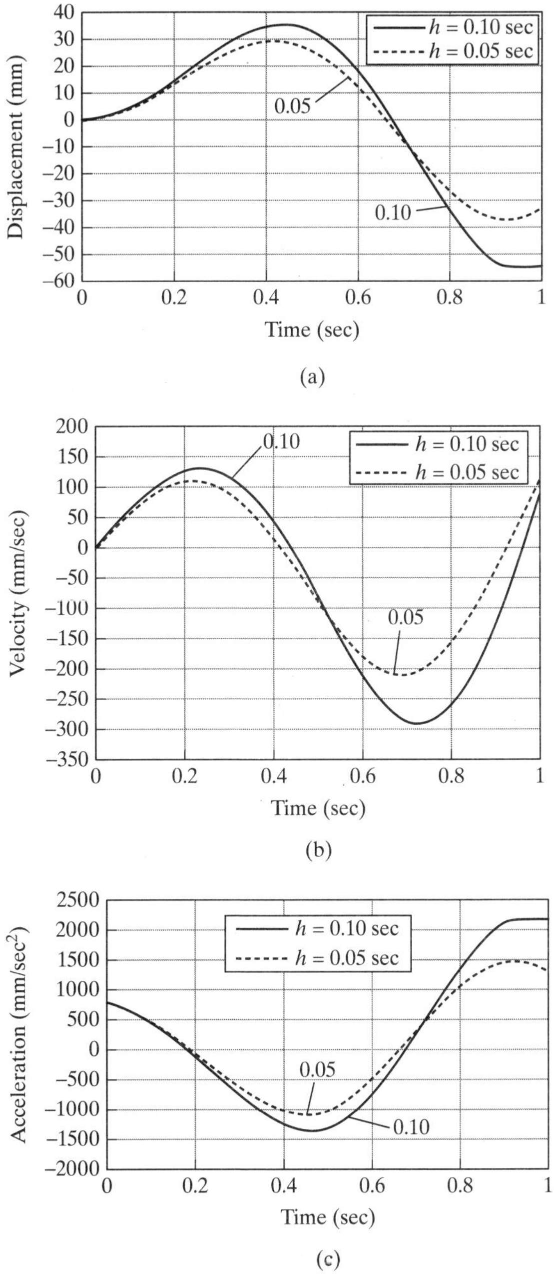

Figure. 7.6 Response of an undamped system using constant acceleration method.

Example 7.2

A damped SDOF system has a mass of 4900 N, stiffness of 20 kN/m and damping ratio of 5%. It is subjected to a triangular force as shown in Figure 7.7. The initial displacement and velocity are zero. Determine the displacement-time history using central difference method.

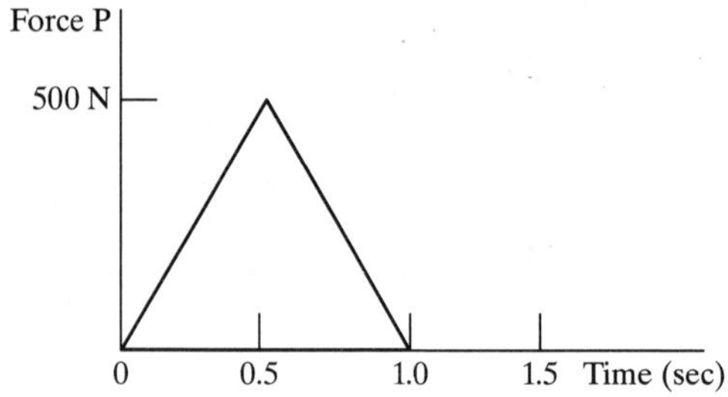

Figure 7.7 Triangular force.

Solution

Acceleration due to gravity = 9.8 m/sec^2
Mass = W/g = 4900/9.8 = 500 kg

Natural frequency of vibration $\omega = \sqrt{\dfrac{k}{m}} = \sqrt{\dfrac{20000}{500}} = 6.32$ rad/sec

Therefore, period of vibration $T = 1$ sec
Damping $c = 2\,m\omega\xi = 2 \times 500 \times 6.32 \times 0.05 = 316$ kg/sec

$$x_0 = 0 \text{ and } \dot{x}_0 = 0$$

$$\ddot{x}_0 = \frac{p_0 - c\dot{x}_0 - kx_0}{m} = 0$$

$$x_{-1} = x_0 - \Delta t\,\dot{x}_0 + \frac{(\Delta t)^2}{2}\ddot{x}_0 = 0$$

$$\bar{k} = \left[\frac{m}{(\Delta t)^2} + \frac{c}{2\Delta t}\right] = \frac{500}{0.1^2} + \frac{316}{0.20} = 51580$$

$$a = \left[\frac{m}{(\Delta t)^2} - \frac{c}{2\Delta t}\right] = 48240$$

$$b = \left[k - \frac{2m}{(\Delta t)^2}\right] = 20000 - \frac{2 \times 500}{0.1^2} = -80000$$

$$\bar{p}_i = p_i - ax_{i-1} - bx_i = p_i - 48240x_{i-1} + 80000x_i$$

$$x_{i+1} = \frac{\bar{p}_i}{\bar{k}} = \frac{\bar{p}_i}{51580}$$

Rest of the calculations can be done in tabular form in MS-EXCEL for convenience as shown in Table 7.2. The displacement response is shown in Figure 7.8. □

TABLE 7.2 CENTRAL DIFFERENCE METHOD

t	p_i	x_{i-1}	x_i	$\bar{p}_i$	x_{i+1}
sec	N	m	m	N	m
0	0	0.0000	0.0000	0.0000	0.0000
0.1	100	0.0000	0.0000	100.0000	0.0019
0.2	200	0.0000	0.0019	355.0989	0.0069
0.3	300	0.0019	0.0069	757.2297	0.0147
0.4	400	0.0069	0.0147	1242.3499	0.0241
0.5	500	0.0147	0.0241	1718.6745	0.0333
0.6	400	0.0241	0.0333	1903.7418	0.0369
0.7	300	0.0333	0.0369	1645.2982	0.0319
0.8	200	0.0369	0.0319	971.3718	0.0188
0.9	100	0.0319	0.0188	67.8277	0.0013
1	0	0.0188	0.0013	−803.2717	−0.0156
1.1	0	0.0013	−0.0156	−1309.3010	−0.0254
1.2	0	−0.0156	−0.0254	−1279.4544	−0.0248
1.3	0	−0.0254	−0.0248	−759.9005	−0.0147
1.4	0	−0.0248	−0.0147	18.0078	0.0003
1.5	0	−0.0147	0.0003	738.6239	0.0143

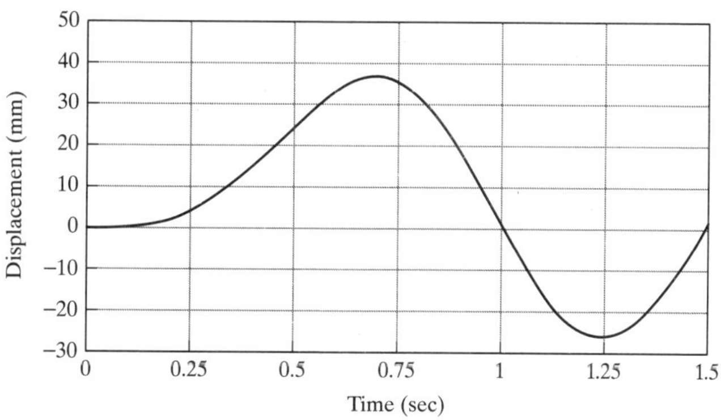

Figure 7.8 Displacement-time history – central difference method.

7.5 INCREMENTAL EQUATION OF MOTION

Let us rewrite the equation of motion in the incremental form for convenience in the solution of implicit algorithms. The equation of motion is written at time steps t_n and t_{n+1}

$$m\ddot{x}_n + c_n\dot{x}_n + k_n x_n = p_n \tag{7.18}$$

and

$$m\ddot{x}_{n+1} + c_{n+1}\dot{x}_{n+1} + k_{n+1}\,x_{n+1} = p_{n+1} \tag{7.19}$$

where,

$$x_{n+1} = x_n + \Delta x \tag{7.20a}$$

$$\dot{x}_{n+1} = \dot{x}_n + \Delta\dot{x} \tag{7.20b}$$

$$\ddot{x}_{n+1} = \ddot{x}_n + \Delta\ddot{x} \tag{7.20c}$$

$$c_{n+1} = c_n + \Delta c \tag{7.20d}$$

$$k_{n+1} = k_n + \Delta k \tag{7.20e}$$

Δx = displacement increment in a time step
$\Delta\dot{x}$ = velocity increment in a time step
$\Delta\ddot{x}$ = acceleration increment in a time step

In nonlinear problems, the damping c and stiffness k may vary with each time step. However, in linear problems, the increments Δc and Δk will be zero. The mass term will always remain constant.

Let us substitute terms from Equation (7.20) in Equation (7.19) and then subtract Equation (7.18), we get

$$m\Delta\ddot{x} + c_n\,\Delta\dot{x} + k_n\,\Delta x + P_2 = P_1 \tag{7.21}$$

where,

$$P_1 = p_{n+1} - m\,\ddot{x}_n - c_n\,\dot{x}_n - k_n\,x_n \tag{7.22a}$$

$$P_2 = \Delta c\,(\dot{x}_n + \Delta\dot{x}) + \Delta k(x_n + \Delta x) \tag{7.22b}$$

For a linear system, $P_2 = 0$ because Δc and Δk are zero. The damping and stiffness terms will remain constant in a linear system.

In general, it is possible to express incremental velocity and acceleration in terms of incremental displacement.

7.6 LINEAR ACCELERATION METHOD

In this method, $\dddot{x} \neq 0$ in the Taylor's series, that is,

$$x(t+h) = x(t) + h\dot{x}(t) + \frac{h^2}{2}\ddot{x}(t) + \frac{h^3}{6}\dddot{x}(t) + \ldots \qquad h << t \tag{7.23}$$

This equation can be re-written by changing symbols as follows:

$$x_{n+1} = x_n + h\dot{x}_n + \frac{h^2}{2}\ddot{x}_n + \frac{h^3}{6}\dddot{x}_n \tag{7.24}$$

On differentiating Equation (7.24),

$$\dot{x}_{n+1} = \dot{x}_n + h\ddot{x}_n + \frac{h^2}{2}\dddot{x}_n \tag{7.25}$$

On differentiating Equation (7.25),

$$\ddot{x}_{n+1} = \ddot{x}_n + h\dddot{x}_n \tag{7.26a}$$

or,

$$\dddot{x}_n = \frac{\ddot{x}_{n+1} - \ddot{x}_n}{h} \tag{7.26b}$$

$$= \frac{\Delta\ddot{x}}{h} \tag{7.26c}$$

or, Equation (7.26a) becomes $\ddot{x}_{n+1} = \ddot{x}_n + \Delta\ddot{x}$ (7.26d)

Equation (7.24) can be written making use of Equation (7.26b) as:

$$x_{n+1} = x_n + h\dot{x}_n + \frac{h^2}{3}\ddot{x}_n + \frac{h^2}{6}\ddot{x}_{n+1} \tag{7.27a}$$

or,

$$x_{n+1} = x_n + h\dot{x}_n + \frac{h^2}{3}\ddot{x}_n + \frac{h^2}{6}(\ddot{x}_n + \Delta\ddot{x}) \tag{7.27b}$$

and Equation (7.25) as:

$$\dot{x}_{n+1} = \dot{x}_n + \frac{h}{2}(\ddot{x}_n + \ddot{x}_{n+1}) \tag{7.28a}$$

or,

$$\dot{x}_{n+1} = \dot{x}_n + \frac{h}{2}(\ddot{x}_n + \ddot{x}_n + \Delta\ddot{x}) \tag{7.28b}$$

Equations (7.27), (7.28) and (7.26d) are shown in Figure 7.9.

It is now possible to express either

(a) $\Delta\dot{x}$ and Δx in terms of $\Delta\ddot{x}$
(b) $\Delta\dot{x}$ and $\Delta\ddot{x}$ in terms of Δx

In either case, only one unknown quantity remains in the incremental equations of equilibrium. It is preferred to express incremental velocity and acceleration in terms of incremental displacement. So far, we have not enforced the condition of dynamic equilibrium. Let us write the equation of motion for time step t_{n+1} as follows:

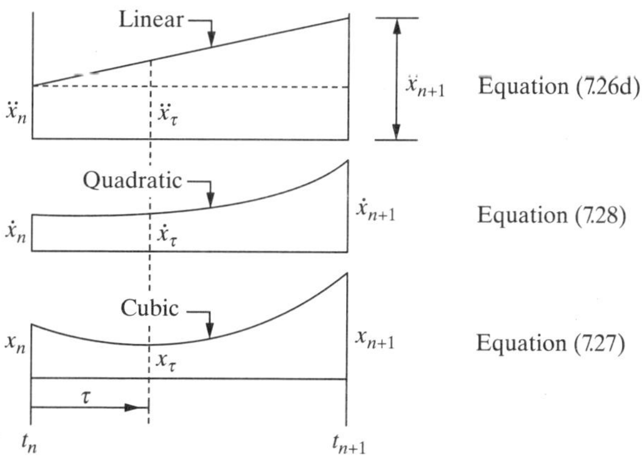

Figure 7.9 Variation of response – linear acceleration method.

$$\ddot{x}_{n+1} = \frac{1}{m}[p_{n+1} - c\dot{x}_{n+1} - kx_{n+1}] \tag{7.29}$$

Making use of the relations:

$$\Delta x = x_{n+1} - x_n$$
$$\Delta \dot{x} = \dot{x}_{n+1} - \dot{x}_n$$
$$\Delta \ddot{x} = \ddot{x}_{n+1} - \ddot{x}_n \tag{7.30}$$

Equation (7.27b) can be re-written as follows:

$$\Delta \ddot{x} = -3\ddot{x}_n - \frac{6}{h}\dot{x}_n + \frac{6}{h^2}\Delta x \tag{7.31}$$

and Equation (7.28b) can be re-written as follows:

$$\Delta \dot{x} = -\frac{h}{2}\ddot{x}_n - 3\dot{x}_n + \frac{3}{h}\Delta x \tag{7.32}$$

Now, the equation of motion can be written in the incremental form:

$$m\Delta\ddot{x} + c\Delta\dot{x} + k\Delta x = P_{n+1} - P_n = \Delta P \tag{7.33}$$

Let us substitute Equations (7.31) and (7.32) into Equation (7.33), we get

$$\bar{k}\Delta x = \overline{\Delta}\overline{P} \tag{7.34}$$

where,

$$\bar{k} = \frac{6m}{h^2} + \frac{3c}{h} + k \tag{7.35a}$$

and

$$\overline{\Delta}\overline{P} = \Delta P + 3m\,(\ddot{x}_n + \frac{2}{h}\dot{x}_n) + c(\frac{h}{2}\ddot{x}_n + 3\dot{x}_n) \tag{7.35b}$$

h = time interval
All values in R.H.S. of Equation (7.35b) are known

Algorithm:

Step 1: Initial displacement and velocity are known as initial conditions of the problem at time $t = 0$

Step 2: Damping c and stiffness k are computed from the system properties

Step 3: Initial acceleration is computed from the equation of motion, Equation (7.29) at time step $t = n$

Step 4: Effective load increment and stiffness increment are computed using Equations (7.35a) and (7.35b)

Step 5: Compute Δx from Equation (7.34) and $\Delta\dot{x}$ from Equation (7.32)

Step 6: Finally total displacement and velocity are computed from Equation (7.30)

Step 7: Repeat steps 3 to 6 for the next time step

7.6.1 Selection of the Time Increment *h*

1. It depends up on the rate of variation of the applied load or ground motion $p(t)$
2. Period of vibration of the structure
3. Accuracy and stability criteria
4. Complexity of nonlinear behaviour of the structure, that is, stiffness K and damping C, if applicable

The linear acceleration method is conditionally stable. It means the step size is governed by Equation (7.10). It is stable only if this equation is satisfied. The implicit schemes require triangularization of the stiffness matrix for solution of a MDOF system.

Example 7.3

An undamped SDOF system has a mass of 4900 N and stiffness of 20 kN/m. It is subjected to a triangular force as shown in Figure 7.5. The initial displacement and velocity are zero. Determine the displacement-time history using linear acceleration method.

Solution

This is the same problem that was solved earlier by constant acceleration method.

$$\Delta\bar{P} = \Delta P + 3m\left(\ddot{x}_n + \frac{2\dot{x}_n}{h}\right) + 0$$

$$= \Delta P + 1500\ddot{x}_n + 30000\dot{x}_n$$

$$\bar{k} = \frac{6m}{h^2} + \frac{3c}{h} + k = 320000 \text{ N/m}$$

$$\Delta x = \Delta\bar{P}/\bar{k}$$

$$\ddot{x}_n = \frac{1}{m}(p_n - c\dot{x}_n - kx_n) = \frac{1}{m}(p_n - 20000x_n)$$

$$\dot{x}_{n+1} = -\frac{h}{2}\ddot{x}_n - 2\dot{x}_n + \frac{3}{h}\Delta x = -0.05\ddot{x}_n - 2\dot{x}_n + 30\Delta x$$

Now it is convenient to carry out the calculations in a tabular form in MS-EXCEL as shown in Table 7.3. Again, the calculations are repeated for a smaller step size $h = 0.05$ sec. The displacement-time history, velocity-time history and acceleration-time history are shown in Figure 7.10. It can be seen that effect of reducing the time step is insignificant in this case. □

TABLE 7.3 LINEAR ACCELERATION METHOD – UNDAMPED SDOF SYSTEM

t	p	x_n	$\dot{x}_n$	$\ddot{x}_n$	Δp	$\overline{\Delta p}$	Δx	$\dot{x}_{n+1}$	x_{n+1}
sec	N	m	m/sec	m/sec²	N	N	m	m/sec	m
(1)	(2)	(3)	(4)	(5)	(6)	(7)	(8)	(9)	(10)
0	400.00	0.0000	0.0000	0.8000	–80	1120.0000	0.0035	0.0650	0.0035
0.1	320.00	0.0035	0.0650	0.5000	–80	2620.0000	0.0082	0.0906	0.0117
0.2	240.00	0.0117	0.0906	0.0125	–80	2657.5000	0.0083	0.0673	0.0200

(Continued)

TABLE 7.3 (CONTINUED)

t	p	x_n	$\dot{x}_n$	$\ddot{x}_n$	Δp	$\overline{\Delta p}$	Δx	$\dot{x}_{n+1}$	x_{n+1}
0.3	160.00	0.0200	0.0673	−0.4797	−80	1218.4375	0.0038	0.0037	0.0238
0.4	80.00	0.0238	0.0037	−0.7920	−80	−1157.5391	−0.0036	−0.0763	0.0202
0.5	0.00	0.0202	−0.0763	−0.8073	0.00	−3499.4385	−0.0109	−0.1351	0.0092
0.6	0.00	0.0092	−0.1351	−0.3699	0.00	−4609.0485	−0.0144	−0.1433	−0.0052
0.7	0.00	−0.0052	−0.1433	0.2063	0.00	−3990.2653	−0.0125	−0.0978	−0.0176
0.8	0.00	−0.0176	−0.0978	0.7050	0.00	−1875.1326	−0.0059	−0.0155	−0.0235
0.9	0.00	−0.0235	−0.0155	0.9394	0.00	943.1748	0.0029	0.0725	−0.0205
1	0.00	−0.0205	0.0725	0.8215	0.00	3407.7916	0.0106	0.1334	−0.0099

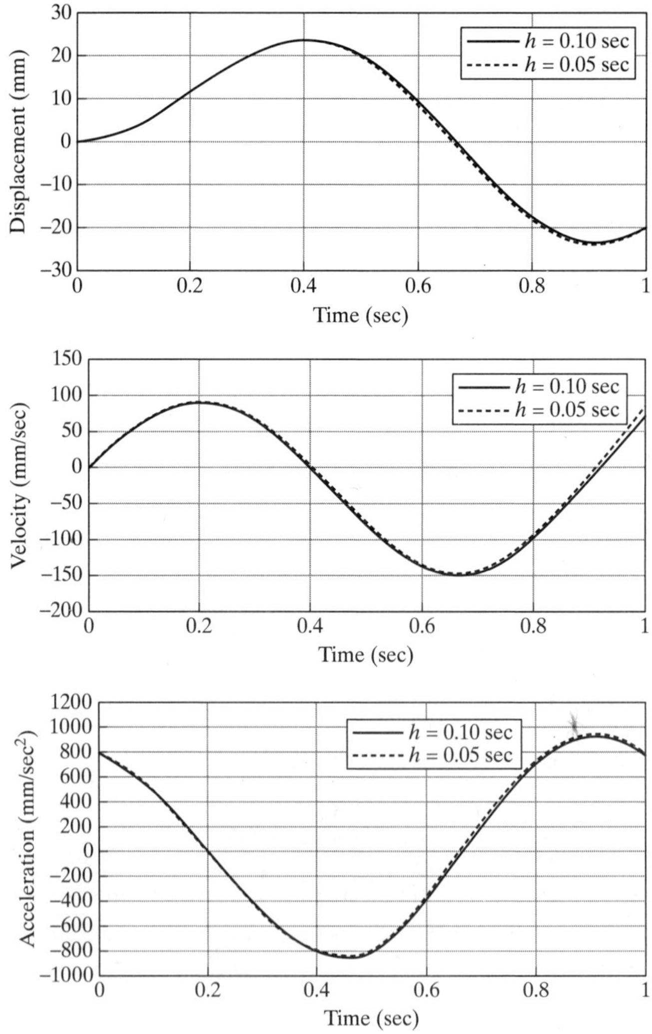

Figure 7.10 Response history – linear acceleration method.

Example 7.4

Let us solve Example 7.3 again by taking 5% damping.

Solution

Damping coefficient $c = 2m\omega\xi = 2 \times 500 \times 6.32 \times 0.05 = 316$ kg/m

$$\Delta\bar{P} = \Delta P + 3m\left(\ddot{x}_n + \frac{2\dot{x}_n}{h}\right) + c\left(\frac{h}{2}\ddot{x}_n + 3\dot{x}_n\right)$$

$$= \Delta P + 1500\ddot{x}_n + 30000\dot{x}_n + 15.8\ddot{x}_n + 948\dot{x}_n$$

$$= \Delta P + 1515.8\ddot{x}_n + 30948\dot{x}_n$$

$$\bar{k} = \frac{6m}{h^2} + \frac{3c}{h} + k = 329480$$

$$\Delta x = \Delta\bar{P}/\bar{k}$$

$$\ddot{x}_n = \frac{1}{m}(p_n - c\dot{x}_n - kx_n) = \frac{1}{m}(p_n - 316\dot{x}_n - 20000x_n)$$

$$\dot{x}_{n+1} = -\frac{h}{2}\ddot{x}_n - 2\dot{x}_n + \frac{3}{h}\Delta x = -0.05\ddot{x}_n - 2\dot{x}_n + 30\Delta x$$

The calculations are shown in Table 7.4. The effect of 5% damping is shown in Figure 7.11. □

TABLE 7.4 LINEAR ACCELERATION METHOD – DAMPED SDOF SYSTEM

t	p	x_n	$\dot{x}_n$	$\ddot{x}_n$	Δp	$\overline{\Delta p}$	Δx	$\dot{x}_{n+1}$	x_{n+1}
sec	N	m	m/sec	m/sec^2	N	N	m	m/sec	m
(1)	(2)	(3)	(4)	(5)	(6)	(7)	(8)	(9)	(10)
0	400.00	0.0000	0.0000	0.8000	−80	1132.6400	0.0034	0.0631	0.0034
0.1	320.00	0.0034	0.0631	0.4626	−80	2574.9429	0.0078	0.0851	0.0113
0.2	240.00	0.0113	0.0851	−0.0239	−80	2516.4274	0.0076	0.0602	0.0189
0.3	160.00	0.0189	0.0602	−0.4737	−80	1064.7706	0.0032	0.0003	0.0221
0.4	80.00	0.0221	0.0003	−0.7250	−80	−1171.1507	−0.0036	−0.0709	0.0186
0.5	0.00	0.0186	−0.0709	−0.6979	0	−3251.8603	−0.0099	−0.1194	0.0087
0.6	0.00	0.0087	−0.1194	−0.2724	0	−4108.4741	−0.0125	−0.1216	−0.0038
0.7	0.00	−0.0038	−0.1216	0.2277	0	−3419.4454	−0.0104	−0.0794	−0.0142
0.8	0.00	−0.0142	−0.0794	0.6162	0	−1524.6698	−0.0046	−0.0107	−0.0188
0.9	0.00	−0.0188	−0.0107	0.7579	0	816.3708	0.0025	0.0579	−0.0163
1	0.00	−0.0163	0.0579	0.6154	0	2725.3652	0.0083	0.1015	0.0080

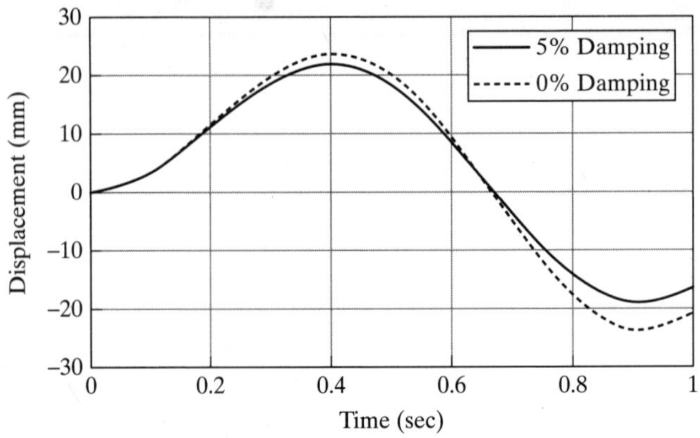

Figure 7.11 Effect of damping – linear acceleration method

7.7 NEWMARK β METHOD

Prof. N. M. Newmark, University of Illinois, Urbana, Champaign in 1959 proposed the following equations for displacement and velocity:

$$x_{n+1} = x_n + \Delta t\dot{x}_n + (0.5 - \beta)(\Delta t)^2\ddot{x}_n + \beta(\Delta t)^2\ddot{x}_{n+1} \tag{7.36}$$

and

$$\dot{x}_{n+1} = \dot{x}_n + (1 - \gamma)\Delta t\ddot{x}_n + \gamma\Delta t\ddot{x}_{n+1} \tag{7.37}$$

β and γ can be selected suitably based on the accuracy and stability criteria.

It is interesting to see that this formulation represents a family of algorithms depending upon the values of γ and β.

$\gamma = 0.5$ and $\beta = 1/6$ leads to linear acceleration method (Figure 7.9)

$\beta = ¼$ leads to constant average acceleration method (Figure 7.12)

$\beta = 0$ leads to explicit method

For $\gamma = 0.5$, Equation (7.37) can be written as:

$$\dot{x}_{n+1} = \dot{x}_n + 0.5\,\Delta t(\ddot{x}_n + \ddot{x}_{n+1}) \tag{7.38}$$

and

$$\ddot{x}_{n+1} = \frac{1}{m}[p_{n+1} - c\dot{x}_{n+1} - kx_{n+1}] \tag{7.39}$$

Iterative Algorithm

Since the new values occur on both sides of the equation, an iterative solution is preferred.

Step 1: Initial displacement and velocity are known as initial conditions of the problem at time $t = 0$

Step 2: Damping c and stiffness k are computed from the system properties

Step 3: Initial acceleration is computed from the equation of motion, Equation (7.39) at time step $t = n$

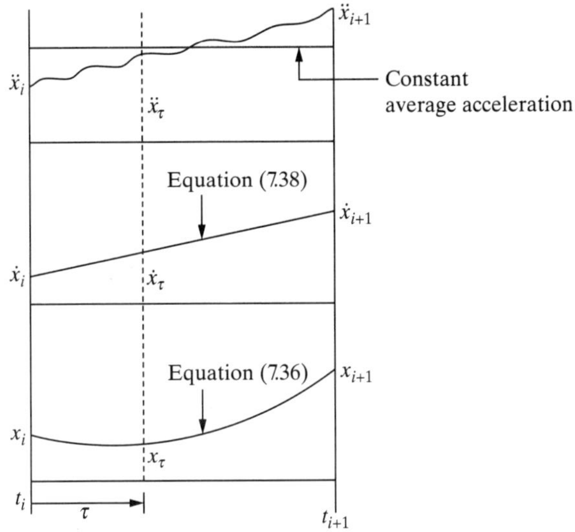

Figure 7.12 Variation of response–Newmark method.

Step 4: Assume a value of acceleration at time step $n + 1$

Step 5: Solve for new displacement and velocity using Equations (7.36) and (7.38)

Step 6: Solve for new acceleration at time n+1 from Equation (7.39)

Step 7: If $\ddot{x}_{n+1}$ from Steps 4 and 6 compare within acceptable accuracy, go to the next time step and repeat Steps 4 to 7; otherwise, revise the assumption for $\ddot{x}_{n+1}$ and repeat Steps 5 to 7

The basic difference between the linear acceleration method and Newmark method is that in the former, acceleration is computed from the incremental equation of equilibrium while in the latter the acceleration is computed from the total equation of equilibrium. In this manner, the former method may accumulate more errors than the latter.

Non-iterative Algorithm

It is possible to re-formulate the Newmark's equations such that there is no need for any iteration.

Step 1: Let us express acceleration $\ddot{x}_{n+1}$ in terms of displacement x_{n+1} and previous values of displacement, velocity and acceleration using Equation (7.36)

$$\ddot{x}_{n+1} = \frac{1}{\beta \Delta t^2}(x_{n+1} - x_n) - \frac{1}{\beta \Delta t}\dot{x}_n - \left(\frac{1}{2\beta} - 1\right)\ddot{x}_n \tag{7.40}$$

Step 2: Substitute it in Equation (7.37) and the velocity $\dot{x}_{n+1}$ can be obtained in terms of displacement x_{n+1}

$$\dot{x}_{n+1} = \dot{x}_n + \Delta t(1-\gamma)\ddot{x}_n + \gamma \Delta t\, \ddot{x}_{n+1} \tag{7.41}$$

Step 3: Now substitute the values of acceleration $\ddot{x}_{n+1}$ and velocity $\dot{x}_{n+1}$ in terms of displacement x_{n+1} in Equation (7.39). This is now in terms of displacement only, and its value can be determined without any iteration. We get,

$$\bar{k}x_{n+1} = \bar{P} \text{ or, } x_{n+1} = \frac{\bar{P}}{\bar{k}} \tag{7.42}$$

where
$$\bar{k} = k + \frac{1}{\beta \Delta t^2} m + \frac{\gamma}{\beta \Delta t} c \tag{7.43}$$

and

$$\bar{P} = P_{n+1} + m\left(\frac{1}{\beta \Delta t^2} x_n + \frac{1}{\beta \Delta t}\dot{x}_n + \left(\frac{1}{2\beta} - 1\right)\ddot{x}_n\right)$$
$$+ c\left(\frac{\gamma}{\beta \Delta t} x_n + \left(\frac{\gamma}{\beta} - 1\right)\dot{x}_n + \frac{\Delta t}{2}\left(\frac{\gamma}{\beta} - 2\right)\ddot{x}_n\right) \tag{7.44}$$

All values in R.H.S. of Equation (7.44) are known.

Step 4: The acceleration $\ddot{x}_{n+1}$ and velocity $\dot{x}_{n+1}$ can be determined using Equations (7.40) and (7.41), respectively

This algorithm can be summarized as follows:

Algorithm:

Step 1: Compute m, c and k for the system

Step 2: Initialize $x(0)$, $\dot{x}(0)$ and $\ddot{x}(0)$, that is, initial displacement and velocity are known. Acceleration at $t = 0$ can be obtained from the equation of motion

Step 3: Select time step Δt, β and γ. Define the following constants:

For γ.GE. 0.50 and β.GE. $0.25(0.50 + \gamma)^2$

$$a_0 = \frac{1}{\beta \Delta t^2},\ a_1 = \frac{\gamma}{\beta \Delta t},\ a_2 = \frac{1}{\beta \Delta t},\ a_3 = \frac{1}{2\beta} - 1$$

$$a_4 = \frac{\gamma}{\beta} - 1,\ a_5 = \frac{\Delta t}{2}\left(\frac{\gamma}{\beta} - 2\right),\ a_6 = \Delta t(1-\gamma),\ a_7 = \gamma \Delta t \tag{7.45}$$

Step 4: Form $\bar{k} = k + a_0 m + a_1 c$ (7.46)

Step 5: For each time step

$$\bar{P} = P_{n+1} + m\,(a_0 x_n + a_2 \dot{x}_n + a_3 \ddot{x}_n) + c\,(a_1 x_n + a_4 \dot{x}_n + a_5 \ddot{x}_n) \tag{7.47}$$

Determine, $x_{n+1} = \bar{P}/\bar{k}$ (7.42)

Step 6: Now determine the new acceleration and velocity using the following equations:

$$\ddot{x}_{n+1} = a_0\,(x_{n+1} - x_n) - a_2 \dot{x}_n - a_3 \ddot{x}_n \tag{7.48}$$

$$\dot{x}_{n+1} = \dot{x}_n + a_6 \ddot{x}_n + a_7 \ddot{x}_{n+1} \tag{7.49}$$

7.7.1 Stability of the Newmark Method

The Newmark method is stable if,

$$\frac{\Delta T}{T} \le \frac{1}{\pi\sqrt{2}\sqrt{\gamma-2\beta}} \tag{7.50a}$$

For $\gamma = 0.5$ and $\beta = ¼$, this condition becomes,

$$\frac{\Delta T}{T} \le \infty \tag{7.50b}$$

This implies that the constant average acceleration method is stable for any h (or Δt) no matter how large it may be. However, for accuracy, Δt should be small enough.

For $\gamma = 0.5$ and $\beta = 1/6$ (i.e. linear acceleration method), $\frac{\Delta T}{T} \le 0.551$

Again a shorter time step is desirable for obtaining accurate solutions.

7.7.2 Newmark Method in Incremental Form

It is more convenient to arrange the Newmark's equations in incremental form.

Consider Equation (7.33)

$$m\Delta\ddot{x} + c\Delta\dot{x} + k\Delta x = P_{n+1} - P_n = \Delta p \tag{7.33}$$

It can be written as

$$m\Delta\ddot{x}_i + c\Delta\dot{x}_i + k\Delta x_i = \Delta p_i \tag{7.51}$$

We know that

$$x_{n+1} = x_n + \Delta t\,\dot{x}_n + (0.5 - \beta)(\Delta t)^2\ddot{x}_n + \beta(\Delta t)^2\ddot{x}_{n+1} \tag{7.36}$$

and

$$\dot{x}_{n+1} = \dot{x}_n + (1-\gamma)\,\Delta t\,\ddot{x}_n + \gamma\Delta t\,\ddot{x}_{n+1} \tag{7.37}$$

Making use of the relations:

$$\begin{aligned} \Delta x &= x_{n+1} - x_n \\ \Delta\dot{x} &= \dot{x}_{n+1} - \dot{x}_n \\ \Delta\ddot{x} &= \ddot{x}_{n+1} - \ddot{x}_n \end{aligned} \tag{7.30}$$

Equation (7.37) can be written as:

$$\Delta\dot{x}_i = \Delta t\,\ddot{x}_i + \gamma\,\Delta t\Delta\ddot{x}_i \tag{7.52a}$$

Equation (7.36) can be written as:

$$\Delta x_i = \Delta t\,\dot{x}_i + \frac{(\Delta t)^2}{2}\ddot{x}_i + \beta(\Delta t)^2\Delta\ddot{x}_i \tag{7.52b}$$

This gives

$$\Delta\ddot{x}_i = \frac{1}{\beta(\Delta t)^2}\Delta x_i - \frac{1}{\beta\Delta t}\dot{x}_i - \frac{1}{2\beta}\ddot{x}_i \tag{7.53}$$

Substituting Equation (7.53) in Equation (7.52a)

$$\Delta \dot{x}_i = \frac{\gamma}{\beta \Delta t}\Delta x_i - \frac{\gamma}{\beta}\dot{x}_i + \Delta t\left(1 - \frac{\gamma}{2\beta}\right)\ddot{x}_i \tag{7.54}$$

Equation (7.53) and (7.54) can be substituted in Equation (7.51)

$$\bar{k} = \frac{\Delta \bar{p}}{\Delta x_i} \tag{7.55}$$

where,

$$\bar{k} = k + \frac{\gamma}{\beta \Delta t}c + \frac{1}{\beta (\Delta t)^2}m \tag{7.56}$$

and

$$\Delta \bar{p}_i = \Delta p_i + \left(\frac{1}{\beta \Delta t}m + \frac{\gamma}{\beta}c\right)\dot{x}_i + \left[\frac{1}{2\beta}m + \Delta t\left(\frac{\gamma}{2\beta} - 1\right)c\right]\ddot{x}_i \tag{7.57}$$

Once Δx_i is known, $\Delta \dot{x}_i$ and $\Delta \ddot{x}_i$ can be computed from Equations (7.54) and (7.53), respectively. The total displacement, velocity and acceleration can be computed from Equation (7.30). Alternatively, the total acceleration can also be computed from Equation (7.39) instead of using Equations (7.53) and (7.30). It should be remembered that Equation (7.39) is required to start the process from the beginning.

Example 7.5

Solve Example 7.3 using Newmark method for $\beta = 1/4$ and $\beta = 1/6$.

Solution

Mass = 500 kg, stiffness = 20000 N/m, damping = 0
Period $T = 1.0$ sec, step size $\Delta t = 0.10$ sec
Newmark constants are:

$$a_0 = \frac{1}{\beta \Delta t^2},\ a_1 = \frac{\gamma}{\beta \Delta t},\ a_2 = \frac{1}{\beta \Delta t},\ a_3 = \frac{1}{2\beta} - 1$$

$$a_4 = \frac{\gamma}{\beta} - 1,\ a_5 = \frac{\Delta t}{2}\left(\frac{\gamma}{\beta} - 2\right),\ a_6 = \Delta t(1-\gamma),\ a_7 = \gamma \Delta t$$

Newmark integration constants:

For $\beta = 0.25$

$a_0 = 400.0000$	$a_4 = 1.0000$
$a_1 = 20.0000$	$a_5 = 0.0000$
$a_2 = 40.0000$	$a_6 = 0.0500$
$a_3 = 1.0000$	$a_7 = 0.0500$

For $\beta = 0.16667$

$a_0 = 600.2401$	$a_4 = 2.0012$
$a_1 = 30.0120$	$a_5 = 0.0501$
$a_2 = 60.0240$	$a_6 = 0.0500$
$a_3 = 2.0012$	$a_7 = 0.0500$

The calculations can be carried out either in MS-EXCEL, MATLAB or in Fortran. The results are shown in Figure 7.13. Since the step size was taken as T/10, the results are very close to each other. □

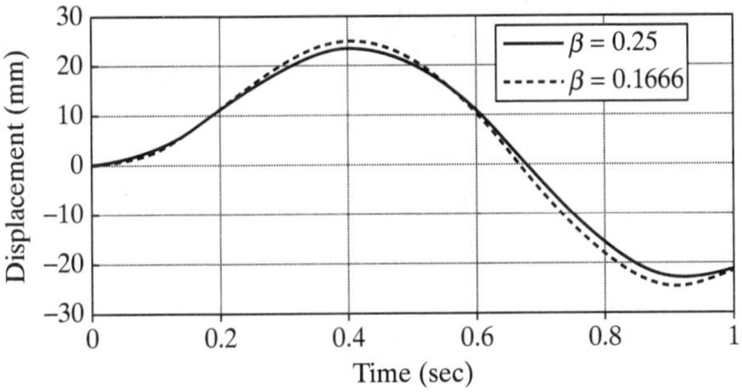

Figure 7.13 Effect of Newmark constant β

Example 7.6

A damped SDOF system has a mass of 10 kg, stiffness of 175 N/m and damping of 2%. It is subjected to a reversed cyclic acceleration force as shown in the table. The initial displacement and velocity are zero. Determine the displacement-time history using Newmark β method.

Acceleration, g	0	0.2	– 0.2	0.4	– 0.4	0.6	– 0.6	0.2	– 0.2	0.1	0	0
Time, sec	0	0.1	0.2	0.3	0.4	0.5	0.6	0.7	0.8	0.9	1.0	5.0

Solution

Let us take $\gamma = 0.5$ and $\beta = 1/4$, $\Delta t = 0.10$ sec

Mass = 10 kg; stiffness = 175 N/m; Natural frequency = 4.18 rad/sec and period $T = 1.5$ sec

Acceleration due to gravity $g = 980$ cm/sec^2

The input ground excitation is shown in Figure 7.14. It needs to be multiplied by mass to get force.

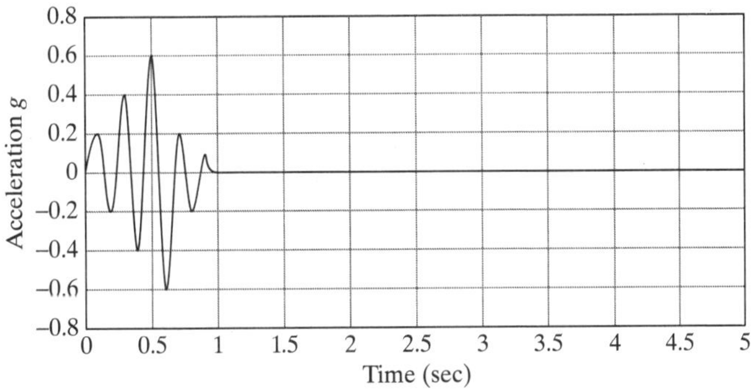

Figure 7.14 Ground acceleration.

$$a_0 = \frac{1}{\beta \Delta t^2},\ a_1 = \frac{\gamma}{\beta \Delta t},\ a_2 = \frac{1}{\beta \Delta t},\ a_3 = \frac{1}{2\beta} - 1$$

$$a_4 = \frac{\gamma}{\beta} - 1,\ a_5 = \frac{\Delta t}{2}\left(\frac{\gamma}{\beta} - 2\right),\ a_6 = \Delta t(1-\gamma),\ a_7 = \gamma \Delta t$$

The integration constants are:

$$a_0 = 400.0000$$

$$a_1 = 20.0000$$

$$a_2 = 40.0000$$
$$a_3 = 1.0000$$
$$a_4 = 1.0000$$
$$a_5 = 0.0000$$
$$a_6 = 0.0500$$
$$a_7 = 0.0500$$
$$\bar{k} = k + a_0 m + a_1 c$$

For each time step,

$$\bar{P} = P_{n+1} + m(a_0 x_n + a_2 \dot{x}_n + a_3 \ddot{x}_n) + c(a_1 x_n + a_4 \dot{x}_n + a_5 \ddot{x}_n)$$
$$x_{n+1} = \bar{P}/\bar{k}$$

The detailed calculations can be done in MS-Excel, MATLAB or in Fortran. The displacement response is shown in Figure 7.15. The same problem was again solved with $\xi = 10\%$. The results are shown in the same figure. □

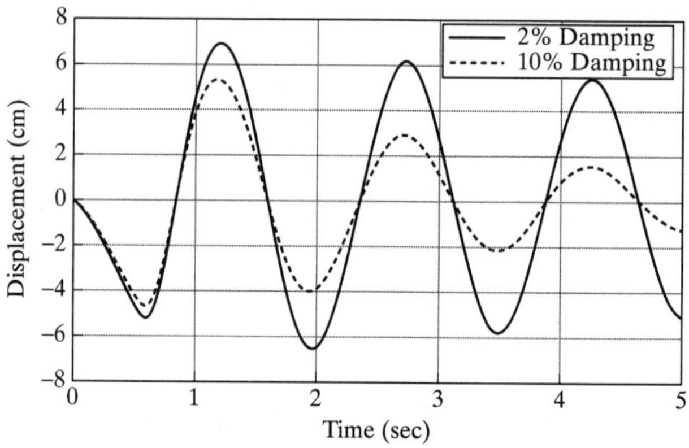

Figure 7.15 Newmark method with $\beta = 0.25$.

Example 7.7

Consider an undamped SDOF system with the following data:
Mass = 2000 kg, stiffness = 20000 N/m, initial displacement = 0, velocity = 0
It is subjected to a constant force = 100 N throughout. Illustrate the effect of step size on stability of Newmark β method.

Solution

Period of vibration = 1.987 sec
Let us find its response with a step size Δt = 0.25 sec and again with 2.5 sec. The results are shown in Table 7.5. Two observations can be made from this table:

- The numerical values do not grow with increase in step size from 0.25 sec to 2.5 sec.
- In the first step, the displacement increases to a very high value from 1.35 mm to 9.4 mm and then it keeps oscillating.
- The maximum displacements in the two cases are 9.96 mm and 9.93 mm.
- The results with step size = 2.5 are not accurate, but it shows that the method is stable and does not depend upon the step size. The values do not grow.

The results are also shown in Figure 7.16. □

TABLE 7.5 EFFECT OF STEP SIZE ON STABILITY OF NEWMARK METHOD

	$\Delta t =$	0.250										
Time	Δt	2 Δt	3 Δt	4 Δt	5 Δt	6 Δt	7 Δt	8 Δt	9 Δt	10 Δt	11 Δt	12 Δt
Displacement	1.35	4.67	8.17	9.96	9.06	5.97	2.35	0.168	0.595	3.4	7.07	9.62
	$\Delta t =$	2.500										
Displacement	9.4	2.26	5.42	7	1.06	9.93	0.266	8.4	3.75	3.8	8.37	0.28

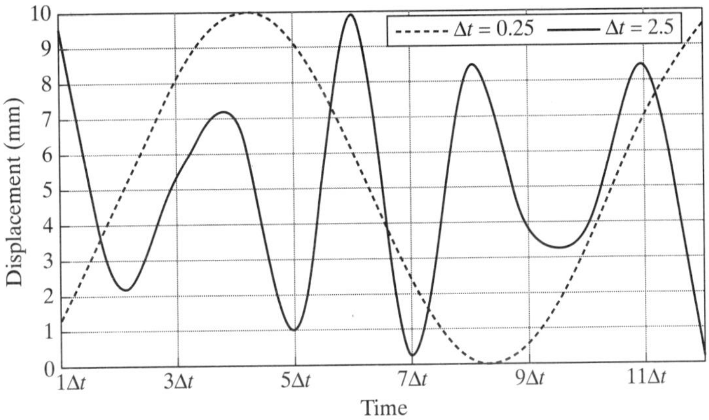

Figure 7.16 Effect of step size on the stability of Newmark β method.

Example 7.8

A two DOF system is subjected to a constant force P. The initial displacement and velocity are zero. Determine the response-time history using Newmark β method.

$$M = \begin{bmatrix} 4 & 0 \\ 0 & 1 \end{bmatrix} K = \begin{bmatrix} 8 & -2 \\ -2 & 6 \end{bmatrix} C = \begin{bmatrix} 0.53 & 0 \\ 0 & 0.25 \end{bmatrix} P = \begin{Bmatrix} 0 \\ 2.5 \end{Bmatrix}$$

Initial conditions are: $\begin{Bmatrix} x_{10} \\ x_{20} \end{Bmatrix} = \begin{Bmatrix} 0 \\ 0 \end{Bmatrix}$ and $\begin{Bmatrix} \dot{x}_{10} \\ \dot{x}_{20} \end{Bmatrix} = \begin{Bmatrix} 0 \\ 0 \end{Bmatrix}$

Solution

The natural frequency and periods for the two DOF system can be computed as discussed in Chapters 9 and 10 and are shown as follows:

$$\begin{Bmatrix} \omega_1 \\ \omega_2 \end{Bmatrix} = \begin{Bmatrix} 1.328 \\ 2.497 \end{Bmatrix} \text{ and } \begin{Bmatrix} T_1 \\ T_2 \end{Bmatrix} = \begin{Bmatrix} 4.73 \\ 2.51 \end{Bmatrix}$$

Newmark β method with $\beta = ¼$ is unconditionally stable. Any step size can be chosen. Let us choose a step size of $\Delta t = 0.25$ sec and $\beta = 1/4$.
Newmark integration constants are:

$$a_0 = \frac{1}{\beta \Delta t^2},\ a_1 = \frac{\gamma}{\beta \Delta t},\ a_2 = \frac{1}{\beta \Delta t},\ a_3 = \frac{1}{2\beta} - 1$$

$$a_4 = \frac{\gamma}{\beta} - 1,\ a_5 = \frac{\Delta t}{2}\left(\frac{\gamma}{\beta} - 2\right),\ a_6 = \Delta t(1-\gamma),\ a_7 = \gamma\Delta t$$

$$a_0 = 64.0$$
$$a_1 = 8.0$$
$$a_2 = 16.0$$
$$a_3 = 1.0$$
$$a_4 = 1.0$$
$$a_5 = 0.0$$
$$a_6 = 0.125$$
$$a_7 = 0.125$$

The effective stiffness matrix can be written as follows:

$$\left[\bar{K}\right] = \begin{bmatrix} 8 & -2 \\ -2 & 6 \end{bmatrix} + a_0\begin{bmatrix} 4 & 0 \\ 0 & 1 \end{bmatrix} + a_1\begin{bmatrix} 0.53 & 0 \\ 0 & 0.25 \end{bmatrix} \tag{7.46}$$

For each time step:
The effective load vector can be written as follows:

$$\{\bar{P}\} = \begin{Bmatrix} 0 \\ 2.5 \end{Bmatrix} + \begin{bmatrix} 4 & 0 \\ 0 & 1 \end{bmatrix}\left(a_0\begin{Bmatrix} x_{1n} \\ x_{2n} \end{Bmatrix} + a_2\begin{Bmatrix} \dot{x}_{1n} \\ \dot{x}_{2n} \end{Bmatrix} + a_3\begin{Bmatrix} \ddot{x}_{1n} \\ \ddot{x}_{2n} \end{Bmatrix}\right) + \begin{bmatrix} 0.53 & 0 \\ 0 & 0.25 \end{bmatrix}\left(a_1\begin{Bmatrix} x_{1n} \\ x_{2n} \end{Bmatrix} + a_4\begin{Bmatrix} \dot{x}_{1n} \\ \dot{x}_{2n} \end{Bmatrix} + a_5\begin{Bmatrix} \ddot{x}_{1n} \\ \ddot{x}_{2n} \end{Bmatrix}\right) \tag{7.47}$$

Solve for $\begin{Bmatrix} x_{1n+1} \\ x_{2n+1} \end{Bmatrix} = \left[\bar{K}\right]^{-1}\{\bar{P}\}$

or, $\{\bar{P}\} = \left[LDL^T\right]\{x_{n+1}\}$

There is no need to determine inverse of effective stiffness matrix. Instead, effective stiffness matrix can be decomposed in a lower triangular matrix, and by using back substitution, a solution for displacement vector can be estimated.
Now, the acceleration and velocity vectors can be estimated at t + Δt step as follows:

$$\begin{Bmatrix} \ddot{x}_{1n+1} \\ \ddot{x}_{2n+1} \end{Bmatrix} = a_0\begin{Bmatrix} x_{1n+1} - x_{1n} \\ x_{2n+1} - x_{2n} \end{Bmatrix} - a_2\begin{Bmatrix} \dot{x}_{1n} \\ \dot{x}_{2n} \end{Bmatrix} - a_3\begin{Bmatrix} \ddot{x}_{1n} \\ \ddot{x}_{2n} \end{Bmatrix} \tag{7.48}$$

and

$$\begin{Bmatrix} \dot{x}_{1n+1} \\ \dot{x}_{2n+1} \end{Bmatrix} = \begin{Bmatrix} \dot{x}_{1n} \\ \dot{x}_{2n} \end{Bmatrix} + a_6\begin{Bmatrix} \ddot{x}_{1n} \\ \ddot{x}_{2n} \end{Bmatrix} + a_7\begin{Bmatrix} \ddot{x}_{1n+1} \\ \ddot{x}_{2n+1} \end{Bmatrix} \tag{7.49}$$

The calculations were carried out in MS-EXCEL and the results are shown in Table 7.6. The displacement response for the two DOF system is shown in Figure 7.17. Similarly, this method can be used for the solution of any MDOF system. The displacement is quite high because of the selection of the data. Normally such a large displacement would be expected if the system becomes inelastic. □

TABLE 7.6 TWO DOF SYSTEM NEWMARK β METHOD

t	x_{1n}	x_{2n}	$\dot{x}_{1n}$	$\dot{x}_{2n}$	$\ddot{x}_{1n}$	$\ddot{x}_{2n}$	Re1	Re2	x_{1n+1}	x_{2n+1}	$\ddot{x}_{1n+1}$	$\ddot{x}_{2n+1}$	$\dot{x}_{1n+1}$	$\dot{x}_{2n+1}$
(1)	(2)	(3)	(4)	(5)	(6)	(7)	(8)	(9)	(10)	(11)	(12)	(13)	(14)	(15)
Δt	0.00	0.00	0.00	0.00	0.00	10.00	0.00	40.00	0.00	0.56	0.27	25.56	0.03	4.45
2 Δt	0.00	0.56	0.03	4.45	0.27	25.56	4.24	134.75	0.03	1.87	0.85	–12.42	0.17	6.09
3 Δt	0.03	1.87	0.17	6.09	0.85	–12.42	22.01	207.33	0.10	2.88	1.12	–20.35	0.42	1.99
4 Δt	0.10	2.88	0.42	1.99	1.12	–20.35	57.76	198.49	0.24	2.76	0.66	–19.14	0.64	–2.94
5 Δt	0.24	2.76	0.64	–2.94	0.66	–19.14	104.07	113.12	0.40	1.58	–0.43	–9.36	0.67	–6.51
6 Δt	0.40	1.58	0.67	–6.51	–0.43	–9.36	143.46	–9.69	0.53	–0.12	–1.69	4.53	0.40	–7.11
7 Δt	0.53	–0.12	0.40	–7.11	–1.69	4.53	155.76	–114.39	0.57	–1.57	–2.53	16.22	–0.12	–4.52
8 Δt	0.57	–1.57	–0.12	–4.52	–2.53	16.22	127.61	–154.21	0.46	–2.13	–2.47	20.45	–0.75	0.07
9 Δt	0.46	–2.13	–0.75	0.07	–2.47	20.45	59.92	–112.22	0.21	–1.55	–1.42	15.35	–1.24	4.54
10 Δt	0.21	–1.55	–1.24	4.54	–1.42	15.35	–30.56	–8.84	-0.11	–0.13	0.29	3.28	–1.38	6.87
11 Δt	–0.11	–0.13	–1.38	6.87	0.29	3.28	–116.43	107.64	-0.42	1.48	2.04	–10.21	–1.09	6.00
12 Δt	–0.42	1.48	–1.09	6.00	2.04	–10.21	–169.72	183.28	-0.61	2.53	3.14	–18.96	–0.44	2.36

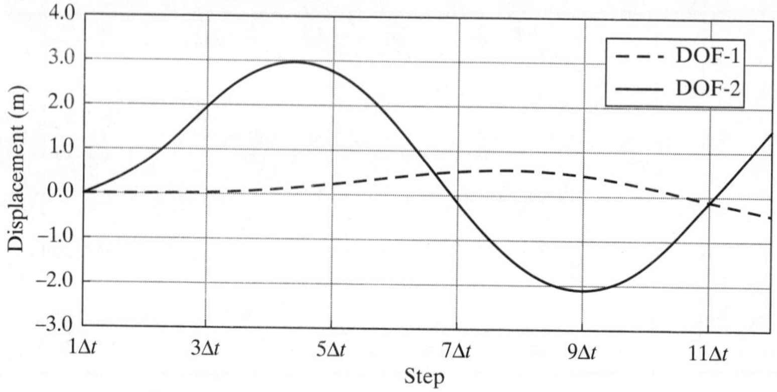

Figure 7.17 Variation of displacement with time step.

7.8 WILSON θ METHOD

This is another algorithm for the solution of incremental equation of equilibrium developed by Prof. E. L. Wilson, University of California, Berkeley. The calculations are carried out over an extended time step $\tau = \theta\Delta t$, where θ is an amplifier for the time step. It assumes that the variation of acceleration over the extended time step remains unchanged, that is, it is still the same as that of the original time step Δt, that is, a linear variation (Figure 7.18).

At time t, acceleration $= \ddot{x}(t)$

At time $t + \Delta t$, the acceleration $= \ddot{x}(t) + \Delta\ddot{x}$ over the normal time step

At time $t + \tau$, the acceleration is $= \ddot{x}(t) + \overline{\Delta\ddot{x}}$ over the extended time step

The equation of motion at the end of $t + \tau$ can be written as follows:

$$m\ddot{x}_{t+\tau} + c_n\dot{x}_{t+\tau} + k_n x_{t+\tau} = R \tag{7.58}$$

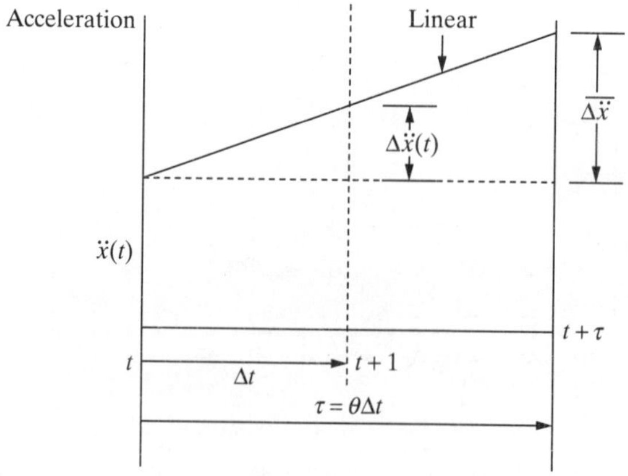

Figure 7.18 Linear acceleration assumption over extended time τ.

where R is the projected load vector given as follows:

$$R = P_n + \theta (P_{n+1} - P_n) \tag{7.59}$$

$$\begin{aligned} x_{t+\tau} &= x_n + \Delta x_\tau \\ \dot{x}_{t+\tau} &= \dot{x}_n + \Delta \dot{x}_\tau \\ \ddot{x}_{t+\tau} &= \ddot{x}_n + \Delta \ddot{x}_\tau \end{aligned} \tag{7.60}$$

Therefore, Equation (7.58) becomes,

$$m\Delta\ddot{x}_\tau + c_n \Delta\dot{x}_\tau + k_n \Delta x_\tau = R - m\ddot{x}_n - c_n \dot{x}_n - k_n x_n \tag{7.61}$$

Thus, by analogy with Equations (7.24, 7.27a) and (7.28b) of the linear acceleration method,

$$\Delta x_\tau = \tau \dot{x}_n + \frac{\tau^2}{2}\ddot{x}_n + \frac{\tau^2}{6}\Delta\ddot{x}_\tau \tag{7.62a}$$

$$\Delta \dot{x}_\tau = \tau \ddot{x}_n + \frac{\tau}{2}\Delta\ddot{x}_\tau \tag{7.62b}$$

Rearranging these equations to express each of them in terms of incremental displacement Δx_τ, we get,

$$\Delta\ddot{x}_\tau = \frac{6}{\tau^2}\Delta x_\tau - \frac{6}{\tau}\dot{x}_n - 3\ddot{x}_n \tag{7.63a}$$

$$\Delta\dot{x}_\tau = \frac{3}{\tau}\Delta x_\tau - 3\dot{x}_n - \frac{\tau}{2}\ddot{x}_n \tag{7.63b}$$

Substituting Equation (7.63) in Equation (7.61) yields,

$$\left[\frac{6}{\tau^2}m + \frac{3}{\tau}c_n + k_n\right]\Delta x_\tau = R - k_n x_n + m\left[\frac{6}{\tau}\dot{x}_n + 2\ddot{x}_n\right] + c_n\left[2\dot{x}_n + \frac{\tau}{2}\ddot{x}_n\right] \tag{7.64a}$$

$$\bar{k}\,\Delta x_\tau = \overline{\Delta P} \tag{7.64b}$$

This gives Δx_τ.

Finally, the acceleration, velocity and displacement at the end of the normal time step Δt are calculated as follows:

$$\ddot{x}_{n+1} = \frac{1}{\theta}\left[\frac{6}{\tau^2}\Delta x_\tau - \frac{6}{\tau}\dot{x}_n + \theta\left(1 - \frac{3}{\theta}\right)\ddot{x}_n\right] \tag{7.65}$$

The velocity and displacements can be computed using Equations (7.28a) and (7.27a) derived for the linear acceleration method, where h is the same as Δt, that is,

$$x_{n+1} = x_n + \Delta t\,\dot{x}_n + \frac{(\Delta t)^2}{3}\ddot{x}_n + \frac{(\Delta t)^2}{6}\ddot{x}_{n+1} \tag{7.66}$$

$$\dot{x}_{n+1} = \dot{x}_n + 0.5\,\Delta t\,(\ddot{x}_n + \ddot{x}_{n+1}) \tag{7.67}$$

Alternatively,

Equation (7.64a) can be re-written as follows:

Let us add and subtract $m\dot{x}_n$ and $c_n\,\dot{x}_n$ on the right-hand side of Equation (7.64a) and re-write as follows:

$$\left[\frac{6}{\tau^2}m+\frac{3}{\tau}c_n+k_n\right]\Delta x_\tau = R-m\ddot{x}_n-c_n\dot{x}_n-k_nx_n$$

$$+m\left[\frac{6}{\tau}\dot{x}_n+3\ddot{x}_n\right]+c_n\left[3\dot{x}_n+\frac{\tau}{2}\ddot{x}_n\right]$$

or,
$$\left[\frac{6}{\tau^2}m+\frac{3}{\tau}c_n+k_n\right]\Delta x_\tau = R_1+m\left[\frac{6}{\tau}\dot{x}_n+3\ddot{x}_n\right]+c_n\left[3\dot{x}_n+\frac{\tau}{2}\ddot{x}_n\right] \tag{7.68a}$$

$$\bar{k}\,\Delta x_\tau = \overline{\Delta P} \tag{7.68b}$$

This gives Δx_τ.

Alternatively,

Equation (7.64a) can again be re-written by adding the following term on both sides:

$$\left[\frac{6}{\tau^2}m+\frac{3}{\tau}c_n+k_n\right]x_n$$

The final equation becomes as follows:

$$\left[\frac{6}{\tau^2}m+\frac{3}{\tau}c_n+k_n\right]x_{t+\tau} = R+m\left[\frac{6}{\tau^2}x_n+\frac{6}{\tau}\dot{x}_n+2\ddot{x}_n\right]+c_n\left[\frac{3}{\tau}x_n+2\dot{x}_n+\frac{\tau}{2}\ddot{x}_n\right] \tag{7.69a}$$

or,
$$\bar{k}\;x_{t+\tau} = \overline{\Delta P} \tag{7.69b}$$

This gives $x_{t+\tau}$.

Algorithm:

Step 1: Compute $\bar{k}$ from $\left[\frac{6}{\tau^2}m+\frac{3}{\tau}c_n+k_n\right]$

Step 2: For each time step

Form $\overline{\Delta P}$

Solve for Δx_τ using Equation (7.64b), or (7.68b), or $x_{t+\tau}$ using Equation (7.69b)

Step 3: Calculate x_{n+1}, $\dot{x}_{n+1}$ and $\ddot{x}_{n+1}$ using Equations (7.65), (7.66) and (7.67).

Step 4: Update c and k.

Step 5: Repeat steps 1 to 4.

It should be noted that in this method, k and c are assumed to remain constant during the extended time step and are updated at the end of the real-time increment Δt.

$\theta = 1$ leads to the linear acceleration method.

It is recommended that θ is taken > 1.37.

7.9 NONLINEAR PROBLEMS

The algorithms for linear acceleration method, Newmark method and Wilson method are capable of analysing nonlinear problems due to material nonlinearity. There is a need to track the system displacement, member spring force and spring stiffness. Appropriate stiffness should be considered in the calculations. The time step needs to be chosen very carefully so that the change in stiffness occurs at the selected time interval. Otherwise, a correction will have to be applied. A detailed treatment of nonlinear analysis is presented in Chapter 15.

REVIEW QUESTIONS

7.1 Discuss the essential features of direct integration methods for the solution of equations of motion.

7.2 What is the significance of the term "direct" in direct integration methods?

7.3 What is the implication of step-by-step numerical integration method for the solution of equation of motion?

7.4 How do you select time step for a direct integration method?

7.5 What are explicit algorithms for the solution of equation of motion?

7.6 What are implicit algorithms for the solution of equation of motion?

7.7 On what basis the constant acceleration method derives its name?

7.8 Develop the constant acceleration method for the solution of equation of motion of a SDOF system.

7.9 Develop the central difference method for the solution of equation of motion of a SDOF system.

7.10 What time step should be chosen for stability of central difference method?

7.11 What is incremental equation of motion? Discuss its merits.

7.12 Develop the linear acceleration method for the solution of equation of motion of a SDOF system.

7.13 How do you select time increment for linear acceleration method?

7.14 What is the implication of triangularization of stiffness matrix in implicit methods?

7.15 Develop the non-iterative algorithm for the Newmark β method for the solution of equation of motion of a SDOF.

7.16 What is the implication of different values of constants β and γ in the Newmark method?

7.17 Discuss the stability of Newmark β method.

7.18 Distinguish between the linear acceleration method and Newmark β method.

7.19 What is the basis of Wilson θ method?

7.20 How do you modify the linear acceleration method for the solution of non-linear problems?

PROBLEMS

7.1 A SDOF system has a mass = 100 kg, stiffness = 4000 N/m and damping $\xi = 5\%$. Determine the response of this system when it is subjected to a triangular pulse force as defined in the table using (a) Constant acceleration method and (b) Central difference method. Take step size = 0.1 sec and plot the displacement, velocity and acceleration time history.

Time, sec	0	0.1	0.2	0.3	0.4	0.5	0.6	1.0
Force, N	0	100	150	90	40	10	0	0

Ans: Period = 1 sec, Step size = 0.1 sec. The results are shown in Figures P7.1.

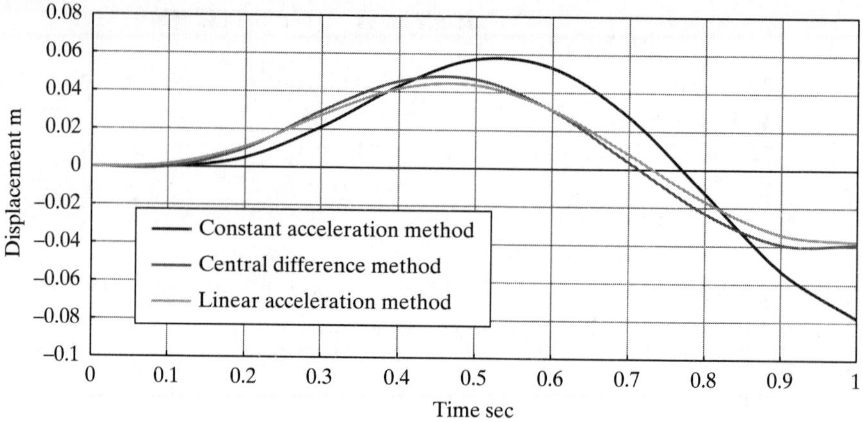

Figure P7.1(a) Displacement – time history

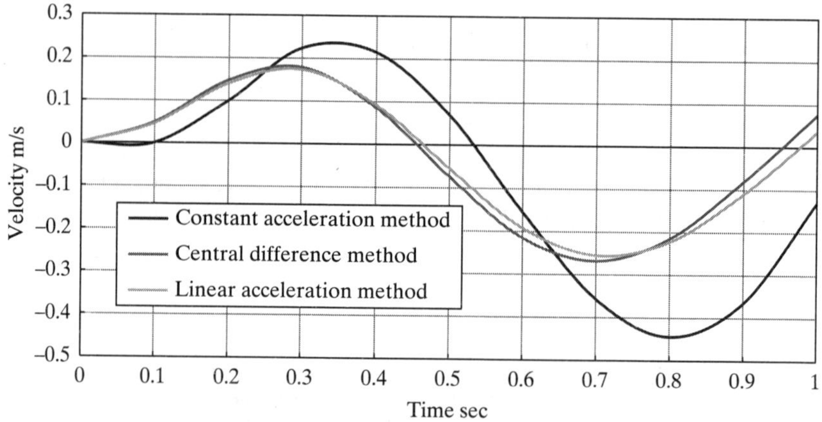

Figure P7.1(b) Velocity – time history

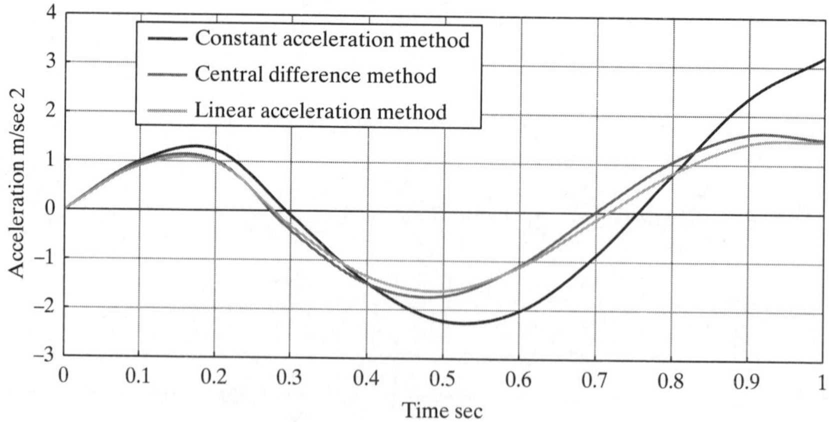

Figure P7.1(c) Acceleration – time history

7.2 Solve Problem 7.1 again using the linear acceleration method with a step size = 0.1 sec and compare the results obtained by using the Constant acceleration and central difference method.

Ans: The results are shown in Figures P7.1.

7.3 Solve Problem 7.1 again with a step size = 0.05 sec and comment on the accuracy and stability of the solution.

7.4 A SDOF system has a mass m = 125 kg and stiffness = 2000 N/m and damping = 7%. Determine the response of this system when it is subjected to a half sine pulse force = 50 sin (3t) N using (a) Constant acceleration method and (b) Central difference method. Take (i) step size = 0.1 sec and (ii) step size = 0.2 sec. Plot the displacement, velocity and acceleration time history, and comment on the stability and accuracy.

7.5 Solve Problem 7.4 using the Newmark β method with $\beta = 0.25$ and compare the results with those obtained in Problem 7.4.

7.6 Solve Problem 7.4 again using the Wilson θ method. Comment on the results.

7.7 A two DOF system has the following properties (kg-N-m units):

$$M = \begin{bmatrix} 5 & 0 \\ 0 & 1 \end{bmatrix}, \; K = \begin{bmatrix} 10 & -2 \\ -2 & 4 \end{bmatrix}, \; C = \begin{bmatrix} 0.53 & 0 \\ 0 & 0.25 \end{bmatrix}, \; P = \begin{Bmatrix} 0 \\ 5 \end{Bmatrix}$$

Initial conditions are: $\begin{Bmatrix} x_{10} \\ x_{20} \end{Bmatrix} = \begin{Bmatrix} 0.05 \\ 0 \end{Bmatrix}$ and $\begin{Bmatrix} \dot{x}_{10} \\ \dot{x}_{20} \end{Bmatrix} = \begin{Bmatrix} 0 \\ 0.01 \end{Bmatrix}$

Determine its response up to 5 sec using the linear acceleration method and Newmark β method with $\beta = ¼$. Compare the results.

8 Elastic Response Spectra

8.1 INTRODUCTION

One of the top priorities of researchers in early 1900s was to develop a methodology to analyse and design buildings that are resistant to earthquakes. But how to estimate the earthquake force was a moot point. How to get the accelerogram of '*the earthquake*' that is likely to occur at a given location? The problem became quite complicated for the following reasons:

(a) Earthquakes do not occur frequently.

(b) Earthquakes cannot be predicted.

(c) It is not possible to instrument each and every possible location to record the earthquake ground motion and maintain these instruments over a period of several decades—24 × 7.

(d) Very meagre database on earthquakes.

(e) An earthquake is a random natural phenomenon. Each earthquake occurring even at the same site is expected to be different.

An earthquake excitation may be described in terms of ground displacement, velocity or acceleration varying with time. The most important characteristics of an earthquake include its magnitude, frequency content, peak ground acceleration and duration. An earthquake motion is recorded in terms of ground acceleration using accelerometers at any location in three mutually perpendicular directions (x, y and z). It is called accelerogram. This accelerogram after applying some corrections can be integrated to get ground velocity-time history and again integrated to obtain ground displacement-time history. The North–South component of the El Centro or Imperial Valley, California earthquake of 18 May 1940, Koyna earthquake of 11 December 1967, Mexico earthquake of 19 September 1985 and Kobe earthquake of 17 January 1995 were some of the very strong earthquakes ever recorded in different continents and were selected for illustration in this chapter. The El Centro earthquake of May 1940 was the first strongest earthquake ever recorded till that point of time and became the natural choice of the researchers all over the world to study the dynamic response of various structures as a bench mark. The main features of these four earthquakes are shown in Table 8.1 and the estimated damage in Table 8.2. The accelerograms of these earthquakes are shown in Figures 8.1 to 8.4. The data for different strong earthquakes is available from

TABLE 8.1 DATA OF THE EARTHQUAKES CONSIDERED

Earthquake	Date	Magnitude	MM Intensity	Epicenter	Depth	Soil type	Peak ground acceleration
El Centro or Imperial valley, USA	19 May 1940	6.9	X	8 km North of Calexico, California	16 km	hard	0.33 g
Koyna, India	11 Dec 1967	6.5	V	1–5 km	27 km	hard	0.67 g
Mexico City	19 Sept 1985	8.1	IX	350 km west of city	20 km	soft	0.18 g
Kobe, Japan or Great Hanshin earthquake	17 Jan 1995	6.9	X	20 km	17 km	hard	0.35 g

TABLE 8.2 ESTIMATED LOSS TO LIFE AND BUILDINGS

Earthquake	Estimated loss and damage
El Centro	9 dead, 25% residential buildings and about 50% commercial buildings collapsed/severely damaged
Koyna	180 dead, 2000 injured, 80% houses damaged, minor cracks in a dam
Mexico	9500 dead, 30,000 injured, 3500 buildings collapsed/demolished and 100,000 seriously damaged
Kobe	6000 dead, 45,000 injured, 200,000 buildings collapsed or severely damaged, 1 km long Hanshin expressway collapsed

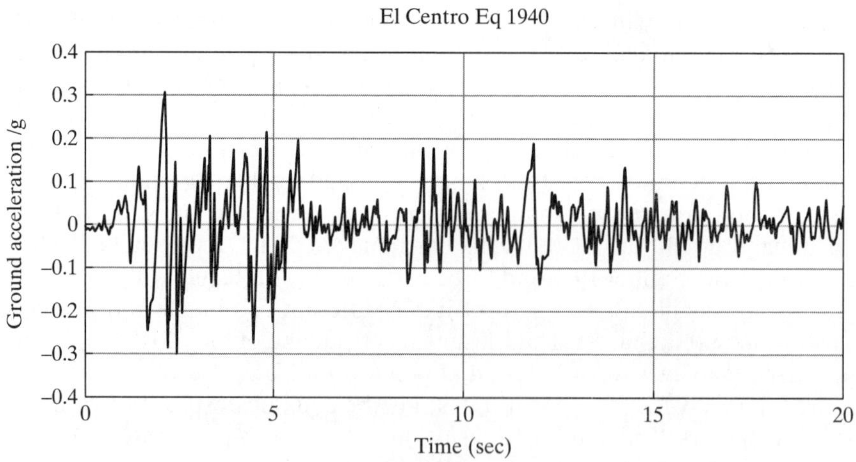

(a) Ground acceleration

Figure 8.1 N–S component of El Centro earthquake, May 1940.

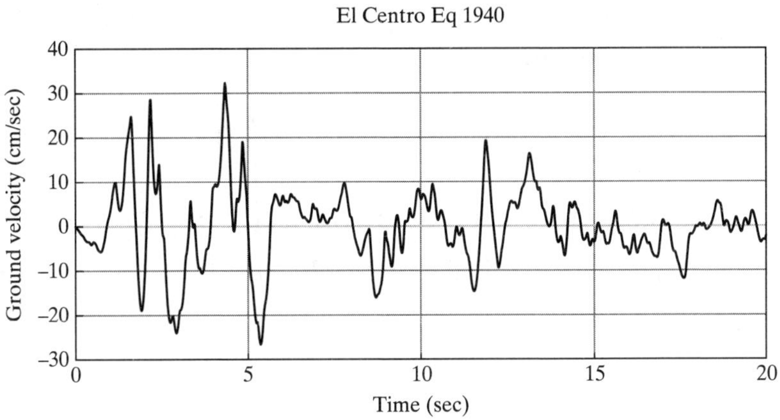

(b) Ground velocity

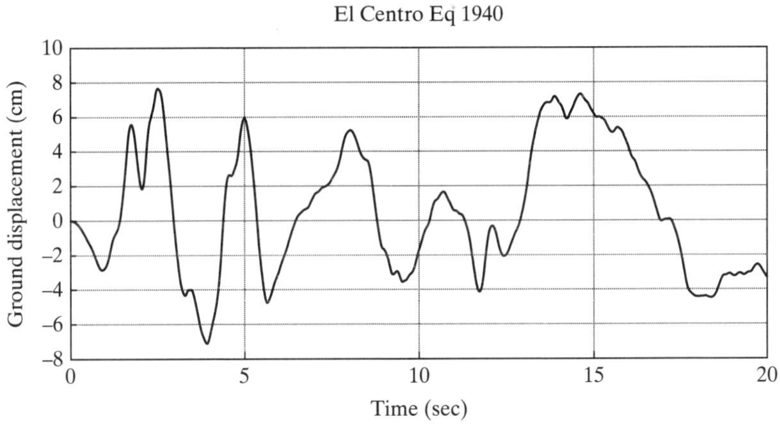

(c) Ground displacement

Figure 8.1 (Continued)

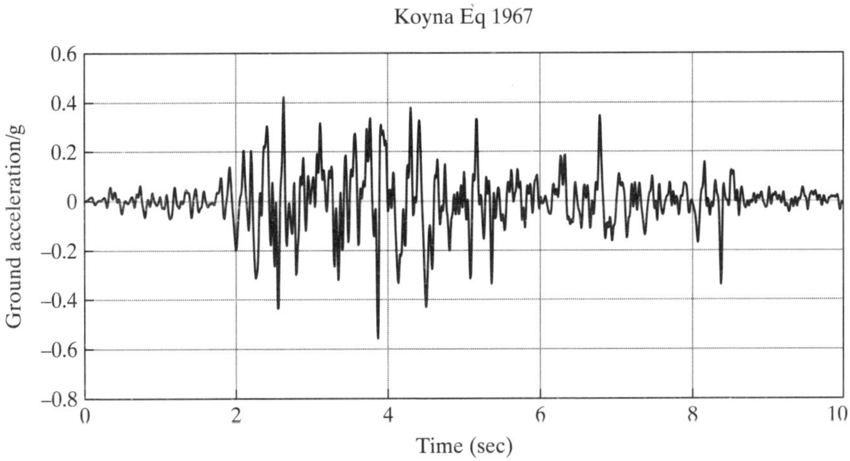

Figure 8.2 Accelerogram of Koyna earthquake 1967, India.

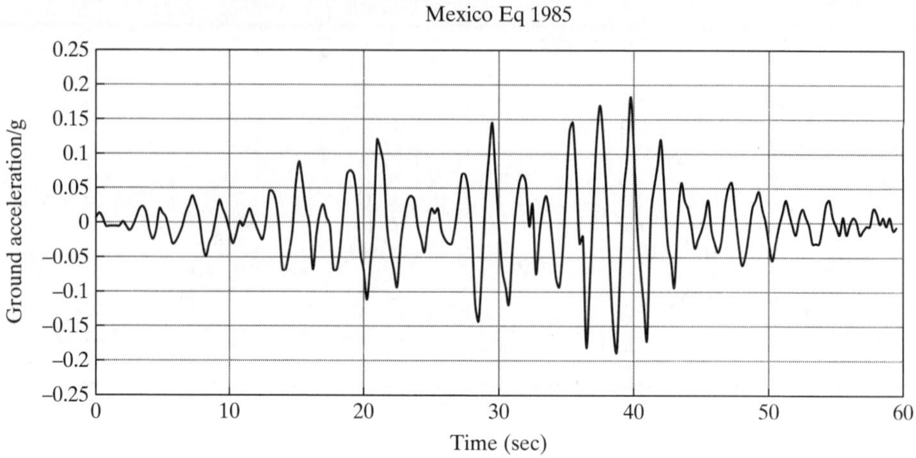

Figure 8.3 Accelerogram of Mexico earthquake 1985, Mexico.

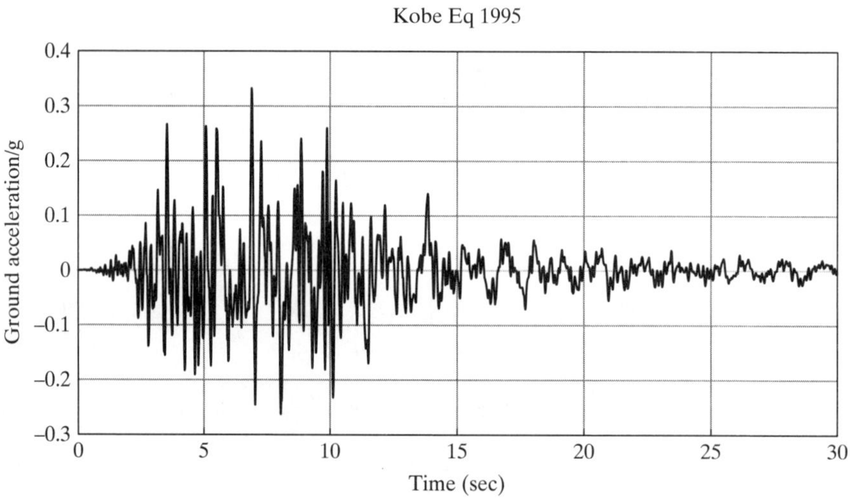

Figure 8.4 Accelerogram of Kobe earthquake 1995, Japan.

the Pacific Earthquake Engineering Research Center (PEER) web site, University of California, Berkeley, USA (peer.berkeley.edu) and USGS web site besides many other web sites.

It should be noted that several different versions of these earthquake records are available from different sources. An earthquake is recorded at several different stations operating in a given region. A variation will arise depending upon which record and which component is being used. The variations among them also arise from differences in how the original analog data was digitized and how the base line correction was applied. It is quite possible that earthquake records for the four sites employed in the present book may differ from those employed by others for the same sites.

In the early 1900s, the dynamic behaviour of structures was being explored. The behaviour of a single-degree-of-freedom (SDOF) system was understood quite well. The researchers focused on developing a methodology to analyse and design a SDOF system for different damping ratio and period of vibration. This chapter deals with the development of elastic response spectra, design response spectra, tripartite graph and tripartite design spectra. The spectra developed for SDOF systems became the basis for design of MDOF systems. It was a revolutionary concept and the structures designed using this concept have performed quite well in severe seismic zones all over the world.

Peak Ground Acceleration PGA and Area under the Accelerogram Curve
Peak Ground Acceleration (PGA) is a source of great confusion among the designers. This PGA is being interpreted as a measure of the severity of ground shaking. The magnitude of the peak ground acceleration by itself is not a significant parameter. Rather it is the area under the curve that is most crucial. It is referred to as the pulse. The higher peak accelerations are generally associated with narrower pulses hence not significant. For example, the pulse recorded at the Pacoima Dam in the 1971 earthquake had a peak acceleration of 1.25g. But it was a narrow pulse. Its area was nearly the same as that under the 0.33g pulse of the El Centro earthquake. Similarly, the PGA recorded during the Koyna earthquake was 0.67g but again the pulse was much smaller. A sudden spike in an accelerogram is a short pulse, that is, having a small area under the curve. In such a situation, the building is unable to "feel" it, and is unable to respond to it due to its inertia. Therefore, there is no need to worry about the PGA alone.

8.2 MATHEMATICAL BACKGROUND

When earthquake excitation is applied to the base of a structure, it produces a time-dependent response in each element of the structure which may be described in terms of displacement, velocity or acceleration. Consider a SDOF system which consists of mass 'm' attached to the ground through a spring of stiffness 'k' and a damper having a coefficient of viscous damping 'c' as shown in Figure 8.5. If such a system is subjected to a ground motion, its equation of motion is given by:

$$m\ddot{x}(t)+c\dot{x}(t)+kx(t)=-m\ddot{y}_g(t) \tag{6.50a}$$

where $\ddot{y}_g(t)$ = ground acceleration

$x(t)$, $\dot{x}(t)$, $\ddot{x}(t)$ = relative displacement, relative velocity and relative acceleration of the mass with respect to ground, respectively.

The solution of the above equation for the relative displacement x at any time t is given by Duhamel's integral as follows:

$$x(t)=(-)\frac{1}{\omega_D}\int_0^t \ddot{y}_g(\tau)e^{-\omega\xi(t-\tau)}\sin\omega_D(t-\tau)\,d\tau \tag{8.1a}$$

or,

$$x(t)=(-)\frac{1}{\omega\sqrt{1-\xi^2}}\int_0^t \ddot{y}_g(\tau)e^{-\omega\xi(t-\tau)}\sin\omega\sqrt{1-\xi^2}(t-\tau)\,d\tau \tag{8.1b}$$

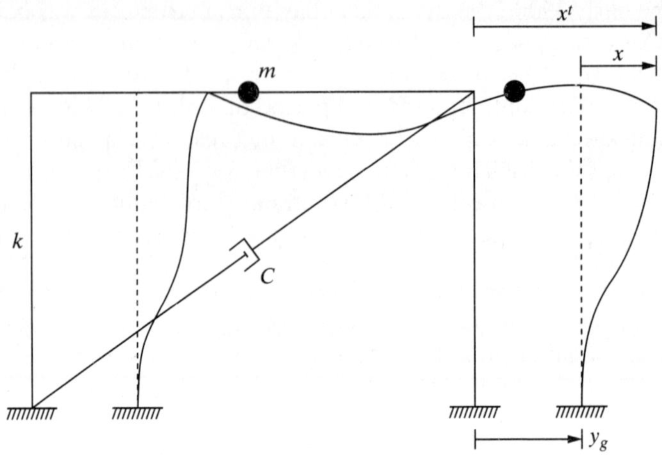

Figure 8.5 A SDOF system subjected to ground excitation.

where,

$\omega = \sqrt{\dfrac{k}{m}}$ = undamped circular frequency of the system.

$\xi = \dfrac{c}{2m\omega}$ = damping ratio.

t and τ are the time parameters.

It is possible to determine the absolute maximum values of the displacement, velocity and acceleration for a given damping and natural frequency of a SDOF system using the above equations. Similarly, a set of such data can be generated for different damping ratios and natural frequencies. Alternatively, any of the direct integration methods discussed earlier can be used to solve the equation of motion for any set of input data, and the absolute maximum response can be estimated.

A flow diagram for the generation of elastic response spectra is shown in Figure 8.6.

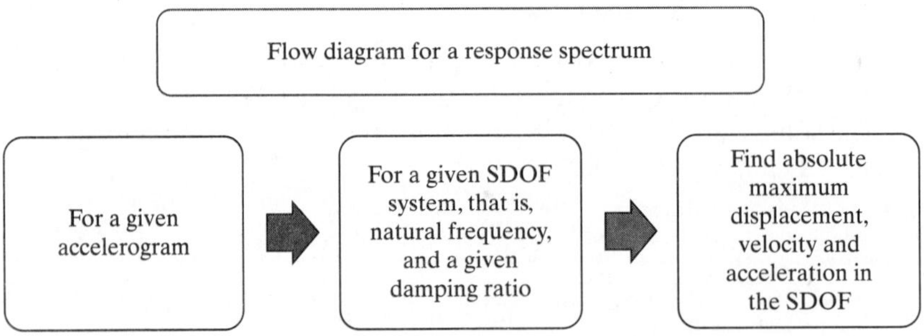

(a) Process 1 – Generation of response spectra

Figure 8.6 Flow diagram for generation of elastic response spectra

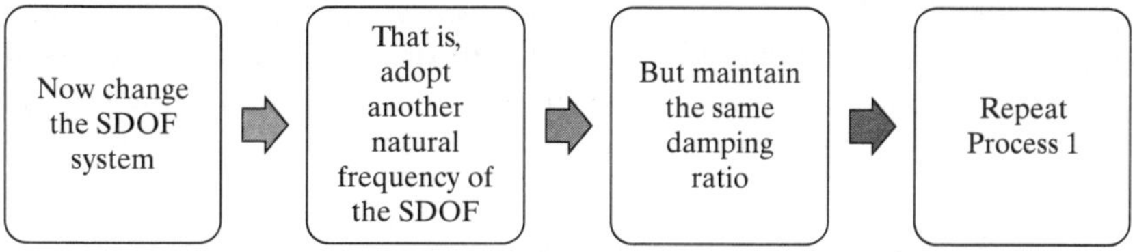

(b) Process 2 – Generation of response spectra

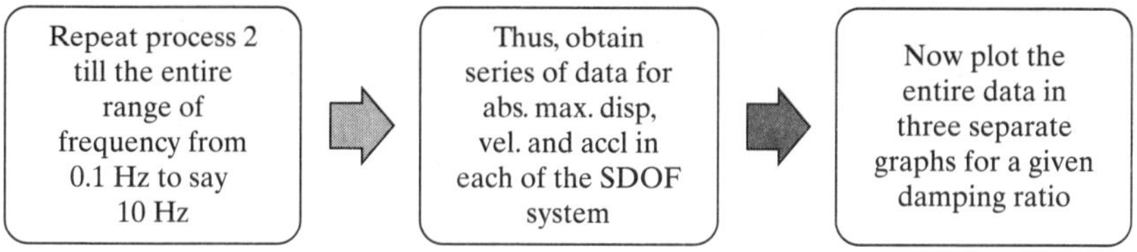

(c) Process 3 – Generation of response spectra

Figure 8.6 (Continued)

8.3 ELASTIC RESPONSE SPECTRA

Each of the three plots consisting of peak relative displacement versus natural frequency, peak relative velocity versus natural frequency and peak acceleration versus natural frequency of a SDOF system for a given damping is referred to as the *elastic response spectrum*. Alternatively, the plots can be drawn with respect to natural periods instead of natural frequency of a SDOF system. A spectrum provides a convenient means of presenting the peak response of all possible linear SDOF systems to a given component of earthquake motion.

For a given SDOF system, knowing its natural frequency or period, and damping, the response spectrum curve will provide peak displacement, peak velocity or peak acceleration. Knowing the mass of the system, it is easy to estimate its acceleration and, therefore, earthquake force. Now it is possible to design the SDOF system to resist this force.

8.3.1 Displacement Response Spectra

The maximum value of relative displacement x of the system with respect to the ground is termed as the *Peak Relative Displacement* and it is denoted by x_0. It is given by

$$x_0(\omega,\xi)=\frac{1}{\omega\sqrt{1-\xi^2}}\left|\int_0^t \ddot{y}_g(\tau)e^{-\omega\xi(t-\tau)}\sin\omega\sqrt{1-\xi^2}(t-\tau)d\tau\right|_{\max} \tag{8.2}$$

x_0 depends not only on the ground motion history but also on the frequency of vibration and the damping of the system. For any given earthquake record, by assuming a suitable value of damping in the structure, it is possible to calculate values of x_0 for a full range of vibration frequencies by making use of Duhamel integral as discused in Chapter 5. A graph showing these peak displacement values plotted as a function of frequency (or its reciprocal quantity, period of vibration) for different damping ratios is called a *Relative Displacement Response Spectrum*. Such a spectrum is very useful in assessing the internal forces in various members of a structure. The internal forces such as bending moment, shear force and axial force, etc. are related to the relative displacements through member stiffness matrix.

8.3.2 Velocity Response Spectra

For the maximum value of $\dot{x}$ the relative velocity of the system with respect to the ground is denoted by $\dot{x}_0$ and it is termed as the *peak relative velocity*. When this is plotted as a function of period of vibration of a system, the plot is known as *Relative Velocity Response Spectrum*.

Upon differentiating Equation (8.1) under the integral sign gives,

$$\dot{x}(t) = -\xi\omega x(t) - \int_0^t \ddot{y}_g(\tau) e^{-\xi\omega(t-\tau)} \cos\omega_D(t-\tau)\,d\tau \tag{8.3}$$

In Equation (8.2), the term $\left|\int_0^t \ddot{y}_g(\tau)e^{-\omega\xi(t-\tau)} \sin\omega_D(t-\tau)d\tau\right|_{\max}$ represents Duhamel integral and can be re-written by replacing ω_D by ω

$$\left|\int_0^t \ddot{y}_g(\tau)e^{-\omega\xi(t-\tau)} \sin\omega(t-\tau)d\tau\right|_{\max} \tag{8.4}$$

This equation has the units of velocity. It may be denoted by S_v and is called *peak pseudo velocity*. The prefix *pseudo* is used because it is not the same as $\dot{x}_0$.

We can calculate the peak relative velocity either from Equation (8.3), which is the exact value or by Equation (8.4) which will be an approximate value. However, for small damping, these two equations are expected to give fairly close results. The comparison between the maximum velocity given by these two methods is shown in Figure 8.7 for the El Centro and Koyna earthquakes for 2% and 20% damping. It can

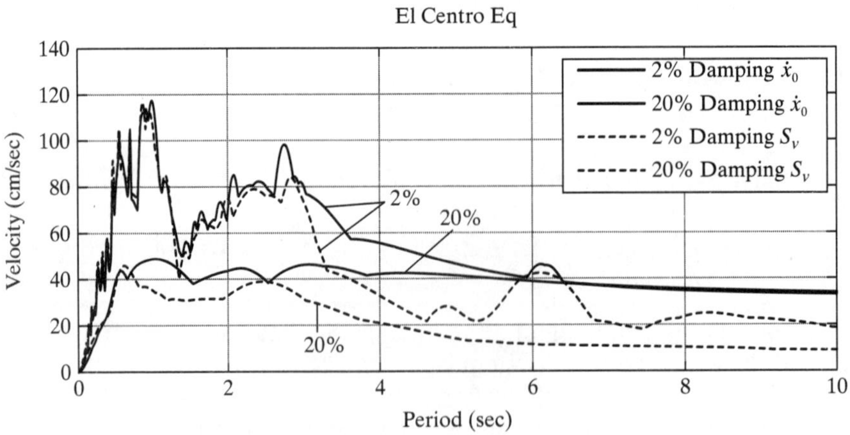

Figure 8.7(a) El Centro earthquake—velocity and pseudo velocity spectra.

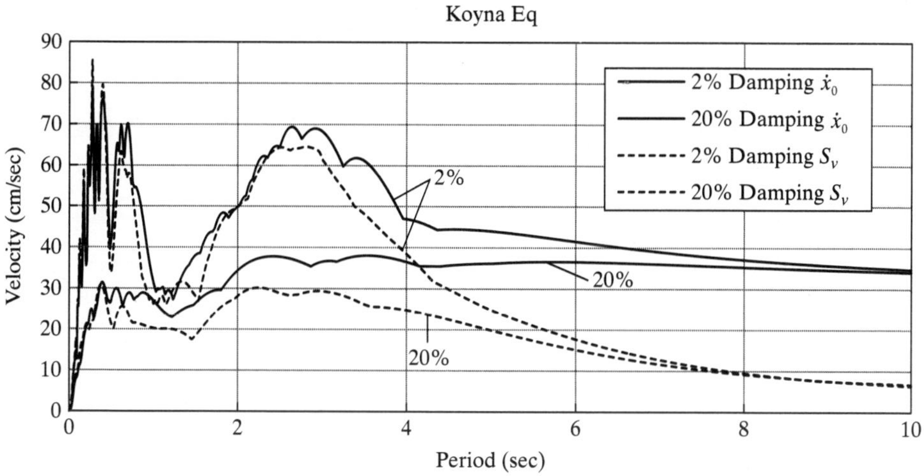

Figure 8.7(b) Koyna earthquake—velocity and pseudo velocity spectra.

be seen that for 2% damping and small periods, the difference in velocity spectra and pseudo velocity spectra is quite small. The difference gets magnified at large damping and longer periods.

Naturally, it is convenient to use Equation (8.4) instead of Equation (8.3). Thus,

$$\dot{x}_0 \approx S_v = \omega S_d \tag{8.5a}$$

or,

$$S_d = \frac{S_v}{\omega} \tag{8.5b}$$

Therefore, it we plot S_v instead of $\dot{x}_0$ as a function of period, for different values of damping, the plot is known as *Pseudo Velocity Response Spectra.*

8.3.3 Acceleration Response Spectra

Let us consider Equation (8.3).

$$\dot{x}(t) = -\xi\omega x(t) - \int_0^t \ddot{y}_g(\tau)e^{-\xi\omega(t-\tau)}\cos\omega_D(t-\tau)\,d\tau \tag{8.3}$$

An equation for relative acceleration $\ddot{x}(t)$ can be obtained by differentiating Equation (8.3). Total acceleration can be obtained by adding the ground acceleration $\ddot{y}_g(t)$. Alternatively, the total acceleration can be obtained by writing the equation of motion as follows:

$$m\ddot{x}_r(t) + c\dot{x}_r(t) + kx_r(t) = -m\ddot{y}_g(t) \tag{6.49b}$$

or,

$$m\ddot{x}_r(t) + m\ddot{y}_g(t) + c\dot{x}_r(t) + kx_r(t) = 0$$

or,

$$m\ddot{x}^t(t) + c\dot{x}_r(t) + kx_r(t) = 0$$

or,

$$m\ddot{x}^t(t) = -c\dot{x}_r(t) - kx_r(t)$$

or,

$$\ddot{x}^t(t) = -2\omega\xi\dot{x}_r(t) - \omega^2 x_r(t) \tag{8.6}$$

where,

$\ddot{x}^t(t)$ = absolute acceleration of the SDOF system ($x_r = x - y$ used in Equation (6.49a))

The maximum value of absolute acceleration or total acceleration of the system $\ddot{x}^t = \ddot{x}_r + \ddot{y}_g$ denoted by $\ddot{x}_0$ is termed as *peak acceleration* and when it is plotted against natural period of vibration of the system, for different damping values, the plot obtained is termed as the *Acceleration Response Spectra*. However, instead of $\ddot{x}_0$, we plot $\omega^2 S_d$ denoted by S_a which has the units of acceleration. Such a response spectra is called *Pseudo Acceleration Response Spectra*. Again for small values of damping $\ddot{x}_0 \approx S_a$. A comparison of maximum acceleration as obtained by these two methods is shown in Figure 8.8 for El Centro and Koyna earthquakes for 2% and 20% damping. It can be seen that the difference in total acceleration and pseudo acceleration spectra for both these earthquakes for 2% damping is very small and is slightly more for 20% damping. This observation is very significant in developing pseudo acceleration spectra for earthquakes.

Most often the dimensionless quantity S_a/g is plotted for acceleration spectra where g denotes acceleration due to gravity. It most of the civil engineering structures the value of damping ratio ξ is very low (normally less than 20%) and therefore, we have the following simple relationships between the three spectral quantities (displacement, velocity and acceleration):

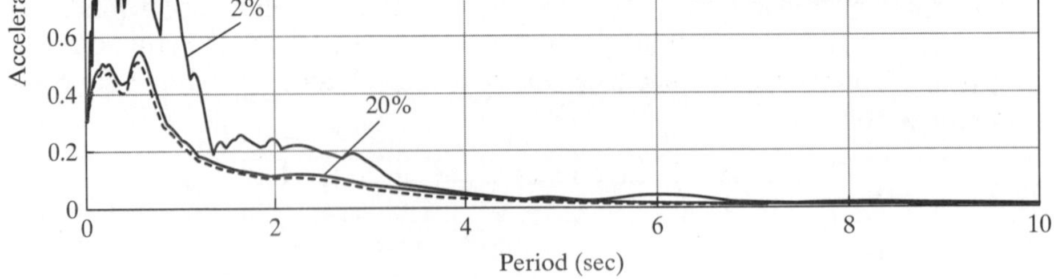

Figure 8.8(a) El Centro earthquake—acceleration and pseudo acceleration spectra.

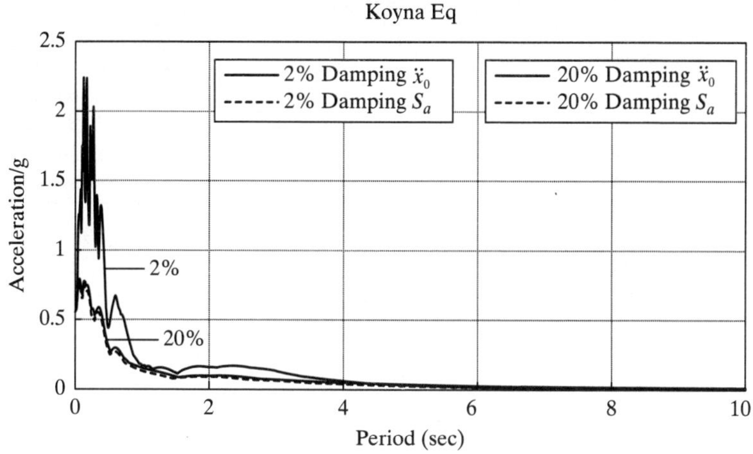

Figure 8.8(b) Koyna earthquake—acceleration and pseudo acceleration spectra.

$$S_v = \omega S_d = \frac{2\pi}{T} S_d \tag{8.7}$$

$$S_a = \omega S_v = \omega^2 S_d = \frac{4\pi^2}{T^2} S_d \tag{8.8a}$$

or,

$$S_v = \frac{S_a}{\omega} = \frac{T}{2\pi} S_a \tag{8.8b}$$

The spectral displacement, pseudo velocity and pseudo acceleration response spectra for 0%, 2%, 5%, 10% and 20% damping for El Centro earthquake (N–S Component)

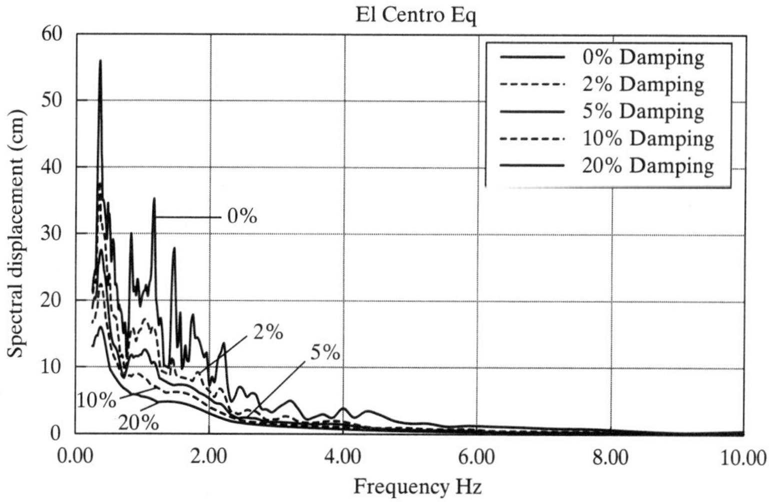

Figure 8.9(a) Spectral displacement spectrum vs. frequency for different damping—El Centro Earthquake.

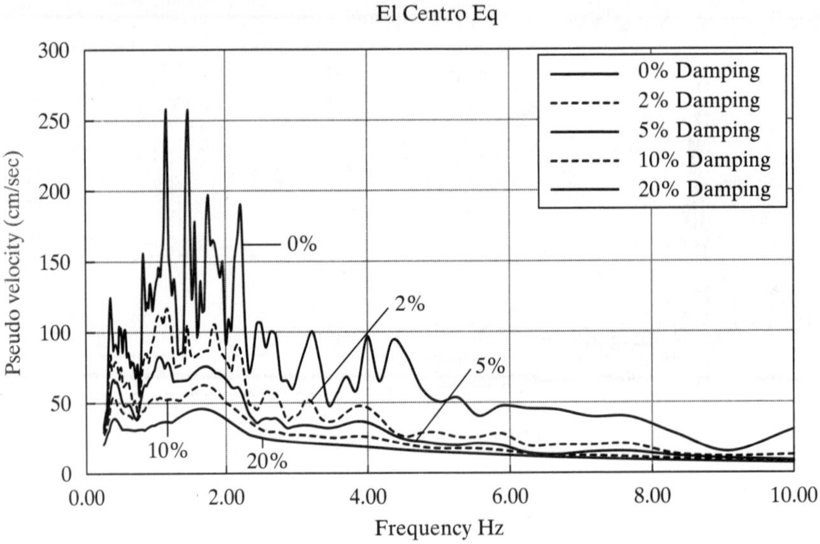

Figure 8.9(b) Pseudo velocity spectrum vs. frequency for different damping—El Centro Earthquake.

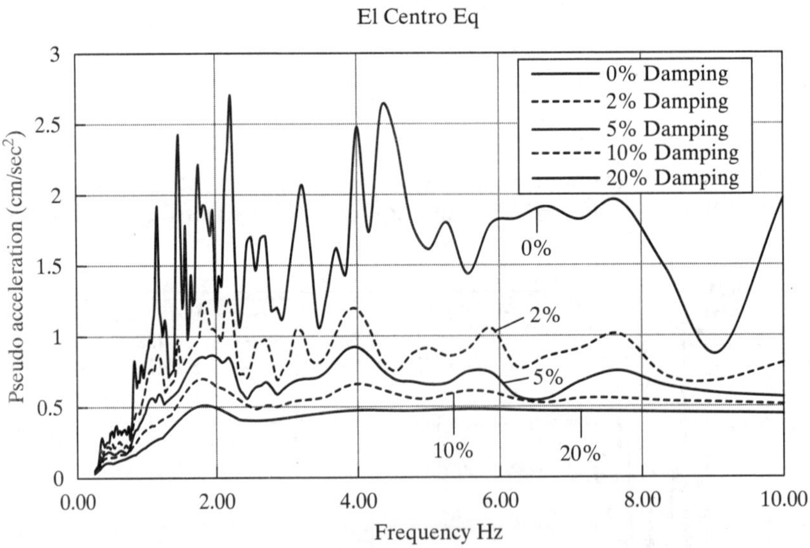

Figure 8.9(c) Pseudo acceleration spectrum vs. frequency for different damping—El Centro Earthquake.

are shown in Figure 8.9 with natural frequency and in Figure 8.10 with natural period. The two plots are mirror image of each other since frequency and period are inverse of each other. The pseudo velocity spectra and pseudo acceleration spectra for Koyna earthquake of 11 December 1967, Mexico earthquake of 19 September 1985 and Kobe earthquake of 17 January 1995 are shown in Figures 8.11 to 8.13.

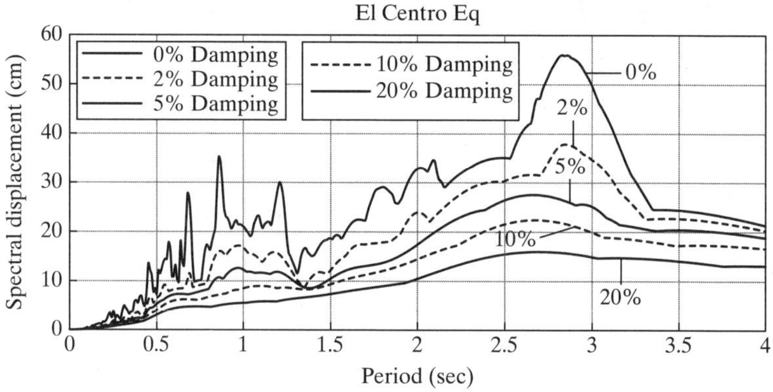

Figure 8.10(a) Spectral displacement spectrum vs. period for different damping—El Centro earthquake.

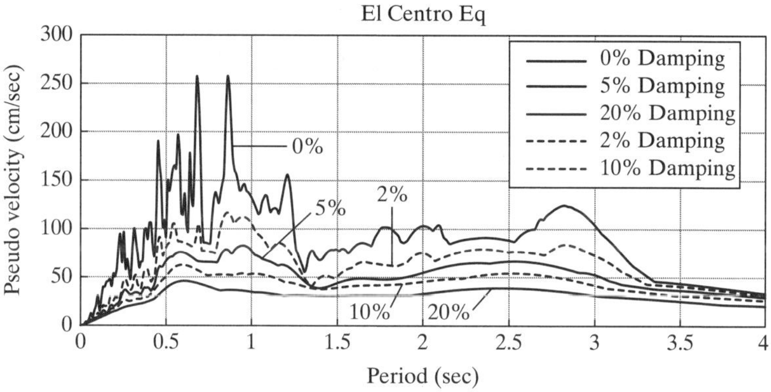

Figure 8.10(b) Pseudo velocity spectrum vs. period for different damping—El Centro earthquake.

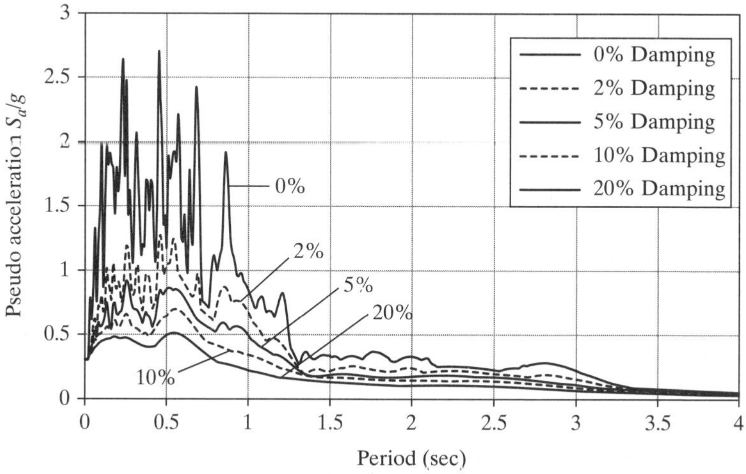

Figure 8.10(c) Pseudo acceleration spectrum vs. period for different damping—El Centro earthquake.

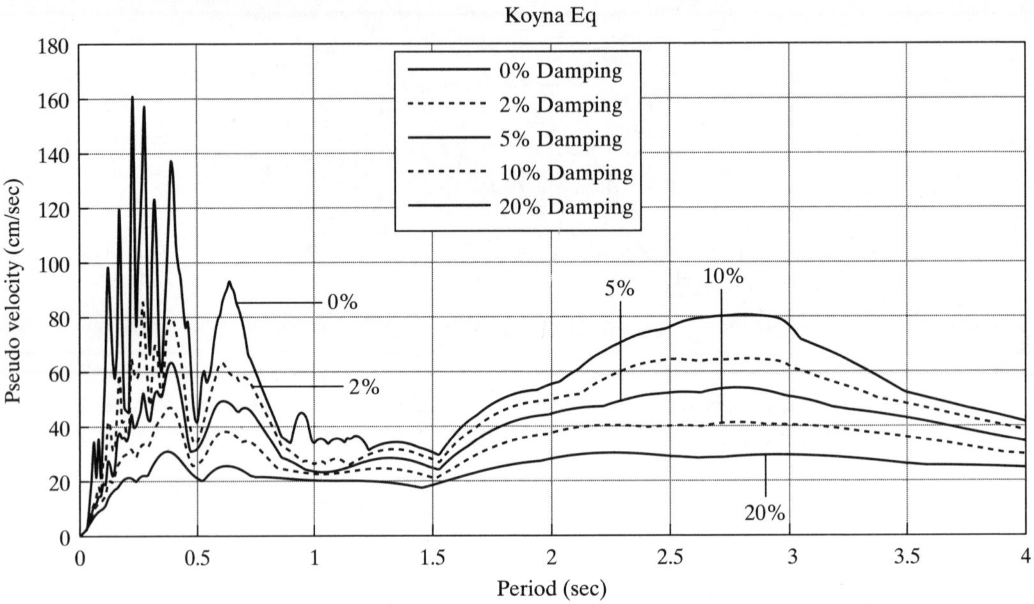

Figure 8.11(a) Pseudo velocity spectrum vs. period for different damping—Koyna earthquake.

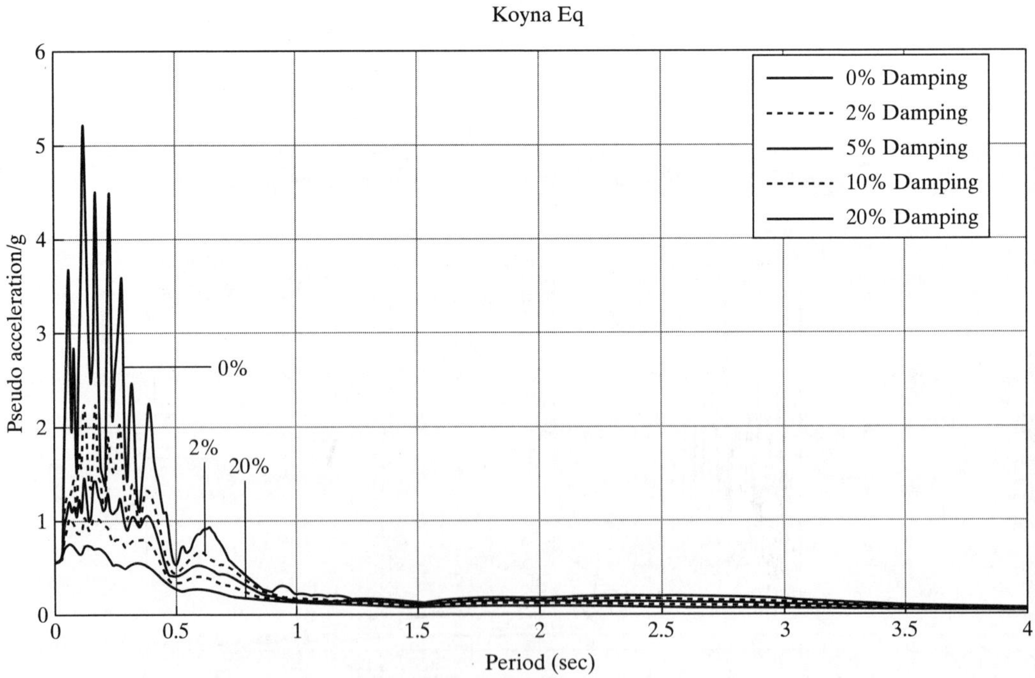

Figure 8.11(b) Pseudo acceleration spectrum vs. period for different damping—Koyna earthquake.

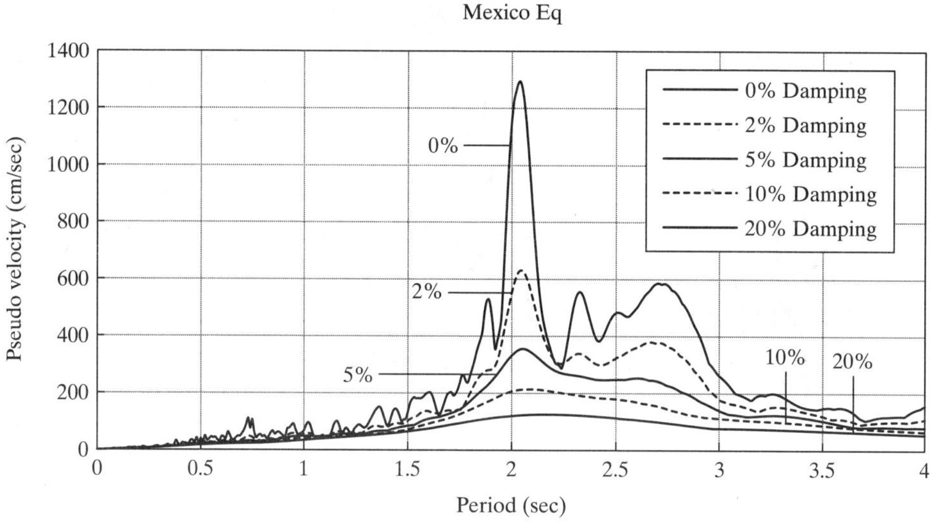

Figure 8.12(a) Pseudo velocity spectrum vs. period for different damping—Mexico earthquake.

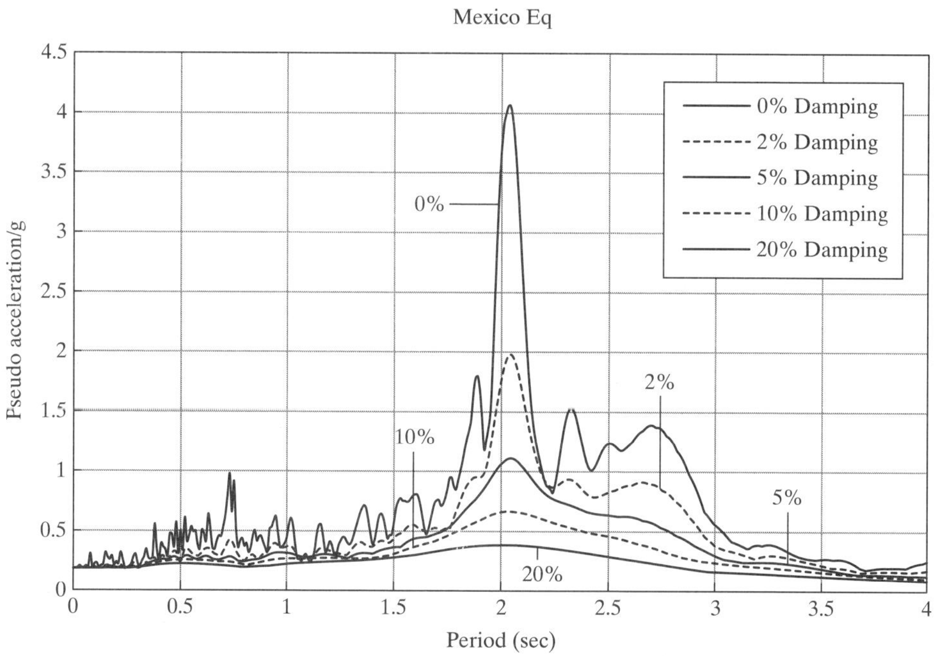

Figure 8.12(b) Pseudo acceleration spectrum vs. period for different damping—Mexico earthquake.

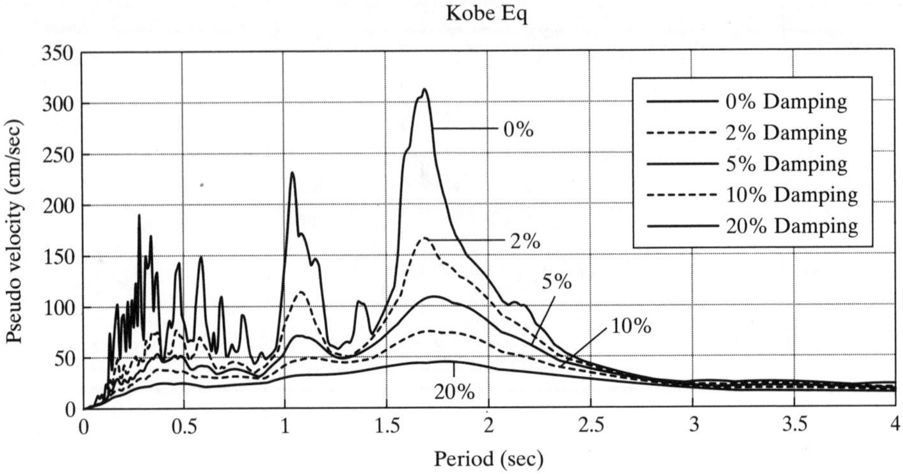

Figure 8.13(a) Pseudo velocity spectrum vs. period for different damping—Kobe earthquake.

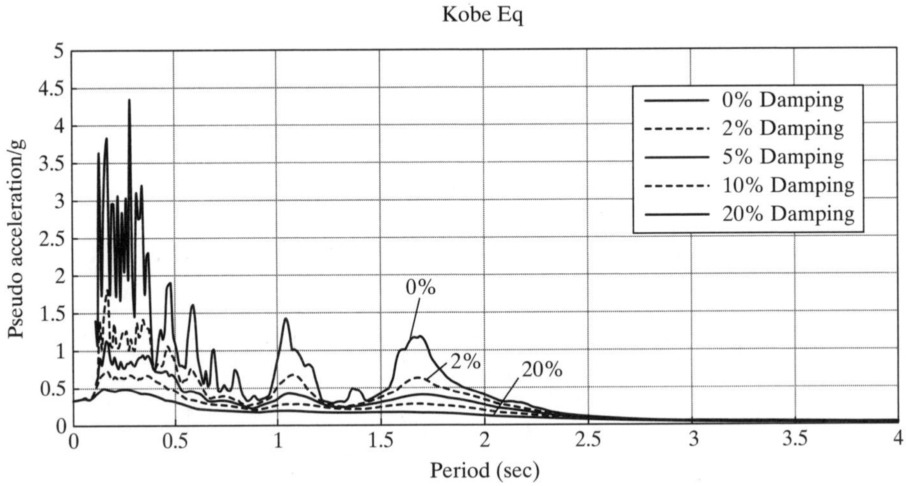

Figure 8.13(b) Pseudo acceleration spectrum vs. period for different damping—Kobe earthquake.

In all these response spectra, the following common features can be seen:

1. There are too many sharp peaks for zero damping.
2. For a slight damping of 2%, the oscillations start becoming less violent. With further increase in damping to 20%, the curves became quite smooth.
3. The acceleration response spectrum has three distinct segments: initial increasing segment, near plateau segment and decreasing segment.

4. Another observation is that peak in the velocity and acceleration response spectra for the Mexico earthquake is quite different from that of the other three earthquakes. The Mexico earthquake was influenced by soft alluvial soil, whereas the other earthquakes occurred on hard soil. In soft soils, the dominating period of an earthquake gets shifted to higher periods. It is quite natural and well expected. Each earthquake is different and depends upon several seismological and geotechnical features. It leads to different *power spectral density* in each earthquake. Therefore, each earthquake spectra may have its own dominating frequency or period.

In practice, commonly used structural materials such as steel and concrete exhibit a damping of 2% and 5%, respectively. At these damping, the zig-zag pattern in the response curves became a big hurdle in design. It was not possible to take an average as the variation was too much, and the number of strong motion records available in the 1950s were very few. If there was an ensemble of 50 or 100 records of earthquakes, then it was possible to draw statistical elastic response spectra for different confidence and damping levels.

8.4 FOURIER AMPLITUDE SPECTRA

Another approach for characterizing the response of a system for a ground motion is provided by Fourier amplitude spectrum, which is a measure of the total energy of an undamped system evaluated at the end of the earthquake (i.e., at time $\tau = t_1$ where duration of earthquake is from $\tau = 0$ to $\tau = t_1$). The Fourier spectrum of a ground motion is defined as:

$$F(\omega) = \int_{\tau=-\infty}^{\infty} \ddot{y}(\tau)\, e^{-i\omega\tau}\, d\tau \tag{8.9}$$

where

$\ddot{y}(\tau)$ = ground motion acceleration
ω = natural frequency of the system
τ = time parameter

If the duration of the ground motion is from $\tau = 0$ to $\tau = t_1$, this can be written as:

$$F(\omega) = \int_0^{t_1} \ddot{y}(\tau)\cos\omega\tau\, d\tau - i\int_0^{t_1} \ddot{y}(\tau)\sin\omega\tau\, d\tau$$

The amplitude of the Fourier Spectrum termed as *Fourier amplitude spectrum* $|F(\omega)|$ will be given by:

$$|F(\omega)| = \left[\left\{\int_0^{t_1} \ddot{y}(\tau)\cos\omega\tau\, d\tau\right\}^2 + \left\{\int_0^{t_1} \ddot{y}(\tau)\sin\omega\tau\, d\tau\right\}^2\right]^{1/2} \tag{8.10}$$

The total energy of a structural system can be obtained by combining expressions for the strain energy and the kinetic energy, that is,

$$E(t)=\frac{1}{2}m\{\dot{x}(t)\}^2+\frac{1}{2}k\{x(t)\}^2 \tag{8.11}$$

where $x(t),\ \dot{x}(t)$ can be determined from Equation (8.2) for undamped system ($\xi = 0$). In practice, it is convenient to express the energy in terms of the square root of twice its value per unit mass, that is:

$$\sqrt{\frac{2E(t)}{m}}=[\{\omega x(t)\}^2+\{\dot{x}(t)\}^2]^{1/2} \tag{8.12}$$

The maximum value of this quantity clearly provides an upper bound to both the pseudo-velocity response spectrum and the time-velocity response spectrum, each of which is represented by one of the terms under the square root sign above. By substituting the values of $x(t)$ and $\dot{x}(t)$ for *undamped case* from Equation (8.2), Equation (8.12) is reduced to:

$$\sqrt{\frac{2E(t)}{m}}=\left[\left\{\int_0^t \ddot{y}(\tau)\cos\omega\tau\ d\tau\right\}^2+\left\{\int_0^t \ddot{y}(\tau)\sin\omega\tau\ d\tau\right\}^2\right]^{1/2} \tag{8.13}$$

Comparison of Equations (8.10) and (8.13) shows that the Fourier amplitude spectrum is a measure of the total energy of an undamped system evaluated at the end of an earthquake as shown in Figure 8.14 for El Centro and Mexico earthquakes. But the maximum response due to a ground motion may occur sometime before the end of the earthquake, therefore, the Fourier amplitude spectrum is not a good approach for design than the response spectrum which represents the maximum response of the structure during the ground motion.

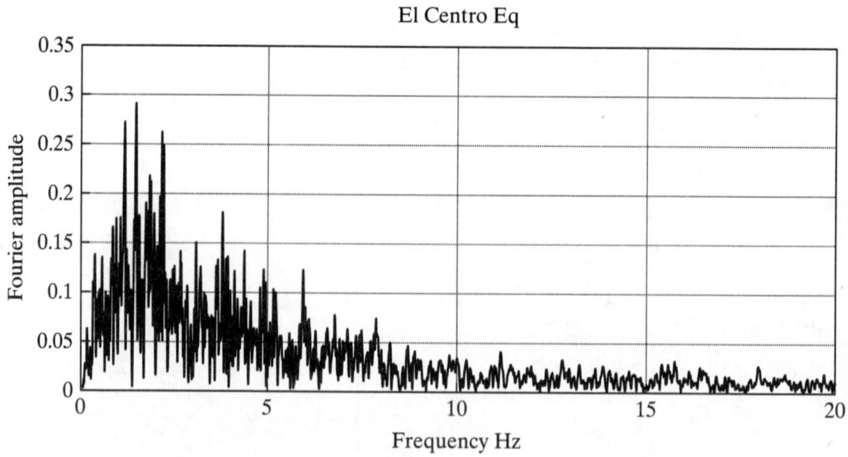

Figure 8.14(a) Fourier amplitude spectra for El Centro earthquake.

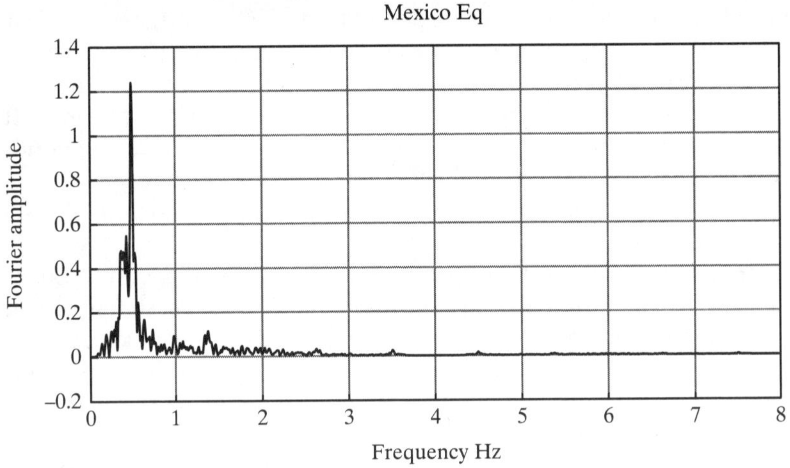

Figure 8.14(b) Fourier amplitude spectra for Mexico earthquake.

8.5 DESIGN RESPONSE SPECTRA

A response spectra is different from a design response spectra. A response spectra represents peak response of a SDOF system for various natural frequencies or periods of vibrations and damping values for a given component of earthquake motion at a given site. Each curve has too many zig-zags. A response value may lie in a valley or a peak of a curve depending upon how accurately natural frequency of the SDOF system has been computed. Moreover, if there are more than one earthquake record for a given site, each record may provide different peak-response value for a given natural frequency and damping. The question arises as to how to use this information in design of a structure? Moreover, there may not be any earthquake data available for a given site. Thus, the question arises as to how to design a structure for earthquake resistance under these circumstances? There is a need to arrive at an average and smoothened response spectrum which exhibits all the basic characteristics and can be adopted in design with reasonable confidence in the absence of realistic data. Such a spectrum is called a *design spectrum*.

For aseismic design of structures, the maximum force experienced by the structure due to the effect of ground motion is required. This maximum force for a SDOF system is given by:

$$\text{Design force} = m\,|\ddot{x}|_{\max}$$

$$= mS_a = \frac{W}{g}S_a$$

or

$$\text{Design Force} = W \cdot \alpha_0 \tag{8.14}$$

where $\alpha_0 = \dfrac{S_a}{g}$ and it is termed as *seismic coefficient*

$W = \text{mg} =$ weight of the system

For a structural system, the seismic coefficient S_a/g for a given earthquake can be directly read from the acceleration response spectra of that earthquake corresponding to the natural period of vibration and damping ratio of the system, and when it is multiplied by the weight of the system, the design seismic force is obtained. If a spectra is generated for different earthquake records for a given site, it can be noticed that there is a difference in the peak ground acceleration, velocity and displacement for various earthquake records as shown in Figures 8.10 to 8.13. The computed response cannot be averaged on an absolute basis.

The pseudo acceleration spectra for 5% damping for the El Centro, Koyna, Mexico and Kobe earthquakes are shown in Figure 8.15. These four earthquakes were recorded in four different continents of the world at different points of time. The Mexico response spectra is different than the rest of the three due to its frequency contents and soft soil attenuation. Figure 8.15 highlights the variations in the response spectra. A zig-zag spectra can be very inconvenient and impractical. The zig-zag in lower damping ratio spectra is very high. It is possible to draw a smooth curve through these data and avoid the zig-zag pattern. A smooth curve can be drawn either by simple inspection and judgement or by using some statistical parameter. It can follow more or less a set pattern in three segments, that is, an ascending straight line, a small plateau, followed by a descending smooth curve. A smoothened curve is also shown in Figure 8.16. This appeared to be a reasonable compromise except of course for the Mexico earthquake. Studies have been carried out by several researchers in the past to develop a simplified elastic spectrum, which can be used for designing. The following are the most popular spectra:

(a) Housner's average spectra
(b) Newmark and Hall's spectra

Such spectra are termed as the smoothened response spectra and makes things easier for a designer. These spectra will be discussed next.

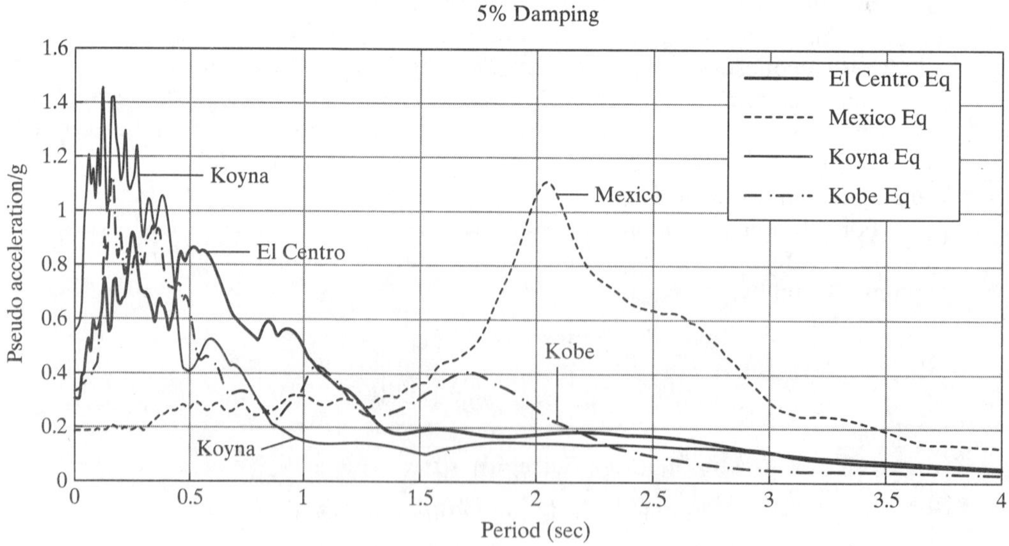

Figure 8.15 Comparison of different earthquake spectra.

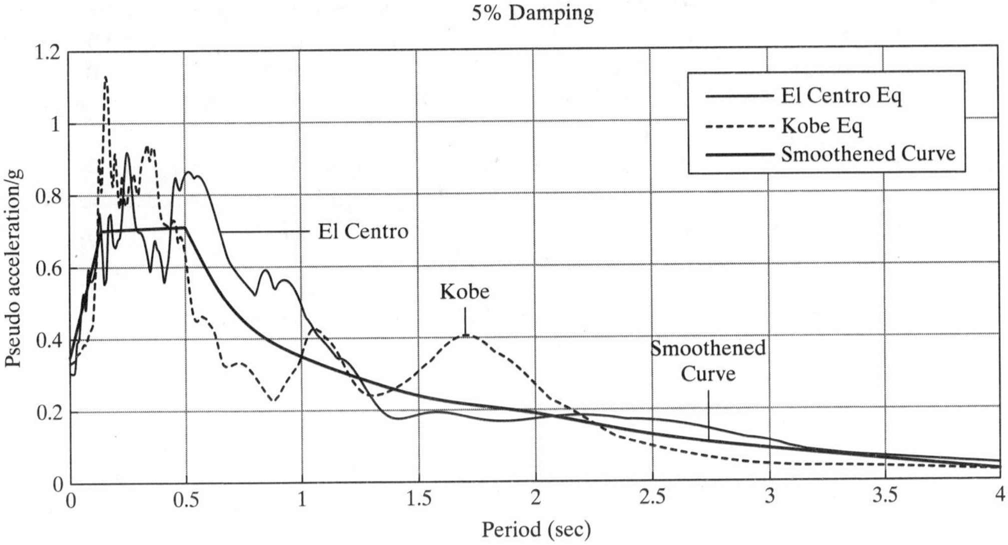

Figure 8.16 El Centro and Kobe pseudo acceleration spectra for 5% damping.

8.6 HOUSNER'S AVERAGE SPECTRA

Each earthquake is different in terms of its frequency content, magnitude and duration. Different earthquakes can be combined by normalizing them to the same scale. Various procedures were used to normalize response spectra before averaging is carried out. Among these procedures, two have been most commonly used:

1. *normalization* according to spectrum intensity where the areas under the spectra between two given frequencies or periods are set equal to each other
2. normalization to peak ground motion where the spectral ordinates are divided by peak ground acceleration, velocity or displacement for the corresponding region of the spectrum.

Normalization to other parameters such as effective peak acceleration and effective peak velocity-related acceleration has also been suggested and used in development of design spectra for seismic codes.

Prof. G. W. Housner, at the CalTech, Pasedena, California, chose to normalize the spectra by keeping the area under the velocity spectrum for 20% damping to be the same. At this damping, the velocity spectrum curve becomes nearly a straight line and the shape between any two period limits becomes a trapezoid. The spectral intensity was computed as follows:

$$SI = \int_{0.1}^{2.5} S_v(T,\xi)\,dt \tag{8.15}$$

For example, let A_1 and A_2 be the areas under the velocity spectrum curves of two different accelerograms. In that case, if the ordinates of the second accelerogram are multiplied by A_1/A_2, then the modified second and the original first record are considered to have been normalized to the same scale. If we plot the response spectra for the above two normalized accelerograms, both the response spectra will be running very close to each other, and the average of these two can be conveniently considered as the spectra depicted by either of the normalized accelerograms. This type of response spectra is termed as *Averaged Spectra*.

Prof. G.W. Housner developed a design spectrum by computing the spectra for two components of each of the four different earthquakes that occurred in the Western USA, and then *normalizing, averaging, scaling and smoothening* the resulting curves. The four earthquake records studied by Housner were:

(a) El Centro earthquake of 1934
(b) El Centro earthquake of 1940
(c) Olympia earthquake of 1949
(d) Taft earthquake of 1952

The spectra were scaled so that the long period value of the undamped spectral velocity was 1 ft/sec (30 cm/sec) at 0% damping. The average smoothened velocity and acceleration spectra obtained by Housner are shown in Figures 8.17(a) and 8.17(b), respectively. It should be noted that the maximum spectral accelerations in this average smoothened spectra are much lower than those obtained in these real earthquakes. It was done purposely in view of a lower probability of occurrence of a strong earthquake in any given zone. This spectrum was used and is still being used as a design response spectrum in many countries even today. It was used in the Indian Code IS:1893 till 2002 when it was replaced with the spectra based on an ensemble of Indian earthquakes.

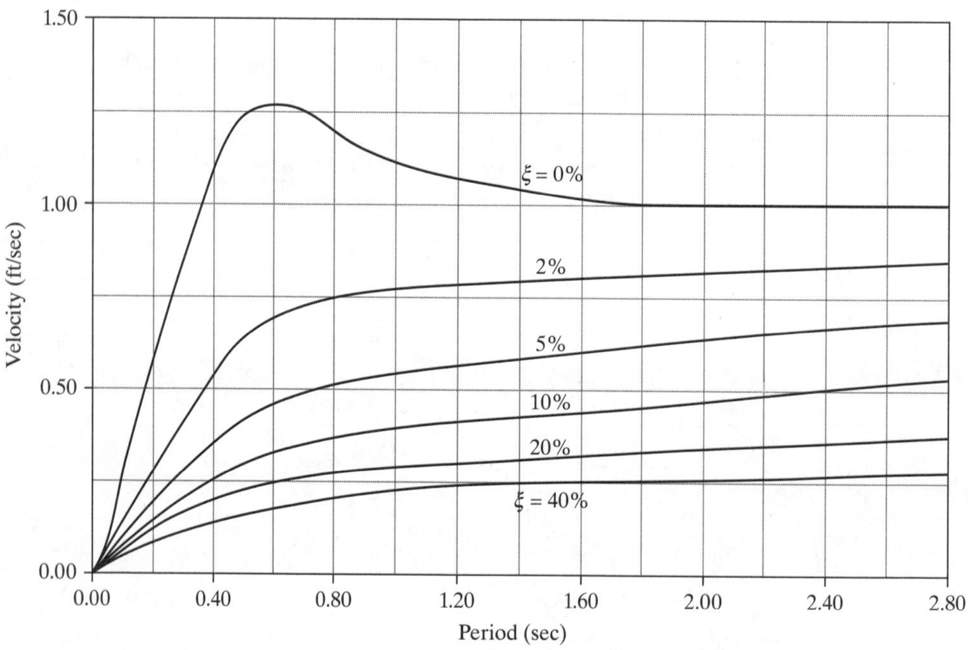

Figure 8.17(a) Housner's average velocity response spectra (1 ft = 30.48 cm).

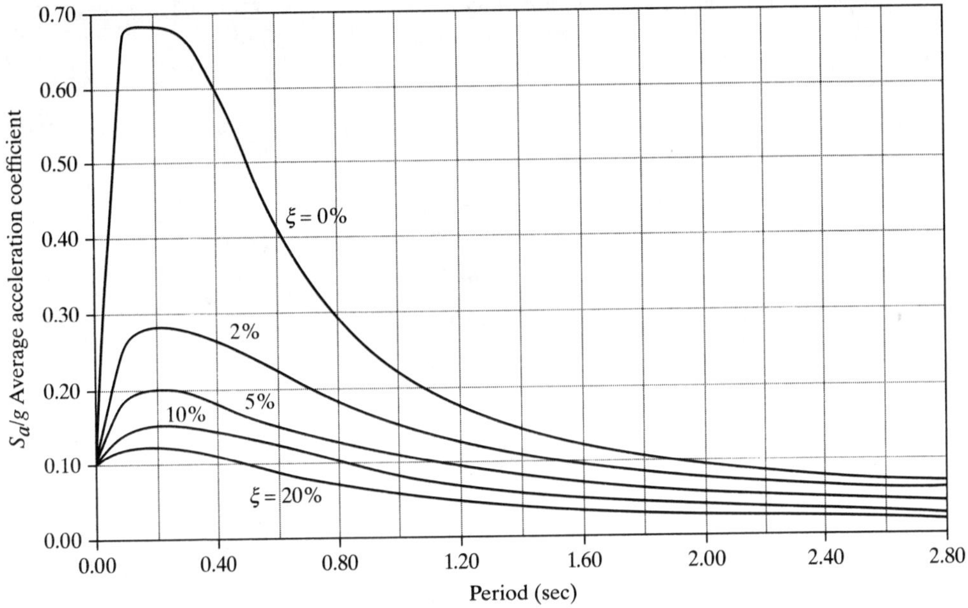

Figure 8.17(b) Housner's average acceleration response spectra.

8.7 TRIPARTITE GRAPH

The displacement, pseudo velocity and pseudo acceleration response spectra for a given earthquake motion virtually provides the same information. The three spectra are different ways to present the same information for a SDOF system. The obvious question is why do we need three spectra? The plots show how each quantity varies with natural frequency of a SDOF directly. Although these three quantities are mathematically related, a plot gives much more clarity directly without having to go through the mathematical equations. The displacement spectra shows the variation of peak displacement of a SDOF system, the pseudo velocity spectra shows the variation of peak kinetic energy (=1/2 mv^2), whereas the pseudo acceleration spectra gives the variation of peak seismic force (mass times acceleration) or base shear. Thus, each spectra contributes to the total response in its own way. Prof. A. S. Veletsos and Prof. N. M. Newmark were the first to propose the concept of combining all the three spectra into a single spectrum in 1960.

A response spectrum should cover a wide range of natural vibration periods or frequencies and several damping ratios so that it provides peak response of all possible structures – very short period as well as very long period, on different soil and geological conditions. Choice of logarithmic scales was obvious.

The simple relationships Equations (8.7) and (8.8) existing among the three spectral quantities (i.e. displacement, velocity and acceleration) make it possible to represent them all in a simple plot on four way log paper. This type of plot is known as *tripartite* plot. The maximum displacement (relative to ground) is designated by the symbol D, the maximum pseudo-velocity (relative to ground) by the symbol V, and the maximum pseudo-acceleration (representing the force in the spring) by the symbol A.

Construction of tripartite spectra with natural frequency as abscissa It has already been shown earlier Equations (8.7) and (8.8b) that:

$$S_v = \omega S_d \tag{8.7a}$$

and

$$S_v = \frac{S_a}{\omega} \tag{8.8b}$$

Taking log of both the above equations,

$$\log S_v = \log \omega + \log S_d \tag{8.7b}$$

and

$$\log S_v = -\log \omega + \log S_a \tag{8.8c}$$

Comparing these two equations with that of a straight line, that is, $y = mx + C$.

In Equation (8.7b), if $\log S_v$ is taken as ordinate and $\log \omega$ is taken as abscissa, and the remaining term $\log S_d$ is taken as constant, then the straight line makes an angle of 45° with the abscissa. Similarly, in Equation (8.8c), the straight line makes an angle of –45° with the abscissa. First the coordinates of the origin are decided, that is, the values of S_v and T or ω along with their maximum values. It will decide the number of log cycles along the period (or frequency) and pseudo velocity axes. For the purpose of plotting the graph, the minimum values of T or ω and S_v may be taken as equal, say 0.01 and 0.01 each. Then, the point of intersection of S_d curve with T or ω is computed using Equation (8.7b). Similarly, the point of intersection of S_a curve with T or ω is computed using Equation (8.8b). The coordinates of the four corners of the graph may be taken as shown in Figures 8.18(a) and 8.18(b) for use in MATLAB code.

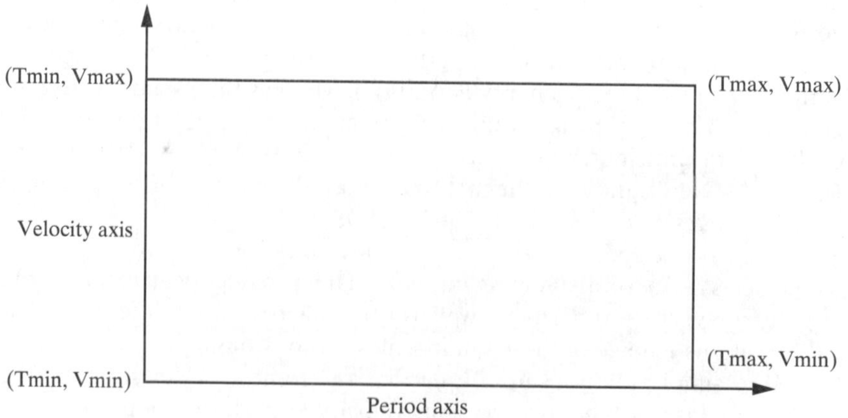

Figure 8.18(a) Coordinates of the corners.

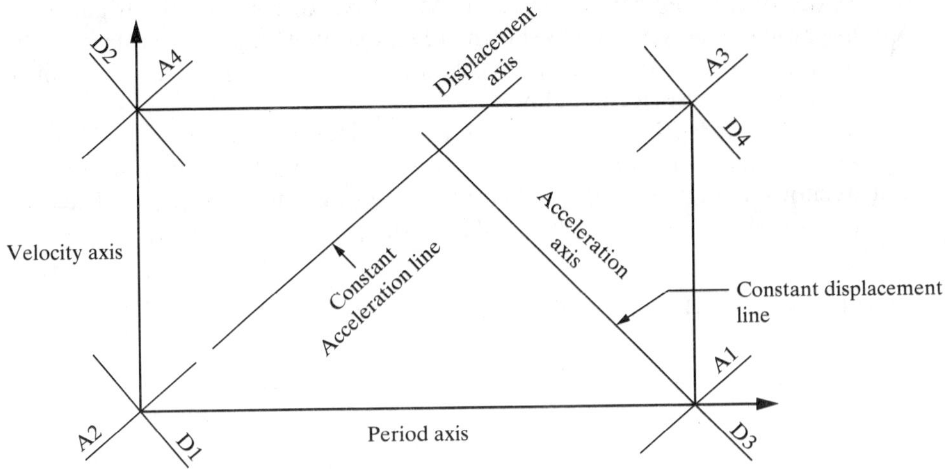

Figure 8.18(b) Coordinates of the corners for diagonals.

Construction of tripartite spectra with natural period as abscissa

It has already been shown earlier Equations (8.7) and (8.8b) that:

$$S_v = \omega S_d = \frac{2\pi}{T} S_d \tag{8.7b}$$

$$S_v = \frac{S_a}{\omega} = \frac{T}{2\pi} S_a \tag{8.8b}$$

Taking log of both the above equations,

$$\log S_v = -\log T + \log S_d + \log 2\pi \tag{8.7d}$$

and

$$\log S_v = \log T + \log S_a - \log 2\pi \tag{8.8d}$$

Comparing these two equations with that of a straight line, that is, $y = mx + C$.

In Equation (8.7d), if $\log S_v$ is taken as ordinate and log T is taken as abscissa, and the remaining terms 2π and $\log S_d$ are taken as constants, then the straight line makes an angle of –45° with the abscissa. Similarly, in Equation (8.8d), the straight line makes an angle of 45° with the abscissa.

Steps for Generating a Tripartite Graph

Step 1: Generate vertical grid lines, that is lines of constant period or frequency in terms of log cycles.

Step 2: Generate horizontal grid lines, that is lines of constant pseudo velocity in terms of log cycles.

Step 3: Compute the limiting values of S_a and S_d at each of the four corners of the graph using Equations (8.7) and (8.8) knowing the coordinates of these corners.

Step 4: Compute the coordinates (T, S_v) corresponding to each of the diagonal grids parallel to acceleration or displacement axes at the two ends of each grid line.

A computer code can be written in MATLAB to generate the tripartite graph. A four-way log scale is plotted as shown in Figure 8.19 with period as absicca. The displacement axis is right angles to the acceleration lines, whereas the acceleration axis is right angles to the displacement lines.

The tripartite spectra for any earthquake can be plotted in MATLAB by importing the pseudo velocity versus period or frequency data for a given set of damping ratio as shown in Figures 8.20 to 8.23 for the four different earthquakes. The response spectra data should be made available in MS-Excel sheet, which will be read by MATLAB.

Note: The MATLAB code DOS8_1 in available on the web.

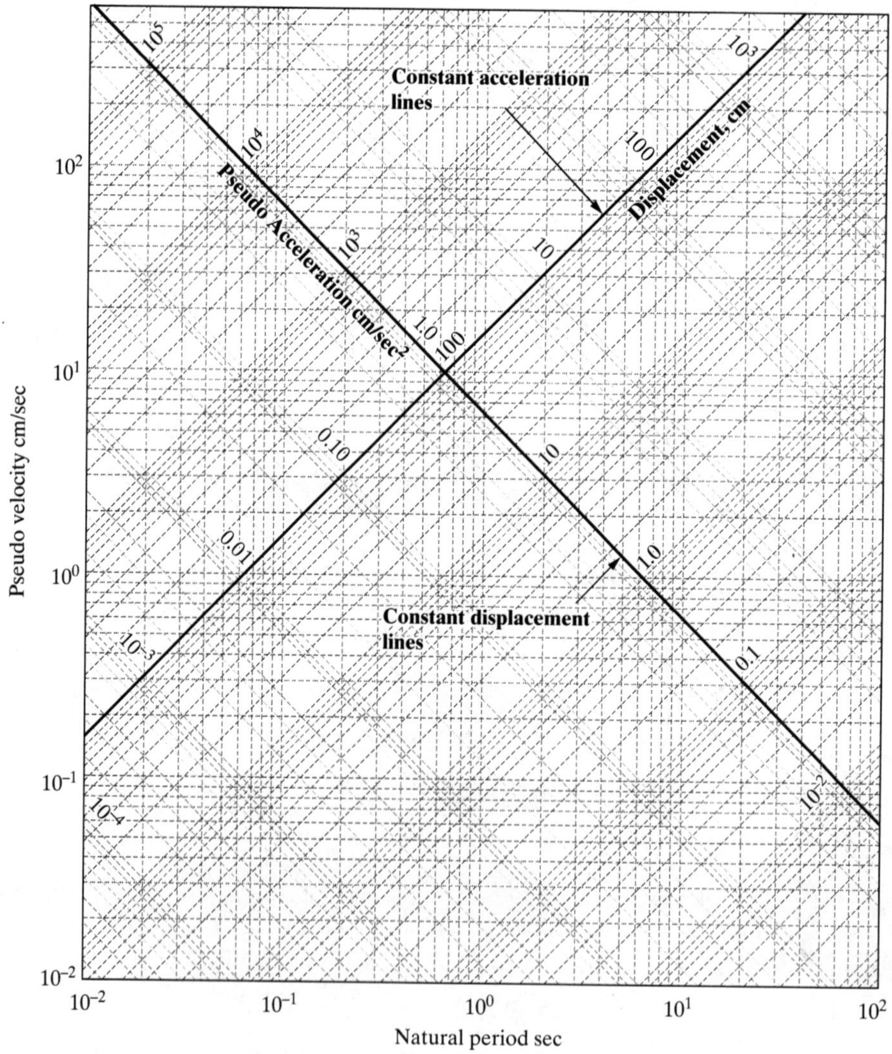

Figure 8.19 Tripartite graph—Period as abscissa.

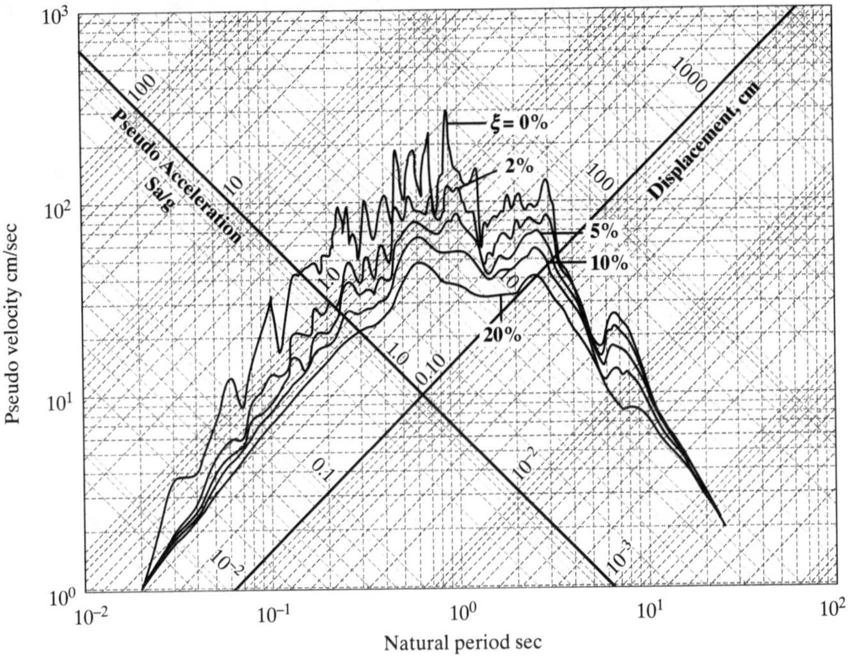

Figure 8.20 Tripartite spectra for El Centro earthquake, 1940.

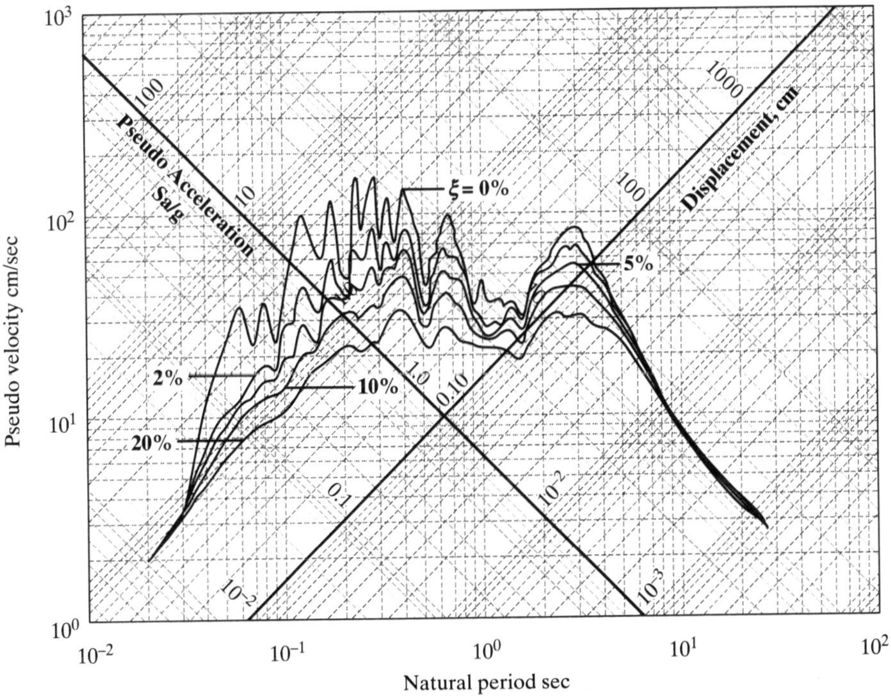

Figure 8.21 Tripartite spectra for Koyna earthquake, 1967.

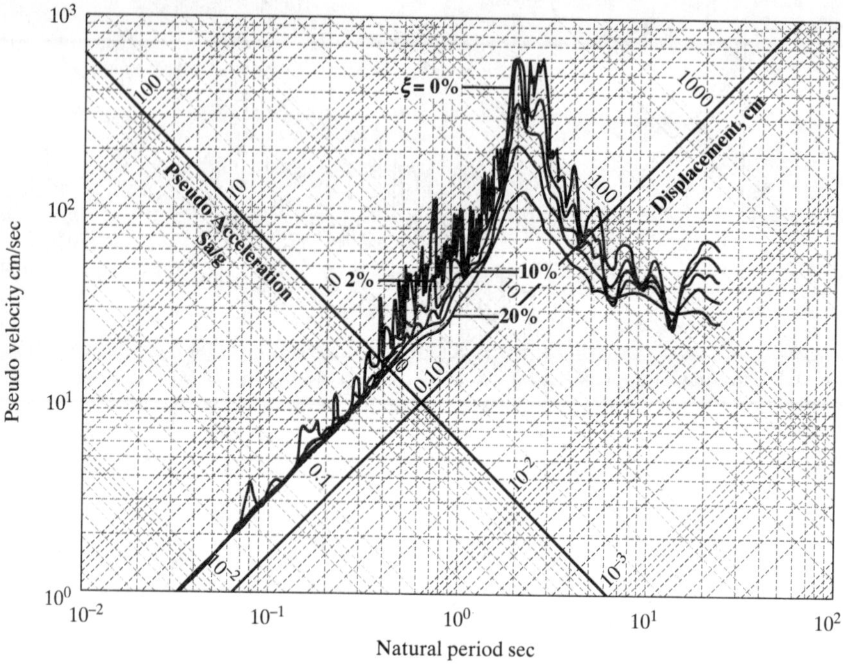

Figure 8.22 Tripartite spectra for Mexico earthquake, 1985.

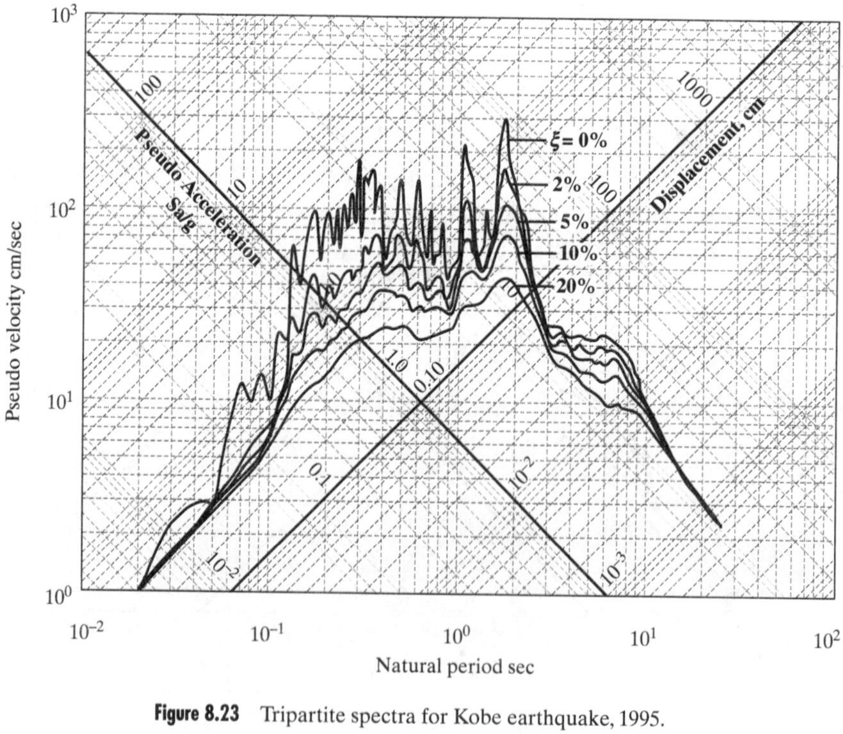

Figure 8.23 Tripartite spectra for Kobe earthquake, 1995.

How to Read the Tripartite Graph?

Let us draw a tripartite graph and consider two points P and Q as shown in Figure 8.24. The period coordinate of P is 0.70 sec and V ordinate point Q is 200 cm/sec. It should be remembered that diagonal grid lines correspond to a constant displacement or constant acceleration value. The diagonal lines passing through point P can be read at P1 and P2 for displacement and acceleration values, respectively. Line P–P1 is parallel to the constant displacement lines and line P–P2 is parallel to the constant acceleration lines. Similarly, diagonal lines passing through point Q can be read at Q1 and Q2 for displacement and acceleration values, respectively. Line Q–Q1 is parallel to the constant displacement lines and line Q–Q2 is parallel to the constant acceleration lines.

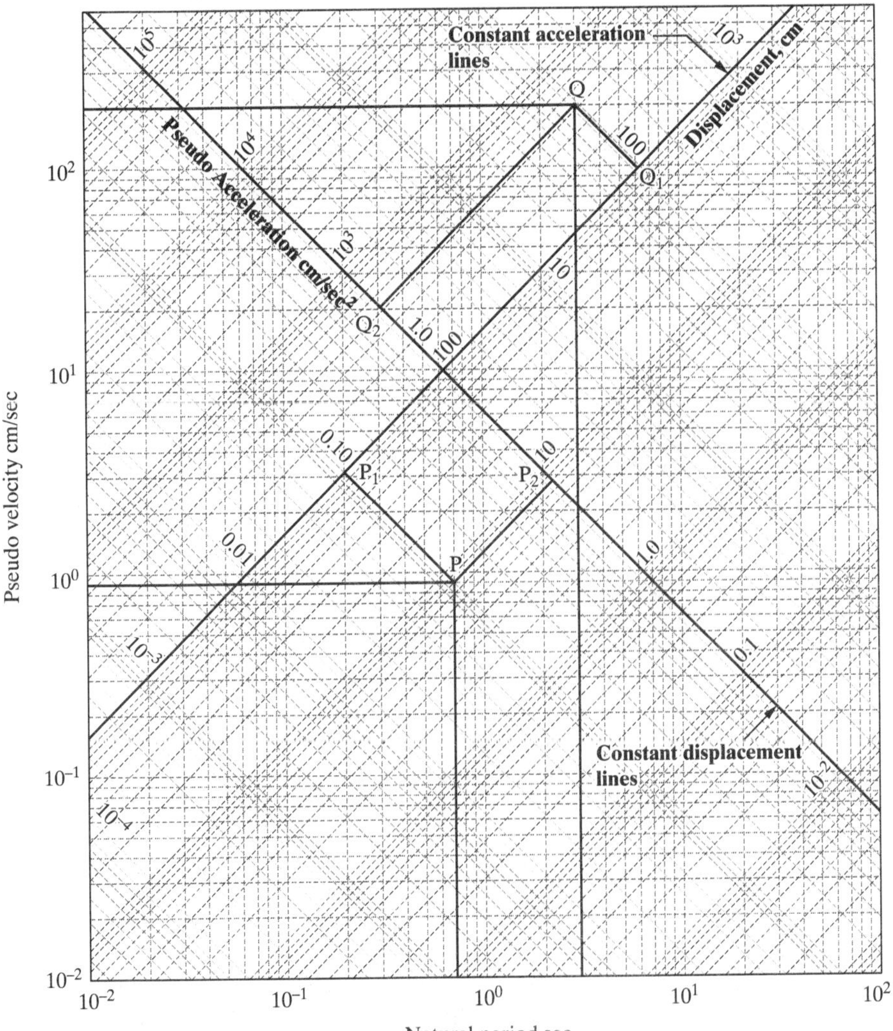

Figure 8.24 Tripartite graph.

The steps to read the displacement D, velocity V and acceleration A coordinates of P and Q are as follows:

Step 1: Draw a vertical line from the time axis at 0.7 sec and then a horizontal line at P to V axis. Read V ordinate as 0.9 cm/sec. The true value is 0.897 cm/sec.

Step 2: Now draw a line normal to the displacement axis through P and read D ordinate as 0.1 cm.

Step 3: Now draw a line normal to the acceleration axis through P and read A ordinate as 8 cm/sec^2. The true value is 8.056 cm/sec^2.

Step 4: Similarly, draw a horizontal line from the V axis at 200 cm/sec and then a vertical line at Q to the time axis. Read T ordinate as 3 sec.

Step 5: Now draw a line normal to the displacement axis through Q and read D ordinate as 95 cm. The true value is 95.49 cm.

Step 6: Now draw a line normal to the acceleration axis through Q and read A ordinate as 420 cm/sec^2. The true value is 418.90 cm/sec^2.

The T, D, V and A coordinates of P and Q are as follows:

Point	T sec	D cm	V cm/sec	A cm/sec^2
P	0.7	0.10	0.90	8
Q	3	95	200	421

8.8 ELASTIC DESIGN TRIPARTITE SPECTRA

Prof. N. M. Newmark and W. J. Hall studied the characteristics of tripartite response spectra of several earthquakes recorded at different sites in different countries having different seismological parameters and noted some common key features. They observed the following characteristics in the response spectra of the horizontal component of the North–South component of El Centro earthquake of 1940 for systems having 0, 2, 5, 10 and 20% of critical damping (Figure 8.20):

1. For high frequency systems, higher than about 2 cycles/sec (or low period systems having T < 0.5 sec), the maximum acceleration response is nearly constant but is a function of damping. The amplification of the response acceleration as compared to the ground acceleration is quite large for lightly damped systems.
2. For extremely high frequency systems (or very low periods), the maximum response acceleration is same as the maximum ground acceleration.
3. For relatively low frequency systems, having frequencies less than about 0.3 cycles/sec (or for high period systems having T > 3 sec), the maximum displacement response is nearly constant and maximum displacement shows only a slight amplification over the maximum ground displacement.
4. For extremely low frequency systems (or extremely high period systems having T > 10 sec), the maximum displacement response is exactly the same as the maximum ground displacement.

5. In the intermediate range of frequencies, the maximum pseudo velocity response is nearly constant, indicating constant energy absorption over the entire range of frequencies from 0.3 to 3 cycles/sec (or T between 0.33 sec and 3 sec). The amplifications are strongly influenced by damping.

A tripartite spectra for El Centro earthquake, Koyna earthquake, Mexico earthquake and Kobe earthquakes for 5% damping is shown in Figure 8.25. These curves also exhibit a behaviour similar to those noticed in Figure 8.20 for the El Centro earthquake.

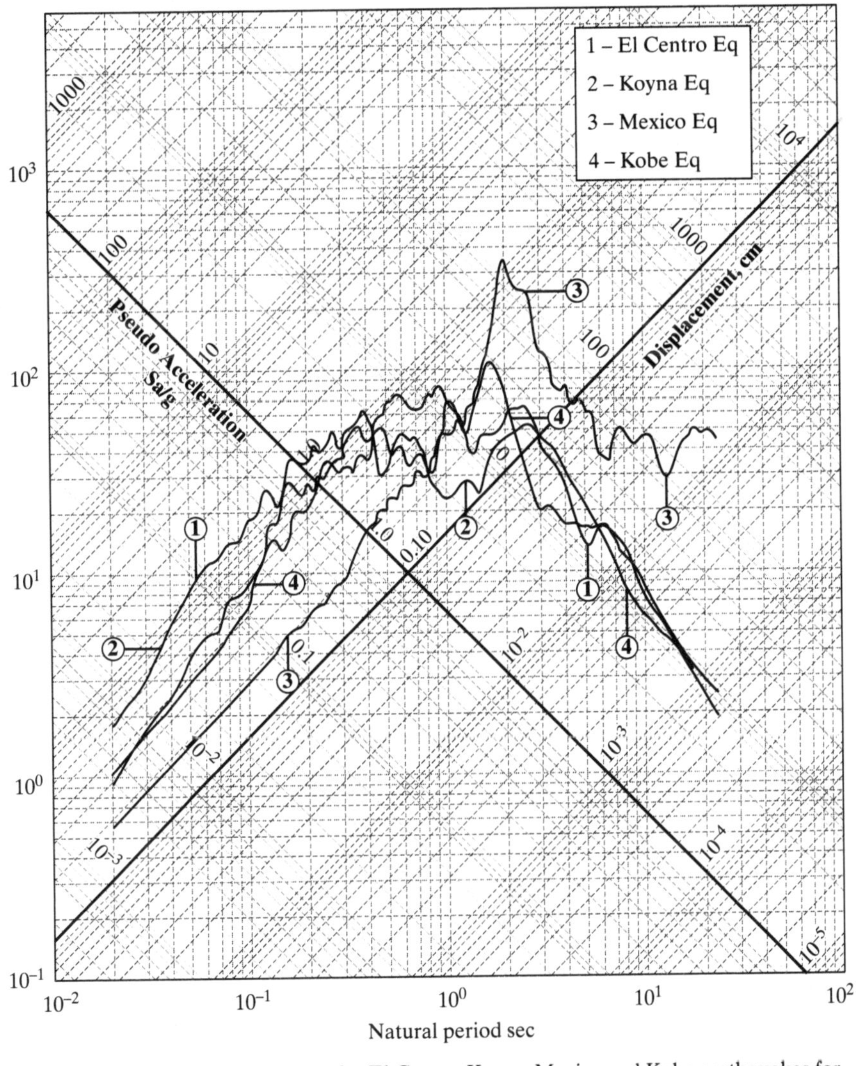

Figure 8.25 Tripartite response spectra for El Centro, Koyna, Mexico and Kobe earthquakes for 5% damping.

Procedure to Generate Simplified Elastic Design Response Spectra Based on these characteristics, they proposed a much simpler method to construct them using the peak values of ground displacement, ground velocity and ground acceleration. It is possible to draw the tripartite response spectra using these three parameters without any more knowledge about the time history of that component of the ground motion. The response spectra for an earthquake can be approximated by using straight line segments in the response spectrum plot, having for the different degrees of damping about the same ratio to the ground motions as the El Centro response spectrum or that of an ensemble of ground motions. The important question was if a normalized, averaged, and smoothened response spectra based on eight components of four earthquakes recorded in USA is acceptable for design, why not make it simpler while retaining the most significant characteristics? They identified three sensitive regions in any tripartite spectra: *acceleration sensitive region, velocity sensitive region* and *displacement sensitive region.*

Region 1a: Maximum acceleration of the SDOF system is equal to maximum ground acceleration.

Region 1b:

(i) Maximum acceleration response of a SDOF system is constant for a given damping.

(ii) It varies with damping—higher for lightly damped system.

Region 2: Constant energy absorption, that is, constant velocity amplification and a function of damping.

Region 3: Maximum displacement response of a SDOF is equal to maximum ground displacement.

The maximum values of ground acceleration $\ddot{x}_{g0}$, velocity $\dot{x}_{g0}$ and displacement x_{g0} are sketched on the tripartite logarithmic chart shown in dash lines in Figure 8.26. These plots give a polygonal curve representing the maximum ground motion values only. The response of items or of equipment, components of structures and complete structures is then determined by amplifying the ground motion values to obtain response spectrum values using amplification factors for various degrees of damping.

Newmark and Hall carried out statistical analysis of a very large number of earthquake records and computed the probability distributions in each of the three sensitive regions for the spectra ordinate, its mean value and its standard deviation at each period. These used lognormal probability distributions. Based on these data, they generated amplification factors in each of the three sensitive regions for different damping ratio (1%, 2%, 5%, 10% and 20%) two different non-exceedance probabilities of 50% (representing mean value of spectra ordinates) and 84.1 per cent (representing mean plus one standard deviation of spectra ordinates) as shown in Table 8.3. Thus, they developed mean response spectrum (having 50% non-exceedance probability) and mean plus one standard deviation response spectrum (having 84.1% non-exceedance probability).

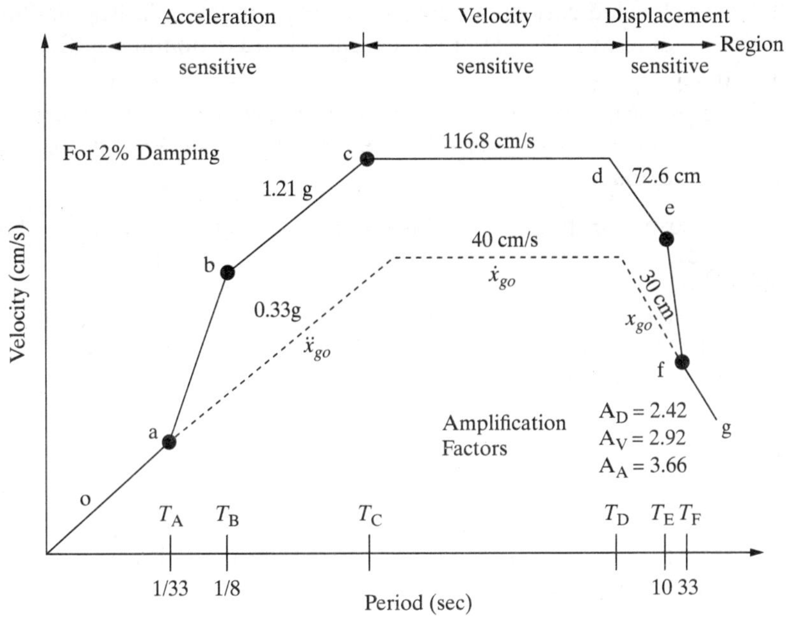

Figure 8.26 Simplified smoothened elastic response spectra for El Centro earthquake for 84.1% non-exceedance probability—Newmark and Hall.

TABLE 8.3 NEWMARK AND HALL AMPLIFICATION FACTORS

	Median (50%)			Mean + SD (84.1%)		
Damping	A	V	D	A	V	D
1%	3.21	2.31	1.82	4.38	3.38	2.73
2%	2.74	2.03	1.63	3.66	2.92	2.42
5%	2.12	1.65	1.39	2.71	2.30	2.01
10%	1.64	1.37	1.20	1.99	1.84	1.69
20%	1.17	1.08	1.01	1.26	1.37	1.38

In the delineation of the complete response spectrum, straight line bounds are used. The procedure for generating a simplified response spectrum is as follows (Figure 8.26):

1. A line c-d is drawn parallel to the horizontal axis by amplifying the ground velocity by factor V from Table 8.3.
2. A line b-c is drawn parallel to the peak ground acceleration line by amplifying the peak ground acceleration by factor A from Table 8.3. The intersection of lines b-c and c-d gives point c.
3. A line d-e is drawn parallel to the peak ground displacement line by amplifying the peak ground displacement by factor D from Table 8.3. The intersection of lines c-d and d-e give point d.

4. Point b is located corresponding to 1/8 sec period. Similarly, point ‘a’ is located corresponding to 1/33 sec period. Line a-b is transition line in the acceleration-sensitive region.
5. Point ‘e’ is located corresponding to 10 sec period. Similarly, point ‘f’ is located corresponding to 33 sec period. Line e-f is transition line in the displacement sensitive region.

The resulting response spectrum o-a-b-c-d-e-f-g is shown in solid lines in Figure 8.26.

Example 8.1

A SDOF system was subjected to the N–S component of the El Centro accelerogram of May 1940. Determine the spectral ordinates for 5% damping if its period was (i) 0.5 sec, (ii) 1 sec and (iii) 3 sec.

Solution

Its solution can be obtained in any of the following three ways:

(i) The set of three spectra—displacement, velocity and acceleration can be used to determine the ordinates corresponding to three different periods for 5% damping.
(ii) The tripartite spectra can be used to determine these ordinates.
(iii) A time history analysis can be carried out for each of the three SDOF systems for the given accelerogram having a period of 0.5, 1 or 3 sec.

Each of these methods will produce nearly the same results as shown in Table 8.4. □

TABLE 8.4 SPECTRAL ORDINATES

Period, sec	Displacement, cm	Velocity, cm/sec	Acceleration, g
0.5	4.43	55.68	0.71
1.0	12.08	75.89	0.48
3.0	22.2	46.5	0.10

8.9 INDIAN CODE:1893 PART 1

In the 1960s, the Housner’s average smoothened response spectra had become available. This spectra was adopted in many countries as well as in the Indian Standard IS:1893 till it was revised in 2002. IS:1893-part 1 adopted an average spectra based on a series of Indian earthquakes as shown in Figure 8.27. This is based on strong motion records of eight Indian earthquakes: Himachal Pradesh 26 April 1986 and 24 March 1995 earthquakes; UP Hills 20 October 1991 and 26 March 1996 earthquakes; N.E. India 10 September 1986, 19 May 1987, 6 February 1988 and 6 August 1988 earthquakes. The average shape of the response spectra was arrived at from an ensemble of total of 92 records (46 sites × 2 components) for rocky sites and 114 records (57 sites × 2 components) for stiff soil. The mean spectra so obtained were smoothened for convenience of use in design. It was called response spectra for Maximum Considered (or Credible) Earthquake (MCE) condition. This elastic response spectrum is divided by a factor 2 to get a Design Basis Earthquake (DBE) response spectra.

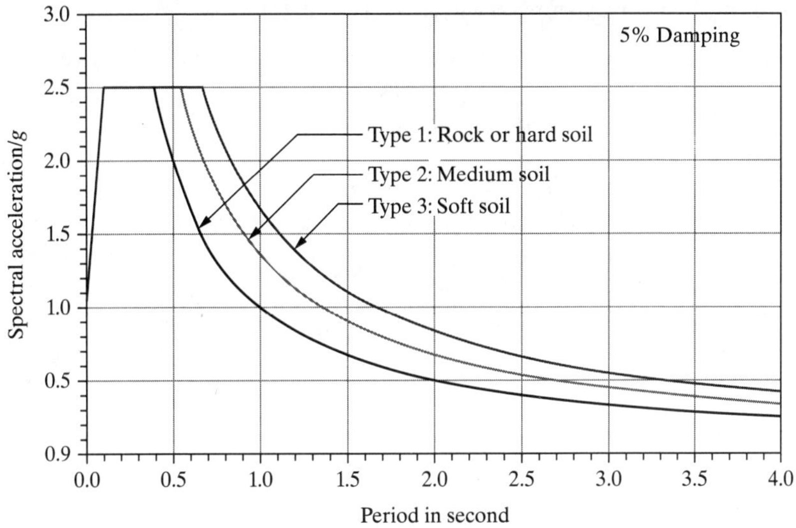

Figure 8.27 Elastic response spectra IS:1893-part 1.

For rocky or hard soils:

$$S_a/g = \begin{cases} 1 + 15\,T & \text{for} \quad 0 \le T \le 0.10 \text{ s} \\ 2.50 & \text{for} \quad 0.10 \le T \le 0.40 \text{ s} \\ 1.0/T & \text{for} \quad 0.40 \le T \le 4.0 \text{ s} \\ 0.25 & \text{for} \quad T > 4.0 \text{ s} \end{cases} \tag{8.16a}$$

For medium soils

$$S_a/g = \begin{cases} 1 + 15\,T & \text{for} \quad 0 \le T \le 0.10 \text{ s} \\ 2.50 & \text{for} \quad 0.10 \le T \le 0.55 \text{ s} \\ 1.36/T & \text{for} \quad 0.55 \le T \le 4.0 \text{ s} \\ 0.34 & \text{for} \quad T > 4.0 \text{ s} \end{cases} \tag{8.16b}$$

For soft soils

$$S_a/g = \begin{cases} 1 + 15\,T & \text{for} \quad 0 \le T \le 0.10 \text{ s} \\ 2.50 & \text{for} \quad 0.10 \le T \le 0.67 \text{ s} \\ 1.67/T & \text{for} \quad 0.67 \le T \le 4.0 \text{ s} \\ 0.42 & \text{for} \quad T > 4.0 \text{ s} \end{cases} \tag{8.16c}$$

The Indian code defines these two terms as follows:

MCE: The most severe earthquake effects considered by this standard

DBE: It is the earthquake which can reasonably be expected to occur at least once during the design life of the structure

The UBC 1997 defined these two terms as follows:

MCE: Largest reasonably conceived earthquake in any zone that appears possible along a recognized fault. It has a 10% probability of being exceeded in 100 years (i.e., a return period = 1000 years)

DBE: Reasonably expected to occur at least once in the design life of the structure. It has a 10% probability of being exceeded in 50 years (i.e., a return period = 475 years)

The IBC 2006 defines these two terms as follows:

MCE: The most severe earthquake effects considered by this code

DBE: The earthquake ground motion that buildings and structures are specifically proportioned to resist

The ASCE 7 2010 defines these two terms as follows:

MCE Ground Motion: The most severe earthquake effects considered by this standard more specifically defined in the following two terms:

Maximum Considered Earthquake Geometric Mean (MCE_G) Peak Ground Acceleration: The most severe earthquake effects considered by this standard determined for geometric mean peak ground acceleration and without adjustment for targeted risk. The MCE_G peak ground acceleration adjusted for site effects (PGA_M) is used in this standard for evaluation of liquefaction, lateral spreading, seismic settlements and other soil related issues.

Risk-Targeted Maximum Considered Earthquake (MCE_R) Ground Motion Response Acceleration: The most severe earthquake effects considered by this standard determined for the orientation that results in the largest maximum response to horizontal ground motions and with adjustment for targeted risk.

Design Earthquake Ground Motion: The earthquake ground motions that are two-thirds of the corresponding MCE_R ground motions.

There is a need to be very careful while using these terms as they may vary from code to code. Nevertheless, the concept behind using these terms remains same. Many countries have developed probability-based response spectra depending upon the risk of earthquakes at a given site.

8.9.1 Design Spectrum

The elastic response spectra for El Centro and Kobe earthquakes and that given in IS:1893-part 1 code for 5% damping are compared in Figure 8.28. It can be seen that the codal spectrum is well below what was obtained during real earthquakes. This is

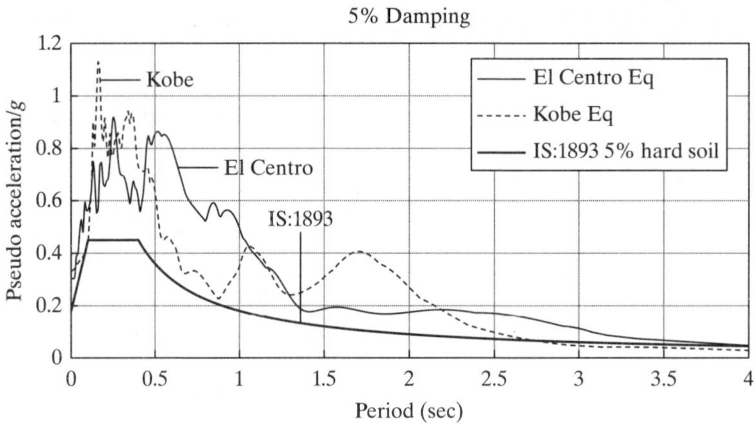

Figure 8.28 El Centro, Kobe and IS:1893–part 1 spectra for 5% damping. (Z = 0.36, I = 1 and R = 1 on hard soil)

a very significant observation. It shows that the code has intentionally provided a spectrum which is well below the forces recorded during real earthquakes. The question arises as to what is the reason behind such a decision? The answer lies in the probability of occurrence of an earthquake of given magnitude and return period at a given site. Therefore, it is desirable to design the building for a lesser force and allow the building to undergo inelastic deformations. This requires provision of sufficient ductility in the structure at all possible locations of the formation of plastic hinges to take care of inelastic deformations. The intention is to design a safe and economical structure.

Example 8.2

Using the Housner's Response spectra (Figure 8.17), determine

(a) The amplitude of spectra acceleration and spectra displacement for a SDOF system having a natural period of 0.2 sec and damping 2%

(b) The amplitude of spectral acceleration and spectral displacement for a SDOF system having a natural period of 1.2 sec and damping 5%

(c) What is the peak ground acceleration of the ground motion represented by the Housner's spectra?

Solution

The Housner's average acceleration spectra is shown in Figure 8.17(b).

(a) For a SDOF system having a period of 0.2 sec and 2% damping, spectral acceleration is 0.28 g

$$\text{Spectral displacement } S_d = \left(\frac{T}{2\pi}\right)^2 S_a$$

$$= \left(\frac{0.2}{2\pi}\right)^2 \times 0.28 \times 9.81 = 0.00278 \text{ m}$$

(b) For a SDOF system having a period of 1.2 sec and 5% damping, spectral acceleration is 0.095g

$$\text{Spectral displacement } S_d = \left(\frac{1.2}{2\pi}\right)^2 \times 0.095 \times 9.81 = 0.034 \text{ m}$$

It shows that although the spectral acceleration for the SDOF system with $T = 1.2$ sec is reduced as compared to that for the $T = 0.2$ sec, but spectral displacement has increased.

(c) One of the conclusions from the study of tripartite response spectra was that for extremely high frequency systems or very low periods, the maximum response acceleration is the same as the peak ground acceleration. The PGA corresponds to zero period acceleration, that is, period below 0.03 sec or frequencies above 33 Hz.

Thus, PGA of the earthquake represented by Housner's average spectra is 0.2 g.

Example 8.3

A RC portal frame is shown in Figure 8.29. Its weight equal to 200 kN is lumped at the rigid roof level. Each column has a cross-section of 30 × 30 cm, length 3 m, Grade of concrete is M30. Its damping may be taken as 5%. Determine the peak roof displacement and bending moment diagram at the instant of peak response using Housner's average response spectra.

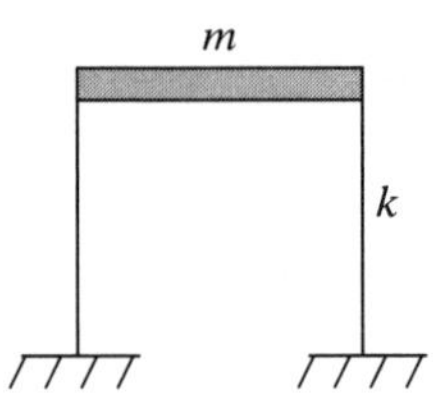

Figure 8.29(a) Portal frame

Solution

The lateral stiffness of the frame $k = \dfrac{2 \times 12\, EI}{L^3}$

Modulus of elasticity of concrete $Ec = 5000\sqrt{f_{ck}} = 5000 \times \sqrt{30} = 27386$ Mpa

Moment of inertia of each column $I = bd^3/12 = 300 \times 300^3/12 = 675 \times 10^6$ mm^4

$$k = \frac{24 \times 27386 \times 675 \times 10^6}{3000^3} = 16430 \text{ N/mm}$$

or,

$$k = 16.43 \times 10^6 \text{ N/m}$$

$$\text{Natural frequency } \omega = \sqrt{\frac{k}{m}} = \sqrt{\frac{16.43 \times 10^6}{200000/9.81}} = 28.38 \text{ rad/sec}$$

$$\text{Natural period } T = \frac{2\pi}{\omega} = \frac{2\pi}{28.38} = 0.22 \text{ sec}$$

Sa/g for 5% damping = 0.2 g

Earthquake force at the level of beam F = mass × acceleration

$$= (200000/9.81) \times 0.2 \times 9.81 = 40000 \text{ N}$$

$$\text{Spectral displacement } S_d = \left(\frac{0.22}{2\pi}\right)^2 \times 0.2 \times 9.81 = 0.0024 \text{ m}$$

Earthquake force at the level of beam F is also given as follows:

Shear in columns of the frame V = stiffness × floor displacement = $16.43 \times 10^6 \times 0.0024$

$$= 39.45 \text{ kN} \approx 40 \text{ kN obtained earlier}$$

The slight difference is due to roundoff error in the stiffness value.
Since the beam is very rigid, the seismic shear will be shared equally by both columns = 20 kN and point of contraflexure will occur at the mid height of each column.
The bending moment in each column

$$= (0.5 \times 40000) \times h/2 = (0.5 \times 40000) \times 3/2 = 30000 \text{ Nm}$$

or 30 kNm. The bending moment in each beam will also be 30 kNm for equilibrium as shown in Figure 8.29(b).

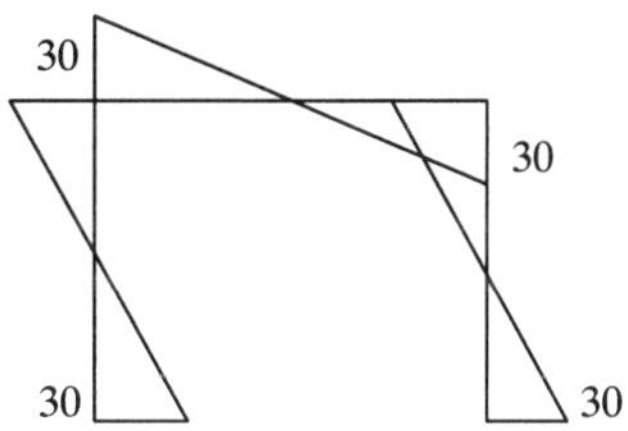

Figure 8.29(b) Bending moment diagram kNm

Example 8.4

A RC portal frame is to be built on a sloping terrain as shown in Figure 8.30(a). Its weight equal to 300 kN is lumped at the rigid roof level. Left column has a circular cross-section of 30 cm dia, length 3 m; right column has a circular cross-section of 35 cm dia and length 5 m. The Grade of concrete is M30. Its damping may be taken as 5%. Determine the peak roof displacement and bending moment diagram at the instant of peak response using the El Centro May 1940 spectral displacement response spectra shown in Figure 8.30(b).

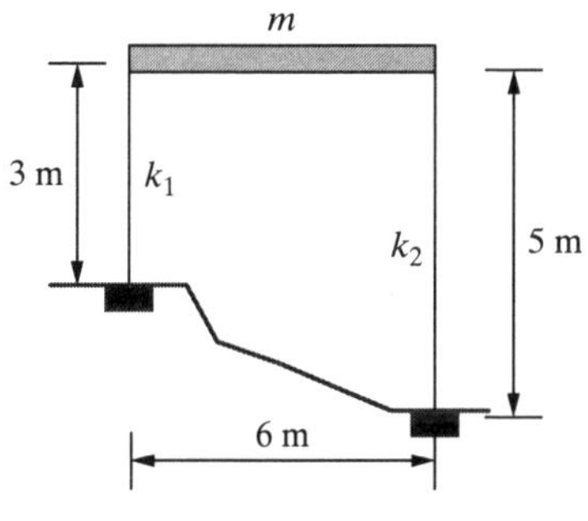

Figure 8.30(a) Portal frame on slope

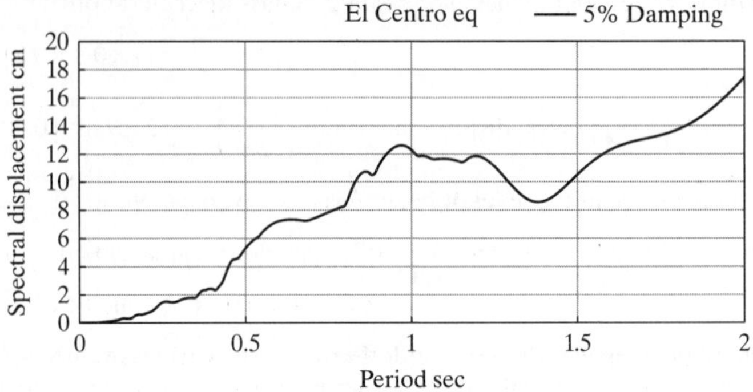

Figure 8.30(b) El Centro May 1940 spectral displacement spectra for 5% damping

Solution

Stiffness of left column $k_1 = 12\ EI/L^3$

$$\text{Moment of inertia } I = \frac{\pi D^4}{64} = \frac{\pi \times 300^4}{64} = 397.6 \times 10^6 \text{ mm}^4$$

Modulus of elasticity of concrete $Ec = 5000\ \sqrt{f_{ck}} = 5000 \times \sqrt{30} = 27386$ Mpa
Stiffness of right column $k_2 = 12\ EI/L^3$

$$\text{Moment of inertia } I = \frac{\pi D^4}{64} = \frac{\pi \times 350^4}{64} = 736.6 \times 10^6 \text{ mm}^4$$

$$\therefore \quad \text{Total stiffness of the frame } k = 12E \times \left(\frac{397.6 \times 10^6}{3000^3} + \frac{736.6 \times 10^6}{5000^3} \right) = 6770 \text{ N/mm}$$

Or, $$k = 6.77 \times 10^6 \text{ N/m}$$

$$\text{Natural frequency } \omega = \sqrt{\frac{k}{m}} = \sqrt{\frac{6.77 \times 10^6}{300000/9.81}} = 14.87 \text{ rad/sec}$$

$$\text{Natural period } T = \frac{2\pi}{\omega} = \frac{2\pi}{14.87} = 0.42 \text{ sec}$$

Spectral displacement S_d for 5% damping = 2.33 cm = 0.0233 m
Since the beam is very rigid, the seismic shear will be shared in proportion to the stiffness of each column.

$$\text{Shear in short column } V_L = k_1 \times 0.0233 = 4.84 \times 10^6 \times 0.0233 = 112770 \text{ N}$$

$$\text{Shear in long column, } V_R = k_2 \times 0.0233 = 1.93 \times 10^6 \times 0.0233 = 44970 \text{ N}$$

$$\text{Total earthquake force} = V_L + V_R = 112770 + 44970 = 157740 \text{ N}$$

The bending moment in short column = $V_L \times h/2 = 112770 \times 3/2 = 169150$ Nm

Or 169.15 kNm.

The bending moment in long column = $V_R \times h/2 = 44970 \times 5/2 = 112400$ Nm

Or 112.40 kNm.

The bending moment diagram is shown in Figure 8.30(c).

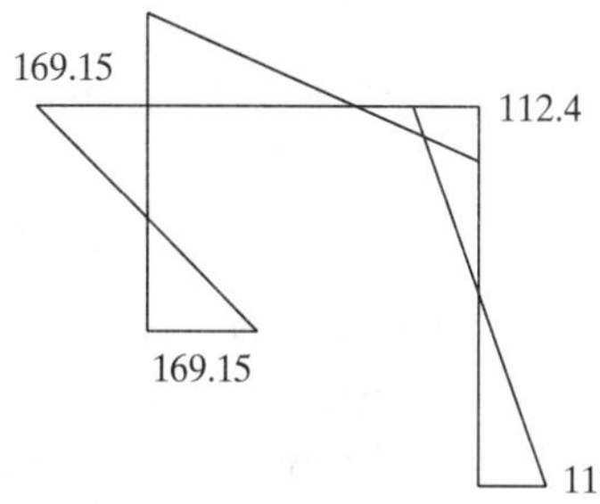

Figure 8.30(c) Bending moment diagram kNm

REVIEW QUESTIONS

8.1 What do you understand by response spectrum for a SDOF system?

8.2 Draw a flow diagram for the generation of elastic response spectra for a SDOF system?

8.3 Discuss the basis of peak relative displacement spectra. How is it useful?

8.4 Discuss the basis of peak relative velocity spectra. How is it useful?

8.5 Discuss the basis of peak relative and absolute acceleration spectra. How is it useful? What is the need of absolute acceleration spectra?

8.6 Explain the terms elastic response spectra and design response spectra.

8.7 Differentiate between velocity response spectra and pseudo velocity response spectra. How is it useful to the designers?

8.8 Explain the difference between elastic spectra and smoothened elastic spectra. How do you normalize a set of spectra?

8.9 Write the relationship between peak pseudo displacement, pseudo velocity, and pseudo acceleration. How this information is useful?

8.10 Discuss the three distinct regions in elastic acceleration response spectra.

8.11 What is the role of viscous damping in response spectra?

8.12 What is the need of a tripartite graph?

8.13 Show that acceleration and displacement axes are inclined at 45° with the velocity axis in a tripartite spectra graph.

8.14 Discuss the salient features of the various regions in tripartite elastic response spectra. How this information is useful to the designers?

8.15 What are the major steps in developing Housner's average response spectra?

8.16 Write a short note on Housner's average response spectra.

8.17 Write a short note on Newmark and Hall's smoothened response spectra.

8.18 Differentiate between a smoothened response spectra and design response spectra.

8.19 Write a short note on Fourier amplitude spectra. How is it useful?

8.20 Discuss the salient features of the El Centro earthquake of May 1940, Koyna earthquake of Dec 1967, and Mexico earthquake of Sept 1985.

8.21 What is the significance of peak ground acceleration of a given accelerogram?

8.22 How do you determine the dominant frequencies of a given accelerogram? How it is use ful to the designers?

8.23 For extremely high frequency systems (or very low periods), what does the spectral accel eration represent?

8.24 For extremely low frequency systems (or very high periods), what does the spectral dis placement represent?

8.25 What maximum credible earthquake is defined?

8.26 How design basis earthquake is defined?

8.27 What are the distinct regions in the European elastic response spectra?

8.28 What are type 1 and type 2 response spectra in Eurocode 8?

8.29 Why the codal design response spectra give lower values than those measured in rea earthquakes in any seismic region?

8.30 Develop an elastic tripartite response spectrum for the following peak ground parameter using the Newmark and Hall amplification factors: maximum ground acceleration, veloc ity and displacement equal to 0.45 g, 40 cm/sec, and 25 cm, respectively. Use a dampin factor of 5%. Plot the graph with frequency as abscissa and again with period as abscissa

REFERENCES

Seismosoft <www.seismosoft.com> *Very powerful programs are available to compute and plc elastic response spectra, Fourier spectra, Ground motion parameters, inelastic constant ductilit spectra, and generate artificial earthquakes and spectrum compatible earthquakes etc.*

ASCE 7 (2022) Minimum Design Loads for Buildings and other Structures, ASCE/SEI Standar ASCE 7–22, American Society of Civil Engineers, Reston, VA.

Eurocode 1998 (2004) Design of Structures for Earthquake Resistance—Part 1: General Rule Seismic Actions and Rules for Buildings, European Standard, Brussels.

Housner, G.W. (1941) Calculating the Response of an Oscillator to Arbitrary Ground Motion Bulletin of Seismological Society of America, Vol 31, pp. 143–149.

IS 1893:2016 (Part 1) Criteria for Earthquake Resistant Design of Structures, Part 1 Genera Provisions and Buildings, Bureau of Indian Standards, New Delhi.

Newmark, N.M. and Hall, W.J., (1973) A Rational Approach to Seismic Design Standards fc Structures, Proc., Vth World Conference on Earthquake Engg, Rome, Vol. 2, pp. 2266–2275.

Newmark, N.M. and Hall, W.J., (1969) Seismic Design Criteria for Nuclear Reactor Facilitie Proc., IVth World Conference on Earthquake Engg, Santiago, Chile, Vol. 2, pp. 37–50.

Part

2

Multi-Degree of Freedom Systems

9 Two-degree of Freedom Systems

9.1 INTRODUCTION

A study of a two-degree of freedom (DOF) system explores how to write and solve the equation of motion, find frequencies and mode shapes and interpret its results. It leads to a very special area of highly practical importance known as *vibration absorbers.* These vibration absorbers are mounted in all kinds of structures where vibrations are a problem, for example, buildings, theater floors, bridges, automobile parts, aircrafts and machines. Tuned mass dampers are special cases of the vibration absorbers. The theory of vibration absorbers and tuned mass dampers are discussed along with real-life applications.

9.2 UNDAMPED FREE VIBRATIONS

Let us consider an undamped two-degree of freedom system as shown in Figure 9.1. Its free body diagrams for the mass m_1 and mass m_2 are also shown. Equations of motion for the two masses can be written as follows:

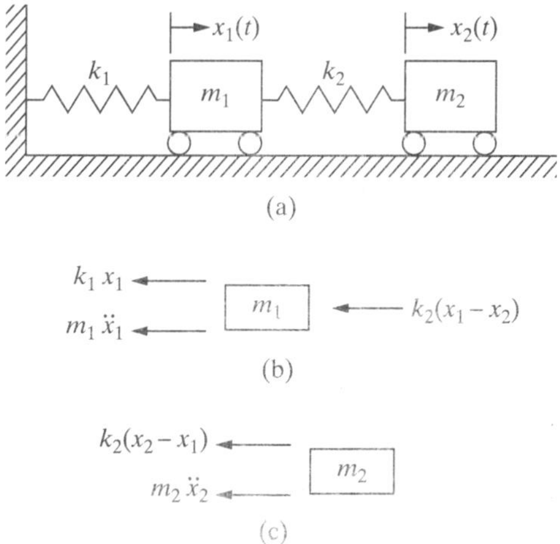

Figure 9.1 Two degree of freedom system – undamped.

$$m_1\ddot{x}_1 + k_1 x_1 + k_2(x_1 - x_2) = 0 \tag{9.1a}$$

and
$$m_2\ddot{x}_2 + k_2(x_2 - x_1) = 0 \tag{9.1b}$$

Let us assume that the masses vibrate in phase with each other. That is, they follow an identical variation with time but with their own characteristic amplitudes.

Let
$$\left.\begin{aligned} x_1 &= X_1 \sin\omega_1 t \\ x_2 &= X_2 \sin\omega_2 t \end{aligned}\right\} \tag{9.2}$$

∴ Substituting Equation (9.2) in Equation (9.1a) gives,

$$-m_1 X_1 \omega_1^2 \sin\omega_1 t + k_1 X_1 \sin\omega_1 t + k_2(X_1 \sin\omega_1 t - X_2 \sin\omega_2 t) = 0$$

or,
$$-m_1 X_1 \omega_1^2 \sin\omega_1 t + (k_1 + k_2) X_1 \sin\omega_1 t = k_2 X_2 \sin\omega_2 t$$

or,
$$\frac{X_1}{X_2} = \frac{k_2 \sin\omega_2 t}{[(k_1 + k_2) - m_1\omega_1^2]\sin\omega_1 t} \tag{9.3}$$

Since X_1 and X_2 are the amplitudes of two harmonic motions, these ratios must be constant and independent of time.

∴
$$\frac{\sin\omega_2 t}{\sin\omega_1 t} = \text{constant} = c \text{ say} \tag{9.4}$$

This should be true at all times

Let us see what happens if $c > 1$

At
$$t = \frac{\pi}{2\omega_1},\ \sin\omega_1 t = \sin\frac{\omega_1\pi}{2\omega_1} = 1$$

∴
$$\frac{\sin\omega_2 t}{\sin\omega_1 t} = \sin\omega_2 t = c > 1$$

or $\sin\omega_2 t > 1$, which is not possible.

Therefore c cannot exceed 1. Similarly, it can be shown that c cannot be less than 1.

Hence, $c = 1$ always

∴
$$\frac{\sin\omega_2 t}{\sin\omega_1 t} = 1 \quad \text{or} \quad \omega_1 = \omega_2 \tag{9.5}$$

Thus, the two harmonic motions, if at all they exist, have to be of same frequency. Let us modify the assumed solution as follows:

$$\left.\begin{aligned} x_1 &= X_1 \sin \omega t \\ x_2 &= X_2 \sin \omega t \end{aligned}\right\} \tag{9.6}$$

Substituting in Equation (9.1), we get

$$\left[-m_1\omega^2 + \left(k_1 + k_2\right)\right] X_1 = k_2 X_2 \tag{9.7a}$$

and

$$\left(-m_2\omega^2 + k_2\right) X_2 = k_2 X_1 \tag{9.7b}$$

Equation (9.7a) can be written as:

$$\therefore \quad \frac{X_1}{X_2} = \frac{k_2}{-m_1\omega^2 + (k_1 + k_2)} = \frac{k_2}{(k_1 + k_2) - m_1\omega^2}$$

and Equation (9.7b) can be written as:

$$\frac{X_1}{X_2} = \frac{k_2 - m_2\omega^2}{k_2}$$

or,

$$\frac{k_2}{(k_1 + k_2) - m_1\omega^2} = \frac{k_2 - m_2\omega^2}{k_2}$$

or,

$$k_2^2 = [(k_1 + k_2) - m_1\omega^2][k_2 - m_2\omega^2]$$

$$= m_1 m_2 \omega^4 - m_1 k_2 \omega^2 - (k_1 + k_2) m_2 \omega^2 + (k_1 + k_2) k_2$$

or,

$$m_1\, m_2\, \omega^4 - [m_1 k_2 + m_2\, (k_1 + k_2)]\omega^2 + k_1 k_2 = 0 \tag{9.8}$$

This gives two positive roots of ω^2, hence two positive values of ω, that is, ω_1^* and ω_2^*. Equation (9.8) is referred to as the characteristic equation of vibration of a two-DOF system.

Let us re-write Equation (9.1) in matrix form as follows:

$$\begin{bmatrix} m_1 & 0 \\ 0 & m_2 \end{bmatrix} \begin{Bmatrix} \ddot{x}_1 \\ \ddot{x}_2 \end{Bmatrix} + \begin{bmatrix} k_1 + k_2 & -k_2 \\ -k_2 & k_2 \end{bmatrix} \begin{Bmatrix} x_1 \\ x_2 \end{Bmatrix} = \begin{Bmatrix} 0 \\ 0 \end{Bmatrix} \tag{9.9}$$

Upon substituting the values of x_1 and x_2 from Equation (9.6), we get

$$\begin{bmatrix} k_1 + k_2 - m_1\omega^2 & -k_2 \\ -k_2 & k_2 - m_2\omega^2 \end{bmatrix} \begin{Bmatrix} X_1 \\ X_2 \end{Bmatrix} = \begin{Bmatrix} 0 \\ 0 \end{Bmatrix} \tag{9.10}$$

Since the vector $\{X_1\ X_2\}$ cannot be zero, the determinant of the term inside the square bracket must be zero. That is,

$$\det \begin{vmatrix} k_1 + k_2 - m_1\omega^2 & -k_2 \\ -k_2 & k_2 - m_2\omega^2 \end{vmatrix} = 0 \tag{9.11a}$$

or, $$[(k_1+k_2)-m_1\omega^2][k_2-m_2\omega^2]-k_2^2=0 \tag{9.11b}$$

or it can be written as:

$$\omega^4-\left(\frac{k_2}{m_2}+\frac{k_1+k_2}{m_1}\right)\omega^2+\frac{k_1}{m_1}\frac{k_2}{m_2}=0 \tag{9.12}$$

This is the same equation as Equation (9.8).

Equation (9.12) can be written as follows:

$$\omega^4-\left(\frac{k_2}{m_1}+\frac{k_1}{m_1}+\frac{k_2}{m_2}\right)\omega^2+\frac{k_1}{m_1}\frac{k_2}{m_2}=0$$

$$\omega^4-\left(\frac{k_1(m_1+m_2)}{m_1(m_1+m_2)}+\frac{k_2}{m_1}+\frac{k_2}{m_2}\right)\omega^2+\frac{k_1}{m_1}\frac{k_2}{m_2}=0$$

or, $$\omega^4-\left(\frac{k_1}{m_1+m_2}+\frac{k_2}{m_2}\right)\left(\frac{m_1+m_2}{m_1}\right)\omega^2+\frac{k_1}{m_1+m_2}\frac{k_2}{m_2}\frac{m_1+m_2}{m_1}=0 \tag{9.13}$$

If $$\bar{\omega}_1^{\,2}=\frac{k_1}{m_1+m_2} \quad \text{and} \quad \bar{\omega}_2^{\,2}=\frac{k_2}{m_2}$$

Let $$\mu=\frac{m_2}{m_1}=\text{mass ratio} \tag{9.14}$$

Equation (9.13) can be written as follows:

$$\omega^4-\omega^2[(\bar{\omega}_1^{\,2}+\bar{\omega}_2^{\,2})(1+\mu)]+\bar{\omega}_1^{\,2}\bar{\omega}_2^{\,2}(1+\mu)=0 \tag{9.15}$$

It again gives four roots of ω, two positive and two negative. Each positive value of ω will give the values of X_1 and X_2 known as eigenvectors.

9.3 UNDAMPED FORCED VIBRATIONS

Now let us consider forced vibrations of undamped two-DOF systems as shown in Figure 9.2.

Equations of motion become:

$$m_1\ddot{x}_1+k_1x_1+k_2(x_1-x_2)=P_0\sin\bar{\omega}t \tag{9.16a}$$

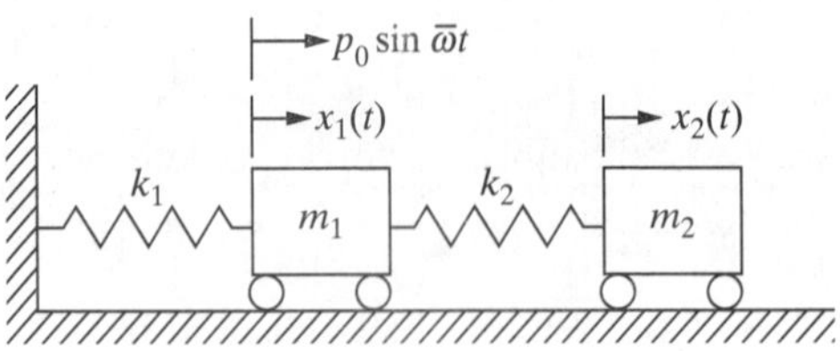

Figure 9.2 Two degree of freedom system.

and $$m_2\ddot{x}_2 + k_2(x_2 - x_1) = 0 \tag{9.16b}$$

Let us rewrite Equation (9.16) in matrix form:

$$\begin{bmatrix} m_1 & 0 \\ 0 & m_2 \end{bmatrix}\begin{Bmatrix} \ddot{x}_1 \\ \ddot{x}_2 \end{Bmatrix} + \begin{bmatrix} k_1 + k_2 & -k_2 \\ -k_2 & k_2 \end{bmatrix}\begin{Bmatrix} x_1 \\ x_2 \end{Bmatrix} = \begin{Bmatrix} P_0 \sin \bar{\omega}t \\ 0 \end{Bmatrix} \tag{9.17}$$

Let $$\left.\begin{aligned} x_1 &= X_1 \sin \bar{\omega}t \\ x_2 &= X_2 \sin \bar{\omega}t \end{aligned}\right\} \text{ for a steady state solution} \tag{9.18}$$

It is known from the differential equations that the forced response of an undamped system is of the form of a harmonic function of the same frequency as the driving force with different amplitude but in phase. $\bar{\omega}$ is the forcing frequency in Equation (9.18).

Substituting in Equation (9.16), we have for steady state response

$$[-m_1\bar{\omega}^2 + (k_1 + k_2)]X_1 - k_2X_2 = P_0 \tag{9.19a}$$

and $$-m_2\bar{\omega}^2X_2 + k_2\,X_2 - k_2X_1 = 0 \tag{9.19b}$$

or, $$k_2X_1 + (m_2\bar{\omega}^2 - k_2)X_2 = 0 \tag{9.19c}$$

These equations can be written in matrix form as follows:

$$\begin{bmatrix} k_1 + k_2 - m_1\bar{\omega}^2 & -k_2 \\ -k_2 & k_2 - m_2\bar{\omega}^2 \end{bmatrix}\begin{Bmatrix} X_1 \\ X_2 \end{Bmatrix} = \begin{Bmatrix} P_0 \\ 0 \end{Bmatrix}$$

or, $$\begin{Bmatrix} X_1 \\ X_2 \end{Bmatrix} = \begin{bmatrix} k_1 + k_2 - m_1\bar{\omega}^2 & -k_2 \\ -k_2 & k_2 - m_2\bar{\omega}^2 \end{bmatrix}^{-1}\begin{Bmatrix} P_0 \\ 0 \end{Bmatrix}$$

or, $$\begin{Bmatrix} X_1 \\ X_2 \end{Bmatrix} = \frac{1}{(k_1 + k_2 - m_1\bar{\omega}^2)\times(k_2 - m_2\bar{\omega}^2) - k_2^2}\begin{bmatrix} k_2 - m_2\bar{\omega}^2 & k_2 \\ k_2 & k_1 + k_2 - m_1\bar{\omega}^2 \end{bmatrix}\begin{Bmatrix} P_0 \\ 0 \end{Bmatrix}$$

or, $$\begin{Bmatrix} X_1 \\ X_2 \end{Bmatrix} = \frac{1}{(k_1 + k_2 - m_1\bar{\omega}^2)\times(k_2 - m_2\bar{\omega}^2) - k_2^2}\begin{Bmatrix} P_0(k_2 - m_2\bar{\omega}^2) \\ P_0k_2 \end{Bmatrix} \tag{9.20}$$

Solving Equation (9.20) gives,

$$X_1 = \frac{[k_2 - m_2\bar{\omega}^2]P_0}{[m_1m_2\bar{\omega}^4 - \{m_1k_2 + m_2(k_1 + k_2)\}\bar{\omega}^2 + k_1k_2]} \tag{9.21a}$$

$$X_2 = \frac{k_2\,P_0}{[m_1m_2\bar{\omega}^4 - \{m_1k_2 + m_2(k_1 + k_2)\}\bar{\omega}^2 + k_1k_2]} \tag{9.21b}$$

The determinant given by Equation (9.11b) can be written as follows:

$$\det = \left(k_1 - m_1\bar{\omega}^2\right)\left(k_2 - m_2\bar{\omega}^2\right) - k_2 m_2 \bar{\omega}^2$$

Equating the determinant to zero, leads to the natural frequencies of the two-DOF system ω_1^* and ω_2^*. The amplitude of vibrations is given by Equation (9.21).

9.4 DAMPED FORCED VIBRATIONS

Let us consider a two-degree-of-freedom system as shown in Figure 9.3(a).

The free body diagrams of the two masses are shown in Figure 9.3(b). The equation of motion for the two masses can be written as follows:

$$m_1\ddot{x}_1 + c_1\dot{x}_1 + k_1x_1 - k_2\left(x_2 - x_1\right) - c_2\left(\dot{x}_2 - \dot{x}_1\right) - p_1 = 0 \tag{9.22a}$$

or,

$$m_1\ddot{x}_1 + \left(c_1 + c_2\right)\dot{x}_1 - c_2\dot{x}_2 + (k_1 + k_2)x_1 - k_2x_2 = p_1 \tag{9.22b}$$

and

$$m_2\ddot{x}_2 + c_2\left(\dot{x}_2 - \dot{x}_1\right) + k_2\left(x_2 - x_1\right) = p_2 \tag{9.22c}$$

In matrix form,

$$\begin{bmatrix} m_1 & 0 \\ 0 & m_2 \end{bmatrix}\begin{Bmatrix} \ddot{x}_1 \\ \ddot{x}_2 \end{Bmatrix} + \begin{bmatrix} c_1 + c_2 & -c_2 \\ -c_2 & c_2 \end{bmatrix}\begin{Bmatrix} \dot{x}_1 \\ \dot{x}_2 \end{Bmatrix} + \begin{bmatrix} k_1 + k_2 & -k_2 \\ -k_2 & k_2 \end{bmatrix}\begin{Bmatrix} x_1 \\ x_2 \end{Bmatrix} = \begin{Bmatrix} p_1 \\ p_2 \end{Bmatrix} \tag{9.23}$$

These are coupled equations and need to be solved simultaneously.

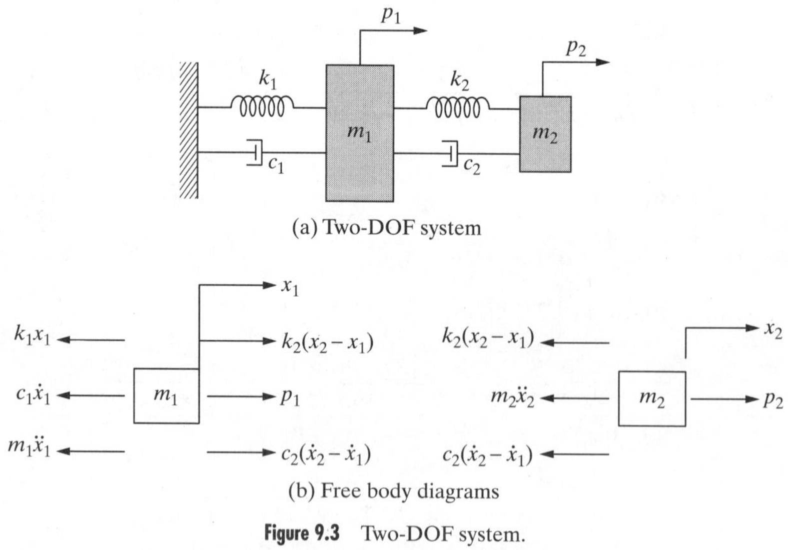

Figure 9.3 Two-DOF system.

9.5 UNDAMPED VIBRATION ABSORBER

Let us again consider two-DOF undamped system of Figure 9.2. Equation (9.21a) can be written as:

$$X_1 = \frac{P_0 k_2 \left[1 - \frac{m_2}{k_2}\bar{\omega}^2\right]}{k_1 k_2 \left[1 - \frac{\bar{\omega}^2}{\omega_1^2}\right]\left[1 - \frac{\bar{\omega}^2}{\omega_2^2}\right] - k_2 m_2 \bar{\omega}^2}$$

or,

$$X_1 = \frac{\frac{P_0}{k_1}\left[1 - \frac{\bar{\omega}^2}{\omega_2^2}\right]}{\left[1 - \frac{\bar{\omega}^2}{\omega_1^2}\right]\left[1 - \frac{\bar{\omega}^2}{\omega_2^2}\right] - \frac{m_1}{m_1}\frac{m_2}{k_1}\bar{\omega}^2}$$

or,

$$D_1 = \frac{\left[1 - \frac{\bar{\omega}^2}{\omega_2^2}\right]}{\left[1 - \frac{\bar{\omega}^2}{\omega_1^2}\right]\left[1 - \frac{\bar{\omega}^2}{\omega_2^2}\right] - \mu \frac{\bar{\omega}^2}{\omega_1^2}} \tag{9.24}$$

where

$$\omega_1^2 = \frac{k_1}{m_1} \quad \text{and} \quad \omega_2^2 = \frac{k_2}{m_2}$$

$$X_{st} = P_0 / k_1$$

$$\omega_1 = \sqrt{\frac{k_1}{m_1}}, \qquad \omega_2 = \sqrt{\frac{k_2}{m_2}}, \qquad \mu = \frac{m_2}{m_1} \tag{9.25}$$

μ = Mass ratio

and D_1 is the dynamic magnification factor for mass m_1.

It is assumed that ω_1 is the natural frequency of a SDOF system consisting of mass m_1 and spring k_1 only. Similarly, ω_2 is the natural frequency of a SDOF system consisting of mass m_2 and spring k_2 only.

It is interesting to know that the denominator of Equation (9.21) is same as the frequency equation of undamped-free vibrations. These two-DOF systems will have two roots or two natural frequencies, ω_1^* and ω_2^*. If the exciting frequency $\bar{\omega}$ is equal to ω_1^* or ω_2^*, the natural frequency of the two-DOF system, there is resonance. The denominator vanishes and the amplitude becomes infinity, that is, $X_1 = \infty = X_2$.

Further, the numerator of X_1 vanishes, when

$$k_2 - m_2 \bar{\omega}^2 = 0$$

or, if forcing frequency

$$\bar{\omega} = \omega_2 = \sqrt{\frac{k_2}{m_2}} \tag{9.26}$$

Then $X_1 = 0$

Thereby, making the mass m_1 motionless at this frequency ($X_1 = 0$).

At this condition, there is no resonance because ω_2 is not a natural frequency of the two mass system. As stated earlier, ω_2 is the natural frequency of a SDOF system consisting of mass m_2 and spring stiffness k_2 only. No such stationary condition (zero displacement) occurs for mass m_2. This formulation gives rise to the concept of *vibration absorber*. Let us assume there is a primary SDOF system consisting of mass m_1 and spring k_1. It will vibrate at its natural frequency ω_1. It is subjected to a forcing function $P(t)$ having a frequency of $\bar{\omega}$. It is now desired to control the vibrations of this primary system. Let us attach another SDOF system called secondary system consisting of mass m_2 and spring k_2 as shown in Figure 9.4. The vibrations of this secondary system are of no consequence to our problem. The object is to control the vibrations of the primary SDOF system. Let the frequency ω_2 be adjusted in such a manner that $\bar{\omega} = \omega_2$. In such a situation, the mass m_1 will have zero vibrations as $X_1 = 0$. Only mass m_2 will vibrate.

The fact that a mass which is being excited can have zero amplitude of vibration under certain conditions by coupling it to another spring mass system, forms the *basis of vibration absorbers*. The second mass continues to vibrate. This type of absorber is extremely effective at one speed only and this is suitable only for constant speed machines or for wind or seismic force acting at a certain frequency.

At

$$\bar{\omega} = \omega_2 \tag{9.27}$$

$$X_2 = -\frac{X_{st}}{\mu \dfrac{\omega_2^2}{\omega_1^2}} = -\frac{P_0}{k_2}$$

or,

$$P_0 = -k_2 X_2 \tag{9.28}$$

This equation shows that spring force $k_2 X_2$ on the main mass due to the amplitude X_2 of the absorber mass is equal and opposite to the exciting force on the main mass resulting in no motion of the main system. The absorber system exerts a force equal and

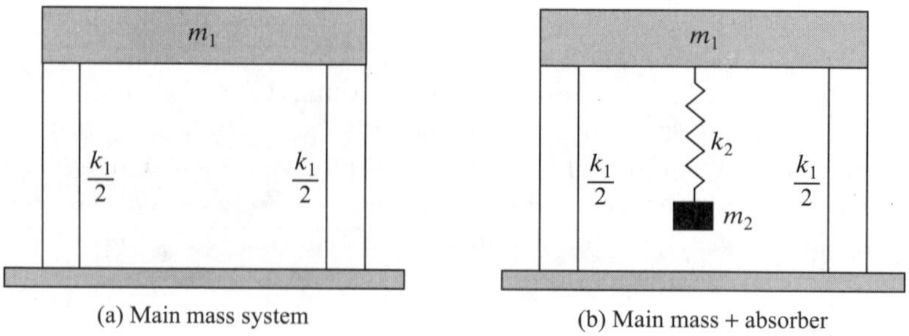

Figure 9.4 Concept of vibration absorber.

opposite to that of the applied force. The main system vibrations have been reduced to zero and these vibrations have been taken up by the absorber system. Hence, the name *vibration absorber*.

The analysis used to design a vibration absorber assumes that it can be constructed without introducing any appreciable damping. If damping is introduced, the equations can not necessarily be decoupled and the magnitude of the displacement of the primary mass will not be zero.

9.6 TUNED VIBRATION ABSORBER

The concept of vibration absorber developed earlier can be further refined. The auxiliary system is much more effective, if the main system is operating at resonance. That is, $\bar{\omega} = \omega_1$

But for absorber to be effective, we have $\bar{\omega} = \omega_2$

that is,

$$\bar{\omega} = \omega_1 = \omega_2 \quad \text{or} \quad \frac{k_2}{m_2} = \frac{k_1}{m_1} \tag{9.29}$$

When this condition is fulfilled, this absorber is known to be a *tuned vibration absorber or tuned mass damper*.

Equations (9.21a) and (9.21b) can be written as follows:

$$\frac{X_1}{X_{ST}} = \frac{1 - \dfrac{\bar{\omega}^2}{\omega_2^2}}{\dfrac{\bar{\omega}^4}{\omega_2^4} - (2+\mu)\dfrac{\bar{\omega}^2}{\omega_2^2} + 1} \tag{9.30a}$$

and

$$\frac{X_2}{X_{ST}} = \frac{1}{\dfrac{\bar{\omega}^4}{\omega_2^4} - (2+\mu)\dfrac{\bar{\omega}^2}{\omega_2^2} + 1} \tag{9.30b}$$

To get resonant frequencies, the denominator of Equations (9.30a) or (9.30b) must be zero,

$$\left(\frac{\bar{\omega}}{\omega_2}\right)^4 - (2+\mu)\left(\frac{\bar{\omega}}{\omega_2}\right)^2 + 1 = 0$$

or,

$$\left(\frac{\bar{\omega}}{\omega_2}\right)^2 = \left(1 + \frac{\mu}{2}\right) \pm \sqrt{\mu + \frac{\mu^2}{4}} \tag{9.31}$$

This equation can be plotted as shown in Figure 9.5. At a given mass ratio, it gives two resonant frequencies corresponding to the two degrees of freedom.

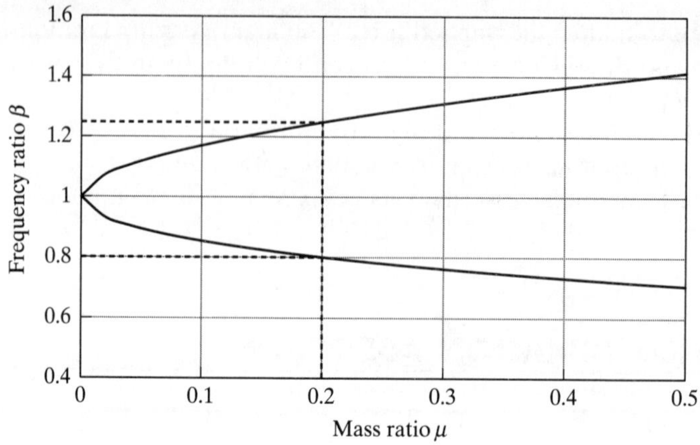

Figure 9.5 Mass ratio vs. resonant frequency ratio ($\bar{\omega}/\omega_2$).

9.6.1 Effect of Mass Ratio on the Amplitude of Primary Mass

In Equation (9.30a), at a frequency ratio of 1.0 ($\beta = \bar{\omega} / \omega_2$) and mass ratio $\mu = 0$, there is resonance and its denominator is zero. The amplitude of primary mass is infinity. This is a highly undesirable situation. If a small mass is attached having a mass ratio equal to 2% only, it is possible to reduce the amplitude of mass m_1 to zero or less than the static displacement. However, it will be very difficult to design a vibration absorber with a frequency ratio equal to 1.0 at which the response of the primary mass will be exactly zero because of the practical difficulties. Therefore, an obvious choice will be to design a vibration absorber such that the amplitude of the primary mass is less than 1.0, that is ($x_1/x_{st} \leq 1.0$). Because the system has two DOF, there will be two frequencies within which this criteria can be satisfied. This bandwidth is known as *operating frequency* of the vibration absorber.

Let us re-write Equation (9.30a) as follows:

$$1 - \frac{\bar{\omega}^2}{\omega_2^2} \leq \frac{\bar{\omega}^4}{\omega_2^4} - (2+\mu)\frac{\bar{\omega}^2}{\omega_2^2} + 1$$

or,

$$\frac{\bar{\omega}^4}{\omega_2^4} - (1+\mu)\frac{\bar{\omega}^2}{\omega_2^2} \geq 0$$

or,

$$\frac{\bar{\omega}^2}{\bar{\omega}_2^2} \geq (1+\mu) \tag{9.32}$$

Equation (9.32) gives only one positive value of the frequency ratio, while the second value gets lost in simplification. It gives the upper frequency ratio. To get the other frequency ratio at which the normalized response of primary mass is less than 1.0, graphical solution is adopted.

Let us examine the effect of different mass ratios ($\mu = 0.02, 0.25$ and 2.0) on the normalized amplitude of the primary mass m_1 and secondary mass m_2 as shown in Figures 9.6 to 9.8 by plotting Equation (9.30). The combined response of primary mass and secondary mass for different mass ratio $\mu = 0.02, 0.05, 0.50$ and 2.0 are shown in Figures 9.9(a) to 9.9(d).

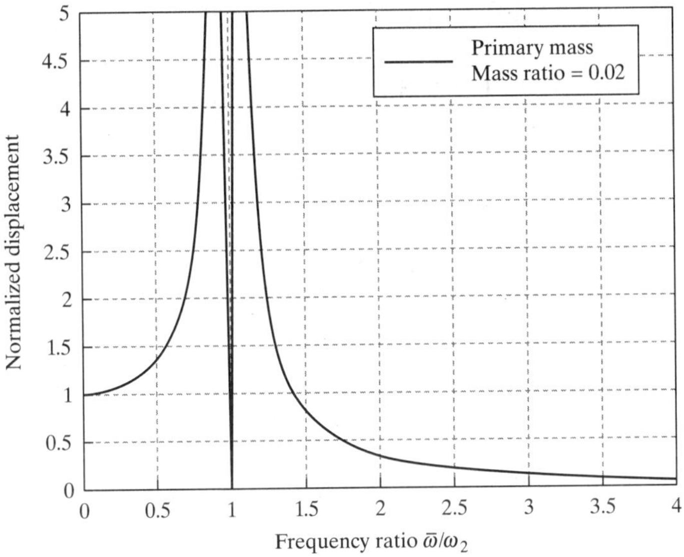

Figure 9.6(a) Normalized amplitude of primary mass vs. normalized driving frequency for $\mu = 0.02$.

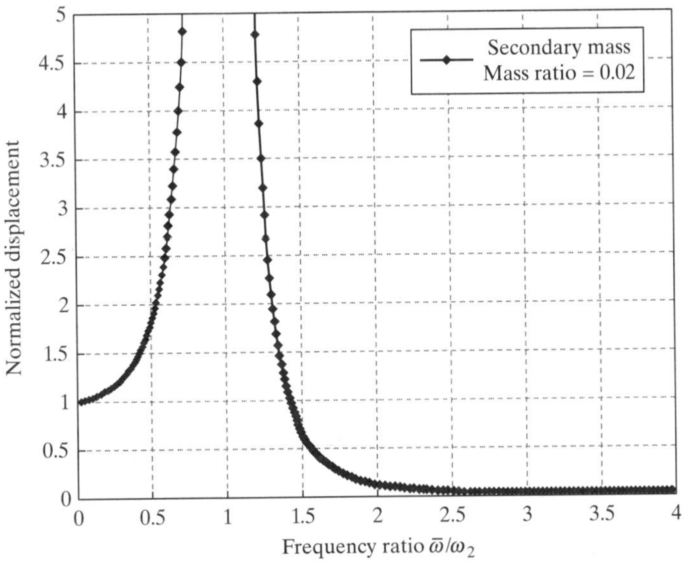

Figure 9.6(b) Normalized amplitude of secondary mass vs. normalized driving frequency for $\mu = 0.02$.

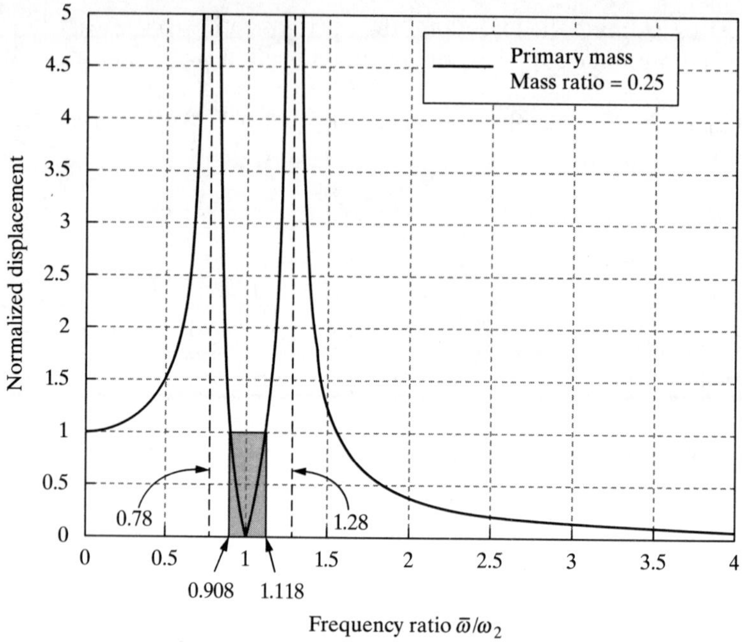

Figure 9.7(a) Normalized amplitude of primary mass vs. normalized driving frequency for $\mu = 0.25$. The shaded area shows the frequency ratios for which the displacement magnification is less than 1.0.

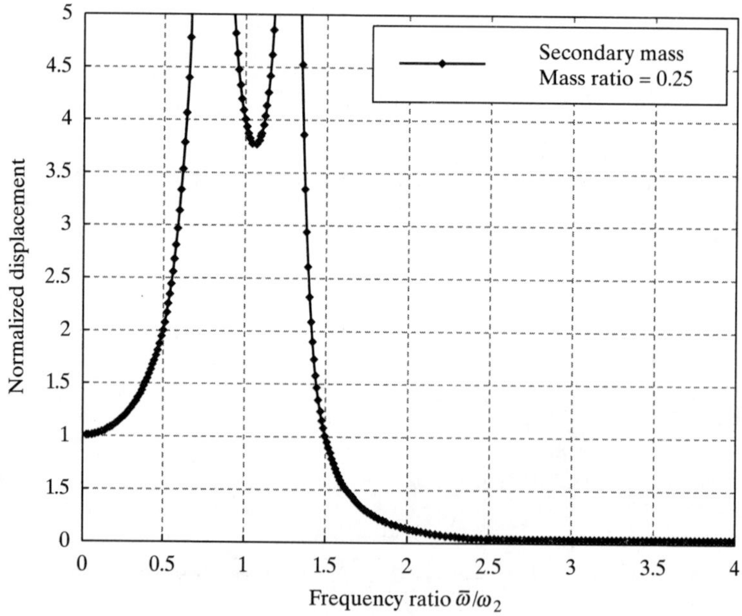

Figure 9.7(b) Normalized amplitude of secondary mass vs. normalized driving frequency for $\mu = 0.25$.

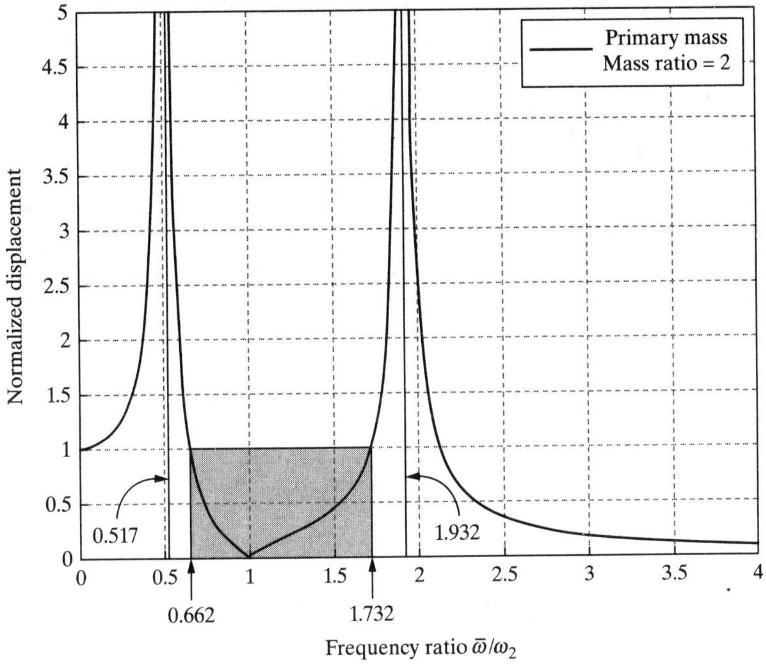

Figure 9.8(a) Normalized amplitude of primary mass vs. normalized driving frequency for $\mu = 2.0$. The shaded area shows the frequency ratios for which the displacement magnification is less than 1.0.

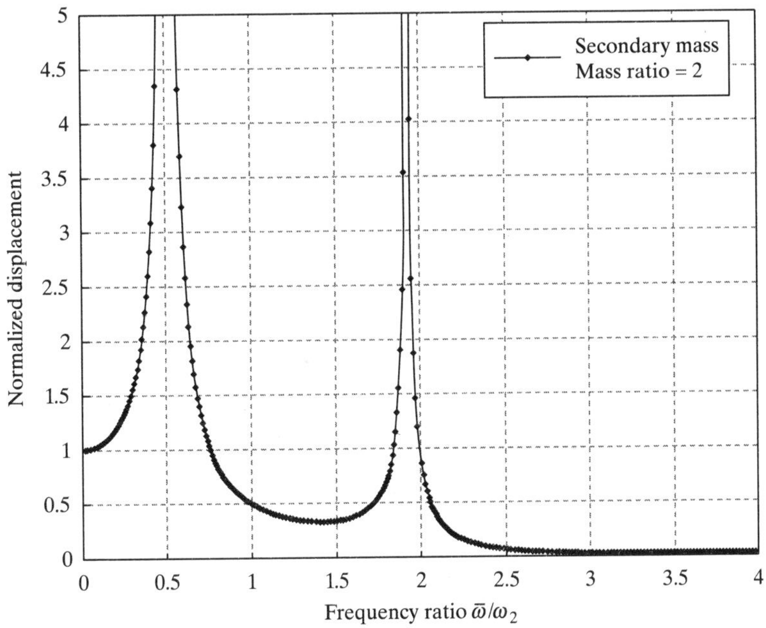

Figure 9.8(b) Normalized amplitude of secondary mass vs. normalized driving frequency for $\mu = 2.0$.

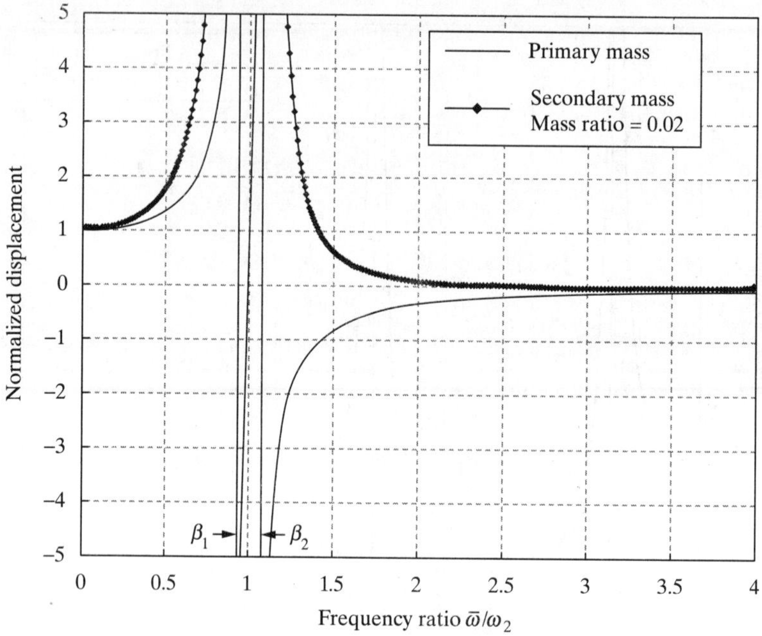

Figure 9.9(a) Normalized amplitude vs. frequency ratio for $\mu = 0.02$.

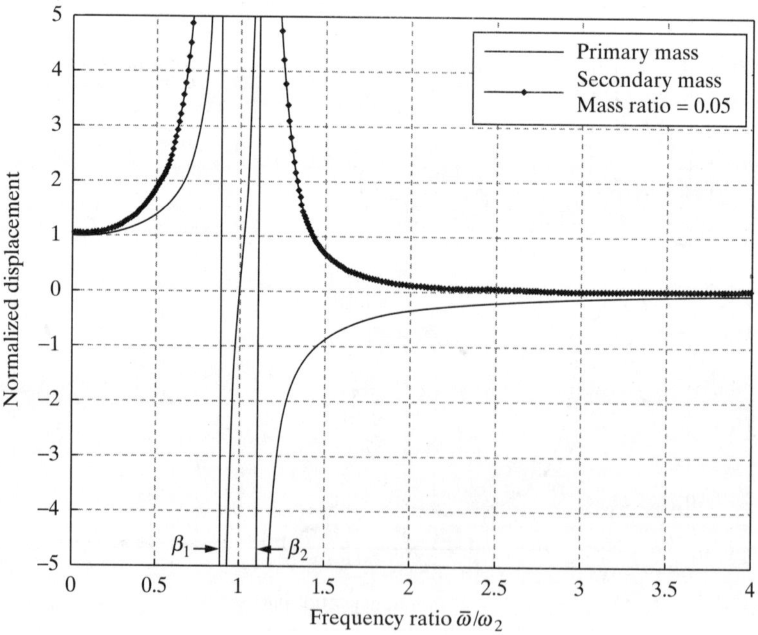

Figure 9.9(b) Normalized amplitude vs. frequency ratio for $\mu = 0.05$.

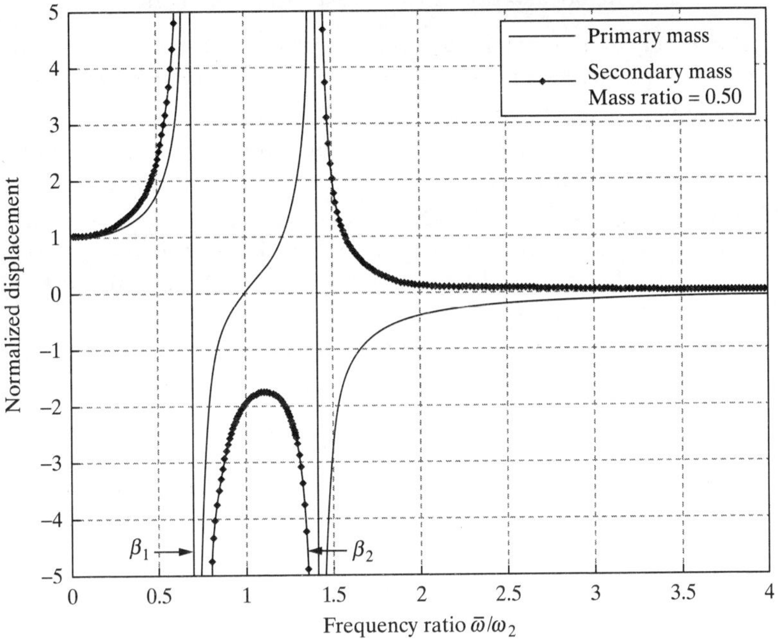

Figure 9.9(c) Normalized amplitude vs. frequency ratio for $\mu = 0.50$.

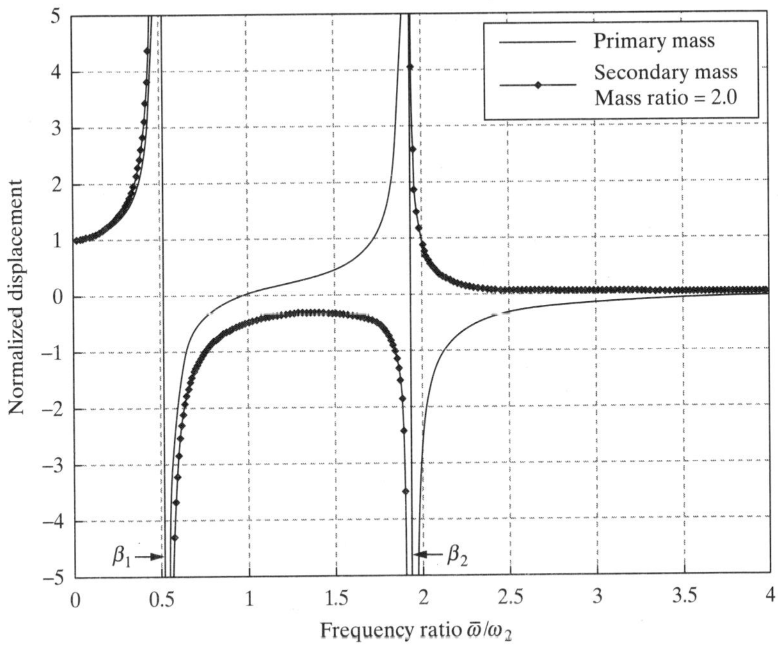

Figure 9.9(d) Normalized amplitude vs. frequency ratio for $\mu = 2.0$.

The following observations can be made in these figures:

- The effect of attaching a secondary mass to the primary mass is to split a single resonant frequency in two resonant peaks corresponding to two natural frequencies of the two DOF systems.
- The spread between the two resonant frequencies keeps increasing with the increase in mass ratio.
- The main purpose of attaching a secondary mass is to reduce the displacement of primary mass. It means the normalized displacement should be less than 1.0. The figures for primary mass show the operating frequency range for which the amplification is less than 1.0.
- Figures 9.6(a) to 9.8(a) give both lower and upper values of the operating frequency ratio. The range of operating frequencies can be seen clearly in Figures 9.7(a) and 9.8(a).
- The advantage of a higher mass ratio is a larger spread in resonant frequencies. It helps in choosing a larger range of operating frequency. However, a higher mass ratio means larger space is required for accommodating the secondary mass, which may not be practically feasible.

The resonant frequencies and operating frequencies for different mass ratios are shown in Table 9.1.

The stiffness ratio of primary mass and secondary mass is given by the following relation:

$$\mu = \frac{m_2}{m_1} \text{ and } \beta^2 = \frac{\omega_2^2}{\omega_1^2} = \frac{k_2}{k_1}\frac{m_1}{m_2}$$

or,

$$\frac{k_2}{k_1} = \mu\beta^2 \tag{9.33}$$

Stiffness of the secondary mass also plays a significant role in selecting an absorber. The displacement of mass m_2 will depend upon its stiffness k_2. If the stiffness k_2 is low, it will undergo very large displacements which again may not be acceptable. There is a need to arrive at a compromise value for the mass ratio as well as stiffness k_2. Mass

TABLE 9.1 RESONANT AND OPERATING FREQUENCY RATIO

Mass Ratio	Resonant Frequency Ratio		Operating Frequency Ratio	
	β_1	β_2	$\bar{\omega}_1/\omega_2$	$\bar{\omega}_2/\omega_2$
0.02	0.931	1.073	0.990	1.010
0.05	0.894	1.118	0.977	1.025
0.25	0.780	1.280	0.908	1.118
0.50	0.707	1.414	0.848	1.225
2.0	0.517	1.932	0.662	1.732

ratio μ is usually kept between 0.02 and 0.25. A mass ratio above 0.50 may not be practically feasible. Charts shown in Figures 9.6 to 9.9 will help arrive at a reasonable and acceptable solution.

9.6.2 Secondary Mass with Viscous Damping

The design of the vibration absorber can be made more efficient under certain conditions by incorporating damping in the secondary mass system as shown in Figure 9.10(a). The free body diagrams of the two masses are shown in Figure 9.10(b). The equation of motion for the two masses can be written as follows:

$$m_1\ddot{x}_1 + k_1x_1 - k_2(x_2 - x_1) - c_2(\dot{x}_2 - \dot{x}_1) - p = 0 \tag{9.34a}$$

or,

$$m_1\ddot{x}_1 + c_2(\dot{x}_1 - \dot{x}_2) + (k_1 + k_2)x_1 - k_2x_2 = p \tag{9.34b}$$

and

$$m_2\ddot{x}_2 + c_2(\dot{x}_2 - \dot{x}_1) + k_2(x_2 - x_1) = 0 \tag{9.34c}$$

In matrix form,

$$\begin{bmatrix} m_1 & 0 \\ 0 & m_2 \end{bmatrix}\begin{Bmatrix} \ddot{x}_1 \\ \ddot{x}_2 \end{Bmatrix} + \begin{bmatrix} c_2 & -c_2 \\ -c_2 & c_2 \end{bmatrix}\begin{Bmatrix} \dot{x}_1 \\ \dot{x}_2 \end{Bmatrix} + \begin{bmatrix} k_1 + k_2 & -k_2 \\ -k_2 & k_2 \end{bmatrix}\begin{Bmatrix} x_1 \\ x_2 \end{Bmatrix} = \begin{Bmatrix} p \\ 0 \end{Bmatrix} \tag{9.35}$$

These are coupled equations and can be solved for steady state condition. The damping of the secondary mass plays a significant role in optimizing the design of vibration absorber. Further discussion is beyond the scope of the present text.

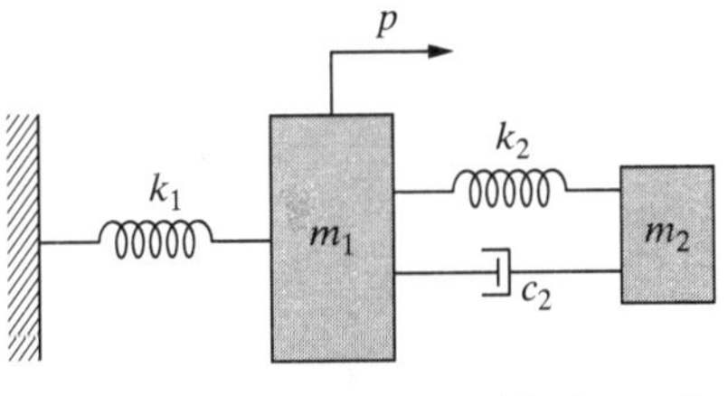

Figure 9.10(a) Tuned mass damper with viscous damping.

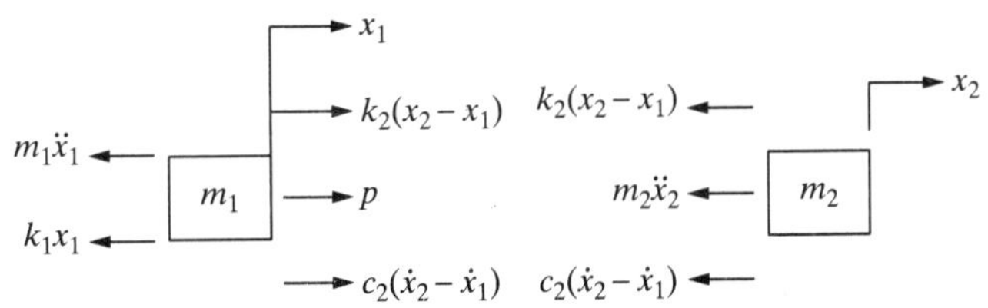

Figure 9.10(b) Free body diagrams.

9.6.3 Applications

Burj-al-Arab, Dubai

It is a hotel building in Dubai built in 1999. Its height is 322 m. It is located 230 m into the sea from the shore and is supported by 40 m deep 230 concrete piles. One of the main problems was to mitigate the vibrations due to strong wind. It is fitted with tuned mass dampers to absorb vibrations due to wind at frequencies varying from 0.75 Hz to 2 Hz. Weight of each damper is 5000 kg. These absorbers were placed inside the vertical steel arms of the building.

Taipei 101, Taiwan

It is the tallest building in Taipei, Taiwan, built in 2004. Its height is 509 m. There are 101 floors above ground and 5 floors below ground. The top floor is at an elevation of 439 m and the roof top is at 448 m. The building was designed to resist a very strong earthquake as well as vibrations due to very strong winds. It is fitted with a 662 metric ton steel pendulum that serves as a tuned mass damper. Suspended from the 92nd to the 88th floor, the pendulum sways to offset movements in the building caused by strong gusts. Its sphere, the largest damper sphere in the world, consists of 41 layered steel plates, each with a height of 125 mm being welded together to form a 5.5 m diameter sphere. Another two tuned mass dampers, each weighing 4.5 tons, sit at the tip of the spire. These prevent cumulative damage to the structure due to strong wind loads.

London Millennium Footbridge

The London Millennium footbridge is sited on the River Thames, London. There were two design constraints:

- maximum height limitation so that tourists would be provided an unobstructed view of the river front
- requirement of the head room to allow marine traffic on the River Thames.

It is a three span bridge with the end span of 80 m on the north, central main span of 144 m between the piers, and end span of 108 m on the south. The bridge deck is 4 m wide, and uses articulated sliding joints spaced at regular intervals along its length. In the bridge lateral suspension cables are located at the level of the bridge deck in view of the constraints. The bridge exhibited severe lateral sway in a frequency band of 0.5 to 1.1 Hz, with lateral accelerations of up to 0.25 g. As many as five natural modes were being excited, and pedestrians found it virtually impossible to walk on the bridge. It was baffling that resonance was occurring without any intentional or expected forced motion or synchronous marching. Extensive investigations revealed a unique phenomenon *synchronous lateral footfall* which resulted in seemingly random walking motions becoming synchronized over time, among members of an unrelated group of people on the bridge. A series of vertical and lateral TMDs were employed to mitigate the problem. There were 50 Vertical TMD, weight @ 1000 to 2000 kg, and frequency 1.20 to 2.2 Hz; and 8 Horizontal TMD weight @ 2500 kg, and frequency 0.45 Hz.

9.7 ILLUSTRATIVE EXAMPLES

Example 9.1

An undamped two DOF system shown in Figure 9.1 has mass $m_1 = m_2 = m$ and stiffness $k_1 = k_2 = k$. Determine its frequencies and mode shapes.

Solution

Let us make use of Equations (9.14) and (9.15).

$$\omega^4 - \omega^2\left[\left(\bar{\omega}_1^{\,2} + \bar{\omega}_2^{\,2}\right)(1+\mu)\right] + \bar{\omega}_1^{\,2}\bar{\omega}_2^{\,2}(1+\mu) = 0 \tag{9.15}$$

where

$$\bar{\omega}_1^{\,2} = \frac{k_1}{m_1 + m_2}, \quad \text{and} \quad \bar{\omega}_2^{\,2} = \frac{k_2}{m_2}$$

$$\mu = \frac{m_2}{m_1} = \text{mass ratio} \tag{9.14}$$

$\therefore$

$$\bar{\omega}_1^{\,2} = \frac{k_1}{m_1 + m_2} \quad \text{or} \quad \bar{\omega}_1^{\,2} = \frac{k}{2m}$$

$$\bar{\omega}_2^{\,2} = \frac{k_2}{m_2} \quad \text{or} \quad \bar{\omega}_2^{\,2} = \frac{k}{m} = 2\bar{\omega}_1^{\,2}$$

Mass ratio $\mu = 1$

$\therefore$ frequency equation is written as follows:

$$\omega^4 - 6\bar{\omega}_1^{\,2}\omega^2 + 4\bar{\omega}_1^{\,2} = 0$$

Or, its roots are $\quad \omega_1^{*2} = 0.764\,\bar{\omega}_1^{\,2} \quad \text{or} \quad \omega_2^{*2} = 5.236\,\bar{\omega}_1^{\,2}$

$\therefore \quad \omega_1^{*} = 0.874\,\bar{\omega}_1 \quad \text{and} \quad \omega_2^{*} = 2.288\,\bar{\omega}_1$

Mode shapes can be determined using Equation (9.10)

$$\begin{bmatrix} k_1 + k_2 - m_1\omega^2 & -k_2 \\ -k_2 & k_2 - m_2\omega^2 \end{bmatrix} \begin{Bmatrix} X_1 \\ X_2 \end{Bmatrix} = \begin{Bmatrix} 0 \\ 0 \end{Bmatrix} \tag{9.10}$$

Substituting $\omega^2 = 0.764\ \bar{\omega}_1^{\,2}$

Equation (9.10) can be written as:

$$\begin{bmatrix} 3.236 & -2 \\ -2 & 1.236 \end{bmatrix} \begin{Bmatrix} X_{11} \\ X_{21} \end{Bmatrix} = \begin{Bmatrix} 0 \\ 0 \end{Bmatrix}$$

or,

$$3.236\,X_{11} - 2\,X_{21} = 0 \quad \text{or} \quad X_{11} = 0.618\,X_{21}$$

Similarly, substituting $\omega^2 = 5.236\ \bar{\omega}_1^{\,2}$

Equation (9.10) can be written as:

$$\begin{bmatrix} -1.236 & -2 \\ -2 & -3.236 \end{bmatrix} \begin{Bmatrix} X_{12} \\ X_{22} \end{Bmatrix} = \begin{Bmatrix} 0 \\ 0 \end{Bmatrix}$$

or, $-1.236\, X_{12} - 2\, X_{22} = 0$ or, $X_{12} = -\,1.618\, X_{22}$

The mode shapes can be plotted as shown in Figure 9.11. □

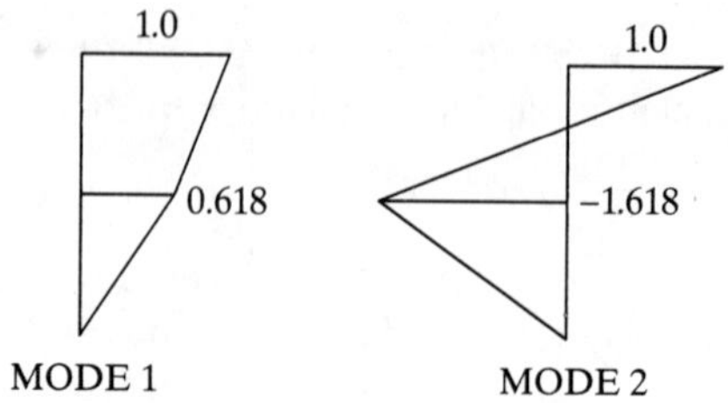

Figure 9.11 Mode shape in two-DOF system.

Example 9.2

An undamped two DOF system is shown in Figure 9.12. Determine its frequencies and mode shapes.

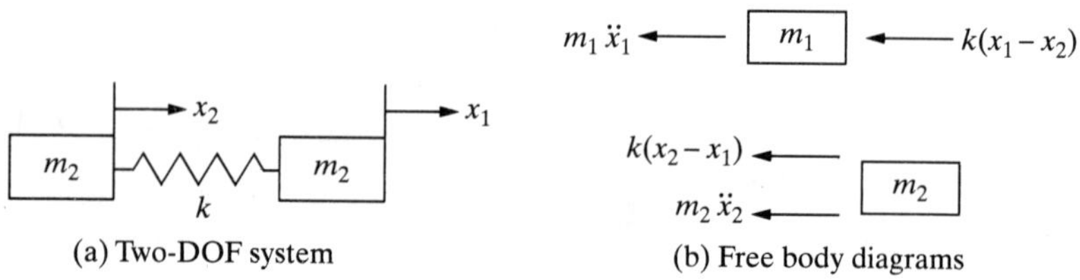

Figure 9.12 Two-DOF system.

Solution

The free body diagrams of the mass m_1 and m_2 are shown in Figure 9.12(b). The equations of motion can be written as:

$$m_1\ddot{x}_1 + k(x_1 - x_2) = 0$$

and

$$m_2\ddot{x}_2 + k(x_2 - x_1) = 0 \tag{i}$$

Let

$$x_1 = x_{10} \sin \omega t \qquad x_2 = x_{20} \sin \omega t \tag{ii}$$

Substituting these values in Equation (i) gives,

$$(-)\begin{bmatrix} m_1\omega^2 & 0 \\ 0 & m_2\omega^2 \end{bmatrix}\begin{Bmatrix} x_{10} \\ x_{20} \end{Bmatrix} + \begin{bmatrix} k & -k \\ -k & k \end{bmatrix}\begin{Bmatrix} x_{10} \\ x_{20} \end{Bmatrix} = \begin{Bmatrix} 0 \\ 0 \end{Bmatrix}$$

or,

$$\begin{bmatrix} k - m_1\omega^2 & -k \\ -k & k - m_2\omega^2 \end{bmatrix}\begin{Bmatrix} x_{10} \\ x_{20} \end{Bmatrix} = \begin{Bmatrix} 0 \\ 0 \end{Bmatrix} \tag{iii}$$

It can be written in short as follows:

$$[[K] - [M]\omega^2]\{X_0\} = \{0\} \tag{iv}$$

where $[K]$ and $[M]$ are stiffness and mass matrices of the system.

Its solution is given by setting the determinant to zero,

$$\det\left|K - M\omega^2\right| = 0 \tag{v}$$

This is referred to as the characteristic equation.
Equations (iv) and (v) are very important for eigenvalue analysis.

or, $$m_1 m_2 \omega^4 - (m_1 + m_2)k\omega^2 = 0$$

Its roots are given by $\omega_1^{*2} = 0$ or $\omega_2^{*2} = \dfrac{(m_1 + m_2)k}{m_1 m_2}$

or, the frequencies are given by $\omega_1^* = 0$ and $\omega_2^* = \sqrt{\left(\dfrac{m_1 + m_2}{m_1 m_2}\right)k}$

Mode shapes
Mode shapes can be obtained by substituting the value of ω in Equation (iii).
Substituting $\omega^2 = 0$ in Equation (iii) gives

$$x_{10} = x_{20} = 1 \quad \text{say}$$

Similarly, substituting the other value,

$$\omega^2 = \frac{(m_1 + m_2)k}{m_1 m_2}$$

$$\left(k - m_1\omega^2\right)x_{10} - kx_{20} = 0$$

or, $$\frac{x_{20}}{x_{10}} = 1 - \frac{m_1}{k}\,\omega^2 = 1 - \frac{m_1 + m_2}{m_2} = -\frac{m_1}{m_2}$$

Thus, if $$x_{10} = 1,\ x_{20} = -\frac{m_1}{m_2}$$

Now the mode shapes can be plotted as shown in Figure 9.13. It can be seen that the spring remain undeformed in Mode 1, that is, Mode 1 is a rigid body displacement mode. □

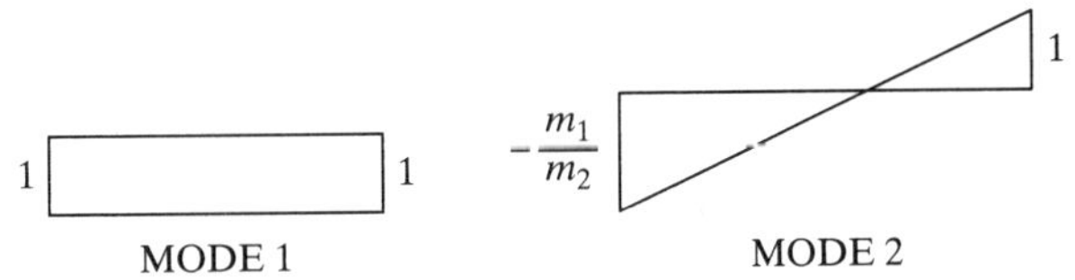

Figure 9.13 Mode shapes.

Example 9.3

A two storey portal frame is shown in Figure 9.14. Develop its equation of motion if it is subjected to an undamped-free vibration. EI_c is the flexural rigidity of the upper storey columns, and $2EI_c$ is the flexural rigidity of the lower storey columns. The flexural rigidity of beams may be treated as very high. Axial deformation in columns can be neglected.

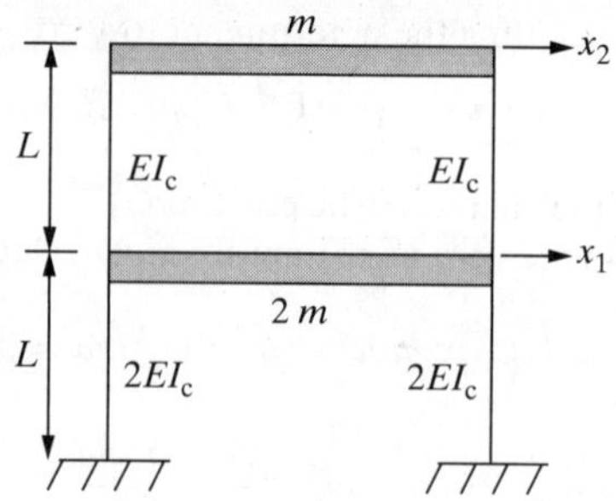

Figure 9.14 Two-DOF portal frame.

Solution

It can be treated as a two DOF system having lateral displacements of the floors x_1 and x_2. The lateral stiffness of each storey can be determined from the basic definition of stiffness. The lateral displacement at the roof level is restrained, that is, $x_2 = 0$, and a unit displacement is given to x_1. Now determine the forces produced in the upper and lower storey columns. Similarly, the first floor lateral displacement is restrained, that is, $x_1 = 0$, and a unit displacement is given to x_2. Now determine the forces produced in the upper storey columns. This can also be explained with the help of diagrams shown in Figure 9.15.

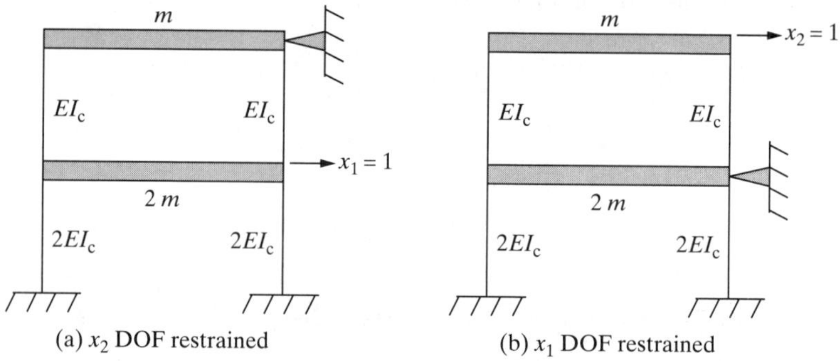

Figure 9.15 Storey lateral stiffness.

The lateral stiffness of each column can be obtained as follows using slope – deflection method:

$k = \dfrac{12EI}{L^3}$ and the total lateral stiffness of a storey can be taken as $2k$.

Thus, lateral stiffness of upper storey

$$k_2 = \frac{24EI_c}{L^3}$$

and
lateral stiffness of lower storey

$$k_1 = \frac{2 \times 24EI_c}{L^3}$$

Now this two storey portal frame can be replaced with a spring mass system having two-degrees of freedom as shown in Figure 9.16(a). Its free body diagram is also shown in Figures 9.16(b) and 9.16(c).

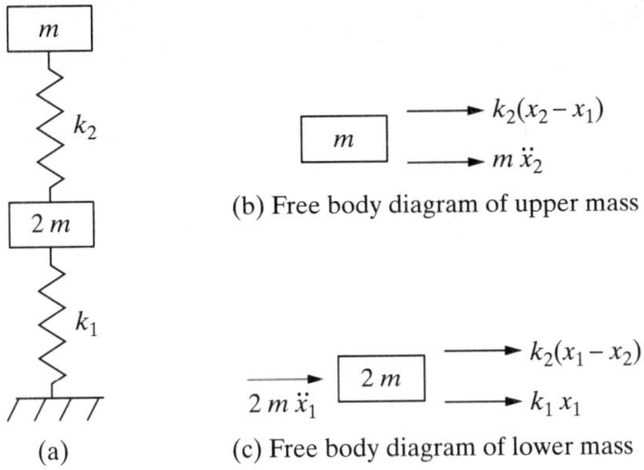

Figure 9.16 Two-DOF spring-mass system

The equations of motion of undamped vibrations can be written as follows:

$$2m\ddot{x}_1 + k_1x_1 + k_2(x_1 - x_2) = 0$$

and

$$m\ddot{x}_2 + k_2(x_2 - x_1) = 0$$

or,
in matrix notation

$$\begin{bmatrix} 2m & 0 \\ 0 & m \end{bmatrix}\begin{Bmatrix} \ddot{x}_1 \\ \ddot{x}_2 \end{Bmatrix} + \begin{bmatrix} k_1 + k_2 & -k_2 \\ -k_2 & k_2 \end{bmatrix}\begin{Bmatrix} x_1 \\ x_2 \end{Bmatrix} = \begin{Bmatrix} 0 \\ 0 \end{Bmatrix}$$

Stiffness matrix will always be a symmetric matrix. On substituting the values of stiffness coefficients, we get

$$\begin{bmatrix} 2m & 0 \\ 0 & m \end{bmatrix}\begin{Bmatrix} \ddot{x}_1 \\ \ddot{x}_2 \end{Bmatrix} + \frac{24EI_c}{L^3}\begin{bmatrix} 3 & -1 \\ -1 & 1 \end{bmatrix}\begin{Bmatrix} x_1 \\ x_2 \end{Bmatrix} = \begin{Bmatrix} 0 \\ 0 \end{Bmatrix}$$

Its frequency and mode shapes can be determined as shown in Example 9.2 using Equations (iv) and (v).

$$\left[[K] - [M]\omega^2\right]\{X_0\} = \{0\} \tag{iv}$$

$$\begin{bmatrix} \dfrac{72EI_c}{L^3} - 2m\omega^2 & -\dfrac{24EI_c}{L^3} \\ -\dfrac{24EI_c}{L^3} & \dfrac{24EI_c}{L^3} - m\omega^2 \end{bmatrix}\begin{Bmatrix} X_{10} \\ X_{20} \end{Bmatrix} = \begin{Bmatrix} 0 \\ 0 \end{Bmatrix}$$

Its solution is given by Equation (v), that is,

$$\det\left|K - M\omega^2\right| = 0 \text{ the characteristic equation} \tag{v}$$

$$\begin{vmatrix} \dfrac{72EI_c}{L^3} - 2m\omega^2 & -\dfrac{24EI_c}{L^3} \\ -\dfrac{24EI_c}{L^3} & \dfrac{24EI_c}{L^3} - m\omega^2 \end{vmatrix} = 0$$

The frequencies and mode shapes can be determined by substituting the numerical values. □

Example 9.4

A cantilever portal frame is shown in Figure 9.17. Develop its equation of motion for undamped-free vibration. EI is the flexural rigidity of the beam as well as that of the column. Axial deformation in the beam and column can be neglected.

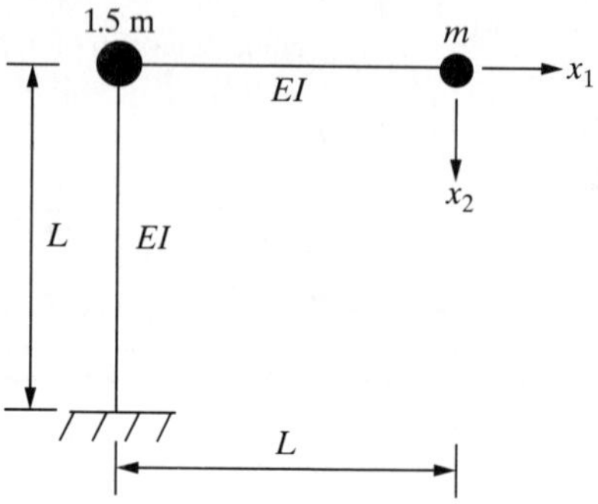

Figure 9.17 Cantilever portal frame.

Solution

Let us derive the stiffness matrix of this cantilever portal frame. It can be derived from its flexibility matrix. There are two degrees of freedom – lateral displacement x_1 at the floor level and vertical displacement x_2 at the free end. The flexibility coefficients f_{ij} can be derived using the influence coefficient method as follows:

$$F = \begin{bmatrix} f_{11} & f_{12} \\ f_{21} & f_{22} \end{bmatrix}$$

Let us first draw bending moment diagram due to a unit force f_1 applied at the free end alone as shown in Figure 9.18. This diagram is known as h_{11} diagram. Now draw bending moment diagram due to a unit force f_2 applied at the free end alone. This diagram is known as h_{12} diagram. The influence coefficients can be computed as follows:

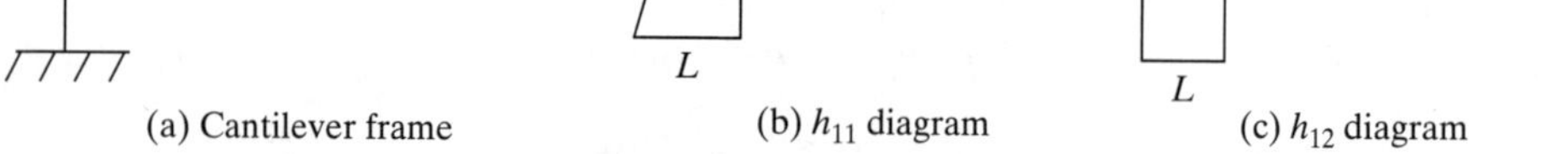

Figure 9.18 h-diagram.

$$f_{11} = \int \frac{h_{11}h_{11}\,dy}{EI} = \frac{L^3}{3EI}$$

$$f_{12} = \int \frac{h_{11}h_{12}\,dy}{EI} = \frac{L^3}{2EI}$$

$$f_{22} = \int \frac{h_{12}h_{12}dy}{EI} = \frac{L^3}{3EI} + \frac{L^3}{EI} = \frac{4L^3}{3EI}$$

The flexibility matrix can be written as follows:

$$[F] = \frac{L^3}{6EI}\begin{bmatrix} 2 & 3 \\ 3 & 8 \end{bmatrix}$$

The flexibility matrix is always a symmetric matrix. The stiffness matrix is the inverse of the flexibility matrix, that is,

$$[K] = [F]^{-1}$$

or,

$$[K] = \frac{6EI}{7L^3}\begin{bmatrix} 8 & -3 \\ -3 & 2 \end{bmatrix}$$

The stiffness matrix is always a symmetric matrix. The mass matrix can be written as follows:

$$[M] = \begin{bmatrix} 2.5m & 0 \\ 0 & m \end{bmatrix}$$

It should be noted that for vibration along the x_1 direction, the two masses will add up. The equation of motion of undamped-free vibrations can be written as follows:

$$[M]\{\ddot{X}\} + [K]\{X\} = \{0\}$$

or,

$$\begin{bmatrix} 2.5m & 0 \\ 0 & m \end{bmatrix}\begin{Bmatrix} \ddot{x}_1 \\ \ddot{x}_2 \end{Bmatrix} + \frac{6EI}{7L^3}\begin{bmatrix} 8 & -3 \\ -3 & 2 \end{bmatrix}\begin{Bmatrix} x_1 \\ x_2 \end{Bmatrix} = \begin{Bmatrix} 0 \\ 0 \end{Bmatrix}$$

Its frequency and mode shapes can be determined as shown in Example 9.2 using Equations (iv) and (v).

$$\left[[K] - [M]\omega^2\right]\{X_0\} = \{0\}$$

Let us denote

$$\frac{6EI}{7L^3} = C, \text{ a constant}$$

or,

$$\begin{bmatrix} 8C - 2.5m\omega^2 & -3C \\ -3C & 2C - m\omega^2 \end{bmatrix}\begin{Bmatrix} x_{10} \\ x_{20} \end{Bmatrix} = \begin{Bmatrix} 0 \\ 0 \end{Bmatrix}$$

Its solution is given by Equation (v), that is,

$$\det\left|K - M\omega^2\right| = 0$$

$$\begin{vmatrix} 8C - 2.5m\omega^2 & -3C \\ -3C & 2C - m\omega^2 \end{vmatrix} = 0$$

By substituting the numerical values, frequency and mode shapes can be determined. □

Example 9.5

A rigid bar of total mass m is supported on two springs as shown in Figure 9.19. Write the equations of motion in terms of end displacements and find natural frequencies and mode shapes.

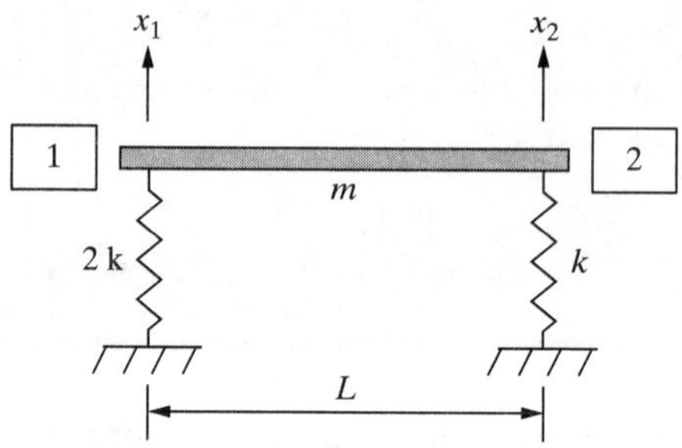

Figure 9.19 Rigid bar on two springs.

Solution

Consider the deflected shape of the bar shown in Figure 9.20(a) The left spring will have a deflection x_1 and the right spring will have a deflection x_2. Since stiffness of the left spring is higher than that of the right spring, the mass will rotate anti-clockwise. This system has the following independent two degrees of freedom:

1. Translational deformation at node 1
2. Translational deformation at node 2

Alternatively, it can have the following independent two degrees of freedom at the center of mass:

1. Translational deformation at the midspan
2. Rotational deformation at the midspan

Yet there can be another alternative,

1. Translational deformation at node 1
2. Rotational deformation at the node 1

The similar two DOFs can be written at node 2 also.

The equations of motion will depend upon the selection of the independent two degrees of freedom. The frequencies and mode shapes will always correspond to the independent degrees of freedom. It means they will change depending upon the selection of the two degrees of freedom. However, final forces in various members to a given set of force will always remain unchanged.

Let us first consider the two translational degrees of freedom x_1 and x_2. At the center of the bar, a rotational inertia force will act in clockwise direction.

$$\text{Inertia force} = \frac{mL^2\ddot{\theta}}{12} = \frac{mL^2(\ddot{x}_2 - \ddot{x}_1)}{12L}$$

It can be resolved as a couple acting on the two springs across a length L. The free body diagram of the two springs is shown in Figures 9.20(b) and (c).

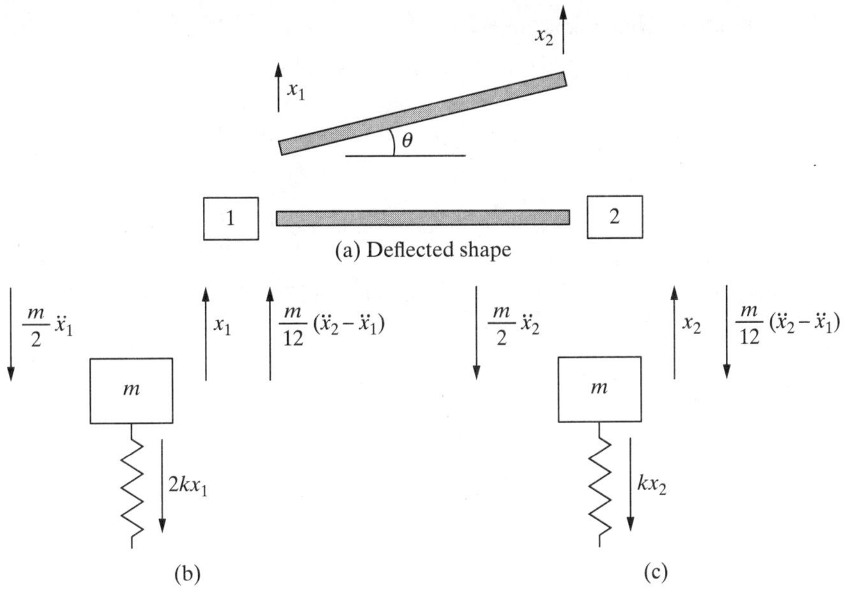

Figure 9.20 Free body diagrams.

∴ The equation of motion at the left spring can be written as follows:

$$\frac{m\ddot{x}_1}{2}-\frac{m}{12}(\ddot{x}_2-\ddot{x}_1)+2kx_1=0$$

Similarly, the equation of motion at the right spring can be written as follows:

$$\frac{m\ddot{x}_2}{2}+\frac{m}{12}(\ddot{x}_2-\ddot{x}_1)+kx_2=0$$

These equations can be re-written as follows:

$$\frac{m}{12}\begin{bmatrix}7 & -1\\ -1 & 7\end{bmatrix}\begin{Bmatrix}\ddot{x}_1\\ \ddot{x}_2\end{Bmatrix}+\begin{bmatrix}2k & 0\\ 0 & k\end{bmatrix}\begin{Bmatrix}x_1\\ x_2\end{Bmatrix}=\begin{Bmatrix}0\\ 0\end{Bmatrix}$$

Two important observations can be made in this equation:

1. The mass matrix is not a diagonal matrix. Rather it is a coupled matrix. The rotational inertia force is acting at the center of the bar and not at the two nodes where degrees of freedom are identified.
2. The stiffness matrix is a diagonal matrix.

The solution is given by the following equation:

$$\left[[K]-[M]\omega^2\right]\{X_0\}=\{0\}$$

or,

$$\begin{bmatrix}2k-7m'\omega^2 & m'\omega^2\\ m'\omega^2 & k-7m'\omega^2\end{bmatrix}\begin{Bmatrix}x_{10}\\ x_{20}\end{Bmatrix}=\begin{Bmatrix}0\\ 0\end{Bmatrix}$$

where $m'=m/12$

Its solution is given by the equation:

$$\det\left|K - M\omega^2\right| = 0$$

$$\left(2k - 7m'\omega^2\right)\left(k - 7m'\omega^2\right) - m'^2\omega^4 = 0$$

or,

$$48m'^2\omega^4 - 21km'\omega^2 + 2k^2 = 0$$

Solving it, we get, $\omega_1^{*2} = 0.297\dfrac{k}{m'}$ or $\omega_1^{*2} = 3.57\dfrac{k}{m}$

Similarly, $\omega_2^{*2} = 0.140\dfrac{k}{m'}$ or $\omega_2^{*2} = 1.68\dfrac{k}{m}$

Mode shape 1 is given by

$$\left(2k - 7m'\omega^2\right)x_{11} + m'\omega^2 x_{21} = 0$$

On substituting $\omega^2 = \omega_1^{*2} = 0.297\dfrac{k}{m'}$

$$\frac{x_{11}}{x_{21}} = \frac{0.297}{0.079} = 3.76$$

Mode shape 2 is given by substituting $\omega^2 = \omega_2^{*2} = 0.140\dfrac{k}{m'}$

$$\frac{x_{12}}{x_{22}} = \frac{-0.14}{1.02} = -0.137$$

The mode shapes are shown in Figure 9.21.

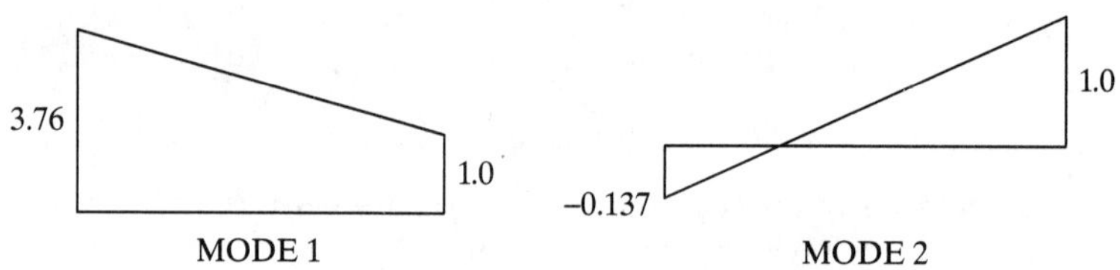

Figure 9.21 Mode shapes.

Alternatively, it can have the following independent two degrees of freedom at the center of mass:

1. Translational deformation at the midspan, x_0
2. Rotational deformation at the midspan, θ

The stiffness coefficients for this system can be determined by drawing free body diagrams for the two cases shown in Figure 9.22 as follows:

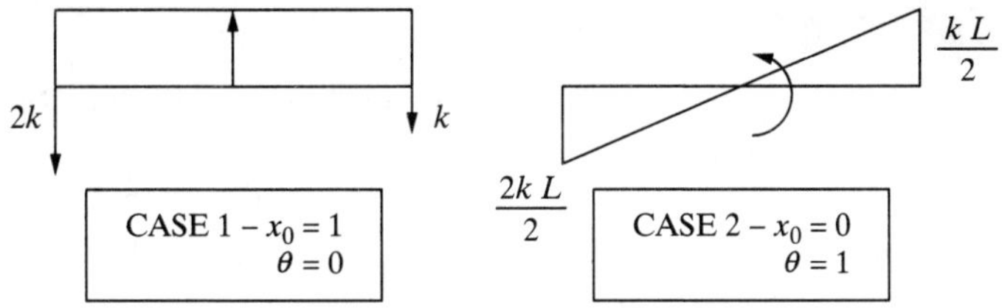

Figure 9.22 Stiffness coefficients.

For Case 1,
Give the unit deformation $x_0 = 1$ keeping $\theta = 0$, the spring forces will develop as shown. Now consider the static equilibrium, we get the stiffness coefficients:

$$k_{xx} = 2k + k = 3k, \qquad \text{and} \qquad k_{x\theta} = 2k\frac{L}{2} - k\frac{L}{2} = k\frac{L}{2}$$

and,
For Case 2,
Give the unit deformation $\theta = 1$ keeping $x_0 = 0$, the spring forces will develop as shown. Now consider the static equilibrium, we get the stiffness coefficients:

$$k_{\theta\theta} = \left(2k\frac{L}{2} + k\frac{L}{2}\right)\frac{L}{2} = 3k\frac{L^2}{4}$$

and

$$k_{x\theta} = 2k\frac{L}{2} - k\frac{L}{2} = k\frac{L}{2}$$

The 2×2 stiffness matrix can be written as follows:

$$K = \begin{bmatrix} k_{xx} & k_{x\theta} \\ k_{x\theta} & k_{\theta\theta} \end{bmatrix} = \begin{bmatrix} 3k & k\frac{L}{2} \\ k\frac{L}{2} & 3k\frac{L^2}{4} \end{bmatrix}$$

An important observation can be made in this equation:

The stiffness matrix is not a diagonal matrix unlike in the first case. Rather it is a coupled matrix. The two springs are located at the two ends that resist the translational as well as rotational forces acting at the center of the bar. Had there been a translational spring and a rotational spring each located at the center of the bar, the stiffness matrix would have been a diagonal matrix.

Similarly, the mass matrix can be generated directly.
The inertia force will be generated along the two degrees of freedom as identified. The translational inertia force will be $m\ddot{x}$ and the rotational inertia force will be $m'\ddot{\theta}$, where m' is mass moment of inertia given as:

$$m' = \frac{mL^2\ddot{\theta}}{12}$$

The mass matrix can be written as follows:

$$[M] = \begin{bmatrix} m & 0 \\ 0 & \frac{mL^2}{12} \end{bmatrix}$$

The mass matrix is a diagonal matrix. It means it has uncoupled terms since the inertia forces have been written directly in terms of the degrees of freedom of the midspan node.

□

Example 9.6

A two-degrees of freedom system is shown in Figure 9.23. Estimate its natural frequencies of vibrations.

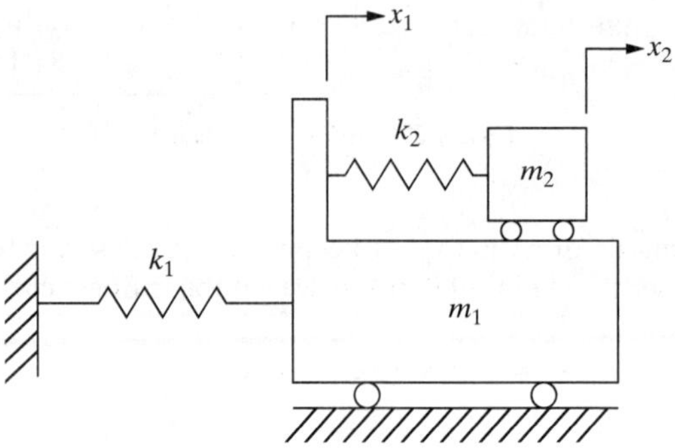

Figure 9.23 Two-DOF system.

Solution

The free body diagrams of the mass m_1 and m_2 can be drawn as shown in Figure 9.24.

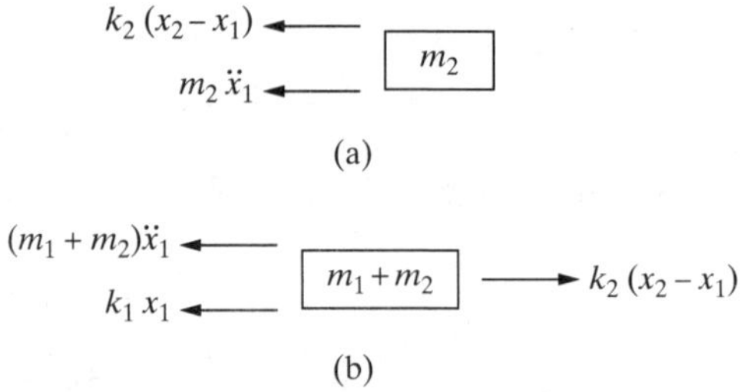

Figure 9.24 Free body diagrams.

Considering the equilibrium of mass m_2 and m_1 gives,

$$m_2\ddot{x}_2 + k_2(x_2 - x_1) = 0$$

or,

$$m_2\ddot{x}_2 + k_2x_2 = k_2x_1 \qquad \text{(i)}$$

and

$$(m_1 + m_2)\ddot{x}_1 + k_1x_1 - k_2(x_2 - x_1) = 0$$

or,

$$(m_1 + m_2)\ddot{x}_1 + (k_1 + k_2)x_1 = k_2x_2 \qquad \text{(ii)}$$

These can be arranged as follows:

$$\begin{bmatrix} m_1 + m_2 & 0 \\ 0 & m_2 \end{bmatrix}\begin{Bmatrix} \ddot{x}_1 \\ \ddot{x}_2 \end{Bmatrix} + \begin{bmatrix} (k_1 + k_2) & -k_2 \\ -k_2 & k_2 \end{bmatrix}\begin{Bmatrix} x_1 \\ x_2 \end{Bmatrix} = \begin{Bmatrix} 0 \\ 0 \end{Bmatrix} \qquad \text{(iii)}$$

The solution is given by the following equation:

$$\left[[K] - [M]\omega^2\right]\{X_0\} = \{0\}$$

or,

$$\begin{bmatrix} (k_1+k_2)-(m_1+m_2)\omega^2 & -k_2 \\ -k_2 & k_2-m_2\omega^2 \end{bmatrix} \begin{Bmatrix} x_{10} \\ x_{20} \end{Bmatrix} = \begin{Bmatrix} 0 \\ 0 \end{Bmatrix}$$

Its solution is given by the equation:

$$\det\left|K - M\omega^2\right| = 0$$

or,

$$\left[(k_1+k_2)-(m_1+m_2)\omega^2\right]\times\left(k_2-m_2\omega^2\right)-k_2^2=0 \quad \text{(iv)}$$

On simplification,

$$(m_1+m_2)m_2\omega^4-\left[m_1k_2+m_2(k_1+2k_2)\right]\omega^2+k_1k_2=0 \quad \text{(v)}$$

This equation gives two positive roots of the natural frequency ω.

If $m_1 = 250$ kg, $k_1 = 50000$ N/m, $m_2 = 75$ kg and $k_2 = 20000$ N/m

The characteristic equation can be written as:

$$24375w^4 - 1175\times10^4\omega^2 + 10^9 = 0$$

The frequencies are 19.27 and 10.50 rad/sec.

For a higher degree polynomial, MATLAB function `ROOTS` can be used to find its roots.

□

Example 9.7

Consider the system shown in Figure 9.25. The supports A and B also move by x_a and x_b, respectively. Write its equation of motion.

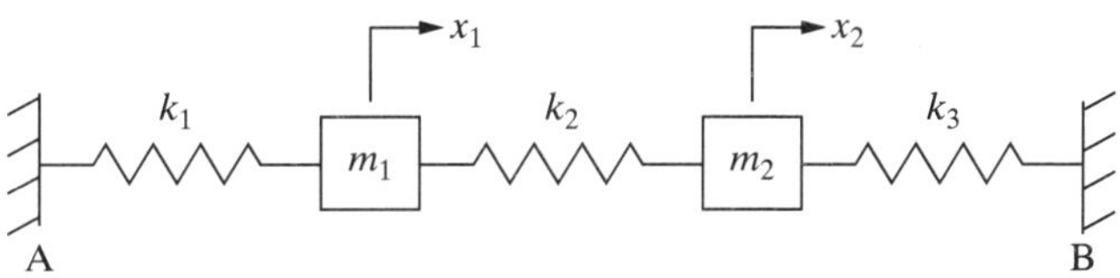

Figure 9.25 Two-DOF system.

Solution

The free body diagrams of the mass m_1 and m_2 can be drawn as shown in Figure 9.26.

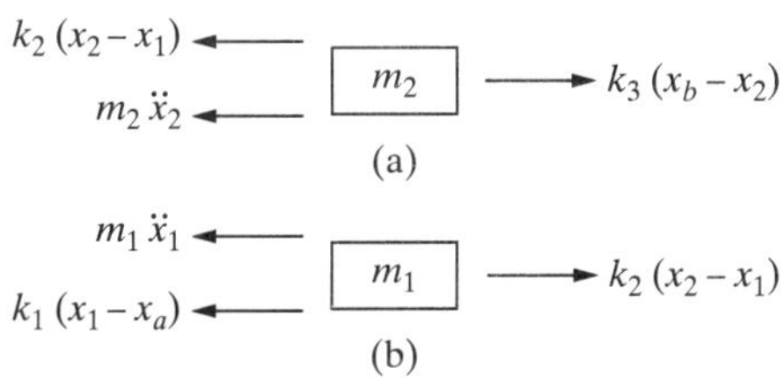

Figure 9.26 Free body diagrams.

Considering the equilibrium of mass m_1,

$$m_1\ddot{x}_1 + k_1(x_1 - x_a) - k_2(x_2 - x_1) = 0$$

or,
$$m_1\ddot{x}_1 + (k_1 + k_2)x_1 - k_2 x_2 = k_1 x_a$$

Similarly, the equilibrium of mass m_2 gives

$$m_2\ddot{x}_2 + k_2(x_2 - x_1) - k_3(x_b - x_2) = 0$$

or,
$$m_2\ddot{x}_2 - k_2 x_1 + (k_2 + k_3)x_2 = k_3 x_b$$

The equation of motion can be written in matrix form

$$\begin{bmatrix} m_1 & 0 \\ 0 & m_2 \end{bmatrix}\begin{Bmatrix} \ddot{x}_1 \\ \ddot{x}_2 \end{Bmatrix} + \begin{bmatrix} k_1 + k_2 & -k_2 \\ -k_2 & k_2 + k_3 \end{bmatrix}\begin{Bmatrix} x_1 \\ x_2 \end{Bmatrix} = \begin{bmatrix} k_1 & 0 \\ 0 & k_3 \end{bmatrix}\begin{Bmatrix} x_a \\ x_b \end{Bmatrix}$$

If the supports are fixed, the right-hand side becomes zero.

In case the system moves statically, the inertia term becomes zero, that is,

$$\begin{bmatrix} k_1 + k_2 & -k_2 \\ -k_2 & k_2 + k_3 \end{bmatrix}\begin{Bmatrix} x_1 \\ x_2 \end{Bmatrix} = \begin{bmatrix} k_1 & 0 \\ 0 & k_3 \end{bmatrix}\begin{Bmatrix} x_a \\ x_b \end{Bmatrix}$$

The solution of this equation yields x_{10} and x_{20}, the static displacements of mass 1 and 2,

$$x_{10} = \frac{\left(\dfrac{1}{k_2} + \dfrac{1}{k_3}\right)x_a + \dfrac{1}{k_1}x_b}{\dfrac{1}{k_1} + \dfrac{1}{k_2} + \dfrac{1}{k_3}}$$

and

$$x_{20} = \frac{\dfrac{1}{k_3}x_a + \left(\dfrac{1}{k_1} + \dfrac{1}{k_2}\right)x_b}{\dfrac{1}{k_1} + \dfrac{1}{k_2} + \dfrac{1}{k_3}}$$

In case the two supports move by an equal amount in the same direction, then

$$x_a = x_b$$

$\therefore$
$$x_{10} = x_{20} = x_a = x_b$$

It means, there will be a rigid body motion under static conditions. □

Example 9.8

A two-DOF system is shown in Figure 9.27. Write its equations of motion.

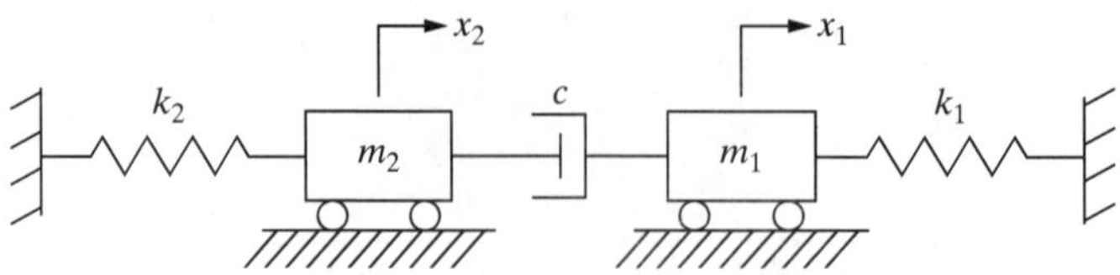

Figure 9.27 Two-DOF systems with a common damper.

Solution

The free body diagrams of the mass m_1 and m_2 can be drawn as shown in Figure 9.28.

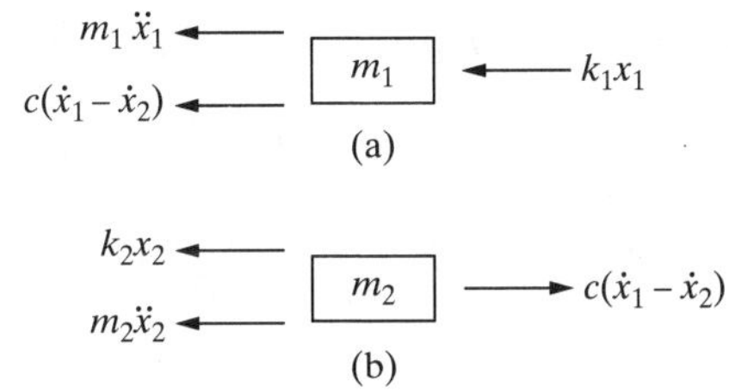

Figure 9.28 Free body diagrams.

Considering the equilibrium of mass m_1,

$$m_1\ddot{x}_1 + k_1x_1 + c(\dot{x}_1 - \dot{x}_2) = 0 \tag{i}$$

Similarly, the equilibrium of mass m_2 gives

$$m_2\ddot{x}_2 + k_2x_2 - c(\dot{x}_1 - \dot{x}_2) = 0 \tag{ii}$$

The equations of motion can be written in matrix form as follows:

$$\begin{bmatrix} m_1 & 0 \\ 0 & m_2 \end{bmatrix}\begin{Bmatrix} \ddot{x}_1 \\ \ddot{x}_2 \end{Bmatrix} + \begin{bmatrix} c & -c \\ -c & c \end{bmatrix}\begin{Bmatrix} \dot{x}_1 \\ \dot{x}_2 \end{Bmatrix} + \begin{bmatrix} k_1 & 0 \\ 0 & k_2 \end{bmatrix}\begin{Bmatrix} x_1 \\ x_2 \end{Bmatrix} = \begin{Bmatrix} 0 \\ 0 \end{Bmatrix} \tag{iii}$$

Its solution is assumed as follows:

$$x_1 = D_1 e^{\omega^* t} \quad \text{and} \quad x_2 = D_2 e^{\omega^* t} \tag{iv}$$

Differentiating these equations twice and substituting in Equations (i) and (ii) gives,

$$\left[m_1 D_1 \omega^{*2} + k_1 D_1 + c\omega^*(D_1 - D_2)\right] e^{\omega^* t} = 0 \tag{v}$$

and

$$\left[m_2 D_2 \omega^{*2} + k_2 D_2 - c\omega^*(D_1 - D_2)\right] e^{\omega^* t} = 0 \tag{vi}$$

For a non-trivial solution,

$$e^{\omega^* t} \neq 0$$

$$\therefore \quad m_1 D_1 \omega^{*2} + k_1 D_1 + c\omega^*(D_1 - D_2) = 0$$

or,

$$m_1\omega^{*2} + c\omega^* + k_1 = c\omega^* \frac{D_2}{D_1} \tag{vii}$$

and

$$m_2 D_2 \omega^{*2} + k_2 D_2 + c\omega^*(D_2 - D_1) = 0$$

or,

$$m_2\omega^{*2} + c\omega^* + k_2 = c\omega^* \frac{D_1}{D_2} \tag{viii}$$

Equations (vii) and (viii) can be written as:

$$\frac{D_1}{D_2} - \frac{c\omega^*}{m_1\omega^{*2} + c\omega^* + k_1} - \frac{m_2\omega^{*2} + c\omega^* + k_2}{c\omega^*} \tag{ix}$$

Equations (ix) yields the characteristic eigenvalue equation, that is,

$$\left(m_1\omega^{*2}+c\omega^*+k_1\right)\times\left(m_2\omega^{*2}+c\omega^*+k_2\right)=\left(c\omega^*\right)^2 \tag{x}$$

This gives four roots of ω^* – two positive and two negative. The natural frequencies of the two DOF system can be obtained.
If $m_1 = m_2 = m$ and $k_1 = k_2 = k$, Equation (x) can be written as

$$\left(m\omega^{*2}+k\right)\times\left(m\omega^{*2}+2c\omega^*+k\right)=0 \tag{xi}$$

Therefore,

$$\left(m\omega^{*2}+k\right)=0,$$

It gives
$$\omega^* = \pm i\sqrt{\frac{k}{m}} \tag{xii}$$

and
$$\left(m\omega^{*2}+2c\omega^*+k\right)=0$$

or,

It gives
$$\omega^* = -\frac{c}{m}\pm\sqrt{\left(\frac{c}{m}\right)^2-\frac{k}{m}} \tag{xiii}$$

Using the relations

$$\omega=\sqrt{\frac{k}{m}} \quad \text{and} \quad \xi=\frac{c}{c_c}=\frac{c}{2m\omega}$$

Equation (xiii) can be written as

$$\omega^* = -2\xi\omega\pm\sqrt{(2\xi\omega)^2-\omega^2}$$

or,

$$\omega^* = \left(-2\xi\pm i\sqrt{1-(2\xi)^2}\right)\omega \quad \text{for low damping} \tag{xiv}$$

The solution of the equations of motion can be given by both Equations (xii) and (xiv). The most general solution can be written as follows:

$$x_1(t)=D_{11}e^{\pm i\omega t}+D_{12}e^{\left(-2\xi\pm i\sqrt{1-(2\xi)^2}\right)\omega t}$$

This can be simplified and written as follows:

$$x_1(t)=A_1\sin\left(\omega t+\theta_1\right)+A_2\ e^{-2\xi\omega t}\sin\left(\sqrt{1-(2\xi)^2}\,\omega t+\theta_2\right) \tag{xv}$$

Similarly,

$$x_2(t)=A_3\sin\left(\omega t+\theta_1\right)+A_4\ e^{-2\xi\omega t}\sin\left(\sqrt{1-(2\xi)^2}\,\omega t+\theta_2\right) \tag{xvi}$$

The constants need to be evaluated using the initial conditions. □

Example 9.9

A 4000 kg machine operates at a frequency of 130 Hz. A mass of 500 kg is attached to absorb the vibrations at the operating frequency. Calculate the frequency range at which the vibration absorber is very effective.

Solution

The main mass $m_1 = 4000$ kg; auxiliary mass $m_2 = 500$ kg, operating frequency $\bar{f} = 130$ Hz.
Mass ratio $\mu = 500/4000 = 0.125$

$$\left(\frac{\bar{\omega}}{\omega_2}\right)^2 = (1+\frac{\mu}{2}) \pm \sqrt{\mu + \frac{\mu^2}{4}} \tag{9.31}$$

$$\therefore \quad \beta^2 = \left(1 + \frac{500}{2\times 4000}\right) \pm \sqrt{0.125 + \frac{0.125^2}{4}}$$

$$\beta^2 = 0.703 \quad \text{or} \quad 1.421$$

or,

$$\beta = 0.838 \quad \text{or} \quad 1.192$$

but

$$\beta = \bar{\omega}/\omega_2$$

∴ The frequency range at which the absorber is most effective is between 130/0.838 = 155.13 Hz and 109.06 Hz.

The displacement magnification factor for the absorber mass X_2

$$\frac{X_2}{X_{ST}} = \frac{1}{\frac{\bar{\omega}^4}{\omega_2^4} - (2+\mu)\frac{\bar{\omega}^2}{\omega_2^2} + 1}$$

It can be re-written as follows:

$$\frac{X_2}{X_{st}} = \frac{1}{(1-\beta^2)^2 - \mu\beta^2} \approx \frac{1}{-\mu\beta^2}$$

For $\beta = 0.838$,

$$\therefore \quad \frac{X_2}{X_{st}} = \frac{1}{0.125\times 0.838^2} = 11.40$$

For $\beta = 1.192$,

$$\frac{X_2}{X_{st}} = \frac{1}{0.125\times 1.192^2} = 5.63$$

At these frequencies, the amplitude ratio of the secondary mass will vary between 5.63 and 11.40. The amplitude ratio of the machine vibration will be zero or nearly zero. □

Example 9.10

A machine operates at a frequency of 5000 rpm, exerts a force of 140 N and produces excessive vibrations. Design a vibration absorber having a maximum displacement of 3.5 mm only.

Solution

$P_0 = 140$ N, operating frequency $\bar{\omega} = 5000$ rpm $= 5000/60 = 83.33$ rad/sec

$$P_0 = -k_2 X_2$$

The spring stiffness $k_2 = 140/(3.5/1000) = 40000$ N/m

$$\left(\frac{\bar{\omega}}{\omega_2}\right)^2 = (1+\frac{\mu}{2}) \pm \sqrt{\mu + \frac{\mu^2}{4}}$$

If the mass ratio = 0.10, let us determine the frequency range in which the absorber will be effective.

$$\beta^2 = (1+0.10/2) \pm \sqrt{0.10 + \frac{0.10^2}{4}} = 1.05 \pm 0.32$$

$$\beta^2 = 0.73 \text{ or } 1.37$$

or,

$$\beta = 0.854 \text{ or } 1.170$$

∴ The frequency range at which the absorber is most effective is between 83.33/0.854 = 97.58 rad/sec and 71.22 rad/sec. The vibration absorber will have a mass ratio of 0.10 and a stiffness of 40000 N/m. The nearest resonance will be about 15% away from the operating frequency. □

Example 9.11

A steel box girder foot bridge may be assumed to be represented by a SDOF system with a mass of 17500 kg and a stiffness of 3×10^6 N/m. The worst case of dynamic loading occurs when two people walk across the bridge in steps in tune with its natural frequency. This is almost equivalent to a sinusoidal loading with a constant amplitude of 0.48 kN. Design a suitable tuned vibration absorber.

Solution

$$m_1 = 17500 \text{ kg}, \quad k_1 = 3 \times 10^6 \text{ N/m}$$

∴

$$\omega_1 = \sqrt{\frac{k_1}{m_1}} = 13.09 \text{ rad/sec}$$

or,

$$f_1 = 2.08 \text{ Hz}$$

Let mass ratio

$$\mu = 0.01$$

∴ $m_2 = 175$ kg – It can be easily accommodated in the box girder.

∴

$$\omega_2 = \omega_1 = 13.09 \text{ rad/sec}$$

or,

$$k_2 = \omega_2^2 m_2 = 13.09^2 \times 175 = 30000 \text{ N/m}$$

Resonant frequencies:

$$\left(\frac{\bar{\omega}}{\omega_2}\right)^2 = \left(1 + \frac{0.01}{2}\right) \pm \sqrt{0.01 + \frac{(0.01)^2}{4}}$$

$$= 1.005 \pm 0.100 \quad \text{or} \quad 0.905 \quad \text{and} \quad 1.105$$

Taking square roots

$$\therefore \qquad \bar{\omega}_1 = 0.951\,\omega_2 = 12.45 \text{ rad/sec}$$

and
$$\bar{\omega}_2 = 1.051\,\omega_2 = 13.76 \text{ rad/sec}$$

For these frequencies, $X_1 = 0$

and
$$X_2 = \frac{F_0}{k_2} = \frac{480}{30000} = 0.016 \text{ m} = 16 \text{ mm}$$

This motion can be easily accommodated within the box girder using coil springs. □

Example 9.12

A two-DOF undamped system (Figure 9.14) consists of the following data: m_1 = 10 kg, k_1 = 25 N/m, m_2 = 1 kg and k_2 = 5 N/m. Find the response of the system for the following initial conditions:

(i) $x(0) = \begin{Bmatrix} 2 \\ 0 \end{Bmatrix}$ mm and $\dot{x}(0) = \begin{Bmatrix} 0 \\ 0 \end{Bmatrix}$ mm/sec

(ii) $x(0) = \begin{Bmatrix} 0 \\ 0 \end{Bmatrix}$ mm and $\dot{x}(0) = \begin{Bmatrix} 2 \\ 0 \end{Bmatrix}$ mm/sec

Solution

The equations of motion of the free vibrations of an undamped two-DOF system are

$$\begin{bmatrix} m_1 & 0 \\ 0 & m_2 \end{bmatrix} \begin{Bmatrix} \ddot{x}_1 \\ \ddot{x}_2 \end{Bmatrix} + \begin{bmatrix} k_1 + k_2 & -k_2 \\ -k_2 & k_2 \end{bmatrix} \begin{Bmatrix} x_1 \\ x_2 \end{Bmatrix} = \begin{Bmatrix} 0 \\ 0 \end{Bmatrix}$$

The frequency equation is given by

$$\left| K - M\omega^2 \right| = 0$$

Where,

$$M = \begin{bmatrix} 10 & 0 \\ 0 & 1 \end{bmatrix} \text{ and } K = \begin{bmatrix} 30 & -5 \\ 5 & 5 \end{bmatrix}$$

Its frequencies and mode shapes are as follows (Figure 9.29):

$$\omega = \begin{Bmatrix} 1.46 \\ 2.42 \end{Bmatrix} \text{rad/sec}, \quad \phi_1 = \begin{Bmatrix} 0.574 \\ 1 \end{Bmatrix} \quad \text{and} \quad \phi_2 = \begin{Bmatrix} -0.174 \\ 1 \end{Bmatrix}$$

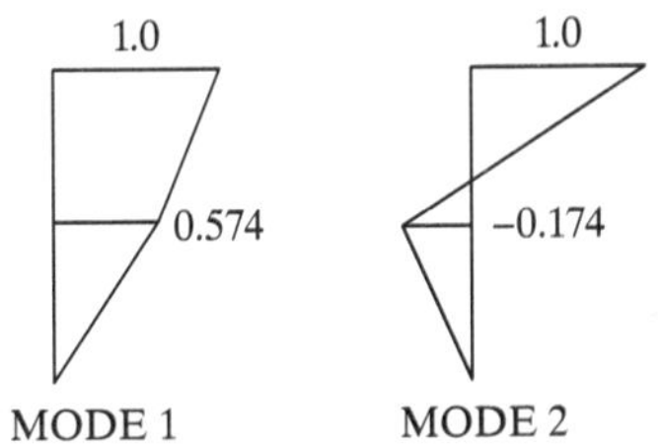

Figure 9.29 Mode shapes.

(i) Solution for the given initial conditions (i)

$$x(0)=\begin{Bmatrix}2\\0\end{Bmatrix}\text{mm and }\dot{x}(0)=\begin{Bmatrix}0\\0\end{Bmatrix}\text{mm/sec}$$

$$\begin{Bmatrix}x_1(t)\\x_2(t)\end{Bmatrix}_{2\times1}=[\{\phi_1\}\ \ \{\phi_2\}]_{2\times2}\begin{Bmatrix}A\sin(\omega_1 t+\theta_1)\\B\sin(\omega_2 t+\theta_2)\end{Bmatrix}_{2\times1}$$

For $t=0$,

or,
$$\begin{Bmatrix}x_1(0)\\x_2(0)\end{Bmatrix}=\begin{Bmatrix}\phi_{11}A\sin\theta_1+\phi_{12}B\sin\theta_2\\\phi_{21}A\sin\theta_1+\phi_{22}B\sin\theta_2\end{Bmatrix}\tag{1a}$$

$$\begin{Bmatrix}2\\0\end{Bmatrix}=\begin{Bmatrix}0.574A\sin\theta_1-0.174B\sin\theta_2\\A\sin\theta_1+B\sin\theta_2\end{Bmatrix}\tag{1b}$$

Equations (1b) can be written as:

$$0.574A\sin\theta_1-0.174B\sin\theta_2=2\tag{1c}$$

and
$$A\sin\theta_1+B\sin\theta_2=0\tag{1d}$$

On differentiating Equation (1a) and substituting the initial values:

$$\begin{Bmatrix}\dot{x}_1(0)\\\dot{x}_2(0)\end{Bmatrix}=\begin{Bmatrix}\phi_{11}A\omega_1\cos\theta_1+\phi_{12}B\omega_2\cos\theta_2\\\phi_{21}A\omega_1\cos\theta_1+\phi_{22}B\omega_2\cos\theta_2\end{Bmatrix}$$

or,
$$\begin{Bmatrix}0\\0\end{Bmatrix}=\begin{Bmatrix}0.574\times1.46A\cos\theta_1-0.174\times2.42B\cos\theta_2\\1.46A\cos\theta_1+2.42B\cos\theta_2\end{Bmatrix}\tag{2a}$$

or,
$$\begin{Bmatrix}0\\0\end{Bmatrix}=\begin{Bmatrix}0.838A\cos\theta_1-0.421B\cos\theta_2\\1.46A\cos\theta_1+2.42B\cos\theta_2\end{Bmatrix}\tag{2b}$$

Equations (2b) can be written as:

$$A\cos\theta_1-0.502B\cos\theta_2=0\tag{2c}$$

and
$$A\cos\theta_1+1.657B\cos\theta_2=0\tag{2d}$$

Solving these two equations, for $B\neq0$ gives,

$$\cos\theta_2=0\text{ or, }\theta_2=\pi/2$$

Similarly, for $A\neq0$,

$$\cos\theta_1=0\text{ or, }\theta_1=\pi/2$$

Using Equations (1c) and (1d),

$$0.574A-0.174B=0$$

and
$$A+B=0$$

$\therefore A=2.674$ and $B=-2.674$

Thus, the final solution is

$$\begin{Bmatrix} x_1(t) \\ x_2(t) \end{Bmatrix}_{2\times1} = \begin{bmatrix} 0.574 & -0.174 \\ 1 & 1 \end{bmatrix}_{2\times2} \begin{Bmatrix} 2.674\sin\left(1.46t + \frac{\pi}{2}\right) \\ -2.674\sin\left(2.42t + \frac{\pi}{2}\right) \end{Bmatrix}_{2\times1}$$

or,

$$x_1(t) = 1.535\cos 1.46t + 0.465\cos 2.42t \tag{3a}$$

and

$$x_2(t) = 2.674\cos 1.46t - 2.674\cos 2.42t \tag{3b}$$

The plots of $x_1(t)$ and $x_2(t)$ are shown in Figures 9.30 (a).

The contribution of the second mode or second frequency ω_2 is small because the coefficient of the second term in Equation (3a) is small.

(ii) Solution for the given initial conditions (ii)

$$x(0) = \begin{Bmatrix} 0 \\ 0 \end{Bmatrix} \text{mm and } \dot{x}(0) = \begin{Bmatrix} 2 \\ 0 \end{Bmatrix} \text{mm/sec}$$

Let us substitute the initial condition in Equation (1a),

$$\begin{Bmatrix} 0 \\ 0 \end{Bmatrix} = \begin{Bmatrix} 0.574A\sin\theta_1 - 0.174B\sin\theta_2 \\ A\sin\theta_1 + B\sin\theta_2 \end{Bmatrix} \tag{1b}$$

Equations (1b) can be written as:

$$0.574A\sin\theta_1 - 0.174B\sin\theta_2 = 0$$

or,

$$A\sin\theta_1 - 0.303B\sin\theta_2 = 0 \tag{1c}$$

and

$$A\sin\theta_1 + B\sin\theta_2 = 0 \tag{1d}$$

Solving these two equations, for $B \neq 0$ gives,
$\sin\theta_2 = 0$ or, $\theta_2 = 0$, also for $A \neq 0$, $\theta_1 = 0$
Similarly, Equation (2a) can be written as

$$\begin{Bmatrix} 2 \\ 0 \end{Bmatrix} = \begin{Bmatrix} 0.574 \times 1.46A\cos\theta_1 - 0.174 \times 2.42B\cos\theta_2 \\ 1.46A\cos\theta_1 + 2.42B\cos\theta_2 \end{Bmatrix} \tag{2b}$$

or,

$$\begin{Bmatrix} 2 \\ 0 \end{Bmatrix} = \begin{Bmatrix} 0.838A\cos\theta_1 - 0.421B\cos\theta_2 \\ 1.46A\cos\theta_1 + 2.42B\cos\theta_2 \end{Bmatrix}$$

or,

$$A\cos\theta_1 - 0.502B\cos\theta_2 = 2.3866 \tag{2c}$$

and

$$A\cos\theta_1 + 1.657B\cos\theta_2 = 0 \tag{2d}$$

Solving these two equations,

$$A = 1.830, \text{ and } B = -1.105$$

The final solution becomes

$$\begin{Bmatrix} x_1(t) \\ x_2(t) \end{Bmatrix}_{2\times1} = \begin{bmatrix} 0.574 & -0.174 \\ 1 & 1 \end{bmatrix}_{2\times2} \begin{Bmatrix} 1.830\sin(1.46t) \\ -1.105\sin(2.42t) \end{Bmatrix}_{2\times1}$$

or, $$x_1(t) = 1.050\sin 1.46t + 0.192\sin 2.42t \quad (3a)$$

and $$x_2(t) = 1.830\sin 1.46t - 1.105\sin 2.42t \quad (3b)$$

The plots of $x_1(t)$ and $x_2(t)$ are shown in Figures 9.30 (b).
The contribution of the second mode or second frequency ω_2 is small because the coefficient of the second term in Equation (3a) is small.
Naturally $x_2(t)$ is more than $x_1(t)$ being the upper floor displacement in both cases.

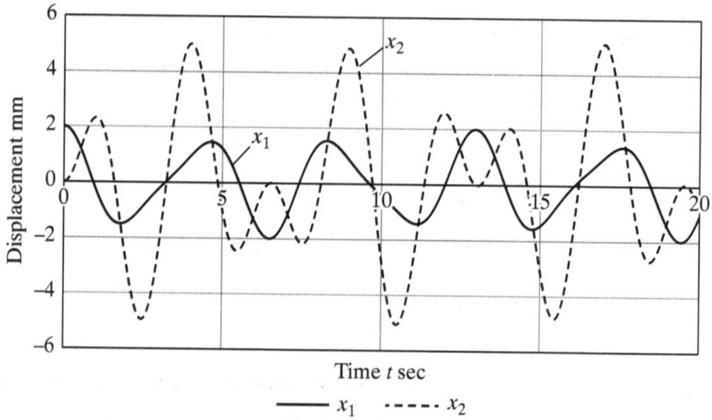

Figure 9.30(a) Displacement response for initial condition (i)

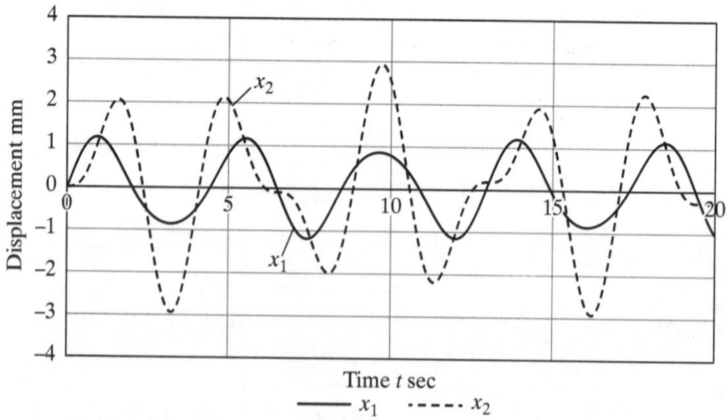

Figure 9.30(b) Displacement response for initial condition (ii)

REVIEW QUESTIONS

9.1. What is interesting about the study of vibrations of a 2-DOF system?

9.2. Write the equations of motion of an undamped free vibration of a 2-DOF system in matrix form. Draw free body diagrams.

9.3. Derive the characteristics equation for determining the frequencies of vibrations of an undamped 2-DOF system.

9.4. What is a vibration absorber?

9.5 What do you understand by vibration absorber? Derive the expression for the amplitude of the absorber mass when the main mass is at rest.

9.6. What is a tuned mass damper?

9.7. Discuss the concept of tuned vibration absorber or tuned mass damper. Plot the variation of frequency ratio vs. mass ratio.

9.8. Discuss the effect of mass ratio on the amplitude of primary mass at resonant frequency.

9.9. Draw a plot for normalized displacement vs. frequency ratio both for primary mass and secondary mass for a mass ratio of 0.25 and 2.0.

9.10. What is band width for a vibration absorber?

9.11. What is operating frequency of a vibration absorber?

PROBLEMS

9.1 An undamped two DOF system shown in Figure 9.1 has a mass $m_1 = m$, mass $m_2 = 2$ m, stiffness $k_1 = k$, and stiffness $k_2 = 2$ k. Determine its natural frequencies and mode shapes.

9.2 An undamped two DOF system has a mass $m_1 = m_2 = 2$ kg, and for the first mode $\omega_1 = 50$ rad/sec and mode shapes $\phi_{11} = 0.6$ and $\phi_{21} = 1.0$. Determine the mode shape and natural frequency of the second mode.

Ans: $\omega = \begin{Bmatrix} 0.517 \\ 1.93 \end{Bmatrix} \sqrt{\dfrac{k}{m}}\ \Phi = \begin{bmatrix} 1 & 1 \\ 0.732 & -2.732 \end{bmatrix}$

9.3 A machine operates at a frequency of 2000 rpm, exerts a force of 350 N and produces excessive vibrations. Design a vibration absorber having a maximum displacement of 3 mm only.

Ans: $\omega_2 = 121$ rad/sec $\phi_2 - \begin{Bmatrix} 1 \\ -1.667 \end{Bmatrix}$

9.4 Plot the frequency response curve for the system shown in Figure 9.2 with $m_1 = 3$ m, $m_2 = m$, $k_1 = 3$ k and $k_2 = k$ subjected to a harmonic force p_0 applied on mass m_1.

Ans: $m_2 = 2.66$ kg, $k_2 = 116666$ N/m

9.5 A steel box girder foot bridge may be assumed to be represented by a SDOF system with a mass of 25000 kg and a stiffness of 5×10^6 N/m. The worst case of dynamic loading occurs when five people walk across the bridge in steps in tune with its natural frequency. This is almost equivalent to a sinusoidal loading with a constant amplitude of 0.75 kN. Design a suitable tuned vibration absorber so that its displacement does not exceed 10 cm.

Ans: $m_2 = 37.5$ kg, $k_2 = 7500$ N/m

9.6 A machine weighing 50 kg runs at a constant speed of 5000 rpm. At this speed, it is known to resonate with the foundation. Design an absorber such that its nearest resonance is at least 20% away from the operating frequency.

9.7 A balcony floor of a theater experiences excessive vibrations when 50 persons walk over it. This is equivalent to a sinusoidal loading with a constant amplitude of 25 kN. Design a suitable tuned vibration absorber so that its displacement does not exceed 5 cm. The balcony floor may be assumed to be represented by a SDOF system with a mass of 50000 kg and a stiffness of 15000 kN/m.

9.8 A two degree freedom system shown in Figure 9.28 has m_1 = 50 kg, m_2 = 75 kg, k_1 = 20000 N/m, k_2 = 30000 N/m and k_3 = 15000 N/m. Estimate its natural frequencies and mode shapes if the supports are rigid.

$$\textbf{Ans: } \omega = \begin{Bmatrix} 16.456 \\ 36.458 \end{Bmatrix} \text{rad/sec} \quad \Phi = \begin{bmatrix} -0.1174 & 0.0789 \\ 0.0644 & 0.0958 \end{bmatrix}$$

9.9 A two DOF system is shown in Figure P9.1. Estimate its natural frequencies and mode shapes, if the supports are rigid. Assume $m_2 = 2m_1$.

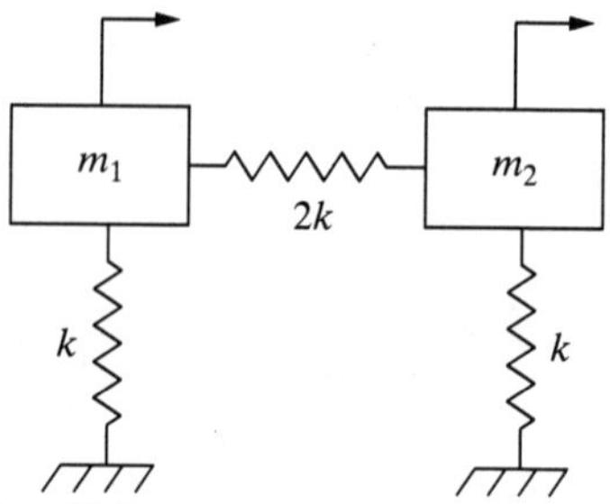

Figure P9.1 Two-degree freedom system

[Hint: Rotate the vertical springs and bring them in a horizontal alignment]

10 Multi-degree of Freedom Systems

10.1 INTRODUCTION

If the physical properties of a system are such that its motion can be described by a single coordinate and no other motion is possible, then it is a SDOF system and its solution can be obtained using any method discussed so far. If, however, the structure has more than one possible mode of displacement and it is reduced mathematically to a SDOF approximation, the solution of the equation of motion is only an approximation to the true dynamic behaviour. The quality of results obtained with a SDOF model depends on several factors, such as, the spatial distribution of mass and stiffness. In general, dynamic response of a flexible structure cannot be determined adequately by a SDOF model. Behaviour of such a structure can be described by more than one degree of freedom, that is, displacement amplitudes of certain selected points in the structure. The number of degrees of freedom (DOF) or displacement components to be considered is left to the judgement of the analyst; greater numbers provide better approximation to the true behaviour. A structure may consist of a discrete system or a distributed mass and elasticity system. Its DOF needs to be identified. If it is a discrete system, it may be analysed using the standard matrix analysis methods. In case, it is a distributed system, it may be analysed using the finite element method. The equations of motion remain same in either case.

The object of this chapter is to develop the equation of motion of a general *multi-degree-of-freedom system* (MDOF) subjected to *forced vibrations*. The MDOF system may be a multi-storey building, a TV tower, a flexural member, a machine foundation, a water retaining structure, a bridge including its super-structure and/or sub-structure, an underground metro station or parking structure or an off-shore oil platform. The forced vibrations may be due to any possible source. Once the equation of motion of a MDOF system is constituted, its solution can be easily obtained using the solution algorithms discussed in Chapter 7 on direct integration methods. However, the direct integration methods have their own limitations. They need time-history of the external loading. This is itself a very challenging problem. Most of the time, such time-histories are not available or not available in sufficient number. Therefore, there is a need to develop other solution techniques that give solutions with reasonable accuracy for any MDOF system. One such solution is called *modal analysis* or *response spectrum analysis*. This method is discussed in detail in this chapter.

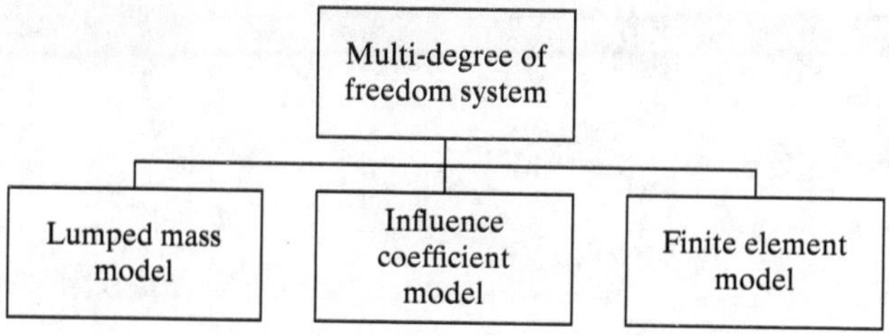

Figure 10.1 Mathematical modeling of a MDOF system

The different types of mathematical models of a multi-degree of freedom system are shown in Figure 10.1.

There are certain methods that are applicable exclusively to discrete systems. One such method is Holzer's method applicable for the analysis of a simple spring-mass system or a lumped-mass system such as a multi-storey building or a steel TV tower. It is a very powerful method for understanding the physical concept of frequency and mode shapes in MDOF systems.

10.2 SPRING MASS MODEL: MDOF SYSTEM

A multistorey building may be represented by a series of springs and masses as shown in Figure 10.2. This is also referred to as a *lumped mass system*. All the masses on a given floor are lumped together. Similarly, stiffness of all the lateral load resisting system in one storey are lumped together. Damping is neglected in the present

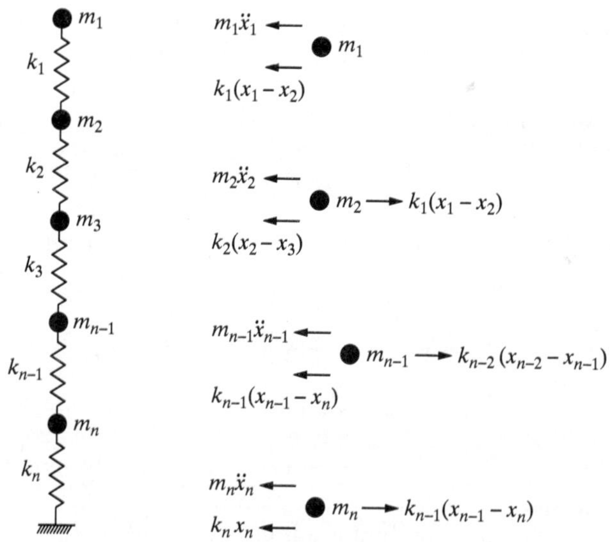

(a) (b) Free body diagrams

Figure 10.2 An undamped multi-degree of freedom system.

formulation. It is assumed that there is only one lateral degree of freedom per floor. If there are 20 storeys in the building, it will have 20-degrees of freedom. If there are *n*-storeys, there will be n-degrees of freedom. If this system is allowed to vibrate freely, it will vibrate in *natural mode or normal mode*. It means the system has exactly the same number of normal modes as the DOF. A *natural frequency* and a *characteristic shape* is associated with each normal mode. A salient feature of this normal mode is that the system could under certain conditions vibrate freely in that mode alone, and during such vibration, the ratio of the displacement of any two masses is constant with time. The complete motion of the system can be obtained by superimposing the independent motions of the individual modes. This forms the basis of the solution of the MDOF system.

Free body diagram of each mass can be considered and equation of dynamic equilibrium may be written for each mass as follows:
For mass m_1,

$$m_1\ddot{x}_1 + k_1(x_1 - x_2) = 0 \tag{A.1}$$

For mass m_2,

$$m_2\ddot{x}_2 + k_2(x_2 - x_3) + k_1(x_2 - x_1) = 0 \tag{A.2}$$

Similarly, for other masses,

$$m_3\ddot{x}_3 + k_3(x_3 - x_4) + k_2(x_3 - x_2) = 0 \tag{A.3}$$

and so on

$$m_n\ddot{x}_n + k_n(x_n) + k_{n-1}(x_n - x_{n-1}) = 0 \tag{A.n}$$

Let this set of n Equations be (A).

This set of n equations can be arranged in matrix form as follows:

$$[M]_{n\times n}\{\ddot{X}\}_{n\times 1} + [K]_{n\times n}\{X\}_{n\times 1} = \{0\}_{n\times 1} \tag{10.1a}$$

where,

$[M]_{n\times n}$ = mass matrix of size $n \times n$

$[K]_{n\times n}$ = stiffness matrix of size $n \times n$

$\{X\}_{n\times 1}$ = displacement vector of size $n \times 1$

$\{\ddot{X}\}_{n\times 1}$ = acceleration vector of size $n \times 1$

n = total active DOF of the system

A square bracket represents a matrix of size $m \times n$, whereas a curly bracket represents a column vector of size $m \times 1$. If it is a square matrix, then rows are equal to columns, that is, $m = n$.

Equation (10.1a) can also be written as follows:

$$\boldsymbol{M\ddot{X}} + \boldsymbol{KX} = \boldsymbol{0} \tag{10.1b}$$

Bold and capital letters are used to represent a matrix. Thus, M and K each represent a matrix. A bold and capital letter X and P represent a column vector.

It can be shown that vibration in a normal mode must always be harmonic. It was already stated earlier that during vibration in a single mode, the displacements of several masses are always in the same proportion, that is, all possible positions are geometrically similar. All masses vibrate in phase with the same natural frequency.

Let us assume that:

$$x_1 = \phi_1 \sin \omega t \quad \text{or} \quad \ddot{x}_1 = -\omega^2 \phi_1 \sin \omega t \tag{B.1}$$

$$x_2 = \phi_2 \sin \omega t \quad \text{or} \quad \ddot{x}_2 = -\omega^2 \phi_2 \sin \omega t \tag{B.2}$$

and so on,

$$x_n = \phi_n \sin \omega t \quad \text{or} \quad \ddot{x}_n = -\phi^2 \phi_n \sin \omega t \tag{B.n}$$

Let this set of n Equations be (B).

This set of n equations can be arranged in matrix form as follows:

$$\{X\}_{n\times 1} = \{\phi\}_{n\times 1} \sin \omega t = \sin \omega t \{\phi\}_{n\times 1} \tag{10.2}$$

and

$$\{\ddot{X}\}_{n\times 1} = -\omega^2 \sin \omega t \{\phi\}_{n\times 1} = -\omega^2 \{X\} \tag{10.3}$$

Now let us substitute Equations of set B in set A, and for $\sin \omega t \neq 0$.

For mass m_1

$$-m_1\omega^2\phi_1 + k_1(\phi_1 - \phi_2) = 0$$

or

$$\phi_1(k_1 - m_1\omega^2) - \phi_2 k_1 = 0 \tag{C.1}$$

for mass m_2

$$-k_1\phi_1 + (k_1 + k_2 - m_2\omega^2)\phi_2 - k_2\phi_3 = 0 \tag{C.2}$$

for mass m_3

$$-k_2\phi_2 + (k_2 + k_3 - m_3\omega^2)\phi_3 - k_3\phi_4 = 0 \tag{C.3}$$

and so on, for mass m_n

$$-k_{n-1}\phi_{n-1} + (k_{n-1} + k_n - m_n\omega^2)\phi_n = 0 \tag{C.n}$$

Let this set of n equations be (C).

The set of Equations (C) can be re-written as follows:

$$\begin{bmatrix} (k_1 - m_1\omega^2) & -k_1 & 0 & 0 & 0 \\ -k_1 & (k_1 + k_2 - m_2\omega^2) & -k_2 & 0 & 0 \\ 0 & -k_2 & (k_2 + k_3 - m_3\omega^2) & -k_3 & 0 \\ 0 & 0 & & & \\ 0 & 0 & 0 & -k_{n-1} & (k_{n-1} + k_n - m_n\omega^2) \end{bmatrix} \begin{Bmatrix} \phi_1 \\ \phi_2 \\ \phi_3 \\ \\ \phi_n \end{Bmatrix} = \{0\} \tag{10.4}$$

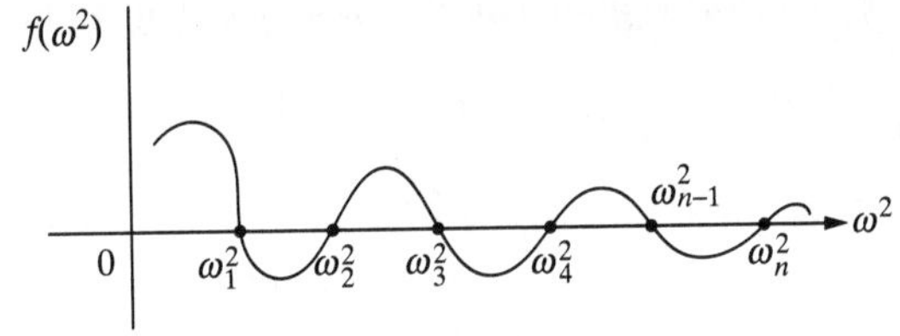

Figure 10.3 Roots of a polynomial.

This set of equations can be arranged in matrix notation as follows:

$$\left[[K]-\omega^2[M]\right]_{n\times n}\{\phi\}_{n\times 1}=\{0\}_{n\times 1} \tag{10.5}$$

There are $(n + 1)$ unknowns: n values of ϕ's and one ω^2. However, there are only n-equations. Thus, it is an under-determined system. The solution of Equation (10.4) or (10.5) gives n-values of ω^2. Each of the frequency ω_1, ω_2, ω_3, etc. is substituted in Equation (10.4) one-by-one, and the corresponding values of vector $\{\phi\}_{n\times 1}$ is determined in terms of any one vector component ϕ_i. Thus, vector $\{\phi\}_{n\times 1}$ is determined as a relative value because this system of equations happen to be an under-determined system. The vector $\{\phi\}_{n\times 1}$ is called *mode shapes*.

For a non-trivial solution, vector $\{\phi\}_{n\times 1} \neq 0$, therefore, determinant of matrix of Equation (10.5) must be zero. This is referred to as the *frequency determinant or characteristic equations*. Upon simplification, it yields a polynomial equation of order n in ω^2, that is,

$$a_n(\omega^2)^n + a_{n-1}(\omega^2)^{n-1} + a_{n-2}(\omega^2)^{n-2} + \ldots + a_0 = 0 \tag{10.6}$$

This gives n values of ω^2, that is, n eigenvalues or n natural frequencies of vibration. A plot of this polynomial is shown in Figure 10.3. The problem is to find these roots at which this polynomial has zero values. This n^{th} order equation can be solved in several ways.

10.3 HOLTZER METHOD

This is an iterative method for computing frequencies of vibration of a MDOF spring mass system. Let us rearrange equations in set C.

Equation (C.1) gives,

$$\phi_2 = \phi_1 - \frac{\omega^2}{k_1} m_1\phi_1 \tag{D.1}$$

Equation (C.2) gives,

$$\phi_3 = \phi_2 - \frac{\omega^2}{k_2}(m_1\phi_1 + m_2\phi_2) \tag{D.2}$$

after substituting for k_1 from Equation (C.1) in Equation (C.2).

Similarly,

$$\phi_n = \phi_{n-1} - \frac{\omega^2}{k_{n-1}}\left(\sum_{i=1}^{n-1} m_i\phi_i\right) \tag{D.n–1}$$

By similarity, the following additional equation can be written:

$$\phi_{n+1} = \phi_n - \frac{\omega^2}{k_n}\left(\sum_{i=1}^{n} m_i\phi_i\right) = 0 \quad \text{since base is fixed.} \tag{D.n}$$

There are n equations. Let this set of n equations be (D). These equations can be solved iteratively using a very simple logic.

Algorithm:

Step 1: Write equations of motion, set A

Step 2: Write set of equations B

Step 3: Write set of equations C

Step 4: Write set of equations D

Step 5: Choose ω^2 (say = 0.1 k/m)

Step 6: Work out ϕ_2 from Equation (D.1) in terms of ϕ_1; then ϕ_3 from Equation (D.2) in terms of ϕ_1; then ϕ_4 from Equation (D.3) in terms of ϕ_1 and so on. Remember that ϕ represents displacement.

Step 7: Compute ϕ_{n+1} from the last equation.

The displacement given by ϕ_{n+1} must turn out to be zero since the base is fixed. If not, choose another value of ω^2 and iterate on ω^2 till ϕ_{n+1} is zero.

It is a very easy, convenient and powerful manual method for estimating eigenvalues and eigenvectors for a MDOF-lumped mass system.

10.4 DYNAMIC EQUILIBRIUM CONDITION: MDOF SYSTEM

The equations of motion of the system shown in Figure 10.4 can be formulated by expressing the equilibrium of the effective forces associated with each of its n-degrees of freedom. It is a general MDOF system. It may be any discrete or distributed system.

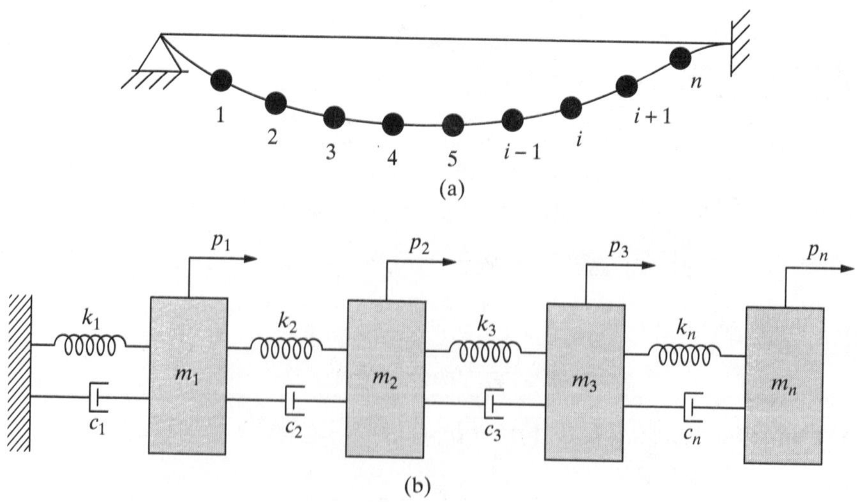

Figure 10.4 A MDOF system.

The choice of selection of DOF depends upon the characteristics of the structure under consideration and the experience and judgement of the structural analyst. The formulation is concerned only with the total active DOF 'n'. There are four types of forces acting at any i^{th} degree of freedom:

1. externally applied load $p_i(t)$
2. elastic force f_{si}
3. damping force f_{di}
4. inertia force f_{ii}

For each of the n-degrees of freedom, the dynamic equilibrium equations may be expressed as:

$$f_{i1} + f_{d1} + f_{s1} = p_1(t)$$

$$f_{i2} + f_{d2} + f_{s2} = p_2(t)$$

$$f_{i3} + f_{d3} + f_{s3} = p_3(t)$$

and so on

$$f_{in} + f_{dn} + f_{sn} = p_n(t) \tag{10.7}$$

Rearranging these n-equations in matrix form:

$$\{f_I\}_{n\times 1} + \{f_D\}_{n\times 1} + \{f_S\}_{n\times 1} = \{p(t)\}_{n\times 1} \tag{10.8}$$

Each of the resisting forces is expressed most conveniently by means of an appropriate set of influence coefficients. In a MDOF system, any displacement applied at i^{th} degree-of-freedom will influence all the remaining $n - 1$ DOF. There is a need to evaluate all these influence coefficients using the standard procedure adopted for the static analysis of a structure using matrix method, that is, *matrix structural analysis*. These coefficients will be determined separately for the inertia, damping and elastic forces. Let us first find the influence coefficients for elastic forces with which we are already familiar in the matrix analysis method.

10.4.1 Elastic Force (Spring Force)

At node 1, let us apply a unit displacement and determine the force produced at each of the remaining $(n - 1)$ degrees of freedom. That is, let us determine the *influence coefficients for stiffness* k_{ij}

where k_{ij} = force produced at node i due to unit displacement applied at node j.

Similarly, let us apply a unit displacement at node 2 and determine the force produced at each of the remaining $(n - 1)$ degrees of freedom. And so on.

If the final displacement at node 1 is x_1, at node 2 is x_2, at node 3 is x_3 and so on, we can get the total spring force produced at each of the n nodes.

Finally, let us collect all the forces acting at node 1, node 2, node 3, etc.

At node 1,

$$f_{s1} = k_{11}x_1 + k_{12}x_2 + k_{13}x_3 + k_{14}x_4 + \cdots + k_{1n}x_n$$

At node 2,

$$f_{s2} = k_{21}x_1 + k_{22}x_2 + k_{23}x_3 + k_{24}x_4 + \cdots + k_{2n}x_n$$

At node 3

$$f_{s3} = k_{31}x_1 + k_{32}x_2 + k_{33}x_3 + k_{34}x_4 + \cdots + k_{3n}x_n$$

and, in general

$$f_{sn} = k_{n1}x_1 + k_{n2}x_2 + k_{n3}x_3 + k_{n4}x_4 + \cdots + k_{nn}x_n$$

In these expressions, it has been assumed that the structural behaviour is linear so that the principle of superposition is applicable.

Let us arrange these n–equations in matrix form:

$$\begin{Bmatrix} f_{s1} \\ f_{s2} \\ \vdots \\ f_{sn} \end{Bmatrix} = \begin{bmatrix} k_{11} & k_{12} & \cdots\cdots & x_{1n} \\ k_{21} & \cdots & \cdots & \cdots \\ \cdots & \cdots & \cdots & \cdots \\ k_{n1} & \cdots & \cdots & k_{nn} \end{bmatrix} \begin{Bmatrix} x_1 \\ x_2 \\ \vdots \\ x_n \end{Bmatrix} \tag{10.9a}$$

or,

$$\{f_s\}_{n\times 1} = [K]_{n\times n}\{X\}_{n\times 1} \tag{10.9b}$$

where

$[K]$ is matrix of stiffness influence coefficients of size $n \times n$.

$\{X\}$ is a displacement vector of size $n \times 1$

10.4.2 Damping Force

If it is assumed that damping depends on the velocity, that is, if it is a viscous type damping, the influence coefficients for damping force can be evaluated in the same manner as for the elastic force.

At node 1, let us apply a unit velocity and determine the damping force produced at each of the remaining $(n - 1)$ degrees of freedom. That is, let us determine the *influence coefficients for damping* c_{ij}

where c_{ij} = force produced at node i due to unit velocity imposed at node j.

The same procedure is repeated at each of the remaining $(n - 1)$ nodes. The final expression can be written in matrix form similar to Equation (10.9).

$$\begin{Bmatrix} f_{d1} \\ f_{d2} \\ f_{d3} \\ \vdots \\ f_{dn} \end{Bmatrix} = \begin{bmatrix} c_{11} & c_{12} & c_{13} & \cdots\cdots & c_{1n} \\ c_{21} & \cdots & \cdots & \cdots & \cdots \\ \vdots & \cdots & \cdots & \cdots & \cdots \\ \vdots & \cdots & \cdots & \cdots & \cdots \\ c_{n1} & \cdots & \cdots & \cdots & c_{nn} \end{bmatrix} \begin{Bmatrix} \dot{x}_1 \\ \dot{x}_2 \\ \dot{x}_3 \\ \vdots \\ \dot{x}_n \end{Bmatrix} \tag{10.10a}$$

or,

$$\{f_D\}_{n\times 1} = [C]_{n\times n}\{\dot{X}\}_{n\times 1} \tag{10.10b}$$

where

[C] is matrix of damping influence coefficients of size $n \times n$.

$\{\dot{X}\}$ is a velocity vector of size $n \times 1$

10.4.3 Inertia Force

The inertia forces may also be expressed by a set of influence coefficients similar to elastic force and damping force coefficients. At node 1, let us apply a unit acceleration and determine the inertia force produced at each of the remaining $(n - 1)$ degrees of freedom. That is, let us determine the *influence coefficients for inertia* m_{ij}
where

m_{ij} = force corresponding to node i due to unit acceleration imposed at node j.

By analogy with damping forces:

$$\begin{Bmatrix} f_{i1} \\ f_{i2} \\ \vdots \\ f_{in} \end{Bmatrix} = \begin{bmatrix} m_{11} & m_{12} & m_{13} & \ldots\ldots m_{1n} \\ m_{21} & \ldots & \ldots & \ldots \\ \ldots & \ldots & \ldots & \ldots \\ m_{n1} & \ldots & \ldots & \ldots\ldots m_{nn} \end{bmatrix} \begin{Bmatrix} \ddot{x}_1 \\ \ddot{x}_2 \\ \vdots \\ \ddot{x}_n \end{Bmatrix} \tag{10.11a}$$

where

$$\{f_I\}_{n\times 1} = [M]_{n\times n}\{\ddot{X}\}_{n\times 1} \tag{10.11b}$$

where

$[M]$ is matrix of mass influence coefficients of size $n \times n$.

$\{\ddot{X}\}$ is acceleration vector of size $n \times 1$

By substituting the values in Equation (10.8), the equation of motion becomes:

$$[M]_{n\times n}\{\ddot{X}(t)\}_{n\times 1} + [C]_{n\times n}\{\dot{X}(t)\}_{n\times 1} + [K]_{n\times n}\{X(t)\}_{n\times 1} = \{p(t)\}_{n\times 1} \tag{10.12a}$$

This equation can also be written as follows:

$$\boldsymbol{M\ddot{X} + C\dot{X} + KX = P(t)} \tag{10.12b}$$

where, the capital and bold letters ***M*, *C*** and ***K*** represents matrices, bold and capital letters ***X***, $\dot{\boldsymbol{X}}$ and $\ddot{\boldsymbol{X}}$ represents displacement, velocity and acceleration vectors; and ***P*** represents a force vector.

In Chapter 6, the equation of motion for a SDOF system subjected to earthquake force was derived as follows:

$$m\,\ddot{x}_r(t) + c\,\dot{x}_r(t) + k\,x_r(t) = -m\ddot{y}_g(t) \tag{6.49b}$$

where, $x_r(t)$ is relative displacement.

Equation (10.12a) can be written in the form of Equation (6.49b) as follows:

$$[M]_{n\times n}\left\{\ddot{X}_r(t)\right\}+[C]_{n\times n}\left\{\dot{X}_r(t)\right\}+[K]_{n\times n}\left\{X_r(t)\right\}=-[M]_{n\times n}\{I\}_{n\times 1}\ddot{y}_g(t) \tag{10.12c}$$

Here $\ddot{y}_g(t)$ is an array of ground accelerations with time. For a given time t, it is a scalar quantity.

The nature of mass matrix, damping matrix and stiffness matrix, whether they are diagonal, banded, full, and real or complex, will depend upon the physical problem. In any case, one thing is for certain. The stiffness matrix will always be a coupled matrix. The mass and damping matrices may be coupled or uncoupled. The solution of equation of motion will depend upon the nature of its constituents and size 'n'.

10.4.4 Solution of the Coupled Equations of Motion

The equation of motion for a MDOF system (Equation (10.12)) can be solved using any of the direct integration methods. Some of them were discussed in Chapter 7. One has to select the most efficient algorithm to suit the given problem. Depending upon the problem, all the supports may be subjected to the same earthquake induced ground motion or different supports may be subjected to different ground motions or multicomponent ground motions. The formulation in Equation (10.12c) is applicable to a single ground motion. It will need modification, if the system is subjected to multiple support excitations.

Time-History Analysis

Selection of accelerogram is a tedious issue in the absence of any or sufficient earthquake records available for a given site. It is recommended that at least three pairs of accelerograms with three components each in the three orthogonal directions of natural or artificial earthquakes should be selected. These accelerograms may be modified to be compatible with the design response spectra as specified in the code.

This solution will provide *displacement – time, velocity – time and acceleration – time history* at all the active DOFs. Knowing the member stiffnesses, it is possible to determine the member internal force – time histories, that is, axial force, shear force, bending moments etc. as a function of time t. The interpretation of the results is likely to be tricky. It is also possible to determine the *absolute positive and negative values* of each response quantity for each member for use in its design. The negative values indicate change in direction of an earthquake. These are precisely the reasons as to why a time-history analysis of a MDOF system is carried out only in special situations.

Eigenvalue Analysis

Besides the various response time histories of a MDOF system, it is also of interest to determine its frequencies or periods and mode shapes in various modes which provide a very useful insight into its dynamic characteristics. It should be remembered that size 'n' of the problem may vary from two to several thousand. Depending upon the problem, it may not be necessary to determine all the n-frequencies and mode shapes. The fundamental frequency or fundamental periods are the most significant parameters.

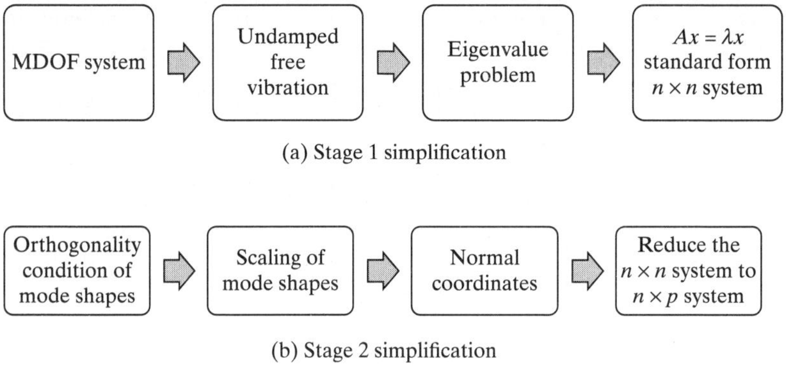

Figure 10.5 Flow diagram of simplification of a MDOF system

Next, it may be sufficient to determine a few lowest frequencies and also a few highest frequencies along with the corresponding mode shapes. Thus, a complete band of frequencies will be available.

The various stages of simplification of a MDOF system are shown in the flow diagram in Figure 10.5.

The determination of natural frequencies and mode shapes of a MDOF system will be discussed in the next section.

10.5 UNDAMPED FREE VIBRATION ANALYSIS

The equation of motion for a freely vibrating undamped system can be obtained by omitting the damping matrix and applied load vector.

$$[M]_{n\times n}\{\ddot{X}\}_{n\times 1}+[K]_{n\times n}\{X\}_{n\times 1}=\{0\}_{n\times 1} \tag{10.13a}$$

or,

$$\boldsymbol{M\ddot{X}}+\boldsymbol{KX}=\boldsymbol{0} \tag{10.13b}$$

The problem of vibration analysis consists of determining the condition under which Equation (10.13) will permit motion to occur. By analogy with SDF systems, it will be assumed that the free vibration motion is simple harmonic, that is

$$\{X(t)\}=\{X_0\}\cos(\omega t+\theta) \tag{10.14a}$$

$$\therefore \quad \{\ddot{X}(t)\}=-\omega^2\{X_0\}\cos(\omega t+\theta)=-\omega^2\{X(t)\} \tag{10.14b}$$

Equation (10.13) can be written as

$$-\omega^2 M\{X_0\}\cos(\omega t+\theta)+K\{X_0\}\cos(\omega t+\theta)=\{0\}$$

or,

$$\left[[K]-\omega^2[M]\right]\{X_0\}=\{0\} \tag{10.15}$$

since $\cos(\omega t+\theta)\neq 0$

Hence, non-trivial solution of Equation (10.15) is possible only if determinant $|K-\omega^2 M|$ vanishes.

or,
$$\det \left|[K]-\omega^2 [M]\right| = 0 \tag{10.16}$$

Re-writing Equation (10.15) as
$$[K]_{n\times n}\{X_0\}_{n\times 1} = \omega^2 [M]_{n\times n}\{X_0\}_{n\times 1} \tag{10.17}$$

or,
$$[M]^{-1}_{n\times n}[K]_{n\times n}\{X_0\}_{n\times 1} = \omega^2 \{X_0\}_{n\times 1} \tag{10.18}$$

or,
$$[A]_{n\times n}\{\phi\}_{n\times 1} = \lambda\{\phi\}_{n\times 1} \tag{10.19a}$$

or,
$$\boldsymbol{A\phi} = \boldsymbol{\lambda\phi} \tag{10.19b}$$

where
$$[A]_{n\times n} = [M]^{-1}_{n\times n}[K]_{n\times n} \text{ and } \lambda = \omega^2 \tag{10.20}$$

$[A]$ = coefficient matrix of size $n \times n$
λ = eigenvalue, a scalar quantity, size 1×1
$\{\phi\}$ = eigenvector corresponding to eigenvalue λ.

Equation (10.19) is known as the *characteristic eigenvalue equation*.

Alternatively, consider Equation (10.17)
$$[K]_{n\times n}\{X_0\}_{n\times 1} = \omega^2 [M]_{n\times n}\{X_0\}_{n\times 1}$$

or,
$$\{X_0\}_{n\times 1} = \omega^2 [K]^{-1}_{n\times n}[M]_{n\times n}\{X_0\}_{n\times 1}$$

or,
$$[K]^{-1}_{n\times n}[M]_{n\times n}\{X_0\}_{n\times 1} = \frac{1}{\omega^2}\{X_0\}_{n\times 1} \tag{10.21}$$

$$[A]_{n\times n}\{\phi\}_{n\times 1} = \lambda\{\phi\}_{n\times 1} \tag{10.22a}$$

or,
$$\boldsymbol{A\phi} = \boldsymbol{\lambda\phi} \tag{10.22b}$$

where
$$[A]_{n\times n} = [K]^{-1}_{n\times n}[M]_{n\times n} \text{ and } \lambda = \frac{1}{\omega^2} \tag{10.23}$$

$[A]$ = coefficient matrix of size $n \times n$
λ = eigenvalue, a scalar quantity, size 1×1
$\{\phi\}$ = eigenvector corresponding to eigenvalue λ.

Equation (10.22) is known as the *characteristic eigenvalue equation*.

There are several standard solutions for this equation depending upon the characteristics of [A]. In Equation (10.19a), the coefficient matrix A consists of product of stiffness matrix K pre-multiplied by the inverse of mass matrix M; and the eigenvalue λ consists of ω^2. In Equation (10.22a), the coefficient matrix A consists of product of mass matrix M pre-multiplied by the inverse of stiffness matrix K; and the eigenvalue λ consists of $1/\omega^2$. Again, matrix A may be symmetric or unsymmetric, full or sparse, real or complex, banded or tri-diagonal, etc. It may be positive definite or not.

The solution of the characteristic eigenvalue problem, Equations (10.19) or (10.22), provides 'n' eigenvalues and corresponding to each eigenvalue λ_i, an eigenvector $\{\phi\}_{n\times 1}$. In turn, eigenvalue λ leads to natural frequency ω and eigenvector $\{\phi\}$ leads to mode shapes of free vibration of the MDOF system. If there are n eigenvalues, λ_1, λ_2, λ_3, etc., there will be 'n', eigenvectors $\{\phi\}$ each of size $n \times 1$. Let us write each of these n-eigenvectors column-wise in a single matrix Φ as follows:

$$[\Phi]_{n\times n} = \left[\{\phi_1\}_{n\times 1} \quad \{\phi_2\}_{n\times 1} \quad \{\phi_3\}_{n\times 1} \quad \cdots \quad \{\phi_n\}_{n\times 1}\right]_{n\times n} \tag{10.24}$$

Thus, Equation (10.24) is a square matrix of size $n \times n$.

It can be shown that for *real, symmetric, positive definite* mass and stiffness matrices which pertain to a stable structural system, all roots of the characteristic equation will always be real and positive. It is only then the frequency, which is given by square root of the eigenvalue λ, will be real and positive.

The solution of Equation (10.19) by power method leads to the highest eigenvalue, that is, highest frequency of vibration or lowest period. Similarly, the solution of Equation (10.22) by the power method leads to the highest eigenvalue, that is, lowest frequency of vibration or highest period. The lowest frequency of vibration is referred to as the *fundamental frequency of vibration*. Similarly, the highest period is referred to as the *fundamental period of vibration*.

10.5.1 Solution of Eigenvalue Problem

There are several algorithms for the solution of an eigenvalue problem depending upon the characteristics of the coefficient matrix A. Some of these algorithms are as follows:

1. Iterative Methods
   (a) Power method
   (b) Matrix deflation method
   (c) Inverse iteration method
2. Transformation-cum-Iterative Methods
   (a) Jacobi method
   (b) Given's method
   (c) Householder method
   (d) LR or QR method

3. For Very Large Systems
   (a) Determinant search technique
   (b) Subspace iteration method

Given's method and Householder method transform an $n \times n$ coefficient matrix in a tri-diagonal matrix. The eigenvalues of a tri-diagonal matrix are same as those of the original matrix. However, its eigenvectors are different. The eigenvalues of a tri-diagonal matrix are determined using Sturm sequence method along with Bisection or Secant iteration method.

Some of these methods will be discussed through examples in this chapter.

Basic Theorems

There are some basic theorems that are very useful in the solution of eigenvalue problems.

1. If $\lambda_1, \lambda_2, \lambda_3, \ldots, \lambda_n$ are eigenvalues of coefficient matrix A, then eigenvalues of A^k are $\lambda_1^k, \lambda_2^k, \lambda_3^k, \ldots, \lambda_n^k$
2. If coefficient matrix A is real and symmetric, all eigenvalues and eigenvectors are real. Moreover, eigenvectors corresponding to distinct eigenvalues are orthogonal.
3. If matrix A is real and positive definite, its eigenvalues will be positive.
4. Any similarity transformation PAP^{-1} or $P^{-1}AP$ applied to coefficient matrix A leaves the eigenvalues of the matrix A unchanged.
5. If A is any coefficient matrix, whose eigenvalues are all distinct, then there exists a similarity transformation such that

$$X^{-1}AX = D$$

where,

D = diagonal matrix whose diagonal elements are the eigenvalues of matrix A.
X = orthogonal matrix

10.5.2 Rayleigh's Quotient

Consider the Characteristic equation

$$\mathbf{A}\boldsymbol{\phi} = \lambda\boldsymbol{\phi}$$

Pre-multiply with $\boldsymbol{\phi}^T$

$$\boldsymbol{\phi}^T \mathbf{A}\boldsymbol{\phi} = \lambda\boldsymbol{\phi}^T\boldsymbol{\phi}$$

or,

$$\lambda = \frac{\phi^T A\phi}{\phi^T \phi} \tag{10.25a}$$

Alternatively,

$$\mathbf{KX} = \lambda\mathbf{MX}$$

Pre-multiplying by X^T gives

$$X^T KX = \lambda X^T MX$$

or,

$$\lambda = \frac{X^T KX}{X^T MX} \tag{10.25b}$$

The quotient λ is called *Rayleigh's quotient*. The positive definiteness of M guarantees that the denominator is non-zero.

If vector $\boldsymbol{\phi}$ or $\boldsymbol{X}$ is an eigenvector of the problem, the Rayleigh's quotient is equal to its eigenvalue λ. Moreover, the Rayleigh's quotient is bounded between its minimum and maximum eigenvalues λ_1 and λ_n.

10.5.3 Orthogonality Condition of Modes

Free vibration mode shapes $[\Phi]$ have certain special properties which are very useful in structural dynamics. These are called *orthogonality conditions*.

$$\{\phi_r\}^T_{1\times n}[M]_{n\times n}\{\phi_s\}_{n\times 1} = 0 \qquad \text{for} \qquad \omega_r \neq \omega_s \tag{10.26}$$

and

$$\{\phi_r\}^T_{1\times n}[K]_{n\times n}\{\phi_s\}_{n\times 1} = 0 \qquad \text{for} \qquad \omega_r \neq \omega_s \tag{10.27}$$

where

$\{\phi_r\}$ = r^{th} mode shape
$\{\phi_s\}$ = s^{th} mode shape

It can be seen that these equations lead to a scalar product.

These two equations represent that vibrating shapes are orthogonal with respect to the mass matrix as well as stiffness matrix. It means, if mass matrix $\boldsymbol{M}$ is pre-multiplied by mode shape vector in r^{th} mode and post-multiplied by mode shape vector in the sth mode, this scalar product will be a zero. Similarly, if stiffness matrix $\boldsymbol{K}$ is pre-multiplied by mode shape vector in r^{th} mode and post-multiplied by mode shape vector in the sth mode, this scalar product will be a zero.

Proof

Let us consider Equation (10.17)

$$[K]_{n\times n}\{X_0\}_{n\times 1} = \omega^2[M]_{n\times n}\{X_0\}_{n\times 1} \tag{10.17}$$

Let us write it for the rth mode

$$[K]\{\phi_r\} = \omega_r^2[M]\{\phi_r\} \tag{10.28}$$

where

ϕ_r = r^{th} mode shape
ω_r = r^{th} frequency

Pre-multiply Equation (10.28) by s^{th} mode shape vector ϕ_s^T, that is, by transposing dimensional compatibility,

$$\{\phi_s\}^T[K]\{\phi_r\} = \omega_r^2\{\phi_s\}^T[M]\{\phi_r\} \tag{10.29}$$

Similarly, let us consider Equation (10.17) for the sth mode shape and pre-multiply it by r^{th} mode shape vector

$$\{\phi_r\}^T[K]\{\phi_s\} = \omega_s^2\{\phi_r\}^T[M]\{\phi_s\} \tag{10.30}$$

Let us re-write Equation (10.29) by taking transpose of both sides as follows:

$$\left[\{\phi_s\}^T[K]\{\phi_r\}\right]^T = \omega_r^2\left[\{\phi_s\}^T[M]\{\phi_r\}\right]^T \tag{10.31}$$

or, it can be written as

$$\{\phi_r\}^T[K]^T\{\phi_s\} = \omega_r^2\{\phi_r\}^T[M]^T\{\phi_s\} \tag{10.32}$$

In structural engineering problems, mass matrix and stiffness matrix are always symmetric for a stable structural system, therefore, Equation (10.32) can be written as:

$$\{\phi_r\}^T[K]\{\phi_s\} = \omega_r^2\{\phi_r\}^T[M]\{\phi_s\} \tag{10.33}$$

Therefore, Equations (10.30) and (10.33) must be equal

$$\omega_s^2\{\phi_r\}^T[M]\{\phi_s\} = \omega_r^2\{\phi_r\}^T[M]\{\phi_s\}$$

or,

$$\left(\omega_s^2 - \omega_r^2\right)\left[\{\phi_r\}^T[M]\{\phi_s\}\right] = 0$$

If the frequencies ω_r and ω_s are not equal, then it follows that

$$\{\phi_r\}^T[M]\{\phi_s\} = 0 \qquad \text{for} \qquad \omega_r \neq \omega_s \tag{10.34}$$

This proves orthogonality of mode shapes in r^{th} and s^{th} modes with respect to mass matrix.

Similarly, orthogonality of mode shapes in r^{th} and s^{th} modes with respect to stiffness matrix can be proved. This is a very crucial property for decoupling the equations of motion in a MDOF system.

The orthogonality of natural modes implies that the following matrices are diagonal:

$$[\Phi]^T[K][\Phi] = \left[\bar{K}\right]$$

also

$$[\Phi]^T[M][\Phi] = \left[\bar{M}\right]$$

where the diagonal elements are given by

$$k_r = \phi_r^T[K]\phi_r \tag{10.35a}$$

and

$$m_r = \phi_r^T[M]\phi_r \tag{10.35b}$$

Since both mass and stiffness matrices are positive definite, the diagonal elements of K and M are positive. They are related by

$$k_r = m_r\omega_r^2 \tag{10.35c}$$

10.5.4 Normalization of Modes

It should be noted that the vibration mode shapes or mode amplitudes obtained from eigen problem solution are arbitrary; any amplitude will satisfy the characteristic of Equation (10.19) or (10.22). The eigen solution is usually carried out iteratively, and in this process, the eigenvectors keep growing due to numerical calculations. If not checked, it may lead to numerical instability of the solution. It also follows that if any vector ϕ satisfies Equation (10.19) or (10.22), any other vector which is proportional to ϕ will also satisfy it.

Hence, it is usual to normalize mode shapes so that

$$\{\phi_r\}^T [M]\{\phi_r\} = 1 \tag{10.36}$$

It can be done by computing a scale factor S_r for r th mode,

$$\{\hat{\phi}_r\}^T [M]\{\hat{\phi}_r\} = S_r \tag{10.37}$$

where $\{\hat{\phi}_r\}$ represents an arbitrarily determined r th modal amplitude.

Now, normalized mode shape is given as

$$\{\phi_r\} = \frac{\{\hat{\phi}_r\}}{\sqrt{S_r}} \tag{10.38}$$

Thus,

$$[\Phi]^T [M][\Phi] = I \tag{10.36}$$

where, I = identity matrix

Equation (10.36) states that the natural modes are not only orthogonal but also normalized with respect to mass. Mode shapes normalized in this fashion are said to be *orthonormal* relative to the mass matrix. These are called *orthonormal mode shapes.*

When the modes are normalized in this manner, Equation (10.35c) can be written as follows:

$$k_r = m_r\omega_r^2 = \omega_r^2 \tag{10.39}$$

10.6 TRANSFORMATION OF EIGENVALUE PROBLEM TO STANDARD FORM

Let us again consider Equations (10.19) and (10.20)

$$\boldsymbol{A}\phi = \lambda\phi \tag{10.19b}$$

where

$$[A]_{n\times n} = [M]^{-1}_{n\times n}[K]_{n\times n} \text{ and } \lambda = \omega^2 \tag{10.20}$$

The mass matrix $\boldsymbol{M}$ and the stiffness matrix $\boldsymbol{K}$ are generally both symmetric in structural engineering problems but the product $\boldsymbol{A}$ given by Equation (10.20) or (10.23) in general is not symmetric. Although Equation (10.19b) or Equation (10.22b) is a standard eigenvalue problem for which many computer codes are readily available, due to unsymmetric nature of matrix $\boldsymbol{A}$, the computational efforts are increased significantly. Let us try to arrive at a symmetric matrix $\boldsymbol{A}$. Consider a diagonal mass matrix $\boldsymbol{M}$ which is positive definite. It means its inverse exists.

Define $M = M^{1/2}M^{1/2}$ (10.40)

or,

$$I = M^{1/2}M^{-1/2} = M^{-1/2}M^{1/2} \tag{10.41}$$

Consider Equation (10.17)

$$[K]_{n\times n}\{X_0\}_{n\times 1} = \omega^2[M]_{n\times n}\{X_0\}_{n\times 1} \tag{10.17}$$

or,

$$\boldsymbol{K\phi} = \omega^2\boldsymbol{M\phi} \tag{10.42}$$

This can be re-written as follows:

$$\boldsymbol{KM^{-1/2}M^{1/2}\phi} = \omega^2\boldsymbol{M^{1/2}M^{1/2}\phi}$$

Pre-multiplying both sides by $\boldsymbol{M^{-1/2}}$ gives

$$\boldsymbol{M^{-1/2}KM^{-1/2}M^{1/2}\phi} = \omega^2\boldsymbol{M^{-1/2}M^{1/2}M^{1/2}\phi} \tag{10.43}$$

or,

$$\boldsymbol{By} = \lambda\boldsymbol{y} \tag{10.44}$$

where

$$\boldsymbol{B} = \boldsymbol{M^{-1/2}KM^{-1/2}} \tag{10.45a}$$

$$\boldsymbol{y} = \boldsymbol{M^{1/2}\phi} \tag{10.45b}$$

and

$$\lambda = \omega^2$$

Equation (10.44) is a standard eigenvalue problem and coefficient matrix B is now symmetric.

10.7 NORMAL COORDINATES

For most applications, there is no need to compute all the n frequencies as well as mode shapes as it may be computationally very expensive. The determination of first few lowest frequencies is generally sufficient in many cases. The normal coordinates serve to uncouple the damped MDOF equations of motion. Let us assume that we need to consider only the lowest p modes out of total n modes in any MDOF system. These p modes will be sequential from mode 1 to p.

The displacement vector $\{X\}_{n\times 1}$ can be written as follows:

$$\{X\}_{n\times 1} = [\Phi]_{n\times p}\{Y\}_{p\times 1} \tag{10.46}$$

or,

$$X = \Phi Y$$

where

$\{X\}$ = displacement vector of size $n \times 1$
Φ = mode shape matrix of size $n \times p$
$\{Y\}$ = displacement vector in generalized or normal coordinates, size $p \times 1$
p = number of desired modes $\leq n$

Thus, the total displacement $\{X\}$ is obtained as the sum of the modal components. In this equation, the mode shape matrix Φ serves to transform *generalized coordinates* $\{Y\}_{p\times 1}$ to the *geometric coordinates* $\{X\}_{n\times 1}$. The generalized coordinates $\{Y\}$ are called the *normal coordinates* of the structure.

10.8 UNCOUPLED EQUATIONS OF MOTION

The equation of motion of a MDOF system is given by Equation (10.12a)

$$[M]_{n\times n}\{\ddot{X}(t)\}_{n\times 1} + [C]_{n\times n}\{\dot{X}(t)\}_{n\times 1} + [K]_{n\times n}\{X(t)\}_{n\times 1} = \{P(t)\}_{n\times 1} \tag{10.12a}$$

or,

$$\boldsymbol{M\ddot{X} + C\dot{X} + KX = P(t)} \tag{10.12b}$$

The influence coefficients for stiffness, damping and inertia forces derived earlier indicate that this equation has coupled terms. Therefore, Equation (10.12a) will have to be solved simultaneously, which is a very tedious task. It is possible to decouple this equation with the help of normal coordinates and orthogonality conditions derived in the previous sections as shown in Figure 10.6. These decoupled equations essentially represent a set of SDOF systems that can be solved using the results derived in Chapters 2, 3 and 7.

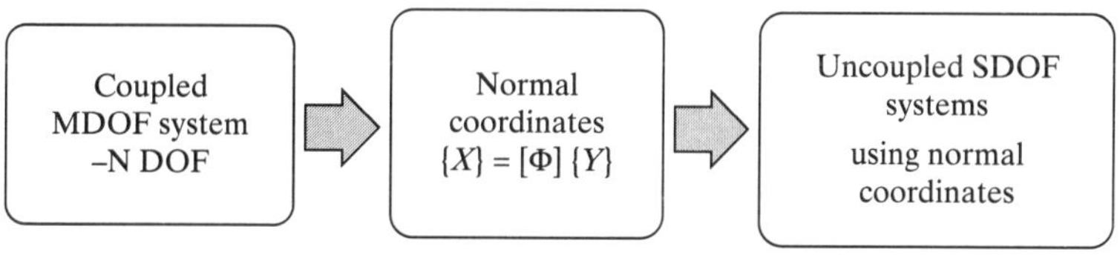

Figure 10.6 Deriving uncoupled SDOF systems from coupled MDOF system

Let us substitute Equation (10.46) in Equation (10.12b)

$$M\Phi\ddot{Y} + C\Phi\dot{Y} + K\Phi Y = P(t)$$

Pre-multiply it by the transpose of the modal shape vector Φ^T,

$$\Phi^T M\Phi\ddot{Y} + \Phi^T C\Phi\dot{Y} + \Phi^T K\Phi Y = \Phi^T P(t) \tag{10.47a}$$

where

$$\Phi^T M \Phi = \Phi^T_{p\times n} M_{n\times n} \Phi_{n\times p} = M_{p\times p}$$

Similarly, damping and stiffness terms can be written.

$$M_{p\times p}\ddot{Y}_{p\times 1} + C_{p\times p}\dot{Y}_{p\times 1} + K_{p\times p}Y_{p\times 1} = \Phi^T_{p\times n}P(t)_{n\times 1} \tag{10.47b}$$

The set of n equations of motion are now reduced to a set of p equations, where p is the desired number of modes considered for the reduced MDOF system. This is referred to as the modal equation of motion.

Orthogonality condition gives

$$\phi_r^T M \phi_s = 0 \quad \text{for} \quad \omega_r \neq \omega_s \tag{10.26}$$

and

$$\phi_r^T K \phi_s = 0 \quad \text{for} \quad \omega_r \neq \omega_s \tag{10.27}$$

ϕ_r = r^{th} mode shape vector, size $n \times 1$
ϕ_s = s^{th} mode shape vector, size $n \times 1$

It is assumed that similar orthogonality relation applies to damping also, provided it is a classical damping

$$\phi_r^T C \phi_s = 0 \quad \text{for} \quad \omega_r \neq \omega_s \tag{10.48}$$

After applying all the orthogonality conditions Equations (10.26), (10.27) and (10.48) in Equation (10.47b), all the terms for mass, stiffness and damping in Equation (10.47b) for which $r \neq s$ will vanish. Therefore, Equation (10.47b) will be reduced to equation of a SDOF system for r^{th} mode:

$$m_r\ddot{y}_r + c_r\dot{y}_r + k_r y_r = p_r(t) \tag{10.49a}$$

where

$$m_r = \phi_r^T M \phi_r \tag{10.49b}$$

Similarly,

$$C_r = \phi_r^T C \phi_r = 2 m_r \omega_r \xi_r \tag{10.49c}$$

and

$$k_r = \phi_r^T K \phi_r = \omega_r^2 m_r \tag{10.49d}$$

where

m_r = generalized mass
c_r = generalized damping
k_r = generalized stiffness
p_r = generalized force = $\phi_r^T P(t)_{n\times 1}$

Equation (10.49a) is the decoupled modal equation of motion of the MDOF system for r^{th} mode. This is equation of a SDOF system since all quantities are scalar. This equation of motion can also be written as:

$$\ddot{y}_r + 2\xi_r\omega_r\,\dot{y}_r + \omega_r^2 y_r = \frac{p_r(t)}{m_r} \tag{10.50}$$

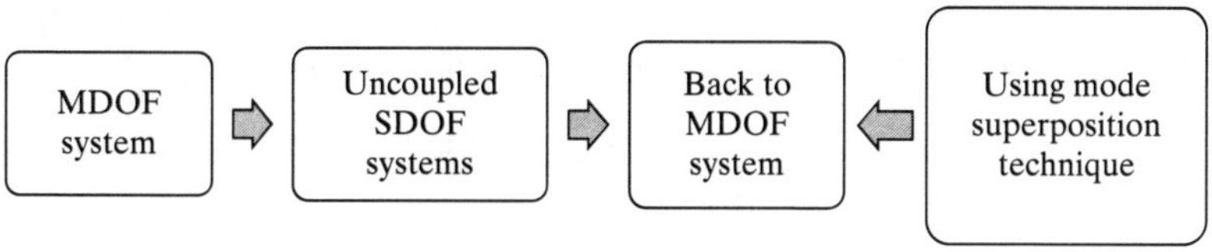

Figure 10.7 Mode superposition technique

where ξ_r = modal damping

Thus, we get p decoupled or independent equations of motion for the p modes. The desired number of modes, p, may be selected equal to the total active degrees of freedom, n, in order to work on the full set of decoupled equations. Alternatively, the desired number of modes, p, may be selected less than n for a reduced but reasonable accuracy. These SDOF equations of motion can be solved by any method discussed earlier. Knowing the generalized displacement in each mode, the geometric displacements can be obtained by making use of normal coordinate transformation in Equation (10.46). This method to obtain the response is referred to as the *mode superposition method* (Figure 10.7). This entire procedure from decoupling the equations of motion and then to find the total response is referred to as the *modal analysis*.

There are two options for carrying out an eigenvector analysis to determine the mode shapes:

- Eigenvalue analysis determines the undamped free vibration mode shapes and frequencies of the system. These can be used for the mode superposition based analytical methods.
- Ritz vector analysis seeks to find modes that are excited by a particular loading. Ritz vectors can provide a better solution than do the eigenvector analysis when used for mode superposition based response spectrum analysis (RSA) or modal time-history analysis (MTHA).

The reason that the Ritz vectors offer better results is that they are generated by taking into account the spatial distribution of the dynamic loading. The natural mode shapes obtained from the eigenvalue analysis lack this feature. Moreover, the Ritz vector algorithm automatically includes the advantages of the numerical techniques of static condensation, and static correction due to higher mode truncation. However, the selection of Ritz vectors carries its own complications. In the present text, only the eigenvalue analysis is discussed.

10.9 SOLUTION OF UNDAMPED FREE VIBRATION ANALYSIS

Once the equations of motion of a MDOF system have been decoupled, it is convenient to determine the solution for undamped free vibration analysis. It was shown in Chapter 2 that for a SDOF system,

$$x(t) = A\sin\omega t + B\cos\omega t$$

or, $$x(t) = \frac{\dot{x}(0)}{\omega}\sin\omega t + x(0)\cos\omega t$$

These equations can be written for the decoupled equations of motion for a set of 'n' SDOF systems.

Let us consider $$\{X\}_{n\times 1} = [\Phi]_{n\times p}\{Y\}_{p\times 1} \tag{10.46}$$

It is possible to evaluate $\{Y\}_{p\times 1}$. Let us multiply both sides by $\boldsymbol{\phi}_r^T \boldsymbol{m}$

$$\{\phi_r\}^T[M]\{X\} = \{\phi_r\}^T[M]_{n\times n}[\Phi]_{n\times p}\{Y\}_{p\times 1}$$

Due to orthogonality condition, this equation will be reduced to

$$\{\phi_r\}^T[M]\{X\} = \{\phi_r\}^T[M]_{n\times n}\{\phi_r\}y_r$$

Thus, $$y_r = \frac{\{\phi_r\}^T[M]\{X\}}{\{\phi_r\}^T[M]_{n\times n}\{\phi_r\}} \tag{10.51}$$

For initial conditions, it can be written as:

$$y_r(0) = \frac{\phi_r^T[M]\{x(0)\}}{\phi_r^T M\phi_r} \tag{10.52a}$$

and

$$\dot{y}_r(0) = \frac{\phi_r^T[M]\{\dot{x}(0)\}}{\phi_r^T M\phi_r} \tag{10.52b}$$

By making use of Equation (10.46), the initial displacement and velocity can also be written as:

$$x(0) = \sum_{r=1}^{n}\phi_r y_r(0) \tag{10.53a}$$

and $$\dot{x}(0) = \sum_{r=1}^{n}\phi_r \dot{y}_r(0) \tag{10.53b}$$

Final solution is given by

$$x(t) = \sum_{r=1}^{n}\phi_r y_r(t) \tag{10.54a}$$

where $$y_r(t) = y_r(0)\cos\omega_r t + \frac{\dot{y}_r(0)}{\omega_r}\sin\omega_r t \tag{10.54b}$$

10.10 SOLUTION OF THE UNCOUPLED EQUATIONS OF MOTION

The solution of the *uncoupled equations of motion* for earthquake ground motion is of utmost importance in structural dynamics. There are two solution techniques:

1. Response Spectrum Analysis (RSA) or Modal analysis (MA) (approximate)
2. Modal Time – History Analysis (MTHA)
   - Numerical integration of FULL SET of *decoupled* equations
   - Numerical integration of PARTIAL SET of *decoupled* equations (approximate)

Remember, the time-history analysis can also be carried out directly on the coupled equations of motion for earthquake ground motion using any of the direct integration methods discussed earlier.

The *response spectrum analysis* (RSA) is carried out in three steps:

- Select a desired response spectrum for the given site based on seismology and geotechnical considerations. Alternatively, use the response spectrum specified in the code.
- Compute the earthquake force for the desired number of modes and at the desired degrees of freedom
- Static analysis of the MDOF system due to the computed earthquake force to obtain the member forces and displacements etc. for the desired number of modes, and then superimpose the modal response to obtain the total response.

The *modal time – history analysis* (MTHA) is carried out in three steps:

- Select or generate an appropriate set of earthquake ground motion time – history for the site under consideration. The selection criteria are available in building and other codes.
- Carry out a time – history analysis for each decoupled equation of motion of a SDOF system for a given set of earthquake ground motion;
- Next, carry out mode superposition of the response across all the desired modes.

For most structures, the contributions of the various modes generally are greatest for the lowest frequencies and tend to decrease for the higher frequencies except under certain conditions. Consequently, it is not necessary to include all modes of vibration in the superposition process. The series of Equation (10.46) can be truncated when the response has been obtained to any desired degree of accuracy.

The modal time – history analysis procedure will be explained with the help of Example 10.15.

Let us develop the response spectrum analysis procedure to determine the response of a structure due to earthquake ground motion *identical at all supports*. The decoupled equation of motion can be written as follows:

$$m_r\ddot{y}_r + c_r\dot{y}_r + k_r y_r = \phi_r^T p(t) = -\phi_r^T MI\ddot{y}_g(t) \tag{10.55a}$$

where, $\ddot{y}_g(t)$ is ground acceleration – time history

The vector I represents a vector of influence coefficients. The i-th element of vector I represents the displacement of ith degree of freedom due to a unit displacement of the base of the structure. It demonstrates that a unit static translation of the base of a structure produces directly a unit displacement of all degrees of freedom.

It is, therefore, a unit vector. This simple relationship is a consequence of the type of support displacement which has been applied as well as of the structural configuration of a multistorey building. For other forms of structures this influence coefficient or static displacement vector would be different.

$$p(t) = -MI\ddot{y}_g(t) \tag{10.56}$$

Equation (10.55a) can be re-written as follows:

$$\ddot{y}_r + 2\xi_r\omega_r\dot{y}_r + \omega_r^2 y_r = \frac{\bar{m}}{m_r}\ddot{y}_g(t) \tag{10.55b}$$

neglecting sign

The term $\bar{m}$ is defined as follows:

$$\bar{m} = \phi_r^T[M]\{I\} \tag{10.57}$$

I = identity vector, size $n \times 1$

The ratio $\dfrac{\bar{m}}{m_r}$ is defined as follows:

$$\Gamma_r = \frac{\phi_r^T[M]\{I\}}{\phi_r^T M\phi_r} \tag{10.58}$$

Where, Γ_r = modal participation factor in r-th mode

The symbol Γ is pronounced as Gamma.

For a lumped mass system or a system having diagonal mass matrix, Equation (10.58) can be written as follows:

$$\Gamma_r = \frac{\sum_{i=1}^{n} m_i\phi_i}{\sum_{i=1}^{n} m_i\phi_i^2} \tag{10.59}$$

It gives the contribution of each mode.

$$y_r = \Gamma_r S_d \tag{10.60}$$

It gives modal displacement for the rth mode.

For a SDOF, it was shown that

$$S_d = \frac{S_v}{\omega} \quad \text{or,} \quad S_v = \omega S_d \tag{8.5b}$$

Thus,

$$|y(t)|_{\max} = S_d$$

and

$$S_a = \omega^2 S_d \tag{8.8a}$$

∴ The geometric displacement vector for the rth mode is given by

$$\{x_r\} = \{\phi_r\}y_r = \{\phi_r\}\Gamma_r S_d \tag{10.61}$$

By modal superposition, the final displacement vector can be obtained.

$$\{X(t)\}_{nx1} = [\Phi]_{nxp}\{Y(t)\}_{px1} = [\Phi]_{nxp}\{\Gamma_r S_d\}_{px1} \tag{10.62}$$

It may be recalled that S_d, S_v and S_a are spectral displacement, pseudo velocity and pseudo acceleration, respectively, (Equation (8.8)). For a given natural period and viscous damping in a given mode of vibration, their values can be obtained from the corresponding response spectra. This is precisely the reason as to why this method of analysis is referred to as the *response spectrum analysis*.

Modal participation factor (MPF) – The *modal participation factor* given by Equation (10.59) has two implications:

- There are, in general, six modal participation factors corresponding to each mode shape along the six global directions of the structure – three translational and three rotational.
- It is a measure of the degree to which each i-th mode participates towards the total response.

However, this definition (Equation (10.59)) has its own drawbacks. MPF depends upon how modes are normalized. This is apparent because the modal scale factor is squared in the denominator but appears only once in the numerator. It means for the same set of mode shapes, different MPF will be obtained depending upon how the modes were normalized. Therefore, the contribution of a mode in the given direction to a response quantity will also be subjective. A negative mode shape leads to a negative MPF. Thus, interpretation of the MPF is confusing. The actual magnitude and signs of the modal participation factors are not important. What is important is the relative values of the six factors for a given mode.

In real structures, in view of the six MPF for each mode, it would be quite difficult to identify the contribution of a given mode in the given global direction. For example, it would be quite difficult to conclude if it is a translational mode in the X-direction or torsional mode or a combination thereof. One has to use his best judgement.

10.10.1 Member Forces

Elastic forces in members of the structure are given by

$$\{f_s(t)\} = [K]\{X(t)\} = [K]\,[\,\Phi\,]\,\{Y(t)\} \tag{10.63}$$

Also, we know that $[K]\,[\,\Phi\,] = [M]\,[\,\Phi\,]\,[\Omega^2]$

$$\therefore \qquad \{f_s(t)\} = [M]\,[\,\Phi\,]\,[\Omega^2]\,\{Y(t)\}$$

or,

$$\{f_s\} = [M]_{n\times n}[\Phi]_{n\times p}\{\Gamma_r \omega_r^2 S_d\}_{p\times 1} \tag{10.64}$$

or, for each mode,

$$\{f_{s,r}(t)\}_{n\times 1} = [M]_{n\times n}\{\phi_r\}_{n\times 1}\Gamma_r \omega_r^2 S_d \tag{10.65}$$

For each ith dof in the rth mode,

$$f_{i,r} = m_i \phi_r^i \Gamma_r \omega_r^2 S_d \tag{10.66a}$$

or,

$$f_{i,r} = m_i g \phi_r^i \Gamma_r \frac{S_a}{g} \tag{10.66b}$$

$$= \frac{S_a}{g} \phi_r^i \Gamma_r W_i \tag{10.67}$$

where

W_i = weight at the ith DOF
φ_r^i = r^{th} mode shape ordinate for the ith DOF

This is the same equation as that of Clause 7.7.5.4 (c) of IS:1893 part 1 Code to compute force at the ith floor in the rth mode of a building. The code accounts for seismicity, importance and ductile behaviour of a structure and modifies S_a/g with these dimensionless parameters while retaining its units.

10.10.2 Modal Mass

Let us re-consider Equation (10.64)

$$\{f_s\}_{n\times 1} = [M]_{n\times n} [\Phi]_{n\times p} \{\Gamma_r \omega_r^2 S_d\}_{p\times 1}$$

where, n = total degrees of freedom
p = number of modes considered in analysis $\leq n$
It can be written as follows:

$$\{f_s\}_{n\times 1} = [M]_{n\times n} [\Phi]_{n\times p} \{\Gamma_r S_a\}_{p\times 1} \tag{10.68}$$

Let us expand only $[M]_{n\times n} [\Phi]_{n\times p}$ for convenience

$$[M]_{n\times n} [\Phi]_{n\times p} = \begin{bmatrix} m_1 & 0 & 0 & 0 & 0 & 0 \\ 0 & m_2 & 0 & 0 & 0 & 0 \\ 0 & 0 & m_3 & 0 & 0 & 0 \\ 0 & 0 & 0 & m_i & 0 & 0 \\ 0 & 0 & 0 & 0 & m_r & 0 \\ 0 & 0 & 0 & 0 & 0 & m_n \end{bmatrix} \times \begin{bmatrix} \phi_{11} & \phi_{12} & \phi_{13} & \phi_{1i} & \phi_{1r} & \phi_{1p} \\ \phi_{21} & \phi_{22} & \phi_{23} & \phi_{2i} & \phi_{2r} & \phi_{2p} \\ \phi_{31} & \phi_{32} & \phi_{33} & \phi_{3i} & \phi_{3r} & \phi_{3p} \\ \phi_{i1} & \phi_{i2} & \phi_{i3} & \phi_{ii} & \phi_{ir} & \phi_{ip} \\ \phi_{r1} & \phi_{r2} & \phi_{r3} & \phi_{ri} & \phi_{rr} & \phi_{rp} \\ \phi_{n1} & \phi_{n2} & \phi_{n3} & \phi_{ni} & \phi_{nr} & \phi_{np} \end{bmatrix}$$

Due to the diagonal nature of mass matrix with all off-diagonals being zero, this product can be written as follows:

$$[M]_{n\times n}[\Phi]_{n\times p} = \begin{bmatrix} m_1\phi_{11} & 0 & 0 & 0 & 0 & 0 \\ 0 & m_2\phi_{22} & 0 & 0 & 0 & 0 \\ 0 & 0 & m_3\phi_{33} & 0 & 0 & 0 \\ 0 & 0 & 0 & m_i\phi_{ii} & 0 & 0 \\ 0 & 0 & 0 & 0 & m_r\phi_{rr} & 0 \\ 0 & 0 & 0 & 0 & 0 & m_n\phi_{np} \end{bmatrix}$$

Thus, Equation (10.68) becomes

$$\{f_s\}_{n\times 1} = \begin{Bmatrix} f_1 \\ f_2 \\ f_3 \\ f_i \\ f_r \\ f_n \end{Bmatrix}_{n\times 1} = \begin{bmatrix} m_1\phi_{11} & 0 & 0 & 0 & 0 & 0 \\ 0 & m_2\phi_{22} & 0 & 0 & 0 & 0 \\ 0 & 0 & m_3\phi_{33} & 0 & 0 & 0 \\ 0 & 0 & 0 & m_i\phi_{ii} & 0 & 0 \\ 0 & 0 & 0 & 0 & m_r\phi_{rr} & 0 \\ 0 & 0 & 0 & 0 & 0 & m_n\phi_{np} \end{bmatrix}_{n\times p} \left\{\sum_{i=1}^{p}\Gamma_i S_{ai}\right\}_{p\times 1}$$

The base shear can be determined by adding all the lateral forces from top downwards:

$$V_{\mathrm{Bi}} = \sum_{i=1}^{n} f_i = \left(\sum m_i\phi_i\right)\left(\Gamma_i S_{ai}\right)$$

$$V_{\mathrm{Bi}} = \left(\sum_{i=1}^{n} m_i\phi_i\right)\left(\frac{\sum_{i=1}^{n} m_i\phi_i}{\sum_{i=1}^{n} m_i\phi_i^2}(S_{ai})\right)$$

or

Base shear in i^{th} mode
$$V_{\mathrm{Bi}} = \left(\frac{\left(\sum_{i=1}^{n} m_i\phi_i\right)^2}{\sum_{i=1}^{n} m_i\phi_i^2}\right)(S_{ai}) \qquad (10.69a)$$

S_{ai} = Spectral acceleration in i^{th} mode corresponding to natural frequency ω_i and damping ξ.

The modal mass in each mode is given by

$$M_r = \left(\frac{\left(\sum_{i=1}^{n} m_i\phi_i\right)^2}{\sum_{i=1}^{n} m_i\phi_i^2}\right) \qquad (10.69b)$$

The expression for the modal mass can also be written as:

$$M_r = \frac{\left[\sum_{i=1}^{n} m_i\phi_i\right]\times\left[\sum_{i=1}^{n} m_i\phi_i\right]}{\left[\sum_{i=1}^{n} m_i\phi_i^2\right]} = \frac{\left[\sum_{i=1}^{n} m_i\phi_i\right]\times\left[\sum_{i=1}^{n} m_i\phi_i\right]}{\left[\sum_{i=1}^{n} m_i\phi_i^2\right]}\times\frac{\left[\sum_{i=1}^{n} m_i\phi_i^2\right]}{\left[\sum_{i=1}^{n} m_i\phi_i^2\right]}$$

or,

$$M_r = \Gamma^2 \times \left[\sum_{i=1}^{n} m_i\phi_i^2\right] \tag{10.69c}$$

- The sum of the effective modal mass for all modes is equal to the total structural mass.
- The value of effective modal mass is *independent* of the manner of mode shape scaling.
- Most codes require to use enough number of modes in the analysis to provide a total effective mass not less than 90% of the total structural mass.

The response of each modal SDOF system need to be determined using response spectra as shown in Figure 10.8.

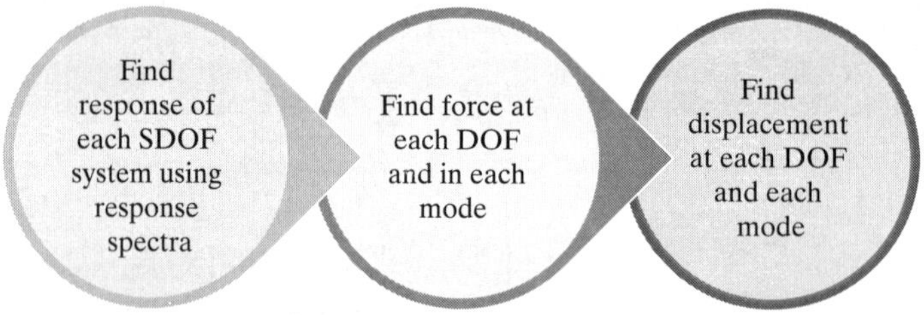

Figure 10.8 Flow diagram to find response at a given DOF

10.10.3 Mode Superposition

In the response spectrum method, there are two distinct stages to get the response. First, to determine the response in a given r^{th} mode. Second, to determine the final or total response. This second stage is referred to as the *mode superposition*. The term response refers to any parameter of interest such as displacement, axial force, shear force, bending moment, storey shear and support reactions. The response spectrum method gives the maximum response or value of a given parameter for each mode. It must then be superimposed to get the total response. The maximum or minimum value of a given parameter in each mode occurs at a different time. If the absolute value of each modal maxima is added numerically, obviously, it will lead to a very conservative upper bound. This assumes that each maxima or minima occurs at the same time which is not true.

$$\Lambda = |\Lambda_1| + |\Lambda_2| + |\Lambda_3| + |\Lambda_4| + \ldots + |\Lambda_n| \tag{10.70}$$

Therefore the absolute sum ABSSUM modal combination rule is not used in structural dynamics

The other alternative is to make use of a probable value of the maximum response, which can be obtained by taking the *square root of the sum of the squares* (SRSS) of a given parameter.

$$\Lambda = \sqrt{\Lambda_1^2 + \Lambda_2^2 + \Lambda_3^2 + \ldots \Lambda_n^2} \tag{10.71}$$

where the symbol Λ is read as lambda.

This is also referred to as the SRSS value of a given parameter. This is based on the assumption that modal components are random variables which is consistent with the random nature of the input, that is earthquake motion. The accuracy of the SRSS value will increase with the increase in number of modes. The SRSS value is recommended by most building codes.

10.10.4 Closely Spaced Modes

In many practical situations, it has been observed that natural frequencies in any two consecutive modes may be equal or very close to each other. The SRSS method of superposition does not give correct estimation of the total response in such situations. Therefore, another method known as *complete quadratic combination* (CQC) method is used. It can be stated as follows:

$$\Lambda = \sqrt{\sum_{i=1}^{r}\sum_{j=1}^{r}\Lambda_i \rho_{ij} \Lambda_j} \tag{10.72}$$

where

r = number of modes being considered
Λ_i = response quantity in i^{th} mode with sign
Λ_j = response quantity in j^{th} mode with sign
ρ_{ij} = cross-correlation coefficient

$$\rho_{ij} = \frac{8\xi^2 (1+\beta)\beta^{1.5}}{\left(1-\beta^2\right)^2 + 4\xi^2\beta(1+\beta)^2} \tag{10.73}$$

β = frequency ratio = ω_i/ω_j
ξ = damping ratio

Any two consecutive modes are treated as closely spaced if the difference in the frequencies is less than 10%.

A plot of the cross-correlation parameter is shown in Figure 10.9 to demonstrate its physical meaning. The CQC method is recommended by most building codes for closely spaced modes.

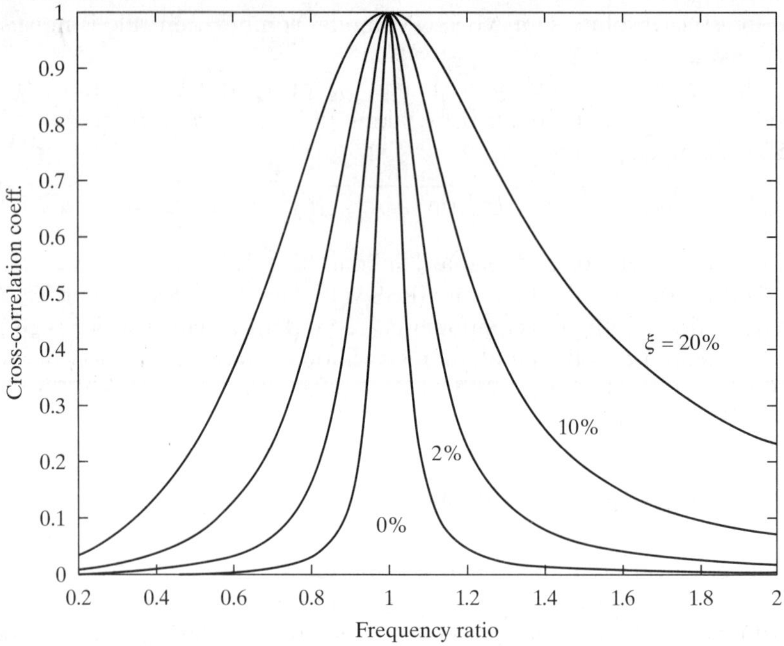

Figure 10.9 Variation of cross-correlation coefficient with frequency ratio and damping.

10.10.5 Minimum Number of Modes

Ideally the response contribution of all the modes must be accounted for in the mode superposition method to obtain an accurate result. The question is how many minimum modes would be sufficient for the modal analysis? In many structures, the contribution of the first p modes would give sufficiently accurate result. The numerical value of p depends upon the dynamic characteristics of a structure. In typical regular symmetric multistoried buildings the response contribution from the first 3 to 5 modes is usually sufficient. In cable roofs the number of modes required is usually very large. The contribution of higher modes is quite significant in many structures and needs to be incorporated. The minimum number of modes may be decided such that the total modal mass considered in any modal analysis is at least 90%.

10.11 ILLUSTRATIVE EXAMPLES

Example 10.1

Consider a three-DOF spring mass system shown in Figure 10.10. Determine its frequencies and mode shapes. Given: $m_1 = 2$ m, $m_2 = 3$ m, $m_3 = 2$ m; $k_1 = k$, $k_2 = 2$ k, $k_3 = 2$ k.

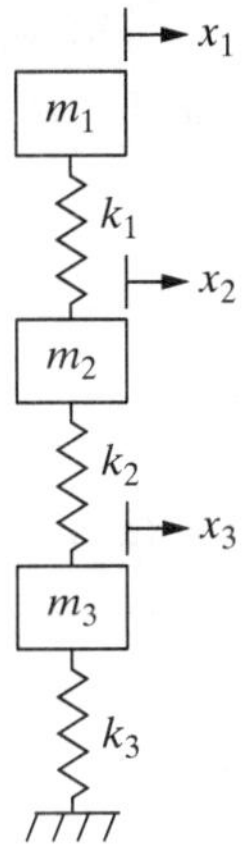

Figure 10.10 Three DOF spring – mass system.

Solution

The equations of motion can be written by considering the dynamic equilibrium of each mass:

$$m_1\ddot{x}_1 + k_1(x_1 - x_2) = 0$$

$$m_2\ddot{x}_2 + k_2(x_2 - x_3) + k_1(x_2 - x_1) = 0 \quad \text{(i)}$$

$$m_3\ddot{x}_3 + k_3x_3 + k_2(x_3 - x_2) = 0$$

It may be noted that the DOF may be numbered either from top or from bottom. In the present case, these have been numbered from top. The equations will change accordingly. The mass matrix can be written as follows:
It is given that: $m_1 = 2$ m, $m_2 = 3$ m, and $m_3 = 2$ m

$$[M] = \begin{bmatrix} 2m & 0 & 0 \\ 0 & 3m & 0 \\ 0 & 0 & 2m \end{bmatrix}$$

The stiffness matrix can be written as follows by rearranging Equation (i) in matrix form:

$$[K] = \begin{bmatrix} k_1 & -k_1 & 0 \\ -k_1 & k_1 + k_2 & -k_2 \\ 0 & -k_2 & k_2 + k_3 \end{bmatrix}$$

Given $k_1 = k$, $k_2 = 2$ k and $k_3 = 2$ k
On substitution, we get

$$[K] = k\begin{bmatrix} 1 & -1 & 0 \\ -1 & 3 & -2 \\ 0 & -2 & 4 \end{bmatrix}$$

$$\det\left|K - m\omega^2\right| = \begin{vmatrix} k - 2m\omega^2 & -k & 0 \\ -k & 3k - 3m\omega^2 & -2k \\ 0 & -2k & 4k - 2m\omega^2 \end{vmatrix}$$

Let k/m = β

The expression for determinant can be written as follows:

$$\det\left|k - m\omega^2\right| = \begin{vmatrix} \beta - 2\omega^2 & -\beta & 0 \\ -\beta & 3\beta - 3\omega^2 & -2\beta \\ 0 & -2\beta & 4\beta - 2\omega^2 \end{vmatrix}$$

Or, it can be expanded as follows:

$$6(\omega^2)^3 - 21\beta(\omega^2)^2 + 16\beta^2(\omega^2) - 2\beta^3 = 0$$

Its three positive roots are given as follows:

$$\{\omega^2\} = \begin{Bmatrix} 2.477\beta \\ 0.866\beta \\ 0.155\beta \end{Bmatrix} \text{ or } \{\omega\} = \begin{Bmatrix} 1.574 \\ 0.93 \\ 0.394 \end{Bmatrix}\sqrt{\frac{k}{m}}$$

Now mode shapes can be determined for each frequency using the following expression:

$$\left[K - m\omega^2\right]\{X\} = \{0\}$$

$$\begin{bmatrix} \beta - 2\omega^2 & -\beta & 0 \\ -\beta & 3\beta - 3\omega^2 & -2\beta \\ 0 & -2\beta & 4\beta - 2\omega^2 \end{bmatrix}\begin{Bmatrix} x_1 \\ x_2 \\ x_3 \end{Bmatrix} = \begin{Bmatrix} 0 \\ 0 \\ 0 \end{Bmatrix} \quad \text{(ii)}$$

Let us obtain the eigenvector corresponding to $\lambda_3 = \omega_3^2 = 2.477\,\beta$. Its value is substituted in Equation (ii), we get

$$\begin{bmatrix} -3.954 & -1 & 0 \\ -1 & -4.431 & -2 \\ 0 & -2 & -0.954 \end{bmatrix}\begin{Bmatrix} x_{13} \\ x_{23} \\ x_{33} \end{Bmatrix} = \begin{Bmatrix} 0 \\ 0 \\ 0 \end{Bmatrix}$$

Upon simplification,

$$-3.954x_{13} - x_{23} + 0 = 0 \quad \text{(iii)}$$

$$-x_{13} - 4.431x_{23} - 2x_{33} = 0 \quad \text{(iv)}$$

$$-2x_{23} - 0.954x_{33} = 0 \quad \text{(v)}$$

Equation (iii) and Equation (v) give,

$$\frac{x_{13}}{x_{23}} = \frac{-1}{3.954} \text{ and } \frac{x_{23}}{x_{33}} = \frac{-0.954}{2} = \frac{-0.477}{1}$$

If the value of x_{33} in terms of x_{23} is substituted in Equation (iv), it gives the same ratio of x_{13} and x_{23} as before.

∴ In such cases, only the ratio of the elements is determined. A numerical value for each element of the eigenvector $\{x_3\}$ may be obtained by arbitrarily assigning any one element as unity. For example, if x_{13} is assigned a unity, then

$$x_{23} = -3.954 \text{ and } x_{33} = 8.289$$

This procedure is repeated for other eigenvalues as well.

For first mode, $\omega_1^2 = 0.155\,\beta$, and $x_{11} = 1$

$$\begin{Bmatrix} x_{11} \\ x_{21} \\ x_{31} \end{Bmatrix} = \begin{Bmatrix} 1.000 \\ 0.689 \\ 0.374 \end{Bmatrix}$$

For second mode, $\omega_2^2 = 0.866\,\beta$, and $x_{12} = 1$

$$\begin{Bmatrix} x_{12} \\ x_{22} \\ x_{32} \end{Bmatrix} = \begin{Bmatrix} 1.364 \\ -1 \\ -0.882 \end{Bmatrix}$$

For third mode $\omega_3^2 = 2.477\,\beta$, and $x_{13} = 1$

$$\begin{Bmatrix} x_{13} \\ x_{23} \\ x_{33} \end{Bmatrix} = \begin{Bmatrix} 1.0 \\ -3.954 \\ 8.289 \end{Bmatrix}$$

Alternatively, it can be normalized with respect to $x_{33} = 1$ instead of $x_{13} = 1$

or,
$$\begin{Bmatrix} x_{13} \\ x_{23} \\ x_{33} \end{Bmatrix} = \begin{Bmatrix} 0.1206 \\ -0.477 \\ 1.0 \end{Bmatrix}$$

The mode shape matrix can be written as follows by arranging them column-wise or row-wise. In this case they have been arranged column-wise.

$$[\Phi] = \begin{bmatrix} \phi_{11} & \phi_{12} & \phi_{13} \\ \phi_{21} & \phi_{22} & \phi_{23} \\ \phi_{31} & \phi_{32} & \phi_{33} \end{bmatrix}$$

where in ϕ_{ij}, i represents DOF and j represents mode number

$$[\Phi] = \begin{bmatrix} 1.000 & 1.364 & 0.121 \\ 0.689 & -1 & -0.477 \\ 0.374 & -0.882 & 1.0 \end{bmatrix}$$

The mode shapes are shown in Figure 10.11.

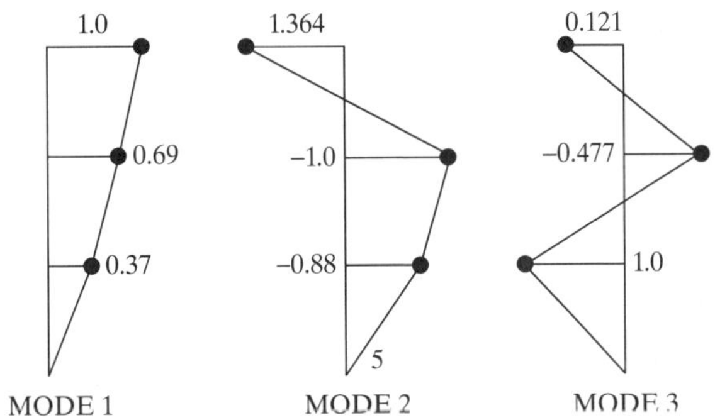

Figure 10.11 Mode shapes.

Let us verify the results using MATLAB.
The command eig(K, M) gives two matrices V and D. Matrix V is for eigenvectors arranged column-wise and matrix D is a diagonal matrix consisting of eigenvalues on the diagonal. The frequencies are obtained as follows:

$$\lambda = \omega^2$$

$>>[V, D] = \text{eig}(K, M)$
$V =$

$$\begin{matrix} -0.5195 & -0.4741 & 0.0734 \\ -0.3582 & 0.3476 & -0.2902 \\ -0.1942 & 0.3066 & 0.6069 \end{matrix}$$

$D =$

$$\begin{matrix} 0.1552 & 0 & 0 \\ 0 & 0.8665 & 0 \\ 0 & 0 & 2.4782 \end{matrix}$$

$$\therefore \qquad \omega^2 = \begin{Bmatrix} 0.1552 \\ 0.8665 \\ 2.4782 \end{Bmatrix} \frac{k}{m} \quad \text{or} \quad \omega = \begin{Bmatrix} 0.394 \\ 0.930 \\ 1.574 \end{Bmatrix} \sqrt{\frac{k}{m}}$$

In this option, the eigenvalues are obtained in increasing order.
Alternatively, the following command can be given in MATLAB.

$>> [V, D] = \text{eig}(M, K)$

It again generates two matrices V and D. Matrix V is for eigenvectors arranged column-wise and matrix D is a diagonal matrix consisting of eigenvalues on the diagonal. The frequencies are obtained as follows:

$$\lambda = 1/\omega^2$$

$>>[V, D] = \text{eig}(M, K)$
$V =$

$$\begin{matrix} -0.0466 & 0.5093 & 1.3185 \\ 0.1844 & -0.3734 & 0.9092 \\ -0.3855 & -0.3294 & 0.4928 \end{matrix}$$

$D =$

$$\begin{matrix} 0.4035 & 0 & 0 \\ 0 & 1.1540 & 0 \\ 0 & 0 & 6.4425 \end{matrix}$$

$$\omega^2 = \begin{Bmatrix} \dfrac{1}{0.4035} \\ \dfrac{1}{1.1540} \\ \dfrac{1}{6.4425} \end{Bmatrix} \frac{k}{m} \quad \text{or} \quad \omega = \begin{Bmatrix} 1.574 \\ 0.93 \\ 0.394 \end{Bmatrix} \sqrt{\frac{k}{m}}$$

In this option, the eigenvalues are obtained in decreasing order. □

Example 10.2

Determine the eigenvalues of the matrix A using the power method and matrix deflation method.

$$[A]=\begin{bmatrix}11 & 5 & 2\\ 5 & 5 & 2\\ 2 & 2 & 2\end{bmatrix}$$

Background

The characteristic eigenvalue problem is defined as follows:

$$[A]_{n\times n}\{X\}_{n\times 1}=\lambda\{X\}_{n\times 1} \tag{10.19a}$$

where,

λ = eigenvalue, a scalar quantity

X = eigenvector

In this equation, λ may be considered as a scale factor. Let us assume that it is unity. We can write it as follows:

$$[A]\{X\}^i=\{X\}^{i+1}$$

The power method is an iterative method. It always converges to the highest eigenvalue of the coefficient matrix [A]. In this method, a value of the vector $\{X\}^i$ on the left-hand side is assumed, it is pre-multiplied with [A] and the right-hand side vector $\{X\}^{i+1}$ is obtained. The right-hand side vector $\{X\}^{i+1}$ is normalized with respect to any term, say $x(1)$. It means, $x(1)$ is taken as a common factor and the remaining vector is expected to be close to the assumed left-hand side vector $\{X\}^i$. The next iteration is carried out with this normalized vector on the left-hand side. The iteration is continued till the two consecutive values of the common factor $x(1)$ are close enough. The common factor $x(1)$ is the eigenvalue. The vector $\{X\}$ is the eigenvector.

The second and subsequent eigenvalues and eigenvectors are obtained after carrying out deflation operation on the coefficient matrix $[A]$ by making use of the orthogonality condition. The entire process is illustrated in the following example.

Solution

Power Method

Let us assume $\{X\} = \{I\}$ unity vector

Now we operate on the left side of the characteristic equation and determine vector on the right side.

$$[A]\{X\}=\begin{bmatrix}11 & 5 & 2\\ 5 & 5 & 2\\ 2 & 2 & 2\end{bmatrix}\begin{Bmatrix}1\\1\\1\end{Bmatrix}=\begin{Bmatrix}18\\12\\6\end{Bmatrix}=18\begin{Bmatrix}1\\0.6667\\0.3334\end{Bmatrix}$$

Let us carryout the iterations in tabular form for convenience.

I Eigenvalue

Iteration	$\{X\}^T$	$\{X\}^T=\{[A]_{n\times n}\{X\}_{n\times 1}\}^T$	λ
1	{1 1 1}	{18 12 6}	18
2	{1 0.666 0.333}	{15 9 4}	15
3	{1 0.600 0.266}	{14.533 8.533 3.733}	14.533
4	{1 0.587 0.257}	{14.45 8.45 3.68}	14.45
7	{1 0.58424 0.25489}		14.4314

Thus, 7th iteration gives eigenvector and the corresponding eigenvalue.

II Eigenvalue

The second eigenvalue can be obtained using the *matrix deflation method*. It makes use of orthogonality condition.

$$\sum x_i^{(r)} x_i^{(s)} = 0$$

where $r \neq s$ mode
Let us assume that II mode eigenvector is $\{x_1 \quad x_2 \quad x_3\}$.
Therefore, let us apply orthogonality condition between mode 1 and mode 2, we get

$$1 \times x_1 + 0.58424 x_2 + 0.25489 x_3 = 0$$

$$\therefore \qquad x_1 = -0.58424 x_2 - 0.25489 x_3$$

$$x_2 = x_2$$

$$x_3 = x_3$$

Let us write these equations in matrix form:

$$\begin{Bmatrix} x_1 \\ x_2 \\ x_3 \end{Bmatrix} = \begin{bmatrix} 0 & -0.58424 & -0.25489 \\ 0 & -1 & 0 \\ 0 & 0 & 1 \end{bmatrix} \begin{Bmatrix} x_1 \\ x_2 \\ x_3 \end{Bmatrix}$$

or,

$$\{x\}_{3\times 1} = [R_1]_{n\times 1} \{x\}_{3\times 1}$$

$[R_1]$ = rotation matrix

$$[A][R_1] = [A_1]$$

$$\begin{bmatrix} 11 & 5 & 2 \\ 5 & 5 & 2 \\ 2 & 2 & 2 \end{bmatrix} \begin{bmatrix} 0 & -0.58424 & -0.25489 \\ 0 & -1 & 0 \\ 0 & 0 & 1 \end{bmatrix} = \begin{bmatrix} 0 & -1.4266 & -0.80379 \\ 0 & 2.0788 & 0.72555 \\ 0 & 0.83152 & 1.49022 \end{bmatrix}$$

Let us now iterate on A_1 as done earlier on A.

Iteration	$\{X\}^T$	$\{X\}^T = \{[A]_{n\times n}\{X\}_{n\times 1}\}^T$	λ
1	$\{1 \quad 1 \quad 1\}$	$\{-2.30 \quad 2.8043 \quad 2.3217\}$	2.23
2	$\{-1 \quad 1.2573 \quad 1.0409\}$	$\{-2.6304 \quad 3.3689 \quad 2.5966\}$	2.63
3	$\{-1 \quad 1.2807 \quad 0.98716\}$	$\{-2.62 \quad 3.3787 \quad 2.5966\}$	2.62
6	$\{-1 \quad 1.2934 \quad 0.9579\}$		2.6158

Thus, 6th iteration gives eigenvector and the corresponding eigenvalue.

III Eigenvalue

III eigenvector is orthogonal to both first and second eigenvectors.

Let III eigenvector be $\{x_1 \quad x_2 \quad x_3\}$.

Therefore, let us apply orthogonality condition between mode 3 and mode 1, we get

$$1 \times x_1 + 0.58424 x_2 + 0.25489 x_3 = 0$$

or,

$$x_1 = -0.58424 x_2 - 0.25489 x_3 \quad \text{(i)}$$

Between mode 3 and mode 2, we get

$$x_1 = 1.29348 x_2 + 0.95797 x_3 \quad \text{(ii)}$$

Solving Equations (i) and (ii), in terms of x_3,

$$\begin{Bmatrix} x_1 \\ x_2 \\ x_3 \end{Bmatrix} = \begin{bmatrix} 0 & 0 & 0.12249 \\ 0 & 0 & -0.64593 \\ 0 & 0 & 1 \end{bmatrix} \begin{Bmatrix} x_1 \\ x_2 \\ x_3 \end{Bmatrix}$$

$$\{x\}_{3\times1} = [R_2]_{n\times1} \{x\}_{3\times1}$$

$[R_2]$ = rotation matrix

$$[A_1][R_2] = [A_2]$$

or,

$$[A][R_1][R_2] = [A_2]$$

$$\therefore \quad [A_2] = \begin{bmatrix} 0 & -1.4266 & -0.80379 \\ 0 & 2.0788 & 0.72555 \\ 0 & 0.83152 & 1.49022 \end{bmatrix} \begin{bmatrix} 0 & 0 & 0.12249 \\ 0 & 0 & -0.64593 \\ 0 & 0 & 1 \end{bmatrix}$$

or,

$$[A_2] = \begin{bmatrix} 0 & 0 & 0.1177 \\ 0 & 0 & -0.6172 \\ 0 & 0 & 0.9531 \end{bmatrix}$$

Let us now iterate on A_2 as done earlier on A and A_1.

Iteration	$\{X\}^T$	$\{X\}^T = \{[A]_{n\times n}\{X\}_{n\times1}\}^T$	λ
1	$\{1 \quad 1 \quad 1\}$	$\{0.1177 \quad -0.6172 \quad 0.9531\}$	0.1177
2	$\{1 \quad -5.2438 \quad 8.0977\}$	$\{0.953 \quad -4.9979 \quad 7.7179\}$	0.953
3	$\{1 \quad -5.2443 \quad 8.0985\}$		0.953

The eigenvalues and eigenvectors are as follows:

$$\{\lambda\} = \begin{Bmatrix} 14.4314 \\ 2.6158 \\ 0.953 \end{Bmatrix} \text{ and } [\Phi] = \begin{bmatrix} 1 & -1 & 1 \\ 0.58424 & 1.2934 & -5.2443 \\ 0.25489 & 0.9579 & 8.0985 \end{bmatrix}$$

The eigenvalues so obtained are not frequencies of the matrix [A].
The eigenvectors are arranged column-wise. □

Example 10.3

Determine the eigenvalues of the Matrix [A] using inverse iteration method.

$$[A]=\begin{bmatrix}2 & 2\\ 2 & 5\end{bmatrix}$$

Background

The characteristic equation of eigenvalue can be written as follows:

$$[A]_{n\times n}\{X\}_{n\times 1}=\lambda\{X\}_{n\times 1} \tag{i}$$

Inverse Iteration Method

The eigenvalue term λ is treated as a scale factor and may be taken as unity. This equation can now be written as:

$$[A]\{X\}^{i+1}=\{X\}^{i} \tag{ii}$$

In this iterative method, the right-hand side vector $\{X\}^i$ is assumed and the left-hand side vector $\{X\}^{i+1}$ is determined. This equation is similar to the solution of linear simultaneous equation

$$[A]\{X\}=\{b\} \tag{iii}$$

where

$\{b\}$ = known R.H.S. vector
$\{x\}$ = unknown L.H.S. vector

We can make use of any method used to solve the set of linear simultaneous equations. Knowing the left-hand side vector, it is normalized with respect to any term, say, $x(1)$. In the subsequent iteration, this normalized vector is assumed on the right-hand side, and the un-normalized vector on the left-hand side is determined. The iterations are repeated till the two consecutive values of the normalized vector $x(1)$ are close enough. This is called *inverse iteration method* because the iterations are carried out in a direction opposite to that used in the power method.

Inverse Iteration Method with Shift

This is a very powerful iterative procedure as it improves the rate of convergence as well as it makes it converge to an eigenpair other than (λ_1, X_1). Let p be the shift in the origin of the eigenvalue axis.

Let $\bar{\lambda}=\lambda-p$, that is, shifted eigenvalue measured from the shifted origin (iv)

Equation (i) can be written as follows:

$$\left([A]-(\bar{\lambda}+p)[I]\right)\{X\}=\{0\}$$

or,

$$([A]-p[I])\{X\}=\bar{\lambda}\{X\} \tag{v}$$

or,

$$[B]_{n\times n}\{X\}_{n\times 1}=\bar{\lambda}\{X\}_{n\times 1} \tag{vi}$$

This method is based on the property that eigenvectors of Equations (i) and (vi) are the same. Knowing the eigenvector, the eigenvalue of Equation (vi) can be obtained using the Rayleigh quotient. Thus, eigenvalue of Equation (i) can be obtained using Equation (iv). The value of shift p can be obtained using Sturm sequence or the Gerschgorin's theorem.

Solution

Let us assume that a root of this matrix lies in the vicinity of 0.9. That is, shift $p = 0.9$

Then

$$\left(\begin{bmatrix} 2 & 2 \\ 2 & 5 \end{bmatrix} - 0.9\begin{bmatrix} 1 & 0 \\ 0 & 1 \end{bmatrix}\right)\begin{Bmatrix} x_1 \\ x_2 \end{Bmatrix}^{(1)} = \begin{Bmatrix} x_1 \\ x_2 \end{Bmatrix}^{(0)}$$

$$\begin{bmatrix} 1.1 & 2 \\ 2 & 4.1 \end{bmatrix}\begin{Bmatrix} x_1 \\ x_2 \end{Bmatrix} = \begin{Bmatrix} x_1 \\ x_2 \end{Bmatrix}^{(0)}$$

$$\begin{Bmatrix} x_1 \\ x_2 \end{Bmatrix}^{(0)} = \text{normalized vector}$$

and

$$\begin{Bmatrix} x_1 \\ x_2 \end{Bmatrix}^{(1)} = \text{un-normalized vector}$$

Let us assume

$\begin{Bmatrix} x_1 \\ x_2 \end{Bmatrix}^{(0)} = \begin{Bmatrix} 1 \\ 1 \end{Bmatrix}$ and solve for the left-hand side vector $\{x\}$.

Matrix $B = \begin{bmatrix} 1.1 & 2 \\ 2 & 4.1 \end{bmatrix}$

Let us carry out the iterations as shown in the table. β is the common factor $x(1)$.

Iteration	Assumed $\{b\}$	$\{x\} = [B]^{-1}\{b\}$	β	Normalized vector
1	$\{1 \quad 1\}$	$\{4.14 \quad -1.17\}$	4.14	$\{1 - 0.428\}$
2	$\{1 \quad -0.428\}$	$\{9.766 \quad -4.870\}$	9.766	$\{1 \quad -0.498\}$
3	$\{1 \quad -0.498\}$	$\{10.021 \quad -5.020\}$	10.021	$\{1 \quad -0.50\}$
4	$\{1 \quad -0.50\}$		10.021	

It should be noted that in determining the L.H.S. vector $\{x\}$, inverse of B was not computed. Instead, Gauss elimination method was used.

$$\beta = (\lambda - p)^{-1} = 10.021$$

or,

$$(\lambda - p) = 10.021^{-1} = 0.10$$

or, eigenvalue $\lambda = 0.9 + 0.1 = 1.0$

This can also be verified using the Rayleigh quotient method:

$$\lambda = \frac{\{x\}^T[A]\{x\}}{\{x\}^T\{x\}} = \frac{\{1 \ \ -0.5\}\begin{bmatrix} 2 & 2 \\ 2 & 5 \end{bmatrix}\begin{Bmatrix} 1 \\ -0.5 \end{Bmatrix}}{\{1 \ \ -0.5\}\begin{Bmatrix} 1 \\ -0.5 \end{Bmatrix}} = 1.0$$

II Eigenvalue

Let second eigenvalue be in the vicinity of 4.

$$\left(\begin{bmatrix} 2 & 2 \\ 2 & 5 \end{bmatrix} - 4\begin{bmatrix} 1 & 0 \\ 0 & 1 \end{bmatrix}\right)\begin{Bmatrix} x_1 \\ x_2 \end{Bmatrix}^{(1)} = \begin{Bmatrix} x_1 \\ x_2 \end{Bmatrix}^{(0)}$$

Let us assume

$\begin{Bmatrix} x_1 \\ x_2 \end{Bmatrix}^{(0)} = \begin{Bmatrix} 1 \\ 1 \end{Bmatrix}$ and solve for the left hand side vector $\{x\}$.

Matrix $B = \begin{bmatrix} -2 & 2 \\ 2 & 1 \end{bmatrix}$

Let us again carry out the iterations in the table. In this case β is the common factor $x(2)$. Any element of $\{x\}$ can be taken as common.

Iteration	Assumed $\{b\}$	$\{x\} = [B]^{-1}\{b\}$	β	Normalized vector
1	$\{1 \ \ 1\}$	$\{0.166 \ \ 0.667\}$	0.667	$\{0.25 \ \ 1.0\}$
2	$\{0.25 \ \ 1.0\}$	$\{0.292 \ \ 0.416\}$	0.416	$\{0.702 \ \ 1.0\}$
3	$\{0.702 \ \ 1.0\}$	$\{0.216 \ \ 0.567\}$	0.567	$\{0.381 \ \ 1.0\}$
10	$\{0.506 \ \ 1.0\}$		0.496	

$$\beta = (\lambda - p)^{-1} = 0.496$$

or,

$$(\lambda - p) = 0.496^{-1} = 2.0$$

or, eigenvalue $\lambda = 2.0 + 4.0 = 6.0$

This can also be verified using the Rayleigh quotient method:

$$\lambda = \frac{\{x\}^T[A]\{x\}}{\{x\}^T\{x\}} = \frac{\{0.506 \ \ 1.0\}\begin{bmatrix} 2 & 2 \\ 2 & 5 \end{bmatrix}\begin{Bmatrix} 0.506 \\ 1.0 \end{Bmatrix}}{\{0.506 \ \ 1.0\}\begin{Bmatrix} 0.506 \\ 1.0 \end{Bmatrix}} = 5.99$$

The eigenvalues and eigenvectors are as follows:

$$\{\lambda\} = \begin{Bmatrix} 1 \\ 6 \end{Bmatrix} \text{ and } [\Phi] = \begin{bmatrix} 1.0 & 0.506 \\ -0.5 & 1.0 \end{bmatrix}$$ □

Example 10.4

Consider a four-DOF undamped lumped mass system as shown in Figure 10.12. Determine its frequencies and mode shapes using Holtzer method.

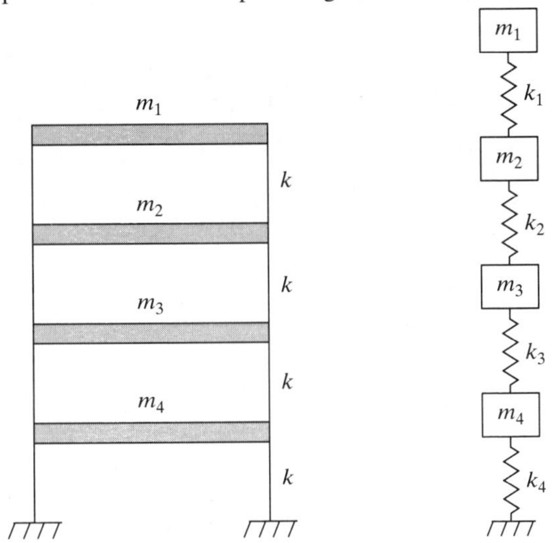

(a) Four-storey portal frame (b) Spring-mass idealization

Figure 10.12 Four-DOF system.

Solution

It is given that all masses are equal (= m) and all spring stiffness are also equal (= k).
The DOF are numbered from the top as shown in the figure.
The Holtzer expression can be written as follows:

$$\phi_{n+1} = \phi_n - \frac{\omega^2}{k_n}\left(\sum_{i=1}^{n} m_i \phi_i\right) = 0 \quad \text{since base is fixed.} \tag{D.n}$$

Trial 1: Let $\omega^2 = 0.1\dfrac{k}{m}$ and $\phi_1 = 1.0$

At the beginning of a trial, it is not possible to predict the mode corresponding to the assumed value of ω^2. It will be known only when the final mode shape in available at the end of the trial.
Let us carryout the calculations shown in Equation (D.n) in tabular form for convenience. The calculations are carried out row-wise in the Table 10.1.
At the end of first row,

$$\phi_2 = \phi_1 - \frac{1}{k}\sum m_i \omega^2 \phi_i = 1.0 - 0.10 = 0.90$$

Now the calculations in row 2 can be done.
At the end of the 4th row calculations, it is found that

$$\phi_s = \phi_4 - \frac{1}{k}\sum m_i \omega^2 \phi_i \quad (\phi_s = \text{displacement of support})$$

or,

$\therefore$ $\phi_s = 0.449 - 0.306 = 0.143 \neq 0$ Hence revise the calculations.

TABLE 10.1 $\omega^2 = 0.10$ k/m

S. No	mass	$m\omega^2$	ϕ	$m\omega^2\phi$	$\sum m_i\omega^2\phi_i$	$\frac{1}{k}$	$\frac{1}{k}\sum m_i\omega^2\phi_i$
1	m	0.1 k	1	0.1 k	0.1 k	1/k	0.10
2	m	0.1 k	0.9	0.09 k	0.19 k	1/k	0.19
3	m	0.1 k	0.71	0.071 k	0.261 k	1/k	0.261
4	m	0.1 k	0.449	0.0449 k	0.36 k	1/k	0.306

Trial 2: Let us assume $\omega^2 = 0.12\frac{k}{m}$ and $\phi_1 = 1.0$

The calculations are shown in Table 10.2.
At the end of the 4th row calculations, it is found that

$$\phi_s = \phi_4 - \frac{1}{k}\sum m_i\omega^2\phi_i$$

or,

$$\phi_s = 0.350 - 0.346 = 0.004 \approx 0 \qquad \text{Hence OK}$$

Thus, frequency is given by

$$\omega_1 = 0.346\sqrt{\frac{k}{m}}$$

and the mode shape is given by column 4. Its plot shows that it corresponds to the first mode.

Trial 3: Let us assume $\omega^2 = 1.0\frac{k}{m}$ and $\phi_1 = 1.0$

The calculations are shown in Table 10.3.
At the end of the 4th row calculations, it is found that

$$\phi_s = \phi_4 - \frac{1}{k}\sum m_i\omega^2\phi_i$$

or, $\phi_s = -1 + 1 = 0$ Hence OK

The mode shapes are given by column 4 of Table 10.3. Its plot shows that it corresponds to the second mode.

The frequency is given by $\omega_2 = \sqrt{\frac{k}{m}}$

Trial 4: Let us assume $\omega^2 = 3.50\frac{k}{m}$ and $\phi_1 = 1.0$

The calculations are shown in Table 10.4.

At the end of the 4th row calculations, it is found that

$$\phi_s = \phi_4 - \frac{1}{k}\sum m_i\omega^2\phi_i$$

or, $\phi_s = -1.625 + 1.3125 = -0.3125 \neq 0$ Hence revise it.

TABLE 10.2 $\omega^2 = 0.12$ k/m

S. No	mass	$m\omega^2$	ϕ	$m\omega^2\phi$	$\sum m_i\omega^2\phi_i$	$\frac{1}{k}$	$\frac{1}{k}\sum m_i\omega^2\phi_i$
1	m	0.12 k	1	0.12 k	0.12 k	1/k	0.12
2	m	0.12 k	0.88	0.1056 k	0.2256 k	1/k	0.2256
3	m	0.12 k	0.654	0.0785 k	0.304 k	1/k	0.304
4	m	0.12 k	0.350	0.042 k	0.346 k	1/k	0.346

TABLE 10.3 $\omega^2 = k/m$

S. No	mass	$m\omega^2$	ϕ	$m\omega^2\phi$	$\sum m_i\omega^2\phi_i$	$\frac{1}{k}$	$\frac{1}{k}\sum m_i\omega^2\phi_i$
1	m	k	1	k	k	1/k	1
2	m	k	0	k	k	1/k	1
3	m	k	–1	–k	0	1/k	0
4	m	k	–1	–k	–k	1/k	–1

TABLE 10.4 $\omega^2 = 3.50$ k/m

S. No	mass	$m\omega^2$	ϕ	$m\omega^2\phi$	$\sum m_i\omega^2\phi_i$	$\frac{1}{k}$	$\frac{1}{k}\sum m_i\omega^2\phi_i$
1	m	3.50 k	1.0	3.5 k	3.5 k	1/k	3.5
2	m	3.50 k	–2.5	–8.75 k	–5.25 k	1/k	–5.25
3	m	3.50 k	2.75	9.625 k	4.375 k	1/k	4.375
4	m	3.50 k	–1.625	–5.6875 k	–1.3125 k	1/k	–1.3125

TABLE 10.5 $\omega^2 = 3.60$ k/m

S. No	mass	$m\omega^2$	ϕ	$m\omega^2\phi$	$\sum m_i\omega^2\phi_i$	$\frac{1}{k}$	$\frac{1}{k}\sum m_i\omega^2\phi_i$
1	m	3.60 k	1.0	3.6 k	3.6 k	1/k	3.6
2	m	3.60 k	–2.6	–9.36 k	–5.76 k	1/k	–5.76
3	m	3.60 k	3.16	11.376 k	5.616 k	1/k	5.616
4	m	3.60 k	–2.456	–8.8416 k	–3.2256 k	1/k	–3.2256

Trial 5: Let us assume $\omega^2 = 3.60\frac{k}{m}$ and $\phi_1 = 1.0$

The calculations are shown in Table 10.5.
At the end of the 4th row calculations, it is found that

$$\phi_s = \phi_4 - \frac{1}{k}\sum m_i\omega^2\phi_i$$

TABLE 10.6 $\omega^2 = 2.35\ \text{k/m}$

S. No	mass	$m\omega^2$	ϕ	$m\omega^2\phi$	$\sum m_i\omega^2\phi_i$	$\frac{1}{k}$	$\frac{1}{k}\sum m_i\omega^2\phi_i$
1	m	2.35 k	1.0	2.35 k	2.35 k	1/k	2.35
2	m	2.35 k	−1.35	−3.1725 k	−0.8225 k	1/k	−0.8225
3	m	2.35 k	−0.5275	−1.2396 k	−2.062 k	1/k	−2.062
4	m	2.35 k	1.5346	3.6063 k	1.544 k	1/k	1.544

or, $\phi_s = -2.456 + 3.2256 = 0.7696 \neq 0$ Hence revise it.

Trials 4 and 5 show that the difference has reversed. That is, if $\omega^2 = 3.50\ \text{k/m}$, then the final difference is −0.3125; while if $\omega^2 = 3.60\ \text{k/m}$, then the final difference is 0.7696; It shows that the true value lies somewhere in between these two values. The correct value is $\omega^2 = 3.532\ \text{k/m}$. It corresponds to mode 4.

Trial 6: Let us assume $\omega^2 = 2.35\frac{k}{m}$ and $\phi_1 = 1.0$

The calculations are shown in Table 10.6.
At the end of the 4th row calculations, it is found that

$$\phi_s = \phi_4 - \frac{1}{k}\sum m_i\omega^2\phi_i$$

or, $\phi_s = 1.5346 - 1.5440 = -0.01 \approx 0$ Hence OK

Frequency and mode shapes are as follows:

$$\{\omega^2\} = \begin{Bmatrix} 0.12 \\ 1 \\ 3.532 \\ 2.35 \end{Bmatrix} \frac{k}{m}$$

Or, re-arranging the frequencies in increasing order,

$$\{\omega\} = \begin{Bmatrix} 0.346 \\ 1 \\ 1.53 \\ 1.88 \end{Bmatrix} \sqrt{\frac{k}{m}}$$

The mode shapes are arranged column-wise as follows:

$$[\Phi] = \begin{bmatrix} 1 & 1 & 1 & 1 \\ 0.88 & 0 & -1.35 & -2.5 \\ 0.654 & -1 & -0.5275 & 2.75 \\ 0.35 & -1 & 1.5346 & -1.625 \end{bmatrix}$$

The first column represents mode 1, second column represents mode 2, third column represents mode 3 and fourth column represents mode 4. These mode shapes may be normalized with respect to any element in the respective column. Thus, 3rd mode shape is

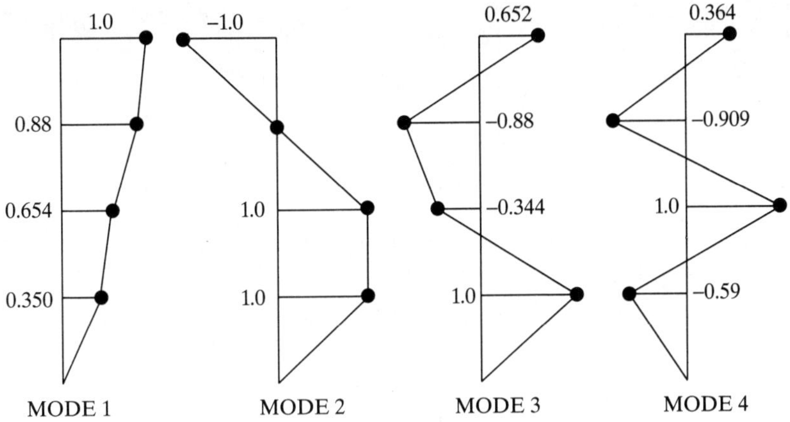

Figure 10.13 Mode shapes.

normalized with respect to 1.5346 while 4th mode shape is normalized with respect to 2.75. The final mode shapes are shown in Figure 10.13.

A mode shape can be identified based on how many times it intersects the mean position, that is, the vertical axis. The first mode shape does not intersect at all; the second mode shape intersects only once; the third mode shape intersects twice; and the fourth mode shape intersects three times. Thus, by looking at the numerical sign of the mode shape, its mode can be easily identified.
Let us verify the results using MATLAB.
MATLAB Solution

The mass matrix $M = m\begin{bmatrix} 1 & 0 & 0 & 0 \\ 0 & 1 & 0 & 0 \\ 0 & 0 & 1 & 0 \\ 0 & 0 & 0 & 1 \end{bmatrix}$

The stiffness matrix $K = \begin{bmatrix} k & -k & 0 & 0 \\ -k & 2k & -k & 0 \\ 0 & -k & 2k & -k \\ 0 & 0 & -k & 2k \end{bmatrix}$

```
>>[V, D] = eig(K, M)          % MATLAB Command

V =
   -0.6565  -0.5774   0.4285  -0.2280
   -0.5774  -0.0000  -0.5774   0.5774
   -0.4285   0.5774  -0.2280  -0.6565
   -0.2280   0.5774   0.6565   0.4285

D =
   0.1206        0        0        0
        0   1.0000        0        0
        0        0   2.3473        0
        0        0        0   3.5321
```

Thus,

$$\{\omega^2\} = \begin{Bmatrix} 0.1206 \\ 1 \\ 2.3473 \\ 3.5321 \end{Bmatrix} \frac{k}{m} \quad \text{or} \quad \{\omega\} = \begin{Bmatrix} 0.346 \\ 1 \\ 1.53 \\ 1.88 \end{Bmatrix} \sqrt{\frac{k}{m}}$$

In this case, the eigenvalues are obtained in increasing order. The mode shapes are available in $[V]$ in the corresponding column.

$>>[V, D] = \text{eig}(M, K)$ % MATLAB Command

$V =$

0.1213	−0.2797	0.5774	1.8904
−0.3072	0.3768	−0.0000	1.6624
0.3493	0.1488	−0.5774	1.2339
−0.2280	−0.4285	−0.5774	0.6565

$D =$

0.2831	0	0	0
0	0.4260	0	0
0	0	1.0000	0
0	0	0	8.2909

Thus,

$$\{\omega^2\} = \begin{Bmatrix} 1/0.2831 \\ 1/0.4260 \\ 1 \\ 1/8.2909 \end{Bmatrix} \frac{k}{m} \quad \text{or} \quad \{\omega\} = \begin{Bmatrix} 1.88 \\ 1.53 \\ 1 \\ 0.346 \end{Bmatrix} \sqrt{\frac{k}{m}}$$

In this case, the eigenvalues are obtained in decreasing order. The mode shape are available in $[V]$ in the corresponding column. □

Example 10.5

Mass and stiffness matrices for a three-DOF system are as follows:

$$[M] = \begin{bmatrix} 2m & 0 & 0 \\ 0 & 3m & 0 \\ 0 & 0 & 2m \end{bmatrix} \quad \text{and} \quad [K] = k\begin{bmatrix} 1 & -1 & 0 \\ -1 & 3 & -2 \\ 0 & -2 & 4 \end{bmatrix}$$

Calculate the coefficient matrix of the standard eigenvalue problem and show if it is a unsymmetric matrix or a symmetric matrix.

Solution

(i) The standard eigenvalue problem is given as follows:

$$\mathbf{A}\phi = \lambda\phi$$

where

$$[A]_{n\times n} = [M]^{-1}_{n\times n}[K]_{n\times n} \text{ and } \lambda = \omega^2$$

Let us find $[M]_{n\times n}^{-1}$

$$[M]_{n\times n}^{-1} = \frac{1}{m}\begin{bmatrix} 0.5 & 0 & 0 \\ 0 & 0.333 & 0 \\ 0 & 0 & 0.5 \end{bmatrix}$$

Thus,

$$[A]_{n\times n} = [M]_{n\times n}^{-1}[K]_{n\times n}$$

$$[A] = \frac{1}{m}\begin{bmatrix} 0.5 & 0 & 0 \\ 0 & 0.333 & 0 \\ 0 & 0 & 0.5 \end{bmatrix} \times k\begin{bmatrix} 1 & -1 & 0 \\ -1 & 3 & -2 \\ 0 & -2 & 4 \end{bmatrix}$$

or,

$$[A] = \frac{k}{m}\begin{bmatrix} 0.5 & -0.5 & 0 \\ -0.333 & 1 & -0.666 \\ 0 & -1 & 2 \end{bmatrix}$$

It can be seen that the coefficient matrix is unsymmetric.

(ii) The coefficient matrix can also be written as follows:

$$[A]_{n\times n} = [K]_{n\times n}^{-1}[M]_{n\times n} \quad \text{and} \quad \lambda = \frac{1}{\omega^2}$$

Let us find $[K]_{n\times n}^{-1}$

$$[K]_{n\times n}^{-1} = \frac{1}{k}\begin{bmatrix} 2 & 1 & 0.5 \\ 1 & 1 & 0.5 \\ 0.5 & 0.5 & 0.5 \end{bmatrix}$$

Thus,

$$[A]_{n\times n} = [K]_{n\times n}^{-1}[M]_{n\times n}$$

$$[A] = \frac{1}{k}\begin{bmatrix} 2 & 1 & 0.5 \\ 1 & 1 & 0.5 \\ 0.5 & 0.5 & 0.5 \end{bmatrix} \times m\begin{bmatrix} 2 & 0 & 0 \\ 0 & 3 & 0 \\ 0 & 0 & 2 \end{bmatrix}$$

$$[A] = \frac{m}{k}\begin{bmatrix} 4 & 3 & 1 \\ 2 & 3 & 1 \\ 1 & 1.5 & 1 \end{bmatrix}$$

It can be seen that the coefficient matrix is again unsymmetric.

(iii) The coefficient matrix can also be written as follows:

$$By = \lambda y$$

where,

$$B = M^{-1/2}KM^{-1/2}$$

$$y = M^{1/2}\phi$$

$$\lambda = \omega^2$$

Let us first find $M^{1/2}$

$$M^{1/2} = \begin{bmatrix} 1.4142 & 0 & 0 \\ 0 & 1.7321 & 0 \\ 0 & 0 & 1.4142 \end{bmatrix}$$

$$M^{-1/2} = \begin{bmatrix} 0.7071 & 0 & 0 \\ 0 & 0.5774 & 0 \\ 0 & 0 & 0.7071 \end{bmatrix}$$

$$B = M^{-1/2} K M^{-1/2}$$

$$M^{-1/2} K = \begin{bmatrix} 0.7071 & -0.7071 & 0 \\ -0.5774 & 1.7321 & -1.1547 \\ 0 & -1.4142 & 2.8284 \end{bmatrix}$$

$$B = M^{-\frac{1}{2}} K M^{-\frac{1}{2}} = \begin{bmatrix} 0.5 & -0.4082 & 0 \\ -0.4082 & 1 & -0.8165 \\ 0 & -0.8165 & 2 \end{bmatrix}$$

It can be seen that the coefficient matrix B is a symmetric matrix. □

Example 10.6

In a previous problem, the following mass matrix and stiffness matrix were employed. The corresponding eigenvalues and eigenvectors are also shown.

$$[M] = m\begin{bmatrix} 2 & 0 & 0 \\ 0 & 3 & 0 \\ 0 & 0 & 2 \end{bmatrix} \text{ and } [K] = k\begin{bmatrix} 1 & -1 & 0 \\ -1 & 3 & -2 \\ 0 & -2 & 4 \end{bmatrix}$$

$$\{\omega^2\} = \begin{Bmatrix} 2.4782\beta \\ 0.8665\beta \\ 0.1552\beta \end{Bmatrix} \qquad [\Phi] = \begin{bmatrix} 0.5195 & -0.4741 & 0.0734 \\ 0.3582 & 0.3476 & -0.2902 \\ 0.1942 & 0.3066 & 0.6069 \end{bmatrix}$$

Check if the eigenvectors are orthogonal and orthonormal.

Solution

In mathematics, two vectors v_1 and v_2 are said to be orthogonal if their dot product is zero, that is,

$$v^T_{1_{1\times n}} v_{2_{n\times 1}} = 0$$

In the dynamics of structures, two mode shapes are said to be orthogonal, if the following relation is satisfied:

$$[\Phi]^T [M][\Phi] = \text{A diagonal matrix} \tag{i}$$

or,

$$\phi_r^T M \phi_s = 0 \text{ for } \omega_r \neq \omega_s \tag{ii}$$

Similar relations exist for stiffness matrix.
Let us check using the dynamics of structures and carry out the following operation:

$$[\Phi]^T[M][\Phi] \tag{i}$$

On substituting the values of Φ and M in Equation (i), we get a diagonal matrix which happens to be an identity matrix.

$$\begin{bmatrix} 1 & 0 & 0 \\ 0 & 1 & 0 \\ 0 & 0 & 1 \end{bmatrix}$$

The orthogonality of mode shapes with respect to mass matrix is proved.
Similarly, consider the following operation:

$$[\Phi]^T[K][\Phi] \tag{iii}$$

On substituting the values of Φ and M in Equation (iii), we get a diagonal matrix.

$$\begin{bmatrix} 0.1552 & 0 & 0 \\ 0 & 0.8665 & 0 \\ 0 & 0 & 2.4782 \end{bmatrix}$$

The orthogonality of mode shapes with respect to stiffness matrix is proved.
Now, consider the first two eigenvectors

$$\phi_1 = \begin{Bmatrix} 0.5195 \\ 0.3582 \\ 0.1942 \end{Bmatrix} \text{ and } \phi_2 = \begin{Bmatrix} -0.4741 \\ 0.3476 \\ 0.3066 \end{Bmatrix}$$

Therefore, if ϕ_1 and ϕ_2 are orthogonal, then,

$$\phi_1^T M \phi_2 = 0 \tag{iv}$$

On substituting the values of mode shapes, we do get a zero.
Similarly, if ϕ_2 and ϕ_3 are orthogonal, then,

$$\phi_2^T M \phi_3 = 0 \tag{v}$$

It again gives a zero.
Similarly, if ϕ_1 and ϕ_3 are orthogonal, then,

$$\phi_1^T M \phi_3 = 0 \tag{vi}$$

It again gives a zero.
It can be concluded that the eigenvectors in the present case are orthogonal.
Similar results are obtained with respect to stiffness matrix.

Check vector norm
The first norm of a vector is denoted by $\|x\|$ and is defined as follows:

$$\|x\| = \sqrt{x^T x} = \left[\sum_1^n (x_i)^2\right]^{1/2}$$

For eigenvector ϕ_1

$$\|\phi_1\| = \left[\sum_1^n (\phi_i)^2\right]^{1/2}$$

or,

$$\|\phi_1\| = \sqrt{0.5195^2 + 0.3582^2 + 0.1942^2} = 0.6596$$

Eigenvector ϕ_1 can be normalized as follows:

$$1 = \|\phi_1\| = \phi_{11}\sqrt{0.5195^2 + 0.3582^2 + 0.1942^2} = \phi_{11}0.66$$

or, $$\phi_{11} = 1/0.66$$

or, $$\phi_{10} = \frac{1}{0.66}\begin{Bmatrix} 0.5195 \\ 0.3582 \\ 0.1942 \end{Bmatrix}$$

This vector ϕ_{10} is called as orthonormal since it was already an orthogonal vector. Now it has also been normalized.

Similarly, eigenvector ϕ_2 can be normalized as follows:

$$1 = \|\phi_2\| = \phi_{21}\sqrt{-0.4741^2 + 0.3476^2 + 0.3066^2} = \phi_{21}0.662$$

or, $$\phi_{21} = 1/0.662$$

or, $$\phi_{20} = \frac{1}{0.662}\begin{Bmatrix} -0.4741 \\ 0.3476 \\ 0.3066 \end{Bmatrix}$$

Similarly, eigenvector ϕ_3 can be normalized as follows:

$$1 = \|\phi_3\| = \phi_{31}\sqrt{(0.0734)^2 + (-0.2902)^2 + 0.6069^2} = \phi_{31}0.676$$

or, $$\phi_{30} = \frac{1}{0.676}\begin{Bmatrix} 0.0734 \\ -0.2902 \\ 0.6069 \end{Bmatrix}$$

Vectors ϕ_{10}, ϕ_{20} and ϕ_{30} are orthonormal vectors. □

Example 10.7

Consider a two storey steel frame as shown in Figure 10.14. The dead load at the roof girder is 10 kN/m^2 and that at the first floor girder is 15 kN/m^2. The dead load due to walls lumped at the top columns is 35 kN each and that lumped at the lower columns is 70 kN each. The bent spacing is 5 m c/c. Determine its frequencies and mode shapes.

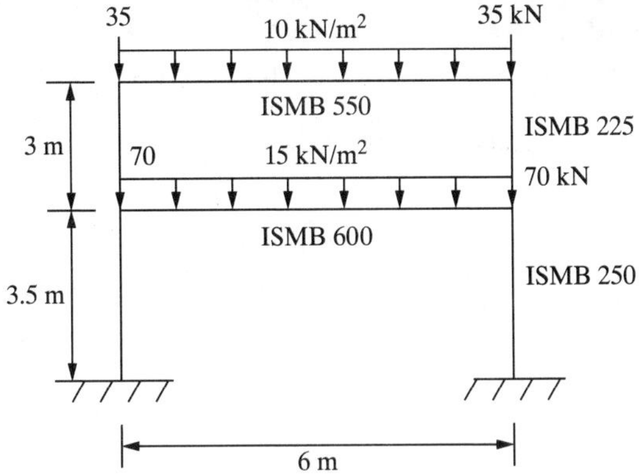

Figure 10.14 Two storey portal frame.

Solution

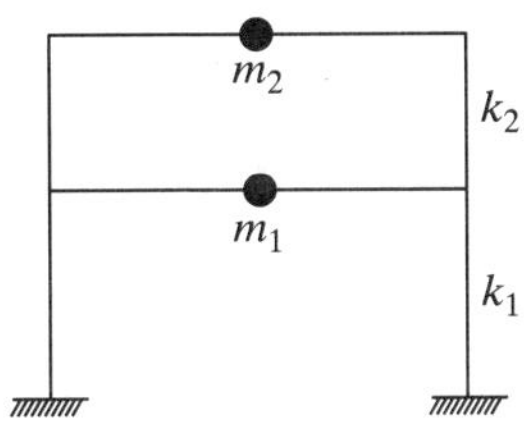

Figure 10.15(a) Idealized lumped mass system.

The properties of the ISMB steel sections used in this frame are as given in Table 10.7.

TABLE 10.7 PROPERTIES OF STEEL SECTIONS

Section	Moment of inertia cm^4	Stiffness I/L	Least radius of gyration, cm	Slenderness ratio L/r
ISMB 225	3441	11.47	9.31	32.2
ISMB 250	5131	14.66	10.39	33.7
ISMB 550	64893	108.15	22.16	27.1
ISMB 600	91813	153.0	24.24	24.75

It can be seen that the girders are very rigid as compared to columns with respect to I/L ratio. The 2-DOF idealized lumped mass system is shown in Figure 10.15(a). Let us determine the storey lateral stiffness. It can be determined by using the basic principles of stiffness method of structural analysis. First, the first floor is held against translation and a unit displacement is given to the roof. Alternatively, an arbitrary load, say 10 kN, is applied at the roof level and the lateral displacement of roof is determined. Next, roof is held against translation, and a unit displacement is given to the first floor. Alternatively, an arbitrary load, say 10 kN, is applied at the floor level and the lateral displacement of the floor is determined. This can be done using any manual method or any computer program for matrix analysis.

It is important to mention here that this method gives better results when the beams are taken as rigid. The ratio of I/L of the beams and columns of a given storey is about 10 in the present case which shows that the beams are very rigid.

Storey Stiffness

Case 1 – First floor is held against translation

The displaced shape of the frame is shown in Figure 10.15(b). The roof displacement is 1.96 mm due to a 10 kN lateral load.

$$\text{Storey stiffness } k_2 = \frac{10}{1.96} = 5.10 \text{ kN/mm}$$

Case 2 – Roof is held against translation

The displaced shape of the frame is shown in Figure 10.15(c). The support lateral reactions are also shown. The floor displacement is 0.98 mm due to a 10 kN lateral load.

Lateral forces in the storeys are shown in Figures 10.15(d) and (e). Net storey shear in second storey is $V_2 = 5.01$ kN.

$$\text{The second storey stiffness } k_2 = \frac{V_2}{\Delta} = \frac{5.01}{0.98} = 5.10 \text{ kN/mm}$$

This is the same value as obtained in the earlier case.

Net storey shear in first storey is $V_1 = 4.99$ kN.

$$\text{The first storey stiffness } k_1 = \frac{V_1}{\Delta} = \frac{4.99}{0.98} = 5.09 \text{ kN/mm} \approx 5.10 \text{ kN/mm}$$

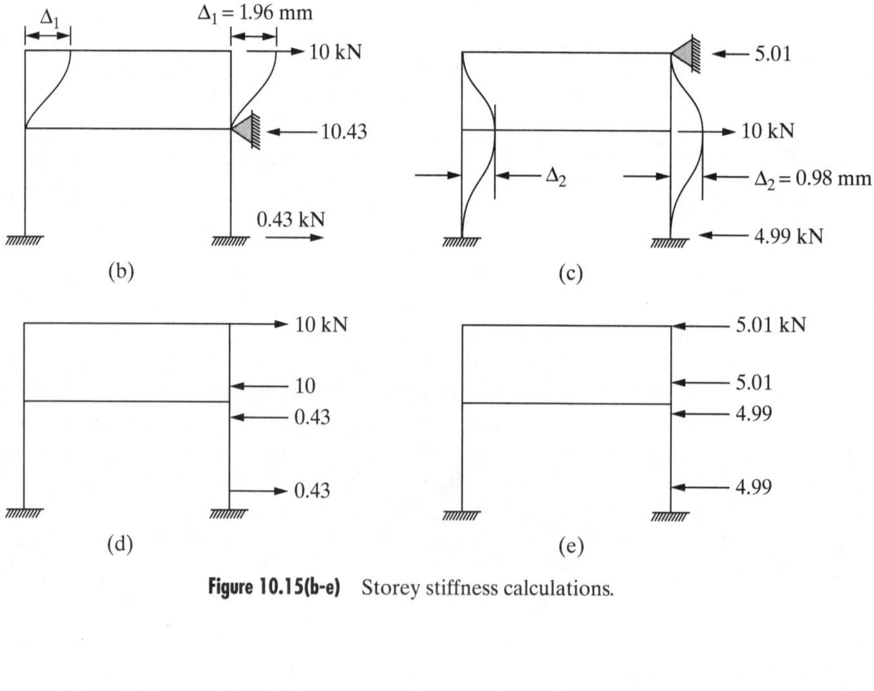

Figure 10.15(b-e) Storey stiffness calculations.

Mass Calculations

Mass of the second storey can be lumped at the roof while that of the first storey can be lumped at the first floor.

$$\text{Mass } m_2 = \frac{35+35+10\times5\times6}{g} = \frac{370}{9.81} = 37.7 \approx 38\frac{\text{kNs}^2}{\text{m}}$$

$$\text{Mass } m_1 = \frac{70+70+15\times5\times6}{g} = \frac{590}{9.81} = 60.14 \approx 60\frac{\text{kNs}^2}{\text{m}}$$

The mass matrix is

$$[M] = \begin{bmatrix} 60 & 0 \\ 0 & 38 \end{bmatrix}$$

and stiffness matrix is

$$[K] = \begin{bmatrix} k_1+k_2 & -k_1 \\ -k_1 & k_2 \end{bmatrix} = \begin{bmatrix} 10.2 & -5.1 \\ -5.1 & 5.1 \end{bmatrix}$$

Now the frequency and mode shapes can be determined by the methods discussed earlier.

$$\omega = \begin{Bmatrix} 6.618 \\ 16.137 \end{Bmatrix} \text{rad/sec} \quad \text{Period T} = \begin{Bmatrix} 0.95 \\ 0.39 \end{Bmatrix} \text{sec}$$

Mode shapes are given by

$$\Phi = \begin{bmatrix} 0.674 & -0.94 \\ 1 & 1 \end{bmatrix}$$

Mode shapes are shown in Figure 10.16.

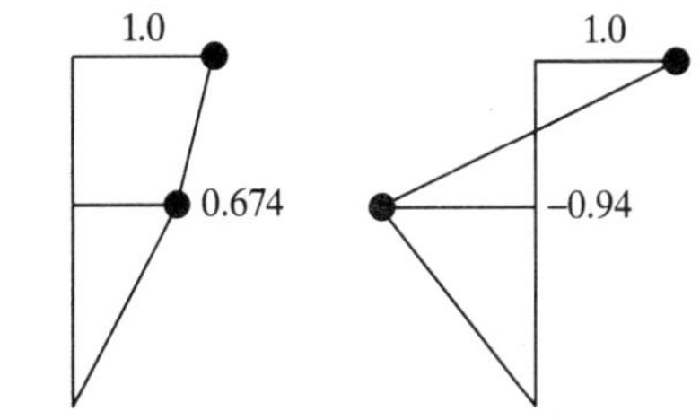

Figure 10.16 Mode shapes.

Let us check their orthogonality

$$\phi_1^T M \phi_2 = \{1 \quad 0.674\} \begin{bmatrix} 38 & 0 \\ 0 & 60 \end{bmatrix} \begin{Bmatrix} 1 \\ -0.94 \end{Bmatrix} = 0.0136 \approx 0 \qquad \text{OK}$$

Let us find the mode participation factors

$$\Gamma_r = \frac{\sum m_i \phi_i}{\sum m_i \phi_i^2}$$

For mode 1:

$$\Gamma_1 = \frac{60\times0.674+38\times1}{60\times0.674^2+38\times1^2} = \frac{78.44}{65.256} = 1.20$$

For mode 2: $$\Gamma_2 = \frac{60\times(-0.94)+38\times1}{60\times0.94^2+38\times1^2} = \frac{-18.4}{91} = -0.20$$

It shows that the participation of the first mode is much higher than that of second mode in the present case. The sign in the mode participation factors does not have any significance. □

Example 10.8

Consider the following two-DOF systems as shown in Figure 10.17 and determine if there is a resonance in each case.

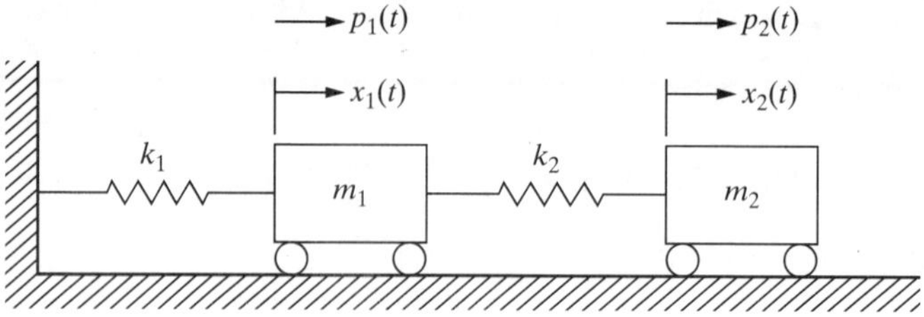

Figure 10.17 A two-DOF system

$$\boldsymbol{M} = \begin{bmatrix} 3 & 0 \\ 0 & 5 \end{bmatrix}, \quad \boldsymbol{K} = \begin{bmatrix} 20+4 & -4 \\ -4 & 4 \end{bmatrix}$$

(a) $P(t) = \begin{Bmatrix} 0.5 \\ 1.5 \end{Bmatrix} \sin 3.5t$

(b) $P(t) = \begin{Bmatrix} 0.2515 \\ 2.3078 \end{Bmatrix} \sin 2.854t$

Solution

Let us find its natural frequencies and mode shapes using MATLAB function eig. Frequencies are:

$$\begin{Bmatrix} \omega_1 \\ \omega_2 \end{Bmatrix} = \begin{Bmatrix} 0.8091 \\ 2.8540 \end{Bmatrix} \text{rad/sec}$$

and mode shapes are:

$$\phi_1 = \begin{Bmatrix} 0.0804 \\ 0.4429 \end{Bmatrix} \quad \text{and} \quad \phi_2 = \begin{Bmatrix} -0.5717 \\ 0.0623 \end{Bmatrix}$$

(a) The external force is given by

$$P(t) = \begin{Bmatrix} 0.5 \\ 1.5 \end{Bmatrix} \sin 3.5t$$

Where, the forcing frequency is 3.5 rad/sec.

In this case, the natural frequency of vibrations in each of the two modes is away from the forcing frequency of 3.5 rad/sec. Hence there is no scope of resonance.

(b) The external force is given by

$$P(t)=\begin{Bmatrix}0.2515\\2.3078\end{Bmatrix}\sin 2.854t$$

Where, the forcing frequency is 2.854 rad/sec.

In this case, the natural frequency of second mode is the same as the forcing frequency of vibration, that is, 2.8540 rad/sec. However, let us examine the uncoupled modal equations to check if this is a sufficient condition to cause resonance.

$$m_r\ddot{y}_r + c_r\dot{y}_r + k_r y_r = p_r(t) \tag{10.49}$$

Where,

$$p_r(t)=\phi_r^T P(t)$$

$$\therefore\ p_2(t)=\{-0.5717 \quad 0.0623\}\begin{Bmatrix}0.2515\\2.3078\end{Bmatrix}\sin 2.854t$$

$$=0$$

It means there is no external force applied in the second mode. That is, the second mode has not been excited. In other words, the vector of applied force distribution is orthogonal to the second mode shape. Therefore, there is no question of a resonance in this problem.

Thus, it is possible to avoid resonance by design. □

Example 10.9

Determine the free vibration response of the two-storey frame shown in Figure 10.18. The initial conditions are as follows:

$$x(0)=\begin{Bmatrix}1\\0.434\end{Bmatrix}\text{cm}, \quad \text{and} \quad \dot{x}(0)=\begin{Bmatrix}0\\0\end{Bmatrix}$$

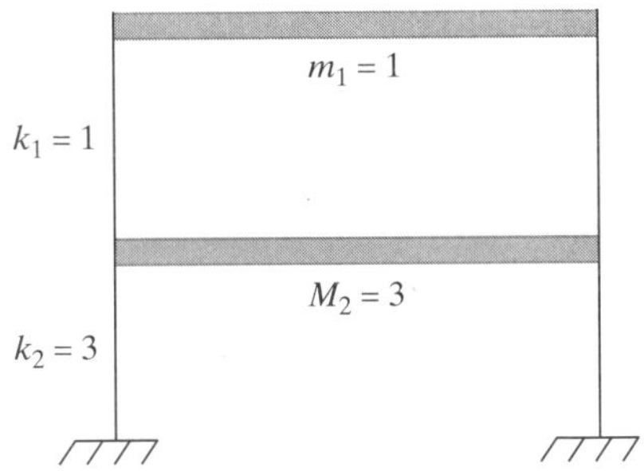

Figure 10.18 Two storey frame

Solution

The mass matrix can be written as

$$\boldsymbol{M}=\begin{bmatrix}1 & 0\\0 & 3\end{bmatrix}$$

The stiffness matrix can be written as

$$\boldsymbol{K} = \begin{bmatrix} 1 & -1 \\ -1 & 4 \end{bmatrix}$$

Its natural frequencies and mode shapes can be written using MATLAB function eig.

Frequencies are:

$$\begin{Bmatrix} \omega_1 \\ \omega_2 \end{Bmatrix} = \begin{Bmatrix} 0.752 \\ 1.330 \end{Bmatrix} \text{rad/sec}$$

and mode shapes are:

$$\phi_1 = \begin{Bmatrix} 1 \\ 0.434 \end{Bmatrix} \quad \text{and} \quad \phi_2 = \begin{Bmatrix} -1 \\ 0.768 \end{Bmatrix}$$

The modal parameters may be written as follows:

$$m_r = \phi_r^T M \phi_r$$

$$m_1 = \{1 \quad 0.434\} \begin{bmatrix} 1 & 0 \\ 0 & 3 \end{bmatrix} \begin{Bmatrix} 1 \\ 0.434 \end{Bmatrix} = 1.565$$

and

$$m_2 = \{-1 \quad 0.768\} \begin{bmatrix} 1 & 0 \\ 0 & 3 \end{bmatrix} \begin{Bmatrix} -1 \\ 0.768 \end{Bmatrix} = 2.769$$

Now, the initial conditions in normal coordinates can be written as

$$y_1(0) = \frac{\phi_r^T M \{x(0)\}}{m_1} = \frac{\{1 \quad 0.434\} \begin{bmatrix} 1 & 0 \\ 0 & 3 \end{bmatrix} \begin{Bmatrix} 1 \\ 0.434 \end{Bmatrix}}{1.565} = 1.0$$

and

$$y_2(0) = \frac{\phi_r^T M \{x(0)\}}{m_2} = \frac{\{-1 \quad 0.768\} \begin{bmatrix} 1 & 0 \\ 0 & 3 \end{bmatrix} \begin{Bmatrix} 1 \\ 0.434 \end{Bmatrix}}{2.769} = 0$$

The modal response can be written as

$$y(t) = \begin{Bmatrix} y_1(t) \\ y_2(t) \end{Bmatrix} = \begin{Bmatrix} y_1(0)\cos\omega_1 t \\ y_2(0)\cos\omega_2 t \end{Bmatrix}$$

That is,

$$y_1(t) = \cos 0.752t \quad \text{and} \quad y_2(t) = 0$$

The second mode displacement is zero because the initial condition at $t = 0$ is proportional to the first mode which is orthogonal to the second mode.

The geometric displacements can be written as

$$x = \Phi y$$

or,

$$x_1(t) = \cos 0.752t \quad \text{and} \quad x_2(t) = 0.434\cos 0.752t$$

It is obvious that the lower floor displacements are lower than those of the top floor.

The plots of modal and geometric displacements are shown in Figure 10.19. □

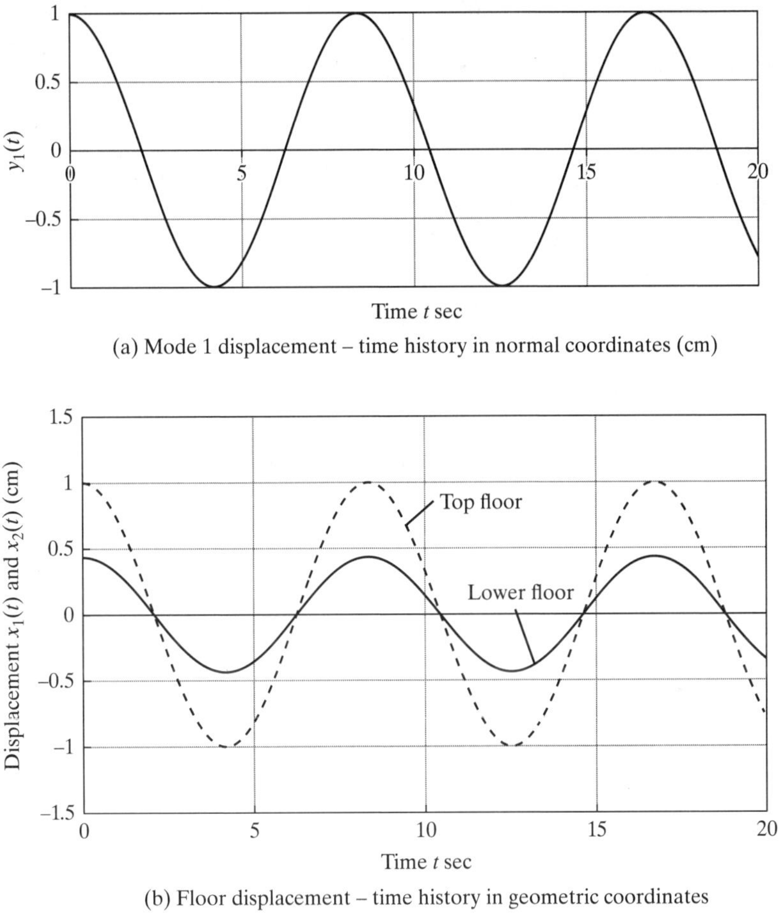

Figure 10.19 Modal and geometric displacement time histories

Example 10.10

Consider the Example 9.12(i) and determine the response of two-DOF undamped system under free vibrations using modal analysis technique.

Solution

$$\boldsymbol{M} = \begin{bmatrix} 10 & 0 \\ 0 & 1 \end{bmatrix} \quad \text{and} \quad \boldsymbol{K} = \begin{bmatrix} 30 & -5 \\ -5 & 5 \end{bmatrix}$$

Its frequencies and mode shapes are as follows:

$$\omega = \begin{Bmatrix} 1.46 \\ 2.42 \end{Bmatrix} \text{rad/sec}, \quad \phi_1 = \begin{Bmatrix} 0.574 \\ 1 \end{Bmatrix} \quad \text{and} \quad \phi_2 = \begin{Bmatrix} -0.174 \\ 1 \end{Bmatrix}$$

The initial conditions were given as:

$$x(0) = \begin{Bmatrix} 2 \\ 0 \end{Bmatrix} \text{mm and } \dot{x}(0) = \begin{Bmatrix} 0 \\ 0 \end{Bmatrix} \text{mm/sec}$$

The modal parameters may be written as follows:

$$m_r = \phi_r^T M \phi_r$$

$$m_1 = \{0.574 \quad 1\} \begin{bmatrix} 10 & 0 \\ 0 & 1 \end{bmatrix} \begin{Bmatrix} 0.574 \\ 1 \end{Bmatrix} = 4.294$$

and

$$m_2 = \{-0.174 \quad 1\} \begin{bmatrix} 10 & 0 \\ 0 & 1 \end{bmatrix} \begin{Bmatrix} -0.174 \\ 1 \end{Bmatrix} = 1.303$$

Now, the initial conditions in normal coordinates can be written as

$$y_1(0) = \frac{\phi_r^T M\{x(0)\}}{m_1} = \frac{\{0.574 \quad 1\} \begin{bmatrix} 10 & 0 \\ 0 & 1 \end{bmatrix} \begin{Bmatrix} 2 \\ 0 \end{Bmatrix}}{4.294} = 2.67$$

And

$$y_2(0) = \frac{\phi_r^T M\{x(0)\}}{m_2} = \frac{\{-0.174 \quad 1\} \begin{bmatrix} 10 & 0 \\ 0 & 1 \end{bmatrix} \begin{Bmatrix} 2 \\ 0 \end{Bmatrix}}{1.303} = -2.67$$

The modal response can be written as follows because the initial velocity is zero.

$$y(t) = \begin{Bmatrix} y_1(t) \\ y_2(t) \end{Bmatrix} = \begin{Bmatrix} y_1(0)\cos\omega_1 t \\ y_2(0)\cos\omega_2 t \end{Bmatrix}$$

That is,

$$y_1(t) = 2.67\cos 1.46t \quad \text{and} \quad y_2(t) = -2.67\cos 2.42t$$

The geometric displacements $x(t)$ can be written as

$$x(t) = \begin{Bmatrix} x_1(t) \\ x_2(t) \end{Bmatrix} = \begin{bmatrix} 0.574 & -0.174 \\ 1 & 1 \end{bmatrix} \times \begin{Bmatrix} 2.67\cos 1.46t \\ -2.67\cos 2.42t \end{Bmatrix}$$

or,

$$x(t) = \begin{Bmatrix} 1.532\cos 1.46t + 0.464\cos 2.42t \\ 2.670\cos 1.46t - 2.670\cos 2.42t \end{Bmatrix}$$

This solution is the same as obtained in Example 9.12 using the basic principles of solution of differential equations but it is much more convenient and faster. □

Example 10.11

Consider the Example 6.3 on drop hammer foundation and determine the response of two-DOF undamped system under free vibrations using modal analysis technique.

Solution

$$\boldsymbol{M} = \begin{bmatrix} 135000 & 0 \\ 0 & 32000 \end{bmatrix} \text{ and } \boldsymbol{K} = \begin{bmatrix} 13.6E08 & -6.1E08 \\ -6.1E08 & 6.1E08 \end{bmatrix}$$

Its frequencies, periods and mode shapes are as follows:

$$\omega = \begin{Bmatrix} 65.24 \\ 157.74 \end{Bmatrix} \text{rad/sec}, \quad \boldsymbol{T} = \begin{Bmatrix} 0.0960 \\ 0.0398 \end{Bmatrix} \text{sec}, \ \phi_1 = \begin{Bmatrix} 0.766 \\ 1 \end{Bmatrix} \text{ and } \phi_2 = \begin{Bmatrix} -0.3 \\ 1 \end{Bmatrix}$$

The initial conditions were given as:

$$x(0) = \begin{Bmatrix} 0 \\ 0 \end{Bmatrix} \text{m and } \dot{x}(0) = \begin{Bmatrix} 0 \\ 0.26 \end{Bmatrix} \text{m/sec}$$

The modal parameters may be written as follows:

$$m_r = \phi_r^T M \phi_r$$

$$m_1 = \{0.766 \quad 1\} \begin{bmatrix} 135000 & 0 \\ 0 & 32000 \end{bmatrix} \begin{Bmatrix} 0.766 \\ 1 \end{Bmatrix} = 111212$$

and

$$m_2 = \{-0.3 \quad 1\} \begin{bmatrix} 135000 & 0 \\ 0 & 32000 \end{bmatrix} \begin{Bmatrix} -0.3 \\ 1 \end{Bmatrix} = 44150$$

Now, the initial conditions in normal coordinates can be written as

$$y_1(0) = \frac{\phi_r^T M \{x(0)\}}{m_1} = 0 = y_2(0)$$

and

$$\dot{y}_1(0) = \frac{\phi_r^T M \{\dot{x}(0)\}}{m_1} = \frac{\{0.766 \quad 1\} \begin{bmatrix} 135000 & 0 \\ 0 & 32000 \end{bmatrix} \begin{Bmatrix} 0 \\ 0.26 \end{Bmatrix}}{111212} = 0.0748$$

$$\dot{y}_2(0) = \frac{\phi_r^T M \{\dot{x}(0)\}}{m_2} = \frac{\{-0.3 \quad 1\} \begin{bmatrix} 135000 & 0 \\ 0 & 32000 \end{bmatrix} \begin{Bmatrix} 0 \\ 0.26 \end{Bmatrix}}{44150} = 0.188$$

The modal velocity is in m/s. The modal response can be written as follows because the initial displacement is zero.

$$y(t) = \begin{Bmatrix} y_1(t) \\ y_2(t) \end{Bmatrix} = \begin{Bmatrix} \dfrac{\dot{y}_1(0)}{\omega_1} \sin \omega_1 t \\ \dfrac{\dot{y}_2(0)}{\omega_2} \sin \omega_2 t \end{Bmatrix}$$

That is,

$$y_1(t) = 1.146 \sin 65.24t \text{ and } y_2(t) = 1.192 \sin 157.74t$$

The modal displacements are in mm. The geometric displacements x(t) can be written as

$$x(t)=\begin{Bmatrix} x_1(t) \\ x_2(t) \end{Bmatrix}=\begin{bmatrix} 0.766 & -0.3 \\ 1 & 1 \end{bmatrix}\times\begin{Bmatrix} 1.146\sin 65.24t \\ 1.192\sin 157.7t \end{Bmatrix}$$

or,

$$x(t)=\begin{Bmatrix} 0.877\sin 65.24t-0.357\sin 157.7t \\ 1.146\sin 65.24t+1.192\sin 157.7t \end{Bmatrix}$$

The results are shown in Figure 10.20(a) for the displacement of anvil and in Figure 10.20(b) for the foundation. This problem could have been solved using the basic principles of differential equations but the modal analysis approach is much more convenient and faster. □

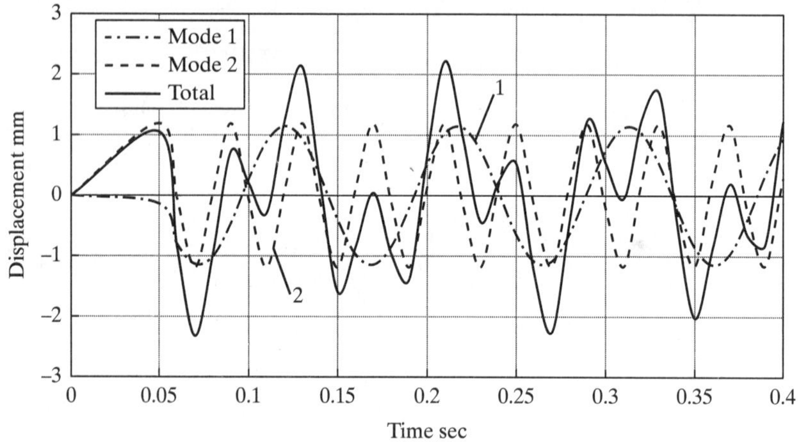

Figure 10.20(a) Displacement of anvil, mm

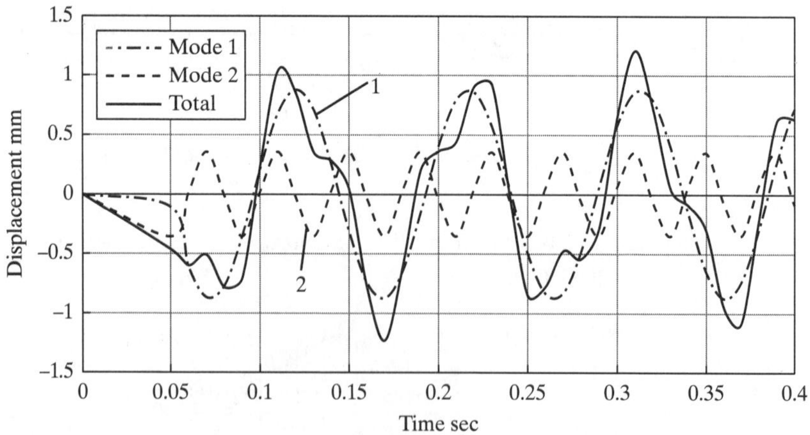

Figure 10.20(b) Displacement of foundation, mm

Example 10.12

Consider the two storey frame shown in Example 10.7. Determine its undamped free response if the initial conditions are as follows:

$$\{x(0)\} = \begin{Bmatrix} 1 \\ -1 \end{Bmatrix} \text{cm} \quad \text{and} \quad \{\dot{x}(0)\} = \begin{Bmatrix} 0 \\ 0 \end{Bmatrix}$$

Solution

Let us find $\{y(0)\}$ and $\{\dot{y}(0)\}$ using Equation (10.52)

$$y_r(0) = \frac{\phi_r^T[M]\{x(0)\}}{\phi_r^T M \phi_r} \quad \text{and} \quad \dot{y}_r(0) = \frac{\phi_r^T[M]\{\dot{x}(0)\}}{\phi_r^T M \phi_r}$$

The mass matrix is

$$[M] = \begin{bmatrix} 60 & 0 \\ 0 & 38 \end{bmatrix}$$

Frequency and mode shapes are as follows:

$$\omega = \begin{Bmatrix} 6.618 \\ 16.137 \end{Bmatrix} \text{rad/sec}$$

Mode shapes are given by

$$\Phi = \begin{bmatrix} 0.674 & -0.94 \\ 1 & 1 \end{bmatrix}$$

Initial conditions in normal coordinates are given by:

$$y_1(0) = \frac{\phi_1^T[M]\{x_1(0)\}}{\phi_1^T M \phi_1} \qquad y_1(0) = \frac{\{1 \quad 0.674\}\begin{bmatrix} 60 & 0 \\ 0 & 38 \end{bmatrix}\begin{Bmatrix} 1 \\ -1 \end{Bmatrix}}{\{1 \quad 0.674\}\begin{bmatrix} 60 & 0 \\ 0 & 38 \end{bmatrix}\begin{Bmatrix} 1 \\ 0.674 \end{Bmatrix}} = 0.445$$

$$y_2(0) = \frac{\{1 \quad -0.94\}\begin{bmatrix} 60 & 0 \\ 0 & 38 \end{bmatrix}\begin{Bmatrix} 1 \\ -1 \end{Bmatrix}}{\{1 \quad -0.94\}\begin{bmatrix} 60 & 0 \\ 0 & 38 \end{bmatrix}\begin{Bmatrix} 1 \\ -0.94 \end{Bmatrix}} = -0.26$$

The initial velocity vector $\{\dot{y}(0)\}$ will be nil as $\{\dot{x}(0)\}$ is also nil.
The solution can be written as Equation (10.54):

$$y_r(t) = y_r(0)\cos\omega_r t + \frac{\dot{y}_r(0)}{\omega_r}\sin\omega_r t$$

or,

$$\{y(t)\} = \begin{Bmatrix} y_1(t) \\ y_2(t) \end{Bmatrix} = \begin{Bmatrix} 0.45\cos(6.618t) \\ -0.26\cos(16.137t) \end{Bmatrix}$$

and

$$X_{2\times1}(t) = \Phi_{2\times2}Y_{2\times1}(t)$$

$$X_{2\times1}(t) = \begin{bmatrix} 0.674 & -0.94 \\ 1 & 1 \end{bmatrix}\begin{Bmatrix} 0.45\cos(6.618t) \\ -0.26\cos(16.137t) \end{Bmatrix}$$

or,

$$X_{2\times1}(t) = \begin{Bmatrix} 0.30\cos(6.618t) + 0.25\cos(16.137t) \\ 0.45\cos(6.618t) - 0.26\cos(16.137t) \end{Bmatrix}$$

The modal displacements and floor displacements are shown in Figure 10.21. These displacements follow free vibration pattern in the absence of any damping. The first mode displacements are higher than those of the second mode. The maximum and minimum values of floor displacements occur at different instants as shown in Table 10.8. □

TABLE 10.8 DISPLACEMENT MAXIMA AND THEIR TIME OF OCCURRENCE

Value	First Floor		Roof	
	Displacement, cm	Time, s	Displacement, cm	Time, s
Maximum	0.547	0	0.70	0.97
Minimum	−0.546	3.31	−0.704	4.28

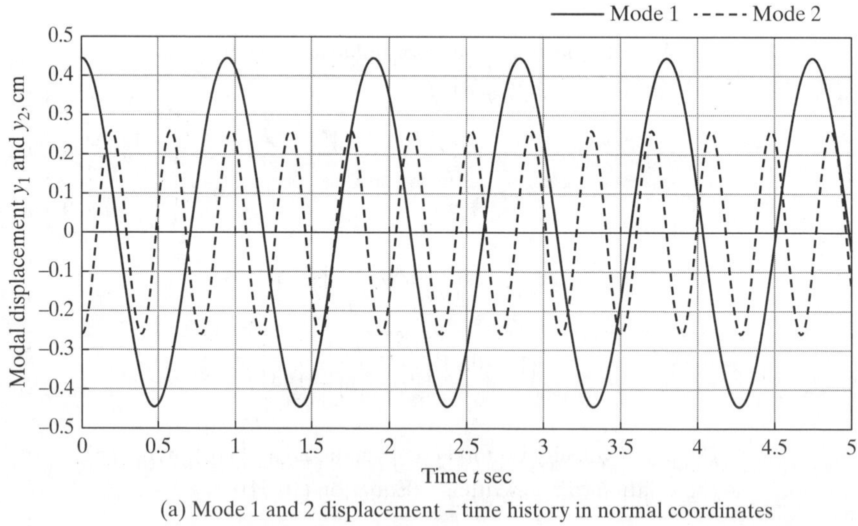

(a) Mode 1 and 2 displacement – time history in normal coordinates

Figure 10.21 Modal and floor displacement – time history under free vibrations

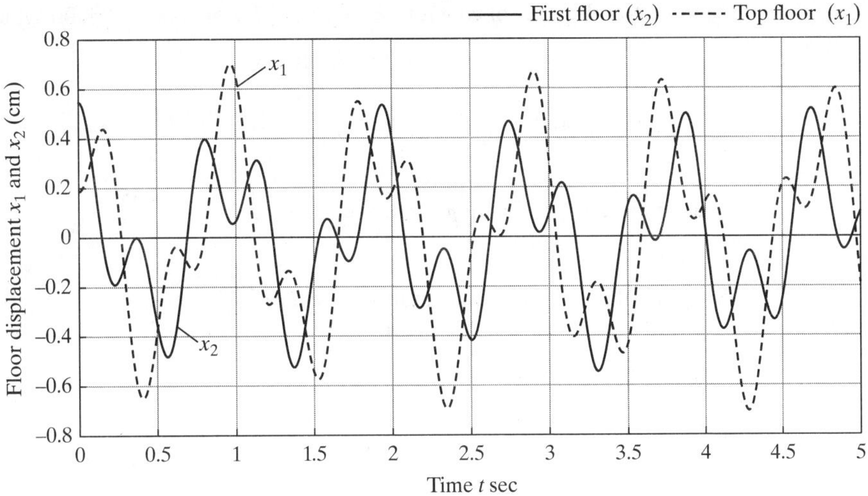

(b) Floor displacement – time history in geometric coordinates

Figure 10.21 (Continued)

Example 10.13

Consider a two bay × three storey RC frame as shown in Figure 10.22(a). The floor is rigid. The mass at the first floor girder, second floor girder and roof is 75, 75 and 50 kN-s²/m, respectively. The column sizes from top are: 300 × 300 mm, 300 × 350 mm, 300 × 400 mm. Determine the storey stiffness, frequencies and mode shapes. Grade of concrete is M25.

Also, compute storey shears and floor forces using an elastic response spectra.

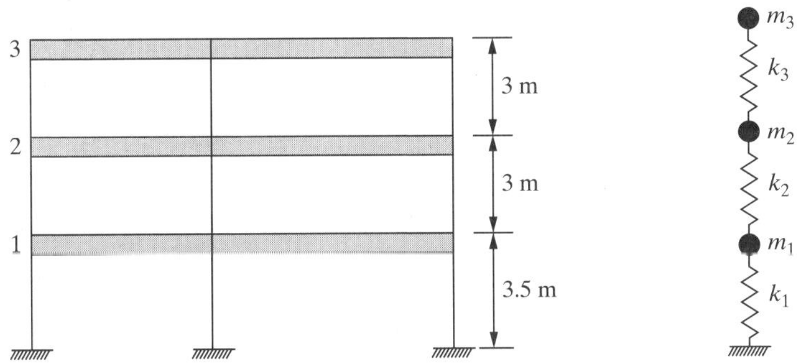

(a) (b) Spring mass idealization

Figure 10.22 Two bay-three storey frame.

Solution

It may be noted that the DOF may be numbered either from top or from bottom. In the present case, these have been numbered from bottom. The equations of motion will change accordingly.

Modulus of elasticity of concrete $E_c = 5000\sqrt{fck} = 5000 \times 5 = 25000$ MPa

or, $E_c = 2500$ kN/cm²

Moment of inertia of top storey column $= \dfrac{bD^3}{12} = \dfrac{30 \times 30^3}{12} = 67500 \text{ cm}^4$

Moment of inertia of middle storey column $= \dfrac{bD^3}{12} = \dfrac{30 \times 35^3}{12} = 107200 \text{ cm}^4$

Moment of inertia of bottom storey column $= \dfrac{bD^3}{12} = \dfrac{30 \times 40^3}{12} = 160000 \text{ cm}^4$

Lateral stiffness of one column $k = \dfrac{12EI}{L^3}$

Lateral stiffness of top storey column $k = \dfrac{12EI}{L^3} = \dfrac{12 \times 2500 \times 67500}{300^3} = 75 \text{ kN/cm}$

Lateral stiffness of middle storey column $k = \dfrac{12EI}{L^3} = \dfrac{12 \times 2500 \times 107200}{300^3} = 119 \text{ kN/cm}$

Lateral stiffness of bottom storey column $k = \dfrac{12EI}{L^3} = \dfrac{12 \times 2500 \times 160000}{350^3} = 112 \text{ kN/cm}$

The total lateral stiffness of top storey $k_3 = 3$ k = 22500 kN/m
The total lateral stiffness of middle storey $k_2 = 3$ k = 35700 kN/m
The total lateral stiffness of bottom storey $k_1 = 3$ k = 33600 kN/m
Now a three DOF mass-spring model of the building can be developed as shown in Figure 10.21(b). Mass and stiffness matrices can be determined as follows:

$$[M] = \begin{bmatrix} m_1 & 0 & 0 \\ 0 & m_2 & 0 \\ 0 & 0 & m_3 \end{bmatrix} \quad [K] = \begin{bmatrix} k_1 + k_2 & -k_2 & 0 \\ -k_2 & k_2 + k_3 & -k_3 \\ 0 & -k_3 & k_3 \end{bmatrix}$$

$$[M] = \begin{bmatrix} 75 & 0 & 0 \\ 0 & 75 & 0 \\ 0 & 0 & 50 \end{bmatrix} \text{ and } [K] = \begin{bmatrix} 69300 & -35700 & 0 \\ -35700 & 58200 & -22500 \\ 0 & -22500 & 22500 \end{bmatrix}$$

$$\{\omega\} = \begin{Bmatrix} 10.30 \\ 25.42 \\ 37.38 \end{Bmatrix} \text{ rad/sec and } [\Phi] = \begin{bmatrix} 0.445 & 0.748 & -2.118 \\ 0.763 & 0.436 & 2.105 \\ 1.0 & -1.0 & -1.0 \end{bmatrix}$$

Mode shapes are shown in Figure 10.23.
Let us find the mode participation factors

$$\Gamma_r = \frac{\sum m_i \phi_i}{\sum m_i \phi_i^2}$$

This can be done in a tabular form for convenience as shown in Table 10.9.

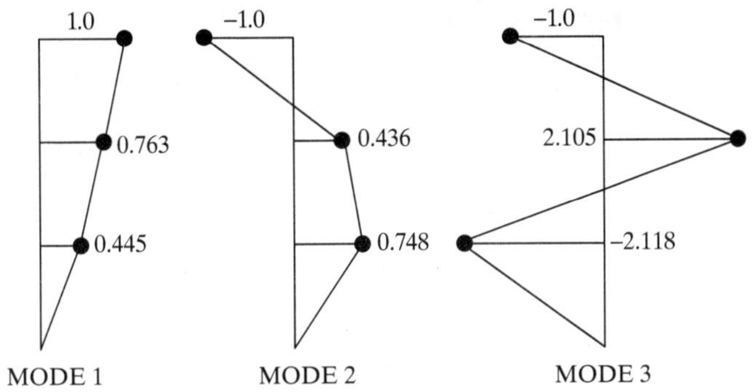

Figure 10.23 Mode shapes.

TABLE 10.9 MODE PARTICIPATION FACTORS

Floor	m_i	Mode 1 ϕ_i	$m_i\phi_i$	$m_i\phi_i^2$	Mode 2 ϕ_i	$m_i\phi_i$	$m_i\phi_i^2$	Mode 3 ϕ_i	$m_i\phi_i$	$m_i\phi_i^2$
Bottom	75	0.445	33.37	14.85	0.748	56.1	41.96	−2.118	−158.85	336.45
Middle	75	0.763	57.22	43.66	0.436	32.7	14.26	2.105	157.87	332.33
Top	50	1.0	50	50	−1.0	−50	50	−1	−50	50
	Σ		140.59	108.51		38.8	106.22		−50.98	718.78

Mode participation factor in mode 1 = 140.59/108.51 = 1.30
Mode participation factor in mode 2 = 38.8/106.22 = 0.365
Mode participation factor in mode 3 = −50.98/718.78 = − 0.071
Two observations can be made from these factors:

1. The participation factor is maximum for mode 1 and thereafter it decreases very rapidly.
2. It may be positive or negative. Negative participation factor has no physical significance.

Let us read the spectral acceleration for 5% damping from Housner's average spectra given in Figure 8.17(b) as shown in Table 10.10.

Let us calculate the floor displacements in different modes, storey drifts and storey shears knowing the storey stiffness as shown in Table 10.11, Table 10.12 and Table 10.13, respectively.

The SRSS values of the floor forces and storey shears are shown in Figure 10.24.

TABLE 10.10 SPECTRAL VALUES

Mode	Frequency ω	Period T sec	MPF	S_a/g	$S_d = \dfrac{S_a}{\omega^2}$ cm	MPF × S_d
1	10.30	0.61	1.30	0.15	1.39	1.81
2	25.42	0.247	0.365	0.20	0.30	0.11
3	37.38	0.168	−0.071	0.20	0.14	−0.01

TABLE 10.11 MODAL DISPLACEMENTS OF FLOORS

	First Floor		Middle Floor		Roof	
Mode	ϕ_i	$\phi_i \Gamma S_d$	ϕ_i	$\phi_i \Gamma S_d$	ϕ_i	$\phi_i \Gamma S_d$
1	0.445	0.805	0.763	1.38	1	1.81
2	0.748	0.082	0.436	0.048	−1	−0.11
3	−2.118	0.021	2.105	−0.021	−1	0.01

TABLE 10.12 MODAL STOREY DRIFTS

	Ground Storey		Middle Storey		Top Storey	
Mode	$\phi_1 \Gamma S_d$	$\lvert x_1 \rvert$	$(\phi_2 - \phi_1)\Gamma S_d$	$\lvert x_2 \rvert$	$(\phi_3 - \phi_2)\Gamma S_d$	$\lvert x_3 \rvert$
1	0.805	0.805	1.38 − 0.805	0.575	1.81 − 1.38	0.43
2	0.082	0.082	0.048 − 0.082	0.034	−0.11 − 0.048	0.16
3	0.021	0.021	−0.021 − 0.021	0.042	−0.01 + 0.021	0.03

TABLE 10.13 STOREY SHEAR USING MODAL STOREY DRIFTS

	Abs Max value		SRSS Value	
Storey	Storey Displacement, cm	Storey Shear kN	Storey Displacement, cm	Storey Shear kN
Top	0.43 + 0.16 + 0.03 = 0.62	140	SQRT($0.43^2 + 0.16^2 + 0.03^2$) = 0.46	104
Middle	0.575 + 0.034 + 0.042 = 0.65	232	SQRT($0.575^2 + 0.034^2 + 0.042^2$) = 0.57	204
Ground	0.805 + 0.082 + 0.021 = 0.91	306	SQRT($0.805^2 + 0.082^2 + 0.021^2$) = 0.81	272

The first mode makes the maximum contribution to storey shears in all cases. The second mode also makes significant contribution to the top storey. In Table 10.13, the base shear is 272 kN using the SRSS method against 306 kN using the absolute sum of modal values. The latter is the upper bound and is not recommended for use in practice. The SRSS values of the floor forces and storey shears are shown in Figure 10.24.

Alternatively, let us determine the storey shears using the modal values of floor forces as shown in Table 10.14. The S_a/g values for different modes were obtained in Table 10.10. Peak floor forces are obtained by making use of absolute sum and SRSS method as shown in Table 10.15. The peak values of storey shears are obtained from the peak values of the floor forces as shown in Table 10.15. The base shear in Table 10.15 is 297 kN while the base shear in Table 10.13 is 272 kN. This method is incorrect. A peak response quantity cannot be obtained from another peak response quantity.

Another quantity of interest is lateral floor accelerations. The modal floor accelerations are shown in Table 10.14. The SRSS value of top floor acceleration is as follows:

$$\text{Top floor lateral acceleration SRSS value} = \sqrt{0.195^2 + 0.073^2 + 0.0142^2} = 0.208\ \text{g}$$

TABLE 10.14 MODAL FLOOR FORCES AND ACCELERATIONS

Mode	First Floor			Middle Floor			Roof		
	ϕ_i	$\phi_i\Gamma S_a/g$	$\phi_i\Gamma S_a m_i$	ϕ_i	$\phi_i\Gamma S_a/g$	$\phi_i\Gamma S_a m_i$	ϕ_i	$\phi_i\Gamma S_a/g$	$\phi_i\Gamma S_a m_i$
1	0.445	0.0867	64	0.763	0.148	110	1	0.195	96
2	0.748	0.0546	41	0.436	0.0318	23	–1	–0.073	–36
3	–2.118	0.03	22	2.105	0.0299	–22	–1	–0.0142	7

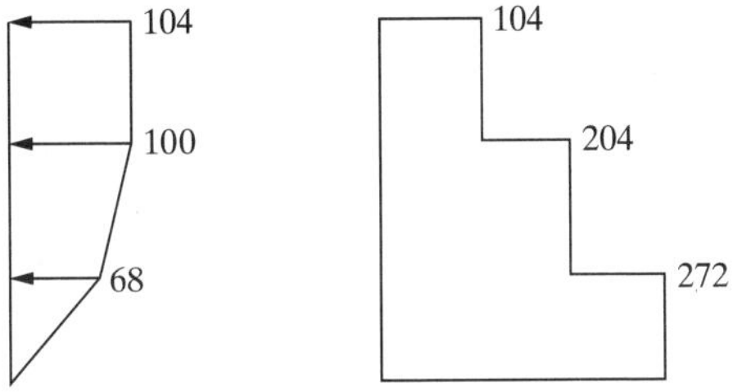

(a) Floor lateral force (kN) (b) Storey shear (kN)

Figure 10.24 Lateral force distribution using SRSS values.

TABLE 10.15 LATERAL FORCES AND STOREY SHEARS – INCORRECT METHOD

	Abs Max Value kN		SRSS Value kN	
Floor	Force F_i	Shear V_i	Force F_i	Shear V_i
Roof	96 + 36 + 7 = 139	139	SQRT($96^2 + 36^2 + 7^2$) = 103	103
Middle	110 + 23 + 22 = 155	294	SQRT($110^2 + 23^2 + 22^2$) = 115	218
First	64 + 41 + 22 = 127	421	SQRT($64^2 + 41^2 + 22^2$) = 79	297

10.12 RAYLEIGH DAMPING

Consider Equation (10.47)

$$\Phi^T M\Phi\ddot{Y} + \Phi^T C\Phi\dot{Y} + \Phi^T K\Phi Y = \Phi^T P(t) \tag{10.47a}$$

$$C_n = \Phi^T C\Phi \tag{10.47b}$$

The square matrix given by Equation (10.47b) may or may not be a diagonal matrix depending upon the nature of matrix C. If C is diagonal, then Equation (10.47a) represents N uncoupled differential equations in normal coordinates. The system possesses the same natural modes as those of the undamped system. The system is said to have *classical damping*. If C is not diagonal matrix, then Equation (10.47a) cannot be uncoupled. The undamped natural modes are not the modes of the damped system. Such a damping is called *nonclassical damping*. Such a system cannot be solved using modal analysis.

Let us consider mass and stiffness proportional damping as follows:

$$\boldsymbol{C} = a_0 \boldsymbol{M} \quad \text{and} \quad \boldsymbol{C} = a_1 \boldsymbol{K} \tag{10.74}$$

In both cases, Equation (10.74) will be a diagonal matrix in view of orthogonal properties of the mode shapes. Thus, Equation (10.74) represents *classical damping*. Let us relate the modal damping ratios for a system with mass proportional damping to the coefficient a_0. The generalized damping for the nth mode is

$$C_n = a_0 M_n$$

We know for a SDOF system,

$$c = 2\,\mathrm{m}\omega\xi$$

$$\therefore \quad C_n = 2M_n\omega_n\xi_n \tag{10.75}$$

$$\therefore \quad \xi_n = \frac{a_0}{2\omega_n} \tag{10.76}$$

The coefficient a_0 can be determined using the specified damping in any mode i

$$a_0 = 2\omega_i\xi_i \tag{10.77}$$

Knowing a_0, damping in any other mode can be obtained using Equation (10.76).

Similarly, the modal damping ratio for a system with stiffness proportional damping can be related to the coefficient a_1 as follows:

$$C_n = a_1 K_n = a_1 \omega_n^2 M_n$$

also,

$$C_n = 2M_n\omega_n\xi_n \tag{10.75}$$

$$\therefore \quad a_1\omega_n = 2\xi_n$$

or,

$$\xi_n = \frac{a_1\omega_n}{2} \tag{10.78}$$

The coefficient a_1 can be determined using the specified damping in any mode i

$$a_1 = \frac{2\xi_i}{\omega_i} \tag{10.79}$$

Thus, modal damping in any mode can be determined using Equation (10.78).

Both mass proportional damping and stiffness proportional damping given by Equation (10.74) are not suitable for use in a MDOF system. The results are not consistent with those obtained experimentally. Therefore, there is a need to develop another formulation called *Rayleigh Damping* given as follows:

$$\boldsymbol{C} = a_0\boldsymbol{M} + a_1\boldsymbol{K} \tag{10.80}$$

The damping ratio for the nth mode is given by

$$\xi_n = \frac{a_0}{2\omega_n} + \frac{a_1\omega_n}{2} \tag{10.81}$$

The coefficients a_0 and a_1 can be determined knowing the damping ratios in any two modes i and j.

Thus, $$\xi_i = \frac{a_0}{2\omega_i} + \frac{a_1\omega_i}{2} \qquad \xi_j = \frac{a_0}{2\omega_j} + \frac{a_1\omega_j}{2}$$

These two relations can be written as:

$$\begin{Bmatrix} \xi_i \\ \xi_j \end{Bmatrix} = \frac{1}{2}\begin{bmatrix} \frac{1}{\omega_i} & \omega_i \\ \frac{1}{\omega_j} & \omega_j \end{bmatrix}\begin{Bmatrix} a_0 \\ a_1 \end{Bmatrix} \tag{10.82a}$$

The coefficients a_0 and a_1 can be determined. In case, any two modes have equal damping ratios, the coefficients are as follows:

$$a_0 = \frac{\omega_i\omega_j}{\omega_i + \omega_j}\xi \tag{10.82b}$$

and $$a_1 = \frac{2\xi}{\omega_i + \omega_j} \tag{10.82c}$$

The two modes i and j should be chosen to ensure reasonable values of damping ratios in all other modes contributing significantly to the overall response. The variation of Rayleigh damping is shown in Figure 10.25.

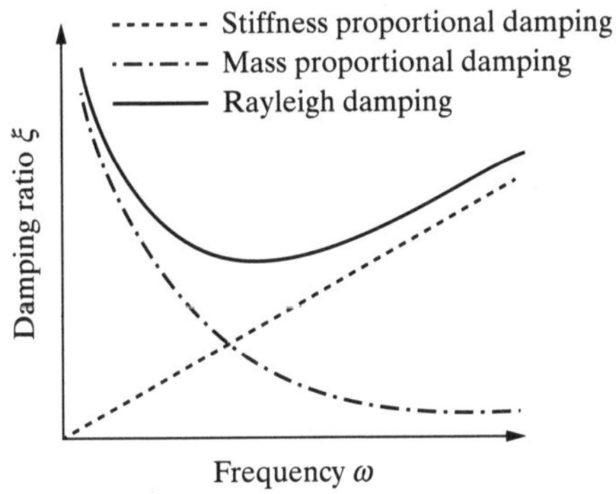

Figure 10.25 Rayleigh damping vs frequency.

Example 10.14

Consider the three storey moment resistant frame of Example 10.13. If the Rayleigh damping in the first two modes is 5% each, determine the damping in the third mode.

Solution

The mass matrix, stiffness, frequency and mode shapes were determined as follows:

$$[M]=\begin{bmatrix}75 & 0 & 0\\ 0 & 75 & 0\\ 0 & 0 & 50\end{bmatrix} \text{ and } [K]=\begin{bmatrix}69300 & -35700 & 0\\ -35700 & 58200 & -22500\\ 0 & -22500 & 22500\end{bmatrix}$$

$$\{\omega\}=\begin{Bmatrix}10.30\\ 25.42\\ 37.38\end{Bmatrix} \text{ rad/sec and } [\Phi]=\begin{bmatrix}0.445 & 0.748 & -2.118\\ 0.763 & 0.436 & 2.105\\ 1.0 & -1.0 & -1.0\end{bmatrix}$$

For any two modes

$$\frac{1}{2}\begin{bmatrix}1/\omega_i & \omega_i\\ 1/\omega_j & \omega_j\end{bmatrix}\begin{Bmatrix}a_0\\ a_1\end{Bmatrix}=\begin{Bmatrix}\xi_i\\ \xi_j\end{Bmatrix}$$

or,

$$\frac{1}{2}\begin{bmatrix}1/10.30 & 10.30\\ 1/25.42 & 25.42\end{bmatrix}\begin{Bmatrix}a_0\\ a_1\end{Bmatrix}=\begin{Bmatrix}0.05\\ 0.05\end{Bmatrix}$$

This equation is of the form

$$[A]\{x\}=\{b\} \quad \text{or} \quad \{x\}=[A]^{-1}\{b\}$$

where,

$$[A]=\begin{bmatrix}a_{11} & a_{12}\\ a_{21} & a_{22}\end{bmatrix}$$

$$\therefore \qquad [A]^{-1}=\frac{1}{(a_{11}\times a_{22}-a_{21}\times a_{12})}\begin{bmatrix}a_{22} & -a_{12}\\ -a_{21} & a_{11}\end{bmatrix}$$

$$\begin{Bmatrix}a_0\\ a_1\end{Bmatrix}=2\begin{bmatrix}12.323 & -4.993\\ -0.019 & 0.0471\end{bmatrix}\begin{Bmatrix}0.05\\ 0.05\end{Bmatrix}=\begin{Bmatrix}0.733\\ 0.0028\end{Bmatrix}$$

Damping matrix $[C]=a_0[M]+a_1[K]$

Or, for the three-DOF system, damping matrix is given by:

$$[C]=0.733\begin{bmatrix}75 & 0 & 0\\ 0 & 75 & 0\\ 0 & 0 & 50\end{bmatrix}+0.0028\begin{bmatrix}69300 & -35700 & 0\\ -35700 & 58200 & -22500\\ 0 & -22500 & 22500\end{bmatrix}$$

$$[C]=\begin{bmatrix}249 & -100 & 0\\ -100 & 218 & -63\\ 0 & -63 & 99.65\end{bmatrix}$$

Damping ratio

$$\xi_3=\frac{a_0}{2}\frac{1}{\omega_3}+\frac{a_1}{2}\omega_3$$

or, $$\xi_3 = \frac{0.733}{2}\frac{1}{37.38} + \frac{0.0028}{2} \times 37.38 = 0.0621$$

or, $$\xi_3 = 6.21\% \text{ in the third mode}.$$ □

Example 10.15

Consider a four storey building frame as shown in Figure 10.26. It is subjected to the first 10 seconds of El Centro earthquake of May 1040. It has 5% damping ratio in the first and the third modes. Determine the response time history using the modal analysis for the frame.

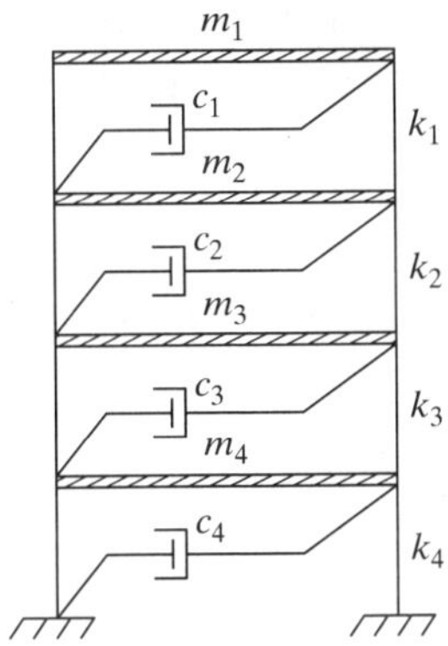

Figure 10.26 Damped 4-storey building model

Solution

The mass matrix and stiffness matrix for the frame can be written as follows:

$$\boldsymbol{M} = \begin{bmatrix} m_1 & 0 & 0 & 0 \\ 0 & m_2 & 0 & 0 \\ 0 & 0 & m_3 & 0 \\ 0 & 0 & 0 & m_4 \end{bmatrix} = \begin{bmatrix} 1000 & 0 & 0 & 0 \\ 0 & 1500 & 0 & 0 \\ 0 & 0 & 2000 & 0 \\ 0 & 0 & 0 & 2500 \end{bmatrix} \text{kg}$$

$$\boldsymbol{K} = \begin{bmatrix} k_1 & -k_1 & 0 & 0 \\ -k_1 & k_1 + k_2 & -k_2 & 0 \\ 0 & -k_2 & k_2 + k_3 & -k_3 \\ 0 & 0 & -k_3 & k_3 + k_4 \end{bmatrix}$$

or,

$$\boldsymbol{K} = \begin{bmatrix} 200 & -200 & 0 & 0 \\ -200 & 450 & -250 & 0 \\ 0 & -250 & 550 & -300 \\ 0 & 0 & -300 & 650 \end{bmatrix} \times 1000 \text{ N/m}$$

The frequencies and mode shapes can be determined using MATLAB function eig.

The frequency vector is

$$\{\omega\} = \begin{Bmatrix} 5.087 \\ 12.402 \\ 18.537 \\ 22.62 \end{Bmatrix} \text{rad/sec} \quad \text{and} \quad \{T\} = \begin{Bmatrix} 1.235 \\ 0.506 \\ 0.339 \\ 0.277 \end{Bmatrix} \text{sec}$$

The mode shapes are as follows:

$$[\Phi] = \{\phi_1 \quad \phi_2 \quad \phi_3 \quad \phi_4\}$$

or,

$$[\Phi] = \begin{bmatrix} -0.0177 & -0.0185 & 0.0150 & -0.0110 \\ -0.0154 & -0.0043 & -0.0108 & 0.0172 \\ -0.0112 & 0.0110 & -0.0092 & -0.0130 \\ -0.0057 & 0.0125 & 0.0132 & 0.0062 \end{bmatrix}$$

It can be normalized with respect to the elements in the first row.

$$[\Phi] = \begin{bmatrix} -1.0 & -1.0 & 1.0 & -1.0 \\ -0.870 & -0.232 & -0.720 & 1.564 \\ -0.633 & 0.595 & -0.613 & -1.182 \\ -0.322 & 0.676 & 0.880 & 0.564 \end{bmatrix}$$

The mode shapes are column-wise for modes 1 to 4.

Next, it is possible to compute generalized mass, stiffness and damping matrices.

$$m_r = \phi_r^T M \phi_r \quad k_r = \phi_r^T K \phi_r \quad \text{and} \quad c_r = \phi_r^T C \phi_r$$

Also, $\bar{m} = \phi_r^T [M]\{I\}$
Where, r varies from 1 to 4.

$$\{m_r\} = \begin{Bmatrix} 3195.938 \\ 2931.226 \\ 4465.138 \\ 8258.632 \end{Bmatrix} \quad \text{and} \quad \{\bar{m}\} = \begin{Bmatrix} -4376 \\ 1532 \\ 894 \\ 392 \end{Bmatrix}$$

The mode participation factors can be written as follows:

$$\{\Gamma\} = \begin{Bmatrix} -1.370 \\ 0.522 \\ 0.200 \\ 0.0474 \end{Bmatrix}$$

Classical Damping

Viscous damping in the first and third mode is 5% of critical. The classical damping is given as follows:

$$\boldsymbol{C} = a_0 \boldsymbol{M} + a_1 \boldsymbol{K}$$

For any two modes,

$$\begin{Bmatrix} a_0 \\ a_1 \end{Bmatrix} = 2\begin{bmatrix} 1/5.087 & 5.087 \\ 1/18.537 & 18.537 \end{bmatrix}^{-1} \begin{Bmatrix} 0.05 \\ 0.05 \end{Bmatrix} = \begin{Bmatrix} 0.3992 \\ 0.0042 \end{Bmatrix}$$

Therefore,

$$\xi_2 = \frac{a_0}{2}\frac{1}{\omega_2} + \frac{a_1}{2}\omega_2 = 0.0421$$

and

$$\xi_4 = \frac{a_0}{2}\frac{1}{\omega_4} + \frac{a_1}{2}\omega_4 = 0.0563$$

Damping matrix is given by

$$C = 0.3992\begin{bmatrix} 1000 & 0 & 0 & 0 \\ 0 & 1500 & 0 & 0 \\ 0 & 0 & 2000 & 0 \\ 0 & 0 & 0 & 2500 \end{bmatrix} + 0.0042\begin{bmatrix} 200 & -200 & 0 & 0 \\ -200 & 450 & -250 & 0 \\ 0 & -250 & 550 & -300 \\ 0 & 0 & -300 & 650 \end{bmatrix} \times 1000$$

or,

$$C = \begin{bmatrix} 1239.2 & -840 & 0 & 0 \\ -840 & 2488.8 & -1050 & 0 \\ 0 & -1050 & 3108.4 & -1260 \\ 0 & 0 & -1260 & 3728 \end{bmatrix}$$

Modal damping is given by

$$C_r = \Phi^T C \Phi \text{ or } c_r = \phi_r^T C \phi_r$$

or,

$$\{c_r\} = \begin{Bmatrix} 1623 \\ 3062 \\ 8228 \\ 21036 \end{Bmatrix}$$

The uncoupled equations of motion can be written as follows:

$$\ddot{y}_r + 2\xi_r\omega_r\dot{y}_r + \omega_r^2 y_r = -\Gamma_r\ddot{y}_g(t)$$

or,

$$\ddot{y}_1 + 2\times 0.05\times 5.087\dot{y}_1 + 5.087^2 y_1 = 1.37\ddot{y}_g(t)$$

$$\ddot{y}_2 + 2\times 0.0421\times 12.402\dot{y}_2 + 12.402^2 y_2 = -0.522\ddot{y}_g(t)$$

$$\ddot{y}_3 + 2\times 0.05\times 18.537\dot{y}_3 + 18.537^2 y_3 = -0.20\ddot{y}_g(t)$$

$$\ddot{y}_4 + 2\times 0.0563\times 22.62\dot{y}_4 + 22.62^2 y_4 = -0.0474\ddot{y}_g(t)$$

These equations can be solved using any of the direct integration methods discussed earlier. In the present case, linear acceleration method was used with a step size of 0.001 sec. The smallest period in the 4th mode is 0.277 sec. For stability and accuracy,

$$\Delta T \leq T/10, \text{ or, } \Delta T \leq 0.277/10 = 0.0277 \text{ sec}$$

Therefore, a step of 0.001 << 0.0277 sec is quite reasonable.

The modal displacement – time histories in normal coordinates are shown in Figures 10.27 (a).

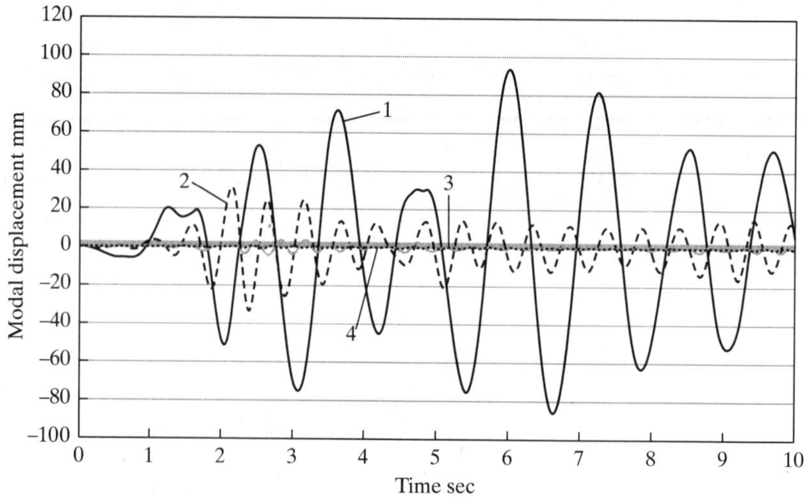

(a) Modal displacement – time history in normal coordinates

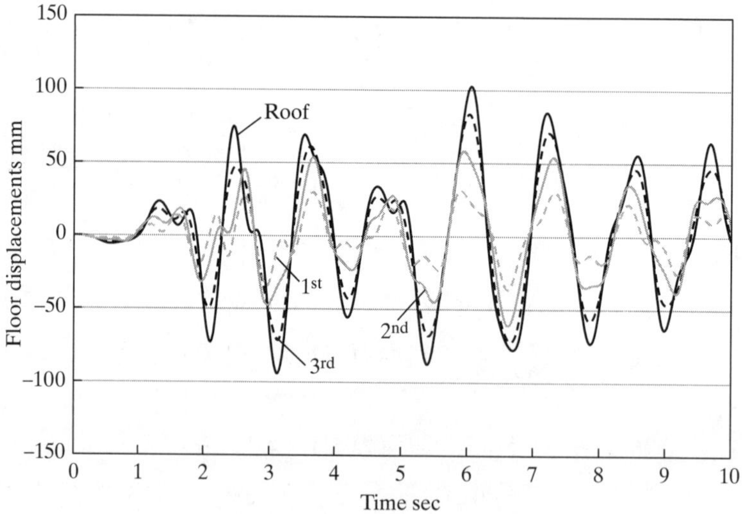

(b) Floor displacement – time history in geometric coordinates

Figure 10.27 Floor displacement – time histories due to the El Centro earthquake motion

The floor displacements can be determined by using the transformation equation

$$\{X\} = [\Phi]\{y_r(t)\}$$

$$\begin{Bmatrix} x_1(t) \\ x_2(t) \\ x_3(t) \\ x_4(t) \end{Bmatrix} = \begin{bmatrix} -1.0 & -1.0 & 1.0 & -1.0 \\ -0.870 & -0.232 & -0.720 & 1.564 \\ -0.633 & 0.595 & -0.613 & -1.182 \\ -0.322 & 0.676 & 0.880 & 0.564 \end{bmatrix} \begin{Bmatrix} y_1(t) \\ y_2(t) \\ y_3(t) \\ y_4(t) \end{Bmatrix}$$

Where, $x_i(t)$ represents displacement in geometric coordinates corresponding to the i-th DOF. In the present case, the lateral DOF were numbered from top floor to bottom floor in Figure 10.26 The floor displacement-time histories are shown in Figure 10.27 (b).

Using the floor displacements, it is possible to calculate storey drifts, that is,

$$\begin{Bmatrix} \Delta x_1(t) \\ \Delta x_2(t) \\ \Delta x_3(t) \\ \Delta x_4(t) \end{Bmatrix} = \begin{Bmatrix} x_1(t) - x_2(t) \\ x_2(t) - x_3(t) \\ x_3(t) - x_4(t) \\ x_4(t) \end{Bmatrix}$$

The storey drifts obtained from the normal coordinates $y(t)$ multiplied by the mode shapes and those obtained from the floor displacements $x(t)$ are the same in view of the linear relationship between the floor displacements and modal displacements.

Knowing the storey drift, it is possible to calculate storey shears by using the storey stiffness as well as the base shear. This will give lateral floor force at each floor. Thus, it is convenient to compute overturning moments knowing the storey heights.

The maximum and minimum values of modal displacements and their time of occurrence are shown in Table 10.16. The displacement values in mm are maximum in Mode 1 and very low in mode 3 and 4. Moreover, they occur at different instants. The positive and negative displacements have no physical significance except that they occur on either side of the mean position.

The maximum and minimum values of floor displacements and their time of occurrence are shown in Table 10.17. The displacement values in mm are maximum at the roof and very low in the lowest floor. Moreover, they occur at different instants.

TABLE 10.16 MODAL DISPLACEMENT (mm) MAXIMA AND THEIR TIME OF OCCURRENCE

Value	Mode 1		Mode 2		Mode 3		Mode 4	
	Disp.	Time, *s*	Disp.	Time, *s*	Disp.	Time, *s*	Disp.	Time, *s*
Maximum	93.46	6.0	31.05	2.16	3.66	3.18	0.68	2.44
Minimum	–86.1	6.64	–33.30	2.40	–4.30	2.66	–0.77	2.58

TABLE 10.17 DISPLACEMENT MAXIMA (mm) AND THEIR TIME OF OCCURRENCE

Value	Floor 1		Floor 2		Floor 3		Roof	
	Disp.	Time, *s*	Disp.	Time, *s*	Disp.	Time, *s*	Disp.	Time, *s*
Maximum	31.34	5.88	58.48	5.94	83.75	6.02	102.8	6.04
Minimum	–36.26	6.6	–61.1	6.62	–72.3	6.66	–93.96	3.12

10.13 TORSION IN SINGLE STOREY SYSTEMS

Let us consider a general single storey system as shown plan in Figure 10.28. Total mass of the building is m and it is uniformly distributed over the entire plan. There are four lateral load resisting frames A, B, C and D. The frames A and B resist lateral forces acting along x-axis; while frames C and D resist lateral forces acting along y-axis. Their stiffness are: k_{Ax} and k_{Bx} about y-axis, and k_{Cy} and k_{Dy} about x-axis, respectively. It is assumed that these elements do not resist lateral forces about their weak axis. For convenience, the lateral force resisting elements are assumed to be placed at the periphery of the diaphragm and their thickness is neglected. The frames are unsymmetric, therefore, torsion is introduced about the vertical axis of the system. By playing with the lateral stiffnesses of these four elements, and their distance from the geometric center of the building, several cases can be developed. If all elements have equal stiffness and are placed symmetrically about the geometric center, it will simulate a symmetric building and there will be no torsion. Of course, accidental torsion will always be there. Alternatively, any one or more of these elements may have a zero stiffness. Let us first consider a general case.

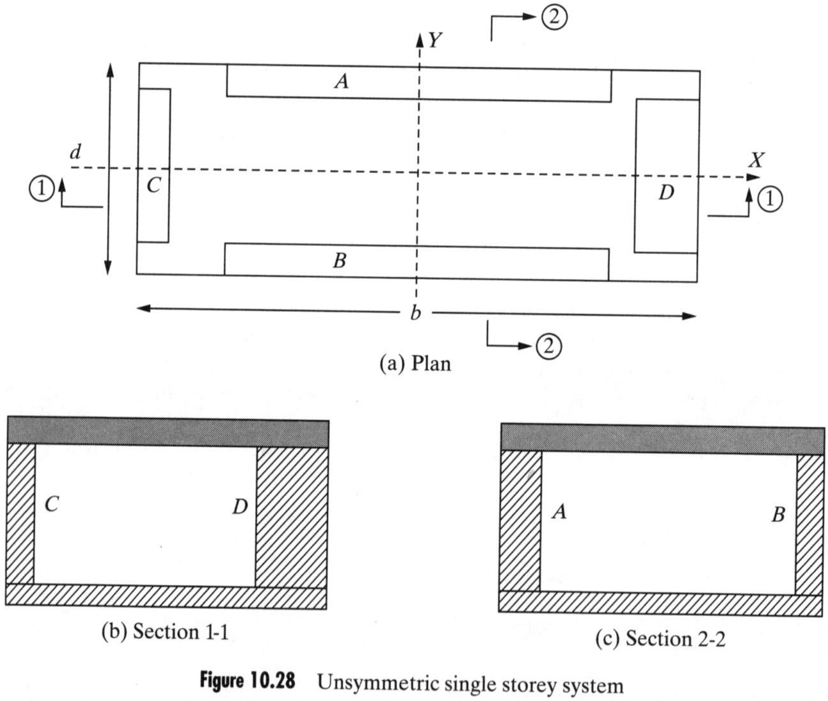

(a) Plan

(b) Section 1-1

(c) Section 2-2

Figure 10.28 Unsymmetric single storey system

There are three global degrees of freedom u_x, u_y and u_θ, respectively located at the center of mass of the floor diaphragm. The force-deformation relation in terms of their stiffness can be written as follows:

$$\boldsymbol{P} = \boldsymbol{K\Delta} \tag{10.74a}$$

$$\begin{Bmatrix} P_x \\ P_y \\ P_\theta \end{Bmatrix} = \begin{bmatrix} k_{xx} & k_{xy} & k_{x\theta} \\ k_{yx} & k_{yy} & k_{y\theta} \\ k_{\theta x} & k_{\theta y} & k_{\theta\theta} \end{bmatrix} \begin{Bmatrix} u_x \\ u_y \\ u_\theta \end{Bmatrix} \tag{10.74b}$$

where,

k_{ij} = force at DOF i due to a unit deformation applied at DOF j in the direction j; stiffness coefficients

P = force vector

Let us determine the 3 × 3 stiffness coefficients by permitting only one degree of freedom while restraining the other two degrees of freedom at a time using the basic principle.

Case 1: $u_x = 1, u_y = 0$ and $u_\theta = 0$ (Figure 10.29 (a))
From the equilibrium of forces along the three directions (Figure 10.29(b)),

$$\begin{aligned} k_{xx} &= k_{Ax} + k_{Bx} \\ k_{yx} &= 0 \\ k_{\theta x} &= (k_{Bx} - k_{Ax})\, d/2 \end{aligned} \tag{10.75a}$$

Case 2: $u_x = 0, u_y = 1$ and $u_\theta = 0$ (Figure 10.29 (c))
From the equilibrium of forces along the three directions (Figure 10.29(d)),

$$\begin{aligned} k_{xy} &= 0 \\ k_{yy} &= k_{Cy} + k_{Dy} \\ k_{\theta y} &= (k_{Dy} - k_{Cy})\, b/2 \end{aligned} \tag{10.75b}$$

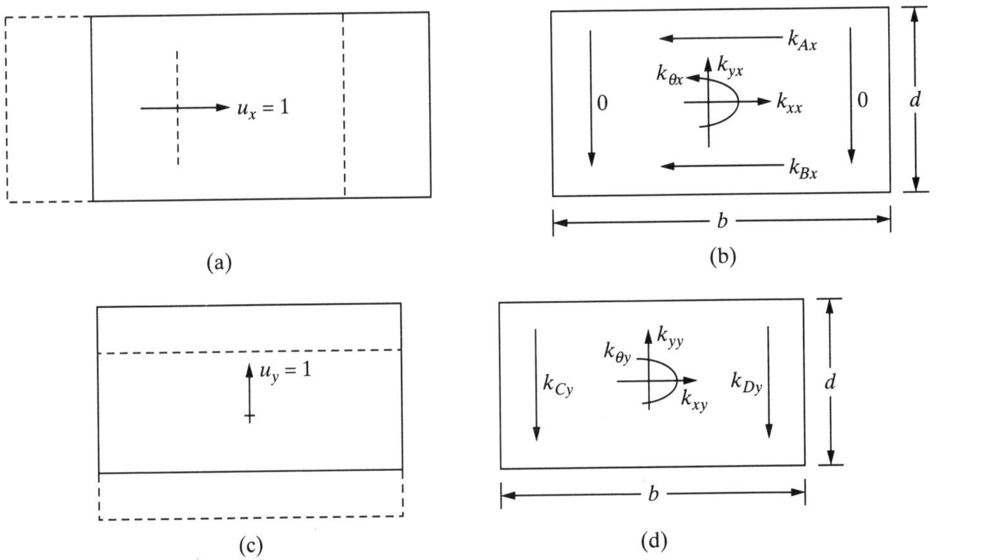

Figure 10.29 Computation of influence coefficients

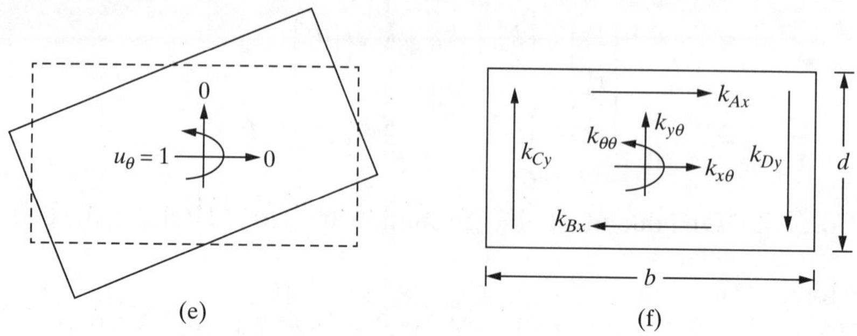

Figure 10.29 (Continued)

Case 3: $u_x = 0, u_y = 0$ and $u_\theta = 1$ (Figure 10.29 (e))
From the equilibrium of forces along the three directions (Figure 10.29 (f)),

$$k_{x\theta} = (k_{Bx} - k_{Ax})\ d/2$$

$$k_{y\theta} = (k_{Dy} - k_{Cy})\ b/2$$

$$k_{\theta\theta} = (k_{Ax} + k_{Bx})\ d^2/4 + (k_{Cy} + k_{Dy})\ b^2/4 \tag{10.75c}$$

The final stiffness matrix of the structure can be obtained by substituting the values from Equations (10.75a) to (10.75c) in [K] shown in Equation (10.74b).

The equations of motion for undamped free vibrations of the structure can be written as follows:

$$\boldsymbol{M\ddot{X}} + \boldsymbol{KX} = \boldsymbol{0} \tag{10.76}$$

where

$$\text{Mass matrix } [M] = \begin{bmatrix} m & 0 & 0 \\ 0 & m & 0 \\ 0 & 0 & m' \end{bmatrix} \tag{10.77a}$$

where,
m = total mass of the diaphragm distributed uniformly over the plan
m' = mass moment of inertia of the diaphragm about the vertical axis passing through the center of mass (CM)
$= m(b^2 + d^2)/12$ (10.77b)

$$[K] = \begin{bmatrix} (k_{Ax} + k_{Bx}) & 0 & (k_{Bx} - k_{Ax})d/2 \\ 0 & (k_{Cy} + k_{Dy}) & (k_{Dy} - k_{Cy})b/2 \\ (k_{Bx} - k_{Ax})d/2 & (k_{Dy} - k_{Cy})b/2 & (k_{Ax} + k_{Bx})d^2/4 + (k_{Cy} + k_{Dy})b^2/4 \end{bmatrix}_{3x3} \tag{10.77c}$$

The inertia force on the structure are:

$$f_{Ix} = m\ddot{u}_x^t; \quad f_{Iy} = m\ddot{u}_y^t; \quad f_{I\theta} = m'\ddot{u}_\theta^t \tag{10.77d}$$

where,

f_{Ix}, f_{Iy} and $f_{I\theta}$ = inertia force along x, y and θ directions

$\ddot{u}_x^t, \ddot{u}_y^t, \ddot{u}_\theta^t = x, y$ and θ components of the total acceleration acting at the center of mass

Let $\ddot{u}_{gx}, \ddot{u}_{gy}$ and $\ddot{u}_{g\theta}$ are the components of the ground acceleration

The total accelerations of the mass are

$$\begin{Bmatrix} \ddot{u}_x^t \\ \ddot{u}_y^t \\ \ddot{u}_\theta^t \end{Bmatrix} = \begin{Bmatrix} \ddot{u}_x \\ \ddot{u}_y \\ \ddot{u}_\theta \end{Bmatrix} + \begin{Bmatrix} \ddot{u}_{gx} \\ \ddot{u}_{gy} \\ \ddot{u}_{g\theta} \end{Bmatrix} \tag{10.77e}$$

Substituting the values of ***M***, ***K***, total acceleration, and displacements in Equation (10.76), we get the equations of motion of the unsymmetric single storey system

$$\begin{bmatrix} m & 0 & 0 \\ 0 & m & 0 \\ 0 & 0 & m' \end{bmatrix} \begin{Bmatrix} \ddot{u}_x + \ddot{u}_{gx} \\ \ddot{u}_y + \ddot{u}_{gy} \\ \ddot{u}_\theta + \ddot{u}_{g\theta} \end{Bmatrix} + \begin{bmatrix} k_{xx} & 0 & k_{x\theta} \\ 0 & k_{yy} & k_{y\theta} \\ k_{\theta x} & k_{\theta y} & k_{\theta\theta} \end{bmatrix} \begin{Bmatrix} u_x \\ u_y \\ u_\theta \end{Bmatrix} = \begin{Bmatrix} 0 \\ 0 \\ 0 \end{Bmatrix}$$

or, it can be written as

$$\begin{bmatrix} m & 0 & 0 \\ 0 & m & 0 \\ 0 & 0 & m' \end{bmatrix} \begin{Bmatrix} \ddot{u}_x \\ \ddot{u}_y \\ \ddot{u}_\theta \end{Bmatrix} + \begin{bmatrix} k_{xx} & 0 & k_{x\theta} \\ 0 & k_{yy} & k_{y\theta} \\ k_{\theta x} & k_{\theta y} & k_{\theta\theta} \end{bmatrix} \begin{Bmatrix} u_x \\ u_y \\ u_\theta \end{Bmatrix} = -\begin{Bmatrix} m\ddot{u}_{gx} \\ m\ddot{u}_{gy} \\ m'\ddot{u}_{g\theta} \end{Bmatrix} \tag{10.78}$$

The solution of this equation can be obtained using an appropriate step-by-step numerical integration technique.

10.13.1 One-way Unsymmetric System

Let us consider a special case of the unsymmetric single storey system shown in Figure 10.28, where

$$k_{Ax} = k_{Bx} = k_x; k_{Cy} = 0; \text{ and } k_{Dy} = k_y$$

Also, the element D has been placed at a distance e from the center of mass along x-axis as shown in Figure 10.29.

This system is symmetric about x-axis but not about y-axis. The equation of motion can be written as follows:

$$\begin{bmatrix} m & 0 & 0 \\ 0 & m & 0 \\ 0 & 0 & m' \end{bmatrix} \begin{Bmatrix} \ddot{u}_x \\ \ddot{u}_y \\ \ddot{u}_\theta \end{Bmatrix} + \begin{bmatrix} 2k_x & 0 & 0 \\ 0 & k_y & ek_y \\ 0 & ek_y & 2k_x\left(\dfrac{d^2}{4}\right) + k_y e^2 \end{bmatrix} \begin{Bmatrix} u_x \\ u_y \\ u_\theta \end{Bmatrix} = -\begin{Bmatrix} m\ddot{u}_{gx} \\ m\ddot{u}_{gy} \\ m'\ddot{u}_{g\theta} \end{Bmatrix} \tag{10.79}$$

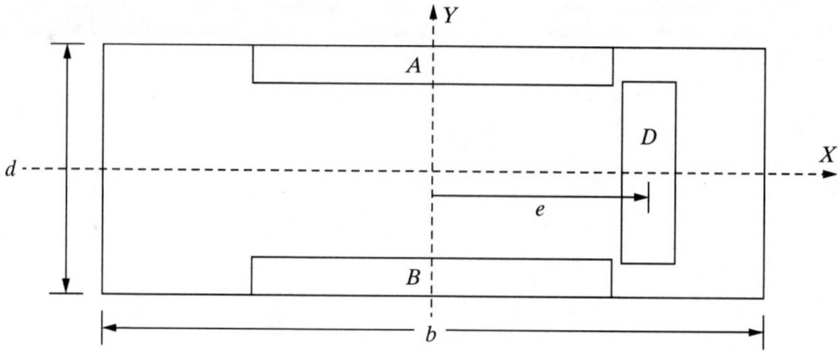

Figure 10.29 One-way unsymmetric system

This equation can be further simplified as follows:

$$m\ddot{u}_x + 2k_x u_x = -m\ddot{u}_{gx} \tag{10.80a}$$

$$\begin{bmatrix} m & 0 \\ 0 & m' \end{bmatrix}\begin{Bmatrix} \ddot{u}_y \\ \ddot{u}_\theta \end{Bmatrix} + \begin{bmatrix} k_y & ek_y \\ ek_y & 2k_x\left(\dfrac{d^2}{4}\right) + k_y e^2 \end{bmatrix}\begin{Bmatrix} u_y \\ u_\theta \end{Bmatrix} = -\begin{Bmatrix} m\ddot{u}_{gy} \\ m'\ddot{u}_{g\theta} \end{Bmatrix} \tag{10.80b}$$

Equation (10.80a) is an uncoupled equation in the x-direction, that is, it is independent of the motion in the y-direction as well as that of the torsional motion. It represents a single-degree-of-freedom system. However, Equation (10.80b) represents a two-degrees-of-freedom system as well as coupled lateral-torsional motion of the structure. These two equations can be solved independently.

In case, the rotational component of the ground motion is absent, then Equation (10.80b) becomes

$$\begin{bmatrix} m & 0 \\ 0 & m' \end{bmatrix}\begin{Bmatrix} \ddot{u}_y \\ \ddot{u}_\theta \end{Bmatrix} + \begin{bmatrix} k_y & ek_y \\ ek_y & 2k_x\left(\dfrac{d^2}{4}\right) + k_y e^2 \end{bmatrix}\begin{Bmatrix} u_y \\ u_\theta \end{Bmatrix} = -\begin{Bmatrix} m\ddot{u}_{gy} \\ 0 \end{Bmatrix} \tag{10.80c}$$

It shows that the ground motion in the y-direction will cause a lateral motion in the y-direction as well as torsional motion about the vertical axis of the system.

10.13.2 Two-way Unsymmetric System

Let us consider a single storey building which is unsymmetrical about both x and y axis in plan as shown in Figure 10.30. It is a very common sight for buildings on a corner plot. It represents a shop with exposed walls on front and side roads.
For the building system shown in Figure 10.28,

$$k_{Ax} = 0, k_{Cy} = 0$$

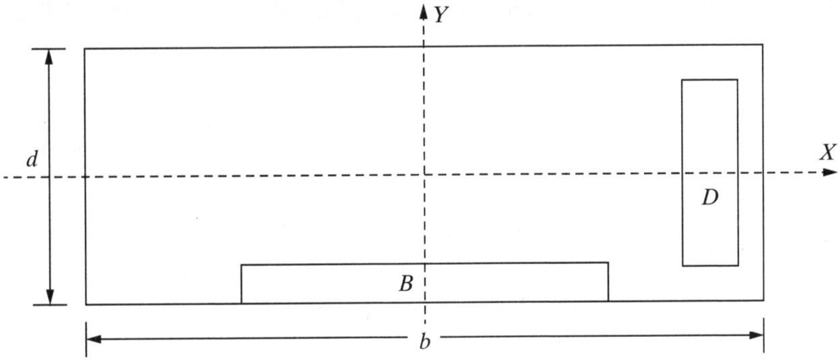

Figure 10.30 Two-way unsymmetric system

The mass matrix remains unchanged as given by Equation (10.77a).

The stiffness matrix for this building can be written by modifying Equation (10.77c) as follows:

$$[K]=\begin{bmatrix} k_{Bx} & 0 & k_{Bx}d/2 \\ 0 & k_{Dy} & k_{Dy}b/2 \\ k_{Bx}d/2 & k_{Dy}b/2 & k_{Bx}d^2/4+k_{Dy}b^2/4 \end{bmatrix}_{3x3}$$

The equation of motion can be written as follows:

$$\begin{bmatrix} m & 0 & 0 \\ 0 & m & 0 \\ 0 & 0 & m' \end{bmatrix}\begin{Bmatrix} \ddot{u}_x \\ \ddot{u}_y \\ \ddot{u}_\theta \end{Bmatrix}+\begin{bmatrix} k_{Bx} & 0 & k_{Bx}d/2 \\ 0 & k_{Dy} & k_{Dy}b/2 \\ k_{Bx}d/2 & k_{Dy}b/2 & k_{Bx}d^2/4+k_{Dy}b^2/4 \end{bmatrix}_{3x3}\begin{Bmatrix} u_x \\ u_y \\ u_\theta \end{Bmatrix}=-\begin{Bmatrix} m\ddot{u}_{gx} \\ m\ddot{u}_{gy} \\ m'\ddot{u}_{g\theta} \end{Bmatrix} \quad (10.81)$$

The solution of this equation can be obtained by using the step-by-step direct integration methods.

REVIEW QUESTIONS

10.1 Discuss the different techniques for mathematical modelling of a multi-degree of freedom system?

10.2 Explain with the help of a flow diagram how to simplify the solution of coupled equations of motion of a MDOF system.

10.3 Discuss the influence coefficient method for writing equations of motion of a MDOF system.

10.4 Discuss the characteristics of global mass matrix of a discrete MDOF system.

10.5 Discuss the characteristics of global stiffness matrix of a discrete MDOF system.

10.6 Derive the characteristic equation for eigenvalue analysis for undamped free vibrations of a MDOF system.

10.7 Differentiate between fundamental frequency of vibration and fundamental period of vibration of a MDOF system.

10.8 Derive and explain the Rayleigh's quotient in MDOF system.

10.9 What do you understand by orthogonality conditions of modes? Derive the various relationships.

10.10 What is normalization of modes? Why is it necessary?

10.11 What are orthonormal mode shapes?

10.12 How do you transform eigenvalue problem to standard form?

10.13 Differentiate between the normal coordinates (or generalized coordinates) and geometric coordinates.

10.14 Write the expressions for generalized mass, generalized stiffness, and generalized damping.

10.15 Discuss the salient features of modal analysis of a MDOF system.

10.16 What do you mean by eigenvalue analysis?

10.17 What are the solution techniques for the uncoupled equations of motion of a MDOF system? Discuss their salient features.

10.18 What is modal participation factor (MPF) in the analysis of a MDOF system?

10.19 What do you understand by modal mass?

10.20 What are the basic steps for carrying out response spectrum analysis (RSA) of a MDOF system?

10.21 What are the basic steps for carrying out modal time-history analysis (MTHA) of a MDOF system?

10.22 How can you account for the initial conditions of the system, $x(0)$ and $\dot{x}(0)$ in response spectrum analysis of a MDOF system?

10.23 What is modal superposition technique in a MDOF system?

10.24 Discuss the salient features of SRSS modal superposition technique.

10.25 Discuss the salient features of CQC modal superposition technique.

10.26 Can you estimate peak value of a response quantity from the peak value of another response quantity? If not, why not?

PROBLEMS

10.1 Consider a five-DOF undamped lumped mass system having equal mass 'm' and spring stiffness 'k' as shown in Figure P10.1. Determine its fundamental frequency and mode shape using (i) Holtzer method and (ii) Power method.

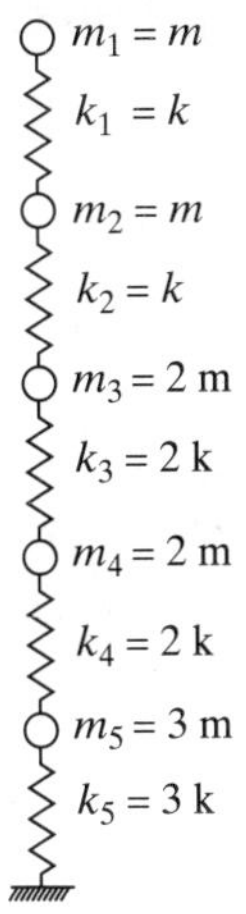

Figure P10.1

Ans: Lowest eigenvalue $\lambda = 16.6264$, or fundamental frequency $\omega = 4.077$ rad/sec,

$$\{\phi\} = \begin{Bmatrix} 0.0147 \\ 0.0128 \\ 0.0094 \\ 0.0065 \\ 0.0028 \end{Bmatrix}$$

10.2 In Problem 10.1,

(a) Determine all frequency and mode shapes using (i) solution of the characteristic polynomial equation, and (ii) using the power method with matrix deflation.

(b) Check if the eigenvectors are orthogonal?

(c) Verify the eigenvalues using the Rayleigh's quotient.

(d) Verify the results using MATLAB.

$$\textbf{Ans: } \omega = \begin{Bmatrix} 4.077 \\ 9.017 \\ 14.26 \\ 18.74 \\ 20.88 \end{Bmatrix} \text{ rad/sec}$$

$$\Phi = \begin{bmatrix} 0.0147 & 0.0156 & 0.0080 & -0.0108 & 0.0057 \\ 0.0128 & 0.0061 & -0.0042 & 0.0177 & -0.0116 \\ 0.0094 & -0.0071 & -0.0100 & -0.0004 & 0.0096 \\ 0.0065 & -0.0094 & 0.0024 & -0.0083 & -0.0113 \\ 0.0028 & -0.0059 & 0.0111 & 0.0057 & 0.0047 \end{bmatrix}$$

10.3 Consider the following coefficient matrix:

$$\begin{bmatrix} 10 & 5 & 0 & 0 \\ 5 & 20 & 5 & 0 \\ 0 & 5 & 20 & 5 \\ 0 & 0 & 5 & 30 \end{bmatrix}$$

Determine its highest and lowest eigenvalues and eigenvectors only using (i) power method and (ii) inverse iteration method with shift = 5 and 30. You may carry out the calculations in MS-EXCEL. Verify the results using MATLAB.

(Hint: Operate on A^{-1} to get its highest eigenvalue or the lowest eigenvalue of A.)

$$\textbf{Ans: } \lambda_1 = 7.5576 \ \{\phi\} = \begin{Bmatrix} 0.8813 \\ -0.4305 \\ 0.1900 \\ -0.0423 \end{Bmatrix} \text{ and } \lambda_4 = 32.4424 \ \{\phi\} = \begin{Bmatrix} 0.0423 \\ 0.1900 \\ 0.4305 \\ 0.8813 \end{Bmatrix}$$

10.4 In a three-DOF system, the mass matrix and stiffness matrix are as follows:

$$[M] = \begin{bmatrix} 5 & 0 & 0 \\ 0 & 10 & 0 \\ 0 & 0 & 15 \end{bmatrix} \text{ and } [K] = \begin{bmatrix} 2 & -1 & 0 \\ -1 & 4 & -2 \\ 0 & -2 & 6 \end{bmatrix}$$

Calculate its frequencies, mode shapes, mode participation factors and modal mass.

$$\textbf{Ans: } \lambda = \begin{Bmatrix} 0.184 \\ 0.400 \\ 0.616 \end{Bmatrix} \ \omega = \begin{Bmatrix} 0.4290 \\ 0.6325 \\ 0.7848 \end{Bmatrix} \ \Phi = \begin{bmatrix} 1 & -1 & -1 \\ 1.0801 & 0 & 1.0801 \\ 0.6667 & 0.5 & -0.6667 \end{bmatrix}$$

Mode participation factors 1.106, 0.286, and – 0.18;
modal mass = 28.527, 0.714, and 0.756
The sum of modal mass = 30 = total mass

10.5 In Problem 10.4, show that the eigenvectors are orthogonal. Normalize each mode so that modal mass is unity.

10.6 (a) A three-storey shear frame is shown in Figure P10.2. The flexural rigidity of beams and columns is shown. The masses are lumped at the floor. Using the mass and stiffness influence coefficients, write the equations of motion. Neglect the axial deformations in all members.

(b) If mass $m = 5000$ kg and $I = 67{,}500$ cm^4, grade of concrete = M30 and storey height is 3.5 m, determine the frequencies, mode shapes, mode participation factors and modal mass.

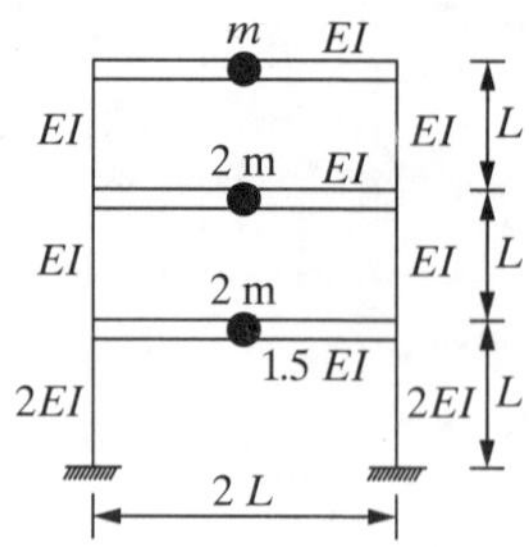

Figure P10.2

10.7 Consider a two bay × three storey RC frame as shown in Figure P10.3. The floor is rigid. The mass at the first floor girder, second floor girder and roof is 50, 50 and 40 kN-s²/m, respectively. The column sizes from top are: 300 × 400 mm, 300 × 500 mm, 300 × 600 mm. Determine the storey stiffness, frequencies and mode shapes. Grade of concrete is M30.

Also, compute storey shears and floor forces using elastic response spectra for 5% damping of El Centro earthquake of May 1940 given in Chapter 8.

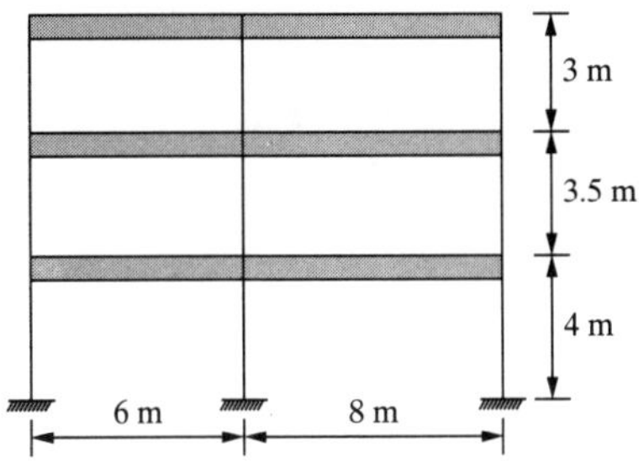

Figure P10.3

10.8 Consider the three-storey frame shown in Problem 10.7. Determine its undamped free response if the initial conditions are as follows:

$$\{x(0)\} = \begin{Bmatrix} 0.1 \\ -0.1 \\ 0.1 \end{Bmatrix} m \quad \text{and} \quad \{\dot{x}(0)\} = \begin{Bmatrix} 0 \\ 0 \\ 0 \end{Bmatrix}$$

10.9 (a) A four storey frame has its mass and storey stiffness from top as follows:

$$[M] = \begin{Bmatrix} 10 \\ 15 \\ 15 \\ 15 \end{Bmatrix} \times 100 \text{ kg} \qquad K = \begin{Bmatrix} 150 \\ 150 \\ 200 \\ 200 \end{Bmatrix} \text{kN/m}$$

Assemble the mass matrix and stiffness matrix of the frame and determine its frequency and mode shapes.

(b) Determine the mode participation factors and modal mass. Check if sum of total modal mass at each floor is equal to the respective mass.

(c) If damping in first mode is 5% and second mode is 7%, determine the damping in the other two modes. Also, determine the Rayleigh damping.

10.10 (a) In Fig. P10.1, if m = 1500 kg, and k = 200 kN/m, determine lateral forces and storey shears at each level using the IS:1893 Part 1 elastic response spectra for 5% damping on hard soil. Plot mode shapes, floor forces and storey shears.

$$\textbf{Ans: } \omega = \begin{Bmatrix} 4.077 \\ 9.017 \\ 14.26 \\ 18.74 \\ 20.88 \end{Bmatrix} \text{ and } T = \begin{Bmatrix} 1.54 \\ 0.696 \\ 0.44 \\ 0.335 \\ 0.301 \end{Bmatrix} \text{ sec}$$

$$\Phi = \begin{bmatrix} 0.0147 & 0.0156 & 0.0080 & -0.0108 & 0.0051 \\ 0.0128 & 0.0061 & -0.0042 & 0.0177 & -0.0116 \\ 0.0094 & -0.0071 & -0.0100 & -0.0004 & 0.0096 \\ 0.0065 & -0.0094 & 0.0024 & -0.0083 & -0.0113 \\ 0.0028 & -0.0059 & 0.0111 & 0.0057 & 0.0047 \end{bmatrix}$$

(b) If the top storey is very flexible with mass $m_1 = 30$ kg and stiffness $k_1 = 700$ N/m only, representing an appendage, again determine lateral forces and storey shears and compare with the results obtained in part (a).

$$\textbf{Ans: } \omega = \begin{Bmatrix} 4.6235 \\ 5.0 \\ 11.55 \\ 15.674 \\ 20.50 \end{Bmatrix} \text{ and } T = \begin{Bmatrix} 1.358 \\ 1.2565 \\ 0.543 \\ 0.400 \\ 0.306 \end{Bmatrix} \text{ sec}$$

$$\Phi = \begin{bmatrix} -0.1259 & 0.1321 & -0.0036 & 0.0013 & 0.0003 \\ -0.0106 & -0.0095 & 0.0172 & -0.0122 & -0.0044 \\ -0.0085 & -0.0082 & 0.0000 & 0.0103 & 0.0094 \\ -0.0061 & -0.0060 & -0.0086 & 0.0026 & -0.0134 \\ -0.0027 & -0.0027 & -0.0086 & -0.0099 & 0.0060 \end{bmatrix}$$

11 Systems with Distributed Mass and Elasticity

11.1 INTRODUCTION

In the previous chapters, we have discussed the dynamics of discrete single degree of freedom (SDOF) and two-DOF systems. There are situations when it is required to determine the vibration characteristics of a system with distributed mass and elasticity or a continuum system such as a chimney or a flexure member having different boundary conditions. The mass and elasticity or stiffness of such systems are distributed along their length. The variation of mass and stiffness may be uniformly distributed or uniformly varying. The dynamic behaviour of a rod, tightly held across a length L, and having a uniform mass, is the simplest example of such a problem. Such a system has infinite degrees of freedom. Now the question arises how to analyze it. Such a system cannot be modeled as a MDOF system in view of infinite DOF, which are very difficult to identify. Moreover, all the DOF may not be necessary to understand its dynamic behaviour. One possible solution is to lump its mass at pre-determined locations along its length and thus discretizing it as a finite MDOF system. If its mass is lumped at three locations, it becomes a three-DOF system; if its mass is lumped at ten locations, it becomes a ten-DOF system. The solution of such a problem is discussed in detail in physics at the higher secondary level of education to create awareness about frequencies and mode shapes. The question arises how to select at how many points its mass should be lumped to get an accurate result? In order to avoid such a situation, it has to be treated as a continuum system or a distributed mass and stiffness system. A general distributed mass and stiffness system can vibrate in different modes, such as axial mode, shear mode, torsional mode or flexural mode. In civil engineering domain, flexural mode is more significant.

This chapter deals with the dynamic behaviour of flexure members having distributed mass and stiffness with different boundary conditions. Rayleigh's method for determining the fundamental frequency of vibration of such systems is also discussed.

11.2 DISTRIBUTED MASS AND STIFFNESS SYSTEMS

Consider forced vibration of a flexure member, that is a beam shown in Figure 11.1(a) subjected to a force $p(x, t)$ varying in space and time. Such a member will undergo transverse vibrations, that is vibrations normal to its length. The free body diagram of its small element is shown in Figure 11.1(b).

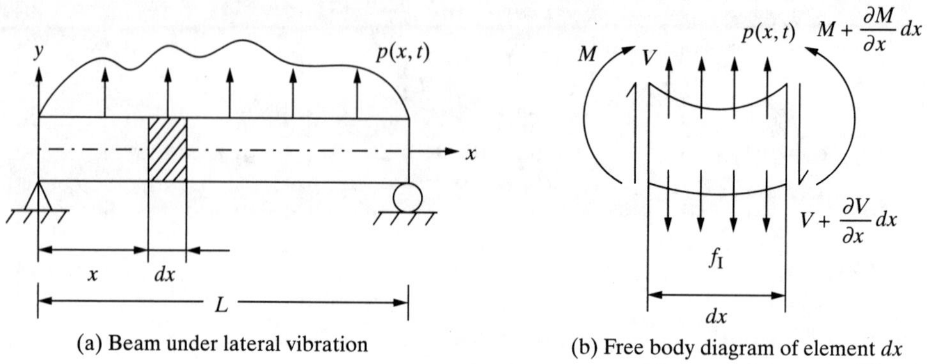

Figure 11.1 Forced vibrations in a beam.

The equation of dynamic equilibrium in the y-direction can be written as follows:

$$\Sigma F_y = 0$$

or,
$$-\left[V + \frac{\partial V}{\partial x} dx\right] + V + p(x,t)\,dx - f_I\,dx = 0 \tag{11.1}$$

but
$$f_I\,dx = (m\,dx)\,\frac{\partial^2 w}{\partial t^2}$$

∴
$$\frac{\partial V}{\partial x} = p(x,t) - f_I = p(x,t) - m\,\frac{\partial^2 w}{\partial t^2} \tag{11.2}$$

where, $w(x, t)$ = vertical deflection at any section
$m(x)$ = mass per unit length
$EI(x)$ = flexural stiffness
f_I = inertia force ($= m\ddot{w}$)
$V(x, t)$ = shear force
$M(x, t)$ = bending moment

Here vertical deflection w, shear force V, bending moment M and the external force p, each of these parameters is a function of position x and time t. It means each of these parameters vary along the length of the flexure member as well as time t. Mass m and moment of inertia I are functions of position x only. For clarity, these parameters will be used without specifying x or t in the subsequent derivations.

The second equilibrium equation is obtained by summing moments about the elastic axis at the right-hand face of the segment, that is,

$$\Sigma M = 0$$

or,
$$M + V\,dx - \left\{M + \frac{\partial M}{\partial x} dx\right\} = 0$$

or,
$$\frac{\partial M}{\partial x} = V \tag{11.3}$$

we know

$$M = -EI\,\frac{\partial^2 w}{\partial x^2}$$

or,
$$M = EI\frac{\partial^2 w}{\partial x^2} \tag{11.4}$$

This is standard relationship for a long slender beam also known as Euler–Bernoulli beam. All the assumptions used in the derivation of Equations (11.3) and (11.4) for the static solution are valid in dynamics too. These are:

1. Beam is uniform along its length and is slender
2. It consists of linear, homogeneous, isotropic and elastic material
3. A cross-section remains plane before and after the application of the force
4. A beam vibrates along the plane of symmetry so that rotation and translation vibrations are decoupled
5. Rotatory inertia and shear deformations can be neglected

It may be noted that the distributed lateral force $p(x, t)$ makes only a second-order contribution to moment. Inertia force does not contribute to the moment equilibrium.

Differentiating Equation (11.3) with respect to x gives

$$\frac{\partial^2 M}{\partial x^2} = \frac{\partial V}{\partial x}$$

and substituting in Equation (11.2) gives:

$$\frac{\partial^2 M}{\partial x^2} + m\frac{\partial^2 w}{\partial t^2} = p(x,t) \tag{11.5}$$

In this case due to sign convention

$$\frac{\partial^2}{\partial x^2}\left(EI\frac{\partial^2 w}{\partial x^2}\right) + m\frac{\partial^2 w}{\partial t^2} = p(x,t) \tag{11.6a}$$

In Equation (11.6a), the flexural stiffness EI is also a function of x, that is it is a distributed stiffness.

or,
$$EI\frac{\partial^4 w}{\partial x^4} + m\frac{\partial^2 w}{\partial t^2} = p(x,t) \tag{11.6b}$$

In Equation (11.6b), the flexural stiffness EI is taken as constant.

This is the equation of motion for undamped forced vibrations of a system with distributed mass and elasticity. The equation for free vibrations is as follows:

$$EI\frac{\partial^4 w}{\partial x^4} + m\frac{\partial^2 w}{\partial t^2} = 0 \tag{11.7}$$

As stated earlier, the transverse deflection w is a function of position x and time t. It means the deflection varies along the length of the beam as well as at any given section, it also varies with time. The solution of Equation (11.7) will require four boundary conditions and two initial conditions in terms of deflection $w(x,t)$, slope $\theta(x,t)$, shear force $V(x,t)$, bending moment $M(x,t)$ and initial conditions displacement and velocity at time $t = t_0$. This solution becomes very tedious. Therefore, the solution of Equation (11.7) is obtained by using separation of variables techniques available in differential calculus.

Let
$$w(x,t) = \phi(x)\, Y(t) \tag{11.8}$$

where, $\phi(x)$ gives the deflected shape and depends only upon the position variable x, and $Y(t)$ gives the displacement and depends only upon at time t. It means at a given time t, the position of the deflected shape of the beam along its length remains constant.

Substituting Equation (11.8) in Equation (11.7) gives,

$$\therefore \qquad Y(t)\,EI\frac{\partial^4\phi(x)}{\partial x^4}+m\phi(x)\,\frac{\partial^2 Y(t)}{\partial t^2}=0$$

or,
$$\frac{EI}{m\phi(x)}\,\frac{\partial^4\phi(x)}{\partial x^4}=-\frac{1}{Y(t)}\,\frac{\partial^2 Y(t)}{\partial t^2}=\text{constant}$$

$$\frac{1}{\phi(x)}\,\frac{\partial^4\phi(x)}{\partial x^4}=(-)\frac{m}{EI\,Y(t)}\cdot\frac{\partial^2 Y(t)}{\partial t^2}=a^4 \quad \text{say}$$

or,
$$\frac{\partial^4\phi(x)}{\partial x^4}-a^4\,\phi(x)=0 \tag{11.9a}$$

and
$$\frac{\partial^2 Y(t)}{\partial t^2}+\frac{a^4\,EI}{m}Y(t)=0 \tag{11.9b}$$

Let
$$\omega^2 = a^4\,\frac{EI}{m}$$

or,
$$\frac{\omega^2 m}{EI}=a^4 \tag{11.10}$$

$\therefore$ Equation (11.9a) becomes

$$\phi^{IV}(x)-a^4\,\phi(x)=0 \tag{11.11a}$$

This is a fourth-order differential equation in $\phi(x)$ and requires four boundary conditions for its solution.

and Equation (11.9b) becomes:

$$\ddot{Y}(t)+\omega^2\,Y(t)=0 \tag{11.11b}$$

This equation is similar to that of an undamped SDOF-free vibration.

For solving Equation (11.11a)

Let
$$\phi(x)=Ce^{sx} \tag{11.12}$$

$\therefore$ Equation (11.11a) gives,

$$(s^4-a^4)\,Ce^{sx}=0$$

or,

$$s=+\,a,+\,ia$$

Hence solution is,

$$\phi(x)=c_1\,e^{iax}+c_2\,e^{-iax}+c_3e^{ax}+c_4\,e^{-ax} \tag{11.13a}$$

or, alternatively,

$$\phi(x) = A_1 \sin ax + A_2 \cos ax + A_3 \sinh ax + A_4 \cosh ax \tag{11.13b}$$

For solving Equation (11.11b)

Let $$Y(t) = A \sin \omega t + B \cos \omega t$$

or, $$Y(t) = \frac{\dot{Y}(0)}{\omega} \sin \omega t + Y(0) \cos \omega t \tag{11.14}$$

where, $Y(0)$ and $\dot{Y}(0)$ represent initial conditions of displacement and velocity at time $t = t_0$.

The complete solution for a given continuum system requires the solution of Equations (11.10), (11.13) and (11.14) with the help of expressions for displacement, slope, moment and shear at the two ends. These relations will yield three constants in terms of the fourth constant and will also yield a frequency equation from which ω can be evaluated. The fourth coefficient expressing amplitude of vibration would require knowledge of the initial conditions of motion.

In the preceding derivation of the equation of motion for the transverse vibration of a beam, the effects of rotational inertia and shear deformation were ignored.

11.3 SIMPLY SUPPORTED BEAM

Let us consider a simply supported beam. The four boundary conditions for this beam are as follows:

At one end, $x = 0$,

Deflection $\phi(0) = 0$ (i)

Bending moment $M(0) = EI\,\phi''(0) = 0$ (ii)

at other end, $x = L$,

Deflection $\phi(L) = 0$ (iii)

Bending moment $M(L) = EI\,\phi''(L) = 0$ (iv)

The general solution is given by Equation (11.13b)

$$\phi(x) = A_1 \sin ax + A_2 \cos ax + A_3 \sinh ax + A_4 \cosh ax \tag{11.13b}$$

Let us substitute the boundary conditions (i) and (ii) in Equation (11.13b),

$$\phi(0) = A_1 \sin 0 + A_2 + A_1 \sin 0 + A_4 = 0$$

or, $$A_2 + A_4 = 0 \tag{v}$$

$$\phi''(0) = a^2 (-A_1 \sin 0 - A_2 \cos 0 + A_3 \sinh 0 + A_4 \cosh 0) = 0$$

or, $$-A_2 + A_4 = 0 \tag{vi}$$

∴ Equations (v) and (vi) give, $A_2 = A_4 = 0$

Similarly, let us substitute the boundary conditions (iii) and (iv) in Equation (11.13b),

$$\phi(L) = A_1 \sin aL + A_3 \sinh aL = 0$$

and
$$\phi''(L) = a^2(-A_1 \sin aL + A_3 \sinh aL) = 0$$

or,
$$A_3 = 0$$

∴
$$\phi(L) = A_1 \sin aL = 0 \tag{vii}$$

A non-trivial solution exists if,

$$\sin aL = 0 \tag{viii}$$

This is known as the *frequency equation or characteristic equation.*

Its solution gives,

$$aL = n\pi$$

or,
$$a = \frac{n\pi}{L}$$

where, $n = 0, 1, 2, \ldots, \infty$

The sine function vanishes when its argument is 0 or any integer multiple of π. There is one solution of the characteristic equation for each value of $n = 0, 1, 2\ 3, \ldots$. Hence, there exists infinite number of values of 'a' that satisfy the condition (viii). Thus, 'a' can be replaced with the notation 'a_n' as follows:

$$a_n = \frac{n\pi}{L} \quad \text{where } n = 1, 2, 3, \ldots$$

The solution at $n = 0$ is ignored because it means zero solution.

but
$$a^4 = \frac{\omega^2 m}{EI} \tag{11.10}$$

or,
$$\omega_n^2 = \left(\frac{n\pi}{L}\right)^4 \frac{EI}{m}$$

or,
$$\omega_n = n^2\pi^2\sqrt{\frac{EI}{mL^4}} \tag{11.15}$$

The mode shape is given by Equation (11.13b).

Because $A_2 = 0 = A_3 = A_4$

$$\phi_n(x) = A_1 \sin\frac{n\pi}{L}x \tag{11.16}$$

Different values of n will give different values of frequency and mode shapes for different modes. First three mode shapes are shown in Figure 11.2.

$$\omega_1 = \pi^2\sqrt{\frac{EI}{mL^4}} \quad \text{and} \quad \phi_1 = \sin\frac{\pi x}{L}$$

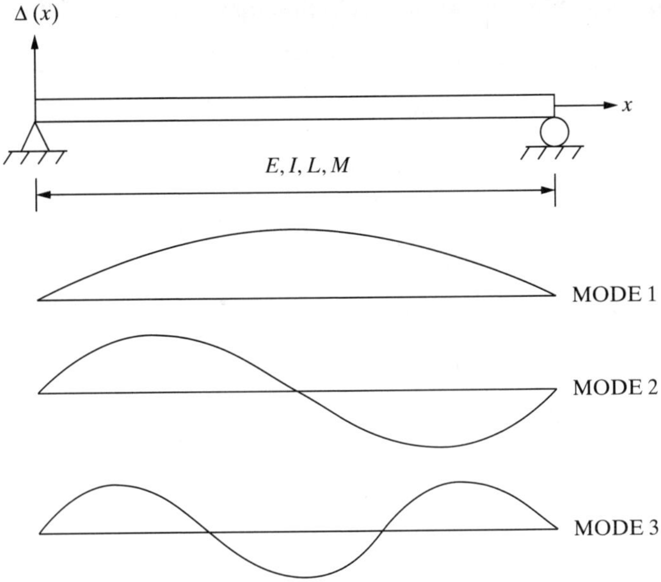

Figure 11.2 Simply supported beam and mode shapes.

$$\omega_2 = 4\pi^2\sqrt{\frac{EI}{mL^4}} \quad \text{and} \quad \phi_2 = \sin\frac{2\pi x}{L}$$

$$\omega_3 = 9\pi^2\sqrt{\frac{EI}{mL^4}} \quad \text{and} \quad \phi_3 = \sin\frac{3\pi x}{L} \tag{11.17}$$

It will be seen that the first mode is one-half sine wave, second mode is one-full sine wave and third mode is one and one-half sine wave.

11.4 CANTILEVER BEAM

Let us consider a cantilever beam fixed at $x = 0$.

Boundary conditions are:

at $x = 0$ (Fixed end)

$$\text{Deflection } \phi(0) = 0 \quad \text{and} \quad \text{slope } \phi'(0) = 0 \tag{i}$$

at $x = L$ (Free end)

$$\text{Moment } M = EI\,\phi''(L) = 0 \quad \text{and} \quad \text{shear } V = EI\,\phi'''(L) = 0 \tag{ii}$$

$$\phi(x) = A_1 \sin ax + A_2 \cos ax + A_3 \sinh ax + A_4 \cosh ax \tag{11.13b}$$

Introducing the boundary conditions in Equation (11.13b),

$$\phi(0) = A_2 + A_4 = 0 \quad \text{or} \quad A_2 = -A_4 \tag{iii}$$

$$\phi'(0) = a(A_1 + A_3) = 0 \quad \text{or} \quad A_1 = -A_3 \tag{iv}$$

$$\phi''(L) = a^2(-A_1 \sin aL - A_2 \cos aL + A_3 \sinh aL + A_4 \cosh aL) = 0 \tag{v}$$

$$\phi'''(L) = a^3(-A_1 \cos aL - A_2 \sin aL + A_3 \cosh aL + A_4 \sinh aL) = 0 \tag{vi}$$

Substituting Equations (iii) and (iv) in (v) and (vi),

$$0 = A_1(\sin aL + \sinh aL) + A_2(\cos aL + \cosh aL)$$

and
$$0 = -A_1(\cos aL + \cosh aL) + A_2(\sin aL - \sinh aL)$$

In matrix form,

$$\begin{bmatrix} \sin aL + \sinh aL & \cos aL + \cosh aL \\ \cos aL + \cosh aL & \sin aL - \sinh aL \end{bmatrix} \begin{Bmatrix} A_1 \\ A_2 \end{Bmatrix} = \{0\} \tag{vii}$$

For non-trivial solution, determinant must be zero, that is:

$$\begin{vmatrix} \sin aL + \sinh aL & \cos al + \cosh aL \\ \cos aL + \cosh aL & \sin aL - \sinh aL \end{vmatrix} = 0$$

or,

$$(\cos aL + \cosh aL)^2 - (\sin^2 aL - \sinh^2 aL) = 0$$

or, On simplification,

$$1 + \cos aL \cosh aL = 0 \tag{11.18a}$$

This is a transcendental equation and gives the value of aL. It must be solved numerically or graphically to get the frequency of vibration. It gives

$a_n L = 1.875, 4.694, 7.855$ and 10.996 for $n = 1, 2, 3$ and 4.

Mode shapes are given by Equation (vii), that is,

$$A_2 = -\left[\frac{\sin aL + \sinh aL}{\cos aL + \cosh aL}\right] A_1 \tag{viii}$$

Substituting Equations (iii), (iv) and (viii) in Equation (11.13b) gives:

$$\phi(x) = A_1\left[\sin ax - \sinh ax + \frac{\sin aL + \sinh aL}{\cos aL + \cosh aL}(\cosh ax - \cos ax)\right] \tag{11.18b}$$

This gives mode shapes.

The solution of Equation (11.18a) gives,

$$\omega_n = \frac{(aL)^2}{L^2}\sqrt{\frac{EI}{m}} \tag{11.19}$$

$$\omega_1 = (1.875)^2 \sqrt{\frac{EI}{mL^4}}$$

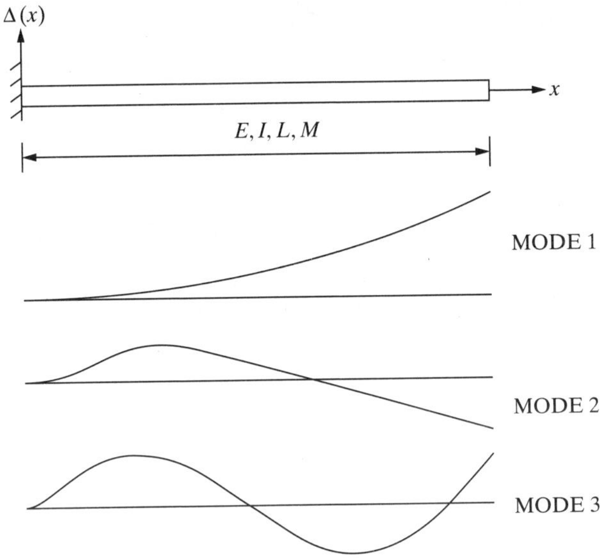

Figure 11.3 Cantilever beam and mode shapes.

$$\omega_2 = (4.694)^2 \sqrt{\frac{EI}{mL^4}}$$

$$\omega_3 = (7.855)^2 \sqrt{\frac{EI}{mL^4}} \tag{11.20}$$

First three mode shapes are shown in Figure 11.3.

Similarly, it is possible to write the expressions for frequency and mode shapes for systems with distributed mass and elasticity having different boundary conditions.

11.5 RAYLEIGH'S PRINCIPLE: CONSERVATION OF ENERGY

The energy in a freely vibrating system must remain constant if no damping forces act to absorb it. That is,

$$\text{Total potential energy} + \text{total kinetic energy} = \text{constant} \tag{11.21}$$

For a SDOF system

$$x = x_0 \sin \omega t$$

or,

$$\frac{dx}{dt} = \dot{x} = x_0\ \omega \cos \omega t$$

Potential energy = strain energy of the spring

$$\text{PE} = \int_0^L kx\,dx$$

$$= \frac{1}{2} k\, x^2 = \frac{1}{2} k\, x_0^2 \sin^2 \omega t \tag{i}$$

= work done on the system by the applied loading.

$$\text{Kinetic energy of the mass} = \frac{1}{2} m\dot{x}^2 = \frac{1}{2} m\, x_0^2\, \omega^2 \cos^2 \omega t \tag{ii}$$

$$\therefore \qquad \frac{1}{2} k{x_0}^2 \sin^2 \omega t + \frac{1}{2} m{x_0}^2 \omega^2 \cos^2 \omega t = \text{constant} \tag{iii}$$

$$\text{Max. PE} = \frac{1}{2} kx_0^2 \quad \text{and} \quad \text{KE} = 0 \ (\text{at } t = \text{T}/4 = \pi/2\omega) \tag{iv}$$

$$\text{Max. KE} = \frac{1}{2} mx_0^2\omega^2 \quad \text{and} \quad \text{PE} = 0 \ (\text{at } t = \text{T}/2 = \pi/\omega) \tag{v}$$

If total energy in a vibrating system remains constant,

then
$$\text{Max. PE} = \text{Max. KE}$$

or,
$$\frac{1}{2} kx_0^2 = \frac{1}{2} mx_0^2\omega^2$$

or,
$$\omega = \sqrt{k/m} \tag{11.22a}$$

This equation can be applied to any structure, which can be represented as a SDOF system through the use of an assumed displacement shape function ϕ of the *fundamental mode*. Even though the assumed mode shape is approximate, the *Rayleigh method* gives fairly accurate value of the fundamental frequency. The best first estimate of the fundamental mode shape is produced by the dead weight or the gravity forces of the structure. Most international building codes specify Rayleigh method to estimate the fundamental frequency of the building as follows:

$$T = 2\pi \sqrt{\frac{\sum_{i=1}^{n} w_i x_i^2}{g \sum_{i=1}^{n} F_i x_i}} \tag{11.22b}$$

where

x_i = elastic horizontal displacements at i^{th} level due to lateral forces F_i ignoring the effect of torsion.

w_i = weight at the ith floor

The lateral force F_i can be taken in proportion to the weight of the ith floor.

11.6 MULTI-DEGREE OF FREEDOM SYSTEM

Consider a flexure member which has infinite numbers of DOF. It is desired to determine its fundamental frequency of vibration. It can be determined by treating it as a continuum system and solving Equation (11.13b). It is convenient to solve this equation

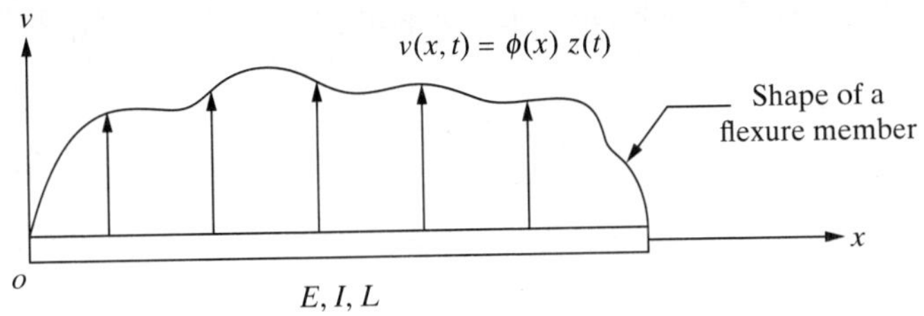

Figure 11.4 Assumed deflected shape in fundamental mode.

for simpler cases. In many practical applications, a member may have a continuously varying cross-section along its length. In such cases, it is convenient to estimate the fundamental frequency of vibration using the Rayleigh's principle. It is necessary to assume the shape which the flexure member will take in its fundamental mode of vibration (Figure 11.4).

Let
$$v(x,t) = \phi(x)\, Z(t) \tag{11.23a}$$

or,
$$v(x,t) = \phi(x)\, Z_0 \sin\omega t \tag{11.23b}$$

This equation assumes that shape of the vibrating beam does not change with time. Only the amplitude of motion does, and it varies harmonically in a free vibration condition. $\phi(x)$ is referred to as the *shape function* or *Ritz function,* which represents the ratio of the displacement at any point x to the *generalized coordinate* $Z(t)$. This assumption of the shape function *effectively reduces* the beam *to a SDOF system.* Thus, the frequency of vibration can be found by equating the maximum strain energy developed during the motion to the maximum kinetic energy.

Strain energy of the flexural system

$$U = \frac{1}{2}\int \frac{M^2 dx}{EI} \tag{11.24a}$$

Potential energy

$$U = \frac{1}{2}\int_0^L EI(x)\left(\frac{\partial^2 v}{\partial x^2}\right)^2 dx \tag{11.24b}$$

Substituting the assumed mode shape and letting the displacement amplitude take its maximum value leads to

$$\text{PE}_{\text{max}} = \frac{1}{2} Z_0^2 \int_0^L EI(x)[\phi''(x)]^2\, dx \tag{11.25}$$

Kinetic energy of non-uniformly distributed mass is

$$\text{KE} = \frac{1}{2}\int_0^L m(x)\,(\dot{v})^2\, dx$$

Equation (11.23b) is differentiated with respect to time to obtain the velocity, and amplitude is allowed to take its maximum value,

$$\text{KE}_{\text{max}} = \frac{1}{2} Z_0^2\, \omega^2 \int_0^L m(x)[\phi(x)]^2\, dx \tag{11.26}$$

Equating the maximum energies, $PE_{max} = KE_{max}$

$$\text{Rayleigh frequency } \omega^2 = \frac{\int_0^L EI(x)[\phi''(x)]^2\,dx}{\int_0^L m(x)[\phi(x)]^2\,dx} \tag{11.27}$$

or,

$$\omega^2 = \sqrt{\frac{k^*}{m^*}} \tag{11.28a}$$

where,

$$m^* = \int_0^L m(x)[\phi(x)]^2\,dx \tag{11.28b}$$

$$k^* = \int_0^L EI(x)[\phi''(x)]^2\,dx \tag{11.28c}$$

In Equation (11.27), the numerator is merely the generalized stiffness of the beam k^* for this assumed displacement shape, while the denominator is its generalized mass m^*. This equation is referred to as the standard Rayleigh frequency equation. The accuracy of the estimation of frequency depends upon the selection of the shape function for its fundamental mode of vibration.

11.7 IMPROVED RAYLEIGH METHOD

A better approximation of the frequency can be made by computing the potential energy from the work done in deflecting the structure by the inertia force associated with the assumed deflection. The distributed inertia force is given by

$$p(t) = m\ddot{x}(t) = m(x)\ddot{x}(t) \tag{11.29a}$$

As a first approximation,

Let

$$v^{(0)}(x,t) = \phi^{(0)}(x)Z^{(0)}(t)$$

or,

$$v^{(0)}(x,t) = \phi^{(0)}(x)Z_0^{(0)}\sin\omega t$$

where,

$$Z^{(0)}(t) = Z_0^{(0)}\sin\omega t$$

$Z_0^{(0)}$ = amplitude of generalized coordinate $Z^{(0)}(t)$

The inertia force can be expressed as

$$p^{(0)}(t) = \omega^2 m(x)v^{(0)}(x,t) \tag{11.29b}$$

$$= \omega^2 m(x)\phi^{(0)}(x)Z^{(0)}(t)$$

The deflection produced by this inertia loading may be written as

$$v^{(1)}(x,t) = \omega^2 \frac{v^{(1)}(x,t)}{\omega^2} = \omega^2 \phi^{(1)}(x) \frac{Z_0^{(1)}(t)}{\omega^2}$$

$$v^{(1)} = \omega^2 \frac{v^{(1)}}{\omega^2} = \omega^2 \phi^{(1)} \frac{Z_0^{(1)}}{\omega^2}$$

or,

$$v^{(1)} = \omega^2 \phi^{(1)} \bar{Z}_0^{(1)} \tag{11.30}$$

where ω^2 is the unknown frequency. The term ω^2 has been brought in so as to determine its value.

$v^{(1)}$ is a better approximation than $v^{(0)}$.

The potential energy of strain produced by this loading is given by

$$\text{PE}_{\text{max}} = \frac{1}{2} \int_0^L p^{(0)} v^{(1)} \, dx \tag{11.31}$$

$$= \frac{Z_0^{(0)} \bar{Z}_0^{(1)}}{2} \omega^4 \int_0^L m(x) \phi^{(0)} \phi^{(1)} dx \tag{11.32a}$$

$$\text{KE}_{\text{max}} = \frac{1}{2} Z_0^2 \, \omega^2 \int_0^L m(x)[\phi(x)]^2 \, dx \tag{11.26}$$

It can be written as

$$\text{KE}_{\text{max}} = \frac{1}{2} Z_0^{(0)2} \omega^2 \int_0^L m(x) \left(\phi^{(0)}(x)\right)^2 dx \tag{11.32b}$$

Equating maximum potential energy to the maximum kinematic energy gives

$$\omega^2 = \frac{Z_0^{(0)}}{\bar{Z}_0^{(1)}} \frac{\int_0^L m(x) \left(\phi^{(0)}\right)^2 dx}{\int_0^L m(x) \phi^{(0)} \phi^{(1)} dx} \tag{11.33}$$

Equation (11.33) gives a better estimation of the fundamental frequency than that of Equation (11.27). It is because this relation avoids the curvature term, which is poorly estimated by differentiation than the shape function $\phi(x)$, which involves no derivative.

11.8 GENERALIZED SDOF SYSTEM

A system with distributed mass and elasticity can be treated as a SDOF system if a suitable displacement shape can be assumed that satisfies its boundary conditions. This approach can be conveniently used to estimate the forces generated in such a system during an earthquake excitation. The generalized force produced due to earthquake needs to be computed. Let us consider a cantilever system with rigid base subjected to an earthquake in the lateral direction as shown in Figure 11.5.

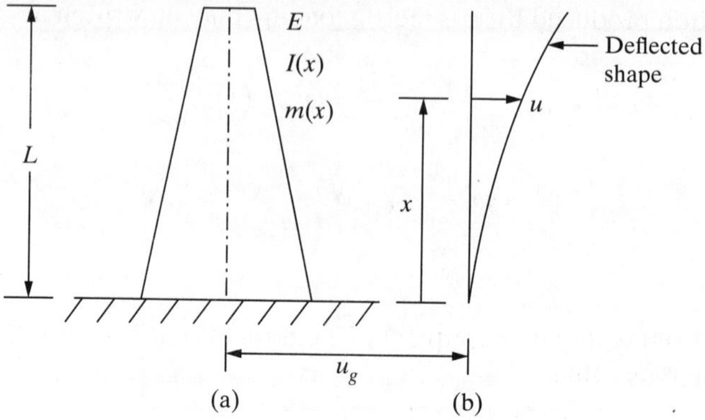

Figure 11.5 Generalized SDOF system.

The equation of motion can be written as follows:

$$f_I(x,t)+f_D(x,t)+f_S(x,t)=0 \tag{11.34}$$

The displacement can be expressed in terms of separation of variables $\phi(x)$ and $z(t)$, that is

$$u(x,t)=\phi(x)\,z(t) \tag{11.23a}$$

Using the principle of virtual work, $\delta u=\phi(x)\delta z$, leads to the equation of dynamic equilibrium

$$f_I^{\,*}\delta z+f_D^{\,*}\delta z+f_S^{\,*}\delta z=0 \tag{11.35}$$

where,

$$\begin{aligned} f_I^{\,*} &= \int_0^L f_I(x,t)\phi(x)\,dx \\ f_D^{\,*} &= \int_0^L f_D(x,t)\phi(x)\,dx \\ f_S^{\,*} &= \int_0^L f_S(x,t)\phi(x)\,dx \end{aligned} \tag{11.36}$$

where,

$$f_D^{\,*}=c^*\dot{z}$$

and

$$f_S^{\,*}=k^*z$$

The inertia force depends upon the total acceleration, that is

$$f_I(x,t)=m(x)\ddot{u}^t(x,t)$$

Since,

$$u^t(x,t)=u(x,t)+u_g(t)=\phi(x)z(t)+u_g(t)$$

where, $u^t(x,t)=$ total displacement

The generalized inertia force can be written as

$$f_I^* = \ddot{z}(t)\int_0^L m(x)(\phi(x))^2\,dx + \ddot{u}_g\int_0^L m(x)\phi(x)\,dx \tag{11.37}$$

Substituting all the generalized force expressions in Equation (11.35) gives the modal equation of motion.

$$m^*\ddot{z}(t)+c^*\dot{z}(t)+k^*z(t) = -\bar{m}\ddot{u}_g(t) \tag{11.38a}$$

or,

$$m^*\ddot{z}(t)+c^*\dot{z}(t)+k^*z(t) = p^*(t) \tag{11.38b}$$

$$\text{Generalized mass } m^* = \int_0^L m(x)[\phi(x)]^2\,dx \tag{11.28b}$$

$$\text{Generalized stiffness } k^* = \int_0^L EI(x)[\phi''(x)]^2\,dx \tag{11.28c}$$

$$\text{Generalized damping } c^* = \int_0^L c(x)[\phi(x)]^2\,dx \tag{11.28d}$$

$$\text{Generalized excitation } p^*(t) = -\bar{m}\ddot{u}_g(t) \tag{11.39a}$$

$$\bar{m} = \int_0^L m(x)\phi(x)dx \tag{11.39b}$$

where,

$\bar{m}$ = extent to which an earthquake motion excites the response in an assumed mode shape $\phi(x)$

By analogy of the analysis of a lumped mass system, Equation (11.38) can be written as

$$\ddot{z}+2\omega\xi\dot{z}+\omega^2 z = -\frac{\bar{m}}{m^*}\ddot{u}_g(t)$$

The solution of the modal equation of motion, that is response $z(t)$ can be obtained by any procedure discussed earlier.

$$z(t) = \frac{\bar{m}}{m^*\omega}v(t) \tag{11.40a}$$

where, $v(t)$ = velocity response at time t.

Its peak response can be estimated using

$$z_0 = \frac{\bar{m}}{m^*\omega}S_V \tag{11.40b}$$

The local displacement at any section x at time t is given by

$$u(x,t) = \phi(x)\,z(t) \tag{11.23a}$$

or,

$$u(x,t) = \frac{\phi(x)\bar{m}}{m^*\omega}v(t) \tag{11.40c}$$

11.9 ILLUSTRATIVE EXAMPLES

Example 11.1

Estimate the fundamental frequency of vibration of a simply supported beam using the Rayleigh's principle. EI = constant, m = constant

Solution

Let us consider a simply supported beam as shown in Figure 11.6.

(i) Let us consider the shape function

$$\phi(x)=\frac{x}{L}\left(\frac{x}{L}-1\right) \tag{i}$$

It satisfies the boundary conditions with respect to deflection. Let us differentiate it twice.

$$\therefore \qquad \phi'(x)=\frac{2x}{L^2}-\frac{1}{L} \tag{ii}$$

$$\therefore \qquad \phi''(x)=\frac{2}{L^2} \tag{iii}$$

Maximum potential energy

$$\text{PE}_{\text{max}}=\frac{1}{2}z_0^2\,EI\int_0^L\left(\frac{2}{L^2}\right)^2 dx=\frac{1}{2}z_0^2\frac{4EI}{L^3}$$

and maximum kinetic energy

$$\text{KE}_{\text{max}}=\frac{1}{2}z_0^2\,\omega^2\,m\int_0^L\left[\frac{x}{L}\left(\frac{x}{L}-1\right)\right]^2 dx$$

$$=\frac{1}{2}z_0^2\,\omega^2\frac{mL}{30}$$

Equating the maximum energies gives,

$$\omega^2=\frac{120\,EI}{mL^4} \tag{iv}$$

(ii) Let us consider an improved shape function.

$$\phi(x)=\sin(\pi x/L) \tag{v}$$

Let us differentiate it twice

$$\therefore \qquad \phi'(x)=\frac{\pi}{L}\cos\left(\frac{\pi x}{L}\right) \tag{vi}$$

$$\therefore \qquad \phi''(x)=(-)\frac{\pi^2}{L^2}\left(\sin\left(\frac{\pi x}{L}\right)\right) \tag{vii}$$

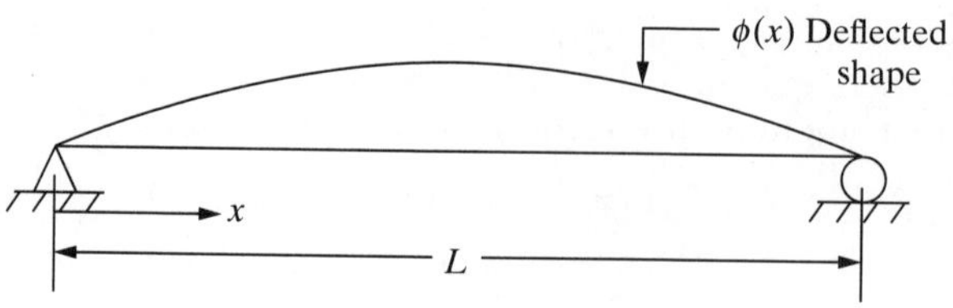

Figure 11.6 Simply supported beam.

Equating the maximum PE and maximum KE and using Equation (11.27)

$$\omega^2 = \frac{\int_0^L EI\left(\frac{\pi^2}{L^2}\right)^2 \sin^2\left(\frac{\pi x}{L}\right)dx}{\int_0^L m \sin^2\left(\frac{\pi x}{L}\right)dx}$$

or,

$$\omega^2 = \frac{\pi^4 EI}{mL^4} = \frac{97.408\,EI}{mL^4} \tag{viii}$$

The second shape function is a much better approximation since it gives a lower value. It also happens to be the true frequency. The mode shape is also a sine curve. □

Example 11.2

A RC chimney 200 m high has a hollow cross-section with 25 m outer diameter linearly tapering to 10 m outer diameter at the top with uniform wall thickness 0.75m in M30 grade as shown in Figure 11.7(a). Estimate the peak displacement, shear force and bending moment due to earthquake motion. It is located in Greater Noida on hard soil.

Solution

Outer diameter at the base = D_1; outer diameter at the top = D_2, wall thickness = t
Let us consider a cross-section at height x above the ground.

$$\text{Outer diameter at height } x,\ D_{ox} = D_1 - (D_1 - D_2)\frac{x}{L} = 25 - 0.075x$$

$$\text{Inner diameter at height } x,\ D_{ix} = D_{ox} - 2t = 23.5 - 0.075x$$

$$\text{Area of cross-section } A(x) = \frac{\pi}{4}\left(D_{ox}^{\ 2} - D_{ix}^{\ 2}\right) = \frac{\pi}{4}(72.75 - 0.225x)$$

$$\text{Moment of inertia } I(x) = \frac{\pi}{64}\left(D_{ox}^4 - D_{ix}^4\right)$$

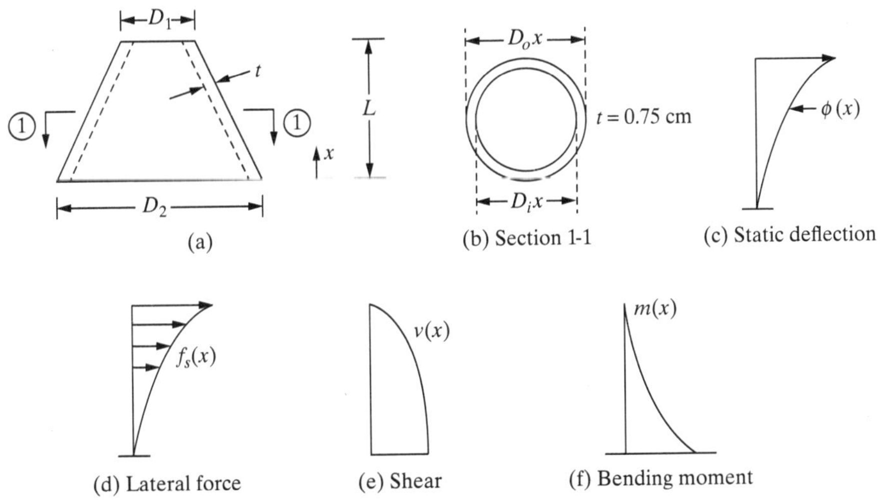

Figure 11.7 R.C. Chimney.

Weight density of concrete $\gamma_c = 25$ kN/m³, mass density of concrete $\rho_c = 2500$ kg/m³
Modulus of elasticity $E = 5000\sqrt{\text{fck}} = 5000\sqrt{30} = 27390$ MPa $= 27390 \times 10^3$ kN/m²

Let us assume its deflected shape in the first mode $\phi(x) = 1 - \cos\dfrac{\pi x}{2L}$ as shown in Figure 11.7(c).
Generalized mass is given by Equation (11.28b),

$$m^* = \int_0^L m(x)[\phi(x)]^2 dx$$

$$m^* = \int_0^L \rho_c \frac{\pi}{4}(72.75 - 0.225x)\left(1 - cos\frac{\pi x}{2L}\right)^2 dx$$

Generalized stiffness is given by Equation (11.28c),

$$k^* = \int_0^L EI(x)[\phi''(x)]^2 dx$$

$$k^* = E\int_0^L \frac{\pi}{64}\left[(25 - 0.075x)^4 - (23.5 - 0.075x)^4\right]\left(\frac{\pi}{2L}\right)^4 cos^2\frac{\pi x}{2L}dx$$

$$\bar{m} = \int_0^L m(x)\phi(x)dx \tag{11.39b}$$

$$\bar{m} = \int_0^L \rho_c \frac{\pi}{4}(72.75 - 0.225x)\left(1 - \cos\frac{\pi x}{2L}\right)dx$$

These integrals can be evaluated using the standard formulae (Appending 3):
Generalized mass $m^* = 3191100$ kg/m
Generalized stiffness $k^* = 25500$ kN/m $= 255 \times 10^5$ N/m

Fundamental frequency $\omega_n = \sqrt{\dfrac{k^*}{m^*}}$

$$\omega_n = \sqrt{\frac{255 \times 10^5}{3191100}} = 2.826 \text{ rad/sec}$$

Fundamental period $T = \dfrac{2\pi}{\omega_n} = 2.22$ sec

Horizontal seismic coefficient is given by clause 16 of IS:1893-part 4 as follows:
Zone factor for zone IV = 0.24, Importance factor $I = 1.50$, Response reduction factor $R = 1.50$
Sa/g for $T = 2.22$ sec on hard rock $= 1/T = 0.45$
Total dead load of chimney = 197250 kN

$$\alpha_h = \frac{Z}{2}\frac{I}{R}\frac{S_a}{g} = \frac{0.24 \times 1.5 \times 0.45}{2 \times 1.50} = 0.054$$

Base shear $V_B = 0.054$ W

$= 0.054 \times 197250 = 10650$ kN

Spectral displacement $S_d = \dfrac{S_a}{\omega_n^2} = \dfrac{0.45 \times g}{2.826^2} = 0.553$ m

Peak value of displacement $z(t) = z_0 = \text{MPF } S_d = \dfrac{\bar{m}}{m^*} S_d$

$$\bar{m} = 5627700 \text{ kg/m}$$

$$\therefore \qquad z_0 = \frac{5627700 \times 0.553}{3191100} = 0.975 \text{ m}$$

Displacement at any section x is given by

$$v(x) = \text{MPF } S_d \, \phi(x) = 0.975\left(1 - \cos\frac{\pi x}{2L}\right)$$

Equivalent static force is given by

$$f_s(x,t) = kv(x,t) = \omega_n^2 m(x)\phi(x)z(t)$$

Peak value of force is given by

$$f_{s,\max}(x) = m(x)\phi(x)\omega_n^2 z_0$$

$$f_{s,\max}(x) = m(x)\phi(x)\text{MPF } S_a$$

$$= \rho_c A(x) \times \left(1 - \cos\frac{\pi x}{2L}\right) \times 1.764 \times 0.45 \text{ g N/m}$$

Shear force at any section can be determined using statics

$$\text{Shear } V(x) = \int_0^x f_s(x)dx$$

$$= \text{MPF} \, S_a \int_0^x m(x)\phi(x)dx$$

Shear at base is given by integrating it from 0 to L.

$$V(0) = \frac{\bar{m}}{m^*} S_a \bar{m} = \frac{\bar{m}^2}{m^*} S_a = \frac{\bar{m}^2}{m^*} \omega_n S_v$$

$$= 1.764 \times 5627700 \times 0.45 \text{ g} = 43823900 \text{ N}$$

Similarly, base moment can be determined using statics

$$\text{Moment } M(x) = \int_0^x f_s(x)x dx$$

$$= \text{MPF} \, S_a \int_0^x m(x)\phi(x)x dx$$

The code specified base shear is only 10650 kN whereas the structural dynamics gives a base shear of 43824 kN. It means the Codal base shear is 24 % of that given by dynamic considerations. It is important to note that:

(1) The Codal base shear is for the design basis earthquake.

(2) The Code requires ductile detailing of the chimney.

(3) The analytical base shear does not consider the effects of factors Z, I and R. □

Example 11.3

An overhead water tank is shown in Figure 11.8. The total mass of the staging is small as compared to the total mass of the tank. It can be modeled as a SDOF system. Find the fundamental frequency of vibration.

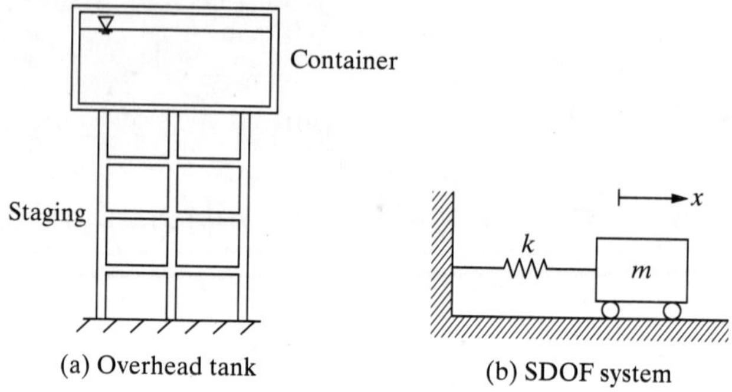

Figure 11.8 Model of a tank.

Solution

Let the total mass of the container including water = m

Let the total mass of the beam and column staging including staircase = m_0

A single-degree-of-freedom model is shown in Figure 11.8(b). The stiffness of the staging or the spring is k. The height of the staging, that is, length of the spring is L.

Total mass of the spring is $m_0 \ll$ total mass of the container

The maximum static deflection of the SDOF system due to the mass m is given by

$$u_0 = \frac{mg}{k} \tag{i}$$

$\therefore$ The deflection at any section x from the fixed support due to the mass m:

$$\phi(x) = u_0\left(\frac{x}{L}\right) \tag{ii}$$

This is the equation of the deflected shape of the spring if the total mass of the staging m_0 is small in comparison to the applied mass m at the free end.

The displacement can be expressed in terms of separation of variables

$$u(x,t) = \phi(x)z(t) \tag{iii}$$

or,

$$u(x,t) = \phi(x)\sin\omega t \tag{iv}$$

And,

$$\dot{u}(x,t) = \phi(x)\omega\cos\omega t \tag{v}$$

For $x = L$,

$$u(L,t) = \phi(L)\sin\omega t$$

or,

$$u(L,t) = u_0\sin\omega t \text{ and } \dot{u}(L,t) = u_0\omega\cos\omega t$$

Kinetic energy of the system is given by

$$\mathrm{KE} = \frac{1}{2}mv^2$$

or,

$$\mathrm{KE} = \frac{1}{2}m\left[\dot{u}(L,t)\right]^2 + \int_0^L \frac{1}{2}\left(\frac{m_0}{L}dx\right)\left[\dot{u}(x,t)\right]^2$$

$$\mathrm{KE} = \frac{1}{2}m\left[u_0\omega\cos\omega t\right]^2 + \int_0^L \frac{1}{2}\left(\frac{m_0}{L}dx\right)\left[\phi(x)\omega\cos\omega t\right]^2$$

$$\mathrm{KE} = \frac{1}{2}m\left[u_0\omega\cos\omega t\right]^2 + \int_0^L \frac{1}{2}\left(\frac{m_0}{L}dx\right)\left[u_0\left(\frac{x}{L}\right)\omega\cos\omega t\right]^2$$

$$\mathrm{KE} = \frac{1}{2}m\left[u_0\omega\cos\omega t\right]^2 + \frac{1}{2}m_0\left[u_0\omega\cos\omega t\right]^2\frac{1}{3}$$

$$\mathrm{KE} = \frac{1}{2}\left(m + \frac{m_0}{3}\right)\left[u_0\omega\cos\omega t\right]^2 \tag{vi}$$

$$\mathrm{KE} = \frac{1}{2}m_{eq}\left(u_0\omega\cos\omega t\right)^2 \tag{vii}$$

where,

$$m_{eq} = \left(m + \frac{m_0}{3}\right) \tag{viii}$$

$$\mathrm{KE}_{\max} = \frac{1}{2}m_{eq}\left(u_0\omega\right)^2$$

Now let us evaluate the potential energy of the system.

By definition,

Strain energy, U = Work done = force × displacement

or, $$dU = kxdx$$

or, $$U = \int kxdx$$

or, $$\mathrm{SE} = \mathrm{PE} = \frac{1}{2}kx^2$$

Where, x = spring elongation

K = spring stiffness

This can be written as $$\mathrm{PE} = \frac{1}{2}k\left[u(x,t)\right]^2 = \frac{1}{2}k\left[\phi(x)\sin\omega t\right]^2 \tag{ix}$$

$$\mathrm{PE} = \frac{1}{2}k\left(u_0\frac{x}{L}\sin\omega t\right)^2$$

$$\mathrm{PE}_{\max} = \frac{1}{2}ku_0^2$$

Now, let us equate the maximum kinetic energy with the maximum potential energy,

$$\frac{1}{2}m_{eq}(u_0\omega)^2 = \frac{1}{2}ku_0^2$$

$$\omega^2 = \frac{k}{m_{eq}}$$

Fundamental frequency of the system is given by

$$\omega = \sqrt{\frac{k}{m_{eq}}} = \sqrt{\frac{k}{(m + m_0/3)}} \tag{x}$$

Equivalent mass is given by

$$m_{eq} = \left(m + \frac{m_0}{3}\right) \tag{xi}$$

□

Example 11.4

A cantilever beam of total mass m_0 carries a point load mg acting at its tip as shown in Figure 11.9. Find the fundamental frequency of vibration. The total mass of the beam is small as compared to the applied mass at the free end but not negligible. EI = constant.

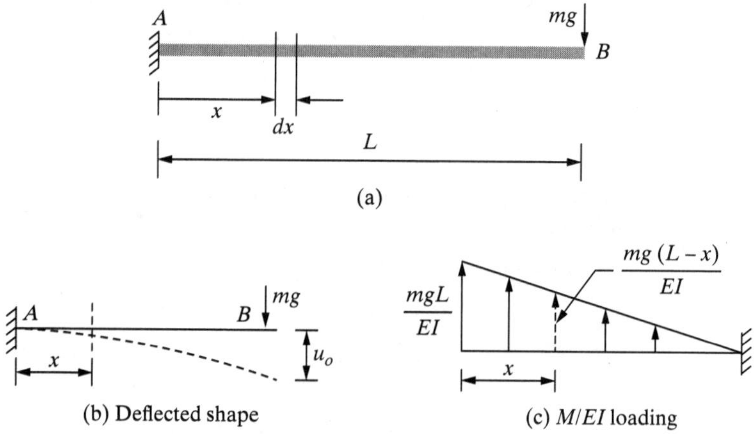

Figure 11.9 Cantilever beam.

Solution

The maximum deflection at the free end of the beam due to the point load mg is given by

$$u_0 = \frac{mgL^3}{3EI} \tag{i}$$

Therefore, stiffness of the beam is

$$k = \frac{3EI}{L^3} \tag{ii}$$

It is given that the mass of the beam is small as compared to the applied mass at the free end but not negligible. Now let us compute deflection at any section x from the fixed support due to the load mg acting at the tip using the conjugate beam method,

$$\phi(x) = \frac{mg(3L-x)x^2}{6EI} = \frac{u_0(3L-x)x^2}{2L^3} \tag{iii}$$

This is the equation of the deflected shape of the beam if the total mass of the beam m_0 is small in comparison to the applied mass m at the free end but not negligible.

The displacement can be expressed in terms of separation of variables

$$u(x,t) = \phi(x)z(t) \tag{iv}$$

or,

$$u(x,t) = \phi(x)\sin\omega t$$

For $x = L$,

$$u(L,t) = \phi(L)\sin\omega t$$

or,

$$u(L,t) = u_0\sin\omega t \text{ and } \dot{u}(L,t) = u_0\omega\cos\omega t \tag{v}$$

Kinetic energy of the system is given by

$$\text{KE} = \frac{1}{2}mv^2 \tag{vi}$$

or,

$$\text{KE} = \frac{1}{2}m\left[\dot{u}(L,t)\right]^2 + \int_0^L \frac{1}{2}\left(\frac{m_0}{L}dx\right)\left[\dot{u}(x,t)\right]^2$$

$$\text{KE} = \frac{1}{2}m(u_0\omega\cos\omega t)^2 + \int_0^L \frac{1}{2}\left(\frac{m_0}{L}dx\right)\left[\frac{u_0(3L-x)x^2}{2L^3}\omega\cos\omega t\right]^2$$

$$\text{KE} = \frac{1}{2}m(u_0\omega\cos\omega t)^2 + \int_0^L \frac{m_0}{8L^7}\left(9L^2x^4 - 6Lx^5 + x^6\right)(u_0\omega\cos\omega t)^2\,dx$$

$$\text{KE} = \frac{1}{2}m(u_0\omega\cos\omega t)^2 + \frac{33}{280}m_0(u_0\omega\cos\omega t)^2$$

$$\text{KE} = \frac{1}{2}\left(m + \frac{33}{140}m_0\right)(u_0\omega\cos\omega t)^2$$

$$\text{KE} = \frac{1}{2}m_{eq}(u_0\omega\cos\omega t)^2 \tag{vii}$$

where,

m_{eq} = equivalent mass of the system

$$m_{eq} = \left(m + \frac{33}{140}m_0\right) = m + 0.2357m_0 \tag{viii}$$

$$\text{KE}_{\max} = \frac{1}{2}m_{eq}(u_0\omega)^2 \tag{ix}$$

Now let us evaluate the potential energy of the system.

$$\text{Strain energy in flexure} = \frac{1}{2}\int \frac{M^2 dx}{EI} \tag{x}$$

or,

$$SE = PE = \frac{1}{2}\int EI\left(\frac{d^2y}{dx^2}\right)^2 dx$$

$$PE = \frac{1}{2}\int_0^L EI\left(\frac{d^2u(x,t)}{dx^2}\right)^2 dx$$

where,

$$\frac{d^2u(x,t)}{dx^2} = \frac{d^2\phi(x)\sin\omega t}{dx^2} = \frac{3u_0}{L^3}(L-x)\sin\omega t$$

$$PE = \frac{1}{2}\int_0^L EI\left[\frac{3u_0}{L^3}(L-x)\sin\omega t\right]^2 dx$$

or,

$$PE = \frac{1}{2}\frac{3EI}{L^3}u_0^2\sin^2\omega t \tag{xi}$$

∴

$$PE_{max} = \frac{1}{2}\frac{3EI}{L^3}u_0^2 = \frac{1}{2}ku_0^2 \tag{xii}$$

Now, let us equate the maximum kinetic energy with the maximum potential energy,

$$\frac{1}{2}m_{eq}(u_0\omega)^2 = \frac{1}{2}ku_0^2$$

or,

$$\omega^2 = \frac{k}{m_{eq}}$$

Fundamental frequency of the system is given by

$$\omega = \sqrt{\frac{k}{m_{eq}}} = \sqrt{\frac{k}{(m + 0.2357m_0)}} \tag{xiii}$$

□

Example 11.5

A simply supported beam of total mass m_0 carries a point load mg acting at its midspan as shown in Figure 11.10. Assume that the mass of the beam is small as compared to the point load but not negligible. Find the fundamental frequency of vibration. Take EI = constant.

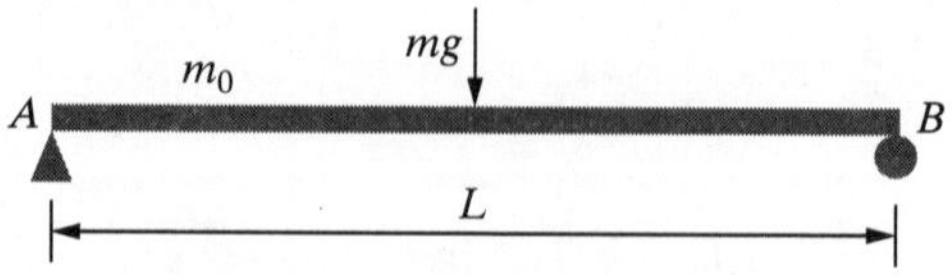

Figure 11.10 Simply supported beam.

Solution

The maximum deflection at the mid span of the beam due to the point load mg is given by

$$u_0 = \frac{mgL^3}{48EI} \tag{i}$$

Therefore, stiffness of the beam is

$$k = \frac{48EI}{L^3} \tag{ii}$$

It is given that the mass of the beam is small as compared to the applied mass at the mid span. It means the deflected shape of the beam can be assumed to be the same as that without the self-weight of the beam.

Now let us compute deflection at any section x from one end of the beam due to the load mg acting at the mid span,

$$\phi(x) = \frac{mg\left(\frac{-x^3}{12} + \frac{xL^2}{16}\right)}{EI} \quad \text{for} \quad x \le L/2 \tag{iii}$$

Alternatively, it may be written as:

$$\phi(x) = u_0\left(\frac{3xL^2 - 4x^3}{L^3}\right) \tag{iv}$$

This is the equation of the deflected shape of the beam if the total mass of the beam m_0 is small in comparison to the applied mass m at the free end but not negligible.

The displacement can be expressed in terms of separation of variables

$$u(x,t) = \phi(x)z(t) \tag{v}$$

or,

$$u(x,t) = \phi(x)\sin\omega t \tag{vi}$$

For $x = L/2$

$$u(L/2,t) = \phi(L/2)\sin\omega t$$

or,

$$u(L/2,t) = u_0 \sin\omega t \text{ and } \dot{u}(L/2,t) = u_0\omega\cos\omega t \tag{vii}$$

Kinetic energy of the system is given by

$$\text{KE} = \frac{1}{2}mv^2$$

or,

$$\text{KE} = \frac{1}{2}m\left[\dot{u}(L/2,t)\right]^2 + \int_0^L \frac{1}{2}\left(\frac{m_0}{L}dx\right)\left[\dot{u}(x,t)\right]^2$$

$$\text{KE} = \frac{1}{2}m(u_0\omega\cos\omega t)^2 + 2\int_0^{L/2} \frac{1}{2}\left(\frac{m_0}{L}dx\right)\left[u_0\left(\frac{3xL^2 - 4x^3}{L^3}\right)\omega\cos\omega t\right]^2$$

or,

$$\text{KE} = \frac{1}{2}\left[m + 2\left(\frac{m_0}{L^7}\right)\int_0^{L/2}\left(3xL^2 - 4x^3\right)^2 dx\right] \times (u_0\omega\cos\omega t)^2$$

or,

$$\text{KE} = \frac{1}{2}(m + 0.4857\, m_0) \times (u_0\omega\cos\omega t)^2$$

$$\text{KE} = \frac{1}{2}m_{eq}\left(u_0\omega\cos\omega t\right)^2 \tag{viii}$$

where,
m_{eq} = equivalent mass of the system

$$m_{eq} = \left(m + 0.4857\, m_0\right) \tag{ix}$$

$$\text{KE}_{\max} = \frac{1}{2}m_{eq}\left(u_0\omega\right)^2 \tag{x}$$

Now let us evaluate the potential energy of the system.

$$\text{Strain energy in flexure} = \frac{1}{2}\int\frac{M^2 dx}{EI}$$

$$\text{SE} = \text{PE} = \frac{1}{2}\int EI\left(\frac{d^2y}{dx^2}\right)^2 dx$$

$$\text{PE} = \frac{1}{2} \times 2\int_0^{L/2} EI\left(\frac{d^2u(x,t)}{dx^2}\right)^2 dx$$

where,

$$\frac{d^2u(x,t)}{dx^2} = \frac{d^2\phi(x)\sin\omega t}{dx^2} = \frac{u_0}{L^3}(-24x)\sin\omega t$$

or,

$$\text{PE} = \int_0^{L/2} EI\left[\frac{u_0}{L^3}(-24x)\sin\omega t\right]^2 dx = 24\, EI\left(u_0\sin\omega t\right)^2 / L^3$$

$$\therefore \quad \text{PE}_{\max} = \frac{24EI}{L^3}u_0^2 = \frac{1}{2}ku_0^2 \tag{xi}$$

Now, let us equate the maximum kinetic energy with the maximum potential energy,

$$\frac{1}{2}m_{eq}\left(u_0\omega\right)^2 = \frac{1}{2}ku_0^2$$

or,

$$\omega^2 = \frac{k}{m_{eq}}$$

Fundamental frequency of the system is given by

$$\omega = \sqrt{\frac{k}{m_{eq}}} = \sqrt{\frac{k}{(m + 0.4857m_0)}} \tag{xii}$$

□

11.10 LUMPED MASS SYSTEM: SHEAR BUILDINGS

It is possible to extend the principle of virtual displacement to discrete lumped mass systems. Let us consider a multi-storey framed building having n-DOF as shown in Figure 11.11. The floor displacements are $x_1, x_2, x_3, x_4, \ldots x_n$. The floor displacements relative to ground can be expressed as follows:

$$x_i(t) = \phi_i z(t) \qquad i = 1, 2, 3, \ldots n \tag{11.41a}$$

where, $x_i(t)$ = displacement of ith floor
ϕ_i = mode shape of ith floor
$z(t)$= generalized displacement as a function of time t

It can be expressed in vector form as follows:

$$\{x(t)\}_{n\times 1} = \{\phi\}_{n\times 1} z(t) \tag{11.41b}$$

where, $\{\phi\}$ = assumed shape vector

A shear building is defined as a building having rigid axial and flexure stiffness and flexible columns. Shear in any i^{th} storey is the sum of shears in all the columns of the storey. The storey shear is related to the storey drift through the storey stiffness as follows:

Storey drift $\qquad \Delta_i = x_i - x_{i-1}$ (11.42a)

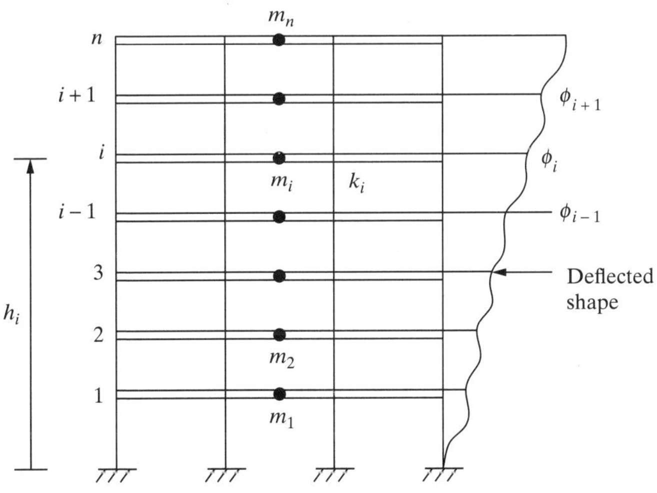

Figure 11.11 Deflected shape of a shear building.

Storey shear $$V_i = \Delta_i k_i \tag{11.42b}$$

where,

Storey stiffness $$k_i = \sum \frac{12EI}{L^3} \tag{11.42c}$$

The summation sign extends over all the columns in a storey.

It can be shown by proceeding as in the previous case that the natural frequency of the shear building is given by

$$\omega^2 = \frac{k^*}{m^*} \tag{11.43}$$

where generalized properties are as follows:

$$k^* = \sum k_i (\phi_i - \phi_{i-1})^2 \tag{11.44a}$$

and

$$m^* = \sum m_i \phi_i^2 \tag{11.44b}$$

The equation of motion of an undamped discrete mass spring model under earthquake motion is given by

$$[M]\{\ddot{X}\} + [K]\{X\} = \{P(t)\} = -[M]\{\ddot{y}_g(t)\}$$

We had earlier defined

$$\{x(t)\}_{n\times 1} = \{\phi\}_{n\times 1} z(t)$$

n = number of storeys

or,

$$x_i(t) = \phi_i z(t)$$

$\therefore$ Equation of motion can be written as:

$$m^* \ddot{z} + k^* z = -\bar{m}\ddot{y}_g(t) \tag{11.45}$$

where,

$$\bar{m} = \{\phi\}^T [M] = \sum m_i \phi_i$$

m_i, k_i, and ϕ_i are properties of the ith storey

It is assumed that the shear building deflects in a shape defined by the shape function ϕ in a given mode. This simplification is best suited for the fundamental mode of vibration as it is difficult to define or assume a shape function for higher modes. This equation can be easily extended to damped shear systems by assuming a modal damping ratio ξ.

Example 11.6

Consider a four-storey shear building as shown in Figure 11.12. Assuming that the floor displacements vary linearly with height, determine its fundamental frequency of vibration.

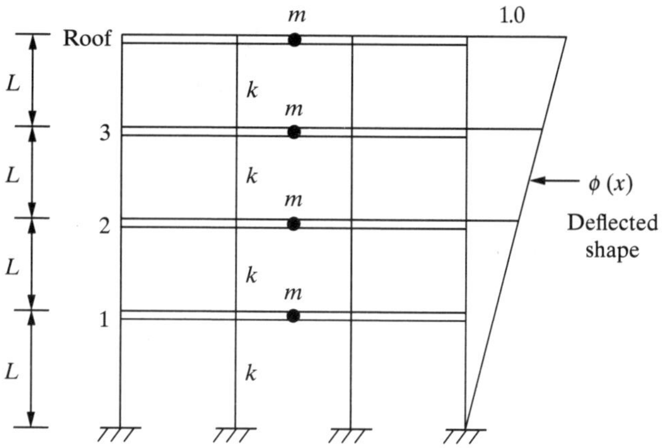

Figure 11.12 Four storey shear building.

Solution

Let us determine the generalized properties of the shear building:

$$m^* = \sum m_i \phi_i^2$$

$$k^* = \sum k_i (\phi_i - \phi_{i-1})^2$$

Let us assume that the top floor displacement is 1.0. The displacements at lower floors can be estimated by linear variation. Thus, the shape function can be written as follows:

$$\{\phi\} = \begin{Bmatrix} 1.0 \\ 0.75 \\ 0.50 \\ 0.25 \end{Bmatrix}$$

Thus,

$$m^* = m\left(1^2 + 0.75^2 + 0.50^2 + 0.25^2\right) = 1.875\text{ m}$$

$$k^* = k\left(0.25^2 + 0.25^2 + 0.25^2 + 0.25^2\right) = 0.25k$$

where,

$$k = \text{total lateral stiffness of a storey}$$

Natural frequency

$$\omega = \sqrt{\frac{0.25k}{1.875m}} = 0.365\sqrt{\frac{k}{m}}$$ □

Example 11.7

Consider the four-storey shear building of Example 11.6. Its mass $m = 4000$ kg, stiffness $k = 1000$ kN/m and storey height = 3 m. Determine the peak displacements, storey shears and floor overturning moments when it is subjected to the average response spectra shown in Figure 8.17(b). Take 5% damping.

Solution

Natural frequency $\omega = 0.365\sqrt{\frac{k}{m}}$

$$\omega = 0.365\sqrt{\frac{1000 \times 1000}{4000}} = 5.77 \text{ rad/sec}$$

Period $T = \frac{2\pi}{5.77} = 1.09$ sec

The spectral acceleration for 5% damping is given as 0.1 g = 0.1 × 981 = 98.1 cm/sec^2.
Spectral displacement $S_d = S_a/\omega^2$

$$S_d = \frac{98.1}{5.77^2} = 2.95 \text{ cm}$$

∴ Equation of motion can be written as:

$$m^*\ddot{z} + k^*z = -\bar{m}\ddot{y}_g(t) \tag{11.45}$$

where,

$$\bar{m} = \{\phi\}^T [M] = \sum m_i\phi_i$$

$$\bar{m} = m(1 + 0.75 + 0.50 + 0.25) = 2.5m = 2.5 \times 4000 = 10000$$

$$\Gamma = \frac{\bar{m}}{m^*} = \frac{10000}{1.875m} = \frac{10000}{1.875 \times 4000} = 1.33$$

∴ Peak displacement = 1.33 × 2.95 = 3.93 cm
∴ Peak floor displacements are given by:

$$\{x\} = \begin{Bmatrix} 3.93 \\ 2.95 \\ 1.97 \\ 0.98 \end{Bmatrix} \text{cm}$$

Lateral force at each floor is given by:

$$f_i = \Gamma m_i\phi_i S_a = 1.33 \times 4000 \times \phi_i \times \frac{98.1}{100} = 5218\phi_i N$$

The floor forces, storey shear and overturning moment calculations are shown in Table 11.1.

TABLE 11.1 LATERAL FORCES AND STOREY SHEARS

Floor	Mode shape, ϕ_i	Floor force, N	Storey shear N	Overturning moment, N-m
Roof	1.0	5218	5218	5218 × 3 = 15654
Third	0.75	3913	9131	5218 × 6 + 3913 × 3 = 43047
Second	0.50	2610	11741	5218 × 9 + 3913 × 6 + 2610 × 3 = 78270
First	0.25	1305	13046	5218 × 12 + 3913 × 9 + 2610 × 6 + 1305 × 3 =117400

The base shear = 13046 N

or, base shear = 13046/(4 × 4000 × 9.81) = 0.083 W

It means the base shear is 8.3% of the weight of the building. □

11.11 BRIDGES UNDER MOVING LOADS

The latest trend is to go for leaner bridges and faster vehicular speeds while ensuring greatest comfort for the vehicle occupants. This is true for highway bridges and railway bridges. It is necessary to understand dynamic analysis of the vehicle-bridge coupled vibration system. There is an increase in the effective force acting on a bridge depending upon the type of bridge, span of bridge, type of vehicle, and speed of vehicle. The effect of impact or dynamic action of a vehicle on the bridge is made by an increment of the live load by an impact allowance expressed as a fraction or percentage of the applied live load. This is known as *impact factor*. As moving vehicles on the bridge vary in both time and space, the problem becomes even more complex. The concept of impact factor for brides is quite old. The specification about *impact factor* (IF) or *dynamic load allowance* (DLA) in most design codes was obtained based on the dynamic load test on real bridges. However, it is a very cumbersome, expensive and time consuming proposition. With the availability of very powerful 3D finite element tools, it is possible to carryout sophisticated analysis to arrive at reasonable impact factors for different kinds of bridges under dynamic loads.

Modeling Aspects

There are wide range of problems involving vibration of bridges subjected to a moving loads. The simplest cases are as follows:

- Simply Supported Girder Bridge Traversed by a Single Moving Constant Load
- Simply Supported Girder Bridge Traversed by a Moving Sprung Mass

If the weight of the vehicle is far smaller than that of the bridge, the inertia force of the vehicle can be ignored. The vehicle-bridge coupled system can be simplified as a simply supported beam traversed by a single moving constant load. The damping may also be ignored. The bridge can be modeled as shown in Figure 11.13(a). It is subjected to a generalized force as shown in Figure 11.13(b). In this model, it is not possible to consider the coupled vibration in the vehicle-bridge system because the mass of the vehicle has been ignored.

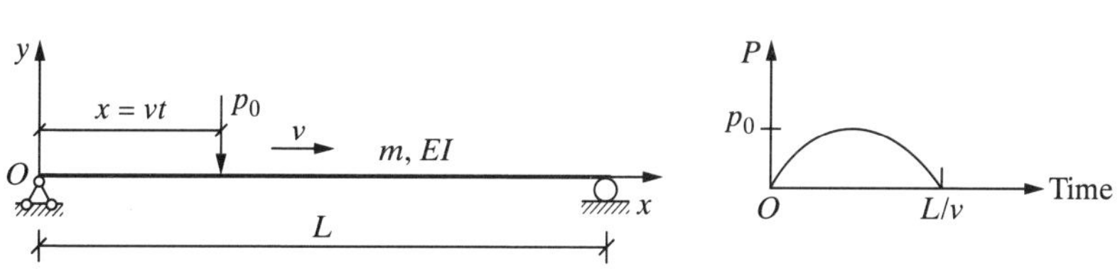

(a) Single moving constant load (b) Generalized force

Figure 11.13 Simply supported girder bridge.

In a vehicle with *suspension* such as an automobile, motorcycle, or a train, sprung mass is the portion of the vehicle's total mass that is supported above the suspension. In such cases, the vehicle body and the portion below the suspension, that is, wheels are modeled separately as shown in Figure 11.14. The vehicle body and the wheel are connected with a spring and a damper. It is assumed that the wheel is always in contact with the bridge and that the bridge vibrates in the first mode only. With these assumptions, it is now possible to write the equations of motion and find their solution.

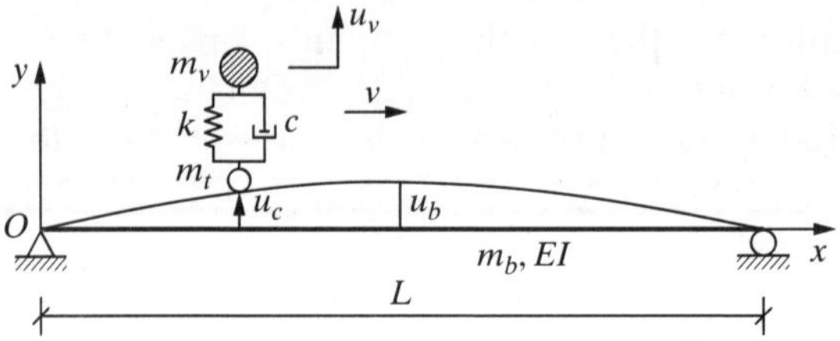

where m_v = mass of vehicle
m_t = mass of wheel
u_c = displacement of the contact point
u_v = displacement of the vehicle
u_b = displacement of the bridge
v = speed of vehicle

Figure 11.14 A moving sprung mass model – improved model.

Similarly, more complex models can be developed to better understand the dynamic response of vehicle-bridge-support-foundation interaction. In the present text, only the dynamic response of a simply supported beam traversed by a single moving constant load will be discussed.

11.11.1 Girder Bridge Under a Single Moving Load

Let us consider the model of a simply supported bridge shown in Figure 11.13(a). Let us assume that the mode shape is given by the shape function

$$\phi(x) = \sin\left(\frac{\pi x}{L}\right) \tag{11.40}$$

A single point load p_0 travels with a speed v across a bridge of span L. It takes time $t_d = L/v$ to cross the bridge. At any time, t, the position of the load is also shown. The moving load can be described mathematically as follows:

$$p(x,t) = \begin{cases} p_0\delta(x - vt) & 0 \le t \le t_d \\ 0 & t \ge t_d \end{cases} \tag{11.41}$$

where,

$\delta(x - vt)$ = Dirac delta function centered at $x = vt$.

The generalized force can be written as

$$p^*(t) = \int_0^L p(x,t)\phi(x)dx$$

$$p^*(t) = \int_0^L p_0\delta(x-vt)\phi(x)dx$$

$$p^*(t) = \int_0^L p_0\delta(x-vt)\sin\left(\frac{\pi x}{L}\right)dx \quad 0 \le t \le t_d \tag{11.42a}$$

$$= 0 \quad t \ge t_d \tag{11.42b}$$

Duration of the force on the bridge $t_d = L/v$

The distance x travelled by the vehicle at any time t is given by $x = vt$. The generalized force can be expressed in terms of velocity of the vehicle, also by making use of the Dirac delta function

$$p^*(t) = p_0 \sin\left(\frac{\pi vt}{L}\right) \quad 0 \le t \le t_d$$

or,

$$p^*(t) = p_0 \sin\left(\frac{\pi t}{t_d}\right) \quad 0 \le t \le t_d \tag{11.43a}$$

$$= 0 \qquad t \ge t_d \tag{11.43b}$$

The generalized force is the half-cycle sine pulse as shown in Figure 11.13(b).

The equation of motion of the generalized system can be written as

$$m^*\ddot{z}(t) + k^*z(t) = p^*(t) = p_0 \sin\left(\frac{\pi t}{t_d}\right) \quad 0 \le t \le t_d \tag{11.44a}$$

$$= 0 \qquad t \ge t_d \tag{11.44b}$$

Initial conditions are $x(0) = 0$ and $\dot{x}(0) = 0$.

The solution of Equation 11.44(a), a forced vibration response, is given by Equation (3.5b).

$$z(t) = \frac{p_0}{k}\frac{1}{1-\beta^2}(\sin\bar{\omega}t - \beta\sin\omega t) \tag{3.5b}$$

The frequency ratio $\beta = \bar{\omega}/\omega$
where,

$$\bar{\omega} = \text{forcing frequency} = \frac{\pi}{t_d}$$

$$\omega = \text{natural frequency of the bridge/beam} = 2\pi/T$$

The solution can be written as

$$z(t)=\frac{p_0}{k}\frac{1}{1-\left(\frac{T}{2t_d}\right)^2}\left[\sin\left(\frac{\pi t}{t_d}\right)-\left(\frac{T}{2t_d}\right)\sin\left(\frac{2\pi}{T}t\right)\right] \quad \text{for} \quad t\le t_d \tag{11.45a}$$

and velocity is given by

$$\dot{z}(t)=\frac{p_0}{k}\frac{1}{1-\left(\frac{T}{2t_d}\right)^2}\left[\cos\left(\frac{\pi t}{t_d}\right)\frac{\pi}{t_d}-\left(\frac{T}{2t_d}\right)\frac{2\pi}{T}\cos\left(\frac{2\pi}{T}t\right)\right] \quad \text{for} \quad t\le t_d \tag{11.45b}$$

The solution after the loading has ceased to zero may be found by the response of the free vibration analysis with proper boundary conditions. It means we need to know the displacement and velocity at the end of the force function, at time t_d.
At $t=t_d$

$$z(t_d)=(-)\frac{p_0}{k}\left\{\frac{1}{1-\left(\frac{T}{2t_d}\right)^2}\right\}\left[\left(\frac{T}{2t_d}\right)\sin\left(\frac{2\pi}{T}t_d\right)\right] \tag{11.46a}$$

and

$$\dot{z}(t_d)=(-)\frac{p_0}{k}\frac{\pi}{t_d}\left\{\frac{1}{1-\left(\frac{T}{2t_d}\right)^2}\right\}\left[1+\cos\left(\frac{2\pi}{T}t_d\right)\right] \tag{11.46b}$$

The solution of Equation 11.44(b), a free vibration response, is given by Equation (2.9a). For $t\ge t_d$

$$z(t)=\frac{\dot{z}(t_d)}{\omega}\sin\omega(t-t_d)+z(t_d)\cos\omega(t-t_d) \quad \text{for} \quad t\ge t_d \tag{11.47}$$

Upon substituting the values of initial conditions at $t=t_d$ from Equations (11.46a) and (11.46b) in Equation (11.47), we obtain

$$z(t)=\frac{p_0}{k}\left[\frac{\left(\frac{T}{2t_d}\right)}{\left(\frac{T}{2t_d}\right)^2-1}\right]\left\{\sin\frac{2\pi}{T}(t-t_d)+\sin\frac{2\pi}{T}(t-t_d)\cos\frac{2\pi}{T}t_d+\cos\frac{2\pi}{T}(t-t_d)\sin\frac{2\pi}{T}t_d\right\}$$

or,
$$z(t)=\frac{p_0}{k}\left[\frac{\left(\frac{T}{2t_d}\right)}{\left(\frac{T}{2t_d}\right)^2-1}\right]\left\{\sin\frac{2\pi}{T}(t-t_d)+\sin\left(\frac{2\pi}{T}(t-t_d)+\frac{2\pi}{T}t_d\right)\right\}$$

or,
$$z(t)=\frac{p_0}{k}\left[\frac{\left(\frac{T}{2t_d}\right)}{\left(\frac{T}{2t_d}\right)^2-1}\right]\left\{\sin\frac{2\pi}{T}(t-t_d)+\sin\left(\frac{2\pi}{T}t\right)\right\} \quad (11.48a)$$

Making use of the identity

$$\sin C\pm\sin D=2\sin\frac{C\pm D}{2}\cos\frac{C\mp D}{2} \quad (i)$$

We obtain

$$z(t)=\frac{p_0}{k}\left[\frac{\left(\frac{T}{t_d}\right)}{\left(\frac{T}{2t_d}\right)^2-1}\right]\left\{\sin 2\pi\left(\frac{t}{T}-\frac{t_d}{2T}\right)\cos\left(\frac{\pi t_d}{T}\right)\right\} \quad \text{for} \quad t\geq t_d \quad (11.48b)$$

Thus, the solution for the forced vibration and free vibration phases are given by Equation (11.45) and (11.48), respectively.

Now let us find the generalized mass and stiffness for the simply supported beam making use of Equations (11.28b) and (11.28c).

$$\text{Shape function } \phi(x)=\sin\frac{\pi x}{L} \text{ and } \phi''(x)=-\left(\frac{\pi}{L}\right)^2\sin\frac{\pi x}{L} \quad (11.40)$$

Generalized mass

$$m^*=\int_0^L m(x)[\phi(x)]^2\,dx$$

$$m^*=\int_0^L m\sin^2\left(\frac{\pi x}{L}\right)dx=\frac{mL}{2} \quad (11.49a)$$

Generalized stiffness

$$k^*=\int_0^L EI\left(\frac{\pi^2}{L^2}\right)^2\sin^2\left(\frac{\pi x}{L}\right)dx=\frac{\pi^4 EI}{2L^3} \quad (11.49b)$$

Fundamental frequency

$$\omega = \sqrt{\frac{k^*}{m^*}} = \frac{\pi^2}{L^2}\sqrt{\frac{EI}{m}} \tag{11.50}$$

Maximum static displacement

$$(z_{st})_0 = \frac{p_0}{k^*} = \frac{p_0}{\dfrac{\pi^4 EI}{2L^3}}$$

or,

$$(z_{st})_0 = \frac{2p_0}{mL\omega^2} \tag{11.51}$$

Now let us rewrite the forced response and free response in terms of speed of vehicle v, that is, replace, t_d by L/v and T by $2\pi/\omega$ for convenience.
We get
Forced vibrations

$$z(t) = \frac{2p_0}{mL\omega^2}\left[\frac{1}{1-\left(\dfrac{\frac{2\pi}{\omega}}{\frac{2L}{v}}\right)^2}\right]\left\{\sin\left(\frac{\pi t v}{L}\right)-\left(\dfrac{\frac{2\pi}{\omega}}{\frac{2L}{v}}\right)\sin\omega t\right\}$$

or,

$$z(t) = \frac{2p_0}{mL}\left[\frac{1}{\omega^2-\left(\dfrac{\pi v}{L}\right)^2}\right]\left\{\sin\left(\frac{\pi v}{L}t\right)-\frac{\pi v}{\omega L}\sin\omega t\right\} \quad \text{for} \quad t \le t_d \tag{11.52a}$$

It can be seen from Equation (11.52a) that there are two parts in the dynamic displacement of the simply supported girder bridge traversed by a single moving constant load. The first part is the forced vibration related to the speed of the moving load, and the second part is the free vibration of the bridge itself.
Free Vibrations

$$z(t) = \frac{2p_0}{mL\omega^2}\left[\frac{\left(\dfrac{\frac{2\pi}{\omega}}{\frac{L}{v}}\right)}{\left(\dfrac{\frac{2\pi}{\omega}}{\frac{2L}{v}}\right)^2-1}\right]\sin\left(t\omega-\frac{L}{2v}\omega\right)\cos\left(\frac{\omega L}{2v}\right)$$

or,
$$z(t)=\left(\frac{2p_0}{mL}\right)\left[\frac{\left(\frac{2\pi v}{\omega L}\right)}{\left(\frac{\pi v}{L}\right)^2-\omega^2}\right]\cos\left(\frac{\omega L}{2v}\right)\sin\left[\omega\left(t-\frac{L}{2v}\right)\right] \quad \text{for} \quad t\geq t_d \tag{11.52b}$$

Equations (11.52a) and (11.52b) are valid provided $\omega \neq \frac{\pi v}{L}$

If the duration of half-cycle sine pulse is greater than $T/2$, the maximum response will occur due to the force vibrations, that is, while the load is still on the bridge.

The deflection at any section x is given by

$$v(x,t)=z(t)\phi(x)$$

$$v(x,t)=z(t)\sin\frac{\pi x}{L} \tag{11.53a}$$

At $x = L/2$,

$$v\left(\frac{L}{2},t\right)=z(t) \tag{11.53b}$$

It means at the midspan, the displacement is the same as the generalized coordinate displacement.

The *dynamic magnification factor* or *impact factor* is given by

$$D = z_{\max}/(z_{st})_0$$

Example 11.8

A single point load p_0 moves across a 30 m simply supported bridge with constant speed. Its mass is 25×10^5 kg/m^2, moment of inertia is 45 m^4, modulus of elasticity is 2.9×10^{10} N/m^2. Determine the impact factors for different speeds of the point load.

Solution

A computer code can be written in MATLAB using Equation (11.52a) and (11.52b). The speed of vehicle was varied between 15 kmph to 200 kmph. The *influence lines* for impact factor at the midspan when a unit load crosses the bridge are shown in Figures 11.15(a) and 11.15(b). The impact factor increases with the speed of load. The maximum value of the impact factor lies in between 1.07 and 1.74, or 7% and 74% for different vehicle speeds and data used in this example.

Impact Factors in IS Codes

Indian Roads Congress Code IRC 6 gives the following simplified expressions for impact factors for different types of vehicles independent of their speeds.

Class A and Class B vehicles

For RC bridges

$$I=\frac{4.5}{6+L} \text{ for } 3\leq L\leq 45 \text{ m} \tag{11.54a}$$

Where, L = span of the simply supported bridge in m

For steel bridges

$$I = \frac{9}{13.5 + L} \text{ for } 3 \le L \le 45 \text{ m} \tag{11.54b}$$

Thus, for a 30 m RC bridge, the impact factor is 0.125 or 12.5%; while for a 30 m steel bridge, the impact factor is 0.207 or 20.7%.

There are two kinds of Class AA or 70 R vehicles: *wheeled and tracked*. For wheeled vehicles over RC bridges, the impact factor is 25% for spans between 9 and 12 m; while for tracked vehicles over RC bridges, the impact factor is 10% for spans between 9 and 40 m.

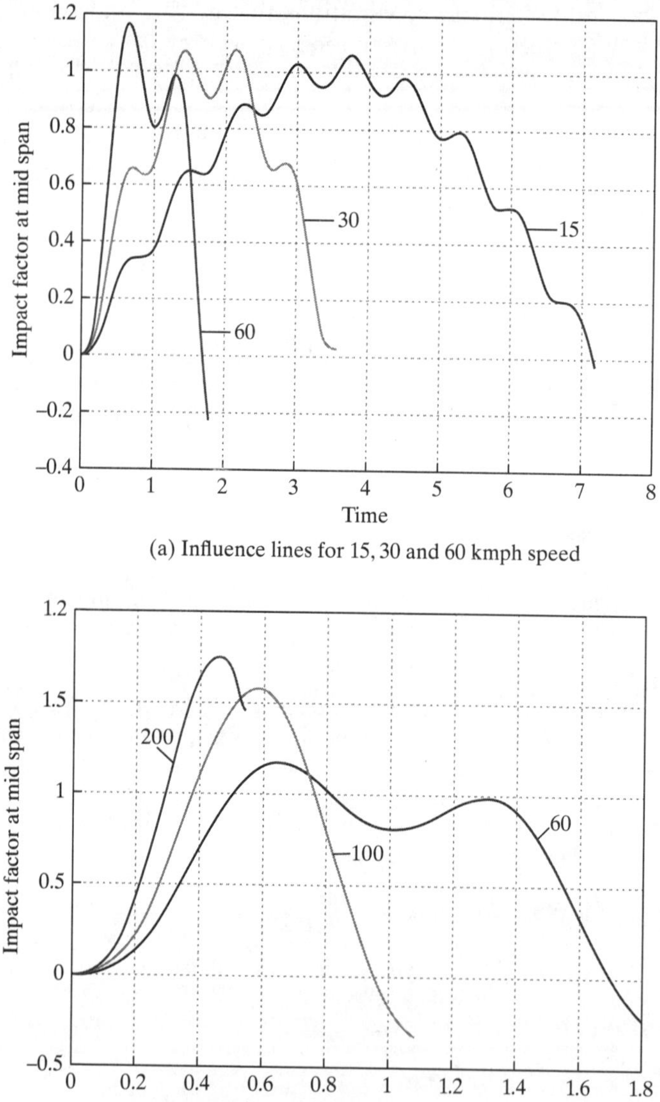

(a) Influence lines for 15, 30 and 60 kmph speed

(b) Influence lines for 60, 100 and 200 kmph speed

Figure 11.15 Influence lines for impact factor at the midspan of a simply supported bridge.

REVIEW QUESTIONS

11.1 State the assumptions for the analysis of a Euler-Bernoulli beam.

11.2 Write the equation of motion for undamped forced vibrations of a beam with distributed mass and elasticity.

11.3 What is separation of variables technique in differential calculus? How is it useful for the vibration analysis of a continuum beam?

11.4 Draw first three mode shapes for the vibration of a (i) simply supported beam, (ii) cantilever beam, and (iii) fixed ended beam.

11.5 Write the equation for estimating the fundamental frequency of a multistorey building using Rayleigh method.

11.6 Write expressions for generalized mass and generalized stiffness.

11.7 Write expressions for potential energy and kinematic energy in terms of shape function.

11.8 Write the equation for estimating the fundamental frequency of a continuum system using Rayleigh method.

11.9 A cantilever beam of total mass m_0 carries a point load mg at its free end. What is the equivalent mass of the SDOF system?

11.10 An overhead water tank has a staging of mass m_0, and mass of the container including water is m. What is the equivalent mass of the SDOF system?

11.11 What is a shear building?

11.12 Describe mathematically a single point load p_0 travelling with a speed of v across a simply supported bridge?

11.13 Express generalized force due to a single point load p_0 moving with a speed v across a simply supported bridge.

11.14 What is impact factor in bridges? Give typical values of impact factor for (i) Class A loading on steel bridges, and (ii) Class AA loading on RC bridges having span less than 9 m.

PROBLEMS

11.1 Calculate the natural frequencies and mode shapes of a flexural member clamped at both ends and plot the first three mode shapes using MATLAB.

11.2 Calculate the natural frequencies and mode shapes of a flexural member hinged at both ends and plot the first three mode shapes using MATLAB.

11.3 Compare the natural frequencies of two identical flexural members made of steel and aluminium each, having boundary conditions as: fixed-free, fixed-hinged and hinged-roller.

11.4 Compare the natural frequency of a SDOF system having a concentrated mass M at its free end with that of a distributed cantilever system having a total mass M along its length L.

11.5 Estimate the fundamental frequency of vibration of a fixed ended beam using Rayleigh's principle. Its mass and elasticity are uniformly distributed along the length. Compare the fundamental frequency with the first natural frequency obtained with the exact standard solution.

11.6 Estimate the fundamental frequency of vibration of a fixed-hinged beam using Rayleigh's principle. Its mass and elasticity are uniformly distributed along the length. Compare the fundamental frequency with the first natural frequency obtained with the exact standard solution.

11.7 Compare the first three mode shapes of a cantilever beam with those of a fixed-hinged beam using MATLAB graphics.

11.8 A beam of length L having uniformly distributed mass and elasticity can be idealized as a five-degree of freedom system by lumping m/5 mass at the centre of each L/5 segment. Determine the first five frequencies and mode shapes by treating it as a discrete system using MATLAB and compare them with those obtained from the exact solution. Take boundary conditions as (i) fixed-fixed and (ii) fixed-hinged.

11.9 A RC chimney 250 m high has a tapered hollow section with 15 m outer diameter at the base and 7.5 m at the top; wall thickness 1m uniform throughout in M35 grade. Assume the shape function

$$\phi(x) = 1 - \cos\frac{\pi x}{2L}$$

where, L is height of the chimney and x is measured from the base. The modulus of elasticity of concrete is given by $5000\sqrt{f_{ck}}$ MPa, where f_{ck} is the characteristic strength of concrete. Unit weight of concrete is 25 kN/m³. Damping may be taken as 5%.

Estimate the peak displacement at its top, shear force and bending moment at its base due to earthquake motion. It is located in Coimbatore, TN, on medium soil. Use the design spectrum specified in IS:1893-part 4.

11.10 A steel chimney 150 m high has a tapered hollow section with 10 m outer diameter at the base and 5 m at the top; wall thickness is 0.25 m uniform throughout. Assume the shape function.

$$\phi(x) = \frac{3}{2}\frac{x^2}{L^2} - \frac{1}{2}\frac{x^3}{L^3}$$

where, L is height of the chimney and x is measured from the base. The modulus of elasticity of steel is 200 GPa. Unit weight of steel is 79kN/m³. Damping may be taken as 2%.

Estimate the peak displacement at its top, shear force and bending moment at its base due to earthquake motion. It is located in Itanagar, Arunachal Pradesh, on soft soil. Use the design spectrum specified in IS:1893-part 4.

REFERENCE

IS:1893:2015 (Part 4) Criteria for Earthquake Resistant Design of Structures, Part 4: Industrial and Stack-like Structures, Bureau of Indian Standards, New Delhi.

Part 3

Application to Earthquake Engineering

12 Analysis of Buildings for Earthquake Force

12.1 INTRODUCTION

A force is defined as the product of mass and acceleration. During an earthquake, the mass is imparted by the building, whereas the acceleration is imparted by the ground disturbance. In order to have a minimum force, the mass of the building should be as low as possible. There can be no control on the ground acceleration, being an act of God! The point of application of this inertial force is the center of gravity of the mass on each floor of the building. Once there is a force, there has to be an equal and opposite reaction to balance this force. The inertial force is resisted by the building and the resisting force acts at the center of rigidity at each floor of the building or shear center of the building at each storey. An earthquake may be classified into one of the three general categories along with the desired behaviour and controlling parameter in a building as shown in Table 12.1. It is referred to as the seismic design criteria for buildings.

It was shown in Chapter 8 that the lateral force computed using the codal response spectra are much lower than those actually recorded during real earthquakes. This is intentional. Depending upon the probability of occurrence of an earthquake in a given region, it is desirable to design the building for a much lesser force and allow the building to undergo inelastic deformations. In the event of a stronger earthquake, the ductility provided at all possible locations in the elements of the building will help dissipate energy hysteretically while undergoing (relatively) large inelastic deformations. The intention is to design an economical, affordable and safe structure. Seismic requirements provide minimum standards for use in building design to

TABLE 12.1 SEISMIC DESIGN CRITERIA

Earthquake	Desired Behaviour	Controlling Parameter
Small	No damage to structural components	Control deflection by providing *stiffness*
Moderate	No significant structural damage, minor cracks in beams and columns, Response should be predominantly elastic	Avoid yielding of members or permanent damage by providing *strength*
Large, catastrophic	No collapse of the system which could cause loss of life	Allow structure to enter into inelastic range and absorb energy by providing *ductility*

maintain public safety in a major earthquake. These requirements safeguard against major failures and loss of life. They are not intended to necessarily limit damage, maintain function or provide for easy repair.

This chapter describes structural systems and irregularity in buildings. How to estimate the seismic force using Indian Standard Code IS:1893-Part 1 in buildings using static and dynamic methods including torsion as well as how to analyze them are explained in detail?

12.2 WHAT IS A BUILDING?

It is very important to know as to what is a building before beginning any discussion on the analysis of buildings. Does the term 'building' cover a residential building, or a commercial building, or an auditorium building, or a stadium, or a bridge or a tower and so on? Neither clause 3 of IS:1893-Part 1 on terminology for earthquake engineering nor clause 4 terminology for earthquake engineering of buildings defines the term 'building'. Clause 6 covers general principles and design criteria for any structure. However, Clause 7 covers only 'buildings' but without defining it. The terms 'structure' and 'building' are being used interchangeably in analysis and design by engineers. There may not be any difference in these two terms for a layman. But this term is causing confusion among many designers in India. The trouble arises in the estimation of the earthquake force which in turn makes use of the fundamental period of vibrations. Clause 7 of IS:1893 gives the empirical formula for estimation of fundamental period of buildings. This formula is being applied for non-buildings as well leading to wrong estimation of the force.

Building *Any structure whose intended use includes shelter of human occupants.*

If this definition is used, then there will be no confusion. The term building in this context includes commercial or office buildings, hospitals, multistorey shopping malls, etc. but excludes auditorium, stadium, bridge or a tower etc. The scope of the present chapter covers only buildings.

Storey *The portion of a structure between the tops of two successive floor surfaces and, for the topmost story, from the top of the floor surface to the top of the roof surface.*

Storey drift *The horizontal deflection at the top of the storey relative to the bottom of the storey.*

Storey shear *The summation of design lateral seismic forces at levels above the storey under consideration.*

Most Desirable Characteristics

A building should have the following attributes in order to perform well in an earthquake:

- Simple structural configuration
- Symmetry with respect to geometry
- Symmetry with respect to mass and stiffness distributions in plan and elevation

- Adequate lateral strength
- Adequate lateral stiffness
- Adequate ductility

12.3 STRUCTURAL SYSTEMS

The purpose of a structural system is to transfer the all loads, vertical as well as lateral, to the soil below without any distress anywhere. Different systems may be employed in a building to carry vertical and lateral loads. A structural system is to be conceived depending upon the functional, architectural, structural and geotechnical requirements. Based on the occupancy and functional requirements, different systems may be required. The following buildings will have different requirements:

(a) Residential building
(b) Office building
(c) Hotel building
(d) Car parking garage

There are basically three types of structural systems for RC and steel buildings (Figure 12.1):

1. Moment-resistant frames
2. Shear wall frames
3. Braced frames

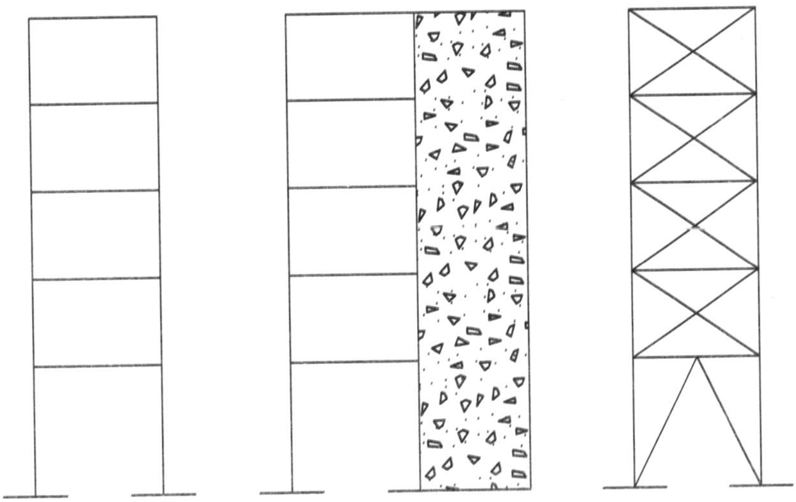

(a) M-R frame (b) Shear wall (c) Braced frame

Figure 12.1 Basic structural systems.

Depending upon their detailing, buildings are further classified as follows:

Reinforced Concrete Buildings

(a) Ordinary moment-resistant frames
(b) Intermediate moment-resistant frames
(c) Special ductile moment-resistant frames
(d) Ordinary shear wall frames
(e) Special ductile shear wall frames

Steel Buildings

(a) Ordinary moment-resistant frames
(b) Special moment-resistant frames
(c) Ordinary concentrically braced frames
(d) Special concentrically braced frames
(e) Ordinary eccentrically braced frames
(f) Special eccentrically braced frames

A braced frame is essentially a vertical truss designed to resist lateral forces. The basic concentric and eccentric-braced configurations are shown in Figures 12.2 and 12.3. Bracing members are pin-ended and can be used in the façade to give aesthetic look to buildings as done in the John Hancock building in Chicago built in the early 1970s. The inverted V configuration in Figure 12.2(a) is also known as *K-brace*. In the concentrically braced frame, the center lines of the bracing members meet the horizontal beam at a single point or beam–column joint. In the eccentrically braced frame, the braces are deliberately designed to frame into a beam a short distance from a beam–column joint or from another diagonal brace. The configuration shown in Figure 12.2(b) is highly undesirable as they may lead to inelasticity in columns and thus collapse of the building. In the eccentric frame, the short piece of beam between the ends of the braces is called a *link beam*. The purpose of the *link beam* is to develop plastic hinges at its ends due to large shear and dissipate energy. Thus, this link beam will help protect rest of the structure. Typical failure mode of an eccentrically braced frame is shown in Figure 12.4.

A bracing member is generally designed to carry only axial forces. In a concentric system, a brace is expected to buckle and start dissipating energy. This is how

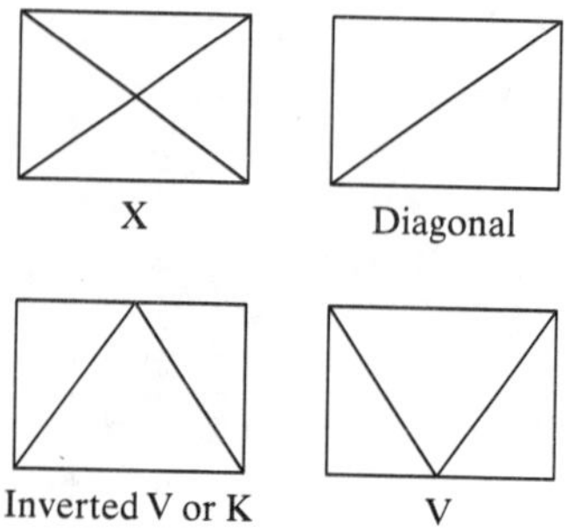

Figure 12.2(a) Concentric-braced configurations.

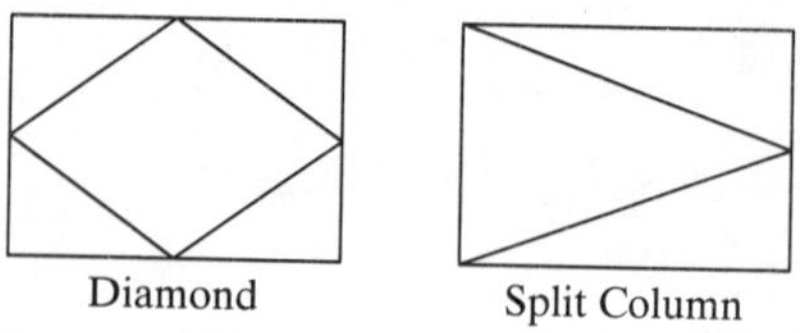

Figure 12.2(b) Undesirable concentric-braced configurations.

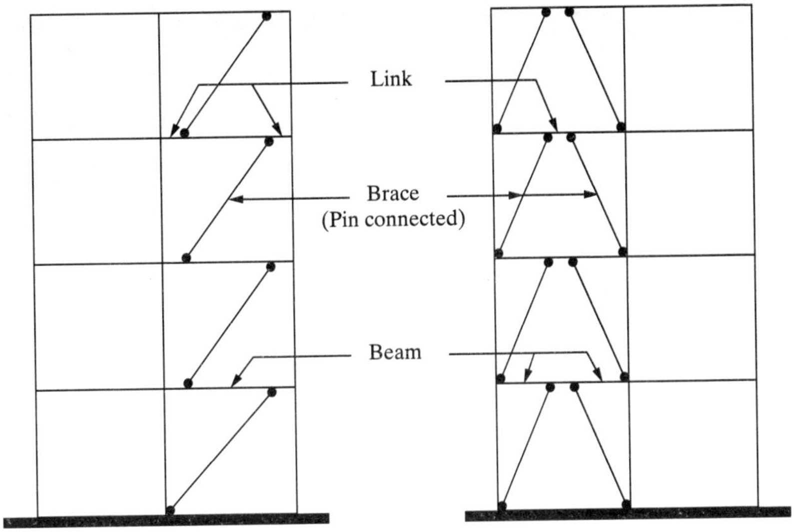

Figure 12.3 Eccentric-braced configurations.

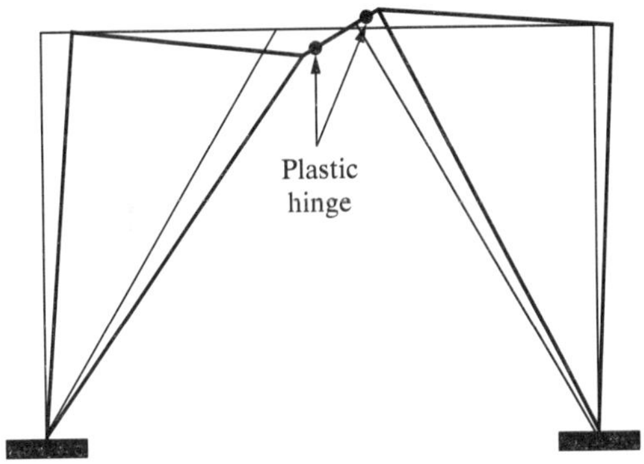

Figure 12.4 Deformations in eccentrically braced frame.

safety of the main frame is ensured. In an eccentric system, a brace is designed to remain elastic and force the formation of plastic hinge in the link beam due to very high shear. It leads to very fat and stable hysteresis loops. This is how safety of the main frame is ensured. In a concentric braced frame, only probable locations of plastic hinges are known. While in an eccentric braced frame, the locations of plastic hinges are well defined.

There is a unique advantage with steel structures over concrete structures because of the flexibility available in designing their connections. In steel frames, the connections can be as follows:

(a) Simple connection
(b) Semi-rigid connection
(c) Moment-resistant connection

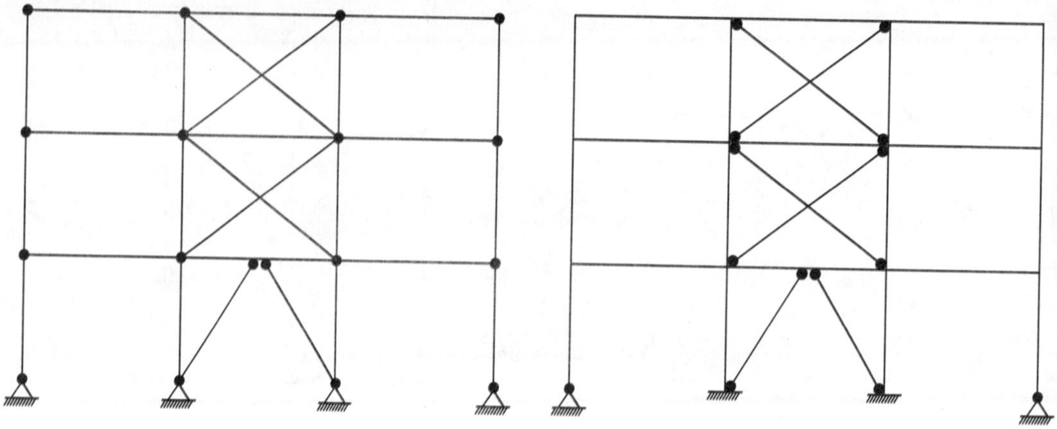

(a) Pin connected frame

(b) Dual frame : Moment resistant + Braced frame

Figure 12.5 Connections in steel frames.

Simple connections in steel structures are designed to carry only shear force, only axial force or both. A moment-resistant connection may carry axial force, shear force in addition to a moment. In concrete frames, in general, all connections are moment resistant. In the structural system shown in Figure 12.5(a), all connections are simple or pin-connected. The columns are continuous. Under lateral loads, such a frame acts as a vertical cantilever and each member carries only axial force. Such a system is very economical and popular especially in less severe earthquake zone. In Figure 12.5(b), all beam to column connections are moment resistant while all braces are connected through simple or pin-connections. The beams carry bending moment, columns carry axial force and bending moment, while braces carry only axial forces. The column bases can be pin-connected that will relieve the foundation from bending moment and transfer it to the superstructure.

By using innovative combinations of the three systems described earlier more systems can be evolved such as:

1. Tubular system
2. Dual system
   - **(a)** Frame with shear wall
   - **(b)** Frame with braces
3. Inverted pendulum-type system
4. Outrigger system

Tubular System The idea behind a tubular system is to increase the lateral and torsional stiffness of a building so as to control its lateral deflections and vibrations due to severe wind and earthquake forces. The columns are placed at the outer periphery at a very close spacing, say 1 m to 2 m clear in order to permit placement of doors and windows. The intention is to let light and air inside the building. This system behaves as a continuous wall around its periphery in plan, that is as a box with very high moment of inertia, and therefore, stiffness. This system was developed for the 411 m high World Trade Center twin towers, New York, in the 1970s that were later destroyed in a terrorist attack on 11 September 2001 (*9/11 attack*).

Dual System There are two structural systems to resist seismic forces: primary system and a secondary system. The former consists of a braced frame or a shear wall frame. In case of failure of the primary system, secondary system resists the lateral forces. For a dual system, the moment frames shall be capable of resisting at least 25% of the design seismic forces. The total seismic force resistance is to be provided by the combination of the moment frames and the shear walls or braced frames in proportion to their rigidities.

Inverted Pendulum-type System In such a system, more than 50 percent of the mass of the structure is concentrated at the top of a slender cantilevered structure as shown in Figure 12.6. The stability of the mass at the top of the structure relies on rotational restraint provided to the top of the cantilever by the lower portion. Supporting columns or piers of inverted pendulum-type structures are designed for the bending moment calculated at the base and varying uniformly to a moment at the top equal to one-half the calculated bending moment at the base. During an earthquake, the dissipation of energy takes place mainly at the base of a single building element.

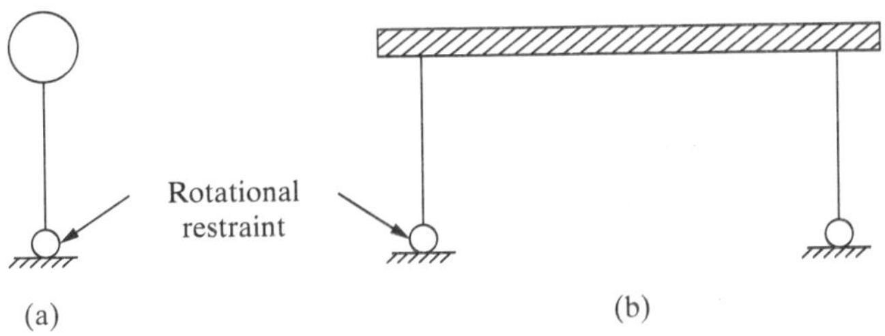

Figure 12.6 Inverted pendulum system

Outrigger System In the outrigger and belt truss system, the external columns are tied to the central core wall with very stiff outriggers and belt (perimeter) truss at one or more levels. The belt truss ties the peripheral column of building while the outriggers engage them with central shear wall or core as shown in Figure 12.7(a). The outriggers are generally in the form of trusses in steel structures, or walls in concrete structures. The outriggers make the whole system to act as a single unit in resisting the lateral load. They serve to reduce the overturning moment in the core that would otherwise act as pure cantilever (Figure 12.7(b)). The reduced moment is transferred to the outer columns in the form of axial tension and compression. Belt trusses are provided to distribute these tensile and compressive forces to a large number of exterior columns. The belt trusses also help in minimizing differential elongation and shortening of columns. The floor space is usually free of columns in between the core and the external columns, thus increasing the functional efficiency of the building.

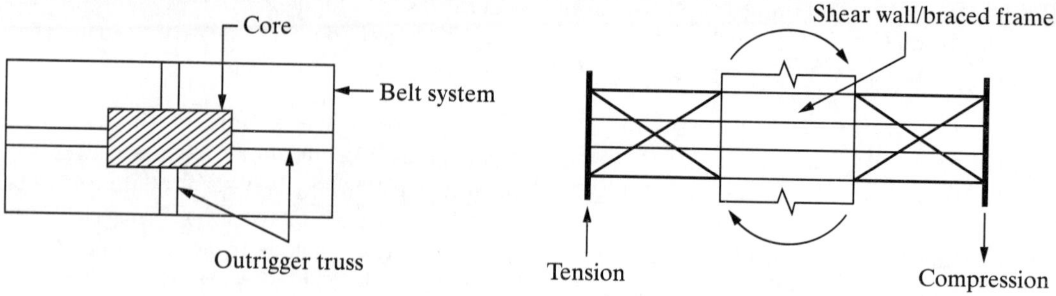

(a) Outrigger truss and belt system in plan (b) Transfer of forces from core to outrigger columns

Figure 12.7

Factors affecting efficiency of the outrigger system:

- Geometry of the tall building
- Stiffness of the central core
- The stiffness and location of the outrigger truss system
- The stiffness and location of the belt truss system
- Connections between outrigger system and central core

In choosing the structural system for a building, large dissimilarities in the stiffness and ductile characteristics of framing systems in the orthogonal directions should be avoided. For example, a moment-resisting ductile frame in one direction and reinforced masonry wall in the other direction would be unsuitable, whereas RC ductile flexural walls and RC walls with nominal ductility in orthogonal directions would be acceptable. The reason for this recommendation is that seismic displacements induced in flexible framing systems would probably cause failure in the relatively brittle and weak directions of the elements that resist the load in orthogonal directions. Choice of a structural system depends upon the building configuration, height, loads and geotechnical considerations. It may have to be evolved for a given building. For example, Burj-al-Arab and Burj-al-Khalifa, Dubai, employed innovative structural systems to meet the specific requirements.

12.3.1 Tall Buildings

Plan Aspect Ratio

The maximum plan aspect ratio (L/B) of the overall building should not exceed 5.0

Height Limit for Structural Systems

The maximum value of height, h above top of base level of buildings with different structural systems for lateral loads is shown in Table 12.2.

Slenderness Ratio for Structural Systems

The maximum values of the ratio of height to minimum base width B shall not exceed values given in Table 12.3.

TABLE 12.2 MAXIMUM VALUE OF HEIGHT OF BUILDINGS WITH DIFFERENT STRUCTURAL SYSTEMS (m)

Seismic Zone	Structural System				
	Moment Frame	Well Distributed Structural Wall	Structural Wall + Moment Frame	Structural Wall + Perimeter Frame	Structural Wall + Tube Frame
V	NA	120	150	150	180
IV	NA	150	200	200	225
III	60	200	225	225	250
II	80	250	250	250	250

TABLE 12.3 MAXIMUM SLENDERNESS RATIO

Seismic Zone	Structural System				
	Moment Frame	Structural Wall	Structural Wall + Moment Frame	Structural Wall + Perimeter Frame	Structural Wall + Tube Frame
V	NA	8	8	9	9
IV	NA	8	8	9	9
III	4	8	8	9	10
II	5	9	9	10	10

12.4 CONCRETE FRAME AND SHEAR WALLS

Consider a wall system with different degrees of openings in Figure 12.8. A solid RC wall is shown in Figure12.8(a), whereas a wall with very large opening is shown in Figure12.8(c). The wall section is shown below the sectional elevation in each frame. The frame in Figure 12.8(a) is a shear wall frame, whereas the frame in Figure 12.8(c) can be said to be a moment resistant frame. The middle frame with intermediate openings can be said to be a coupled shear wall frame.

The moment resistant frame and shear wall frame deform in different modes under lateral loads as shown in Figure 12.9. A wall deflects in *flexure mode* just like a vertical cantilever deflects under the same set of loads. Therefore, in the literature, a shear wall is now referred to as a *flexure wall* rather than a *shear wall.* Similarly, a building deflects in *shear mode*. Its columns have very high axial stiffness but flexible flexural stiffness, and the beam-slab floor system (or floor diaphragm) has very high axial and flexural stiffnesses. The storey shear is related to the storey drift through the storey stiffness as discussed in Chapter 11. In fact, in buildings, it is safe to assume that there are only three degrees-of-freedom per floor, that is, two translational about the two orthogonal axis in the horizontal plane, and one rotational about the vertical axis. Thus, a building is referred to as a *shear building* provided it has rigid floor diaphragms.

Quite often, the frame and shear walls are used in combination. Such a system exhibits frame – shear wall interaction which depends upon the relative stiffness of frame and shear wall. Because of different modes of deformation, they tend to push

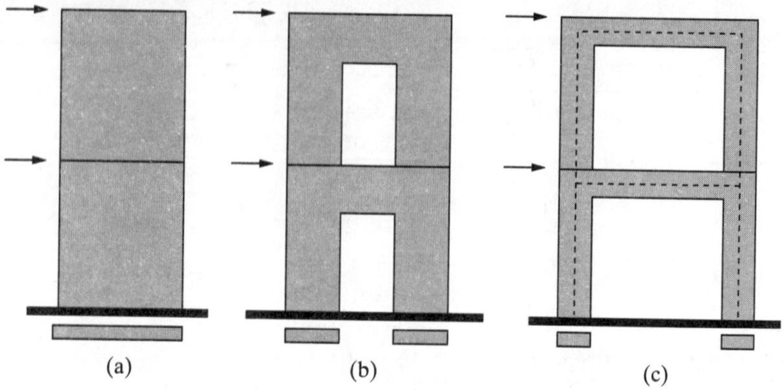

Figure 12.8 RC wall with different degrees of openings.

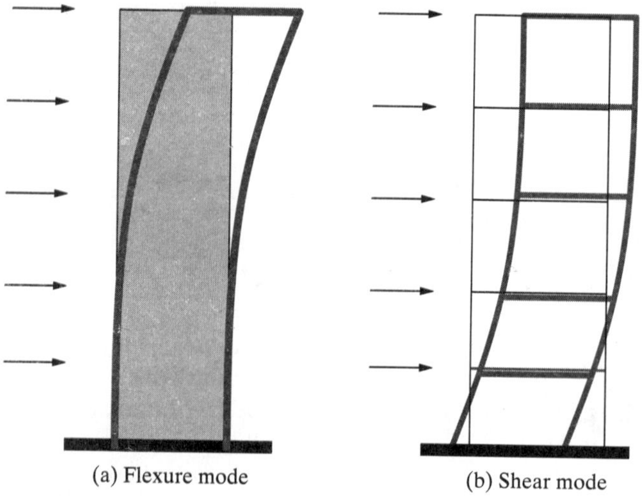

Figure 12.9 Deflection modes.

each other in the lower storeys while trying to pull each other in the upper storeys. There is a need to carefully examine the member forces in the upper storeys where some of them may be in tension due to the interaction.

Moment-resistant Frame

- Deforms predominantly in a shear mode
- Lateral resistance is due to rigidity of beam–column/slab joints

Shear Wall

- Deforms essentially in bending mode
- Only low shear walls with H/W ratio <1 fail in shear
- Behave mostly like a slender vertical cantilever
- Designed to resist the combined effect of axial, shear and bending about strong axis

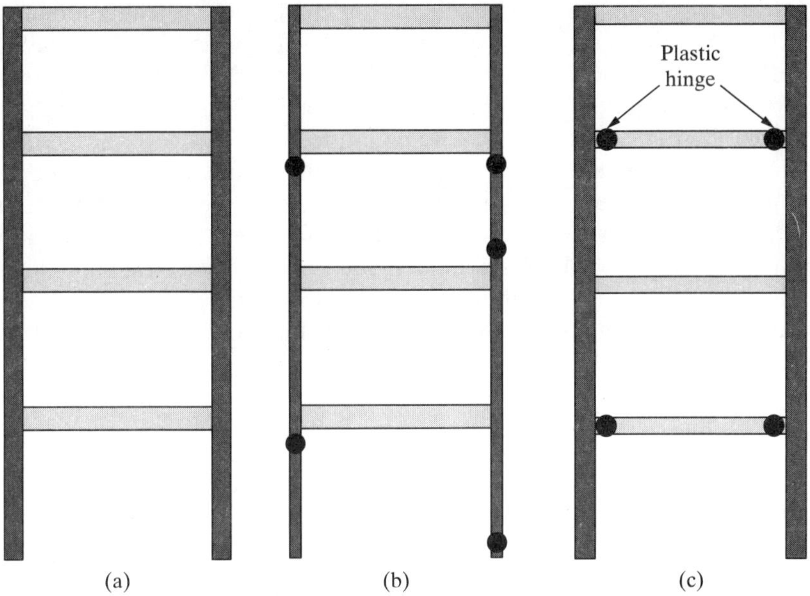

Figure 12.10 Member proportions.

12.5 MEMBER PROPORTIONS

One of the most difficult decisions while designing a building is how to proportion the various members relatively. Each beam and column can be designed only after knowing the member forces from analysis after considering various load combinations. However, there is a need to keep a watch on their relative proportions. It may lead to the following two situations in a moment resistant frame (Figure 12.10(a)):

1. Strong beam–weak column proportions (Figure 12.10(b))
2. Weak beam–strong column proportions (Figure 12.10(c))

A frame with strong beam–weak column proportions will develop plastic hinges in columns first in the event of a severe force. Inelasticity even in a few columns may eventually lead to early collapse of the whole frame. A frame with weak beam–strong column will develop plastic hinges in beams first. Inelasticity in a beam will eventually lead to a local failure in that bay only. Thus, it is a local failure, whereas, it is a global failure in the former case. Obviously, a local failure is always preferred over a global failure.

12.6 IRREGULARITY IN CONFIGURATIONS OF BUILDINGS

The simplest form of a building is cubical, that is symmetric about each of its three axes. It is easy to analyse, design, construct and has a much better performance in the event of severe loadings. It is called a regular building. However, architects prefer to be innovative and come up with all kinds of configurations leading to unsymmetry in the plan, elevation or both. These irregularities may also be in the mass distribution or stiffness distribution in the building. An irregularity leads to stress concentration in certain areas and torsion about the vertical axis of the building. Both these factors influence the performance of a building in the event of a severe earthquake, besides making the analysis and design quite complicated. A regular building vibrates in translational mode, whereas an irregular building vibrates in translational and torsional mode. Many structures collapsed due to irregularity during the past earthquakes in various parts of the world. A torsional mode imposes a very high ductility demand on the flexible side columns of the building which generally exceeds the ductility capacity and leads to immediate collapse. Some of the worst irregularities are as follows (Figures 12.11 and 12.12):

(a) Re-entrant corners
(b) Soft and weak storeys
(c) Discontinuous shear walls
(d) Variations in perimeter strength and stiffness

Detailed diagrams for different types of irregularities are available in IS:1893-Part 1. The term *irregularity* gives rise to two new terms: *center of mass* (CM) and *center of stiffness or rigidity* (CR). These are defined for each floor of a building in each of the two orthogonal directions. Center of mass is defined as the center of gravity of all the masses acting on a floor. It includes 50% of the mass above and below the floor under consideration acting through the columns or walls. Similarly, center of rigidity is defined as the center of gravity of stiffness of all the lateral load resisting elements on a floor. The distance between the center of mass and center of rigidity on a given floor is called *eccentricity*. A regular building is expected to have a nearly zero eccentricity.

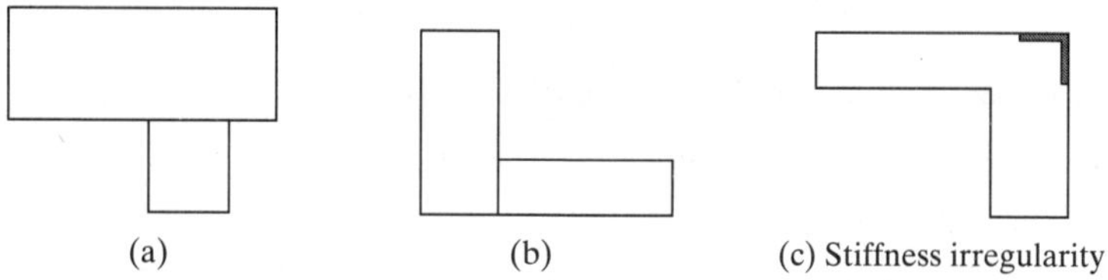

Figure 12.11 Typical plan irregularity—re-entrant corners.

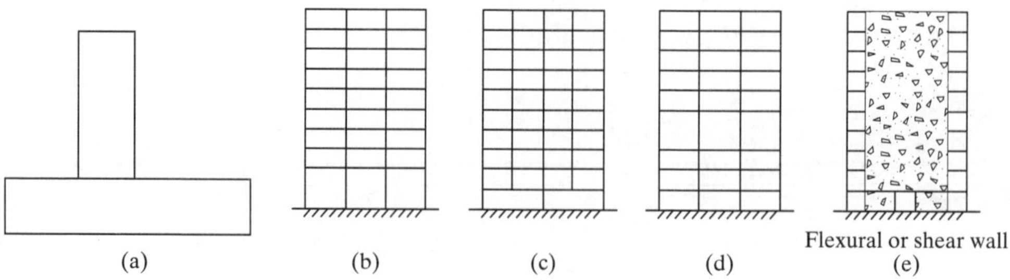

Figure 12.12 Vertical irregularity—stiffness.

The terms *re-entrant corner, soft storey* and *weak storey* are defined as follows (IS:1893-Part 1):

- Plan configurations of a structure and its lateral force resisting system contain re-entrant corners where both projections of the structure beyond the entrant corner are greater than 15% of its plan dimension in the given direction.
- A soft storey is one in which the lateral stiffness is less than 70% of that in the storey above or less than 80% of the average lateral stiffness of the three storeys above.
- A weak storey is one in which the storey lateral strength is less than 80% of that in the storey above. The storey lateral strength is the total strength of all seismic force resisting elements sharing the storey shear in the given direction.

Different situations of soft and or weak storey are shown in Figures 12.12(b), (c), (d) and Figure 12.13 where storey heights are significantly different, or a column, shear wall or bracing members are discontinued. The mechanism of failure in a soft storey is shown in Figure 12.14. It deflects essentially in sway mode leading to stress concentration at the upper ends of the columns of the corresponding storey and thus complete collapse. There were number of buildings up to G+12 having weak column-strong girder proportions, and weak or soft storeys in Turkey. They were in violation of the local building code. These buildings collapsed during the twin earthquakes and aftershocks of Feb 6, 2023. The loss to property and human lives was enormous.

A regular building configuration provides the following advantages:

(a) Uniform strength and stiffness distribution

(b) Minimum eccentricity between center of mass and center of stiffness thus minimizing torsion

(c) Minimum stress concentration

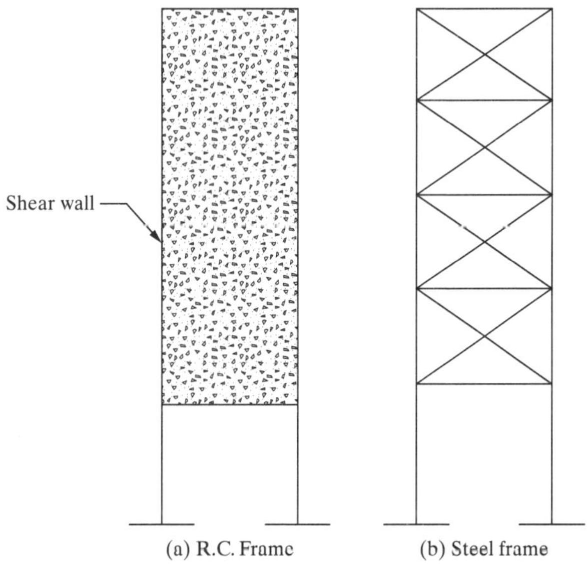

Figure 12.13 Soft/weak storey—ground level.

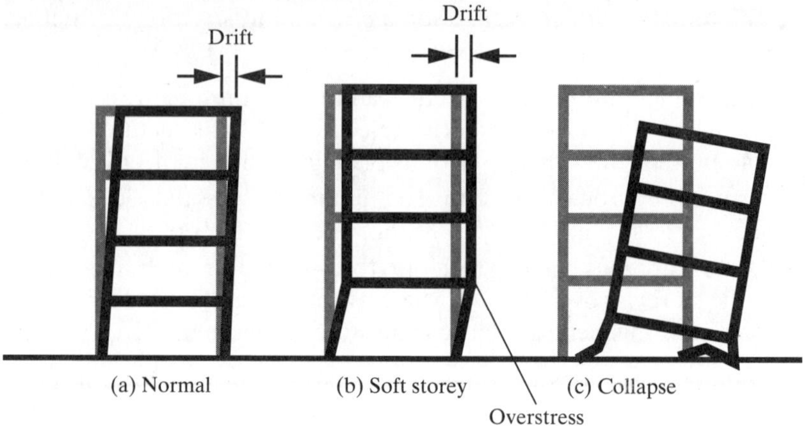

Figure 12.14 Failure mechanism in a soft storey.

(d) Continuous load path up to the foundation

(e) Ease in design and construction of beams, columns, bracing members and shear walls.

12.7 MODELLING OF A BUILDING

A building is a space structure and consists of any of the various kinds of structural systems. The term *modelling of a building* means how to idealize a building for convenience in analysis and design? There are two kinds of elements in any building: structural elements and non-structural elements. Non-structural elements do not participate in the load carrying mechanism. These elements need to be identified and removed from the building for the purpose of analysis. Only their self-weight needs to be considered. The modelling will depend upon the shape, size, configuration, loads, proposed structural system and geotechnical conditions. A building may be modelled as a series of 2D plane frames in two orthogonal directions. In each plane frame, masses may be lumped at the floor levels, with each mass having one degree of freedom, that of lateral displacement in the direction under consideration. At each floor, 50% of the mass of the storey above this floor and 50% of the mass from the storey below this floor under consideration is lumped at this floor. Similarly, on each vertical frame, 50% of the mass is lumped from the adjoining frame on its left, and 50% of the mass is lumped from the adjoining frame on its right.

A building may be modeled as a 3D space frame with each floor having three degrees of freedom—two orthogonal translations and one rotation—all in the horizontal plane. A building may also be modelled as a space frame with six degrees of freedom at each node or joint. In case, soil is weak, soil-structure interaction also needs to be considered. Choice of a model will depend essentially upon the judgement and experience of the designer. The following salient features of modelling must be kept in mind:

1. A building may be considered to consist of a number of vertical and lateral load resisting systems connected by horizontal diaphragms. The diaphragm may be rigid or flexible in a given case and should be modelled suitably.

2. The model must adequately represent the distribution of mass and stiffness so that all significant mode shapes and inertia forces are properly accounted.
3. The model should account for the contribution of joint regions to the deformability of the building, for example the end zones in beams or columns of frame type structures. These end zones are also modelled as rigid links. The rigid links become critical in case the frame has shear walls also.
4. The mass and stiffness of non-structural elements such as in-fill walls, which may significantly influence the response of the structure, should also be modelled.
5. When the floor diaphragms of the building are taken as being rigid in their own planes, the masses at each floor may be lumped at the center of gravity (CM).
6. In concrete buildings and in composite steel-concrete buildings, the stiffness of the load bearing elements should, in general, be evaluated taking into account the effect of cracking. Such stiffness should correspond to the initiation of yielding of the reinforcement.
7. RC Members may be modeled as cracked or uncracked sections depending on their stress levels due to the most severe seismic load combination. It is important to appropriately model the cracked stiffness of the beams, columns and joints, as this stiffness determines the resulting building periods, base shear, story drifts, and internal force distributions. The stiffness modifiers as shown in Table 12.4 may be adopted:

TABLE 12.4 STIFFNESS MODIFIERS FOR RC BUILDINGS

Structural Element	Unfactored Loads		Factored Loads	
	Area	Moment of inertia	Area	Moment of inertia
Slab	Gross area	0.35 Ig	Gross area	0.25 Ig
Beam	Gross area	0.70 Ig	Gross area	0.35 Ig
Column	Gross area	0.90 Ig	Gross area	0.70 Ig
Shear wall	Gross area	0.90 Ig	Gross area	0.70 Ig

Effects of Stiffness Modifiers

There are two profound effects of introducing stiffness modifiers on the response of a RC building:

(a) A reduced lateral stiffness means a higher lateral displacement and storey drift

(b) A reduced lateral stiffness means a higher natural period

If the original period of a building, that is, without using stiffness modifiers, was more than about 1 sec, then it will lead to a reduction in the base shear. Moreover, both the lateral displacements and storey drift need to be under control.

8. For steel moment frame systems, the contribution of panel zone deformations to overall story drift must be included. Also, consider gross moment of inertia for beams and columns.

12.7.1 RC Building with Brick Infill Panels

Infill A panel of masonry placed within a steel or concrete frame. Panels separated from the surrounding frame by a *minimum gap* are termed *isolated infills*. Panels that are in tight contact with a frame around its full perimeter are termed *shear infills*.

Unreinforced Masonry (URM) Wall A masonry wall containing less than the minimum amounts of reinforcement as defined for masonry walls. An unreinforced wall is assumed to resist gravity and lateral loads solely through resistance of the masonry materials.

Reinforced concrete frame buildings with masonry infill panels make up a significant portion of the buildings constructed all around the world. The behaviour of such frames is quite complex in view of various factors such as strength of infill and mortar, connection or gap between the infill and frame, interaction between the frame and the infill, and degree of cracking in the infill during an earthquake. Due to the initial high stiffness of the infill relative to that of the frame, the infill walls will attract most of the seismic shear. In many cases, because these walls are unreinforced or lightly reinforced, their strength and ductility may be inadequate to resist the design force. Once there is extensive damage to the infill, the bare frame will resist the lateral force. Therefore, there is a growing need to carry out a detailed evaluation of their seismic performance. Deformation of an infill frame panel and formation of a compression strut are shown in Figure 12.15.

Behavior of cracked concrete frames with masonry infills may be represented by a diagonally braced frame model in which the columns act as vertical chords, the beams act as horizontal ties, and the infill is modeled using the equivalent compression strut analogy. In frames with full height masonry infills, the evaluation may include the effect of strut compression forces applied to the column and beam, concentric or eccentric from the beam-column joint as shown in Figure 12.16(a) and 12.16(b). The thickness of the strut normal to the plane of the infill is taken equal to the thickness of the infill. The depth of the strut is usually taken as one-third of the diagonal length

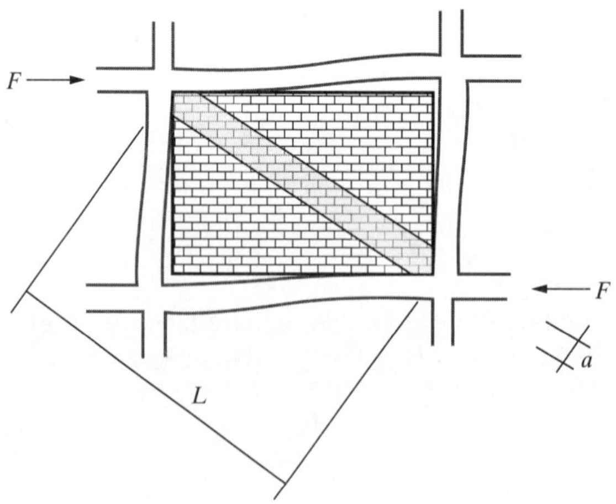

Figure 12.15 Deformation in an infill panel under lateral shear

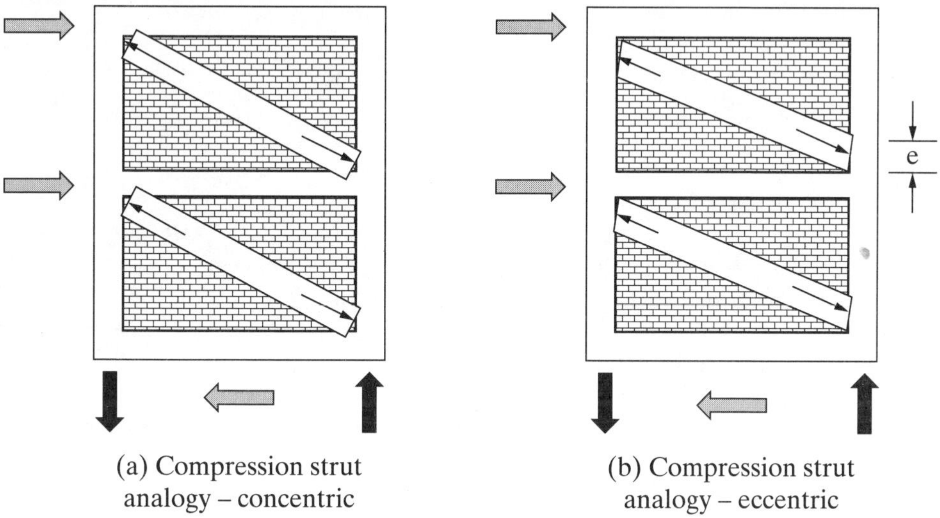

Figure 12.16 Compression strut analogy

of the strut. The modulus of elasticity of the strut (in MPa) is taken same as that of the infill as follows:

Masonry wall replaced with diagonal strut
Variables are: strut width, thickness, and E value
Different models give different results ?

Modulus of elasticity of masonry prism E_m is as follows:

$$E_m = 0.433 f_b^{0.64} f_{mo}^{0.36} \text{ Mpa}$$

where,

f_b = compressive strength of brick Mpa
f_{mo} = compressive strength of mortar Mpa

Width of an equivalent diagonal struct is given by the following equation:

$$w_{ds} = 0.175\,\alpha_h^{-0.4}$$

where,

$$\alpha_h = h\left(\sqrt[4]{\frac{E_m t \sin 2\theta}{4E_t I_c h}}\right)$$

E_m and E_t = Modulii of elasticity of material of URM infill and RC MRF
t and h = Thickness and height of in-fill wall
I_c = Moment of inertia of adjoining column of the frame
$\theta = \tan^{-1}(h/L)$

Thickness of equivalent diagonal strut is such that it behaves as a short member, that is,

$$h/t < 12 \text{ and } l/t < 12$$

where,

h = clear height of URM infill wall

l = clear length of URM infill between the vertical RC columns/walls

A linear dynamic analysis of the frame can now be carried out.

12.7.2 Shear Lag

In a *framed tube* system, there are closely spaced columns and deep spandrel beams rigidly connected together throughout the exterior frames in a building. The spacing of exterior columns generally varies from 1.5 m to 4.5 m c/c. The depth of the spandrel beams varies from 0.60 m to 1.2 m. The axial stresses in columns when the framed tube system is subjected to lateral loads due to wind or earthquake are shown in Figure 12.17. The axial stress distribution due to cantilever action is linear for both flange columns and web columns. However, the actual stress distribution is non-linear for both the web frame columns (that is, frame parallel to wind), and the flange frame columns (that is, frame perpendicular to wind). The axial stress is maximum in the corner columns. This is because the axial forces in the columns toward the middle of the flange frames lag behind those near the corner due to the nature of a framed tube which is different from a solid-wall tube. This phenomenon is known as *shear lag*. This nonlinear stress distribution must be taken into consideration while designing the structural system. Efforts should be made to minimize the shear lag effect and aim for more cantilever-type behavior of the structure.

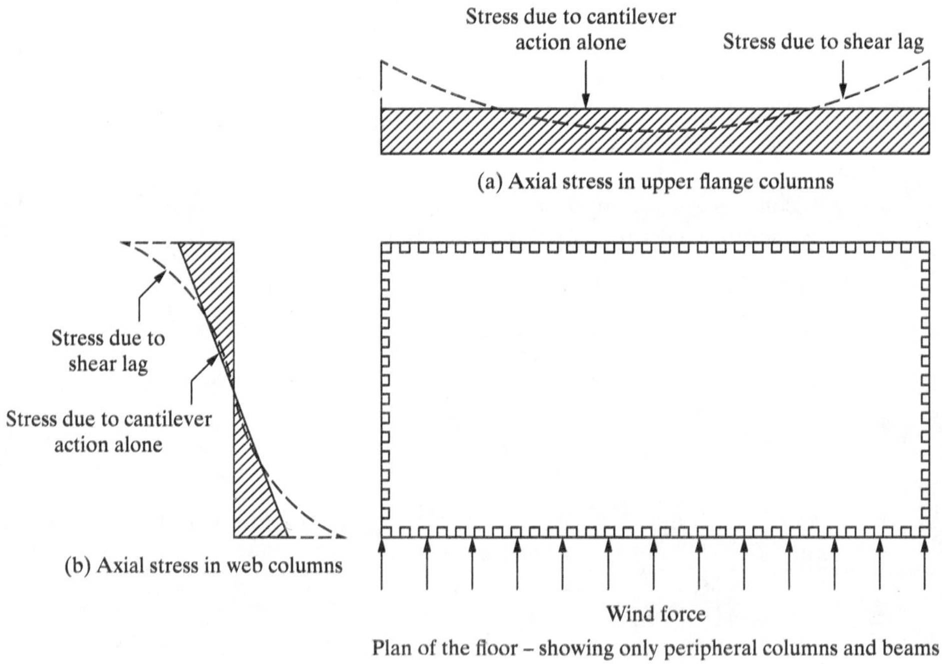

Figure 12.17 Shear lag effect

12.8 BASE SHEAR IN A BUILDING

In the event of an earthquake, the seismic waves travel in all directions inside earth and thus shake it. It is, therefore, natural that an earthquake force is determined at the base of a building in the form of base shear. The base shear is given by the following equation (IS1893-Part 1):

$$V_b = \alpha_h W \tag{12.1a}$$

$$\alpha_h = \frac{Z}{2}\frac{I}{R}\frac{S_a}{g} \tag{12.1b}$$

where α_h = horizontal seismic coefficient
Z = zone factor for MCE condition, Table 12.5
I = importance factor, Table 12.6
R = response reduction factor
S_a = spectral acceleration depending upon the period of vibration and damping
g = acceleration due to gravity
W = seismic weight of building

The zone factor Z depends upon the seismicity of a given area. It reflects more realistic values of effective peak ground acceleration considering Maximum Considered Earthquake (MCE) and service life of structure in each seismic zone.

The factor 2 in the denominator is used to reduce the peak ground acceleration to Design Basis Earthquake (DBE). Its value differs in different international codes. The importance factor of a building depends upon its post-earthquake utility, that is consequence of its collapse on the rescue and rehabilitation programme of the community, as well as on its safety and life. Response reduction factor in discussed later in this chapter.

Various response spectra were generated and discussed in Chapter 8. Equation (12.1) is applicable to any structure—building or a non-building. However, the rest of the treatment of the subject in the following sections is applicable to buildings only.

TABLE 12.5 ZONE FACTOR

Zone	II	III	IV	V
Zone Factor	0.10	0.16	0.24	0.36

TABLE 12.6 IMPORTANCE FACTOR

Structure	Importance Factor
Important service and community centers—hospital, power house, schools, water tanks, telephone exchange, TV station, assembly halls, etc.	1.5
Residential or commercial buildings with occupancy more than 200 persons	1.2
Other buildings, but I/R .LE. 1	1.0

Seismic Weight of Floors The seismic weight of each floor is its full dead load plus any other permanent load, and appropriate amount of imposed load. While computing the seismic weight of each floor, the weight of columns and walls in any storey is equally distributed to the floors above and below the storey.

Seismic Weight of Building The seismic weight of the whole building is the sum of the seismic weights of all the floors.

It is known that an earthquake force is essentially an inertia force. The reasoning behind considering only a part of the imposed load present on a floor is that only the mass that is fixed to the floor contributes to the inertia term ($m\ddot{x}$). The imposed load by definition is a live load whose magnitude and location on a floor will change with time. Therefore, it is quite logical to consider only a part of the total imposed load contributing to the inertia force. The code requires that for imposed loads up to 3 kN/m^2, consider only 25% load and above that only 50% of the total load. Imposed load present on the roof is ignored. It should be remembered that any load that is fixed to the floor or columns or walls must be considered 100%.

12.9 FUNDAMENTAL PERIOD OF VIBRATION

The fundamental period of any building may be determined either by frequency analysis or eigenvalue problem using any commercially available software. The fundamental period of vibration of a structure can also be determined using the Rayleigh method.

$$T = 2\pi \sqrt{\frac{\sum_{i=1}^{n} w_i x_i^2}{g \sum_{i=1}^{n} F_i x_i}} \tag{12.2}$$

where, x_i = elastic horizontal displacements at i^{th} level due to lateral forces F_i ignoring the effect of torsion

w_i = weight at the ith floor

This equation gives fairly reasonable estimate of the period because it takes account of mass and stiffness distribution in the building. The eigenvalue analysis may not give a correct fundamental period of a building because of modelling issues. It is a general practice not to model non-structural elements, that is in-fill masonry walls. Thus, the model considers mass of such walls but ignores their stiffness. This results in a longer period of vibration leading to a lower estimation of the spectral acceleration (S_a/g) from the elastic response spectrum. Therefore, most building codes put a restriction on the period or frequency estimated from the eigenvalue analysis to take care of modelling lacuna.

IS:1893-Part 1 requires that period of a building must also be determined by the following empirical relation:

$$T = 0.075\ H^{0.75} \quad \text{for a RC moment-resistant building} \tag{12.3a}$$

$$T = 0.085\ H^{0.75} \quad \text{for a steel moment-resistant building} \tag{12.3b}$$

where, T = fundamental period of the building (in first mode) in seconds
H = height of the building in meter. This excludes the basement storeys where basement walls are connected with the ground floor deck or fitted between the building columns.

The fundamental period of a RC framed building with masonry in-fill walls may be determined by the following empirical relation:

$$T = \frac{0.09H}{\sqrt{D}} \tag{12.3c}$$

where, D = depth of building in meter in the direction of the earthquake force.

It should be noted that Equations (12.3) are not applicable to an auditorium building, industrial building, metro station, stadium or aircraft hangar etc. The period of vibration in such cases need to be estimated using the eigenvalue problem as discussed in Chapter 10.

These equations were intended to give a quick estimate of the period. These are based only upon the height and plan dimensions of a building. Equations (12.3a) and (12.3b) were based on number of tests carried out on real RC and steel buildings in USA. The period so computed gives the lower bound of time period. The upper bound varies up to about 25%. The lower bound gives a higher base shear whereas, the upper bound gives lower base shear. Equation (12.3c) was introduced in the Uniform Building Code of America in its 1970 edition. Later, it was found that it results in increase in earthquake force by a factor of about two or more. Most International codes have discontinued it.

The empirical computation of period of structures is quite debatable. Let us look at some of the other International code stipulations.

ASCE 7 Clause 12.8.2.1 requires that approximate period may be calculated from the following equation:

$$T_a = C_t H_n^x \tag{12.4}$$

where, the constant C_t and exponent x are given in Table 12.7.
H_n = total height of a building above the basement

The fundamental period of the structure, T, in the direction under consideration should be established using the structural properties and deformational characteristics of the resisting elements in a properly substantiated analysis. It has also provided a table for another coefficient C_u for different design spectral acceleration parameter S_{D1}. It requires that the fundamental period, T, shall not exceed the product of the coefficient for upper limit on calculated period (C_u) and the approximate fundamental

TABLE 12.7 APPROXIMATE PERIOD CALCULATION COEFFICIENTS

	Constant C_t	Exponent x
Steel M-R frames	0.0724	0.80
Concrete M-R frames	0.0466	0.90
Eccentrically braced steel frames and Steel buckling restrained frames	0.0731	0.75
All other structural systems	0.0488	0.75

period, T_a, is determined in accordance with Equation (12.4). Alternatively, it is permitted to use the approximate building period, T_a directly.

Alternatively, for RC or steel buildings up to 12 stories high whose average storey height is at least 3 m, the approximate fundamental period can also be calculated using the following equation:

$$T_a = 0.1\ \mathrm{N} \tag{12.5}$$

where, N = number of storeys above the base

Equation (12.5) was one of the earliest empirical equations to estimate the period of a building. It is no doubt the simplest equation and gives a fairly reasonable estimate. No strings are attached to this equation except that it should not be used for buildings beyond 12 stories.

The approximate fundamental period, T_a, for masonry or concrete shear wall structures is permitted to be determined from Equation (12.6a) as follows:

$$T_a = \frac{0.00058}{\sqrt{C_w}} H_n \tag{12.6a}$$

$$C_w = \frac{100}{A_B} \sum_{i=1}^{x} \left(\frac{H_n}{H_i}\right)^2 \frac{A_i}{\left(1 + 0.83\left(\frac{H_i}{D_i}\right)^2\right)} \tag{12.6b}$$

where A_B = area of base of structure, m^2
A_i = web area of shear wall i in m^2
D_i = length of shear wall i in m
H_i = height of shear wall i in m
x = number of shear walls in the building effective in resisting lateral forces in the direction under consideration

EUROCODE 1998-Part 1 Clause 4.3.3.2.2 of EC8-Part 1 permits the use of the Rayleigh method (Equation (12.2)) for the determination of the fundamental period of vibration for a building.

Alternatively, for a RC moment-resistant building and eccentrically braced steel frames

$$T = 0.075\ H^{0.75} \tag{12.3a}$$

For a steel moment-resistant building

$$T = 0.085\ H^{0.75} \tag{12.3b}$$

$$T = 0.050\ H^{0.75} \text{ for other buildings} \tag{12.3d}$$

where, H = Height of the building from the foundation or from top of a rigid basement, in *m*

However, the total height of buildings for use in Equations (12.3) is restricted to 40 m.

Alternatively, for structures with concrete or masonry shear walls, the approximate fundamental natural period of vibration (T_a) in seconds may be estimated by the empirical expression:

$$T_a = \frac{0.075}{\sqrt{A_c}} H^{0.75} \tag{12.7a}$$

where,

$$A_c = \sum_{i=1}^{N_w} \left\{ A_i \times \left(0.2 + \left(\frac{l_{wi}}{H} \right)^2 \right) \right\} \tag{12.7b}$$

A_c = total effective area of shear walls in the first storey of the building in m^2

A_i = effective cross-sectional area of the shear wall i in the direction considered in the first storey of the building in m^2

l_{wi} = length of the shear wall i in the first storey in the direction parallel to the applied forces, in *m*, with the restriction that l_{wi}/H should not exceed 0.90

N_w = number of shear walls in the first storey

12.10 HOW TO ESTIMATE AND ANALYZE FOR EARTHQUAKE FORCE?

There are four methods to estimate earthquake force and analyze a building:

(a) Seismic coefficient method (SCM), equivalent lateral force method (ELF) or static method

(b) Response spectrum method (RSM) or modal analysis method or dynamic method,

(c) Modal time-history analysis (MTHA) method, and

(d) Linear Time-History analysis (LTH) method.

The *seismic coefficient method* (SCM) is generally applicable to buildings those are symmetrical in plan and elevation with respect to geometry, mass and stiffness distributions. In other words, the eccentricity between the center of mass (CM) and center of rigidity (CR) should be nearly zero. The seismic coefficient method is a static method of analysis and does not account for mass and stiffness distribution in a building. It is based on the first mode deflected shape of the building and assumes 100% mass participation in the first mode. Obviously, it is an overestimation. The effect of higher modes in the seismic coefficient method is taken care of by the codes to some extent. IS 1893 code assumes a parabolic distribution of the base shear in the vertical direction. Similarly, ASCE 7 assumes a linear to parabolic distribution for different time periods. For most practical purposes, static method of seismic analysis gives reasonable estimate of member forces.

The simplifications inherent in the seismic coefficient method (SCM) result in approximations that are likely to be inadequate if the lateral motions in two orthogonal directions and the torsional motion are strongly coupled. Such would be the case if the building were irregular in its plan configuration or if it had a regular plan but its lower natural frequencies were nearly equal.

Response spectrum analysis is applicable for calculating the linear response of complex, multi-degree-of-freedom structures and is based on the fact that the response is the superposition of the responses of individual natural modes of vibration, each mode responding with its own particular pattern of deformation (the mode shape), with its own frequency (the modal frequency), and with its own modal damping. It requires at least three degrees of freedom per floor: two for translational motion and one for torsional motion. This method can be generalized further to model the effect of diaphragm flexibility, soil-structure interaction, etc. In the most general form, the idealization would take the form of large number of mass points, each with six degrees of freedom (three translational and three rotational) connected by generalized stiffness elements. The response of the structure, therefore, can be modeled by the response of number of uncoupled single-degree-of-freedom systems with properties chosen to be representative of the mode and the degree to which the mode is excited by the earthquake motion. The modal analysis method was discussed in detail in chapter 10.

The *modal time-history analysis method* (MTHA) and *linear time-history analysis method* (LTH) are the other methods of earthquake analysis. They require one or more accelerograms for the specific site under consideration. The equation of motion of the entire system ($n \times n$) is solved using step-by-step integration scheme discussed in Chapter 7. This method is usually chosen for a major project as it involves seismological studies at the site and development of site specific accelerograms or an ensemble of accelerograms. It is a time-consuming process as well as quite expensive. The interpretation of results needs a lot of experience. ASCE 7 and Eurocode 1998-Part 1 give detailed requirements for time-history analysis.

In order to account for strength and stiffness degradation and estimate ductility requirements, performance of a building in a severe earthquake, a non-linear time-history analysis with appropriate hysteresis models and damping properties needs to be carried out as discussed in Chapters 15 and 16.

Direction of Earthquake Force

In any building code, it is assumed that the earthquake force acts along any one orthogonal axis in the horizontal plane of the building at a time. Thus, two analyses are required—one along each of the two orthogonal axes. If it is desired to apply the earthquake force in more than one direction simultaneously, then the code gives combination rules. In case, a building has a non-orthogonal plan, an appropriate combination rule can be applied. The kind of seismic analysis and design procedure for different types of buildings is listed in Table 12.8.

TABLE 12.8 EARTHQUAKE ANALYSIS AND DESIGN PROCEDURES

Method of Analysis	Material Behaviour	Type of Configuration	Design Philosophy
Static analysis—linear	Elastic	Regular	Limit state design for serviceability
	Inelastic	Regular	Limit state design for collapse
Dynamic analysis—linear	Elastic	Regular or irregular	Limit state design for serviceability
	Inelastic	Regular or irregular	Limit state design for collapse
Dynamic analysis—nonlinear time-history	Inelastic—reversed cyclic using hysteresis behaviour	Regular or irregular	Limit state design for collapse

12.10.1 Seismic Coefficient Method

This procedure is useful in preliminary design of all structures and is allowed for final design of the vast majority of structures depending upon regularity, seismic zone and height.

Once the fundamental period of vibration has been estimated using the IS code or eigenvalue analysis, it is possible to estimate the base shear using Equation (12.1). The next step is to distribute this base shear along the height of the building and then laterally to the various frames arranged in the horizontal x- and y-directions.

Vertical Distribution of Base Shear The lateral force at each floor can be estimated using Equation (12.8a), which assumes a parabolic distribution of the force along the height of the building:

$$Q_i = \frac{w_i h_i^2}{\sum_{j=1}^{n} w_j h_j^2} V_b \tag{12.8a}$$

where, Q_i = lateral force at the ith floor

h_i, h_j = height of ith floor or j^{th} floor measured above the base

w_i, w_j = seismic weight of the ith or j^{th} floor

n = total number of storeys

Clause 12.8.3 of ASCE 7 requires the calculation of vertical distribution of the base shear as follows:

$$Q_i = \frac{w_i h_i^k}{\sum_{j=1}^{n} w_j h_j^k} V_b \tag{12.8b}$$

where, the exponent k is a function of fundamental period of the structure

$k = 1$ if $T \leq 0.5$ sec

$= 2$ if $T \geq 2.5$ sec

For T between 0.5 and 2.5 sec, k needs to be linearly interpolated between 1 and 2.

Horizontal Distribution of Shear The lateral force estimated at a given floor now needs to be distributed to the various frames of the building in proportion to their rigidities considering rigidity of the diaphragm. It is assumed that the floor is very rigid in its own plane. Thus,

$Q_{ik} \propto$ distance of the frame from the center of gravity of the mass at a floor

where, Q_{ik} = lateral force in k^{th} frame at the ith floor

In other words, the frames farthest from the center of gravity will carry the maximum lateral force. It is a very time consuming and laborious procedure if carried out manually. Therefore, it is much more convenient to make use of a software. There are many user-friendly softwares with very powerful graphical user interface (GUI) both for pre-processing and post-processing of data. Only the base shear parameters including period, the level of top of the rigid basement or foundation and top of the building need to be specified along with the computer model, and rest of the calculations are done by the software.

12.10.2 Response Spectrum Method

The detailed steps are as follows:

(1) Estimate or assign preliminary sections to each beam, column and masonry and RC wall in the building.

(2) Compute lumped mass at each floor level.

(3) The inertial force is applied at the center of gravity of mass (CM) of each floor The direction of the response spectra is specified along X or Y or Z directions, or even all the three directions simultaneously, if required.

(4) The 3D dynamic analysis takes care of the horizontal and vertical distribution of lateral forces on the entire building assuming the floor diaphragm is very rigid The equation of motion is given by the following equation:

$$[M]\{\ddot{X}\}+[C]\{\dot{X}\}+[K]\{X\}=-[M]\{\ddot{Y}\} \quad (10.12c)$$

This equation is decoupled by making use of the condition of orthogonality of modes.

Carry out an undamped free vibration analysis to evaluate eigenvalues and eigenvectors, that is, natural periods of vibration and the corresponding mode shapes in the first 'p' modes as discussed in Chapter 10.

$$\boldsymbol{M\ddot{X}} + \boldsymbol{KX} = \boldsymbol{0} \quad (10.13b)$$

Or,

$$\boldsymbol{A}\phi = \lambda\phi \quad (10.19)$$

(5) Evaluate mode participation factor $\Gamma^{(r)}$ in the rth mode :

$$\Gamma^{(r)} = \frac{\left[\sum_{i=1}^{n} m_i \phi_i^{(r)}\right]}{\sum_{i=1}^{n} m_i \left[\phi_i^{(r)}\right]^2} \tag{10.59}$$

where n = number of total storeys in the building

m_i = mass lumped at the ith floor

$\phi_i^{(r)}$ = mode shape coefficient at ith floor level in rth mode of vibration

(6) Evaluate $\alpha_h^{(r)}$ design horizontal acceleration spectrum value in the rth mode of vibration corresponding to the natural period of vibration in each mode.

(7) Design lateral force at each floor in each mode is given by the following equation (based on Equation (10.67)):

$$Q_i^{(r)} = \alpha_h^{(r)}\, \phi_i^{(r)}\, \Gamma^{(r)}\, m_i\, g \tag{12.9}$$

(8) Storey shear in each mode is given by :

$$V_i^{(r)} = \sum_{j=i+1}^{n} Q_j^{(r)} \tag{12.10}$$

(9) Modal Combinations

The peak response quantities such as storey shears, member forces and displacements may be combined using the square root of sum of squares (SRSS) method or complete quadratic combination (CQC) method.

If the modes are well separated from each other, as defined earlier, the SRSS method of mode superposition may be used.

$$\lambda = \sqrt{\sum_{i=1}^{p} \lambda_i^2} \tag{10.71}$$

λ = peak response quantity

Otherwise, CQC method will have to be used.

$$\lambda = \sqrt{\sum_{i=1}^{p}\sum_{j=1}^{p} \lambda_i \rho_{ij} \lambda_j} \tag{10.72}$$

where

λ = peak response quantity

λ_i = response quantity in mode i

λ_j = response quantity in mode j

p = number of modes being considered (less than or equal to i)

ρ_{ij} = cross correlation coefficient

$$\rho_{ij} = \frac{8\xi^2(1+\beta)\beta^{1.5}}{(1-\beta^2)^2 + 4\xi^2\beta(1+\beta)^2} \tag{10.73}$$

β = frequency ratio = ω_j / ω_i

ξ = modal damping ratio

(10) Lateral force at each floor due to all modes considered is computed as follows:

$$F_{roof} = V_{roof} \tag{12.11a}$$

and

$$F_i = V_i - V_{i+1} \tag{12.11b}$$

where

F_i = lateral force at i-th floor

V_i, V_{i+1} = storey shears at i-th and i+1 th storeys

(11) Carry out a 3D frame analysis for dead loads, live loads and lateral forces F_i in each mode and get the member forces for the specified load combinations. Finally, find the response quantities of interest, that is, member forces and displacements.

(12) Check the frame for storey drift.

12.10.3 Linear Time-history Analysis Method

Linear time history analysis method is a numerically involved technique in which the response of a structural model to a specific earthquake ground motion accelerogram is determined through a process of numerical integration of the equation of motion. Its details were discussed in Chapter 10.

Recorded accelerograms, or accelerograms generated through a numerical simulation of source and travel path mechanisms may be used provided that the samples used are adequately qualified about the seismological features of the sources and to the soil conditions appropriate to the site, and their values are scaled for the seismic zone under consideration. Some codes require that such accelerograms should be compatible with the design response spectrum. It has its own merits and demerits.

The main advantage of using *T-H* analysis is that signs (positive–negative bending moments, tension–compression brace/column axial forces) are preserved, whereas they are lost in forming the SRSS and CQC combination in LRS analysis. Further, it provides a time dependent history of the response of the structure to a specific ground motion, and stress and deformation state of the structure throughout the duration of response. A response spectrum analysis, however, indicates only the maximum response quantities and does not indicate the time of occurrence of these events.

12.10.4 Important Considerations in Response Spectrum Analysis

Scaling of Base Shear

The base shear is calculated by using Equation (12.1) for use in the seismic coefficient method (SCM) wherein the period is calculated using an empirical formula as discussed earlier. The period so calculated is on the conservative side so as to give very high value of the base shear. The base shear is also calculated in the response spectrum analysis method by using the stiffness and mass distribution in the model. As mentioned earlier, most of the time lateral stiffness of the non-structural elements are ignored in the modelling leading to a higher period of vibration. Thus, RSA generally gives a lower base shear as compared to that calculated using the empirical formula because of more accurate representation of the mass and stiffness distribution. Different building codes deal with this situation differently. IS 1893 requires that the dynamic base shear must not be less than that calculated using the empirical method to avoid excessive flexible building resulting due to inaccuracies in the calculation of stiffness of non-structural elements in the analysis, and to ensure minimum strength of earthquake resisting elements. ASCE 7 also has a similar requirement. However, ASCE 7 permits adjustment of period of vibration computed using the approximate formula (T_a) and modal analysis (T_m) within a specified range, and thus, ensures that the static base shear is reasonably higher than the dynamic base shear in most cases. In reality, each of these formulae have a lower and upper bound as determined by field measurements on several buildings in the USA. But IS 1893 only makes use of the lower bound so as to get a very high base shear and completely ignores the upper bound on the time period.

In certain cases where higher modes are significant, the base shear calculated using the RSA may turn out to be higher than that given by the SCM. In such cases, one has to use higher dynamic base shear.

To summarize, where RSA predicts response quantities corresponding to a total base shear less than that which is computed using the SCM procedure, all response results must be scaled up to that level. Where RSA predicts response quantities in excess of those predicted by the SCM procedure, this is likely the result of significant higher mode participation and reduction to the values obtained from the SCM procedure is not permitted.

Loss of Sign for Computed Quantities

For a given direction of loading, the displacement in each mode is determined from the corresponding spectral acceleration, modal participation, and mode shape. In the process of mode superposition using either SRSS or CQC method, the sign of the response quantities, that is, member forces and displacements is lost. The final forces are obtained as follows:

$$\text{Static member forces} + \text{abs (dynamic forces)}$$

$$\text{Static member forces} - \text{abs (dynamic forces)}$$

The loss of signs for computed quantities leads to problems in interpreting force results where seismic effects are combined with gravity effects, produce forces that are not in static equilibrium, and make it impossible to plot deflected shapes of the structure. Nevertheless, statistical combination of modal responses (SRSS or CQC) produces reasonably accurate estimates of displacements and component forces.

Number of Modes

The analysis should include a sufficient number of modes to obtain a combined modal mass participation of at least 90 percent of the actual mass in each of the orthogonal horizontal directions of response considered by the model. The modal mass in any mode is given by Equation (10.69b)

$$M^{(r)} = \frac{\left[\sum_{i=1}^{n} m_i \varphi_i^{(r)}\right]^2}{\sum_{i=1}^{n} m_i \left[\varphi_i^{(r)}\right]^2} \tag{10.69b}$$

Closely Spaced Modes

If any two consecutive modes are closely spaced in a given lateral direction, it means the translational and torsional modes are highly correlated. Otherwise, they are independent of each other. Most building codes specify a difference of 10% of the larger value for the period in any two modes to be considered as close. Alternatively, the response in two vibration modes i and j (including both translational and torsional modes) may be taken as independent of each other, if their periods T_i and T_j satisfy (with $T_j \le T_i$) the following condition:

$$T_j \ge 0.9\, T_i \qquad 1 \le i < j \le p \tag{12.12}$$

In case the modes are independent of each other, the SRSS method may be used for modal combination. Otherwise, CQC method must be used. These statistical methods were discussed in Chapter 10.

Modal Combination

Any peak response quantity must be computed by combining the peak values of the modal contribution of the same quantity. For example, peak value of storey drift must be calculated from the modal contributions of the storey drift and not from the peak values of floor displacements. Similarly, peak value of base shear must be computed from the modal contributions of the lateral force at each floor in each mode rather than from the peak values of static force at each floor. In computing the peak value, sign of the response quantity is lost, that is why, it is a must to make use of the modal contributions of each response quantity.

12.10.5 Orientation of Lateral Load Resisting Elements

All members of the structure, including those not part of the seismic force-resisting system, are designed using the seismic load effects such as axial force, shear force, and bending moments resulting from application of horizontal and vertical seismic forces applied on the structure. The directions of application of seismic forces used in the design must be those which will produce the most critical load effects.

Buildings with Orthogonal Lateral Load Resisting Elements

For structures with orthogonal seismic force-resisting systems, the most critical load effects can typically be computed using a pair of orthogonal directions that coincide with the principal axes of the structure. For such buildings the design seismic forces are permitted to be applied in one horizontal direction at a time, independently in each of the two orthogonal directions and orthogonal interaction effects are permitted to be ignored.

Buildings with Non-orthogonal Lateral Load Resisting Elements

Seismic forces are delivered to a building through ground accelerations that may approach from any direction relative to the orthogonal directions of the building; therefore, seismic effects are expected to develop in both directions simultaneously. Structures with non-parallel or non-orthogonal systems may require a set of orthogonal direction pairs to determine the most critical load effects. If a three-dimensional mathematical model is used, the analyst must be attentive to the orientation of the global axes in the model in relation to the principal axes of the structure.

Any of the following two methods can be used as convenient:

(a) *Independent application of orthogonal ground motion*

The structure can be analyzed using any of the methods discussed earlier with the loading applied independently in any two orthogonal directions. The most critical load effect due to direction of application of seismic forces on the structure is permitted to be assumed to be satisfied if components and their foundations are designed for the following combination of prescribed loads:

100 percent of the forces for one direction plus 30 percent of the forces for the perpendicular direction; the combination requiring the maximum component strength shall be used.

For instance

$$\pm EL_x \pm 0.30\ EL_y \text{ or } \pm 0.30\ EL_x \pm EL_y$$

where the individual directional results have been combined by SRSS or CQC, as appropriate.

When response from the three earthquake components are to be considered, the response due to each component may be combined using the assumption that when the maximum response from one component occurs, the responses from the other two components are 30% of their maximum. All possible combinations of the three components (EL_x, EL_y and EL_z) including variations in sign (plus or minus) should be considered, Thus, the response due earthquake force (EL) is the maximum of the following three cases:

$$\pm EL_x \pm 0.30\ EL_y \pm 0.30\ EL_z$$

$$\pm 0.30\ EL_x \pm EL_y \pm 0.30\ EL_z$$

$$\pm 0.30\ EL_x \pm 0.30\ EL_y \pm EL_z \qquad (12.13)$$

The entire process of design eccentricity, modal analysis, mode superimposition, non-orthogonal combinations and other load combinations as specified in a given design code is carried out seamlessly by the computer programs. Only the appropriate data is to be supplied through GUI.

(b) *Simultaneous application of orthogonal ground motion*

The structure must be analyzed using the linear time – history method with orthogonal pairs of ground motion acceleration histories applied simultaneously.

For horizontal structural elements such as beams and slabs, orthogonal effects may be minimal; however, for vertical elements of the seismic-force-resisting system that participate in both orthogonal directions, the design likely will be governed by these combinations. Orthogonal combinations should not be confused with modal combinations such as the square root of the sum of the squares (SRSS) or complete quadratic combination (CQC) technique.

12.11 TORSION

It is important to know the point of application of the earthquake force in a building. It acts at the *center of mass* (CM) of each floor. It is resisted by the building by applying an equal and opposite reaction through the *center of rigidity* (CR) at each floor. The distance between the center of mass and center of rigidity at each floor is referred to as the *structural eccentricity*. Lateral force times the eccentricity at each floor give rise to torsion about the vertical axis of the building. Torsion in a building is highly undesirable force and may lead to partial or complete collapse of the building in the event of a strong earthquake as experienced in the past several earthquakes all over the world. Therefore, it needs to be taken very seriously. Most building codes give a pair of equations to define design eccentricity e_d

$$e_{da} = \alpha e + \beta b \tag{12.14a}$$

$$e_{db} = \delta e - \beta b \tag{12.14b}$$

where e = structural eccentricity, that is distance between the center of mass (CM) and center of stiffness (CR) at a floor

b = maximum dimension of the building perpendicular to the direction of earthquake under consideration

α and δ = dynamic magnification factors

β = accidental eccentricity factor

The eccentricity e is to be measured both along x-and y-direction in a building at each floor. In case of a symmetric building, eccentricity e is zero. Even then this building will be analyzed for accidental eccentricity. The purpose of dynamic magnification factors is to account for the possibility of the increase in in-plane torsion due to dynamic effects. These are prescribed when a static analysis is performed for torsion. The *accidental eccentricity* intends to take account of unforeseeable differences between computed and actual values of stiffness, yield strength and dead load masses, uncertainties in the unfavorable distribution of live load mass and rotational components of earthquake motion about a vertical axis. The accidental eccentricity is applicable in both static and dynamic analyses.

IS:1893-Part 1 The eccentricity of the applied force is given by the following equations:

$$e_{da} = 1.5e + 0.05b \tag{12.15a}$$

$$e_{db} = e - 0.05b \tag{12.15b}$$

where, e_{da}, e_{db} = design eccentricity
e = computed eccentricity between the center of rigidity and center of mass at each floor

Again, different codes account for torsion differently. The physical interpretation of Equations (12.15) is illustrated in Figure 12.18. The earthquake force acts through the CM at each floor while the building resists it through equal and opposite force acting through CR at each floor. It develops a twisting moment $T = Ve_{da}$ or Ve_{db}. In columns and shear walls farthest from the center of rigidity, the demand on strain becomes very critical due to torsion as seen in Figure 12.18(d) and may lead to complete collapse of the building.

If the direction of earthquake reverses, the building will twist in the opposite direction.

ASCE 7 Clause 12.8.4.2 of ASCE 7 specifies that a building with rigid diaphragm will be subjected to an accidental eccentricity of ±5% of the dimension of the building perpendicular to the direction of the applied forces.

$$e_a = e + 0.05b \tag{12.16a}$$

$$e_b = e - 0.05b \tag{12.16b}$$

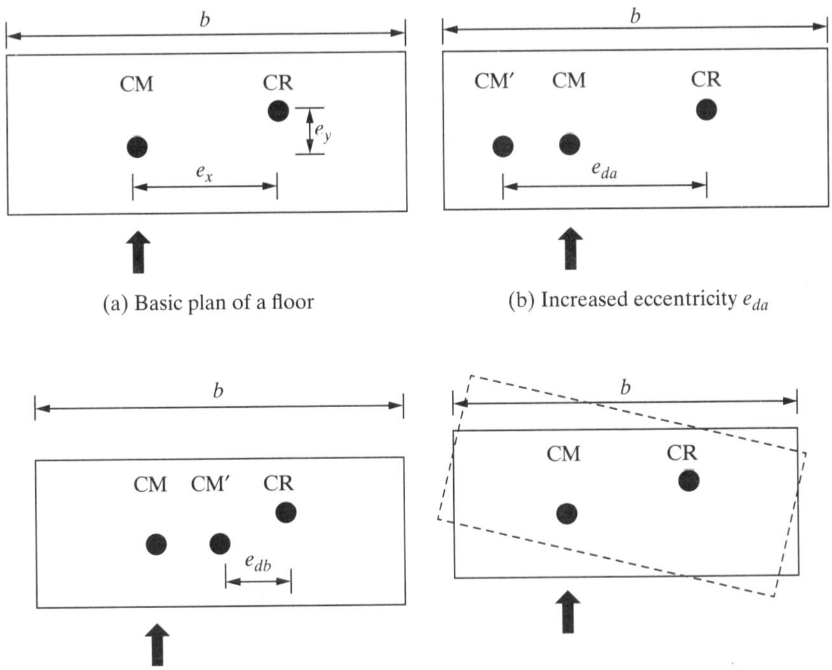

(a) Basic plan of a floor

(b) Increased eccentricity e_{da}

(c) Decreased eccentricity e_{db}

(d) Rotation about CR

CM = Computed center of mass; CM′ = Modified center of mass

Figure 12.18 Design eccentricities in a floor plan in x-direction.

Clause 4.3.2 of the Eurocode 1998-Part 1 also makes use of Equation (12.16).

The stiffness matrix formulation of a structure takes care of the structural eccentricity "*e*" automatically. In case, structural eccentricity needs to be magnified by a factor α or δ as in Equation (12.14) or (12.15), then it is advisable to carryout static analysis of building due to torsion alone and superimpose the results.

How to Account for Accidental Eccentricity in Dynamic Analysis?

The accidental eccentricity in Equation (12.16) can be easily incorporated in the dynamic analysis methods discussed earlier. A set of three dynamic analyses of a building is carried out in each of the two orthogonal directions by shifting the *center of mass*. Initially, with the mass at the original center of mass of each floor, complete analysis is carried out. Next, the center of mass is shifted by +/– 0.05b on either side of the original CM, and analysis is carried out. Thus, a set of three analyses is carried out in each of the two orthogonal directions. Finally, envelope of the forces produced by these three dynamic analyses in each direction is considered for design.

What if the First Mode is Torsion?

Sometimes, the frequency analysis tells that the first mode of a building is torsional mode or first and third mode are torsional modes. Studies of damage to buildings due to earthquakes during the past more than 100 years concluded that torsional mode of vibration was responsible for most of the failures or complete collapse of buildings. Therefore, torsional mode of vibration must be avoided in the first few modes. This may require changes in the architectural layout of the building or in the structural layout or both. This exercise may require a few iterations. Moreover, each building code requires that the minimum number of modes considered in the analysis is such that at least 90% of the translational modal mass must participate. In a regular building, first three modes are usually sufficient to fulfill this condition. Otherwise, a large number of modes are required.

12.11.1 Rigid and Flexible Floor Diaphragms

The purpose of a *floor diaphragm* in a building is to distribute the lateral force acting at the floor level to all the lateral load resisting vertical elements in that floor. This lateral distribution depends if the floor diaphragm is *rigid or flexible*. In a rigid floor diaphragm, the lateral force is distributed to the various vertical elements in proportion to their distance from the center of rotation of the diaphragm. However, this is not so if the floor diaphragm is flexible. In general, if there are large cutouts in a floor, then it is likely to be a flexible diaphragm.

Lateral force is applied along a given horizontal direction and the lateral displacement at the two ends of a floor is determined in the same direction. If the maximum lateral displacement is more than 50% of that of the minimum lateral displacement, the floor is said to have torsional irregularity as shown in Figure 12.19(a).

A floor diaphragm is flexible if it deforms such that the maximum lateral displacement measured from the chord of the deformed shape at any point of diaphragm is more than 1.2 times the average displacement of the entire diaphragm as shown in Figure 12.19(b). In such a situation, it is essential to model the semi-rigid stiffness of the floor diaphragm in the model for seismic analysis. Collector elements must be capable of transferring the seismic forces originating in other portions of the structure to the element providing the resistance to those forces.

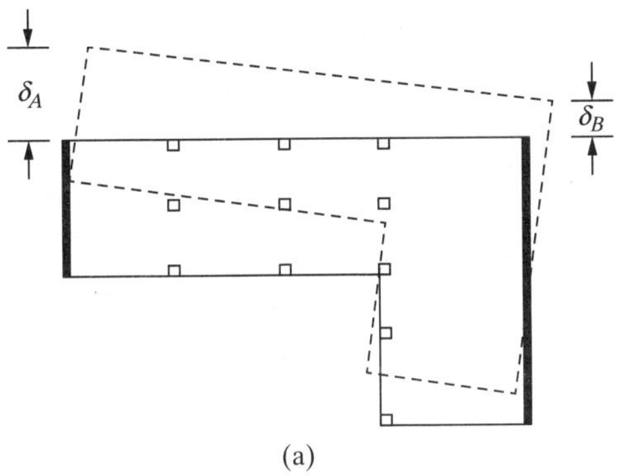

Figure 12.19(a) Deflection due to Torsion in plan

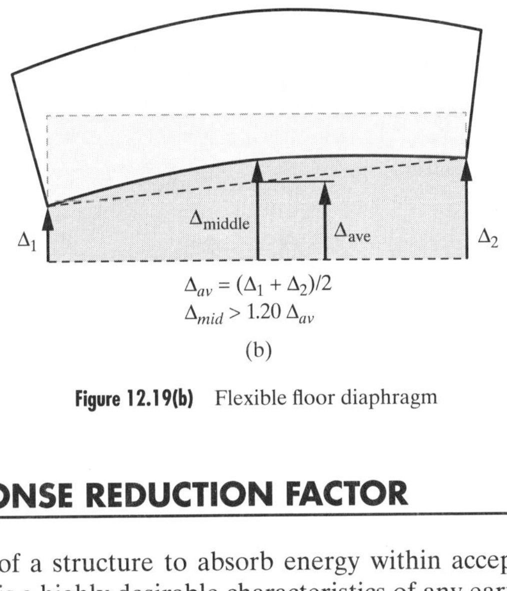

Figure 12.19(b) Flexible floor diaphragm

12.12 RESPONSE REDUCTION FACTOR

The capability of a structure to absorb energy within acceptable deformations and without failure is a highly desirable characteristics of any earthquake resistant design. Let us consider a multistorey framed building as shown in Figure 12.20(a). It is subjected to lateral loads due to earthquake force at each floor level. These loads are increased gradually from zero till its collapse. The circles represent formation of plastic hinges at different locations at the ends of beams and columns. At a certain stage, there is a significant yielding in the frame. The *first significant yield* is the level of force that causes complete plastification of at least one of the most critical regions of the structure. Let us plot *base shear* versus *roof displacement* in Figure 12.20(b) and the corresponding plastic hinges are also marked in the figure. The first significant yield point is shown by a dark circle in Figures 12.20(a) and 12.20(b). The strength corresponding

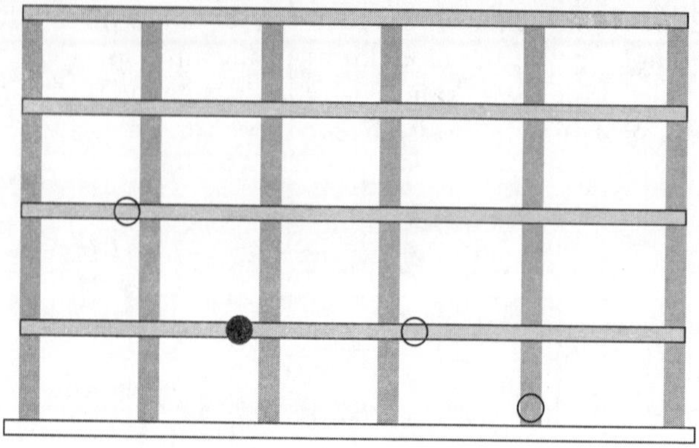

(a) Formation of plastic hinges in a RC framed building

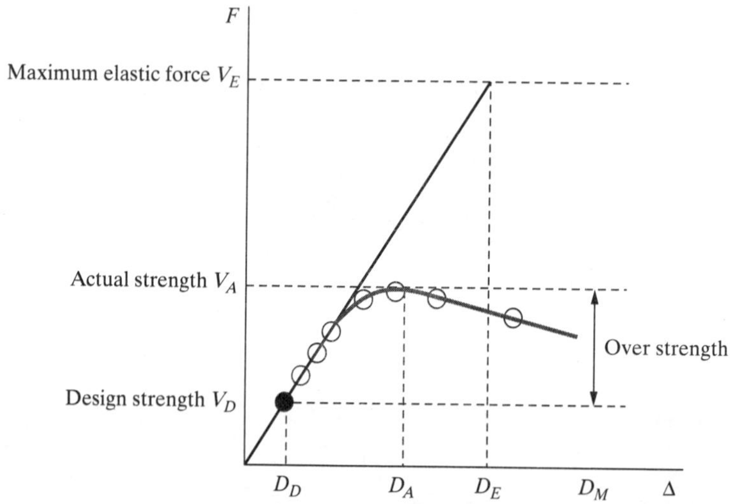

(b) Base shear vs roof displacement until collapse

Figure 12.20

to the first significant yield represents the design strength of the building V_D and the corresponding roof displacement D_D.

As the lateral force increases with time, more plastic hinge form at various locations till collapse of the building or withdrawal of the earthquake force. The final base shear vs roof displacements plot is curvilinear. The maximum base shear is referred to as the actual strength V_A of the building and the corresponding roof displacement is D_A. It also shows the maximum elastic force V_E and the corresponding roof displacement D_E. The maximum roof displacement at collapse is referred to as D_M.

Thus, two force ratios can be defined.

$$R_1 = \frac{V_E}{V_D} > 1.0 \tag{12.17a}$$

$$R_2 = \frac{V_E}{V_A} > 1.0 \tag{12.17b}$$

R_1 represents the ratio of elastic force to the specified design force for a given design earthquake motion. It is always greater than 1.0. R_2 represents the ratio of elastic force to the fully plastic or significant yield force. One more factor can be defined which is known as over strength factor as follows:

$$R_3 = \frac{\text{Apparent or actual strength}}{\text{Design strength}} = \frac{V_A}{V_D} > 1.0 \tag{12.17c}$$

Overstrength is introduced in a structure by means of the following factors:

- Material overstrength (actual vs specified yield)
- Strain hardening
- Increase in size of a member over its design value
- Increase in reinforcement in a member over its design value
- Structures where the proportioning is controlled by the seismic drift limits
- Sequential yielding of critical regions
- Capacity reduction factors

A structure is designed for a force level that is always lower than V_E. The level of significant yield force always exceeds the prescribed design force. Thus, a structure is forced to enter into the inelastic state and make use of its available reserve energy. The design for a reduced force in intentional due to the following reasons:

(a) The probability of occurrence of a severe earthquake during the life of a building is usually low.

(b) As the structure begins to yield and deform inelastically, the effective period of response of the structure tends to lengthen, which for many structures, results in a reduction in strength demand. It can be verified from the shape of the response spectrum curves for S_a/g.

(c) The inelastic action results in a significant amount of energy dissipation also known as hysteretic damping.

(d) Presence of overstrength and ductility in a structure.

Thus, a *response reduction factor* R_1 can be expressed as follows:

$$R_1 = R_2 R_3 \tag{12.18}$$

The combined effect, which is also known as the *ductility,* explains why a properly designed structure with a fully yielded strength that is significantly lower than the elastic seismic force demand is expected to provide a satisfactory performance under the design earthquake motion.

The question is how to assign a value to response reduction factor R for a given structural system, such as an ordinary RC frame, ductile MR frame, shear wall frame, concentrically braced frame, or eccentrically braced frame. It can be done based on experimental evidence on reversed cyclic loading on such frames and plotting their

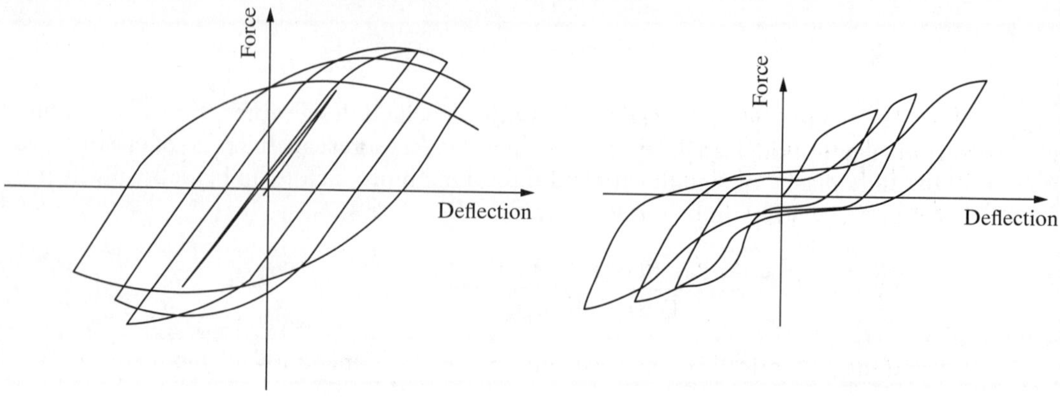

(a) Ductile hysteresis loops (b) Pinched hysteresis loops

Figure 12.21 Hysteresis behaviour for different systems

hysteresis loops as seen in Figure 12.21. A nonlinear analysis of a SDOF system having such a hysteretic characteristic can be carried out under different earthquakes and estimating the available ductility. Thus, response reduction factors for different structural systems having different ductile detailing and therefore, hysteretic characteristics, can be estimated. Reduction factor spectra is discussed in Chapter 15.

In practice, the response reduction factor *R* is used to account for a series of effects such as:

- Anticipated ductility supply
- Overstrength
- Damping (if different than 5% of critical)
- Past performance of similar systems
- Redundancy
- Calibration between the current and the proposed design seismic coefficient

It is quite difficult to isolate the effect of each of the above factors. Therefore, in practice, the values of R factors are chosen empirically. These factors are not unique across different international building codes. Different international codes deal with this aspect differently. The values of factor *R* are given in Table 12.9 for buildings as per the IS 1893-1 code.

12.12.1 Need for Redundancy

The gravity and lateral load resisting system in a tall building should be made as redundant as possible within the functional parameters of the building to take care of unforeseen extreme events. Redundancy, that is, degree of static indeterminacy, plays an important role in determining the ability of the building to resist these

TABLE 12.9 RESPONSE REDUCTION FACTOR R

S. No.	Lateral Load Resisting System	R
(1)	*Framed Building*	
	RCC moment-resisting frame – ordinary (OMRF)	3
	RCC moment-resisting frame – special, that is, with ductile detailing (SMRF)	5
	Ordinary moment-resisting steel frame (OMRF)	3
	Special moment-resisting steel frame (SMRF)	5
(2)	*Braced Steel Frame*	
	Ordinary steel frame with concentric braces (OCBF)	4
	Special steel frame with concentric braces (SCBF)	4.5
	Special steel frame with eccentric braces (SCBF)	5
(3)	*Building with Flexural (Shear) Walls*	
	Load bearing masonry wall building	
	(a) Unreinforced	1.5
	(b) Reinforced with horizontal bands	2
	(c) Reinforced with both vertical steel and horizontal bands	3
	RC flexural wall—ordinary	3
	RC flexural wall—ductile	4
(4)	*Dual System*	
	Ordinary flexural wall with ordinary M-R frame	3
	Ordinary flexural wall with ductile M-R frame	4
	Ductile flexural wall with ordinary M-R frame	4.5
	Ductile wall with ductile M-R frame	5
(5)	*Flat Slab – Structural Wall System*	
	RC building with (a) Ductile shear walls that are designed to resist 100% lateral force, and (b) Perimeter RC special moment resisting frames designed to independently resist 25% of the design lateral force Maximum lateral sway at the roof not to exceed 0.1%	3

forces in the event of an unforeseen situation by letting some members enter in their non-linear or plastic state. In a *statically determinate system* every component must remain elastic in order to preserve the integrity of the structure. On the contrary, in a highly *statically indeterminate system*, a few redundant components may plastify and undergo extensive damage and still leave a structural system which retains its integrity and continue to resist these extreme forces although with reduced effectiveness.

Clause 12.3.4 of ASCE 7 has introduced a *redundancy factor* for structures in Seismic Design Categories D, E, and F to quantify redundancy. The value of this factor is either 1.0 or 1.3. This factor has an effect of reducing the response reduction factor

R for less redundant structures, thereby increasing the seismic demand. The value of redundancy factor ρ is 1.3 unless one of the following two conditions is met, whereby ρ is permitted to be taken as 1.0:

(a) Each story resisting more than 35 percent of the base shear in the direction of interest shall comply with the following conditions:
- removal of an element or connection thereto, would not result in more than a 33% reduction in story strength,
- nor does the resulting system have an extreme torsional irregularity.

(b) Structures that are regular in plan at all levels provided that the seismic force-resisting systems consist of at least two bays of seismic force-resisting perimeter framing on each side of the structure in each orthogonal direction at each story resisting more than 35 percent of the base shear. The number of bays for a shear wall shall be calculated as the length of shear wall divided by the story height or two times the length of shear wall divided by the story height for light-frame construction.

Eurocode 8 – part 1 defines a *behaviour factor* which is similar to the *response reduction factor* in IS:1893 and ASCE 7. This factor is used for design purposes to reduce the forces obtained from a linear analysis, in order to account for the non-linear response of a structure, associated with the material, the structural system, redundancy and the design procedures. A high degree of redundancy accompanied by redistribution capacity is sought, enabling a more widely spread energy dissipation and an increased total dissipated energy. Consequently, structural systems of lower static indeterminacy are assigned lower behaviour factors. The necessary redistribution capacity is achieved through the use of ductility rules.

12.13 BUILDING ON STILTS

It is a common practice to design a multi-storey building with parking at the ground floor or in one or more basements. There are usually no walls in such floors but only columns. This is a perfect example of a soft storey (loss of stiffness). It may also be a case of weak storey (loss of storey shear strength). The building on soft storey or on stilts needs special precaution in order to avoid the formation of sway mechanism and, therefore, collapse as shown in Figure 12.14. Several buildings having soft storeys have collapsed during the past earthquakes. The collapse of the Olive View Hospital building in San Fernando Earthquake 1971 is widely reported. A number of buildings on stilts collapsed during the twin earthquakes and multiple aftershocks of Turkey-Syria earthquake of Feb 6, 2023. Such unsafe buildings are still being widely built in the Himalayan hills as shown in Figure 12.22.

It should be possible to provide shear walls or diagonal braces in one or both directions at certain locations aligned with the columns so that there is no hindrance to the movement of vehicles and at the same time there is no soft storey as discussed earlier. Such elements must be provided in such a manner so as to maintain regularity of the building in plan and elevation.

(a) (b)

Figure 12.22 Buildings on stilts in Himalayan Hills (Uttarakhand).

12.14 STOREY DRIFT AND SEPARATION OF BUILDINGS

The design gravity loads and lateral seismic forces are applied to the computer model of the physical structure to determine lateral displacement at each floor. The model should include the stiffness and strength of all elements that are significant to the distribution of forces and deformations in the structure. The model should also comply with the following:

- Stiffness properties of reinforced concrete and masonry elements should consider the effects of cracked sections, and
- For steel moment resisting frame systems, the contribution of panel zone deformations to overall story drift should be included.

A linear elastic analysis is carried out to determine member forces and lateral displacements. Once the lateral displacements at each floor are known, the storey drifts can be determined as inter-storey displacement, that is, relative displacement between two consecutive floors. The storey drift is a measure of discomfort to the occupants at serviceability limit state. The maximum permissible lateral drift under earthquake force is 0.4% of the storey height at serviceability as per IS 1893-part 1. The lateral displacements or storey drifts at the limit state of collapse have no design relevance. There can be very large lateral displacements, say 4 to 5% of the height, along with severe plastification depending upon the ductility in the structure at the limit state of collapse. The only condition is that there should be no collapse of the structural system. This is to ensure that the occupants can be evacuated safely.

Here two points must be noted:

(1) The lateral displacements of the floors must be calculated without scaling the dynamic base shear (so as to make it equal to that of the static base shear). The storey drifts so calculated should not exceed 0.4% of the storey height. If dynamic base shear is scaled, both the lateral displacements and storey drifts are scaled by the same factor.

(2) The lateral displacements must be calculated for serviceability limit state, that is, by using a partial safety factors on loads as 1.0. The concept of storey drift is meaningful at the serviceability limit state so as to ensure comfort to the occupants during its service life.

In case it is decided to connect two adjacent buildings together, the method of connection should take into account the mass, stiffness, strength, ductility and anticipated motion of the connected building and the character of the connection. The connected buildings should be assumed to have the lowest R value of the building connected unless the use of a higher value can be justified by rational analysis. The non-structural components should be designed so as not to transfer to the structural system any forces unaccounted for in the design.

The Eurocode 1998-part 1 defines the design interstorey drifts as follows:

Δs = design interstorey drift = $q\,\Delta$

Δ = computed storey drift from elastic analysis

q = behavior factor which is analogous to response reduction factor R

ν = reduction factor which takes into account the lower return period of the seismic action associated with the level of seismic hazard and importance of the property

= 0.4 or 0.5 depending upon the importance of the building

It gives the requirements for design interstorey drifts ($\nu\,\Delta s$) as shown in Table 12.10.

Pounding Between Two Buildings

The other aspect of lateral displacements is the separation between two adjacent buildings that may or may not belong to the same property. In many cities around the world such as Hong Kong and Mexico City, there is acute shortage of land and very tall

TABLE 12.10 PERMISSIBLE INTERSTOREY DRIFT

Structure	Permissible storey drift
Buildings having non-structural elements of brittle materials attached to the structure	0.005 h
Buildings having ductile non-structural elements	0.0075 h
For buildings having non-structural elements fixed in a way so as not to interfere with structural deformations, or without non-structural elements	0.01 h

h = storey height

buildings are located very close to each other. A similar situation can be seen in many of the Indian cities as well. Adjacent structures may vibrate in phase or out of phase with each other during an earthquake depending upon their individual characteristics. If they vibrate out of phase, then there is a chance that they may pound on each other leading to severe damage or even collapse. This pounding effect has been observed in many earthquakes where the adjacent buildings were at arm length, for example in Mexico City during 1985 earthquake and in the Turkey-Syria earthquake of Feb 6, 2023. Adjacent structures should be separated by at least the sum of their individual deflections or should be connected to each other. This is to prevent collapse due to pounding. Remember, the magnitude of earthquake force was reduced by a factor R in order to push the structure in inelastic region. These lateral deflections obtained from an elastic analysis should be multiplied with the same factor R to give realistic values of the anticipated deflections in the event of collapse.

In case of separation between two adjacent buildings of the same property, the minimum seismic gap should be as follows:

$$\text{Seismic gap} \geq R_1\Delta_1 + R_2\Delta_2 \tag{12.19a}$$

where, Δ_1 and Δ_2 are maximum absolute elastic lateral deflections of the two adjacent buildings, at the corresponding level, and R_1 and R_2 are the response reductions factors of the two adjacent buildings.

These two adjacent buildings or blocks may or may not belong to the same property. The elastic lateral displacements must include torsional effects.

In case of buildings, or structurally independent units, that do not belong to the same property, the distance from the property line to the potential points of impact should be as follows:

$$\text{Seismic gap} \geq R_1\Delta_1 \tag{12.19b}$$

The Eurocode 1998-part 1 gives the following requirements for protection against pounding:

Buildings shall be protected from earthquake-induced pounding from adjacent structures or between structurally independent units of the same building. This is presumed to have been satisfied:

(a) for buildings, or structurally independent units, that do not belong to the same property, if the distance from the property line to the potential points of impact is not less than the maximum horizontal displacement of the building at the corresponding level

(b) for buildings, or structurally independent units, belonging to the same property, if the distance between them is not less than the square root of the sum of the squares (SRSS) of the maximum horizontal displacements of the two buildings or units at the corresponding level

(c) If the floor elevations of the building or independent unit under design are the same as those of the adjacent building or unit, the above referred minimum distance may be reduced by a factor of 0.7.

The ASCE 7 gives different requirements for storey drifts depending upon the type of structure and risk category. The permissible storey drifts vary from 1% to 2% of the storey height.

12.15 APPENDAGES ON THE ROOF

In a tall building, it is a common practice to provide small tanks, towers, parapets, bill boards, smoke stacks (chimney), cornices, balconies, or ornamentations projecting out of the roof. Such a small cantilever structure may be oriented either vertically or horizontally. The mass and stiffness of such a system is usually very small as compared to that of any floor or roof of the building. If there are '*n*' lateral DOF up to the roof level, then there will be an additional DOF due to the appendage. An eigenvalue analysis will reveal very high lateral displacement at the level of this $(n + 1)^{\text{th}}$ DOF. The stability of the appendage could be a serious issue. Therefore, most building codes require a special attention to the treatment and design of an appendage to the roof. IS 1893-part 1 requires that the vertical appendage must be designed for five times the design horizontal seismic coefficient; while a horizontal appendage (for example, cornices and balconies) must be designed for five times the design vertical seismic coefficient, that is, $5 \times 2/3 = 10/3$ times the design horizontal seismic coefficient. These increased design forces are only for designing the projecting parts and their connections with the main structure. Clause 12.2 of ASCE 7 gives detailed treatment of such appendages.

12.16 ILLUSTRATIVE EXAMPLES

Example 12.1

A 10-storey moment-resistant RC residential building has a plan dimension 20 m × 30 m and has 32 m height above the ground. It is located in Lucknow. Estimate the fundamental period of vibration and base shear coefficient if it is supported on medium soil.

Solution

The fundamental period of vibration can be estimated using the empirical equation given in IS:1893-Part 1 code.

$$T = 0.075\, H^{0.75}$$

$$= 0.075 \times 32^{0.75} = 1 \text{ sec}$$

For a moment-resistant building, the empirical period of vibration is independent of its plan dimensions. Therefore, it will have the same period in both the horizontal directions. Lucknow is located in seismic zone III. The spectral acceleration value S_a/g for 5% damping and 1 sec period can be estimated from the IS:1893 spectra given in Figure 8.27, Chapter 8.

Seismic zone $Z = 0.16, I = 1.0$, and $S_a/g = 1.36$

If the response reduction factor is taken as 5 for a ductile M-R frame building, then

$$\alpha_h = \frac{Z}{2}\frac{I}{R}\frac{S_a}{g} = \frac{0.16}{2} \times \frac{1}{5} \times 1.36$$

or,

$$\alpha_h = 0.02176$$

□

Example 12.2

If the building in Example 12.1 has a period of vibration of 0.6 sec and 0.15 sec in second and third modes of vibrations, estimate the seismic coefficient in these modes.

Solution

The spectral acceleration value S_a/g for 5% damping and 0.6 sec and 0.15 sec periods can be estimated from the IS:1893-Part 1 spectra (Figure 8.27):

$$S_a/g = 1.36/T = 1.36/0.6 = 2.27 \quad \text{for} \quad T = 0.6 \text{ sec}$$

and

$$S_a/g = 2.50 \quad \text{for} \quad T = 0.15 \text{ sec}$$

The seismic coefficient α_h in the 2nd mode is 0.036 and the 3rd mode is 0.04. □

Example 12.3

Find the period of vibration of the shear wall buildings and framed building shown in Figures 12.23(a) and 12.23(b) using the ASCE 7, Eurocode 8 and IS 1893 codal provisions.

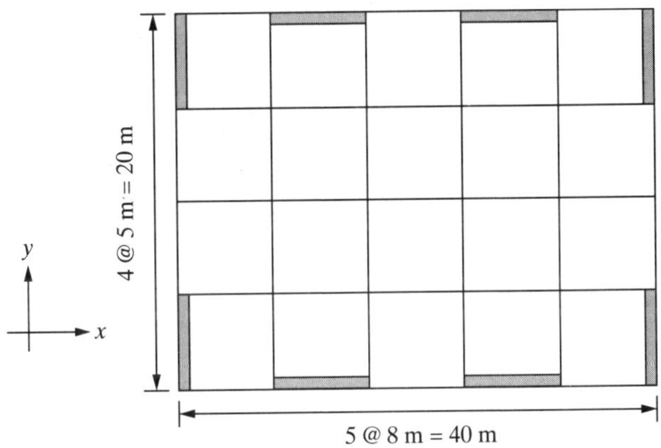

Figure 12.23(a) Shear wall building in plan (wall thickness = 30 cm).

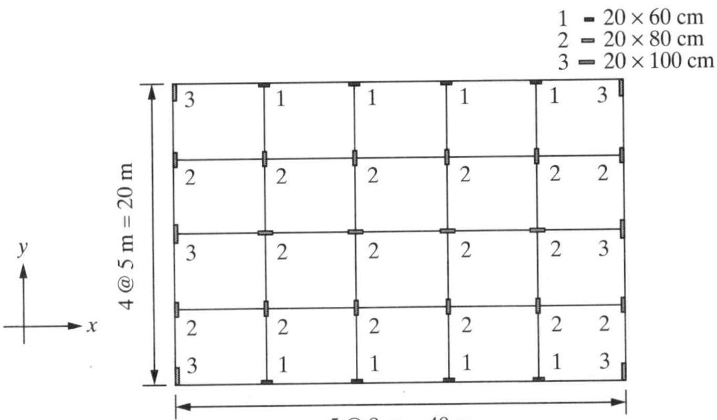

Figure 12.23(b) Framed building in plan.

Solution

In building A, there are 4 shear walls in each direction. In building B, there are large numbers of elongated columns in each direction. These elongated columns fall outside the geometric definition of a column. IS:13920 requires that in a column, the ratio of shortest cross-sectional dimension to the perpendicular dimension is not less than 0.4.
In the present case, in building B, the width of each column = 200 mm.

$$\therefore \quad D < 200/0.4 = 500 \text{ mm.}$$

∴ All elongated columns are to be treated as shear walls in the present case.

ASCE Formula

$$T_a = \frac{0.00058}{\sqrt{C_w}} H_n \tag{12.6a}$$

$$C_w = \frac{100}{A_B} \sum_{i=1}^{x} \left(\frac{H_n}{H_i}\right)^2 \frac{A_i}{\left(1 + 0.83\left(\frac{H_i}{D_i}\right)^2\right)} \tag{12.6b}$$

If height of both the buildings is 30 m and height of all walls and columns is also 30 m, the periods in the x-direction are given as follows:

Building A

$H_n = 30$ m, $H_i = 30$ m, $D_i = 8$ m, $A_B = 40 \times 20 = 800$ m^2, $A_i = 0.3 \times 8 = 2.4$ m^2
$x = 4$
$C_w = 0.095$ and $T = 0.608$ sec

Building B

$H_n = 30$ m, $H_i = 30$ m, $A_B = 40 \times 20 = 800$ m^2
$A_i = 0.2 \times 0.6 = 0.12$ m^2, $D_i = 0.6$ m, $x = 8$ walls
$A_i = 0.2 \times 0.8 = 0.16$ m^2, $D_i = 0.8$ m, $x = 4$ walls
$C_w = 0.00013$ and $T = 1.53$ sec

Eurocode EC8 and IS 1893-1

$$T_a = \frac{0.075}{\sqrt{A_c}} H^{0.75} \tag{12.7a}$$

where,

$$A_c = \sum \left\{ A_i \times \left(0.2 + \left(\frac{l_{wi}}{H}\right)^2\right)\right\} \tag{12.7b}$$

Building A

$H = 30$ m, $l_{wi} = 8$ m, $A_i = 0.3 \times 8 = 2.4$ m^2, no. of walls in x-direction = 4
$A_c = 2.603$, $T = 0.596$ sec

Building B

$H = 30$ m, $l_{wi} = 0.6$ m, $A_i = 0.2 \times 0.6 = 0.12$ m^2, no. of walls in x-direction = 8
$H = 30$ m, $l_{wi} = 0.8$ m, $A_i = 0.2 \times 0.8 = 0.16$ m^2, no. of walls in x-direction = 4
$A_c = 0.32$, $T = 1.70$ sec

A comparison of all the results for these two buildings is shown in Table 12.11.

TABLE 12.11 COMPARISON OF PERIODS, SEC

	ASCE 7	EC 8 / IS:1893-Part 1
Building A	0.608	0.596
Building B	1.53	1.70

The computation of fundamental period of buildings using the empirical equations given in the codes need to be carried out carefully. In the present case, the result are quite close. □

Example 12.4

A 4-storey building having moment-resistant frame with in-fill walls is located in Srinagar, J&K and has the following data:

Floor	Seismic Weight, kN	Storey Height, m
Roof	5500	3.25
3rd	7250	3.25
2nd	7800	3.25
1st	6500	3.75

Its plan dimensions are 15 × 20 m. Determine the base shear if it is located on soft soil and has a special ductile detailing. Also, determine the lateral force acting at each floor.

Solution

Base shear $$V_B = \alpha_h W$$

$$\alpha_h = \frac{Z}{2}\frac{I}{R}\frac{S_a}{g}$$

Fundamental period $$T = \frac{0.09H}{\sqrt{D}}$$

Along the short direction, $T_1 = \dfrac{0.09 \times 13.50}{\sqrt{15}} = 0.314$ sec

Along the long direction, $T_2 = \dfrac{0.09 \times 13.50}{\sqrt{20}} = 0.272$ sec

In case the period of vibration is estimated using Equation (12.3d),

$$T = 0.05\ H^{0.75} = 0.05 \times 13.50^{0.75} = 0.352 \text{ sec}$$

$\therefore\ S_a/g = 2.5$ in both directions since $0.10 \le T \le 0.67$ sec for soft soil
For seismic zone V, $Z = 0.36$, $I = 1.0$, total seismic weight $W = 25250$ kN

Base shear $$V_B = \frac{0.36}{2} \times \frac{1}{5} \times 2.5 \times 25250 = 2272.5 \text{ kN}$$

The vertical distribution of base shear can be determined using the following equation:

$$Q_i - \frac{W_i h_i^2}{\sum_{j=1}^{n} W_j h_j^2} V_B$$

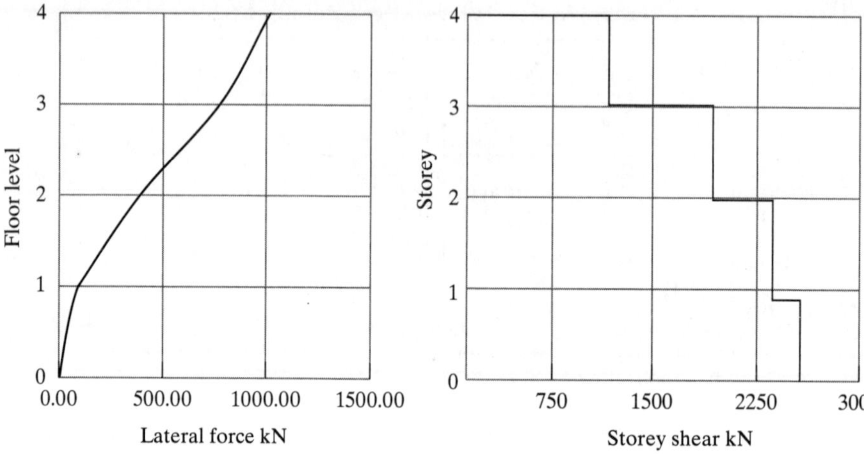

Figure 12.24 Lateral force and storey shears.

The distribution of earthquake force on different floors is shown in Table 12.12.

TABLE 12.12 LATERAL FORCES AND STOREY SHEARS

Floor	W_i kN	h_i m	$W_i h_i^2$	F_i kN	V_i kN
Roof	5500	13.50	1002375	1017.97	1017.97
3rd	7250	10.25	761703	773.55	1791.53
2nd	7800	7.0	382200	388.15	2179.67
1st	6500	3.75	91406	92.83	2272.50
		Σ	2237684	2272.50	

The lateral force and storey shear distributions are shown in Figure 12.24. □

Example 12.5

An industrial steel building (Category 2 as per IS:1893-Part 4) is located in Bhopal on hard rock. Its seismic weight is 15000 kN and period from dynamic analysis is 0.7 sec. Estimate its base shear.

Solution

Bhopal is located in seismic zone II. $Z = 0.10$
As per the frequency analysis, its period is 0.7 sec. It satisfies clause 9.3.

$$\therefore \quad Sa/g = 1/T = 1.428$$

Clause 8.1 of IS:1893-Part 4 defines a Category 2 structure as follows:
Structures whose failure can cause conditions that can lead to direct or indirect serious fire threat or extensive structural damage within the plant complex. Structures, which are required to handle emergencies immediately after an earthquake, also are included.

Table 3 requires that importance factor for Category 2 structure should be taken as 1.5.

Clause 9.4 requires that damping for a steel structure under DBE condition should be taken as 2%.

Table 15 gives the multiplying factor for 2% damping as 1.40.

This industrial building consists of steel moment resistant frame designed in accordance with clause 12.11 of IS:800-2007. It is a special M-R frame. Therefore, response reduction factor R is 5.

For DBE shaking, the design horizontal seismic coefficient α_h shall be estimated as:

$$\alpha_h = \frac{Z}{2} \times \frac{I}{R} \times \frac{S_a}{g}$$

$$\alpha_h = \frac{0.10}{2} \times \frac{1.5}{5} \times 1.428 \times 1.40 = 0.03 \text{ or } 3\%$$

Table 2 of IS:1893-Part 4 requires that an industrial building located in seismic zone II must be designed for a minimum lateral force of 1.5% of its seismic weight.

$$\text{Base shear} = 0.03\text{ W} > 0.015\text{ W} \qquad \text{OK}$$

For MCE shaking, the design horizontal seismic coefficient α_h shall be estimated as:

$$\alpha_h = Z \times \frac{I}{R} \times \frac{S_a}{g}$$

The damping ratio will be taken as 4%. The damping multiplier will be 1.13.

$$\alpha_h = 0.10 \times \frac{1.5}{5} \times 1.428 \times 1.13 = 0.048 \text{ or } 4.8\%$$

□

Example 12.6

A single-storey building is shown in Figure 12.25(a). There are two M-R frames along grid lines A and D with lateral stiffness k and there are two shear walls along grid lines 1 and 4 with lateral stiffness $5k$. Estimate the static lateral forces if the earthquake force acts in y-direction.

Solution

There are two main features of this building:

(a) It carries only self weight of the roof slab. It is a uniformly distributed load. During earthquake, there will be no live load on the roof.

(b) It is symmetric in plan along x-direction but unsymmetric along y-direction. There are two 5 m long walls along y-direction at grid 1-1 and 4-4.

By inspection, the center of mass of the building will be at the center of gravity of the mass on the roof. It will coincide with the geometric center of the plan on grid 3. The center of rigidity will lie midway between grids 1-1 and 4-4 as shown in Figure 12.25(a).

∴ The distance between CM and CR, that is, eccentricity $e = 3$ m along x-direction. Eccentricity along y-direction is zero.

Consider the static lateral force V due to earthquake in y-direction. Design eccentricities are given as follows:

$$e_{da} = 1.5\, e + 0.05\, b \qquad (12.15a)$$

$$e_{db} = e - 0.05\, b \qquad (12.15b)$$

$$b = 24 \text{ m}$$

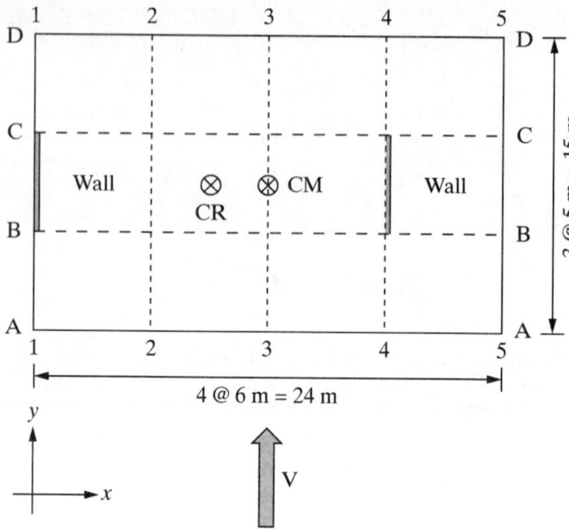

Figure 12.25(a) Plan of a single-storey building.

∴
$$e_{da} = 1.5 \times 3 + 0.05 \times 24 = 5.7 \text{ m}$$
$$e_{db} = 0.5 \times 3 - 0.05 \times 24 = 0.3 \text{ m}$$

Shear due to torsion along each axis resisted by a particular element is proportional to the lateral stiffness of the element relative to the total torsional stiffness of the storey and its distance from the center of rigidity. The total torsional stiffness of the storey I_p about Z-axis passing through the center of rigidity is given by

$$I_p = \sum K_{yi} x_i^2 + \sum K_{xi} y_i^2$$

where K_{xi} is lateral stiffness of element i along x-direction (about y-axis)
K_{yi} is lateral stiffness of element i along y-direction (about x-axis)
I_p is similar to polar moment of inertia of a rivet group about its centroid.

Polar moment of inertia I_p calculation in y-direction

Line	K_y	x, m	$K_y x^2$
1-1	5 k	–9	405 k
4-4	5 k	+9	405 k
			Σ810 k

x is measured from CR to the c.g. of the wall.

Polar moment of inertia I_p calculation in x-direction

Line	K_x	y, m	$K_x y^2$
A-A	k	–7.5	56.25 k
D-D	k	+7.5	56.25 k
			Σ112.5 k

y is measured from CR to the c.g. of the wall.

$\therefore$ Polar moment of inertia $I_p = 810 + 112.5 = 922.5$ k

Consider the frames in the x-direction due to earthquake shear in y-direction:

Additional shear on any frame or column line due to torsion T is given by

$$V'_{xj} = \frac{TK_{xj}y_j}{I_p}$$

where $T = V \times e_x = V \times e_{da} = 5.7$ V anti-clockwise

It should be remembered that the earthquake shear V will act through the center of mass, whereas the resisting shear, equal and opposite to V, will act through the center of rigidity. The torsion will change its direction with the change in the direction of earthquake. At the center of rigidity, there is a net force V and an anti-clockwise moment 5.7 V.

Consider Frame A-A, $e_{da} = 5.7$ m

$$V'_{xA} = \frac{V \times 5.7 \times k \times (-7.5)}{922.5k} = -0.046 \text{ V}$$

and on Frame D-D

$$V'_{xD} = \frac{V \times 5.7 \times k \times (7.5)}{922.5k} = 0.046 \text{ V}$$

Now consider frames in y-direction due to earthquake shear in y-direction:

Additional shear due to torsion $T = Ve_{da}$ is given by

$$V'_{yj} = \frac{TK_{yj}x_j}{I_p}$$

$\therefore$ Net shear

$$V_{yj} = \frac{VK_{yj}}{\sum K_{yj}} \pm V'_{yj}$$

Consider Frame 1-1

$$V_{y1} = \frac{V5k}{10k} - \frac{V \times 5.7 \times 5k \times 9}{922.5k} = (0.50 - 0.278)\,V = 0.222 \text{ V}$$

Frame 4-4

$$V_{y4} = (0.50 + 0.278)V = 0.778 \text{ V}$$

Thus, wall 4–4 carries maximum shear.

Direction of the shear acting on various lateral load-resisting elements

The earthquake direction is reversible. Therefore, the torsion can be assumed to be either clockwise positive or negative. It would not make any difference. The additional shear due to torsion is computed as ± 0.278 V. Thus, under an anti-clockwise torsion, the forces on the Frames 1-1 and 4-4 will look as shown in Figure 12.25(b), and under a clockwise torsion, the forces will look as shown in Figure 12.25(c). In any case, Frame 4-4 will continue to carry more shear, that is equal to 0.778 V.

The total shears on each of the four lateral force resisting elements are shown in Figure 12.25(d) under an anti-clockwise torsion.

Similarly, calculations for $e_{db} = 0.3$ m can be made. □

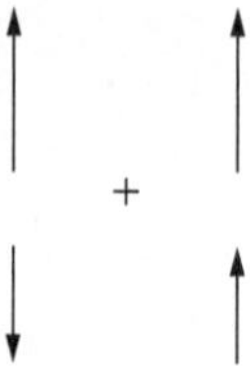

Figure 12.25(b)

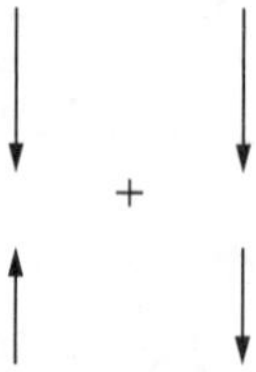

Figure 12.25(c)

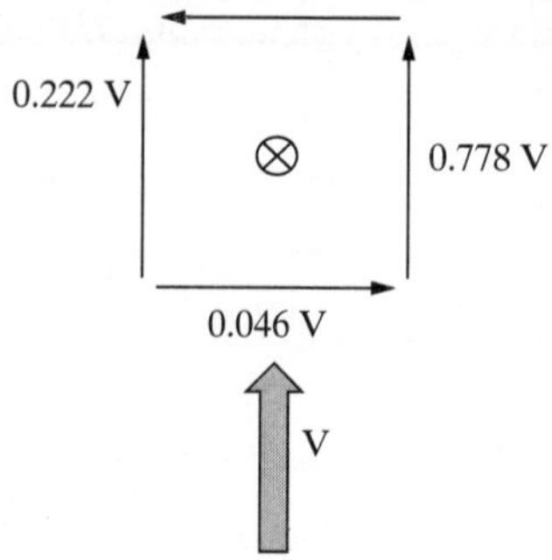

Figure 12.25(d) Total lateral shears on frames/walls.

Example 12.7

A single-storey RC frame building is shown in Figure 12.26. It is enclosed with 230 mm thick brick masonry walls on three sides up to 3 m high and 16 no. RC columns 230 × 230 mm and 3.9 m high. There are 230 × 450 mm deep beams along A-A, B-B, C-C and D-D. The slab thickness is 125 mm and water proofing layer is 100 mm thick over the slab. A section *x-x* through the wall is shown in Figure 12.26(b). Analyse the building for torsion and short column effects in seismic zone IV assuming ductile RC frames. The building is resting on hard soil.

Solution

There are two main features of this building:

(a) It is unsymmetric in plan about *x*-axis, therefore, it carries torsion when the earthquake force acts along *x*-direction.

(b) The columns along the periphery will act as short column of 0.9 m height because they are restrained by the masonry walls.

Let us estimate the static forces in these columns by taking the effect of torsion and short column effect.

Dead load

Density of brick masonry = 20 kN/m^3

Density of concrete = 25 kN/m^3

Density of water proofing material = 20 kN/m^3

Dead load of roof = $0.125 \times 25 + 0.10 \times 20 = 5.125$ kN/m^2

∴ Total dead load of roof = $5.125 \times 12 \times 12 = 738$ kN

Weight of 230 mm wall = $0.23 \times 12 \times 3 \times 20 = 165.6$ kN

∴ Total weight of 3 walls = $3 \times 165.6 = 497$ kN

Beams, 4 no. = $0.325 \times 0.23 \times 12 \times 25 \times 4 = 89.7$ kN

3.9 m high columns, 6 no. = $0.23 \times 0.23 \times 3.9 \times 25 \times 6 = 31$ kN

0.9 m high columns, 10 no. = $0.23 \times 0.23 \times 0.9 \times 25 \times 10 = 11.9$ kN

∴ Total weight of building = 1370 kN

Although all the 16 columns are in RCC and 9.3 m high, the weight of 10 columns enclosed within the masonry is included in the weight of the walls. There will be slight error on account of difference in material density but it can be ignored.

Seismic weight = $738 + 0.5 \times 497 + 89.7 + 11.9 + 0.5 \times 31 = 1200$ kN

Period of building = 0.1 sec

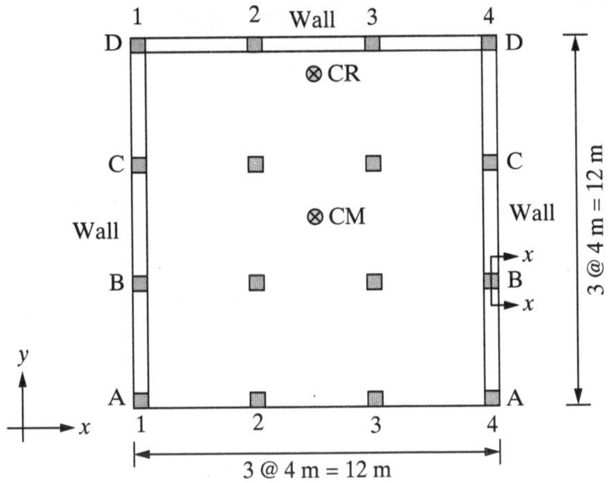

Figure 12.26(a) Plan of a single-storey building.

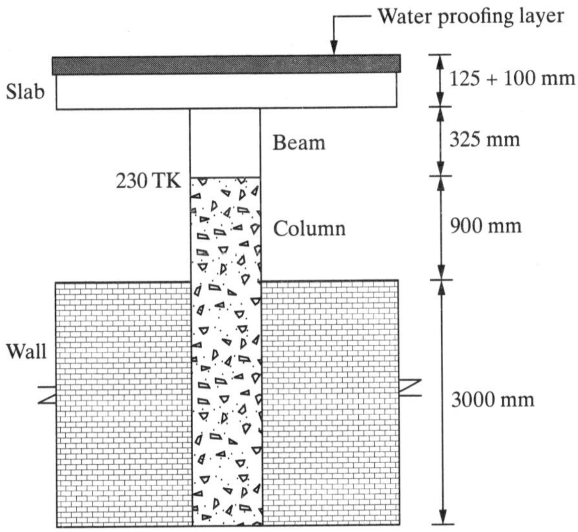

Figure 12.26(b) Section through x-x.

Base shear $$V_B = \frac{Z}{2}\frac{I}{R}\frac{S_a}{g}W_{\text{effective}}$$

For zone IV, $Z = 0.24$, $I = 1.25$, $R = 4$ for ductile M-R frame although the code permits $R = 5$.

For 5% damping, $S_a/g = 2.5$

$$\therefore \quad \text{Base shear} = \frac{0.24}{2}\times\frac{1.25}{4}\times 2.50\times 1200 = 112.5 \text{ say } 120 \text{ kN}$$

Let us consider earthquake force along y-axis.

The building is symmetric about the y-axis. Hence, lateral force on each frame along 1-1 and 4-4 will be 60 kN each as shown in Figure 12.26(c).

By visual inspection, the center of mass CM will be at the center of gravity of the building while the center of rigidity CR will lie at mid center of D-D.

Thus, eccentricity e = 6 m. Let us take it as a design eccentricity also for the purpose of this example.

If the earthquake force acts along *x*-axis, there will be a torsion equal to $120 \times 6 =$ 720 kNm

It will be resisted by the three masonry walls being very stiff. The equilibrium of forces is shown in Figure 12.26(c). Now member forces in Frame D-D can be computed manually or by using any software for the forces shown in Figure 12.26(d).

Area of cross-section of a column = $0.23 \times 0.23 = 0.0530$ m^2

Moment of inertia of a column I = 2.33×10^{-4} m^4

Area of cross-section of a beam = $0.23 \times 0.45 = 0.1035$ m^2

Moment of inertia of a beam I = 17.46×10^{-4} m^4

Modulus of elasticity $E = 5000\sqrt{25} = 25000$ MPa for M25 concrete

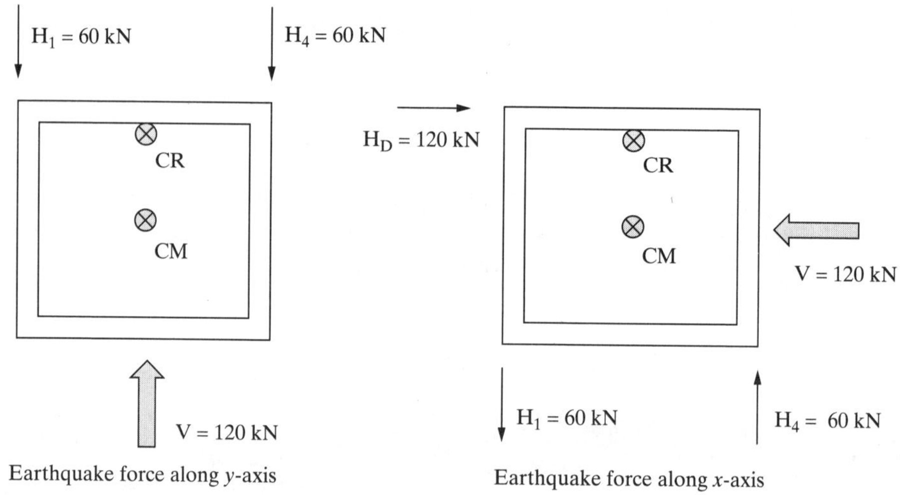

Figure 12.26(c) Earthquake shear and equilibrium forces.

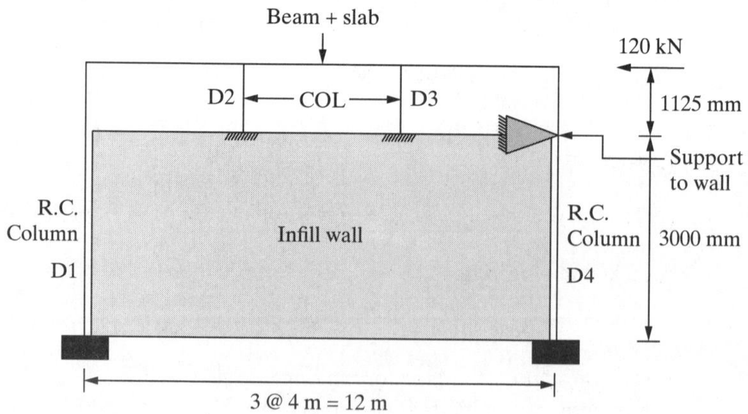

Figure 12.26(d) Frame D-D in elevation.

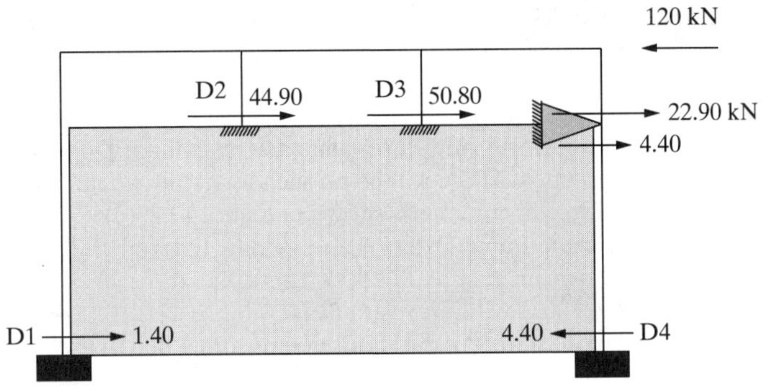

Figure 12.26(e) Forces acting on Frame D-D with short column action.

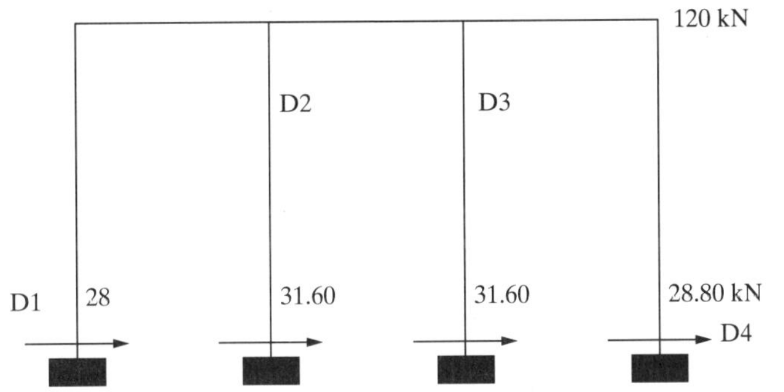

Figure 12.26(f) Forces acting on Frame D-D – without short column action.

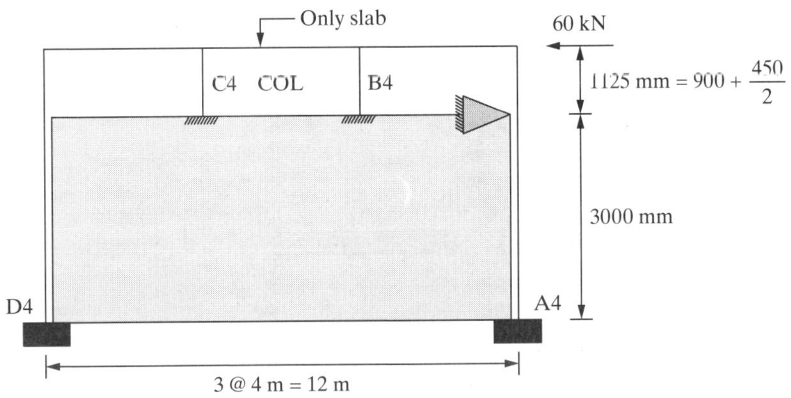

Figure 12.26(g) Frame D-A.

Moment of inertia of slab (width = 3 Depth) $I = (12.5 \times 3) \times 12.5^3/12 = 6100\ cm^4$

or, $$I = 0.61 \times 10^{-4}\ m^4$$

Frame D1-D4 as shown in Figure 12.26(d) can be analysed using the above data. It should be noted that the wall will offer a restraint to the column D4 when the frame wants to deflect along x-direction. There will be no such restraint to column D1.

The shear force in columns is shown in Figure 12.26(e).

Now if the same frame D1-D4 is analysed by ignoring the masonry walls, the member forces are shown in Figure 12.26(f). The shear force in column D3 with masonry restraint is 50.8 kN and without restraint is 31.6 kN. The increase in shear due to short column effect is 61%. Similarly, the short column effect due to the masonry walls on frame A4-D4 as shown in Figure 12.26(g) can be estimated.

The short column effect in earthquakes is a very common form of failure in buildings in most earthquakes all over the world. □

Example 12.8

A 4-storey steel frame is shown in Figure 12.27. It is located in seismic zone V on soft soil. The super imposed dead load SIDL on each floor is 10 kN/m and on the roof is 5 kN/m. Determine the member forces due to earthquake using dynamic analysis in IS:1893-Part 1 code.

Solution

$$\text{Moment of inertia of columns } I = \begin{Bmatrix} 30390 \\ 30390 \\ 45218 \\ 64893 \end{Bmatrix} cm^4$$

Modulus of elasticity of steel = 200 GPa = 200000 MPa

Mass calculation

Let us first consider mass of the top floor

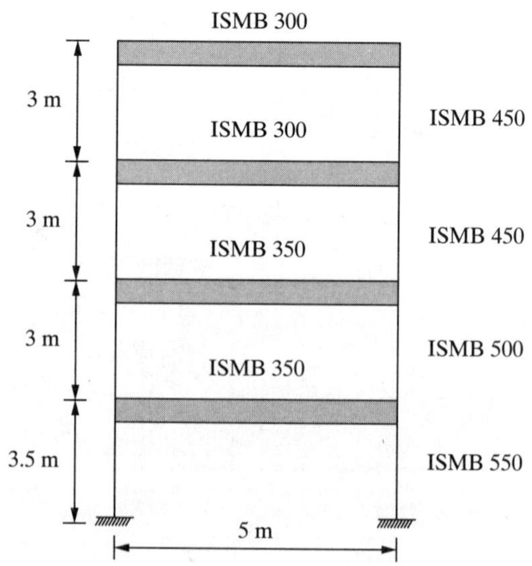

Figure 12.27 Steel frame.

Beam – ISMB 300 – Area = 5.626×10^{-3} m^2, weight density = 76.97 kN/m^3
Column – ISMB 450 – Area = 9.227×10^{-3} m^2, weight density = 76.97 kN/m^3
SIDL = 5 kN/m

The span of beam is 5 m, and there are two columns of 3 m height. However, only 1.5 m height will contribute towards mass on the roof.
Contribution of mass from ISMB 300 = $5.626 \times 10^{-3} \times 76.97 \times 5/9.81 = 0.22$ kN-s^2/m
Contribution of mass from ISMB 450 = $9.227 \times 10^{-3} \times 76.97 \times (3/2) \times 2/9.81 = 0.22$ kN-s^2/m
Contribution of mass from SIDL = $5 \times 5/9.81 = 2.548$ kN-s^2/m
Total mass on roof = $2.988 \approx 3.0$ kN-s^2/m
Similarly, mass on other floors can be calculated.

$$\text{Mass } \{M\} = \begin{Bmatrix} 3.0 \\ 6.0 \\ 6.0 \\ 6.0 \end{Bmatrix} \text{ kN-s}^2\text{/m}$$

Now the stiffness matrix of the frame can be assembled using the procedure described in Chapter 10. It has four lateral degrees of freedom, that is one translation per floor. Node numbers in the frame are shown in Figure 12.28. Its frequency and mode shapes can be determined using the procedure explained in Chapter 10. Alternatively, the frame can be analysed using a stiffness matrix-based software. The mode shapes are shown in Figures 12.29.

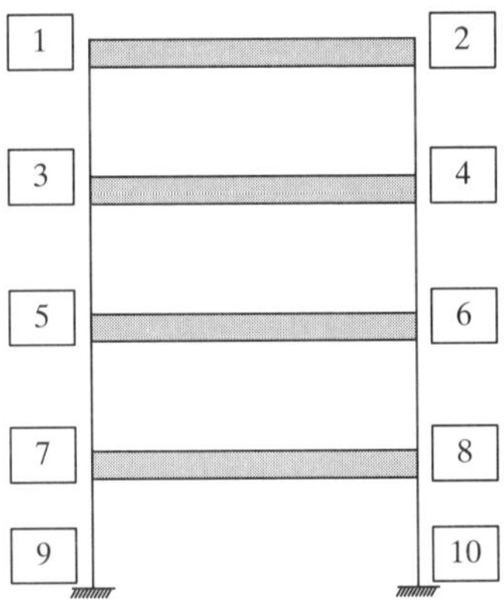

Figure 12.28 Node numbers.

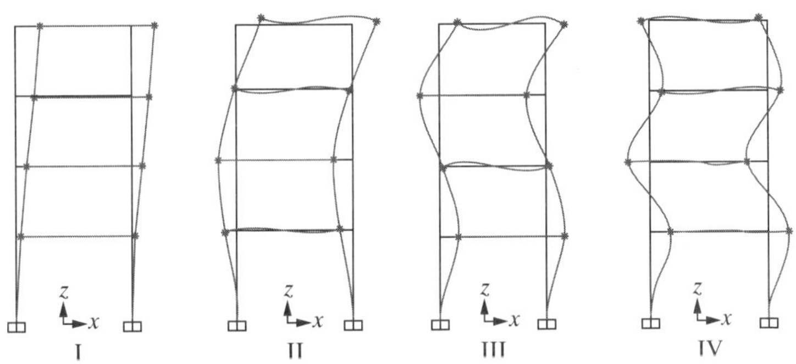

Figure 12.29 Mode shapes.

$$\text{Period } \{T\} = \begin{Bmatrix} 0.39 \\ 0.12 \\ 0.06 \\ 0.038 \end{Bmatrix} \text{sec} \quad \text{Mode shapes } \Phi = \begin{bmatrix} 1 & 1 & 1 & 1 \\ 0.769 & -0.099 & -1.011 & -1.700 \\ 0.464 & -0.749 & 0.168 & 2.723 \\ 0.177 & -0.490 & 0.966 & -2.698 \end{bmatrix}$$

Clause 7.6.2 of IS:1893-Part 1 for moment resistant steel buildings gives,

$$T = 0.085\, H^{0.75}$$

$$T = 0.085 \times 12.5^{0.75} = 0.565 \text{ sec}$$

The eigenvalue analysis is giving a lower period of vibration as compared to that of the empirical formula. In many other cases, it has been noted that the empirical formula gives a lower period. Let us calculate its modal mass, mode participation factors and spectral acceleration for 2% damping using the IS:1893-Part 1 response spectra.

Mode participation factor $\Gamma_r = \dfrac{\sum m_i \phi_i}{\sum m_i \phi_i^2}$

This can be done in a tabular form for convenience. The calculations are shown in Table 12.13.

$Z = 0.36$, $R = 5.0$ for a special M-R frame, $I = 1.0$, damping factor = 1.40

$$\alpha_h = \frac{Z}{2}\frac{I}{R}\frac{S_a}{g} = \frac{0.36}{2}\times\frac{1}{5}\times\frac{S_a}{g} = 0.036\frac{S_a}{g}$$

Mode participation factor in mode 1 = 11.47/8.03 = 1.4274
Mode participation factor in mode 2 = –5.04/7.87 = –0.6396
Mode participation factor in mode 3 = 3.74/14.89 = 0.2509
Mode participation factor in mode 4 = –7.05/108.54 = –0.065

$$\text{Modal mass} = \frac{\left(\sum_{i=1}^{n} m_i \phi_i\right)^2}{\sum_{i=1}^{n} m_i \phi_i^2}$$

Modal mass in mode 1 = $(11.47)^2/8.03 = 16.37$
Modal mass in mode 2 = $(5.04)^2/7.87 = 3.22$
Modal mass in mode 3 = $(3.74)^2/14.89 = 0.937$
Modal mass in mode 4 = $(7.05)^2/108.54 = 0.458$
Total modal mass = 20.99 = Total mass of the frame OK
Corresponding to periods of vibration in different modes, the values of spectral accelerations are obtained from the response spectra of IS:1893-Part 1 for 2% damping and shown in Table 12.14.

$\alpha_0 = \Gamma \alpha_h 1.4g = 0.036(S_a/g)\Gamma 1.4g$ can be computed for each mode.

Now modal forces at each floor can be computed for each mode as shown in Table 12.15.

These floor modal forces are shown in Figure 12.30 for each mode for a clear understanding of the magnitude and direction of forces. A static analysis of the frame is carried out in each mode and the member forces are determined using a software. These member forces are shown in Table 12.16.

Next, SRSS values of member forces are computed by combining the member forces in each mode for each force component individually. SRSS values for bending moment in beams and columns are shown in Table 12.16. The moment in right-hand columns of the

TABLE 12.13 MODAL MASS AND MODE PARTICIPATION FACTORS

		Mode 1			Mode 2			Mode 3			Mode 4		
Floor	m_i	ϕ_i	$m_i\phi_i$	$m_i\phi_i^2$	ϕ_i	$m_i\phi_i$	$m_i\phi_i^2$	ϕ_i	$m_i\phi_i$	$m_i\phi_i^2$	ϕ_i	$m_i\phi_i$	$m_i\phi_i^2$
Top	3	1.00	3.00	3.00	1.00	3.00	3.00	1.00	3.00	3.00	1.00	3.00	3.00
3rd	6	0.77	4.62	3.55	−0.10	−0.60	0.06	−1.01	−6.06	6.13	−1.70	−10.20	17.34
2nd	6	0.46	2.79	1.29	−0.75	−4.50	3.37	0.17	1.01	0.17	2.72	16.34	44.51
1st	6	0.18	1.07	0.19	−0.49	−2.94	1.44	0.97	5.79	5.59	−2.70	−16.19	43.69
	Σ		11.47	8.03		−5.04	7.87		3.74	14.89		−7.05	108.54

TABLE 12.14 SPECTRAL VALUES

Mode	Period T sec	S_a/g	MPF = Γ	$\Gamma \times S_a/g$	$\alpha_0 = \Gamma \times \alpha_h \times 1.4 \times g$
1	0.39	2.5	1.42	3.550	1.755
2	0.12	2.5	–0.64	–1.600	–0.791
3	0.06	1.9	0.25	0.475	0.235
4	0.038	1.57	–0.065	–0.102	–0.051

$g = 9.81$ m/s^2

TABLE 12.15 MODAL FORCES

		Mode 1		Mode 2		Mode 3		Mode 4	
Floor	m_i	ϕ_i	$\phi_i\alpha_0 m_i$	ϕ_i	$\phi_i\alpha_0 m_i$	ϕ_i	$\phi_i\alpha_0 m_i$	ϕ_i	$\phi_i\alpha_0 m_i$
Roof	3	1.000	5.27	1.000	–2.37	1.000	0.70	1.000	–0.15
3	6	0.769	8.10	–0.099	0.47	–1.011	–1.42	–1.700	0.51
2	6	0.464	4.89	–0.750	3.56	0.168	0.24	2.724	–0.82
1	6	0.178	1.87	–0.491	2.33	0.965	1.36	–2.698	0.82

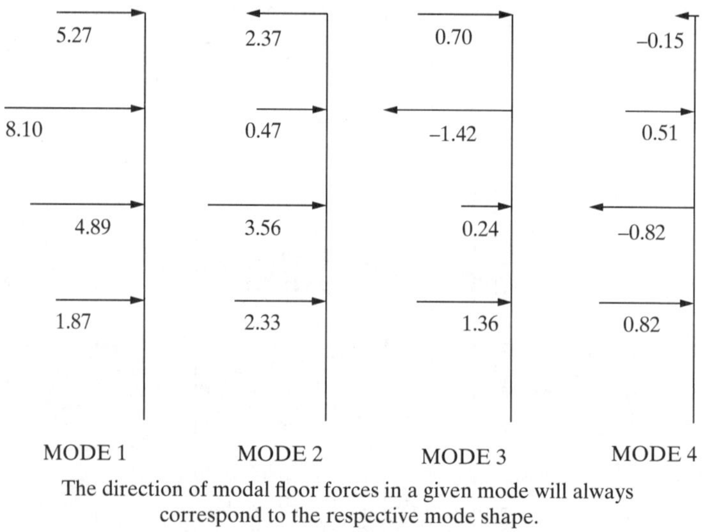

Figure 12.30 Floor modal forces (kN).

TABLE 12.16 BENDING MOMENT IN MEMBERS AT NODE I

Member ID		Node	Mode 1	Mode 2	Mode 3	Mode 4	SRSS Value
Beam	1–2	1	7.61	–1.72	0.28	–0.04	7.81
	3–4	3	11.23	–1.67	0.02	0.04	11.35
	5–6	5	19.16	–0.19	–0.33	–0.02	19.17
	7–8	7	15.69	1.44	0.03	–0.02	15.75

(Continued)

TABLE 12.16 (CONTINUED)

Member ID		Node	Mode 1	Mode 2	Mode 3	Mode 4	SRSS Value
Column	1–3	1	7.61	–1.72	0.28	–0.04	7.81
		3	–0.20	1.84	–0.83	0.21	2.04
	3–5	3	11.03	0.17	–0.81	0.25	11.06
		5	–9.13	3.07	0.32	–0.37	9.65
	5–7	5	10.03	2.89	–0.01	–0.38	10.44
		7	–17.34	0.37	0.74	0.39	17.37
	7–9	7	–1.66	1.81	0.77	0.38	2.60
		9	–36.92	–5.27	–0.85	–0.33	37.30

+ve moment: Clockwise; –ve moment: anti-clockwise.

TABLE 12.17 FINAL BENDING MOMENT IN MEMBERS, KNM

				SRSS Value	Net Moment	
Member Number		Node	SIDL	±	SIDL+SRSS	SIDL–SRSS
Beam	1–2	1	–9.70	7.81	–1.90	17.52
	3–4	3	–20.00	11.35	–8.72	31.43
	5–6	5	–19.90	19.17	–0.75	39.08
	7–8	7	–20.0	15.75	–4.26	35.77
Column	1–3	1	9.70	7.81	–1.90	17.52
		3	10.0	2.04	12.06	–7.98
	3–5	3	10.0	11.06	1.01	21.12
		5	8.98	9.65	18.64	0.66
	5–7	5	10.93	10.44	–0.48	21.37
		7	10.38	17.37	27.74	6.99
	7–9	7	9.64	2.60	–7.04	12.24
		9	4.09	37.30	41.39	33.22

Moments due to dead load of the frame are also to be tabulated.

frame can be obtained by anti-symmetry in each mode. The SRSS values in right-hand side columns will be the same as on the left-hand side columns of the frame.

Next, the gravity load member forces are combined with those of the earthquake forces as shown in Table 12.17. The earthquake force is reversal. Therefore, each member will be designed for both maximum sagging and maximum hogging forces.

The following observations can be made in the various results presented in this problem:

1. The role of dynamic analysis is to determine the frequency and mode shapes of the structure and then estimate spectral accelerations in each mode. Modal forces can be computed in each mode.
2. Now onwards, the remaining analysis is purely static. Static analysis of the frame is carried out for each mode and member forces are determined. The floor forces are to be applied in appropriate directions. The static equilibrium of forces is satisfied at each joint in each mode.

3. The contribution of higher modes in member forces keeps decreasing depending upon the mode participation factors.
4. SRSS value is computed for each force component in each member. Each SRSS value is absolute. Similarly, SRSS value is also computed for each displacement component.
5. Since earthquake force is reversible, the SRSS values are added and subtracted from the gravity forces to get a set of two forces for each member. The static equilibrium of joints gets lost at this stage because of mode superposition.
6. The shape of bending moment diagram for the frame in each mode depends upon the relative stiffness of the various members.
7. The absolute bending moment, shear force and axial force in each member due to earthquake force depend upon the contributory area of each frame from the earthquake point of view. Larger the contributory area, larger will be the member forces and the displacements. The frame may require special considerations in order to limit the lateral displacements.
8. The storey shears can be estimated from the corresponding column shears in each mode and then superimposed.
9. Appropriate load combinations must be considered as per the relevant codal provisions. Also, for limit state design, appropriate partial safety factors must be considered.
10. Each member must be designed for the worst set of forces. □

Example 12.9

In a four storey building, modal floor forces were computed as shown in Table 12.18. Determine the storey shears and base shear.

Solution

The modal storey shears are computed from the modal floor forces as shown in Table 12.18.

TABLE 12.18 COMPUTATION OF MODAL STOREY SHEARS KN

Floor	Mode 1		Mode 2		Mode 3		Mode 4	
	Modal floor force	Modal storey shear	Modal floor force	Modal storey shear	Modal floor force	Modal storey shear	Modal floor force	Modal storey shear
Top	42.2	42.2	–18.4	–18.4	5.6	5.6	–1.34	–1.34
3rd	32.4	74.5	2	–16.4	–5.68	–0.08	2.1	0.76
2nd	19.56	94.06	14.25	–2.15	1	0.92	–3.5	–2.74
1st	7.48	101.54	9.32	7.17	5.44	6.36	4.5	1.76

The peak storey shears are computed using SRSS technique from the modal storey shears as shown in Table 12.19. Peak floor forces are computed from the peak storey shears. The base shear is 102 kN.

An incorrect way to compute peak storey shears from peak floor forces are shown in Table 12.20. It gives the base shear as 117.87 kN. It is 15.6% higher than that obtained in Table 12.19. In this approach the sign of the modal floor forces is lost, hence, a higher storey shears. A peak response value cannot be computed from another peak response value.

TABLE 12.19 COMPUTATION OF PEAK STOREY SHEARS

Storey	Peak Storey Shears	SRSS	Peak Floor force
Top	sqrt $(42.2^2 + 18.4^2 + 5.6^2 + 1.34^2)$	46.39	46.39
3rd	sqrt $(74.5^2 + 16.4^2 + 0.08^2 + 0.76^2)$	76.28	29.89
2nd	sqrt $(94.06^2 + 2.15^2 + 0.92^2 + 2.74^2)$	94.12	18.04
1st	sqrt $(101.54^2 + 7.17^2 + 6.36^2 + 1.76^2)$	102	7.88

TABLE 12.20 INCORRECT WAY TO CALCULATE PEAK STOREY SHEARS, KN

Floor	Peak Floor Force	SRSS	Peak Storey Shears
Top	sqrt $(42.2^2 + 18.4^2 + 5.6^2 + 1.34^2)$	46.39	46.39
3rd	sqrt$(32.4^2 + 2^2 + 5.68^2 + 2.1^2)$	33.02	79.41
2nd	sqrt $(19{,}56^2 + 14.25^2 + 1^2 + 3.5^2)$	24.47	103.88
1st	sqrt $(7.68^2 + 9.32^2 + 5.44^2 + 4.5^2)$	13.99	117.87

Example 12.10

A 20-storey office building has a floor plan as shown in Figure 12.31(a) and basement plan as shown in Figure 12.31(b). It is symmetric in both directions in plan as well as in elevation. It has two basements as shown in Figure 12.31(c). Determine the points of application of the earthquake force.

Solution

Its plan dimension = 42 m × 26 m, columns are placed @ 8 m c/c. Column size = 800 × 800 mm.

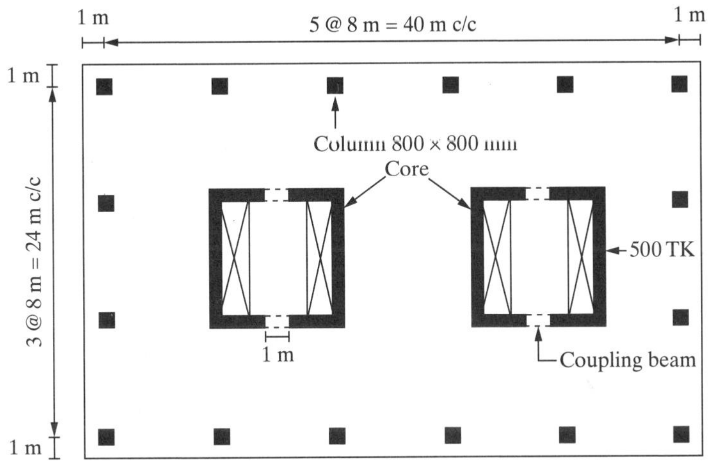

Figure 12.31(a) Building plan.

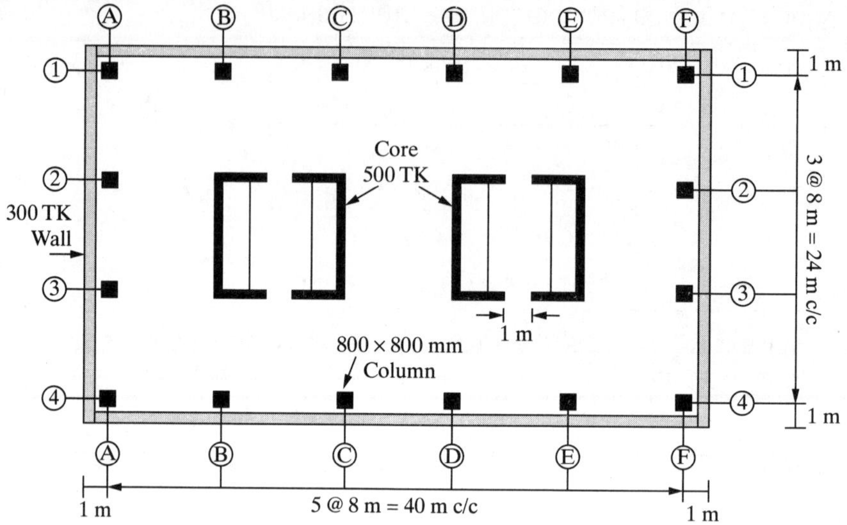

Figure 12.31(b) Basement plan.

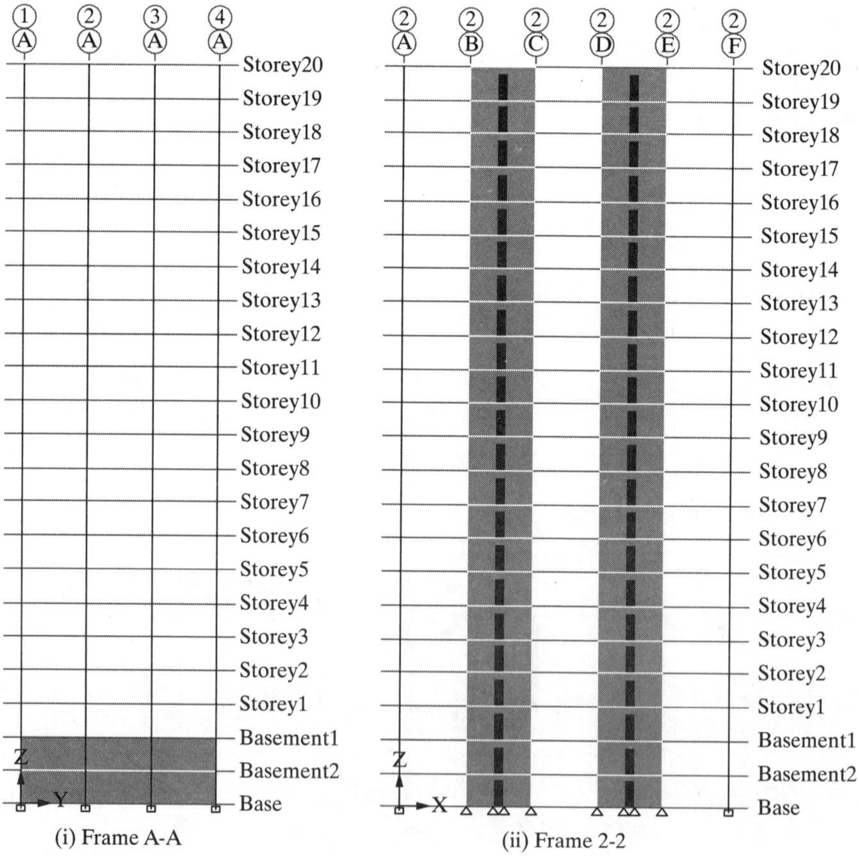

Figure 12.31(c) Sectional elevation.

Slab size = 250 mm thick; coupling beam thickness = 1.25 m, Core wall thickness = 500 mm, door opening = 1 m, storey height = 4 m, total height = 80 m above the ground level. There are no beams.

A 3D dynamic analysis will be carried out to determine the member forces under various loads and load combinations. Lateral load is resisted by the core walls in both directions.

The center of mass of the building is at its axis of symmetry about both directions. Although the building is symmetric, it will still experience accidental torsion. The design eccentricity is given by

$$E_d = \pm\, 0.05b \text{ because } e = 0 \text{ due to symmetry.}$$

If the earthquake force acts normal to the 42 m face, design eccentricity = $0.05 \times 42 = 2.1$ m
If the earthquake force acts normal to the 26 m face, design eccentricity = $0.05 \times 26 = 1.3$ m
Thus, a set of six 3D dynamic analyses will be carried out as follows:

Earthquake force along x-direction (that is normal to 26 m face)
Case 1: No change in the center of mass and carry out the response spectrum analysis
Case 2: Shift the center of mass along y-direction by +1.3 m and carry out the response spectrum analysis
Case 3: Shift the center of mass along y-direction by –1.3 m and carry out the response spectrum analysis

Earthquake force along y-direction (that is normal to 42 m face)
Case 1: No change in the center of mass and carry out the response spectrum analysis
Case 2: Shift the center of mass along x-direction by +2.1 m and carry out the response spectrum analysis
Case 3: Shift the center of mass along x-direction by –2.1 m and carry out the response spectrum analysis

Carry out the load combination analysis with appropriate load factors as per the relevant code (IS:456, IS:1893). Get member forces from all load combinations. The worst load combination for each member will govern its design. □

Example 12.11

Determine the lateral forces in the 20-storey office building shown in Figure 12.31 as per IS:1893-Part 1 if it is situated in seismic zone III. Assume hard soil.

Solution

Floor slab thickness = 250 mm
Column size = 800 × 800 mm
Basement wall thickness = 300 mm
Superimposed dead load on each floor = 2.5 kN/m^2
Live load = 3 kN/m^2
Lateral load resisting system along x-direction = core walls and coupling beams
Lateral load resisting system along y-direction = core walls only
Typical floor area = $26 \times 42 = 1092$ m^2
Total area of columns = $0.8 \times 0.8 \times 16$ no. = 10.24 m^2
Coupling beam size = 0.5 m wide × 1.25 m deep × 1 m long
Core wall thickness = 500 mm
Area of core walls = $8 \times 8 \times 0.5 - 4 \times 1 \times 0.5 = 30$ m^2
Grade of concrete = M30

Item	Dead Load, kN	Live Load, kN
Floor slab	$1092 \times 0.25 \times 25 = 6825$	$1092 \times 3 = 3276$
Columns	$10.24 \times 4 \times 25 = 1024$	
Core walls	$30 \times 4 \times 25 = 3000$	

Total dead load per floor = 6825 + 1024 + 3000 + 1092 × 2.5 (SIDL) = 13579 kN
Total live load on roof = nil
Total live load per floor = 1092 × 3 = 3276 kN

Floor	Elevation, m	Load, kN
Roof	80	13579 (DL)
Floors 2 to 19	4 to 76	13579 + 3276 = 16855 (DL + LL)
Ground floor	0	13579 + 3276 = 16855 (DL + LL)
Basement 1	–4	13579 + 3276 = 16855 (DL + LL)
Basement 2	–8	

Seismic weight $W = 13579 + 13579 \times 19 + 3276 \times 19 \times 0.25 = 287141$ kN (only 25% of live load)
Zone factor $Z = 0.16$, importance factor $I = 1.0$, Response reduction factor $R = 3$ assuming it to be an ordinary shear wall framed building.

Period of vibration $T = \dfrac{0.075}{\sqrt{A_c}} H^{0.75}$

$$A_c = \sum_{i=1} \left\{ A_i \times \left[0.2 + \left(\frac{l_{wi}}{H} \right)^2 \right] \right\}$$

Along x-direction
Area of each shear wall $A_i = (8 - 1) \times 0.5 = 3.5\ \text{m}^2$
Length of each shear wall = 8 – 1 = 7 m

$$A_c = 4\left\{ 3.5 \times \left[0.2 + \left(\frac{7}{80} \right)^2 \right] \right\} = 2.907 \quad T_x = \frac{0.075}{\sqrt{2.907}} \times 80^{0.75} = 1.18\ \text{sec}; \quad S_a/g = 0.847$$

Along y-direction
Area of each shear wall $A_i = 8 \times 0.5 = 4\ \text{m}^2$
Length of each shear wall = 8 m

$$A_c = 4\left\{ 4 \times \left[0.2 + \left(\frac{8}{80} \right)^2 \right] \right\} = 3.36 \quad T_y = \frac{0.075}{\sqrt{3.36}} \times 80^{0.75} = 1.09\ \text{sec}; \quad S_a/g = 0.917$$

Seismic coefficient along x-direction, $\alpha_{hx} = \dfrac{0.16}{2} \times \dfrac{1}{3} \times 0.847 = 0.023$

Seismic coefficient along y-direction, $\alpha_{hy} = \dfrac{0.16}{2} \times \dfrac{1}{3} \times 0.917 = 0.025$

Base shear in x-direction $V_{bx} = 0.023 \times 287141 = 6600$ kN
Base shear in y-direction $V_{by} = 0.025 \times 287141 = 7178 \approx 7200$ kN

A 3D dynamic analysis was carried out and the periods of vibrations in the first 12 modes are as shown in the table.

Mode	1	2	3	4	5	6	7	8	9	10	11	12
Period, sec	2.642	2.62	1.023	0.45	0.445	0.321	0.178	0.176	0.175	0.116	0.102	0.101

The lateral force distribution in the *x*- and *y*-directions is shown in Figures 12.32(a), and storey shear is shown in Figure 12.32(b). The contribution of each mode in the total base shear is shown in Figure 12.32(c).
There are four important observations:

1. The contribution of basements that are underground is not considered in the calculation of seismic weight.
2. Only 25% contribution of live load is considered if it is less than or equal to 3 kN/m^2
3. The seismic base shear computed at the ground floor must be transferred to the lowest basement floor and thereby to the foundation
4. The periods of vibration are too close in modes 1–2, 4–5, 7–8 and 11–12. These will qualify for closely spaced modes. Therefore, mode superposition in dynamic analysis must be carried out using CQC method rather than SRSS method. □

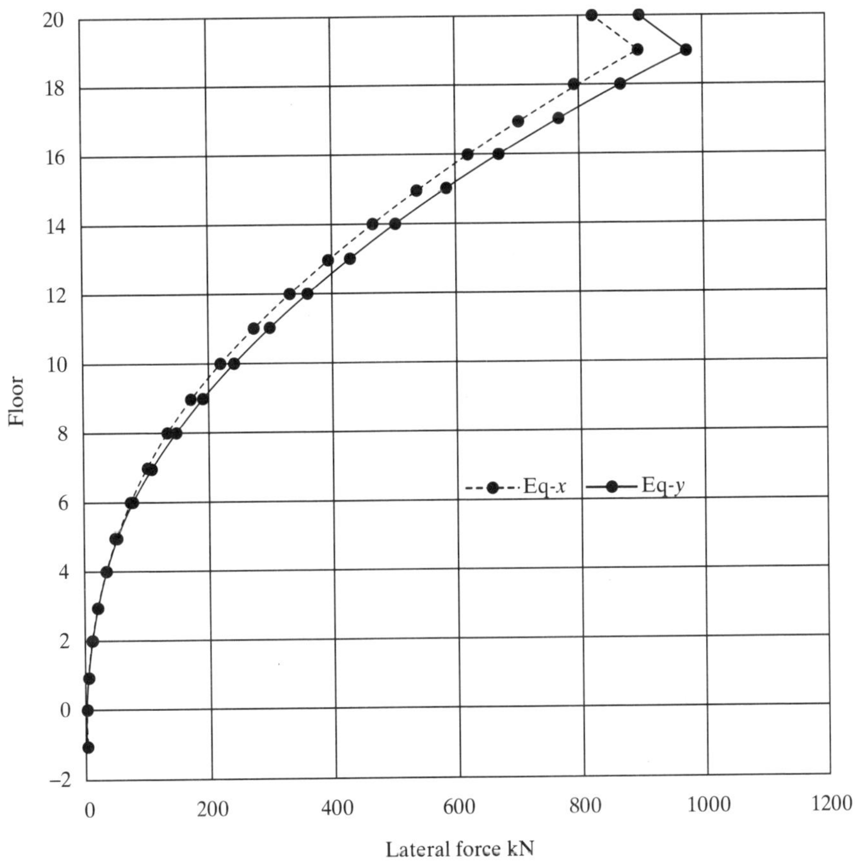

Figure 12.32(a) Lateral force distribution, kN.

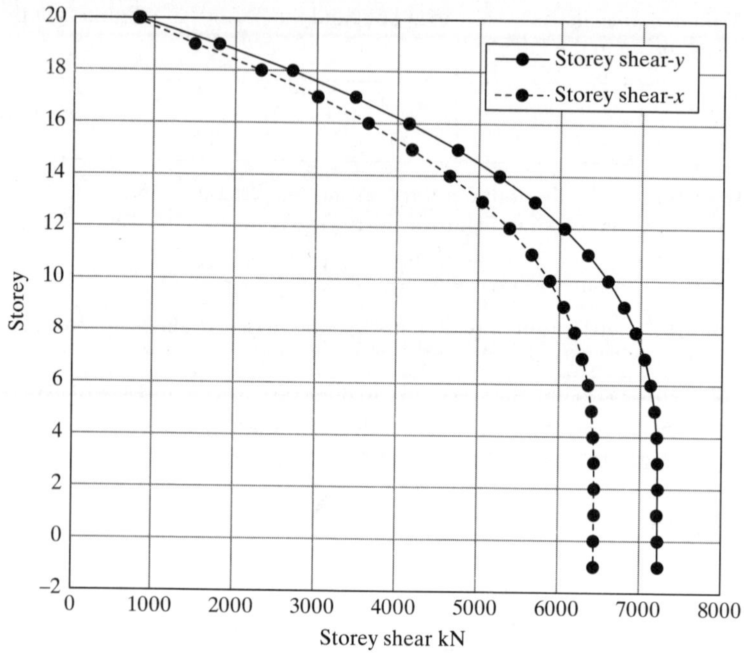

Figure 12.32(b) Storey shear distribution, kN.

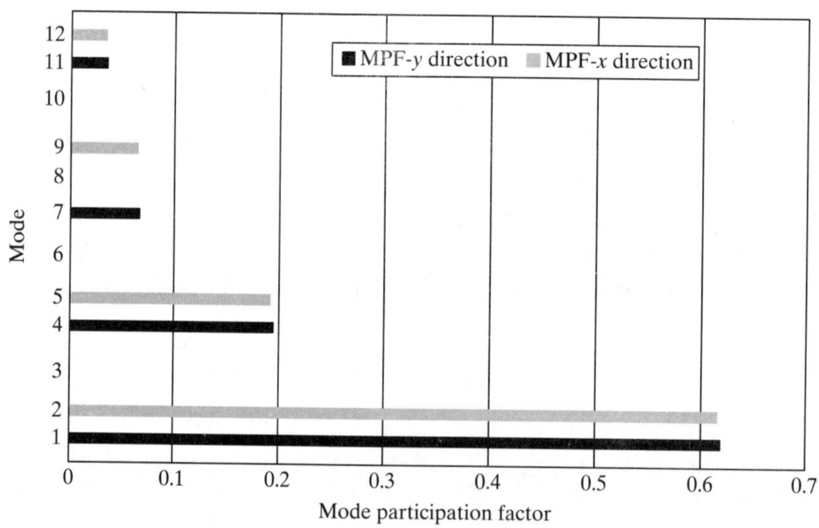

Figure 12.32(c) Contribution of different modes in x- and y-directions.

Example 12.12

A 4-storey building is shown in Figure 10.12. Determine the frequencies, mode shapes, mode participation factors, and storey shears using the absolute and SRSS techniques. The spectral displacements can be determined using the El Centro May 1940 response spectra for 5% damping as shown in Figure 12.33. The mass at each flow is 250 kN-S²/m and each storey stiffness is 25000 kN/m.

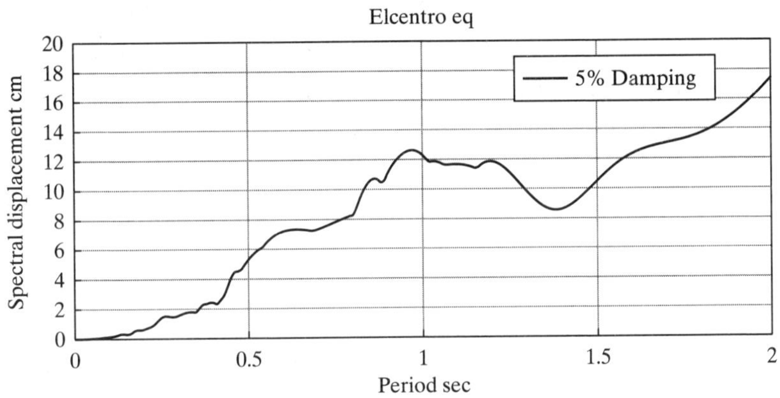

Figure 12.33 El Centro May 1940 Spectral displacement spectrum

$$\text{Mass } [M] = \begin{bmatrix} 250 & 0 & 0 & 0 \\ 0 & 250 & 0 & 0 \\ 0 & 0 & 250 & 0 \\ 0 & 0 & 0 & 250 \end{bmatrix}$$

$$\text{Stiffness } [K] = \begin{bmatrix} 25000 & -25000 & 0 & 0 \\ -25000 & 50000 & -25000 & 0 \\ 0 & -25000 & 50000 & -25000 \\ 0 & 0 & -25000 & 50000 \end{bmatrix}$$

Solution

The frequency, mode shapes and periods can be determined using MATLAB function `eig`.

$$\text{Frequency } \{\omega^2\} = \begin{Bmatrix} 12.06 \\ 100 \\ 234.73 \\ 353.21 \end{Bmatrix} \text{ and period } \{T\} = \begin{Bmatrix} 1.814 \\ 0.628 \\ 0.41 \\ 0.334 \end{Bmatrix} \text{sec}$$

The mode shapes are shown in Table 12.21. Since masses are constant on each floor, the computation of MPF becomes simple as shown in the same table. A negative participation factor has no significance, therefore, only absolute values are considered.

TABLE 12.21 MODE SHAPES AND MODAL PARTICIPATION FACTORS

	Mode 1	Mode 2	Mode 3	Mode 4
Mode shapes	4.1523	3.6515	2.7102	–1.4421
	3.6515	0	–3.6515	3.6515
	2.7102	–3.6515	–1.4421	–4.1523
	1.4421	–3.6515	4.1523	2.7102
SUM	11.9561	–3.6515	1.7689	0.7673
SUM of squares	39.999	40.000	39.999	39.999
Abs (MPF)	0.298	0.091	0.044	0.019

The spectral displacements are read in the Figure 12.33 and the values are as follows:

$$\{S_d\} = \begin{Bmatrix} 13.870 \\ 7.330 \\ 2.332 \\ 1.783 \end{Bmatrix} \text{cm}$$

The floor displacements are obtained from modal displacements shown in Table 12.22 using mode superposition method. Both absolute value and SRSS value techniques are used. The results are shown in Table 12.23.

TABLE 12.22 MODAL DISPLACEMENTS OF FLOORS, cm

Mode	First floor		Second Floor		Third Floor		Roof	
	ϕ_i	$\phi_i \Gamma S_d$	ϕ_i	$\phi_i \Gamma S_d$	ϕ_i	$\phi_i \Gamma S_d$	ϕ_i	$\phi_i \Gamma S_d$
1	1.4421	5.979	2.7102	11.236	3.6515	15.138	4.1523	17.215
2	–3.6515	–2.443	–3.6515	–2.443	0	0.000	3.6515	2.443
3	4.1523	0.428	–1.4421	–0.149	–3.6515	–0.377	2.7102	0.279
4	2.7102	0.093	–4.1523	–0.142	3.6515	0.125	–1.4421	–0.049

TABLE 12.23 FLOOR DISPLACEMENTS, cm

Floor	Abs Value		SRSS value	
	Floor Displacement cm		Floor Displacement cm	
		cm		cm
Roof	(0.049+0.279+2.44+17.214)	19.982	sqrt $(0.049^2+0.279^2+2.44^2+17.214^2)$	17.388
Third	(0.124+0.376+0+15.138)	15.638	sqrt $(0.124^2+0.376^2+0+15.138^2)$	15.143
Second	(0.142+0.148+2.443+11.235)	13.968	sqrt $(0.142^2+0.148^2+2.443^2+11.235^2)$	11.5
First	(0.092+0.428+2.443+5.978)	8.941	sqrt $(0.092^2+0.428^2+2.44^2+5.97^2)$	6.46

The interstorey modal drifts as shown in Table 12.24 are computed using the modal displacements in Table 12.22.

TABLE 12.24 MODAL INTERSTOREY DRIFTS, cm

Mode	Ground storey	First Storey	Second Storey	Top storey
	$(x1 - 0)$	$(x2 - x1)$	$(x3 - x2)$	$(x4 - x3)$
1	5.979	5.257	3.902	2.076
2	2.443	0.000	–2.443	–2.443
3	0.428	–0.577	–0.228	0.656
4	0.093	–0.235	0.267	–0.174

The modal interstory drifts will be used to compute modal story shears. Note that the interstory drifts are NOT obtained from the SRSSed displacements shown in Table 12.23. The modal interstorey drifts are multiplied by the corresponding storey stiffness to obtain modal storey shears as shown in Table 12.25.

TABLE 12.25 MODAL STOREY SHEARS, kN

Mode	Ground storey		First Storey		Second Storey		Top storey	
	Abs drift	Storey shear	Abs drift	Storey shear	Abs drift	Storey shear	Abs drift	Storey shear
1	5.979	1494.661	5.257	1314.319	3.902	975.608	2.076	519.053
2	2.443	610.833	0.000	0.000	2.443	610.833	2.443	610.833
3	0.428	107.054	0.577	144.234	0.228	56.962	0.656	164.016
4	0.093	23.174	0.235	58.679	0.267	66.727	0.174	43.553
Abs sum		2235.722		1517.231		1710.131		1337.456
SRSS value		1618.371		1323.511		1154.394		819.348

The storey shears are obtained by using the mode superposition techniques: both *absolute as well as SRSS*. It will be seen that the SRSS values are lower than those given by the absolute method. It is obvious because the maxima in each mode will occur at different instants and not at the same time. The exact analysis indicates that the SRSS values are closer. □

Example 12.13

A 30-storey building has a total height of 100 m above the ground level. There are two such blocks to be built adjacent to each other. The storey drifts in each block is within 0.4%. What should be the minimum clear gap between these two blocks from earthquake considerations? The response reduction factor was considered as 5.0.

Solution

The maximum lateral displacement at roof level = $100 \times 0.004 = 0.4$ m

If the floors in these two blocks are at the same levels, then minimum clear gap between these two blocks is given by

Seismic gap $\geq (\Delta_1 + \Delta_2) \times 0.50\,R$ (IS:1893-Part 1)

$> (0.4 + 0.4) \times 0.5 \times 5 = 2$ m

In case the floors in these two blocks are not at the same levels, then minimum clear gap between these two blocks is given by

$$\text{Seismic gap} \geq (\Delta_1 + \Delta_2) \times R$$
$$\geq (0.4 + 0.4) \times 5 = 4 \text{ m}$$

□

12.17 DETAILING FOR DUCTILITY

Once a RC building has been designed and reinforcement have been calculated, the next step is to develop structural drawings and show the exact reinforcement details. Recall that the entire analysis and design were based on the premise that the building will undergo non-linear plastic excursions in the event of a severe earthquake. It is time to implement this concept of non-linear response into reality. Typical failures in 12 storey RC buildings at Ahmedabad during the Bhuj earthquake of Jan 26, 2001 are shown in Figures 12.34 and 12.35. Members and connections in such systems must therefore be detailed to accommodate these deformations in a ductile manner. The intention is to encourage a designer to provide ductile detailing and design it for a smaller earthquake force. Numerous experimental studies have been conducted all over the world to understand and develop reinforcement details to ensure development of stable plastic hinges in beams, columns, shear walls, beam-column joints, and foundations. IS 456, IS 13920, ACI 318 and Eurocode 8 provides detailing of reinforcement for ductility in such elements. The central idea is to provide *confinement of concrete* by steel reinforcement to improve the maximum strain at failure, and hence *ductility*. It is discussed in detail in Chapter 16.

Figure 12.34 Collapse of a 12-storey Mansi Tower, Ahmedabad, January 2001.

Figure 12.35 12-storey Shikhar Tower, Ahmedabad, January 2001.

The detailing of reinforcement for individual structural elements consists of the following steps:

- Limits on grade of concrete and steel,
- Limits on geometry,
- Minimum and maximum reinforcement,
- Bar diameter, spacing, rules for curtailment and splicing,
- Rules for confinement of concrete, and
- Anchorage of reinforcement.

A RC framed structure with rigid joints must be designed to have weak girder – strong column proportions. The idea is to develop inelasticity within beams only. The columns are designed to remain elastic as far as possible. Care must be taken to ensure that there is no inelastic activity within a beam-column joint. Only salient features are discussed here.

12.17.1 Beams

A beam is a structural member in which the factored axial compressive stress does not exceed 0.08 f_{ck}, otherwise, it is to be treated as a column.

In beams, two points need to be remembered:

- Section must be designed as under-reinforced, and
- Shear failure is a brittle failure and must be avoided.

In order to avoid a shear failure, the shear force capacity must be more than the following criteria:

- Factored shear force as per structural analysis, and
- Factored gravity shear force + equilibrium shear force when plastic hinges are formed at both ends of a beam.

It is assumed that the ratio of actual ultimate tensile stress to the actual tensile strength of a steel bar is not less than 1.25. At locations, where yielding of longitudinal reinforcement is expected, a 1.25 multiplier is applied to account for the likelihood that the actual yield strength exceeds the specified yield strength of the bar, as well as the influence of strain hardening and cyclic load reversals. The actual yield stress at collapse will be as follows:

$$\frac{1.25f_y}{0.87} = 1.43f_y \approx 1.40f_y$$

There will be two situations, when a frame sways to right and it sways to left as shown in Figure 12.36. Accordingly, there will be two plastic shears at each end of the beam as given by Equation (12.20a) to (12.20d).

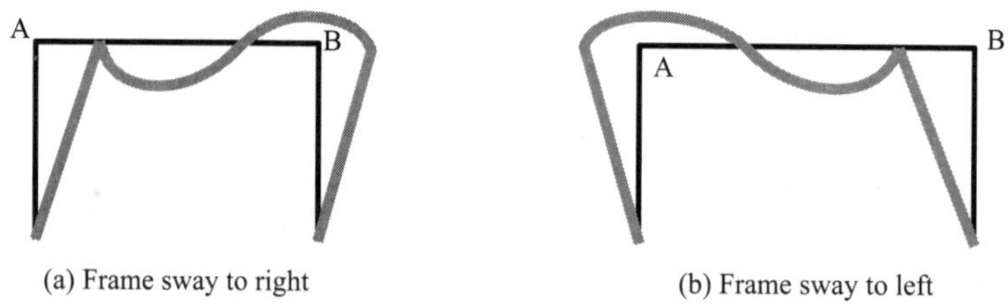

Figure 12.36

Frame sway to right

$$V_a = 0.5wL_c - 1.4\left[\frac{M_u^{As} + M_u^{Bh}}{L_c}\right] \tag{12.20a}$$

$$V_b = 0.5wL_c + 1.4\left[\frac{M_u^{As} + M_u^{Bh}}{L_c}\right] \tag{12.20b}$$

Frame sway to left

$$V_a = 0.5wL_c + 1.4\left[\frac{M_u^{Ah} + M_u^{Bs}}{L_c}\right] \tag{12.20c}$$

$$V_b = 0.5wL_c - 1.4\left[\frac{M_u^{Ah} + M_u^{Bs}}{L_c}\right] \tag{12.20d}$$

where, w = factored gravity load ($DL + LL$) on beam
L_c = clear span of beam AB
M_u = moment of resistance of the section

Symbols s and h represent sagging moment and hogging moment, respectively. Symbols A and B represent end A and B, respectively, of the beam AB.

The design shear strength at end A of the beam must be larger of the two values of V_a computed above. Similarly, design shear demand at end B must be larger than the two values of V_b computed above. Further, the spacing of shear stirrups over a length of 2 times effective depth of the beam at either end should not exceed $d/4$, 6 times the diameter of the smallest longitudinal bar and 100 mm.

12.17.2 Columns

The axial force – bending moment interaction curve for a RC column is shown in Figure 12.37. If the axial force is very high as at point A, the corresponding moment capacity of the column is very low. If the axial force is at B, the moment capacity is maximum. However, if the axial force is at C, the moment capacity is still quite high. In the event of a very severe earthquake, it is quite possible that the axial force in a column is several times higher than anticipated in the design. In that case, its moment capacity will be drastically reduced. Therefore, the factored axial compressive stress considering all load combinations involving earthquake loads is limited to 0.40 f_{ck} in columns.

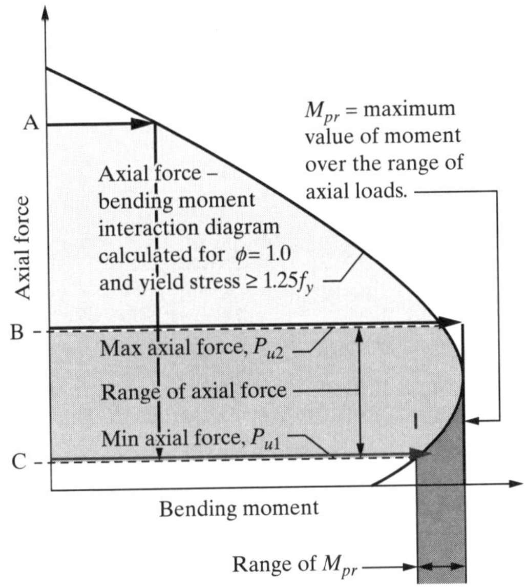

Figure 12.37 Axial force – bending moment interaction curve for a column

In order to avoid a shear failure, the shear force capacity must be more than the following criteria:

- Factored shear force as per structural analysis, and
- Factored equilibrium shear force when plastic hinges are formed at each face of beams meeting at a joint.

Let us consider an inner beam-column joint as shown in Figure 12.38. Under certain conditions, a plastic hinge will develop at each face of the beam meeting at this joint. The moments in both the upper and lower columns will remain elastic. If the distance between the points of contraflexure in the upper and lower storey is h_c, the shear in columns can be determined by considering the joint equilibrium as given by Equations 12.21(a) and 12.21(b).

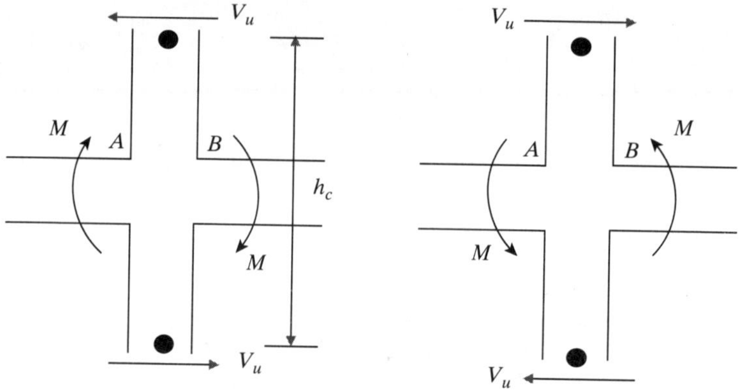

(a) Sway to right (b) Sway to left

Figure 12.38

Frame sway to right

$$V_u = 1.4\left[\frac{M_u^{As} + M_u^{Bh}}{h_c}\right] \tag{12.21a}$$

Frame sway to left

$$V_u = 1.4\left[\frac{M_u^{Ah} + M_u^{Bs}}{h_c}\right] \tag{12.21b}$$

Special Confinement Reinforcement

Circular column

The minimum area of special confining reinforcement must be at least given by each of the two equations:

$$A_{sh} = 0.09SD_c\left(\frac{A_g}{A_c} - 1\right)\frac{f_{ck}}{f_y} \tag{12.22a}$$

$$= 0.024SD_c\frac{f_{ck}}{f_y} \tag{12.22b}$$

A_{sh} = area of the cross-section of a bar forming spiral or a column tie
S = pitch of spiral or spacing of ties

D_c = diameter of core of circular column measured to outside of spiral/tie

f_y = yield strength of steel used in spiral or ties

Rectangular column

The minimum area of special confining reinforcement (Figure 12.39) must be at least given by each of the two equations:

$$A_{sh} = 0.18Sh\left(\frac{A_g}{A_c} - 1\right)\frac{f_{ck}}{f_y} \tag{12.23a}$$

$$= 0.05\,Sh\frac{f_{ck}}{f_y} \tag{12.23b}$$

where,

h = longer dimension of the rectangular confining hoop measured to its outside but does not exceed 300 mm

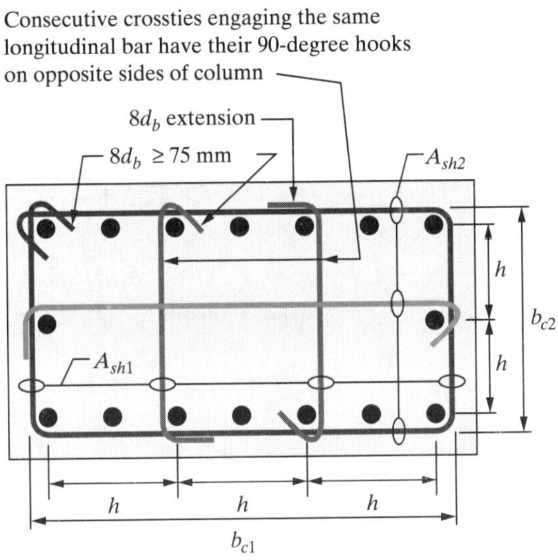

Figure 12.39 Confinement reinforcement in a rectangular column

12.17.3 Weak Girder – Strong Column Proportions

At each beam-column joint of a moment-resisting frame (Figure 12.40), the sum of the moment capacities of columns for the design factored axial load must be at least 1.4 times the sum of the moment capacities of beams meeting at that joint along each principal plane.

$$\sum M_{col} \geq 1.40\ M_{beam} \tag{12.24}$$

A beam-column joint is designed for diagonal tension so that inelastic activity remains outside the panel zone.

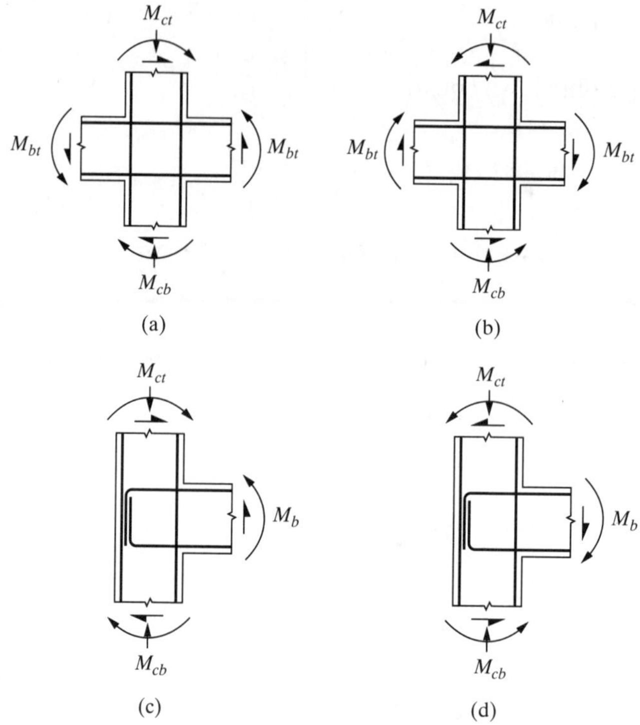

Figure 12.40 Weak girder – strong column proportions under reversed loading

12.17.4 Shear Walls

A reinforced concrete wall is subjected to the same set of forces as a RC column due to wind or earthquake loads. Therefore, the design of a shear wall is similar to that of a column. However, in view of its small thickness, 100 mm to 300 mm in general, it is designed only for in-plane forces in a given direction. Thus, at least two pairs of shear walls are required in each direction and must be placed symmetrically in plan. Each set of shear walls resist axial force, in-plane lateral force and in-plane bending moment. A shear wall may have different configurations in plan as per requirement as shown in Figure 12.41. The highlighted area in each wall represents boundary element. These are critical regions where concentrated flexural plastic hinges are expected to form. The requirement for minimum longitudinal reinforcement in the ends of the wall is to promote the formation of well-distributed secondary flexural cracks in the wall plastic hinge region to achieve the required deformation capacity during earthquakes. Special confinement reinforcement is also provided around the longitudinal reinforcement as discussed earlier with reference to columns.

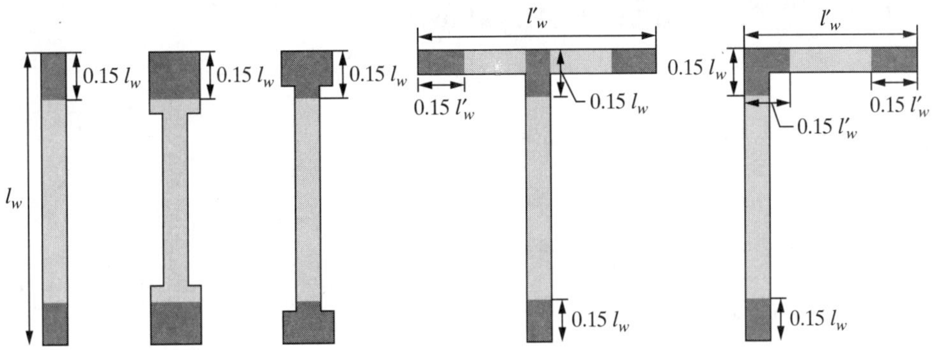

Figure 12.41 Typical shear wall cross-sections in plan and boundary elements

A shear wall may be classified in a squat wall, intermediate wall or a slender wall depending upon the ratio of overall height to length as follows:

Squat wall $$\frac{h_w}{L_w} < 1 \qquad (12.25a)$$

Intermediate wall $$1 \le \frac{h_w}{L_w} \le 2 \qquad (12.25b)$$

Slender wall $$\frac{h_w}{L_w} > 2 \qquad (12.25c)$$

The inelastic response of each of these walls and the failure mechanism under severe earthquake force is different. That is why, there are different minimum reinforcement requirements for different types of walls.

12.18 SPECIAL DEVICES

Nowadays with increasing challenges to improve the performance and life of buildings and other structures after a strong earthquake, there is increasing trend to fit them with special devices to absorb the energy or reduce the base shear. These devices are classified as follows:

- Passive Control Devices
- Active Control Devices

Passive control devices do not need any source of power supply, whereas the active control systems do require. It is absolutely essential to guarantee the availability of power even in the event of a severe earthquake in order to ensure smooth and desired functioning of the active control system. Therefore, passive control systems are being widely used. Details of analysis and design of such systems are available in ASCE 7, FEMA 450, 451, P1050 and other documents.

12.18.1 Passive Control Systems

Various passive control systems are as follows:

- Seismic Base Isolation Devices
  - Elastomeric bearing
  - Sliding bearing
- Energy Absorbing Devices
  - Viscous dampers
  - Metallic dampers
  - Tuned mass dampers (TMD)

Objectives of Seismic Base Isolation Devices

- Enhance performance of structures at all hazard levels by minimizing interruption of use of facility
- Reducing the base shear or acceleration response
- Reducing damaging deformations in structural and non-structural components by cutting off the transmission of base excitation to superstructure. In other words, the entire deformation is absorbed by the base isolation system. Nothing is transferred to the superstructure. The superstructure undergoes rigid body displacements under controlled conditions.

The principle of seismic isolation system is illustrated in Figures 12.42(a) through (d). There is a shift in the period of a structure supported on base isolation devices as shown in Figure 12.42(c). It helps reduce the acceleration and therefore base shear. However, this increase in period is beneficial if the structure is supported on hard soil rather than on soft soil as shown in Figure 12.42(d). The effect of base isolation on the mode shapes and period of a single-storey building is shown in Figure 12.43. The base isolation system increases the lateral degree of freedom by one. The storey drift in a building without base isolation is quite large, whereas it is negligible in a building with base isolation. Here lies the advantage of base isolation.

The use of base isolators had been made mandatory in large hospitals in Turkey since 2013. Four large state hospitals built in Turkey in Kahramanmaras, Hatay and Malatya provinces on seismic base isolators did not suffer any damage what-so-ever during the twin earthquakes and multiple aftershocks of Turkey-Syria earthquake of Feb 6, 2023. These hospitals were fitted with 250 to 600 base isolator devices depending upon their plinth area and gravity load. For buildings located in a severe seismic zone and expected to survive multiple earthquakes/aftershocks within a short period of few hours to few days, base isolators provide the most efficient solution in terms of performance and economy.

Base isolation may be achieved through bearings of different types:

- Elastomeric bearings
  - Laminated lead rubber bearings
  - High damping laminated rubber bearings
  - Low damping laminated rubber bearings

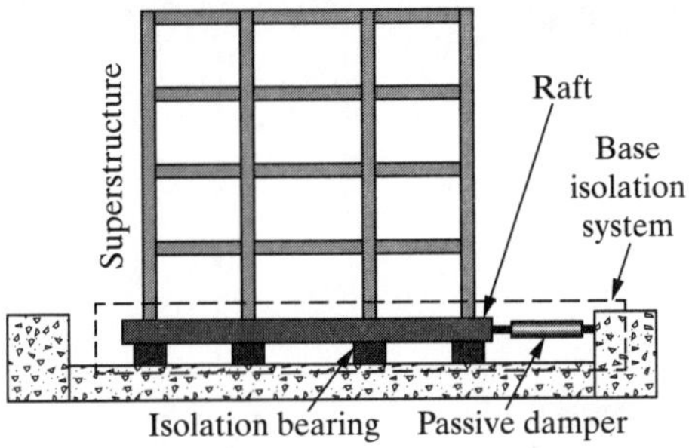

Figure 12.42(a) A building supported on seismic isolation system (adapted from FEMA 451).

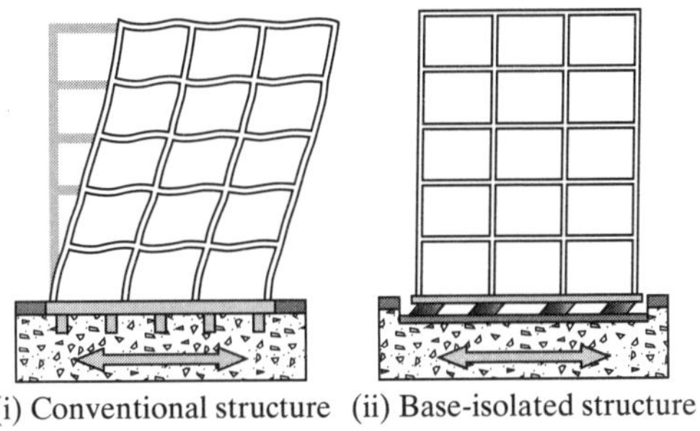

Figure 12.42(b) Response of a building without and with base isolation (adapted from FEMA 451).

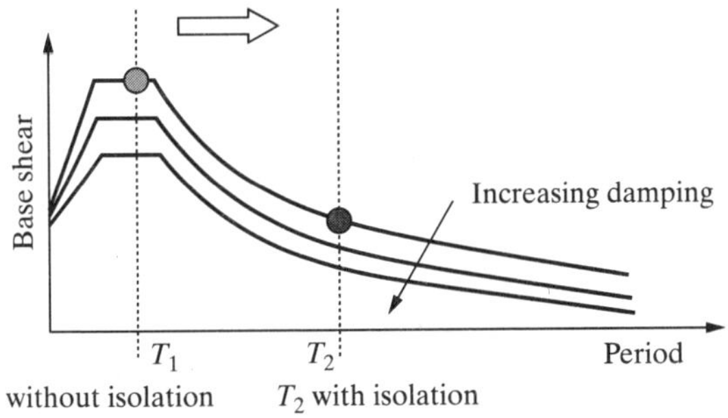

Figure 12.42(c) Shift in period of a base isolated structure to reduce base shear.

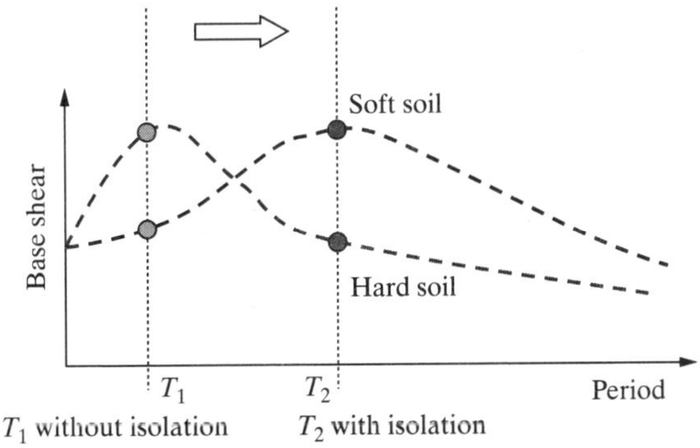

Figure 12.42(d) Effect of soil on the shift of period and therefore base shear.

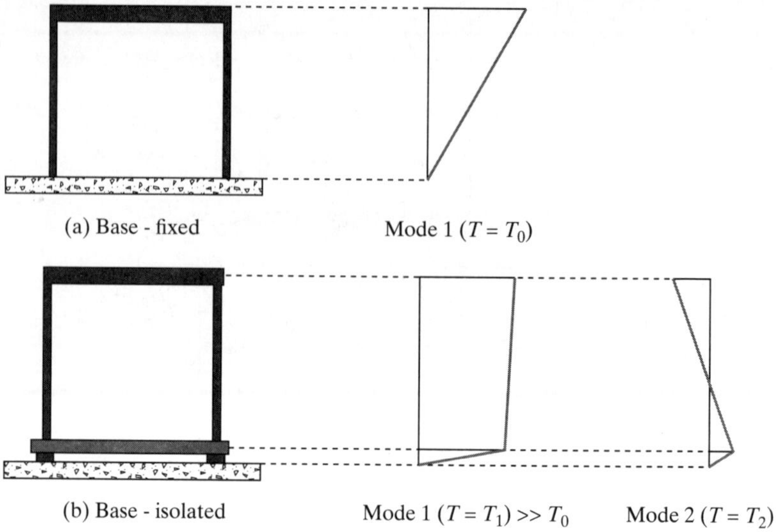

Figure 12.43 Effect of base isolation on mode shapes and period of a single-storey building.

- Friction sliding bearings
  - Flat sliding bearing
  - Friction pendulum bearing
  - Spherical sliding bearing
- Roller bearings

The concept of base isolation is equally applicable to bridges as depicted in Figure 12.44.

Elastomeric isolators act as follows:

- Adds flexibility to the structure and thus lengthens natural period
- Imparts energy dissipation through damping
- Re-centers the structure when ground motion due to earthquake ceases
- May be used to provide necessary rigidity under low service loads, e.g., wind, braking, etc.
- Perform under all service loads and slow displacements due to thermal action and secondary effects, offering moderately low resistance

The hysteresis behaviour of elastomeric bearings of different types is illustrated in Figure 12.45. It is discussed in more detail in Chapters 15 and 16.

Energy Dissipating Devices

Different types of dampers used for dissipating the seismic energy are discussed in Chapter 15. More details are available in ASCE 7 and FEMA P1050. The nonlinear seismic analysis of structures fitted with these special devices can be conveniently carried out using commercial software such as ANSYS, SAP2000 and ETABS.

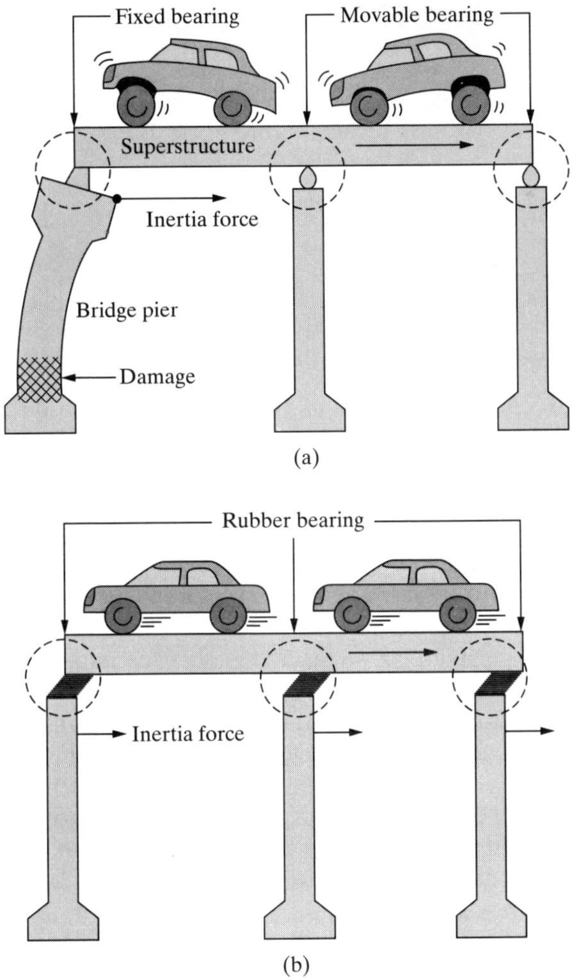

Figure 12.44 Response of a bridge without and with base isolation (rubber bearings).

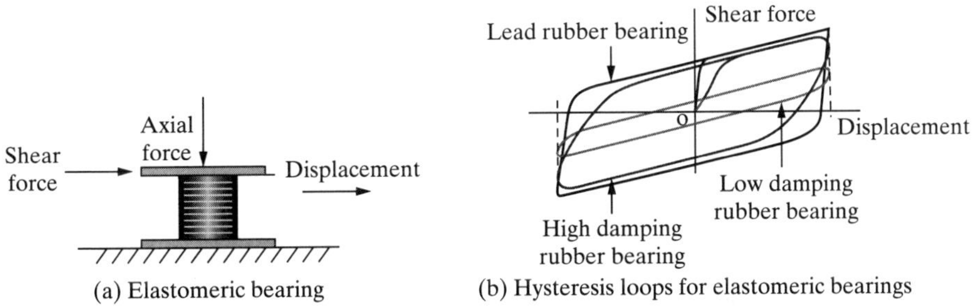

Figure 12.45 Hysteresis behaviour of elastomeric bearing of different types.

12.18.2 Active Control Systems

Active control systems can be classified as follows:

- Active control systems (Dynamic Intelligent Building)
  - Active mass damping
  - Active bracing
- Semi-active control systems
- Hybrid control systems

The basic configuration of an active control system is schematically shown in Figure 12.46. The system consists of three basic elements:

- Sensors to measure external excitation and/or structural response
- Computer hardware and software to compute control forces on the basis of observed excitation and/or structural response
- Hydraulic actuators to provide the necessary control forces

Thus, an active system has to necessarily have an external energy input to drive the actuators and the control system. On the other hand, passive systems do not required external energy and their efficiency depends on tunings of system to expected excitation and structural behaviour. As a result, the passive systems are effective only for the modes of the vibrations for which these are tuned. The advantage of an active system lies in its much wider range of applicability since the control forces are worked out on the basis of actual excitation and structural behaviour. In the active system, when only external excitation is measured system is said to be in open-looped. However, when the structural response is used as input, the system is in closed loop control. In certain instances, the excitation and response both are used, and it is termed as open-closed loop control. The solution of such systems can be obtained with the help of linear control theory, MATLAB, and direct integration techniques. A detailed discussion on the active control system is beyond the scope of the present text book.

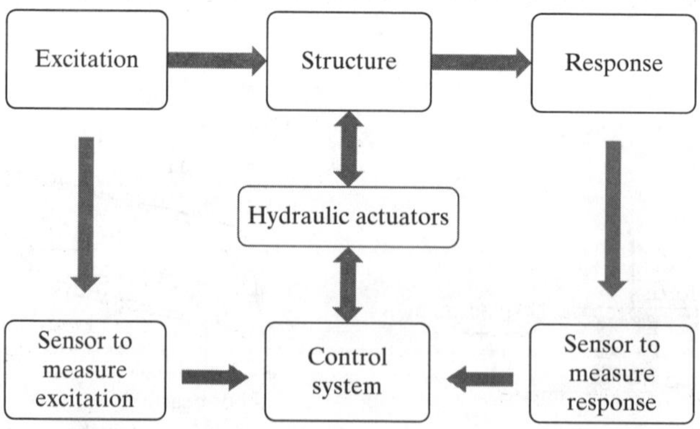

Figure 12.46 Basic configuration of active control system.

REVIEW QUESTIONS

12.1 Explain the following terms:
- Building
- Shear building
- Shear wall or flexural wall
- Storey drift
- Storey shear
- Most desirable characteristics of a building
- Structural system
- Irregularity in configurations of buildings
- Mass irregularity
- Stiffness irregularity
- Plan irregularity
- Elevation irregularity
- Soft storey
- Weak storey
- Concentrically braced frame
- Eccentrically braced frame
- Tubular system
- Dual system
- Inverted pendulum system
- Outrigger system
- Stiffness modifiers
- Shear lag
- Unreinforced brick masonry infills (URM)

12.2 What is the implication of stiffness modifiers on the behaviour of a building?

12.3 Explain the following terms:
- Zone factor
- Importance factor
- Response reduction factor
- Significance of numeral 2 in the base shear equation
- Maximum credible earthquake (MCE)
- Design basis earthquake (DBE)

12.4 Discuss the various failure mechanisms in buildings with neat sketches.

12.5 Discuss the action of masonry infill on the enclosing RC frame during an earthquake. Sketch the different failure patterns.

12.6 How do you model a brick masonry wall in a building?

12.7 Discuss the structural systems for RC buildings for carrying vertical loads and lateral loads with neat sketches. What is the most desirable configuration of lateral load resisting elements?

12.8 Discuss the structural systems for steel buildings for carrying vertical loads and lateral loads with neat sketches. Explain the concentric and eccentric bracing systems.

12.9 Which is the most suitable system for a low rise building and also for a very tall building in steel?

12.10 Explain the various vertical and horizontal irregularities in buildings with neat sketches. Discuss the ASCE 7, IS 1893 and Eurocode 1998 provisions.

12.11 What do you understand by a dual frame system? Explain with sketches.

12.12 Explain the terms MCE and DBE as adopted in IS-1893-Part 1, ASCE-7 and Eurocode 1998-Part 1.

12.13 Discuss the salient features of empirical formulae to determine the fundamental periods of buildings.

12.14 Why empirical formulae for the determination of fundamental time periods are not applicable for industrial buildings?

12.15 What are the seismic design criteria for buildings?

12.16 Elaborate on different earthquake analysis and design procedures for buildings.

12.17 Write a short note on seismic coefficient method (SCM).

12.18 Write a short note on response spectrum method (RSM).

12.19 Write a short note on linear time-history analysis method (LTHM)

12.20 What is the idea behind scaling of base shear obtained using the modal analysis?

12.21 Explain center of mass, center of rigidity, accidental eccentricity, and design eccentricity.

12.22 What is the implication of two equations for computing design eccentricities in a building?

12.23 How do you implement the effect of accidental eccentricity in the dynamic analysis of buildings?

12.24 What is the implication of a rigid diaphragm and flexible diaphragm?

12.25 What is the need for redundancy in tall buildings?

12.26 Explain what is hysteresis behaviour of different structural systems.

12.27 How orientation of lateral load resisting elements affects the response of buildings?

12.28 Why a soft or weak storey in a multistorey building is critical?

12.29 Why the first mode as a torsional mode is critical in buildings?

12.30 Explain the 30% combination rule for member forces.

12.31 What is the need of having minimum separation gap between two adjacent buildings?

12.32 Discuss the implication of the formation of plastic hinges in beams and columns of a building.

12.33 Explain the salient features of base shear vs roof displacement curve when a building is subjected to gradually increasing lateral loads until collapse.

12.34 What is first significant yield point in a building?

12.35 What do you understand by over strength factor in a building?

12.36 What is the concept behind response reduction factor R in a building?

12.37 What is the concept behind detailing of reinforcement in buildings?

12.38 Why the maximum design axial force in RC columns is restricted to about 40% of its capacity?

12.39 How do you differentiate between a beam and a column?

12.40 How do you differentiate between a RC column and a RC shear wall?

12.41 What is the meaning of confinement of concrete?

12.42 How do you achieve ductility in RC beams? Show with neat sketches.

12.43 How do you achieve ductility in RC columns? Show with neat sketches.

12.44 What are the minimum and maximum reinforcement ratios in a RC beam for seismic considerations?

12.45 How do you carryout detailing of shear reinforcement in RC beams?

12.46 How do you carryout curtailment of longitudinal reinforcement in RC beams?

12.47 How do you carryout curtailment of longitudinal reinforcement in RC columns?

12.48 Write a short note on passive control devices.

12.49 Write a short note on active control devices.

12.50 Discuss the concept behind base isolation.

PROBLEMS

12.1 A single-storey 3.5 m high RC building is pulled at the roof level with a lateral force of 75 kN and undergoes a lateral displacement of 10 mm. It has a net weight of 30 kN. It is situated in Chennai on medium soil. Estimate its natural frequency, natural period and base shear if damping is 5% and response reduction factor $R = 3$.

How will the base shear change if its damping is (i) 2% and (ii) 10%?

Ans: Mass $m = 30000/9.81$, stiffness $k = 7500000$ N/m

Natural frequency = 49.52 rad/sec; period $T = 0.126$ sec

(a) For 5% damping, base shear = 0.0667 W

(b) For 2% damping, base shear = 0.0933 W

(c) For 10% damping, base shear = 0.0534 W

12.2 A 15 m high overhead water tank on RC shaft has an effective weight of 1000 kN and is situated in seismic zone V on soft soil. It is pulled at the top with a lateral force of 100 kN and undergoes a lateral displacement of 35 mm. Estimate its period of vibration and base shear if the response reduction factor is 3.5. Also, determine the shear and overturning moment along the height of the shaft.

Ans: Mass $m = 101936$ kg, stiffness $k = 2857140$ N/m

Natural frequency = 5.294 rad/sec; period $T = 1.186$ sec; base shear = 108.5 kN

12.3 A four-storey steel building has a plan dimension of 20 m × 10 m and each storey is 3.5 m high. It is situated in Kolkata on soft soil. The dead load per floor is 20 kN/m^2 and live load is 6 kN/m^2. It is symmetrically braced along the short direction only. Estimate its period of vibration and base shears in both the lateral directions. Also, plot the lateral force distribution along the height.

12.4 A single-storey building has a plan as shown in Figure P12.1. There are two RC walls 200 mm thick each along 1-1 and A-A grids. There are three RC columns 200 × 200 mm at B-1, B-2 and A-2. There are two beams 200 × 450 mm deep along 2-2 and B-B. Estimate the lateral force on the walls and the frames due to earthquake force along the two directions. Assume 4.5 m height and a uniform load on the roof.

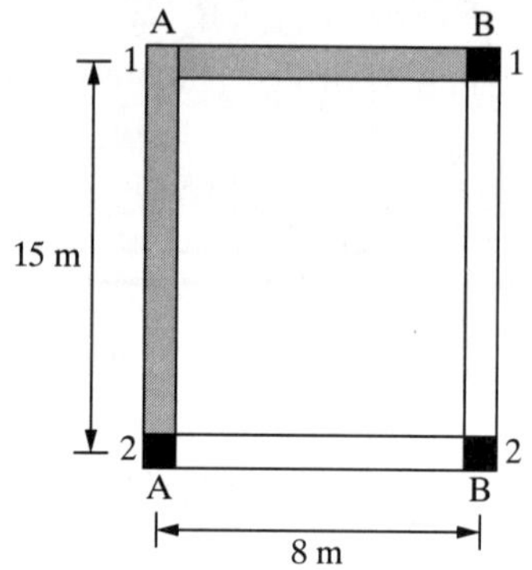

Figure P12.1

12.5 A 10-storey RC building has a moment-resistant frame with 5 bays @ 6 m c/c. The height of the first storey is 4.5 m c/c while rest of the storeys are 3.5 m c/c. The columns are 300 × 500 mm and beams are 300 × 600 mm. The slab thickness is 125 mm including the finish. Imposed load on the floors is 4.5 kN/m^2 and the lateral spacing of the frames is 5 m c/c. The building is located in seismic zone IV on soft soil.

(a) Determine the fundamental period of vibration using the Rayleigh method.

(b) Determine the period of vibrations in the first 3 modes and the corresponding mode shape.

(c) Analyse the frame in each mode and determine the column shears. Thus, estimate the storey shears, base shears and their SRSS values.

(d) Determine the lateral floor forces along the height in each mode and display graphically.

Hint: Use any software to determine the displacements and member forces, etc. Use MS-EXCEL to estimate the storey shears.

12.6 A 15-storey building plan is shown in Figure P12.2. The width of the shear walls is 200 mm each. Each wall continues up to the roof. The height of first storey is 4.5 m and subsequent storeys are 3.5 m high. Column size is 500 × 500 mm, beam size is 300 × 500 mm and slab thickness is 125 mm. Column is placed at each intersection of grid. Estimate the period of vibration in each direction using the IS 1893-Part 1, ASCE-7 and Eurocode 1998-Part 1 codes.

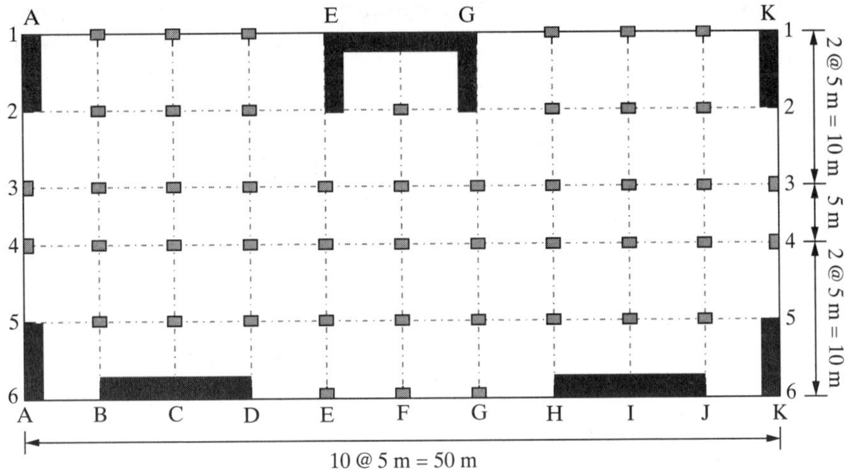

Figure P12.2 Plan of a 15-storey building.

REFERENCES

Agarwal, J. (2001) Earthquake Response of Buildings Fitted with Vibration Isolators, M Tech Thesis, I.I.T. Roorkee.

AISC 341 (2016) Seismic Provisions for Structural Steel Buildings,American Institute of Steel Construction, Chicago.

ASCE 7 (2022) Minimum Design Loads for Buildings and Other Structures, American Society of Civil Engineers, Reston, Virginia.

Eurocode 8-1 (2004) Design of Structures for Earthquake Resistance – Part 1: General Rules, Seismic Actions and Rules for Buildings, incorporating corrigendum 2013, European Committee for Standardization, Brussels.

FEMA 273 (1997) NEHRP Guidelines for the Seismic Rehabilitation of Buildings, Federal Emergency Management Agency, Washington, DC.

FEMA 356 (2000) Pre-standard and Commentary for the Seismic Rehabilitation of Buildings, Federal Emergency Management Agency, Washington, DC.

FEMA 451B (2006) 2003 NEHRP Recommended Seismic Provisions – Design Examples, Federal Emergency Management Agency, Washington, D.C.

FEMA 464 (2006) Designing for Earthquakes: a Manual for Architects, Washington. D.C.

FEMA P-749 (2010) Earthquake-Resistant Design Concepts, An Introduction to the NEHRP Recommended Seismic Provisions for New Buildings and Other Structures, Federal Emergency Management Agency, Washington, DC.

FEMA P-750 (2009) NEHRP Recommended Seismic Provisions for New Buildings and Other Structures, Federal Emergency Management Agency, Washington, DC.

FEMA P-1050 (2015) 2015 NEHRP Recommended Seismic Provisions for New Buildings and Other Structures, Federal Emergency Management Agency, Washington, DC

IS: 16700 (2017) Criteria for structural safety of tall RC buildings, Bureau of Indian Standards, New Delhi.

IS:1893-Part 1 (2016) Criteria for Earthquake Resistant Design of Structures, Part 1, General Provisions and Buildings, Bureau of Indian Standards, New Delhi.

IS:1893-Part 2 (2014) Criteria for Earthquake Resistant Design of Structures, Part 2, Liquid Retaining Tanks, Bureau of Indian Standards, New Delhi.

IS:1893-Part 3 (2014) Criteria for Earthquake Resistant Design of Structures, Part 3, Bridges and Retaining Walls, Bureau of Indian Standards, New Delhi.

IS:1893-Part 4 (2015) Criteria for Earthquake Resistant Design of Structures, Part 4, Industrial and Stack-Like Structures, Bureau of Indian Standards, New Delhi.

IS:13920 (2016) Ductile Detailing of Reinforced Concrete Structures Subjected to Seismic Forces, Bureau of Indian Standards, New Delhi.

Jain, A.K. (2012) Reinforced Concrete – Limit State Design, 7th Ed., Nem Chand & Bros., Roorkee.

Moehle, Jack P., Hooper John D., and Lubke, Chris D. (2008) Seismic Design of Reinforced Concrete Special Moment Frames: A Guide for Practicing Engineers, NEHRP Seismic Design Technical Brief No. 1, NIST, Gaithersburg, MD, USA.

Moehle, Jack P. et al (2012) Seismic Design of Cast-in-Place Concrete Special Structural Walls and Coupling Beams, A Guide for Practicing Engineers, NEHRP Seismic Design Technical Brief No. 6, NIST, Gaithersburg, MD, USA.

Naeim, F. and Kelly, J. M. (1999) Design of Seismic Isolated Structures: From theory to practice, John Wiley & Sons, New York.

NZS 1170-5 (2004) Structural Design Actions – Part 5: Earthquake Actions – New Zealand, Standards New Zealand, Wellington.

NZS 1170-5 (S1) (2004) Structural Design Actions – Part 5: Earthquake actions – New Zealand, Commentary, Standards New Zealand, Wellington.

PEER 5 (2010) Seismic Design Guidelines for Tall Buildings, Pacific Earthquake Engineering Research Center (PEER), Berkeley.

Rafael Sabelli, R., Roeder, C. W. and Hajjar, J. F. (2013) Seismic Design of Steel Special Concentrically Braced Frame Systems, A Guide for Practicing Engineers, U.S. Dept. of Commerce National Institute of Standards and Technology Engineering Laboratory, Gaithersburg, MD.

Satyanarayana, J. (2003) Dynamic Behaviour of Base Isolated Buildings, M Tech Thesis, I.I.T. Roorkee.

Willford, M., Whittaker, A. and Klemencic, R. (2008) Recommendations for the Seismic Design of High-Rise Buildings, The Council on Tall Buildings and Urban Habitat, Chicago.

13 Analysis of Bridges for Earthquake Force

13.1 INTRODUCTION

The primary purpose of a bridge is to be able to negotiate an obstacle for the purpose of transport of men, materials, electric or communication cables, liquids or gaseous. The obstacle may be in the form of river, canal, valley, another highway, or railway or some other natural or artificial obstacle. Now-a-days, elevated highways/expressways are very common in mega cities in view of very heavy congestion and paucity of land. These are also known as viaducts. The bridges are made of different materials such as timber, masonry, concrete and steel. The timber bridges are constructed over small spans only and for temporary purposes or in remote areas. The masonry bridges are used to cover small spans. Reinforced concrete is probably the most popular material for permanent bridges. Simple R.C. culverts can be used up to 10 m supported on opposite ends only. Balanced cantilever bridges, prestressed concrete girder bridges, or box girder bridges can be used for spans up to 80 m. Concrete arch has been used for spans of 200 m. Steel truss bridges are very common for use in highways and railways for spans up to 150 m. Steel plate girder bridges are very common for heavy loads for spans up to 50 m. A steel bridge may have a single deck or a double deck. It may carry a highway on one floor and a railway on another floor. Suspension bridges, extra dozed bridges, and cable stayed bridges are used across very large spans.

A bridge may be classified in several different ways depending upon the choice of materials, span, type of superstructure and substructure, structural arrangements, connections, type of supports, and type of construction. It may be cast-in-situ or precast. Some of these classifications are as follows:

(a) Purpose of a bridge – highway, railway, pedestrian, utility, canal, syphon aqueduct

(b) Type of material – Masonry, reinforced concrete, steel, timber, composite materials

(c) Type of structural arrangement – T-beam bridge, box girder bridge, Steel truss bridge, plate girder bridge, cable stayed bridge, suspension bridge, arch bridge

- Live load on lower chord
- Live load on upper chord
- Single deck bridge
- Double deck bridge

(d) Number of spans – single span or multiple spans

(e) Type of support
- Simply supported bridge or multi-span simply supported bridge
- Continuous bridge, or
  - Girders and deck slab. Both are continuous
  - Continuity is only through deck slab
- Integral bridge.

(f) Type of geometry in plan
- Straight bridge
- Skewed bridge
- Curved bridge

(g) Type of construction
- Cast-in-situ bridge
- Precast bridge
- Segmental precast bridge

(h) Fixed bridge or movable bridge

For bridges having one span, the following types of structures may be used:

- Simply supported deck slab or T-beam deck
- Girder with cantilevers
- Integral bridge
- Arch

The simply supported structures are statically determinate, are easiest to design, and construct. When unyielding foundation is attainable, girder with cantilevers may be preferred. Arch bridge is considered for long span and unyielding supports.

For a bridge with several spans, the following arrangements are considered:

- Number of simply supported T-beam spans or box girder spans
- Number of balanced cantilever spans; that is, a girder with cantilevers on both sides, and a central simply supported short span resting on these cantilevers
- Continuous girders supported by independent piers
- Integral bridges

Under certain conditions, where there are unequal spans, it may be economical to go for continuous bridges. It is important to understand the sequence of construction in such bridges. The designer must clearly state the whole erection and construction process. When the foundation is rocky or very rigid, it may be economical to go for integral bridges, that is, combined super and sub structure. There are no bearings and expansion joints. The cost of maintenance is reduced as well as the quality of ride is much better. The most appropriate bridge type is selected by evaluating the various factors in bridge planning including economy, time factor, durability, vertical alignment, environmental impacts, aesthetics, constructability, and maintainability.

For the last few decades, the trend is to design a very slender bridge across large spans. Such bridges are susceptible to vibrations due to traffic and wind. Sometimes, the geometry of a bridge is very complicated curvilinear curve in space. It makes the analysis, design and construction of such a bridge very challenging. A multi-span simply supported viaduct curved in space is shown in Figure 13.1 (a) and (b). There is a 6-lane post-tensioned box girder bridge in Figure 13.1(a), whereas, there are 8-steel plate girders over the railway span in the same viaduct as shown in Figure 13.1(b). The sub-structure consists of single column pier, double bent pier or triple bent pier in Figure 13.1 and 13.2. The height of the piers is also varying from span to span from 6 m to 12 m in this segment of the bridge. The pier cap is also different on different piers. Such situations make the behaviour of the bridge quite complex. It becomes essential to carry out a non-linear dynamic analysis of such a bridge.

There are two main components of a bridge:

- Superstructure
- Substructure including foundation

(a) (b)

Figure 13.1 A viaduct curved in space multi-spanimply supported.

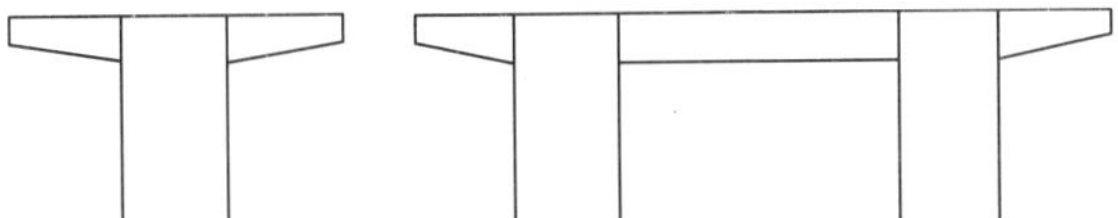

(a) Single pier (b) Portal frame pier

Figure 13.2 Different arrangements of piers.

Typical cross-sections of superstructure and substructure of bridges are shown in Figures 13.3.

Superstructure

(a) Floor slab, solid slab or voided slab
(b) I Girders or box girder
(c) Footpath/median
(d) Cross-beams or diaphragm
(e) Crash barrier and railing
(f) Bearings
(g) Seismic restrainers

A cross-section of superstructure of a T-beam bridge is shown in Figure 13.4. A beam-slab system can also be analyzed and designed as a composite section as shown in Figure 13.5. Shear studs are provided at the top of a beam so that these steel studs resist shear force during composite action of the beam and slab. Composite

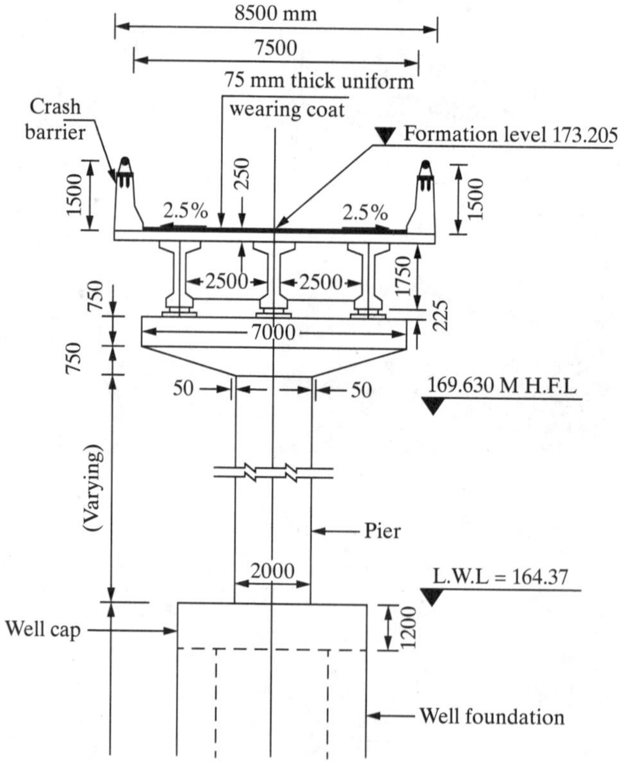

(a)

Figure 13.3(a) A typical T-beam girder bridge on a single pier and well foundation.

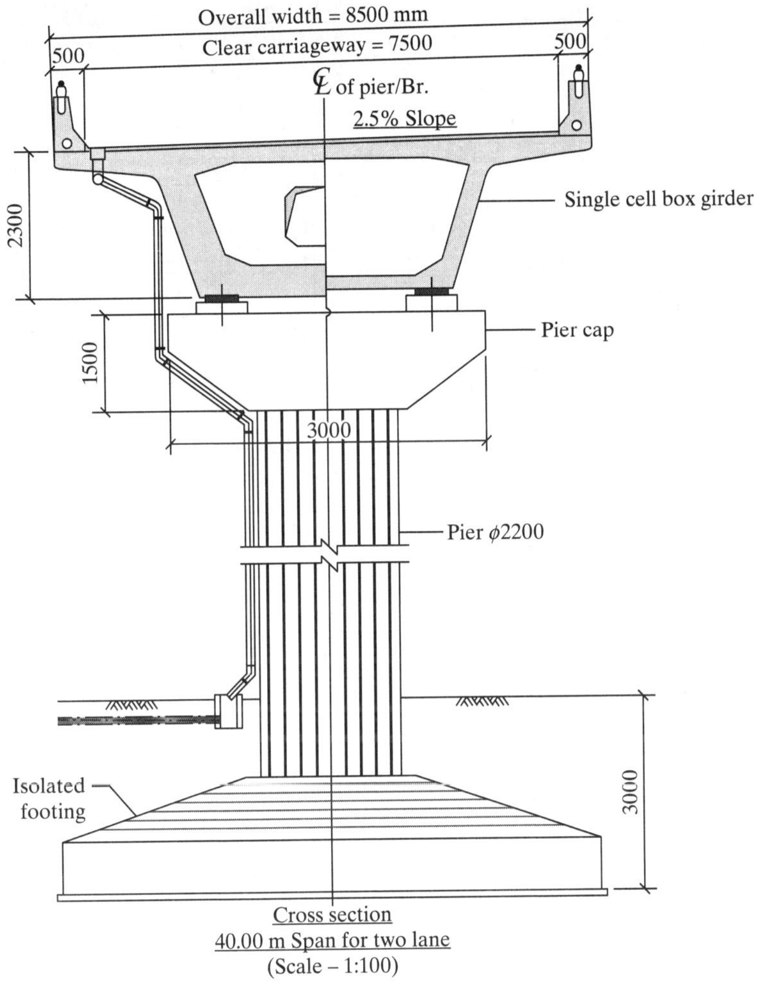

Figure 13.3(b) A typical 2-lane box girder bridge on a single pier and isolated footing.

action can be ensured both in reinforced concrete as well as steel bridges. The basic components of the cross-section of a box girder superstructure are as follows (Figure 13.6):

- Top slab – the entire width of the concrete deck, including the portions between the webs and the overhangs outside of the webs.
- Overhangs (cantilever wings) – the overhanging portion of the top slab
- Webs – vertical or inclined, exterior or interior
- Bottom slab

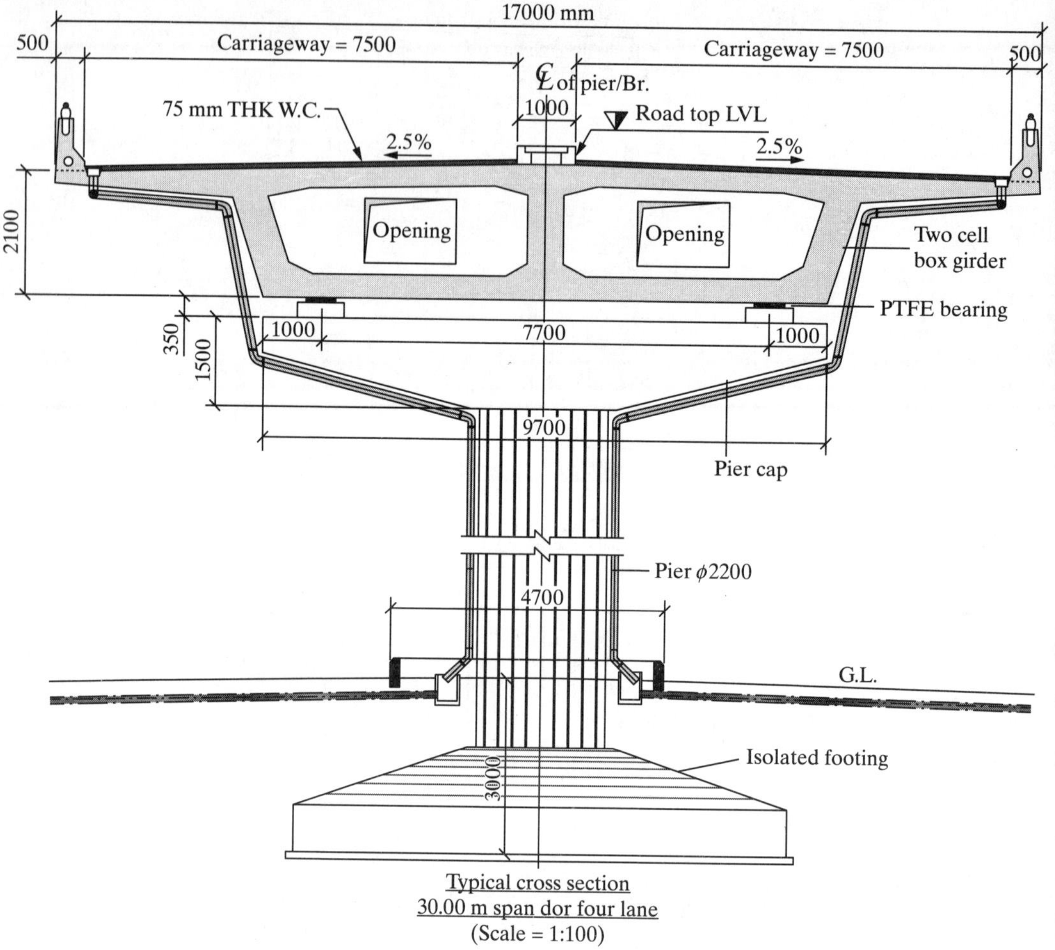

Figure 13.3(c) A typical 4-lane box girder bridge on a single pier and isolated footing.

Multi-cell box girder cross-section as shown in Figure 13.6(b) can be used for bridges of nearly any width, by varying the spacing between, and/or, changing the number of webs. Widths of single cell box girders typically range from 7.5 m to 20 m, though there are single cell box girder cross-sections as wide as 25 m. This wide range of widths of single cell box girders is achieved through the use of transverse post-tensioning within the top slab to control tensile stresses under the action of the permanent dead and live wheel loads plus impact effects as shown in Figure 13.7.

Substructure

- **(a)** Pier and pier cap
- **(b)** Pile cap and pile; or well cap and well
- **(c)** Abutment
- **(d)** Protection works

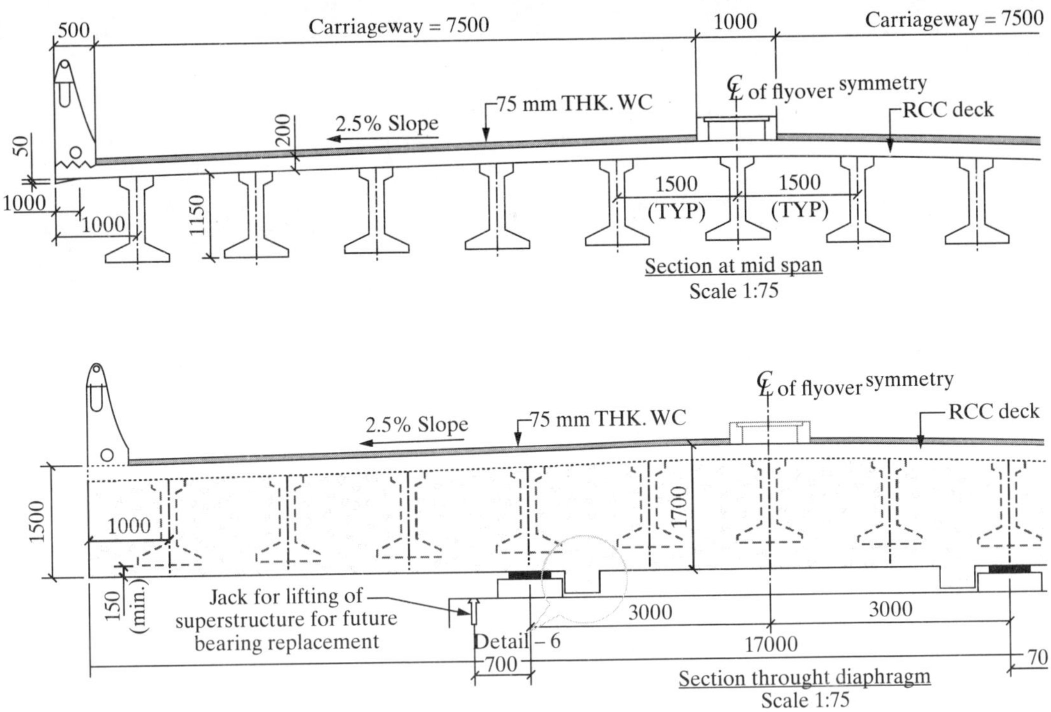

Figure 13.4 Cross-section of a superstructure for 4-lane – 20 m span, T-beam girder bridge.

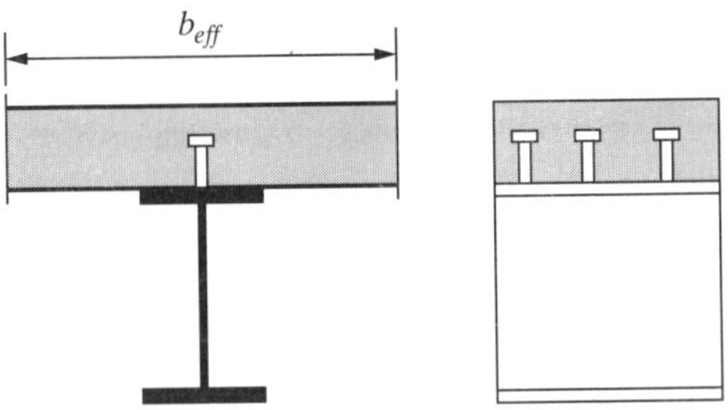

Figure 13.5 Composite construction - studs.

Different types of substructures were shown in Figures 13.1 and 13.2. Typical components of a substructure were shown in Figure 13.3. A pier may carry a free bearing, guided bearing or a fixed bearing depending upon the design requirements. The body of the pier may be made in reinforced concrete, solid in the same material or cellular with filling material inside. Piers of varied design in slender reinforced concrete column type are employed. The pier cap is generally made in reinforced cement concrete of M25 to M45 or even higher grade. The function of the pier cap is to distribute the load of the superstructure on to the pier. The bearings of the bridge rest on the cap and are held to it by means of steel bolts. The pier cap also serves as a coping and is kept projecting beyond the pier by 150

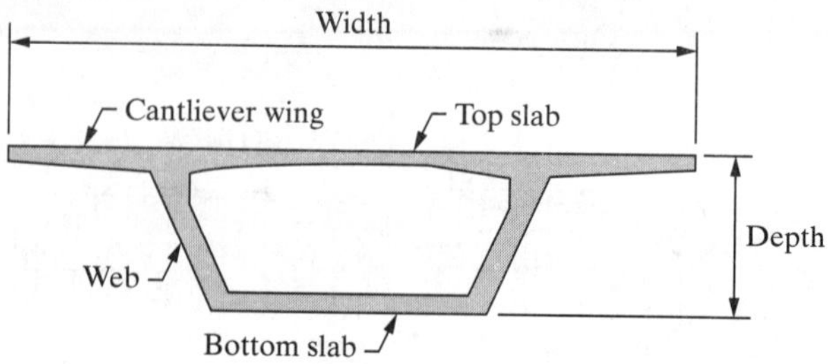

(a) Single cell box girder cross-section

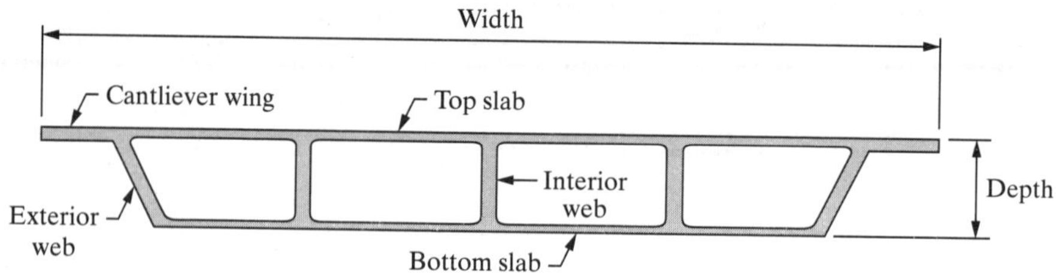

(b) Multi-cell box gorder cross-section

Figure 13.6 A typical box girder bridge cross-section.

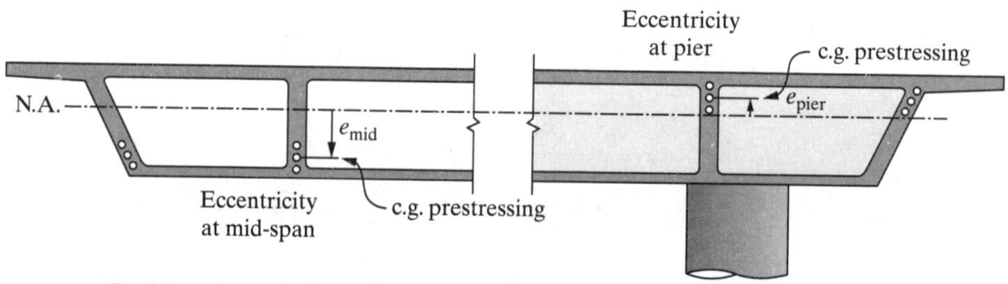

Figure 13.7 Tendon locations within the box girder cross-section.

to 300 mm. The size of pier cap and pier are decided by the vertical, longitudinal and lateral loads transferred to it from the superstructure. The top width and length of the pier cap are usually governed by the requirements of bridge seat. The top width should be sufficient to accommodate the bearings over it plus seismic restrainers. Similarly, the maximum length of the pier cap will be from outer-to-outer edges of bearings of the outer beams or girders of the superstructure.

The shape and size of the pier will depend upon the design loads, geometry of the road alignment in horizontal and vertical planes as well as aesthetics. A pier may rest on an isolated footing, combined footing, pile foundation or well foundation depending upon the soil properties and if situated in a river, then velocity of water current and scour depth etc. Well foundations have been extensively used in India on all major bridges across various rivers.

This chapter primarily deals with bridge loadings, frame proportions, modeling of bridges, design requirements, and analysis of bridges for earthquake force. Long span bridges are beyond the scope of the present text. Non-linear analysis of bridges is covered in Chapters 15 and 16.

13.2 DESIGN LOADS

The following types of loads act on the superstructure of a bridge:

1. Dead load
2. Live load
3. Impact factor on vehicular live load
4. Impact due to floating bodies or vessels
5. Centrifugal force
6. Wind load
7. Longitudinal forces caused by tractive effort of vehicles or braking of vehicles
8. Earthquake force
9. Secondary effects
10. Erection effects
11. Snow load
12. Vehicle collision load
13. Water current
14. Buoyancy
15. Earth pressure including live load surcharge, if any
16. Temperature effect
17. Deformation effects
18. Wave pressure
19. Grade effect

These loads are to be used with appropriate partial safety factors and combinations. There are two types of live loads on a bridge:

- Highway loadings
- Railway loadings.

Each country specifies its own loadings. In India, the *Indian Roads Congress* (IRC), New Delhi, under the Ministry of Surface Transport, specifies the highway loadings in IRC 6, while *Research Designs and Standards Organization* (RDSO), Lucknow, of the Indian Railways, specifies the railway loading in Bridge Rules. The *American Association of State Highway and Transportation Officials* (AASHTO)specifies loadings and other specifications in AASHTO LRFD Bridge Design Specifications.

In addition to the various loads listed earlier, it is assumed that due to some unforeseen reason, one of the spans of a highway bridge has dislodged off the pier/abutment. Similarly, in a railway bridge, *derailment loads* are also to be considered.

Wind loads on highway bridges are covered in Chapter 17.

13.2.1 Highway Loading

The IRC specifies different types of standard vehicles. The following loadings are very common (Figure 13.8):

- Class 70R tracked or wheeled loadings
- Class A or B loadings
- Class AA tracked or wheeled loading.
- Special vehicle

The maximum type pressure in different types of loadings in most cases is 5.273 kg/cm^2.

Class 70R vehicle

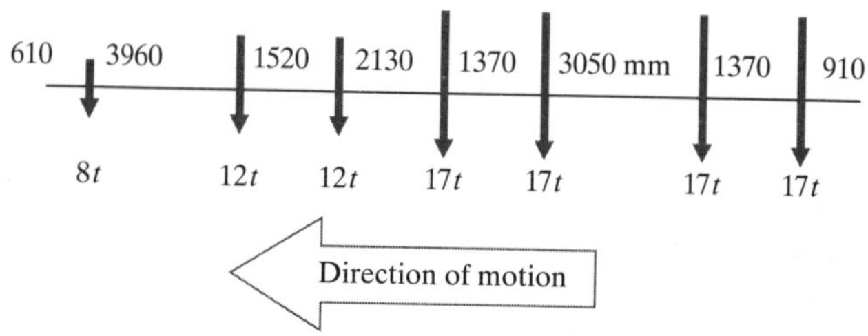

Overall nose to tail length = 14.92 m; Wheel to wheel length = 13.4 m; Total load = 100 t

Class A vehicle

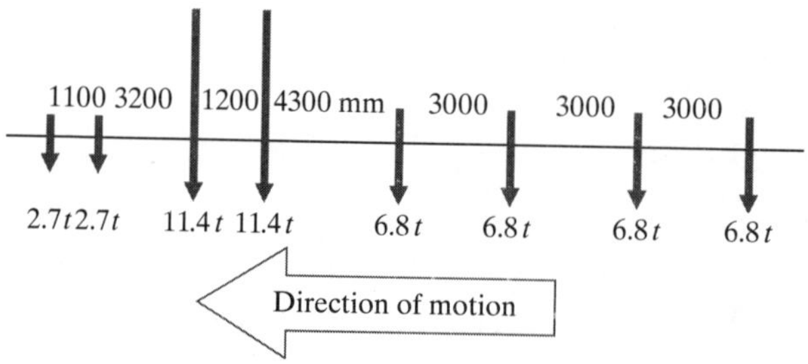

Overall nose to tail length = 20.3 m; Wheel to wheel length = 18.8 m; Total load = 55.4 t

Figure 13.8 Class 70R and Class A loading.

Class B vehicle: Same as Class A vehicle, the only difference is that loading is 2/3rd of class A, rest is same.

Special Vehicle
In view of very heavy vehicles with long trailers, a special vehicle has been introduced. The trailer unit has 20 axles @ 1.5 m c/c and 18 t load each.

13.2.2 Railway Loading

The RDSO Bridge Rules provide different loadings for different railway gauges. A gauge means the distance between the two rails of a track. There are three different railway gauges: broad gauge – 1676 mm, meter gauge – 1000 mm and narrow gauge – 762 mm or 610 mm. On most of the Indian rails and metros, broad gauge is the most prevalent. There are two types of live loadings for broad gauge railways:

- 25 t Loading – 2008 with a maximum axle load of 245.2 kN (25.0 t) for the locomotives and a train load of 91.53 kN/m (9.33 t/m) on both sides of the locomotives
- 32.5 t Loading – *Dedicated Freight Corridor Loading*, or (DFC) Loading – with a maximum axle load of 245.25 kN (25.0 t) for the locomotives and a train load of 118.99 kN/m (12.13 t/m) on both sides of the locomotives. The maximum axle load of wagons are 318.825 kN (32.5t).

(1 ton = 1000 kg, 1 kg = 9.81 N)

For convenience, the Bridge Rules provide diagrams of standard loading and Equivalent Uniformly Distributed Loads (EUDL) on each track for calculating bending moment and shear force.

The Equivalent Uniformly Distributed Load (EUDL) for Bending Moment (BM),

- for spans up to 10m, is that uniformly distributed load which produces the BM at the center of the span equal to the absolute maximum BM developed under the standard loads.
- for spans above 10m, the EUDL for BM is that uniformly distributed load which produces the BM at one-sixth of the span equal to the BM developed at that section under the standard loads.

EUDL for Shear Force (SF) is that uniformly distributed load which produces SF at the end of the span equal to the maximum SF developed under the standard loads at that section.

DFC Loading

- Combination 1 - Double headed diesel loco
- Combination 2 - Double headed electric loco
- Combination 3 - Electric loco
- Combination 4 - Double headed 25 t loco
- Combination 5 - Double headed 22.5 t loco

13.2.3 Combination of Vehicles on a Multi-lane Carriageway

On a multilane bridge, there can be number of combinations of vehicles on the bridge at any given point of time. The question arises how to consider the vehicle load combinations as well as pedestrian load combinations in various lanes of the bridge. IRC 6 provides minimum clearances between outer edge of the wheel and the roadway face of the kerb; and the minimum clearance between the outer edges of passing or crossing vehicles on multi-lane bridges as given in Table 13.1. IRC 5 defines *width of a carriageway* as the minimum clear width measured at right angles to the longitudinal center line of the bridge, between inside faces of the crash barrier/kerbs/median.

TABLE 13.1 CARRIAGEWAY LIVE LOAD COMBINATION IRC 6

S. No.	Carriageway width (CW)	Number of lanes for design purpose	Load combination
1	Less than 5.3 m	1	One lane of Class A considered to occupy 2.3 m. The remaining carriageway shall be loaded with 500 kg/m^2
2	5.3 m < CW < 9.6 m	2	One lane of Class 70R or two lanes of Class A
3	9.6 m < CW < 13.1 m	3	One lane of Class 70R for every two lanes, with one lane of Class A on the remaining lane, or three lanes of Class A
4	13.1 m < CW < 16.6 m	4	One lane of Class 70R for every two lanes, with one lane of Class A on the remaining lane, if any, OR one lane of Class A for each lane
5	16.6 m < CW < 20.1 m	5	
6	20.1 m < CW < 23.6 m	6	

The minimum width of two-lane carriageway shall be 7.5 m.

A series of longitudinal analysis of the bridge is carried out with different load combinations by placing the various vehicles in different lanes to determine the axial force, shear force, bending moment and torsional forces in the superstructure and bearings. Torsional forces in the superstructure arise due to the lateral placing of loads in outer lanes, and also due to pedestrian loading in the footpaths.

13.2.4 Combination of Vehicles for Railways

The analysis and design will be carried out for all possible cases of rolling train loads. All the supporting structures, such as superstructure, bearings, substructure and foundations must be checked for the following four cases:

- One track of one span is loaded (OTOS)
- One track of both spans is loaded (OTBS)
- Two tracks of one span are loaded (BTOS)
- Two tracks of both spans are loaded (BTBS)

A railway track consists of the rails, fasteners, sleepers and ballast (or slab track), plus the underlying subgrade. There are two types of tracks:

Ballasted Track

A ballasted track form worldwide consists of flat-bottom steel rails supported on timber or pre-stressed concrete sleepers, which are themselves, laid on crushed stone ballast. The purpose of crushed angular stone ballast is to support the sleepers and allow some adjustment of their position, while allowing free drainage.

Ballastless Track

In a ballastless track, the rails are attached directly to a reinforced concrete slab through a resilient base plate. There are no sleepers and crushed stone ballast. Such a track has very long life cycles, top speed, ride comfort, and great load-carrying capability. Practically maintenance free, ballastless track systems ensure very long durability and cost-effective solution over the long run.

Rail-Structure Interaction

Earlier, most railways consisted of a series of rails having finite length and separated by a small gap of 5 mm. They were free to expand and contract under the thermal stresses due to the movement of the train. This resulted in heavy wear and tear to the rails as well as to the train wheels, besides a very poor quality of ride for the users. In such cases, analysis of effects of various loads on rails and bridges was carried out separately.

Now most railway tracks consist of *continuous welded rails* (CWR). This has resulted in very high speed tracks with a very good ride quality. Continuous welded rails include a central zone where expansion and contraction are completely prevented and two "breather" zones at each end about 150 m long. Expansion devices at the ends of the CWR have a variation of opening of 50 mm and permit the free movement of ends of the CWR. The thermal effects generated are as shown in Figure 13.9(a).

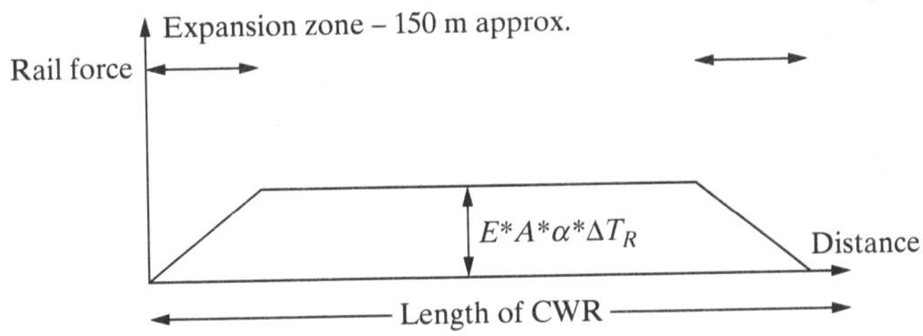

Figure 13.9(a) Behaviour of CWR under thermal changes.

Introducing a bridge under a CWR track means that it is resting on surface subjected to deformation and movements, hence causing displacement of the track. Since both track and the bridge are able to move, any force or displacement that acts on any one of them will induce forces in the other. There is an interaction between them as follows (Figure 13.9b):

- Forces applied to a CWR track induce additional forces into the track and/or into the bearings supporting the deck and movements of the track and of the deck;
- Any movement of the deck induces a movement of the track and an additional force in the track, indirectly, in the bridge bearings.

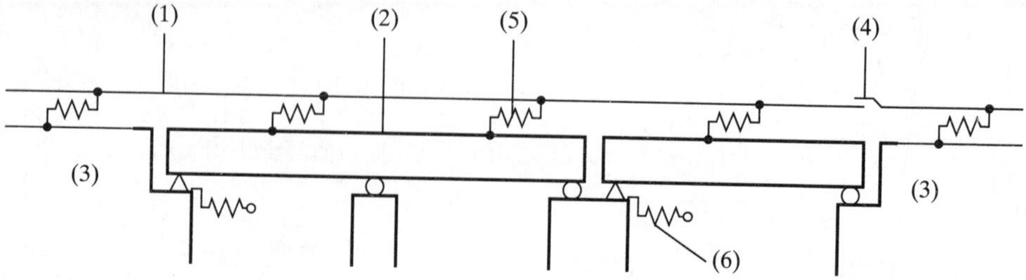

Figure 13.9(b) Model of a track/structure system.

Where,

1. Track
2. Superstructure (a single deck comprising two spans and a single deck with one span shown)
3. Embankment
4. Rail expansion device (if present)
5. Longitudinal non-linear springs reproducing the longitudinal load/displacement behaviour of the track
6. Longitudinal springs reproducing the longitudinal stiffness K of a fixed support to the deck taking into account the stiffness of the foundation, piers and bearings etc.

The extra stresses in the rail are induced by thermal expansion/contraction of bridge deck(s)/tracks, deflection of sub-structure under tractive/braking forces from the trains and the end rotations caused by vertical bending under vertical train loads. The magnitude of these extra stresses in the CWR mainly depends on the stiffness of various elements of bridge, resistance offered by the track structure to deformation and the boundary condition of rails (i.e. whether these are continuous or have expansion joint(s) in between).

Therefore, in a railway bridge, there is a need to analyze the bridge for *rail-structure interaction* (RSI) in accordance with UIC 774-3R code (2001) and RDSO Guidelines for RSI (2014).

13.2.5 Impact Factor (Dynamic Effect) IRC 6

The dynamic effect of the moving load is taken care of by increasing the live load by a certain factor, called *impact factor*. This factor depends on many variables like the type of loading, speed, type of the structure, material of the structure, loaded length as discussed in Chapter 11. It is difficult to have a single expression involving all the variables. Design codes generally give empirical expressions for impact factor for different bridges. IRC 6 gives the following impact factors for different situations.

Impact Factor Fraction

(A) For class A or class B loading

(i) *RCC Bridge*

For span 3 m or less	0.5	
For span 3 m to 45 m	$4.5/(6 + L)$	(11.54a)

(ii) *Steel bridge*

For span 3 m or less	0.545	
For span 3 m to 45 m	$9/(13.5 + L)$	(11.54b)

(B) For class AA or class 70R loading

(a) For spans less than 9 m

(i) For tracked vehicles	0.25 up to 5m linearly reducing to 0.10 for span of 9 m
(ii) For wheeled vehicles	0.25

(b) For spans of 9 m or more

(i) *RCC Bridge*

(i) For tracked vehicles	0.10 up to 40 m and in accordance to curve given in IRC 6 for span in excess of 40 m.
(ii) For wheeled vehicles	0.25 up to 12 m and in accordance to curve given in IRC 6 for span in excess of 12 m.

(ii) *Steel Bridge*

(i) For tracked vehicles	0.10
(ii) For wheeled vehicles	0.25 up to 23 m and in accordance to curve given in IRC 6 for span in excess of 23 m.

13.2.6 Impact Factor (Dynamic Effect) IRS Bridge Rules

IRS Bridge Rules give impact factors, referred to as *Coefficient of Dynamic Augment (CDA)*for different situations.

For Broad Gauge Railway: The augmentation in load due to dynamic effects should be considered by adding a load Equivalent to a *Coefficient of Dynamic Augment (CDA)* multiplied by the live load giving the maximum stress in the member under consideration. The CDA should be obtained as follows and would be applicable up to 160 km/h on BG.

For single track spans,

$$\text{CDA} = 0.15 + \frac{8}{6+L} \leq 1.0 \tag{13.1}$$

where L is

- the loaded length of span in meter for the position of the train giving the maximum stress in the member under consideration, or
- 1.5 times the cross-girder spacing in the case of stringers (rail bearers) and
- 2.5 times the cross girder spacing in the case of cross girders.

For double track spans,
For main girders of double track spans with 2 girders, CDA as calculated above may be multiplied by a factor of 0.72 and shall be subject to a maximum of 0.72.

13.3 LONGITUDINAL FORCES ON HIGHWAY BRIDGES

In all bridges provision should be made for longitudinal forces along the direction of traffic arising from any one or more of the following causes:

(a) Tractive effort caused through acceleration of the driving wheels,
(b) Braking effect resulting from the application of the brakes to braked wheels, and
(c) Frictional resistance offered to the movement of free bearings due to change of temperature or any other cause.

The braking effect is invariably greater than the tractive effort in highway bridges. The braking effect on a simply supported span or a continuous unit of spans or on any other type of highway bridge unit will be assumed to have the following value:

In the case of a single lane or a two-lane bridge –

- 20% of the first train load plus 10% of the load of the succeeding trains or part thereof, the train loads in one lane only being considered for the purpose of this subclause.
- Where the entire first train is not on the full span, the braking force shall be taken as equal to 20% of the loads actually on the span or continuous unit of spans.

In the case of bridges having more than two-lanes – As above for the first two lanes plus 5% of the loads on the lanes in excess of two.

The force due to braking effect is assumed to act along a line parallel to the roadway and 1.2 m above it. While transferring the force to the bearings, the change in the vertical reaction at the bearings should be taken into account. The distribution of longitudinal horizontal forces among the bridge bearings depends on the horizontal deformation of bridges, and interaction between the bearings, piers and foundations.

13.3.1 Spans on Unyielding Supports

Simply Supported Spans
For a simply supported span with fixed and free bearings (other than elastomeric type) on stiff supports, horizontal forces at the bearing level in the longitudinal direction shall be greater of the two values given below:

Fixed Bearing

$$F_h - \mu\left(R_g + R_q\right) \tag{13.2a}$$

or,

$$\frac{F_h}{2} + \mu\left(R_g + R_q\right) \tag{13.2b}$$

Free Bearing

$$\mu\left(R_g + R_q\right) \tag{13.2c}$$

Where, F_h = applied horizontal force
R_g = reaction at free end due to dead load
R_q = reaction at free end due to live load
μ = coefficient of friction at the movable bearing which may be assumed to have the following values:

- For steel roller bearings = 0.03
- For concrete roller bearings = 0.05
- For sliding bearings
    - Steel on cast iron or steel on steel = 0.40
    - Concrete over concrete with bitumen layer in between = 0.50
    - Teflon on stainless steel 0.03 or 0.05 whichever is governing

(b) For a simply supported span sitting on identical elastomeric bearings at each end resting on unyielding supports, the force at each end is given by

$$\frac{F_h}{2} + V_r l_{tc} \tag{13.3}$$

Where, V_r = shear rating of the elastomeric bearings (as discussed later)
l_{tc} = movement of deck above bearing other than that due to applied forces

Continuous Bridges with One Fixed Bearing and Other Free Bearings

A typical 4-span continuous bridge with boundary conditions at pier top is shown in Figure 13.10. There is only one fixed support at *E*, whereas, all the remaining supports are free. The entire longitudinal force in the direction of the traffic for this 4-span continuous bridge acts at the fixed bearings at *E* alone. The lateral force in the transverse direction of the traffic will act at each fixed and free bearing corresponding to a given pier span.

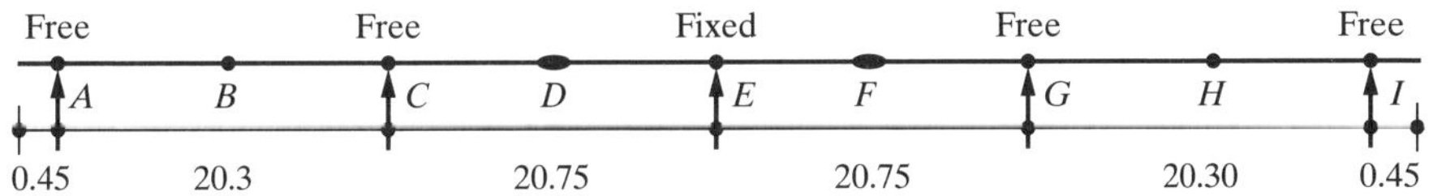

Figure 13.10 A 4-span continuous bridge with support conditions at pier top.

The support reactions at the fixed bearing and free bearings are as follows:

Fixed Bearing

Case 1: $(\mu R - \mu L) +$ ve; F_h acting in + ve direction

If $F_h > 2\mu R$

$$F_h - \mu(R + L) \tag{13.4a}$$

If $F_h < 2\mu R$

$$\frac{F_h}{1+\sum n_R}+(\mu R-\mu L) \quad (13.4b)$$

Case 2: $(\mu R-\mu L)+$ ve; F_h acting in – ve direction

If $F_h > 2\mu L$

$$F_h-\mu(R+L) \quad (13.4c)$$

If $F_h < 2\mu L$

$$\frac{F_h}{1+\sum n_L}+(\mu R-\mu L) \quad (13.4d)$$

Free Bearing

$$\mu R_x \quad (13.4e)$$

Where, n_L or n_R = number of free bearings to the left or right of fixed bearings, respectively

μL or μR = the total horizontal force developed at the free bearings to the left or right of the fixed bearing, respectively, due to friction

μR_x = the net horizontal force developed at any one of the free bearings considered to the left or right of the fixed bearings

In seismic areas, the fixed bearing must also be checked for full earthquake force and braking/tractive force. The structure under the fixed bearing must be designed to withstand the full earthquake and design braking/tractive force.

13.3.2 Spans on Flexible Supports

The term *flexible supports* here mean elastomeric bearings. *Shear rating* of an elastomeric bearing is the horizontal force required to move the top of the support through a unit distance taking into account horizontal deformation of the bridges, flexibility of the support and rotation of the foundation. The distribution of *the applied longitudinal horizontal forces* (for example, braking force, earthquake force, wind force etc.) depends solely on shear ratings of the supports and may be estimated in proportion to the ratio of individual shear ratings of a support to the sum of the shear ratings of all the supports.

The distribution of self-induced horizontal force caused by deck movement (owing to temperature, shrinkage, creep, elastic shortening, etc.) depends not only on shear ratings of the supports but also on the location of the *zero movement point* in the deck.

13.3.3 Reduction in the Longitudinal Effect

The IRC 6 code permits a reduction in the longitudinal effect on bridges carrying more than two lanes in view of low probability that all the lanes will be subjected to the maximum load simultaneously. It is given as shown in Table 13.2.

TABLE 13.2 REDUCTION IN LONGITUDINAL EFFECTS

Number of lanes	Load combination	Reduction factor
For two lanes	1 class 70R or 2 class A	1
For three lanes	1 class 70R + 1 class A or 3 class A	0.9
For four lanes	2 class 70R or 4 class A	0.8
For five or more lanes	1 class 70R per 2 lane + 1 class A per remaining lane or 1 class A per each lane	0.8

13.4 LONGITUDINAL FORCES ON RAILWAY BRIDGES

The longitudinal forces on railway bridges are specified by the Bridge Rules as shown in Table 13.3 for DFC loading. The braking effect is invariably smaller than the tractive effort of the driving wheels of locomotives in railway bridges unless the loaded length is very large as specified in IRS Bridge Rules. For twin tracked decks carrying traffic in opposite directions, consideration should be given to braking forces from one train and traction forces from other train, acting simultaneously, which will be the maximum longitudinal loading on the deck.

TABLE 13.3 LONGITUDINAL FORCES – BRIDGE RULES

Item	Combination 1	Combination 2	Combination 3	Combination 4 and 5
Tractive effort per loco	63 t	52 t	84 t	50 t
Braking force per loco axle	25%	25%	25%	25%
Braking force of train load	13.4%	13.4%	13.4%	13.4%

The longitudinal force on bearings can be determined similar to that in the highway bridges discussed earlier.

13.5 EARTHQUAKE FORCE

The horizontal earthquake force to be resisted by the bridge structure

$$F_{\text{eq}} = \alpha_h W_e$$

Where W_e = Effective dead load and live load on the bridge

The horizontal seismic coefficient for a bridge is same as discussed in Chapter 12:

$$\alpha_h = \frac{Z}{2} \times I \times \frac{S_a}{g} \tag{13.5}$$

Both in the Indian Highway Code IRC 6 and in the Indian Railway code on Seismic Design of Bridges, the factor R is taken as 1 in the computation of design base shear or design seismic force. Later, the member forces are divided by the corresponding values of R to get the design member forces. The displacements are not to be modified with the R factor.

The earthquake ground motion is a random phenomenon and it can be resolved in three mutually perpendicular directions. The components of the ground motion are considered to act simultaneously, but independently. The two horizontal components of earthquake are taken as of equal magnitude, while the vertical component is taken as two third of the horizontal component.

13.5.1 Period of Vibration

The following approximation can be used to compute the fundamental period of vibration of a bridge as per IRC 6:

$$T = 2\pi\sqrt{\frac{m}{k}} = 2\pi\sqrt{\frac{W_e/g}{1000K}} \tag{13.6a}$$

$$\approx 2\sqrt{\frac{W_e}{1000K}} \tag{13.6b}$$

Where, m = mass of the superstructure in kg corresponding to appropriate dead load and live load

k = lateral stiffness of the bridge in N/m

W_e = appropriate dead load and live load in kN

K = stiffness in kN/mm

Or, 1000 K = stiffness in kN/m

g = acceleration due to gravity in m/sec^2

Buoyancy and uplift should be ignored in the calculation of seismic weight.

The full weight of superstructure and pile cap along with 1/3rd weight of piers are included in dead load. In order to calculate the lateral stiffness of the bridge, an arbitrary force of 10 kN is applied at the center of mass of the superstructure and the corresponding lateral deflection is calculated by static analysis. The force/lateral deflection gives the desired stiffness. The moment of inertia of concrete sections should be considered on cracked basis to estimate stiffness.

The Indian railway code BS 118 has the following stipulation:

W_e = full weight of the superstructure, 80% weight of the pier, and appropriate amount of live load in kN

The fundamental period of a bridge can also be calculated using the eigenvalue method discussed in Chapter 10.

13.5.2 Contribution of Live Load for Earthquake Analysis

The earthquake force will act in the three orthogonal directions on the bridge. The contribution of live load in the estimation of earthquake force along these three directions in highway bridges is considered as follows:

- The earthquake force due to live load shall not be considered when acting in the direction of traffic, but shall be considered in the direction perpendicular to the traffic.
- The horizontal earthquake force in the direction perpendicular to the traffic shall be calculated using 20 percent of live load.
- The vertical earthquake force shall be calculated using 20 percent of live load.

The contribution of live load in the estimation of earthquake force along these three directions *in railway bridges* is considered as follows:

- The earthquake force due to live load shall not be considered when acting in the direction of traffic, but shall be considered in the direction perpendicular to the traffic.
- The horizontal earthquake force in the direction perpendicular to the traffic shall be calculated using 50 percent of live load (excluding impact effect).
- The vertical earthquake force shall be calculated using 50 percent of live load (excluding impact effect).

13.5.3 Importance Factor

The importance of a bridge depends whether it is classified as an essential bridge or a critical bridge that, in turn, will depend on one or more of the following factors:

- Extent of disturbance to traffic and possibility of providing temporary diversion
- Availability of alternative routes
- Cost of repairs and time involved, which depend on the extent of damages – minor or major
- Cost of replacement, and time involved in reconstruction in case of failure, and
- Indirect economic loss due to its partial or full non-availability, Importance factors are given in Table 13.4 for different types of bridges.

13.5.4 Response Reduction Factor

The physical significance of response reduction factor was discussed in detail in Chapter 12 with respect to buildings. The same is applicable to bridges and other structures. Different response reduction factors are applicable for different components of a bridge as shown in Table 13.5.

TABLE 13.4 IMPORTANCE FACTOR

Seismic Class	Description	Importance factor I
Normal bridge	All bridges except those mentioned below.	1.0
Essential bridge	(a) River bridges and flyovers inside cities (b) Bridges on national and state highways (c) Bridges serving traffic near ports etc. (d) Bridges crossing railway lines (e) It should be usable by emergency/defense purposes immediately after the safety evaluation	1.25
Critical bridge	(a) Bridges more than 1 km length (b) Bridges for which alternate routes are not available (c) It should be usable by emergency/defense purposes immediately after the safety evaluation	1.5

TABLE 13.5 RESPONSE REDUCTION FACTORS (IRC 6)

Bridge Component	R with ductile detailing
Superstructure	
(a) Superstructure of integral/Semi integral bridge/Framed bridges	2.0
(b) Other types of Superstructure, including precast segmental constructions	1.0
Substructure	
(i) Masonry/PCC Piers, Abutments	1.0
(ii) RCC wall piers and abutments in transverse direction (where plastic hinge cannot develop)	1.0
(iii) RCC wall piers and abutments in longitudinal direction (where hinges can develop)	3.0
(iv) RCC Single Column	3.0
(v) RCC/PSC Frames	3.0
(vi) Steel Framed Construction	3.0
(vii) Steel Cantilever Pier	1.5
Bearings and Connections	1.0
Stoppers (Reaction Blocks) Those restraining dislodgement or drifting away of bridge elements	1.0

The Railway code on reinforced concrete bridges gives R factors for railway bridge components.

13.6 BRIDGE GEOMETRY AND PROPORTIONS

The simplest way to increase likelihood of a bridge structure responding to a seismic event in its fundamental mode of vibration is to balance its stiffness and mass distribution. Irregularities in geometry lead to complex nonlinear response that cannot be predicted by elastic modeling or plane frame nonlinear static modeling.

13.6.1 Balanced Stiffness

The distributions of stiffness and mass are included in the model for dynamic analysis. The discretization of the model must account for geometric and material variation in stiffness and mass. Most of the mass of a bridge is in the superstructure. Four to five elements per span are generally sufficient to represent the mass and stiffness distribution of the superstructure. For spine models of the superstructure, the line of elements should be located at the locus of the mass centroid. Rigid links can be used to represent the geometric location of mass relative to the spine elements in the model. For single-column piers, C-bents, or unusual pier configurations, the rotational mass moment of inertia of the superstructure about the longitudinal axis should be included. The inertia of live loads need not be included in the earthquake analysis. However, the probability of a large live load being on the bridge during an earthquake should be considered when designing bridges with high live-to-dead-load ratios that are located in heavy traffic congestion areas.

The following should be considered when calculating effective stiffness of a frame: *framing effects, end conditions, column height, percentage of longitudinal and transverse column steel, column diameter, and foundation flexibility*. Some of the consequences of not meeting the relative stiffness requirements defined above include:

- Increased damage in the stiffer elements
- An unbalanced distribution of inelastic response throughout the structure
- Increased column torsion generated by rigid body rotation of the superstructure

The ratio of effective stiffness between any two bents within a frame or between any two columns within a bent, or between adjacent bents within a frame or between adjacent columns within a bent must satisfy the conditions given in Table 13.6. An increase in superstructure mass along the length of the frame should be accompanied by a reasonable increase in column stiffness as shown in Figure 13.11. For variable width frames the tributary mass supported by each bent or column should be included in the stiffness comparisons as specified in the same table.

13.6.2 Balanced Frame Geometry

For bridges with multiple frames, which are separated by expansion bearings or hinges, it is unnecessary to model and analyze the entire bridge for earthquake loads. Each frame is expected to have sufficient strength to resist inertia loads from its own mass.

TABLE 13.6 COLUMN/BENT STIFFNESS RATIOS FOR FRAMES

Column/Bent	Stiffness ratio for	
	Constant width frame	**Variable width frame**
For any two bents in the frame or, any two columns in a bent	$\frac{k_i}{k_j} \geq 0.50$	$2 \geq \frac{\frac{k_i}{m_i}}{\frac{k_j}{m_j}} \geq 0.50$
For adjacent bents in a frame or, adjacent columns in a bent	$\frac{k_i}{k_j} \geq 0.75$	$1.33 \geq \frac{\frac{k_i}{m_i}}{\frac{k_j}{m_j}} \geq 0.75$

Where, k_i = smaller effective bent or column stiffness
k_j = larger effective bent or column stiffness
m_i = tributary mass of column or bent i
m_j = tributary mass of column or bent j

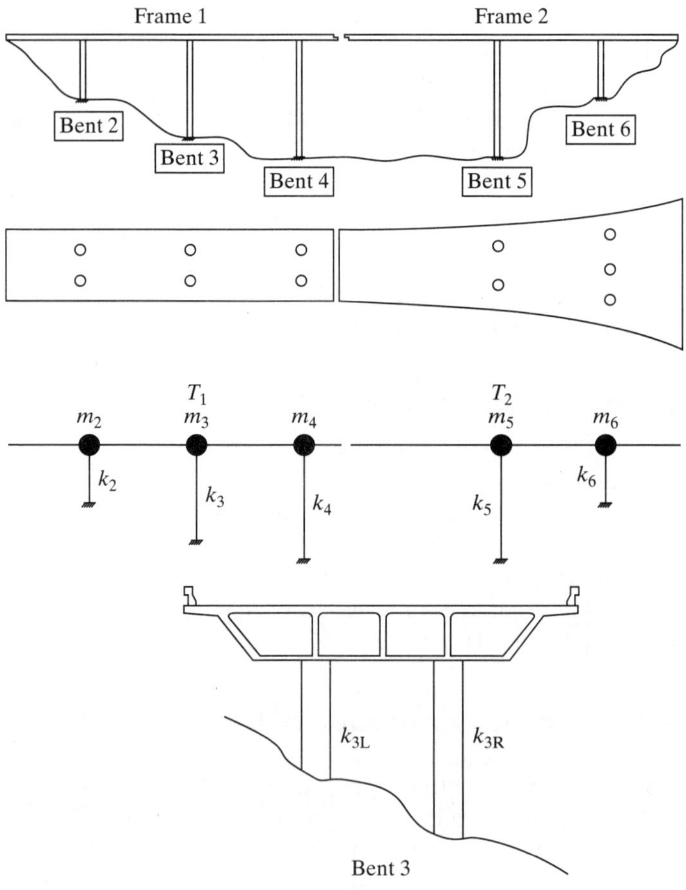

Figure 13.11 Balanced Stiffness (Caltrans 2019).

However, when adjacent frames have large differences in vibration period, the frame with the longer period may increase the earthquake load on the frame with the shorter period by impact across the bearing or hinge, or by transverse forces through shear keys. To account for these effects, the number of frames included in a model depends on the ratio of vibration period of the frames. For bridges in which the period ratio of adjacent frames is less than 0.70 (shortest period frame divided by longest period frame), it is recommended to limit a model to five frames. The first and fifth frames in the model are considered to be boundary frames, representing the interaction with the remainder of the structure. The response of the three interior frames can be used for design of those frames. For a bridge with more than five frames, several different models may be used in the design. For bridges with period ratios of frames between 0.70 and 1.0, fewer than five frames may be used in a model.

The ratio of fundamental periods of vibration for adjacent frames in the longitudinal and transverse direction shall satisfy Equation (13.7)

$$\frac{T_i}{T_j} \geq 0.70 \tag{13.7}$$

T_i = natural period of the less flexible frame

T_j = natural period of the more flexible frame

The consequences of not meeting the fundamental period requirements of Equation (13.7) include a greater likelihood of out-of-phase response between adjacent frames leading to large relative displacements that increase the probability of longitudinal unseating and collision between frames at the expansion joints. The collision and relative transverse translation of adjacent frames will transfer the seismic demand from one frame to the next, which can be detrimental to the stand-alone capacity of the frame receiving the additional seismic demand.

In the case of bridges with a continuous deck and with transverse stiffness of the abutments and of the adjacent piers which is very high compared to that of the other piers, it may be preferable to use transversally sliding or elastomeric bearings over the short piers or the abutments. This is preferable in order to avoid unfavourable distribution of the transverse seismic action among the piers and the abutments as shown in Figure 13.12.

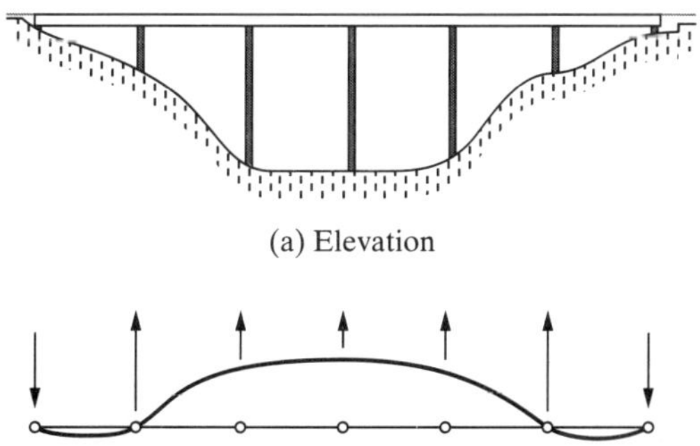

(a) Elevation

(b) Plan

Figure 13.12 Unfavourable distribution of transverse seismic action.

13.7 BEARINGS IN BRIDGES

A bearing is a structural device that transmits loads while facilitating translation and/or rotation. The bearings play a very significant role in transferring the entire load from superstructure to the top of piers. This load includes dead load, superimposed dead load, live load, longitudinal effects, lateral load due to wind and earthquake, and centrifugal force etc. Bearings are designed and detailed for service loads. However, the bearings should be checked for their capacity and mode of failure to be consistent with the assumptions made in the analysis. Distribution of vertical load among bearings may adversely affect individual bearings. This is particularly critical when the girders are stiff in bending and torsion, and bearings are stiff in compression, and the construction method does not allow minor misalignments to be corrected.

Bridge movements arise from number of different causes. Curved and skewed bridges have transverse as well as longitudinal movement due to temperature effects and creep or shrinkage. Transverse movement of the superstructure relative to the substructure may become significant for very wide bridges. Relatively wide curved and skewed bridges often undergo significant diagonal thermal movement, which introduces large transverse movements or large transverse forces if the bridge is restrained against such movements. Rotations caused by permissible levels of misalignment during installation should also be considered, and in many cases they will be larger than the live load rotations.

The bearings should be detailed in such a manner that they can be easily inspected for any damage, and replaced or repaired after an earthquake. A bearing may permit translation in one or more of the three orthogonal directions, or restrain all translations. There are at least two bearings at each pier cap. However, the actual number will depend upon the nature and type of superstructure. The boundary conditions at each bearing need to be assigned very carefully consistent with the desired behaviour during normal and earthquake loading, in the longitudinal and lateral directions in plan. Different types of bridge bearings are as follows (IRC 83):

- Steel bearings – Roller and rocker
- Elastomeric bearings
- Pot, Pot cum PTFE bearings

Steel roller and rocker bearings are classical bearings used in steel bridges for more than 150 years. Elastomeric and Pot, Pot cum PTFE bearings are relatively new and are widely used throughout the world. PTFE is also known as Teflon. *Pot Bearing is a* bearing that carries vertical load by compression of an elastomeric disc confined in a steel cylinder and that accommodates rotation by deformation of the disc. These bearings ae used for supporting very heavy loads.

Symbols for different bearings are shown in Figure 13.13. Typical arrangements of bearings in different bridges are shown in Figure 13.14.

Pin Bearing A type of pot bearing which along with vertical load, bears and transmits horizontal force in any direction and allows rotation about any axis in horizontal plane, without permitting any movement in horizontal plane. It is also referred to as a fixed bearing.

Bearing Type	**Symbol**	**Bearing Type**	**Boundary conditions (Non-zero Reactions)**
Type 1		Pin bearing	*Fx* and *Fy*
Type 2		Metallic bearing	*Fx* and *Fz*
Type 3		Transverse sliding bearing	*Fy* and *Fz*
Type 4		Free bearing	*Fz*

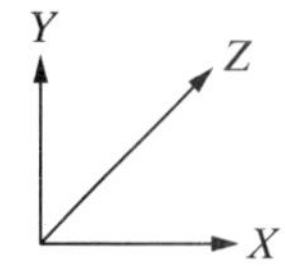

(X and Y are in horizontal plane)

Figure 13.13 Symbols (in plan) to represent degrees of freedom in bearings and the corresponding reactions.

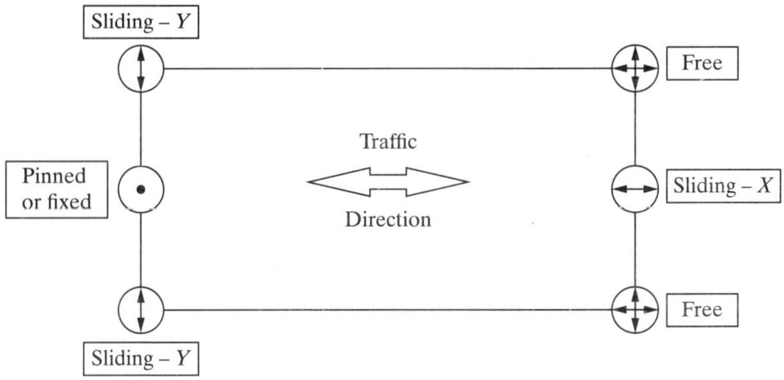

(a) Typical arrangement of bearings in a simply supported bridge (Plan)

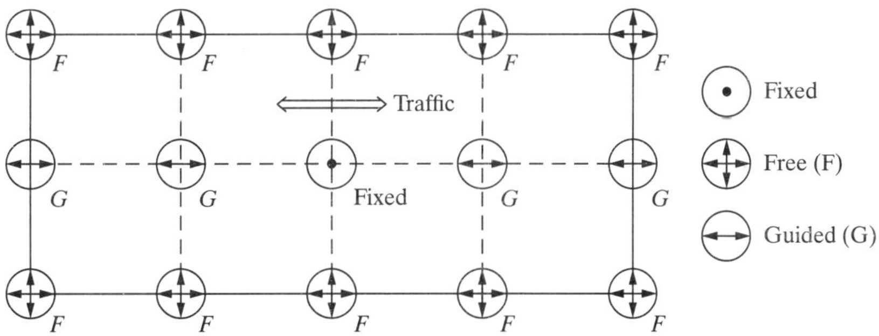

(b) Arrangement of bearings in straight continuous bridge – plan

Figure 13.14 Typical arrangement of bearings in bridges (plan).

Free Bearing A type of pot bearing which along with vertical load, bears and transmits horizontal force in any direction and allows movement in any direction in the horizontal plane and permits rotation about any axis in horizontal plane.

Guided Bearing A type of pot bearing which along with vertical load, bears and transmits horizontal force in any one direction only and allows movement perpendicular to that direction and permits rotation about any axis in horizontal plane.

In any bridge, there must be at least one pin or fixed bearing to anchor the superstructure to the abutments/piers.

Figure 13.14(a) shows a simply supported span. There is one sliding-X or guided-X bearing which permits movement in X-direction only, and resists the force in Y direction. Similarly, there are two sliding-Y or guided-Y bearings that permit movement in Y-direction only, and resist the forces in X direction. There is one pin bearing and two free bearings.

Figure 13.14(b) shows bearing layout for a straight 4-span continuous bridge. There is one pin bearing, 4-guided bearings along X-direction, and rest of the bearings are free bearings. Thus, the entire lateral force in Y-direction is borne by the pin bearing and the guided bearings. The entire longitudinal force is borne by the pin bearing alone. Thus, the design of the pin bearing becomes critical. The bearings must be chosen very carefully so that they are compatible with the nature of the bridge.

Deformations at Bearings

There is a further need to compute translational movements (strains) along longitudinal and transverse directions due to shrinkage, creep, and temperature in concrete of the deck. Also, rotation due to self weight of girder, SIDL, and live load need to be computed (IRC 83-part 2). These deformations must be accommodated by the bearings.

13.8 MODELING OF A BRIDGE

A global model should capture the response of the entire bridge system. The model of the bridge and the selection of the dynamic degrees of freedom should represent the distribution of stiffness and mass so that all significant deformation modes and inertia forces are activated under the design earthquake excitation. It is usually sufficient to use two separate models in the analysis, one for modeling the response in the longitudinal direction of the bridge, and the other for the transverse direction. The following information is required for the modeling of the basic bridge structural geometry:

- Total length of the bridge
- Number of spans and length of each superstructure span
- Total superstructure width
- Superstructure cross-sectional geometry
- Number and clear height of each column bent
- Column cross-sectional dimension in the direction of interest
- Distance from column top to center of gravity of superstructure
- Length of cab beam to centroid of column

- Cap beam width
- Location of expansion joints
- Support details for boundary conditions

In addition, the following data are also required:

- Foundation soil geotechnical properties
- Abutment general arrangement drawings
- Number and properties of abutment bearing pads
- Size of expansion joints

For earthquake analysis of highway bridges,3-D beam column elements (line or frame elements) with corresponding cross-sectional properties are used to represent the superstructure and the components of the bents, that is, columns and pile cap beams. The geometry, nodes, and connectivity of the elements in the model will be determined by the local topography and the structural system. In this 3-D spine model of the bridge structure, it is assumed that the line elements are located at the centroid of the cross section, and follow the alignment of the bridge.

The superstructure elements will be modeled as linear-elastic beam-column elements with material properties corresponding to cracked reinforced concrete. The elevation (node height) of the superstructure frame elements will be defined at the elevation of the superstructure centroid. The values of the cross-sectional area (A), torsional constant (J), moments of inertia (I_{22} and I_{33}), shear areas (A_2 and A_3), elastic and plastic section moduli (S_{22}, S_{33}, Z_{22}, and Z_{33}), and radii of gyration (r_{22} and r_{33}) in the vertical and transverse directions of the superstructure must be estimated accurately.

Skew and curved bridges pose special problems in terms of torsion and uplift. Therefore, they need to be modeled very carefully so as to capture their characteristic behaviour.

The pile cap beam is a concrete element connecting the superstructure and the column bents, helping a multi-column bent bridge resist, through frame action, lateral loads or displacements applied primarily in the transverse direction of the bridge. For single-column bent bridges, the cap beam is built to facilitate the connection of the bent to the superstructure and reinforce the joint. It is again modeled using a line beam-column element with a solid rectangular cross section with dimensions according to plans.

No nonlinearities are considered for the superstructure elements for an overall analysis of the bridge, since other elements such as the columns and abutments are designed to undergo inelastic excursions, while the superstructure is protected by a capacity design and is expected to remain in the elastic range of response. There are three modelling options for a typical T-girder bridge:

- Line beam or spine model
- Grillage model
- Finite element model

A line beam or spine model is a fairly simple tool. It does not account for transverse distribution of loads; it gives no output for transverse design (e.g. slab or bracing) and does not consider skew effects. It cannot be recommended for detail design, but is a useful tool for preliminary design. Grillage model is suitable in many situations and is being used extensively for the analysis of T-girder, deck slab, and voided slab bridges. The finite element model is very powerful as it accounts for varying cross-sections of the bridge geometry and gives more accurate results.

Typical spine models with single column bent and double column bents are shown in Figures 13.15. Modeling of bridges having unequal piers, curved in plan, and having curvilinear geometry in space are discussed in PEER (2008) and Caltrans (2019).

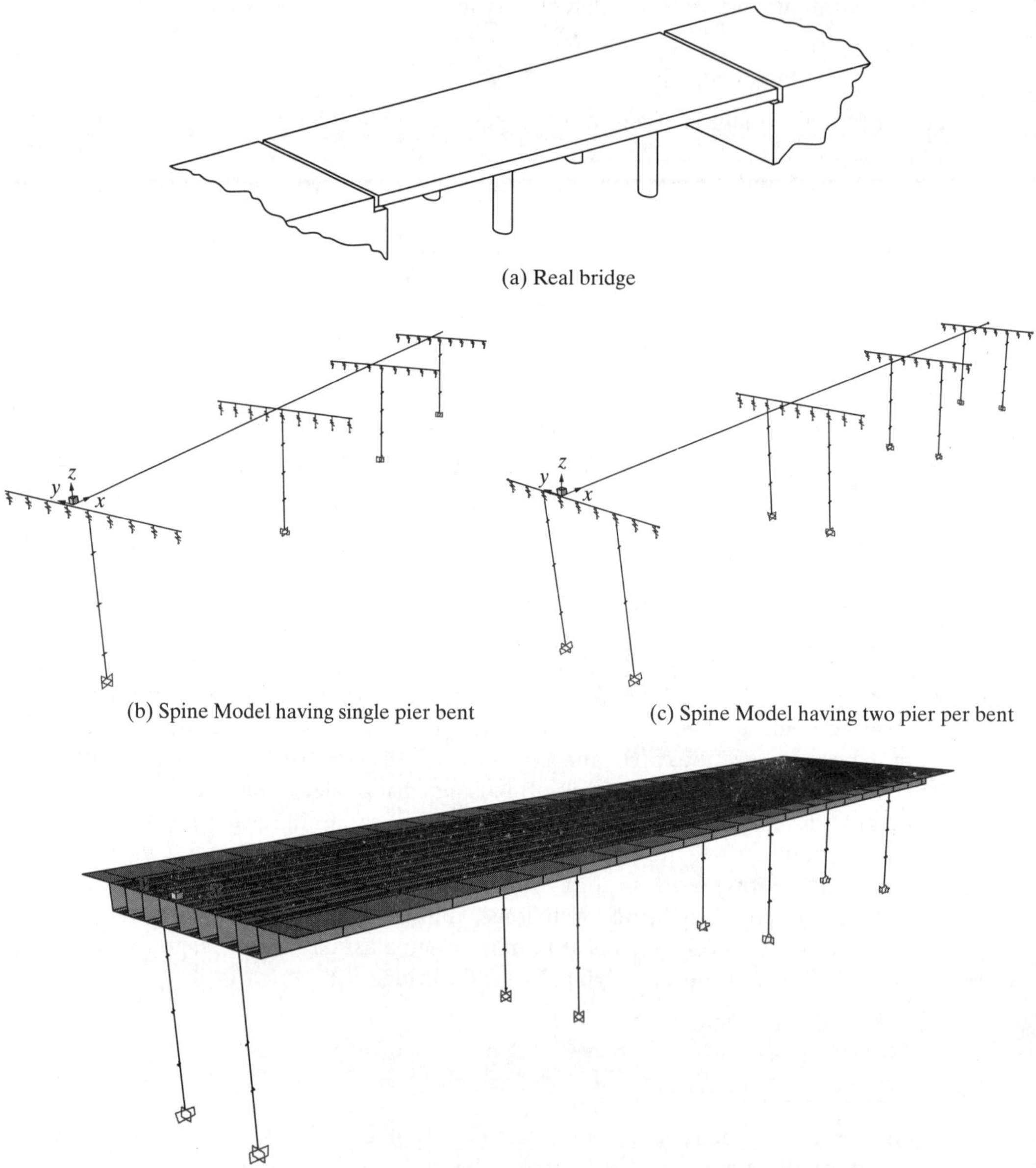

(a) Real bridge

(b) Spine Model having single pier bent

(c) Spine Model having two pier per bent

(d) FEM or Area object model having two pier per bent

Figure 13.15 Modeling of a bridge having single or double pier per bent.

13.9 WHEN TO USE EARTHQUAKE ANALYSIS TOOLS?

The earthquake response of a bridge includes the development of an analytical model followed by the response analysis of the analytical model to predict the resulting dynamic response for the structure. Both the development of the analytical model and the selected analysis procedure are dependent on the earthquake hazard, selected earthquake design strategy and the complexity of the bridge. There are various levels or degrees of refinement in the analytical model and analytical procedures that are available to the designer. The purpose of earthquake analysis is to assess the force and deformation demands, and capacities on the structural system and its individual components.

Seismic Coefficient Method (SCM) or Equivalent Lateral Force Method (ELF), and *Response Spectrum Analysis Method (RSM), or Linear Time-History Method* (LTH) are the analytical tools for estimating the displacement demands for normal bridges. These procedures were discussed earlier in Chapters 10 and 12. *Non-linear Static Analysis* (NSA) or *Pushover Analysis* is an analytical tool for establishing the displacement capacities for most bridges. Under certain conditions, *Non-linear Time-History Analysis Method* (NLTH) may have to be carried out. These procedures will be discussed in Chapters 15 and 16.

The objective of a displacement analysis is to determine the displacement of an individual pier when its deformation capacity (that of the inelastic earthquake resisting element) is reached. The displacement capacity must be greater than the displacement demand. The accuracy of the demand and capacity analyses depend on the assumption of the model related to the geometry, boundary conditions, material properties, and energy dissipation incorporated in the model. Very flexible bridges must be analyzed accounting for the $P - \Delta$ effect. The need for modeling of foundations and abutments depends on the sensitivity of the structure to foundation flexibility and associated displacements. This in turn depends on whether the foundation is a spread footing, pile footing with pile cap, or a pile bent.

Requirements for single span bridges are not as rigorous as for multi-span bridges because of their favorable response to earthquake loads in past earthquakes. Thus, single span bridges need not be analyzed for earthquake loads, regardless of the earthquake hazard. Design requirements are limited to minimum seat widths and connection forces. Adequate seat widths must be provided in both the transverse and longitudinal directions. These reduced requirements are also based on the assumption that there are no vulnerable substructures (no columns) and that a rigid (or near rigid) superstructure is in place to distribute the in-plane loads to the abutments.

It is the responsibility of the designer to assess the reasonableness of a model in representing the behavior of the structure at the level of forces and deformations expected for the earthquake excitation.

13.10 LOAD COMBINATIONS AND PARTIAL LOAD FACTORS

Highway Loading

Load combinations under different limit states in accordance with IRC 6 are given as follows:

(a) Equilibrium of structure, that is,
- Sliding
- Overturning
- Uplifting

Check equilibrium under the following load combinations
- Basic Combination
- Accidental Combination
- Seismic Combination

(b) Limit State of Collapse or Ultimate limit State

Check strength under the following load combinations
- Basic Combination
- Accidental Combination
- Seismic Combination

These load combinations can be illustrated for the following loads and partial load factors as follows:
- Basic combination 1 = 1.35 DL + 1.35 CB + 1.75 WC + 1.5 EP + 1.5 LL + 0.9 WL + 1.2 LLS
- Basic combination 2 = 1.35 DL + 1.35 CB + 1.75 WC + 1.5 EP + 1.1 5LL + 1.5 WL + 1.2 LLS
- Accidental combination = 1.0 DL + 1.0 CB + 1.0 WC + 1.0 EP + 0.75 LL + 0.2 LLS
- Seismic combination = 1.35 DL + 1.35 CB + 1.75 WC + 1.0 EP + 0.2 LL + 1.5 EQ + 0.2 LLS

(c) Limit State of Serviceability

Check under the following load combinations
- Rare Combination: Check stresses only
- Frequent Combination: Check deflection, vibration, and *crack width in PSC structures*
- Quasi-permanent Combination: Check *crack width in RCC structures,* settlement, creep effects and to estimate the permanent stress in the structure,

These load combinations can be illustrated for the following loads and partial load factors as follows:
- Rare combination 1 = 1.0 DL + 1.0 CB + 1.2 WC + 1.0 EP + 1.0 LL + 0.6 WL + 0.8 LLS
- Rare combination 2 = 1.0 DL + 1.0 CB + 1.2 WC + 1.0 EP + 0.75 LL + 1.0 WL + 0.8 LLS

- Quasi permanent combination = 1.0 DL + 1.0 CB + 1.2 WC + 1.0 EP
  CB = crash barrier
  WC = wearing course
  EP = earth pressure
  WL = wind load
  EQ = seismic load
  LLS = LL surcharge

(d) Base Pressure and Design of Foundation
Check the base pressure under foundation, and estimate the structural strength *under the following load combinations*

Ultimate Limit State for Retaining Wall

Basic combination 1 = 1.35 DL + 1.35 CB + 1.75 WC + 1.5 EP + 1.5 LL + 0.9 WL + 1.2 LLS

Basic combination 2 = 1.35 DL + 1.35 CB + 1.75 WC + 1.5 EP + 1.15 LL + 1.5 WL + 1.2 LLS

Accidental combination = 1.0 DL + 1.0 CB + 1.0 WC + 1.0 EP + 0.75 LL + 0.2 LL

Seismic combination = 1.35 DL + 1.35 CB + 1.75 WC + 1.0 EP + 0.2 LL + 1.5 EQ + 0.2 LLS

Serviceability Limit State for Retaining Wall

Rare combination 1 = 1.0 DL + 1.0 CB + 1.2 WC + 1.0 EP + 1.0 LL + 0.6 WL + 0.8 LLS

Rare combination 2 = 1.0 DL + 1.0 CB + 1.2 WC + 1.0 EP + 0.75 LL + 1.0 WL + 0.8 LLS

Quasi-Permanent Combination = 1.0 DL + 1.0 CB + 1.2 WC + 1.0 EP

In case some more loads are acting on the structure than those considered in the above illustrations, then they will also be included with appropriate partial load factors. The detailed analysis of a highway bridge for static loads is available in Jain (2012).

Railway Loading
Load combinations under different limit states in accordance with IRS Reinforced Concrete bridges are given as follows:

Limit State of Collapse
There are three load combinations:

Combination 1 = 1.25 DL + 1.50 SIDL + 1.7 EP + 1.5 EQ + 1.4 PS

Combination 2 = 1.25 DL + 1.5 SIDL + 0.5 (LL + LLF) + 1.2 EQ + 1.7 EP+ 1.4 PS + 1.4 HY + 1.4 BO

Combination 3 = 0.9 DL+0.8 SIDL + 1.5 EQ + 1.4 PS + 1.7 EP

Limit State of Serviceability

There are two load combinations.

Combination 1 = 1.0 DL + 1.2 SIDL + 1.0 EQ + 1.0 EP + 1.0 PS + 1.0 HY + 1.0 BO

Combination 2 = 1.0 DL + 1.2 SIDL + 0.5 (LL + LLF) + 1.0 EQ +1.0 EP + 1.0 PS + 1.0 HY + 1.0 BO

During Construction Stage

Combination 1 = 1.0 DL + 1.2 SIDL + 0.8 EQ + 1.0 ER + 1.3 EP + 1.0 PS + 1.0 HY + 1.0 BO

PS = prestressing load
HY = hydrodynamic load
BO = buoyancy load
ER = erection load such as cranes, machines etc.
LLF = live load on footpath

13.10.1 Combination of Component Motions – 30% Rule

Clause 219.4 of IRC 6 specifies a combination rule when two orthogonal components of an earthquake need to be considered in the analysis. For this purpose, two separate analyses must be performed for design seismic forces along the two orthogonal horizontal directions. The design seismic force resultants (that is, axial force, bending moment etc.) at any cross-section of a bridge component resulting from the above analyses should be combined as follows:

(a) $\pm r_1 \pm 0.3\, r_2$
(b) $\pm 0.3\, r_1 \pm r_2$

where,

r_1 = force resultant due to full design force along global X-direction
r_2 = force resultant due to full design force along global Y-direction

Similarly, the effect of vertical component of an earthquake can be considered. This is referred to as the 30% rule. The combination rules for design moments in the two local orthogonal directions are shown in Table 13.7.

TABLE 13.7 DESIGN MOMENTS FOR ORTHOGONAL SEISMIC FORCES

	Moments for earthquake along global X-axis	Moments for earthquake along global Y-axis
Design moments	$M_p = M_p^X + 0.3M_p^Y$	$M_q = M_q^X + 0.3\, M_q^Y$
	$M_p = 0.3\, M_p^X + M_p^Y$	$M_q = 0.3\, M_q^X + M_q^Y$

where,

M_p = absolute moment in the local p-axis at a cross-section of the bridge
M_q = absolute moment in the local q-axis at a cross-section of the bridge

13.11 ILLUSTRATIVE EXAMPLES

Example 13.1

Determine the period of vibration of a highway bridge along longitudinal and transverse directions for the following data:
Dead load of superstructure of bridge = 7900 kN
Superimposed dead load incl. wearing course = 1350 kN
Live load reaction = 2550 kN
Dead load of pier cap (4.5 m × 2.8 m × 1.3 m in taper) = 320 kN
Dead load of pier wall (2.1 × 1.7 m) = 800 kN
Height of pier = 9 m above the pier cap
Stiffness of pier about strong axis = 65 kN/mm (in transverse direction)
Stiffness of pier about weak axis = 25 kN/mm (in longitudinal direction)
Also, estimate the base shear at the base of the pier in both directions, if the bridge is located in seismic zone IV on medium soil. It is an important bridge.

Solution

Period of vibration $T = 2\pi\sqrt{\dfrac{m}{k}} = 2\sqrt{\dfrac{W_e}{1000K}}$

Importance factor for bridge = 1.2 for important bridge

Longitudinal Direction
Effective weight of the bridge in the longitudinal direction = Dead load of superstructure + Nil live load

$$= 7900 + 1350 + 0 = 9250 \text{ kN}$$

∴ Period of vibration T_L in longitudinal direction $= 2\sqrt{\dfrac{9250}{1000 \times 25}} = 1.216$ sec

Corresponding S_a/g for 5% damping on medium soil = 1.36/1.216 = 1.118
Response reduction factor in longitudinal direction for RCC wall pier with ductile detailing = 3
Design seismic coefficient $\alpha_h = \dfrac{Z}{2}\dfrac{I}{R}\dfrac{S_a}{g} = \dfrac{0.24}{2} \times \dfrac{1.2}{3} \times 1.118 = 0.0536$

∴ Design seismic force in the wall pier in longitudinal direction = 0.0536 × (9250 + 320 + 800/3) = 527 kN

Transverse Direction
Effective weight of the bridge in the transverse direction = Dead load of superstructure + 20% live load

$$= 7900 + 1350 + 0.20 \times 2550 = 9760 \text{ kN}$$

Similarly, period of vibration T_T in transverse direction $= 2\sqrt{\dfrac{9760}{1000 \times 65}} = 0.775$ sec

Corresponding S_a/g for 5% damping on medium soil = 1.36/0.775 = 1.754
In the transverse direction, a plastic hinge cannot form due to very high lateral stiffness and strength, IRC 6 says *R* factor is not applicable. However, in order to determine the design seismic force in the transverse direction for the design of pier and piles, *R* factor is taken as 1 which means this member will remain elastic.

Design seismic coefficient $\alpha_h = \frac{Z}{2}\frac{I}{R}\frac{S_a}{g} = \frac{0.24}{2} \times \frac{1.2}{1} \times 1.754 = 0.252$

∴ Design seismic force in the wall pier in transverse direction = 0.252 × (9760 + 320 + 800/3) = 2610 kN □

Example 13.2

A 3-lane simply supported bridge has a 11 m carriage way. The center-to-center distance between the bearings is 16.04 m with 0.98 m overhangs on either side as shown in Figure 13.16. Determine the forces acting at bearings due to dead load and three lanes of Class A loading using the following data:

Dead load reaction at either end = 2100 kN

Superimposed DL due to 65 mm thick wearing coat at either end = 155 kN

Center of gravity of the Class A loading from the extreme left end = 5.71 m (when it is moving from right to left)

Height of the top of surfacing above the level of bearing = 1650 + 65 = 1715 mm

Center of gravity of the superstructure above the top of the bearing = 1150 mm

Height of pedestal for placing bearings = 250 mm

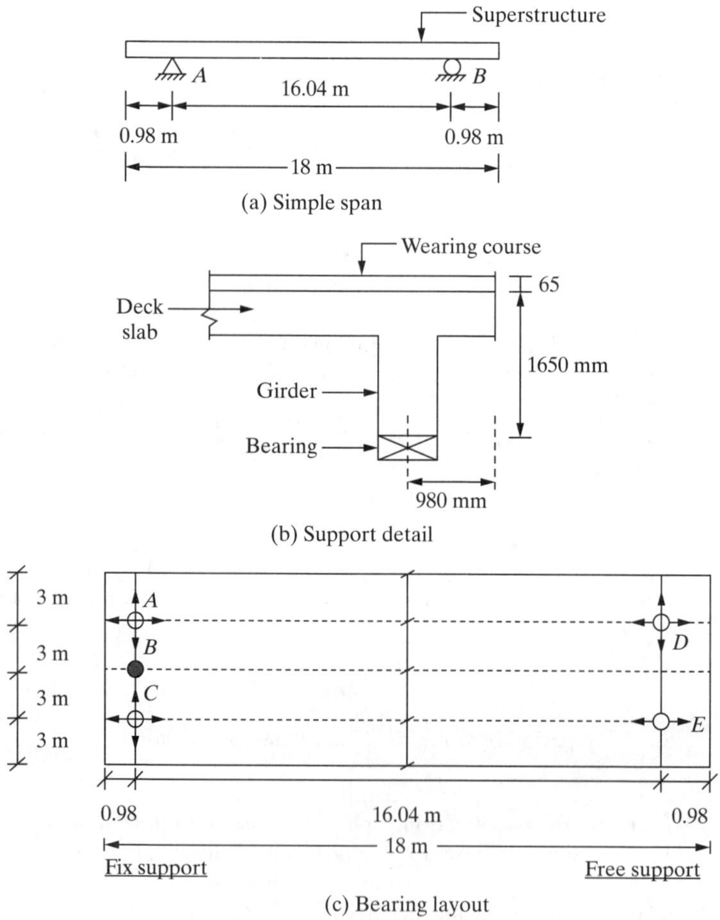

Figure 13.16 18 m span bridge.

Legend

Bearing Type	Fixity		Box
	Longitudinal	Transverse	
A, C, D	Free	Free	Outer
B	Fixed	Fixed	Center
E	Free	Fixed	Outer

Figure 13.16 (Continued)

Solution

IRC 6 – Annexure B, Table B.2, *Basic Combination*
Partial safety factor for permanent load for verification of structural strength = 1.35
Partial safety factor for *SIDL* due to surfacing for verification of structural strength = 1.75
Partial safety factor for variable load due to vehicles for verification of structural strength = 1.50

At a fixed bearing, horizontal force in longitudinal direction is greater of the following two values (Cl. 211.5.1.1 of IRC 6)

$$H_1 = F_h - \mu(R_g + R_q)$$
$$H_2 = 0.5\,F_h + \mu(R_g + R_q)$$

At a free bearing, horizontal force in longitudinal direction is as follows:

$$H = \mu(R_g + R_q)$$

where, F_h = applied horizontal force
R_g = reaction at the free end due to dead (permanent) load
R_q = reaction at the free end due to live (variable) load
μ = coefficient of friction at the movable bearing = 0.03 or 0.05 whichever gives worst effect.

Dead load reaction at either end = 2100 kN
SIDL due to surfacing reaction at either end = 155 kN

Class A loading
Since all the three lanes are loaded with Class A load, there is no transverse eccentricity, hence, no additional load on bearings due to torsion.
Total load due to one-class A vehicle = 500 kN
Vertical reaction at fixed support due to live load

$$= \frac{500 \times (16.04 + 0.98 - 5.71)}{16.04} = 352.55 \text{ kN}$$

Total vertical reaction at *fixed support* due to 3-Class A vehicles = 3 × 352.55 = 1058 kN
This will be shared by bearing A and C equally.
Total vertical reaction at *free support* due to 3-Class A vehicles = 1500 – 1058 = 442 kN
This will be shared by bearing D and E equally.

SUMMARY OF VERTICAL REACTIONS AT BEARINGS, kN

Reaction due to	Bearing A	Bearing C	Bearing D	Bearing E
Self weight	1050	1050	1050	1050
SIDL	77.5	77.5	77.5	77.5
3-Class A	529	529	221	221
Total	1657	1657	1349	1349

Horizontal braking load = 20% of load in lane 1 + nil of load in lane 2 + 5% of the load in lane 3

$$F_h = 0.20 \times 500 + 0.05 \times 500 = 125 \text{ kN}$$

It is given that braking force acts at 1200 mm above the wearing surface (Cl. 211.3 of IRC 6).

Additional vertical reaction at *either support* due to braking

$$= \pm \frac{125 \times (1.715 + 1.2)}{16.04} = \pm 22.7 \text{ kN}$$

This will be shared by bearing A and C equally, that is, $11.4 \approx 11$ kN each.

Similarly, it will be shared equally by bearing D and E, that is, $11.4 \approx 11$ kN each.

Total vertical reaction at fixed support due to vehicles, $R_A = 1058 + 22.7 = 1080$ kN

$\therefore$ Total vertical reaction at free support $R_B = 3 \times 500 - 1080 = 420$ kN

At Free Bearing

Horizontal force due to friction $F = H = \mu(R_g + R_q)$

$$= 0.05 \times (1.35 \times 2100 + 1.75 \times 155 + 1.5 \times 420)$$

$$= 186.8 \text{ kN}$$

At Fixed Bearing

Horizontal force due to friction $F = H_1 = F_h - \mu(R_g + R_q)$

$$H_1 = 1.5 \times 125 - 0.03 \times (1.35 \times 2100 + 1.75 \times 155 + 1.5 \times 420) = 75.40 \text{ kN}$$

and $H_2 = 0.5\, F_h + \mu(R_g + R_q)$

$$H_2 = 0.5 \times 1.5 \times 125 + 0.05 \times (1.35 \times 2100 + 1.75 \times 155 + 1.5 \times 420) = 280.5 \text{ kN}$$

$\therefore$ Design horizontal reaction due to friction $H = 280.5 \text{ kN} > H_1$ OK

SUMMARY OF BEARING FORCES FOR NORMAL CASE, kN

	Free bearings A, C and D		Pin bearing B		Guided bearing E	
	Vertical	Horizontal	Vertical	Horizontal	Vertical	Horizontal
Minimum	1338	0	0	62.5	1338	62.5
Maximum	1668	0	0	281	1668	187

Remember, earthquake forces are *reversible*. □

Example 13.3

Consider the bridge data as given in Example 13.2. If the bridge is located in seismic zone IV, on soft soil, estimate the earthquake forces at the bearings. Importance factor $I = 1.2$, $S_a/g = 2.5$. Distance between the bearings in lateral direction = 6 m c/c.
Also, if vertical component of earthquake acts along with the horizontal component of earthquake simultaneously, then estimate the bearing forces.

Solution

Clause 219.5.2 of IRC 6 states that earthquake force due to live load shall not be considered when acting in the direction of the traffic. However, only 20% live load is considered when the earthquake occurs in the transverse direction of the bridge.
Design horizontal seismic coefficient is given by

$$\alpha_h = \frac{Z}{2} \times I \times \frac{S_a}{g} = \frac{0.24}{2} \times 1.2 \times 2.5 = 0.36$$

Table 20 of IRC 6 gives different R factors for different components.
For the design of bearings, $R = 1$, that is, they must remain elastic.
For RCC wall piers and abutments in transverse direction (where plastic hinge cannot develop), $R = 1$
For RCC wall piers and abutments in longitudinal direction (where hinges can develop), $R = 3$ for ductile detailing
At present, for the design of bearings, $R = 1$,
∴ Design horizontal seismic coefficient = 0.36 and design vertical seismic coefficient α_v = (2/3) of 0.36 = 0.24

Case 1: *Horizontal Component of Earthquake in Longitudinal Direction*
Earthquake force due to dead load of superstructure

$$= 0.36 \times 2 \times (2100 + 155) = 1624 \text{ kN}$$

Earthquake force due to live load of superstructure = Nil
Total earthquake force F_h = 1624 kN
This force will be shared equally by bearing B and E, that is, 812 kN each.
This force will act at the center of gravity of the superstructure, that is, at 1.15 m above the bearing level.
Additional vertical reaction at each support due to seismic force on dead load

$$= \pm \frac{1624 \times 1.15}{16.04} = \pm 116.4 \text{ kN}$$

Bearings A and C will carry 116.4/2 = 58 kN equally, and bearings D and E will also share 116.4/2 = 58 kN equally.

Case 2: *Horizontal Component of Earthquake in Transverse Direction*
Earthquake force due to dead load of superstructure

$$= 0.36 \times 2 \times (2100 + 155) = 1624 \text{ kN}$$

Earthquake force due to live load of superstructure = $0.36 \times 2 \times (0.2 \times 1500)$ = 216 kN
Total applied horizontal force F_h = 1624 + 216 = 1840 kN
This will be shared equally by bearings B and E, that is, 920 kN each.

Case 3: *Vertical Component of Earthquake*
Vertical earthquake force due to dead load of superstructure

$$= 0.24 \times 2 \times (2100 + 155) = 1083 \text{ kN}$$

Bearings A, C, D and E will carry 1083/4 = ±271 kN equally.

SUMMARY OF VERTICAL FORCES IN BEARINGS, kN

Reaction due to	Bearing A	Bearing C	Bearing D	Bearing E
Self weight	1050	1050	1050	1050
SIDL	77.5	77.5	77.5	77.5
3-Class A	529	529	221	221
Earthquake-Longitudinal	±58	±58	±58	±58
Earthquake-Vertical	±271	±271	±271	±271

SUMMARY OF BEARING FORCES FOR HORIZONTAL COMPONENT OF EARTHQUAKE CASE, kN

Loading condition	Free bearings A, C and D		Pin bearing B	Guided bearing E		
	Vertical		Horizontal	Vertical		Horizontal
	Min	Max		Min	Max	
Eq – Long	1280	1726	812	1280	1726	812
Eq – Trans	1338	1668	920	1338	1668	920

Combination of horizontal and vertical components of earthquake

Let all the three components of earthquake act simultaneously: longitudinal, transverse, and vertical. The net forces acting at each of the bearings can be estimated by making use of the 30% combination rule as discussed in Chapter 12. □

Example 13.4

A 45 m cantilever pier has a tapered hollow cross-section as shown in Figure 13.17. It is located in seismic zone III on medium soil. Determine the shear force distribution along the lateral and longitudinal axes using response spectrum analysis.

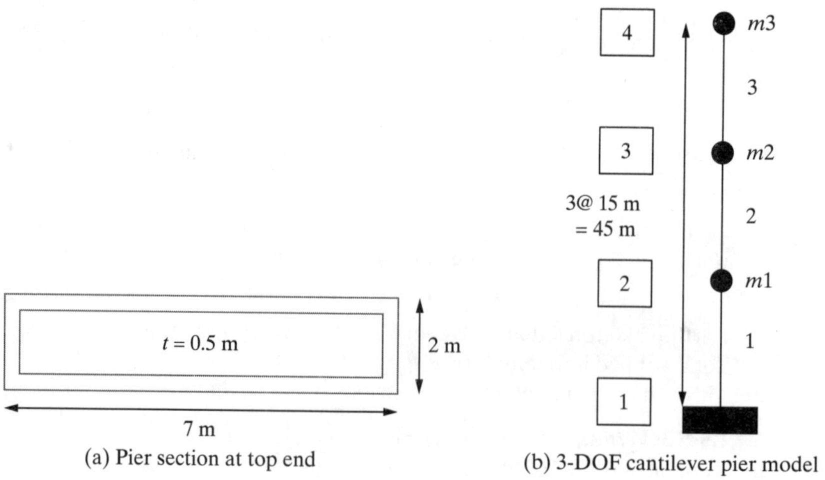

Figure 13.17 Vertical cantilever pier.

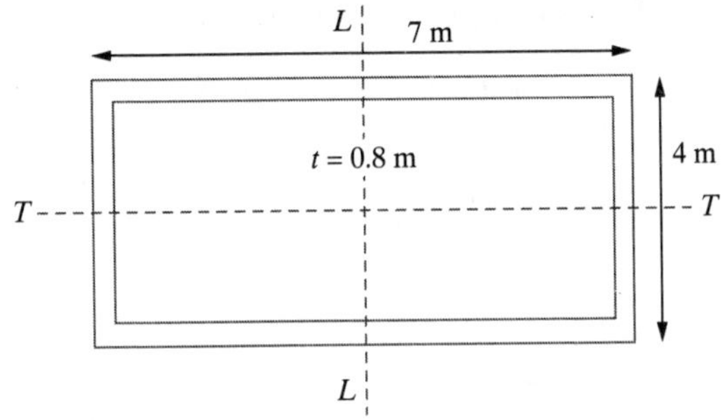

(c) Pier section at bottom end

Figure 13.17 (Continued)

Assume the following data:
Dead load of superstructure + SIDL = 10000 kN
Dead load of pier cap = 1200 kN
Carriageway live load on superstructure = 1500 kN
Importance factor $I = 1.2$, Response reduction factor $R = 3$
Grade of concrete = M35, Modulus of elasticity of concrete $Ec = 2.96 \times 10^7$ kN/m^2

Solution

The 45 m tall pier can be discretized in three parts @ 15 m as shown in Figure 13.17(b). The section properties can be compiled as shown in Table 13.8 for manual calculations. The lateral stiffness of each of three segments, and storey shears can be estimated as discussed in Chapter 10. Alternatively, the 45 m cantilever pier can be modeled as a tapered section in any software for dynamic analysis.

TABLE 13.8 SECTION PROPERTIES

Location	width	depth	thickness	Area	I_{L-L}	I_{T-T}	Red I_{L-L}	Red I_{T-T}
height	b	D	t				75%	75%
m	m	m	m	m^2	m^4	m^4	m^4	m^4
45	7	2	0.5	8.00	39.17	4.17	29.38	3.13
37.5	7	2.33	0.55	9.05	45.55	6.46	34.16	4.85
30	7	2.667	0.6	10.16	52.38	9.54	39.28	7.15
22.5	7	3	0.65	11.31	59.51	13.42	44.64	10.06
15	7	3.33	0.7	12.50	66.94	18.19	50.20	13.64
7.5	7	3.667	0.75	13.75	74.77	24.10	56.08	18.08
0	7	4	0.8	15.04	82.84	31.11	62.13	23.33

A mass corresponding to superstructure DL + SIDL + pier cap is assigned along T- and L-directions to the top node. A mass corresponding to 20% of CWLL is assigned to the top node along T-T axis.
The mass was lumped at 15 m interval as shown in Table 13.9.

TABLE 13.9 LUMPED MASS (kN-s²/m)

Level m	Mass-X	Mass-Y
45	1340.54	1310.54
15	485.24	485.24
30	395.53	395.53
0	272.52	272.52
Total	2494	2464

Period of vibrations in the first 5 modes are as shown in Table 13.10.

TABLE 13.10 PERIODS OF VIBRATIONS

Mode	Period sec
1	1.84
2	1.07
3	0.23
4	0.12
5	0.09

Seismic coefficient corresponding to first mode with a period of 1.84 sec along L-L direction is 0.0236, and effective weight is 21484 kN. Thus, SCM base shear = 507 kN
Seismic coefficient corresponding to second mode with a period of 1.07 sec along T-T direction is 0.0404 and effective weight is 21778 kN. Thus, SCM base shear = 880 kN
The shear distribution obtained by computer analysis along the T-T and L-L directions are shown in Table 13.11 and Figure 13.18. The overturning moments at the base are 29857 kNm and 17172 kNm in T-T and L-L directions, respectively. The SCM base shears are higher because it assumes 100% contribution of the first mode along L-L direction, and 100% contribution of the second mode along T-T direction.

TABLE 13.11 SHEAR IN PIER kN

Segment	T-T	L-L
3	612	363
2	690	404
1	768	493

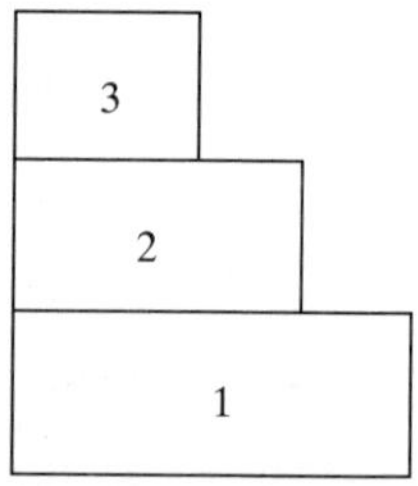

Figure 13.18 Shear distribution in pier segments. □

Example 13.5

A cantilever pier-pile system is shown in Figure 13.19. It is located in seismic zone III on medium soil. The pier has 2.5 m diameter, 18.5 m height, and 2.8 × 4.5 m × 1.5 m deep pier cap. It is supported on a 5.1 × 5.1 × 1.8 m deep pile cap; and 4-piles having 1.2 m diameter each. Determine the mode shapes and base shear using response spectrum analysis. Consider the following data:

Item	From	To	Unit
Bearing	27.8	28.05	m
Pier Cap	26.3	27.8	m
Pier	7.8	26.3	m
Pile Cap	6	7.8	m
Pile fixity	0	6	m

Dead load of superstructure = 10000 kN

Dead load of crash barrier = 960 kN

Dead load of wearing course = 1140 kN

Importance factor $I = 1.2$, Response reduction factor $R = 3$

Grade of concrete = M35, Modulus of elasticity of concrete $E_c = 2.96 \times 10^7$ kN/m^2

Solution

The pier stiffness is taken as 75% in each direction to take care of cracking effect. The weight of various items are shown in Table 13.12. There are 4-piles at 3 m c/c in each direction. The dynamic model is shown in Figure 13.19.

The mass of the superstructure and SIDL are lumped at the bearing level. The mass of the pile cap is lumped at mid height of the pile cap.

Total weight up to the pile cap = 12100 + 472.5 + 0.5 × 2269.14 = 13707 kN

Seismic coefficient along T-T direction

$$= \alpha_h = \frac{Z}{2} \times I \times \frac{S_a}{g} = \frac{0.16}{2} \times 1.2 \times \frac{0.649}{g} = 0.0621\,g$$

Static base shear at the base of pier = (0.0621/3) × 13707 = 284.8 kN

TABLE 13.12 WEIGHT CALCULATIONS

Item	Height	Weight		Total weight kN	Total mass kN-S^2/m
At Bearing	0.25	12100 kN		12100	1233.4
Pier Cap	1.5	472.5 kN		472.5	48.2
Pier	18.5	122.6563 kN/m		2269.14	231.3
Pile Cap	1.8	1170.45 kN		1170.45	119.3
Pile	6	28.26 kN/m		678.24	69.1
			Total	16690.33	1701.4

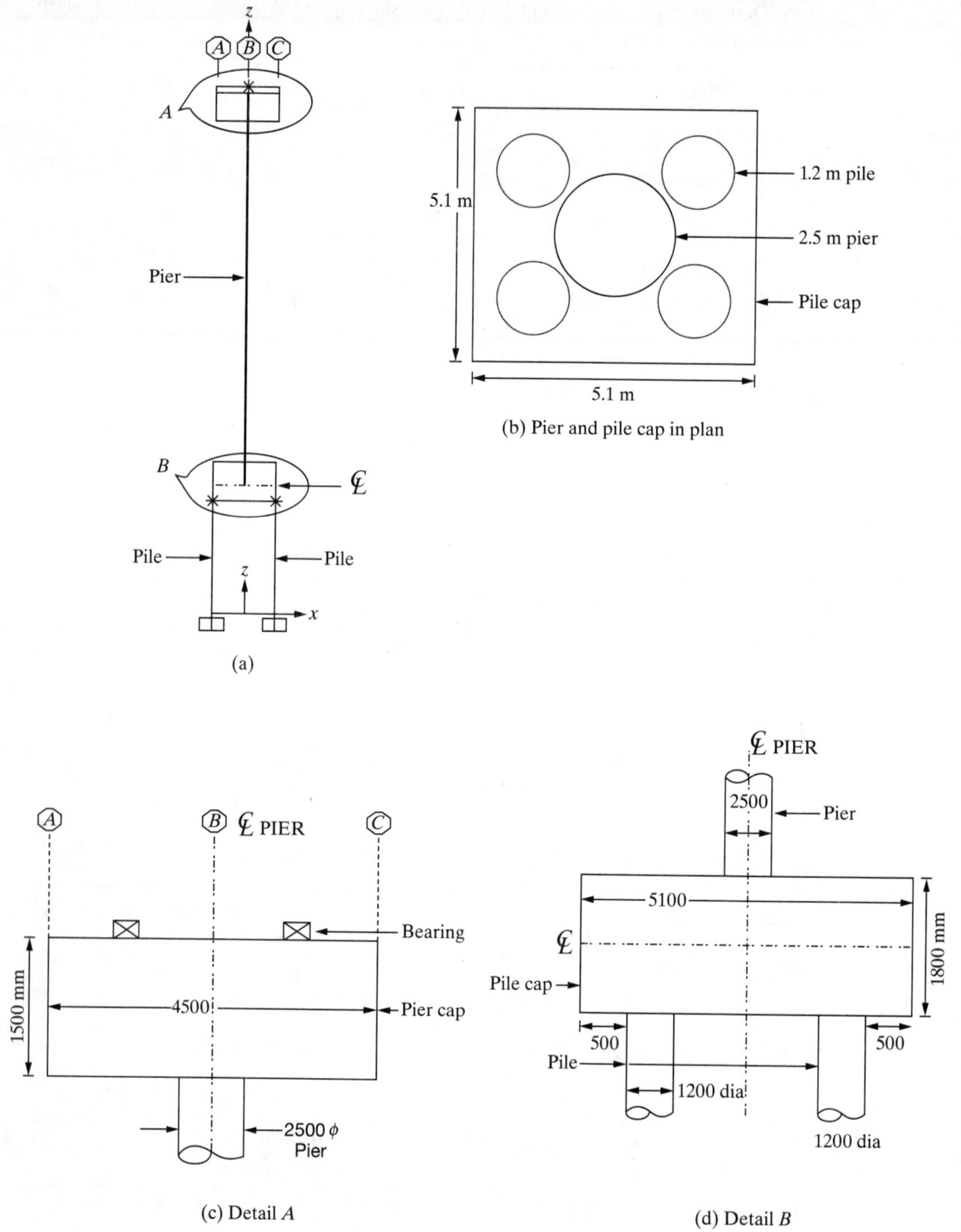

Figure 13.19 Pier system model (Along T-T).

Where, $R = 3$ for the design of a RCC pier.

Dynamic base shear along T-T at the base of pier = 289.3 kN

Both values are very close to each other.

The overturning moment at the base of pier = 5812 kNm.

The first two mode shapes are shown in Figure 13.20.

Time periods in the first three modes and mode participation mass ratios are shown in Table 13.13

TABLE 13.13 TIME PERIODS IN FIRST 3 MODES

Mode	Period	Modal Participation mass ratio	
	Sec	UX (T-T)	UY (L-L)
1	2.094	0.853	0
2	0.144	0.146	0
3	0.048	0	0.886

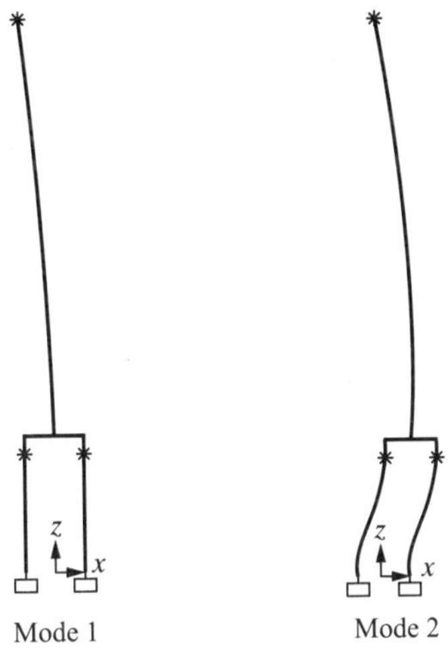

Figure 13.20 Mode shapes.

□

Example 13.6

A 2-span simply supported bridge is supported on the middle pier B and on the abutments A and C as shown in Figure 13.21. There are three lanes on 11 m wide carriage way. The pier is rectangular with 1700 × 2100 mm cross-section. Grade of concrete for superstructure is M45 including piers. Estimate the seismic base shears if the bridge is located in seismic zone IV with $I = 1.2$ and $R = 3$ on soft soil. There are two fixed bearings at B and rest of the bearings are free.

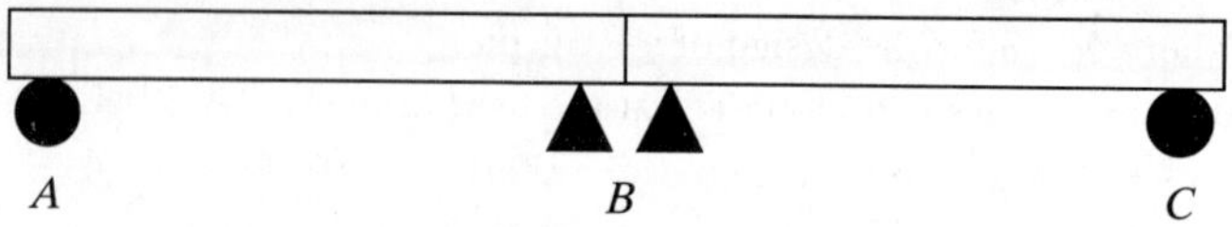

(a) Two span simply supported bridge

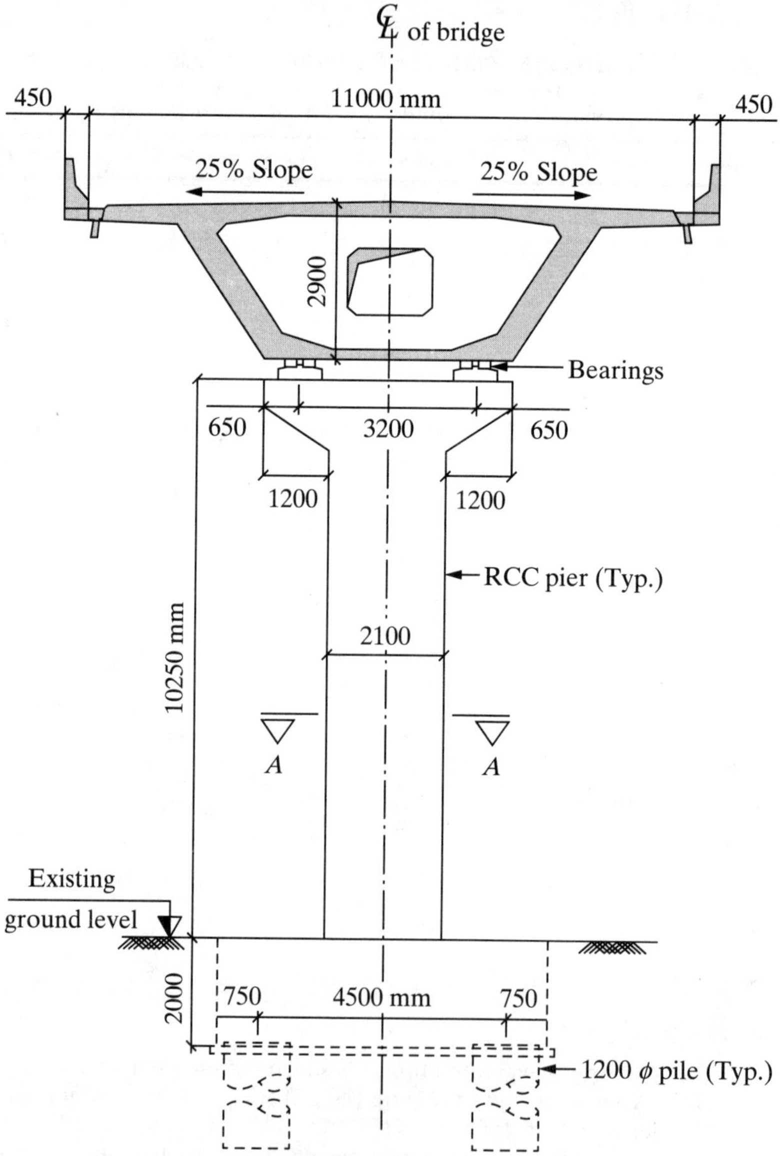

(b) Section transverse direction

Figure 13.21 2-span simple bridge.

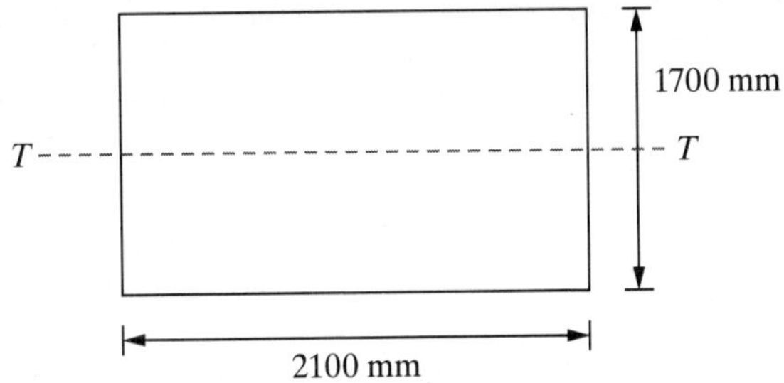

(c) Cross-section of pier at *A-A*

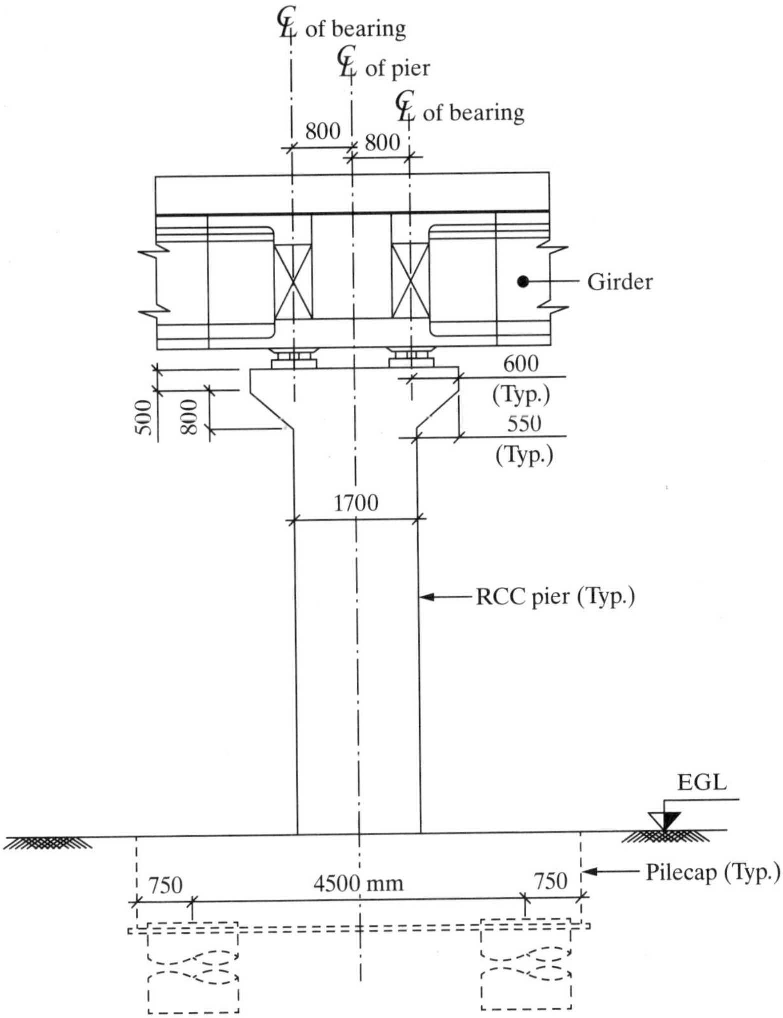

(d) *L*-section at the pier

Figure 13.21 (Continued)

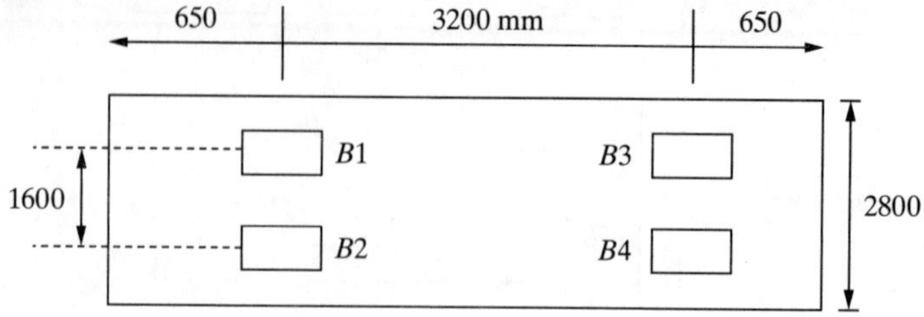

(e) Plan of pier cap showing bearing arrangement

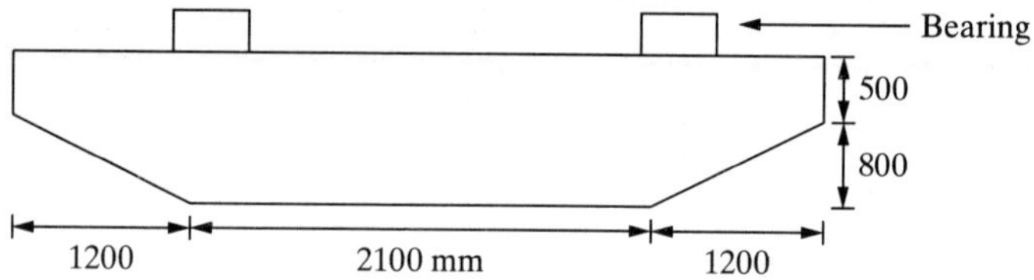

(f) Longitudinal section of pier cap

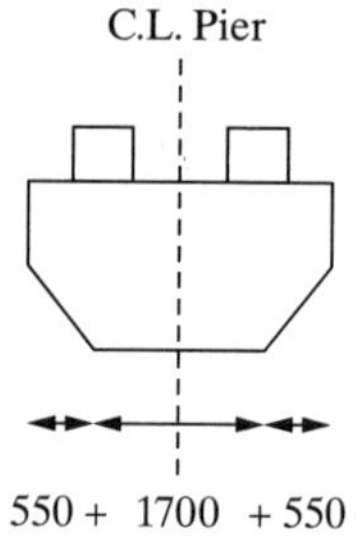

(g) Transverse section of pier cap

Figure 13.21 (Continued)

Solution

Each span = 50 m
Dead Load superstructure, each span = 7700 kN
SIDL - permanent SIDL-Fixed, each span = 700 kN
SIDL - permanent SIDL-Variable, each span = 650 kN
Braking force at the pier = 300 kN
Dead load of the pier cap = 320 kN. Its center of gravity above the pier top = 0.741 m
Height of pier = 8.95 m
There are 2-trains of Class 70R on each span. Weight of each 70R train = 1000 kN

Case 1: *Longitudinal period of vibration*

$$T_L = 2\sqrt{\frac{W}{1000 \times K}}$$

Where, W = dead load of the superstructure + appropriate live load
Live load = 0 in the direction of traffic

$\therefore$
$$W = 2 \times 9050 = 18100 \text{ kN}$$

Under seismic condition, the entire lateral force will be resisted by the fixed bearing at the pier.

$K = F$ = Horizontal force applied at the top of bearings to get 1 mm deflection at the top of pier in the longitudinal direction of the horizontal force

Deflection at top of pier,

$$\Delta = \frac{F \times H^3}{3EI_L} \tag{1a}$$

Or, lateral stiffness

$$F = \frac{3EI_L\Delta}{H^3} \tag{1b}$$

Where, $\Delta = 0.001$ m

$E = 5000\ \sqrt{45}\ = 33541$ MPa $= 3.35 \times 10^7$ kN/m²

z = Distance from top of pier cap to CG of the superstructure = 0.25 + 1.5 = 1.75 m

where, thickness of bearing pad = 0.25 m

H = Height of pier above pilecap to the top of pier cap = 8.95 + 1.3 = 10.25 m

I_L = Moment of inertia of the cracked pier section about longitudinal bending (weak axis) = 0.859 m⁴ and with 75% cracking, $I_L = 0.644$ m⁴

$$\therefore \qquad F = 60.25 \text{ kN and } T_L = 2\sqrt{\frac{18100}{1000 \times 60.25}} = 1.096 \text{ sec}$$

S_a/g on soft soil = 1.67/T = 1.523

Seismic coefficient

$$\alpha_h = \frac{Z}{2} \times I \times \frac{S_a}{g} = \frac{0.24}{2} \times 1.2 \times \frac{1.523}{g} = 0.219 \text{ g}$$

Seismic coefficient for the design of pier ($R = 3$), = 0.073 g

Case 2: *Transverse period of vibration*

Dead load will be shared by both the abutments and pier in the transverse direction. Thus, dead load at the pier = 9050 kN

Live load = 20% of LL transverse to the direction of the traffic

$$= 0.2 \times 2 \times 2150 = 860 \text{ kN}$$

50% of this load will be shared by the pier and the rest by the two abutments.

Thus, $W = 9050 + 430 = 9480$ kN

$$\Delta = 0.001 \text{ m}$$

I_T = Moment of inertia of the cracked pier section about transverse bending (strong axis) = 1.312 m⁴ and with 75% cracking, $I_T = 0.984$ m⁴

F = Horizontal force applied at the CM of the superstructure to get 1 mm deflection at the top of pier in the transverse direction

Deflection at the top of pier is

$$\Delta = \frac{F \times z \times H^2}{2EI_T} \tag{2a}$$

Or,

$$= \frac{F \times H^2}{6EI_T}(3z + 2H) \tag{2b}$$

$$\therefore \qquad F = 74.19 \text{ kN and } T_T = 2\sqrt{\frac{9480}{1000 \times 74.19}} = 0.715 \text{ sec}$$

S_a/g on soft soil = $1.67/T = 2.34$

Horizontal seismic coefficient

$$\alpha_h = \frac{Z}{2} \times I \times \frac{S_a}{g} = \frac{0.24}{2} \times 1.2 \times \frac{2.34}{g} = 0.337 \text{ g}$$

Seismic coefficient for the design of pier ($R = 3$), = 0.337/3 = 0.112 g
Vertical seismic coefficient $\alpha_v = (2/3)$ of α_h in each direction
Seismic forces due to each component of the bridge along L-L and T-T directions is shown in Table 13.14.

TABLE 13.14 COMPUTATION OF SEISMIC FORCE DUE TO EACH COMPONENT

Weight/Reaction		**Seismic force**		**C.G. above pier base**
	kN	**HL**	**HT**	
		kN	**kN**	**m**
DL	7700	562.1	862.4	10.5
SIDL-F	700	51.1	78.4	10.5
SIDL-V	650	47.45	72.8	10.5
Pier Cap	320	23.36	35.84	10.25 – 1.3 + 0.741 = 9.691
Pier	800	58.4	89.6	(10.25 – 1.3)/2 = 4.475
Pmax LL	2150	0	48.2	10.25 + 0.25 = 10.5

□

Placement of Live Load on the Bridge

The live load (Q) on the bridge due to different classes of vehicles and in different lanes at different times will lead to number of situations such as:

- Maximum vertical reaction at the bearings at the Pier B (Q_1)
- Maximum vertical reaction at the two bearings (B1 and B2) and (B3 and B4), on either side of the center line of the pier, to cause maximum longitudinal bending moment in the pier (Q_2)
- Maximum vertical reaction at the two bearings, (B1 and B3) and (B2 and B4), on either side of the center line of the bridge, to cause maximum transverse bending moment in the pier (Q_3)

All possible combinations must be considered to get the worst effect in the pier in both longitudinal and transverse directions. In the present example, this exercise is beyond its scope.

Let us assume that the maximum vertical reaction in the pier is 2150 kN. It will produce no horizontal seismic force in the longitudinal direction but only 20% force will contribute towards horizontal seismic force in the transverse direction as shown in Table 13.15.

Let us compute *unfactored seismic shear* at the base of the pier.

Longitudinal direction
Due to superstructure = 2 × (562.1 + 51.1 + 47.45) = 1321.2 kN
Due to pier cap and pier = 23.36 + 58.4 = 81.76 kN
Due to LL = 0
Total unfactored shear = 1321.2 + 81.76 = 1403 kN

Transverse direction
Due to superstructure = (862.4 + 78.4 + 72.8) = 1013.6 kN
Due to pier cap and pier = 35.84 + 89.6 = 125.44 kN
Due to LL = 48.2 kN
Total unfactored shear = 1013.6 + 125.44 + 48.2 = 1187 kN

Let us compute the total factored forces at the base of the pier under seismic conditions from the above data. The partial load factors are taken from the seismic combination given in Table B.2 of IRC 6.

Longitudinal Direction

P_{Lu} = 1.35 (DL + SIDL-F + PierCap + Pier) + 1.75 (SIDL-V) = 13990 kN

M_{Lu} = 1.5 * alphaH[2* (DL+SIDL-F)*a_1 + 2* (SIDL-V)*a_1 + PierCap*a_2 + Pier *a_3] = 21542 kNm

H_{Lu} = 1.5*alphaH*2*SUM(DL + SIDL-F+SIDL-V)+1.5*SUM(PierCap + Pier) = 2105 kN

Lateral Direction

P_{Tu} = 1.35 (DL + SIDL-F + PierCap + Pier) + 1.75 (SIDL-V) + 0.2 (Q_1) = 14420 kN

M_{Tu} = 1.5 * alphaH[DL+ SIDL-F)*a_1 + SIDL-V*a_1 + PierCap*a_2 + Pier *a_3 + 0.2 Q_1 *a_1] = 17188 kNm

H_{Tu} = 1.5*alphaH*SUM(DL + SIDL-F + SIDL-V) + 1.5*SUM(PierCap + Pier + 0.2 Q_1) = 1780 kN

where, a_1, a_2 and a_3 are corresponding lever arm.
By making use of 30% combination rule as discussed in 13.10.1 and Table 13.7, moment MT along EQ-L and moment ML along EQ-T can be estimated.

Thus, MT = 0.3 × 17187.76 = 5156.33 kNm

and ML = 0.3 × 21542.06 = 6462.62 kNm

The summary of forces is shown in Table 13.15.

TABLE 13.15 SUMMARY OF FACTORED SEISMIC FORCES AT THE BASE OF PIER

	P	HL	HT	ML	MT
	kN	kN	kN	kNm	kNm
EQ-L	13989.50	2104.59	0.00	21542.06	5156.33
EQ-T	14419.50	0	1780	6462.62	17187.76

13.12 BASIC DESIGN REQUIREMENTS

Bridges should be designed to avoid undesirable structural or psychological effects due to their deformations. Service load deformations may cause deterioration of wearing surfaces and local cracking in concrete slabs and in metal bridges that could impair serviceability and durability, even if not a potential source of collapse.

The design of a bridge should satisfy the following two limit states:

- Limit state of serviceability – *minimum damage*
- Limit state of collapse – *no collapse*

Limit State of Serviceability

A seismic action with a high probability of occurrence may cause only minor damage to secondary components and to those parts of the bridge intended to contribute to energy dissipation. All other parts of the bridge should remain undamaged.

Limit State of Collapse

- After occurrence of the design seismic action, the bridge must retain its structural integrity and adequate residual resistance, although at some parts of the bridge considerable damage may occur.
- Flexural yielding of specific sections, that is, formation of plastic hinges, is allowed to occur in the piers. When no seismic isolation is provided, such flexural yielding is in general necessary in regions of high seismicity, in order to reduce the design seismic action to a level corresponding to a reasonable increase of the additional construction cost, compared to a bridge not designed for earthquake resistance.
- The bridge deck should in general be designed to avoid damage, other than locally to secondary components such as expansion joints, continuity slabs or parapets.

The principles of capacity design require that the strength of those members that are not part of the primary energy-dissipating system should be stronger than the overstrength capacity of the primary energy dissipating members. The intent is to avoid any damage to those members that are expected to remain elastic during the earthquake motion. The non-linearity is forced to occur only in those members that have been intentionally designed and detailed for ductility, for example, columns with plastic hinges at their ends.

Ductile Behaviour

- It is preferable to design a bridge for ductile behaviour, that is, to provide it with reliable means to dissipate a significant amount of the input energy under severe earthquakes. This is accomplished by providing for the formation of an intended configuration of flexural plastic hinges or by using base isolating devices. This makes sense both from economic and safety reasons.
- The bridge deck should remain within the elastic range.
- Bridges for ductile behaviour should be designed so that partial or full mechanisms can develop in the structure through the formation of flexural plastic hinges. These hinges normally form in the piers (top, bottom or both) and act as the primary energy dissipating components. To achieve this objective, all members connected to the columns, the shear capacity of the column and all

members in the load path from the superstructure to the foundation, must be capable of transmitting the maximum (overstrength) force effects developed by plastic hinges in the columns.

- As far as practicable, the location of plastic hinges should be selected at points accessible for inspection and repair.
- Flexural plastic hinges need not necessarily form in all piers. However, an optimum post-elastic seismic behaviour of a bridge is achieved if plastic hinges develop approximately simultaneously in as many piers as possible.
- The global force-displacement relationship should exhibit a significant force plateau at yield and should ensure hysteretic energy dissipation over at least five inelastic deformation cycles.
- Superstructure and substructure components and their connections to columns that are designed not to yield (that is, must remain elastic) should be designed to resist overstrength moments and shears of ductile columns using *Capacity Design Procedure.*
- Supporting members (piers or abutments) connected to the deck through sliding or flexible mountings (sliding bearings or flexible elastomeric bearings) should, in general, remain within the elastic range.

There is a need to calculate forces in the superstructure for longitudinal direction loading, and forces in the bent cap and foundation for both longitudinal and transverse loading.

Single Columns and Piers

Design shear forces and moments in the superstructure, bent caps, and the foundation structure should be calculated for the two principal axes of a column and in the weak direction of a pier or bent.

Bents with Two or More Columns

The forces for bents with two or more columns should be calculated both in the plane of the bent and perpendicular to the plane of the bent. The forces in the plane perpendicular to the plane of the bent should be calculated as for single columns. The effects of axial load redistribution due to overturning forces should be considered when calculating the plastic moment capacity for multi-column bents in the transverse direction.

Pier Walls

Pier walls should be designed to perform in a ductile manner longitudinally (about the weak axis), and to remain essentially elastic in the transverse direction (about the strong axis). The large difference in stiffness between the strong and weak axis of pier walls leads to complex foundation behavior. Typically, it is not economical to design pier wall-pile foundations to resist the transverse seismic shear. Essentially elastic response of the wall in the strong direction will induce large foundation demands that may cause inelastic response in the foundation. If this occurs, piles will incur some damage from transverse demands most likely near the pile head/pile cap connection. Methods for reducing the inelastic damage in pier wall and pile foundations include:

- Utilizing ductile pile head details
- Pinning the pier wall-footing connection in the weak direction to reduce the weak axis demand on the piles that may be damaged by transverse demands
- Pinning the pier wall-soffit connection, thereby limiting the demands imparted to the substructure
- Use a ductile system in lieu of the traditional pier wall. For example, columns or pile extensions with isolated shear walls

P-Δ Effects

The dynamic effects of gravity loads acting through lateral displacements should be included in the design. The magnitude of displacements associated with P-Δ effects can only be accurately captured with step-by-step time history analysis.

Foundation Capacity

The foundation must have sufficient strength to ensure the column has moved well beyond its elastic capacity prior to the foundation reaching its expected nominal capacity.

13.12.1 Minimum Seat Width

Unseating of girders at abutments and piers must be avoided in all circumstances. The requirement for minimum seat width (Figure 13.22) accounts for:

- relative displacement due to out-of-phase ground motion of the piers,
- rotation of pier footings, and
- longitudinal and transverse deformation of the pier.

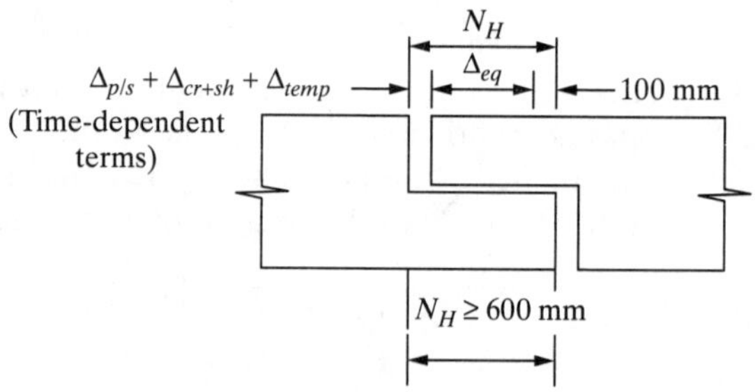

Figure 13.22 Seat width requirement.

where N_H = Minimum seat width normal to the centerline of bearing

$\Delta p/s$ = Displacement attributed to pre-stress shortening

Δ_{temp} = Displacement attributed to thermal expansion and contraction

Δ_{cr+sh} = Displacement attributed to creep and shrinkage

Δ_{eq} = Relative longitudinal earthquake displacement demand

Different codes give different seating requirements.

13.13 WHAT IS CAPACITY DESIGN PROCEDURE?

All components of a building or a bridge are designed using the limit state design philosophy. Where ever, a plastic hinge is likely to form in a member, ductile detailing is carried out. In case, it is desired that a plastic hinge must form only at a specified location and not anywhere else in a given region, this procedure does not ensure any guarantee. This is where *capacity design procedure* is helpful.

An overall dissipative and ductile behavior can be assured in a structure if concentration of plastic hinges in columns of a single storey of a multistorey building, shear failure of structural elements, failure of beam-column joints, yielding of foundations or premature formation of unstable mechanisms can be prevented. This procedure is used to ensure that an appropriate hierarchy of resistance exists within the various structural components at all possible locations of intended plastic activity. The design forces of selected regions are derived from equilibrium conditions at a given joint, assuming that plastic hinges have developed an upper fractile of their flexural resistance (overstrength) in their adjacent areas. This process is repeated at all the joints of the desired regions in the structure, one by one. Since it is a localized exercise, the sequence of selection of joints is immaterial.

Capacity protected concrete components such as superstructure, bent cap beams, joints, and footings must be designed flexurally to remain essentially elastic during their entire design life. A plastic hinge is preferred in columns, that is, piers. It may form either at its top, or bottom or both. A hinge may also form at the top and bottom of piles. Structural components that are desired to remain elastic are designed for higher forces than the normal design forces obtained using the various limit state design load combinations. In order to determine force demands on essentially elastic members, an overstrength magnifier is applied to the plastic moment capacity of a column to account for:

- Material strength variations between the column and adjacent members (e.g. superstructure, bent cap, and footings)
- Column moment capacities greater than the idealized plastic moment capacity

Clause 7.3 of IRC SP 114 describes the procedure for capacity design in bridges.

$$M_o^{col} = 1.35\, M_p^{col} \tag{13.8a}$$

or,

$$\sum M_{beam} \gg \gamma M_P^{col} \tag{13.8b}$$

Where, $\gamma = 1.35$ over strength factor

Thus, no plastic hinge can form in the bridge superstructure as shown in Figure 13.23. Remember, the pier is designed for M_P^{col}. The superstructure is designed for γM_P^{col}.

The seismic shear demand is based on the overstrength shear V_o associated with the overstrength capacities of the connected ductile components, that is,

$$V_n > V_0 = \frac{\sum \gamma M_P^{col}}{h} \tag{13.9}$$

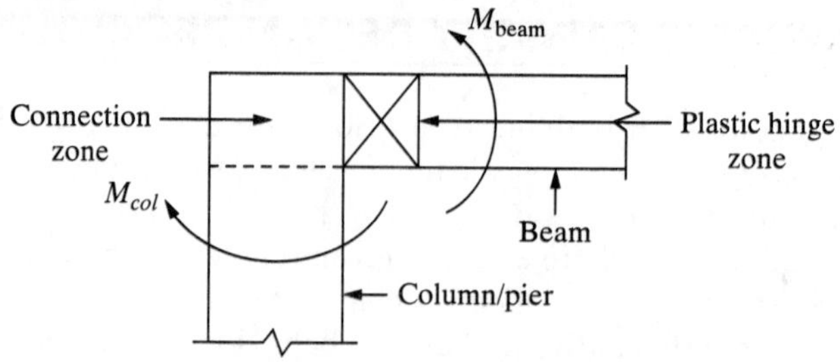

Figure 13.23 Capacity design to ensure no plastic hinge forms in beam.

It is to ensure that a member will not fail in shear before it fails in flexure.

$\sum \gamma M_P^{Col}$ = sum of the overstrength moment capacities of the hinges resisting lateral loads, as detailed.

In case of twin pier this would be the sum of the overstrength moment capacities at the top and bottom of the column; For single stem piers the overstrength moment capacity at the bottom only should be used.

h = clear height of the column in the case of a column in double curvature; height to calculated point of contra-flexure in the case of a column in single curvature.

The possible locations of plastic hinges in piers and piles during earthquakes are shown in Figure 13.24.

Plastic Hinge Region

The plastic hinge region, L_p defines the portion of the column or pier that requires enhanced lateral confinement. L_p is defined by the larger of the following:

- 1.5 times the cross sectional dimension in the direction of bending
- The region of column where the moment exceeds 75% of the maximum plastic moment, M_p^{col}
- 0.25 times length of column from the point of maximum moment to the point of contra-flexure

Example 13.7

Design the RCC pier of Example 13.6 for the design forces computed in Table 13.13 in accordance with IRC 112-2020 and IRC SP 114-2018. Consider M45 concrete, and Fe500 grade steel.
Also, consider the following data:
Maximum longitudinal moment under vertical loads = 265 kNm
Maximum lateral moment under vertical loads = 3200 kNm
Maximum braking load = 325 kN

Solution

The cross-section of the RCC pier is shown in Figure 13.25. Let us change the notation for bending moments in accordance with those of the theory of bending. MuL now becomes MuT, and MuT becomes MuL, that is, bending ABOUT the axis of bending not ALONG the axis.

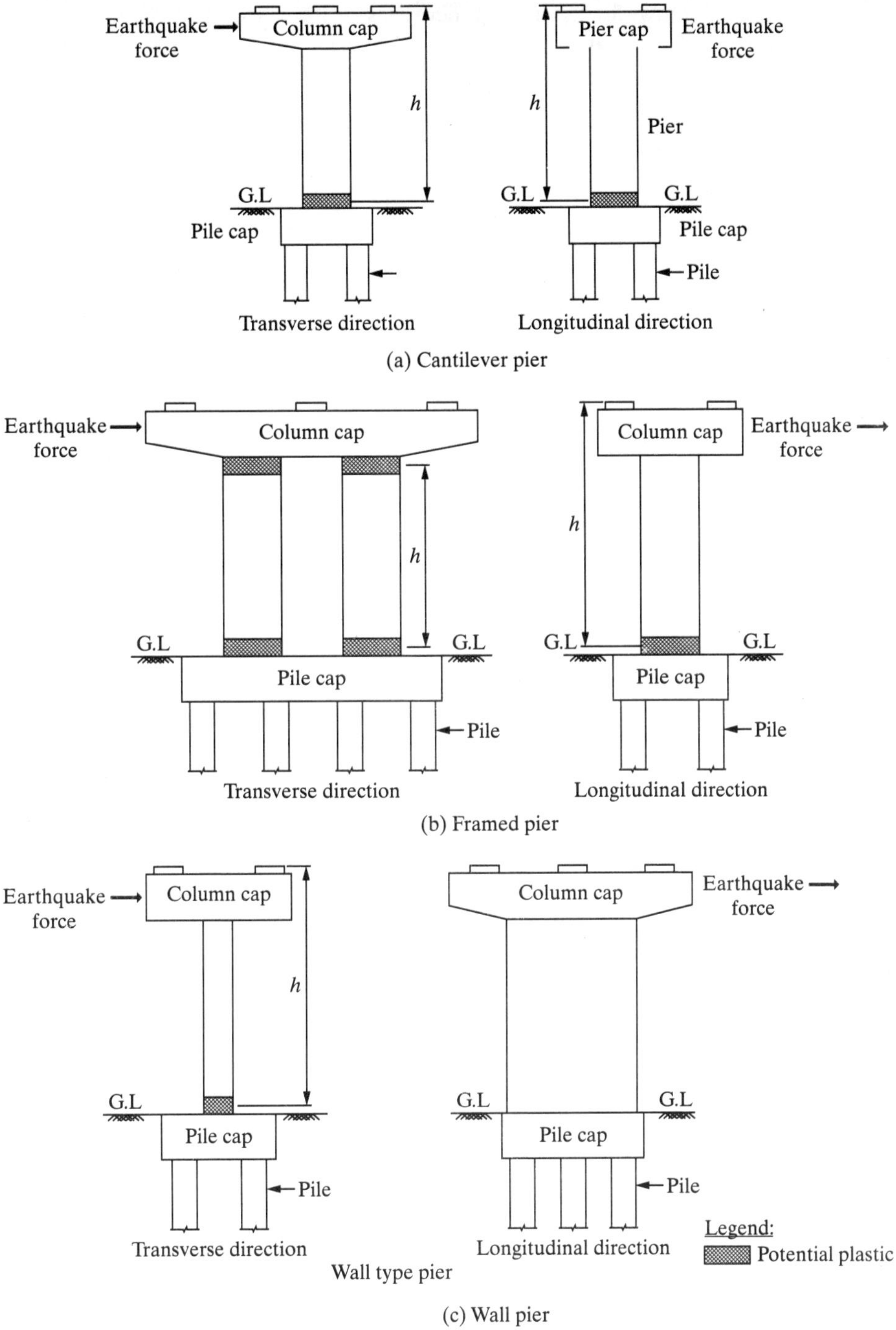

Figure 13.24 Possible locations of plastic hinges in different types of substructures.

Let us apply various checks as per Clause 8.3.2 of IRC 112.

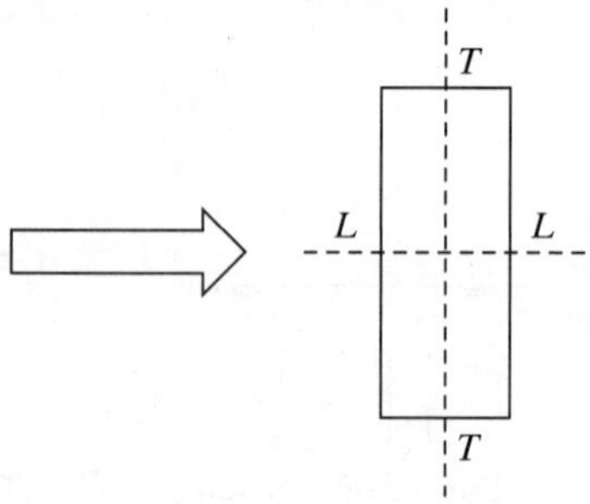

Figure 13.25 Cross-section of RCC pier.

$b = 2100$ mm
$D = 1700$ mm
$A = 3570000$ mm^2
$I_{LL} = 1.312\text{E+}12$ mm^4
$I_{TT} = 8.5978\text{E+}11$ mm^4
$r_L = 606.22$ mm
$r_T = 490.75$ mm
$L = 10250.00$ mm
Slenderness ratio $\lambda_{LL} = 16.91$
Slenderness ratio $\lambda_{TT} = 20.89$

Eccentricity $e_{LL} = M_{uT}/N_{Ed}$	21,542.00/13,990.00	1539.81 mm
Eccentricity $e_{TT} = M_{uL}/N_{Ed}$	17,188.00/14,420.00	1191.96 mm
	$b_{eq} = rL \times \text{sqrt}(12)$	2100 mm
	$D_{eq} = rT \times \text{sqrt}(12)$	1700 mm

$$\frac{e_L/D_{eq}}{e_T/b_{eq}} = 1.596 > 0.20 \quad \text{Not Good} \tag{1}$$

Similarly,

$$\frac{e_T/b_{eq}}{e_L/D_{eq}} = 0.627 > 0.20 \quad \text{Not Good} \tag{2}$$

Therefore, there is a need to apply the bi-axial interaction check.

(1) Bending about transverse axis,

$$\frac{P_u}{\sigma_{ck} bD} = 13{,}990.00 \times 10^{-3}/(45 \times 2.1 \times 1.7) = 0.0871$$

$$\frac{M_{uT}}{\sigma_{ck} bD^2} = 21{,}542.00 \times 10^{-3}/(45 \times 2.1 \times 1.7^2) = 0.0789$$

Standards design charts give for $d'/D = 0.05$, steel $p = 0.675$ %

(2) Bending about longitudinal axis,

$$\frac{P_u}{\sigma_{ck} bD} = 14{,}420.00 \times 10^{-3}/(45 \times 1.7 \times 2.1) = 0.0898$$

$$\frac{M_{uL}}{\sigma_{ck}bD^2} = 17188.00 \times 10^{-3}/(45 \times 1.7 \times 2.1^2) = 0.0509$$

Standards design charts for $d'/D = 0.05$ give $p = 0.1$ % steel

Minimum steel in wall type piers is 0.24% and maximum steel is 4%. Let us provide 3% steel distributed on all the four faces.

Reinforcement provided along 1.7 m face each = 30 no. 28 mm bars.

Reinforcement provided along 2.1 m face each = 34 no. 40 mm bars.

Total steel provided = $4 \times [15 \times 6.16 + 17 \times 12.56] = 1223.7$ cm^2

Let us apply interaction check and calculate moment of resistance about the strong and weak axes of the section for 3% steel.

$$\therefore \quad p/\sigma_{ck} = 0.067$$

$$P_u/\sigma_{ck}\, bD = 0.087$$

$$M_{RdT}/\sigma_{ck}bD^2 = 0.14,$$

$$\therefore \quad M_{RdT} = 38234 \text{ kNm}$$

and

$$\therefore \quad p/\sigma_{ck} = 0.067$$

$$P_u/\sigma_{ck}\, bD = 0.0897$$

$$M_{RdL}/\sigma_{ck}Db^2 = 0.14$$

$$\therefore \quad M_{RdL} = 47231 \text{ kNm}$$

Let us calculate design axial resistance of the section N_{Rd}.

$$N_{Rd} = A_c f_{cd} + A_s f_{yd} \tag{3}$$

$$N_{Rd} = 0.67 \times \sigma_{ck}/1.5 \times b \times D + \sigma_y/1.15 \times p \times b \times D = 118322 \text{ kN}$$

where, $f_{cd} = \dfrac{\alpha f_{ck}}{\gamma_m} = \dfrac{0.67 f_{ck}}{1.5}$

$$f_{yd} = \frac{f_{yk}}{1.15}$$

Design value of axial force $N_{Ed} = 14420$ kN

$$N_{Ed}/N_{Rd} = 14420.00/118322.22 = 0.122$$

$$\therefore \quad \alpha = 1.0$$

Interaction equation is as follows:

$$\left(\frac{M_{EdL}}{M_{RdL}}\right)^{\alpha} + \left(\frac{M_{EdT}}{M_{RdT}}\right)^{\alpha} \tag{4}$$

$(17188.00/47231.10)^{1.00} + (21542.00/38234.7)^{1.00} = 0.93 < 1.0$ OK □

Now, let us carryout non-linear analysis of the pier section to derive M-ϕ curve, plastic moment capacity and M-P interaction. Confined concrete is assumed in accordance with Mander's formulation. Analysis is done using MATLAB as discussed in

Chapter 16. The stress-strain curve for concrete is shown in Figures 13.26(a). Moment-curvature curve is shown in Figure 13.26(b).

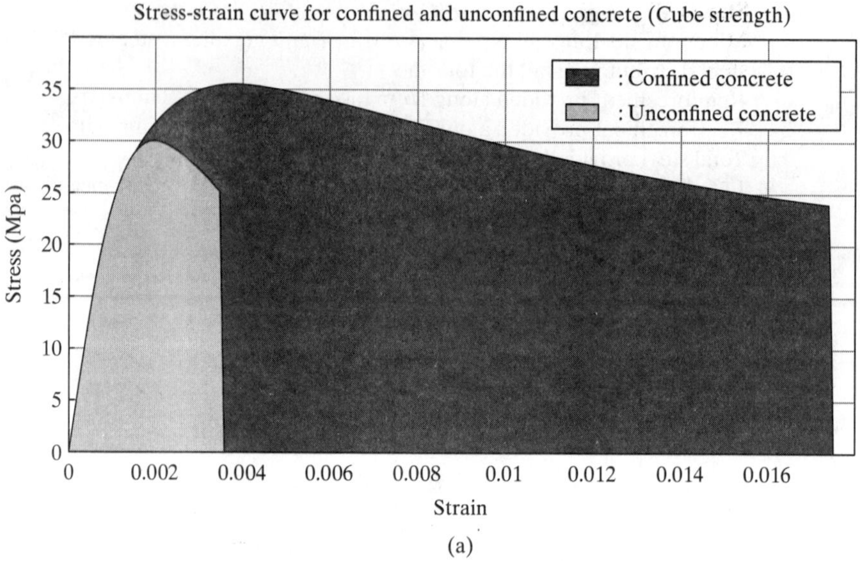

Figure 13.26(a) Stress-strain curve for concrete.

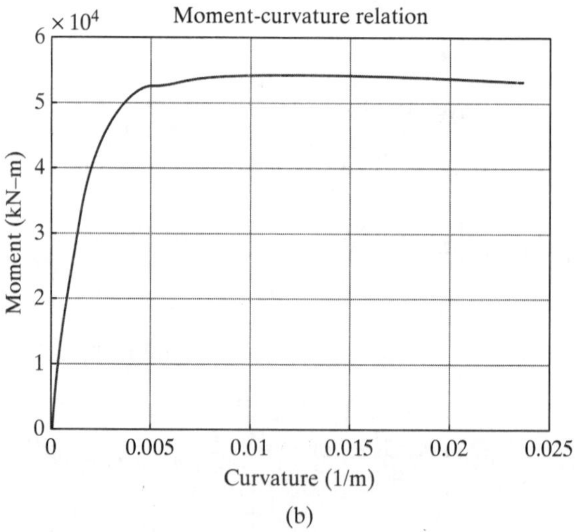

Figure 13.26(b) Moment-curvature curve for the cross-section about strong axis (L-L).

$$\text{Plastic moment } M_{PL} = 54200 \text{ kNm}$$

Similarly, plastic moment about the weak axis can be determined.

$$\text{Plastic moment } M_{PT} = 50700 \text{ kNm}$$

The axial force – moment interaction curve has been determined using the stress-strain curve for unconfined concrete as shown in Figure 13.26(c) and (d).

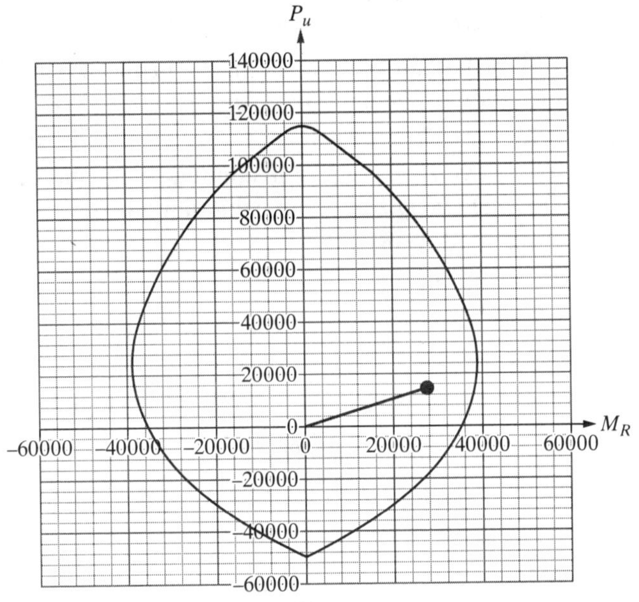

(d)

Figure 13.26(c) $M_R - P_u$ interaction curve, where M_R = 27564 kNm resultant moment, (27564, 14420).

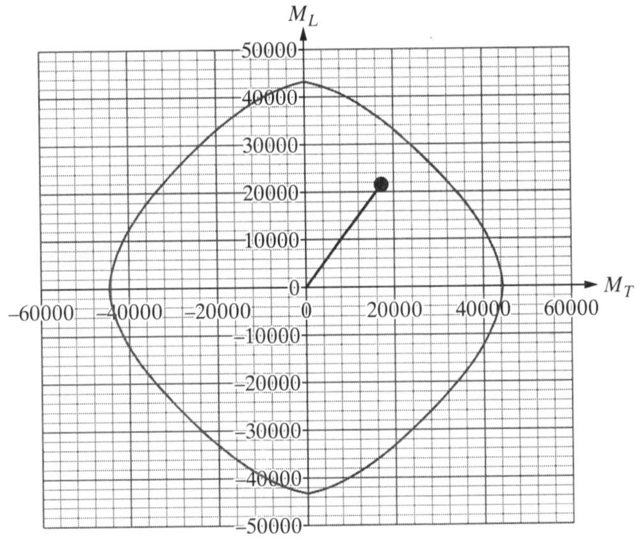

(d)

Figure 13.26(d) M_T-M_L interaction curve, (17200, 21500 kNm).

These curves show that the assumed reinforcement of 3% is safe. The moment capacity ratio is 0.7.

Length of Plastic Hinge

Clause 17.2.1.4 of IRC 112-2011 gives length of plastic hinge as follows:

When $\eta_k = N_{ED}/A_c f_{ck} \leq 0.30$, length of plastic hinge L_p is greater of the following

(i) the depth of the pier section within the plane of bending (perpendicular to the axis of rotation of the hinge) = 1.7 m
Or,

(ii) the distance from the point of maximum design moment to the point where the design moment is 80% of the maximum moment
$= (0.2 \times 10.25 = 2.05 \text{ m})$
$= 2.05$ m say 2.1 m.

When $0.6 \geq \eta_k \geq 0.3$, the design length of the potential plastic hinge as determined above should be increased by 50%.

Different Codes give different expressions to compute the length of plastic hinge

Curtailment of Reinforcement in the Pier

Let us curtail the reinforcement in the pier from 3% to 2% at 5 m above the base of the pier.

Provide $2 \times 15 - 28$ mm bars along each short face
Provide $2 \times 21 - 40$ mm bars along each long face
Total steel = 712 cm^2

MATLAB gives $M_{PL} = 40700$ kNm and $M_{PT} = 37900$ kNm plastic moment capacities.

The moment-rotation curve about the strong axis is shown in Figure 13.26(e).

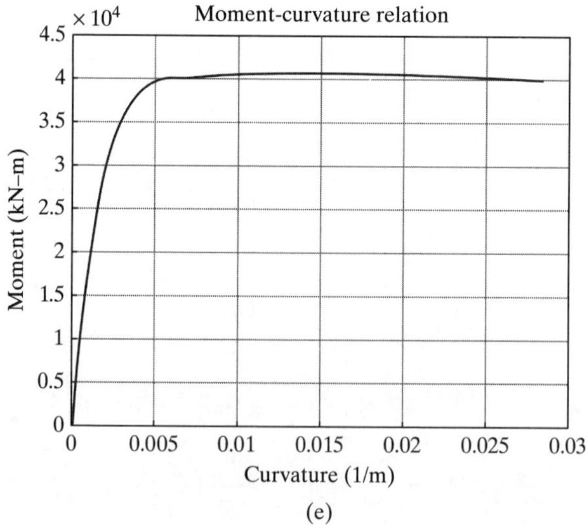

Figure 13.26(e) Moment-curvature curve at the curtailed section.

Over strength factor for concrete = 1.35
Overstrength moment at the base $M_{oL} = 1.35 \times 54200 = 73170$ kNm

Overstrength moment at the base $M_{oT} = 1.35 \times 50700 = 68445$ kNm
Over strength required at 5 m height are given by

$$M_{oL} = 73170 \times (10.25 - 5)/10.25 = 37477 \text{ kNm}$$

$$M_{PL} = 40700 > M_{oL} \quad \text{OK}$$

$$M_{oT} = 68445 \times (10.25 - 5)/10.25 = 35057 \text{ kNm}$$

$$M_{PT} = 37900 > M_{oT} \quad \text{OK}$$

At the curtailed section, the plastic moment capacity is higher than the demand originating from the over strength of plastic hinge. OK

Shear Resistance of the Base of the Pier

Clause 7.5.3.2 of IRC SP 114 read with Cl. 10 of IRC 112

Let us calculate factored moments for non-seismic actions:
Maximum longitudinal moment under vertical loads = 265 kNm
Maximum lateral moment under vertical loads = 3200 kNm
Maximum braking force = 325 kN
Factored forces under seismic conditions are as follows:
Load factor = 0.2 for seismic combination
Factored BM due to live load in longitudinal direction = 0.2 × 265 = 53 kNm
Factored max. braking force = 0.2 × 325 = 65 kN
∴ Total factored BM in longitudinal direction = 53 + 10.25 × 65 = 719.25 say 720 kNm
Factored BM due to live load in transverse direction = 0.2 × 3200 = 640 kNm

Thus, Net increase in plastic moment over the non-seismic moments are as follows:

- along longitudinal direction, $DM_L = 68445 - 720 = 67725$ kNm
- along transverse direction, $DM_T = 73170 - 640 = 72530$ kNm

Shear corresponding to this increase in plastic moment is given by

$$\Delta V = \frac{\Sigma \Delta M}{h}$$

along longitudinal direction = 67725.75/10.25 = 6607 kN (i)

along transverse direction = 72530/10.25 = 7076 kN (ii)

Seismic Base shear at the base of pier obtained earlier with $R = 1$ are (Cl. 7.3.4.2 (f) IRC SP 114)

along longitudinal direction = 3 × 2105 = 6315 kN (iii)

along transverse direction = 3 × 1780 = 5340 kN (iv)

Since values given by (i) and (ii) are more than those given by (iii) and (iv), the higher values will govern the shear design.

The reinforcement in the pier section at its base is shown in Figure 13.27. Ductile detailing should be done in accordance with IRC SP 114.

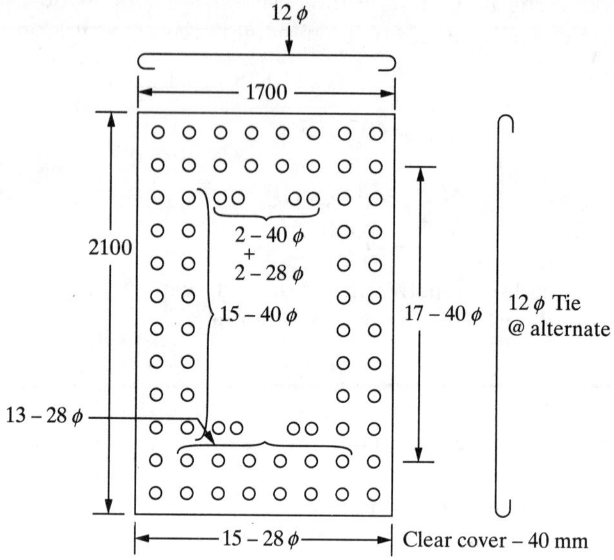

Figure 13.27 Reinforcement detail at the bottom cross-section of pier.

REVIEW QUESTIONS

13.1 Discuss different classifications of bridges.

13.2 For a single span bridge, what are the various options for the superstructure? Draw neat sketches.

13.3 For a multi-span bridge, what are the various options for the superstructure? Draw neat sketches.

13.4 Identify various components of a superstructure of a T-beam bridge with a neat sketch.

13.5 Identify various components of a substructure of a T-beam bridge with a neat sketch.

13.6 Discuss different arrangements of piers with neat sketches.

13.7 Draw a neat sketch of a cross-section of a typical 4-lane box girder bridge.

13.8 Differentiate between wheeled loading and tracked loading for highways.

13.9 Discuss the live load combinations for a bridge having (i) 6 m carriageway, (ii) 11 m carriageway, and (iii) 18 m carriageway. What are the permissible reductions?

13.10 Draw a sketch of a rail-structure interaction model and discuss the salient features.

13.11 What is an impact factor? For a Class 70R tracked vehicle, what is the impact factor for a 30 m span?

13.12 What do you understand by longitudinal forces in a bridge? Explain tractive effort and braking effect.

13.13 Discuss the longitudinal forces acting at the bearings of a simply supported bridge.

13.14 Discuss the longitudinal forces acting at the bearings of a continuous bridge.

13.15 What is the reduction in the longitudinal effect on a multi-lane bridge?

13.16 What is the purpose of grillage analysis of the deck of a bridge?

13.17 Discuss the contribution of live load for the estimation of earthquake force.

13.18 Discuss the importance factor with regard to railway bridges.

13.19 Discuss response reduction factor with reference to bridge components.

13.20 How do you proportion the geometry of a bridge to improve its response in the event of an earthquake?

13.21 Discuss different types of bridge bearings and their relative merits.

13.22 What information is required for modeling a highway bridge?

13.23 What information is required for modeling a railway bridge?

13.24 Discuss modeling of piers of a bridge with respect to its dynamic analysis.

13.25 Discuss modeling of superstructure along with piers and abutments of a bridge with respect to its dynamic analysis.

13.26 What do you understand by design vibration units of a bridge? Explain with neat sketches.

13.27 Discuss modeling of a bridge curved in plan with respect to its dynamic analysis.

13.28 What is a shock transmission unit in a bridge?

13.29 Under what conditions seismic coefficient method can be used for the analysis of a bridge?

13.30 Under what conditions response spectrum analysis method should be used for the analysis of a bridge?

13.31 Write a short note on partial load factors for the analysis of a highway bridge.

13.32 Write a short note on load combinations for the analysis of a highway bridge.

13.33 Discuss the basic design requirements of a bridge for limit state of collapse.

13.34 What is capacity design procedure? Discuss in detail.

13.35 Sketch the possible locations of plastic hinges in different types of piers.

REFERENCES

AASHTO (2020) LRFD Bridge Design Specifications, American Association of State Highway and Transportation Officials, Washington, DC.

Agrawal, S. (2009) Nonlinear Seismic Analysis of Multi-Span Simply Supported Viaduct, M. Tech. Thesis, Indian Institute of Technology Roorkee, Roorkee.

Agrawal, S. and Jain, A.K. (2010) Non-linear Modeling of Expansion Joints in Multi-span Simply Supported Bridges, Proc. Asian Conference on Earthquake Engineering, Paper no. ACEE-A-007, AIT Bangkok, Dec.

Agrawal, S. and Jain, A.K. (2010) Non-linear Modeling and Seismic Performance of a Multi-Span Simply Supported Viaduct, Proc., 5th Int Conf. on Earthquake Engineering. (5ICEE and 7CUEE), Tokyo Institute of Technology, Tokyo, March.

Caltrans (2019) Seismic Design Criteria, Version 2, California Department of Transportation, Sacramento, California.

Eurocode 1998 – Part 2 (2005) Design of Structures for Earthquake Resistance–Bridges incorporating corrigendum 2012, European Committee for Standardization, Brussels.

Gangal, S. A. (2011) Seismic Response of RC Bridges with Viscous Dampers, M. Tech. Thesis, Indian Institute of Technology Roorkee, Roorkee.

IS:1893-Part 1 (2016) Criteria for Earthquake Resistant Design of Structures – General Provisions and Buildings, Bureau of Indian Standards, New Delhi.

IS:1893-Part 3 (2014) Criteria for Earthquake Resistant Design of Structures – Bridges and Retaining Walls, Bureau of Indian Standards, New Delhi.

IRC 5 (2015) Section 1 – General Features of Design, Indian Roads Congress, New Delhi.

IRC 6 (2017) Section 2 – Loads and Load Combinations, with latest amendments, Indian Roads Congress, New Delhi.

IRC 24 (2010) Steel Bridges, Indian Roads Congress, New Delhi.

IRC 78 (2020) Limit State Design of Foundations, Indian Roads Congress, New Delhi.

IRC 83 (2015) Part I, Bearings – Roller & Rocker Bearings, Indian Roads Congress, New Delhi.

IRC 83 (2018) Part II, Bearings – Elastomeric Bearings, Indian Roads Congress, New Delhi.

IRC 83 (2008) Part III, Bearings – POT, POT-CUM-PTFE bearings, Pin and Metallic Guide Bearings, Indian Roads Congress, New Delhi.

IRC 112 (2020) Concrete Bridges, Indian Roads Congress, New Delhi.

IRC SP 114 (2018) Guidelines for Seismic Design of Road Bridges, with latest amendments, Indian Roads Congress, New Delhi.

BS 112 (2014) Guidelines for Planning of Road over Bridges (ROB), Research Designs and Standards Organisation, Ministry of Railways, Lucknow.

IRS Bridge Rules (2008) Research Designs and Standards Organisation, Ministry of Railways, Lucknow.

IRS Concrete Bridge Code (2003) Research Designs and Standards Organisation, Ministry of Railways, Lucknow.

Jain, A. K. (2012) Reinforced Concrete - Limit State Design, 7th ed, Nem Chand & Bros, Roorkee.

Lokhandwala, S. (2012) Nonlinear Analysis of Bridges for Seismic Loading, M. Tech. Thesis, Indian Institute of Technology Roorkee, Roorkee.

PEER 3 (2008) Guidelines for Nonlinear Analysis of Bridge Structures in California, Report UCB/PEER 2008/03, University of California, Berkeley, California.

RDSO Guidelines for Carrying out Rail-Structure Interaction Studies on Metro Systems (2014), Research Designs and Standards Organisation, Ministry of Railways, Lucknow.

RDSO Guidelines for Seismic Design of Railway Bridges (2015), Report no. BS-118, Research Designs and Standards Organisation, Ministry of Railways, Lucknow.

UIC 772-2R (1989) Code for the Use of Rubber Bearings for Rail Bridges, International Union of Railways, Paris.

UIC 774-3R (2001) Track/Bridge Interaction, Recommendations for Calculations, International Union of Railways, Paris.

14 Analysis of Liquid Retaining Structures for Earthquake Force

14.1 INTRODUCTION

Liquid retaining tanks are used in industry to store different kinds of liquids, such as, water, gaseous, petroleum products, chemicals, and other products. In India, they are used extensively to store and supply drinking water to the community. These tanks are made of reinforced concrete, prestressed concrete, or steel. These tanks can be classified as follows:

- Tanks supported on ground
- Overhead tanks
- Underground tanks

They are further classified based on their geometry:

- Rectangular tanks
- Circular or polygon tanks

The circular tanks consist of a combination of cylindrical, spherical, and conical thin shells. Ring beams are provided at the junction of shells.

Ground supported tanks may also be classified based on the wall-base joint type:

- Fixed or rigid joint
- Hinged Joint
- Flexible or sliding joint

Generally, the shape and size of elevated concrete tanks depend upon the functional requirements such as:

- Capacity of tank
- Height of staging
- Maximum depth for water in the container
- Geotechnical conditions including depth of water table
- Geographical location in terms of seismicity and wind loads
- Type of suitable foundation
- Aesthetic considerations
- Other local site conditions

An elevated tank may be supported on any of the two distinct staging:

- Beam-column framed staging
- Cylindrical or curvilinear shell, also referred to as a shaft staging

The height of staging depends upon the local terrain and loss of head during supply of the liquid.

Typical elevated concrete tanks are shown in Figure 14.1 and 14.2, and ground supported steel tanks are shown in Figure 14.3. A collapse of a conical water tank on shaft while testing for first water filling is shown in Figure 14.4.

(a) (b)

Figure 14.1 Typical overhead RC water tanks.

Concrete tanks are designed using the limit state design philosophy for collapse and serviceability in accordance with IS 3370 parts 1 and 2. Although design for serviceability will generally dominate, design for strength must be considered to ensure that the load capacity and slenderness ratios for members of the structure are within acceptable limits. The serviceability limit state corresponds to the following:

- Cracking
- Deflection
- Durability

The maximum surface width of cracks for direct tension and flexure, or restrained temperature and moisture effects is a function of ratio of the hydrostatic head (h) to the wall thickness (t) of the containing structure. For $h/t \leq 5$, the crack width should not exceed 0.2 mm with specified cover; while for $h/t > 35$, the crack width should not exceed 0.05 mm with specified cover. The maximum stress in reinforcing steel must

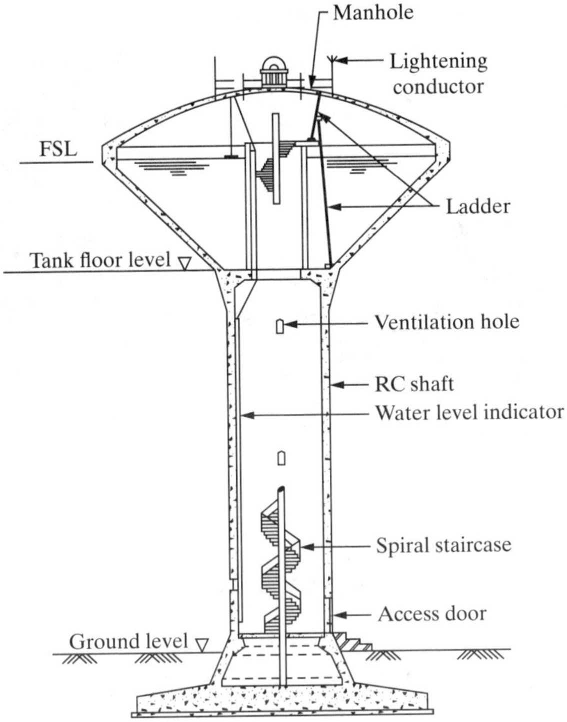

Figure 14.2 Cross-section of a typical conical tank on cylindrical shell staging.

(a) Typical steel tanks

(b) Foundation of a 10000 MT Ammonia Tank

Figure 14.3 Typical steel tanks supported on ground (pile foundation not visible).

be such that the maximum strain in concrete, that is, cracks in concrete remain within the permissible limit. The considered system, including a specified set of accessory elements integrated with it, must remain fully serviceable and leak proof under the relevant seismic action. Usually, all concrete would permit the passage of small quantities of liquids and gases by diffusion.

(a) Conical container

(b) Container dome

(c) Bottom of conical container

Figure 14.4 Collapse of a 650 kL conical tank over 20 m shaft staging during initial testing.

To provide adequate assurance for structures of liquid tightness so that cracks do not pass through the full width of a section, the design value of the depth of the compression zone should be at least x_{min} calculated for the long term combination of actions. The recommended value for x_{min} is the lesser of 50 mm or $0.2t$ where t is the element thickness.

Steel tanks are also designed using the limit state design philosophy. The serviceability limit state corresponds to the following:

- Stability (buckling)
- Deflection

It must be verified that local buckling, if it occurs, does not trigger collapse and is reversible.

Adequate freeboard should be provided in the tanks under the maximum vertical displacement of the liquid surface, in order to prevent damage to the roof due to the pressure of the sloshing liquid or, if the tank has no rigid roof, to prevent undesirable effects of spilling of the liquid. Further, the hydraulic systems which are part of, or are connected to the tank, must be verified to accommodate stresses and distortions due to relative displacements between tanks or between tanks and soil, without their functions being impaired.

The overall stability of the tank must be verified in accordance with IS 456. The overall stability refers to rigid body behaviour and may be impaired by sliding or overturning. A limited amount of sliding may be accepted, if tolerated by the pipe system and if the tank is not anchored to the foundation.

Liquid retaining tanks are designed for hydrostatic pressure due to the contained liquid. When a tank is subjected to horizontal acceleration due to an earthquake, it will experience inertia forces generated by the acceleration of the structure itself, and the hydrodynamic forces generated by the horizontal acceleration of the contained liquid. The analysis of the circular tanks for hydrostatic force can be done using the conventional *membrane theory*. The *effect of continuity* due to secondary forces is carried out using compatibility conditions. The analysis of rectangular tanks for hydrostatic force can be done using the conventional *theory of strength of materials*. The analysis of overhead and under-ground concrete tanks due to earthquake force is discussed in the present chapter.

14.2 DYNAMIC MODELING OF TANKS

The model to be used for the determination of the seismic effects should reproduce the stiffness, strength, damping, mass and geometrical properties of the containment structure, and must account for the hydrodynamic response of the contained liquid and, where necessary, for the effects of the interaction with the foundation soil.

When a tank containing liquid with a free surface is subjected to horizontal earthquake ground motion, tank wall and liquid are subjected to hydrodynamic pressures. The liquid in the lower region of tank behaves like a mass that is rigidly connected to tank wall. This mass is termed as *impulsive liquid mass* which accelerates along with the wall and induces impulsive hydrodynamic pressure on tank wall and base. Liquid mass in the upper region of tank undergoes sloshing motion. This mass is termed as *convective liquid mass* and it exerts convective hydrodynamic pressure on tank wall and base. The equivalent hydrodynamic mass comprises two components:

1. The impulsive mass representing the portion of the contents accelerating with the tank, and
2. The convective mass representing the portion of the contents oscillating in the tank.

The *impulsive pressures* are not the same impulse loading as discussed in Chapter 5. These are associated with the inertia forces produced by the accelerations of the walls of the container. The *convective pressures* are those produced by the oscillations of the liquid and are, therefore, the consequences of the impulsive pressures. A dynamic model of the tank-liquid system should represent these two liquid masses suitably.

For thin walled circular tanks ($t/R < 0.03$) non-symmetrical loads (i.e. temperature loads and hydrodynamic seismic pressures) may be considered to be rotationally symmetric and equal to the value at the section under consideration.

Housner (1963) and others studied the dynamic behaviour of tanks, and computed impulsive pressures and convective pressures on the walls and base slab of tanks with flat base slab. They used a single degree-of-freedom as well as two degrees-of-freedom model to study the dynamic behaviour of tanks.

14.2.1 Ground Supported Tanks

Such tanks can be idealized using spring and mass model as shown in Figure 14.5. In this model, the mass m_i is the equivalent mass of the oscillating liquid that produces impulsive pressures on the tank walls. The mass m_i is rigidly connected to the tank walls at a height h_i above the tank bottom, which corresponds to the location of the resultant impulsive force P_i. The mass m_i moves with the tank walls as they respond to the ground acceleration. The impulsive force P_i is evenly divided into a pressure force on the wall accelerating into the liquid, and a suction force on the wall accelerating away from the liquid. During an earthquake, the force P_i changes its direction several times corresponding to the change in direction of the ground motion. Thus, the overturning moment generated by the force P_i is unable to overturn the tank.

The mass m_c is the equivalent mass of the oscillating liquid that produces convective pressures on the tank walls with the resultant force P_c which acts at a height h_c above the tank bottom. In this model, the mass m_c is connected to the tank walls by springs. The sloshing pressures or convective pressures on the tank walls result from the motion of the liquid associated with the oscillations of the waves. The period of oscillation of the sloshing depends on the ratio of the depth of liquid to tank diameter. It may last for several seconds. The overturning moment exerted by P_c acts for a sufficient time to tend to lift the tank wall, if there is insufficient counter weight or anchorage.

The impulsive and convective forces P_i and P_c, act independently but simultaneously on the tank. The force P_i essentially acts to stress the tank wall, whereas, the force P_c acts essentially to uplift the tank wall. The vertical vibrations of the ground are also transmitted to the liquid producing additional pressures on the walls. The duration of the fluctuations of the force P_i is 10 to 15 seconds, whereas, that of the fluctuation of the force P_c is 20 to 40 seconds, for a stronger earthquake. The effect of sloshing is usually smaller than that of the impulsive effect, but it will tend to uplift the tank if there is not enough dead weight.

Two cases of overturning of the tank are considered: *excluding base pressure* and *including base pressure*. The term excluding base pressure (EBP) refers to the hydrodynamic design in which the overturning of the wall is considered with respect to the tank floor excluding the pressure acting on the base. This case is used to determine the need for anchorage of the tank in non-fixed base tanks. The term including base pressure (IBP) refers to the hydrodynamic design in which the overturning of the entire tank is considered with respect to the foundation. The IBP accounts for the overturning moment effects due to dynamic liquid pressures on the bottom of the tank by increasing the effective vertical lever arm to the applied forces.

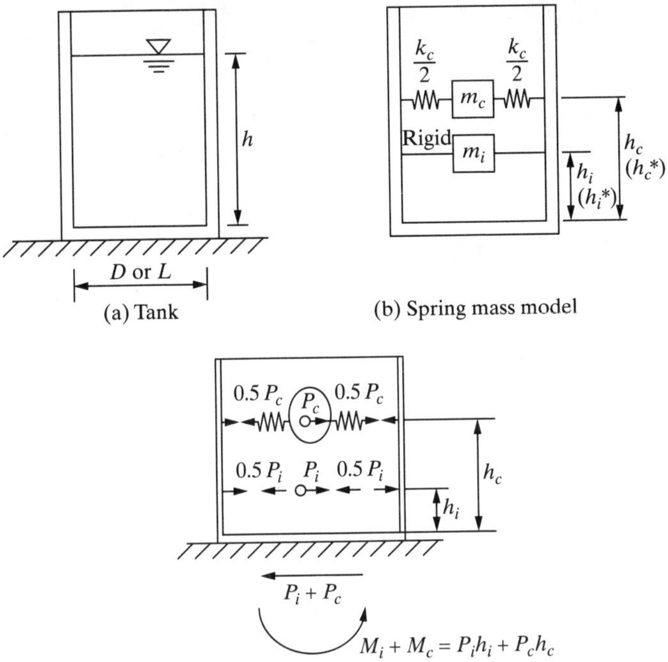

(c) Dynamic equilibrium of horizontal forces

In this figure,

m_i = equivalent impulsive mass of liquid, denotes the mass of the contained fluid which moves together with the walls

m_c = equivalent convective mass of liquid

Height h_w = height of wall above the base of the tank

Height h = height of liquid above the base of the tank wall

Height h_i = height of center of gravity of the impulsive lateral force on the wall above the base of the tank wall for the case excluding base pressure (EBP)

Height h_i^* = equivalent height of center of gravity of the impulsive lateral force on the wall above the base of the tank wall for the case including base pressure (IBP). In other words, the equivalent height at which the impulsive force is placed to give the total overturning moment arising from pressures on both the walls and base.

Height h_c = height of center of gravity of the convective lateral force on the wall above the base of the tank wall for the case excluding base pressure (EBP)

Height h_c^* = equivalent height of center of gravity of the convective lateral force on the wall above the base of the tank wall for the case including base pressure (IBP). In other words, the equivalent height at which the convective force is placed to give the total overturning moment arising from pressures on both the walls and base.

Convective spring stiffness k_c = Stiffness of spring by which the convective mass is attached to the tank wall at height h_c or h_c^*

Heights h_i^* and h_c^* can be outside the tank body as they are equivalent heights.

Figure 14.5 Spring mass model for ground supported circular and rectangular tanks.

14.2.2 Elevated Tanks

The dynamic behaviour of an elevated tank during horizontal earthquake motion is similar to that of a ground supported tank discussed earlier. An elevated tank can be idealized using the spring mass model as shown in Figure 14.6. The model shown in Figure 14.6(c) is known as a two-mass model having two degrees of freedom. It can be analyzed as discussed in Chapter 9. It is observed that for most overhead tanks, the natural periods in the two modes are well separated ($T_1/T_2 > 2.5$). Therefore, this system can be treated as two uncoupled SDOF systems as shown in Figure 14.6(d).

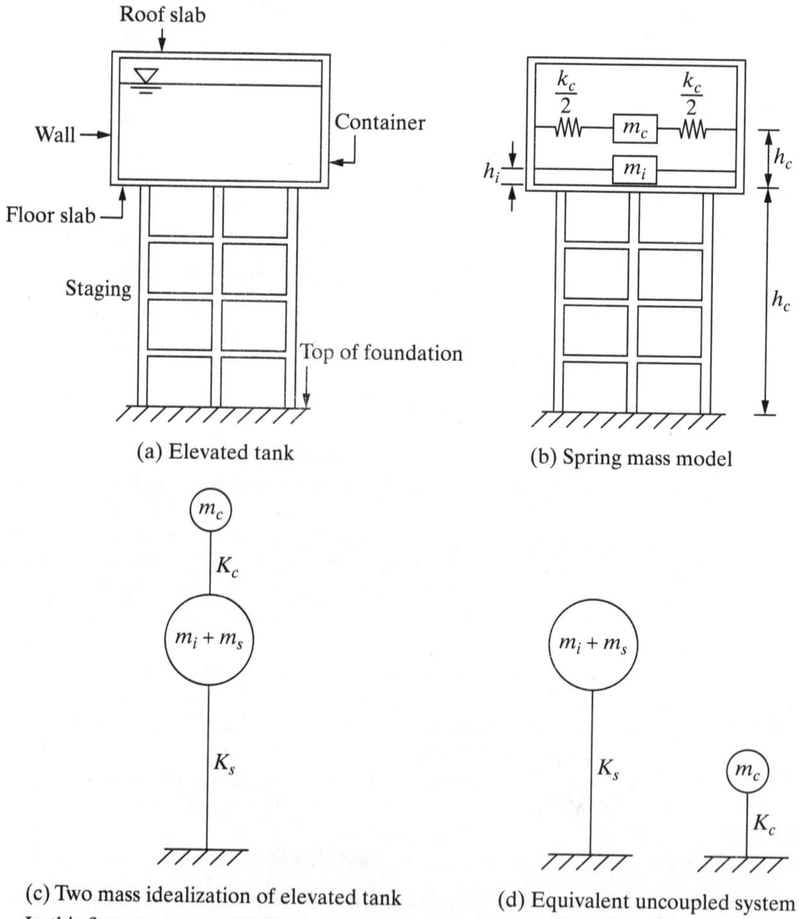

In this figure,
m_s = structural mass = mass of empty container + [mass of the staging including staircase]/3
k_s = lateral stiffness of the staging, N/m

Figure 14.6 Spring mass idealization of elevated tank.

Lateral stiffness of the staging is defined as the lateral force required to produce a unit displacement at the center of gravity of the tank. Height of staging is measured above the average ground level up to the top of the bottom ring beam of the tank. In other words, height of staging is the difference between the lowest supply level of tank and the average ground level at the tank site.

14.3 PARAMETERS FOR DYNAMIC MODELS

The parameters for defining dynamic models for concrete tanks can be determined with the help of internal plan dimensions of the tank (diameter D, or length L) and height h of liquid inside the tank (ACI 350.3).

14.3.1 Rectangular Tanks

Equivalent Mass of the Accelerating Liquid

$$\frac{m_i}{m} = \frac{\tan h\left(0.866\dfrac{L}{h}\right)}{0.866\dfrac{L}{h}} \tag{14.1a}$$

$$\frac{m_c}{m} = 0.264\frac{\tan h\left(3.16\dfrac{h}{L}\right)}{\dfrac{h}{L}} \tag{14.1b}$$

where, m = total mass of the liquid in tank = $LBh\,\rho_L$

ρ_L = mass density of liquid

L = inner length of the tank parallel to the direction of the earthquake force

B = inner width of the tank at right angles to the direction of the earthquake force

Height of Center of Gravity EBP

For tanks with $\dfrac{h}{L} < 0.75$

$$\frac{h_i}{h} = 0.375 \tag{14.1c}$$

For tanks with $\dfrac{h}{L} > 0.75$

$$\frac{h_i}{h} = 0.5 - \frac{0.09375}{\dfrac{h}{L}} \tag{14.1d}$$

For all tanks

$$\frac{h_c}{h} = 1 - \frac{\cos h\left(3.16\frac{h}{L}\right) - 1}{3.16\left(\frac{h}{L}\right)\sin h\left(3.16\frac{h}{L}\right)} \tag{14.1e}$$

Height of Center of Gravity IBP

For tanks with $\frac{h}{L} < 1.33$

$$\frac{h_i^*}{h} = \frac{0.866\frac{L}{h}}{2\tan h\left(0.866\frac{L}{h}\right)} - 0.125 \tag{14.1f}$$

For tanks with $\frac{h}{L} > 1.33$

$$\frac{h_i^*}{h} = 0.45 \tag{14.1g}$$

For all tanks

$$\frac{h_c^*}{h} = 1 - \frac{\cos h\left(3.16\frac{h}{L}\right) - 2.01}{3.16\left(\frac{h}{L}\right)\sin h\left(3.16\frac{h}{L}\right)} \tag{14.1h}$$

14.3.2 Circular Tanks

Equivalent Mass of the Accelerating Liquid

$$\frac{m_i}{m} = \frac{\tan h\left(0.866\frac{D}{h}\right)}{0.866\frac{D}{h}} \tag{14.2a}$$

$$\frac{m_c}{m} = 0.230\frac{\tan h\left(3.68\frac{h}{D}\right)}{\frac{h}{D}} \tag{14.2b}$$

Height of Center of Gravity EBP

For tanks with $\frac{h}{D} < 0.75$

$$\frac{h_i}{h} = 0.375 \tag{14.2c}$$

For tanks with $\frac{h}{D} > 0.75$

$$\frac{h_i}{h} = 0.5 - \frac{0.09375}{\frac{h}{D}} \tag{14.2d}$$

For all tanks

$$\frac{h_c}{h} = 1 - \frac{\cos h\left(3.68\frac{h}{D}\right) - 1}{3.68\left(\frac{h}{D}\right)\sin h\left(3.68\frac{h}{D}\right)} \tag{14.2e}$$

Height of Center of Gravity IBP

For tanks with $\frac{h}{D} < 1.33$

$$\frac{h_i^*}{h} = \frac{0.866\frac{D}{h}}{2\tan h\left(0.866\frac{D}{h}\right)} - 0.125 \tag{14.2f}$$

For tanks with $\frac{h}{D} > 1.33$

$$\frac{h_i^*}{h} = 0.45 \tag{14.2g}$$

For all tanks

$$\frac{h_c^*}{h} = 1 - \frac{\cos h\left(3.68\frac{h}{D}\right) - 2.01}{3.68\left(\frac{h}{D}\right)\sin h\left(3.68\frac{h}{D}\right)} \tag{14.2h}$$

These parameters can be plotted against h/D as shown in Figure 14.7 for circular tanks. Similar curves can be generated for rectangular tanks.

14.4 PERIOD OF VIBRATION

The natural periods of vibration of tanks are calculated for the following conditions:

(a) Tank empty

(b) Tank full

- Impulsive mode
- Convective mode

When the tank is empty, there is no convective mode.

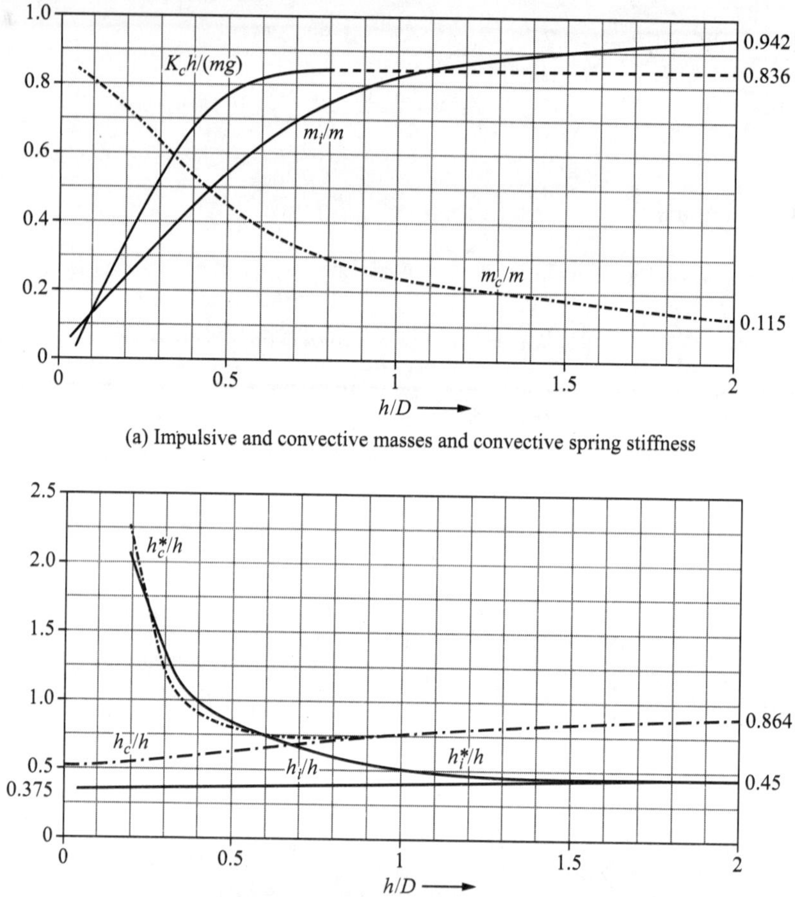

(a) Impulsive and convective masses and convective spring stiffness

(b) Heights of Impulsive and convective masses

Figure 14.7 Parameters of the spring mass model for circular tanks.

14.4.1 Impulsive Mode

Ground Supported Circular Tanks

The expression for period of vibration for the impulsive mode was developed for roofless steel tanks fixed at base and filled with water. This expression was derived based on the assumption that mass of the tank is quite small as compared to the mass of the fluid stored in the tank. This assumption is true for steel tanks. However, as an approximation, it may also be used for concrete tanks.

$$T_i = C_i \frac{h\sqrt{\rho_L}}{\sqrt{\frac{t_w}{D}}\sqrt{E}} \tag{14.3a}$$

where, T_i = fundamental period of vibration of the tank (plus the impulsive component of the contents)

C_i = coefficient for period of vibration for impulsive mode, Eurocode 1998-part 4

h = maximum depth of liquid

D = inner diameter of circular tank

t_w = average wall thickness

E = modulus of elasticity of tank wall

ρ_L = mass density of liquid

$$C_i = \frac{1}{\sqrt{\frac{h}{D}}\left[0.46 - \frac{0.3h}{D} + 0.067\left(\frac{h}{D}\right)^2\right]} \qquad (14.3b)$$

Ground Supported Rectangular Tanks

$$T_i = 2\pi\sqrt{\frac{m}{k}} \qquad (14.4a)$$

or,

$$= 2\pi\sqrt{\frac{\Delta}{g}} \qquad (14.4b)$$

where,

$$m = 0.5\, m_i + m_{w1} \qquad (14.4c)$$

One-half of the impulsive mass of the contained liquid acts on each of the two walls at right angles to the direction of the earthquake force.

m_{w1} = mass of one wall at right angles to the direction of the earthquake

$$m_{w1} = B\, h_w\, t_w\, \rho_c \qquad (14.4d)$$

ρ_c = mass density of concrete = 2500 kg/m³

k = flexural stiffness of a rectilinear tank wall

For a fixed-base, free top cantilever wall, such as in open-top tanks, flexural stiffness for a unit width of wall may be approximated using the following equation (Figure 14.8):

$$k = 3\frac{EI}{L^3} = 3\frac{E_c}{\bar{h}^3}\left(\frac{1 \times t_w^3}{12}\right) = \frac{1}{4}E_c\left(\frac{t_w}{\bar{h}}\right)^3 \qquad (14.4e)$$

The height of the cantilever is assumed as $\bar{h}$,
where, $\bar{h}$ = height of combined center of gravity of half impulsive mass of liquid and mass of one wall

$$\bar{h} = \frac{\left(\frac{m_i}{2}h_i + m_{w1}\frac{h}{2}\right)}{\left(\frac{m_i}{2} + m_{w1}\right)} \qquad (14.4f)$$

Since, stiffness k is computed per unit width of the wall, therefore, mass m for use in Equation (14.4(a)) should also be taken per unit width of the wall, that is, equal to m/B.

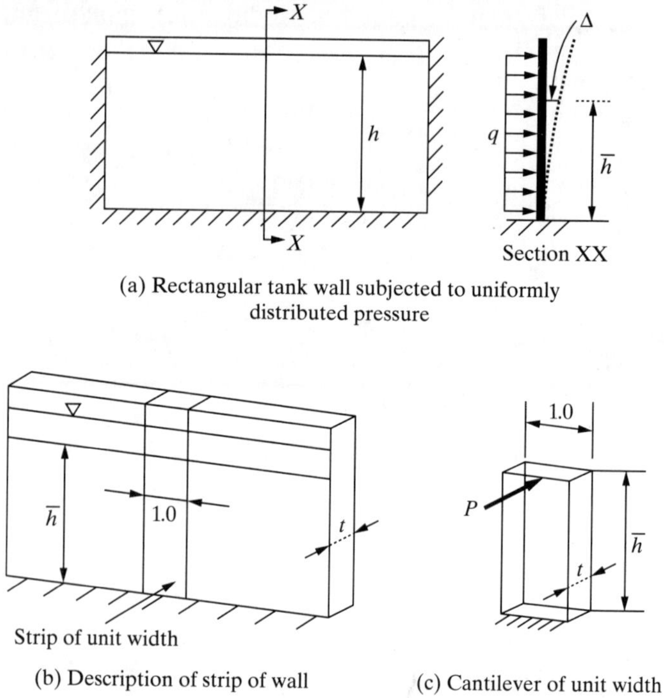

Figure 14.8 Idealization of a unit cantilever beam.

Alternatively,

Δ = deflection of tank wall on the vertical center line at a height $\bar{h}$, when loaded by uniform pressure distribution of intensity q_y given by

$$q_y = \frac{\left(\frac{m_i}{2} + \bar{m}_w\right)g}{Bh} \text{ in kN/m}^2 \tag{14.4g}$$

The total load P is equal to $(q_y \times h)$ in kN/m length. Therefore, deflection Δ is given by

$$\Delta = \frac{P\bar{h}^3}{3E_c I_w} \tag{14.4h}$$

Both the expressions in Equation (14.4(a) and (b)) will naturally give the same result.

NZ 3106 code requires that unless calculated using a more rigorous analysis, the period of the fundamental impulsive modes is to be taken as follows:

(a) Ground supported circular or rectangular tanks horizontal mode, assume $T_i = 0.1$ sec.

(b) Ground supported circular or rectangular tanks vertical mode, assume $T_i = 0.1$ sec

(c) Fully ground-embedded circular or rectangular tank: $T_i = 0$ sec, use peak ground acceleration.

(d) The natural period of elevated tank and supporting structure should be calculated by considering the strength and stiffness of the staging. The flexibility of the tank walls may be neglected.

The potentially higher seismic loading will be offset by allowing higher steel stresses, up to yield stress. It is expected that in most cases service loads rather than ultimate limit state will govern the reinforcing design.

14.4.2 Convective Mode

Time period of ground supported tanks in the convective mode are calculated using the following equations:

Circular Tank

$$T_c = C_c \sqrt{\frac{D}{g}} \tag{14.5a}$$

$$C_c = \frac{2\pi}{\sqrt{3.68 \tanh\left(\frac{3.68h}{D}\right)}} \tag{14.5b}$$

where, C_c = Coefficient of time period for convective mode

Rectangular Tank

$$T_c = C_c \sqrt{\frac{L}{g}} \tag{14.6a}$$

$$C_c = \frac{2\pi}{\sqrt{3.16 \tanh\left(\frac{3.16h}{L}\right)}} \tag{14.6b}$$

L = inside length of the tank parallel to the direction of seismic force

14.4.3 Elevated Tank

The period of the OHT will be determined under two conditions:

- Tank empty
- Tank full

The formula remains same under each condition. However, the impulsive mass is different.

$$T_i = 2\pi \sqrt{\frac{m_i + \frac{m_s}{3}}{k_s}} \tag{14.7}$$

m_s = structural mass = mass of empty container + [mass of the staging including staircase]/3

k_s = stiffness of staging, it can be determined using a 3-D space frame analysis.

The time period of overhead tanks in the convective mode are calculated using the same equations as for the ground supported tanks, that is, Equation (14.5) and (14.6).

Beam-Column Frame Staging

The container of the tank is supported on a series of columns spread on the periphery of a polygon. These columns are interconnected at a few levels through beams or braces to provide lateral stiffness to the columns. These beams again form a polygon in plan. For very large capacity tanks, say above 2500 kL, it is desirable to adopt two concentric polygons in plan. A 3-D model can be developed to represent the strength and stiffness of the staging using the stiffness matrix method. The mass of the container is lumped at the top of columns. A provision is made at the top of the columns to apply lateral forces through the center of gravity of the container through a rigid frame. The staging can be analyzed for gravity loads, and lateral loads due to wind and earthquake. A response spectrum analysis can also be carried out for both horizontal and vertical components of an earthquake. The lateral loads must be applied in a direction so as to produce maximum forces in braces as well as columns. This will require at least two load cases as shown in Figure 14.9. Effective length of columns must be calculated as per IS 456 or IS 800.

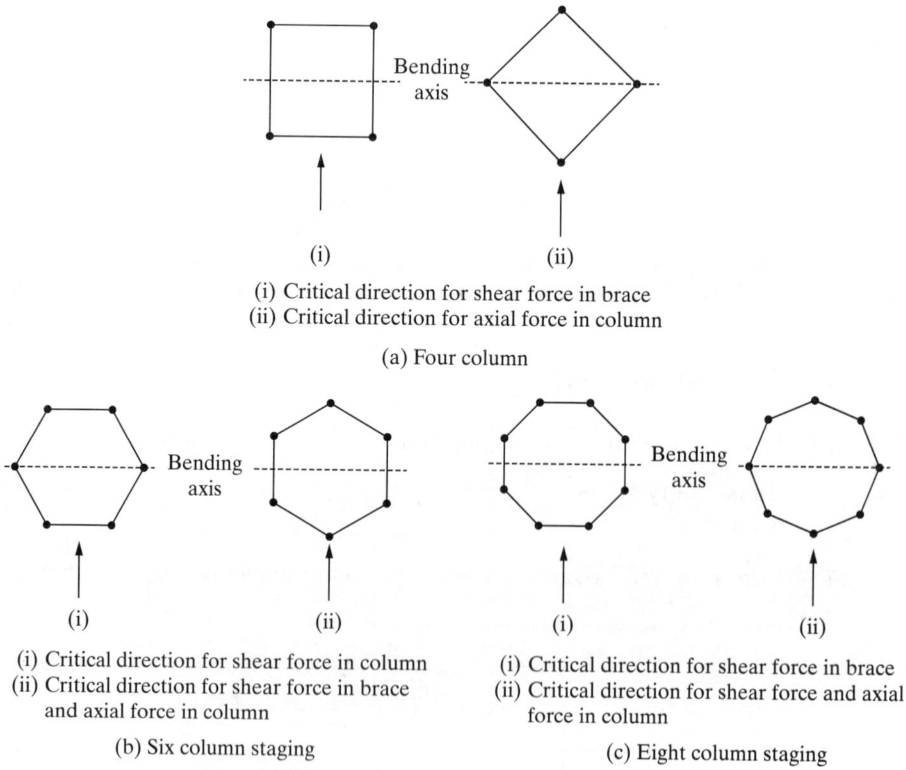

Figure 14.9 Critical directions of seismic force for staging of OHT.

Shaft Type Staging

The staging may be in the form of single shaft, circular or polygonal in plan, and may be tapering. A door is provided at the bottom of the shaft, and a few ventilators at different heights to let natural light and air inside the shaft as shown in Figure 14.2. These openings make the analysis of the shaft for lateral loads somewhat complicated. A 3-D finite element analysis may be carried out of the complete tank to determine the stresses due to various load cases and load combinations. Alternatively, an approximate analysis may be carried out of the shaft for lateral loads as explained in IS 11682.

The staging is designed using the limit state of collapse, and detailing of reinforcement in the RC staging is carried out in accordance with IS 456, IS 1893-part 2, and IS 13920. The design and detailing of steel staging is carried out in accordance with IS 800.

14.5 DESIGN SEISMIC COEFFICIENT

The design horizontal seismic coefficient was discussed in detail in Chapter 12.

$$\alpha_h = \frac{Z}{2}\frac{I}{R}\frac{S_a}{g} \tag{14.8a}$$

$\alpha_h = \alpha_{h,i}$ design horizontal seismic coefficient in impulsive or $(= \alpha_{h,c})$ convective mode, depending upon the corresponding time period

R = response modification factors given in IS 1893-part 2 for ground supported tanks and elevated tanks.

The design vertical seismic coefficient is given as follows:

$$\alpha_v = \frac{2}{3} \times \alpha_h \tag{14.8b}$$

Different codes specify different values of factor R for the same structural system because each code adopts its own philosophy to estimate the seismic force. Thus, factor R is not a standard value. IS 1893-part 2 does not give separate response reduction factors for impulsive mode and convective modes. It means the same factor is to be used for both cases. However, ACI 350.3 and NZ 3106 specify a response reduction factor equal to unity for convective mode for all types of tanks.

14.6 HYDRODYNAMIC PRESSURE DISTRIBUTION

Both the tank wall and base slab are subjected to hydrodynamic pressure normal to the corresponding surface during lateral seismic excitation. Both exact and approximate linear distribution of the impulsive and convective pressures on the tank wall are shown in Figure 14.10. The expressions for impulsive and convective pressures for circular and rectangular tanks were developed by Housner (1963) and are also available in IS 1893-part 2.

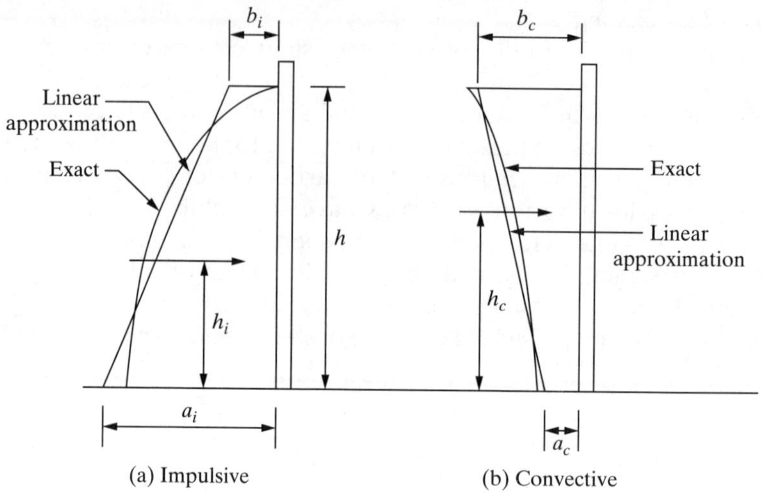

Figure 14.10 Linear pressure distribution on tank walls.

Circular Tanks

The dynamic forces acting on a circular tank are as follows:

(i) The cylindrical walls of circular tanks are loaded by the wall's own inertia force distributed uniformly around the entire circumference as shown by f_i

(ii) one-half of the impulsive force P_i is applied symmetrically about $\theta = 0°$ and acting outward on one-half of the wall's circumference, and one-half P_i is applied symmetrically about $\theta = 180°$ and acting inward on the opposite half of the wall's circumference (Figure 14.11),

(iii) one-half of the convective force P_c is applied on one-half of the wall's circumference symmetrically about $\theta = 0°$, and one-half P_c is applied symmetrically about $\theta = 180°$ and acting inward on the opposite half of the wall's circumference; and

(iv) Dynamic earth and groundwater pressure against the trailing half of the buried portion of the wall.

On these lateral unbalanced forces, the axisymmetric lateral hydrodynamic force resulting from the hydrodynamic pressure $P_v(y)$ due to the vertical component of earthquake acting on the tank wall will be superimposed.

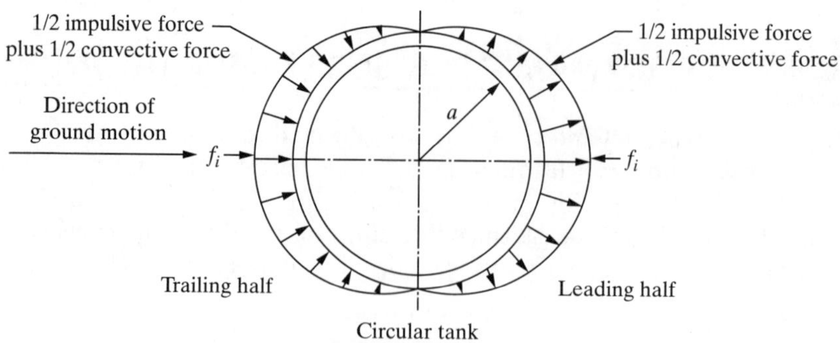

Figure 14.11 Lateral force distribution in a circular tank.

Rectangular Tanks

The dynamic forces acting on a rectangular tank are as follows:

(i) Walls perpendicular to the ground motion being investigated and in the leading half of the tank are loaded perpendicular to their plane (dimension B) by the wall's own inertia force P_w, one-half of the impulsive force P_i, and one-half of the convective force P_c (Figure 14.12)

(ii) Walls perpendicular to the ground motion being investigated and in the trailing half of the tank shall be loaded perpendicular to their plane (dimension B) by the wall's own inertia force P_w, one-half of the impulsive force P_i; one-half of the convective force P_c, and

(iii) Dynamic earth and ground water pressure against the buried portion of the wall.

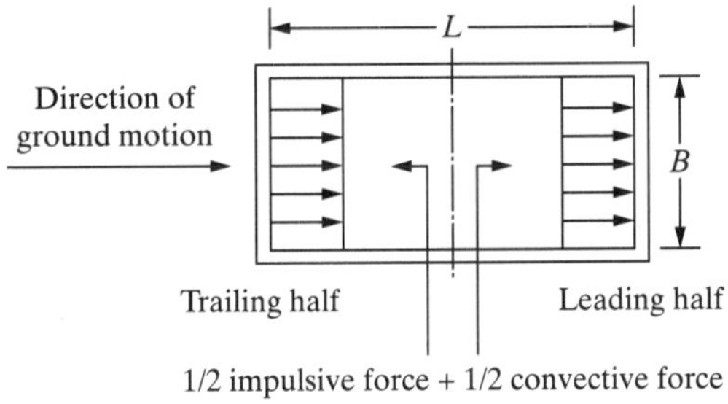

Figure 14.12 Lateral force distribution in a rectangular tank.

Similarly, walls parallel to the direction of the ground motion being investigated are loaded in their plane (dimension L) by: (a) the wall's own in-plane inertia force P_w and the in-plane forces corresponding to the edge reactions from the abutting wall(s). On these lateral unbalanced forces, the lateral hydrodynamic force resulting from the hydrodynamic pressure due to the effect of vertical acceleration $P_v(y)$ acting on each wall will be superimposed.

14.6.1 Exact Hydrodynamic Pressure Distribution

Impulsive hydrodynamic pressure on the wall (P_{iw}) and base slab (P_{ib}) are given as follows:

(a) Impulsive pressure in circular tanks (Figure 14.13)

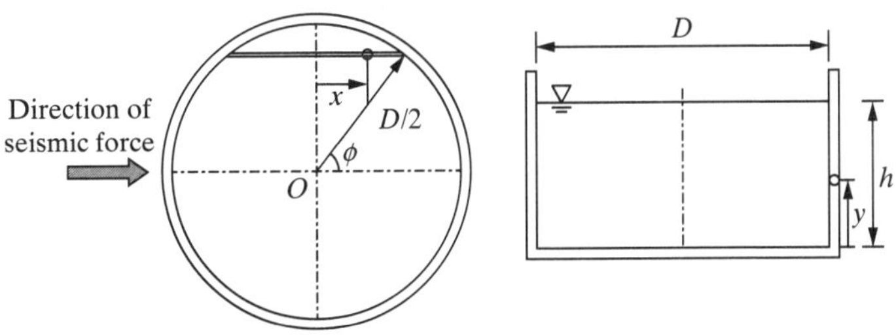

Figure 14.13 Geometry of circular tank.

Impulsive pressure exerted by the liquid on the tank wall

$$p_{iw}(x) = Q_{iw}(y)\alpha_{hi}\rho g h \cos\phi \tag{14.7a}$$

where, ϕ = circumferential angle

y = vertical distance of the point on the tank wall measured from bottom of the wall

$$Q_{iw}(y) = \frac{\sqrt{3}}{2}\left[1-\left(\frac{y}{h}\right)^2\right]\tan h\left(\frac{\sqrt{3}}{2}\frac{D}{h}\right) \tag{14.7b}$$

Impulsive pressure exerted by the liquid on the base slab on a strip of width l' (= $D\cos\phi$) in vertical direction

at $y = 0$,

$$p_{ib}(x) = \alpha_{hi}\rho g h\frac{\sqrt{3}}{2}\times\left[\frac{\sin h\left(\sqrt{3}\frac{x}{h}\right)}{\cos h\left(\frac{\sqrt{3}}{2}\frac{D\cos\phi}{h}\right)}\right] \tag{14.7c}$$

or,

$$p_{ib}(x) = \alpha_{hi}\rho g h\times 0.866\times\left[\frac{\sin h\left(1.732\frac{x}{h}\right)}{\cos h\left(0.866\frac{l'}{h}\right)}\right] \tag{14.7d}$$

x = horizontal distance of a point on the base of the tank from the center, in the direction of the seismic force

(b) Impulsive pressure in rectangular tanks (Figure 14.14)

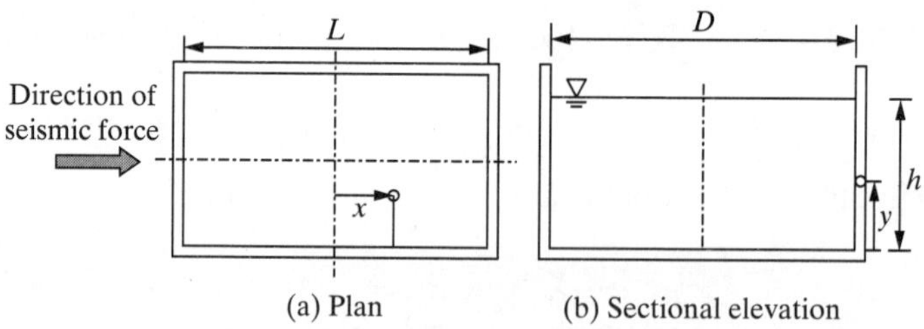

Figure 14.14 Geometry of rectangular tank.

Impulsive pressure exerted by the liquid on the tank wall

$$p_{iw}(y) = Q_{iw}(y)\alpha_{hi}\,\rho g h \tag{14.8a}$$

where,

$$Q_{iw}(y) = \frac{\sqrt{3}}{2} \times \left[1 - \left(\frac{y}{h}\right)^2\right] \times \frac{\sinh\left(\sqrt{3}\frac{x}{h}\right)}{\cosh\left(\frac{\sqrt{3}}{2}\frac{L}{h}\right)} \tag{14.8b}$$

For $x = L/2$

$$Q_{iw}(y) = 0.866\left[1 - \left(\frac{y}{h}\right)^2\right] \tanh\left(0.866\frac{L}{h}\right) \tag{14.8c}$$

Impulsive pressure exerted by the liquid on the base slab in vertical direction at $y = 0$,

$$p_{ib}(x) = Q_{ib}(x)\alpha_{hi}\,\rho g h \tag{14.8d}$$

where

$$Q_{ib}(x) = \frac{\sqrt{3}}{2} \times \frac{\sinh\left(\sqrt{3}\frac{x}{h}\right)}{\cosh\left(\frac{\sqrt{3}}{2}\frac{L}{h}\right)} \tag{14.8e}$$

(c) Convective pressure in circular tank (Figure 14.13)
Convective pressure exerted by the liquid on the tank wall

$$p_{cw}(y) = Q_{cw}(y)\alpha_{hc}\,\rho g D\left(1 - \frac{\cos^2\phi}{3}\right)\cos\phi \tag{14.9a}$$

where,

$$Q_{cw}(y) = 0.5625 \times \frac{\cosh\left(3.674\frac{y}{D}\right)}{\cosh\left(3.674\frac{h}{D}\right)} \tag{14.9b}$$

Convective pressure exerted by the liquid on the base slab in vertical direction at $y = 0$,

$$p_{cb}(x) = Q_{cb}(x)\alpha_{hc}\,\rho g D \tag{14.9c}$$

where,

$$Q_{cb}(x) = 1.125\left[\frac{x}{D} - \frac{4}{3} \times \left(\frac{x}{D}\right)^3\right] \operatorname{sech}\left(3.674\frac{h}{D}\right) \tag{14.9d}$$

(d) Convective pressure in rectangular tank (Figure 14.14)
Convective pressure exerted by the liquid on the tank wall

$$p_{cw}(y) = Q_{cw}(y)\alpha_{hc}\,\rho g L \tag{14.10a}$$

where,

$$Q_{cw}(y) = 0.4165 \times \frac{\cos h\left(3.162\frac{y}{L}\right)}{\cos h\left(3.162\frac{h}{L}\right)} \tag{14.10b}$$

Convective pressure exerted by the liquid on the base slab in vertical direction at $y = 0$,

$$p_{cb}(x) = Q_{cb}(x)\alpha_{hc}\rho g L \tag{14.10c}$$

where,

$$Q_{cb}(x) = 1.25\left[\frac{x}{L} - \frac{4}{3}\times\left(\frac{x}{L}\right)^3\right]\text{sech}\left(3.162\frac{h}{L}\right) \tag{14.10d}$$

14.6.2 Simplified Hydrodynamic Pressure Distribution

The exact hydrodynamic pressure due to the horizontal seismic excitation varies along the circumference of a circular tank as shown in Figure 14.11. For thin walled circular tanks ($t/R < 0.03$) non-symmetrical loads (i.e. temperature loads and hydrodynamic seismic pressures) may be considered to be rotationally symmetric and equal to the value at the section under consideration. In other words, it may be approximated by an outward pressure distribution of intensity equal to that of the maximum hydrodynamic pressure as shown in Figure 14.15.

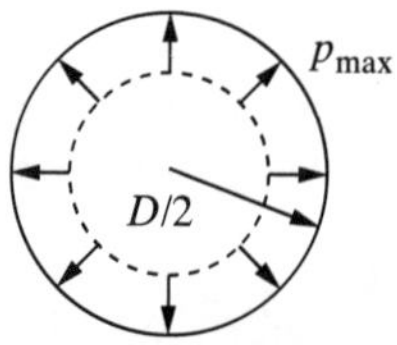

Figure 14.15 Simplified hydrodynamic pressure distribution for circular tank wall analysis.

The exact hydrodynamic pressure due to the horizontal seismic excitation varies along the height of a tank as shown in Figure 14.10. It is applicable both to circular as well as rectangular tanks. Instead of a curvilinear hydrodynamic pressure distribution on the walls of a tank, it may be simplified as a linear distribution such that it gives the same base shear and bending moment at the bottom of the wall as shown in the same figure.

For Circular and Rectangular Tanks

Lateral hydrodynamic *impulsive pressure* on the wall at any height y is given as follows:

$$P_i(y) = \frac{1}{2}[Q_i(y)]\alpha_{h,i}\, m_i g \ \text{ in N/m height of the wall} \tag{14.11a}$$

where,

$$Q_i(y) = \frac{1}{h^2}\left[4h - 6h_i - (6h - 12h_i)\left(\frac{y}{h}\right)\right] \tag{14.11b}$$

For y = 0, at the base of a wall

$$P_i(0) = a_i = \frac{\alpha_{h,i} m_i g}{2h^2}(4h - 6h_i) \tag{14.11c}$$

For y = h, at the top of a wall

$$P_i(h) = b_i = \frac{\alpha_{h,i} m_i g}{2h^2}(6h_i - 2h) \tag{14.11d}$$

The impulsive pressure distribution on a wall is shown in Figure 14.16(a).

Pressure intensity at height y across the width B of the wall is given by

$$p_{iy} = P_i(y)/B \text{ in N/m}^2 \tag{14.11e}$$

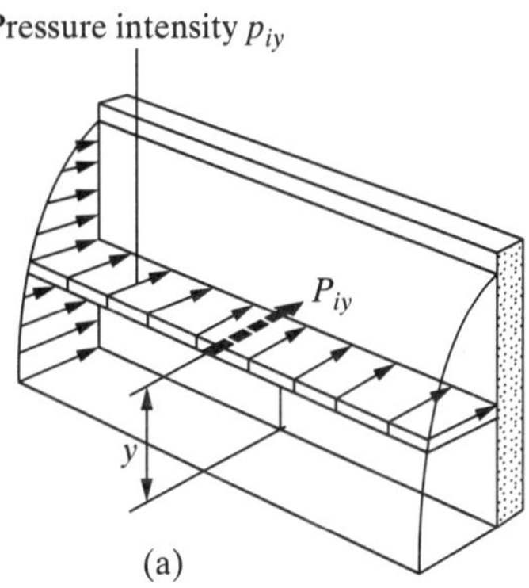

Figure 14.16(a) Impulsive pressure distribution on wall.

Lateral hydrodynamic convective pressure on the wall at any height y is given as follows:

$$P_c(y) = \frac{1}{2}[Q_c(y)]\alpha_{h,c}\, m_c\, g \text{ in N/m height of the wall} \tag{14.12a}$$

where,

$$Q_c(y) = \frac{1}{h^2}\left[4h - 6h_c - (6h - 12h_c)\left(\frac{y}{h}\right)\right] \tag{14.12b}$$

For y = 0, at the base of a wall

$$P_c(0) = a_c = \frac{\alpha_{h,c} m_c g}{2h^2}(4h - 6h_c) \tag{14.12c}$$

For y = h, at the top of a wall

$$P_c(h) = b_c = \frac{\alpha_{h,c} m_c g}{2h^2}(6h_c - 2h) \tag{14.12d}$$

Pressure intensity at height y across the width B of the wall is given by

$$p_{cy} = P_c(y)/B \text{ in N/m}^2 \tag{14.12e}$$

The convective pressure distribution on a wall is shown in Figure 14.16(b).

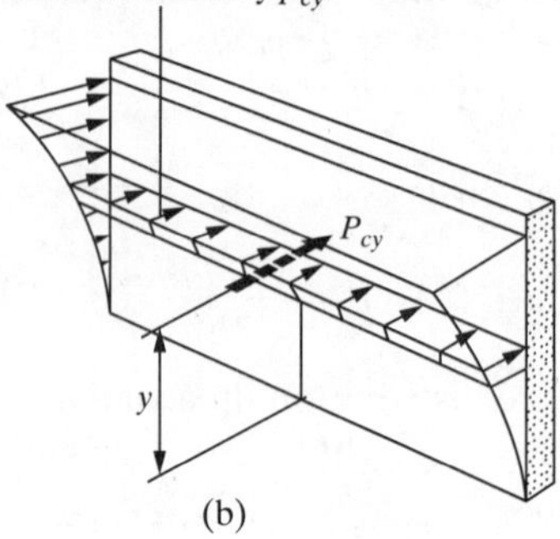

Figure 14.16(b) Convective pressure distribution on wall.

Various notations are explained in Figure 14.10.

The simplified hydrodynamic pressure distribution can be used in all cases without introducing any appreciable error in the structural design of tanks.

14.6.3 Hydrostatic Pressure Distribution on wall

The hydrostatic pressure distribution on a wall is shown in Figure 14.16(c).

$$P_{hs}(y) = \frac{1}{2}\rho g h^2 B \tag{14.13a}$$

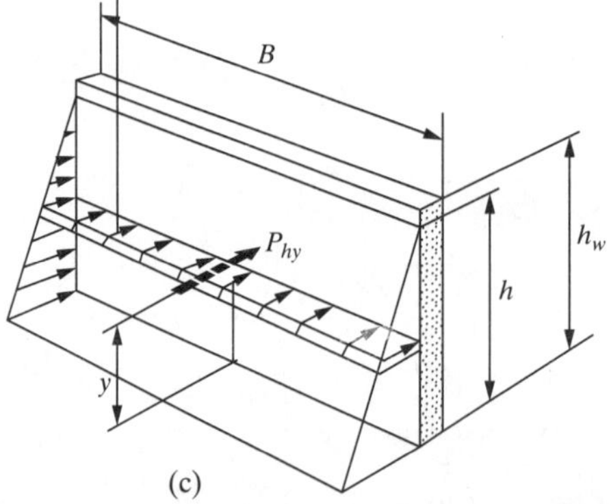

Figure 14.16(c) Hydrostatic pressure distribution on wall.

Pressure intensity at height y above base is given by

$$p_{hs}(y) = \rho g h\left(1 - \frac{y}{h}\right) \text{ in N/m}^2 \tag{14.13b}$$

or, $$p_{hs}(y)B \text{ in N/m height of wall} \tag{14.13c}$$

The dynamic force on the leading half of the tank will be additive to the hydrostatic force on the wall, whereas, the dynamic force on the trailing half of the tank will reduce the effect of the hydrostatic force on the wall.

14.6.4 Pressure Due to Wall Inertia

Pressure on the tank wall due to its inertia is given by (Figure 14.16(d))

$$P_w(y) = \alpha_{h,i}\, \rho_c\, g\, t_w\, B \text{ in N/m height of wall} \quad (14.14a)$$

or,

$$p_w(y) = P_w(y)/B \text{ in N/m}^2 \quad (14.14b)$$

where, ρ_c = mass density of the tank wall

t_w = wall thickness

It is a uniform load across the height of the wall.

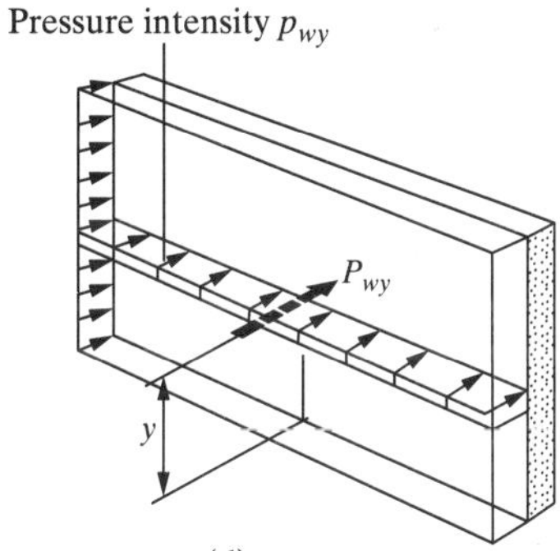

(d)

Figure 14.16(d) Pressure distribution due to wall inertia.

14.6.5 Effect of Vertical Ground Acceleration

There is additional pressure due to the vertical component of the ground acceleration acting on each wall. It can be expressed as:

$$p_v(y) = \alpha_v \rho g h\left(1 - \frac{y}{h}\right) \text{ in N/m}^2 \quad (14.15a)$$

or,

$$P_v(y) = p_v(y)\,B \text{ in N/m height of wall} \quad (14.15b)$$

where,

$$\alpha_v = \frac{2}{3}\frac{Z}{2}\frac{I}{R}\frac{S_a}{g} \quad (14.8b)$$

$$\rho g h = \text{hydrostatic pressure at the base} \quad (14.15c)$$

The period of vibration in the vertical mode of vibration may be obtained from eigen-value analysis, or taken as 0.3 sec for all types of tanks.

14.6.6 Resultant Hydrodynamic Pressure

The periods of vibrations of the inertia and convective responses are generally widely separated, the impulsive period being much shorter than the convective period. When responses are widely separated, near simultaneous occurrence of peak values is a likely possibility. However, the convective response takes much longer to build up than the impulsive response, therefore, the impulsive component is likely to be subsiding by the time the convective component reaches its peak. Therefore, the resultant hydrodynamic pressure on the walls of a tank, at any height y from the base due to various effects may be obtained using the SRSS rule as follows:

$$P_{hd}(y) = \sqrt{\left(P_{iy} + P_{wy}\right)^2 + P_{cy}^2 + \left(P_{vy}\right)^2} \tag{14.16}$$

in N/m height of wall

14.7 DYNAMIC LATERAL FORCES

The walls of the liquid retaining structures need to be designed for the following dynamic forces in addition to the static pressures determined in accordance with IS 3370:

- Inertia force on the accelerating walls P_w
- Inertia force on the roof P_r
- Inertia force on the empty container and staging of elevated tank P_s
- Hydrodynamic impulsive force P_i from the contained liquid
- Hydrodynamic convective force P_c from the contained liquid
- The effects of vertical acceleration.

Inertia forces are parallel to the horizontal seismic action, inducing a pressure normal to the surface of the tank. The inertia forces of the tank wall and roof may be taken equal to the total mass of the tank walls and roof, times the acceleration of the ground.

The expressions for various dynamic lateral forces are as follows:

$$P_w = \alpha_{hi} m_w g \text{ acting @} 0.5h_w \text{ above the base of walls}$$

$$P_r = \alpha_{hi} m_r g \text{ acting @} \left(h_w + 0.5t_r\right) \text{ above the base of walls}$$

$$P_i = \alpha_{hi} m_i g \text{ acting @} h_i \text{ above the base of walls}$$

$$P_i^* = \alpha_{hi} m_i g \text{ acting @} h_i^* \text{ above the base of walls}$$

$$P_s = \alpha_{hi} m_s g \text{ acting @} \left(\bar{h} + h_s + h_d\right) \text{ above the bottom of footing}$$

Force on the empty container plus staging of the elevated tanks, acting at h_{cg} of the empty tank $\left(= \bar{h} + h_s + h_d\right)$ above the bottom of footing,

$$m_s = \text{mass of empty container of the tank} + \frac{\text{mass of staging}}{3}$$

$$P_c = \alpha_{hc} m_c g \text{ acting @} h_c \text{ above the base of walls}$$

$$P_c^* = \alpha_{hc} m_c g \text{ acting @} h_c^* \text{ above the base of walls}$$

where, h_w = Height of a wall above the base of the tank in ground supported tanks

$\bar{h}$ = height of center of gravity of the empty container of the elevated tank above the base slab of the container

h_s = height of staging of elevated tanks above the ground level

h_d = depth of foundation below the ground level

t_r = thickness of roof slab

IS 1893-part 2 does not differentiate between the response modification factors for impulsive mode and convective mode. For the convective mode, ACI 350.3 gives a factor equal to unity for all types of tanks.

The base shear will be simply the addition of all the applicable lateral forces in a given tank, in a given mode. The total base shear can be computed by using the SRSS rule in impulsive and convective modes, that is,

$$V = \sqrt{V_i^2 + V_c^2} \tag{14.17a}$$

or,

$$V = \sqrt{(P_i + P_w + P_r)^2 + P_c^2} \text{ for ground supported tanks} \tag{14.17b}$$

or,

$$V = \sqrt{(P_i + P_s)^2 + P_c^2} \text{ for elevated tanks} \tag{14.17c}$$

14.7.1 Overturning Moment at Base

The overturning moment on the entire cross-section of the tank due to seismic forces can be computed for two cases:

- Just above the base of the tank wall excluding base pressure (EBP)
- At the bottom of the base slab of the tank including base pressure (IBP)

Excluding Base Pressure

The total overturning moment acting at the level of the base of the wall immediately above the floor slab on the entire cross-section of the tank due to various components is given as follows:

$$\left.\begin{aligned} M_w &= P_w h_w/2 \\ M_i &= P_i h_i \\ M_r &= P_r (h_w + 0.5\, t_r) \\ M_c &= P_c h_c \end{aligned}\right\} \tag{14.18}$$

Including Base Pressure

The total overturning moment acting on the floor slab from the hydrodynamic loads on the walls and floor (IBP) is given as follows:

Ground Supported Tanks

$$\left.\begin{aligned} M_w &= P_w\,(h_w/2 + t_b) \approx P_w\,h_w/2 \\ M_i^* &= P_i\,(h_i^* + t_b) \approx P_i\,h_i^* \\ M_r &= P_r\,(h_w + 0.5\,t_r + t_b) \approx P_r\,(h_w + 0.5\,t_r) \\ M_c^* &= P_c\,(h_c^* + t_b) \approx P_c\,h_c^* \\ M_b &= P_b\left(0.5t_b\right) \end{aligned}\right\} \quad (14.19)$$

P_b = inertia force on the base slab of the ground supported tanks
t_b = thickness of the base slab

It must be noted that only IS 1893-part 2 requires the contribution M_b of the floor slab; while ACI 350.3, NZ 3106 and Eurocode 1998-part 4 do not consider it. Also, the thickness of the base slab t_b is too small as compared to other height terms and can be neglected.

Elevated Tanks

Total overturning moment at the foundation level of the tank including supporting structure (IBP) is given as follows:

$$\left.\begin{aligned} M_i^* &= P_i\,(h_i^* + h_s + h_d) \\ M_s &= P_s\left(\bar{h} + h_s + h_d\right) \\ M_c^* &= P_c\,(h_c^* + h_s + h_d) \end{aligned}\right\} \quad (14.20)$$

h_d = depth of foundation below the ground level

The resultant overturning moment can be computed by using the SRSS rule in impulsive and convective modes.

For ground supported tanks under EBP

$$M = \sqrt{(M_i + M_w + M_r)^2 + M_c^2} \quad (14.21a)$$

This moment, with ordinary beam theory, can be used to calculate the axial force at the base of the wall and hence on the wall footing.

For ground supported tanks under IBP

$$M^* = \sqrt{(M_i^* + M_w + M_r)^2 + (M_c^*)^2} \quad (14.21b)$$

Moment M^* can be used to calculate the bearing pressures on the ground beneath the floor slab.

For elevated tanks

$$M^* = \sqrt{(M_i^* + M_s)^2 + (M_c^*)^2} \qquad (14.21c)$$

14.7.2 Damping

Clause 4.4 of IS 1893-2 requires that damping in the impulsive mode should be taken as 2% of the critical for steel tanks, and 5% of the critical for concrete or masonry tanks. Damping in the convective mode for all types of liquids and for all types of tanks should be taken as 0.5% of the critical. Clause 4.5.2 of IS 1893-2 specifies multiplying factors for design horizontal seismic coefficients for different damping ratios. For 5%, 2% and 0.5% damping, the multiplying factors are 1, 1.4 and 1.75, respectively.

14.8 SLOSHING WAVE HEIGHT

- A freeboard is provided in all types of tanks to take care of overflow and other effects.
- Freeboard at least equal to the calculated height of the slosh waves shall be provided, if the contents are toxic, or if spilling could cause damage to piping or scouring of the foundation.
- Freeboard less than the calculated height of the slosh waves may be sufficient, if the roof is designed for the associated uplift pressure or if an overflow spillway is provided to control spilling.
- Damping devices, as for example grillages or vertical partitions, may be used to reduce sloshing.

Maximum sloshing wave height can be computed using the following equation:

$$h_{sl} = \alpha_{h,c} R \frac{D}{2} \qquad (14.22)$$

where, $\alpha_{h,c}$ = design horizontal seismic coefficient in convective mode

D = inner diameter of the tank

= length of the tank for rectangular tanks, parallel to the direction of seismic force

R = response reduction factor

14.9 FOUNDATION

A tank may be supported on interconnected isolated column footings, a raft, or a pile foundation depending upon the site conditions. Both the staging including the staircase and the foundation is designed using the limit state of collapse.

14.10 CRACKS AND CRACK WIDTH

Cracks in liquid retaining structures may occur due to following reasons:

1. Excessive direct or flexural tension in concrete due to external loads and temperature gradients due to solar radiations may cause cracking in concrete.
2. Changes in the moisture content of concrete may cause dimensional changes and may result in cracking of concrete.
3. Heat is evolved as cement hydrates and the temperature will rise for a day or more after casting and then fall towards ambient. Cracking usually occurs at this stage while the concrete is still weak.
4. Due to corrosion in reinforcing steel.

The cracking of concrete is controlled using one or more of the following methods:

1. By avoiding or reducing the gradient of steep changes in temperature and moisture of especially the early age concrete. Type of shuttering, de-shuttering procedure and curing method may affect the changes in temperature and moisture. Curing should be done for a minimum of 14 days in accordance with IS:3370-part 1.
2. The risk of cracking due to overall temperature and shrinkage effects may be minimized by limiting the changes in moisture content and temperature to which the structure is subjected.
3. Cracking may be controlled by reducing the restraint on the free expansion or contraction of the structure as well as provision of the movement joints.
4. Due attention must be given to durability aspects of concrete.
5. The detailing of reinforcement in members and joints should be done very carefully with adequate clear cover.

Limiting crack width has been defined based on tightness class of a structure. There are three class of tightness:

Tightness Class 1: Limiting crack width for cracks expected to pass through the full thickness of the element is limited to 0.2 mm.

Tightness Class 2: *Limiting crack width is 0.2 mm* and cracks should not pass through the full thickness of the element using appropriate measures.

Tightness Class 3: *Limiting crack width is 0.1 mm* and cracks should not pass through the full thickness of the element as well as a compression zone of at least 50 mm must be available.

Crack width and spacing between cracks in concrete can be calculated as per the provisions given in IS 3370 -part 2. There are three situations:

1. Crack width due to temperature and moisture in immature concrete
2. Crack Width in Mature Concrete
    - Crack Width in Flexure
    - Crack Width in Direct Tension

After calculating the design forces due to static and dynamic forces in various elements of the structure, reinforcement is provided. The next step is to check the crack width in concrete.

Crack Width Due to Temperature and Moisture in Immature Concrete

The width of fully developed crack due to drying shrinkage and the heat of hydration contraction in lightly reinforced restrained walls and slabs may be calculated using the equation:

$$W_{max} = S_{max}\,\varepsilon \tag{14.23a}$$

or,

$$W_{max} = S_{max}\,(\varepsilon_{cs} + \varepsilon_{te} - 100 \times 10^{-6}) \tag{14.23b}$$

where, S_{max} = maximum spacing of cracks

ε_{cs} = estimated shrinkage strain

ε_{te} = estimated total thermal contraction after peak temperature due to heat of hydration

Crack Width in Mature Concrete in Flexure

The crack width of surface cracks may be computed from the equation:

$$w = \frac{3a_{cr}\,\varepsilon_m}{1+\dfrac{2(a_{cr}-C_{min})}{D-x}} \quad \text{For } \varepsilon_{st} \le 0.6\,\sigma_{y/Es} \text{ and } \sigma_{ct} \le 0.4\,\sigma_{ck} \tag{14.24a}$$

where, w = design surface crack width

a_{cr} = distance from the point considered to the surface of the nearest longitudinal bar

C_{min} = minimum cover to tension steel

x = depth of neutral axis

σ_{ct} = direct tensile strength of immature concrete

ε_m = average strain at the level where cracking is being considered

$$= \varepsilon_1 - \varepsilon_2 \tag{14.24b}$$

D = Overall depth of the member

Under certain conditions, it is possible that $\varepsilon_2 > \varepsilon_1$. It means the surface crack width w is negative. In other words, it means there is no cracking.

Crack Width in Mature Concrete in Direct Tension

The design surface width in sections subjected to direct tension may be estimated using the equation:

$$w = 3\,a_{cr}\,\varepsilon_m = 3\,a_{cr}\,(\varepsilon_1 - \varepsilon_2) \tag{14.25a}$$

where,

$$\text{Apparent strain in tension steel } \varepsilon_1 = \frac{\sigma_{st}}{E_s} = \frac{T}{A_{st}E_s} \tag{14.25b}$$

T = direct tension in section
A_{st} = area of steel

If steel is provided on each face, take $0.5T$ on each face, and area of steel provided on the face under consideration.

a_{cr} = distance from the point considered to the surface of the nearest longitudinal bar

The strain due to the stiffening effect is calculated using the following equations:

$$\varepsilon_2 = \frac{2}{3}\frac{b_t D}{E_s A_{st}} \text{ for a limiting design surface crack width of 0.2 mm} \quad (14.25c)$$

$$\varepsilon_2 = \frac{b_t D}{E_s A_{st}} \text{ for a limiting design surface crack width of 0.1 mm} \quad (14.25d)$$

b_t = width of the section at the centroid of tension steel

14.11 MINIMUM REINFORCEMENT

The minimum reinforcement in liquid retaining structures depend upon the type of element and its length. The reinforcement in provided in two directions at right angles to each other on each face. The minimum high strength reinforcement in walls, floors, and roof in each of the two directions at right angles within each *surface zone* should not be less than that specified in Table 14.1 for HSD bars. For intermediate lengths, the reinforcement may be determined by linear interpolation. In case length of an element exceeds 40 m, then an expansion joint must be provided. Alternatively, advanced analysis must be carried out to take care of the *effects of temperature and shrinkage strains.*

TABLE 14.1 MINIMUM REINFORCEMENT FOR FE415 OR FE 500 GRADE STEEL

Elevated Tanks with Length		Ground Supported Tanks with Length	
≤ 14 m	≥ 28 m	≤ 14 m	≥ 22 m
0.28%	0.42%	0.24%	0.36%

The surface zones are defined in Figure 14.17.

(i) For $D < 500$ mm, each reinforcement face controls 0.5 D of concrete.
(ii) For $D \geq 500$ mm, each reinforcement face controls 250 mm depth of concrete, ignoring any central core beyond this surface depth.

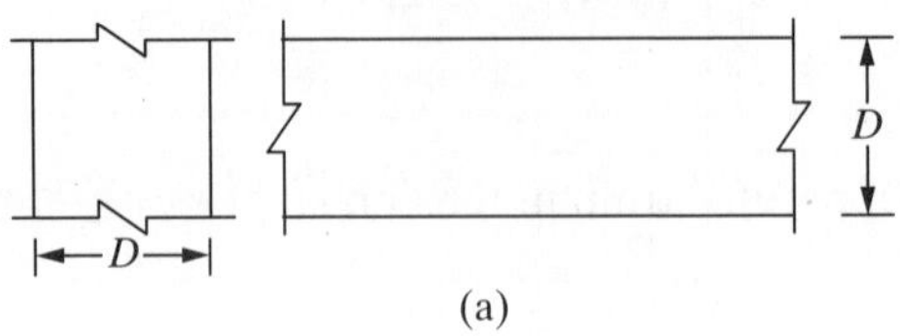

(a)

Figure 14.17(a) Surface zones – walls and suspended slabs.

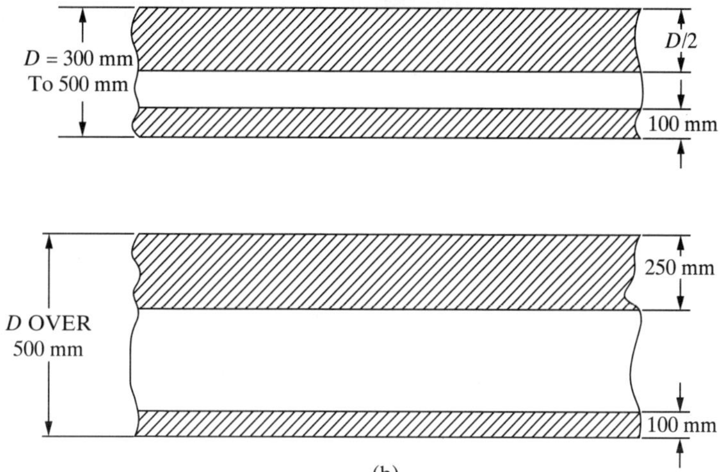

(b)

Figure 14.17(b) Surface zones – ground slabs.

1. In walls of less than 160 mm thickness, the calculated amount of reinforcement may be placed in one face with appropriate cover.
2. In slabs less than 180 mm thickness, the calculated reinforcement should be placed in one face as near as possible to the upper surface with appropriate cover.
3. When reinforcement is placed in two layers, the two layers of reinforcing steel should be placed one near each face of the section to make up the minimum reinforcement.
4. For liquid faces of parts of members either in contact with the liquid or enclosing the space above the liquid, the minimum clear cover to all reinforcement should be determined based on durability criteria.

14.12 ILLUSTRATIVE EXAMPLES

EXAMPLE 14.1

A rectangular liquid retaining tank has a capacity of 2000 kL, and it is placed on the ground as shown in Figure 14.18. It is open from top. The tank is in Kohima (seismic zone *V*, on hard soil).

The concrete grades are as follows:

Container – M30; Foundation – M30.

The grade of steel is Fe500. Weight density of concrete = 25 kN/m^3 and water = 10 kN/m^3

Acceleration due to gravity = 10 m/sec^2 (9.81 m/sec^2 is rounded)

Mass density of concrete = 2500 kg/m^3; Mass density of water = 1000 kg/m^3

Analyze the tank for seismic forces.

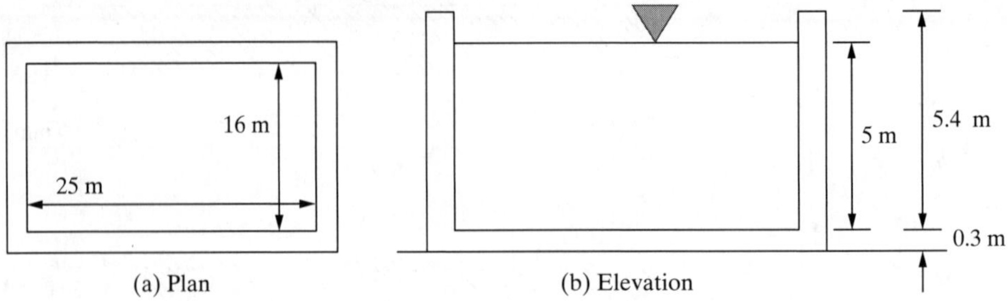

(a) Plan (b) Elevation

Figure 14.18 Rectangular tank.

Solution

Wall thickness = 35 cm, floor thickness = 30 cm

Weight of tank walls – 4 no. = 2 × (25.35 + 16.35) × 0.35 × 5.4 × 25 = 3940.65 kN

Weight of base slab = 25.7 × 16.7 × 0.3 × 25 = 3219.925 kN

Capacity of tank = 2000 kL

Weight of water = 25 × 16 × 5 × 10 = 20000 kN

∴ Mass of tank walls m_w = 3940.65 × 1000/10 = 394060 kg

∴ Mass of base slab m_b = 3219.925 × 1000/10 = 321990 kg

∴ Mass of water m = 20000 × 1000/10 = 2000000 kg

Let us analyze the tank in x-direction, that is, along the longer direction of the tank, due to earthquake force.

∴ Length L = 25 m, width B = 16 m (inside dimensions), h = 5 m (depth of water)

Spring Mass Model

For $h/L = 5/25 = 0.2$

$$\frac{m_i}{m} = \frac{\tan h\left(0.866\dfrac{L}{h}\right)}{0.866\dfrac{L}{h}} = \frac{\tan h4.33}{4.33} = 0.2309$$

∴ $$m_i = 461800 \text{ kg}$$

$$\frac{m_c}{m} = 0.264\frac{\tan h\left(3.16\dfrac{h}{L}\right)}{\dfrac{h}{L}} = 0.264\frac{\tan h0.632}{0.2}$$

or, $$\frac{m_c}{m} = 0.738$$

∴ $$m_c = 1476000 \text{ kg}$$

$$\frac{h_i}{h} = 0.375$$

or, $$h_i = 1.875 \text{ m}$$

$$\frac{h_c}{h} = 1 - \frac{\cos h\left(3.16\dfrac{h}{L}\right) - 1}{3.16\left(\dfrac{h}{L}\right)\sin h\left(3.16\dfrac{h}{L}\right)}$$

$$\frac{h_c}{h} = 1 - \frac{0.2064}{0.4265} = 0.516$$

or, $$h_c = 2.58 \text{ m}$$

$$\frac{h_i^*}{h} = \frac{0.866\dfrac{L}{h}}{2\tan h\left(0.866\dfrac{L}{h}\right)} - 0.125$$

$$\frac{h_i^*}{h} = \frac{4.33}{2\tan h 4.33} - 0.125 = 2.040$$

or, $$h_i^* = 10.2 \text{ m}$$

$$\frac{h_c^*}{h} = 1 - \frac{\cos h\left(3.16\dfrac{h}{L}\right) - 2.01}{3.16\left(\dfrac{h}{L}\right)\sin h\left(3.16\dfrac{h}{L}\right)}$$

$$\frac{h_c^*}{h} = 1 - \frac{-0.803}{0.4265} = 2.884$$

$$h_c^* = 14.42 \text{ m}$$

Weight of one wall normal to the direction of earthquake,

$$W_{w1} = 16 \times 5.4 \times 0.35 \times 25 = 756 \text{ kN}$$

∴ $$m_{w1} = 756 \times \frac{1000}{10} = 75600 \text{ kg}$$

The height of center of gravity of the inertia force on liquid and the front wall is given by

$$\bar{h} = \frac{\left(\dfrac{m_i}{2}h_i + m_{w1}\dfrac{h}{2}\right)}{\left(\dfrac{m_i}{2} + m_{w1}\right)}$$

$$\bar{h} = \frac{(461800/2) \times 1.875 + 75600 \times 5.4/2}{461800/2 + 75600} = 2.078 \text{ m}$$

The stiffness k of the cantilever beam of unit width is given by

$$k = \frac{1}{4}E_c\left(\frac{t_w}{h}\right)^3$$

$$E_c = 5000\sqrt{30} = 27386 \text{ N/mm}^2$$

or, $$E_c = 27.39 \times 10^6 \text{ kN/m}^2$$

∴ $$k = \frac{1}{4} \times 27.39 \times 10^6 \times \left(\frac{0.35}{2.078}\right)^3 = 32719 \text{ kN/m}$$

Mass of the cantilever beam of unit width is given by

$$m = [0.5\, m_i + m_{w1}]/B$$

or, $$m = [0.5 \times 461800 + 75600]/16 = 19156 \text{ kg}$$

The period of vibration in impulsive mode is given by

$$T_i = 2\pi\sqrt{\frac{19156}{32719 \times 1000}} = 0.152 \text{ sec}$$

The seismic coefficient in impulsive mode for 5% damping is given by

$$\alpha_{hi} = \frac{Z}{2} \times \frac{I}{R} \times \frac{S_a}{g}$$

where, $Z = 0.36, I = 1.5, R = 2.5$ and $S_a/g = 2.5$,

$$\therefore \qquad \alpha_{hi} = \frac{0.36}{2} \times \frac{1.5}{2.5} \times 2.5 = 0.27$$

Let us compute the period of vibration in convective mode,

$$T_c = C_c\sqrt{\frac{L}{g}}$$

$$C_c = \frac{2\pi}{\sqrt{3.16 \tan h\left(\frac{3.16h}{L}\right)}}$$

$$C_c = \frac{2\pi}{\sqrt{3.16 \tan h\left(3.16 \times \frac{5}{25}\right)}} = 4.725$$

$$\therefore \qquad T_c = 4.725 \times \sqrt{\frac{25}{10}} = 7.47 \text{ sec}$$

The seismic coefficient in convective mode for 0.5% damping is given by

$$\alpha_{hc} = \frac{Z}{2} \times \frac{I}{R} \times \frac{S_a}{g}$$

where, $Z = 0.36, I = 1.5, R = 2.5$ and $S_a/g = 0.25$,

$$\therefore \qquad \alpha_{hc} = \frac{0.36}{2} \times \frac{1.5}{2.5} \times 0.25 \times 1.75 = 0.0473$$

where, 1.75 is multiplying factor for 0.5% damping vide Clause 4.5.2 of IS 1893-2.

Exact Pressure Distribution

Let us calculate the hydrodynamic pressures on the wall.

Impulsive pressure

For y = 0, at the base of a wall

$$p_{iw}(y) = Q_{iw}(y)\alpha_{hi}\rho g h$$

where,

$$Q_{iw}(y) = 0.866\left[1 - \left(\frac{y}{h}\right)^2\right]\tan h\left(0.866\frac{L}{h}\right)$$

For y = 0, at the base of a wall

$$Q_{iw}(0) = 0.866 \times \tan h\left(0.866 \times \frac{25}{5}\right) = 0.866$$

$$p_{iw}(0) = 0.866 \times 0.27 \times 1000 \times 10 \times 5 = 11690 \text{ N/m}^2$$

or, $$P_{iw}(0) = 11690 \times B = 11690 \times 16 = 187040 \text{ N/m}$$

For y = h, at the top of a wall

$$p_{iw}(h) = 0$$

Convective pressure
For y = 0, at the base of a wall

$$p_{cw}(y) = Q_{cw}(y)\alpha_{hc}\rho g L$$

where,

$$Q_{cw}(y) = 0.4165 \times \frac{\cos h\left(3.162\frac{y}{L}\right)}{\cos h\left(3.162\frac{h}{L}\right)}$$

$$Q_{cw}(y) = 0.4165 \times \frac{1}{\cos h\left(3.162 \times \frac{5}{25}\right)} = 0.3451$$

∴ $$p_{cw}(0) = 0.3451 \times 0.0473 \times 1000 \times 10 \times 25 = 4080 \text{ N/m}^2$$

or, $$P_{cw}(0) = 4080 \times B = 4080 \times 16 = 65280 \text{ N/m}$$

For y = h, at the top of a wall

$$Q_{cw}(y) = 0.4165$$

∴ $$p_{cw}(h) = 0.4165 \times 0.0473 \times 1000 \times 10 \times 25 = 4923 \text{ N/m}^2$$

or, $$P_{cw}(h) = 4923 \times B = 4923 \times 16 = 78770 \text{ N/m}$$

Simplified Pressure Distribution
Impulsive pressure
For y = 0, at the base of a wall

$$P_i(0) = a_i = \frac{\alpha_{h,i} m_i g}{2h^2}(4h - 6h_i)$$

$$P_i(0) = \left(\frac{0.27 \times 461800 \times 10}{2 \times 5^2}\right)(4 \times 5 - 6 \times 1.875) = 218200 \text{ N/m}$$

For y = h, at the top of a wall

$$P_i(h) = b_i = \frac{\alpha_{h,i} m_i g}{2h^2}(6h_i - 2h)$$

$$P_i(h) = \left(\frac{0.27 \times 461800 \times 10}{2 \times 5^2}\right)(6 \times 1.875 - 2 \times 5) = 31170 \text{ N/m}$$

Convective pressure
For y = 0, at the base of a wall

$$P_c(0) = a_c = \frac{\alpha_{h,c} m_c g}{2h^2}(4h - 6h_c)$$

$$P_c(0) = \left(\frac{0.0473 \times 1476000 \times 10}{2 \times 5^2}\right)(4 \times 5 - 6 \times 2.58) = 63110 \text{ N/m}$$

For y = h, at the top of a wall

$$P_c(h) = b_c = \frac{\alpha_{h,c} m_c g}{2h^2}(6h_c - 2h)$$

$$P_c(h) = \left(\frac{0.0473 \times 1476000 \times 10}{2 \times 5^2}\right)(6 \times 2.58 - 2 \times 5) = 76517 \text{ N/m}$$

Comparison of exact and simplified pressure distributions on the walls

Location	Impulsive Pressure (N/m)		Convective Pressure (N/m)	
	Exact	Simplified	Exact	Simplified
Top of wall	0	31170	78770	76517
Bottom of wall	187040	218200	65280	63110

The pressures computed using the simplified analysis are comparable to those obtained using the exact analysis.
Pressure due to wall inertia

$$P_{ww} = \alpha_{h,i} t_w \rho_c g B$$

$$P_{ww} = 0.27 \times 0.35 \times 2500 \times 10 \times 16 = 37800 \text{ N/m}$$

Lateral pressure due to vertical ground excitation

$$P_v(y) = \alpha_v \rho g h\left(1 - \frac{y}{h}\right) \times B$$

where,
$$\alpha_v = \frac{2}{3} \times \frac{Z}{2} \times \frac{I}{R} \times \frac{S_a}{g}$$

$$\alpha_v = \frac{2}{3} \times \frac{0.36}{2} \times \frac{1.5}{2.5} \times 2.5 = 0.181$$

$$P_v(0) = 0.181 \times 1000 \times 10 \times 5 \times 16 = 144800 \text{ N/m}$$

Gross pressure on the base of wall is given by

$$P_{hd}(0) = \sqrt{(P_{iw} + P_{ww})^2 + P_{cw}{}^2 + P_v{}^2}$$

or,
$$P_{hd}(0) = \sqrt{(218.2 + 37.8)^2 + 63.11^2 + 144.8^2} = 300.8 \text{ N/m}$$

or,
$$p_{hd}(0) = \frac{300.8}{16} = 18.8 \text{ kN/m}^2$$

The maximum hydrostatic pressure on the base of the wall

$$p_{hs}(0) = \rho g h = 1000 \times 10 \times 5 = 50000 \text{ N/m}^2$$

or, $$p_{hs}(0) = 50 \text{ kN/m}^2$$

Thus, the hydrodynamic pressure is (18.8 × 100/50 =) 37.6% of the hydrostatic pressure.

Dynamic lateral forces excluding base pressure

Let us determine the dynamic lateral forces just above the base slab of the tank.

$$P_w = \alpha_{hi} m_w g \text{ acting } @0.5h_w \text{ above the base of walls}$$

$$P_w = 0.27 \times 394060 \times 10 = 1063900 \text{ N acting } @ 2.7 \text{ m}$$

$$P_i = \alpha_{hi} m_i g \text{ acting } @h_i \text{ above the base of walls}$$

$$P_i = 0.27 \times 461800 \times 10 = 1246860 \text{ N acting } @1.875 \text{ m}$$

$$P_c = \alpha_{hc} m_c g \text{ acting } @h_c \text{ above the base of walls}$$

$$P_c = 0.0473 \times 1476000 \times 10 = 698150 \text{ N acting } @2.58 \text{ m}$$

Base shear in impulsive mode, $V_{Bi} = 1063.9 + 1246.86 = 2310.76$ kN

Base shear in convective mode, $V_{Bc} = 698.15$ kN

Resultant dynamic base shear just above the base slab = $\sqrt{2310.76^2 + 698.15^2} = 2414$ kN

Total weight of the liquid tank when full, excluding base slab = 3940 + 20000 = 23940 kN

Thus, the effective base shear = 2414/23940 = 10% of the weight of the tank OK

Overturning Moment at the bottom of wall

Overturning moment at the level of the base of the wall immediately above the floor slab can be calculated using Equations (14.18).

$$M_w = P_w h_w/2 = 1063.9 \times 5.4/2 = 2872 \text{ kNm}$$

$$M_i = P_i h_i = 1246.86 \times 1.875 = 2338 \text{ kNm}$$

$$M_c = P_c h_c = 698.15 \times 2.58 = 1801 \text{ kNm}$$

∴ Overturning moment in impulsive mode = 2872 + 2338 = 5210 kNm

Resultant overturning moment for the entire wall at the base of walls =

$$M = \sqrt{5210^2 + 1801^2} = 5512 \text{ kNm}$$

Axial force just below the 16 m wide vertical walls = 5512/25.35 = 217.5 kN

or, $$217.5/16.35 = 13.3 \text{ kN/m length}$$

Center-to-center length of the walls are 25.35 m and 16.35 m.

The support below the tank wall must be designed for this force.

Dynamic lateral forces including the base pressure

$$P_w = \alpha_{hi} m_w g \text{ acting } @0.5h_w \text{ above the bottom of base slab}$$

$$P_w = 1063.9 \text{ kN acting } @(0.5 \times 5.4) = 2.7 \text{ m}$$

$$P_i = \alpha_{hi} m_i g \text{ acting } @h_i^* \text{ above the bottom of base slab}$$

$$P_i = 1246.86 \text{ kN acting } @10.2 \text{ m}$$

$$P_c = \alpha_{hc} m_c g \text{ acting } @h_c^* \text{ above the bottom of base slab}$$

$$P_c = 698.15 \text{ kN acting } @14.42 \text{ m}$$

Overturning moment on the floor slab

The total overturning moment acting on the floor slab from the hydrodynamic loads on the floor and the walls can be determined by:

$$M_w = 1063.9 \times 2.7 = 2872.5 \text{ kNm}$$

$$M_i^* = 1246.86 \times 10.2 = 12718 \text{ kNm}$$

$$M_c^* = 698.15 \times 14.42 = 10068 \text{ kNm}$$

Resultant overturning moment on the floor slab

$$M = \sqrt{(2872.5 + 12718)^2 + 10068^2} = 18559 \text{ kNm}$$

Pressure on the base due to this moment can be determined using the rigid beam theory:

$$\sigma = \frac{M}{I} y$$

Moment of inertia of the floor slab $I = 16 \times 25^3/12 = 20833 \text{ m}^4$

$$\therefore \text{ Maximum and minimum pressure on the floor slab} = \pm\frac{18559}{20833} \times 12.5 = \pm 11.1 \text{ kN/m}^2$$

This pressure needs to be superimposed with the pressure due to the fluid in the tank

$$= \gamma h = 10 \times 5 = 50 \text{ kN/m}^2$$

This pressure will be transferred to the soil below directly through bearing.
There is a need to determine the following forces:

1. The forces in the wall and base slab due to static and dynamic lateral earth pressure when the tank is empty and full,
2. The vertical load at the base of the walls under gravity.

The pressure due to the overturning moment will be superimposed and the foundation of the tank will be designed.

Sloshing Wave Height

$$h_{sl} = \alpha_{h,c} R \frac{L}{2} = 0.0473 \times 2.5 \times \frac{25}{2}$$

$$h_{sl} = 1.478 \text{ m} > 0.5 \text{ m free board}$$

In the present case, it is not feasible to provide a free board of 1.5 m. Therefore, water will splash outside the tank.

Anchorage Requirement

$$\text{Overturning moment} = 19559 \text{ kNm}$$

$$\text{Restoring moment} = (\text{Total weight} \times \text{Lever arm})$$

$$= (3940.65 + 20000) \times 25.7/2 = 307640 \text{ kNm}$$

$$>> \text{OTM} \qquad \text{Safe}$$

No need to provide any anchorage.
Similarly, the tank can be analyzed due to seismic force in the y-direction. □

EXAMPLE 14.2

An Intze overhead water tank has a capacity of 1250 kL. It is supported on a 20 m high RCC staging having 12 columns @ 550 mm dia, and bracings @ 200 × 600 mm at three levels as shown in Figure 14.19. The water tank is in Noida, UP, seismic zone IV, on soft soil. The concrete grades are as follows:

Container – M30; Staging – M25; Foundation – M30.

Acceleration due to gravity $g = 10$ m/s^2 (9.81 m/s^2 is rounded off)

The grade of steel is Fe500.

Analyze the water tank for seismic forces.

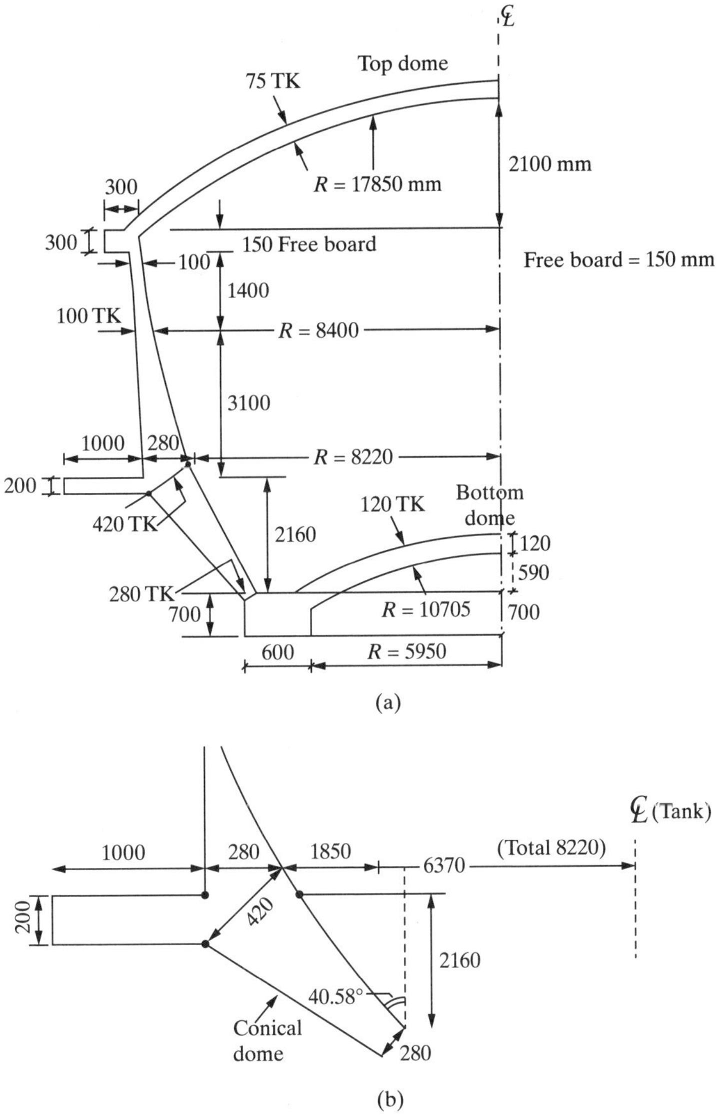

Figure 14.19 Overhear Water Tank.

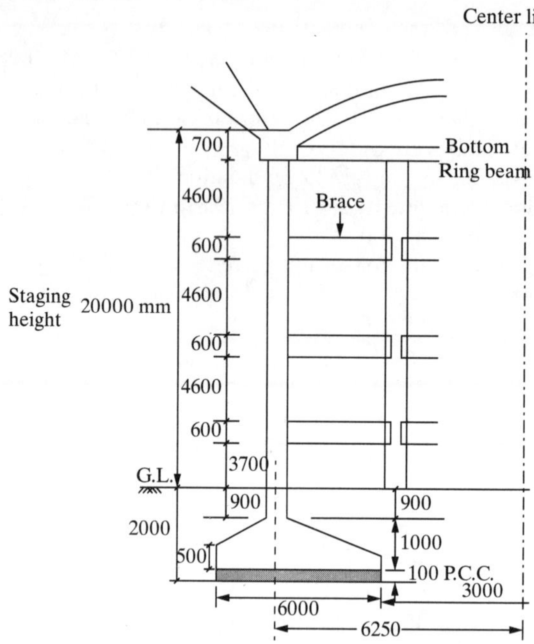

(c) Section of staging

Figure 14.19 (Continued)

Solution

Free board = 150 mm

Density of concrete = 25 kN/m^3

The data for various components of the tank are shown in Table 14.2.

TABLE 14.2 DATA FOR OVERHEAD TANK

S. No.	Component	Size, mm
1	Top dome	75 mm thick; rise of inner surface = 2100 mm Radius of inner surface = 17850 mm
2	Top ring beam	300 × 300 mm; inner radius = 8400 mm
3	Cylindrical wall	100 mm thick in top 1400 mm, and taper to 280 mm at the base in 3100 mm depth; Radius up to 1400 mm depth = 8400 mm; Radius at 3100 mm depth = 8220 mm
4	Middle ring beam	1000 × 200 mm – it will also serve as balcony for inspection
5	Conical dome	420 mm thickness at top, taper to 280 mm at the bottom, vertical depth 2160 mm; Inclination of inner surface with vertical = 40.58° Inclination of cone = 88.59° Radius of inner surface at top = 8220 mm

(*Continued*)

S. No.	Component	Size, mm
		Radius of inner surface at bottom = 6370 mm Inclined length of inner surface of cone = 2843.96 mm Length of center line of cone = 2843.10 mm Radius of center of cone at top = 8220 + 210 sin 48.01 = 8376.08 mm Radius of center of cone at bottom = 6370 + 140 sin 48.01 = 6474.06 mm Mean radius of center of cone = 7425.07 mm
6	Bottom dome	120 mm thick near center; Thickness near the edges in 1200 mm length tapered from 120 mm to 240 mm Radius of bottom surface = 10705 mm
7	Bottom ring beam	600 × 700 mm; inner radius = 5950 mm; Center line radius = 6250 mm
8	Columns	550 mm dia – 12 no.; center line radius = 6250 mm
9	Braces	200 × 600 mm at three levels
10	Staircase	On two independent columns @ 300 mm dia, connected to the main staging through 250 × 300 mm beams (B1) at each flight; Riser = 188.9 mm, tread = 250 mm
11	Pile Foundation	Depth of foundation below GL = 2000 mm

Weight calculations are shown in Table 14.3.

TABLE 14.3 WEIGHT CALCULATIONS

S. No.	Component	Calculations	Weight (kN)
1	Top dome	$W = 2\pi Rht\,\gamma_c$ $= 2 \times \pi \times (17.85 + 0.0375) \times (2.1 + 0.0375) \times 0.075 \times 25 = 450.5$	451.0
2	Top ring beam	$2\pi \times (8.4 + 0.15) \times 0.3 \times 0.3 \times 25 = 120.90$	121.0
3	**Cylindrical wall:** Let us break the vertical wall in two components: 100 mm constant depth up to 4350 mm; triangular shape in 3100 mm depth	$W_1 = 2\pi (8.4 + 0.05) \times (3.1 + 1.4 - 0.15) \times 0.1 \times 25 = 577.38$ $W_2 = (0.5 \times 0.18 \times 3.1) \times 2\pi \times (8.22 + 2/3 \times 0.18) \times 25 = 365.53$	943.0
4	Middle ring beam	$2\pi \times (8.22 + 0.28 + 0.5) \times 0.2 \times 1.0 \times 25 = 282.75$	283.0
5	Conical dome	$2\pi \times 7.425 \times 0.3 \times 2.843 \times 25 = 1160.54$	1161.0

(Continued)

S. No.	Component	Calculations	Weight (kN)
6	**Bottom dome:** Let us break the bottom dome in two components: 120 mm uniform thickness throughout; Triangular thickness in 1200 mm length near edges from zero to 120 mm on the outer surface	$W_1 = 2\pi \times (10.705 + 0.06) \times (1.59 + 0.06) \times 0.12 \times 25 = 334.81$ $W_2 = 2\pi \times (0.5 \times 1.2 \times 0.12) \times (5.95 - 0.4) \times 25 = 62.77$	398.0
7	Bottom ring beam	$0.6 \times 0.7 \times 2\pi \times 6.25 \times 25 = 412.33$	412.0
8	Columns	$\pi \times 0.275^2 \times (20 + 0.9 - 0.7) \times 25 \times 12 = 1439.75$	1440.0
9	Braces	$0.2 \times 0.6 \times 2.685 \times 12 \times 3 \times 25 = 289.98$	290.0
10	Staircase and connected beams	100.0	100.0

Capacity of the container

Capacity of cylinder

The net volume enclosed by the cylinder can be calculated in two parts just like its weight was calculated.

$$V_1 = \pi 8.4^2 \times 4.5 = 997.518 \text{ m}^3$$

$$V_2 = (0.5 \times 0.18 \times 3.1) \times 2\pi \times (8.22 + 2/3 \times 0.18) = 14.62 \text{ m}^3$$

Net volume enclosed by cylinder $= V_1 - V_2 = 997.518 - 14.62 = 982.897 \text{ m}^3$

Capacity of cone

$$V_3 = \frac{1}{3} \times h \times \left(A_1 + A_2 + \sqrt{A_1 \times A_2}\right)$$

$$= \frac{1}{3} \times 2.16 \times \left(\pi 8.22^2 + \pi 6.37^2 + \sqrt{\pi 8.22^2 \times \pi 6.37^2}\right) = 363.066 \text{ m}^3$$

Capacity replaced by bottom dome

$$V_4 = \pi (1.59+0.12)^2 \times (10.705 + 0.12 - 1.71/3) = 94.206 \text{ m}^3$$

Net capacity of container $= 982.897 + 363.066 - 94.206 = 1251.757 \text{ m}^3 > 1250 \text{ m}^3$ required OK

Weight of empty container $= 451 + 121 + 943 + 283 + 1161 + 398 + 412 = 3769$ kN
Weight of staging $= 1440 + 290 + 100 = 1830$ kN
Hence effective seismic weight when tank is empty $= 3769 + 1830/3 = 4379$ kN
Total weight of water $= 1251.8 \times 10 = 12518$ kN
Mass of water $= 12518 \times 1000/g = 12518 \times 1000/10 = 1251800$ kg

Center of gravity of empty container

Let us find the center of gravity of the empty tank above the top of bottom ring beam.
C.G. of the top dome above the top of bottom ring beam =

$$\bar{y} = \frac{R^2}{4h}(\cos 2\alpha + 3 - 4\cos\alpha)$$

Mean radius of top dome = 17.85 + 0.075/2 = 17.8875 m
Mean rise = 2.1 + 0.075/2 = 2.1375 m

Semi-vertex angle, $\tan\alpha = \dfrac{8.4}{17.85 - 2.1} = 0.533$

or, $\alpha = 28.07°$

$$\therefore \quad \bar{y} = \frac{17.8875^2}{4\times 2.1375}(\cos 56.14 + 3 - 4\times\cos 28.07) = 1.0355 \text{ m}$$

C.G. of the top dome above the top of bottom ring beam = 7.85 m
C.G. of the top ring beam above the top of bottom ring beam = 6.66 m
C.G. of the vertical wall above the top of bottom ring beam = 4.335
C.G. of the middle ring beam above the top of bottom ring beam = 2.06 m
C.G. of the cone above the top of bottom ring beam =

$$\bar{y} = \frac{h}{3}\left[\frac{2R_1 + R_2}{R_1 + R_2}\right]$$

Thickness of cone is very small as compared to its radii.

$$R_1 = 8.22 + 0.156 = 8.376 \text{ m}$$

$$R_2 = 6.37 + 0.104 = 6.474 \text{ m}$$

$$h = 2.16 \text{ m}$$

$$\therefore \quad \bar{y} = \frac{2.16}{3}\left[\frac{2\times 8.376 + 6.474}{8.376 + 6.474}\right] = 1.126 \text{ m}$$

C.G. of the bottom dome above the top of bottom ring beam = 0.78 m

C.G. of the entire empty container above the top of bottom ring beam $\bar{h}$

$$= \frac{451\times 7.85 + 121\times 6.66 + 943\times 4.335 + 283\times 2.06 + 1161\times 1.126 + 398\times 0.78 - 412\times 0.35}{3769}$$

$$\bar{h} = 2.78 \text{ m}$$

C.G. of the entire empty container above the base of footing

$$= h_d + h_s + \bar{h}$$

$$= 2 + 20 + 2.78 = 24.78 \text{ m}$$

where, h_d = depth of foundation below G.L.
h_s = height of staging above G.L.

It is assumed that the center of gravity of the full container and that of the empty container are at the same height. However, exact value can also be easily determined.
Equivalent circular cylinder having the same volume and same inner diameter 16.8 m,

$$\pi\frac{D^2}{4}h = 1251.757$$

or, $h = 5.65$ m

$$\frac{h}{D} = \frac{5.65}{16.8} = 0.336$$

Equivalent mass of the accelerating liquid

Impulsive mass

$$\frac{m_i}{m} = \frac{\tan h\left(0.866\dfrac{D}{h}\right)}{0.866\dfrac{D}{h}}$$

$$\frac{m_i}{m} = \frac{\tan h\left(0.866\times\dfrac{16.8}{5.65}\right)}{\left(0.866\times\dfrac{16.8}{5.65}\right)} = 0.3838$$

or, Impulsive mass $m_i = 0.3838\text{ m} = 0.3838 \times 1251800 = 480440\text{ kg}$

Convective mass

$$\frac{m_c}{m} = 0.230\times\frac{\tan h\left(3.68\dfrac{h}{D}\right)}{\dfrac{h}{D}}$$

$$\frac{m_c}{m} = 0.230\times\frac{\tan h(3.68\times 0.336)}{0.336} = 0.5777$$

or, convective mass $m_c = 0.5777\text{ m} = 0.5777 \times 1251800 = 723165\text{ kg}$

Height of center of gravity EBP

For tanks with $\dfrac{h}{D} < 0.75, \dfrac{h_i}{h} = 0.375$

or, $$h_i = 2.118\text{ m}$$

$$\frac{h_c}{h} = 1-\frac{\cos h\left(3.68\dfrac{h}{D}\right)-1}{3.68\left(\dfrac{h}{D}\right)\sin h\left(3.68\dfrac{h}{D}\right)}$$

$$\frac{h_c}{h} = 1-\frac{\cos h(3.68\times 0.336)-1}{3.68\times 0.336\times \sin h(3.68\times 0.336)} = 0.5553$$

or, $h_c = 3.137\text{ m}$

Height of center of gravity IBP

For tanks with $\dfrac{h}{D} < 1.33$

$$\frac{h_i^*}{h} = \frac{0.866\dfrac{D}{h}}{2\tan h\left(0.866\dfrac{D}{h}\right)} - 0.125$$

$$\frac{h_i^*}{h} = \frac{0.866\times 2.973}{2\tan h(0.866\times 2.973)} - 0.125 = 1.1775$$

or, $h_i^* = 6.653\text{ m}$

For all tanks,

$$\frac{h_c^*}{h} = 1 - \frac{\cosh\left(3.68\frac{h}{D}\right) - 2.01}{3.68\left(\frac{h}{D}\right)\sinh\left(3.68\frac{h}{D}\right)}$$

$$\frac{h_c^*}{h} = 1 - \frac{\cosh(3.68 \times 0.336) - 2.01}{3.68 \times 0.336 \times \sinh(3.68 \times 0.336)} = 1.0734$$

or, $$h_c^* = 6.064 \text{ m}$$

Period of Tank

Let us estimate the stiffness of the tank staging. A 3D model was developed using the matrix stiffness method. The container was idealized as a rigid link at its c.g. (= 2.78 m) above the bottom ring beam. The weight of the empty container was lumped at each of the 12 columns at the level of the bottom ring beam. A lateral load of 100 kN was applied at the c.g. of the container along a diagonal. The lateral displacement equal to 9.77 × 10^{-3} m was obtained.

∴ Lateral stiffness of the empty OHT $= \frac{P}{\Delta} = \frac{100}{9.77 \times 10^{-3}} = 10235$ kN/m

$$T_i = 2\pi\sqrt{\frac{m_i + \frac{m_s}{3}}{k_s}}$$

m_s = structural mass = mass of empty container + [mass of the staging including staircase]/3

Period of the empty tank

$$T_e = 2\pi\sqrt{\frac{376900 + \frac{183000}{3}}{10235 \times 1000}} = 1.30 \text{ sec}$$

The 3-D matrix analysis gives the period of the empty tank as 1.408 sec in the first mode and 1.03 sec in the second mode.

Period in Impulsive Mode – Tank full

$$T_i = 2\pi\sqrt{\frac{480440 + 376900 + \frac{183000}{3}}{10235 \times 1000}} = 1.88 \text{ sec}$$

Period in Convective Mode – Tank full

$$T_c = C_c\sqrt{\frac{D}{g}}$$

$$C_c = \frac{2\pi}{\sqrt{3.68\tanh\left(\frac{3.68h}{D}\right)}}$$

$$C_c = \frac{2\pi}{\sqrt{3.68\tanh\left(3.68 \times \frac{5.65}{16.8}\right)}} = 3.56$$

$$\therefore \qquad T_c = 3.56 \times \sqrt{\frac{16.8}{10}} = 4.61 \text{ sec}$$

Design Horizontal Seismic Coefficient

The seismic coefficient in impulsive mode for 5% damping is given by

$$\alpha_{hi} = \frac{Z}{2} \times \frac{I}{R} \times \frac{S_a}{g}$$

where, $Z = 0.24, I = 1.5, R = 4,$

For $T_i = 1.88$ sec, 5% damping, $Sa/g = 1.67/T = 0.888$

$$\therefore \qquad \alpha_{hi} = \frac{0.24}{2} \times \frac{1.5}{4} \times 0.888 = 0.04 \text{ or, } 4\%$$

The seismic coefficient in convective mode for 0.5% damping

For $T_c = 4.61$ sec, 0.5% damping, $Sa/g = 1.67/T = 0.362$

$$\therefore \qquad \alpha_{hc} = \frac{0.24}{2} \times \frac{1.5}{4} \times 0.362 \times 1.75 = 0.028 \text{ or, } 2.8\%$$

where, 1.75 is multiplying factor for 0.5% damping vide Clause 4.5.2 of IS 1893-2.

Hydrodynamic Pressure on Walls

Impulsive pressure at the base of walls

$$P_i(0) = a_i = \frac{\alpha_{h,i} m_i g}{2h^2}(4h - 6h_i) \text{ in N/m height of wall}$$

$$P_i(0) = \frac{0.04 \times 480440 \times 10}{2 \times 5.65^2}(4 \times 5.65 - 6 \times 2.118) = 29770 \text{ N/m}$$

Convective pressure at the base of walls

$$P_c(0) = a_c = \frac{\alpha_{h,c} m_c g}{2h^2}(4h - 6h_c) \text{ in N/m height of wall}$$

$$P_c(0) = \frac{0.028 \times 723165 \times 10}{2 \times 5.65^2}(4 \times 5.65 - 6 \times 3.137) = 11980 \text{ N/m}$$

Hydrostatic pressure intensity at height y above base

$$p_{hs}(y) = \rho g h \left(1 - \frac{y}{h}\right) \text{ in N/m}^2$$

or,
$$P_{hs}(y) B \text{ in N/m height of wall}$$

$$P_{hs}(0) = 1000 \times 10 \times 5.65 \times 1 = 56500 \text{ N/m}$$

Pressure on the tank wall due to its inertia

$$P_w(y) = \alpha_{h,i} \rho_c g t_w B \text{ in N/m height of wall}$$

or,
$$p_w(y) = P_w(y)/B \text{ in N/m}^2$$

$$P_w(0) = 0.04 \times 2500 \times 10 \times \left[\frac{0.1 + 0.28}{2}\right] \times 1 = 190 \text{ N/m}$$

Pressure due to vertical ground acceleration

$$p_v(y) = \alpha_v \rho g h \left(1 - \frac{y}{h}\right) \text{ in N/m}^2$$

or, $$P_v(y) = p_v(y)B \text{ in N/m height of wall}$$

where,

$$\alpha_v = \frac{2}{3}\frac{Z}{2}\frac{I}{R}\frac{S_a}{g}$$

$$\rho gh = \text{hydrostatic pressure at the base}$$

$$P_v(0) = \frac{2}{3} \times 0.04 \times 1000 \times 10 \times 5.65 \times 1 = 1500 \text{ N/m}$$

Gross hydrodynamic pressure at the base of wall

$$P_{hd}(y) = \sqrt{\left(P_{iy} + P_{wy}\right)^2 + P_{cy}^2 + \left(P_{vy}\right)^2} \text{ in N/m height of wall}$$

$$P_{hd}(0) = \sqrt{(29.77 + 0.19)^2 + 11.98^2 + 1.5^2} = 32.30 \text{ kN/m}$$

Hydrostatic pressure at the base of wall

$$P_{hs}(0) = 56.5 \text{ kN/m}$$

In the present case, the hydrodynamic pressure at the base of the wall is 57% of the hydrostatic pressure.

Base Shear when tank is full

The expressions for various dynamic lateral forces are as follows:

$$P_i = \alpha_{hi} m_i g \text{ acting @} h_i \text{ above the base of walls}$$

$$P_i^* = \alpha_{hi} m_i g \text{ acting @} h_i^* \text{ above the base of walls}$$

$$P_s = \alpha_{hi} m_s g \text{ acting @} \left(\bar{h} + h_s + h_d\right) \text{ above the bottom of footing}$$

Force on the empty container plus staging of the elevated tanks, acting at h_{cg} of the empty tank $\left(= \bar{h} + h_s + h_d\right)$ above the bottom of footing,

$$m_s = \text{mass of empty container of the tank} + \frac{\text{mass of staging}}{3}$$

$$P_c = \alpha_{hc} m_c g \text{ acting @} h_c \text{ above the base of walls}$$

$$P_c^* = \alpha_{hc} m_c g \text{ acting @} h_c^* \text{ above the base of walls}$$

Impulsive Mode

Force on liquid

$$P_i = 0.04 \times 480440 \times 10 = 192170 \text{ N}$$

Force on empty tank

$$P_s = 0.04 \times \left(376900 + \frac{183000}{3}\right) \times 10 = 175160 \text{ N}$$

Convective Mode

$$P_c = 0.028 \times 723165 \times 10 = 202480 \text{ N}$$

Total base shear at the bottom of the staging

$$V = \sqrt{(P_i + P_s)^2 + P_c^2}$$

$$V = \sqrt{(192.1 + 175.16)^2 + 202.48^2} = 419.4 \text{ kN}$$

Total weight of the OHT = 3769 + 1830 + 12518 = 18117 kN
Thus, the total base shear = 2.3% of the gross weight of the tank.

Overturning Moment at the Base of Staging
Total overturning moment at the foundation level of the tank including due to pressure on the base slab of the container (IBP) is given as follows:

$$M_i^* = P_i\,(h_i^* + h_s + h_d)$$

$$M_i^* = 192.17 \times (6.653 + 20 + 2) = 5506 \text{ kNm}$$

$$M_s = P_s\left(\bar{h} + h_s + h_d\right)$$

$$M_s = 175.16 \times (2.78 + 20 + 2) = 4340 \text{ kNm}$$

$$M_c^* = P_c\,(h_c^* + h_s + h_d)$$

$$M_c^* = 202.48 \times (6.064 + 20 + 2) = 5680 \text{ kNm}$$

The total overturning moment is given by

$$M^* = \sqrt{(M_i^* + M_s)^2 + (M_c^*)^2}$$

$$M^* = \sqrt{(5506 + 4340)^2 + 5680^2} = 11366 \text{ kNm}$$

Restoring moment due to weight of tank when full is given by

$$M_r = (3769 + 1830 + 12518) \times 6.25 = 113230 \text{ kNm}$$

$$>> 11366 \text{ kNm}$$

∴ Tank is safe against overturning

Base Shear when tank is empty
Design Horizontal Seismic Coefficient
The seismic coefficient in impulsive mode for 5% damping is given by

$$\alpha_{hi} = \frac{Z}{2} \times \frac{I}{R} \times \frac{S_a}{g}$$

where, $Z = 0.24$, $I = 1.5$, $R = 4$,
For $T_i = 1.3$ sec, 5% damping, $Sa/g = 1.67/T = 1.285$

∴ $$\alpha_{hi} = \frac{0.24}{2} \times \frac{1.5}{4} \times 1.285 = 0.058 \text{ or, } 5.8\%$$

$$V_B = P_s = 0.058 \times \left(376900 + \frac{183000}{3}\right) \times 10 = 254000 \text{ N}$$

Overturning moment under empty condition is given by

$$M = P_s\left(\bar{h} + h_s + h_d\right)$$

$$M = 254 \times (2.78 + 20 + 2) = 6295 \text{ kNm}$$

Restoring moment due to weight of tank when empty is given by

$$M_r = (3769 + 1830) \times 6.25 = 34990 \text{ kNm}$$

$$>> 6295 \text{ kNm}$$

∴ Tank is safe against overturning

Both base shear and OTM under the empty tank conditions are less than those under tank full condition. Therefore, tank full condition will govern.

Sloshing Wave Height

$$h_{sl} = \alpha_{h,c} R \frac{D}{2}$$

$$h_{sl} = 0.028 \times 4 \times \frac{16.8}{2} = 0.94 \text{ m}$$

There is a free board of 15 cm, and the rise of the top dome is 2.1 m. Still, the top dome will experience upward pressure due to sloshing. □

14.13 UNDERGROUND RECTANGULAR TANKS

The underground water tanks are generally built for very large capacities. The walls are designed as earth retaining walls due to earth pressure from outside, and hydrostatic pressure from the liquid stored inside the tank. The design philosophy for such tanks is the same as discussed earlier except that being underground, the inward soil pressure on walls and uplift pressure on base slab need also to be considered. Such tanks are not designed for hydrodynamic pressure but the walls are designed for dynamic earth pressure. The members must be doubly reinforced to resist both outward water pressure when tank is full and inward pressure when tank is empty. The roof cover may be rigidly connected or with a sliding type joint to tank walls. The bottom can be a flat slab like in a storage tank or sloping as in a swimming pool or a slab as in a waste treatment plant. The wall may be designed as a T-wall, counterfort wall or buttress wall as shown in Figure 14.20 depending upon the requirements. A retaining wall may retain earth or liquid as per requirement.

An underground reservoir is designed for two conditions:

1. Tank empty
2. Tank full

Under tank full condition, the earth pressure and liquid pressure act in opposite directions. Therefore, tank empty condition governs the design.

Forces on wall of reservoir

- Self weight
- Static and dynamic earth pressures
- Water table – hydrostatic pressure
- Pressure due to retained material
- Surcharge due to moving load, if any
- Blast pressure, if any

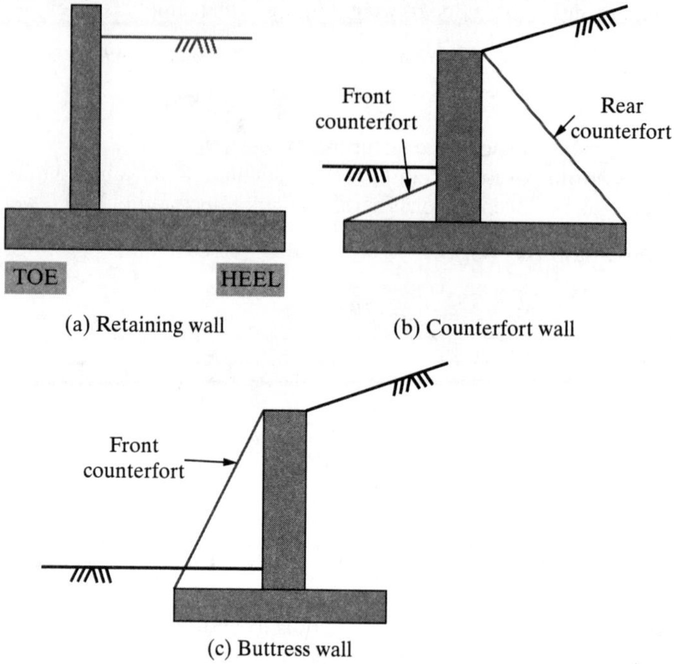

Figure 14.20 Different types of retaining walls – retained material: earth or liquid.

Safety requirements

- Bearing pressure under toe and heel
- Safety against overturning
- Safety against sliding
- Safety against uplift

In this section, the emphasis is on the computation of earth pressure on the tank walls during an earthquake. Rest of the calculations are as discussed earlier.

14.13.1 Definitions

Let us understand some of the terms associated with underground structures.

Active Earth Pressure The earth pressure exerted on the retaining wall by the retained soil. It may be greater than the fully active earth pressure (Figure 14.21).

Disturbing Force The force exerted by retained soil on a retaining wall, tending to cause the wall to move. It includes the surcharge loads, external loads and water pressure. The minimum value is the fully active earth pressure

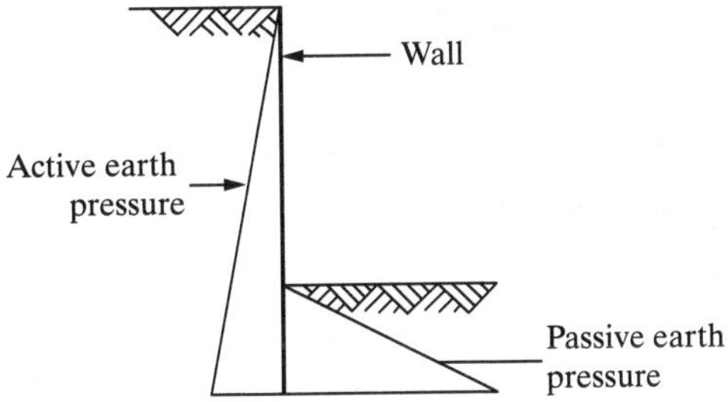

Figure 14.21 Active and passive earth pressures.

Fully Active Earth Pressure The minimum value of the active earth pressure, which occurs after sufficient movement or deflection of the retaining wall; the necessary movement is usually within the serviceability limit state of the wall

Fully Passive Earth Resistance The maximum value of the passive earth resistance, which occurs after sufficient movement or deflection of the retaining wall. The necessary movement is often outside the serviceability limit state of the wall

Passive Earth Resistance The earth pressure generated by the soil when it resists movement of a retaining wall (Figure 14.21).

The *design of water retaining structures* requires consideration of the interaction between the water, earth, and the structure. It requires the performance of two sets of calculations:

1. a set of *equilibrium calculations* to determine the overall proportions and the geometry of the structure necessary to achieve equilibrium under the relevant earth pressures and forces;
2. *structural design calculations* to determine the size and properties of the structural sections necessary to resist the bending moments and shear forces determined from the equilibrium calculations.

Both sets of calculations are carried out for specific design situations in accordance with the principles of limit state design. The selected design situations should be sufficiently severe and varied so as to encompass all reasonable conditions which can be foreseen during the period of construction and the life of the retaining wall.

Limit states are classified into:

(a) Ultimate limit states
(b) Serviceability limit states

Ultimate limit states include:

(a) Instability of the structure or any part of it, including supports and foundations, considered as a rigid body;
(b) Failure by rupture of the structure or any part of it, including supports and foundations.

Serviceability limit states include:

(a) Cracking of concrete
(b) Substantial deformation of the structure;
(c) Substantial movement of the ground.

$$\text{Lateral force due to earth pressure} = \frac{1}{2} C_a \gamma_s h^2 \tag{14.26}$$

The coefficient of earth pressure C_a may be computed using either Coulomb theory or Rankine theory depending upon the assumed failure condition.

14.13.2 Coulomb's Theory of Earth Pressure

The assumptions for Coulomb theory to estimate earth pressure on walls are as follows:

1. Soil is homogeneous and isotropic. It has both internal friction and cohesion.
2. It is a plane strain problem.
3. The rupture surface is a plane surface (BC in Figure 14.22(a)) and the backfill surface is planar.
4. The failure wedge is a rigid body.
5. The friction resistance is distributed uniformly along the rupture surface.
6. The soil-to-soil friction coefficient $f = \tan \phi$.
7. There is wall friction between soil and wall, equal to δ. As the failure wedge move with respect to the back face of the wall, a friction force develops between soil and wall.

The conditions at failure and force triangle are shown in Figure 14.22.

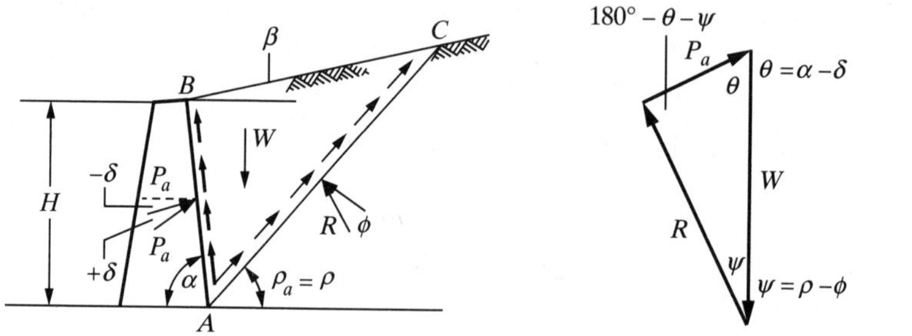

(a) Assumed conditions for failure (b) Force triangle to establish P_a

Figure 14.22 Coulomb active pressure wedge.

The main objections to the Coulomb theory are that soil is assumed to be ideal and the rupture zone is a plane.

Active pressure coefficient

$$C_a = \frac{\sin^2(\alpha_0 + \phi)}{\sin^2\alpha_0 \sin(\alpha_0 - \delta)\left[1 + \sqrt{\dfrac{\sin(\phi+\delta)\sin(\phi-\beta)}{\sin(\alpha_0-\delta)\sin(\alpha_0+\beta)}}\right]^2} \tag{14.27a}$$

The Coulomb equation are valid for both (+) β and (–) β.

For a smooth vertical wall,
$\alpha_0 = 90°$ vertical wall
$\beta = 0$, horizontal backfill,
$\delta = 0$, nil wall friction between soil and wall
ϕ = soil to soil friction coefficient, or $f = \tan \phi$

The active pressure coefficient reduces to

$$C_a = \frac{\sin^2(90+\phi)}{[1+\sin\phi]^2} \tag{14.27b}$$

14.13.3 Rankins's Theory of Earth Pressure

Rankine made the same assumptions as Coulomb except that he assumed no wall friction or soil cohesion. Rankine active pressure wedge and force triangle are shown in Figure 14.23.

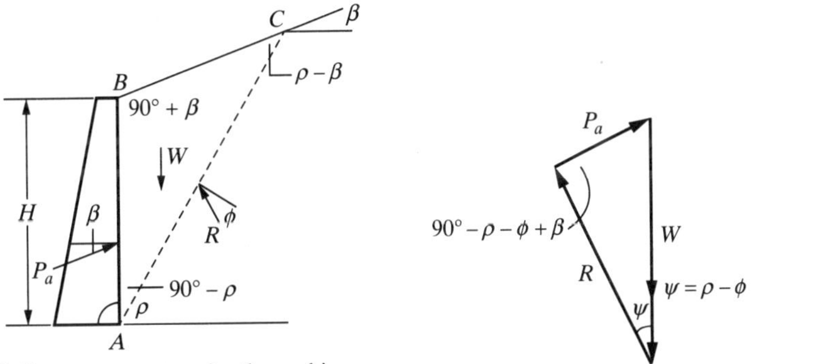

(a) Soil-structure system for the rankine solution for $\alpha = 90°$

(b) Force triangle to establish P_a

Figure 14.23 Rankine active earth pressure wedge.

Active pressure coefficient

$$C_a = \cos\beta\left[\frac{\cos\beta - \sqrt{\cos^2\beta - \cos^2\phi}}{\cos\beta + \sqrt{\cos^2\beta - \cos^2\phi}}\right] \tag{14.28a}$$

For a horizontal backfill, $\beta = 0$

The active pressure coefficient reduces to

$$C_a = \frac{1-\sin\phi}{1+\sin\phi} \tag{14.28b}$$

The calculations for earth pressure on walls under different soil strata, under static conditions are illustrated for better understanding.

14.14 ILLUSTRATIVE EXAMPLES

Example 14.3

For the vertical, smooth wall shown in Figure 14.24, determine the active lateral earth pressure using the Coulomb equation. The water table is at 4 m above the base of the wall.

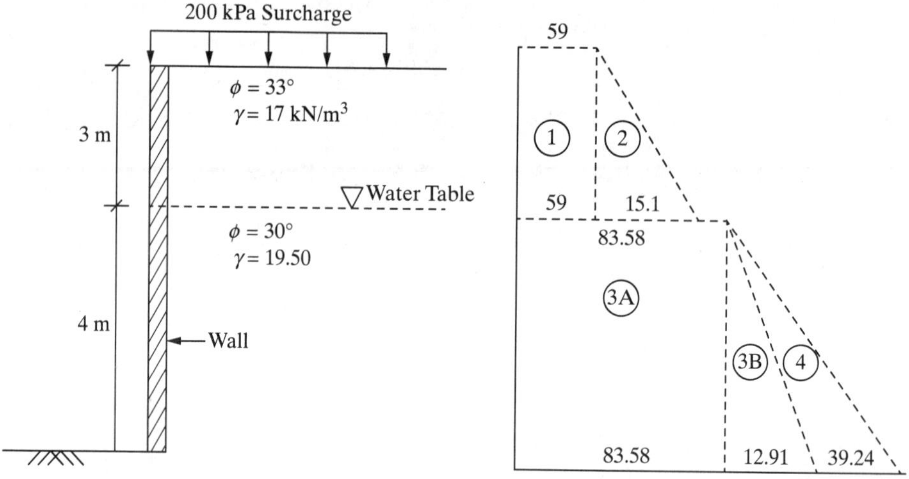

Figure 14.24 Soil data and Earth Pressure.

Solution

Let us consider a unit width of the wall normal to the plane of the paper. The Coulomb equation for active pressure coefficient is given as follows:

$$C_a = \frac{\sin^2(90+\phi)}{[1+\sin\phi]^2}$$

For angle of repose, $\phi = 30°$, $C_a = 0.333$; and $\phi = 33°$, $C_a = 0.295$

At $z = 0$, Top of wall where surcharge acts,

Pressure $p_1 = \gamma_1 z_0 C_a = qC_{a1} = 200 \times 0.295 = 59$ kPa

At the interface of top soil stratum, $z = 3$ m

Pressure $p_2 = (\gamma_1 z_0 + \gamma_1 z_1)C_{a1} = (200 + 17 \times 3)0.295 = 59 + 15.1 = 74.1$ kPa

The surcharge gives a constant or rectangular pressure diagram, whereas, increasing depth of soil gives a triangular pressure diagram with 15.1 kPa at the base.

At the interface with soil 2, a water table is encountered. Just at the interface,

$$p_2' = (\gamma_1 z_0 + \gamma_1 z_1 + (\gamma_2 - \gamma_w) \times 0)C_{a2}$$

$$p_2' = (200 + 17 \times 3 + (19.5 - 9.81) \times 0)0.333 = 83.58 \text{ kPa}$$

At the bottom of the wall,

$$p_3 = (\gamma_1 z_0 + \gamma_1 z_1 + (\gamma_2 - \gamma_w) \times z_2)C_{a2}$$

$$p_3 = (200 + 17 \times 3 + (19.5 - 9.81)4)0.333$$

$$p_3 = (66.6 + 16.98 + 12.02) = 83.58 + 12.91 \text{ kPa}$$

or, $$p_3 = 96.49 \text{ kPa}$$

Here, 83.58 pressure is rectangular and 12.91 is triangular.

Pressure due to water alone is given by

$$p_4 = \gamma_w z_2 = 9.81 \times 4 = 39.24 \text{ kPa}$$

The lateral pressure distribution on the wall is shown in Figure 14.24(b).

The total lateral force on the wall can be calculated from the triangular and rectangular pressure diagrams.

$$P_1 = 59 \times 3 = 177 \text{ kN acting at } 4 + 3/2 = 5.5 \text{ m above the base of wall}$$

$$P_2 = \frac{1}{2} \times 15.1 \times 3 = 22.65 \text{ kN acting at } 4 + 3/3 = 5 \text{ m}$$

$$P_{3A} = 83.58 \times 4 = 334.32 \text{ kN acting at } 4/2 = 2 \text{ m}$$

$$P_{3B} = \frac{1}{2} \times 12.91 \times 4 = 25.82 \text{ kN acting at } 4/3 = 1.33 \text{ m}$$

$$P_4 = \frac{1}{2} \times 39.24 \times 4 = 78.48 \text{ kN acting at } 4/3 = 1.33 \text{ m}$$

Total lateral force $P = 638.27$ kN

The point of application of the resultant lateral force on the wall can be determined as follows:

$$\bar{z} = \frac{177 \times 5.5 + 22.65 \times 5 + 334.32 \times 2 + 25.82 \times 1.33 + 78.48 \times 1.33}{638.27}$$

$$\bar{z} = \frac{1894.11}{638.27} = 2.97 \text{ m above the base of wall.}$$ □

Example 14.4

For the vertical wall and soil data shown in Figure 14.25, determine the active lateral earth pressure using the Rankine equation. The wall carries a surcharge of 75 kPa as shown. The water table is at 7.15 m above the base of the wall. Density of water is 9.81 kN/m³.

Solution

Let us consider a unit width of the wall normal to the plane of the paper. Rankine active pressure coefficient is given by

$$C_a = \frac{1 - \sin\phi}{1 + \sin\phi}$$

For a c-ϕ soil, the lateral pressure is given by $2c\sqrt{C_a}$.

Let us calculate the pressure coefficients for different angles of repose as follows:

ϕ	C_a	$\sqrt{C_a}$
0°	1	1
12°	0.6557	0.8098
22°	0.4549	0.6745
34°	0.2827	0.5317

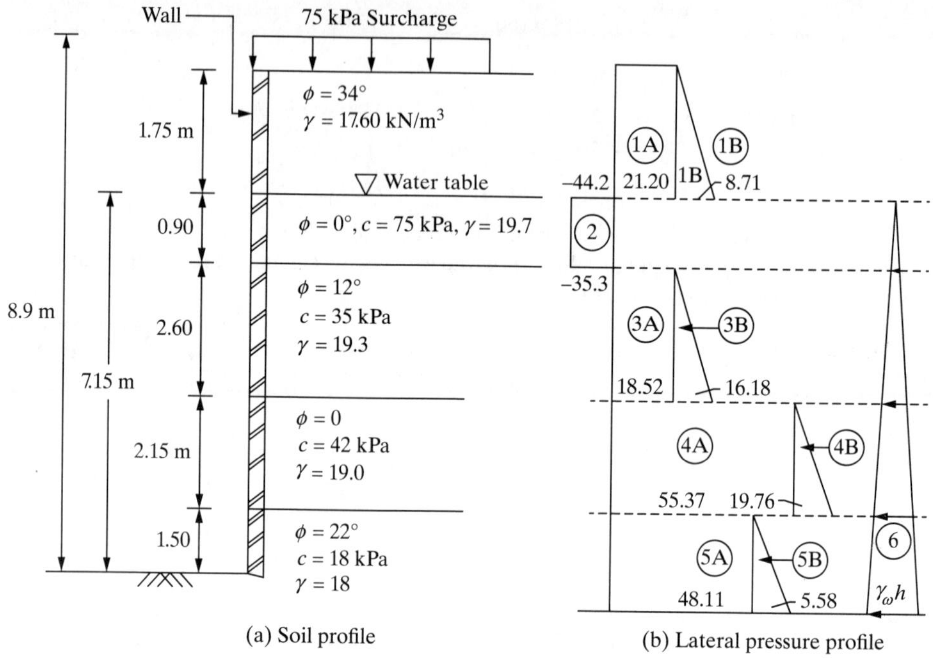

Figure 14.25 Soil data and Earth pressure on the wall.

Let us compute the lateral pressure at different depths of soil profile.

TABLE 14.4 LATERAL PRESSURE ON THE WALL AT THE BOUNDARIES OF DIFFERENT STRATA

Depth from top, *m*	γ_h, kPa	C_a	$\sqrt{C_a}$	Lateral earth pressure on wall, kPa
0	75	0.2827	0.5317	$75 \times 0.2827 = 21.2$
1.75^-	$75 + 17.6 \times 1.75 = 105.8$	0.2827	0.5317	$105.8 \times 0.2827 = 29.91$
1.75^+	$75 + 17.6 \times 1.75 + (19.7 - 9.81) \times 0 = 105.8$	1	1	$105.8 \times 1 - 2 \times 75 \times 1 = -44.2$
2.65^-	$105.8 + (19.7 - 9.81) \times 0.9 = 114.7$	1	1	$114.7 \times 1 - 2 \times 75 \times 1 = -35.3$
2.65^+	114.7	0.6557	0.8098	$114.7 \times 0.6557 - 2 \times 35 \times 0.8098 = 18.52$
5.25^-	$114.7 + (19.3 - 9.81) \times 2.6 = 139.37$	0.6557	0.8098	$139.37 \times 0.6557 - 2 \times 35 \times 0.8098 = 34.7$
5.25^+	139.27	1	1	$139.27 \times 1 - 2 \times 42 \times 1 = 55.37$
7.40^-	$139.27 + (19 - 9.81) \times 2.15 = 159.13$	1	1	$159.13 \times 1 - 2 \times 42 \times 1 = 75.13$
7.40+	159.13	0.4549	0.6745	$159.13 \times 0.4549 - 2 \times 18 \times 0.6745 = 48.11$
8.9	$159.13 + (18 - 9.81) \times 1.5 = 171.42$	0.4549	0.6745	$171.42 \times 0.4549 - 2 \times 18 \times 0.6745 = 53.69$

Lateral pressure due to water at the base of the wall = (1/2) × 9.81 × 7.15 = 70.14 kPa
The lateral pressure distribution on the wall is shown in Figure 14.25(b).
In the second strata below top, there is tension on the wall. If it is included in the calculations, it will reduce the total lateral force acting on the wall. To be on the conservative side, let us ignore tension.
Let us calculate the total lateral force in each strata by separating the rectangles and triangles.

$P_{1A} = 21.2 \times 1.75 = 37.1$ kN acting at 7.15 + 1.75/2 = 8.025 m above the base of wall
$P_{1B} = ½ \times 8.71 \times 1.75 = 7.62$ kN acting at 7.15 + 1.75/3 = 7.73 m
$P_{3A} = 18.52 \times 2.6 = 48.15$ kN acting at 3.65 + 2.6/2 = 4.95 m
$P_{3B} = ½ \times 16.18 \times 2.6 = 21.03$ kN acting at 3.65 + 2.6/3 = 4.52 m
$P_{4A} = 55.37 \times 2.15 = 119.04$ kN acting at 1.5 + 2.15/2 = 2.575 m
$P_{4B} = ½ \times 19.76 \times 2.15 = 21.24$ kN acting at 1.5 + 2.15/3 = 2.217 m
$P_{5A} = 48.11 \times 1.5 = 72.16$ kN acting at 0.75 m
$P_{5B} = ½ \times 5.58 \times 1.5 = 4.18$ kN acting at 1.5/3 = 0.5 m
$P_6 = ½ \times 70.14 \times 7.15 = 250.75$ kN acting at 7.15/3 = 2.38 m

Resultant lateral earth force = 330.52 kN without force due to water.
This resultant lateral force on the wall acts at 3.28 m above the base of the wall.
With water, the total lateral force = 581.27 kN
This resultant lateral force on the wall acts at 2.92 m above the base of the wall.
The lateral force due to water is quite high. It may be desirable to drain out this water by providing weep holes of appropriate size and spacing. □

14.15 DYNAMIC ACTIVE EARTH PRESSURE

The dynamic lateral earth pressure on a retaining wall having dry/moist cohesion less earth fill is as follows (IS 1893-part 3):

$$C_a = \frac{(1 \pm \alpha_v)\cos^2(-90 + \phi - \lambda + \alpha_0)}{\cos\lambda \cos^2(90 - \alpha_0)\cos(90 + (\delta - \alpha_0 + \lambda))} \times \left[\frac{1}{1 + \sqrt{\dfrac{\sin(\phi + \delta)\sin(\phi - \beta - \lambda)}{\cos(90 - \alpha_0 - \beta)\cos(90 + \delta - \alpha_0 + \lambda)}}}\right]^2 \quad (14.29a)$$

or,

$$C_a = \frac{(1 \pm \alpha_v)\sin^2(\phi - \lambda + \alpha_0)}{\cos\lambda \sin^2\alpha_0 \sin(\alpha_0 - \delta - \lambda)} \times \left[\frac{1}{1 + \sqrt{\dfrac{\sin(\phi + \delta)\sin(\phi - \beta - \lambda)}{\sin(\alpha_0 + \beta)\sin(\alpha_0 - \delta - \lambda)}}}\right]^2 \quad (14.29b)$$

nere, α_v = vertical seismic coefficient – Its direction being taken consistently throughout the stability analysis of wall, and equal to 2/3 α_h

$$\lambda = \tan^{-1}\left[\frac{\alpha_h}{1 \pm \alpha_v}\right] \quad (14.29c)$$

ϕ = angle of internal friction
β = slope of earth fill
δ = angle of friction between wall and earth fill
α_0 = angle the earth-face of the wall makes with the horizontal

The active pressure coefficient has two values corresponding to $\pm\ \alpha_v$. In the design, larger of the two values must be considered.

Point of Application
From the total earth pressure as given by the above equation, subtract the static active pressure component obtained by putting $\alpha_h = \alpha_v = \lambda = 0$ in the same equation. The remainder is the dynamic increment. The static component of the total pressure acts at $h/3$ above the base of the wall; while the dynamic increment pressure is assumed to act at $h/2$ above the base.

Similar expression for the passive dynamic pressure is given in IS 1893-part 3.

14.15.1 Active Pressure due to Uniform Surcharge

The active pressure against the wall due to a uniform surcharge of intensity q N/m^2 of the inclined earthfill surface is given as follows:

$$\left(P_{aq}\right)_{dyn} = \frac{C_a qh \sin\alpha}{\sin(\alpha + \beta)} \quad (14.30)$$

The dynamic increment in active pressure due to uniform surcharge will be applied at an elevation of $0.66h$ above the base of the wall. The static component will be applied at mid height of the wall.

14.15.2 Effect of Saturation

Saturated Earthfill
The saturated unit weight of the soil should be used in the above equations.

Submerged Earthfill
The dynamic increment in active earth pressure due to submerged earthfill can be estimated with the following modifications:

(a) The value of wall friction between soil and wall, δ, will be taken as one-half of δ for dry/moist backfill.

(b) The value of λ will be taken as follows:

$$\lambda = \tan^{-1}\left(\frac{\gamma_s}{\gamma_s - 10}\right)\left(\frac{\alpha_h}{1 \pm \alpha_v}\right) \quad (14.31)$$

where, γ_s = saturated unit weight of soil in kN/m^3

(c) The buoyant unit weight of earth must be adopted in earth pressure calculations.

(d) Again, from the value of the dynamic earth pressure determined as above, subtract the value of static earth pressure determined by putting $\alpha_h = \alpha_v = \lambda = 0$ in the same equation. The remainder will be dynamic increment.

Example 14.5

An underground RC tank (15 m × 15 m in plan) is placed at 8 m below the ground level as shown in Figure 14.26. Its height is 6.85 m including top of roof. Free board is 45 cm and thickness of roof is 40 cm. The soil has a dry density of 18 kN/m³ and angle of repose is 31°. There is a surcharge of 1.5 m of earth on the tank. It is located in seismic zone IV on medium soil. The wall of the tank may be treated as smooth. Determine the earth pressure and moment at the base of the wall.

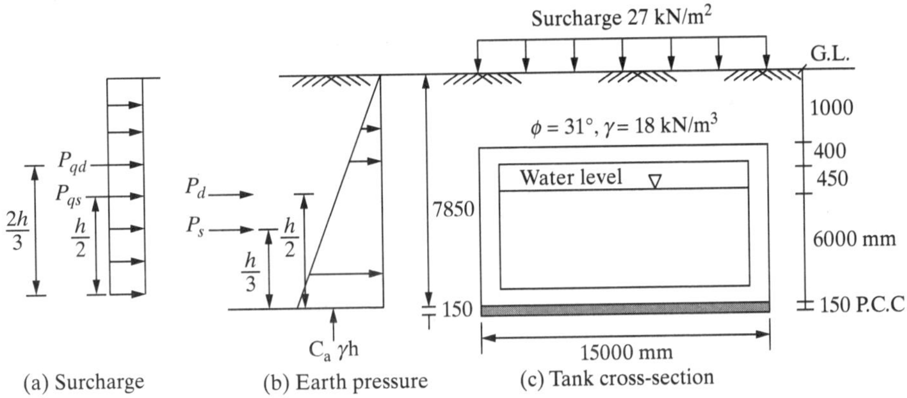

Figure 14.26 Underground water tank.

Solution

The total earth pressure for a depth h is given by

$$P_a = \frac{1}{2} C_a \gamma_s h^2$$

The static earth pressure acts at a height of $h/3$ above the base, while dynamic earth pressure acts at a height of $h/2$ above the base of the tank.

The coefficient of active dynamic earth pressure is given by

$$C_a = \frac{(1 \pm \alpha_v)\sin^2(\phi - \lambda + \alpha_0)}{\cos\lambda \sin^2\alpha_0 \sin(\alpha_0 - \delta - \lambda)} \times \left[\frac{1}{1 + \sqrt{\dfrac{\sin(\phi + \delta)\sin(\phi - \beta - \lambda)}{\sin(\alpha_0 + \beta)\sin(\alpha_0 - \delta - \lambda)}}} \right]^2$$

where, $\alpha_0 = 90°, \beta = 0, \phi = 31°, \delta = 0$ for a smooth vertical surface of tank

Horizontal seismic coefficient α_h is given by

$$\alpha_h = \frac{Z}{2} \frac{I}{R} \frac{S_a}{g}$$

and vertical seismic coefficient α_v is equal to (2/3) α_h.

$Z = 0.24$ for zone IV, $I = 1.5$, $R = 4$ for underground RC tank, $Sa/g = 2.5$

$$\therefore \qquad \alpha_h = \frac{Z}{2}\frac{I}{R}\frac{S_a}{g} = \frac{0.24}{2} \times \frac{1.5}{4} \times 2.5 = 0.1125$$

However, as per IS 1893-part 3, $\alpha_h \not< \dfrac{Z}{2} = 0.12$

$$\therefore \qquad \alpha_h = 0.12$$

and vertical seismic coefficient $\alpha_v = (2/3)\ \alpha_h = 0.08$

$$\lambda = \tan^{-1}\left(\frac{\alpha_h}{1 \pm \alpha_v}\right)$$

Case 1:

$$\lambda = \tan^{-1}\left(\frac{\alpha_h}{1+\alpha_v}\right) = \tan^{-1}\left(\frac{0.12}{1+0.08}\right) = 6.34°$$

Case 2:

$$\lambda = \tan^{-1}\left(\frac{\alpha_h}{1-\alpha_v}\right) = \tan^{-1}\left(\frac{0.12}{1-0.08}\right) = 7.43°$$

For case 1, the coefficient of active earth pressure is given by

$$C_a = \frac{(1+0.08)\sin^2(31-6.34+90)}{\cos(6.34)\sin^2 90\,\sin(90-6.34)} \times \left[\frac{1}{1+\sqrt{\dfrac{\sin(31)\sin(31-6.34)}{\sin(90)\sin(90-6.34)}}}\right]^2$$

$$C_a = 0.421$$

For case 2, the coefficient of active earth pressure is given by

$$C_a = \frac{(1-0.08)\sin^2(31-7.43+90)}{\cos(7.43)\sin^2 90\,\sin(90-7.43)} \times \left[\frac{1}{1+\sqrt{\dfrac{\sin(31)\sin(31-7.43)}{\sin(90)\sin(90-7.43)}}}\right]^2$$

$$C_a = 0.371$$

For static case,

$$C_a = \frac{\sin^2(90+\phi)}{[1+\sin\phi]^2}$$

$$C_a = \frac{\sin^2(90+31)}{[1+\sin 31]^2} = 0.32$$

Total static earth pressure is given by

$$P_s = \frac{1}{2}C_a \gamma h^2 = \frac{1}{2} \times 0.32 \times 18 \times 7.85^2 = 177.5\frac{\text{kN}}{\text{m}} \text{ width of tank wall}$$

It acts at $7.85/3 = 2.616$ m above base of tank.

Total earth pressure during an earthquake is given by

$$P_d = \frac{1}{2} C_a \gamma h^2 = \frac{1}{2} \times 0.421 \times 18 \times 7.85^2 = 233.5 \frac{\text{kN}}{\text{m}} \text{width of tank wall}$$

Therefore, dynamic increment in pressure is given by

$$= 233.5 - 177.5 = 56 \text{ kN/m}$$

acting @ 7.85/2 = 3.925 m above base of tank

Effect of Surcharge

$$\left(P_q\right)_d = \frac{C_a qh \sin\alpha}{\sin(\alpha + \beta)}$$

For $\alpha = 90°$ and $\beta = 0$, and Surcharge per unit area $q = 1.5 \times 18 = 27$ kN/m²

$$\left(P_q\right)_d = C_a qh$$

$$\left(P_q\right)_d = 0.421 \times 27 \times 7.85 = 89.2 \text{ kN/m width of wall}$$

$$\left(P_q\right)_s = 0.32 \times 27 \times 7.85 = 67.8 \text{ kN/m width of wall}$$

It acts at $0.5h = 3.925$ m above the base of tank.
Dynamic increment = 89.2 – 67.8 = 21.4 kN/m
It acts at $0.66h = 5.18$ m above the base of tank.

Bending moment at the base of the tank
Due to earth pressure

$$177.5 \times 2.626 + 56 \times 3.925 = 686 \text{ kN-m/m width of tank}$$

Due to surcharge

$$67.8 \times 3.925 + 21.4 \times 5.18 = 377 \text{ kN-m/m width of tank.}$$

$$\text{Total BM} = 686 + 377 = 1063 \text{ kN-m/m width of tank.}$$

The wall of tank must be designed for this bending moment causing tension on the outside of the tank when it is empty. □

REVIEW QUESTIONS

14.1 Elaborate the effect of earthquake on the liquid stored in a tank.

14.2 What are the serviceability requirements of a liquid retaining structure?

14.3 Explain impulsive and convective hydrodynamic pressures in a tank.

14.4 Discuss the spring mass model of a ground supported tank.

14.5 Define height of staging in an overhead tank.

14.6 Discuss one-mass and two-mass idealizations of an overhead tank.

14.7 Write a short note on:

- Equivalent impulsive mass of liquid
- Equivalent convective mass of liquid

- Height of center of gravity of the impulsive lateral force on the wall above the base excluding base pressure (EBP)
- Height of center of gravity of the impulsive lateral force on the wall above the base including base pressure (IBP)
- Height of center of gravity of the convective lateral force on the wall above the base excluding base pressure (EBP)
- Height of center of gravity of the convective lateral force on the wall above the base including base pressure (IBP)

14.8 Discuss the conditions under which natural period of vibration of ground supported tanks are calculated.

14.9 Discuss the conditions under which natural period of vibration of elevated tanks are calculated.

14.10 Why the time period of vibrations in convective mode same for ground supported tanks and overhead tanks?

14.11 Discuss the critical direction of lateral loads on the 4-column, 6-column, and 8-column staging.

14.12 Elaborate the hydrodynamic pressure distribution in circular tanks.

14.13 Elaborate the hydrodynamic pressure distribution in rectangular tanks.

14.14 Compare the exact and linear approximate pressure distributions on tank walls under impulsive and convective modes.

14.15 Elaborate the dynamic forces for which walls of a circular tank need to be designed with neat sketches.

14.16 Elaborate the dynamic forces for which walls of a rectangular tank need to be designed with neat sketches.

14.17 How do you calculate the resultant hydrodynamic pressure in a tank due to earthquake force?

14.18 How do you calculate the resultant base shear in an elevated tank due to earthquake force?

14.19 How do you calculate the resultant base shear in a ground supported tank due to earthquake force?

14.20 Discuss damping in convective mode in a tank.

14.21 Briefly explain sloshing wave height in a tank.

14.22 What are the causes of cracks in tanks?

14.23 How do you control cracking in tanks?

14.24 How do you measure crack width due to different causes in immature or fresh concrete?

14.25 How do you measure crack width due to different causes in mature concrete under direct tension?

14.26 How do you measure crack width due to different causes in mature concrete under flexure tension?

14.27 List the forces acting on the walls of an underground tank.

14.28 What is the basis of determining the overall proportions of an underground tank?

14.29 What is the design criterion for underground tanks?

14.30 List the assumptions for Coulomb's theory of earth pressure.

14.31 Sketch the active failure wedge and the forces acting on it for use in Coulomb's theory.

14.32 Sketch the active failure wedge and the forces acting on it for use in Rankine's theory.

14.33 Write a short note on Coulomb's theory of earth pressure.

14.34 Write a short note on Rankins's theory of earth pressure.

14.35 How do you estimate the dynamic earth pressure on the wall of an underground tank?

14.36 Where are the points of application of static and dynamic earth pressures on a retaining wall?

14.37 How do you consider the effect of vertical component of earthquake for the analysis of underground tank?

14.38 What is the expression for active pressure due to uniform surcharge of the inclined earthfill surface?

14.39 How do you account for the effect of saturation on the pressure due to earthfill on the retaining wall?

14.40 How do you account for the effect of submerged earthfill on the active pressure on the retaining wall?

PROBLEMS

14.1 A rectangular water tank of 1500 kL capacity is placed on the ground. It is open from the top. Analyze the tank for seismic forces if it is situated in seismic zone IV. Its internal dimensions are 20 × 18.75 × 4.4 m. Base thickness is 300 mm and wall thickness is 350 mm. Grade of concrete and steel are M35 and Fe 500, respectively.

14.2 A circular water tank of 2500 kL capacity is placed on the ground with its top open. Its internal dia. is 28 m and height 4.5 m. Base thickness is 300 mm and wall thickness 350 mm. Analyze the tank for seismic forces if it is situated in seismic zone V. Grade of concrete and steel are M35 and Fe 500, respectively.

14.3 A fully underground rectangular water tank has 5000 kL capacity. Its internal dimensions are: 35 × 30 × 5 m. It has a surcharge of 2 m of earth. The soil has dry density of 17 kN/m^3 and angle of repose is 32°. Design the water tank if it is situated in seismic zone IV on medium soil. The safe bearing capacity of the tank is 150 kN/m^2. The water table is up to the ground level. Assume suitable data and prepare structural drawings.

14.4 A circular overhead water tank of 1000 kL capacity has a 20 m high staging. Its internal dia is 18 m and height 5 m. Base slab is flat having 300 mm thickness and wall thickness is 175 mm. It is covered with a dome having an internal rise of 1.25 m and thickness 150 mm. There are two ring beams: at the top and bottom of the wall. The staging consists of 8 columns @ 500 mm dia. and bracing at 4 levels having 200 × 500 mm depth. It has a 900 mm wide balcony. The dia. of staging is 18.175 m. Analyze the tank for seismic forces if it is situated in seismic zone V. Grade of concrete and steel are M35 and Fe 500, respectively. Assume suitable data.

14.5 A square overhead water tank of 500 kL capacity has a 25 m high staging. Its internal dimensions are 10 × 10 × 5.5 m. Base slab is flat having 300 mm thickness with cross-beams and wall thickness is 250 mm. Roof slab is also flat having 300 mm thickness with cross-beams. The staging consists of 12 columns @ 500 mm dia. placed at the periphery and bracing at 5 levels having 250 × 500 mm depth. It has a 900 mm wide balcony. Analyze the tank for seismic forces if it is situated in seismic zone V. Grade of concrete and steel are M35 and Fe 500, respectively. Assume suitable data.

REFERENCES

ACI 350.3-20 (2021) Seismic Analysis and Design of Liquid-Containing Concrete Structures & Commentary, American Concrete Institute, Michigan.

Bowles, J. E. (1997) Foundation Analysis and Design, 5th ed., McGraw Hill International Edition, Singapore.

EN 1998-4 (2006) Design of structures for earthquake resistance – Part 4: Silos, tanks and pipelines, European Committee for Standardization, Brussels.

Housner, G.W. (1963) The Dynamic Behaviour of Water Tanks, Bulletin of Seismological Society of America, Vol. 53, No. 2, pp. 381-387.

Housner, G.W. (1963) Dynamic Pressure on Fluid Containers, Report no. TID 7024, U.S. Atomic Energy Commission, Washington, DC.

IS 3370 (2021) Code of Practice for Concrete Structures for the Storage of Liquids, Parts 1 and 2, Bureau of Indian Standard, New Delhi.

IS 456 (2000) Code of Practice for Plain and Reinforced Concrete, Bureau of Indian Standard, New Delhi.

IS 1983-Part 1 (2016) Earthquake Resistant Design of Structures – General provisions and Buildings and amendments, Bureau of Indian Standard, New Delhi.

IS 1983-Part 2 (2014) Earthquake Resistant Design of Structures – Liquid Retaining Tanks and amendments, Bureau of Indian Standard, New Delhi.

IS 1983-Part 3 (2014) Earthquake Resistant Design of Structures- Bridges and Retaining Walls and amendments, Bureau of Indian Standard, New Delhi.

IS 11682 (1985) Criteria for Design for RCC Staging for Overhead Water Tanks, Bureau of India Standard, New Delhi

Jain, A. K. (2012) Reinforced Concrete - Limit State Design, 7th ed., Nem Chand & Bros., Roorkee.

NZ 3106 (2009) Design of Concrete Structures for the Storage of Liquids, Standards New Zealand, Wellington.

A1 Measuring Earthquakes: Magnitude and Intensity

Once an earthquake occurs, it is important to know where the seismic event took place, how intense it was and its impact on the built environment, that is buildings, transportation structures, utilities and communication lines. Magnitude refers to the total energy released. Intensity refers to the extent of damage and loss of life.

A1.1 MAGNITUDE

Earthquake magnitude is typically measured by the Richter Scale, which is based on the maximum ground amplitude at a location 100 km from the epicenter. The Richter Scale was developed by Charles F. Richter in 1935 to measure the magnitude of an earthquake. It is a logarithmic measurement of the amount of energy released by an earthquake. Earthquakes with a magnitude of at least 4.5 are strong enough to be recorded by sensitive seismographs all over the world. An increase of 1 point means a 10-fold increase in the characteristic amplitude and an approximately 31-fold increase in the energy released.

In India, several hundred shocks of varying sizes occur annually. Some of the major earthquakes in the world are listed in Table A1.1.

TABLE A1.1 MAJOR WORLD EARTHQUAKES

S. No.	Earthquake	Date	Magnitude
1	Chile	22 May 1960	9.5
2	Great Alaska, USA	28 March 1964	9.2
3	Northern Sumatra	26 Dec 2004	9.2
4	Honshu, Japan	11 March 2011	9.0
5	Assam, India	15 Aug 1950	8.6
6	Sichuan, China	12 May 2008	7.9
7	Kathmandu, Nepal	25 April 2015	7.8
8	Gaziantep,Turkey (Syria border)	6 Feb, 2023 @01:18 GMT	7.8
9	Kahramanmaras, Turkey (Syria border)	6 Feb, 2023 @10:25 GMT	7.5
10	Tangshan, China	28 July, 1976	7.5

A1.2 INTENSITY

Modified Mercalli Intensity scale (MMI) measures the intensity or impact of an earthquake on people and the built environment. The intensity of a quake is evaluated according to the observed severity of the quake at specific locations. The Mercalli scale rates the intensity on a Roman numeral scale that ranges from I to XII.

In some countries, the comprehensive scale also called MSK 64 proposed by UNESCO is also used.

TABLE A1.2 MODIFIED MERCALLI INTENSITY SCALE

MMI Scale	Summary Damage description	Full Description
I		Not felt. Marginal and long period effects of large earthquakes.
II		Felt by persons at rest, on upper floors, or favorably placed.
III		Felt indoors. Hanging objects swing. Vibration like passing of light trucks. Duration estimated. May not be recognized as an earthquake.
IV		Hanging objects swing. Vibration-like passing of heavy trucks; or sensation of a jolt like a heavy ball striking the walls. Standing motor cars rock. Windows, dishes, doors rattle. Glasses clink. Crockery clashes. In the upper range of IV, wooden walls and frame creak.
V	Picture move	Felt outdoors; direction estimated. Sleepers wakened. Liquids disturbed, some spilled. Small unstable objects displaced or upset. Doors swing, close, open. Shutters, pictures move. Pendulum clocks stop, start, change rate.
VI	Object fall	Felt by all. Many frightened and run outdoors. Persons walk unsteadily. Windows, dishes, glassware broken. Knickknacks, books, etc., off shelves. Pictures off walls. Furniture moved or overturned. Weak plaster and masonry D cracked. Small bells ring (church, school). Trees, bushes shaken (visibly, or heard to rustle).
VII	Nonstructural damage	Difficult to stand. Noticed by drivers of motor cars. Hanging objects quiver. Furniture broken. Damage to masonry D, including cracks. Weak chimneys broken at roof line. Fall of plaster, loose bricks, stones, tiles, cornices (also unbraced parapets and architectural ornaments). Some cracks in masonry C. Waves on ponds; water turbid with mud. Small slides and caving in along sand or gravel banks. Large bells ring. Concrete irrigation ditches damaged.
VIII	Moderate damage	Steering of motor cars affected. Damage to masonry C; partial collapse. Some damage to masonry B; none to masonry A. Fall of stucco and some masonry walls. Twisting, fall of chimneys, factory stacks, monuments, towers, elevated tanks. Frame houses moved on foundations if not bolted down; loose panel walls thrown out. Decayed piling broken off. Branches broken from trees. Changes in flow or temperature of springs and wells. Cracks in wet ground and on steep slopes.

(Continued)

TABLE A1.2 (CONTINUED)

MMI Scale	Summary Damage description	Full Description
IX	Heavy damage	General panic. Masonry D destroyed; masonry C heavily damaged, sometimes with complete collapse; masonry B seriously damaged. (General damage to foundations.) Frame structures, if not bolted, shifted off foundations. Frames racked. Serious damage to reservoirs. Underground pipes broken. Conspicuous cracks in ground. In alluvial areas sand and mud ejected, earthquake fountains, sand craters.
X	Heavy damage	Most masonry and frame structures destroyed with their foundations. Some well-built wooden structures and bridges destroyed. Serious damage to dams, dikes, embankments. Large landslides. Water thrown on banks of canals, rivers, lakes, etc. Sand and mud shifted horizontally on beaches and flat land. Rails bent slightly.
XI	Extreme damage	Rails bent greatly. Underground pipelines completely out of service.
XII		Damage nearly total. Large rock masses displaced. Lines of sight and level distorted. Objects thrown into the air.

Masonry A: Good workmanship, mortar and design; reinforced, especially laterally and bound together by using steel, concrete, etc.; designed to resist lateral forces.

Masonry B: Good workmanship and mortar; reinforced but not designed in detail to resist lateral forces.

Masonry C: Ordinary workmanship and mortar; no extreme weaknesses like failing to tie in at corners but neither reinforced nor designed against horizontal forces.

Masonry D: Weak materials, such as adobe; poor mortar; low standards of workmanship; weak horizontally.

A2 MATLAB Basics

A2.1 MATLAB BASICS

MATLAB provides several standard functions. In addition, there are several toolboxes or collections of functions and procedures available as part of the MATLAB package. MATLAB offers the option of developing customized toolboxes. Many such tools are available worldwide. MATLAB is case sensitive, so the commands and programming variables must be used very carefully. It means A + B is not the same as $a + b$. The MATLAB prompt (>>) will be used to indicate where the commands are entered. Anything written after this prompt denotes user input (i.e., a command) followed by a carriage return (i.e., the "enter" key).

A2.1.1 Help Command

MATLAB provides help on any command or topic by typing the help command on the prompt:

```
>> help help
```

HELP Display help text in Command Window. HELP, by itself, lists all primary help topics. Each primary topic corresponds to a directory name on the MATLAB PATH.

```
>> help sum   % It provides help on the command sum
>> help paren % It provides help on different types of parenthesis;
   ( ); { }; [ ]
>> help arith % It provides help on all arithmetic operators
```

Comment It can be seen that on any command line, any information typed after the "%" sign is treated as a comment and is ignored by the MATLAB.

The MATLAB also provides a very exhaustive documentation along with the software for each toolbox. In addition, more information on various aspects is available on MATLAB user groups on the web.

A2.1.2 Parenthesis

In MATLAB, parenthesis ( ); braces { }; and brackets [ ] have specific meanings which is not so in FORTRAN or visual C++.

( ) Parentheses are used to indicate precedence in arithmetic expressions and to enclose arguments of functions in the usual way. They are used to enclose subscripts of vectors and matrices in a manner somewhat more general than the usual way. Parenthesis can also enclose logical (or 0–1) subscripts.

For example:

```
X = [4   -5   2.50   10]
```

(i) X(3) It is the third element of X.

(ii) X([1 2 3]) It is the first three elements of X.

```
ans =
    4.0000   -5.0000    2.5000
```

(iii) If X has N components, X(N:–1:1) reverses them. Thus, X(4:–1:1) gives

```
ans =
    10.0000    2.5000   -5.0000    4.0000
```

(iv) X(X > 2.0) returns those elements of X that are greater than 2.0.

```
ans =
    4.0000    2.5000   10.0000
```

{ } Braces are used to form cell arrays. Braces are also referred to as the curly brackets. They are similar to brackets [ ] except that nesting levels are preserved. Braces are also used for content addressing of cell arrays. They are similar to parentheses in this case except that the contents of the cell are returned.

[ ] Brackets are used in forming vectors and matrices. It is also referred to as the square brackets.

```
A = [2 4 0]               %A is a row vector
B = [ -4 10 SQRT(-5)]     %It is a vector with three elements
```

A2.1.3 Defining Variables

The basic variable types in MATLAB are scalar, vector and matrix. Variables are defined by typing the name of the variable followed by an equal sign and the value of the variable. The values of a vector or matrix are enclosed by square brackets, and rows of matrices are separated by semicolons.

For example:

```
A = 1                      % A is a scalar
```

Vectors

(i) Let us define a row vector

```
>>X = [4 -5 2.50 -10]
X =
  4.0000 -5.0000   2.5000 -10.0000
```

Note that an equal sign was used for assigning the variable name 'X' to the vector, square brackets to enclose its entries and spaces to separate them. It was possible to use commas (,) instead of spaces to separate the entries or even a combination of the two.

There is one more observation. MATLAB repeats what was typed in after processing the command. Quite often, we do not think the need to 'see' the output of a specific command. This output can be suppressed by using a semicolon (;) *at the end of the command line.*

(ii) Let us define a column vector

To create a column vector, either use semicolons (;) to separate the entries or first define a row vector and then take its *transpose* to obtain a column vector. Let us define a column vector D with entries (10 15 −12 0 0.50) using both techniques.

Case (a)

```
>>D= [10; 15; -12;0;0.50]              % It defines a column vector
D =
      10
      15
     -12
      0
      0.50
```

Case (b)

```
>>D = [10, 15, -12, 0,0.50]            % First define a row vector
D =
10 15 -12 0 0.50
>>D'                                   % Now take transpose of vector D
ans =
      10
      15
     -12
      0
      0.50
```

Case (c)

```
>>E = transpose (D) % it will give the same result as
above.
```

A single quote is used to take the *transpose* of a vector (or a matrix).

A2.1.4 Define a Matrix

```
C = [1 2 3; 4 5 6; 7 8 9]              % C is a 3 × 3 matrix
C =
```

$$\begin{bmatrix} 1 & 2 & 3 \\ 4 & 5 & 6 \\ 7 & 8 & 9 \end{bmatrix}$$

You can extract the numbers from the matrix using the convention A(*row* #, *col* #).

```
Try
>>C(1,3)                 % Element at first row and third column
ans
      3.0000
>>C(3,2)                 % Element at third row and second column
ans
      8.0000
```

You can also assign values of individual array elements

```
>>C(1,2) =100
```

Matrices with regularly increasing or decreasing values can be created as follows:

```
F = [1:6]            % create a vector with entries 1  2  3  4  5  6
G = [1:0.1:2]        % create a vector with entries from 1 to 2
                       incremented by 0.1
```

We can build a matrix from row vectors

```
row1 = [1 2 3]; row2 = [4 5 6]; row3 = [7 8 9];
C = [row1; row2; row3]
```

or from column vectors.

```
column1 = [1; 4; 7]; column2 = [2; 5; 8]; column3 = [3; 6; 9];
D = [column1 column2 column3]
```

Serveral matrices can be joined to create a larger one.

```
M = [A B; C D]
```

Displaying Data in a Matrix The values of a variable can be displayed by simply typing the variable name. In matrix case, a specific element, row or column of a matrix can be examined separately. A single element of a matrix can be addressed by typing the name of the matrix followed by the row and column indices of the element in parentheses. To address an entire column or row, a colon can be substituted for either index. For example:

```
A(1,1)        display the element in the 1st row, 1st column of A
A(:,1)        display the 1st column of A
A(2,:)        display the 2nd row of A
```

A2.1.5 Special Matrices

There are some short-cuts for creating special matrices. Try the following:

```
>>B = ones(1,8)             and,   >> B = ones(8)
>>C = eye(6,8)              and,   >> eye(8)
>>D = zeros(3,4)            and,   >> zeros(4)
>>E = diag([1  2  3])       % create a matrix whose diagonal is 1 2 3
```

The ‘eye’ command creates the ‘identity matrix’ – this is the matrix version of the number 1.

A2.1.6 Variable Name "ans"

MATLAB automatically assigns the variable name "ans" to anything that has not been assigned a name. The variable "ans", however, gets re-cycled each time a command is entered without assigning a variable name, and "ans" gets that value.

A2.1.7 Who and Whos Commands

Sometimes it is necessary to keep track of which variables have been defined and occupy the workspace. MATLAB does it for us through the command "who" or "whos" that give all sorts of information on which variables are active.

```
>>who          % List current variables only
>>whos         % Lists more information about each variable
```

A2.1.8 Operators

The operators in MATLAB are arithmetic operators, relational operators and logic operators.
The relational operators are as follows:

```
<      less than
>      greater than
<=     less than or equal
>=     greater than or equal
= =    equal
~ =    not equal
```

Note that "=" is used in an assignment statement while "= =" is used in a relation. Relations may be connected or quantified by the logical operators

```
&      and    xor
|      or     all
~      not    any
```

A2.1.9 Functions

Scalar functions Certain MATLAB functions operate essentially on scalars but operate element-wise when applied to a matrix. The most common functions are as follows:

```
sin    asin   exp                  abs    round
cos    acos   log (natural log)    sqrt   floor
tan    atan   rem (remainder)      sign   ceil
```

Vector functions MATLAB functions operate essentially on a vector (row or column) but act on a m-by-n matrix ($m \geq 2$) in a column-by-column fashion to produce a row vector containing the results of their application to each column. Row-by-row action can be obtained by using the transpose; for example mean(A′)′.

A few of these functions are:

```
max     sum     median    any
min     prod    mean      all
sort    std
```

Matrix functions Much of MATLAB's power comes from its matrix functions. Some of the useful ones are as follows:

det	determinant
size	size
norm	1-norm, 2-norm, F-norm, ∞-norm
cond	condition number in the 2-norm
rank	rank
chol	cholesky factorization
svd	singular value decomposition
inv	inverse
lu	LU factorization
qr	QR factorization
hess	hessenberg form
expm	matrix exponential
sqrtm	matrix square root
poly	characteristic polynomial
eig	eigenvalues and eigenvectors; solution of $[A]\{X\} = \lambda\{X\}$; where λ is eigenvalue and $\{X\}$ is eigenvector.

Matrix building functions Convenient matrix building functions are as follows:

eye	identity matrix
zeros	matrix of zeros
ones	matrix of ones
diag	diagonal matrix
triu	upper triangular part of a matrix
tril	lower triangular part of a matrix
rand	randomly generated matrix
hilb	Hilbert matrix
magic	magic square

Example 1

zeros(m,n) produces a m-by-n matrix of zeros.

```
>>>>zeros(3,4)
ans =
      0     0     0     0
      0     0     0     0
      0     0     0     0
```

□

Example 2

If x is a vector, diag(x) is the diagonal matrix with x down the diagonal.

```
>> x=[4 6 8]
```

```
x =
      4     6     8
>>diag(x)
ans =
      4     0     0
      0     6     0
      0     0     8
```

□

Example 3

If C is a square matrix, then diag(C) is a vector consisting of the diagonal of C.

```
>> C =[1 2 3;4 5 6;7 8 9]
C =
      1     2     3
      4     5     6
      7     8     9
>>diag(C)
ans =
      1
      5
      9
```

MAGIC – A magic square is an arrangement of numbers (usually integers) in a square grid, where the numbers in each row and in each column, and the numbers that run diagonally in both directions, all add up to the same number. The constant that is the sum of every row, column and diagonal is called the *magic constant or magic sum*, *S*. Every normal magic square has a unique constant determined solely by the value of size of the matrix *n*. □

Example 4

```
>>magic(4)
ans =
     16     2     3    13
      5    11    10     8
      9     7     6    12
      4    14    15     1
```

The sum is 34 in each case. It is a magic matrix. □

A2.1.10 Matrix Arithmetic and Functions

MATLAB is able to calculate simple functions.

For example,

```
det(A)          calculate the determinant of A
inv(A)          calculate the inverse of A
rank(A)         calculate the rank of A
```

The following matrix operations are available in MATLAB:

+	addition	e.g. A + B
–	subtraction	e.g. A - B

*	multiplication	e.g. A × B
^	power	e.g. A ^ 2
'	transpose	e.g. A′
\	left division or back slash	e.g. A\b
/	right division or slash	e.g. b/A

The matrix division operators "back slash" and "slash" have the following meanings:

X = A\B is the solution of linear simultaneous equations AX = Band,

X = B/A is the solution of XA = B

A is a coefficient matrix, X is unknown matrix, and B is known matrix. Matrix A need not be a square matrix.

In practice, linear equations of the form AX = B occur more frequently than those of the form XA = B. Consequently, the backslash is used far more frequently than the slash.

Example 5

$$[A] = \begin{bmatrix} 24 & 15 & 10 \\ 35 & 20 & 0 \\ 56 & -20 & 45 \end{bmatrix} \qquad [B] = \begin{bmatrix} 34 & -20 & 0 \\ 25 & 45 & -9 \\ 67 & -9 & 22 \end{bmatrix}$$

Using MATLAB, Find

(i) A + B = C **(ii)** A – B = C

(iii) A B = C **(iv)** AB + B = C

Solution

Matrix Addition

```
>>A = [24   15  10;  35  20   0;  56  -20  45];
>>B = [34  -20   0;  25  45  -9;  67   -9  22];
>>C = A + B
C =
      58   -5   10
      60   65   -9
     123  -29   67
```

Matrix Subtraction

```
>>C = A - B
C =
     -10    35   10
      10   -25    9
     -11   -11   23
```

Matrix Multiplication

```
>>C = A × B
C =
    1861     105     85
    1690     200   -180
    4419   -2425   1170
```

Matrix Multiplication and Addition

```
>>C = A × B + B
C =
    1895      85     85
    1715     245   -189
    4486   -2434   1192
```

□

Example 6

(a) Determine the inverse and determinant of the following matrix using MATLAB.

$$A = \begin{bmatrix} 50 & 20 & 0 \\ 20 & 75 & -10 \\ 0 & -10 & 100 \end{bmatrix}$$

(b) Find the eigenvalues of A.

Solution

(a)

```
>>A = [50      20     0;   20     75     -10;    0     -10     100];
% The matrix A is defined
>>INV(A)     % Find the inverse of A using MATLAB function INV
ans =
        0.0224    -0.0061    -0.0006
       -0.0061     0.0152     0.0015
       -0.0006     0.0015     0.0102
>>det(A)     % Find the determinant of A using MATLAB function
               det
ans =
       330000
```

(b)

```
>>eig(A)     % Find the eigenvalues of A using MATLAB function
               eig
ans =
        38.5225
        81.9673
       104.5102
```

□

Example 7

Determine the solution of the following linear simultaneous equations using MATLAB.

$$A = \begin{bmatrix} 5 & 2 & 3 \\ 4 & 5 & 4 \\ 7 & 0 & 9 \end{bmatrix}, \qquad B = \begin{Bmatrix} 10 \\ 13 \\ 16 \end{Bmatrix}$$

Solution

```
>> A = [5 2 3;4 5 4;7 0 9]    % define matrix A
```

```
A =
       5       2       3
       4       5       4
       7       0       9
>> b = [10 13 16]          % define b vector as a row
b =
      10      13      16
>> A\b'   % find solution by taking transpose of b, that is, column
           vector
ans =
      1.0000
      1.0000
      1.0000
```

It makes use of Gaussian elimination method. □

A2.1.11 Eigenvalues and Eigenvectors

The command eig(K,M) gives two matrices V and D. Matrix V is for eigenvectors arranged column-wise and matrix D is a diagonal matrix consisting of eigenvalues on the diagonal. The frequencies are obtained as follows:

$$\lambda = \omega^2$$

```
>>[V,D] = eig(K,M)
```

Alternatively, the following command can be given in MATLAB.

```
>>eig(M,K)
```

It again generates two matrices V and D. Matrix V is for eigenvectors arranged column-wise, and matrix D is a diagonal matrix consisting of eigenvalues on the diagonal. The frequencies are obtained as follows:

$$\lambda = 1/\omega^2$$

```
>>[V,D] = eig(M,K)
```

More options for this function are illustrated in Chapter 10.

A2.2 WORKING WITH MS EXCEL FILES

Data between MS Excel file and MATLAB can be easily exchanged using some simple commands. There are two options:

(a) The data can be exchanged using the following commands:

```
xlsfinfo
xlsread
xlswrite
```

For example

```
num = xlsread (filename, sheet)
num = xlsread (filename, sheet, x1Range)
[num, text, raw] = xlsread(filename, sheet, x1Range)
```

The `xlsread` function optionally returns the text fields in cell array `txt`, the unprocessed data (numbers and text) in cell array `raw`.

(b) Copy from Excel row or column and paste in MATLAB array

Copy and paste each column from excel sheet to an array in MATLAB.

In MATLAB create an array:

```
array =[ ];
```

Select the column in excel, choose copy, then go to MATLAB window and place the cursor between the square brackets above.

Then paste the column data.

Repeat above with different array numbers for each column.

You can save all the var in MATLAB as

save filename var name1 var name 2, … .

It will be saved as a mat file named filename.mat.

Example 8

```
filename='DOS-A2.xlsx';
sheet=2;
x1Range='C2:C7';
Data=xlsread(filename,sheet,x1Range)

% MATLAB will print the EXCEL data as follows:

Data =

   1
   2
   -3
   0
   5
   21
```

□

Example 9

```
filename='DOS-A2.xlsx';
[num,txt,raw]=xlsread(filename);
xArray=cell(raw(:,1))
yArray=cell(raw(:,2))
```

This EXCEL file contains data in first two columns: A and B. MATLAB will read data from column A in xArray and column B in yArray.

```
xArray
   1
   2
   -3
   0
   5
   21
yArray
   3
   5
   0
   -1
   7
   9
```

It is also possible to specify the cell nos as in the previous example.

Example 10

The EXCEL file DOS_A3.xlsx looks like as follows:

A	B	C	D	E	F
1		JAN	FEB	MAR	APR
2					
3		1	2	3	4
4		5	6	7	8

The MATLAB program is as follows:

```
filename='DOS-A3.xlsx';
sheet=2;
[NDATA,TXT,ALLDATA]=xlsread(filename,sheet)

NDATA =             % numerical data
      1      2      3      4
      5      6      7      8

TXT =               % text data
     'JAN'     'FEB'     'MAR'     'APR'

ALLDATA =           % all data
     'JAN'     'FEB'     'MAR'     'APR'
     [NaN]     [NaN]     [NaN]     [NaN]
[   1]     [   2]     [   3]     [   4]
[   5]     [   6]     [   7]     [   8]
```

Similarly, xlswrite function can be used.

xlswrite(FILE,ARRAY,SHEET,RANGE) writes to the specified SHEET and RANGE.

A2.3 CONDITIONAL STATEMENTS

Like any other programming language, MATLAB also makes use of the FOR, WHILE and IF conditional statements. The general structure of these statements is illustrated through the flow diagrams shown in Figures A2.1–A2.3.

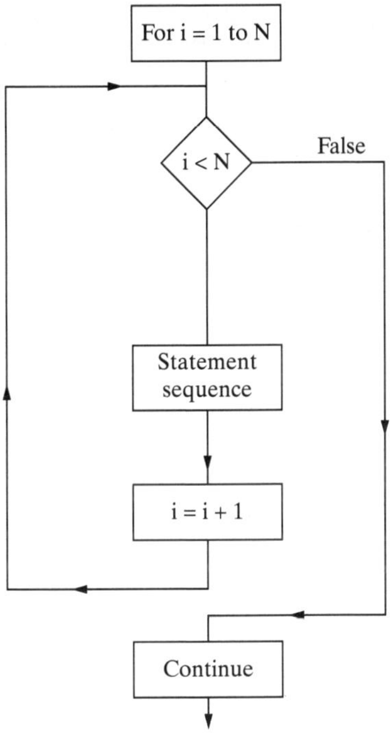

Figure A2.1 For loop

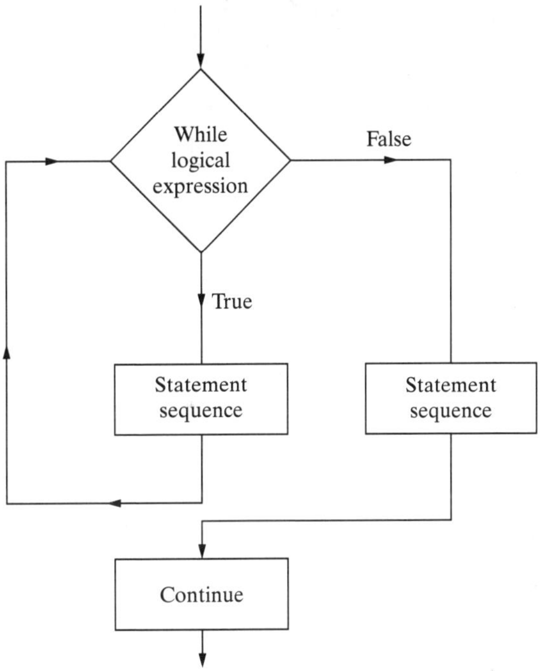

Figure A2.2 While loop

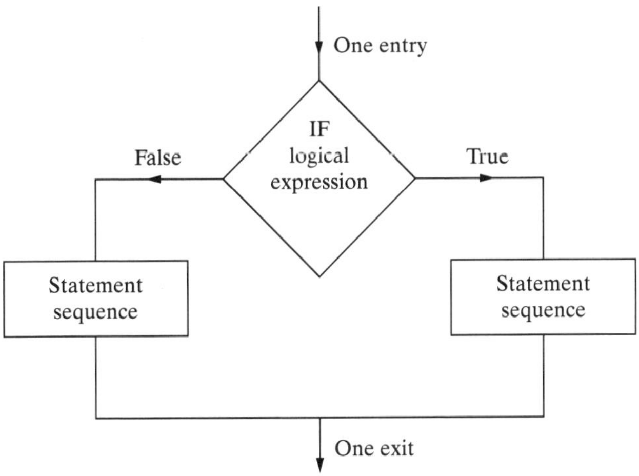

(a)

Figure A2.3 IF loop (Continued)

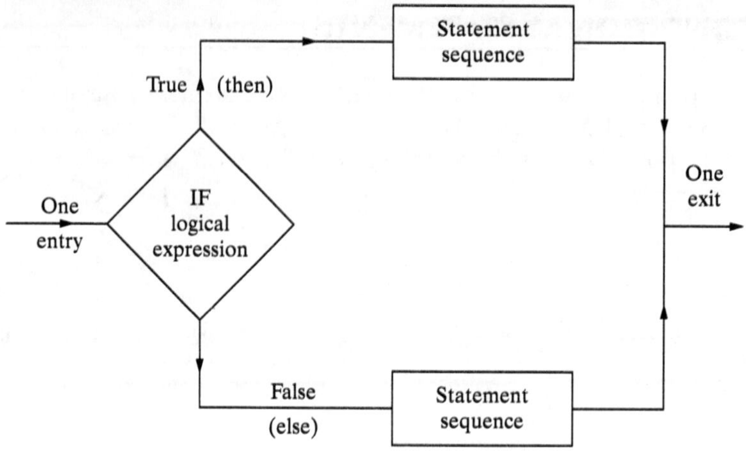

(b) IF loop

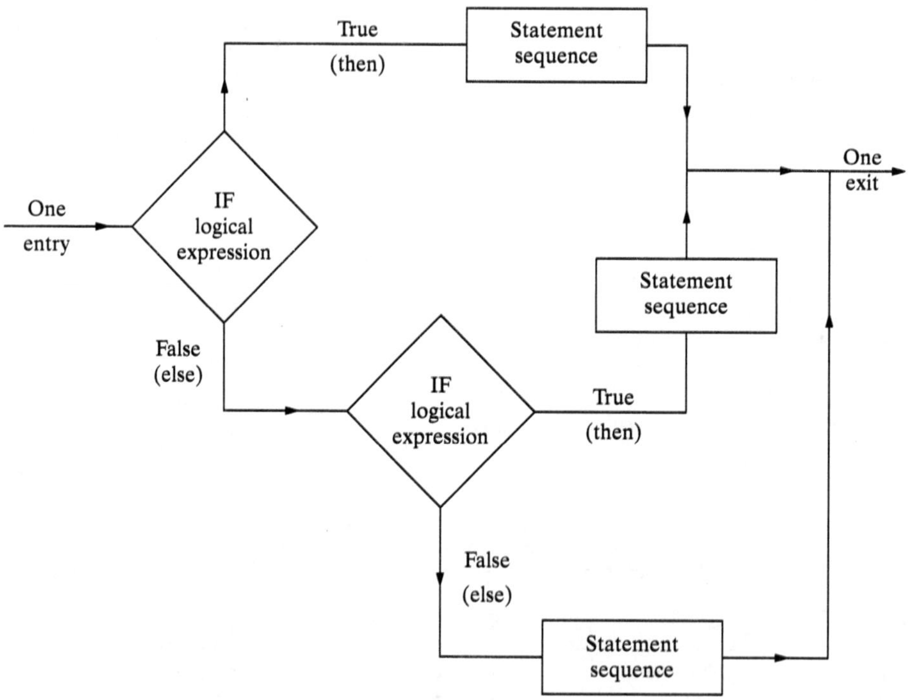

(c) Nested if statement

Figure A2.3 IF loop.

For Statement For Repeat statements a specific number of times.

The general form of a for statement is:

```
for variable = expr,
statements
       END
```

While Statement While Repeat statements an indefinite number of times.

The general form of a while statement is:

```
while expression
statements
       END
```

If Statement If Conditionally execute statements.

The general form of the if statement is

```
if expression
statements
       ELSEIF expression
statements
       ELSE
statements
       END
```

The statements are executed if the real part of the expression has all non-zero elements. The ELSE and ELSEIF parts are optional.

A2.4 BASIC GRAPHING ROUTINES

```
2D plots
>> plot (x,y)
>> plot (t,y(:,1))
>> grid on;
>> grid off;

>> hold ON;      % holds the current plot and all axis properties so
                 that subsequent graphing commands add to the existing
                 graph.
>> hold OFF;     % returns to the default mode whereby PLOT commands
                 erase the previous plots and reset all axis properties
                 before drawing new plots.

>> title ('This is the title')
>> axis ([xmin   xmax   ymin   ymax])   % sets scaling for the x- and
                                        y-axes on the current plot.
>> figure;     % creates a new figure window
```

```
3D plots

mesh   grid      cartesian grid in 2-D/3-D space

create a colored mesh plot:
>> figure; mesh (xx,yy,z1); xlabel ('x'); ylabel ('y'); zlabel ('z');
>> title ('This is the title');

create a colored surface plot:
>> figure; surf (xx,yy,z1); xlabel ('x'); ylabel ('y'); zlabel ('z');
>> title ('This is the title');

create a contour plot:
>> figure; contour (xx,yy,z1); xlabel('x'); ylabel('y'); zlabel ('z');
>> title ('This is the title');

>> clear all
```

A2.5 MATLAB PROGRAMS WITH THIS BOOK

Several programs have been written for this book to perform various calculations. These programs can be stored in any directory and it should be on the path of the MATLAB. The following help command will give a brief description of any program say, DOS2_3:

```
>> help DOS2_3
```

Similarly, help about other programs can be obtained.
MATLAB source codes developed in this text can be obtained from the publisher website.

A3 Standard Mathematical Formulae

Series Expansion

$$(1-x)^n = 1 - nx + \frac{n(n-1)}{\lfloor 2}x^2 - \frac{n(n-1)(n-2)}{\lfloor 3}x^3 + \ldots\ldots \quad \text{for } x < 1 \qquad \text{(i)}$$

$$(a+b)^n = {}^nC_0\, a^n + {}^nC_1\, a^{n-1}\, b^1 + {}^nC_2\, a^{n-2}\, b^2 + {}^nC_3\, a^{n-3}\, b^3 + \ldots + {}^nC_r\, a^{n-r}\, b^r + \ldots + {}^nC_n\, b^n \qquad \text{(ii)}$$

where,

$${}^nC_r = \frac{\lfloor n}{\lfloor r \lfloor n-r} \quad \text{for} \quad 0 \le r \le n \qquad \text{(iii)}$$

n = number of terms
r = number of terms chosen at a time

$$(a-b)^4 = a^4 - 4a^3b + 6a^2b^2 - 4ab^3 + b^4 \qquad \text{(iv)}$$

Trigonometric Functions

$$\sin C \pm \sin D = 2\sin\frac{C \pm D}{2}\cos\frac{C \mp D}{2} \qquad \text{(i)}$$

$$\cos(\pi - x) = -\cos x;\ \sin(\pi - x) = \sin x \qquad \text{(ii)}$$

$$\cos(\pi + x) = -\cos x;\ \sin(\pi + x) = -\sin x \qquad \text{(iii)}$$

$$\cos 2x = 2\cos^2 x - 1 = 1 - 2\sin^2 x \qquad \text{(iv)}$$

$$e^{\pm ix} = \cos x \pm i \sin x \qquad \text{(v)}$$

$$\sin(C + D) = \sin C \cos D + \cos C \sin D \qquad \text{(vi)}$$

$$\cos(C + D) = \cos C \cos D - \sin C \sin D \qquad \text{(vii)}$$

Integrations

$$\int \cos(a + bx)\, dx = \frac{1}{b}\sin(a + bx) \qquad \text{(i)}$$

$$\int x \cos ax\, dx = \frac{\cos ax}{a^2} + \frac{x}{a}\sin ax \qquad \text{(ii)}$$

$$\int x^2 \sin ax\, dx = \frac{2x}{a^2}\sin ax + \frac{2-a^2x^2}{a^3}\cos ax \quad \text{(iii)}$$

$$\int \cos^2 ax\, dx = \frac{x}{2} + \frac{1}{4a}\sin 2ax \quad \text{(iv)}$$

$$\int x\cos^2 ax dx = \frac{x^2}{4} + \frac{x}{4a}\sin 2ax + \frac{1}{8a^2}\cos 2ax \quad \text{(v)}$$

$$\int x^2\cos^2 ax dx = \frac{x^3}{6} + \left(\frac{x^2}{4a} - \frac{1}{8a^3}\right)\sin 2ax + \frac{x}{4a^2}\cos 2ax \quad \text{(vi)}$$

$$\int \sin mx \cos nx dx = -\frac{\cos(m-n)x}{2(m-n)} - \frac{\cos(m+n)x}{2(m+n)} \quad \text{(vii)}$$

$$\int \sin mx \sin nx dx = \frac{\sin(m-n)x}{2(m-n)} - \frac{\sin(m+n)x}{2(m+n)} \quad \text{(viii)}$$

Formula for integration by parts:

$$\int f(x)g(x)dx = f(x)G(x) - \int f'(x)G(x)dx \quad \text{(ix)}$$

Or, $$\int udv = uv - \int vdu$$

= first function x integrate the second function – ∫ differentiate the first function x integrate the second function

Thus,

$$\int x^3 \cos ax dx = \int udv = uv - \int vdu \quad \text{(x)}$$

If $u = x^3$ and $dv = \cos ax$

Then $du = 3x^2 dx$ and $v = \frac{1}{a}\sin ax$

Units

1 Pa = 1 N/m^2
1 kPa = 10^3 N/m^2 = 10^3 Pa
1 Mpa = 10^6 N/m^2 = 10^6 Pa
1 kN/m^2 = 1/10^3 N/mm^2
Mass unit is kg
Force unit is N, that is, 1 N = 1 kg × 1 m/s^2
1 kgf = 9.81 N ≈ 10 N
10 kg/cm^2 = 1 N/mm^2 = 1 MPa

Index

C

D

E

F

G

H

I

K

L

M

N